C# 2008 FOR PROGRAMMERS

THIRD

DEITEL

Deitel® Ser

Deitel® Developer Series

AJAX, Rich Internet Applications, and Web Development
   for Programmers

Visual Basic® 2008 for Programmers

C# 2008 for Programmers, 3/E

Visual Basic® 2005 for Programmers, 3/E

C# for Programmers, 2/E

How to Program Series

Visual C#® 2008 How to Program, 3/E

Visual Basic® 2008 How to Program

Visual C++® 2008 How to Program, 2/E

Java How to Program, 7/E

C++ How to Program, 6/E

Internet & World Wide Web How to Program, 4/E

C How to Program, 5/E

Small C++ How to Program, 5/E

Small Java™ How to Program, 6/E

Simply Series

Simply Visual Basic® 2008, 3/E: An
   Application-Driven Tutorial
   Approach

Simply C++: An Application-Driven
   Tutorial Approach

Simply Java™ Programming: An
   Application-Driven Tutorial
   Approach

Simply C#: An Application-Driven
   Tutorial Approach

ies Page

CourseSmart Web Books

www.deitel.com/books/CourseSmart/

Visual C# 2008 How to Program, 3/E

Visual Basic 2008 How to Program

Visual C++ 2008 How to Program, 2/E

Java How to Program, 6/E & 7/E

C++ How to Program, 5/E & 6/E

Internet & World Wide Web How to Program, 4/E

C How to Program, 5/E

Small Java How to Program, 6/E

Simply Visual Basic 2008: An Application-Driven Tutorial Approach, 3/E

Visual Basic 2005 How to Program, 3/E

Visual C# 2005 How to Program, 2/E

Simply C++: An Application-Driven Tutorial Approach

Simply Visual Basic 2005: An Application-Driven Tutorial Approach, 2/E

LiveLessons Video Learning Products

www.deitel.com/books/LiveLessons/

Java Fundamentals Parts 1 and 2

C# Fundamentals Parts 1 and 2

To follow the Deitel publishing program, register for the free *Deitel® Buzz Online* e-mail newsletter at:

> www.deitel.com/newsletter/subscribe.html

To communicate with the authors, send e-mail to deitel@deitel.com.

For information on government and corporate *Dive-Into® Series* on-site seminars offered by Deitel & Associates, Inc. worldwide, visit:

> www.deitel.com/training/

or write to deitel@deitel.com.

For continuing updates on Prentice Hall/Deitel publications visit:

> www.deitel.com
> www.prenhall.com/deitel

Check out our Resource Centers for valuable web resources that will help you master C# 2008, other important programming languages, software and web-related topics:

> www.deitel.com/ResourceCenters.html

C# 2008 FOR PROGRAMMERS
THIRD EDITION
DEITEL® DEVELOPER SERIES

Paul J. Deitel
Deitel & Associates, Inc.

Harvey M. Deitel
Deitel & Associates, Inc.

PRENTICE
HALL

Upper Saddle River, NJ • Boston • Indianapolis • San Francisco
New York • Toronto • Montreal • London • Munich • Paris • Madrid
Capetown • Sydney • Tokyo • Singapore • Mexico City

The publisher offers excellent discounts on this book when ordered in quantity for bulk purchases or special sales, which may include electronic versions and/or custom covers and content particular to your business, training goals, marketing focus, and branding interests. For more information, please contact:

U. S. Corporate and Government Sales
(800) 382-3419
corpsales@pearsontechgroup.com

For sales outside the U. S., please contact:

International Sales
international@pearsoned.com

Visit us on the Web: informit.com/ph

Library of Congress Cataloging-in-Publication Data

On file

© 2009 Pearson Education, Inc.

ISBN-10: 0-13-714415-6
ISBN-13: 978-0-13-714415-0

Text printed in the United States on recycled paper at R.R . Donnelley in Crawfordsville, Indiana.
First printing, September 2008

Trademarks

DEITEL, the double-thumbs-up bug and Dive Into are registered trademarks of Deitel & Associates, Inc.

Microsoft, Windows, Silverlight, SQL Server, Visual Studio, Visual Basic and Visual Web Developer are either registered trademarks or trademarks of Microsoft Corporation in the United States and/or other countries.

Deitel Resource Centers

Our Resource Centers focus on the vast amounts of mostly free content available online. Find downloads, tutorials, whitepapers, documentation, books, e-books, journals, articles, blogs, podcasts, videos, RSS feeds, tools, forums and more on many of today's hottest programming and technology topics. For the most up-to-date list of our Resource Centers, visit:

> www.deitel.com/ResourceCenters.html

Let us know what other Resource Centers you'd like to see! Also, please register for the free *Deitel® Buzz Online* e-mail newsletter at:

> www.deitel.com/newsletter/subscribe.html

Programming
ADO.NET
Adobe Flex
Ajax
Amazon Web Services
Apex
ASP.NET
ASP.NET 3.5
ASP.NET AJAX
C
C++
C++ Boost Libraries
C++ Game Programming
C#
Cloud Computing
Code Search Engines and Code Sites
Computer Game Programming
CSS 2.1
Dojo
Facebook Developer Platform
Flash 9
Google Web Toolkit (GWT)
Java
Java Certification and Assessment Testing
Java Design Patterns
Java EE 5
Java SE 6
Java SE 7 (Dolphin) Resource Center
JavaFX
JavaScript
JSON
Microsoft LINQ
Microsoft Popfly
MySpace Developer Platform
.NET
.NET 3.0
.NET 3.5
OpenGL
Open Social
Perl
PHP
Programming Projects
Python
Refactoring
Regular Expressions
REST Web Services
Ruby
Ruby on Rails
Service-Oriented Architecture (SOA)
Silverlight

Silverlight 2
Visual Basic
Visual Basic 2008
Visual C++
Visual C# 2008 and C# 3.0
Visual Studio Team System
Web 3D Technologies
Web Services
Windows Communication Foundation
Windows Presentation Foundation
XHTML
XAML
XML

Computer Science
Regular Expressions

Games and Game Programming
Computer Game Programming
Computer Games
Mobile Gaming
Sudoku

Internet Business
Affiliate Programs
Competitive Analysis
Facebook Social Ads
Google AdSense
Google Analytics
Google Services
Government Business
Internet Advertising
Internet Business Initiative
Internet Public Relations
Link Building
Location-Based Services
Online Lead Generation
Podcasting
Search Engine Optimization
Selling Digital Content
Sitemaps
Web Analytics
Website Monetization
YouTube

Java
Java
Java Certification and Assessment Testing
Java Design Patterns
Java EE 5

Java SE 6
Java SE 7 (Dolphin)
JavaFX

Microsoft
ASP.NET
ASP.NET 3.5
ASP.NET AJAX
C#
DotNetNuke (DNN)
Internet Explorer 7 (IE7)
Microsoft LINQ
Microsoft Popfly
.NET
.NET 3.0
.NET 3.5
SharePoint
Silverlight
Silverlight 2
SQL Server 2008
Visual Basic
Visual Basic 2008
Visual C++
Visual C# 2008 and C# 3.0
Visual Studio Team System
Windows Communication Foundation
Windows Presentation Foundation
Windows Vista
XAML

Open Source & LAMP Stack
Apache
DotNetNuke (DNN)
Eclipse
Firefox
Linux
MySQL
Open Source
Perl
PHP
Python
Ruby

Software
Apache
DotNetNuke (DNN)
Eclipse
Firefox
Firefox 3
Internet Explorer 7 (IE7)
Linux
MySQL
Open Source

Search Engines
SharePoint
Skype
SQL Server 2008
Web Servers
Wikis
Windows Vista

Web 2.0
Alert Services
Avatars
Attention Economy
Blogging
Building Web Communities
Community-Generated Content
Facebook Developer Platform
Facebook Social Ads
Google Base
Google Video
Google Web Toolkit (GWT)
Internet Video
Joost
KNOL
Location-Based Services
Mashups
Microformats
Recommender Systems
RSS
Social Graph
Social Media
Social Networking
Software as a Service (SaaS)
Virtual Worlds
Web 2.0
Web 3.0
Widgets

Dive Into® Web 2.0 eBook
Web 2 eBook

Database
MySQL
SQL Server 2008

Other Topics
Computer Games
Computing Jobs
Gadgets and Gizmos
Ring Tones
Sudoku

Contents

Preface   **xxiii**

Before You Begin   **xxxix**

1   Introduction   1

1.1	Introduction	2
1.2	Microsoft's Windows® Operating System	2
1.3	C, C++ and Java	3
1.4	Visual C#	4
1.5	Key Software Trend: Object Technology	5
1.6	The Internet and the World Wide Web	5
1.7	Extensible Markup Language (XML)	7
1.8	Introduction to Microsoft .NET	7
1.9	The .NET Framework and the Common Language Runtime	8
1.10	Test-Driving a C# **Advanced Painter** Application	9
1.11	(Only Required Section of the Case Study) Software Engineering Case Study: Introduction to Object Technology and the UML	11
1.12	Wrap-Up	16
1.13	Web Resources	16

2   Dive Into® Visual C# 2008 Express   18

2.1	Introduction	19
2.2	Overview of the Visual Studio 2008 IDE	19
2.3	Menu Bar and Toolbar	25
2.4	Navigating the Visual Studio IDE	28
	2.4.1 **Solution Explorer**	30
	2.4.2 **Toolbox**	31
	2.4.3 **Properties** Window	32
2.5	Using Help	33
2.6	Using Visual Programming to Create a Simple Program that Displays Text and an Image	35
2.7	Wrap-Up	47
2.8	Web Resources	48

3   Introduction to C# Applications   **49**

3.1   Introduction   50
3.2   A Simple C# Application: Displaying a Line of Text   50
3.3   Creating a Simple Application in Visual C# Express   55
3.4   Modifying Your Simple C# Application   63
3.5   Formatting Text with `Console.Write` and `Console.WriteLine`   65
3.6   Another C# Application: Adding Integers   66
3.7   Arithmetic   70
3.8   Decision Making: Equality and Relational Operators   71
3.9   (Optional) Software Engineering Case Study: Examining the ATM
       Requirements Document   76
3.10   Wrap-Up   85
3.11   Web Resources   85

4   Introduction to Classes and Objects   **86**

4.1   Introduction   87
4.2   Classes, Objects, Methods, Properties and Instance Variables   87
4.3   Declaring a Class with a Method and Instantiating an Object of a Class   89
4.4   Declaring a Method with a Parameter   93
4.5   Instance Variables and Properties   96
4.6   UML Class Diagram with a Property   102
4.7   Software Engineering with Properties and `set` and `get` Accessors 102
4.8   Auto-Implemented Properties   104
4.9   Value Types vs. Reference Types   105
4.10   Initializing Objects with Constructors   107
4.11   Floating-Point Numbers and Type `decimal`   110
4.12   (Optional) Software Engineering Case Study: Identifying the Classes
       in the ATM Requirements Document   116
4.13   Wrap-Up   123

5   Control Statements: Part 1   **125**

5.1   Introduction   126
5.2   Control Structures   126
5.3   `if` Single-Selection Statement   129
5.4   `if...else` Double-Selection Statement   130
5.5   `while` Repetition Statement   134
5.6   Counter-Controlled Repetition   135
5.7   Formulating Algorithms: Sentinel-Controlled Repetition   139
5.8   Formulating Algorithms: Nested Control Statements   144
5.9   Compound Assignment Operators   147
5.10   Increment and Decrement Operators   148
5.11   Simple Types   151

5.12   (Optional) Software Engineering Case Study: Identifying Class
       Attributes in the ATM System   151
5.13   Wrap-Up   156

6   Control Statements: Part 2   157

6.1   Introduction   158
6.2   Essentials of Counter-Controlled Repetition   158
6.3   for Repetition Statement   160
6.4   Examples Using the for Statement   164
6.5   do...while Repetition Statement   168
6.6   switch Multiple-Selection Statement   170
6.7   break and continue Statements   178
6.8   Logical Operators   180
6.9   (Optional) Software Engineering Case Study: Identifying Objects'
       States and Activities in the ATM System   186
6.10   Wrap-Up   190

7   Methods: A Deeper Look   192

7.1   Introduction   193
7.2   Packaging Code in C#   193
7.3   static Methods, static Variables and Class Math   194
7.4   Declaring Methods with Multiple Parameters   197
7.5   Notes on Declaring and Using Methods   201
7.6   Method-Call Stack and Activation Records   202
7.7   Argument Promotion and Casting   203
7.8   The .NET Framework Class Library   205
7.9   Case Study: Random-Number Generation   206
       7.9.1   Scaling and Shifting Random Numbers   210
       7.9.2   Random-Number Repeatability for Testing and Debugging   211
7.10   Case Study: A Game of Chance (Introducing Enumerations)   212
7.11   Scope of Declarations   217
7.12   Method Overloading   220
7.13   Recursion   223
7.14   Passing Arguments: Pass-by-Value vs. Pass-by-Reference   226
7.15   (Optional) Software Engineering Case Study: Identifying Class
       Operations in the ATM System   229
7.16   Wrap-Up   237

8   Arrays   238

8.1   Introduction   239
8.2   Arrays   239

8.3	Declaring and Creating Arrays	241
8.4	Examples Using Arrays	242
8.5	Case Study: Card Shuffling and Dealing Simulation	251
8.6	foreach Statement	255
8.7	Passing Arrays and Array Elements to Methods	257
8.8	Passing Arrays by Value and by Reference	259
8.9	Case Study: Class GradeBook Using an Array to Store Grades	263
8.10	Multidimensional Arrays	268
8.11	Case Study: Class GradeBook Using a Rectangular Array	273
8.12	Variable-Length Argument Lists	279
8.13	Using Command-Line Arguments	280
8.14	(Optional) Software Engineering Case Study: Collaboration Among Objects in the ATM System	282
8.15	Wrap-Up	290

9 Introduction to LINQ and Generic Collections   292

9.1	Introduction	293
9.2	Querying an Array Using LINQ	294
9.3	Introduction to Collections	303
9.4	Querying a Generic Collection Using LINQ	306
9.5	Wrap-Up	308
9.6	Deitel LINQ Resource Center	308

10 Classes and Objects: A Deeper Look   309

10.1	Introduction	310
10.2	Time Class Case Study	311
10.3	Controlling Access to Members	315
10.4	Referring to the Current Object's Members with the this Reference	316
10.5	Indexers	318
10.6	Time Class Case Study: Overloaded Constructors	321
10.7	Default and Parameterless Constructors	327
10.8	Composition	328
10.9	Garbage Collection and Destructors	331
10.10	static Class Members	332
10.11	readonly Instance Variables	336
10.12	Software Reusability	338
10.13	Data Abstraction and Encapsulation	339
10.14	Time Class Case Study: Creating Class Libraries	341
10.15	internal Access	345
10.16	**Class View** and **Object Browser**	347
10.17	Object Initializers	348
10.18	Time Class Case Study: Extension Methods	351
10.19	Delegates	354

10.20	Lambda Expressions	357
10.21	Anonymous Types	360
10.22	(Optional) Software Engineering Case Study: Starting to Program the Classes of the ATM System	362
10.23	Wrap-Up	368

11 Object-Oriented Programming: Inheritance 370

11.1	Introduction	371
11.2	Base Classes and Derived Classes	372
11.3	protected Members	374
11.4	Relationship between Base Classes and Derived Classes	375
	11.4.1 Creating and Using a CommissionEmployee Class	376
	11.4.2 Creating a BasePlusCommissionEmployee Class without Using Inheritance	381
	11.4.3 Creating a CommissionEmployee–BasePlusCommissionEmployee Inheritance Hierarchy	385
	11.4.4 CommissionEmployee–BasePlusCommissionEmployee Inheritance Hierarchy Using protected Instance Variables	388
	11.4.5 CommissionEmployee–BasePlusCommissionEmployee Inheritance Hierarchy Using private Instance Variables	394
11.5	Constructors in Derived Classes	399
11.6	Software Engineering with Inheritance	405
11.7	Class object	406
11.8	Wrap-Up	407

12 Polymorphism, Interfaces and Operator Overloading 408

12.1	Introduction	409
12.2	Polymorphism Examples	411
12.3	Demonstrating Polymorphic Behavior	412
12.4	Abstract Classes and Methods	415
12.5	Case Study: Payroll System Using Polymorphism	417
	12.5.1 Creating Abstract Base Class Employee	418
	12.5.2 Creating Concrete Derived Class SalariedEmployee	420
	12.5.3 Creating Concrete Derived Class HourlyEmployee	422
	12.5.4 Creating Concrete Derived Class CommissionEmployee	423
	12.5.5 Creating Indirect Concrete Derived Class BasePlusCommissionEmployee	425
	12.5.6 Polymorphic Processing, Operator is and Downcasting	426
	12.5.7 Summary of the Allowed Assignments Between Base-Class and Derived-Class Variables	431
12.6	sealed Methods and Classes	432
12.7	Case Study: Creating and Using Interfaces	433
	12.7.1 Developing an IPayable Hierarchy	434

12.7.2	Declaring Interface `IPayable`	435
12.7.3	Creating Class `Invoice`	435
12.7.4	Modifying Class `Employee` to Implement Interface `IPayable`	437
12.7.5	Modifying Class `SalariedEmployee` for Use with `IPayable`	438
12.7.6	Using Interface `IPayable` to Process `Invoices` and `Employees` Polymorphically	440
12.7.7	Common Interfaces of the .NET Framework Class Library	442
12.8	Operator Overloading	443
12.9	(Optional) Software Engineering Case Study: Incorporating Inheritance and Polymorphism into the ATM System	446
12.10	Wrap-Up	455

13 Exception Handling   456

13.1	Introduction	457
13.2	Exception-Handling Overview	458
13.3	Example: Divide by Zero without Exception Handling	458
13.4	Example: Handling `DivideByZeroExceptions` and `FormatExceptions`	461
13.4.1	Enclosing Code in a `try` Block	464
13.4.2	Catching Exceptions	464
13.4.3	Uncaught Exceptions	464
13.4.4	Termination Model of Exception Handling	465
13.4.5	Flow of Control When Exceptions Occur	466
13.5	.NET Exception Hierarchy	466
13.5.1	Class `SystemException`	467
13.5.2	Determining Which Exceptions a Method Throws	467
13.6	`finally` Block	468
13.7	`Exception` Properties	476
13.8	User-Defined Exception Classes	481
13.9	Wrap-Up	484

14 Graphical User Interfaces with Windows Forms: Part 1   485

14.1	Introduction	486
14.2	Windows Forms	487
14.3	Event Handling	490
14.3.1	A Simple Event-Driven GUI	490
14.3.2	Another Look at the Visual Studio Generated Code	492
14.3.3	Delegates and the Event-Handling Mechanism	493
14.3.4	Other Ways to Create Event Handlers	494
14.3.5	Locating Event Information	495
14.4	Control Properties and Layout	497
14.5	`Labels`, `TextBoxes` and `Buttons`	500
14.6	`GroupBoxes` and `Panels`	503

14.7	CheckBoxes and RadioButtons	507
14.8	PictureBoxes	515
14.9	ToolTips	518
14.10	NumericUpDown Control	520
14.11	Mouse-Event Handling	522
14.12	Keyboard-Event Handling	525
14.13	Wrap-Up	528

15 Graphical User Interfaces with Windows Forms: Part 2   530

15.1	Introduction	531
15.2	Menus	531
15.3	MonthCalendar Control	541
15.4	DateTimePicker Control	542
15.5	LinkLabel Control	545
15.6	ListBox Control	549
15.7	CheckedListBox Control	553
15.8	ComboBox Control	556
15.9	TreeView Control	560
15.10	ListView Control	565
15.11	TabControl Control	571
15.12	Multiple Document Interface (MDI) Windows	576
15.13	Visual Inheritance	584
15.14	User-Defined Controls	587
15.15	Wrap-Up	592

16 GUI with Windows Presentation Foundation   593

16.1	Introduction	594
16.2	Windows Presentation Foundation (WPF)	595
16.3	XML Basics	596
16.4	Structuring Data	599
16.5	XML Namespaces	604
16.6	Declarative GUI Programming Using XAML	608
16.7	Creating a WPF Application in Visual C# Express	610
16.8	Laying Out Controls	612
	16.8.1 General Layout Principles	612
	16.8.2 Layout in Action	613
16.9	Event Handling	618
16.10	Commands and Common Application Tasks	625
16.11	WPF GUI Customization	630
16.12	Using Styles to Change a Control's Appearance	631
16.13	Customizing Windows	636
16.14	Defining a Control's Appearance with Control Templates	639

16.15 Data-Driven GUIs with Data Binding   644
16.16 Wrap-Up   650
16.17 Web Resources   650

17 WPF Graphics and Multimedia   651

17.1   Introduction   652
17.2   Controlling Fonts   652
17.3   Basic Shapes   654
17.4   Polygons and Polylines   656
17.5   Brushes   659
17.6   Transforms   665
17.7   WPF Customization: A Television GUI   668
17.8   Animations   677
17.9   (Optional) 3-D Objects and Transforms   680
17.10 Wrap-Up   687

18 Strings, Characters and Regular Expressions   688

18.1   Introduction   689
18.2   Fundamentals of Characters and Strings   690
18.3   string Constructors   691
18.4   string Indexer, Length Property and CopyTo Method   692
18.5   Comparing strings   693
18.6   Locating Characters and Substrings in strings   697
18.7   Extracting Substrings from strings   699
18.8   Concatenating strings   700
18.9   Miscellaneous string Methods   701
18.10 Class StringBuilder   702
18.11 Length and Capacity Properties, EnsureCapacity Method and
       Indexer of Class StringBuilder   704
18.12 Append and AppendFormat Methods of Class StringBuilder   705
18.13 Insert, Remove and Replace Methods of Class StringBuilder   708
18.14 Char Methods   710
18.15 Card Shuffling and Dealing Simulation   713
18.16 Introduction to Regular-Expression Processing   717
       18.16.1 Simple Regular Expressions and Class Regex   718
       18.16.2 Complex Regular Expressions   723
       18.16.3 Validating User Input with Regular Expressions and LINQ 724
       18.16.4 Regex Methods Replace and Split   729
18.17 Wrap-Up   731

19 Files and Streams   732

19.1   Introduction   733
19.2   Data Hierarchy   733

19.3   Files and Streams   735
19.4   Classes `File` and `Directory`   736
19.5   Creating a Sequential-Access Text File   745
19.6   Reading Data from a Sequential-Access Text File   755
19.7   Case Study: Credit Inquiry Program Using LINQ   760
19.8   Serialization   766
19.9   Creating a Sequential-Access File Using Object Serialization   766
19.10   Reading and Deserializing Data from a Binary File   773
19.11   Wrap-Up   777

20   XML and LINQ to XML   778

20.1   Introduction   779
20.2   Document Type Definitions (DTDs)   779
20.3   W3C XML Schema Documents   783
20.4   Extensible Stylesheet Language and XSL Transformations   790
20.5   LINQ to XML: Document Object Model (DOM)   799
20.6   LINQ to XML Class Hierarchy   803
20.7   LINQ to XML: Namespaces and Creating Documents   812
20.8   XSLT with Class `XslCompiledTransform`   815
20.9   Wrap-Up   817
20.10   Web Resources   818

21   Databases and LINQ to SQL   819

21.1   Introduction   820
21.2   Relational Databases   821
21.3   Relational Database Overview: `Books` Database   822
21.4   SQL   826
        21.4.1   Basic `SELECT` Query   826
        21.4.2   `WHERE` Clause   827
        21.4.3   `ORDER BY` Clause   829
        21.4.4   Retrieving Data from Multiple Tables: `INNER JOIN`   831
        21.4.5   `INSERT` Statement   832
        21.4.6   `UPDATE` Statement   833
        21.4.7   `DELETE` Statement   834
21.5   LINQ to SQL   835
21.6   LINQ to SQL: Extracting Information from a Database   836
        21.6.1   Creating LINQ to SQL Classes   836
        21.6.2   Creating Data Bindings   837
21.7   More Complex LINQ Queries and Data Binding   840
21.8   Retrieving Data from Multiple Tables with LINQ   845
21.9   Creating a Master/Detail View Application   848
21.10   Programming with LINQ to SQL: Address-Book Case Study   853
21.11   Wrap-Up   859
21.12   Tools and Web Resources   859

22 ASP.NET 3.5 and ASP.NET AJAX   861

22.1	Introduction	862
22.2	Simple HTTP Transactions	863
22.3	Multitier Application Architecture	867
22.4	Creating and Running a Simple Web-Form Example	868
	22.4.1 Examining an ASPX File	868
	22.4.2 Examining a Code-Behind File	870
	22.4.3 Relationship Between an ASPX File and a Code-Behind File	871
	22.4.4 How the Code in an ASP.NET Web Page Executes	872
	22.4.5 Examining the XHTML Generated by an ASP.NET Application	872
	22.4.6 Building an ASP.NET Web Application	874
22.5	Web Controls	882
	22.5.1 Text and Graphics Controls	883
	22.5.2 AdRotator Control	889
	22.5.3 Validation Controls	892
22.6	Session Tracking	899
	22.6.1 Cookies	900
	22.6.2 Session Tracking with HttpSessionState	908
22.7	Case Study: Connecting to a Database in ASP.NET	915
	22.7.1 Building a Web Form That Displays Data from a Database	916
	22.7.2 Modifying the Code-Behind File for the Guestbook Application	923
22.8	Case Study: Secure Books Database Application	924
	22.8.1 Examining the Completed Secure Books Database Application	925
	22.8.2 Creating the Secure Books Database Application	928
22.9	ASP.NET AJAX	952
	22.9.1 Traditional Web Applications	952
	22.9.2 Ajax Web Applications	953
	22.9.3 Examining an ASP.NET AJAX Application	953
22.10	New ASP.NET 3.5 Data Controls	960
22.11	Wrap-Up	961
22.12	Web Resources	962

23 Windows Communication Foundation (WCF) Web Services   963

23.1	Introduction	964
23.2	WCF Services Basics	965
23.3	Simple Object Access Protocol (SOAP)	965
23.4	Representational State Transfer (REST)	966
23.5	JavaScript Object Notation (JSON)	966
23.6	Publishing and Consuming SOAP-Based Web Services	967
	23.6.1 Creating a WCF Web Service	967
	23.6.2 Code for the WelcomeSOAPXMLService	967
	23.6.3 Building a SOAP-Based Web Service	968
	23.6.4 Deploying the WelcomeSOAPXMLService	971

23.6.5 Creating a Client to Consume the `WelcomeSOAPXMLService` 973
23.6.6 Consuming the `WelcomeSOAPXMLService` 975
23.7 Publishing and Consuming REST-Based XML Web Services 976
23.7.1 Creating a REST-Based XML Web Service 976
23.7.2 Consuming a REST-Based XML Web Service 979
23.8 Publishing and Consuming REST-Based JSON Web Services 980
23.8.1 Creating a REST-Based JSON Web Service 980
23.8.2 Consuming a REST-Based JSON Web Service 982
23.9 Blackjack Web Service: Using Session Tracking in a SOAP-Based
Web Service 984
23.9.1 Creating a Blackjack Web Service 984
23.9.2 Consuming the Blackjack Web Service 988
23.10 Airline Reservation Web Service: Database Access and Invoking a
Service from ASP.NET 997
23.11 Equation Generator: Returning User-Defined Types 1002
23.11.1 Creating the REST-Based XML **EquationGenerator** Web Service 1005
23.11.2 Consuming the REST-Based XML **EquationGenerator**
Web Service 1006
23.11.3 Creating the REST-Based JSON `EquationGenerator`
Web Service 1010
23.11.4 Consuming the REST-Based JSON `EquationGenerator`
Web Service 1011
23.12 Wrap-Up 1014
23.13 Deitel Web Services Resource Centers 1015

24 Silverlight, Rich Internet Applications and Multimedia 1016

24.1 Introduction 1017
24.2 Platform Overview 1018
24.3 Silverlight Runtime and Tools Installation 1019
24.4 Building a Silverlight **WeatherViewer** Application 1019
24.4.1 GUI Layout 1022
24.4.2 Obtaining and Displaying Weather Forecast Data 1024
24.4.3 Custom Controls 1028
24.5 Animations and the **FlickrViewer** 1031
24.6 Images and Deep Zoom 1037
24.6.1 Getting Started With Deep Zoom Composer 1040
24.6.2 Creating a Silverlight Deep Zoom Application 1042
24.7 Audio and Video 1050
24.8 Isolated Storage 1055
24.9 Silverlight Demos and Web Resources 1056
24.10 Wrap-Up 1057

25 Data Structures 1059

25.1 Introduction 1060
25.2 Simple-Type structs, Boxing and Unboxing 1060
25.3 Self-Referential Classes 1061
25.4 Linked Lists 1062
25.5 Stacks 1075
25.6 Queues 1079
25.7 Trees 1082
    25.7.1 Binary Search Tree of Integer Values 1083
    25.7.2 Binary Search Tree of IComparable Objects 1090
25.8 Wrap-Up 1095

26 Generics 1097

26.1 Introduction 1098
26.2 Motivation for Generic Methods 1099
26.3 Generic-Method Implementation 1101
26.4 Type Constraints 1103
26.5 Overloading Generic Methods 1106
26.6 Generic Classes 1107
26.7 Wrap-Up 1116

27 Collections 1118

27.1 Introduction 1119
27.2 Collections Overview 1120
27.3 Class Array and Enumerators 1122
27.4 Nongeneric Collections 1125
    27.4.1 Class ArrayList 1126
    27.4.2 Class Stack 1130
    27.4.3 Class Hashtable 1132
27.5 Generic Collections 1137
    27.5.1 Generic Class SortedDictionary 1137
    27.5.2 Generic Class LinkedList 1140
27.6 Wrap-Up 1144

A Operator Precedence Chart 1145

B Simple Types 1147

C Number Systems 1149

C.1 Introduction 1150
C.2 Abbreviating Binary Numbers as Octal and Hexadecimal Numbers 1153
C.3 Converting Octal and Hexadecimal Numbers to Binary Numbers 1154
C.4 Converting from Binary, Octal or Hexadecimal to Decimal 1154
C.5 Converting from Decimal to Binary, Octal or Hexadecimal 1155
C.6 Negative Binary Numbers: Two's Complement Notation 1157

D ATM Case Study Code 1159

D.1 ATM Case Study Implementation 1159
D.2 Class ATM 1160
D.3 Class Screen 1166
D.4 Class Keypad 1166
D.5 Class CashDispenser 1167
D.6 Class DepositSlot 1168
D.7 Class Account 1169
D.8 Class BankDatabase 1171
D.9 Class Transaction 1174
D.10 Class BalanceInquiry 1176
D.11 Class Withdrawal 1177
D.12 Class Deposit 1181
D.13 Class ATMCaseStudy 1183
D.14 Wrap-Up 1183

E UML 2: Additional Diagram Types 1185

E.1 Introduction 1185
E.2 Additional Diagram Types 1185

F ASCII Character Set 1187

G Unicode® 1188

G.1 Introduction 1189
G.2 Unicode Transformation Formats 1190
G.3 Characters and Glyphs 1191
G.4 Advantages/Disadvantages of Unicode 1191
G.5 Using Unicode 1192
G.6 Character Ranges 1194

H Using the Visual C# 2008 Debugger 1196

H.1 Introduction 1197

H.2	Breakpoints and the **Continue** Command	1197
H.3	*DataTips* and Visualizers	1203
H.4	The **Locals** and **Watch** Windows	1204
H.5	Controlling Execution Using the **Step Into, Step Over, Step Out** and **Continue** Commands	1207
H.6	Other Debugging Features	1210
	H.6.1 **Edit** and **Continue**	1210
	H.6.2 **Exception Assistant**	1212
	H.6.3 **Just My Code**™ Debugging	1213
	H.6.4 Other Debugger Features	1213
H.7	Wrap-Up	1213

Index 1215

Preface

"Live in fragments no longer, only connect."
—Edgar Morgan Forster

Welcome to Visual C#® 2008, C# 3.0 and the world of Microsoft® Windows® and Internet and web programming with Microsoft's .NET Framework 3.5 platform! This book presents leading-edge computing technologies for professional software developers.

We use the Deitel signature "live-code approach," presenting most concepts in the context of complete working Visual C# 2008 programs, rather than using code snippets. Each code example is immediately followed by one or more sample executions. All the source code is available at www.deitel.com/books/csharpfp3/.

At Deitel & Associates, we write programming-language professional books and textbooks for Prentice Hall, deliver our Dive Into® Series professional corporate training courses worldwide and develop Web 2.0 Internet businesses. We have updated the previous edition of this book to Visual Studio 2008 and .NET 3.5, and added extensive new materials on the latest Microsoft technologies.

New and Updated Features

Here are the updates we've made for *C# 2008 for Programmers, 3/e*:

- *LINQ.* Many Microsoft technical evangelists say that LINQ (Language Integrated Query) is the single most important new feature in C# 2008. LINQ provides a uniform syntax for querying data. Strong typing enables Visual Studio to provide *IntelliSense* support for LINQ operations and results. LINQ can be used on different types of data sources, including collections and files (LINQ to Objects, Chapters 9 and 19, respectively), databases (LINQ to SQL, Chapters 21–23) and XML (LINQ to XML, Chapters 20 and 24).

- *Early Introduction to LINQ and Generic Collections.* We introduce LINQ early in the book so that you can begin using it as soon as you've been introduced to data structures—our LINQ coverage begins immediately after Chapter 8 on arrays. To enable you to work with more flexible data structures throughout the book, we also now introduce the List generic collection—a dynamic data structure—in close proximity to arrays. This enables us to demonstrate the power of LINQ and how it can be applied to most data structures. In addition, the List class is a generic collection, which provides strong compile-time type safety—ensuring that all elements of the collection are of the appropriate type.

- *Databases.* We use the free Microsoft SQL Server Express Edition and real-world applications to teach the fundamentals of database programming. Chapters 21–23 discuss database and LINQ to SQL fundamentals, presented in the context of an address-book desktop application, a web-based bookstore application and a web-based airline reservation system, respectively. Chapter 21 also demonstrates using the Visual Studio tools to build a GUI application that accesses a database using LINQ to SQL.

- *Windows Presentation Foundation (WPF) GUI and Graphics.* Graphical user interfaces (GUIs) and graphics make applications fun to create and easier to use. We begin our GUI discussion with the traditional Windows Forms controls in Chapters 14–15. We extend our coverage in Chapters 16 and 17 with an introduction to Windows Presentation Foundation (WPF)—Microsoft's new framework that integrates GUI, graphics and multimedia capabilities. To demonstrate WPF GUI and graphics capabilities we present many examples, including a painting application, a text editor, a color chooser, a book-cover viewer, a television video player, a 3-D rotating pyramid and various animations.

- *Windows Communication Foundation (WCF) Web Services.* Microsoft's .NET strategy embraces the Internet and web as integral to software development and deployment. Web-services technology enables information sharing, e-commerce and other interactions using standard Internet protocols and technologies, such as Hypertext Transfer Protocol (HTTP), Extensible Markup Language (XML) and Simple Object Access Protocol (SOAP). Web services enable programmers to package application functionality in a manner that turns the web into a library of reusable software components. We replaced our treatment of ASP.NET web services from the previous edition with a discussion of Windows Communication Foundation (WCF) services in Chapter 23. WCF is a set of technologies for building distributed systems in which system components communicate with one another over networks. In earlier versions of .NET, the various types of communication used different technologies and programming models. WCF uses a common framework for all communication between systems, so you need to learn only one programming model. Chapter 23 focuses on WCF web services that use either the SOAP protocol or REST (Representational State Transfer) architecture. The REST examples transmit both XML (eXtensible Markup Language) and JSON (JavaScript Object Notation).

- *ASP.NET 3.5 and ASP.NET AJAX.* The .NET platform enables developers to create robust, scalable web-based applications. Microsoft's .NET server-side technology, ASP.NET 3.5, allows programmers to build web documents that respond to client requests. To enable interactive web pages, server-side programs process information that users input into HTML forms. ASP.NET provides enhanced visual programming capabilities, similar to those used in building Windows Forms for desktop programs. Programmers can create web pages visually, by dragging and dropping web controls onto web forms. Chapter 22 introduces these powerful technologies. We present a sequence of examples in which you build several web applications, including a web-based bookstore. The chapter culminates with an example that demonstrates the power of AJAX. Chapter 22 also discusses the ASP.NET Development Server (which enables you to test your web applications on your local computer), multitier architecture and web transactions. The chapter uses ASP.NET 3.5 and LINQ to build a guestbook application that retrieves information from a database and displays it in a web page. We use the new LinqDataSource from a web application to manipulate a database. We use ASP.NET AJAX controls to add AJAX functionality to web applications to improve their responsiveness—in particular, we use the UpdatePanel control to perform partial-page updates.

- *Silverlight.* In Chapter 24, we introduce Silverlight, Microsoft's technology for building Rich Internet Applications (RIA). Silverlight, a competitor to JavaFX and Adobe's Flash and Flex technologies, allows programmers to create visually stunning, multimedia-intensive user interfaces for web applications using .NET languages such as Visual C#. Silverlight is a subset of WPF that runs in a web browser using a plug-in. One of Silverlight's most compelling features is its ability to stream high-definition video. The chapter presents powerful multimedia applications, including a weather viewer, Flickr™ photo viewer, deep zoom book-cover collage and video viewer.

- *New Language Features to Support LINQ.* Many of the new Visual C# language features we cover in Chapter 10 were introduced to support LINQ. We show how to use extension methods to add functionality to a class without modifying the class's source code. We enhanced our discussion of delegates (objects that hold method references) to support our discussion of C#'s new lambda expressions, which define anonymous functions. Lambda expressions can be used wherever delegates are needed—typically as arguments to method calls or to help create more powerful LINQ queries. You'll see how to use anonymous types to create simple classes that store data without writing a class definition—a feature used frequently in LINQ.

- *Implicitly Typed Local Variables.* When you initialize a local variable in its declaration, you can now omit the variable's type—the compiler infers it from the type of the initializer value (introduced in Chapter 8). This is another feature used frequently in LINQ.

- *Object and Collection Initializers.* When creating a new object, you can use the new object initializer syntax to assign values to the new object's properties (introduced in Chapter 10). Similarly, you can use the new collection initializer syntax (discussed in Chapter 9) to specify values for the elements of collections, just as you do with arrays.

- *Auto-Implemented Properties.* For cases in which a property of a class has a get accessor that simply returns a private instance variable's value and a set accessor that simply assigns a value to the instance variable, C# now provides automatically implemented properties (also known as auto-implemented properties; introduced in Chapter 4). With an auto-implemented property, the C# compiler automatically creates a private instance variable and the get and set accessors for manipulating it. This gives you the software engineering benefits of having a property, but enables you to implement the property trivially.

We updated the book to reflect the latest release of Visual C# 2008. New items include:

- Screenshots updated to the Visual C# 2008 Express IDE.

- Updated keywords table (Chapter 3) to include the new contextual keywords—words that are considered keywords only in certain contexts. Outside those contexts, such keywords can still be used as valid identifiers. This minimizes the chance that older Visual C# code will break when upgrading to Visual C# 2008. Many of these contextual keywords are used with LINQ.

- Pointing out additional ways in which the IDE's *IntelliSense* helps you write code.

- Using implicitly typed local variables to determine the types of the control variables in many `foreach` statements.

- Using *DataTips* and visualizers to view object contents in the code window during debugging.

- Using LINQ to Objects to manipulate data in two file-processing examples.

- Using LINQ to SQL in all database-driven examples.

All of this has been carefully reviewed by distinguished academics and industry developers who worked with us on *C# 2008 for Programmers, 3/e*. We believe that this book will give professional programmers an informative, interesting, challenging and entertaining C# educational experience.

As you read the book, if you have questions, send an e-mail to deitel@deitel.com; we'll respond promptly. For updates on this book and the status of all supporting C# software, and for the latest news on all Deitel publications and services, visit www.deitel.com. Sign up at www.deitel.com/newsletter/subscribe.html for the free *Deitel® Buzz Online* e-mail newsletter and check out our growing list of C# and related Resource Centers at www.deitel.com/ResourceCenters.html. Each week we announce our latest Resource Centers in the newsletter.

Features

Early Classes and Objects Approach
We introduce basic object-technology concepts and terminology in Chapter 1. Chapter 4 provides a carefully crafted, friendly introduction to classes and objects that gets you working with object oriented C# comfortably from the start. Chapters 5–8 have been carefully written with a friendly "early classes and objects approach."

Tuned Treatment of Object-Oriented Programming in Chapters 10–12
We performed a high-precision upgrade for *C# 2008 for Programmers, 3/e*. This edition is clearer and more accessible—especially if you are new to object-oriented programming.

Case Studies
We include many case studies, some spanning multiple sections and chapters:

- `GradeBook` class in Chapters 4–8.

- Optional OOD/UML ATM system in the Software Engineering sections of Chapters 1, 3–8, 10 and 12. The complete code for the ATM is included in Appendix D.

- Time class in several sections of Chapter 10.
- Employee payroll application in Chapters 11–12.
- WPF painter application in Chapter 16.
- WPF text-editor application in Chapter 16.
- WPF color-chooser application in Chapter 16.
- WPF book cover viewer application in Chapter 16.
- WPF television application in Chapter 17.
- Address-book application in Chapter 21.
- Guestbook ASP.NET application in Chapter 22.
- Secure-books database ASP.NET application in Chapter 22.
- Airline reservation web service in Chapter 23.
- Blackjack web service in Chapter 23.
- Equation-generator web service and math-tutor application in Chapter 23.
- Silverlight weather-viewer application in Chapter 24.
- Silverlight Flickr™ photo-viewer application in Chapter 24.
- Silverlight deep zoom book-cover collage application in Chapter 24.
- Silverlight video-viewer application in Chapter 24.

Integrated GradeBook Case Study

To reinforce our early coverage of classes, we present an integrated case study using classes and objects in Chapters 4–8. We incrementally build a GradeBook class that represents an instructor's grade book and performs various calculations based on a set of student grades—finding the average, finding the maximum and minimum, and printing a bar chart. Our goal is to familiarize you with the important concepts of objects and classes through a real-world example of a substantial class. We develop this class from the ground up, constructing methods from control statements and carefully developed algorithms, and adding instance variables and arrays as needed to enhance the functionality of the class.

The Unified Modeling Language (UML)—Using the UML 2.0 to Develop an Object-Oriented Design of an ATM

The Unified Modeling Language™ (UML™) has become the preferred graphical modeling language for designing object-oriented systems. All the UML diagrams in the book comply with the UML 2.0 specification. We use UML class diagrams to visually represent classes and their inheritance relationships, and we use UML activity diagrams to demonstrate the flow of control in each of C#'s control statements.

This edition continues to include an optional (but highly recommended) case study on object-oriented design using the UML. The case study was reviewed by a distinguished team of OOD/UML academic and industry professionals, including leaders in the field from Rational (the creators of the UML and now a division of IBM) and the Object Management Group (responsible for maintaining and evolving the UML). In the case study, we design and fully implement the software for a simple automated teller machine (ATM).

The Software Engineering Case Study sections at the ends of Chapters 1, 3–8, 10 and 12 present a carefully paced introduction to object-oriented design using the UML. We introduce a concise, simplified subset of the UML 2.0, then guide you through a first design experience intended for the novice object-oriented designer/programmer. The case study is not an exercise; rather, it is an end-to-end learning experience that concludes with a detailed walkthrough of the complete C# code.

The Software Engineering Case Study sections help you develop an object-oriented design to complement the object-oriented programming concepts you begin learning in Chapter 1 and implementing in Chapter 4. In the first of these sections at the end of Chapter 1, we introduce basic OOD concepts and terminology. In the optional Software Engineering Case Study sections at the ends of Chapters 3–8, we consider more substantial issues, as we undertake a challenging problem with the techniques of OOD. We analyze a typical requirements document that specifies the system to be built; we determine the classes needed to implement that system, determine the attributes the classes need to have, determine the behaviors the classes need to exhibit and specify how the classes must interact with one another to meet the system requirements. In Appendix D, we include a complete C# implementation of the object-oriented system that we design in the earlier chapters. We employ a carefully developed, incremental object-oriented design process to produce a UML model for our ATM system. From this design, we produce a substantial working C# implementation using key programming notions, including classes, objects, encapsulation, visibility, composition, inheritance and polymorphism.

Object-Oriented Programming

Object-oriented programming is today's most widely employed technique for developing robust, reusable software. This text offers a rich treatment of C#'s object-oriented programming features. Chapter 4 introduces how to create classes and objects. These concepts are extended in Chapter 10. Chapter 11 discusses how to create powerful new classes quickly by using inheritance to "absorb" the capabilities of existing classes. Chapter 12 familiarizes you with the crucial concepts of polymorphism, abstract classes, concrete classes and interfaces, all of which facilitate powerful manipulations among objects belonging to an inheritance hierarchy.

Visual Studio 2008 Debugger

In Appendix H, we explain how to use key debugger features, such as setting "breakpoints" and "watches" and stepping into and out of methods. Most of the material in this appendix can be covered after Chapter 4. One example uses the conditional AND (&&) operator, which is explained in Chapter 6.

Dependency Chart

Figure 1 (on the next page) illustrates the dependencies among chapters in the book. An arrow pointing into a chapter indicates that it depends on the content of the chapter from which the arrow points. Though other approaches may work for you, we recommend that you study all of a given chapter's dependencies before studying that chapter. Some of the dependencies apply only to sections of chapters, so we advise readers to browse the material before designing a course of study. We've commented on some additional dependencies in the diagram's footnotes.

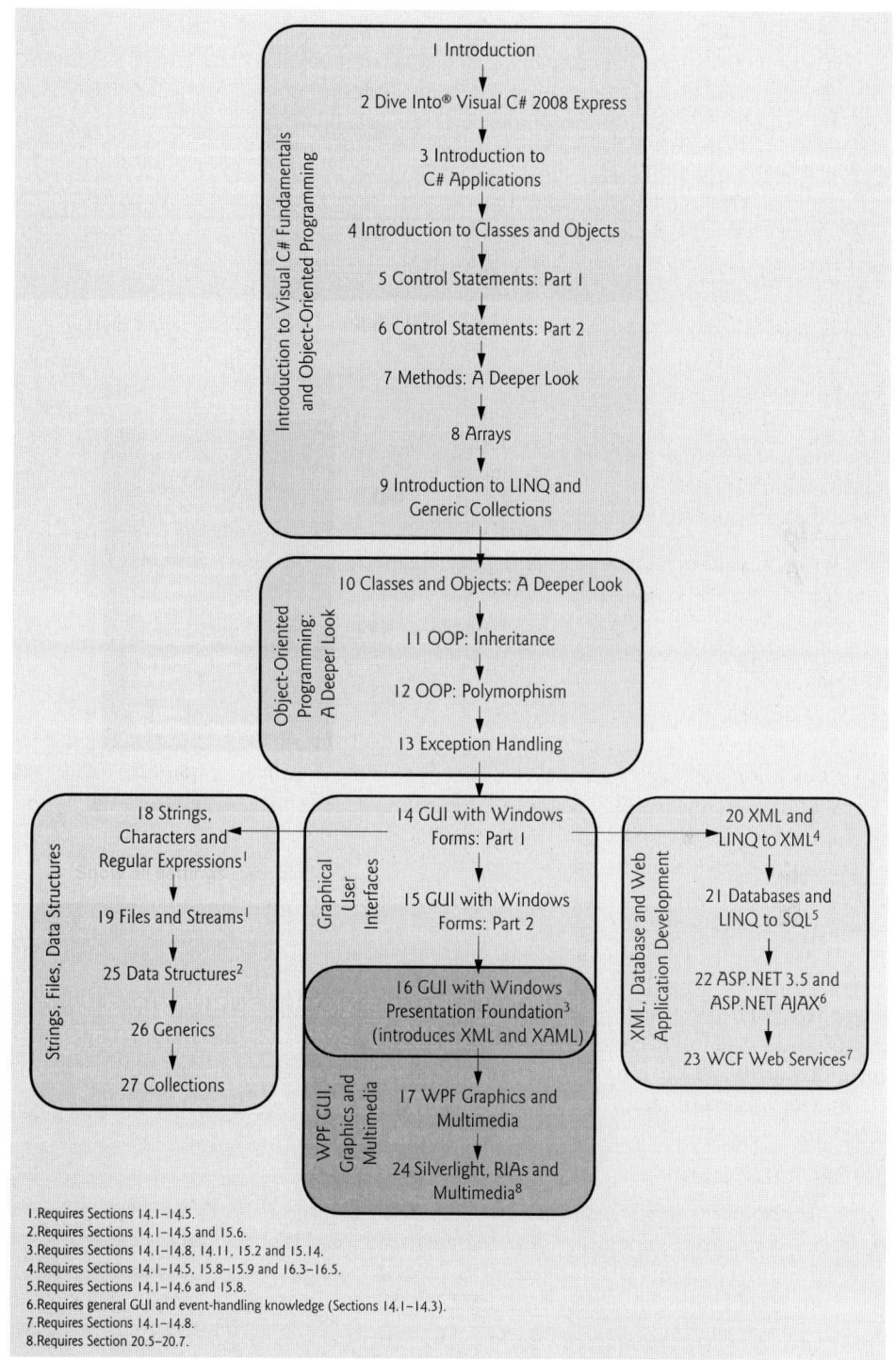

Fig. I | *C# 2008 for Programmers, 3/e* chapter dependency chart.

Teaching Approach

C# 2008 for Programmers, 3/e, contains a rich collection of examples. The book concentrates on the principles of good software engineering and stresses program clarity. We teach by example. We are educators who teach leading-edge topics in industry classrooms worldwide. Dr. Harvey M. Deitel has 20 years of experience in college teaching and 19 years in industry teaching. Paul Deitel has taught 17 years in industry. The Deitels have taught courses at all levels to government, industry, military and academic clients of Deitel & Associates.

Live-Code Approach. C# 2008 for Programmers, 3/e, is loaded with "live-code" examples. By this we mean that each new concept is presented in the context of a complete working C# program, followed immediately by one or more actual executions showing the program's inputs and outputs. This style exemplifies the way we teach and write about programming; we call it the "live-code approach."

Syntax Shading. We syntax-shade all the C# code, similar to the way Visual C# 2008 Express and Visual Studio syntax-color code. This greatly improves code readability—an especially important goal, given that this book contains approximately 20,000 lines of code. Our syntax-shading conventions are as follows:

```
comments appear in italic
keywords appear in bold italic
errors and ASP.NET script delimiters appear in bold black
constants and literal values appear in bold gray
all other code appears in plain black
```

Code Highlighting. We place white rectangles around the key code segments in each program.

Programming Tips. We include programming tips to help you focus on important aspects of program development. These tips and practices represent the best we have gleaned from a combined six decades of programming and teaching experience. One of our students— a mathematics major—likens this approach to the highlighting of axioms, theorems and corollaries in mathematics books; it provides a basis on which to build good software.

Good Programming Practice

Good Programming Practices *will help you produce programs that are clearer, more understandable and more maintainable.*

Common Programming Error

Programmers tend to make certain kinds of errors frequently. Pointing out these Common Programming Errors *reduces the likelihood that you'll make the same mistakes.*

Error-Prevention Tip

These tips contain suggestions for exposing bugs and removing them from your programs; many describe aspects of C# that prevent bugs from getting into programs in the first place.

Performance Tip

Programmers like to "turbocharge" their programs. These tips highlight opportunities for making your programs run faster or minimizing the amount of memory that they occupy.

Portability Tip

We include Portability Tips *to help you write code that will run on a variety of platforms and to explain how C# achieves its high degree of portability.*

Software Engineering Observation

The Software Engineering Observations *highlight architectural and design issues that affect the construction of software systems, especially large-scale systems.*

Look-and-Feel Observation

We provide Look-and-Feel Observations *to highlight graphical-user-interface conventions. These observations help you design attractive, user-friendly graphical user interfaces that conform to industry norms.*

Using Fonts for Emphasis. We place the key terms and the index's page reference for each defining occurrence in *bold italic* text for easier reference. We emphasize on-screen components in the **bold Helvetica** font (e.g., the **File** menu) and C# program text in the Lucida font (e.g., int x = 5).

Web Access. All of the source-code examples for *C# 2008 for Programmers, 3/e* are available for download from:

www.deitel.com/books/csharpfp3/

Site registration is quick and easy. Download all the examples, then run each program as you read the corresponding text discussions. Making changes to the examples and seeing the effects of those changes is a great way to enhance your C# learning experience.

Objectives. Each chapter begins with a statement of objectives. This lets you know what to expect and gives you an opportunity, after reading the chapter, to determine if you have met the objectives.

Quotations. The learning objectives are accompanied by quotations. Some are humorous; some are philosophical; others offer interesting insights. We hope that you enjoy relating the quotations to the chapter material.

Outline. The chapter outline helps you approach the material in a top-down fashion, so you can anticipate what is to come and set an effective learning pace.

Illustrations/Figures. Abundant charts, tables, line drawings, programs and program output are included. We model the flow of control in control statements with UML activity diagrams. UML class diagrams model the fields, constructors and methods of classes. We make extensive use of six major UML diagram types in the optional OOD/UML 2 ATM case study.

Wrap-Up Section. Each chapter ends with a brief "wrap-up" section that recaps the chapter content and transitions to the next chapter.

Thousands of Index Entries. We have included a comprehensive index, which is especially useful when you use the book as a reference.

"Double Indexing" of Live-Code Examples. For every source-code program in the book, we index the figure caption both alphabetically and as a subindex item under "Examples." This makes it easier to find examples using particular features.

A Tour of the Optional Case Study on Object-Oriented Design with the UML

This section tours the book's optional case study on object-oriented design with the UML. We preview the contents of the Software Engineering Case Study sections (in Chapters 1, 3–8, 10, 12 and Appendix D). After completing this case study, you'll be thoroughly familiar with an object-oriented design and implementation for a significant C# application.

The design presented in the ATM case study was developed at Deitel & Associates, Inc., and scrutinized by a distinguished developmental review team of industry professionals and academics. We crafted this design to meet the requirements of introductory course sequences. Real ATM systems used by banks and their customers worldwide are based on more sophisticated designs that take into consideration many more issues than we have addressed here. Our primary goal was to create a simple design that would be clear to OOD and UML novices, while still demonstrating key OOD concepts and the related UML modeling techniques. We worked hard to keep the design and the code relatively small so that they would work well in the introductory course sequence.

Section 1.11—(Required) Software Engineering Case Study: Introduction to Object Technology and the UML—introduces the object-oriented design case study with the UML. The section presents basic concepts and terminology of object technology, including classes, objects, encapsulation and inheritance. We discuss the history of the UML. This is the only required section of the case study.

Section 3.9—(Optional) Software Engineering Case Study: Examining the ATM Requirements Document—discusses a *requirements document* specifying the requirements for a system that we'll design and implement the software for a simple automated teller machine (ATM). We investigate the structure and behavior of object-oriented systems in general. We discuss how the UML will facilitate the design process in subsequent Software Engineering Case Study sections by providing several additional types of diagrams to model our system. We include a list of URLs and book references on object-oriented design with the UML. We discuss the interaction between the ATM system and its user. Specifically, we investigate the scenarios that may occur between the user and the system itself—these are called *use cases*. We model these interactions, using UML *use case diagrams*.

Section 4.12—(Optional) Software Engineering Case Study: Identifying the Classes in the ATM Requirements Documents—begins to design the ATM system. We identify its classes by extracting the nouns and noun phrases from the requirements document. We arrange these classes into a UML class diagram that describes the class structure of our simulation. The diagram also describes relationships, known as *associations*, among the classes.

Section 5.12—(Optional) Software Engineering Case Study: Identifying Class Attributes in the ATM System—focuses on the attributes of the classes discussed in Section 3.9. A class contains both *attributes* (data) and *operations* (behaviors). As we see in later sections, changes in an object's attributes often affect its behavior. To determine the attributes for the classes in our case study, we extract the adjectives describing the nouns and noun phrases (which defined our classes) from the requirements document, then place the attributes in the class diagram we created in Section 4.12.

Section 6.9—(Optional) Software Engineering Case Study: Identifying Objects' States and Activities in the ATM System—discusses how an object, at any given time, occupies a specific condition called a *state*. A *state transition* occurs when the object receives a message to change state. The UML provides the *state machine diagram*, which identifies the set of possible states that an object may occupy and models that object's state transitions. An object also has an *activity*—the work it performs in its lifetime. The UML provides the *activity diagram*—a flowchart that models an object's activity. This section uses both diagram types to model behavioral aspects of our ATM system, such as how it carries out a withdrawal transaction and how it responds when the user is authenticated.

Section 7.15—(Optional) Software Engineering Case Study: Identifying Class Operations in the ATM System—identifies the operations, or services, of our classes. We extract from the requirements document the verbs and verb phrases that specify the operations for each class. We then modify the class diagram of Section 4.12 to include each operation with its associated class. At this point in the case study, we will have gathered all information possible from the requirements document. As future chapters introduce such topics as inheritance, we'll modify our classes and diagrams.

Section 8.14—(Optional) Software Engineering Case Study: Collaboration Among Objects in the ATM System—provides a "rough sketch" of the model for our ATM system. In this section, we see how it works. We investigate the behavior of the simulation by discussing *collaborations*—messages that objects send to each other to communicate. The class operations that we identified in Section 7.15 turn out to be the collaborations among the objects in our system. We determine the collaborations, then collect them into a *communication diagram*—the UML diagram for modeling collaborations. This diagram reveals which objects collaborate and when. We present a communication diagram of the collaborations among objects to perform an ATM balance inquiry. We then present the UML *sequence diagram* for modeling interactions in a system. This diagram emphasizes the chronological ordering of messages. A sequence diagram models how objects in the system interact to carry out withdrawal and deposit transactions.

Section 10.22—(Optional) Software Engineering Case Study: Starting to Program the Classes of the ATM System—takes a break from designing the behavior of our system. We begin the implementation process to emphasize the material discussed in Chapter 8. Using the UML class diagram of Section 4.12 and the attributes and operations discussed in Section 5.12 and Section 7.15, we show how to implement a class in C# from a design. We do not implement all classes—because we have not completed the design process. Working from our UML diagrams, we create code for the `Withdrawal` class.

Section 12.9—(Optional) Software Engineering Case Study: Incorporating Inheritance and Polymorphism into the ATM System—continues our discussion of object-oriented programming. We consider inheritance: classes sharing common characteristics may inherit attributes and operations from a "base" class. In this section, we investigate how our ATM system can benefit from using inheritance. We document our discoveries in a class diagram that models inheritance relationships—the UML refers to these relationships as *generalizations*. We modify the class diagram of Section 4.12 by using inheritance to group classes with similar characteristics. This section concludes the design of the model portion of our simulation.

Appendix D—ATM Case Study Code—The majority of the case study involves designing the model (i.e., the data and logic) of the ATM system. In this appendix, we fully implement that model in C#, using all the UML diagrams we created. We apply the concepts of object-oriented design with the UML and object-oriented programming in C# that you learned in the chapters. By the end of this appendix, you'll have completed the design and implementation of a real-world system and should feel confident tackling larger systems.

Appendix E—UML 2: Additional Diagram Types—overviews the UML 2 diagram types not discussed in the OOD/UML Case Study.

Software for the Book

We use Microsoft Visual Studio 2008 development tools, including the free Visual C#® 2008 Express Edition, Visual Web Developer™ 2008 Express Edition and SQL Server 2005 Express Edition. Per Microsoft's website, Microsoft Express Editions are "lightweight, easy-to-use and easy-to-learn tools for the hobbyist, novice and student developer." The Express Editions provide rich functionality and can be used to build robust .NET applications. They are appropriate for professionals who do not have access to a complete version of Visual Studio 2008.

You may use the Express Editions to compile and execute all the example programs in the book (with the exception of Chapter 24, whose software requirements are presented below in the Other Software Requirements section). You may also use the full Visual Studio product to build and run the examples. All of the features supported by the Express Editions are also available in the complete Visual Studio 2008 editions.

You can download the latest versions of the Express Edition tools from:

    www.microsoft.com/express/

When you install the software (discussed in the Before You Begin section that follows this Preface), you also should install the help documentation and SQL Server Express. Microsoft provides a dedicated forum for help using the Express Editions at:

    forums.microsoft.com/msdn/ShowForum.aspx?siteid=1&ForumID=24

As this book was sent to publication, Microsoft released SQL Server 2008 Express. The instructions we provide for using SQL Server 2005 Express with our examples also apply to the new version.

Windows Vista and Windows XP

You can use either Windows Vista or Windows XP. We used Windows Vista while developing the book. We use the Windows Vista Segoe UI font in the graphical user interfaces. This font is accessible to Windows XP users—we tell you how to get it in the Before You Begin section. Several of our reviewers tested all the programs on Windows XP and reported no problems. If any Windows XP-specific issues arise after the book is published, we'll post them at www.deitel.com/books/csharpfp3/ with appropriate instructions. Write to us at deitel@deitel.com if you encounter any problems, and we'll respond promptly.

Other Software Requirements

For Chapters 21–23, you'll need the SQL Server 2005 Express Edition or SQL Server 2008 Express Edition. Chapters 22 and 23 require Visual Web Developer 2008 Express (or a full Visual Studio 2008 edition).

We present Microsoft Silverlight in Chapter 24. At the time of this writing Silverlight 2 was in beta, and the tools for developing Silverlight applications were available only for Visual Studio 2008 (not Express Editions); tools for developing Silverlight applications with the Express Editions will be available soon. When the final tools become available, we'll post updates at www.deitel.com/books/csharpfp3/.

For updates on the software used in this book, subscribe to our free e-mail newsletter at www.deitel.com/newsletter/subscribe.html and visit the book's website at www.deitel.com/books/csharpfp3/. Also, be sure to visit our Visual C# 2008 Resource Center (www.deitel.com/VisualCSharp2008/) frequently for new Visual C# 2008 resources. We've created Resource Centers for all of the major technologies discussed in this book (www.deitel.com/resourcecenters.html)—each week we announce our latest Resource Centers in the newsletter.

Deitel® Buzz Online Free E-mail Newsletter

Each week, the *Deitel® Buzz Online* newsletter announces our latest Resource Center(s) and includes commentary on industry trends and developments, links to free articles and resources from our published books and upcoming publications, product-release schedules, errata, challenges, anecdotes, information on our corporate instructor-led training courses and more. It's also a good way for you to keep posted about issues related to *C# 2008 for Programmers, 3/e*. To subscribe, visit

> www.deitel.com/newsletter/subscribe.html

The Deitel Online Resource Centers

Our website www.deitel.com provides more than 100 Resource Centers on various topics including programming languages, software development, Web 2.0, Internet business and open-source projects—see the complete list of Resource Centers in the first few pages of this book or visit www.deitel.com/ResourceCenters.html. The Resource Centers evolve out of the research we do to support our books and business endeavors. We've found many exceptional resources online, including tutorials, documentation, software downloads, articles, blogs, podcasts, videos, code samples, books, e-books and more—most of them are free. Each week we announce our latest Resource Centers in our newsletter, the *Deitel® Buzz Online* (www.deitel.com/newsletter/subscribe.html). The following Resource Centers may be of interest to you as you study *C# 2008 for Programmers, 3/e*:

- Visual C# 2008
- ASP.NET
- ASP.NET 3.5
- ASP.NET AJAX
- Visual Studio Team System
- Code Search Engines and Code Sites
- Computer Game Programming
- Computing Jobs
- LINQ
- Popfly
- Open Source
- Programming Projects
- .NET
- .NET 3.0
- .NET 3.5
- Silverlight
- Silverlight 2.0
- SQL Server 2008
- Web Services
- Windows Communication Foundation
- Windows Presentation Foundation
- Windows Vista

Acknowledgments

It's a pleasure to acknowledge the efforts of people whose names do not appear on the cover, but whose hard work, cooperation, friendship and understanding were crucial to the book's production. Many people at Deitel & Associates, Inc., devoted long hours to this project—thanks especially to Abbey Deitel and Barbara Deitel.

We would also like to thank the participants of our Honors Internship and Co-op programs who contributed to this publication—Greg Ayer, a Computer Science major at Northeastern University; Nicholas Doiron, an Electrical and Computer Engineering major at Carnegie Mellon University; Joseph Itkis, a Mathematics major (Computer Science track) at Yeshiva University; David Keyworth, an Information Technology major at Rochester Institute of Technology; Jehhal Liu, an Electrical and Computer Engineering major at Cornell University; Matthew Pearson, a Computer Science major at Cornell University; Bruce Tu, an Information Science major at Cornell University; Scott Wehrwein, a Computer Science major at Middlebury College; and H. Shawn Xu, a Biomedical Engineering and Economics double major at Johns Hopkins University.

We are fortunate to have worked on this project with the talented and dedicated team of publishing professionals at Prentice Hall. We appreciate the extraordinary efforts of Marcia Horton, Editorial Director of Prentice Hall's Engineering and Computer Science Division, Mark Taub, Editor-in-Chief of Prentice Hall Professional, and John Fuller, Managing Editor of Prentice Hall Professional. Carole Snyder, Lisa Bailey and Dolores Mars did a remarkable job recruiting the book's large review team and managing the review process. Sandra Schroeder did a wonderful job designing the book's cover. Scott Disanno, Robert Engelhardt and Marta Samsel did a marvelous job managing the book's production.

This book was adapted from our book *Visual C# 2008 How to Program, 3/e*. We wish to acknowledge the efforts of our reviewers on that book. Adhering to a tight time schedule, they scrutinized the text and the programs, providing countless suggestions for improving the accuracy and completeness of the presentation.

C# 2008 for Programmers, 3/e, *Reviewers*

Academic Reviewers: Mingsheng Hong (Cornell University), Stan Kurkovsky, Ph.D. (Central Connecticut State University), Markus Lumpe (Swinburne University of Technology), and Gavin Osborne (Saskatchewan Institute of Applied Science and Technology). **Microsoft Reviewers:** Vinay Ahuja (Architect), Dan Crevier, Marcelo Guerra Hahn, Helena Kotas, Eric Lippert, Kyrylo Osenkov (Visual C#) and Alex Turner (Visual C# Compiler Program Manager). **Industry Reviewers:** Rizwan Ahmed a.k.a. RizwanSharp (C# MVP, Sr. Software Engineer, TEO), José Alarcón-Aguín (ASP.NET MVP, Krasis.com), Mostafa Arafa (C# MVP, Agility Logistics), Bonnie Berent (Microsoft C# MVP), Peter Bromberg (Senior Architect Merrill Lynch and C# MVP), Adam Calderon (C# MVP, InterKnowlogy), Stochio Goutsev (Independent Consultant, writer and developer and C# MVP), Octavio Hernandez (C# MVP, Plain Concepts), Ged Mead (DevCity.Net, Microsoft VB MVP—Visual Developer) and José Antonio González Seco (Parliament of Andalusia).

C# for Programmers, 2/e, *Reviewers*

Academic Reviewers: Rekha Bhowmik (California Lutheran University), Ayad Boudiab (Georgia Perimiter College), Harlan Brewer (University of Cincinnati), Sam Gill (San Francisco State University), Gavin Osborne (Saskatchewan Institute of Applied Science and Technology) and Catherine Wyman (DeVry-Phoenix). **Microsoft Reviewers:** George Bullock (Program Manager, Microsoft.com Community Team), Dharmesh Chauhan,

Shon Katzenberger, Matteo Taveggia and Matt Tavis. **Industry Reviewers:** Alex Bondarev (Investor's Bank and Trust), Peter Bromberg (Senior Architect Merrill Lynch and C# MVP), Vijay Cinnakonda (TrueCommerce, Inc.), Jay Cook (Alcon Laboratories), Jeff Cowan (Magenic, Inc.), Ken Cox (Independent Consultant, Writer and Developer and ASP.NET MVP), Stochio Goutsev (Independent Consultant, writer and developer and C# MVP), James Huddleston (Independent Consultant), Rex Jaeschke (Independent Consultant and Editor of the *C# Standard ECMA-334, 2005*, produced by committee Ecma TC39/TG2), Saurabh Nandu (AksTech Solutions Pvt. Ltd.), Simon North (Quintiq BV), Mike O'Brien (State of California Employment Development Department), José Antonio González Seco (Andalucia's Parliament), Devan Shepard (XMaLpha Technologies), Pavel Tsekov (Caesar BSC), John Varghese (UBS) and Stacey Yasenka (Software Developer at Hyland Software and C# MVP).

Well, there you have it! Visual C# 2008 is a powerful programming language that will help you write programs quickly and effectively. It scales nicely into the realm of enterprise-systems development to help organizations build their business-critical and mission-critical information systems. As you read the book, we would sincerely appreciate your comments, criticisms, corrections and suggestions for improvement. Please address all correspondence to:

deitel@deitel.com

We'll respond promptly, and we'll post corrections and clarifications on the book's website:

www.deitel.com/books/csharpfp3/

We hope you enjoy reading *C# 2008 for Programmers, 3/e,* as much as we enjoyed writing it!

Paul J. Deitel
Dr. Harvey M. Deitel

About the Authors

Paul J. Deitel, CEO and Chief Technical Officer of Deitel & Associates, Inc., has 21 years of experience in the computer field. Paul is a graduate of MIT's Sloan School of Management, where he studied Information Technology. Through Deitel & Associates, Inc., he has delivered C#, Visual Basic, C++, C and Java courses to industry clients, including Cisco, IBM, Sun Microsystems, Dell, Lucent Technologies, Fidelity, NASA at the Kennedy Space Center, White Sands Missile Range, the National Severe Storm Laboratory, Rogue Wave Software, Boeing, Stratus, Hyperion Software, Adra Systems, Entergy, CableData Systems, Nortel Networks, Puma, iRobot, Invensys and many more. He holds the Sun Certified Java Programmer and Java Developer certifications and has been designated by Sun Microsystems as a Java Champion. He has lectured on Java and C++ for the Boston Chapter of the Association for Computing Machinery. He and his father, Dr. Harvey M. Deitel, are the world's best-selling programming-language textbook authors.

Dr. Harvey M. Deitel, Chairman and Chief Strategy Officer of Deitel & Associates, Inc., has 47 years of experience in the computer field. Dr. Deitel earned B.S. and M.S. degrees from MIT and a Ph.D. from Boston University. He has extensive college teaching experience, including earning tenure and serving as the Chairman of the Computer Science Department at Boston College before founding Deitel & Associates, Inc., with his son, Paul J. Deitel. Harvey and Paul are the co-authors of dozens of books and multimedia packages and they are writing many more. The Deitels' texts have earned international recognition with translations published in Japanese, German, Russian, Spanish, Traditional Chinese, Simplified Chinese, Korean, French, Polish, Italian, Portuguese, Greek, Urdu and Turkish. Dr. Deitel has delivered hundreds of professional seminars to major corporations, academic institutions, government organizations and the military.

About Deitel & Associates, Inc.

Deitel & Associates, Inc., is an internationally recognized corporate training and authoring organization specializing in computer programming languages, Internet and web software technology, object-technology education and Internet business development through its Web 2.0 Internet Business Initiative. The company provides instructor-led courses on major programming languages and platforms, such as Visual C#, Visual Basic, Visual C++, C++, Java, C, XML, object technology, Internet and web programming, and a growing list of additional programming and software-development related courses. The founders of Deitel & Associates, Inc., are Paul J. Deitel and Dr. Harvey M. Deitel. The company's clients include many of the world's largest companies, government agencies, branches of the military, and academic institutions. Through its 32-year publishing partnership with Prentice Hall, Deitel & Associates, Inc., publishes leading-edge programming textbooks, professional books, interactive multimedia *Cyber Classrooms*, *LiveLessons* DVD-based and web-based video courses, and e-content for popular course-management systems. Deitel & Associates, Inc., and the authors can be reached via e-mail at:

    deitel@deitel.com

To learn more about Deitel & Associates, Inc., its publications and its worldwide *Dive Into® Series* Corporate Training curriculum, see the last few pages of this book or visit:

    www.deitel.com

and subscribe to the free *Deitel® Buzz Online* e-mail newsletter at:

    www.deitel.com/newsletter/subscribe.html

Individuals wishing to purchase Deitel books, *LiveLessons* DVD and web-based training courses can do so through:

    www.deitel.com

Bulk orders by corporations, the government, the military and academic institutions should be placed directly with Prentice Hall. For more information, visit

    www.prenhall.com/mischtm/support.html#order

Before You Begin

This section contains information you should review before using this book and instructions to ensure that your computer is set up properly for use with this book. We'll post updates to this Before You Begin section (if any) on the book's website:

www.deitel.com/books/csharpfp3/

Font and Naming Conventions

We use fonts to distinguish between features, such as menu names, menu items, and other elements that appear in the program-development environment. Our convention is to emphasize IDE features in a sans-serif bold Helvetica font (for example, **Properties** window) and to emphasize program text in a sans-serif Lucida font (for example, bool x = true).

A Note Regarding Software for the Book

This book was developed using Visual C#® 2008 Express Edition, Visual Web Developer™ 2008 Express Edition and SQL Server 2005 Express Edition. As this book was sent to publication, Microsoft released SQL Server 2008 Express. The instructions we provide for using SQL Server 2005 Express also apply to the new version. The latest versions of the Express Edition tools can be downloaded from www.microsoft.com/express. The Express Editions are fully functional, and there is no time limit for using the software. We discuss the setup of this software shortly.

Hardware and Software Requirements for the Visual Studio 2008 Express Editions

To install and run the Visual Studio 2008 Express Editions, Microsoft recommends these minimum requirements:

- **Operating System:** Windows XP Service Pack 2 (or above), Windows Server 2003 Service Pack 1 (or above), Windows Server 2003 R2 (or above), Windows Vista or Windows Server 2008.

- **Processor:** Computer with a 1.6 GHz or faster processor (2.2 GHz or higher recommended—2.4 GHz on Vista).

- **RAM minimum:** 192 MB; Microsoft recommends 384 MB (768 MB on Vista).

- **Hard Drive:** 1.3 GB for complete install.

- **Display:** 1024 by 768 (1280 by 1024 recommended).

- To test and build the examples in Chapter 21 and some of the examples in Chapters 22–23, **you must install Microsoft's SQL Server 2005 or 2008 Express.** You can choose SQL Server 2008 Express as an installation option during the installation of each Express Edition.

- To test and build the examples in Chapters 22–23, **you must install Microsoft's Visual Web Developer 2008 Express.**

Desktop Theme Settings for Windows Vista Users

If you are using Windows Vista, we assume that your theme is set to **Windows Vista**. Follow these steps to set **Windows Vista** as your desktop theme:

1. Right click the desktop, then click **Personalize**.
2. Click the **Theme** item. Select **Windows Vista** from the **Theme:** drop-down list.
3. Click **Apply** to save the settings.

Desktop Theme Settings for Windows XP Users

If you are using Windows XP, the windows you see on the screen will look slightly different from the screen captures in the book. We assume that your theme is set to **Windows XP**. Follow these steps to set **Windows XP** as your desktop theme:

1. Right click the desktop, then click **Properties**.
2. Click the **Themes** tab. Select **Windows XP** from the **Theme:** drop-down list.
3. Click **OK** to save the settings.

Viewing File Extensions

Several screenshots in *C# 2008 for Programmers, 3/e* display file names with file-name extensions (e.g., .txt, .cs or .png). Your system's settings may need to be adjusted to display file-name extensions. Follow these steps to configure your computer:

1. In the **Start** menu, select **All Programs**, then **Accessories**, then **Windows Explorer**.
2. In Windows Vista, press *Alt* to display the menu bar, then select **Folder Options...** from **Windows Explorer**'s **Tools** menu. In Windows XP, simply select **Folder Options...** from **Windows Explorer**'s **Tools** menu.
3. In the dialog that appears, select the **View** tab.
4. In the **Advanced settings:** pane, uncheck the box to the left of the text **Hide extensions for known file types**. [*Note:* If this item is already unchecked, no action needs to be taken.]

Notes to Windows XP Users Regarding the Segoe UI Font Used in Many Applications

As part of Windows Vista, Microsoft has released a new font called Segoe UI to make graphical user interfaces (GUIs) more readable. Many of our GUI examples use this font, which is not available by default on Windows XP. You can get it by installing Windows Live Mail—a free download from get.live.com/wlmail/overview.

You must also enable ClearType on your system; otherwise, the font will not display correctly. ClearType is a technology for smoothing the edges of fonts displayed on the screen. To enable ClearType, perform the following steps:

1. Right click your desktop and select **Properties...** from the popup menu to view the **Display Properties** dialog.
2. In the dialog, click the **Appearance** tab, then click the **Effects...** button to display the **Effects** dialog.
3. In the **Effects** dialog, ensure that the **Use the following method to smooth edges of screen fonts** checkbox is checked, then select **ClearType** from the combobox below the checkbox.
4. Click **OK** to close the **Effects** dialog. Click **OK** to close the **Display Properties** dialog.

Obtaining the Code Examples

The examples for *C# 2008 for Programmers, 3/e* are available for download at

> www.deitel.com/books/csharpfp3/

If you are not already registered at our website, go to www.deitel.com and click the **Register** link below our logo in the upper-left corner of the page. Fill in your information. There is no charge to register, and we do not share your information with anyone. We send you only account-management e-mails unless you register separately for our free e-mail newsletter at www.deitel.com/newsletter/subscribe.html. After registering, you'll receive a confirmation e-mail with your verification code. You need this code to sign in at www.deitel.com for the first time.

Next, go to www.deitel.com and sign in using the **Login** link below our logo in the upper-left corner of the page. Go to www.deitel.com/books/csharpfp3/. Click the **Examples** link to download the Examples.zip file to your computer. Write down the location where you choose to save the file on your computer.

We assume the examples are located at C:\Examples on your computer. Extract the contents of Examples.zip using a tool such as WinZip (www.winzip.com) or the built-in capabilities of Windows XP and Windows Vista.

Installing the Software

Before you can run the applications in *C# 2008 for Programmers, 3/e* or build your own applications, you must install a development environment. We used Microsoft's free Visual C# 2008 Express Edition in the examples for most chapters and Visual Web Developer 2008 Express Edition for Chapters 22–23. Chapters 21–23 also require SQL Server Express Edition. Chapter 24, Silverlight, Rich Internet Applications and Multimedia, currently requires a full Visual Studio 2008 edition. We'll post information on the book's website when Silverlight support for the Express Editions becomes available. All of the Visual Studio Express Editions can be downloaded from:

> www.microsoft.com/express/

To install the Visual C# 2008 and Visual Web Developer 2008 Express Editions:

1. Go to www.microsoft.com/express/download/ to display the downloads page.

2. Click the **Download** link next to **Visual C# 2008 Express Edition**. When the download dialog appears, click **Run** to download and run the web-based installer. When the setup dialog appears, click **Next >**.

3. Carefully read the license agreement. Click the **I have read and accept the license terms** radio button to agree to the terms, then click **Next >**. [*Note:* If you do not accept the license agreement, the software will not install and you will not be able to create or execute Visual C# applications.]

4. Select the **MSDN Express Library for Visual Studio 2008, Microsoft SQL Server 2005 Express Edition (x86)** and **Microsoft Silverlight Runtime** options to install. Click **Next >**. [*Note:* Installing the MSDN documentation is not required but is highly recommended.]

5. Click **Next >**, then click **Finish >** to continue with the installation. The installer will now begin copying the files required by Visual C# 2008 Express Edition and

SQL Server 2008 Express Edition. Wait for the installation to complete before proceeding—the installation process can be quite lengthy. When the installation completes, click **Exit**.

6. On the downloads page, click the **Download** link next to **Visual Web Developer 2008 Express Edition**. When the download dialog appears, click **Run** to download and run the web-based installer. When the setup dialog appears, click **Next >**.

7. Carefully read the license agreement. Click the **I have read and accept the license terms** radio button to agree to the terms, then click **Next >**. [*Note:* If you do not accept the license agreement, the software will not install and you will not be able to create or execute web applications with Visual Web Developer.]

8. Click **Install >** to continue with the installation. The installer will now begin copying the files required by Visual Web Developer 2008 Express Edition. This portion of the install process should be much faster, since you've already installed most of the supporting software and files required by Visual Web Developer.

Miscellaneous Notes

- Some people like to change the workspace layout in the development tools. You can return the tools to their default layouts by selecting **Window > Reset Window Layout**.

- There are differences between the full Visual Studio 2008 products and the Express Edition products we use in this book, such as additional menu items. One key difference is that the **Database Explorer** we refer to in Chapters 20–22 is called the **Server Explorer** in the full Visual Studio 2008 products.

- Many of the menu items we use in the book have corresponding icons shown with each menu item in the menus. Many of the icons also appear on one of the toolbars at the top of the development environment. As you become familiar with these icons, you can use the toolbars to help speed up your development time. Similarly, many of the menu items have keyboard shortcuts (also shown with each menu item in the menus) for accessing commands quickly.

You are now ready to learn Visual C# with *C# 2008 for Programmers, 3/e*. We hope you enjoy the book!

Introduction

OBJECTIVES

In this chapter you'll learn:

- The history of the Visual C# programming language.
- Some basics of object technology.
- The history of the UML—the industry-standard object-oriented system modeling language.
- The history of the Internet and the World Wide Web.
- The motivation behind and an overview of Microsoft's .NET initiative, which involves the Internet in developing and using software systems.
- To test-drive a Visual C# 2008 application that enables you to draw on the screen.

Outline

1.1   Introduction

1.2   Microsoft's Windows® Operating System

1.3   C, C++ and Java

1.4   Visual C#

1.5   Key Software Trend: Object Technology

1.6   The Internet and the World Wide Web

1.7   Extensible Markup Language (XML)

1.8   Introduction to Microsoft .NET

1.9   The .NET Framework and the Common Language Runtime

1.10   Test-Driving a C# **Advanced Painter** Application

1.11   (Only Required Section of the Case Study) Software Engineering Case Study: Introduction to Object Technology and the UML

1.12   Wrap-Up

1.13   Web Resources

1.1 Introduction

Welcome to Visual C# 2008! We've worked hard to provide you with accurate and complete information regarding this powerful computer programming language—which, we'll frequently refer to simply as C# (pronounced "C Sharp"). C# is appropriate for programmers to use in building substantial information systems. We hope that working with *C# 2008 for Programmers, 3/e* will be an informative, challenging and entertaining learning experience for you.

We emphasize achieving program clarity through the proven techniques of object-oriented programming (OOP) and event-driven programming. Experienced developers get a rigorous explanation of C# and may improve their programming styles. Perhaps most important, the book presents hundreds of complete, working C# programs and depicts their inputs and outputs. We call this the *live-code approach*. All of the book's examples may be downloaded from www.deitel.com/books/csharpfp3/.

We hope that you'll enjoy learning with *C# 2008 for Programmers, 3/e*. You are embarking on a challenging and rewarding path. As you proceed, if you have any questions, send e-mail to

deitel@deitel.com

To keep current with C# developments at Deitel & Associates and to receive updates to this book, register for our free e-mail newsletter, the *Deitel® Buzz Online*, at

www.deitel.com/newsletter/subscribe.html

Check out our growing list of C# and related Resource Centers at

www.deitel.com/ResourceCenters.html

1.2 Microsoft's Windows® Operating System

Microsoft Corporation became the dominant software company in the 1980s and 1990s. In 1981, Microsoft released the first version of its DOS for the IBM Personal Computer

(DOS is an acronym for "Disk Operating System"). In the mid-1980s, Microsoft developed the *Windows operating system*, a graphical user interface built on top of DOS. Microsoft released Windows 3.0 in 1990; this new version featured a user-friendly interface and rich functionality. The Windows operating system became incredibly popular after the 1993 release of Windows 3.1, whose successors, Windows 95 and Windows 98, virtually cornered the desktop operating-systems market by the late 1990s. These operating systems, which borrowed from many concepts (such as icons, menus and windows) popularized by early Apple Macintosh operating systems after being initially devised at Xerox's Palo Alto Research Center (PARC), enabled users to navigate multiple applications simultaneously. Microsoft entered the corporate operating-systems market with the 1993 release of Windows NT®. Windows XP, which is based on the Windows NT operating system, was released in 2001 and combines Microsoft's corporate and consumer operating-system lines. Windows Vista, released in 2007, is Microsoft's latest operating-system offering. This book is intended for Windows XP and Windows Vista users. Windows today is by far the world's most widely used operating system.

The biggest competitor to the Windows operating system is Linux. The name Linux derives from Linus (after Linus Torvalds, who developed Linux) and UNIX (the operating system on which Linux is based). UNIX was developed at Bell Laboratories and was written in the C programming language. Linux is a free, open-source operating system, unlike Windows, which is proprietary (owned and controlled by Microsoft). The source code for Linux is freely available to users, and they can modify it to fit their needs.

Another popular operating system is Apple Computer's Mac OS X. One of its interesting features for developers is that they can run Windows, Linux and Mac OS X on the same computer (using so-called *virtualization software*). This means that Mac users can develop applications for all three platforms. Virtualization software is offered by many of today's leading software vendors.

1.3 C, C++ and Java

C
The *C* programming language was invented and implemented by Dennis Ritchie at Bell Laboratories in 1973. C first gained widespread recognition as the development language of the UNIX operating system. C is a hardware-independent language, and, with careful design, it is possible to write C programs that are portable to most computers.

C++
C++ was developed by Bjarne Stroustrup in the early 1980s at Bell Laboratories. C++ provides a number of features that "spruce up" the C language, but, more important, it provides capabilities for *object-oriented programming (OOP)*. Many of today's major operating systems are written in C or C++. At a time when the demand for new and more powerful software is soaring, the ability to build software quickly, correctly and economically remains an elusive goal. This problem can be addressed in part through the use of *objects,* or reusable software *components* that model items in the real world (we'll discuss object technology in Section 1.11). A modular, object-oriented approach to design and implementation can make software-development groups much more productive than is possible using earlier programming techniques. Furthermore, object-oriented programs are often easier to understand, correct and modify.

Java

Microprocessors are having a profound impact in intelligent consumer electronic devices. Recognizing this, Sun Microsystems in 1991 funded an internal corporate research project that resulted in the development of a C++-based language. When a group of Sun people visited a local coffee shop, the name *Java* was suggested and it stuck. As the World Wide Web exploded in popularity in 1993, Sun saw the possibility of using Java to add *dynamic content* (e.g., interactivity, animations and the like) to web pages. Sun formally announced the language in 1995. This generated immediate interest in the business community because of the commercial potential of the web. Java is now used to develop large-scale enterprise applications, to enhance the functionality of web servers (the computers that provide the content we see in our web browsers), to provide applications for consumer devices (such as cell phones, pagers and personal digital assistants) and for many other purposes. Visual C# is similar in capability to Java.

1.4 Visual C#

Advancements in programming tools and consumer electronic devices (e.g., cell phones and PDAs) created problems and new requirements. Integrating software components from various languages proved difficult, and installation problems were common because new versions of shared components were incompatible with old software. Developers also discovered they needed web-based applications that could be accessed and used via the Internet. As a result of the popularity of mobile devices, software developers realized that their clients were no longer restricted to desktop computers. Developers recognized the need for software that was accessible to anyone and available via almost any device. To address these needs, in 2000, Microsoft announced the *C#* programming language. Developed at Microsoft by a team led by Anders Hejlsberg and Scott Wiltamuth, C# was designed specifically for the .NET platform (which is discussed in Section 1.8) as a language that would enable programmers to migrate easily to .NET. It has roots in C, C++ and Java, adapting the best features of each and adding new features of its own. C# is object oriented and has access to a powerful *class library* of prebuilt components, enabling programmers to develop applications quickly—the .NET Framework Class Library is discussed in Section 1.9.

Visual C# is an event-driven, visual programming language in which programs are created using an IDE. You'll write programs that respond to timer expirations and user-initiated *events* such as mouse clicks and keystrokes. In addition to writing program statements to build portions of your C# applications, you'll also use Visual Studio to conveniently drag and drop predefined objects like buttons and textboxes into place on your screen, and label and resize them. Visual Studio will write much of the GUI code for you. With the IDE, a programmer can create, run, test and debug C# programs conveniently, thereby producing a working program in a fraction of the time it would have taken without the IDE.

Microsoft introduced its .NET (pronounced "dot-net") strategy in 2000. The *.NET platform*—the set of software components that enables .NET programs to run—allows applications to be distributed to a variety of devices (such as cell phones) as well as to desktop computers. The .NET platform offers a programming model that allows software components created in different programming languages (such as C# and Visual Basic) to communicate with one another. We discuss .NET in more detail in Section 1.8.

The original C# programming language was standardized by Ecma International (www.ecma-international.org) in December, 2002, as *Standard ECMA-334: C# Lan-*

guage Specification (located at www.ecma-international.org/publications/standards/ Ecma-334.htm). Since that time, Microsoft has proposed several language extensions that have been adopted as part of the revised Ecma C# standard. In this book, we discuss Visual C# 2008 and C# 3.0—the latest version of the language, which is included in Visual Studio 2008. This new version provides great new features that we'll discuss throughout this book. You can find a link to the Microsoft version of the C# Language Specification at msdn.microsoft.com/en-us/vcsharp/aa336809.aspx. This version provides annotations that are geared toward developers working with Visual C#.

1.5 Key Software Trend: Object Technology

As the benefits of structured programming were realized in the 1970s, improved software technology began to appear. Not until object-oriented programming became widely used in the 1980s and 1990s, however, did software developers feel they had the tools to dramatically improve the software-development process.

What are objects, and why are they special? *Object technology* is a packaging scheme for creating meaningful software units. There are date objects, time objects, invoice objects, automobile objects, people objects, audio objects, video objects, file objects and so on. In fact, almost any noun can be reasonably represented as a software object. Objects have *properties* (also called *attributes*), such as color, size and weight; and perform *actions* (also called *behaviors* or *methods*), such as moving, sleeping or drawing. *Classes* are types of related objects. For example, all cars belong to the "car" class, even though individual cars vary in make, model, color and options packages. A class specifies the general format of its objects, and the properties and actions available to an object depend on its class. An object is related to its class in much the same way as a building is related to the blueprint from which it is constructed. Contractors can build many buildings from the same blueprint; programmers can instantiate (create) many objects from the same class.

With object technology, properly designed classes can be reused on future projects. Using class libraries can greatly reduce the effort required to implement new systems. Some organizations report that the key benefit they get from object-oriented programming is not, in fact, software reusability. Rather, it is the production of software that is more understandable because it is better organized and has fewer maintenance requirements.

Object orientation allows you to focus on the "big picture." Instead of worrying about the minute details of how reusable objects are implemented, you can focus on the behaviors and interactions of objects. A road map that showed every tree, house and driveway would be difficult, if not impossible, to read. When such details are removed and only the essential information (roads) remains, the map becomes easier to understand. In the same way, an application that is divided into objects is easy to understand, modify and update because it hides much of the detail.

It is clear that object-oriented programming will be the key programming methodology for the next several decades. C# is one of the world's most widely used object-oriented languages.

1.6 The Internet and the World Wide Web

In the late 1960s, ARPA—the Advanced Research Projects Agency of the Department of Defense—rolled out plans to network the main computer systems of approximately a dozen ARPA-funded universities and research institutions. The computers were to be connected with communications lines operating at a then-stunning 56 Kbps (1 Kbps is equal to 1,024 bits per second), at a time when most people (of the few who even had networking access) were connecting over telephone lines to computers at a rate of 110 bits per second. Academic research was about to take a giant leap forward. ARPA proceeded to implement what quickly became known as the *ARPAnet*, the grandparent of today's *Internet*.

Things worked out differently from the original plan. Although the ARPAnet enabled researchers to network their computers, its main benefit proved to be the capability for quick and easy communication via what came to be known as electronic mail (e-mail). This is true even on today's Internet, with e-mail, instant messaging and file transfer allowing more than a billion people worldwide to communicate with each other.

The protocol (in other words, the set of rules) for communicating over the ARPAnet became known as the *Transmission Control Protocol (TCP)*. TCP ensured that messages, consisting of pieces called "packets," were properly routed from sender to receiver, arrived intact and were assembled in the correct order.

In parallel with the early evolution of the Internet, organizations worldwide were implementing their own networks for both intraorganization (that is, within an organization) and interorganization (that is, between organizations) communication. A huge variety of networking hardware and software appeared. One challenge was to enable these different networks to communicate with each other. ARPA accomplished this by developing the *Internet Protocol (IP)*, which created a true "network of networks," the current architecture of the Internet. The combined set of protocols is now called *TCP/IP*.

Businesses rapidly realized that by using the Internet, they could improve their operations and offer new and better services to their clients. Companies started spending large amounts of money to develop and enhance their Internet presence. This generated fierce competition among communications carriers and hardware and software suppliers to meet the increased infrastructure demand. As a result, bandwidth—the information-carrying capacity of communications lines—on the Internet has increased tremendously, while hardware costs have plummeted.

The *World Wide Web* is a collection of hardware and software associated with the Internet that allows computer users to locate and view multimedia-based documents (documents with various combinations of text, graphics, animations, audios and videos) on almost any subject. Even though the Internet was developed more than three decades ago, the introduction of the World Wide Web (WWW) was a relatively recent event. In 1989, Tim Berners-Lee of CERN (the European Organization for Nuclear Research) began to develop a technology for sharing information via "hyperlinked" text documents. He called his invention the *HyperText Markup Language (HTML)*. He also wrote communication protocols such as *HyperText Transfer Protocol (HTTP)* to form the backbone of his new hypertext information system, which he referred to as the World Wide Web.

In October 1994, Berners-Lee founded an organization, called the *World Wide Web Consortium* (*W3C*, www.w3.org), devoted to developing technologies for the World Wide Web. One of the W3C's primary goals is to make the web universally accessible to everyone regardless of disabilities, language or culture.

The Internet and the web will surely be listed among the most important creations of humankind. In the past, most computer applications ran on "stand-alone" computers (computers that were not connected to one another). Today's applications can be written with the aim of communicating among the world's computers—this is the focus of Microsoft's .NET strategy. The Internet and the web make information instantly and conveniently accessible to large numbers of people, enabling even individuals and small businesses to achieve worldwide exposure. They are profoundly changing the way we do business and conduct our personal lives.

1.7 Extensible Markup Language (XML)

As the popularity of the web exploded, HTML's limitations became apparent. HTML's lack of *extensibility* (the ability to change or add features) frustrated developers, and its ambiguous definition allowed erroneous HTML to proliferate. The need for a standardized, fully extensible and structurally strict language was apparent. As a result, XML was developed by the W3C.

Data independence, the separation of content from its presentation, is the essential characteristic of XML. Because XML documents describe data, any application conceivably can process them. Software developers are integrating XML into their applications to improve web functionality and interoperability.

XML is not limited to web applications. For example, it is increasingly being employed in databases—the structure of an XML document enables it to be integrated easily with database applications. As applications become more web enabled, it is likely that XML will become the universal technology for data representation. All applications employing XML will be able to communicate with one another, provided that they can understand their respective XML markup schemes, or *vocabularies*.

The *Simple Object Access Protocol* (*SOAP*) is a technology for the transmission of objects (marked up as XML) over the Internet. Microsoft's .NET technologies (discussed in the next two sections) use XML and SOAP to mark up and transfer data over the Internet. XML and SOAP are at the core of .NET—they allow software components to interoperate (i.e., communicate easily with one another). Since SOAP's foundations are in XML and HTTP (HyperText Transfer Protocol—the key communication protocol of the web), it is supported on most types of computer systems. We discuss XML in Chapter 20, XML and LINQ to XML, and SOAP in Chapter 23, Windows Communication Foundation (WCF) Web Services. Chapter 23 also discusses the newer Representational State Transfer (REST) architecture—a way to implement web services using web standards such as HTTP. In particular, you'll learn how to transmit XML-based content using REST-based web services.

1.8 Introduction to Microsoft .NET

In June 2000, Microsoft announced its *.NET initiative* (www.microsoft.com/net), a broad new vision for using the Internet and the web in the development, engineering, distribution and use of software. Rather than forcing developers to use a single programming language, the .NET initiative lets them create .NET applications in any .NET-compatible language (such as C#, Visual C++, Visual Basic and others). Part of the initiative includes Microsoft's *ASP.NET* technology, which allows you to create web applications. You'll use ASP.NET 3.5 (the current version) to build the web-based secure-books database application later in the book.

The .NET strategy extends the idea of software reuse to the Internet by allowing programmers to concentrate on their specialties without having to implement every component of every application. Visual programming (which you'll learn throughout this book) has become popular because it enables programmers to create Windows and web applications easily, using such prepackaged controls as buttons, textboxes and scrollbars.

The Microsoft *.NET Framework* is at the heart of the .NET strategy. This framework executes applications and web services, contains a class library (called the *.NET Framework Class Library*) and provides many other programming capabilities that you'll use to build C# applications. Steve Ballmer, Microsoft's CEO, has stated that Microsoft is "betting the company" on .NET. Such a dramatic commitment surely indicates a bright future for C# programmers.

1.9 The .NET Framework and the Common Language Runtime

The *Common Language Runtime (CLR)* is the central part of the .NET Framework—it executes .NET programs. Programs are compiled into machine-specific instructions in two steps. First, the program is compiled into *Microsoft Intermediate Language* (*MSIL*), which defines instructions for the CLR. Code converted into MSIL from other languages and sources can be woven together by the CLR. The MSIL for an application's components is placed into the application's executable file. When the application executes, another compiler (known as the *just-in-time compiler* or *JIT compiler*) in the CLR translates the MSIL in the executable file into machine-language code (for a particular platform), then the machine-language code executes on that platform.

The .NET Framework is needed to run a .NET program and consists mainly of the Common Language Runtime (CLR) and the Framework Class Library. If the .NET Framework exists (and is installed) for a platform, that platform can run any .NET program. The ability of a program to run (without modification) across multiple platforms is known as *platform independence*. Code written once can be used on another type of computer without modification, saving time and money. In addition, software can target a wider audience—previously, companies had to decide whether converting their programs to different platforms (sometimes called *porting*) was worth the cost. With .NET, porting programs is no longer an issue (at least once .NET itself has been made available on the platforms).

The .NET Framework also provides a high level of *language interoperability*. Programs written in different languages (e.g., C# and Visual Basic) are all compiled into MSIL—the different parts can be combined to create a single unified program. MSIL allows the .NET Framework to be *language independent*, because .NET programs are not tied to a particular programming language. Any language that can be compiled into MSIL is called a .NET-aware language.

The .NET Framework Class Library can be used by any .NET language. The library contains a variety of reusable components, saving programmers the trouble of creating new components. This book explains how to develop .NET software with C#.

The details of the .NET Framework are found in the *Common Language Infrastructure* (*CLI*), which contains information about the storage of data types (i.e., data that has predefined characteristics such as a date, percentage or currency amount), objects and so

on. The CLI has been standardized by Ecma International, making it easier to create the
.NET Framework for other platforms. This is like publishing the blueprints of the framework—anyone can build it by following the specifications. The specification is available
from www.ecma-international.org/publications/standards/Ecma-335.htm.

1.10 Test-Driving a C# **Advanced Painter** Application

In this section, you'll "test-drive" a C# application that enables you to draw on the screen
using the mouse. You'll run and interact with the working application. You'll build a similar application in Chapter 16, GUI with Windows Presentation Foundation.

The **Advanced Painter** application allows you to draw with different brush sizes and
colors. The elements and functionality you see in this application are typical of what you'll
learn to program in this book. We use fonts to distinguish between IDE features (such as
menu names and menu items) and other elements that appear in the IDE. Our convention
is to emphasize IDE features (such as the **File** menu) in a bold **sans-serif Helvetica** font and
to emphasize other elements, such as file names (e.g., Form1.cs), in a sans-serif Lucida
font. The following steps show you how to test-drive the application.

1. *Checking your setup.* Confirm that you have set up your computer properly by
   reading the *Before You Begin* section located after the *Preface.*

2. *Locating the application directory.* Open a Windows Explorer window and navigate to the C:\Examples\ch01 directory (Fig. 1.1) or the directory where you
   saved the chapter's examples.

3. *Running the **Advanced Painter** application.* Now that you are in the proper directory, double click the file name AdvancedPainter.exe (Fig. 1.1) to run the application (Fig. 1.2).

   In Fig. 1.2, several graphical elements—called *controls*—are labeled. The
   controls include GroupBoxes, RadioButtons, a Panel and Buttons (these controls
   are discussed in depth later in the book). The application allows you to draw with

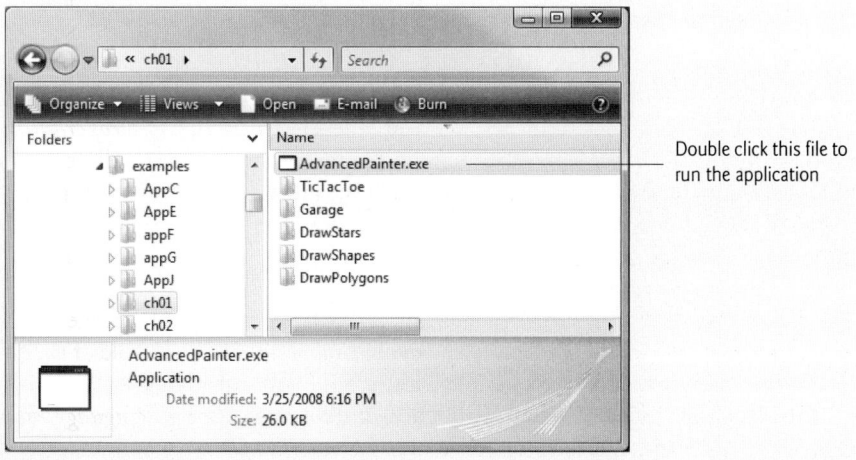

Fig. 1.1 | Contents of C:\Examples\ch01.

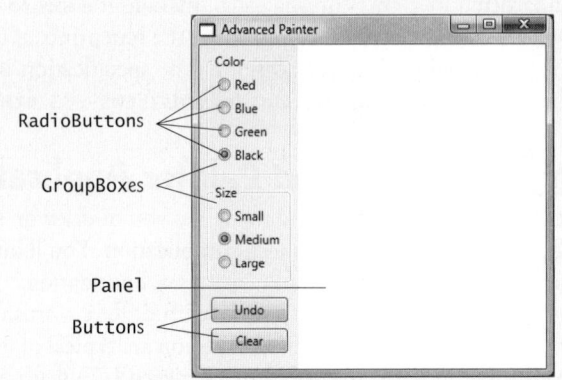

Fig. I.2 | **Advanced Painter** application.

a red, blue, green or black brush of small, medium or large size. You'll explore these options in this test-drive. You can also undo your previous operation or clear the drawing to start from scratch.

By using preexisting controls—which are objects—you can create powerful applications in Visual C# much faster than if you had to write all the code yourself. In this book, you'll learn how to use many preexisting controls, as well as how to write your own program code to customize your applications.

The brush's properties, selected in the RadioButtons labeled **Black** and **Medium**, are default settings—the initial settings you see when you first run the application. You include default settings to provide visual cues for users to choose their own settings. Now you'll choose your own settings.

4. *Changing the brush color and size.* Click the RadioButton labeled **Red** to change the brush's color and **Small** to change its size. Position the mouse over the white Panel, then press and hold down the left mouse button to draw with the brush. Draw flower petals, as shown in Fig. 1.3. Then click the RadioButton labeled **Green** to change the color of the brush again.

Fig. I.3 | Drawing with a new brush color.

5. *Changing the brush size.* Click the RadioButton labeled **Large** to change the size of the brush. Draw grass and a flower stem, as shown in Fig. 1.4.

6. *Finishing the drawing.* Click the **Blue** and **Medium** RadioButtons. Draw raindrops, as shown in Fig. 1.5, to complete the drawing.

7. *Closing the application.* Close your running application by clicking its *close box*,  (Fig. 1.5).

Fig. 1.4 | Drawing with a new brush size.

Fig. 1.5 | Finishing the drawing.

1.11 (Only Required Section of the Case Study) Software Engineering Case Study: Introduction to Object Technology and the UML

Now we begin our early introduction to object orientation, a natural way of thinking about the world and writing computer programs. Chapters 1, 3–8, 10 and 12 each end with a brief Software Engineering Case Study section, in which we present a carefully paced introduction to object orientation. Our goal here is to help you develop an object-oriented way of thinking and to introduce you to the *Unified Modeling Language*™ *(UML*™*)*—a graphical language that allows people who design object-oriented software systems to use an industry-standard notation to represent them.

In this, the only required section of the case study (because it contains foundational information for all readers), we introduce basic object-oriented concepts and terminology. The optional case study sections in Chapters 3–8, 10 and 12, and in Appendix D present an object-oriented design and implementation of the software for a simple automated teller machine (ATM) system. The Software Engineering Case Study sections at the ends of Chapters 3–8:

- analyze a typical requirements document that describes a software system (the ATM) to be built
- determine the objects required to implement that system
- determine the attributes the objects will have
- determine the behaviors these objects will exhibit
- specify how the objects will interact with one another to meet the system requirements

The Software Engineering Case Study sections at the ends of Chapters 8, 10 and 12 modify and enhance the design presented in Chapters 3–7. Appendix D contains a complete, working C# implementation of the object-oriented ATM system.

Although our case study is a scaled-down version of an industry-level problem, we nevertheless cover many common industry practices. You'll experience a solid introduction to object-oriented design with the UML. Also, you'll sharpen your code-reading skills by touring a complete, straightforward and well-documented C# implementation of the ATM.

Basic Object-Technology Concepts

We begin our introduction to object orientation with some key terminology. Everywhere you look in the real world you see *objects*—people, animals, plants, cars, planes, buildings, computers and so on. Humans think in terms of objects. Telephones, houses, traffic lights, microwave ovens and water coolers are just a few more objects we see around us every day.

We sometimes divide objects into two categories: animate and inanimate. Animate objects are "alive" in some sense—they move around and do things. Inanimate objects do not move on their own. Objects of both types, however, have some things in common. They all have *attributes* (e.g., size, shape, color and weight), and they all exhibit *behaviors* (e.g., a ball rolls, bounces, inflates and deflates; a baby cries, sleeps, crawls, walks and blinks; a car accelerates, brakes and turns; a towel absorbs water). We'll study the kinds of attributes and behaviors that software objects have.

Humans learn about objects by studying their attributes and observing their behaviors. Different objects can have similar attributes and can exhibit similar behaviors. Comparisons can be made, for example, between babies and adults and between humans and chimpanzees.

Object-oriented design (OOD) models software in terms similar to those that people use to describe real-world objects. It takes advantage of class relationships, where objects of a certain class, such as a class of vehicles, have the same characteristics—cars, trucks, little red wagons and roller skates have much in common. OOD takes advantage of *inheritance* relationships, where new classes of objects are derived by absorbing characteristics of existing classes and adding unique characteristics of their own. An object of class "convertible" certainly has the characteristics of the more general class "automobile," but more specifically, the roof goes up and down.

Object-oriented design provides a natural and intuitive way to view the software-design process—namely, modeling objects by their attributes, behaviors and interrelationships, just as we describe real-world objects. OOD also models communication between objects. Just as people send *messages* to one another (e.g., a sergeant commands a soldier to stand at attention), objects also communicate via messages. A bank-account object may receive a message to decrease its balance by a certain amount because the customer has withdrawn that amount of money.

OOD *encapsulates* (i.e., wraps) attributes and *operations* (behaviors) into objects—an object's attributes and operations are intimately tied together. Objects have the property of *information hiding*. This means that objects may know how to communicate with one another across well-defined *interfaces*, but normally they are not allowed to know how other objects are implemented—implementation details are hidden within the objects themselves. You can drive a car effectively, for instance, without knowing the details of how engines, transmissions, brakes and exhaust systems work internally—as long as you know how to use the accelerator pedal, the brake pedal, the steering wheel and so on. Information hiding, as you'll see, is crucial to good software engineering.

Languages like C# are *object oriented*. Programming in such a language is called *object-oriented programming (OOP)*, and it allows computer programmers to conveniently implement an object-oriented design as a working software system. Languages like C, on the other hand, are *procedural*, so programming tends to be *action oriented*. In C, the unit of programming is the *function*. In C#, the unit of programming is the *class* from which objects are eventually *instantiated* (an OOP term for "created"). C# classes contain *methods* (C#'s equivalent of C's functions) that implement operations, and data that implements attributes. Message passing between objects is implemented through method calls.

Classes, Fields and Methods

C# programmers concentrate on creating their own *user-defined types* called *classes*. Each class contains data as well as the set of methods that manipulate that data and provide services to *clients* (i.e., other classes that use the class). The data components of a class are called attributes or *fields*. For example, a bank-account class might include an account number and a balance. The operation components of a class are called *methods*. For example, a bank-account class might include methods to make a deposit (increase the balance), make a withdrawal (decrease the balance) and inquire what the current balance is. Programmers use built-in types and user-defined types as the "building blocks" for constructing new user-defined types (classes). The *nouns in a system specification* help the C# programmer determine the set of classes from which objects are created that work together to implement the system.

Classes are to objects as blueprints are to houses—a class is a "plan" for building objects of the class. Just as we can build many houses from one blueprint, we can instantiate (create) many objects from one class. You cannot cook meals in the kitchen of a blueprint, but you can cook meals in the kitchen of a house. You cannot sleep in the bedroom of a blueprint, but you can sleep in the bedroom of a house.

Classes can have relationships with other classes. For example, in an object-oriented design of a bank, the "bank teller" class needs to relate to other classes, such as the "customer" class, the "cash drawer" class, the "safe" class, and so on. These relationships are called *associations*.

Packaging software as classes makes it possible for future software systems to *reuse* the classes. Groups of related classes often are packaged as reusable *components*. Just as realtors often say that the three most important factors affecting the price of real estate are "location, location and location," people in the software-development community often say that the three most important factors affecting the future of software development are "reuse, reuse and reuse."

Software Engineering Observation 1.1

Reuse of existing classes when building new classes and programs saves time, money and effort. Reuse also helps programmers build more reliable and effective systems, because existing classes and components often have gone through extensive testing, debugging and performance tuning.

Indeed, with object technology, you can build much of the new software you'll need by combining existing classes, just as automobile manufacturers combine interchangeable parts. Each new class you create will have the potential to become a valuable software asset that you and other programmers can reuse to speed and enhance the quality of future software-development efforts.

Introduction to Object-Oriented Analysis and Design (OOAD)

Soon you'll be writing programs in C#. How will you create the code for your programs? Perhaps you'll simply turn on your computer and start typing. This approach may work for small programs (like the ones we present in the early chapters of the book), but what if you were asked to create a software system to control thousands of automated teller machines for a major bank? Or what if you were asked to work on a team of 1000 software developers building the next generation of the U.S. air traffic control system? For projects so large and complex, you could not simply sit down and start writing programs.

To create the best solutions, you should follow a detailed process for *analyzing* your project's *requirements* (i.e., determining *what* your system is supposed to do) and developing a *design* that satisfies them (i.e., deciding *how* your system should do it). Ideally, you would go through this process and carefully review the design (and have your design reviewed by other software professionals) before writing any code. If this process involves analyzing and designing your system from an object-oriented point of view, it is called *object-oriented analysis and design* (*OOAD*). Proper analysis and design help avoid an ill-planned system-development approach that has to be abandoned partway through its implementation, possibly wasting considerable time, money and effort.

OOAD is the generic term for analyzing a problem and developing an approach for solving it. Small problems, such as the ones discussed in the first few chapters of this book, do not require an exhaustive OOAD process. As problems and the groups of people solving them increase in size, OOAD quickly becomes appropriate. Ideally, a group should agree on a strictly defined process for solving its problem and a uniform way of communicating the results of that process to one another. Although many different

OOAD processes exist, a single graphical language for communicating the results of *any* OOAD process has come into wide use. This language, known as the Unified Modeling Language (UML), was developed in the mid-1990s under the initial direction of three software methodologists: Grady Booch, James Rumbaugh and Ivar Jacobson.

History of the UML

In the 1980s, many organizations began using OOP to build their applications, and a need developed for a standard object-oriented analysis and design (OOAD) process. Many methodologists—including Grady Booch, James Rumbaugh and Ivar Jacobson—individually produced and promoted separate processes to satisfy this need. Each process had its own notation, or "language" (in the form of graphical diagrams), to convey the results of analysis (i.e., determining *what* a proposed system is supposed to do) and design (i.e., determining *how* a proposed system should be implemented to do what it is supposed to do).

By the early 1990s, different organizations were using their own unique processes and notations. At the same time, these organizations also wanted to use software tools that would support their particular processes. Software vendors found it difficult to provide tools for so many processes. A standard notation and standard process were needed.

In 1994, James Rumbaugh joined Grady Booch at Rational Software Corporation (now a division of IBM), and the two began working to unify their popular processes. They soon were joined by Ivar Jacobson. In 1996, the group released early versions of the UML to the software engineering community and requested feedback. Around the same time, an organization known as the Object Management Group™ (OMG™) invited submissions for a common modeling language. The OMG (`www.omg.org`) is a nonprofit organization that promotes the standardization of object-oriented technologies by issuing guidelines and specifications, such as the UML. Several corporations—among them HP, IBM, Microsoft, Oracle and Rational Software—had already recognized the need for a common modeling language. In response to the OMG's request for proposals, these companies formed the UML Partners—the consortium that developed the UML version 1.1 and submitted it to the OMG. The OMG accepted the proposal and, in 1997, assumed responsibility for the continuing maintenance and revision of the UML. We present the current UML 2 terminology and notation throughout this book.

What Is the UML?

The *Unified Modeling Language* (*UML*) is the most widely used graphical representation scheme for modeling object-oriented systems. It has indeed unified the various popular notational schemes. Those who design systems use the language (in the form of diagrams, many of which we discuss throughout our ATM case study and other portions of the book) to model their systems.

An attractive feature of the UML is its flexibility. The UML is *extensible* (i.e., capable of being enhanced with new features) and is independent of any particular OOAD process. UML modelers are free to use various processes in designing systems, but all developers can now express their designs with one standard set of graphical notations.

The UML is a feature-rich graphical language. In our subsequent (and optional) Software Engineering Case Study sections on developing the software for an automated teller machine (ATM), we present a simple, concise subset of these features. We then use this subset to guide you through a first design experience with the UML. We sincerely hope you enjoy working through it.

Section 1.11 Self-Review Exercises

1.1   List three examples of real-world objects that we did not mention. For each object, list several attributes and behaviors.

1.2   The UML is used primarily to _____.
   a) test object-oriented systems
   b) design object-oriented systems
   c) implement object-oriented systems
   d) Both a and b

Answers to Section 1.11 Self-Review Exercises

1.1   [*Note:* Answers may vary.] a) A television's attributes include the size of the screen, the number of colors it can display, and its current channel and volume. A television turns on and off, changes channels, displays video and plays sounds. b) A coffee maker's attributes include the maximum volume of water it can hold, the time required to brew a pot of coffee and the temperature of the heating plate under the coffee pot. A coffee maker turns on and off, brews coffee and heats coffee. c) A turtle's attributes include its age, the size of its shell and its weight. A turtle crawls, retreats into its shell, emerges from its shell and eats vegetation.

1.2   b.

1.12 Wrap-Up

This chapter introduced basic object-technology concepts, including classes, objects, attributes and behaviors. We presented a brief history of Microsoft's Windows operating system. We discussed the history of the Internet and the web. We presented the history of C# programming and Microsoft's .NET initiative, which allows you to program Internet and web-based applications using C# (and other languages). You learned the steps for executing a C# application. You test-drove a sample C# application similar to the types of applications you'll learn to program in this book. You learned about the history and purpose of the UML—the industry-standard graphical language for modeling software systems. We launched our early objects and classes presentation with the first of our Software Engineering Case Study sections (and the only one which is required). The remaining (all optional) sections of the case study use object-oriented design and the UML to design the software for our simplified automated teller machine system. We present the complete C# code implementation of the ATM system in Appendix D.

   In the next chapter, you'll use the Visual Studio IDE (Integrated Development Environment) to create your first C# application, using the techniques of visual programming. You'll also learn about Visual Studio's help features.

1.13 Web Resources

The Internet and the web are extraordinary resources. This section includes links to interesting and informative websites. Reference sections like this one are included where appropriate throughout the book.

www.deitel.com/VisualCSHarp2008/

Our C# Resource Center focuses on the enormous amount of C# content available online. Search for resources, downloads, tutorials, documentation, books, e-books, journals, articles, blogs and more that will help you develop C# applications.

www.deitel.com/ResourceCenters.html

Deitel.com has a growing list of C# and related Resource Centers, including ASP.NET, ASP.NET 3.5, ASP.NET AJAX, Microsoft LINQ, Microsoft Popfly, .NET 3.0, .NET 3.5, Silverlight 2, SQL Server 2008, Visual C# 2008, Visual C++, Visual Basic 2008 and C# 3.0 Resource Center, Windows Communication Foundation, Windows Presentation Foundation, Windows Vista, XAML and many more.

msdn.microsoft.com/en-us/vcsharp/aa336809.aspx

Thia Microsoft website provides a quick tour of C#. It contains links to various reference information, including Microsoft's version of the C# Language Specification 3.0. This version of the specification is annotated with information for developers.

www.ecma-international.org/publications/standards/Ecma-334.htm

You can download the C# Language Specification in PDF format from here. This version of the specification is geared toward compiler developers.

www.deitel.com

Visit this site for code downloads, updates, corrections and additional resources for Deitel & Associates publications, including *C# 2008 for Programmers, 3/e*, errata, Frequently Asked Questions (FAQs), hot links and code downloads.

www.prenhall.com/deitel

The Deitel & Associates page on the Prentice Hall website contains information about our publications and code downloads for this book.

2

Dive Into®
Visual C# 2008
Express

Seeing is believing.
—Proverb

Form ever follows function.
—Louis Henri Sullivan

OBJECTIVES

In this chapter you'll learn:

- The basics of the Visual Studio Integrated Development Environment (IDE) that assists you in writing, running and debugging your C# programs.

- Visual Studio's help features.

- Key commands contained in the IDE's menus and toolbars.

- The purpose of the various kinds of windows in the Visual Studio 2008 IDE.

- What visual programming is and how it simplifies and speeds program development.

- To create, compile and execute a simple C# program that displays text and an image using the Visual Studio IDE and the technique of visual programming.

Intelligence ... is the faculty of making artificial objects, especially tools to make tools.
—Henri-Louis Bergson

Outline

2.1 Introduction

2.2 Overview of the Visual Studio 2008 IDE

2.3 Menu Bar and Toolbar

2.4 Navigating the Visual Studio IDE

    2.4.1 Solution Explorer

    2.4.2 Toolbox

    2.4.3 **Properties** Window

2.5 Using Help

2.6 Using Visual Programming to Create a Simple Program that Displays Text and an Image

2.7 Wrap-Up

2.8 Web Resources

2.1 Introduction

Visual Studio® 2008 is Microsoft's Integrated Development Environment (IDE) for creating, running and debugging programs (also called *applications*) written in various .NET programming languages. This chapter provides an overview of the Visual Studio 2008 IDE and shows how to create a simple Visual C# program by dragging and dropping predefined building blocks into place—a technique called *visual programming*. This chapter is specific to Visual C#—Microsoft's implementation of Ecma standard C#.

2.2 Overview of the Visual Studio 2008 IDE

There are many Visual Studio 2008 editions available. The book's examples are based on the *Microsoft Visual C# 2008 Express Edition*, which supports only the Visual C# programming language. See the Before You Begin section that follows the Preface for information on installing the software. Microsoft also offers several full versions of Visual Studio 2008, which include support for other languages in addition to Visual C#, such as Visual Basic and Visual C++. Our screen captures and discussions focus on the IDE of the Visual C# 2008 Express Edition. We assume that you have some familiarity with Windows. If you're generally familiar with Visual Studio 2008 you can skip this chapter.

We use fonts to distinguish between IDE features (such as menu names and menu items) and other elements that appear in the IDE. We emphasize IDE features in a sans-serif bold **Helvetica** font (e.g., **File** menu) and emphasize other elements, such as file names (e.g., Form1.cs) and program code in a sans-serif Lucida font.

Introduction to Microsoft Visual C# 2008 Express Edition

To start Microsoft Visual C# 2008 Express Edition, select **Start > All Programs > Microsoft Visual C# 2008 Express Edition**. Once the Express Edition begins execution, the ***Start Page*** displays (Fig. 2.1) Depending on your version of Visual Studio, your **Start Page** may look different. For programmers unfamiliar with Visual C#, the **Start Page** contains a list of links to Visual Studio 2008 IDE resources and web-based resources. From this point forward, we'll refer to the Visual Studio 2008 IDE simply as "Visual Studio" or "the IDE." For experienced developers, this page provides links to the latest Visual C# developments (such as updates and bug fixes) and to information on advanced programming topics. At

New Project button   **Start Page** tab

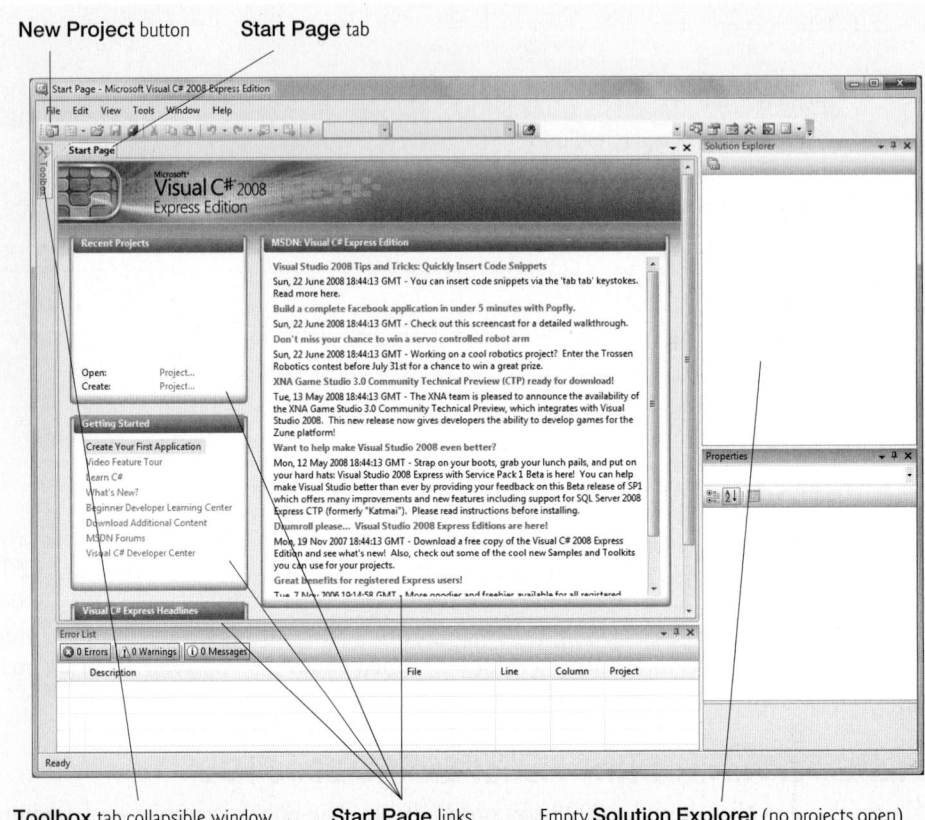

Toolbox tab collapsible window   **Start Page** links   Empty **Solution Explorer** (no projects open)

Fig. 2.1 | **Start Page** in Visual C# 2008 Express Edition.

any time, you can return to the **Start Page** by selecting **View > Other Windows > Start Page**. We use the > character to indicate the selection of a menu item from a menu. For example, we use the notation **File > Open File** to indicate that you should select the **Open File** menu item from the **File** menu.

Links on the Start Page

The **Start Page** links are organized into sections—**Recent Projects, Getting Started, Visual C# Express Headlines** and **MSDN: Visual C# Express Edition**—that contain links to helpful programming resources. Clicking any link on the **Start Page** displays relevant information associated with the specific link. We refer to *single clicking* with the left mouse button as *selecting* or *clicking*; we refer to double clicking with the left mouse button simply as *double clicking*.

The **Recent Projects** section contains information on projects you have recently created or modified. You can also open existing projects or create new ones by clicking the links in the section. The **Getting Started** section focuses on using the IDE for creating programs, learning Visual C#, connecting to the Visual C# developer community (i.e., other software developers with whom you can communicate through newsgroups and websites) and providing various development tools.

If you are connected to the Internet, the **Visual C# Express Headlines** and **MSDN: Visual C# Express Edition** sections provide links to information about programming in Visual C#, including online courses and the latest Visual C# news. To access more extensive information on Visual Studio, you can browse the *MSDN* (*Microsoft Developer Network*) online library at `msdn.microsoft.com/library` (or you can choose to install the documentation when you install Visual C# 2008 Express). The MSDN site contains articles, downloads and tutorials on technologies of interest to Visual Studio developers. You can also browse the web from the IDE using the IDE's *internal web browser*. To request a web page, type its URL into the location bar (Fig. 2.2) and press the *Enter* key—your computer, of course, must be connected to the Internet. (If the location bar is not already displayed, select **View > Other Windows > Web Browser** or type *Ctrl + Alt + R*.) The web page that you wish to view appears as another *tab*, which you can select, inside the Visual Studio IDE (Fig. 2.2).

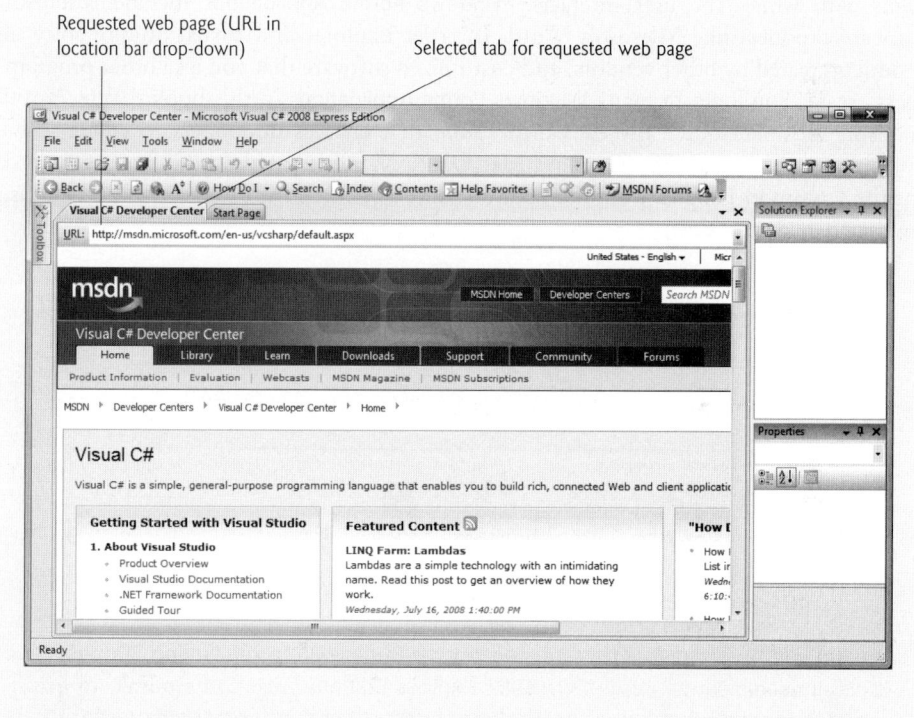

Fig. 2.2 | Displaying a web page in Visual Studio.

Customizing the IDE and Creating a New Project

To begin programming in Visual C#, you must create a new project or open an existing one. To do so, select either **File > New Project...** to create a new project or **File > Open Project...** to open an existing project. From the **Start Page**, under the **Recent Projects** section, you can also click the links **Create: Project...** or **Open: Project...** A *project* is a group of related files, such as the Visual C# code files and any images that might make up a program. Visual Studio 2008 organizes programs into *solutions*, which can contain one or more projects. Multiple-project solutions are used to create large-scale applications. Most programs we create in this book consist of a single project.

When you select **File > New Project...** or click the **Create: Project...** link on the **Start Page**, the ***New Project*** *dialog* (Fig. 2.3) displays. Dialogs are windows that facilitate user–computer communication. We discuss the detailed process of creating new projects momentarily.

Visual Studio provides several templates (Fig. 2.3). ***Templates*** are the project types users can create in Visual C#—Windows Forms applications, console applications, WPF applications and others. Users can also create their own custom application templates. In this chapter, we build a **Windows Forms Application**. We discuss the **Console Application** template in Chapter 3, Introduction to C# Applications. We use a WPF application in Chapter 16, GUI with Windows Presentation Foundation. A ***Windows Forms application*** is a program that executes within a Windows operating system (e.g., Windows XP or Windows Vista) and typically has a ***graphical user interface*** (***GUI***)—the visual part of the program with which the user interacts. **Windows Forms Application**s include Microsoft software products like Microsoft Word, Internet Explorer and Visual Studio; software products created by other vendors; and customized software that you and other programmers create. You'll create many **Windows Forms Application**s in this book. [*Note:* Novell sponsors an open-source project called ***Mono*** that enables developers to create .NET applications for Linux, Windows and Mac OS X. Mono is based on the Ecma standards for the Common Language Infrastructure (CLI). For more information on Mono, visit www.mono-project.com.]

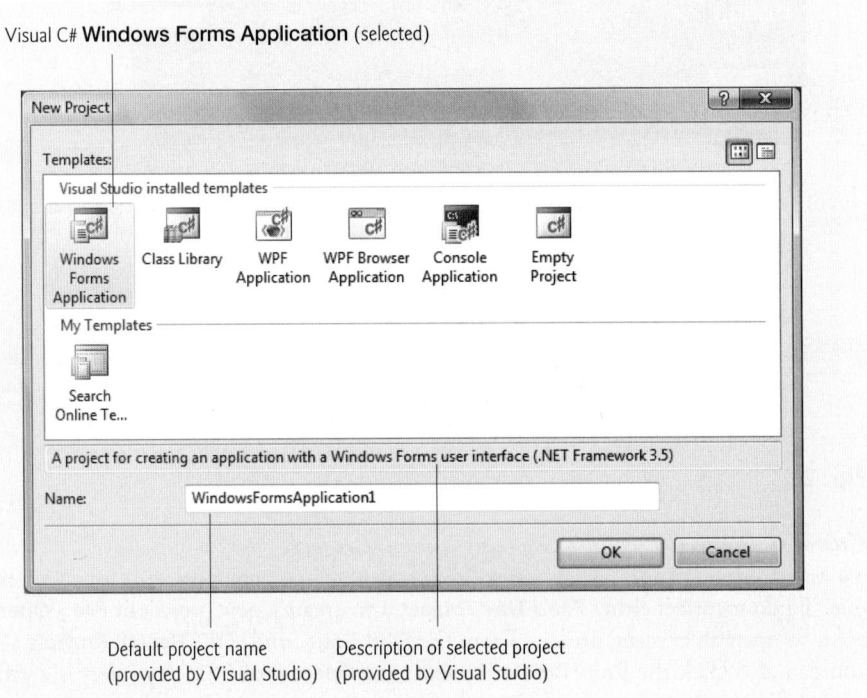

Fig. 2.3 | **New Project** dialog.

By default, Visual Studio assigns the name **WindowsFormsApplication1** to a new Windows Forms Application project and solution (Fig. 2.3). Soon you'll change the name of the project and the location where it is saved. Click **OK** to display the IDE in *Design view* (Fig. 2.4), which contains the features that enable you to create programs. The IDE's **Design** view is also known as the *Windows Form Designer*.

The gray rectangle titled **Form1** (called a *Form*) represents the main window of the Windows Forms application that you are creating. C# applications can have multiple Forms (windows)—however, most applications you'll create in this book use only one Form. You'll learn how to customize the Form by adding controls (i.e., reusable components)—in this example, you'll add a Label and a PictureBox (Fig. 2.26). A *Label* typically contains descriptive text (e.g., "Welcome to Visual C#!"), and a *PictureBox* displays an image, such as the Deitel bug mascot. Visual C# Express has many preexisting controls you can use to build and customize your programs. Many of these controls are discussed and used throughout the book. Other controls are available from third parties.

In this chapter, you'll work with preexisting controls from the .NET Framework Class Library. As you place controls on the Form, you'll be able to modify their properties (discussed in Section 2.4). To modify a control's properties, you first select the control on the Form. Figure 2.5 shows where the Form's name can be modified in the **Properties** window, and Fig. 2.6 shows a dialog in which a control's font properties can be modified.

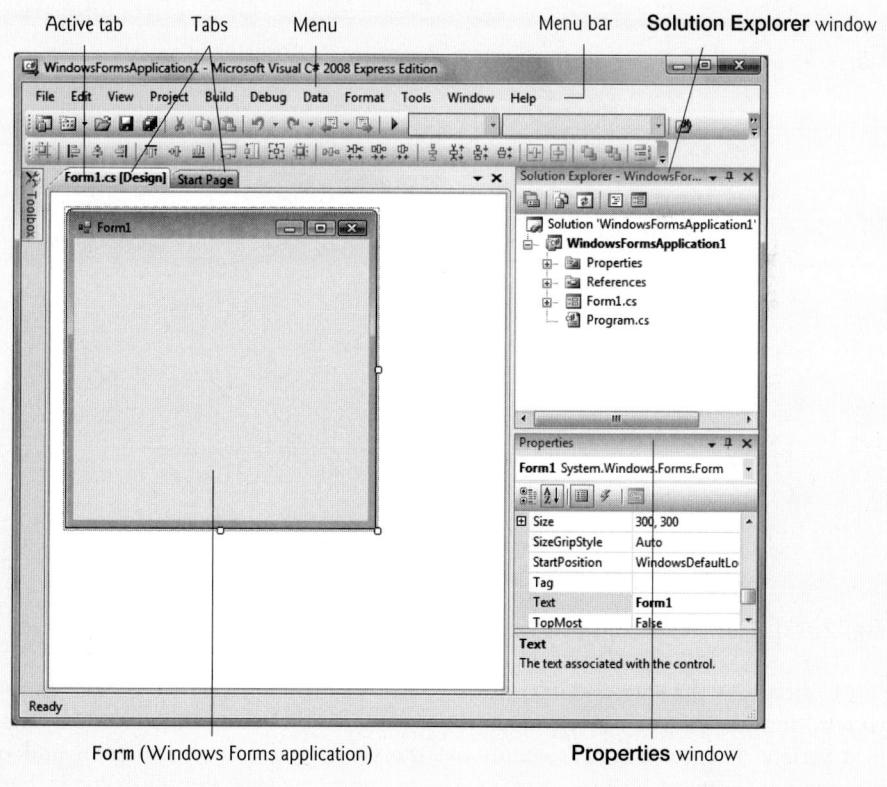

Fig. 2.4 | **Design** view of the IDE.

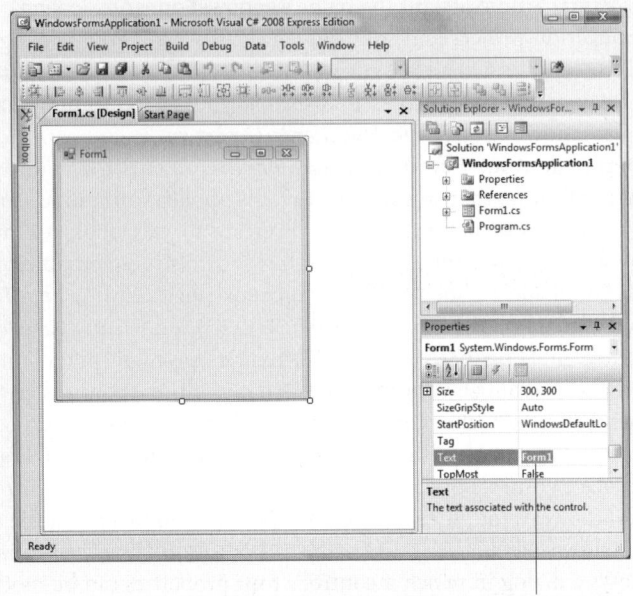

Text box (displaying the Form's name,
Form1) which can be modified

Fig. 2.5 | Textbox control for modifying a property in the Visual Studio IDE.

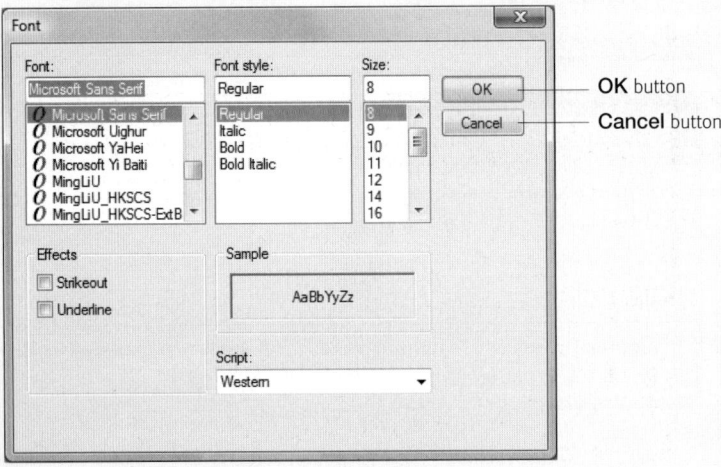

Fig. 2.6 | Dialog for modifying a control's font properties in the Visual Studio IDE.

Collectively, the Form and its controls constitute the program's GUI. Users enter data (*inputs*) into the program by typing at the keyboard, by clicking the mouse buttons and in a variety of other ways. Programs use the GUI to display instructions and other information (*outputs*) for users to read. For example, the **New Project** dialog in Fig. 2.3 presents a GUI where the user clicks the mouse button to select a template type, then inputs a project name from the keyboard (note that the figure is still showing the default project name **WindowsFormsApplication1** supplied by Visual Studio).

Each open document's name is listed on a tab—in Fig. 2.4, the open documents are **Form1.cs [Design]** and the **Start Page**. To view a document, click its tab. Tabs facilitate easy access to multiple open documents. The *active tab* (the tab of the document currently displayed in the IDE) is displayed in bold text (e.g., **Form1.cs [Design]** in Fig. 2.4) and is positioned in front of all the other tabs.

2.3 Menu Bar and Toolbar

Commands for managing the IDE and for developing, maintaining and executing programs are contained in *menus*, which are located on the *menu bar* of the IDE (Fig. 2.7). The set of menus displayed depends on what you are currently doing in the IDE and what version of Visual Studio you are using (for example, a full version or an Express edition).

Menus contain groups of related commands (also called *menu items*) that, when selected, cause the IDE to perform specific actions (e.g., open a window, save a file, print a file and execute a program). For example, new projects are created by selecting **File > New Project...**. The menus depicted in Fig. 2.7 are summarized in Fig. 2.8. In Chapter 14, Graphical User Interfaces with Windows Forms: Part 1, we discuss how to create and add your own menus and menu items to your programs.

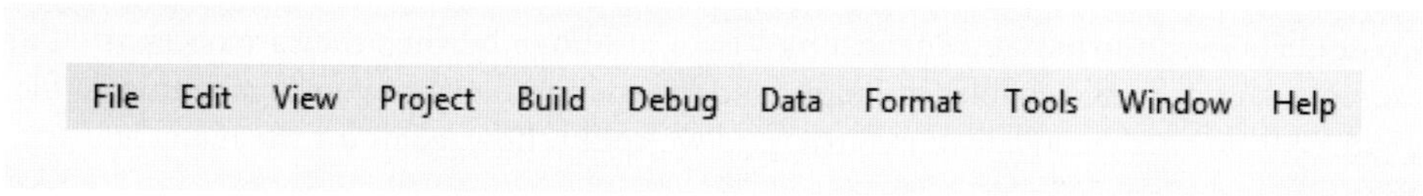

| File   Edit   View   Project   Build   Debug   Data   Format   Tools   Window   Help |

Fig. 2.7 | Visual Studio menu bar.

Menu	Description
File	Contains commands for opening, closing, adding and saving projects, as well as printing project data and exiting Visual Studio.
Edit	Contains commands for editing programs, such as cut, copy, paste, undo, redo, delete, find and select.
View	Contains commands for displaying IDE windows (e.g., **Solution Explorer, Toolbox, Properties** window) and for adding toolbars to the IDE.
Project	Contains commands for managing projects and their files.
Build	Contains commands for compiling Visual C# programs.
Debug	Contains commands for debugging and running programs.
Data	Contains commands for interacting with databases (i.e., organized collections of data stored on computers), which we discuss in Chapter 21, Databases and LINQ to SQL.

Fig. 2.8 | Summary of Visual Studio 2008 IDE menus. (Part 1 of 2.)

Menu	Description
Format	Contains commands for arranging and modifying a Form's controls. Note that the Format menu appears only when a GUI component is selected in Design view.
Tools	Contains commands for accessing additional IDE tools and options that enable customization of the IDE.
Window	Contains commands for hiding, opening, closing and displaying IDE windows.
Help	Contains commands for accessing the IDE's help features.

Fig. 2.8 | Summary of Visual Studio 2008 IDE menus. (Part 2 of 2.)

Rather than navigating the menus from the menu bar, you can access many of the more common commands from the *toolbar* (Fig. 2.9), which contains graphics, called *icons*, that graphically represent commands. By default, the standard toolbar is displayed when you run Visual Studio for the first time—it contains icons for the most commonly used commands, such as opening a file, adding an item to a project, saving and running a program. The icons that appear on the standard toolbar may vary, depending on the version of Visual Studio you are using. Some commands are initially disabled (or unavailable to use). These commands are enabled by Visual Studio only when they are necessary. For example, Visual Studio enables the command for saving a file once you begin editing a file. Figure 2.9 shows the toolbar in two parts, so we could show labels for the many icons.

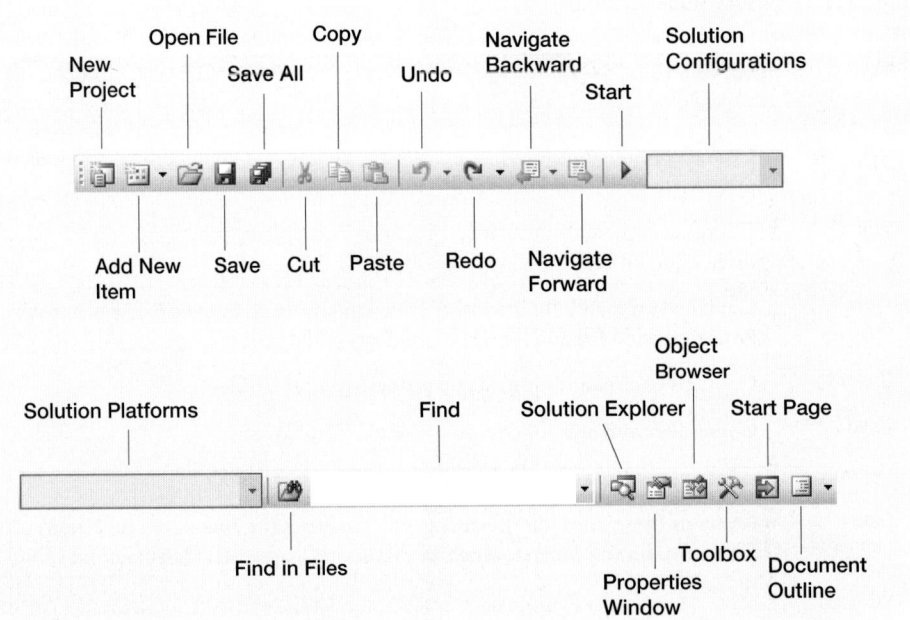

Fig. 2.9 | Standard Visual Studio toolbar.

You can customize the IDE by adding more toolbars. Select **View > Toolbars** (Fig. 2.10). Each toolbar you select is displayed with the other toolbars at the top of the Visual Studio window. To execute a command via the toolbar, click its icon. Some icons contain a down arrow that you can click to display related commands, as shown in Fig. 2.11.

It's difficult to remember what each toolbar icon represents. Positioning the mouse pointer over an icon highlights it and, after a brief pause, displays a description of the icon called a *tool tip* (Fig. 2.12). *Tool tips* help programmers become familiar with the IDE's features and serve as useful reminders for each toolbar icon's functionality. You'll learn how to create tool tips for your own applications in Section 14.9.

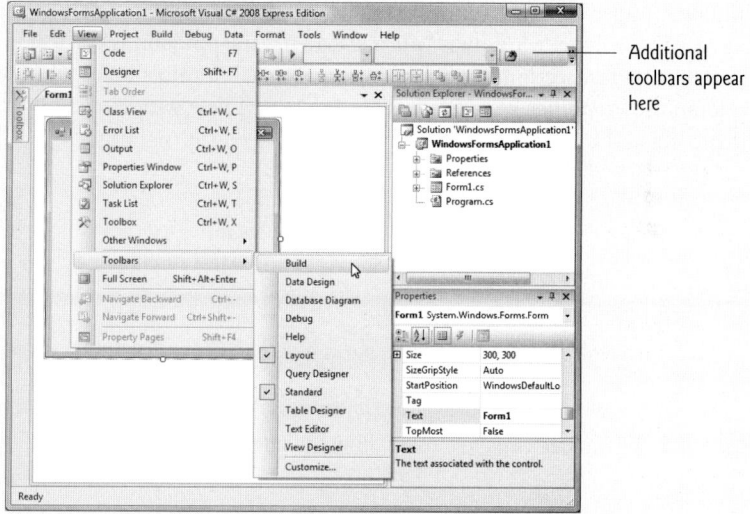

Fig. 2.10 | Adding the **Build** toolbar to the IDE.

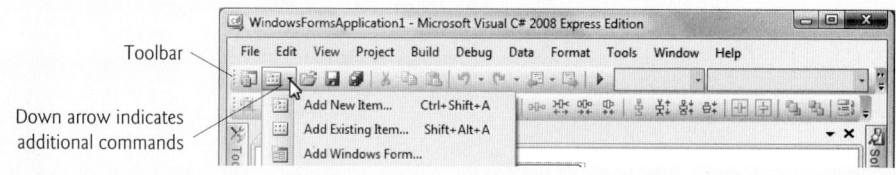

Fig. 2.11 | IDE toolbar icon showing additional commands.

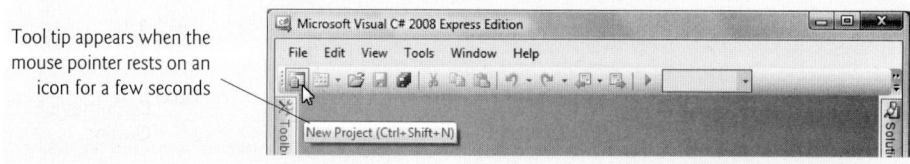

Fig. 2.12 | Tool tip demonstration.

2.4 Navigating the Visual Studio IDE

The IDE provides windows for accessing project files and customizing controls. This section introduces several windows that you'll use frequently when developing Visual C# programs. These windows can be accessed via the toolbar icons (Fig. 2.13) or by selecting the desired window's name in the **View** menu.

Visual Studio provides a space-saving feature called *auto-hide*. When auto-hide is enabled, a tab appears along either the left or right edge of the IDE window (Fig. 2.14). This tab contains one or more icons, each identifying a hidden window. Placing the mouse pointer over one of these icons displays that window (Fig. 2.15). The window is hidden again when the mouse pointer is moved outside the window's area. To "pin down" a window (i.e., to disable auto-hide and keep the window open), click the pin icon in the window's upper-right corner. When auto-hide is enabled, the pin icon is horizontal (Fig. 2.15)—when a window is "pinned down," the pin icon is vertical (Fig. 2.16).

The next few sections overview three of Visual Studio's main windows—the **Solution Explorer**, the **Properties** window and the **Toolbox**. These windows show information about the project and include tools that help you build your programs.

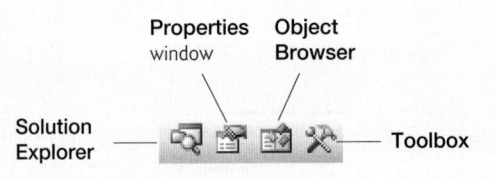

Fig. 2.13 | Toolbar icons for Visual Studio windows.

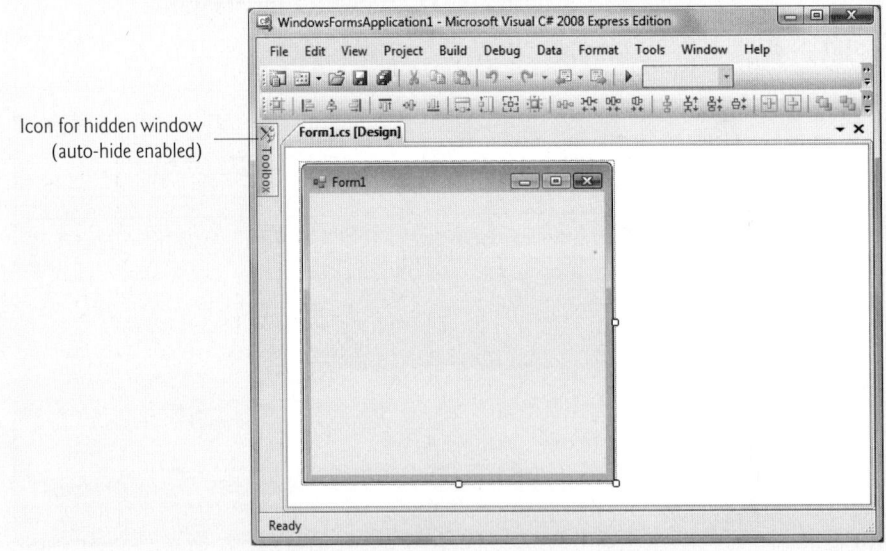

Fig. 2.14 | Auto-hide feature demonstration.

Horizontal orientation for pin icon when auto-hide is enabled

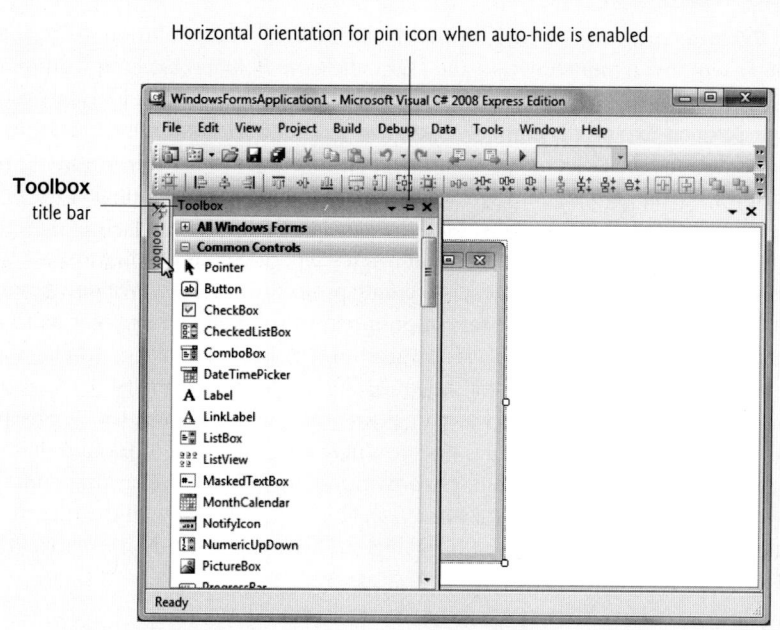

Fig. 2.15 | Displaying a hidden window when auto-hide is enabled.

Toolbox "pinned down"   Vertical orientation for pin icon when window is pinned down

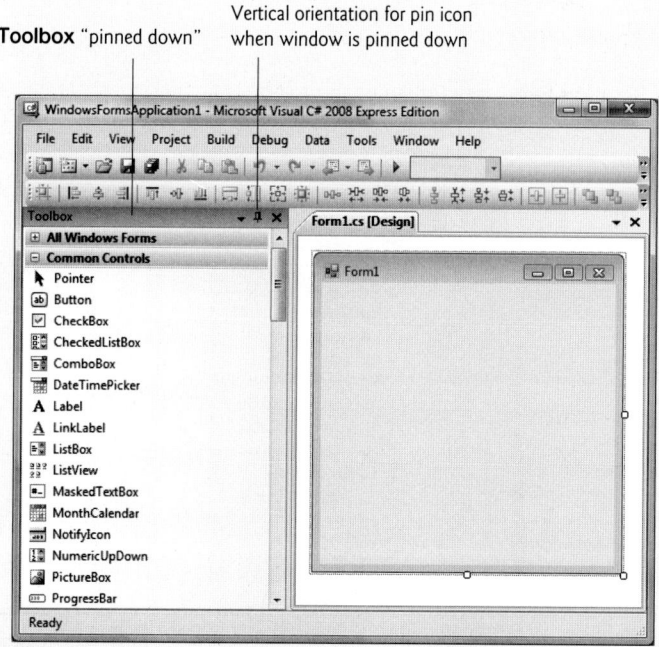

Fig. 2.16 | Disabling auto-hide ("pinning down" a window).

2.4.1 Solution Explorer

The **Solution Explorer** window (Fig. 2.17) provides access to all of the solution's files. If the Solution Explorer window is not shown in the IDE, click the **Solution Explorer** icon in the IDE (Fig. 2.13), select **View > Solution Explorer** or type *Ctrl + Alt + L*. When Visual Studio is first run, the **Solution Explorer** is empty—there are no files to display. Once you open a new or existing solution, the **Solution Explorer** displays the contents of the solution.

The solution's *startup project* runs when you select **Debug > Start Debugging** (or press *F5*). If you have multiple projects in a solution, you can specify the startup project by right-clicking the project name in the **Solution Explorer**, then selecting **Set as StartUp Project**. For a single-project solution, the startup project is the only project (in this case, **WindowsForms-Application1**), and the project name appears in bold text in the **Solution Explorer** window. Files associated with the project are displayed beneath the project name (Fig. 2.17).

The file that corresponds to the Form shown in Fig. 2.4 is named Form1.cs (selected in Fig. 2.17). Visual C# files use the .cs file-name extension, which is short for "C Sharp."

By default, the IDE displays only files that you may need to edit—other files that the IDE generates are hidden. The **Solution Explorer** window includes a toolbar that contains several icons. When clicked, the **Show All Files icon** (Fig. 2.17) displays all the files in the solution, including those generated by the IDE (Fig. 2.18). The plus and minus boxes that

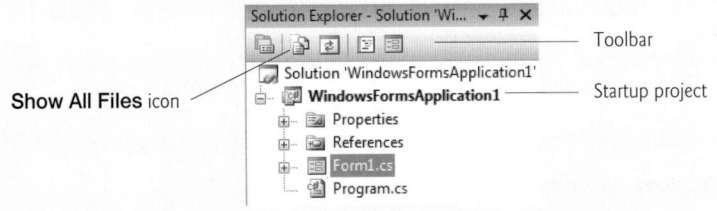

Fig. 2.17 | **Solution Explorer** with an open project.

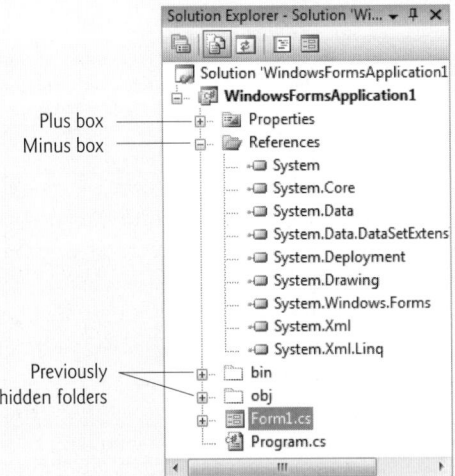

Fig. 2.18 | **Solution Explorer** showing plus boxes and minus boxes for expanding and collapsing the tree to reveal or hide project files, respectively.

appear can be clicked to expand and collapse the project tree, respectively. Click the plus box to the left of **Properties** to display items grouped under the heading to the right of the plus box (Fig. 2.19)—click the minus box to collapse the tree from its expanded state (Fig. 2.20). Other Visual Studio windows also use this plus-box/minus-box convention.

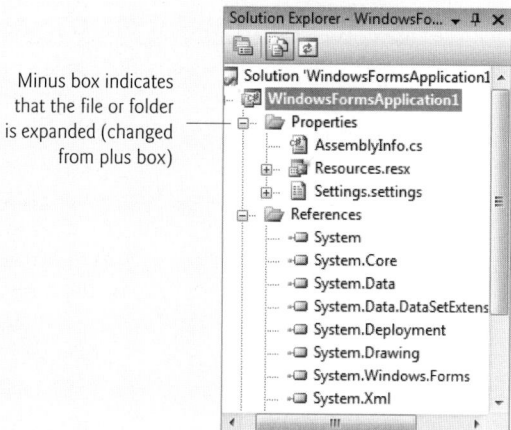

Minus box indicates that the file or folder is expanded (changed from plus box)

Fig. 2.19 | **Solution Explorer** expanding the **Properties** file after you click its plus box.

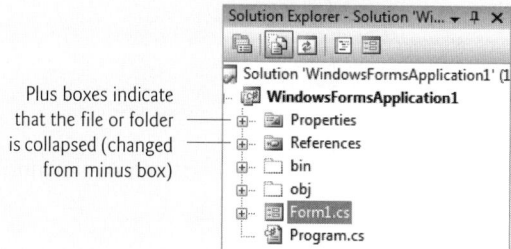

Plus boxes indicate that the file or folder is collapsed (changed from minus box)

Fig. 2.20 | **Solution Explorer** collapsing all files after you click any minus boxes.

2.4.2 Toolbox

The **Toolbox** contains icons representing controls used to customize Forms (Fig. 2.21). Using visual programming, you can "drag and drop" controls onto the Form, which is faster and simpler than building them by writing GUI code (we discuss writing this type of code in Chapter 5, Control Statements: Part 1). Just as you do not need to know how to build an engine to drive a car, you do not need to know how to build controls to use them. Reusing preexisting controls saves time and money when you develop programs. You'll use the **Toolbox** when you create your first program later in the chapter.

The **Toolbox** groups the prebuilt controls into categories—**All Windows Forms**, **Common Controls**, **Containers**, **Menus & Toolbars**, **Data**, **Components**, **Printing**, **Dialogs**, **WPF Interoperability** and **General** are listed in Fig. 2.21. Again, note the use of plus and minus boxes, which can expand or collapse a group of controls. We discuss many of the **Toolbox**'s controls and their functionality throughout the book.

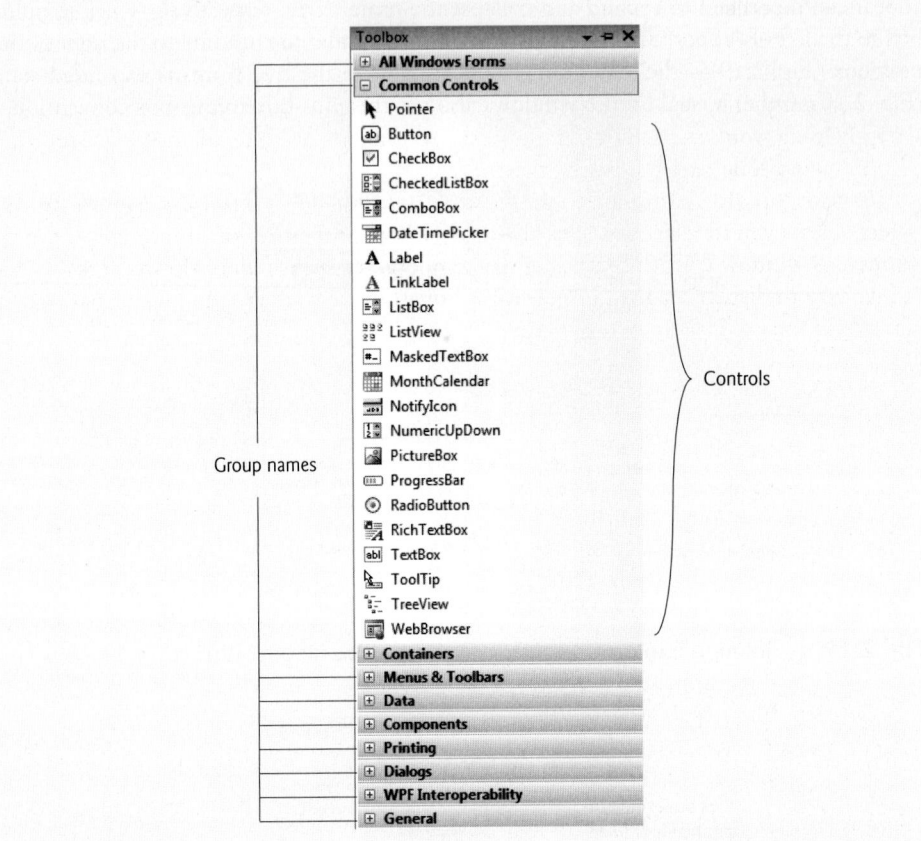

Fig. 2.21 | **Toolbox** window displaying controls for the **Common Controls** group.

2.4.3 Properties Window

To display the **Properties** window, select **View > Properties Window**, click the **Properties** window icon shown in Fig. 2.13, or press the *F4* key. The *Properties window* displays the properties for the currently selected Form (Fig. 2.22), control or file in **Design** view. *Properties* specify information about the Form or control, such as its size, color and position. Each Form or control has its own set of properties—a property's description is displayed at the bottom of the **Properties** window whenever that property is selected.

Figure 2.22 shows Form1's **Properties** window. The left column lists the Form's properties—the right column displays the current value of each property. You can sort the properties either alphabetically by clicking the ***Alphabetical icon*** or categorically by clicking the ***Categorized icon***—these icons are located at the top of the **Properties** window. The properties can be sorted alphabetically from A–Z—sorting by category groups the properties according to their use (i.e., **Appearance**, **Behavior**, **Design**, and so on). Depending on the size of the **Properties** window, some of the properties may be hidden from view on the screen. Users can scroll through the list of properties by dragging the *scrollbox* up or down inside the *scrollbar*, or by clicking the arrows at the top and bottom of the scrollbar. We show how to set individual properties later in this chapter.

The **Properties** window is crucial to visual programming—it allows you to modify a control's properties visually, without writing code. You can see which properties are available for modification and, in many cases, can learn the range of acceptable values for a given property. The **Properties** window displays a brief description of the selected property, helping you understand its purpose. A property can be set quickly using this window—no code needs to be written.

At the top of the **Properties** window is the *component selection drop-down list*, which allows you to select the Form or control whose properties you wish to display in the **Properties** window (Fig. 2.22). Using the component selection drop-down list is an alternative way to display a Form's or control's properties without selecting the actual Form or control in the GUI.

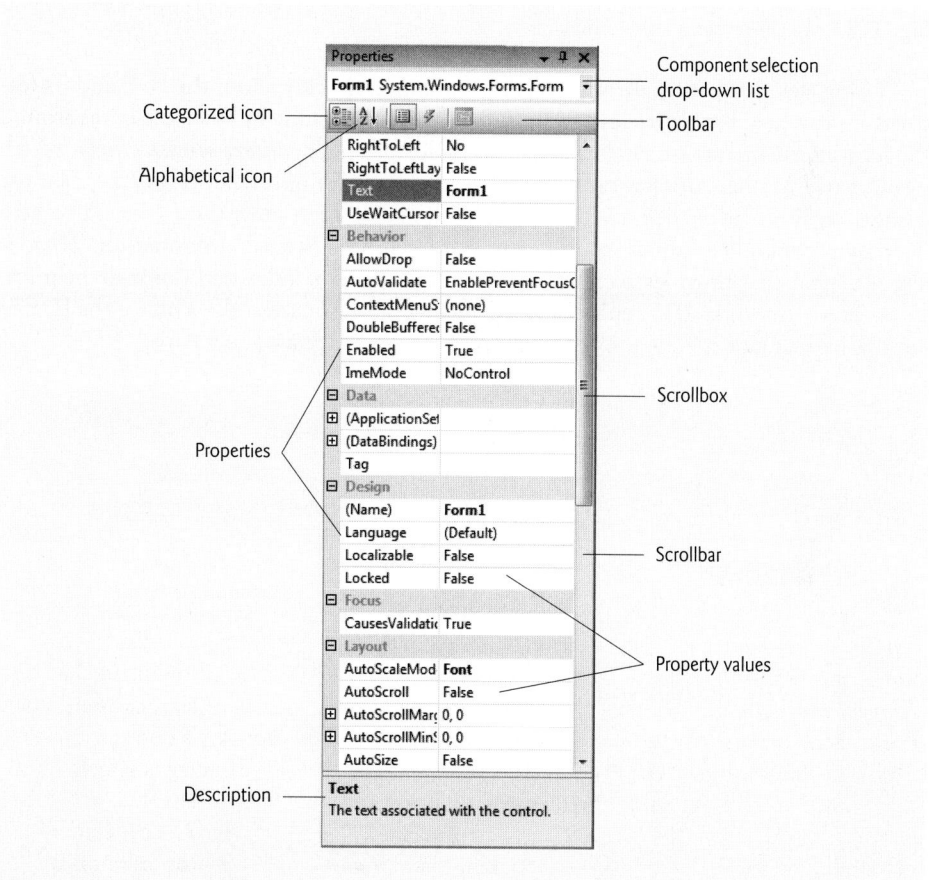

Fig. 2.22 | **Properties** window showing the description of the selected property.

2.5 Using Help

Visual Studio provides extensive help features. The ***Help menu*** commands are summarized in Fig. 2.23.

Command	Description
How Do I?	Contains links to relevant topics, including how to upgrade programs and learn more about web services, architecture and design, files and I/O, data, debugging and more.
Search	Finds help articles based on search keywords.
Index	Displays an alphabetized list of topics you can browse.
Contents	Displays a categorized table of contents in which help articles are organized by topic.

Fig. 2.23 | **Help** menu commands.

Using **Help** is an excellent way to get information quickly about the IDE and its features. It provides a list of articles pertaining to the "current content" (i.e., the items around the location of the mouse cursor). Visual C# also provides *context-sensitive help*, which displays relevant help articles rather than a generalized list of articles (Fig. 2.24). To use context-sensitive help, click an item, such as the Form, then press the *F1* key. The help window provides help topics, code samples and "Getting Started" information. There is also a toolbar that provides access to the **How Do I**, **Search**, **Index** and **Contents** help features. To return to the IDE, either close the help window or select the icon for the IDE in your Windows task bar. Figure 2.24 displays help articles related to a Form.

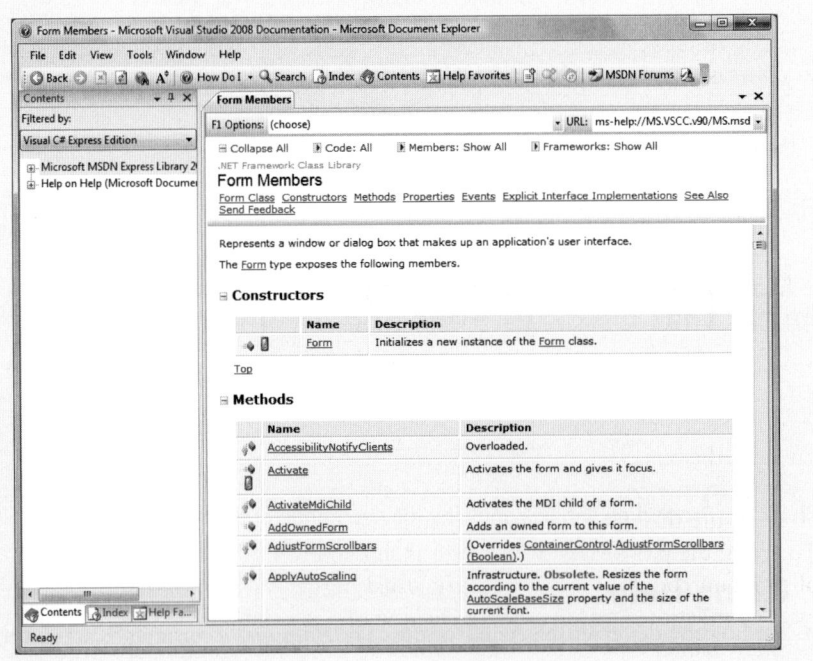

Fig. 2.24 | Using context-sensitive help to show help articles related to a Form.

The **Help** options can be set in the **Options** dialog (accessed by selecting **Tools > Options...**). To display all the settings that you can modify (including the settings for the **Help** options), make sure that the **Show all settings** checkbox in the lower-left corner of the dialog is checked (Fig. 2.25). To change whether the **Help** is displayed in the IDE window or in a separate window, select **Help** on the left, then locate the **Show Help using:** drop-down list on the right. Depending on your preference, selecting **External Help Viewer** displays a relevant help article in a separate window outside the IDE (some programmers like to view web pages separately from the project on which they are working in the IDE)—selecting **Integrated Help Viewer** displays a help article as a tabbed window inside the IDE.

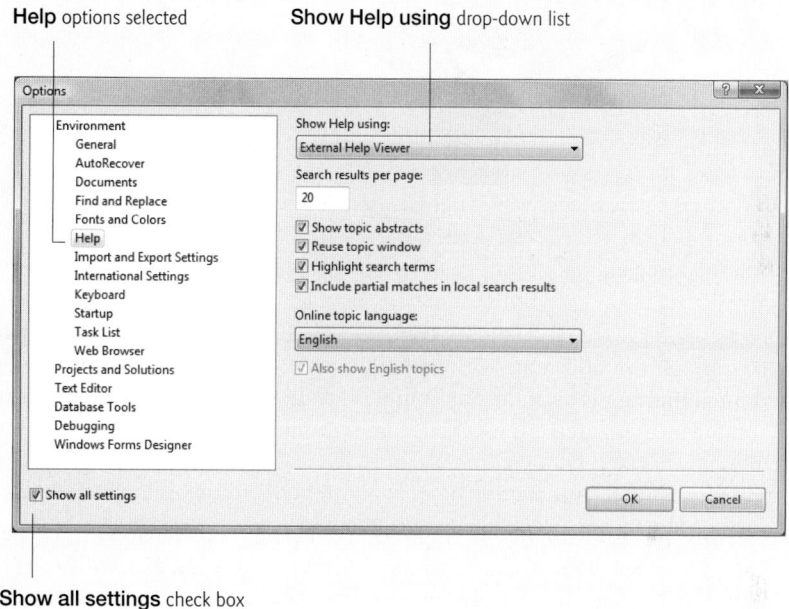

Fig. 2.25 | **Options** dialog displaying **Help** settings.

2.6 Using Visual Programming to Create a Simple Program that Displays Text and an Image

Next, we create a program that displays the text "Welcome to Visual C#!" and an image of the Deitel & Associates bug mascot. The program consists of a single Form that uses a Label and a PictureBox. Figure 2.26 shows the result of the program as it executes. The program and the bug image are available with this chapter's examples. You can download the examples from www.deitel.com/books/csharpfp3/. Please read the Before You Begin section to ensure that you install the examples correctly on your computer.

To create the program whose output is shown in Fig. 2.26, you won't write a single line of program code. Instead, you'll use visual programming techniques. Visual Studio processes your actions (such as mouse clicking, dragging and dropping) to generate program code. Chapter 3 begins our discussion of writing program code. Throughout the book, you produce increasingly substantial and powerful programs that usually include a

Fig. 2.26 | Simple program executing.

combination of code written by you and code generated by Visual Studio. The generated code can be difficult to understand, but you'll rarely need to look at it.

Visual programming is useful for building GUI-intensive programs that require a significant amount of user interaction. Visual programming cannot be used to create programs that do not have GUIs—you must write such code directly.

To create, run and terminate this first program, perform the following steps:

1. *Creating the new project.* If a project is already open, close it by selecting **File > Close Solution**. A dialog asking whether to save the current project might appear. Click **Save** to save any changes. To create a new Windows Forms application for the program, select **File > New Project...** to display the **New Project** dialog (Fig. 2.27). From the template options, select **Windows Forms Application**. Name the project **ASimpleProgram** and click **OK**. [*Note:* File names must conform to certain rules. For example, file names cannot contain symbols (e.g., ?, :, *, <, >, # and %) or Unicode® control characters (Unicode is a special character set described in Appendix G). Also, file names cannot be system reserved names, such as CON, PRN, AUX and COM1, or . and .., and cannot be longer than 256 characters in length.] We mentioned earlier in this chapter that you must set the directory in which the project is saved. In the complete Visual Studio, you do this in the **New Project** dialog. To specify the directory in Visual C# 2008 Express, select **File > Save All** to display the ***Save Project dialog*** (Fig. 2.28). To set the project location, click the **Browse...** button, which opens the ***Project Location dialog*** (Fig. 2.29). Navigate through the directories, select one in which to place the project (in our example, we use a directory named **MyProjects**) and click **Select Folder** (**OK** in Windows XP) to close the dialog. Click **Save** in the **Save Project** dialog (Fig. 2.28) to save the project and close the dialog.

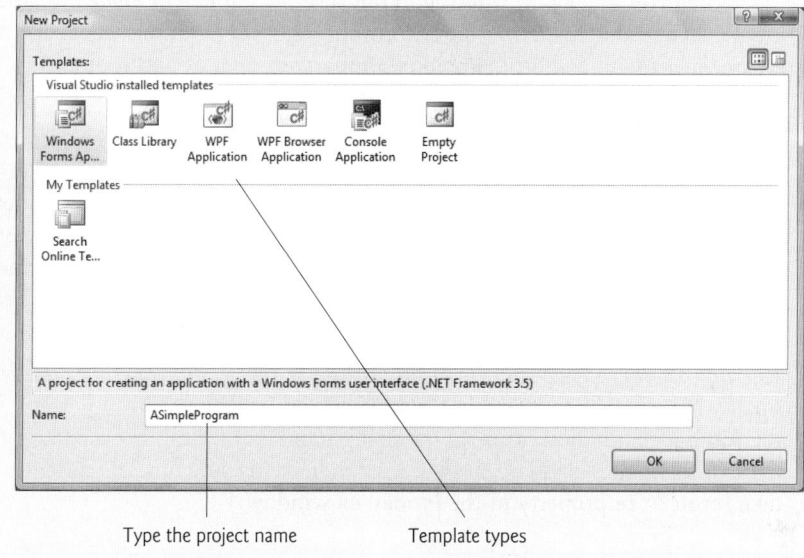

Type the project name   Template types

Fig. 2.27 | **New Project** dialog.

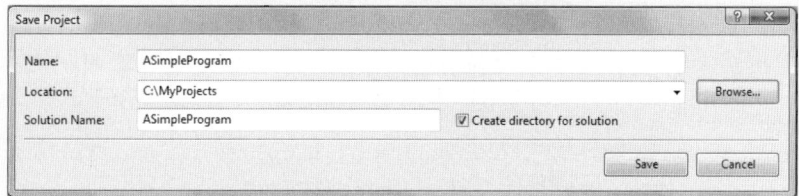

Fig. 2.28 | **Save Project** dialog.

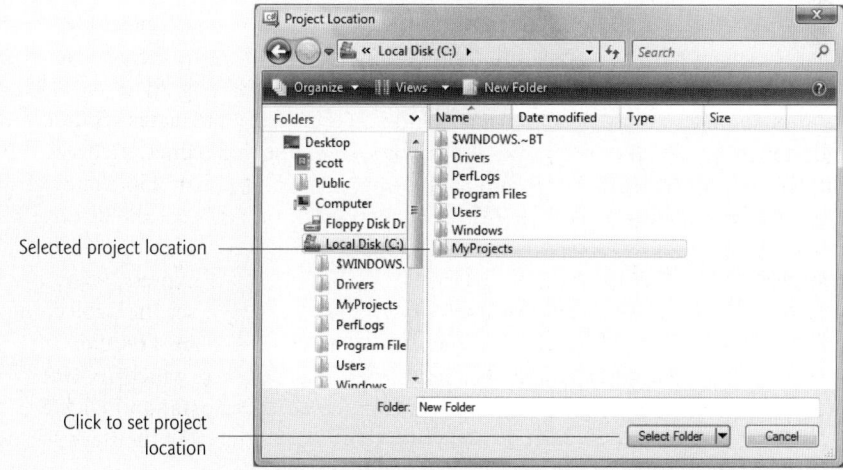

Selected project location

Click to set project
location

Fig. 2.29 | Setting the project location in the **Project Location** dialog.

When you first begin working in the IDE, it is in *design mode* (i.e., the program is being designed and is not executing) and programmers can access all the environment windows (e.g., **Toolbox**, **Properties**), menus and toolbars, as you'll see shortly.

2. *Setting the text in the Form's title bar.* The text in the Form's title bar is determined by the Form's **Text** *property* (Fig. 2.30). If the **Properties** window is not open, click the properties icon in the toolbar or select **View > Properties Window** (or press *F4*). Click anywhere in the Form to display the Form's properties in the **Properties** window. Click in the textbox to the right of the Text property box and type "A Simple Program," as in Fig. 2.30. Press the *Enter* key (*Return* key) when finished—the Form's title bar is updated immediately (Fig. 2.31).

3. *Resizing the Form.* Click and drag one of the Form's *enabled sizing handles* (the small white squares that appear around the Form, as shown in Fig. 2.31). Using the mouse, select the bottom-right sizing handle and drag it down and to the right to make the Form larger (Fig. 2.32). Alternatively, you can select the Form, then set its Size property in the **Properties** window.

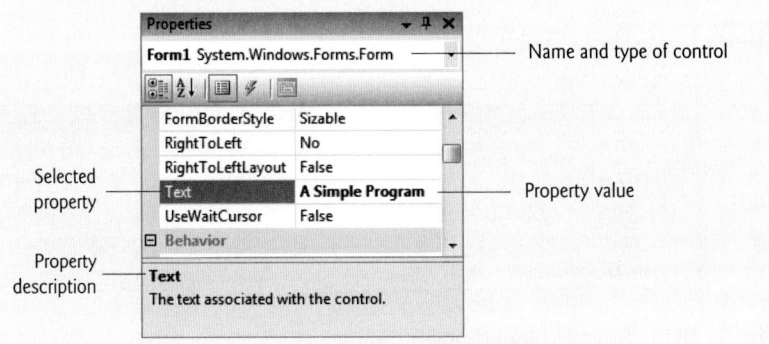

Fig. 2.30 | Setting the Form's Text property in the **Properties** window.

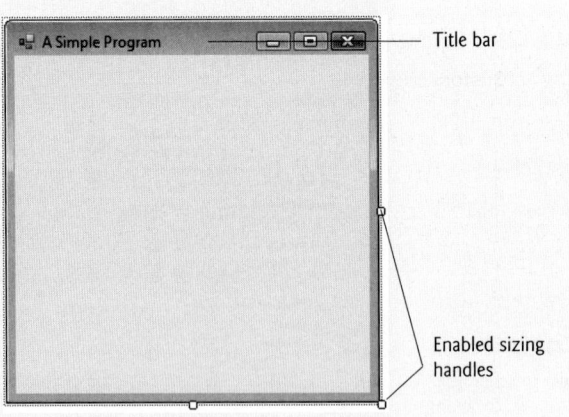

Fig. 2.31 | Form with enabled sizing handles.

Fig. 2.32 | Resized Form.

4. *Changing the Form's background color.* The **BackColor** *property* specifies a Form's or control's background color. Clicking BackColor in the **Properties** window causes a down-arrow button to appear next to the value of the property (Fig. 2.33). When clicked, the down-arrow button displays a set of other options, which vary depending on the property. In this case, the arrow displays tabs for **Custom, Web** and **System** (the default) colors. Click the **Custom** *tab* to display the *palette* (a grid of colors). Select the box that represents light blue. Once you select the color, the palette closes and the Form's background color changes to light blue (Fig. 2.34).

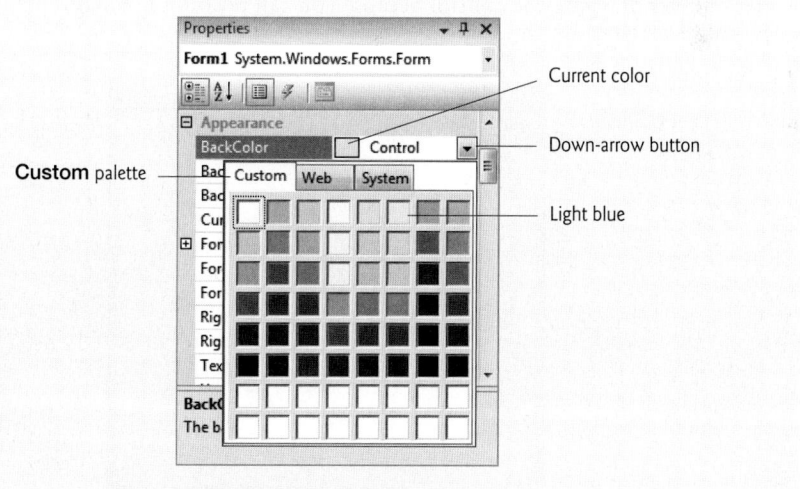

Fig. 2.33 | Changing the Form's BackColor property.

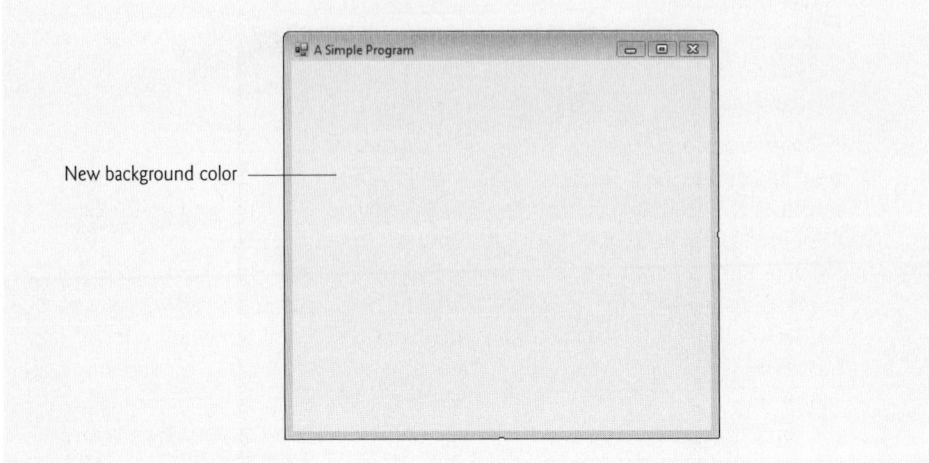

New background color

Fig. 2.34 | Form with new `BackColor` property applied.

5. *Adding a Label control to the Form.* If the **Toolbox** is not already open, select **View > Toolbox** to display the set of controls you'll use for creating your programs. For the type of program we are creating in this chapter, the typical controls we use are located in either the **All Windows Forms** category of the **Toolbox** or the **Common Controls** group. If either group name is collapsed, expand it by clicking the plus sign (the **All Windows Forms** and **Common Controls** groups are shown in Fig. 2.21). Next, double click the `Label` control in the **Toolbox**. This action causes a `Label` to appear in the upper-left corner of the Form (Fig. 2.35). [*Note:* If the Form is behind the **Toolbox**, you may need to hide or close the **Toolbox** to see the `Label`.] Although double clicking any **Toolbox** control places the control on the Form, you also can "drag" controls from the **Toolbox** to the Form (you may prefer dragging the control because you can position it wherever you want). Our

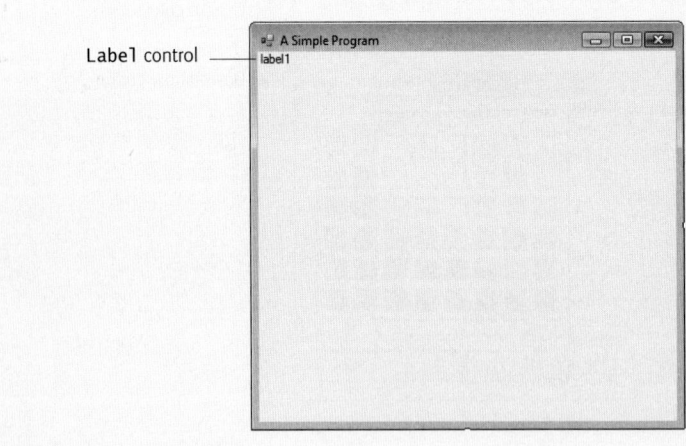

Label control

Fig. 2.35 | Adding a `Label` to the Form.

Label displays the text **label1** by default. Note that the Label's background color is the same as the Form's background color. When a control is added to the Form, its BackColor property is set to the Form's BackColor. You can change the Label's background color by changing its BackColor property.

6. *Customizing the Label's appearance.* Select the Label by clicking it. Its properties now appear in the **Properties** window (Fig. 2.36). The Label's Text property determines the text (if any) that the Label displays. The Form and Label each have their own Text property—Forms and controls can have the same types of properties (such as BackColor, Text) without conflict. Set the Label's Text property to **Welcome to Visual C#!**. Note that the Label resizes to fit all the typed text on one line. By default, the ***AutoSize property*** of the Label is set to true, which allows the Label to update its size to fit all of the text if necessary. Set the AutoSize property to false (Fig. 2.36) so that you can resize the Label on your own. Move the Label to the top center of the Form by dragging it or by using the keyboard's left and right arrow keys to adjust its position (Fig. 2.37). Alternatively, when the Label is selected, you can center the Label control horizontally by selecting **Format > Center In Form > Horizontally**.

7. *Setting the Label's font size.* To change the font type and appearance of the Label's text, select the value of the ***Font property***, which causes an ***ellipsis button*** to appear next to the value (Fig. 2.38). When the ellipsis button is clicked, a dialog that provides additional values—in this case, the ***Font dialog*** (Fig. 2.39)—is displayed. You can select the font name (the font options may be different, depending on your system), font style (**Regular, Italic, Bold**, and so on) and font size in this dialog. The text in the **Sample** area provides sample text with the selected font settings. Under **Font**, select **Segoe UI**, Microsoft's recommended font for user interfaces. Under **Size**, select **24** points and click **OK**. If the Label's text does not fit on a single line, it wraps to the next line. Resize the Label if it's not large enough to hold the text.

8. *Aligning the Label's text.* Select the Label's ***TextAlign*** property, which determines how the text is aligned within the Label. A three-by-three grid of buttons representing alignment choices is displayed (Fig. 2.40). The position of each button

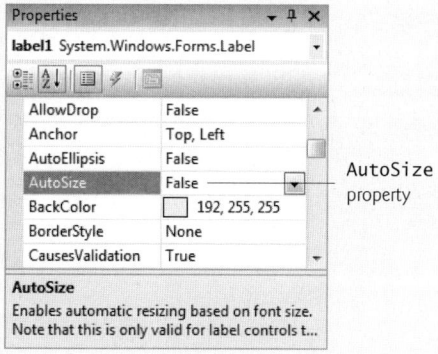

Fig. 2.36 | Changing the Label's AutoSize property to false.

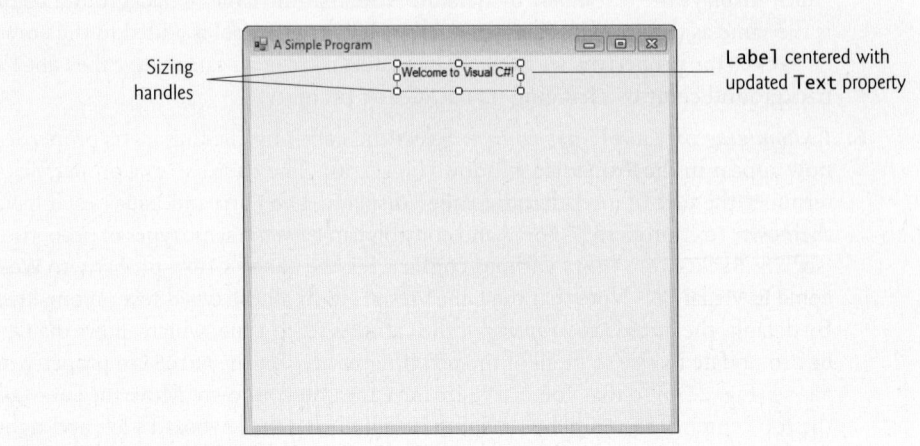

Sizing handles

Label centered with updated Text property

Fig. 2.37 | GUI after the Form and Label have been customized.

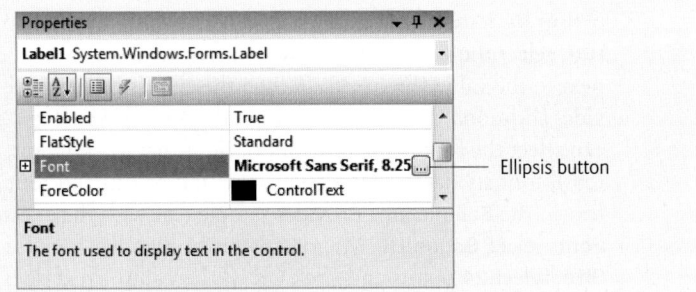

Ellipsis button

Fig. 2.38 | **Properties** window displaying the Label's properties.

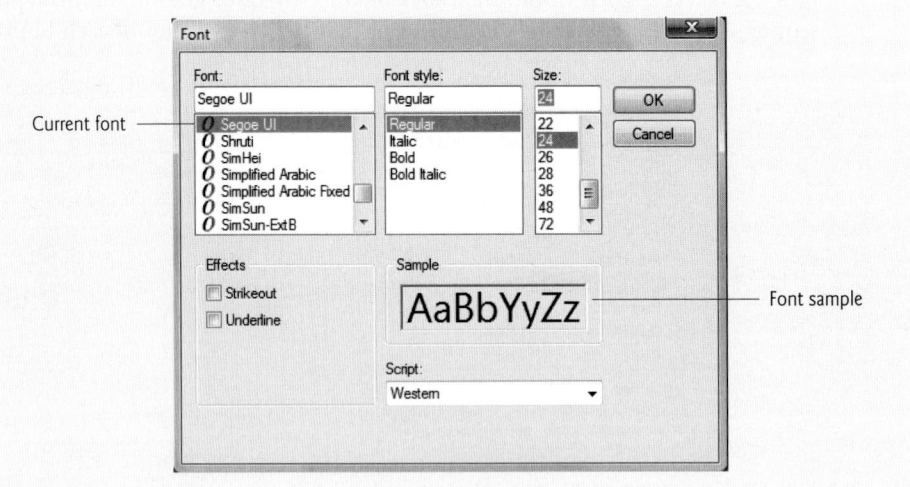

Current font

Font sample

Fig. 2.39 | **Font** dialog for selecting fonts, styles and sizes.

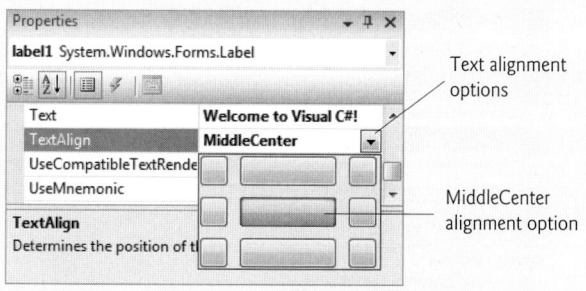

Fig. 2.40 | Centering the Label's text.

corresponds to where the text appears in the Label. For this program, set the TextAlign property to MiddleCenter in the three-by-three grid—this selection causes the text to appear centered in the middle of the Label, with equal spacing from the text to all sides of the Label. The other TextAlign values, such as Top-Left, TopRight, and BottomCenter, can be used to position the text anywhere within a Label. Certain alignment values may require that you resize the Label larger or smaller to better fit the text.

9. *Adding a PictureBox to the Form.* The PictureBox control displays images. The process involved in this step is similar to that of *Step 5*, in which we added a Label to the Form. Locate the PictureBox in the **Toolbox** (Fig. 2.21) and double click it to add it to the Form. When the PictureBox appears, move it underneath the Label, either by dragging it or by using the arrow keys (Fig. 2.41).

10. *Inserting an image.* Click the PictureBox to display its properties in the **Properties** window (Fig. 2.42). Locate the *Image property*, which displays a preview of the image, if one exists. No picture has been assigned, so the value of the Image property displays **(none)**. Click the ellipsis button to display the **Select Resource**

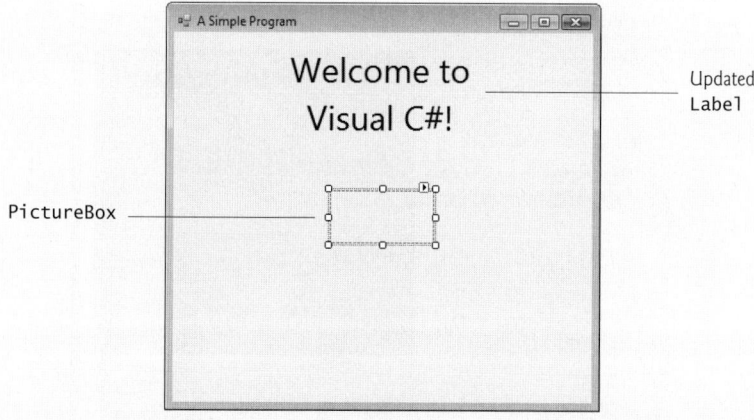

Fig. 2.41 | Inserting and aligning a PictureBox.

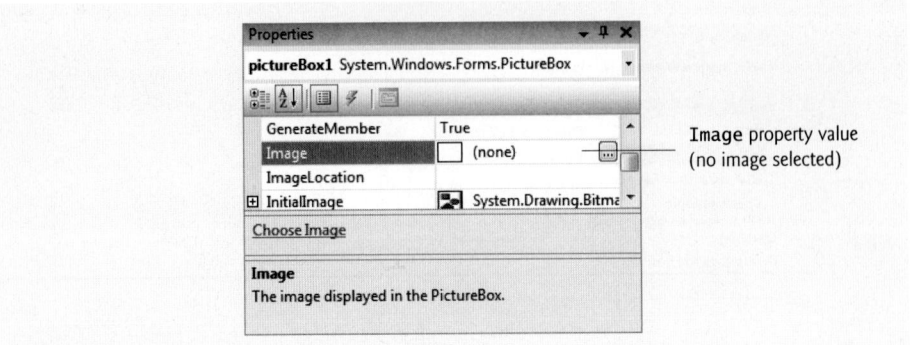

Fig. 2.42 | Image property of the `PictureBox`.

dialog (Fig. 2.43). This dialog is used to import files, such as images, to a program. Click the **Import...** button to browse for an image to insert. In our case, the picture is `bug.png` (located in the folder for this chapter's examples). In the dialog that appears, locate the image file, select it and click **OK**. The image is previewed in the **Select Resource** dialog (Fig. 2.44). Click **OK** to place the image in your program. Supported image formats include PNG (Portable Network Graphics), GIF (Graphic Interchange Format), JPEG (Joint Photographic Experts Group) and BMP (Windows bitmap). Creating a new image requires image-editing software, such as Corel® Paint Shop Pro® (www.corel.com), Adobe® Photoshop™ Elements (www.adobe.com) or Microsoft® Paint (provided with Windows). To size the image to the `PictureBox`, change the *SizeMode property* to *StretchImage* (Fig. 2.45), which scales the image to the size of the `PictureBox`. Resize the `PictureBox`, making it larger (Fig. 2.46).

11. *Saving the project.* Select **File > Save All** to save the entire solution. The solution file contains the name and location of its project, and the project file contains the names and locations of all the files in the project.

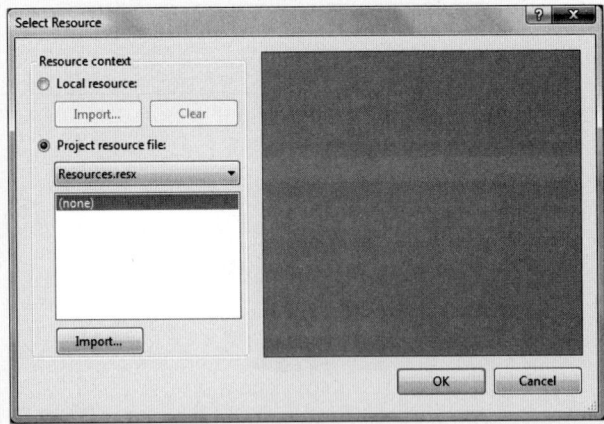

Fig. 2.43 | **Select Resource** dialog to select an image for the `PictureBox`.

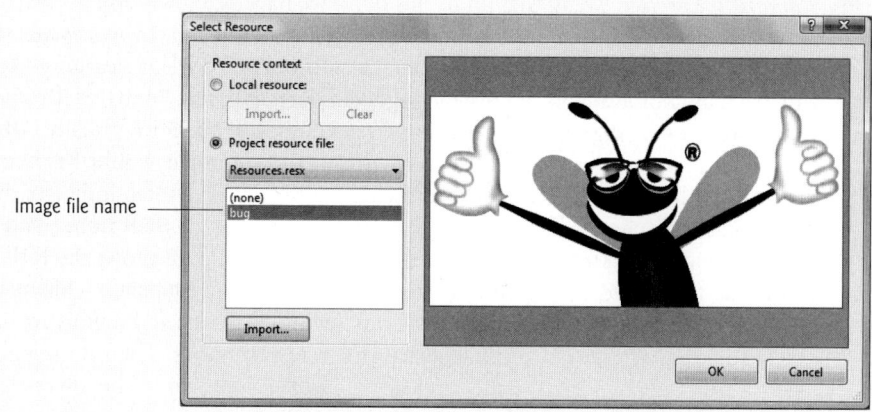

Image file name

Fig. 2.44 | **Select Resource** dialog displaying a preview of selected image.

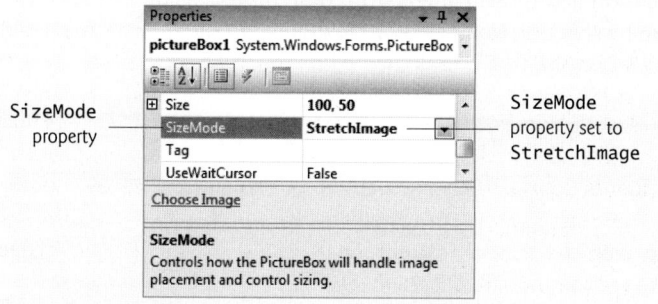

SizeMode property

SizeMode property set to StretchImage

Fig. 2.45 | Scaling an image to the size of the PictureBox.

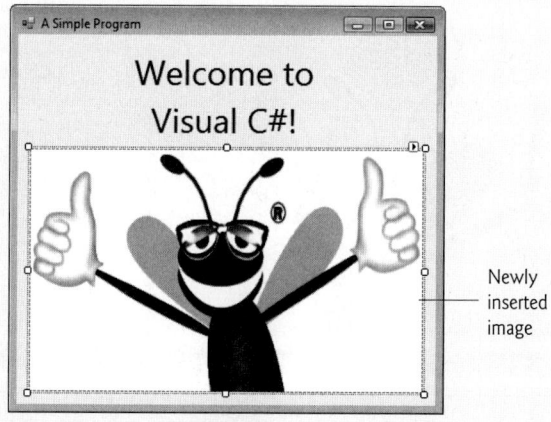

Newly inserted image

Fig. 2.46 | PictureBox displaying an image.

12. *Running the project.* Recall that up to this point we have been working in the IDE design mode (i.e., the program being created is not executing). In **run mode**, the program is executing, and you can interact with only a few IDE features—features that are not available are disabled (grayed out). The text **Form1.cs [Design]*** in the project tab (Fig. 2.47) means that we are designing the Form visually rather than programmatically. If we had been writing code, the tab would have contained only the text **Form1.cs**. The * at the end of the text in the tab indicates that the file has been changed and should be saved. Select **Debug > Start Debugging** to execute the program (or you can press the *F5* key). Figure 2.48 shows the IDE in run mode (indicated by the title-bar text **ASimpleProgram (Running) – Microsoft Visual C# 2008 Express Edition**). Note that many toolbar icons and menus are disabled, since they cannot be used while the program is running. The running program appears in a separate window outside the IDE, as shown in the lower-right portion of Fig. 2.48.

13. *Terminating execution.* Click the running program's close box (the **X** in the top-right corner of the running program's window). This action stops the program's execution and returns the IDE to design mode. You can also terminate the program by selecting **Debug > Stop Debugging** in the IDE or by pressing the stop button (■) on the IDE's toolbar.

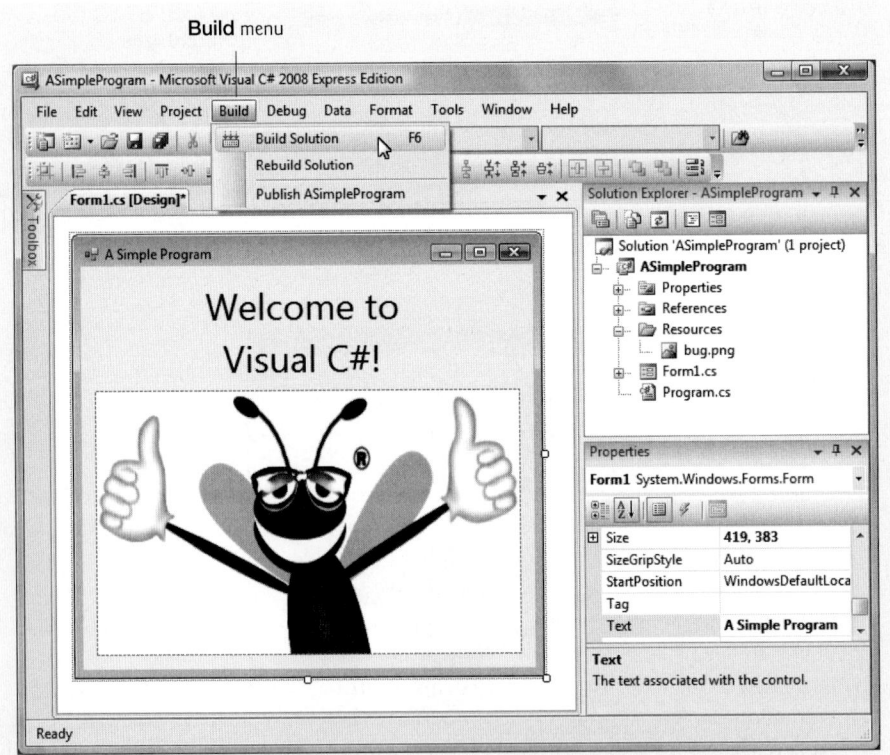

Fig. 2.47 | Building a solution.

IDE displays text **Running**, which
signifies that the program is executing

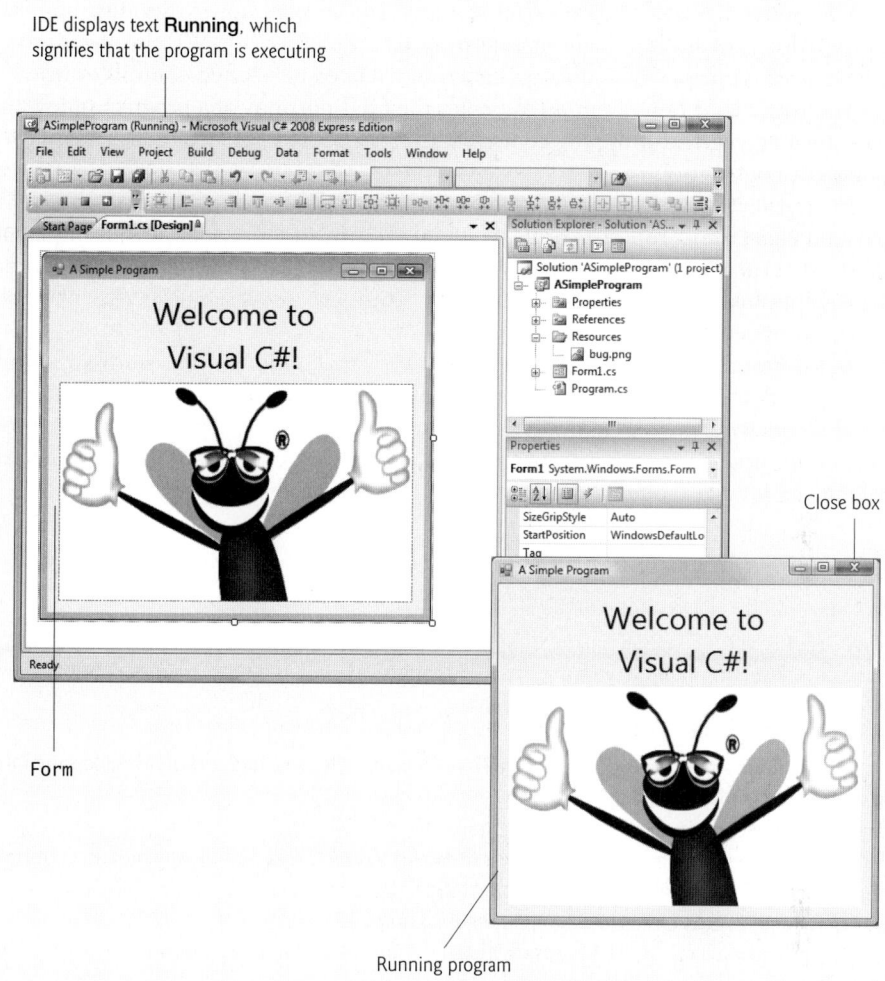

Close box

Form

Running program

Fig. 2.48 | IDE in run mode, with the running program in the foreground.

2.7 Wrap-Up

In this chapter, we introduced key features of the Visual Studio Integrated Development Environment (IDE). You used the technique of visual programming to create a working Visual C# program without writing a single line of code. Visual C# programming is a mixture of the two styles—visual programming allows you to develop GUIs easily and avoid tedious GUI programming; conventional programming (which we introduce in Chapter 3) allows you to specify the behavior of your programs.

You created a Visual C# Windows Forms application with one Form. You worked with the **Solution Explorer, Toolbox** and **Properties** windows, which are essential to developing Visual C# programs. The **Solution Explorer** window allows you to manage your solution's files visually. The **Toolbox** window contains a rich collection of controls for creating GUIs. The **Properties** window allows you to set the attributes of a Form and controls.

You explored Visual Studio's help features. You learned how to set **Help** options to display help resources internally or externally in a web browser. We also demonstrated context-sensitive help, which displays help topics related to selected controls or text.

You used visual programming to design the GUI portions of a program quickly and easily, by dragging-and-dropping controls (a `Label` and a `PictureBox`) onto a `Form` or by double clicking controls in the **Toolbox**.

In creating the **ASimpleProgram** program, you used the **Properties** window to set the `Text` and `BackColor` properties of the `Form`. You learned that `Label` controls display text and that `PictureBox`es display images. You displayed text in a `Label` and added an image to a `PictureBox`. You also worked with the `AutoSize`, `TextAlign` properties of a `Label` and the `SizeMode` property of a `PictureBox`.

In the next chapter, we discuss "nonvisual," or "conventional," programming—you'll create your first programs that contain Visual C# code that you write, instead of having Visual Studio write the code. You'll study console applications (programs that display only text and do not have a GUI). You'll also learn memory concepts, arithmetic, decision making and how to use a dialog to display a message.

2.8 Web Resources

Please take a moment to visit each of these sites briefly.

`www.deitel.com/VisualCSharp2008/`
The Deitel Visual C# 2008 Resource Center is a collection of links to online articles, tutorials, webcasts, forums, introductions and resource sites.

`msdn.microsoft.com/vstudio`
This site is the home page for Microsoft Visual Studio. The site includes news, documentation, downloads and other resources.

`msdn.microsoft.com/vcsharp/default.aspx`
This site provides information on the newest release of Visual C#, including downloads, community information and resources.

`msdn.microsoft.com/en-us/vcsharp/cc546586.aspx`
This site provides access to the Microsoft Visual C# forums, which you can use to get your Visual C# language and IDE questions answered.

`msdn.microsoft.com/msdnmag/`
This is the Microsoft Developer Network Magazine site. It provides articles and code on many Visual C# and .NET programming topics. There is also an archive of past issues.

3

Introduction to C# Applications

What's in a name?
That which we call a rose
by any other name
would smell as sweet.
—William Shakespeare

When faced with a decision,
I always ask, "What would
be the most fun?"
—Peggy Walker

"Take some more tea," the
March Hare said to Alice,
very earnestly. "I've had
nothing yet," Alice replied in
an offended tone, "so I can't
take more." "You mean you
can't take less," said the
Hatter: "it's very easy to take
more than nothing."
—Lewis Carroll

OBJECTIVES

In this chapter you'll learn:

- To write simple C# applications using code rather than visual programming.

- To write input/output statements.

- To declare and use data of various types.

- To store and retrieve data from memory.

- To use arithmetic operators.

- To determine the order in which operators are applied.

- To write decision-making statements.

- To use relational and equality operators.

- To use message dialogs to display messages.

Outline

3.1 Introduction
3.2 A Simple C# Application: Displaying a Line of Text
3.3 Creating a Simple Application in Visual C# Express
3.4 Modifying Your Simple C# Application
3.5 Formatting Text with `Console.Write` and `Console.WriteLine`
3.6 Another C# Application: Adding Integers
3.7 Arithmetic
3.8 Decision Making: Equality and Relational Operators
3.9 (Optional) Software Engineering Case Study: Examining the ATM Requirements Document
3.10 Wrap-Up
3.11 Web Resources

3.1 Introduction

In this chapter, we introduce *console applications*—these input and output text in a *console window*, which in Windows XP and Windows Vista is known as the **Command Prompt**. We use live-code examples to demonstrate input/output, text formatting and arithmetic, equality and relational operators. The optional Software Engineering Case Study section examines the requirements document that specifies what our ATM must do.

3.2 A Simple C# Application: Displaying a Line of Text

Let's consider an application that displays a line of text. (Later in this section we discuss how to compile and run an application.) The application and its output are shown in Fig. 3.1. The application illustrates several important C# language features. For your convenience, each program we present in this book includes line numbers, which are not part of actual C# code. In Section 3.3 we show how to display line numbers for your C# code in the IDE. We'll soon see that line 10 does the real work of the application—namely, displaying the phrase `Welcome to C# Programming!` on the screen. We now do a code walkthrough.

Line 1

```
// Fig. 3.1: Welcome1.cs
```

begins with `//`, indicating that the remainder of the line is a comment. We begin every application with a comment indicating the figure number and the name of the file in which the application is stored.

A comment that begins with `//` is called a *single-line comment*, because it terminates at the end of the line on which it appears. A `//` comment also can begin in the middle of a line and continue until the end of that line (as in lines 7, 11 and 12).

Delimited comments such as

```
/* This is a delimited comment.
   It can be split over many lines */
```

can be spread over several lines. This type of comment begins with the delimiter `/*` and ends with the delimiter `*/`. All text between the delimiters is ignored by the compiler. C#

```
1   // Fig. 3.1: Welcome1.cs
2   // Text-displaying application.
3   using System;
4
5   public class Welcome1
6   {
7      // Main method begins execution of C# application
8      public static void Main( string[] args )
9      {
10        Console.WriteLine( "Welcome to C# Programming!" );
11     } // end Main
12  } // end class Welcome1
```

```
Welcome to C# Programming!
```

Fig. 3.1 | Text-displaying application.

incorporated delimited comments and single-line comments from the C and C++ programming languages, respectively. In this book, we use only single-line comments in our programs.

Common Programming Error 3.1

Forgetting one of the delimiters of a delimited comment is a syntax error.

Line 2

```
// Text-displaying application.
```

is a single-line comment that describes the purpose of the application.
Line 3

```
using System;
```

is a ***using directive*** that tells the compiler where to look for a class that is used in this application. A great strength of Visual C# is its rich set of predefined classes that you can reuse rather than "reinventing the wheel." These classes are organized under ***namespaces***—named collections of related classes. Collectively, .NET's namespaces are referred to as the *.NET Framework Class Library*. Each using directive identifies a namespace containing predefined classes that a C# application should be able to use. The using directive in line 3 indicates that this example uses classes from the System namespace, which contains the predefined Console class (discussed shortly) used in line 10, and many other useful classes.

Error-Prevention Tip 3.1

Forgetting to include a using directive for a namespace that contains a class used in your application typically results in a compilation error, containing a message such as "The name 'Console' does not exist in the current context." When this occurs, check that you provided the proper using directives and that the names in the using directives are spelled correctly, including proper use of uppercase and lowercase letters.

For each new .NET class we use, we indicate the namespace in which it is located. This information is important, because it helps you locate descriptions of each class in the .NET documentation. A web-based version of this documentation can be found at

> msdn.microsoft.com/en-us/library/ms229335.aspx

This can also be found in the Visual C# Express documentation under the **Help** menu. You can also place the cursor on the name of any .NET class or method, then press the *F1* key to get more information.

Line 4 is simply a blank line. Blank lines, space characters and tab characters are *whitespace*. Space characters and tabs are known specifically as *whitespace characters*. Whitespace is ignored by the compiler. We use whitespace to enhance application readability.

Line 5

> ```
> public class Welcome1
> ```

begins a *class declaration* for the class `Welcome1`. Every application consists of at least one class declaration that is defined by the programmer. These are known as *user-defined classes*. The **class** *keyword* introduces a class declaration and is immediately followed by the *class name* (`Welcome1`). Keywords (also called *reserved words*) are reserved for use by C# and are always spelled with all lowercase letters. The complete list of C# keywords is shown in Fig. 3.2.

C# Keywords and contextual keywords

abstract	as	base	bool	break
byte	case	catch	char	checked
class	const	continue	decimal	default
delegate	do	double	else	enum
event	explicit	extern	false	finally
fixed	float	for	foreach	goto
if	implicit	in	int	interface
internal	is	lock	long	namespace
new	null	object	operator	out
override	params	private	protected	public
readonly	ref	return	sbyte	sealed
short	sizeof	stackalloc	static	string
struct	switch	this	throw	true
try	typeof	uint	ulong	unchecked
unsafe	ushort	using	virtual	void
volatile	while			

Contextual Keywords

add	alias	ascending	by	descending
equals	from	get	global	group
into	join	let	on	orderby

Fig. 3.2 | C# keywords and contextual keywords. (Part 1 of 2.)

C# Keywords and contextual keywords				
partial	*remove*	*select*	*set*	*value*
var	*where*	*yield*		

Fig. 3.2 | C# keywords and contextual keywords. (Part 2 of 2.)

By convention, all class names begin with a capital letter and capitalize the first letter of each word they include (e.g., SampleClassName). This is frequently referred to as *Pascal casing*. A class name is an *identifier*—a series of characters consisting of letters, digits and underscores (_) that does not begin with a digit and does not contain spaces. Some valid identifiers are Welcome1, identifier, _value and m_inputField1. The name 7button is not a valid identifier because it begins with a digit, and the name input field is not a valid identifier because it contains a space. Normally, an identifier that does not begin with a capital letter is not the name of a class. C# is *case sensitive*—that is, uppercase and lowercase letters are distinct, so a1 and A1 are different (but both valid) identifiers. Identifiers may also be preceded by the @ character. This indicates that a word should be interpreted as an identifier, even if it is a keyword (e.g., @int). This allows C# code to use code written in other .NET languages where an identifier might have the same name as a C# keyword. The *contextual keywords* in Fig. 3.2 can be used as identifiers outside the contexts in which they are keywords, but for clarity this is not recommended.

Good Programming Practice 3.1

By convention, always begin a class name's identifier with a capital letter and start each subsequent word in the identifier with a capital letter.

Common Programming Error 3.2

C# is case sensitive. Not using the proper uppercase and lowercase letters for an identifier normally causes a compilation error.

In Chapters 3–9, every class we define begins with the keyword **public**. For now, we'll simply require this keyword. You'll learn more about public and non-public classes in Chapter 10, Classes and Objects: A Deeper Look. When you save your public class declaration in a file, the file name is usually the class name followed by the .cs file-name extension. For our application, the file name is Welcome1.cs.

Good Programming Practice 3.2

By convention, a file that contains a single public class should have a name that is identical to the class name (plus the .cs extension) in both spelling and capitalization. Naming your files in this way makes it easier for other programmers (and you) to determine where the classes of an application are located.

A *left brace* (in line 6 in Fig. 3.1), {, begins the *body* of every class declaration. A corresponding *right brace* (in line 12), }, must end each class declaration. Note that lines 7–11 are indented. This indentation is one of the spacing conventions mentioned earlier. We define each spacing convention as a *Good Programming Practice*.

Error-Prevention Tip 3.2

Whenever you type an opening left brace, {, in your application, immediately type the closing right brace, }, then reposition the cursor between the braces and indent to begin typing the body. This practice helps prevent errors due to missing braces.

Good Programming Practice 3.3

Indent the entire body of each class declaration one "level" of indentation between the left and right braces that delimit the body of the class. This format emphasizes the class declaration's structure and makes it easier to read. You can let the IDE format your code by selecting Edit > Advanced > Format Document.

Good Programming Practice 3.4

*Set a convention for the indent size you prefer, then uniformly apply that convention. The **Tab** key may be used to create indents, but tab stops vary among text editors. We recommend using three spaces to form each level of indentation. We show how to do this in Section 3.3.*

Common Programming Error 3.3

It is a syntax error if braces do not occur in matching pairs.

Line 7

```
// Main method begins execution of C# application
```

is a comment indicating the purpose of lines 8–11 of the application. Line 8

```
public static void Main( string[] args )
```

is the starting point of every application. The ***parentheses*** after the identifier Main indicate that it is an application building block called a method. Class declarations normally contain one or more methods. Method names usually follow the same Pascal casing capitalization conventions used for class names. For each application, one of the methods in a class must be called Main (which is typically defined as shown in line 8); otherwise, the application will not execute. Methods are able to perform tasks and return information when they complete their tasks. Keyword ***void*** (line 8) indicates that this method will not return any information after it completes its task. Later, we'll see that many methods do return information. You'll learn more about methods in Chapters 4 and 7. We discuss the contents of Main's parentheses in Chapter 8. For now, simply mimic Main's first line in your applications.

The left brace in line 9 begins the ***body of the method declaration***. A corresponding right brace must end the method's body (line 11 of Fig. 3.1). Note that line 10 in the body of the method is indented between the braces.

Good Programming Practice 3.5

As with class declarations, indent the entire body of each method declaration one "level" of indentation between the left and right braces that define the method body. This format makes the structure of the method stand out and makes the method declaration easier to read.

Line 10

```
Console.WriteLine( "Welcome to C# Programming!" );
```

displays the *string* of characters contained between the double quotation marks. White-space characters in strings are *not* ignored by the compiler.

Class **Console** provides *standard input/output* capabilities that enable applications to read and display text in the console window from which the application executes. The **Console.WriteLine** *method* displays a line of text in the console window. The string in the parentheses in line 10 is the argument to the method. Method Console.WriteLine displays its argument in the console window. When Console.WriteLine completes its task, it positions the screen cursor at the beginning of the next line in the console window.

The entire line 10, including Console.WriteLine, the parentheses, the argument "Welcome to C# Programming!" in the parentheses and the *semicolon (;)*, is called a *statement*. Most statements end with a semicolon. When the statement in line 10 executes, it displays the string Welcome to C# Programming! in the console window. A method is typically composed of one or more statements that perform the method's task.

Error-Prevention Tip 3.3

When the compiler reports a syntax error, the error may not be in the line indicated by the error message. First, check the line for which the error was reported. If that line does not contain syntax errors, check several preceding lines.

Some programmers find it difficult when reading or writing an application to match the left and right braces ({ and }) that delimit the body of a class declaration or a method declaration. For this reason, we include a comment after each closing right brace (}) that ends a method declaration and after each closing right brace that ends a class declaration. For example, line 11

```
} // end Main
```

specifies the closing right brace of method Main, and line 12

```
} // end class Welcome1
```

specifies the closing right brace of class Welcome1. Each of these comments indicates the method or class that the right brace terminates. Visual Studio can help you locate matching braces in your code. Simply place the cursor immediately in front of the left brace or immediately after the right brace, and Visual Studio will highlight both.

Good Programming Practice 3.6

Following the closing right brace of a method body or class declaration with a comment indicating the method or class declaration to which the brace belongs improves application readability.

3.3 Creating a Simple Application in Visual C# Express

Now that we have presented our first console application (Fig. 3.1), we provide a step-by-step explanation of how to compile and execute it using Visual C# Express.

Creating the Console Application

After opening Visual C# 2008 Express, select **File > New Project...** to display the **New Project** dialog (Fig. 3.3), then select the **Console Application** template. In the dialog's **Name** field, type Welcome1. Click **OK** to create the project. The IDE now contains the open console application, as shown in Fig. 3.4. Note that the editor window already contains some

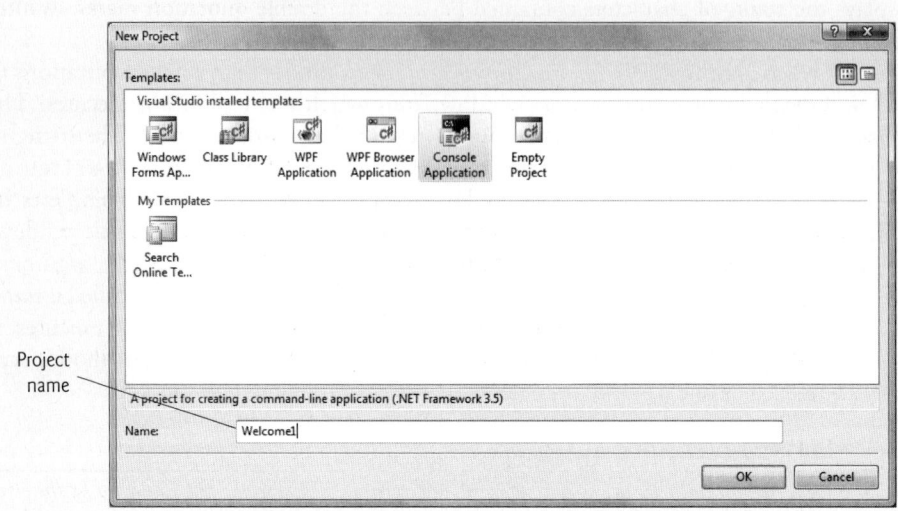

Fig. 3.3 | Creating a **Console Application** with the **New Project** dialog.

code provided by the IDE. Some of this code is similar to that of Fig. 3.1. Some is not, and uses features that we have not yet discussed. The IDE inserts this extra code to help organize the application and to provide access to some common classes in the .NET Framework Class Library—at this point in the book, this code is neither required nor relevant to the discussion of this application; delete all of it.

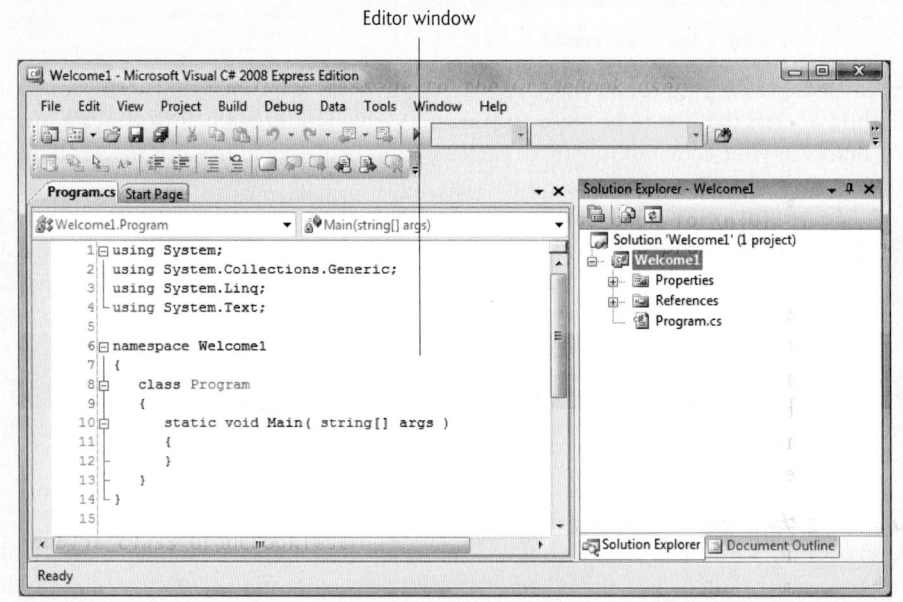

Fig. 3.4 | IDE with an open console application.

The code coloring scheme used by the IDE is called *syntax-color highlighting* and helps you visually differentiate application elements. For example, keywords appear in blue, and comments appear in green. When present, comments are green. In this black-and-white book, we syntax-shade our code similarly—bold italic for keywords, italic for comments, bold gray for literals and constants, and black for other text. One example of a literal is the string passed to `Console.WriteLine` in line 10 of Fig. 3.1. You can customize the colors shown in the code editor by selecting **Tools > Options...**. This displays the **Options** dialog. Then expand the **Environment** node and select **Fonts and Colors**. Here you can change the colors for various code elements.

Modifying the Editor Settings to Display Line Numbers

Visual C# Express provides many ways to personalize your coding experience. In this step, you'll change the settings so that your code matches that of this book. To have the IDE display line numbers, select **Tools > Options...**. In the dialog that appears (Fig. 3.5), click the **Show all settings** checkbox on the lower left of the dialog, then expand the **Text Editor** node in the left pane and select **All Languages**. On the right, check the **Line numbers** checkbox. Keep the **Options** dialog open.

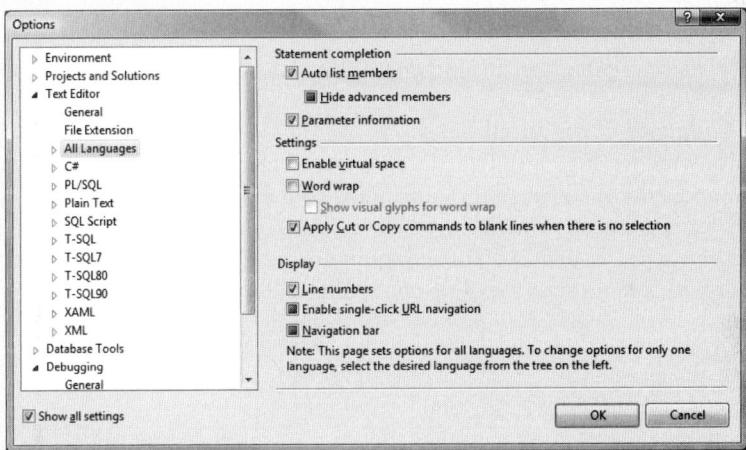

Fig. 3.5 | Modifying the IDE settings.

Setting Code Indentation to Three Spaces per Indent

In the **Options** dialog that you opened in the previous step (Fig. 3.5), expand the C# node in the left pane and select **Tabs**. Make sure that the option **Insert spaces** is selected. Enter **3** for both the **Tab size** and **Indent size** fields. Any new code you add will now use three spaces for each level of indentation. Click **OK** to save your settings, close the dialog and return to the editor window.

Changing the Name of the Application File

For applications we create in this book, we change the default name of the application file (i.e., `Program.cs`) to a more descriptive name. To rename the file, click `Program.cs` in the **Solution Explorer** window. This displays the application file's properties in the **Properties** window (Fig. 3.6). Change the ***File Name*** *property* to `Welcome1.cs`.

Solution Explorer

Click **Program.cs** to display its properties

Properties window

File Name property

Type **Welcome1.cs** here to rename the file

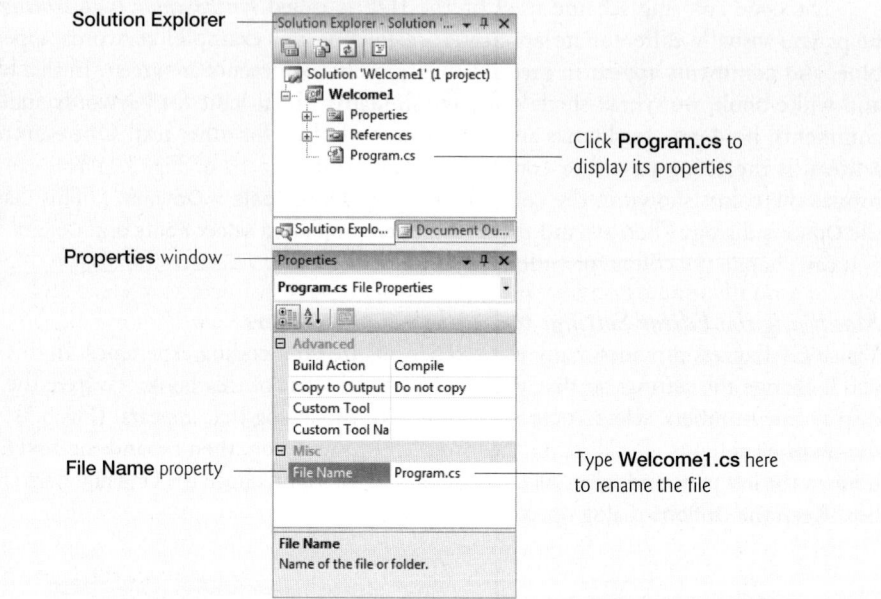

Fig. 3.6 | Renaming the program file in the **Properties** window.

Writing Code and Using IntelliSense

In the editor window (Fig. 3.4), type the code from Fig. 3.1. In line 10, after you type the class name and a dot (i.e., `Console.`), a window containing a scrollbar appears (Fig. 3.7). This IDE feature, called *IntelliSense*, lists a class's *members*, which include method names. As you type, Visual C# Express highlights the first member that matches all the characters typed, and displays a tool tip containing a description of that member. You can

Partially typed member

Member list

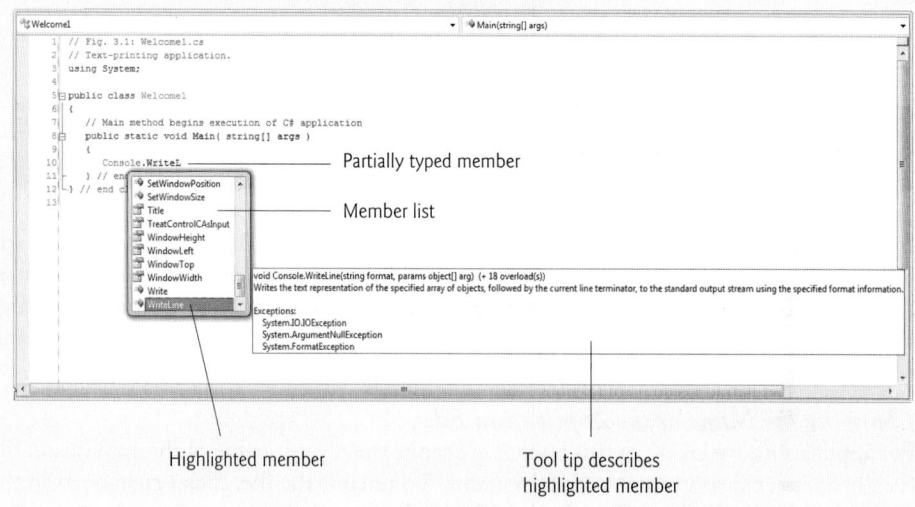

Highlighted member

Tool tip describes highlighted member

Fig. 3.7 | *IntelliSense* feature of Visual C# Express.

type the complete member name (e.g., WriteLine), double click the member name in the list or press the *Tab* key to complete the name. Once the complete name is provided, the *IntelliSense* window closes. While the *IntelliSense* window is displayed, pressing the *Ctrl* key makes the window transparent so you can see the code behind the window.

When you type the dot (.) after Console, the *IntelliSense* window reappears and shows only the members of class Console that can be used on the right side of the dot. When you type the left parenthesis, (, after Console.WriteLine, the *Parameter Info* window appears (Fig. 3.8) and shows information about the method's parameters. As you'll learn in Chapter 7, a class can define several methods that have the same name, as long as they have different numbers and/or types of parameters—a concept known as overloaded methods. Such methods normally perform similar tasks. The *Parameter Info* window indicates how many versions of the selected method are available and enables you to scroll through the different versions. For example, there are 19 versions of the WriteLine method—we use one of these 19 versions in our application. The *Parameter Info* window is one of many features provided by the IDE to facilitate application development. In the next several chapters, you'll learn more about the information displayed in these windows. The *Parameter Info* window is especially helpful when you want to see the different ways in which a method can be used. From the code in Fig. 3.1, we already know that we intend to display one string with WriteLine, so, because you know exactly which version of WriteLine you want to use, you can simply close the *Parameter Info* window by pressing the *Esc* key.

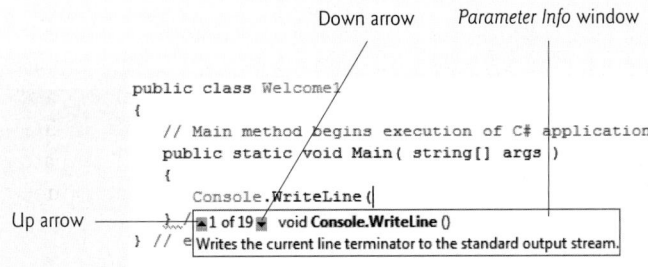

Fig. 3.8 | *Parameter Info* window.

Saving the Application

Select **File > Save All** to display the **Save Project** dialog (Fig. 3.9). In the **Location** textbox, specify the directory where you want to save this project. We chose the MyProjects directory on the C: drive. Select the **Create directory for solution** checkbox and click **Save**.

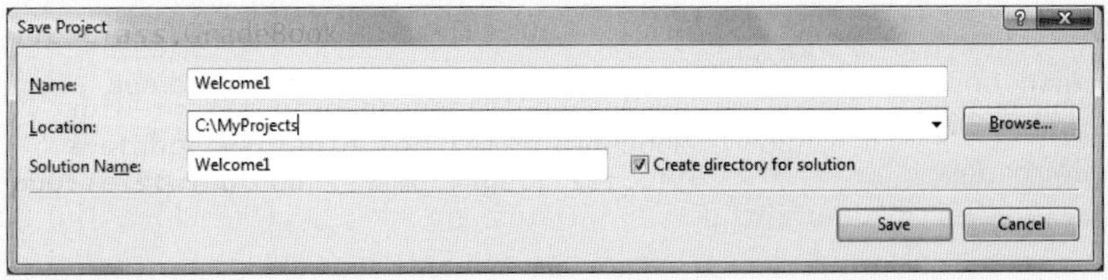

Fig. 3.9 | **Save Project** dialog.

Compiling and Running the Application

You're now ready to compile and execute your application. Depending on its type, the compiler may compile the code into files with a *.exe* (*executable*) *extension*, a *.dll* (*dynamically linked library*) *extension* or one of several other extensions. Such files are called *assemblies* and are the packaging units for compiled C# code. These assemblies contain the Microsoft Intermediate Language (MSIL) code for the application.

To compile the application, select **Build > Build Solution**. If the application contains no syntax errors, this will compile your application and build it into an executable file (named `Welcome1.exe`, in one of the project's subdirectories). To execute it, select **Debug > Start Without Debugging** (or type *Ctrl + F5*), which invokes the `Main` method (Fig. 3.1). The statement in line 10 of `Main` displays `Welcome to C# Programming!`. Figure 3.10 shows the results of executing this application, displayed in a console (**Command Prompt**) window. Leave the application's project open in Visual C# Express; we'll go back to it later in this section. [*Note:* If you attempt to run the application before building it, the IDE will build the application first, then run it only if there are no compilation errors.]

Error-Prevention Tip 3.4

When learning how to program, sometimes it is helpful to "break" a working application so you can familiarize yourself with the compiler's syntax-error messages. Try removing a semicolon or brace from the code of Fig. 3.1, then recompiling the application to see the error messages generated by the omission.

Console window

Fig. 3.10 | Executing the application shown in Fig. 3.1.

Running the Application from the Command Prompt

As we mentioned at the beginning of the chapter, you can execute applications outside the IDE in a **Command Prompt**. This is useful when you simply want to run an application rather than open it for modification. To open the **Command Prompt**, select **Start > All Programs > Accessories > Command Prompt**. The window (Fig. 3.11) displays copyright information, followed by a prompt that indicates the current directory. By default, the prompt specifies the current user's directory on the local machine (in our case, `C:\Users\paul`; this would be `C:\Documents and Settings\paul` on Windows XP). On your machine, the folder name `paul` will be replaced with your username. Enter the command `cd` (which stands for "change directory"), followed by the `/d` flag (to change drives if

Default prompt displays when
Command Prompt is opened

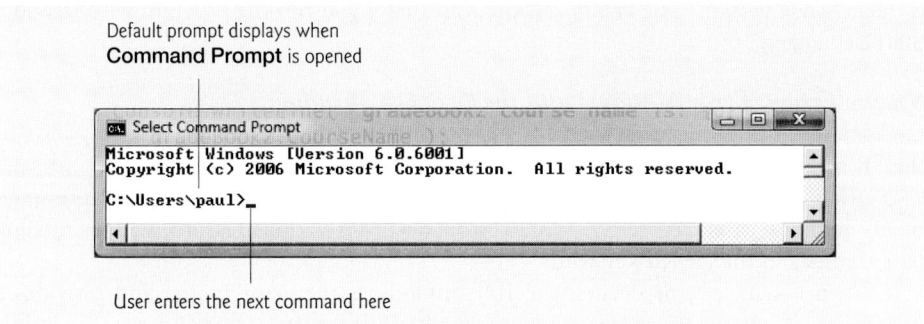

User enters the next command here

Fig. 3.11 | **Command Prompt** window when it is initially opened.

necessary), then the directory where the application's `.exe` file is located (i.e., your application's `bin\Debug` or `bin\Release` directory). For example, the command

```
cd /d C:\MyProjects\Welcome1\Welcome1\bin\Release
```

(Fig. 3.12) changes the current directory, to the `Welcome1` application's `Release` directory on the `C:` drive. The next prompt displays the new directory. After changing to the proper directory, you can run the compiled application by entering the name of the `.exe` file (i.e., `Welcome1`). The application will run to completion, then the prompt will display again, awaiting the next command. To close the **Command Prompt**, type `exit` (Fig. 3.12) and press *Enter*. [*Note:* Many environments show **Command Prompt** windows with black backgrounds and white text. We adjusted these settings in our environment to make our screen captures more readable.]

Note that Visual C# 2008 Express maintains a `Debug` and a `Release` directory in each project's `bin` directory. The `Debug` directory contains a version of the application that can be used with the debugger (see Appendix H, Using the Visual C# 2008 Debugger). The `Release` directory contains an optimized version that you could provide to your clients. In the complete Visual Studio 2008, you can select the specific version you wish to build from the **Solution Configurations** drop-down list in the toolbars at the top of the IDE. The default

Updated prompt showing   Type this to change to the
the new current directory   application's directory

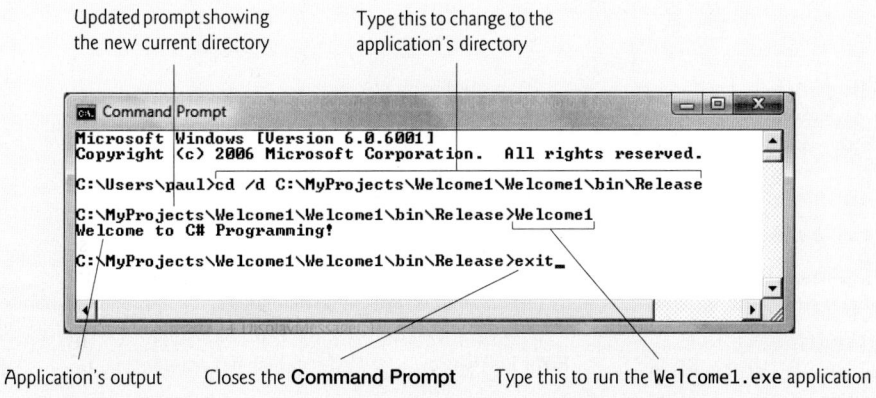

Application's output   Closes the **Command Prompt**   Type this to run the **Welcome1.exe** application

Fig. 3.12 | Executing the application shown in Fig. 3.1 from a **Command Prompt** window.

is the Release version. The Debug version is created if you run the program with **Debug > Start Debugging**.

Syntax Errors, Error Messages and the Error List *Window*

Go back to the application in Visual C# Express. As you type code, the IDE responds either by applying syntax-color highlighting or by generating a *syntax error*, which indicates a violation of Visual C#'s rules for creating correct applications (i.e., one or more statements are not written correctly). Syntax errors occur for various reasons, such as missing parentheses and misspelled keywords.

When a syntax error occurs, the IDE underlines the error in red and provides a description of it in the ***Error List*** *window* (Fig. 3.13). If the **Error List** window is not visible in the IDE, select **View > Error List** to display it. In Figure 3.13, we intentionally omitted the first parenthesis in line 10. The first error contains the text "**; expected**" and specifies that the error is in column 25 of line 10. This error message appears when the compiler thinks that the line contains a complete statement, followed by a semicolon, and the beginning of another statement. The second error contains the same text, but specifies that this error is in column 54 of line 10, because the compiler thinks that this is the end of the second statement. The third error has the text "**Invalid expression term ')'**", because the compiler is confused by the unmatched right parenthesis. Although we're attempting to

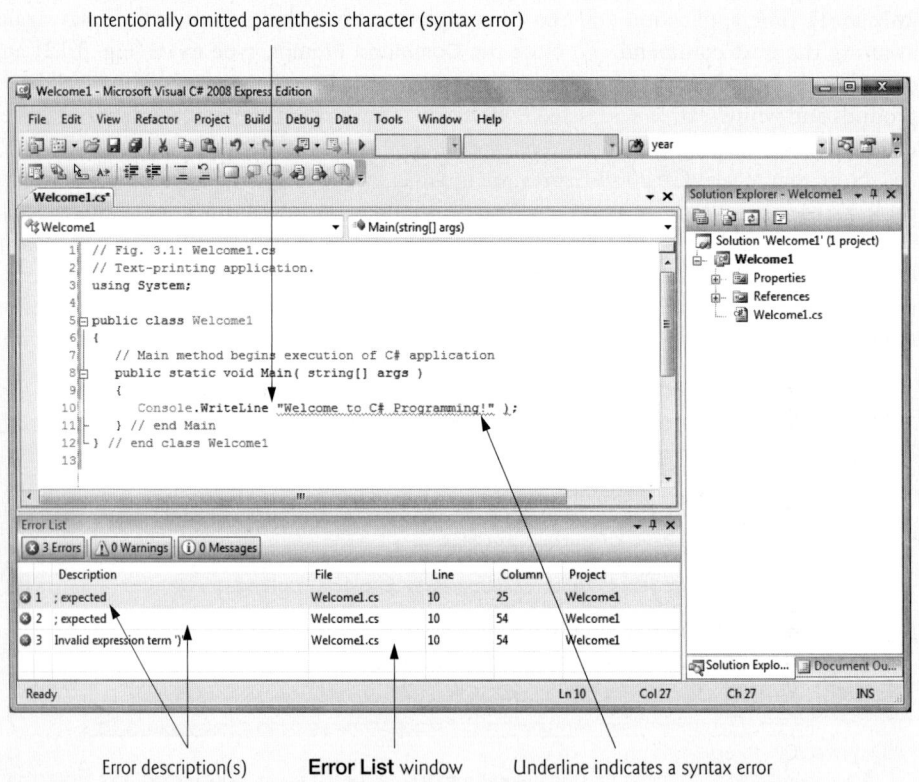

Fig. 3.13 | Syntax errors indicated by the IDE.

include only one statement in line 10, the missing left parenthesis causes the compiler to incorrectly assume that there is more than one statement on that line, to misinterpret the right parenthesis and to generate *three* error messages. You can double click an error message in the **Error List** to jump to the place in the code that caused the error.

Error-Prevention Tip 3.5

One syntax error can lead to multiple entries in the **Error List** *window. Each error that you address could eliminate several subsequent error messages when you recompile your application. So when you see an error you know how to fix, correct it and recompile—this may make several other errors disappear.*

3.4 Modifying Your Simple C# Application

This section continues our introduction to C# programming with two examples that modify the example of Fig. 3.1 to display text on one line by using several statements and to display text on several lines by using only one statement.

Displaying a Single Line of Text with Multiple Statements

"Welcome to C# Programming!" can be displayed several ways. Class Welcome2, shown in Fig. 3.14, uses two statements to produce the same output as that shown in Fig. 3.1. From this point forward, we highlight the new and key features in each code listing, as shown in lines 10–11 of Fig. 3.14.

The application is almost identical to Fig. 3.1. We discuss only the changes here. Line 2

```
// Displaying one line of text with multiple statements.
```

is a comment stating the purpose of this application. Line 5 begins the Welcome2 class declaration.

Lines 10–11 of method Main

```
Console.Write( "Welcome to " );
Console.WriteLine( "C# Programming!" );
```

```
1   // Fig. 3.14: Welcome2.cs
2   // Displaying one line of text with multiple statements.
3   using System;
4
5   public class Welcome2
6   {
7      // Main method begins execution of C# application
8      public static void Main( string[] args )
9      {
10         Console.Write( "Welcome to " );
11         Console.WriteLine( "C# Programming!" );
12      } // end Main
13   } // end class Welcome2
```

```
Welcome to C# Programming!
```

Fig. 3.14 | Displaying one line of text with multiple statements.

display one line of text in the console window. The first statement uses Console's method *Write* to display a string. Unlike WriteLine, after displaying its argument, Write does not position the screen cursor at the beginning of the next line in the console window—the next character the application displays will appear immediately after the last character that Write displays. Thus, line 11 positions the first character in its argument (the letter "C") immediately after the last character that line 10 displays (the space character before the string's closing double-quote character). Each Write statement resumes displaying characters from where the last Write statement displayed its last character.

Displaying Multiple Lines of Text with a Single Statement

A single statement can display multiple lines by using newline characters, which indicate to Console methods Write and WriteLine when they should position the screen cursor to the beginning of the next line in the console window. Like space characters and tab characters, newline characters are whitespace characters. The application of Fig. 3.15 outputs four lines of text, using newline characters to indicate when to begin each new line.

Most of the application is identical to the applications of Fig. 3.1 and Fig. 3.14, so we discuss only the changes here. Line 2

```
// Displaying multiple lines with a single statement.
```

is a comment stating the purpose of this application. Line 5 begins the Welcome3 class declaration.

Line 10

```
Console.WriteLine( "Welcome\nto\nC#\nProgramming!" );
```

displays four separate lines of text in the console window. Normally, the characters in a string are displayed exactly as they appear in the double quotes. Note, however, that the two characters \ and n (repeated three times in the statement) do not appear on the screen. The *backslash* (\) is called an *escape character*. It indicates to C# that a "special character" is in the string. When a backslash appears in a string of characters, C# combines the next

```
 1    // Fig. 3.15: Welcome3.cs
 2    // Displaying multiple lines with a single statement.
 3    using System;
 4
 5    public class Welcome3
 6    {
 7       // Main method begins execution of C# application
 8       public static void Main( string[] args )
 9       {
10          Console.WriteLine( "Welcome\nto\nC#\nProgramming!" );
11       } // end Main
12    } // end class Welcome3
```

```
Welcome
to
C#
Programming!
```

Fig. 3.15 | Displaying multiple lines with a single statement.

character with the backslash to form an *escape sequence.* The escape sequence \n represents the *newline character.* When a newline character appears in a string being output with `Console` methods, the newline character causes the screen cursor to move to the beginning of the next line in the console window. Figure 3.16 lists several common escape sequences and describes how they affect the display of characters in the console window.

Escape sequence	Description
\n	Newline. Positions the screen cursor at the beginning of the next line.
\t	Horizontal tab. Moves the screen cursor to the next tab stop.
\r	Carriage return. Positions the screen cursor at the beginning of the current line—does not advance the cursor to the next line. Any characters output after the carriage return overwrite the characters previously output on that line.
\\	Backslash. Used to place a backslash character in a string.
\"	Double quote. Used to place a double-quote character (") in a string—e,g., `Console.Write( "\"in quotes\"" );` displays `"in quotes"`

Fig. 3.16 | Some common escape sequences.

3.5 Formatting Text with `Console.Write` and `Console.WriteLine`

`Console` methods `Write` and `WriteLine` also have the capability to display formatted data. Figure 3.17 outputs the strings `"Welcome to"` and `"C# Programming!"` with `WriteLine`.

```
1   // Fig. 3.17: Welcome4.cs
2   // Displaying multiple lines of text with string formatting.
3   using System;
4
5   public class Welcome4
6   {
7      // Main method begins execution of C# application
8      public static void Main( string[] args )
9      {
10         Console.WriteLine( "{0}\n{1}", "Welcome to", "C# Programming!" );
11      } // end Main
12   } // end class Welcome4
```

```
Welcome to
C# Programming!
```

Fig. 3.17 | Displaying multiple lines of text with string formatting.

Line 10

```
Console.WriteLine( "{0}\n{1}", "Welcome to", "C# Programming!" );
```

calls method `Console.WriteLine` to display the application's output. The method call specifies three arguments. When a method requires multiple arguments, the arguments appear in a *comma-separated list*.

Good Programming Practice 3.7

Place a space after each comma (,) in an argument list to make applications more readable.

Remember that most statements end with a semicolon (;). Therefore, line 10 represents only one statement. Large statements can be split over many lines, but there are some restrictions.

Common Programming Error 3.4

Splitting a statement in the middle of an identifier or a string is a syntax error.

Method `WriteLine`'s first argument is a *format string* that may consist of *fixed text* and *format items*. Fixed text is output by `WriteLine`, as we demonstrated in Fig. 3.1. Each format item is a placeholder for a value. Format items also may include optional formatting information.

Format items are enclosed in curly braces and contain a sequence of characters that tell the method which argument to use and how to format it. For example, the format item `{0}` is a placeholder for the first additional argument (because C# starts counting from 0), `{1}` is a placeholder for the second, and so on. The format string in line 10 specifies that `WriteLine` should output two arguments and that the first one should be followed by a newline character. So this example substitutes `"Welcome to"` for the `{0}` and `"C# Programming!"` for the `{1}`. The output shows that two lines of text are displayed. Note that because braces in a formatted string normally indicate a placeholder for text substitution, you must type two left braces (`{{`) or two right braces (`}}`) to insert a single left or right brace into a formatted string, respectively. We introduce additional formatting features as they are needed in our examples.

3.6 Another C# Application: Adding Integers

Our next application reads (or inputs) two integers (whole numbers, like –22, 7, 0 and 1024) typed by a user at the keyboard, computes the sum of the values and displays the result. This application keeps track of the numbers supplied by the user in *variables*. The application of Fig. 3.18 demonstrates these concepts. In the sample output, we highlight data the user enters at the keyboard in bold.

Lines 1–2

```
// Fig. 3.18: Addition.cs
// Displaying the sum of two numbers input from the keyboard.
```

state the figure number, file name and purpose of the application.

```
 1   // Fig. 3.18: Addition.cs
 2   // Displaying the sum of two numbers input from the keyboard.
 3   using System;
 4
 5   public class Addition
 6   {
 7      // Main method begins execution of C# application
 8      public static void Main( string[] args )
 9      {
10         int number1; // declare first number to add
11         int number2; // declare second number to add
12         int sum; // declare sum of number1 and number2
13
14         Console.Write( "Enter first integer: " ); // prompt user
15         // read first number from user
16         number1 = Convert.ToInt32( Console.ReadLine() );
17
18         Console.Write( "Enter second integer: " ); // prompt user
19         // read second number from user
20         number2 = Convert.ToInt32( Console.ReadLine() );
21
22         sum = number1 + number2; // add numbers
23
24         Console.WriteLine( "Sum is {0}", sum ); // display sum
25      } // end Main
26   } // end class Addition
```

```
Enter first integer: 45
Enter second integer: 72
Sum is 117
```

Fig. 3.18 | Displaying the sum of two numbers input from the keyboard.

Line 5

```
public class Addition
```

begins the declaration of class Addition. Remember that the body of each class declaration starts with an opening left brace (line 6) and ends with a closing right brace (line 26).

The application begins execution with method Main (lines 8–25). The left brace (line 9) marks the beginning of Main's body, and the corresponding right brace (line 25) marks the end of Main's body. Note that method Main is indented one level within the body of class Addition and that the code in the body of Main is indented another level for readability.

Line 10

```
int number1; // declare first number to add
```

is a *variable declaration statement* (also called a *declaration*) that specifies the name and type of a variable (number1) used in this application. Variables are typically declared with a name and a type before they are used. The name of a variable can be any valid identifier. (See Section 3.2 for identifier naming requirements.) Declaration statements end with a semicolon (;).

The declaration in line 10 specifies that the variable named number1 is of type *int*—it will hold integer values . The range of values for an int is –2,147,483,648 (int.Min-Value) to +2,147,483,647 (int.MaxValue). We'll soon discuss types *float*, *double* and *decimal*, for specifying real numbers, and type *char*, for specifying characters. Real numbers contain decimal points, as in 3.4, 0.0 and –11.19. Variables of type float and double store approximations of real numbers in memory. Variables of type decimal store real numbers precisely (to 28–29 significant digits), so decimal variables are often used with monetary calculations. Variables of type char represent individual characters, such as an uppercase letter (e.g., A), a digit (e.g., 7), a special character (e.g., * or %) or an escape sequence (e.g., the newline character, \n). Types such as int, float, double, decimal and char are called *simple types*. Simple-type names are keywords and must appear in all lowercase letters. Appendix B summarizes the characteristics of the thirteen simple types (bool, byte, sbyte, char, short, ushort, int, uint, long, ulong, float, double and decimal).

The variable declaration statements at lines 11–12

```
int number2; // declare second number to add
int sum; // declare sum of number1 and number2
```

similarly declare variables number2 and sum to be of type int.

Variable declaration statements can be split over several lines, with the variable names separated by commas (i.e., a comma-separated list of variable names). Several variables of the same type may be declared in one declaration or in multiple declarations. For example, lines 10–12 can also be written as follows:

```
int number1, // declare first number to add
    number2, // declare second number to add
    sum; // declare sum of number1 and number2
```

 Good Programming Practice 3.8

Declare each variable on a separate line. This format allows a comment to be easily inserted next to each declaration.

 Good Programming Practice 3.9

*Choosing meaningful variable names helps code to be **self-documenting** (i.e., one can understand the code simply by reading it rather than by reading documentation manuals or viewing an excessive number of comments).*

 Good Programming Practice 3.10

*By convention, variable-name identifiers begin with a lowercase letter, and every word in the name after the first word begins with a capital letter. This naming convention is known as **camel casing**.*

Line 14

```
Console.Write( "Enter first integer: " ); // prompt user
```

uses Console.Write to display the message "Enter first integer: ". This message is a prompt—it directs the user to take a specific action.

Line 16

```
number1 = Convert.ToInt32( Console.ReadLine() );
```

first calls the Console's ***ReadLine*** method. This method waits for the user to type a string of characters at the keyboard and press the *Enter* key. As we mentioned earlier in this chapter, some methods perform a task, then return the result of that task. In this case, ReadLine returns the text the user entered. Then, the string is used as an argument to class ***Convert***'s ***ToInt32*** method, which converts this sequence of characters into data of an type int. In this case, method ToInt32 returns the int representation of the user's input.

Technically, the user can type anything as the input value. ReadLine will accept it and pass it off to the ToInt32 method. This method assumes that the string contains a valid integer value. In this application, if the user types a noninteger value, a runtime logic error will occur and the application will terminate. Chapter 13, Exception Handling, discusses how to make your applications more robust by enabling them to handle such errors and continue executing.

In line 16, the result of the call to method ToInt32 (an int value) is placed in variable number1 by using the ***assignment operator***, =. The statement is read as "number1 gets the value returned by Convert.ToInt32." Operator = is called a ***binary operator***, because it works on two pieces of information. These are known as its ***operands***—in this case, the operands are number1 and the result of the method call Convert.ToInt32. This statement is called an ***assignment statement***, because it assigns a value to a variable. Everything to the right of the assignment operator, =, is always evaluated before the assignment is performed.

 Good Programming Practice 3.11

Place spaces on either side of a binary operator to make it stand out and make the code more readable.

Line 18

```
Console.Write( "Enter second integer: " ); // prompt user
```

prompts the user to enter the second integer. Line 20

```
number2 = Convert.ToInt32( Console.ReadLine() );
```

reads a second integer and assigns it to the variable number2.

Line 22

```
sum = number1 + number2; // add numbers
```

calculates the sum of the variables number1 and number2 and assigns the result to variable sum. In the preceding statement, the addition operator is a binary operator—its two operands are number1 and number2. Portions of statements that contain calculations are called *expressions*. In fact, an expression is any portion of a statement that has a value associated with it. For example, the value of the expression number1 + number2 is the sum of the numbers. Similarly, the value of the expression Console.ReadLine() is the string of characters typed by the user. After the calculation has been performed, line 24

```
Console.WriteLine( "Sum is {0}", sum ); // display sum
```

uses method Console.WriteLine to display the sum. The format item {0} is a placeholder for the first argument after the format string. Other than the {0} format item, the remaining characters in the format string are all fixed text. So method WriteLine displays "Sum is ", followed by the value of sum (in the position of the {0} format item) and a newline.

Calculations can also be performed inside output statements. We could have combined the statements in lines 22 and 24 into the statement

```
Console.WriteLine( "Sum is {0}", ( number1 + number2 ) );
```

3.7 Arithmetic

The *arithmetic operators* are summarized in Fig. 3.19. Note the various special symbols not used in algebra. The *asterisk* (*) indicates multiplication, and the *percent sign* (%) is the *remainder operator* (called modulus in some languages), which we'll discuss shortly. The arithmetic operators in Fig. 3.19 are binary operators—for example, the expression f + 7 contains the binary operator + and the two operands f and 7.

Integer division yields an integer quotient—for example, the expression 7 / 4 evaluates to 1, and the expression 17 / 5 evaluates to 3. Any fractional part in integer division is simply discarded (i.e., truncated)—no rounding occurs. C# provides the remainder operator, %, which yields the remainder after division. The expression x % y yields the remainder after x is divided by y. Thus, 7 % 4 yields 3, and 17 % 5 yields 2. This operator is most commonly used with integer operands but can also be used with floats, doubles, and decimals. We will consider several interesting applications of the remainder operator, such as determining whether one number is a multiple of another.

Arithmetic expressions must be written in *straight-line form* to facilitate entering applications into the computer. Thus, expressions such as "a divided by b" must be written as a / b, so that all constants, variables and operators appear in a straight line. The following algebraic notation is generally not acceptable to compilers:

$$\frac{a}{b}$$

Parentheses are used to group terms in C# expressions in the same manner as in algebraic expressions. For example, to multiply a times the quantity b + c, we write

```
a * ( b + c )
```

If an expression contains *nested parentheses*, such as

```
( ( a + b ) * c )
```

the expression in the innermost set of parentheses (a + b in this case) is evaluated first.

C# operation	Arithmetic operator	Algebraic expression	C# expression
Addition	+	$f + 7$	f + 7
Subtraction	−	$p - c$	p - c
Multiplication	*	$b \cdot m$	b * m
Division	/	x / y or $\frac{x}{y}$ or $x \div y$	x / y
Remainder	%	$r \bmod s$	r % s

Fig. 3.19 | Arithmetic operators.

C# applies the operators in arithmetic expressions in a precise sequence determined by the following ***rules of operator precedence***, which are generally the same as those followed in algebra (Fig. 3.20).

These rules enable C# to apply operators in the correct order.[1] When we say that operators are applied from left to right, we're referring to their ***associativity***. You'll see that some operators associate from right to left. Figure 3.20 summarizes these rules of operator precedence. We expand this table as additional operators are introduced. Appendix A provides the complete precedence chart.

Operators	Operations	Order of evaluation (associativity)
Evaluated first		
*	Multiplication	If there are several operators of this
/	Division	type, they are evaluated from left to
%	Remainder	right.
Evaluated next		
+	Addition	If there are several operators of this
-	Subtraction	type, they are evaluated from left to
		right.

Fig. 3.20 | Precedence of arithmetic operators.

3.8 Decision Making: Equality and Relational Operators

This section introduces a simple version of C#'s ***if statement*** that allows an application to make a decision based on the value of a condition. For example, the condition "grade is greater than or equal to 60" determines whether a student passed a test. If the condition in an if statement is true, the body of the if statement executes. If the condition is false, the body does not execute. We'll see an example shortly.

Conditions in if statements can be formed by using the ***equality operators*** (== and !=) and ***relational operators*** (>, <, >= and <=) summarized in Fig. 3.21. The two equality operators (== and !=) each have the same level of precedence, the relational operators (>, <, >= and <=) each have the same level of precedence, and the equality operators have lower precedence than the relational operators. They all associate from left to right.

Common Programming Error 3.5

Confusing the equality operator, ==, with the assignment operator, =, can cause a logic error or a syntax error. The equality operator should be read as "is equal to," and the assignment operator should be read as "gets" or "gets the value of." To avoid confusion, some people read the equality operator as "double equals" or "equals equals."

---

1. We discuss simple examples here to explain the order of evaluation of expressions. More subtle order of evaluation issues occur in the increasingly complex expressions you'll encounter later in the book. For additional information on order of evaluation, see the following blog posts from Microsoft's Eric Lippert: `blogs.msdn.com/ericlippert/archive/2008/05/23/precedence-vs-associativity-vs-order.aspx` and `blogs.msdn.com/oldnewthing/archive/2007/08/14/4374222.aspx`.

Standard algebraic equality and relational operators	C# equality or relational operator	Sample C# condition	Meaning of C# condition
Equality operators			
=	==	x == y	x is equal to y
≠	!=	x != y	x is not equal to y
Relational operators			
>	>	x > y	x is greater than y
<	<	x < y	x is less than y
≥	>=	x >= y	x is greater than or equal to y
≤	<=	x <= y	x is less than or equal to y

Fig. 3.21 | Equality and relational operators.

Figure 3.22 uses six if statements to compare two integers entered by the user. If the condition in any of these if statements is true, the assignment statement associated with that if statement executes. The application uses class Console to prompt for and read two lines of text from the user, extracts the integers from that text with the ToInt32 method of class Convert, and stores them in variables number1 and number2. Then the application compares the numbers and displays the results of the comparisons that are true.

```csharp
1   // Fig. 3.22: Comparison.cs
2   // Comparing integers using if statements, equality operators,
3   // and relational operators.
4   using System;
5
6   public class Comparison
7   {
8      // Main method begins execution of C# application
9      public static void Main( string[] args )
10     {
11        int number1; // declare first number to compare
12        int number2; // declare second number to compare
13
14        // prompt user and read first number
15        Console.Write( "Enter first integer: " );
16        number1 = Convert.ToInt32( Console.ReadLine() );
17
18        // prompt user and read second number
19        Console.Write( "Enter second integer: " );
20        number2 = Convert.ToInt32( Console.ReadLine() );
```

Fig. 3.22 | Comparing integers using if statements, equality operators and relational operators. (Part 1 of 2.)

```
21
22                    if ( number1 == number2 )
23                        Console.WriteLine( "{0} == {1}", number1, number2 );
24
25                    if ( number1 != number2 )
26                        Console.WriteLine( "{0} != {1}", number1, number2 );
27
28                    if ( number1 < number2 )
29                        Console.WriteLine( "{0} < {1}", number1, number2 );
30
31                    if ( number1 > number2 )
32                        Console.WriteLine( "{0} > {1}", number1, number2 );
33
34                    if ( number1 <= number2 )
35                        Console.WriteLine( "{0} <= {1}", number1, number2 );
36
37                    if ( number1 >= number2 )
38                        Console.WriteLine( "{0} >= {1}", number1, number2 );
39          } // end Main
40      } // end class Comparison
```

```
Enter first integer: 42
Enter second integer: 42
42 == 42
42 <= 42
42 >= 42
```

```
Enter first integer: 1000
Enter second integer: 2000
1000 != 2000
1000 < 2000
1000 <= 2000
```

```
Enter first integer: 2000
Enter second integer: 1000
2000 != 1000
2000 > 1000
2000 >= 1000
```

Fig. 3.22 | Comparing integers using if statements, equality operators and relational operators. (Part 2 of 2.)

The declaration of class Comparison begins at line 6

```
public class Comparison
```

The class's Main method (lines 9–39) begins the execution of the application.
Lines 11–12

```
int number1; // declare first number to compare
int number2; // declare second number to compare
```

declare the int variables used to store the values entered by the user.

Lines 14–16

```
// prompt user and read first number
Console.Write( "Enter first integer: " );
number1 = Convert.ToInt32( Console.ReadLine() );
```

prompt the user to enter the first integer and input the value. The input value is stored in variable number1.

Lines 18-20

```
// prompt user and read second number
Console.Write( "Enter second integer: " );
number2 = Convert.ToInt32( Console.ReadLine() );
```

perform the same task, except that the input value is stored in variable number2.

Lines 22–23

```
if ( number1 == number2 )
    Console.WriteLine( "{0} == {1}", number1, number2 );
```

compare the values of the variables number1 and number2 to determine whether they are equal. An if statement always begins with keyword if, followed by a condition in parentheses. An if statement expects one statement in its body. The indentation of the body statement shown here is not required, but it improves the code's readability by emphasizing that the statement in line 23 is part of the if statement that begins in line 22. Line 23 executes only if the numbers stored in variables number1 and number2 are equal (i.e., the condition is true). The if statements in lines 25–26, 28–29, 31–32, 34–35 and 37–38 compare number1 and number2 with the operators !=, <, >, <= and >=, respectively. If the condition in any of the if statements is true, the corresponding body statement executes.

Common Programming Error 3.6

Forgetting the left and/or right parentheses for the condition in an if statement is a syntax error—the parentheses are required.

Common Programming Error 3.7

Reversing the operators !=, >= and <=, as in =!, => and =<, can result in syntax or logic errors.

Common Programming Error 3.8

It is a syntax error if the operators ==, !=, >= and <= contain spaces between their symbols, as in = =, ! =, > = and < =, respectively.

Good Programming Practice 3.12

Indent an if statement's body to make it stand out and to enhance application readability.

Note that there is no semicolon (;) at the end of the first line of each if statement. Such a semicolon would result in a logic error at execution time. For example,

```
if ( number1 == number2 ); // logic error
    Console.WriteLine( "{0} == {1}", number1, number2 );
```

would actually be interpreted by C# as

```
if ( number1 == number2 )
  ; // empty statement

Console.WriteLine( "{0} == {1}", number1, number2 );
```

where the semicolon in the line by itself—called the ***empty statement***—is the statement to execute if the condition in the if statement is true. When the empty statement executes, no task is performed in the application. The application then continues with the output statement, which always executes, regardless of whether the condition is true or false, because the output statement is not part of the if statement.

Common Programming Error 3.9

Placing a semicolon immediately after the right parenthesis of the condition in an if statement is normally a logic error.

Note the use of whitespace in Fig. 3.22. Recall that whitespace characters, such as tabs, newlines and spaces, are normally ignored by the compiler. So statements may be split over several lines and may be spaced according to your preferences without affecting the meaning of an application. It is incorrect to split identifiers, strings, and multicharacter operators (like >=). Ideally, statements should be kept small, but this is not always possible.

Good Programming Practice 3.13

Place no more than one statement per line in an application. This format enhances readability.

Good Programming Practice 3.14

A lengthy statement can be spread over several lines. If a single statement must be split across lines, choose breaking points that make sense, such as after a comma in a comma-separated list, or after an operator in a lengthy expression. If a statement is split across two or more lines, indent all subsequent lines until the end of the statement.

Figure 3.23 shows the precedence of the operators introduced in this chapter. The operators are shown from top to bottom in decreasing order of precedence. All these operators, with the exception of the assignment operator, =, associate from left to right. Addition is left associative, so an expression like x + y + z is evaluated as if it had been written as (x + y) + z. The assignment operator, =, associates from right to left, so an expression like x = y = 0 is evaluated as if it had been written as x = (y = 0), which, as you'll soon see, first assigns the value 0 to variable y then assigns the result of that assignment, 0, to x.

Operators				Associativity	Type
*	/	%		left to right	multiplicative
+	-			left to right	additive
<	<=	>	>=	left to right	relational
==	!=			left to right	equality
=				right to left	assignment

Fig. 3.23 | Precedence and associativity of operations discussed so far.

Good Programming Practice 3.15

Refer to the operator precedence chart (the complete chart is in Appendix A) when writing expressions containing many operators. Confirm that the operations in the expression are performed in the order you expect. If you're uncertain about the order of evaluation in a complex expression, use parentheses to force the order, as you would do in algebraic expressions. Observe that some operators, such as assignment, =, associate from right to left rather than from left to right.

3.9 (Optional) Software Engineering Case Study: Examining the ATM Requirements Document

Now we begin our optional object-oriented design and implementation case study. The Software Engineering Case Study sections at the ends of this and the next several chapters will ease you into object orientation. We'll develop software for a simple automated teller machine (ATM) system, providing you with a concise, carefully paced, complete design and implementation experience. In Chapters 4–8, 10 and 12, we'll perform the various steps of an object-oriented design (OOD) process using the UML, while relating these steps to the object-oriented concepts discussed in the chapters. Appendix D implements the ATM using the techniques of object-oriented programming (OOP) in C# and presents the complete case study solution. This is not an exercise; rather, it is an end-to-end learning experience that concludes with a detailed walkthrough of the complete C# code that implements our design. It will begin to acquaint you with the kinds of substantial problems encountered in industry and their solutions.

We begin our design process by presenting a *requirements document* that specifies the overall purpose of the ATM system and *what* it must do. Throughout the case study, we refer to the requirements document to determine precisely what functionality the system must include.

Requirements Document
A small local bank intends to install a new automated teller machine (ATM) to allow users (i.e., bank customers) to perform basic financial transactions (Fig. 3.24). For simplicity, each user can have only one account at the bank. ATM users should be able to view their account balance, withdraw cash (i.e., take money out of an account) and deposit funds (i.e., place money into an account).

The user interface of the automated teller machine contains the following hardware components:

- a screen that displays messages to the user
- a keypad that receives numeric input from the user
- a cash dispenser that dispenses cash to the user
- a deposit slot that receives deposit envelopes from the user

The cash dispenser begins each day loaded with 500 $20 bills. [*Note:* Owing to the limited scope of this case study, certain elements of the ATM described here simplify various aspects of a real ATM. For example, a real ATM typically contains a device that reads a user's account number from an ATM card, whereas this ATM asks the user to type an account number on the keypad (which you'll simulate with your personal computer's keypad).

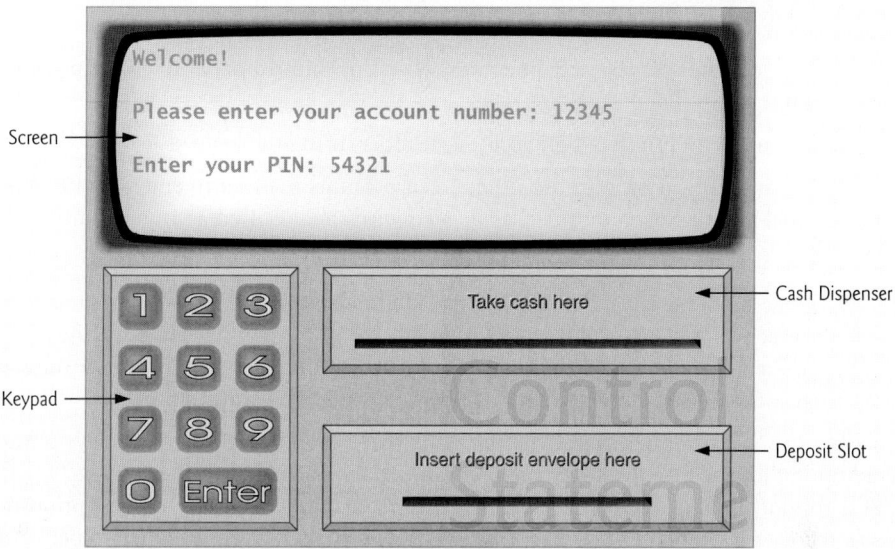

Screen

Keypad

Cash Dispenser

Deposit Slot

Fig. 3.24 | Automated teller machine user interface.

Also, a real ATM usually prints a paper receipt at the end of a session, but all output from this ATM appears on the screen.]

The bank wants you to develop software to perform the financial transactions initiated by bank customers through the ATM. The bank will integrate the software with the ATM's hardware at a later time. The software should simulate the functionality of the hardware devices (e.g., cash dispenser, deposit slot) in software components, but it need not concern itself with how these devices perform their duties. The ATM hardware has not been developed yet, so instead of writing your software to run on the ATM, you should develop a first version of the software to run on a personal computer. This version should use the computer's monitor to simulate the ATM's screen and the computer's keyboard to simulate the ATM's keypad.

An ATM session consists of authenticating a user (i.e., proving the user's identity) based on an account number and personal identification number (PIN), followed by creating and executing financial transactions. To authenticate a user and perform transactions, the ATM must interact with the bank's account information database. [*Note:* A database is an organized collection of data stored on a computer.] For each bank account, the database stores an account number, a PIN and a balance indicating the amount of money in the account. [*Note:* The bank plans to build only one ATM, so we do not need to worry about multiple ATMs accessing the database at the same time. Furthermore, we assume that the bank does not make any changes to the information in the database while a user is accessing the ATM. Also, any business system like an ATM faces reasonably complicated security issues that go well beyond the scope of this book. We make the simplifying assumption, however, that the bank trusts the ATM to access and manipulate the information in the database without significant security measures.]

Upon approaching the ATM, the user should experience the following sequence of events (see Fig. 3.24):

1. The screen displays a welcome message and prompts the user to enter an account number.

2. The user enters a five-digit account number, using the keypad.

3. For authentication purposes, the screen prompts the user to enter the PIN (personal identification number) associated with the specified account number.

4. The user enters a five-digit PIN, using the keypad.

5. If the user enters a valid account number and the correct PIN for that account, the screen displays the main menu (Fig. 3.25). If the user enters an invalid account number or an incorrect PIN, the screen displays an appropriate message, then the ATM returns to *Step 1* to restart the authentication process.

After the ATM authenticates the user, the main menu (Fig. 3.25) displays a numbered option for each of the three types of transactions: balance inquiry (option 1), withdrawal (option 2) and deposit (option 3). The main menu also displays an option that allows the user to exit the system (option 4). The user then chooses either to perform a transaction (by entering 1, 2 or 3) or to exit the system (by entering 4). If the user enters an invalid option, the screen displays an error message, then redisplays the main menu.

If the user enters 1 to make a balance inquiry, the screen displays the user's account balance. To do so, the ATM must retrieve the balance from the bank's database.

The following actions occur when the user enters 2 to make a withdrawal:

1. The screen displays a menu (shown in Fig. 3.26) containing standard withdrawal amounts: $20 (option 1), $40 (option 2), $60 (option 3), $100 (option 4) and

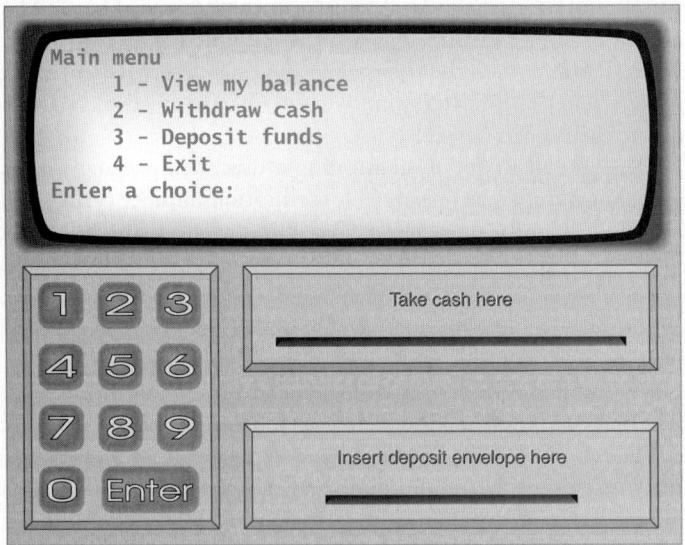

Fig. 3.25 | ATM main menu.

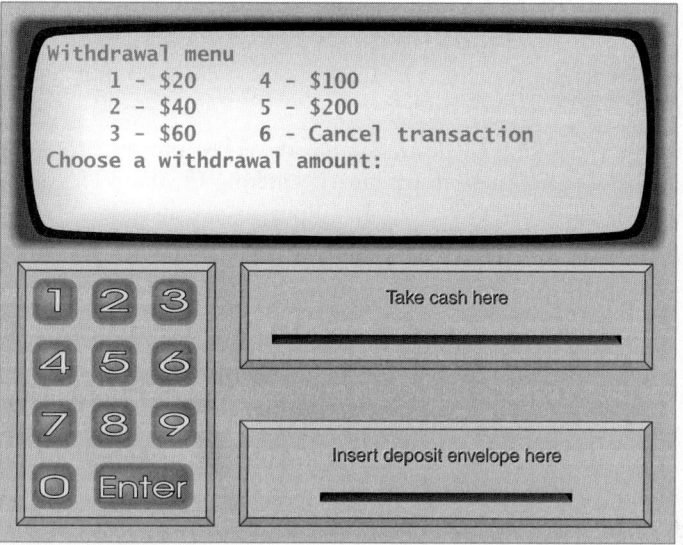

Fig. 3.26 | ATM withdrawal menu.

$200 (option 5). The menu also contains option 6, which allows the user to cancel the transaction.

2. The user enters a menu selection (1–6) using the keypad.

3. If the withdrawal amount chosen is greater than the user's account balance, the screen displays a message stating this and telling the user to choose a smaller amount. The ATM then returns to *Step 1*. If the withdrawal amount chosen is less than or equal to the user's account balance (i.e., an acceptable withdrawal amount), the ATM proceeds to *Step 4*. If the user chooses to cancel the transaction (option 6), the ATM displays the main menu (Fig. 3.25) and waits for user input.

4. If the cash dispenser contains enough cash to satisfy the request, the ATM proceeds to *Step 5*. Otherwise, the screen displays a message indicating the problem and telling the user to choose a smaller withdrawal amount. The ATM then returns to *Step 1*.

5. The ATM debits (i.e., subtracts) the withdrawal amount from the user's account balance in the bank's database.

6. The cash dispenser dispenses the desired amount of money to the user.

7. The screen displays a message reminding the user to take the money.

The following actions occur when the user enters 3 (from the main menu) to make a deposit:

1. The screen prompts the user to enter a deposit amount or to type 0 (zero) to cancel the transaction.

2. The user enters a deposit amount or 0, using the keypad. [*Note:* The keypad does not contain a decimal point or a dollar sign, so the user cannot type a real dollar amount (e.g., $147.25). Instead, the user must enter a deposit amount as a number of cents (e.g., 14725). The ATM then divides this number by 100 to obtain a number representing a dollar amount (e.g., $14725 \div 100 = 147.25$).]

3. If the user specifies a deposit amount, the ATM proceeds to *Step 4*. If the user chooses to cancel the transaction (by entering 0), the ATM displays the main menu (Fig. 3.25) and waits for user input.

4. The screen displays a message telling the user to insert a deposit envelope into the deposit slot.

5. If the deposit slot receives a deposit envelope within two minutes, the ATM credits (i.e., adds) the deposit amount to the user's account balance in the bank's database. [*Note:* This money is not immediately available for withdrawal. The bank first must verify the amount of cash in the deposit envelope, and any checks in the envelope must clear (i.e., money must be transferred from the check writer's account to the check recipient's account). When either of these events occurs, the bank appropriately updates the user's balance stored in its database. This occurs independently of the ATM system.] If the deposit slot does not receive a deposit envelope within two minutes, the screen displays a message that the system has canceled the transaction due to inactivity. The ATM then displays the main menu and waits for user input.

After the system successfully executes a transaction, the system should redisplay the main menu (Fig. 3.25) so that the user can perform additional transactions. If the user chooses to exit the system (by entering option 4), the screen should display a thank-you message, then display the welcome message for the next user.

Analyzing the ATM System

The preceding statement presented a simplified requirements document. Typically, such a document is the result of a detailed process of *requirements gathering* that might include interviews with potential users of the system and specialists in fields related to the system. For example, a systems analyst who is hired to prepare a requirements document for banking software (e.g., the ATM system described here) might interview financial experts and people who have used ATMs to gain a better understanding of *what* the software must do. The analyst would use the information gained to compile a list of *system requirements* to guide systems designers.

The process of requirements gathering is a key task of the first stage of the software life cycle. The *software life cycle* specifies the stages through which software evolves from the time it is conceived to the time it is retired from use. These stages typically include analysis, design, implementation, testing and debugging, deployment, maintenance and retirement. Several software life-cycle models exist, each with its own preferences and specifications for when and how often software engineers should perform the various stages. *Waterfall models* perform each stage once in succession, whereas *iterative models* may repeat one or more stages several times throughout a product's life cycle.

The analysis stage of the software life cycle focuses on precisely defining the problem to be solved. When designing any system, one must certainly *solve the problem right*, but of equal importance, one must *solve the right problem.* Systems analysts collect the requirements that indicate the specific problem to solve. Our requirements document describes our simple ATM system in sufficient detail that you do not need to go through an extensive analysis stage—it has been done for you.

To capture what a proposed system should do, developers often employ a technique known as *use case modeling.* This process identifies the *use cases* of the system, each of which represents a different capability that the system provides to its clients. For example, ATMs typically have several use cases, such as "View Account Balance," "Withdraw Cash," "Deposit Funds," "Transfer Funds Between Accounts" and "Buy Postage Stamps." The simplified ATM system we build in this case study requires only the first three use cases (Fig. 3.27).

Each use case describes a typical scenario in which the user uses the system. You have already read descriptions of the ATM system's use cases in the requirements document; the lists of steps required to perform each type of transaction (i.e., balance inquiry, withdrawal and deposit) actually described the three use cases of our ATM—"View Account Balance," "Withdraw Cash" and "Deposit Funds."

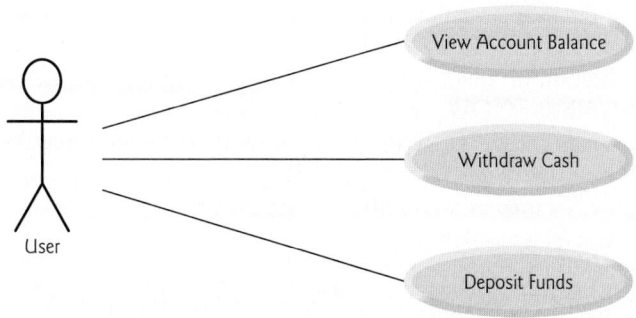

Fig. 3.27 | Use case diagram for the ATM system from the user's perspective.

Use Case Diagrams

We now introduce the first of several UML diagrams in our ATM case study. We create a *use case diagram* to model the interactions between a system's clients (in this case study, bank customers) and the system. The goal is to show the kinds of interactions users have with a system without providing the details—these are shown in other UML diagrams (which we present throughout the case study). Use case diagrams are often accompanied by informal text that describes the use cases in more detail—like the text that appears in the requirements document. Use case diagrams are produced during the analysis stage of the software life cycle. In larger systems, use case diagrams are simple but indispensable tools that help system designers focus on satisfying the users' needs.

Figure 3.27 shows the use case diagram for our ATM system. The stick figure represents an *actor*, which defines the roles that an external entity—such as a person or another system—plays when interacting with the system. For our automated teller machine, the actor is a User who can view an account balance, withdraw cash and deposit funds using the ATM. The User is not an actual person, but instead comprises the roles that a real person—when playing the part of a User—can play while interacting with the ATM. Note that a use case diagram can include multiple actors. For example, the use case diagram for a real bank's ATM system might also include an actor named Administrator who refills the cash dispenser each day.

We identify the actor in our system by examining the requirements document, which states, "ATM users should be able to view their account balance, withdraw cash and deposit funds." The actor in each of the three use cases is simply the User who interacts with the ATM. An external entity—a real person—plays the part of the User to perform financial transactions. Figure 3.27 shows one actor, whose name, User, appears below the actor in the diagram. The UML models each use case as an oval connected to an actor with a solid line.

Software engineers (more precisely, systems designers) must analyze the requirements document, or a set of use cases, and design the system before programmers implement it in a particular programming language. During the analysis stage, systems designers focus on understanding the requirements document to produce a high-level specification that describes *what* the system is supposed to do. The output of the design stage—a *design specification*—should specify *how* the system should be constructed to satisfy these requirements. In the next several Software Engineering Case Study sections, we perform the steps of a simple OOD process on the ATM system to produce a design specification containing a collection of UML diagrams and supporting text. Recall that the UML is designed for use with any OOD process. Many such processes exist, the best known being the Rational Unified Process™ (RUP) developed by Rational Software Corporation (now a division of IBM). RUP is a rich process for designing "industrial-strength" applications. For this case study, we present a simplified design process.

Designing the ATM System

We now begin the design stage of our ATM system. A *system* is a set of components that interact to solve a problem. For example, to perform the ATM system's designated tasks, our ATM system has a user interface (Fig. 3.24), contains software that executes financial transactions and interacts with a database of bank-account information. *System structure* describes the system's objects and their interrelationships. *System behavior* describes how the system changes as its objects interact with one another. Every system has both structure and behavior—designers must specify both. There are several distinct types of system structures and behaviors. For example, the interactions among objects in the system differ from those between the user and the system, yet both constitute a portion of the system behavior.

The UML 2 specifies 13 diagram types for documenting system models. Each diagram type models a distinct characteristic of a system's structure or behavior—six relate to system structure and seven to system behavior. We list here only the six types of diagrams used in our case study—of which one (the class diagram) models system structure and five model system behavior. We overview the remaining seven UML diagram types in Appendix E, UML 2: Additional Diagram Types.

1. *Use case diagrams*, such as the one in Fig. 3.27, model the interactions between a system and its external entities (actors) in terms of use cases (system capabilities, such as "View Account Balance," "Withdraw Cash" and "Deposit Funds").

2. *Class diagrams*, which you'll study in Section 4.12, model the classes, or "building blocks," used in a system. Each noun, or "thing," described in the requirements document is a candidate to be a class in the system (e.g., "account," "keypad"). Class diagrams help us specify the structural relationships between parts of the system. For example, the ATM system class diagram will, among other things, specify that the ATM is physically composed of a screen, a keypad, a cash dispenser and a deposit slot.

3. *State machine diagrams*, which you'll study in Section 6.9, model the ways in which an object changes state. An object's *state* is indicated by the values of all its attributes at a given time. When an object changes state, it may subsequently behave differently in the system. For example, after validating a user's PIN, the ATM transitions from the "user not authenticated" state to the "user authenticated" state, at which point the ATM allows the user to perform financial transactions (e.g., view account balance, withdraw cash, deposit funds).

4. *Activity diagrams*, which you'll also study in Section 6.9, model an object's *activity*—the object's workflow (sequence of events) during program execution. An activity diagram models the actions the object performs and specifies the order in which it performs them. For example, an activity diagram shows that the ATM must obtain the balance of the user's account (from the bank's account-information database) before the screen can display the balance to the user.

5. *Communication diagrams* (called collaboration diagrams in earlier versions of the UML) model the interactions among objects in a system, with an emphasis on *what* interactions occur. You'll see in Section 8.14 that these diagrams show which objects must interact to perform an ATM transaction. For example, the ATM must communicate with the bank's account-information database to retrieve an account balance.

6. *Sequence diagrams* also model the interactions among the objects in a system, but unlike communication diagrams, they emphasize *when* interactions occur. You'll see in Section 8.14 that these diagrams help show the order in which interactions occur in executing a financial transaction. For example, the screen prompts the user to enter a withdrawal amount before cash is dispensed.

In Section 4.12, we continue designing our ATM system by identifying the classes from the requirements document. We accomplish this by extracting key nouns and noun phrases from the requirements document. Using these classes, we develop our first draft of the class diagram that models the structure of our ATM system.

Web Resources
The following URLs provide information on object-oriented design with the UML.

`www-306.ibm.com/software/rational/offerings/design.html`
Provides information about IBM Rational software available for designing systems. Provides downloads of 30-day trial versions of several products, such as IBM Rational Application Developer.

`www.borland.com/us/products/together/index.html`
Provides a free 30-day license to download a trial version of Borland® Together® ControlCenter™—a software-development tool that supports the UML.

`argouml.tigris.org`
Contains information and downloads for ArgoUML, a free open-source UML tool written in Java.

`www.objectsbydesign.com/books/booklist.html`
Lists books on the UML and object-oriented design.

`www.objectsbydesign.com/tools/umltools_byCompany.html`
Lists software tools that use the UML, such as IBM Rational Rose, Embarcadero Describe, Sparx Systems Enterprise Architect, I-Logix Rhapsody and Gentleware Poseidon for UML.

`www.ootips.org/ood-principles.html`
Provides answers to the question, "What Makes a Good Object-Oriented Design?"

`parlezuml.com/tutorials/umlforjava.htm`
Provides a UML tutorial for Java developers that presents UML diagrams side by side with the Java code that implements them.

`www.cetus-links.org/oo_uml.html`
Introduces the UML and provides links to numerous UML resources.

`www.agilemodeling.com/essays/umlDiagrams.htm`
Provides in-depth descriptions and tutorials on each of the 13 UML-2 diagram types.

Recommended Readings
The following books provide information on object-oriented design with the UML.

Booch, G. *Object-Oriented Analysis and Design with Applications.* 3rd ed. Boston: Addison-Wesley, 2004.

Eriksson, H., et al. *UML 2 Toolkit.* Hoboken, NJ: John Wiley & Sons, 2003.

Fowler, M. *UML Distilled.* 3rd ed. Boston: Addison-Wesley Professional, 2004.

Kruchten, P. *The Rational Unified Process: An Introduction.* Boston: Addison-Wesley, 2004.

Larman, C. *Applying UML and Patterns: An Introduction to Object-Oriented Analysis and Design.* 2nd ed. Upper Saddle River, NJ: Prentice Hall, 2002.

Roques, P. *UML in Practice: The Art of Modeling Software Systems Demonstrated Through Worked Examples and Solutions.* Hoboken, NJ: John Wiley & Sons, 2004.

Rosenberg, D. and K. Scott. *Applying Use Case Driven Object Modeling with UML: An Annotated e-Commerce Example.* Reading, MA: Addison-Wesley, 2001.

Rumbaugh, J., I. Jacobson and G. Booch. *The Complete UML Training Course.* Upper Saddle River, NJ: Prentice Hall, 2000.

Rumbaugh, J., I. Jacobson and G. Booch. *The Unified Modeling Language Reference Manual.* Reading, MA: Addison-Wesley, 1999.

Rumbaugh, J., I. Jacobson and G. Booch. *The Unified Software Development Process.* Reading, MA: Addison-Wesley, 1999.

Schneider, G. and J. Winters. *Applying Use Cases: A Practical Guide.* 2nd ed. Boston: Addison-Wesley Professional, 2002.

Software Engineering Case Study Self-Review Exercises
3.1 Suppose we enabled a user of our ATM system to transfer money between two bank accounts. Modify the use case diagram of Fig. 3.27 to reflect this change.

3.2 _____ model the interactions among objects in a system with an emphasis on *when* these interactions occur.
   a) Class diagrams

   b) Sequence diagrams
   c) Communication diagrams
   d) Activity diagrams

3.3 Which of the following choices lists stages of a typical software life cycle in sequential order?
   a) design, analysis, implementation, testing
   b) design, analysis, testing, implementation
   c) analysis, design, testing, implementation
   d) analysis, design, implementation, testing

Answers to Software Engineering Case Study Self-Review Exercises

3.1 Figure 3.28 contains a use case diagram for a modified version of our ATM system that also allows users to transfer money between accounts.

3.2 b.

3.3 d.

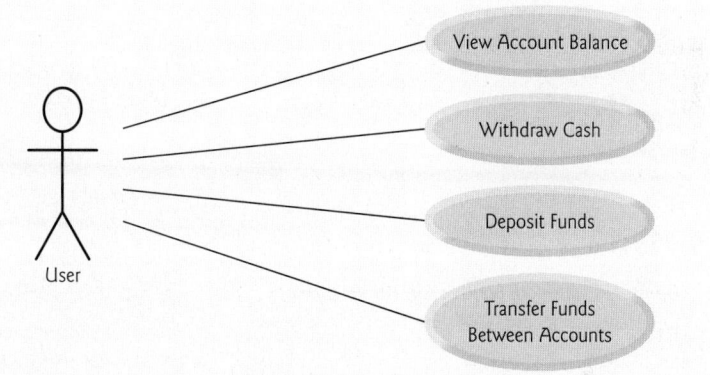

Fig. 3.28 | Use case diagram for a modified version of our ATM system that also allows users to transfer money between accounts.

3.10 Wrap-Up

You learned many important features of C# in this chapter, including displaying data in a Command Prompt, inputting data from the keyboard, performing calculations and making decisions. The applications presented here introduced you to basic programming concepts. As you'll see in Chapter 4, C# applications typically contain just a few lines of code in method Main—these statements normally create the objects that perform the work of the application. In Chapter 4, you'll learn how to implement your own classes and use objects of those classes in applications.

3.11 Web Resources

www.deitel.com/VisualCSharp2008/
The Deitel Visual C# 2008 Resource Center contains links to some of the best Visual C# information on the web, with categorized links to tutorials, references, code examples, videos, and more.

4

Introduction to Classes and Objects

Nothing can have value without being an object of utility.
—Karl Marx

Your public servants serve you right.
—Adlai E. Stevenson

Knowing how to answer one who speaks,
To reply to one who sends a message.
—Amenemope

You'll see something new. Two things. And I call them Thing One and Thing Two.
—Dr. Theodor Seuss Geisel

OBJECTIVES

In this chapter you'll learn:

- What classes, objects, methods and instance variables are.

- How to declare a class and use it to create an object.

- How to implement a class's behaviors as methods.

- How to implement a class's attributes as instance variables and properties.

- How to call an object's methods to make them perform their tasks.

- The differences between instance variables of a class and local variables of a method.

- How to use a constructor to ensure that an object's data is initialized when the object is created.

- The differences between value types and reference types.

Outline

4.1 Introduction

4.2 Classes, Objects, Methods, Properties and Instance Variables

4.3 Declaring a Class with a Method and Instantiating an Object of a Class

4.4 Declaring a Method with a Parameter

4.5 Instance Variables and Properties

4.6 UML Class Diagram with a Property

4.7 Software Engineering with Properties and `set` and `get` Accessors

4.8 Auto-Implemented Properties

4.9 Value Types vs. Reference Types

4.10 Initializing Objects with Constructors

4.11 Floating-Point Numbers and Type `decimal`

4.12 (Optional) Software Engineering Case Study: Identifying the Classes in the ATM Requirements Document

4.13 Wrap-Up

4.1 Introduction

We introduced the basic terminology and concepts of object-oriented programming in Section 1.11. In Chapter 3, you began to use those concepts to create simple applications that displayed messages to the user, obtained information from the user, performed calculations and made decisions. One common feature of every application in Chapter 3 was that all the statements that performed tasks were located in method `Main`. Typically, the applications you develop in this book will consist of two or more classes, each containing one or more methods. Development teams in industry might work on applications that contain hundreds, or even thousands, of classes. In this chapter, we present a simple framework for organizing object-oriented applications in C#.

First, we explain the concept of classes using a real-world example. Then we present five complete working applications to demonstrate how to create and use your own classes. The first four of these examples begin our case study on developing a grade-book class that instructors can use to maintain student test scores. This case study is enhanced over the next several chapters, culminating with the version presented in Chapter 8, Arrays. The last example introduces the type `decimal` and uses it to declare monetary amounts in the context of a bank-account class that maintains a customer's balance.

4.2 Classes, Objects, Methods, Properties and Instance Variables

Let's begin with a simple analogy to help you understand classes and their contents. Suppose you want to drive a car and make it go faster by pressing down on its accelerator pedal. What must happen before you can do this? Well, before you can drive a car, someone has to design it. A car typically begins as engineering drawings, similar to the blueprints used to design a house. These engineering drawings include the design for an accelerator pedal to make the car go faster. The pedal "hides" the complex mechanisms that actually make the car go faster, just as the brake pedal "hides" the mechanisms that slow the car and the steering wheel "hides" the mechanisms that turn the car. This enables people with little or no knowledge of how engines work to drive a car easily.

Unfortunately, you can't drive the engineering drawings of a car. Before you can drive a car, it must be built from the engineering drawings that describe it. A completed car will have an actual accelerator pedal to make the car go faster, but even that's not enough—the car will not accelerate on its own, so the driver must press the accelerator pedal.

Now let's use our car example to introduce the key programming concepts of this section. Performing a task in an application requires a method. The *method* describes the mechanisms that actually perform its tasks. The method hides from its user the complex tasks that it performs, just as the accelerator pedal of a car hides from the driver the complex mechanisms of making the car go faster. In C#, we begin by creating an application unit called a *class* to house (among other things) a method, just as a car's engineering drawings house (among other things) the design of an accelerator pedal. In a class, you provide one or more methods that are designed to perform the class's tasks. For example, a class that represents a bank account might contain one method to deposit money in an account, another to withdraw money from an account and a third to inquire what the current account balance is.

Just as you cannot drive an engineering drawing of a car, you cannot "drive" a class. Just as someone has to build a car from its engineering drawings before you can actually drive a car, you must build an *object* of a class before you can get an application to perform the tasks the class describes. That is one reason C# is known as an object-oriented programming language.

When you drive a car, pressing its gas pedal sends a message to the car to perform a task—make the car go faster. Similarly, you send *messages* to an object—each message is known as a *method call* and tells a method of the object to perform its task.

Thus far, we've used the car analogy to introduce classes, objects and methods. In addition to a car's capabilities, it also has many *attributes*, such as its color, the number of doors, the amount of gas in its tank, its current speed and its total miles driven (i.e., its odometer reading). Like the car's capabilities, these attributes are represented as part of a car's design in its engineering diagrams. As you drive a car, these attributes are always associated with the car. Every car maintains its own attributes. For example, each car knows how much gas is in its own gas tank, but not how much is in the tanks of other cars. Similarly, an object has attributes that are carried with the object as it's used in an application. These attributes are specified as part of the object's class. For example, a bank-account object has a balance attribute that represents the amount of money in the account. Each bank-account object knows the balance in the account it represents, but not the balances of the other accounts in the bank. Attributes are specified by the class's *instance variables*.

Notice that these attributes are not necessarily accessible directly. The car manufacturer does not want drivers to take apart the car's engine to observe the amount of gas in its tank. Instead, the driver can check the fuel gauge on the dashboard. The bank does not want its customers to walk into the vault to count the amount of money in an account. Instead, the customers talk to a bank teller or check personalized online bank accounts. Similarly, you do not need to have access to an object's instance variables in order to use them. You can use the *properties* of an object. Properties contain *get accessors* for reading the values of variables, and *set accessors* for storing values into them.

The remainder of this chapter presents examples that demonstrate the concepts we introduced here in the context of the car analogy. The first five examples, summarized below, incrementally build a GradeBook class:

1. The first example presents a GradeBook class with one method that simply displays a welcome message when it is called. We show how to *create an object* of that class and call the method so that it displays the welcome message.

2. The second example enhances the first by allowing the method to receive a course name as an "argument" and by displaying the name in the welcome message.

3. The third example shows how to store the course name in a GradeBook object. For this version of the class, we also show how to use properties to set the course name and obtain the course name.

4. The fourth example shows how to use C#'s new auto-implemented properties to create the property for the course name.

5. The fifth example demonstrates how the data in a GradeBook object can be initialized when the object is created—the initialization is performed by the class's constructor.

The last example in the chapter presents an Account class that reinforces the concepts presented in the first five examples and introduces the decimal type—a decimal number can contain a decimal point, as in 0.0345, −7.23 and 100.7, and is used for precise calculations, especially those involving monetary values. For this purpose, we present an Account class that represents a bank account and maintains its decimal balance. The class contains a method to credit a deposit to the account, thus increasing the balance, and a property to retrieve the balance and ensure that all values assigned to the balance are nonnegative. The class's constructor initializes the balance of each Account object as the object is created. We create two Account objects and make deposits into each to show that each object maintains its own balance. The example also demonstrates how to input and display decimal numbers.

4.3 Declaring a Class with a Method and Instantiating an Object of a Class

We begin with an example that consists of classes GradeBook (Fig. 4.1) and GradeBook-Test (Fig. 4.2). Class GradeBook (declared in file GradeBook.cs) will be used to display a message on the screen (Fig. 4.2) welcoming the instructor to the grade-book application. Class GradeBookTest (declared in the file GradeBookTest.cs) is a testing class in which the Main method will create and use an object of class GradeBook. By convention, we declare classes GradeBook and GradeBookTest in separate files, such that each file's name matches the name of the class it contains.

To start, select **File > New Project...** to open the **New Project** dialog, then create a GradeBook **Console Application**. Rename the Program.cs file to GradeBook.cs. Delete all the code provided automatically by the IDE and replace it with the code in Fig. 4.1.

Class GradeBook

The GradeBook *class declaration* (Fig. 4.1) contains a DisplayMessage method (lines 8–11) that displays a message on the screen. Line 10 of the class displays the message. Recall

```
 1    // Fig. 4.1: GradeBook.cs
 2    // Class declaration with one method.
 3    using System;
 4
 5    public class GradeBook
 6    {
 7       // display a welcome message to the GradeBook user
 8       public void DisplayMessage()
 9       {
10          Console.WriteLine( "Welcome to the Grade Book!" );
11       } // end method DisplayMessage
12    } // end class GradeBook
```

Fig. 4.1 | Class declaration with one method.

that a class is like a blueprint—we need to make an object of this class and call its method to get line 10 to execute and display its message—we do this in Fig. 4.2.

The class declaration begins in line 5. The keyword public is an *access modifier*. Access modifiers determine the accessibility of an object's properties and methods to other methods in an application. For now, we simply declare every class public. Every class declaration contains keyword class followed by the class's name. Every class's body is enclosed in a pair of left and right braces ({ and }), as in lines 6 and 12 of class GradeBook.

In Chapter 3, each class we declared had one method named Main. Class GradeBook also has one method—DisplayMessage (lines 8–11). Recall that Main is a special method that is always called automatically when you execute an application. Most methods do not get called automatically. As you'll soon see, you must call method DisplayMessage to tell it to perform its task.

The method declaration begins with keyword public to indicate that the method is "available to the public"—that is, it can be called from outside the class declaration's body by methods of other classes. Keyword void—known as the method's *return type*—indicates that this method will not return (i.e., give back) any information to its *calling method* when it completes its task. When a method that specifies a return type other than void is called and completes its task, the method returns a result to its calling method. For example, when you go to an automated teller machine (ATM) and request your account balance, you expect the ATM to give you back a value that represents your balance. If you have a method Square that returns the square of its argument, you'd expect the statement

```
int result = Square( 2 );
```

to return 4 from method Square and assign 4 to variable result. If you have a method Maximum that returns the largest of three integer arguments, you'd expect the statement

```
int biggest = Maximum( 27, 114, 51 );
```

to return the value 114 from method Maximum and assign the value to variable biggest. You have already used methods that return information—for example, in Chapter 3 you used Console method ReadLine to input a string typed by the user at the keyboard. When ReadLine inputs a value, it returns that value for use in the application.

The name of the method, DisplayMessage, follows the return type (line 8). Generally, methods are named as verbs or verb phrases while classes are named as nouns. By convention, method names begin with an uppercase first letter, and all subsequent words in the name begin with an uppercase letter. This naming convention is referred to as Pascal case. The parentheses after the method name indicate that this is a method. An empty set of parentheses, as shown in line 8, indicates that this method does not require additional information to perform its task. Line 8 is commonly referred to as the *method header*. Every method's body is delimited by left and right braces, as in lines 9 and 11.

The body of a method contains statement(s) that perform the method's task. In this case, the method contains one statement (line 10) that displays the message "Welcome to the Grade Book!", followed by a newline in the console window. After this statement executes, the method has completed its task.

Next, we'd like to use class GradeBook in an application. As you learned in Chapter 3, method Main begins the execution of every application. Class GradeBook cannot begin an application because it does not contain Main. This was not a problem in Chapter 3, because every class you declared had a Main method. To fix this problem for the Grade-Book, we must either declare a separate class that contains a Main method or place a Main method in class GradeBook. In preparation for the larger applications we'll encounter later in this book, we use a separate class (GradeBookTest in this example) containing method Main to test each new class we create in this chapter.

Adding a Class to a Visual C# Project

For each example in this chapter, you'll add a class to your console application. To do this, right click the project name in the **Solution Explorer** and select **Add > New Item...** from the pop-up menu. In the **Add New Item** dialog that appears, select **Code File** and enter the name of your new file—in this case, GradeBookTest.cs. A new, blank file will be added to your project. Add the code from Fig. 4.2 to this file.

Class GradeBookTest

The GradeBookTest class declaration (Fig. 4.2) contains the Main method that controls our application's execution. Any class that contains a Main method (as shown in line 6)

```
1   // Fig. 4.2: GradeBookTest.cs
2   // Create a GradeBook object and call its DisplayMessage method.
3   public class GradeBookTest
4   {
5      // Main method begins program execution
6      public static void Main( string[] args )
7      {
8         // create a GradeBook object and assign it to myGradeBook
9         GradeBook myGradeBook = new GradeBook();
10
11        // call myGradeBook's DisplayMessage method
12        myGradeBook.DisplayMessage();
13     } // end Main
14  } // end class GradeBookTest
```

```
Welcome to the Grade Book!
```

Fig. 4.2 | Create a GradeBook object and call its DisplayMessage method.

can be used to execute an application. This class declaration begins in line 3 and ends in line 14. The class contains only a Main method, which is typical of many classes that simply begin an application's execution.

Lines 6–13 declare method Main. A key part of enabling the method Main to begin the application's execution is the static keyword (line 6), which indicates that Main is a static method. A static method is special because it can be called without first creating an object of the class (in this case, GradeBookTest) in which the method is declared. We explain static methods in Chapter 7, Methods: A Deeper Look.

In this application, we'd like to call class GradeBook's DisplayMessage method to display the welcome message in the console window. Typically, you cannot call a method that belongs to another class until you create an object of that class, as shown in line 9. We begin by declaring variable myGradeBook. Note that the variable's type is GradeBook—the class we declared in Fig. 4.1. Each new class you create becomes a new type in C# that can be used to declare variables and create objects. New class types will be accessible to all classes in the same project. You can declare new class types as needed; this is one reason why C# is known as an *extensible language*.

Variable myGradeBook (line 9) is initialized with the result of the *object-creation expression* new GradeBook(). The new operator creates a new object of the class specified to the right of the keyword (i.e., GradeBook). The parentheses to the right of the Grade-Book are required. As you'll learn in Section 4.10, those parentheses in combination with a class name represent a call to a constructor, which is similar to a method, but is used only at the time an object is created to initialize the object's data. In that section you'll see that data can be placed in parentheses to specify initial values for the object's data. For now, we simply leave the parentheses empty.

We can now use myGradeBook to call its method DisplayMessage. Line 12 calls the method DisplayMessage (lines 8–11 of Fig. 4.1) using variable myGradeBook followed by a *member access (.) operator*, the method name DisplayMessage and an empty set of parentheses. This call causes the DisplayMessage method to perform its task. This method call differs from the method calls in Chapter 3 that displayed information in a console window—each of those method calls provided arguments that specified the data to display. At the beginning of line 12, "myGradeBook." indicates that Main should use the GradeBook object that was created in line 9. The empty parentheses in line 8 of Fig. 4.1 indicate that method DisplayMessage does not require additional information to perform its task. For this reason, the method call (line 12 of Fig. 4.2) specifies an empty set of parentheses after the method name to indicate that no arguments are being passed to method DisplayMe-ssage. When method DisplayMessage completes its task, method Main continues executing at line 13. This is the end of method Main, so the application terminates.

UML Class Diagram for Class GradeBook

Figure 4.3 presents a *UML class diagram* for class GradeBook of Fig. 4.1. Recall from Section 1.11 that the UML is a graphical language used by programmers to represent their object-oriented systems in a standardized manner. In the UML, each class is modeled in a class diagram as a rectangle with three compartments. The top compartment contains the name of the class centered horizontally in boldface type. The middle compartment contains the class's attributes, which correspond to instance variables and properties in C#. In Fig. 4.3, the middle compartment is empty because the version of class GradeBook in

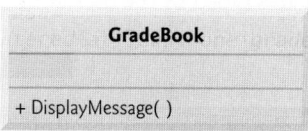

Fig. 4.3 | UML class diagram indicating that class GradeBook has a public DisplayMessage operation.

Fig. 4.1 does not have any attributes. The bottom compartment contains the class's operations, which correspond to methods in C#. The UML models operations by listing the operation name followed by a set of parentheses. Class GradeBook has one method, DisplayMessage, so the bottom compartment of Fig. 4.3 lists one operation with this name. Method DisplayMessage does not require additional information to perform its tasks, so there are empty parentheses following DisplayMessage in the class diagram, just as they appeared in the method's declaration in line 8 of Fig. 4.1. The plus sign (+) in front of the operation name indicates that DisplayMessage is a public operation in the UML (i.e., a public method in C#). The plus sign is sometimes called the ***public visibility symbol***. We'll often use UML class diagrams to summarize a class's attributes and operations.

4.4 Declaring a Method with a Parameter

In our car analogy from Section 4.2, we discussed the fact that pressing a car's gas pedal sends a message to the car to perform a task—make the car go faster. But how fast should the car accelerate? As you know, the farther down you press the pedal, the faster the car accelerates. So the message to the car actually includes both the task to be performed and additional information that helps the car perform the task. This additional information is known as a ***parameter***—the value of the parameter helps the car determine how fast to accelerate. Similarly, a method can require one or more parameters that represent additional information it needs to perform its task. A method call supplies values—called arguments—for each of the method's parameters. For example, the Console.WriteLine method requires an argument that specifies the data to be displayed in a console window. Similarly, to make a deposit into a bank account, a Deposit method specifies a parameter that represents the deposit amount. When the Deposit method is called, an argument value representing the deposit amount is assigned to the method's parameter. The method then makes a deposit of that amount, by increasing the account's balance.

Our next example declares class GradeBook (Fig. 4.4) with a DisplayMessage method that displays the course name as part of the welcome message. (See the sample execution in Fig. 4.5.) The new DisplayMessage method requires a parameter that represents the course name to output.

Before discussing the new features of class GradeBook, let's see how the new class is used from the Main method of class GradeBookTest (Fig. 4.5). Line 12 creates an object of class GradeBook and assigns it to variable myGradeBook. Line 15 prompts the user to enter a course name. Line 16 reads the name from the user and assigns it to the variable nameOfCourse, using Console method ReadLine to perform the input. The user types the course name and presses *Enter* to submit the course name to the application. Note that pressing *Enter* inserts a newline character at the end of the characters typed by the user.

Method ReadLine reads characters typed by the user until the newline character is encountered, then returns a string containing the characters up to, but not including, the newline. The newline character is discarded.

```
1  // Fig. 4.4: GradeBook.cs
2  // Class declaration with a method that has a parameter.
3  using System;
4
5  public class GradeBook
6  {
7     // display a welcome message to the GradeBook user
8     public void DisplayMessage( string courseName )
9     {
10        Console.WriteLine( "Welcome to the grade book for\n{0}!",
11           courseName );
12     } // end method DisplayMessage
13  } // end class GradeBook
```

Fig. 4.4 | Class declaration with a method that has a parameter.

```
1  // Fig. 4.5: GradeBookTest.cs
2  // Create a GradeBook object and pass a string to
3  // its DisplayMessage method.
4  using System;
5
6  public class GradeBookTest
7  {
8     // Main method begins program execution
9     public static void Main( string[] args )
10    {
11       // create a GradeBook object and assign it to myGradeBook
12       GradeBook myGradeBook = new GradeBook();
13
14       // prompt for and input course name
15       Console.WriteLine( "Please enter the course name:" );
16       string nameOfCourse = Console.ReadLine(); // read a line of text
17       Console.WriteLine(); // output a blank line
18
19       // call myGradeBook's DisplayMessage method
20       // and pass nameOfCourse as an argument
21       myGradeBook.DisplayMessage( nameOfCourse );
22    } // end Main
23  } // end class GradeBookTest
```

```
Please enter the course name:
CS101 Introduction to C# Programming

Welcome to the grade book for
CS101 Introduction to C# Programming!
```

Fig. 4.5 | Create GradeBook object and pass a string to its DisplayMessage method.

Line 21 calls myGradeBook's DisplayMessage method. The variable nameOfCourse in parentheses is the argument that is passed to method DisplayMessage so that the method can perform its task. Variable nameOfCourse's value in Main becomes the value of method DisplayMessage's parameter courseName in line 8 of Fig. 4.4. When you execute this application, notice that method DisplayMessage outputs the name you type as part of the welcome message (Fig. 4.5).

Software Engineering Observation 4.1

Normally, objects are created with new. *One exception is a string literal that is contained in quotes, such as* "hello". *String literals are references to* string *objects that are implicitly created by C#.*

More on Arguments and Parameters

When you declare a method, you must specify in the method's declaration whether the method requires data to perform its task. To do so, you place additional information in the method's *parameter list*, which is located in the parentheses that follow the method name. The parameter list may contain any number of parameters, including none at all. Each parameter is declared as a variable with a type and identifier in the parameter list. Empty parentheses following the method name (as in Fig. 4.1, line 8) indicate that a method does not require any parameters. In Fig. 4.4, DisplayMessage's parameter list (line 8) declares that the method requires one parameter. Each parameter must specify a type and an identifier. In this case, the type string and the identifier courseName indicate that method DisplayMessage requires a string to perform its task. At the time the method is called, the argument value in the call is assigned to the corresponding parameter (in this case, courseName) in the method header. Then, the method body uses the parameter courseName to access the value. Lines 10–11 of Fig. 4.4 display parameter courseName's value, using the {0} format item in WriteLine's first argument. Note that the parameter variable's name (Fig. 4.4, line 8) can be the same or different from the argument variable's name (Fig. 4.5, line 21).

A method can specify multiple parameters by separating each parameter from the next with a comma. The number of arguments in a method call must match the number of parameters in the parameter list of the called method's declaration. Also, the types of the arguments in the method call must be consistent with the types of the corresponding parameters in the method's declaration. (As you'll learn in subsequent chapters, an argument's type and its corresponding parameter's type are not always required to be identical.) In our example, the method call passes one argument of type string (nameOfCourse is declared as a string in line 16 of Fig. 4.5), and the method declaration specifies one parameter of type string (line 8 in Fig. 4.4). So the type of the argument in the method call exactly matches the type of the parameter in the method header.

Common Programming Error 4.1

A compilation error occurs if the number of arguments in a method call does not match the number of parameters in the method declaration.

Common Programming Error 4.2

A compilation error occurs if the types of the arguments in a method call are not consistent with the types of the corresponding parameters in the method declaration.

Updated UML Class Diagram for Class GradeBook

The UML class diagram of Fig. 4.6 models class GradeBook of Fig. 4.4. Like Fig. 4.4, this GradeBook class contains public operation DisplayMessage. However, this version of DisplayMessage has a parameter. The UML models a parameter a bit differently from C# by listing the parameter name, followed by a colon and the parameter type in the parentheses following the operation name. The UML has several data types that are similar to the C# types. For example, UML types String and Integer correspond to C# types string and int, respectively. Unfortunately, the UML does not provide types that correspond to every C# type. For this reason, and to avoid confusion between UML types and C# types, *we use only C# types in our UML diagrams*. Class Gradebook's method Display-Message (Fig. 4.4) has a string parameter named courseName, so Fig. 4.6 lists the parameter courseName : string between the parentheses following DisplayMessage.

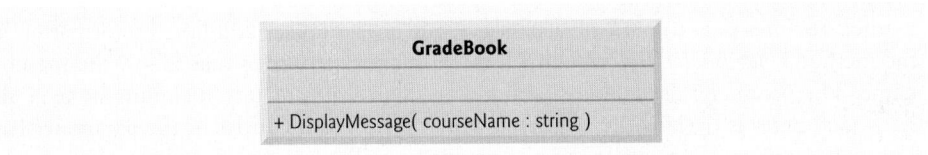

Fig. 4.6 | UML class diagram indicating that class GradeBook has a public DisplayMessage operation with a courseName parameter of type string.

Notes on using Directives

Notice the using directive in Fig. 4.5 (line 4). This indicates to the compiler that the application uses classes in the System namespace, like the Console class. Why do we need a using directive to use class Console, but not class GradeBook? There is a special relationship between classes that are compiled in the same project, like classes GradeBook and GradeBookTest. By default, such classes are considered to be in the same namespace. A using directive is not required when one class in a namespace uses another in the same namespace—such as when class GradeBookTest uses class GradeBook. You'll see in Section 10.14 how to declare your own namespaces with the namespace keyword. For simplicity, our examples in this chapter do not declare a namespace. Any classes that are not explicitly placed in a namespace are implicitly placed in the so-called *global namespace*.

Actually, the using directive in line 4 is not required if we always refer to class Console as System.Console, which includes the full namespace and class name. This is known as the class's *fully qualified class name*. For example, line 15 could be written as

```
System.Console.WriteLine( "Please enter the course name:" );
```

Most C# programmers consider using fully qualified names to be cumbersome, and instead prefer to use using directives. The code generated by the Visual C# Form Designer uses fully qualified names.

4.5 Instance Variables and Properties

In Chapter 3, we declared all of an application's variables in the application's Main method. Variables declared in the body of a method are known as *local variables* and can be used only in that method. When a method terminates, the values of its local variables are lost. Recall from Section 4.2 that an object has attributes that are carried with the object as it is used in an application. Such attributes exist before a method is called on an object and after the method completes execution.

Attributes are represented as variables in a class declaration. Such variables are called *fields* and are declared inside a class declaration but outside the bodies of the class's method declarations. When each object of a class maintains its own copy of an attribute, the field that represents the attribute is also known as an instance variable—each object (instance) of the class has a separate instance of the variable. [*Note:* In Chapter 10, Classes and Objects: A Deeper Look, we discuss another type of field called a static variable, where all objects of the same class share one variable.]

A class normally contains one or more properties that manipulate the attributes that belong to a particular object of the class. The example in this section demonstrates a GradeBook class that contains a courseName instance variable to represent a particular GradeBook object's course name, and a CourseName property to manipulate courseName.

GradeBook Class with an Instance Variable and a Property

In our next application (Figs. 4.7–4.8), class GradeBook (Fig. 4.7) maintains the course name as an instance variable so that it can be used or modified at any time during an application's execution. The class also contains one method—DisplayMessage (lines 24–30)—and one property—CourseName (line 11–21). Recall from Chapter 2 that properties are used to manipulate an object's attributes. For example, in that chapter, we used a Label's Text property to specify the text to display on the Label. In this example, we use a property in code rather than in the **Properties** window of the IDE. To do this, we first declare a property as a member of the GradeBook class. As you'll soon see, the GradeBook's CourseName property can be used to store a course name in a GradeBook (in instance variable courseName) or retrieve the GradeBook's course name (from instance variable courseName). Method DisplayMessage—which now specifies no parameters—still displays a welcome message that includes the course name. However, the method now uses the CourseName property to obtain the course name from instance variable courseName.

A typical instructor teaches more than one course, each with its own course name. Line 8 declares courseName as a variable of type string. Line 8 is a declaration for an instance variable, because the variable is declared in the class's body (lines 7–31) but outside the bodies of the class's method (lines 24–30) and property (lines 11–21). Every instance (i.e., object) of class GradeBook contains one copy of each instance variable. For

```
1   // Fig. 4.7: GradeBook.cs
2   // GradeBook class that contains a courseName instance variable,
3   // and a property to get and set its value.
4   using System;
5
6   public class GradeBook
7   {
8       private string courseName; // course name for this GradeBook
9
```

Fig. 4.7 | GradeBook class that contains a private instance variable, courseName and a public property to get and set its value. (Part 1 of 2.)

```
10        // property to get and set the course name
11        public string CourseName
12        {
13           get
14           {
15              return courseName;
16           } // end get
17           set
18           {
19              courseName = value;
20           } // end set
21        } // end property CourseName
22
23        // display a welcome message to the GradeBook user
24        public void DisplayMessage()
25        {
26           // use property CourseName to get the
27           // name of the course that this GradeBook represents
28           Console.WriteLine( "Welcome to the grade book for\n{0}!",
29              CourseName ); // display property CourseName
30        } // end method DisplayMessage
31     } // end class GradeBook
```

Fig. 4.7 | GradeBook class that contains a private instance variable, courseName and a public property to get and set its value. (Part 2 of 2.)

example, if there are two GradeBook objects, each object has its own copy of courseName. All the methods and properties of class GradeBook can directly manipulate its instance variable courseName, but it is considered good practice for methods of a class to use that class's properties to manipulate instance variables (as we do in line 29 of method DisplayMessage). The software engineering reasons for this will soon become clear.

Access Modifiers public and private
Most instance-variable declarations are preceded with the keyword private (as in line 8). Like public, keyword private is an access modifier. Variables, properties or methods declared with access modifier private are accessible only to properties and methods of the class in which they are declared. Thus, variable courseName can be used only in property CourseName and method DisplayMessage of class GradeBook.

Software Engineering Observation 4.2
Precede every field and method declaration with an access modifier. Generally, instance variables should be declared private and methods and properties should be declared public. If the access modifier is omitted before a member of a class, the member is implicitly declared private. (We'll see that it is appropriate to declare certain methods private, if they will be accessed only by other methods of the class.)

Software Engineering Observation 4.3
Declaring the instance variables of a class as private and the methods of the class as public facilitates debugging, because problems with data manipulations are localized to the class's methods and properties, since the private instance variables are accessible only to these methods and properties.

Good Programming Practice 4.1

We prefer to list the fields of a class first, so that, as you read the code, you see the names and types of the variables before you see them used in the methods of the class. It is possible to list the class's fields anywhere in the class outside its method declarations, but scattering them can make code difficult to read.

Good Programming Practice 4.2

Placing a blank line between method and property declarations enhances code readability.

Declaring instance variables with access modifier `private` is known as *information hiding*. When an application creates (instantiates) an object of class `GradeBook`, variable `courseName` is encapsulated (hidden) in the object and can be accessed only by methods and properties of the object's class. In class `GradeBook`, the property `CourseName` manipulates the instance variable `courseName`.

Setting and Getting the Values of `private` Instance Variables

How can we allow a program to manipulate a class's `private` instance variables but ensure that they remain in a valid state? We need to provide controlled ways for programmers to "get" (i.e., retrieve) the value in an instance variable and "set" (i.e., modify) the value in an instance variable. For these purposes, programmers using languages other than C# normally use *get* and *set* methods. These methods typically are made `public`, and provide ways for the client to access or modify `private` data. Historically, these methods begin with the words "Get" and "Set"—in our class `GradeBook`, for example, if we were to use such methods they might be called `GetCourseName` and `SetCourseName`, respectively.

Although you can define methods like `GetCourseName` and `SetCourseName`, C# properties provide a more elegant solution. Next, we show how to declare and use properties.

GradeBook *Class with a Property*

The `GradeBook` class's `CourseName` *property declaration* is located in lines 11–21 of Fig. 4.7. The property begins in line 11 with an access modifier (in this case, `public`), followed by the type that the property represents (`string`) and the property's name (`CourseName`). Properties use the same naming conventions as methods and classes.

Properties contain *accessors* that handle the details of returning and modifying data. A property declaration can contain a `get` accessor, a `set` accessor or both. The `get` accessor (lines 13–16) enables a client to read the value of `private` instance variable `courseName`; the `set` accessor (lines 17–20) enables a client to modify `courseName`.

After defining a property, you can use it like a variable in your code. For example, you can assign a value to a property using the = (assignment) operator. This executes the code in the property's `set` accessor to set the value of the corresponding instance variable. Similarly, referencing the property to use its value (for example, to display it on the screen) executes the code in the property's `get` accessor to obtain the corresponding instance variable's value. We show how to use properties shortly. By convention, we name each property with the capitalized name of the instance variable that it manipulates (e.g., `CourseName` is the property that represents instance variable `courseName`)—C# is case sensitive, so these are distinct identifiers.

get *and* set *Accessors*

Let us look more closely at property CourseName's get and set accessors (Fig. 4.7). The get accessor (lines 13–16) begins with the identifier **get** and is delimited by braces. The accessor's body contains a ***return statement***, which consists of the keyword ***return*** followed by an expression. The expression's value is returned to the client code that uses the property. In this example, the value of courseName is returned when the property Course-Name is referenced. For example, in the following statement

```
string theCourseName = gradeBook.CourseName;
```

the expression gradeBook.CourseName (where gradeBook is an object of class GradeBook) executes property CourseName's get accessor, which returns the value of instance variable courseName. That value is then stored in variable theCourseName. Note that property CourseName can be used as simply as if it were an instance variable. The property notation allows the client to think of the property as the underlying data. Again, the client cannot directly manipulate instance variable courseName because it is private.

The set accessor (lines 17–20) begins with the identifier **set** and is delimited by braces. When the property CourseName appears in an assignment statement, as in

```
gradeBook.CourseName = "CS100 Introduction to Computers";
```

the text "CS100 Introduction to Computers" is assigned to the set accessor's contextual keyword named ***value*** and the set accessor executes. Note that value is implicitly declared and initialized in the set accessor—it is a compilation error to declare a local variable value in this body. Line 19 stores the contents of value in instance variable courseName. A set accessor does not return any data when it completes its task.

The statements inside the property in lines 15 and 19 (Fig. 4.7) each access course-Name even though it was declared outside the property. We can use instance variable courseName in the methods and properties of class GradeBook, because courseName is an instance variable of the class. The order in which methods and properties are declared in a class does not determine when they are called at execution time, so you can declare method DisplayMessage (which uses property CourseName) before you declare property CourseName. Within the property itself, the get and set accessors can appear in any order, and either accessor can be omitted. In Chapter 10, we discuss how to omit either a set or get accessor to create so-called "read-only" and "write-only" properties, respectively.

Using Property CourseName *in Method* DisplayMessage

Method DisplayMessage (lines 24–30 of Fig. 4.7) does not receive any parameters. Lines 28–29 output a welcome message that includes the value of instance variable courseName. We do not reference courseName directly. Instead, we access property CourseName (line 29), which executes the property's get accessor, returning the value of courseName.

GradeBookTest Class That Demonstrates Class GradeBook

Class GradeBookTest (Fig. 4.8) creates a GradeBook object and demonstrates property CourseName. Line 11 creates a GradeBook object and assigns it to local variable myGrade-Book of type GradeBook. Lines 14–15 display the initial course name using the object's CourseName property—this executes the property's get accessor, which returns the value of courseName.

```
 1    // Fig. 4.8: GradeBookTest.cs
 2    // Create and manipulate a GradeBook object.
 3    using System;
 4
 5    public class GradeBookTest
 6    {
 7       // Main method begins program execution
 8       public static void Main( string[] args )
 9       {
10          // create a GradeBook object and assign it to myGradeBook
11          GradeBook myGradeBook = new GradeBook();
12
13          // display initial value of CourseName
14          Console.WriteLine( "Initial course name is: '{0}'\n",
15             myGradeBook.CourseName );
16
17          // prompt for and read course name
18          Console.WriteLine( "Please enter the course name:" );
19          myGradeBook.CourseName = Console.ReadLine(); // set CourseName
20          Console.WriteLine(); // output a blank line
21
22          // display welcome message after specifying course name
23          myGradeBook.DisplayMessage();
24       } // end Main
25    } // end class GradeBookTest
```

```
Initial course name is: ''

Please enter the course name:
CS101 Introduction to C# Programming

Welcome to the grade book for
CS101 Introduction to C# Programming!
```

Fig. 4.8 | Create and manipulate a GradeBook object.

Note that the first line of the output shows an empty name (marked by `''`). Unlike local variables, which are not automatically initialized, every field has a *default initial value*—a value provided by C# when you do not specify the initial value. Thus, fields are not required to be explicitly initialized before they are used in an application—unless they must be initialized to values other than their default values. The default value for an instance variable of type string (like courseName) is null. When you display a string variable that contains the value null, no text is displayed on the screen. We'll discuss the significance of null in Section 4.9.

Line 18 prompts the user to enter a course name. Line 19 assigns the course name entered by the user to object myGradeBook's CourseName property. When a value is assigned to CourseName, the value specified (which is returned by ReadLine in this case) is assigned to implicit parameter value of CourseName's set accessor (lines 17–20, Fig. 4.7). Then parameter value is assigned by the set accessor to instance variable courseName (line 19 of Fig. 4.7). Line 20 (Fig. 4.8) displays a blank line, then line 23 calls myGradeBook's DisplayMessage method to display the welcome message containing the course name.

4.6 UML Class Diagram with a Property

Figure 4.9 contains an updated UML class diagram for the version of class GradeBook in Fig. 4.7. We model properties in the UML as attributes—the property (in this case, CourseName) is listed as a public attribute—as indicated by the plus (+) sign—preceded by the word "property" in *guillemets* (« and »). Using descriptive words in guillemets (called *stereotypes* in the UML) helps distinguish properties from other attributes and operations. The UML indicates the type of the property by placing a colon and a type after the property name. The get and set accessors of the property are implied, so they are not listed in the UML diagram. Class GradeBook also contains one public method Display-Message, so the class diagram lists this operation in the third compartment. Recall that the plus (+) sign is the public visibility symbol.

In the preceding section, you learned how to declare a property in C# code. You saw that we typically name a property the same as the instance variable it manipulates, but with a capital first letter (e.g., property CourseName manipulates instance variable courseName). A class diagram helps you design a class, so it is not required to show every implementation detail of the class. Since an instance variable that is manipulated by a property is really an implementation detail of that property, our class diagram does not show the courseName instance variable. A programmer implementing the GradeBook class based on this class diagram would create the instance variable courseName as part of the implementation process (as we did in Fig. 4.7).

In some cases, you may find it necessary to model the private instance variables of a class. Like properties, instance variables are attributes of a class and are modeled in the middle compartment of a class diagram. The UML represents instance variables as attributes by listing the attribute name, followed by a colon and the attribute type. To indicate that an attribute is private, a class diagram would list the *private visibility symbol*—a minus sign (-)—before the attribute's name. For example, the instance variable course-Name in Fig. 4.7 would be modeled as "- courseName : string" to indicate that it is a private attribute of type string.

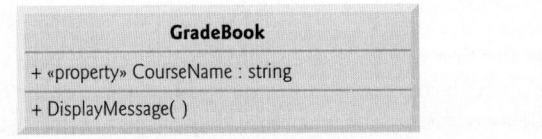

Fig. 4.9 | UML class diagram indicating that class GradeBook has a public CourseName property of type string and one public method.

4.7 Software Engineering with Properties and set and get Accessors

Using properties as described earlier in this chapter would seem to violate the notion of private data. Although providing a property with get and set accessors may appear to be the same as making its corresponding instance variable public, this is not the case. A public instance variable can be read or written by any property or method in the program. If an instance variable is private, the client code can access the instance variable only indirectly through the class's non-`private` properties or methods. This allows the class to control the manner in which the data is set or returned. For example, `get` and `set` accessors can translate between the format of the data used by the client and the format stored in the `private` instance variable.

Consider a `Clock` class that represents the time of day as a `private int` instance variable `time`, containing the number of seconds since midnight. Suppose the class provides a `Time` property of type `string` to manipulate this instance variable. Although `get` accessors typically return data exactly as it is stored in an object, they need not expose the data in this "raw" format. When a client refers to a `Clock` object's `Time` property, the property's `get` accessor could use instance variable `time` to determine the number of hours, minutes and seconds since midnight, then return the time as a `string` of the form `"HH:MM:SS"`. Similarly, suppose a `Clock` object's `Time` property is assigned a `string` of the form `"HH:MM:SS"`. Using the `string` capabilities presented in Chapter 18, Strings, Characters and Regular Expressions, and the method `Convert.ToInt32` presented in Section 3.6, the `Time` property's `set` accessor can convert this `string` to an `int` number of seconds since midnight and store the result in the `Clock` object's `private` instance variable `time`. The `Time` property's `set` accessor can also provide *data-validation* capabilities that scrutinize attempts to modify the instance variable's value to ensure that the value it receives represents a valid time (e.g., `"12:30:45"` is valid but `"42:85:70"` is not). We demonstrate data validation in Section 4.11. So, although a property's accessors enable clients to manipulate `private` data, they carefully control those manipulations, and the object's `private` data remains safely encapsulated (i.e., hidden) in the object. This is not possible with `public` instance variables, which can easily be set by clients to invalid values.

Properties of a class should also be used by the class's own methods to manipulate the class's `private` instance variables, even though the methods can directly access the `private` instance variables. Accessing an instance variable via a property's accessors—as in the body of method `DisplayMessage` (Fig. 4.7, lines 28–29)—creates a more robust class that is easier to maintain and less likely to malfunction. If we decide to change the representation of instance variable `courseName` in some way, the declaration of method `Display-Message` does not require modification—only the bodies of property `CourseName`'s `get` and `set` accessors that directly manipulate the instance variable will need to change. For example, suppose we want to represent the course name as two separate instance variables—`courseNumber` (e.g., `"CS101"`) and `courseTitle` (e.g., `"Introduction to C# Programming"`). The `DisplayMessage` method can still use property `CourseName`'s `get` accessor to obtain the full course name to display as part of the welcome message. In this case, the `get` accessor would need to build and return a `string` containing the `courseNumber`, followed by the `courseTitle`. Method `DisplayMessage` would continue to display the complete course title "CS101 Introduction to C# Programming," because it is unaffected by the change to the class's instance variables.

Software Engineering Observation 4.4

Accessing private data through set and get accessors not only protects the instance variables from receiving invalid values, but also hides the internal representation of the instance variables from that class's clients. Thus, if representation of the data changes (often to reduce the amount of required storage or to improve performance), only the properties' implementations need to change—the clients' implementations need not change as long as the services provided by the properties are preserved.

4.8 Auto-Implemented Properties

In Fig. 4.7, we created a version of class GradeBook with a private courseName instance variable and a public CourseName property to enable client code to access the courseName. When you look at the definition of the CourseName property (Fig. 4.7, lines 11–21), notice that the get accessor simply returns private instance variable courseName's value and the set accessor simply assigns a value to the instance variable—no other logic appears in the accessors. For such cases, C# now provides *automatically implemented properties* (also known as *auto-implemented properties*). With an auto-implemented property, the C# compiler automatically creates a private instance variable, and the get and set accessors for returning and modifying the private instance variable. Unlike a user-defined property, an auto-implemented property, must have both a get and a set accessor. This gives you the software engineering benefits of having a property, but enables you to implement the property trivially. If you later decide to implement other logic in the get or set accessors, you can simply reimplement the property as shown in Fig. 4.7. Figure 4.10 redefines class GradeBook with an auto-implemented CourseName property (line 9), which replaces lines 8–21 of Fig. 4.7. The test program in Fig. 4.11 is the same as that of Fig. 4.8 to show that the auto-implemented property CourseName works identically to the CourseName property in Fig. 4.7.

```
1   // Fig. 4.10: GradeBook.cs
2   // GradeBook class with an auto-implemented property.
3   using System;
4
5   public class GradeBook
6   {
7       // auto-implemented property CourseName implicitly creates
8       // an instance variable for this GradeBook's course name
9       public string CourseName { get; set; }
10
11      // display a welcome message to the GradeBook user
12      public void DisplayMessage()
13      {
14          // use auto-implemented property CourseName to get the
15          // name of the course that this GradeBook represents
16          Console.WriteLine( "Welcome to the grade book for\n{0}!",
17              CourseName ); // display auto-implemented property CourseName
18      } // end method DisplayMessage
19  } // end class GradeBook
```

Fig. 4.10 | GradeBook class with an auto-implemented property.

```
1   // Fig. 4.11: GradeBookTest.cs
2   // Create and manipulate a GradeBook object.
3   using System;
4
5   public class GradeBookTest
6   {
```

Fig. 4.11 | Create and manipulate a GradeBook object. (Part 1 of 2.)

```
 7      // Main method begins program execution
 8      public static void Main( string[] args )
 9      {
10         // create a GradeBook object and assign it to myGradeBook
11         GradeBook myGradeBook = new GradeBook();
12
13         // display initial value of CourseName
14         Console.WriteLine( "Initial course name is: '{0}'\n",
15            myGradeBook.CourseName );
16
17         // prompt for and read course name
18         Console.WriteLine( "Please enter the course name:" );
19         myGradeBook.CourseName = Console.ReadLine(); // set CourseName
20         Console.WriteLine(); // output a blank line
21
22         // display welcome message after specifying course name
23         myGradeBook.DisplayMessage();
24      } // end Main
25   } // end class GradeBookTest
```

```
Initial course name is: ''

Please enter the course name:
CS101 Introduction to C# Programming

Welcome to the grade book for
CS101 Introduction to C# Programming!
```

Fig. 4.11 | Create and manipulate a GradeBook object. (Part 2 of 2.)

Code Snippets for Auto-implemented Properties

The IDE has a feature called *code snippets* that allows you to insert predefined code templates into your source code. One such snippet enables you to insert a public auto-implemented property by typing the word "prop" in the code window and pressing the *Tab* key twice. Certain pieces of the inserted code are highlighted for you to easily change the property's type and name. You can press the *Tab* key to move from one highlighted piece of text to the next in the inserted code. By default, the new property's type is int and its name is MyProperty. To get a list of all available code snippets, type *Ctrl + k*, *Ctrl + x*. This displays the **Insert Snippet** window in the code editor. You can navigate through the snippet folders with the mouse to see the snippets. This feature can also be accessed by right clicking in the source code editor and selecting the **Insert Snippet...** menu item.

4.9 Value Types vs. Reference Types

Types in C# are divided into two categories—*value types* and *reference types*. C#'s simple types are all value types. A variable of a value type (such as int) simply contains a value of that type. For example, Fig. 4.12 shows an int variable named count that contains the value 7. Value types are implemented as structs, which are similar to classes and are discussed in more detail in Chapter 18.

By contrast, a variable of a reference type (sometimes called a *reference*) contains the address of a location in memory where the data referred to by that variable is stored. Such a variable is said to **refer to an object** in the program. Line 11 of Fig. 4.8 creates a Grade-Book object, places it in memory and stores the object's reference in variable myGradeBook of type GradeBook as shown in Fig. 4.13. Note that the GradeBook object is shown with its courseName instance variable.

Reference-type instance variables (such as myGradeBook in Fig. 4.13) are initialized by default to the value **null**. string is a reference type. For this reason, string variable courseName is shown in Fig. 4.13 with an empty box representing the null-valued variable. Note that a string variable with the value null is not an empty string, which is represented by "" or **string.Empty**. The value null represents a reference that does not refer to an object. The empty string is a string object with no characters in it.

A client of an object must use a variable that refers to the object to **invoke** (i.e., call) the object's methods and access the object's properties. In Fig. 4.8, the statements in Main use variable myGradeBook, which contains the GradeBook object's reference, to send messages to the GradeBook object. These messages are calls to methods (like DisplayMessage) or references to properties (like CourseName) that enable the program to interact with GradeBook objects. For example, the statement (in line 19 of Fig. 4.8)

```
myGradeBook.CourseName = Console.ReadLine(); // set CourseName
```

uses the reference myGradeBook to set the course name by assigning a value to property CourseName. This sends a message to the GradeBook object to invoke the CourseName property's set accessor. The message includes as an argument the value read from the user's input (in this case, "CS101 Introduction to C# Programming") that CourseName's set accessor requires to perform its task. The set accessor uses this information to set the courseName instance variable. In Section 7.14, we discuss value types and reference types in detail.

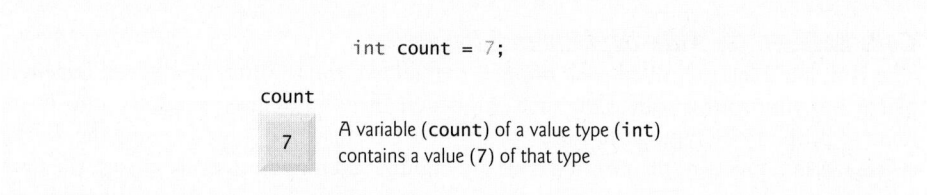

Fig. 4.12 | Value-type variable.

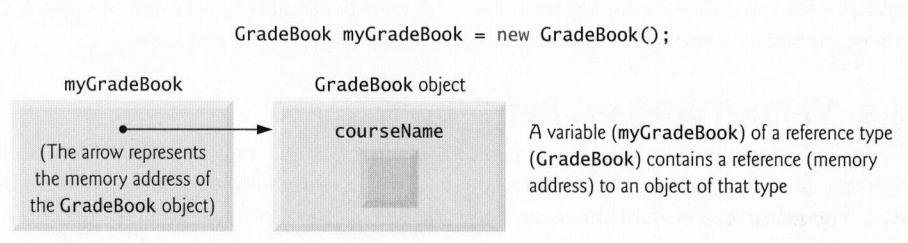

Fig. 4.13 | Reference-type variable.

> **Software Engineering Observation 4.5**
>
> *A variable's declared type (e.g., int, double or GradeBook) indicates whether the variable is of a value or a reference type. If a variable's type is not one of the thirteen simple types (Appendix B), or an enum or a struct type (which we discuss in Section 7.10 and Chapter 18, respectively), then it is a reference type. For example, Account account1 indicates that account1 is a variable that can refer to an Account object.*

4.10 Initializing Objects with Constructors

As mentioned in Section 4.5, when a GradeBook (Fig. 4.7) object is created, its instance variable courseName is initialized to null by default. This is also true of the private instance variable that the compiler creates for the auto-implemented CourseName property in Fig. 4.10. What if you want to provide a course name when you create a GradeBook object? Each class can provide a *constructor* that can be used to initialize an object of a class when the object is created. In fact, C# requires a constructor call for every object that is created. The new operator calls the class's constructor to perform the initialization. The constructor call is indicated by the class name, followed by parentheses. For example, line 11 of Fig. 4.11 first uses new to create a GradeBook object. The empty parentheses after "new GradeBook()" indicate a call without arguments to the class's constructor. The compiler provides a **public *default constructor*** with no parameters in any class that does not explicitly define a constructor, so *every* class has a constructor. The default constructor does not modify the default values of the instance variables.

When you declare a class, you can provide your own constructor (or several constructors, as you'll learn in Chapter 10) to specify custom initialization for objects of your class. For example, you might want to specify a course name for a GradeBook object when the object is created, as in

```
GradeBook myGradeBook =
    new GradeBook( "CS101 Introduction to C# Programming" );
```

In this case, the argument "CS101 Introduction to C# Programming" is passed to the GradeBook object's constructor and used to initialize the CourseName. Each time you create a new GradeBook object, you can provide a different course name. The preceding statement requires that the class provide a constructor with a string parameter. Figure 4.14 contains a modified GradeBook class with such a constructor.

```
1    // Fig. 4.14: GradeBook.cs
2    // GradeBook class with a constructor to initialize the course name.
3    using System;
4
5    public class GradeBook
6    {
7        // auto-implemented property CourseName implicitly created an
8        // instance variable for this GradeBook's course name
9        public string CourseName { get; set; }
10
```

Fig. 4.14 | GradeBook class with a constructor to initialize the course name. (Part 1 of 2.)

```
11      // constructor initializes auto-implemented property
12      // CourseName with string supplied as argument
13      public GradeBook( string name )
14      {
15         CourseName = name; // set CourseName to name
16      } // end constructor
17
18      // display a welcome message to the GradeBook user
19      public void DisplayMessage()
20      {
21         // use auto-implemented property CourseName to get the
22         // name of the course that this GradeBook represents
23         Console.WriteLine( "Welcome to the grade book for\n{0}!",
24            CourseName );
25      } // end method DisplayMessage
26   } // end class GradeBook
```

Fig. 4.14 | GradeBook class with a constructor to initialize the course name. (Part 2 of 2.)

Lines 13–16 declare the constructor for class GradeBook. A constructor must have the same name as its class. Like a method, a constructor specifies in its parameter list the data it requires to perform its task. When you use new to create an object, you place this data in the parentheses that follow the class name. Unlike a method, a constructor doesn't specify a return type (not even void). Line 13 indicates that class GradeBook's constructor has a parameter called name of type string. In line 15, the name passed to the constructor is used to initialize auto-implemented property CourseName via its set accessor.

Figure 4.15 demonstrates initializing GradeBook objects using this constructor. Lines 12–13 create and initialize a GradeBook object. The constructor of class GradeBook is called with the argument "CS101 Introduction to C# Programming" to initialize the course name. The object-creation expression to the right of = in lines 12–13 returns a reference to the new object, which is assigned to variable gradeBook1. Lines 14–15 repeat

```
1    // Fig. 4.15: GradeBookTest.cs
2    // GradeBook constructor used to specify the course name at the
3    // time each GradeBook object is created.
4    using System;
5
6    public class GradeBookTest
7    {
8       // Main method begins program execution
9       public static void Main( string[] args )
10      {
11         // create GradeBook object
12         GradeBook gradeBook1 = new GradeBook( // invokes constructor
13            "CS101 Introduction to C# Programming" );
14         GradeBook gradeBook2 = new GradeBook( // invokes constructor
15            "CS102 Data Structures in C#" );
16
```

Fig. 4.15 | GradeBook constructor used to specify the course name at the time each GradeBook object is created. (Part 1 of 2.)

```
17              // display initial value of courseName for each GradeBook
18              Console.WriteLine( "gradeBook1 course name is: {0}",
19                 gradeBook1.CourseName );
20              Console.WriteLine( "gradeBook2 course name is: {0}",
21                 gradeBook2.CourseName );
22           } // end Main
23        } // end class GradeBookTest
```

```
gradeBook1 course name is: CS101 Introduction to C# Programming
gradeBook2 course name is: CS102 Data Structures in C#
```

Fig. 4.15 | GradeBook constructor used to specify the course name at the time each GradeBook object is created. (Part 2 of 2.)

this process for another GradeBook object, this time passing the argument "CS102 Data Structures in C#" to initialize the course name for gradeBook2. Lines 18–21 use each object's CourseName property to obtain the course names and show that they were indeed initialized when the objects were created. In Section 4.5, you learned that each instance (i.e., object) of a class contains its own copy of the class's instance variables. The output confirms that each GradeBook maintains its own course name.

Like methods, constructors also can take arguments. However, an important difference between constructors and methods is that constructors cannot return values—in fact, they cannot specify a return type. Normally, constructors are declared public. If a class does not explicitly define a constructor, the class's instance variables are initialized to their default values—0 for numeric types, false for bools and null for reference types. If you declare any constructors for a class, C# will not create a default constructor for that class.

Error-Prevention Tip 4.1

Unless default initialization of your class's instance variables is acceptable, provide a constructor to ensure that your class's instance variables are properly initialized with meaningful values when each new object of your class is created.

Adding the Constructor to Class GradeBook's UML Class Diagram

The UML class diagram of Fig. 4.16 models class GradeBook of Fig. 4.14, which has a constructor that has a name parameter of type string. Like operations, the UML models constructors in the third compartment of a class in a class diagram. To distinguish a constructor from a class's operations, the UML places the word "constructor" between guillemets (« and ») before the constructor's name. It is customary to list constructors before other operations in the third compartment.

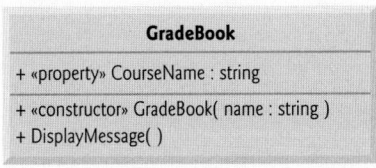

Fig. 4.16 | UML class diagram indicating that class GradeBook has a constructor with a name parameter of type string.

4.11 Floating-Point Numbers and Type `decimal`

In our next application, we depart temporarily from our `GradeBook` case study to declare a class called `Account` that maintains the balance of a bank account. Most account balances are not whole numbers (such as 0, −22 and 1024). For this reason, class `Account` represents the account balance as a real number (i.e., a number with a decimal point, such as 7.33, 0.0975 or 1000.12345). C# provides three simple types for storing real numbers—`float`, *double*, and `decimal`. Types `float` and `double` are called *floating-point* types. The primary difference between them and `decimal` is that `decimal` variables store a limited range of real numbers precisely, whereas floating-point variables store only approximations of real numbers, but across a much greater range of values. Also, `double` variables can store numbers with larger magnitude and finer detail (i.e., more digits to the right of the decimal point—also known as the number's *precision*) than `float` variables. A key application of type `decimal` is representing monetary amounts.

Real-Number Precision and Storage Requirements

Variables of type `float` represent *single-precision floating-point numbers* and have seven significant digits. Variables of type `double` represent *double-precision floating-point numbers*. These require twice as much storage as `float` variables and provide 15–16 significant digits—approximately double the precision of `float` variables. Furthermore, variables of type `decimal` require twice as much storage as `double` variables and provide 28–29 significant digits. In some applications, even variables of type `double` and `decimal` will be inadequate—such applications are beyond the scope of this book.

Most programmers represent floating-point numbers with type `double`. In fact, C# treats all real numbers you type in an application's source code (such as 7.33 and 0.0975) as `double` values by default. Such values in the source code are known as *floating-point literals*. To type a *decimal literal*, you must type the letter "M" or "m" (which stands for "money") at the end of a real number (for example, 7.33M is a `decimal` literal rather than a `double`). Integer literals are implicitly converted into type `float`, `double` or `decimal` when they are assigned to a variable of one of these types. See Appendix B, Simple Types, for the ranges of values for variables of types `float`, `double`, `decimal` and all the other simple types.

Although floating-point numbers are not always 100% precise, they have numerous applications. For example, when we speak of a "normal" body temperature of 98.6, we do not need to be precise to a large number of digits. When we read the temperature on a thermometer as 98.6, it may actually be 98.5999473210643. Calling this number simply 98.6 is fine for most applications involving body temperatures. Due to the imprecise nature of floating-point numbers, type `decimal` is preferred over the floating-point types whenever the calculations need to be exact, as with monetary calculations. In cases where approximation is enough, `double` is preferred over type `float` because `double` variables can represent floating-point numbers more accurately. For this reason, we use type `decimal` throughout the book for dealing with monetary amounts and type `double` for other real numbers.

Real numbers also arise as a result of division. In conventional arithmetic, for example, when we divide 10 by 3, the result is 3.3333333…, with the sequence of 3s repeating infinitely. The computer allocates only a fixed amount of space to hold such a value, so clearly the stored floating-point value can be only an approximation.

Common Programming Error 4.3

Using floating-point numbers in a manner that assumes they are represented precisely can lead to logic errors.

Account Class with an Instance Variable of Type decimal

Our next application (Figs. 4.17–4.18) contains an oversimplified class named Account (Fig. 4.17) that maintains the balance of a bank account. A typical bank services many accounts, each with its own balance, so line 7 declares an instance variable named balance of type decimal. Variable balance is an instance variable because it is declared in the body of the class (lines 6–36) but outside the class's method and property declarations (lines 10–13, 16–19 and 22–35). Every instance (i.e., object) of class Account contains its own copy of balance.

```csharp
1  // Fig. 4.17: Account.cs
2  // Account class with a constructor to
3  // initialize instance variable balance.
4
5  public class Account
6  {
7     private decimal balance; // instance variable that stores the balance
8
9     // constructor
10    public Account( decimal initialBalance )
11    {
12       Balance = initialBalance; // set balance using property
13    } // end Account constructor
14
15    // credit (add) an amount to the account
16    public void Credit( decimal amount )
17    {
18       Balance = Balance + amount; // add amount to balance
19    } // end method Credit
20
21    // a property to get and set the account balance
22    public decimal Balance
23    {
24       get
25       {
26          return balance;
27       } // end get
28       set
29       {
30          // validate that value is greater than or equal to 0;
31          // if it is not, balance is left unchanged
32          if ( value >= 0 )
33             balance = value;
34       } // end set
35    } // end property Balance
36 } // end class Account
```

Fig. 4.17 | Account class with a constructor to initialize instance variable balance.

```
 1    // Fig. 4.18: AccountTest.cs
 2    // Create and manipulate Account objects.
 3    using System;
 4
 5    public class AccountTest
 6    {
 7       // Main method begins execution of C# application
 8       public static void Main( string[] args )
 9       {
10          Account account1 = new Account( 50.00M ); // create Account object
11          Account account2 = new Account( -7.53M ); // create Account object
12
13          // display initial balance of each object using a property
14          Console.WriteLine( "account1 balance: {0:C}",
15             account1.Balance ); // display Balance property
16          Console.WriteLine( "account2 balance: {0:C}\n",
17             account2.Balance ); // display Balance property
18
19          decimal depositAmount; // deposit amount read from user
20
21          // prompt and obtain user input
22          Console.Write( "Enter deposit amount for account1: " );
23          depositAmount = Convert.ToDecimal( Console.ReadLine() );
24          Console.WriteLine( "adding {0:C} to account1 balance\n",
25             depositAmount );
26          account1.Credit( depositAmount ); // add to account1 balance
27
28          // display balances
29          Console.WriteLine( "account1 balance: {0:C}",
30             account1.Balance );
31          Console.WriteLine( "account2 balance: {0:C}\n",
32             account2.Balance );
33
34          // prompt and obtain user input
35          Console.Write( "Enter deposit amount for account2: " );
36          depositAmount = Convert.ToDecimal( Console.ReadLine() );
37          Console.WriteLine( "adding {0:C} to account2 balance\n",
38             depositAmount );
39          account2.Credit( depositAmount ); // add to account2 balance
40
41          // display balances
42          Console.WriteLine( "account1 balance: {0:C}", account1.Balance );
43          Console.WriteLine( "account2 balance: {0:C}", account2.Balance );
44       } // end Main
45    } // end class AccountTest
```

```
account1 balance: $50.00
account2 balance: $0.00

Enter deposit amount for account1: 49.99
adding $49.99 to account1 balance
```

Fig. 4.18 | Create and manipulate an Account object. (Part 1 of 2.)

```
account1 balance: $99.99
account2 balance: $0.00

Enter deposit amount for account2: 123.21
adding $123.21 to account2 balance

account1 balance: $99.99
account2 balance: $123.21
```

Fig. 4.18 | Create and manipulate an Account object. (Part 2 of 2.)

Class Account contains a constructor, a method, and a property. Since it is common for someone opening an account to place money in the account immediately, the constructor (lines 10–13) receives a parameter initialBalance of type decimal that represents the account's starting balance. Line 12 assigns initialBalance to the property Balance, invoking Balance's set accessor to initialize the instance variable balance.

Method Credit (lines 16–19) does not return any data when it completes its task, so its return type is void. The method receives one parameter named amount—a decimal value that is added to the property Balance. Line 18 uses both the get and set accessors of Balance. The expression Balance + amount invokes property Balance's get accessor to obtain the current value of instance variable balance, then adds amount to it. We then assign the result to instance variable balance by invoking the Balance property's set accessor (thus replacing the prior balance value).

Property Balance (lines 22–35) provides a get accessor, which allows clients of the class (i.e., other classes that use this class) to obtain the value of a particular Account object's balance. The property has type decimal (line 22). Balance also provides an enhanced set accessor.

In Section 4.5, we introduced properties whose set accessors allow clients of a class to modify the value of a private instance variable. In Fig. 4.7, class GradeBook defines property CourseName's set accessor to assign the value received in its parameter value to instance variable courseName (line 19). This CourseName property does not ensure that courseName contains only valid data.

The application of Figs. 4.17–4.18 enhances the set accessor of class Account's property Balance to perform this validity checking. Line 32 (Fig. 4.17) ensures that value is nonnegative. If the value is greater than or equal to 0, the amount stored in value is assigned to instance variable balance in line 33. Otherwise, balance is left unchanged.

AccountTest Class to Use Class Account

Class AccountTest (Fig. 4.18) creates two Account objects (lines 10–11) and initializes them respectively with 50.00M and -7.53M (the decimal literals representing the real numbers 50.00 and -7.53). Note that the Account constructor (lines 10–13 of Fig. 4.17) references property Balance to initialize balance. In previous examples, the benefit of referencing the property in the constructor was not evident. Now, however, the constructor takes advantage of the validation provided by the set accessor of the Balance property. The constructor simply assigns a value to Balance rather than duplicating the set accessor's validation code. When line 11 of Fig. 4.18 passes an initial balance of -7.53 to the Account constructor, the constructor passes this value to the set accessor of property Balance, where the actual initialization occurs. This value is less than 0, so the set accessor does not modify balance, leaving this instance variable with its default value of 0.

Lines 14–17 in Fig. 4.18 output the balance in each Account by using the Account's Balance property. When Balance is used for account1 (line 15), the value of account1's balance is returned by the get accessor in line 26 of Fig. 4.17 and displayed by the Console.WriteLine statement (Fig. 4.18, lines 14–15). Similarly, when property Balance is called for account2 from line 17, the value of the account2's balance is returned from line 26 of Fig. 4.17 and displayed by the Console.WriteLine statement (Fig. 4.18, lines 16–17). Note that the balance of account2 is 0 because the constructor ensured that the account could not begin with a negative balance. The value is output by WriteLine with the format item {0:C}, which formats the account balance as a monetary amount. The : after the 0 indicates that the next character represents a *format specifier*, and the C format specifier after the : specifies a monetary amount (C is for currency). The cultural settings on the user's machine determine the format for displaying monetary amounts. For example, in the United States, 50 displays as $50.00. In Germany, 50 displays as 50,00€. Figure 4.19 lists a few other format specifiers in addition to C.

Line 19 declares local variable depositAmount to store each deposit amount entered by the user. Unlike the instance variable balance in class Account, the local variable depositAmount in Main is *not* initialized to 0 by default. However, this variable does not need to be initialized here because its value will be determined by the user's input. Note that the compiler does not allow a local variable's value to be read until it is initialized.

Line 22 prompts the user to enter a deposit amount for account1. Line 23 obtains the input from the user by calling the Console class's ReadLine method, then passing the string entered by the user to the Convert class's *ToDecimal* method, which returns the decimal value in this string. Lines 24–25 display the deposit amount. Line 26 calls object

Format specifier	Description
C or c	Formats the string as currency. Displays an appropriate currency symbol ($ in the United States) next to the number. Separates digits with an appropriate separator character (comma in the United States) and sets the number of decimal places to two by default.
D or d	Formats the string as a decimal. Displays number as an integer.
N or n	Formats the string with a thousands separator and a default of two decimal places.
E or e	Formats the number using scientific notation with a default of six decimal places.
F or f	Formats the string with a fixed number of decimal places (two by default).
G or g	Formats the number normally with decimal places or using scientific notation, depending on context. If a format item does not contain a format specifier, format G is assumed implicitly.
X or x	Formats the string as hexadecimal.

Fig. 4.19 | string format specifiers.

account1's `Credit` method and supplies `depositAmount` as the method's argument. When the method is called, the argument's value is assigned to parameter `amount` of method `Credit` (lines 16–19 of Fig. 4.17), then method `Credit` adds that value to the `balance` (line 18 of Fig. 4.17). Lines 29–32 (Fig. 4.18) output the balances of both Accounts again to show that only account1's balance changed.

Line 35 prompts the user to enter a deposit amount for `account2`. Line 36 obtains the input from the user by calling method `Console.ReadLine`, and passing the return value to the `Convert` class's `ToDecimal` method. Lines 37–38 display the deposit amount. Line 39 calls object account2's `Credit` method and supplies `depositAmount` as the method's argument, then method `Credit` adds that value to the balance. Finally, lines 42–43 output the balances of both Accounts again to show that only account2's balance changed.

set *and* get *Accessors with Different Access Modifiers*
By default, the `get` and `set` accessors of a property have the same access as the property—for example, for a `public` property, the accessors are `public`. It is possible to declare the `get` and `set` accessors with different access modifiers. In this case, one of the accessors must implicitly have the same access as the property and the other must be declared with a more restrictive access modifier than the property. For example, in a `public` property, the `get` accessor might be `public` and the `set` accessor might be `private`. We demonstrate this feature in Section 10.6.

Error-Prevention Tip 4.2
The benefits of data integrity are not automatic simply because instance variables are made `private`—you must provide appropriate validity checking and report the errors.

Error-Prevention Tip 4.3
set accessors that set the values of `private` data should verify that the intended new values are proper; if they are not, the `set` accessors should leave the instance variables unchanged and indicate an error. We demonstrate how to indicate errors in Chapter 13, Exception Handling.

UML *Class Diagram for Class* Account
The UML class diagram in Fig. 4.20 models class `Account` of Fig. 4.17. The diagram models the `Balance` property as a UML attribute of type `decimal` (because the corresponding C# property had type `decimal`). The diagram models class Account's constructor with a parameter `initialBalance` of type `decimal` in the third compartment of the class. The diagram models operation `Credit` in the third compartment with an `amount` parameter of type `decimal` (because the corresponding method has an `amount` parameter of C# type `decimal`).

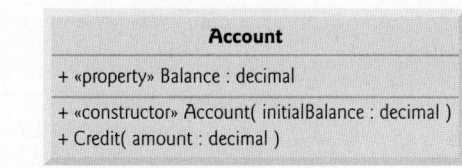

Fig. 4.20 | UML class diagram indicating that class `Account` has a `public Balance` property of type `decimal`, a constructor and a method.

4.12 (Optional) Software Engineering Case Study: Identifying the Classes in the ATM Requirements Document

Now we begin designing the ATM system that we introduced in Chapter 3. In this section, we identify the classes that are needed to build the ATM system by analyzing the nouns and noun phrases that appear in the requirements document. We introduce UML class diagrams to model the relationships between these classes. This is an important first step in defining the structure of our system.

Identifying the Classes in a System

We begin our object-oriented design (OOD) process by identifying the classes required to build the ATM system. We'll eventually describe these classes using UML class diagrams and implement these classes in C#. First, we review the requirements document of Section 3.9 and find key nouns and noun phrases to help us identify classes that comprise the ATM system. We may decide that some of these nouns and noun phrases are attributes of other classes in the system. We may also conclude that some of the nouns and noun phrases do not correspond to parts of the system and thus should not be modeled at all. Additional classes may become apparent to us as we proceed through the design process. Figure 4.21 lists the nouns and noun phrases in the requirements document.

We create classes only for the nouns and noun phrases that have significance in the ATM system. We do not need to model "bank" as a class, because the bank is not a part of the ATM system—the bank simply wants us to build the ATM. "User" and "customer" also represent entities outside of the system—they are important because they interact with our ATM system, but we do not need to model them as classes in the ATM system. Recall that we modeled an ATM user (i.e., a bank customer) as the actor in the use case diagram of Fig. 3.27.

We do not model "$20 bill" or "deposit envelope" as classes. These are physical objects in the real world, but they are not part of what is being automated. We can adequately represent the presence of bills in the system using an attribute of the class that models the cash dispenser. (We assign attributes to classes in Section 5.12.) For example, the cash dispenser maintains a count of the number of bills it contains. The requirements document does not say anything about what the system should do with deposit envelopes

Nouns and noun phrases in the requirements document		
bank	money / funds	account number
ATM	screen	PIN
user	keypad	bank database
customer	cash dispenser	balance inquiry
transaction	$20 bill / cash	withdrawal
account	deposit slot	deposit
balance	deposit envelope	

Fig. 4.21 | Nouns and noun phrases in the requirements document.

after it receives them. We can assume that simply acknowledging the receipt of an envelope—an *operation* performed by the class that models the deposit slot—is sufficient to represent the presence of an envelope in the system. (We assign operations to classes in Section 7.15.)

In our simplified ATM system, representing various amounts of "money," including the "balance" of an account, as attributes of other classes seems most appropriate. Likewise, the nouns "account number" and "PIN" represent significant pieces of information in the ATM system. They are important attributes of a bank account. They do not, however, exhibit behaviors. Thus, we can most appropriately model them as attributes of an account class.

Though the requirements document frequently describes a "transaction" in a general sense, we do not model the broad notion of a financial transaction at this time. Instead, we model the three types of transactions (i.e., "balance inquiry," "withdrawal" and "deposit") as individual classes. These classes possess specific attributes needed to execute the transactions they represent. For example, a withdrawal needs to know the amount of money the user wants to withdraw. A balance inquiry, however, does not require any additional data if the user is authenticated. Furthermore, the three transaction classes exhibit unique behaviors. A withdrawal involves dispensing cash to the user, whereas a deposit involves receiving a deposit envelope from the user. [*Note:* In Section 12.9, we "factor out" common features of all transactions into a general "transaction" class using the object-oriented concepts of abstract classes and inheritance.]

We determine the classes for our system based on the remaining nouns and noun phrases from Fig. 4.21. Each of these refers to one or more of the following:

- ATM
- screen
- keypad
- cash dispenser
- deposit slot
- account
- bank database
- balance inquiry
- withdrawal
- deposit

The elements of this list are likely to be classes we'll need to implement our system, although it's too early in our design process to claim that this list is complete.

We can now model our system's classes based on the list we've created. We capitalize class names in the design process—a UML convention—as we'll do when we write the C# code that implements our design. If the name of a class contains more than one word, we run the words together and capitalize each word (e.g., `MultipleWordName`). Using these conventions, we create classes `ATM`, `Screen`, `Keypad`, `CashDispenser`, `DepositSlot`, `Account`, `BankDatabase`, `BalanceInquiry`, `Withdrawal` and `Deposit`. We construct our system using all of these classes as building blocks. Before we begin building the system, however, we must gain a better understanding of how the classes relate to one another.

Modeling Classes

The UML enables us to model, via *class diagrams*, the classes in the ATM system and their interrelationships. Figure 4.22 represents class ATM. In the UML, each class is modeled as a rectangle with three compartments. The top compartment contains the name of the class, centered horizontally and appearing in boldface. The middle compartment contains the class's attributes. (We discuss attributes in Section 5.12 and Section 6.9.) The bottom compartment contains the class's operations (discussed in Section 7.15). In Fig. 4.22, the middle and bottom compartments are empty, because we've not yet determined this class's attributes and operations.

Class diagrams also show the relationships between the classes of the system. Figure 4.23 shows how our classes ATM and Withdrawal relate to one another. For the moment, we choose to model only this subset of the ATM classes for simplicity. We present a more complete class diagram later in this section. Notice that the rectangles representing classes in this diagram are not subdivided into compartments. The UML allows the suppression of class attributes and operations in this manner, when appropriate, to create more readable diagrams. Such a diagram is said to be an *elided diagram*—one in which some information, such as the contents of the second and third compartments, is not modeled. We'll place information in these compartments in Section 5.12 and Section 7.15.

In Fig. 4.23, the solid line that connects the two classes represents an *association*—a relationship between classes. The numbers near each end of the line are *multiplicity* values, which indicate how many objects of each class participate in the association. In this case, following the line from one end to the other reveals that, at any given moment, one ATM object participates in an association with either zero or one Withdrawal objects—zero if the current user is not performing a transaction or has requested a different type of transaction, and one if the user has requested a withdrawal. The UML can model many types of multiplicity. Figure 4.24 explains the multiplicity types.

An association can be named. For example, the word Executes above the line connecting classes ATM and Withdrawal in Fig. 4.23 indicates the name of that association. This part of the diagram reads "one object of class ATM executes zero or one objects of class Withdrawal." Note that association names are directional, as indicated by the filled arrowhead—so it would be improper, for example, to read the preceding association from right to left as "zero or one objects of class Withdrawal execute one object of class ATM."

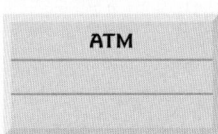

ATM

Fig. 4.22 | Representing a class in the UML using a class diagram.

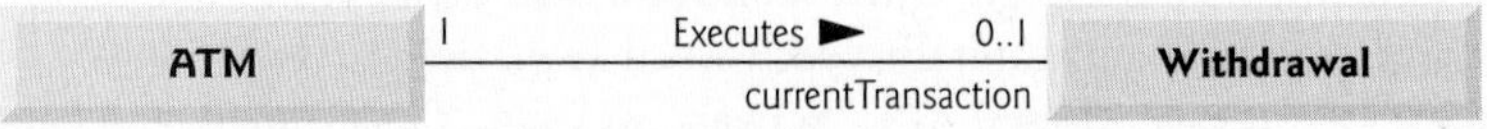

| ATM | 1 | Executes ▶ | 0..1 | Withdrawal |

currentTransaction

Fig. 4.23 | Class diagram showing an association among classes.

Symbol	Meaning
0	None
1	One
m	An integer value
0..1	Zero or one
m, n	m or n
$m..n$	At least m, but not more than n
*	Any nonnegative integer (zero or more)
0..*	Zero or more (identical to *)
1..*	One or more

Fig. 4.24 | Multiplicity types.

The word `currentTransaction` at the `Withdrawal` end of the association line in Fig. 4.23 is a *role name*, which identifies the role the `Withdrawal` object plays in its relationship with the `ATM`. A role name adds meaning to an association between classes by identifying the role a class plays in the context of an association. A class can play several roles in the same system. For example, in a college personnel system, a person may play the role of "professor" when relating to students. The same person may take on the role of "colleague" when participating in a relationship with another professor, and "coach" when coaching student athletes. In Fig. 4.23, the role name `currentTransaction` indicates that the `Withdrawal` object participating in the `Executes` association with an object of class `ATM` represents the transaction currently being processed by the ATM. In other contexts, a `Withdrawal` object may take on other roles (e.g., the previous transaction). Notice that we do not specify a role name for the `ATM` end of the `Executes` association. Role names are often omitted in class diagrams when the meaning of an association is clear without them.

In addition to indicating simple relationships, associations can specify more complex relationships, such as objects of one class being composed of objects of other classes. Consider a real-world automated teller machine. What "pieces" does a manufacturer put together to build a working ATM? Our requirements document tells us that the ATM is composed of a screen, a keypad, a cash dispenser and a deposit slot.

In Fig. 4.25, the *solid diamonds* attached to the association lines of class `ATM` indicate that class `ATM` has a *composition* relationship with classes `Screen`, `Keypad`, `CashDispenser` and `DepositSlot`. Composition implies a whole/part relationship. The class that has the composition symbol (the solid diamond) on its end of the association line is the whole (in this case, `ATM`), and the classes on the other end of the association lines are the parts—in this case, classes `Screen`, `Keypad`, `CashDispenser` and `DepositSlot`. The compositions in Fig. 4.25 indicate that an object of class `ATM` is formed from one object of class `Screen`, one object of class `CashDispenser`, one object of class `Keypad` and one object of class `DepositSlot`—the ATM "has a" screen, a keypad, a cash dispenser and a deposit slot. The *has-a relationship* defines composition. (We'll see in the Software Engineering Case Study section in Chapter 12 that the *is-a* relationship defines inheritance.)

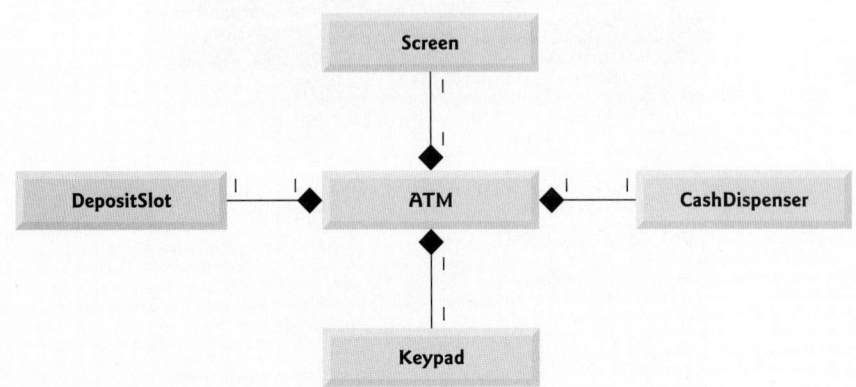

Fig. 4.25 | Class diagram showing composition relationships.

According to the UML specification, composition relationships have the following properties:

1. Only one class in the relationship can represent the whole (i.e., the diamond can be placed on only one end of the association line). For example, either the screen is part of the ATM or the ATM is part of the screen, but the screen and the ATM cannot both represent the whole in the relationship.

2. The parts in the composition relationship exist only as long as the whole, and the whole is responsible for creating and destroying its parts. For example, the act of constructing an ATM includes manufacturing its parts. Furthermore, if the ATM is destroyed, its screen, keypad, cash dispenser and deposit slot are also destroyed.

3. A part may belong to only one whole at a time, although the part may be removed and attached to another whole, which then assumes responsibility for the part.

The solid diamonds in our class diagrams indicate composition relationships that fulfill these three properties. If a *has-a* relationship does not satisfy one or more of these criteria, the UML specifies that hollow diamonds be attached to the ends of association lines to indicate *aggregation*—a weaker form of composition. For example, a personal computer and a computer monitor participate in an aggregation relationship—the computer "has a" monitor, but the two parts can exist independently, and the same monitor can be attached to multiple computers at once, thus violating the second and third properties of composition.

Figure 4.26 shows a class diagram for the ATM system. This diagram models most of the classes that we identified earlier in this section, as well as the associations between them that we can infer from the requirements document. [*Note:* Classes BalanceInquiry and Deposit participate in associations similar to those of class Withdrawal, so we've chosen to omit them from this diagram for simplicity. In Chapter 12, we expand our class diagram to include all the classes in the ATM system.]

Figure 4.26 presents a graphical model of the structure of the ATM system. This class diagram includes classes BankDatabase and Account and several associations that were not present in either Fig. 4.23 or Fig. 4.25. The class diagram shows that class ATM has a *one-to-one relationship* with class BankDatabase—one ATM object authenticates users against

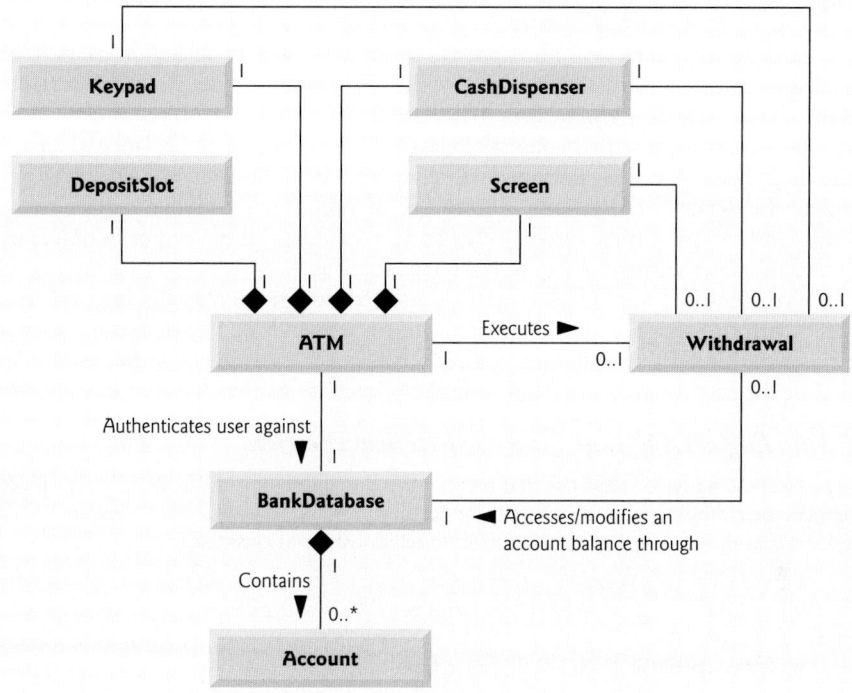

Fig. 4.26 | Class diagram for the ATM system model.

one BankDatabase object. In Fig. 4.26, we also model the fact that the bank's database contains information about many accounts—one object of class BankDatabase participates in a composition relationship with zero or more objects of class Account. Recall from Fig. 4.24 that the multiplicity value 0..* at the Account end of the association between class BankDatabase and class Account indicates that zero or more objects of class Account take part in the association. Class BankDatabase has a *one-to-many relationship* with class Account—the BankDatabase can contain many Accounts. Similarly, class Account has a *many-to-one relationship* with class BankDatabase—there can be many Accounts in the BankDatabase. Recall from Fig. 4.24 that the multiplicity value * is identical to 0..]

Figure 4.26 also indicates that if the user is performing a withdrawal, "one object of class Withdrawal accesses/modifies an account balance through one object of class Bank-Database." We could have created an association directly between class Withdrawal and class Account. The requirements document, however, states that the "ATM must interact with the bank's account-information database" to perform transactions. A bank account contains sensitive information, and systems engineers must always consider the security of personal data when designing a system. Thus, only the BankDatabase can access and manipulate an account directly. All other parts of the system must interact with the database to retrieve or update account information (e.g., an account balance).

The class diagram in Fig. 4.26 also models associations between class Withdrawal and classes Screen, CashDispenser and Keypad. A withdrawal transaction includes prompting the user to choose a withdrawal amount and receiving numeric input. These actions require the use of the screen and the keypad, respectively. Dispensing cash to the user requires access to the cash dispenser.

Classes `BalanceInquiry` and `Deposit`, though not shown in Fig. 4.26, take part in several associations with the other classes of the ATM system. Like class `Withdrawal`, each of these classes associates with classes `ATM` and `BankDatabase`. An object of class `Balance-Inquiry` also associates with an object of class `Screen` to display the balance of an account to the user. Class `Deposit` associates with classes `Screen`, `Keypad` and `DepositSlot`. Like withdrawals, deposit transactions require use of the screen and the keypad to display prompts and receive inputs, respectively. To receive a deposit envelope, an object of class `Deposit` associates with an object of class `DepositSlot`.

We've identified our ATM system's classes, although we may discover others as we proceed with the design and implementation. In Section 5.12, we determine each class's attributes, and in Section 6.9, we use these attributes to examine how the system changes over time. In Section 7.15, we determine the operations of the classes in our system.

Software Engineering Case Study Self-Review Exercises

4.1   Suppose we have a class `Car` that represents a car. Think of some of the different pieces that a manufacturer would put together to produce a whole car. Create a class diagram (similar to Fig. 4.25) that models some of the composition relationships of class `Car`.

4.2   Suppose we have a class `File` that represents an electronic document in a stand-alone, non-networked computer represented by class `Computer`. What sort of association exists between class `Computer` and class `File`?
  a) Class `Computer` has a one-to-one relationship with class `File`.
  b) Class `Computer` has a many-to-one relationship with class `File`.
  c) Class `Computer` has a one-to-many relationship with class `File`.
  d) Class `Computer` has a many-to-many relationship with class `File`.

4.3   State whether the following statement is *true* or *false*. If *false*, explain why: A UML class diagram in which a class's second and third compartments are not modeled is said to be an elided diagram.

4.4   Modify the class diagram of Fig. 4.26 to include class `Deposit` instead of class `Withdrawal`.

Answers to Software Engineering Case Study Self-Review Exercises

4.1   Figure 4.27 presents a class diagram that shows some of the composition relationships of a class `Car`.

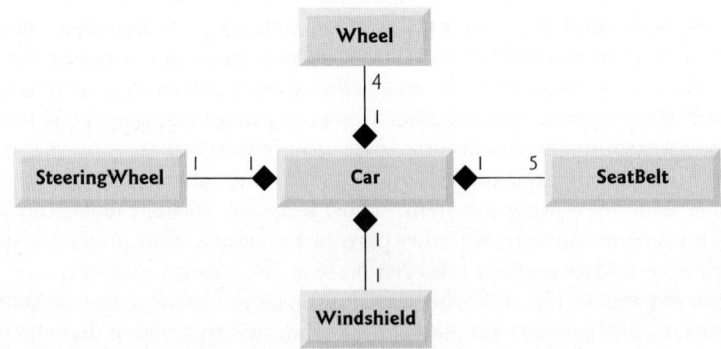

Fig. 4.27 | Class diagram showing some composition relationships of a class `Car`.

4.2   c. In a computer network, this relationship could be many-to-many.

4.3   True.

4.4   Figure 4.28 presents a class diagram for the ATM including class `Deposit` instead of class `Withdrawal` (as in Fig. 4.26). Note that class `Deposit` does not associate with class `CashDispenser` but does associate with class `DepositSlot`.

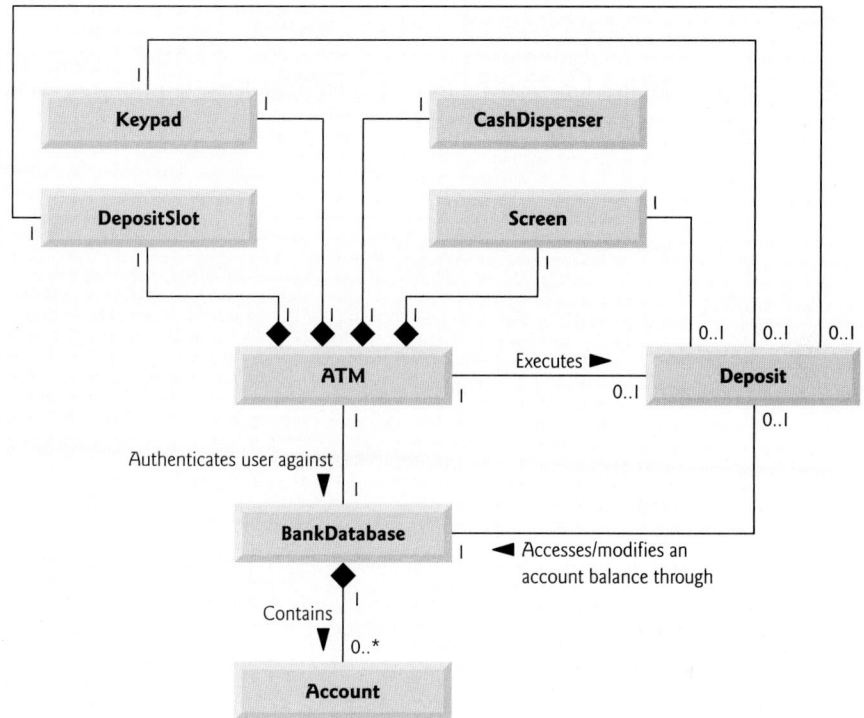

Fig. 4.28 | Class diagram for the ATM system model including class `Deposit`.

4.13 Wrap-Up

In this chapter, you learned the basic object-oriented concepts of classes, objects, methods, instance variables and properties—these will be used in most substantial C# applications you create. You learned how to declare instance variables of a class to maintain data for each object of the class, how to declare methods that operate on that data, and how to declare properties to obtain and set that data. We demonstrated how to call a method to tell it to perform its task and how to pass information to methods as arguments. We discussed the difference between a local variable of a method and an instance variable of a class and that only instance variables are initialized automatically. We discussed the difference between a value type and a reference type. You learned how to create auto-implemented properties. You also learned how to use a class's constructor to specify the initial values for an object's instance variables. We discussed some of the differences between value types and reference types. You learned about the value types `float`, `double` and `decimal` for storing real numbers.

Throughout the chapter, we showed how the UML can be used to create class diagrams that model the constructors, methods, properties and attributes of classes. You learned the value of declaring instance variables `private` and using `public` properties to manipulate them. For example, we demonstrated how `set` accessors in properties can be used to validate an object's data and ensure that the object is maintained in a consistent state. You learned how to create auto-implemented properties.

In the next chapter we begin our introduction to control statements, which specify the order in which an application's actions are performed. You'll use these in your methods to specify how they should perform their tasks.

5

Control Statements: Part 1

Let's all move one place on.
—Lewis Carroll

The wheel is come full circle.
—William Shakespeare

How many apples fell on Newton's head before he took the hint!
—Robert Frost

All the evolution we know of proceeds from the vague to the definite.
—Charles Sanders Peirce

OBJECTIVES

In this chapter you'll learn:

- To use the `if` and `if...else` selection statements to choose between alternative actions.

- To use the `while` repetition statement to execute statements in an application repeatedly.

- To use counter-controlled repetition and sentinel-controlled repetition.

- To use the increment, decrement and compound assignment operators.

Outline

5.1 Introduction
5.2 Control Structures
5.3 if Single-Selection Statement
5.4 if...else Double-Selection Statement
5.5 while Repetition Statement
5.6 Counter-Controlled Repetition
5.7 Formulating Algorithms: Sentinel-Controlled Repetition
5.8 Formulating Algorithms: Nested Control Statements
5.9 Compound Assignment Operators
5.10 Increment and Decrement Operators
5.11 Simple Types
5.12 (Optional) Software Engineering Case Study: Identifying Class Attributes in the ATM System
5.13 Wrap-Up

5.1 Introduction

In this chapter, we introduce C#'s if, if...else and while control statements,. We devote a portion of the chapter (and Chapters 6 and 8) to further developing the GradeBook class we introduced in Chapter 4. In particular, we add a method to the GradeBook class that uses control statements to calculate the average of a set of student grades. Another example demonstrates additional ways to combine control statements to solve a similar problem. We introduce C#'s compound assignment operators and explore its increment and decrement operators. These additional operators abbreviate and simplify many statements. Finally, we present an overview of C#'s simple types. In Chapter 6, Control Statements: Part 2, we present most of C#'s remaining control statements. Then we present C#'s last control statement, foreach, in Chapter 8, Arrays.

5.2 Control Structures

Normally, statements in an application are executed one after the other in the order in which they're written—this process is called sequential execution. Various C# statements, which we'll soon discuss, enable you to specify that the next statement to execute is not necessarily the next one in sequence—this is called transfer of control.

During the 1960s, it became clear that the indiscriminate use of transfers of control was the root of much difficulty experienced by software-development groups. The blame was pointed at the ***goto statement*** (used in most programming languages of the time), which allows programmers to specify a transfer of control to one of a wide range of possible destinations in an application (creating what is often called "spaghetti code"). The notion of so-called ***structured programming*** became almost synonymous with "goto elimination." We recommend that you avoid C#'s goto statement.

The research of Bohm and Jacopini[1] had demonstrated that applications could be written without goto statements. The challenge of the era for programmers was to shift their styles to "goto-less programming." Not until the 1970s did programmers start taking structured programming seriously. The results were impressive. Software-development groups reported shorter development times, more frequent on-time delivery of systems and more frequent within-budget completion of software projects. The key to these successes was that structured applications were clearer, easier to debug and modify, and more likely to be bug free in the first place.

Bohm and Jacopini's work demonstrated that all applications could be written in terms of only three control structures—the *sequence structure*, the *selection structure* and the *repetition structure*. The term "control structures" comes from the field of computer science. When we introduce C#'s implementations of control structures, we'll refer to them in the terminology of the *C# Language Specification* as "control statements."

Sequence Structure in C#
The sequence structure is built into C#. Unless directed otherwise, the computer executes C# statements are executed one after the other in the order in which they're written—that is, in sequence. The UML *activity diagram* in Fig. 5.1 illustrates a typical sequence structure in which two calculations are performed in order. C# lets you have as many actions as you want in a sequence structure. As you'll soon see, anywhere a single action may be placed, you may place several actions in sequence.

An activity diagram models the *workflow* (also called the *activity*) of a portion of a software system. Such workflows may include a portion of an algorithm, such as the sequence structure in Fig. 5.1. Activity diagrams are composed of special-purpose symbols, such as *action-state symbols* (rectangles with their left and right sides replaced with arcs curving outward), *diamonds* and *small circles*. These symbols are connected by *transition arrows*, which represent the flow of the activity—that is, the order in which the actions should occur. Activity diagrams help you develop and represent algorithms. They also clearly show how control structures operate.

Consider the activity diagram for the sequence structure in Fig. 5.1. It contains two *action states* that represent actions to perform. Each action state contains an *action expression*—for example, "add grade to total" or "add 1 to counter"—that specifies a particular action to perform. Other actions might include calculations or input/output oper-

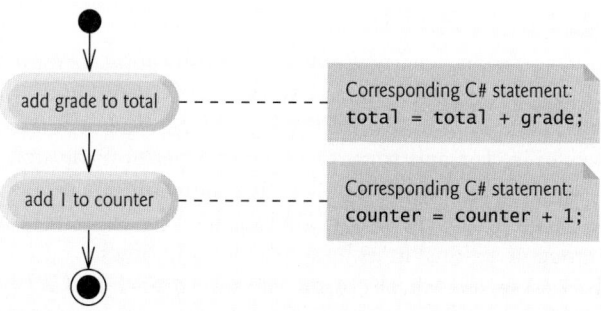

Fig. 5.1 | Sequence structure activity diagram.

---

1. Bohm, C., and G. Jacopini, "Flow Diagrams, Turing Machines, and Languages with Only Two Formation Rules," *Communications of the ACM*, Vol. 9, No. 5, May 1966, pp. 336–371.

ations. The arrows in the activity diagram represent *transitions*, which indicate the order in which the actions represented by the action states occur. The portion of the application that implements the activities illustrated by the diagram in Fig. 5.1 first adds `grade` to `total`, then adds `1` to `counter`.

The *solid circle* at the activity diagram's top represents the activity's *initial state*—the beginning of the workflow before the application performs the modeled actions. The *solid circle surrounded by a hollow circle* that appears at the bottom of the diagram represents the *final state*—the end of the workflow after the application performs its actions.

Figure 5.1 also includes rectangles with the upper-right corners folded over. These are UML *notes* (like comments in C#)—explanatory remarks that describe the purpose of symbols in the diagram. Figure 5.1 uses UML notes to show the C# code associated with each action state in the activity diagram. A *dotted line* connects each note with the element that the note describes. Activity diagrams normally do not show the C# code that implements the activity. We use notes for this purpose here to illustrate how the diagram relates to C# code. For more information on the UML, see our optional case study, which appears in the Software Engineering Case Study sections at the ends of Chapters 1, 3–8, 10 and 12, and visit our UML Resource Center (`www.deitel.com/UML/`) and `www.uml.org`.

Selection Structures in C#

C# has three types of selection structures, which from this point forward we shall refer to as *selection statements*. These are discussed in this chapter and Chapter 6. The *if statement* either performs (selects) an action if a condition is true or skips the action if the condition is false. The *if...else* statement performs an action if a condition is true or performs a different action if the condition is false. The `switch` statement (Chapter 6) performs one of many different actions, depending on the value of an expression.

The `if` statement is called a *single-selection statement* because it selects or ignores a single action (or, as we'll soon see, a single group of actions). The `if...else` statement is called a *double-selection statement* because it selects between two different actions (or groups of actions). The `switch` statement is called a *multiple-selection statement* because it selects among many different actions (or groups of actions).

Repetition Structures in C#

C# provides four repetition structures, which from this point forward we shall refer to as *repetition statements*—these are the `while`, `do...while`, `for` and `foreach` statements. (Chapter 6 presents the do...while and for statements. Chapter 8 discusses the `foreach` statement.) The `while`, `for` and `foreach` statements perform the action (or group of actions) in their bodies zero or more times—if the loop-continuation condition is initially false, the action (or group of actions) will not execute. The do...while statement performs the action (or group of actions) in its body one or more times.

The words `if`, `else`, `switch`, `while`, `do`, `for` and `foreach` are C# keywords. Recall that keywords are used to implement various C# features, such as control statements. Keywords cannot be used as identifiers, such as variable names. A complete list of C# keywords appears in Fig. 3.2.

Summary of Control Statements in C#

C# has only three kinds of structured control statements: the sequence statement, selection statement (three types) and repetition statement (four types). We combine as many of each type of statement as necessary to make the program flow and work as required. As with the sequence statement in Fig. 5.1, we can model each control statement as an activity diagram. Each diagram contains one initial state and one final state that represent a control statement's entry point and exit point, respectively. ***Single-entry/single-exit control statements*** make it easy to build applications—the control statements are "attached" to one another by connecting the exit point of one to the entry point of the next. We call this ***control-statement stacking***. There is only one other way in which control statements may be connected: ***control-statement nesting***, in which one control statement appears inside another. Thus, algorithms in C# applications are constructed from only three kinds of structured control statements, combined in only two ways. This is the essence of simplicity.

5.3 if Single-Selection Statement

Applications use selection statements to choose among alternative courses of action. For example, suppose that the passing grade on an exam is 60. The C# statement

```
if ( grade >= 60 )
    Console.WriteLine( "Passed" );
```

determines whether the condition grade >= 60 is true or false. If the condition is true, "Passed" is displayed, and the next C# statement in order is performed. If the condition is false, the output statement is ignored, and the next C# statement in order is performed. The indentation of the second line of this selection statement is optional, but recommended, because it emphasizes the inherent structure of the if statement.

Figure 5.2 illustrates the single-selection if statement. This UML activity diagram contains what is perhaps the most important symbol in an activity diagram—the diamond, or ***decision symbol***, which indicates that a decision is to be made. The workflow will continue along a path determined by the symbol's associated ***guard conditions***, which can be true or false. Each transition arrow emerging from a decision symbol has a guard condition (specified in square brackets next to the transition arrow). If a guard condition is true, the workflow enters the action state to which the transition arrow points. In Fig. 5.2, if grade >= 60 is true, the application displays "Passed", then transitions to the final state of this activity. If grade < 60 is true, the application immediately transitions to the final state without displaying a message.

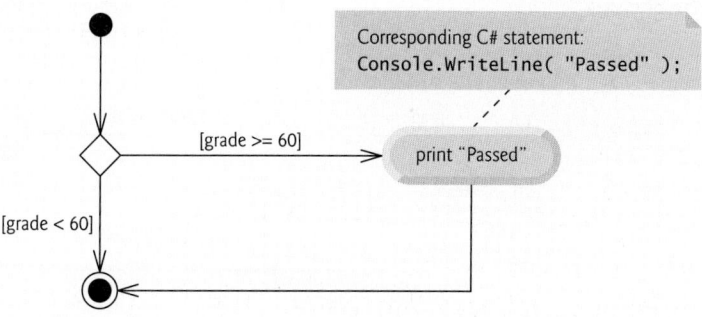

Fig. 5.2 | if single-selection statement UML activity diagram.

The if statement is a single-entry/single-exit control statement. The activity diagrams for the remaining control statements also contain initial states, transition arrows, action states that indicate actions to perform and decision symbols (with associated guard conditions) that indicate decisions to be made, and final states.

5.4 if...else Double-Selection Statement

The if single-selection statement performs an indicated action only when the condition is true; otherwise, the action is skipped. The if...else double-selection statement allows you to specify an action to perform when the condition is true and a different action when the condition is false. For example, the C# statement

```
if ( grade >= 60 )
    Console.WriteLine( "Passed" );
else
    Console.WriteLine( "Failed" );
```

displays "Passed" if grade >= 60 is true, but displays "Failed" if grade < 60 is true. In either case, after displaying occurs, the next statement in sequence is performed. Note that the body of the else part is also indented. Whatever indentation convention you choose should be applied consistently throughout your applications. It is difficult to read applications that do not obey uniform spacing conventions.

 Good Programming Practice 5.1

Indent both body statements of an if...else statement.

 Good Programming Practice 5.2

If there are several levels of indentation, each level should be indented the same additional amount of space.

Figure 5.3 illustrates the flow of control in the if...else statement. Once again, the symbols in the UML activity diagram (besides the initial state, transition arrows and final state) represent action states and a decision.

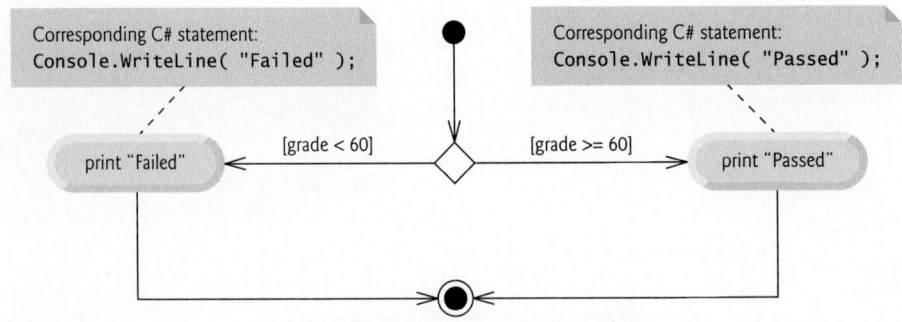

Fig. 5.3 | if...else double-selection statement UML activity diagram.

Conditional Operator (?:)

C# provides the *conditional operator* (*?:*), which can be used in place of an if...else statement. This is C#'s only *ternary operator*—it takes three operands. Together, the operands and the ?: symbols form a *conditional expression.* The first operand (to the left of the ?) is a *boolean* expression (i.e., an expression that evaluates to a bool-type value—***true*** or ***false***), the second operand (between the ? and :) is the value of the conditional expression if the boolean expression is true and the third operand (to the right of the :) is the value of the conditional expression if the boolean expression is false. For example, the statement

```
Console.WriteLine( grade >= 60 ? "Passed" : "Failed" );
```

displays the value of WriteLine's conditional-expression argument. The conditional expression in this statement evaluates to the string "Passed" if the boolean expression grade >= 60 is true and evaluates to the string "Failed" if the boolean expression is false. Thus, this statement with the conditional operator performs essentially the same function as the if...else statement shown earlier in this section. You'll see that conditional expressions can be used in some situations where if...else statements cannot.

Good Programming Practice 5.3

Conditional expressions are more difficult to read than if...else statements and should be used to replace only simple if...else statements that choose between two values.

Good Programming Practice 5.4

When a conditional expression is inside a larger expression, it's good practice to parenthesize the conditional expression for clarity. Adding parentheses may also prevent operator-precedence problems that could cause syntax errors.

Nested if...else Statements

An application can test multiple cases by placing if...else statements inside other if...else statements to create *nested if...else statements.* For example, the following nested if...else statement displays A for exam grades greater than or equal to 90, B for grades in the range 80 to 89, C for grades in the range 70 to 79, D for grades in the range 60 to 69 and F for all other grades:

```
if ( grade >= 90 )
   Console.WriteLine( "A" );
else
   if ( grade >= 80 )
      Console.WriteLine( "B" );
   else
      if ( grade >= 70 )
         Console.WriteLine( "C" );
      else
         if ( grade >= 60 )
            Console.WriteLine( "D" );
         else
            Console.WriteLine( "F" );
```

If grade is greater than or equal to 90, the first four conditions will be true, but only the statement in the if-part of the first if...else statement will execute. After that statement executes, the else-part of the "outermost" if...else statement is skipped. Most C# programmers prefer to write the preceding if...else statement as

```
if ( grade >= 90 )
   Console.WriteLine( "A" );
else if ( grade >= 80 )
   Console.WriteLine( "B" );
else if ( grade >= 70 )
   Console.WriteLine( "C" );
else if ( grade >= 60 )
   Console.WriteLine( "D" );
else
   Console.WriteLine( "F" );
```

The two forms are identical except for the spacing and indentation, which the compiler ignores. The latter form is popular because it avoids deep indentation of the code to the right—such indentation often leaves little room on a line of code, forcing lines to be split and decreasing the readability of your code.

Dangling-else Problem
The C# compiler always associates an else with the immediately preceding if unless told to do otherwise by the placement of braces ({ and }). This behavior can lead to what is referred to as the *dangling-else problem*. For example,

```
if ( x > 5 )
   if ( y > 5 )
      Console.WriteLine( "x and y are > 5" );
else
   Console.WriteLine( "x is <= 5" );
```

appears to indicate that if x is greater than 5, the nested if statement determines whether y is also greater than 5. If so, the string "x and y are > 5" is output. Otherwise, it appears that if x is not greater than 5, the else part of the if...else outputs the string "x is <= 5".

Beware! This nested if...else statement does not execute as it appears. The compiler actually interprets the statement as

```
if ( x > 5 )
   if ( y > 5 )
      Console.WriteLine( "x and y are > 5" );
   else
      Console.WriteLine( "x is <= 5" );
```

in which the body of the first if is a nested if...else. The outer if statement tests whether x is greater than 5. If so, execution continues by testing whether y is also greater than 5. If the second condition is true, the proper string—"x and y are > 5"—is displayed. However, if the second condition is false, the string "x is <= 5" is displayed, even though we know that x is greater than 5.

To force the nested if...else statement to execute as it was originally intended, we must write it as follows:

```
if ( x > 5 )
{
   if ( y > 5 )
      Console.WriteLine( "x and y are > 5" );
}
else
   Console.WriteLine( "x is <= 5" );
```

The braces ({}) indicate to the compiler that the second if statement is in the body of the first if and that the else is associated with the *first* if.

Blocks

The if statement normally expects only one statement in its body. To include several statements in the body of an if (or the body of an else for an if...else statement), enclose the statements in braces ({ and }). A set of statements contained within a pair of braces is called a **block**. A block can be placed anywhere in an application that a single statement can be placed.

The following example includes a block in the else-part of an if...else statement:

```
if ( grade >= 60 )
   Console.WriteLine( "Passed" );
else
{
   Console.WriteLine( "Failed" );
   Console.WriteLine( "You must take this course again." );
}
```

In this case, if grade is less than 60, the application executes both statements in the body of the else and displays

```
Failed.
You must take this course again.
```

Note the braces surrounding the two statements in the else clause. These braces are important. Without the braces, the statement

```
Console.WriteLine( "You must take this course again." );
```

would be outside the body of the else-part of the if...else statement and would execute regardless of whether the grade was less than 60.

Common Programming Error 5.1

Forgetting one or both of the braces that delimit a block can lead to syntax errors or logic errors in an application.

Good Programming Practice 5.5

Always using braces in an if...else (or other) statement helps prevent their accidental omission, especially when adding statements to the if-part or the else-part at a later time. To avoid omitting one or both of the braces, some programmers type the beginning and ending braces of blocks before typing the individual statements within them.

Just as a block can be placed anywhere a single statement can be placed, it is also possible to have an empty statement. Recall from Section 3.8 that the empty statement is represented by placing a semicolon (;) where a statement would normally be.

Common Programming Error 5.2

Placing a semicolon after the condition in an if *or* if...else *statement leads to a logic error in single-selection* if *statements and a syntax error in double-selection* if...else *statements (when the* if*-part contains an actual body statement).*

5.5 while Repetition Statement

A *repetition statement* allows you to specify that an application should repeat an action while some condition remains true. The statement(s) contained in the **while** *repetition statement* constitute its body, which may be a single statement or a block. Eventually, the condition will become false. At this point, the repetition terminates, and the first statement after the repetition statement executes.

Consider a code segment designed to find the first power of 3 larger than 100. When the following while statement finishes executing, product contains the result:

```
int product = 3;

while ( product <- 100 )
   product = 3 * product;
```

When this while statement begins execution, the value of variable product is 3. Each repetition of the while statement multiplies product by 3, so product takes on the subsequent values 9, 27, 81 and 243 successively. When variable product becomes 243, the while statement condition—product <= 100—becomes false. This terminates the repetition, so the final value of product is 243. At this point, application execution continues with the next statement after the while statement.

Common Programming Error 5.3

Not providing in the body of a while *statement an action that eventually causes the condition in the* while *to become false normally results in a logic error called an* **infinite loop**, *in which the loop never terminates.*

The UML activity diagram in Fig. 5.4 illustrates the flow of control that corresponds to the preceding while statement. Once again, the symbols in the diagram (besides the initial state, transition arrows, the final state and three notes) represent an action state and a decision. This diagram also introduces the UML's *merge symbol*. The UML represents both the merge symbol and the decision symbol as diamonds. The merge symbol joins two flows of activity into one. In this diagram, the merge symbol joins the transitions from the initial state and the action state, so they both flow into the decision that determines whether the loop should begin (or continue) executing. The decision and merge symbols can be distinguished by the number of "incoming" and "outgoing" transition arrows. A decision symbol has one transition arrow pointing to the diamond and two or more transition arrows pointing out from the diamond to indicate possible transitions from that point. Each transition arrow pointing out of a decision symbol has a guard condition next to it. A merge symbol has two or more transition arrows pointing to the diamond and only one transition arrow pointing from the diamond, to indicate multiple activity flows merging to continue the activity. None of the transition arrows associated with a merge symbol have guard conditions.

Figure 5.4 clearly shows the repetition of the while statement discussed earlier in this section. The transition arrow emerging from the action state points back to the merge, from which program flow transitions back to the decision that is tested at the beginning of each repetition of the loop. The loop continues to execute until the guard condition product > 100 becomes true. Then the while statement exits (reaches its final state), and control passes to the next statement in sequence in the application.

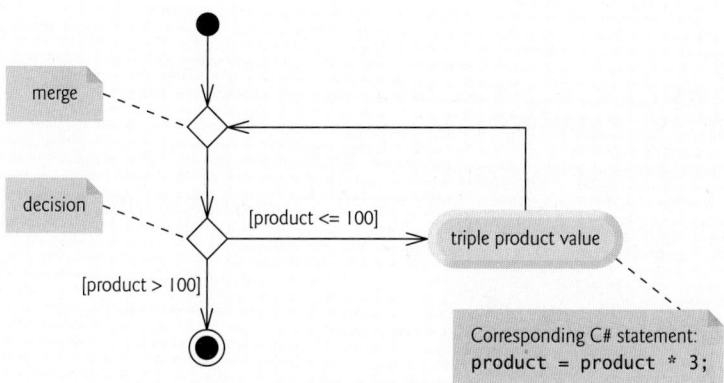

Fig. 5.4 | while repetition statement UML activity diagram.

5.6 Counter-Controlled Repetition

Next, we modify the GradeBook class of Chapter 4 to solve two variations of a problem that averages student grades. Consider the following problem statement:

> *A class of 10 students took a quiz. The grades (integers in the range 0 to 100) for this quiz are available to you. Determine the class average on the quiz.*

The class average is equal to the sum of the grades divided by the number of students. The algorithm for solving this problem must input each grade, keep track of the total of all grades input, perform the averaging calculation and display the result.

Implementing Counter-Controlled Repetition in Class GradeBook

Class GradeBook (Fig. 5.5) contains a constructor (lines 12–15) that assigns a value to the instance variable created by auto-implemented property CourseName in line 9. Lines 18–23 declare method DisplayMessage. Lines 26–52 declare method DetermineClassAverage, which meets the requirements of the problem statement.

```
1   // Fig. 5.5: GradeBook.cs
2   // GradeBook class that solves class-average problem using
3   // counter-controlled repetition.
4   using System;
5
```

Fig. 5.5 | GradeBook class that solves the class-average problem using counter-controlled repetition. (Part 1 of 2.)

```
6    public class GradeBook
7    {
8        // auto-implemented property CourseName
9        public string CourseName { get; set; }
10
11       // constructor initializes CourseName property
12       public GradeBook( string name )
13       {
14           CourseName = name; // set CourseName to name
15       } // end constructor
16
17       // display a welcome message to the GradeBook user
18       public void DisplayMessage()
19       {
20           // property CourseName gets the name of the course
21           Console.WriteLine( "Welcome to the grade book for\n{0}!\n",
22               CourseName );
23       } // end method DisplayMessage
24
25       // determine class average based on 10 grades entered by user
26       public void DetermineClassAverage()
27       {
28           int total; // sum of the grades entered by user
29           int gradeCounter; // number of the grade to be entered next
30           int grade; // grade value entered by the user
31           int average; // average of the grades
32
33           // initialization phase
34           total = 0; // initialize the total
35           gradeCounter = 1; // initialize the loop counter
36
37           // processing phase
38           while ( gradeCounter <= 10 ) // loop 10 times
39           {
40               Console.Write( "Enter grade: " ); // prompt the user
41               grade = Convert.ToInt32( Console.ReadLine() ); // read grade
42               total = total + grade; // add the grade to total
43               gradeCounter = gradeCounter + 1; // increment the counter by 1
44           } // end while
45
46           // termination phase
47           average = total / 10; // integer division yields integer result
48
49           // display total and average of grades
50           Console.WriteLine( "\nTotal of all 10 grades is {0}", total );
51           Console.WriteLine( "Class average is {0}", average );
52       } // end method DetermineClassAverage
53   } // end class GradeBook
```

Fig. 5.5 | GradeBook class that solves the class-average problem using counter-controlled repetition. (Part 2 of 2.)

Lines 28–31 declare local variables total, gradeCounter, grade and average to be of type int. In this example, variable total accumulates the sum of the grades entered and gradeCounter counts the number of grades entered. Variable grade stores the most recent grade value entered (line 41). Variable average stores the average grade.

The declarations (in lines 28–31) appear in method DetermineClassAverage's body. Recall that variables declared in a method body are local variables and can be used only from the line of their declaration to the closing right brace of the block in which they are declared. A local variable's declaration must appear before the variable is used in that method. A local variable cannot be accessed outside the method in which it is declared.

In the versions of class GradeBook in this chapter, we simply read and process a set of grades. The averaging calculation is performed in method DetermineClassAverage using local variables—we do not preserve any information about student grades in instance variables of the class. In later versions of the class (in Chapter 8), we store the grades using an instance variable that refers to an array. This allows a GradeBook object to perform various calculations on the same set of grades without requiring the user to enter the grades multiple times.

Good Programming Practice 5.6

Separate declarations from other statements in methods with a blank line for readability.

We say that a variable is ***definitely assigned*** when it is guaranteed to be assigned a value before it is used. Notice that each local variable declared in lines 28–31 is definitely assigned before it is used in calculations. The assignments (in lines 34–35) initialize total to 0 and gradeCounter to 1. Variables grade and average (for the user input and calculated average, respectively) need not be initialized here—their values are assigned as they're input or calculated later in the method.

Common Programming Error 5.4

Using the value of a local variable before it is definitely assigned results in a compilation error. All local variables must be definitely assigned before their values are used in expressions.

Error-Prevention Tip 5.1

Initialize each counter and total, either in its declaration or in an assignment statement. Totals are normally initialized to 0. Counters are normally initialized to 0 or 1, depending on how they're used (we'll show examples of each).

Line 38 indicates that the while statement should continue looping as long as the value of gradeCounter is less than or equal to 10. While this condition remains true, the while statement repeatedly executes the statements between the braces that delimit its body (lines 39–44).

Line 40 displays the prompt "Enter grade: ". Line 41 reads the grade entered by the user and assigns it to variable grade. Then line 42 adds the new grade entered by the user to the total and assigns the result to total, which replaces its previous value.

Line 43 increments gradeCounter to indicate that the application has processed a grade and is ready to input the next grade from the user. Incrementing gradeCounter eventually causes gradeCounter to exceed 10. At that point the while loop terminates, because its condition (line 38) becomes false.

When the loop terminates, line 47 performs the averaging calculation and assigns its result to the variable average. Line 50 uses Console's WriteLine method to display the text "Total of all 10 grades is " followed by variable total's value. Line 51 then displays the text "Class average is " followed by variable average's value. Method DetermineClassAverage returns control to the calling method (i.e., Main in GradeBookTest of Fig. 5.6) after reaching line 52.

Class GradeBookTest

Class GradeBookTest (Fig. 5.6) creates an object of class GradeBook (Fig. 5.5) and demonstrates its capabilities. Lines 9–10 of Fig. 5.6 create a new GradeBook object and assign it to variable myGradeBook. The string in line 10 is passed to the GradeBook constructor (lines 12–15 of Fig. 5.5). Line 12 calls myGradeBook's DisplayMessage method to display a welcome message to the user. Line 13 then calls myGradeBook's DetermineClassAverage method to allow the user to enter 10 grades, for which the method then calculates and displays the average.

```
 1   // Fig. 5.6: GradeBookTest.cs
 2   // Create GradeBook object and invoke its DetermineClassAverage method.
 3   public class GradeBookTest
 4   {
 5      public static void Main( string[] args )
 6      {
 7         // create GradeBook object myGradeBook and
 8         // pass course name to constructor
 9         GradeBook myGradeBook = new GradeBook(
10            "CS101 Introduction to C# Programming" );
11
12         myGradeBook.DisplayMessage(); // display welcome message
13         myGradeBook.DetermineClassAverage(); // find average of 10 grades
14      } // end Main
15   } // end class GradeBookTest
```

```
Welcome to the grade book for
CS101 Introduction to C# Programming!

Enter grade: 88
Enter grade: 79
Enter grade: 95
```

```
Enter grade: 100
Enter grade: 48
Enter grade: 88
Enter grade: 92
Enter grade: 83
Enter grade: 90
Enter grade: 85

Total of all 10 grades is 848
Class average is 84
```

Fig. 5.6 | Create GradeBook object and invoke its DetermineClassAverage method.

Notes on Integer Division and Truncation

The averaging calculation performed by method DetermineClassAverage in response to the method call at line 13 in Fig. 5.6 produces an integer result. The application's output indicates that the sum of the grade values in the sample execution is 848, which, when divided by 10, should yield the floating-point number 84.8. However, the result of the calculation total / 10 (line 47 of Fig. 5.5) is the integer 84, because total and 10 are both integers. Dividing two integers results in integer division—any fractional part of the calculation is lost (i.e., truncated, not rounded). We'll see how to obtain a floating-point result from the averaging calculation in the next section.

Common Programming Error 5.5

Assuming that integer division rounds (rather than truncates) can lead to incorrect results. For example, 7 ÷ 4, which yields 1.75 in conventional arithmetic, truncates to 1 in integer arithmetic, rather than rounding to 2.

5.7 Formulating Algorithms: Sentinel-Controlled Repetition

Let us generalize Section 5.6's class-average problem. Consider the following problem:

Develop a class-averaging application that processes grades for an arbitrary number of students each time it is run.

In the previous class-average example, the problem statement specified the number of students, so the number of grades (10) was known in advance. In this example, no indication is given of how many grades the user will enter during the application's execution. The application must process an arbitrary number of grades. How can it determine when to stop the input of grades? How will it know when to calculate and display the class average?

One way to solve this problem is to use a special value called a *sentinel value* (also called a *signal value*, a *dummy value* or a *flag value*) to indicate "end of data entry." The user enters grades until all legitimate grades have been entered. The user then types the sentinel value to indicate that no more grades will be entered. *Sentinel-controlled repetition* is often called *indefinite repetition* because the number of repetitions is not known by the application before the loop begins executing.

Clearly, a sentinel value must be chosen that cannot be confused with an acceptable input value. Grades on a quiz are nonnegative integers, so –1 is an acceptable sentinel value for this problem. Thus, a run of the class-average application might process a stream of inputs such as 95, 96, 75, 74, 89 and –1. The application would then compute and display the class average for the grades 95, 96, 75, 74 and 89. Since –1 is the sentinel value, it should not enter into the averaging calculation.

Common Programming Error 5.6

Choosing a sentinel value that is also a legitimate data value is a logic error.

Implementing Sentinel-Controlled Repetition in Class GradeBook

Figure 5.7 shows the C# class GradeBook containing method DetermineClassAverage that meets the requirements of the problem statement. Although each grade is an integer, the averaging calculation is likely to produce a number with a decimal point—in other

```
1   // Fig. 5.7: GradeBook.cs
2   // GradeBook class that solves class-average problem using
3   // sentinel-controlled repetition.
4   using System;
5
6   public class GradeBook
7   {
8      // auto-implemented property CourseName
9      public string CourseName { get; set; }
10
11     // constructor initializes the CourseName property
12     public GradeBook( string name )
13     {
14        CourseName = name; // set CourseName to name
15     } // end constructor
16
17     // display a welcome message to the GradeBook user
18     public void DisplayMessage()
19     {
20        Console.WriteLine( "Welcome to the grade book for\n{0}!\n",
21           CourseName );
22     } // end method DisplayMessage
23
24     // determine the average of an arbitrary number of grades
25     public void DetermineClassAverage()
26     {
27        int total; // sum of grades
28        int gradeCounter; // number of grades entered
29        int grade; // grade value
30        double average; // number with decimal point for average
31
32        // initialization phase
33        total = 0; // initialize total
34        gradeCounter = 0; // initialize loop counter
35
36        // processing phase
37        // prompt for and read a grade from the user
38        Console.Write( "Enter grade or -1 to quit: " );
39        grade = Convert.ToInt32( Console.ReadLine() );
40
41        // loop until sentinel value is read from the user
42        while ( grade != -1 )
43        {
44           total = total + grade; // add grade to total
45           gradeCounter = gradeCounter + 1; // increment counter
46
47           // prompt for and read the next grade from the user
48           Console.Write( "Enter grade or -1 to quit: " );
49           grade = Convert.ToInt32( Console.ReadLine() );
50        } // end while
51
```

Fig. 5.7 | GradeBook class that solves the class-average problem using sentinel-controlled repetition. (Part 1 of 2.)

```
52          // termination phase
53          // if the user entered at least one grade...
54          if ( gradeCounter != 0 )
55          {
56              // calculate the average of all the grades entered
57              average = ( double ) total / gradeCounter;
58
59              // display the total and average (with two digits of precision)
60              Console.WriteLine( "\nTotal of the {0} grades entered is {1}",
61                  gradeCounter, total );
62              Console.WriteLine( "Class average is {0:F}", average );
63          } // end if
64          else // no grades were entered, so output error message
65              Console.WriteLine( "No grades were entered" );
66      } // end method DetermineClassAverage
67  } // end class GradeBook
```

Fig. 5.7 | GradeBook class that solves the class-average problem using sentinel-controlled repetition. (Part 2 of 2.)

words, a real number or floating-point number. The type int cannot represent such a number, so this class uses type double to do so.

In this example, we see that control statements may be stacked on top of one another (in sequence)—the while statement (lines 42–50) is followed in sequence by an if...else statement (lines 54–65). Much of the code in this application is identical to the code in Fig. 5.5, so we concentrate on the new features and issues.

Line 30 declares double variable average. This variable allows us to store the calculated class average as a floating-point number. Line 34 initializes gradeCounter to 0, because no grades have been entered yet. Remember that this application uses sentinel-controlled repetition to input the grades from the user. To keep an accurate record of the number of grades entered, the application increments gradeCounter only when the user inputs a valid grade value.

Program Logic for Sentinel-Controlled Repetition vs. Counter-Controlled Repetition
Compare the program logic for sentinel-controlled repetition in this application with that for counter-controlled repetition in Fig. 5.5. In counter-controlled repetition, each repetition of the while statement (e.g., lines 38–44 of Fig. 5.5) reads a value from the user, for the specified number of repetitions. In sentinel-controlled repetition, the application reads the first value (lines 38–39 of Fig. 5.7) before reaching the while. This value determines whether the application's flow of control should enter the body of the while. If the condition of the while is false, the user entered the sentinel value, so the body of the while does not execute (because no grades were entered). If, on the other hand, the condition is true, the body begins execution, and the loop adds the grade value to the total (line 44) and adds 1 to gradeCounter (line 45). Then lines 48–49 in the loop's body input the next value from the user. Next, program control reaches the closing right brace of the body at line 50, so execution continues with the test of the while's condition (line 42). The condition uses the most recent grade input by the user to determine whether the loop's body should execute again. Note that the value of variable grade is always input from the user immediately before the application tests the while condition. This allows the application

to determine whether the value just input is the sentinel value *before* the application processes that value (i.e., adds it to the total). If the sentinel value is input, the loop terminates; the application does *not* add -1 to the total.

Good Programming Practice 5.7

In a sentinel-controlled loop, the prompts requesting data entry should explicitly remind the user of the sentinel value.

After the loop terminates, the if...else statement at lines 54–65 executes. The condition at line 54 determines whether any grades were input. If none were input, the else part (lines 64–65) of the if...else statement executes and displays the message "No grades were entered", and the method returns control to the calling method.

Error-Prevention Tip 5.2

When performing division by an expression whose value could be zero, explicitly test for this possibility and handle it appropriately in your application (e.g., by displaying an error message) rather than allowing the error to occur.

Notice the while statement's block in Fig. 5.7 (lines 43–50). Without the braces, the loop would consider its body to be only the first statement, which adds the grade to the total. The last three statements in the block would fall outside the loop's body, causing the computer to interpret the code incorrectly as follows:

```
while ( grade != -1 )
    total = total + grade; // add grade to total
gradeCounter = gradeCounter + 1; // increment counter

// prompt for input and read next grade from user
Console.Write( "Enter grade or -1 to quit: " );
grade = Convert.ToInt32( Console.ReadLine() );
```

The preceding code would cause an infinite loop in the application if the user did not enter the sentinel -1 at line 39 (before the while statement).

Error-Prevention Tip 5.3

Omitting the braces that delimit a block can lead to logic errors, such as infinite loops. To prevent this problem, some programmers enclose the body of every control statement in braces even if the body contains only a single statement.

Explicitly and Implicitly Converting Between Simple Types

If at least one grade was entered, line 57 of Fig. 5.7 calculates the average of the grades. Recall from Fig. 5.5 that integer division yields an integer result. Even though variable average is declared as a double (line 30), the calculation

```
average = total / gradeCounter;
```

loses the division's fractional part before the result is assigned to average. This occurs because total and gradeCounter are both integers, and integer division yields an integer result. To perform a floating-point calculation with integer values, we must temporarily treat these values as floating-point numbers for use in the calculation. C# provides the *unary cast operator* to accomplish this task. Line 57 uses the *(double)* cast operator—which has higher precedence than the arithmetic operators—to create a *temporary* floating-point copy of its operand `total` (which appears to the right of the operator). Using a cast operator in this manner is called *explicit conversion*. The value stored in `total` is still an integer.

The calculation now consists of a floating-point value (the temporary `double` version of `total`) divided by the integer `gradeCounter`. C# knows how to evaluate only arithmetic expressions in which the operands' types are identical. To ensure that the operands are of the same type, C# performs an operation called *promotion* (or *implicit conversion*) on selected operands. For example, in an expression containing values of the types `int` and `double`, the `int` values are promoted to `double` values for use in the expression. In this example, the value of `gradeCounter` is promoted to type `double`, then floating-point division is performed and the result of the calculation is assigned to `average`. As long as the `(double)` cast operator is applied to any variable in the calculation, the calculation will yield a `double` result. Later in this chapter, we discuss all the simple types. You'll learn more about the promotion rules in Section 7.7.

Common Programming Error 5.7

A cast operator can be used to convert between simple numeric types, such as int and double, and between related reference types (as we discuss in Chapter 12, Polymorphism, Interfaces and Operator Overloading). Casting to the wrong type may cause compilation or runtime errors.

Cast operators are available for all simple types. (We'll discuss cast operators for reference types in Chapter 12.) The cast operator is formed by placing parentheses around the name of a type. This operator is a *unary operator* (i.e., an operator that takes only one operand). In Chapter 3, we discussed the binary arithmetic operators. C# also supports unary versions of the plus (+) and minus (–) operators, so you can write expressions like +5 or -7. Cast operators associate from right to left and have the same precedence as other unary operators, such as unary + and unary -. This precedence is one level higher than that of the *multiplicative operators* *, / and %. (See the operator precedence chart in Appendix A.) We indicate the cast operator with the notation (*type*) in our precedence charts, to indicate that any type name can be used to form a cast operator.

Line 62 outputs the class average. In this example, we decided that we'd like to display the class average rounded to the nearest hundredth and output the average with exactly two digits to the right of the decimal point. The format specifier F in `WriteLine`'s format item (line 62) indicates that variable `average`'s value should be displayed as a real number. By default, numbers output with F have two digits to the right of the decimal point. The number of decimal places to the right of the decimal point is also known as the number's *precision*. Any floating-point value output with F will be rounded to the hundredths position—for example, 123.457 will be rounded to 123.46, and 27.333 will be rounded to 27.33. In this application, the three grades entered during the sample execution of class `GradeBookTest` (Fig. 5.8) total 263, which yields the average 87.66666…. The format item rounds the average to the hundredths position, and the average is displayed as 87.67.

```
1   // Fig. 5.8: GradeBookTest.cs
2   // Create GradeBook object and invoke its DetermineClassAverage method.
3   public class GradeBookTest
4   {
```

Fig. 5.8 | Create `GradeBook` object and invoke `DetermineClassAverage` method. (Part 1 of 2.)

```
 5        public static void Main( string[] args )
 6        {
 7            // create GradeBook object myGradeBook and
 8            // pass course name to constructor
 9            GradeBook myGradeBook = new GradeBook(
10                "CS101 Introduction to C# Programming" );
11
12            myGradeBook.DisplayMessage(); // display welcome message
13            myGradeBook.DetermineClassAverage(); // find average of grades
14        } // end Main
15    } // end class GradeBookTest
```

```
Welcome to the grade book for
CS101 Introduction to C# Programming!

Enter grade or -1 to quit: 96
Enter grade or -1 to quit: 88
Enter grade or -1 to quit: 79
Enter grade or -1 to quit: -1

Total of the 3 grades entered is 263
Class average is 87.67
```

Fig. 5.8 | Create GradeBook object and invoke DetermineClassAverage method. (Part 2 of 2.)

5.8 Formulating Algorithms: Nested Control Statements

We have seen that control statements can be stacked on top of one another (in sequence). In this case study, we examine the only other structured way control statements can be connected, namely, by *nesting* one control statement within another.

Consider the following problem statement:

> *A college offers a course that prepares students for the state licensing exam for real estate brokers. Last year, 10 of the students who completed this course took the exam. The college wants to know how well its students did on the exam. You've been asked to write an application to summarize the results. You've been given a list of these 10 students. Next to each name is written a 1 if the student passed the exam or a 2 if the student failed.*

> *Your application should analyze the results of the exam as follows:*

> 1. *Input each test result (i.e., a 1 or a 2). Display the message "Enter result" on the screen each time the application requests another test result.*

> 2. *Count the number of test results of each type.*

> 3. *Display a summary of the test results indicating the number of students who passed and the number who failed.*

> 4. *If more than eight students passed the exam, display the message "Raise tuition."*

After reading the problem statement, we make the following observations:

1. The application must process test results for 10 students. A counter-controlled loop can be used because the number of test results is known in advance.

2. Each test result has a numeric value—either a 1 or a 2. Each time the application reads a test result, the application must determine whether the number is a 1 or a 2. We test for a 1 in our algorithm. If the number is not a 1, we assume that it is a 2.

3. Two counters are used to keep track of the exam results—one to count the number of students who passed the exam and one to count the number of students who failed the exam.

4. After the application has processed all the results, it must determine whether more than eight students passed the exam.

The C# class that meets these requirements is shown in Fig. 5.9, and two sample executions appear in Fig. 5.10. Lines 10–13 of Fig. 5.9 declare the variables that method ProcessExamResults of class Analysis uses to process the examination results. Several of these declarations use C#'s ability to incorporate variable initialization into declarations (passes is assigned 0, failures is assigned 0 and studentCounter is assigned 1).

```csharp
1   // Fig. 5.9: Analysis.cs
2   // Analysis of examination results, using nested control statements.
3   using System;
4
5   public class Analysis
6   {
7      public void ProcessExamResults()
8      {
9         // initialize variables in declarations
10        int passes = 0; // number of passes
11        int failures = 0; // number of failures
12        int studentCounter = 1; // student counter
13        int result; // one exam result from user
14
15        // process 10 students using counter-controlled repetition
16        while ( studentCounter <= 10 )
17        {
18           // prompt user for input and obtain a value from the user
19           Console.Write( "Enter result (1 = pass, 2 = fail): " );
20           result = Convert.ToInt32( Console.ReadLine() );
21
22           // if...else nested in while
23           if ( result == 1 ) // if result 1,
24              passes = passes + 1; // increment passes
25           else // else result is not 1, so
26              failures = failures + 1; // increment failures
27
28           // increment studentCounter so loop eventually terminates
29           studentCounter = studentCounter + 1;
30        } // end while
31
```

Fig. 5.9 | Analysis of examination results, using nested control statements. (Part 1 of 2.)

```
32          // termination phase; prepare and display results
33          Console.WriteLine( "Passed: {0}\nFailed: {1}", passes, failures );
34
35          // determine whether more than 8 students passed
36          if ( passes > 8 )
37              Console.WriteLine( "Raise Tuition" );
38      } // end method ProcessExamResults
39  } // end class Analysis
```

Fig. 5.9 | Analysis of examination results, using nested control statements. (Part 2 of 2.)

The while statement (lines 16–30) loops 10 times. During each repetition, the loop inputs and processes one exam result. Notice that the if...else statement (lines 23–26) for processing each result is nested in the while statement. If the result is 1, the if...else statement increments passes; otherwise, it assumes the result is 2 and increments failures. Line 29 increments studentCounter before the loop condition is tested again at line 16. After 10 values have been input, the loop terminates and line 33 displays the number of passes and the number of failures. Lines 36–37 determine whether more than eight students passed the exam and, if so, outputs the message "Raise Tuition".

Error-Prevention Tip 5.4

Initializing local variables when they're declared helps you avoid compilation errors that might arise from attempts to use uninitialized data. While C# does not require that local-variable initializations be incorporated into declarations, it does require that local variables be initialized before their values are used in an expression.

AnalysisTest Class That Demonstrates Class Analysis

Class AnalysisTest (Fig. 5.10) creates an Analysis object (line 7) and invokes the object's ProcessExamResults method (line 8) to process a set of exam results entered by the user. Figure 5.10 shows the input and output from two sample executions of the application. During the first sample execution, the condition at line 36 of method ProcessExamResults in Fig. 5.9 is true—more than eight students passed the exam, so the application outputs a message indicating that the tuition should be raised.

```
1   // Fig. 5.10: AnalysisTest.cs
2   // Test application for class Analysis.
3   public class AnalysisTest
4   {
5       public static void Main( string[] args )
6       {
7           Analysis application = new Analysis(); // create Analysis object
8           application.ProcessExamResults(); // call method to process results
9       } // end Main
10  } // end class AnalysisTest
```

Fig. 5.10 | Test application for class Analysis. (Part 1 of 2.)

```
Enter result (1 = pass, 2 = fail): 1
Enter result (1 = pass, 2 = fail): 2
Enter result (1 = pass, 2 = fail): 1
Enter result (1 = pass, 2 = fail): 1
Enter result (1 = pass, 2 = fail): 1
Enter result (1 = pass, 2 = fail): 1
Enter result (1 = pass, 2 = fail): 1
Enter result (1 = pass, 2 = fail): 1
Enter result (1 = pass, 2 = fail): 1
Enter result (1 = pass, 2 = fail): 1
Passed: 9
Failed: 1
Raise Tuition
```

```
Enter result (1 = pass, 2 = fail): 1
Enter result (1 = pass, 2 = fail): 2
Enter result (1 = pass, 2 = fail): 2
Enter result (1 = pass, 2 = fail): 2
Enter result (1 = pass, 2 = fail): 1
Enter result (1 = pass, 2 = fail): 1
Enter result (1 = pass, 2 = fail): 1
Enter result (1 = pass, 2 = fail): 1
Enter result (1 = pass, 2 = fail): 2
Enter result (1 = pass, 2 = fail): 2
Passed: 5
Failed: 5
```

Fig. 5.10 | Test application for class `Analysis`. (Part 2 of 2.)

5.9 Compound Assignment Operators

C# provides several *compound assignment operators* for abbreviating assignment expressions. Any statement of the form

> *variable = variable operator expression;*

where *operator* is one of the binary operators +, -, *, / or % (or others we discuss later in the text) can be written in the form

> *variable operator= expression;*

For example, you can abbreviate the statement

```
c = c + 3;
```

with the *addition compound assignment operator*, +=, as

```
c += 3;
```

The += operator adds the value of the expression on the right of the operator to the value of the variable on the left of the operator and stores the result in the variable on the left of the operator. Thus, the assignment expression c += 3 adds 3 to c. Figure 5.11 shows the arithmetic compound assignment operators, sample expressions using the operators and explanations of what the operators do.

Assignment operator	Sample expression	Explanation	Assigns
Assume: **int** c = 3, d = 5, e = 4, f = 6, g = 12;			
+=	c += 7	c = c + 7	**10** to c
-=	d -= 4	d = d - 4	**1** to d
*=	e *= 5	e = e * 5	**20** to e
/=	f /= 3	f = f / 3	**2** to f
%=	g %= 9	g = g % 9	**3** to g

Fig. 5.11 | Arithmetic compound assignment operators.

5.10 Increment and Decrement Operators

C# provides two unary operators for adding 1 to or subtracting 1 from the value of a numeric variable. These are the unary *increment operator*, **++**, and the unary *decrement operator*, **--**, respectively, which are summarized in Fig. 5.12. An application can increment by 1 the value of a variable called c using the increment operator, ++, rather than the expression c = c + 1 or c += 1. An increment or decrement operator that is prefixed to (placed before) a variable is referred to as the *prefix increment operator* or *prefix decrement operator*, respectively. An increment or decrement operator that is postfixed to (placed after) a variable is referred to as the *postfix increment operator* or *postfix decrement operator*, respectively.

Incrementing (or decrementing) a variable with the prefix increment (or prefix decrement) operator causes it to be incremented (or decremented) by 1; then the new value of the variable is used in the expression in which it appears. Incrementing (or decrementing) the variable with the postfix increment (or postfix decrement) operator causes the variable's current value to be used in the expression in which it appears; then the variable's value is incremented (or decremented) by 1.

Operator	Called	Sample expression	Explanation
++	prefix increment	++a	Increments a by 1, then uses the new value of a in the expression in which a resides.
++	postfix increment	a++	Uses the current value of a in the expression in which a resides, then increments a by 1.
--	prefix decrement	--b	Decrements b by 1, then uses the new value of b in the expression in which b resides.
--	postfix decrement	b--	Uses the current value of b in the expression in which b resides, then decrements b by 1.

Fig. 5.12 | Increment and decrement operators.

Good Programming Practice 5.8

Unlike binary operators, the unary increment and decrement operators should (by convention) be placed next to their operands, with no intervening spaces.

Figure 5.13 demonstrates the difference between the prefix increment and postfix increment versions of the ++ increment operator. The decrement operator (--) works similarly. Note that this example contains only one class, with method Main performing all the class's work. In this chapter and in Chapter 4, you've seen examples consisting of two classes—one class containing methods that perform useful tasks and one containing method Main, which creates an object of the other class and calls its methods. In this example, we simply want to show the mechanics of the ++ operator, so we use only one class declaration containing method Main. Occasionally, when it makes no sense to try to create a reusable class to demonstrate a simple concept, we'll use a mechanical example contained entirely within the Main method of a single class.

```csharp
 1   // Fig. 5.13: Increment.cs
 2   // Prefix increment and postfix increment operators.
 3   using System;
 4
 5   public class Increment
 6   {
 7      public static void Main( string[] args )
 8      {
 9         int c;
10
11         // demonstrate postfix increment operator
12         c = 5; // assign 5 to c
13         Console.WriteLine( c ); // display 5
14         Console.WriteLine( c++ ); // display 5 again, then increment
15         Console.WriteLine( c ); // display 6
16
17         Console.WriteLine(); // skip a line
18
19         // demonstrate prefix increment operator
20         c = 5; // assign 5 to c
21         Console.WriteLine( c ); // display 5
22         Console.WriteLine( ++c ); // increment, then display
23         Console.WriteLine( c ); // display 6 again
24      } // end Main
25   } // end class Increment
```

```
5
5
6

5
6
6
```

Fig. 5.13 | Prefix increment and postfix increment operators.

Line 12 initializes the variable c to 5, and line 13 outputs c's initial value. Line 14 outputs the value of the expression c++. This expression performs the postfix increment operation on the variable c, so c's original value (5) is output, then c's value is incremented. Thus, line 14 outputs c's initial value (5) again. Line 15 outputs c's new value (6) to prove that the variable's value was indeed incremented in line 14.

Line 20 resets c's value to 5, and line 21 outputs c's value. Line 22 outputs the value of the expression ++c. This expression performs the prefix increment operation on c, so its value is incremented; then the new value (6) is output. Line 23 outputs c's value again to show that the value of c is still 6 after line 22 executes.

The arithmetic compound assignment operators and the increment and decrement operators can be used to simplify statements. For example, the three assignment statements in Fig. 5.9 (lines 24, 26 and 29)

```
passes = passes + 1;
failures = failures + 1;
studentCounter = studentCounter + 1;
```

can be written more concisely with compound assignment operators as

```
passes += 1;
failures += 1;
studentCounter += 1;
```

and even more concisely with prefix increment operators as

```
++passes;
++failures;
++studentCounter;
```

or with postfix increment operators as

```
passes++;
failures++;
studentCounter++;
```

When incrementing or decrementing a variable in a statement by itself, the prefix increment and postfix increment forms have the same effect, and the prefix decrement and postfix decrement forms have the same effect. It is only when a variable appears in the context of a larger expression that the prefix increment and postfix increment have different effects (and similarly for the prefix decrement and postfix decrement).

Common Programming Error 5.8

Attempting to use the increment or decrement operator on an expression other than one to which a value can be assigned is a syntax error. For example, writing ++(x + 1) is a syntax error, because (x + 1) is not a variable.

Figure 5.14 shows the precedence and associativity of the operators introduced so far. The operators are shown from top to bottom in decreasing order of precedence. The second column describes the associativity of the operators at each level of precedence. The conditional operator (?:); the unary operators prefix increment (++), prefix decrement (--), plus (+) and minus (-); the cast operators; and the assignment operators =, +=, -=, *=, /= and %= associate from right to left. All the other operators in the operator precedence chart in Fig. 5.14 associate from left to right. The third column names the groups of operators.

Operators					Associativity	Type
.	new	++*(postfix)*	--*(postfix)*		left to right	highest precedence
++	--	+	-	(*type*)	right to left	unary prefix
*	/	%			left to right	multiplicative
+	-				left to right	additive
<	<=	>	>=		left to right	relational
==	!=				left to right	equality
?:					right to left	conditional
=	+=	-=	*=	/= %=	right to left	assignment

Fig. 5.14 | Precedence and associativity of the operators discussed so far.

5.11 Simple Types

The table in Appendix B, lists the 13 *simple types* in C#. Like its predecessor languages C and C++, C# requires all variables to have a type. For this reason, C# is referred to as a *strongly typed language*.

In C and C++, programmers frequently have to write separate versions of applications to support different computer platforms, because the simple types are not guaranteed to be identical from computer to computer. For example, an int value on one machine might be represented by 16 bits (2 bytes) of storage, while an int value on another machine might be represented by 32 bits (4 bytes) of storage. In C#, int values are always 32 bits (4 bytes). In fact, *all* C# numeric types have fixed sizes, as is shown in Appendix B.

Each type in Appendix B is listed with its size in bits (there are eight bits to a byte) and its range of values. Because the designers of C# want it to be maximally portable, they use internationally recognized standards for both character formats (Unicode; for more information, see Appendix G, Unicode®) and floating-point numbers (IEEE 754; for more information, visit grouper.ieee.org/groups/754/).

Recall from Section 4.5 that variables of simple types declared outside of a method as fields of a class are automatically assigned default values unless explicitly initialized. Instance variables of types char, byte, sbyte, short, ushort, int, uint, long, ulong, float, double, and decimal are all given the value 0 by default. Instance variables of type bool are given the value false by default. Similarly, reference-type instance variables are initialized by default to the value null.

5.12 (Optional) Software Engineering Case Study: Identifying Class Attributes in the ATM System

In Section 4.12, we began the first stage of an object-oriented design (OOD) for our ATM system—analyzing the requirements document and identifying the classes needed to implement the system. We listed the nouns and noun phrases in the requirements document and identified a separate class for each one that plays a significant role in the ATM system. We then modeled the classes and their relationships in a UML class diagram (Fig. 4.26).

Classes have attributes (data) and operations (behaviors). Class attributes are implemented in C# programs as instance variables and properties, and class operations are implemented as methods and properties. In this section, we determine many of the attributes needed in the ATM system. In Section 6.9, we examine how these attributes represent an object's state. In Section 7.15, we determine the operations for our classes.

Identifying Attributes

Consider the attributes of some real-world objects: A person's attributes include height, weight and whether the person is left-handed, right-handed or ambidextrous. A radio's attributes include its station setting, its volume setting and its AM or FM setting. A car's attributes include its speedometer and odometer readings, the amount of gas in its tank and what gear it is in. A personal computer's attributes include its manufacturer (e.g., Dell, HP, Sun, Apple or IBM), type of screen (e.g., LCD or CRT), main memory size and hard-disk size.

We can identify many attributes of the classes in our system by looking for descriptive words and phrases in the requirements document. For each one we find that plays a significant role in the ATM system, we create an attribute and assign it to one or more of the classes identified in Section 4.12. We also create attributes to represent any additional data that a class may need, as such needs become clear throughout the design process.

Figure 5.15 lists the words or phrases from the requirements document that describe each class. For example, the requirements document describes the steps taken to obtain a "withdrawal amount," so we list "amount" next to class Withdrawal.

Class	Descriptive words and phrases
ATM	user is authenticated
BalanceInquiry	account number
Withdrawal	account number amount
Deposit	account number amount
BankDatabase	[no descriptive words or phrases]
Account	account number PIN balance
Screen	[no descriptive words or phrases]
Keypad	[no descriptive words or phrases]
CashDispenser	begins each day loaded with 500 $20 bills
DepositSlot	[no descriptive words or phrases]

Fig. 5.15 | Descriptive words and phrases from the ATM requirements document.

Figure 5.15 leads us to create one attribute of class ATM. This class maintains information about the state of the ATM. The phrase "user is authenticated" describes a state of the ATM (we discuss states in detail in Section 6.9), so we include userAuthenticated as an *attribute* of type bool (i.e., an attribute that has a value of either true or false). This attribute indicates whether the ATM has successfully authenticated the current user—user-Authenticated must be true for the system to allow the user to perform transactions and access account information. This attribute helps ensure the security of the data in the system.

Classes BalanceInquiry, Withdrawal and Deposit share one attribute. Each transaction involves an "account number" that corresponds to the account of the user making the transaction. We assign integer attribute accountNumber to each transaction class to identify the account to which an object of the class applies.

Descriptive words and phrases in the requirements document also suggest some differences in the attributes required by each transaction class. The requirements document indicates that to withdraw cash or deposit funds, users must enter a specific "amount" of money to be withdrawn or deposited, respectively. Thus, we assign to classes Withdrawal and Deposit an attribute amount to store the value supplied by the user. The amounts of money related to a withdrawal and a deposit are defining characteristics of these transactions that the system requires for them to take place. Recall that C# represents monetary amounts with type decimal. Note that class BalanceInquiry does not need additional data to perform its task—it requires only an account number to indicate the account whose balance should be retrieved.

Class Account has several attributes. The requirements document states that each bank account has an "account number" and a "PIN," which the system uses for identifying accounts and authenticating users. We assign to the Account class two integer attributes: accountNumber and pin. The requirements document also specifies that an account maintains a "balance" of the amount of money in the account, and that the money the user deposits does not become available for a withdrawal until the bank verifies the amount of cash in the deposit envelope and any checks in the envelope clear. An account must still record the amount of money that a user deposits, however. Therefore, we decide that an account should represent a balance using two attributes of type decimal—availableBalance and totalBalance. Attribute availableBalance tracks the amount of money that a user can withdraw from the account. Attribute totalBalance refers to the total amount of money that the user has "on deposit" (i.e., the amount of money available, plus the amount of cash deposits waiting to be verified or the amount of checks waiting to be cleared). For example, suppose an ATM user deposits $50.00 in cash into an empty account. The totalBalance attribute would increase to $50.00 to record the deposit, but the availableBalance would remain at $0 until a bank employee counts the amount of cash in the envelope and confirms the total. [*Note:* We assume that the bank updates the availableBalance attribute of an Account soon after the ATM transaction occurs, in response to confirming that $50 worth of cash was found in the deposit envelope. We assume that this update occurs through a transaction that a bank employee performs using a bank system other than the ATM. Thus, we do not discuss this transaction in our case study.]

Class CashDispenser has one attribute. The requirements document states that the cash dispenser "begins each day loaded with 500 $20 bills." The cash dispenser must keep track of the number of bills it contains to determine whether enough cash is on hand to satisfy withdrawal requests. We assign to class CashDispenser integer attribute count, which is initially set to 500.

For real problems in industry, there is no guarantee that requirements documents will be rich enough and precise enough for the object-oriented systems designer to determine all the attributes, or even all the classes. The need for additional classes, attributes and behaviors may become clear as the design process proceeds. As we progress through this case study, we too will continue to add, modify and delete information about the classes in our system.

Modeling Attributes

The class diagram in Fig. 5.16 lists some of the attributes for the classes in our system—the descriptive words and phrases in Fig. 5.15 helped us identify these attributes. For simplicity, Fig. 5.16 does not show the associations among classes—we showed these in Fig. 4.26. Systems designers commonly do this. Recall that in the UML, a class's attributes are placed in the middle compartment of the class's rectangle. We list each attribute's name and type separated by a colon (:), followed in some cases by an equal sign (=) and an initial value.

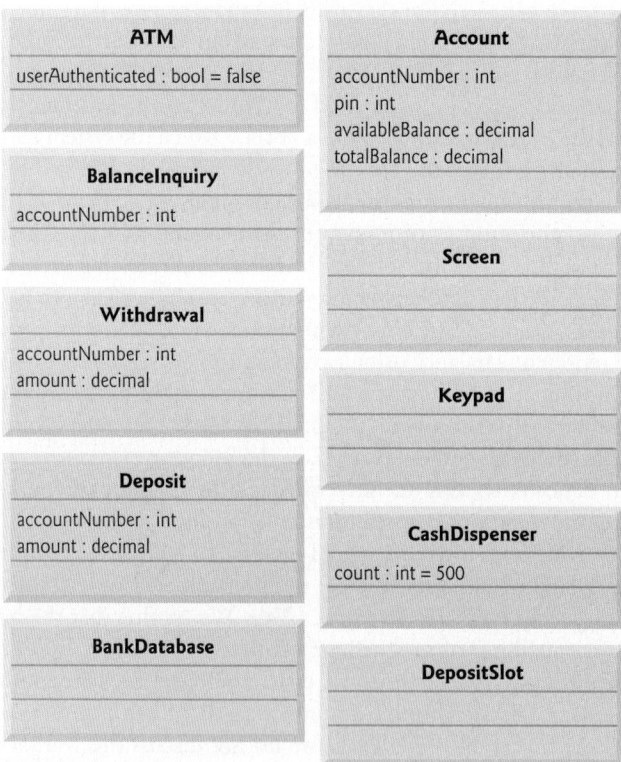

Fig. 5.16 | Classes with attributes.

Consider the `userAuthenticated` attribute of class `ATM`:

```
userAuthenticated : bool = false
```

This attribute declaration contains three pieces of information about the attribute. The *attribute name* is `userAuthenticated`. The *attribute type* is `bool`. In C#, an attribute can be represented by a simple type, such as `bool`, `int`, `double` or `decimal`, or a class type—as discussed in Chapter 4. We have chosen to model only simple-type attributes in Fig. 5.16—we discuss the reasoning behind this decision shortly.

We can also indicate an initial value for an attribute. Attribute `userAuthenticated` in class `ATM` has an initial value of `false`. This indicates that the system initially does not consider the user to be authenticated. If an attribute has no initial value specified, only its name and type (separated by a colon) are shown. For example, the `accountNumber` attribute of class `BalanceInquiry` is an `int`. Here we show no initial value, because the value of this attribute is a number that we do not yet know. This number will be determined at execution time based on the account number entered by the current ATM user.

Figure 5.16 does not contain attributes for classes `Screen`, `Keypad` and `DepositSlot`. These are important components of our system for which our design process simply has not yet revealed any attributes. We may discover some, however, in the remaining phases of design or when we implement these classes in C#. This is perfectly normal.

Software Engineering Observation 5.1

Early in the design process, classes often lack attributes (and operations). Such classes should not be eliminated, however, because attributes (and operations) may become evident in the later phases of design and implementation.

Note that Fig. 5.16 also does not include attributes for the `BankDatabase` class. We have chosen to include only simple-type attributes in Fig. 5.16 (and in similar class diagrams throughout the case study). A class-type attribute is modeled more clearly as an association (in particular, a composition) between the class with the attribute and the attribute's own class. For example, the class diagram in Fig. 4.26 indicates that class `BankDatabase` participates in a composition relationship with zero or more `Account` objects. From this composition, we can determine that when we implement the ATM system in C#, we'll be required to create an attribute of class `BankDatabase` to hold zero or more `Account` objects. Similarly, we'll assign attributes to class `ATM` that correspond to its composition relationships with classes `Screen`, `Keypad`, `CashDispenser` and `DepositSlot`. These composition-based attributes would be redundant if modeled in Fig. 5.16, because the compositions modeled in Fig. 4.26 already convey the fact that the database contains information about zero or more accounts and that an ATM is composed of a screen, keypad, cash dispenser and deposit slot. Software developers typically model these whole/part relationships as composition associations rather than as attributes required to implement the relationships.

The class diagram in Fig. 5.16 provides a solid basis for the structure of our model, but the diagram is not complete. In Section 6.9 we identify the states and activities of the objects in the model, and in Section 7.15 we identify the operations that the objects perform. As we present more of the UML and object-oriented design, we'll continue to strengthen the structure of our model.

Software Engineering Case Study Self-Review Exercises

5.1   We typically identify the attributes of the classes in our system by analyzing the _____ in the requirements document.
a) nouns and noun phrases
b) descriptive words and phrases
c) verbs and verb phrases
d) All of the above

5.2   Which of the following is not an attribute of an airplane?
a) length
b) wingspan
c) fly
d) number of seats

5.3   Describe the meaning of the following attribute declaration of class `CashDispenser` in the class diagram in Fig. 5.16:

```
count : int = 500
```

Answers to Software Engineering Case Study Self-Review Exercises

5.1   b.

5.2   c. Fly is an operation or behavior of an airplane, not an attribute.

5.3   This declaration indicates that attribute `count` is an `int` with an initial value of 500; `count` keeps track of the number of bills available in the `CashDispenser` at any given time.

5.13 Wrap-Up

Only three types of control structures—sequence, selection and repetition—are needed to develop any problem-solving algorithm. Specifically, this chapter demonstrated the `if` single-selection statement, the `if...else` double-selection statement and the `while` repetition statement. We used control-statement stacking to compute the total and the average of a set of student grades with counter- and sentinel-controlled repetition, and we used control-statement nesting to analyze and make decisions based on a set of exam results. We introduced C#'s compound assignment operators, unary cast operators, as well as its increment and decrement operators. Finally, we discussed the simple types available to C# programmers. In Chapter 6, Control Statements: Part 2, we continue our discussion of control statements, introducing the `for`, `do...while` and `switch` statements.

6

Control
Statements:
Part 2

*Not everything that can be
counted counts, and not
everything that counts can
be counted.*
—Albert Einstein

Who can control his fate?
—William Shakespeare

*The used key is always
bright.*
—Benjamin Franklin

*Every advantage in the past
is judged in the light of the
final issue.*
—Demosthenes

OBJECTIVES

In this chapter you'll learn:

- The essentials of counter-controlled repetition.

- To use the `for` and `do...while` repetition statements to execute statements in an application repeatedly.

- To understand multiple selection using the `switch` selection statement.

- To use the `break` and `continue` program-control statements to alter the flow of control.

- To use the logical operators to form complex conditional expressions in control statements.

Outline

6.1 Introduction

6.2 Essentials of Counter-Controlled Repetition

6.3 for Repetition Statement

6.4 Examples Using the for Statement

6.5 do...while Repetition Statement

6.6 switch Multiple-Selection Statement

6.7 break and continue Statements

6.8 Logical Operators

6.9 (Optional) Software Engineering Case Study: Identifying Objects' States and Activities in the ATM System

6.10 Wrap-Up

6.1 Introduction

In this chapter, we introduce all but one of C#'s remaining control statements (the foreach statement is introduced in Chapter 8, Arrays). The control statements we study here and in Chapter 5 are helpful in building and manipulating objects.

In this chapter, we demonstrate C#'s for, do...while and switch statements. Through a series of examples using while and for, we explore the essentials of counter-controlled repetition. We devote a portion of the chapter (and Chapter 8) to expanding the GradeBook class presented in Chapters 4 and 5. In particular, we create a version of class GradeBook that uses a switch statement to count the number of A, B, C, D and F grade equivalents in a set of numeric grades entered by the user. We introduce the break and continue program-control statements. We discuss C#'s logical operators, which enable you to use more complex conditional expressions in control statements.

6.2 Essentials of Counter-Controlled Repetition

This section uses the while *repetition statement* to formalize the elements required to perform counter-controlled repetition. Counter-controlled repetition requires

1. a *control variable* (or loop counter)

2. the *initial value* of the control variable

3. the *increment* (or *decrement*) by which the control variable is modified each time through the loop (also known as each *iteration of the loop*)

4. the *loop-continuation condition* that determines whether to continue looping.

To see these elements of counter-controlled repetition, consider the application of Fig. 6.1, which uses a loop to display the numbers from 1 through 10. Note that Fig. 6.1 contains only one method, Main, which does all of the class's work. For most applications in Chapters 4 and 5, we have encouraged the use of two separate files—one that declares a reusable class (e.g., Account) and one that instantiates one or more objects of that class (e.g., AccountTest) and demonstrates their functionality. Occasionally, however, it is more appropriate simply to create one class whose Main method concisely illustrates a basic concept. Throughout this chapter, we use several one-class examples like Fig. 6.1 to demonstrate the mechanics of various C# control statements.

```
 1   // Fig. 6.1: WhileCounter.cs
 2   // Counter-controlled repetition with the while repetition statement.
 3   using System;
 4
 5   public class WhileCounter
 6   {
 7      public static void Main( string[] args )
 8      {
 9         int counter = 1; // declare and initialize control variable
10
11         while ( counter <= 10 ) // loop-continuation condition
12         {
13            Console.Write( "{0}  ", counter );
14            ++counter; // increment control variable
15         } // end while
16
17         Console.WriteLine(); // output a newline
18      } // end Main
19   } // end class WhileCounter
```

```
1  2  3  4  5  6  7  8  9  10
```

Fig. 6.1 | Counter-controlled repetition with the `while` repetition statement.

In method `Main` of Fig. 6.1 (lines 7–18), the elements of counter-controlled repetition are defined in lines 9, 11 and 14. Line 9 declares the control variable (`counter`) as an `int`, reserves space for it in memory and sets its initial value to 1.

Line 13 in the `while` statement displays control variable `counter`'s value during each iteration of the loop. Line 14 increments the control variable by 1 for each iteration of the loop. The loop-continuation condition in the `while` (line 11) tests whether the value of the control variable is less than or equal to 10 (the final value for which the condition is `true`). Note that the application performs the body of this `while` even when the control variable is 10. The loop terminates when the control variable exceeds 10 (i.e., `counter` becomes 11).

Common Programming Error 6.1

Because floating-point values may be approximate, controlling loops with floating-point variables may result in imprecise counter values and inaccurate termination tests.

Error-Prevention Tip 6.1

Control counting loops with integers.

Good Programming Practice 6.1

Place blank lines above and below repetition and selection control statements, and indent the statement bodies to enhance readability.

The application in Fig. 6.1 can be made more concise by initializing `counter` to 0 in line 9 and incrementing `counter` in the `while` condition with the prefix increment operator as follows:

```
while ( ++counter <= 10 ) // loop-continuation condition
   Console.Write( "{0}  ", counter );
```

This code saves a statement (and eliminates the need for braces around the loop's body), because the while condition performs the increment before testing the condition. (Recall from Section 5.10 that the precedence of ++ is higher than that of <=.) Code written in such a condensed fashion might be more difficult to read, debug, modify and maintain.

Software Engineering Observation 6.1

"Keep it simple" is good advice for most of the code you'll write.

6.3 for Repetition Statement

Section 6.2 presented the essentials of counter-controlled repetition. The while statement can be used to implement any counter-controlled loop. C# also provides the **for repetition statement**, which specifies the elements of counter-controlled-repetition in a single line of code. In general, counter-controlled repetition should be implemented with a for statement. Figure 6.2 reimplements the application in Fig. 6.1 using the for statement.

The application's Main method operates as follows: when the for statement (lines 11–12) begins executing, control variable counter is declared and initialized to 1. (Recall from Section 6.2 that the first two elements of counter-controlled repetition are the control variable and its initial value.) Next, the application checks the loop-continuation condition, counter <= 10, which is between the two required semicolons. Because the initial value of counter is 1, the condition initially is true. Therefore, the body statement (line 12) displays control variable counter's value, which is 1. After executing the loop's body, the application increments counter in the expression counter++, which appears to the right of the second semicolon. Then the loop-continuation test is performed again to determine whether the application should continue with the next iteration of the loop. At this point, the control-variable value is 2, so the condition is still true (the final value is not exceeded)—and the application performs the body statement again (i.e., the next iteration

```
1    // Fig. 6.2: ForCounter.cs
2    // Counter-controlled repetition with the for repetition statement.
3    using System;
4
5    public class ForCounter
6    {
7       public static void Main( string[] args )
8       {
9          // for statement header includes initialization,
10         // loop-continuation condition and increment
11         for ( int counter = 1; counter <= 10; counter++ )
12            Console.Write( "{0}  ", counter );
13
14         Console.WriteLine(); // output a newline
15      } // end Main
16   } // end class ForCounter
```

```
1  2  3  4  5  6  7  8  9  10
```

Fig. 6.2 | Counter-controlled repetition with the for repetition statement.

of the loop). This process continues until the numbers 1 through 10 have been displayed and the counter's value becomes 11, causing the loop-continuation test to fail and repetition to terminate (after 10 repetitions of the loop body at line 12). Then the application performs the first statement after the for—in this case, line 14.

Note that Fig. 6.2 uses (in line 11) the loop-continuation condition counter <= 10. If you incorrectly specified counter < 10 as the condition, the loop would iterate only nine times—a common logic error called an *off-by-one error*.

Common Programming Error 6.2

Using an incorrect relational operator or an incorrect final value of a loop counter in the loop-continuation condition of a repetition statement often causes an off-by-one error.

Good Programming Practice 6.2

Using the final value in the condition of a while or for statement with the <= relational operator helps avoid off-by-one errors. For a loop that displays the values 1 to 10, the loop-continuation condition should be counter <= 10, rather than counter < 10 (which causes an off-by-one error) or counter < 11 (which is correct). Many programmers prefer so-called zero-based counting, in which, to count 10 times, counter would be initialized to zero and the loop-continuation test would be counter < 10.

Figure 6.3 takes a closer look at the for statement in Fig. 6.2. The for's first line (including the keyword for and everything in parentheses after for)—line 11 in Fig. 6.2—is sometimes called the ***for statement header***, or simply the ***for header***. Note that the for header "does it all"—it specifies each of the items needed for counter-controlled repetition with a control variable. If there is more than one statement in the body of the for, braces are required to define the body of the loop.

The general format of the for statement is

> ***for*** (*initialization*; *loopContinuationCondition*; *increment*)
>   *statement*

where the *initialization* expression names the loop's control variable and provides its initial value, the *loopContinuationCondition* is the condition that determines whether looping should continue and the *increment* modifies the control variable's value (whether an increment or decrement), so that the loop-continuation condition eventually becomes false. The two semicolons in the for header are required. Note that we don't include a semico-

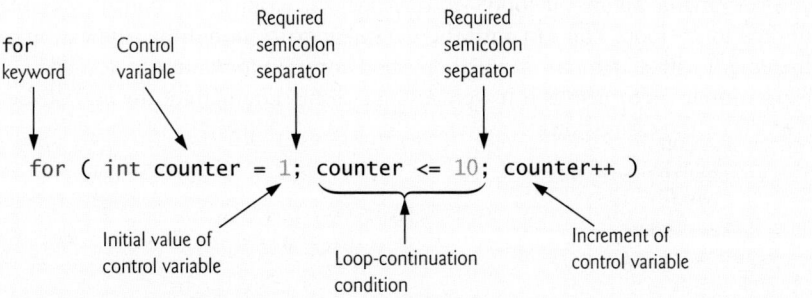

Fig. 6.3 | for statement header components.

lon after *statement*, because the semicolon is already assumed to be included in the notion of a *statement*.

Common Programming Error 6.3

Using commas instead of the two required semicolons in a for header is a syntax error.

In most cases, the for statement can be represented with an equivalent while statement as follows:

> *initialization*;
>
> **while** (*loopContinuationCondition*)
> {
>   *statement*
>   *increment*;
> }

In Section 6.7, we discuss a case in which a for statement cannot be represented with an equivalent while statement.

Typically, for statements are used for counter-controlled repetition, and while statements are used for sentinel-controlled repetition. However, while and for can each be used for either repetition type.

If the *initialization* expression in the for header declares the control variable (i.e., the control variable's type is specified before the variable name, as in Fig. 6.2), the control variable can be used only in that for statement—it will not exist outside it. This restricted use of the name of the control variable is known as the variable's *scope*. The scope of a variable defines where it can be used in an application. For example, a local variable can be used only in the method that declares the variable and only from the point of declaration through the end of the block in which the variable has been declared. Scope is discussed in detail in Chapter 7, Methods: A Deeper Look.

Common Programming Error 6.4

When a for statement's control variable is declared in the initialization section of the for's header, using the control variable after the for's body is a compilation error.

All three expressions in a for header are optional. If the *loopContinuationCondition* is omitted, C# assumes that the loop-continuation condition is always true, thus creating an infinite loop. You can omit the *initialization* expression if the application initializes the control variable before the loop—in this case, the scope of the control variable will not be limited to the loop. You can omit the *increment* expression if the application calculates the increment with statements in the loop's body or if no increment is needed. The increment expression in a for acts as if it were a stand-alone statement at the end of the for's body. Therefore, the expressions

```
counter = counter + 1
counter += 1
++counter
counter++
```

are equivalent increment expressions in a for statement. Many programmers prefer counter++ because it is concise and because a for loop evaluates its increment expression after its body executes—so the postfix increment form seems more natural. In this case, the variable being incremented does not appear in a larger expression, so the prefix and postfix increment operators have the same effect.

Performance Tip 6.1

There is a slight performance advantage to using the prefix increment operator, but if you choose the postfix increment operator because it seems more natural (as in a for header), optimizing compilers will generate MSIL code that uses the more efficient form anyway.

Good Programming Practice 6.3

In many cases, the prefix and postfix increment operators are both used to add 1 to a variable in a statement by itself. In these cases, the effect is exactly the same, except that the prefix increment operator has a slight performance advantage. Given that the compiler typically optimizes your code to help you get the best performance, use the idiom (prefix or postfix) with which you feel most comfortable in these situations.

Common Programming Error 6.5

Placing a semicolon immediately to the right of the right parenthesis of a for header makes that for's body an empty statement. This is normally a logic error.

Error-Prevention Tip 6.2

Infinite loops occur when the loop-continuation condition in a repetition statement never becomes false. *To prevent this situation in a counter-controlled loop, ensure that the control variable is incremented (or decremented) during each iteration of the loop. In a sentinel-controlled loop, ensure that the sentinel value is eventually input.*

The initialization, loop-continuation condition and increment portions of a for statement can contain arithmetic expressions. For example, assume that x = 2 and y = 10; if x and y are not modified in the body of the loop, then the statement

```
for ( int j = x; j <= 4 * x * y; j += y / x )
```

is equivalent to the statement

```
for ( int j = 2; j <= 80; j += 5 )
```

The increment of a for statement may also be negative, in which case it is a decrement, and the loop counts downward.

If the loop-continuation condition is initially false, the application does not execute the for statement's body. Instead, execution proceeds with the statement following the for.

Applications frequently display the control variable value or use it in calculations in the loop body, but this use is not required. The control variable is commonly used to control repetition without being mentioned in the body of the for.

Error-Prevention Tip 6.3

Although the value of the control variable can be changed in the body of a for loop, avoid doing so, because this practice can lead to subtle errors.

The for statement's UML activity diagram is similar to that of the while statement (Fig. 5.4). Figure 6.4 shows the activity diagram of the for statement in Fig. 6.2. The dia-

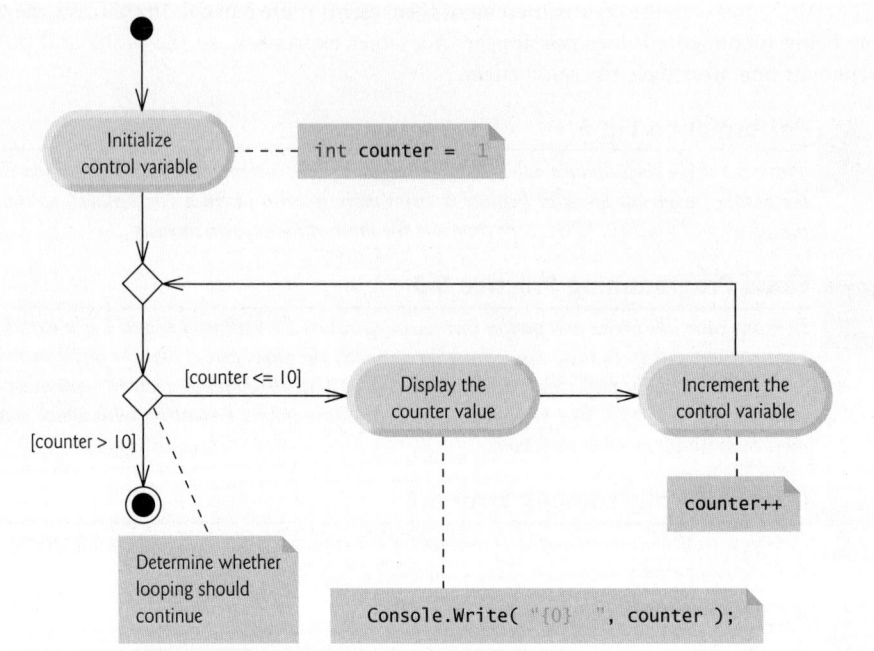

Fig. 6.4 | UML activity diagram for the for statement in Fig. 6.2.

gram makes it clear that initialization occurs only once before the loop-continuation test is evaluated the first time, and that incrementing occurs each time through the loop after the body statement executes.

6.4 Examples Using the for Statement

The following examples show techniques for varying the control variable in a for statement. In each case, we write the appropriate for header. Note the change in the relational operator for loops that decrement the control variable.

a) Vary the control variable from 1 to 100 in increments of 1.

```
for ( int i = 1; i <= 100; i++ )
```

b) Vary the control variable from 100 to 1 in decrements of 1.

```
for ( int i = 100; i >= 1; i-- )
```

c) Vary the control variable from 7 to 77 in increments of 7.

```
for ( int i = 7; i <= 77; i += 7 )
```

d) Vary the control variable from 20 to 2 in decrements of 2.

```
for ( int i = 20; i >= 2; i -= 2 )
```

e) Vary the control variable over the following sequence of values: 2, 5, 8, 11, 14, 17, 20.

```
for ( int i = 2; i <= 20; i += 3 )
```

f) Vary the control variable over the following sequence of values: 99, 88, 77, 66, 55, 44, 33, 22, 11, 0.

```
for ( int i = 99; i >= 0; i -= 11 )
```

Common Programming Error 6.6

Not using the proper relational operator in the loop-continuation condition of a loop that counts downward (e.g., using i <= 1 instead of i >= 1 in a loop counting down to 1) is a logic error.

Application: Summing the Even Integers from 2 to 20

We now consider two sample applications that demonstrate simple uses of for. The application in Fig. 6.5 uses a for statement to sum the even integers from 2 to 20 and store the result in an int variable called total.

The *initialization* and *increment* expressions can be comma-separated lists that enable you to use multiple initialization expressions or multiple increment expressions. For example, you could merge the body of the for statement in lines 12–13 of Fig. 6.5 into the increment portion of the for header by using a comma as follows:

```
for ( int number = 2; number <= 20; total += number, number += 2 )
    ; // empty statement
```

Good Programming Practice 6.4

Limit the size of control-statement headers to a single line if possible.

Good Programming Practice 6.5

Place only expressions involving the control variables in the initialization and increment sections of a for statement. Manipulations of other variables should appear either before the loop (if they execute only once, like initialization statements) or in the body of the loop (if they execute once per iteration of the loop, like increment or decrement statements).

```
 1   // Fig. 6.5: Sum.cs
 2   // Summing integers with the for statement.
 3   using System;
 4
 5   public class Sum
 6   {
 7      public static void Main( string[] args )
 8      {
 9         int total = 0; // initialize total
10
11         // total even integers from 2 through 20
12         for ( int number = 2; number <= 20; number += 2 )
13            total += number;
14
15         Console.WriteLine( "Sum is {0}", total ); // display results
16      } // end Main
17   } // end class Sum
```

Fig. 6.5 | Summing integers with the for statement. (Part 1 of 2.)

```
Sum is 110
```

Fig. 6.5 | Summing integers with the `for` statement. (Part 2 of 2.)

Application: Compound-Interest Calculations

The next application uses the `for` statement to compute compound interest. Consider the following problem:

> *A person invests $1,000 in a savings account yielding 5% interest, compounded yearly. Assuming that all the interest is left on deposit, calculate and display the amount of money in the account at the end of each year for 10 years. Use the following formula to determine the amounts:*

$$a = p\,(1 + r\,)^n$$

where

> *p* is the original amount invested (i.e., the principal)
> *r* is the annual interest rate (e.g., use 0.05 for 5%)
> *n* is the number of years
> *a* is the amount on deposit at the end of the *n*th year.

This problem involves a loop that performs the indicated calculation for each of the 10 years the money remains on deposit. The solution is the application shown in Fig. 6.6. Lines 9–11 in method `Main` declare `decimal` variables `amount` and `principal`, and `double` variable `rate`. Lines 10–11 also initialize `principal` to 1000 (i.e., $1000.00) and `rate` to 0.05. C# treats real-number constants like 0.05 as type `double`. Similarly, C# treats whole-number constants like 7 and 1000 as type `int`. When `principal` is initialized to 1000, the value 1000 of type `int` is promoted to a `decimal` type implicitly—no cast is required.

Line 14 outputs the headers for the application's two columns of output. The first column displays the year, and the second column displays the amount on deposit at the end of that year. Note that we use the format item {0,20} to output the `string` "Amount on deposit". The integer 20 after the comma indicates that the value output should be displayed with a *field width* of 20—that is, `WriteLine` displays the value with at least 20 character positions. If the value to be output is less than 20 character positions wide (17 characters in this example), the value is *right justified* in the field by default (in this case the value is preceded by three blanks). If the year value to be output were more than four character positions wide, the field width would be extended to the right to accommodate the entire value—this would push the amount field to the right, upsetting the neat columns of our tabular output. To indicate that output should be *left justified*, simply use a negative field width.

The `for` statement (lines 17–25) executes its body 10 times, varying control variable `year` from 1 to 10 in increments of 1. This loop terminates when control variable `year` becomes 11. (Note that `year` represents *n* in the problem statement.)

Classes provide methods that perform common tasks on objects. In fact, most methods must be called on a specific object. For example, to output a greeting in Fig. 4.2, we called method `DisplayMessage` on the `myGradeBook` object. Many classes also provide methods that perform common tasks and do not need to be called on objects. Such methods are called **static** *methods*. For example, C# does not include an exponentiation operator, so

```
 1   // Fig. 6.6: Interest.cs
 2   // Compound-interest calculations with for.
 3   using System;
 4
 5   public class Interest
 6   {
 7      public static void Main( string[] args )
 8      {
 9         decimal amount; // amount on deposit at end of each year
10         decimal principal = 1000; // initial amount before interest
11         double rate = 0.05; // interest rate
12
13         // display headers
14         Console.WriteLine( "Year{0,20}", "Amount on deposit" );
15
16         // calculate amount on deposit for each of ten years
17         for ( int year = 1; year <= 10; year++ )
18         {
19            // calculate new amount for specified year
20            amount = principal *
21               ( ( decimal ) Math.Pow( 1.0 + rate, year ) );
22
23            // display the year and the amount
24            Console.WriteLine( "{0,4}{1,20:C}", year, amount );
25         } // end for
26      } // end Main
27   } // end class Interest
```

```
Year    Amount on deposit
   1          $1,050.00
   2          $1,102.50
   3          $1,157.63
   4          $1,215.51
   5          $1,276.28
   6          $1,340.10
   7          $1,407.10
   8          $1,477.46
   9          $1,551.33
  10          $1,628.89
```

Fig. 6.6 | Compound-interest calculations with for.

the designers of C#'s Math class defined static method Pow for raising a value to a power. You can call a static method by specifying the class name followed by the member access (.) operator and the method name, as in

ClassName.methodName(arguments)

Note that Console methods Write and WriteLine are static methods. In Chapter 7, you'll learn how to implement static methods in your own classes.

We use static method Pow of class Math to perform the compound-interest calculation in Fig. 6.6. Math.Pow(x, y) calculates the value of x raised to the yth power. The method receives two double arguments and returns a double value. Lines 20–21 perform the calculation $a = p(1 + r)^n$, where a is the amount, p is the principal, r is the rate and *n* is the year. Notice that, in this calculation, we need to multiply a decimal value (principal) by a double value (the return value of Math.Pow). C# will not implicitly convert double to a decimal type, or vice versa, because of the possible loss of information in either conversion, so line 21 contains a (decimal) cast operator that explicitly converts the double return value of Math.Pow to a decimal.

After each calculation, line 24 outputs the year and the amount on deposit at the end of that year. The year is output in a field width of four characters (as specified by {0,4}). The amount is output as a currency value with the format item {1,20:C}. The number 20 in the format item indicates that the value should be output right justified with a field width of 20 characters. The format specifier C specifies that the number should be formatted as currency.

Notice that we declared the variables amount and principal to be of type decimal rather than double. Recall that we introduced type decimal for monetary calculations in Section 4.11. We also use decimal in Fig. 6.6 for this purpose. You may be curious as to why we do this. We are dealing with fractional parts of dollars and thus need a type that allows decimal points in its values. Unfortunately, floating-point numbers of type double (or float) can cause trouble in monetary calculations. Two double dollar amounts stored in the machine could be 14.234 (which would normally be rounded to 14.23 for display purposes) and 18.673 (which would normally be rounded to 18.67 for display purposes). When these amounts are added, they produce the internal sum 32.907, which would normally be rounded to 32.91 for display purposes. Thus, your output could appear as

```
   14.23
 + 18.67
 -------
   32.91
```

but a person adding the individual numbers as displayed would expect the sum to be 32.90. You have been warned!

Good Programming Practice 6.6

Do not use variables of type double (or float) to perform precise monetary calculations; use type decimal instead. The imprecision of floating-point numbers can cause errors that will result in incorrect monetary values.

Note that the body of the for statement contains the calculation 1.0 + rate, which appears as an argument to the Math.Pow method. In fact, this calculation produces the same result each time through the loop, so repeating the calculation in every iteration of the loop is wasteful.

Performance Tip 6.2

In loops, avoid calculations for which the result never changes—such calculations should typically be placed before the loop. [Note: Optimizing compilers will typically place such calculations outside loops in the compiled code.]

6.5 do...while Repetition Statement

The ***do...while repetition statement*** is similar to the while statement. In the while, the application tests the loop-continuation condition at the beginning of the loop, before executing the loop's body. If the condition is false, the body never executes. The do...while statement tests the loop-continuation condition *after* executing the loop's body; therefore, the body always executes at least once. When a do...while statement terminates, execution continues with the next statement in sequence. Figure 6.7 uses a do...while (lines 11–15) to output the numbers 1–10.

Line 9 declares and initializes control variable counter. Upon entering the do...while statement, line 13 outputs counter's value, and line 14 increments counter. Then the application evaluates the loop-continuation test at the bottom of the loop (line 15). If the condition is true, the loop continues from the first body statement in the do...while (line 13). If the condition is false, the loop terminates, and the application continues with the next statement after the loop.

Figure 6.8 contains the UML activity diagram for the do...while statement. This diagram makes it clear that the loop-continuation condition is not evaluated until after the loop performs the action state at least once. Compare this activity diagram with that of the while statement (Fig. 5.4). It is not necessary to use braces in the do...while repetition statement if there is only one statement in the body. However, most programmers include the braces to avoid confusion between the while and do...while statements. For example,

> *while* (*condition*)

is normally the first line of a while statement. A do...while statement with no braces around a single-statement body appears as:

> *do*
>> *statement*
> *while* (*condition*);

```
1   // Fig. 6.7: DoWhileTest.cs
2   // do...while repetition statement.
3   using System;
4
5   public class DoWhileTest
6   {
7      public static void Main( string[] args )
8      {
9         int counter = 1; // initialize counter
10
11        do
12        {
13           Console.Write( "{0}  ", counter );
14           ++counter;
15        } while ( counter <= 10 ); // end do...while
16
17        Console.WriteLine(); // outputs a newline
18     } // end Main
19  } // end class DoWhileTest
```

```
1  2  3  4  5  6  7  8  9  10
```

Fig. 6.7 | do...while repetition statement.

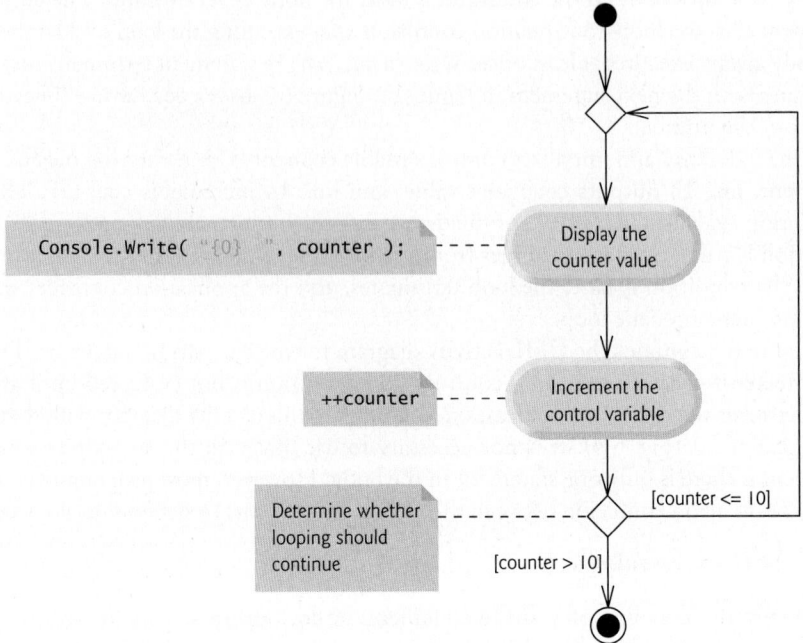

Fig. 6.8 | do...while repetition statement UML activity diagram.

which can be confusing. Some people misinterpret the last line—while(*condition*);—as a while statement containing an empty statement (the semicolon by itself). Thus, a do...while statement with one body statement is written as follows:

```
do
{
    statement
} while ( condition );
```

 Error-Prevention Tip 6.4

Always include braces in a do...while statement, even if they are not necessary. This helps eliminate ambiguity between while statements and do...while statements containing only one statement.

6.6 switch Multiple-Selection Statement

We discussed the if single-selection statement and the if...else double-selection statement in Chapter 5. C# provides the *switch multiple-selection* statement to perform different actions based on the possible values of an expression. Each action is associated with the value of a *constant integral expression* or a *constant string expression* that the variable or expression on which the switch is based may assume. A constant integral expression is any expression involving character and integer constants that evaluates to an integer value—i.e., values of type sbyte, byte, short, ushort, int, uint, long, ulong and char, or a constant from an enum type (enum is discussed in Section 7.10). A constant string expression is any expression composed of string literals that always results in the same string.

GradeBook Class with switch Statement to Count A, B, C, D and F Grades.

Figure 6.9 contains an enhanced version of the GradeBook class introduced in Chapter 4 and further developed in Chapter 5. The version of the class we now present not only calculates the average of a set of numeric grades entered by the user, but uses a switch statement to determine whether each grade is the equivalent of an A, B, C, D or F and to increment the appropriate grade counter. The class also displays a summary of the number of students who received each grade. Figure 6.10 shows sample input and output of the GradeBookTest application that uses class GradeBook to process a set of grades.

```csharp
1   // Fig. 6.9: GradeBook.cs
2   // GradeBook class uses switch statement to count letter grades.
3   using System;
4
5   public class GradeBook
6   {
7      private int total; // sum of grades
8      private int gradeCounter; // number of grades entered
9      private int aCount; // count of A grades
10     private int bCount; // count of B grades
11     private int cCount; // count of C grades
12     private int dCount; // count of D grades
13     private int fCount; // count of F grades
14
15     // automatic property CourseName
16     public string CourseName { get; set; }
17
18     // constructor initializes automatic property CourseName;
19     // int instance variables are initialized to 0 by default
20     public GradeBook( string name )
21     {
22        CourseName = name; // set CourseName to name
23     } // end constructor
24
25     // display a welcome message to the GradeBook user
26     public void DisplayMessage()
27     {
28        // CourseName gets the name of the course
29        Console.WriteLine( "Welcome to the grade book for\n{0}!\n",
30           CourseName );
31     } // end method DisplayMessage
32
33     // input arbitrary number of grades from user
34     public void InputGrades()
35     {
36        int grade; // grade entered by user
37        string input; // text entered by the user
```

Fig. 6.9 | GradeBook class that uses a switch statement to count A, B, C, D and F grades. (Part 1 of 3.)

```
38
39        Console.WriteLine( "{0}\n{1}",
40           "Enter the integer grades in the range 0-100.",
41           "Type <Ctrl> z and press Enter to terminate input:" );
42
43        input = Console.ReadLine(); // read user input
44
45        // loop until user enters the end-of-file indicator (<Ctrl> z)
46        while ( input != null )
47        {
48           grade = Convert.ToInt32( input ); // read grade off user input
49           total += grade; // add grade to total
50           ++gradeCounter; // increment number of grades
51
52           // call method to increment appropriate counter
53           IncrementLetterGradeCounter( grade );
54
55           input = Console.ReadLine(); // read user input
56        } // end while
57     } // end method InputGrades
58
59     // add 1 to appropriate counter for specified grade
60     private void IncrementLetterGradeCounter( int grade )
61     {
62        // determine which grade was entered
63        switch ( grade / 10 )
64        {
65           case 9: // grade was in the 90s
66           case 10: // grade was 100
67              ++aCount; // increment aCount
68              break; // necessary to exit switch
69           case 8: // grade was between 80 and 89
70              ++bCount; // increment bCount
71              break; // exit switch
72           case 7: // grade was between 70 and 79
73              ++cCount; // increment cCount
74              break; // exit switch
75           case 6: // grade was between 60 and 69
76              ++dCount; // increment dCount
77              break; // exit switch
78           default: // grade was less than 60
79              ++fCount; // increment fCount
80              break; // exit switch
81        } // end switch
82     } // end method IncrementLetterGradeCounter
83
84     // display a report based on the grades entered by the user
85     public void DisplayGradeReport()
86     {
87        Console.WriteLine( "\nGrade Report:" );
```

Fig. 6.9 | GradeBook class that uses a switch statement to count A, B, C, D and F grades. (Part 2 of 3.)

```
88
89        // if user entered at least one grade...
90        if ( gradeCounter != 0 )
91        {
92            // calculate average of all grades entered
93            double average = ( double ) total / gradeCounter;
94
95            // output summary of results
96            Console.WriteLine( "Total of the {0} grades entered is {1}",
97                gradeCounter, total );
98            Console.WriteLine( "Class average is {0:F}", average );
99            Console.WriteLine( "{0}A: {1}\nB: {2}\nC: {3}\nD: {4}\nF: {5}",
100               "Number of students who received each grade:\n",
101               aCount, // display number of A grades
102               bCount, // display number of B grades
103               cCount, // display number of C grades
104               dCount, // display number of D grades
105               fCount ); // display number of F grades
106       } // end if
107       else // no grades were entered, so output appropriate message
108           Console.WriteLine( "No grades were entered" );
109    } // end method DisplayGradeReport
110 } // end class GradeBook
```

Fig. 6.9 | GradeBook class that uses a switch statement to count A, B, C, D and F grades. (Part 3 of 3.)

Class GradeBook (Fig. 6.9) declares instance variables total (line 7) and gradeCounter (line 8), which keep track of the sum of the grades entered by the user and the number of grades entered, respectively. Lines 9–13 declare counter variables for each grade category. Class GradeBook maintains total, gradeCounter and the five letter-grade counters as instance variables so that they can be used or modified in any of the class's methods.

Like earlier versions of the class, class GradeBook declares automatic property CourseName (line 16) and method DisplayMessage (lines 26–31) to display a welcome message to the user. The class also contains a constructor (lines 20–23) that initializes the course name. Note that the constructor sets only the course name—the remaining seven instance variables are ints and are initialized to 0 by default.

Class GradeBook contains three additional methods—InputGrades, IncrementLetterGradeCounter and DisplayGradeReport. Method InputGrades (lines 34–57) reads an arbitrary number of integer grades from the user using sentinel-controlled repetition and updates instance variables total and gradeCounter. Method InputGrades calls method IncrementLetterGradeCounter (lines 60–82) to update the appropriate letter-grade counter for each grade entered. Class GradeBook also contains method DisplayGradeReport (lines 85–109), which outputs a report containing the total of all grades entered, the average of the grades and the number of students who received each letter grade. Let's examine these methods in more detail.

Lines 36–37 in method InputGrades declare variables grade and input, which will first store the user's input as a string (in the variable input), then convert it to an int to store in the variable grade. Lines 39–41 prompt the user to enter integer grades and to type *Ctrl* + *z*, then press *Enter* to terminate the input. The notation *Ctrl* + *z* means to simultaneously press both the *Ctrl* key and the *z* key when typing in a **Command Prompt**. *Ctrl* + *z* is the Windows key sequence for typing the ***end-of-file indicator***. This is one way to inform an application that there is no more data to input. If *<Ctrl> z* is entered while the application is awaiting input with a ReadLine method, null is returned. (The end-of-file indicator is a system-dependent keystroke combination. On many non-Windows systems, end-of-file is entered by typing *Ctrl* + *d*.) In Chapter 19, Files and Streams, we'll see how the end-of-file indicator is used when an application reads its input from a file. [*Note:* Windows typically displays the characters ^Z in a **Command Prompt** when the end-of-file indicator is typed, as shown in the output of Fig. 6.10.]

Line 43 uses the ReadLine method to get the first line that the user entered and store it in variable input. The while statement (lines 46–56) processes this user input. The condition at line 46 checks whether the value of input is a null reference. The Console class's ReadLine method will return null only if the user typed an end-of-file indicator. As long as the end-of-file indicator has not been typed, input will not contain a null reference, and the condition will pass.

Line 48 converts the string in input to an int type. Line 49 adds grade to total. Line 50 increments gradeCounter. The class's DisplayGradeReport method uses these variables to compute the average of the grades. Line 53 calls the class's IncrementLetterGradeCounter method (declared in lines 60–82) to increment the appropriate letter-grade counter, based on the numeric grade entered.

Method IncrementLetterGradeCounter contains a switch statement (lines 63–81) that determines which counter to increment. In this example, we assume that the user enters a valid grade in the range 0–100. A grade in the range 90–100 represents A, 80–89 represents B, 70–79 represents C, 60–69 represents D and 0–59 represents F. The switch statement consists of a block that contains a sequence of **case** *labels* and an optional **default** *label*. These are used in this example to determine which counter to increment based on the grade.

When the flow of control reaches the switch statement, the application evaluates the expression in the parentheses (grade / 10) following keyword switch—this is called the ***switch expression***. The application attempts to match the value of the switch expression with one of the case labels. The switch expression in line 63 performs integer division, which truncates the fractional part of the result. Thus, when we divide any value in the range 0–100 by 10, the result is always a value from 0 to 10. We use several of these values in our case labels. For example, if the user enters the integer 85, the switch expression evaluates to int value 8. If a match occurs between the switch expression and a case (case 8: at line 69), the application executes the statements for that case. For the integer 8, line 70 increments bCount, because a grade in the 80s is a B. The ***break statement*** (line 71) causes program control to proceed with the first statement after the switch—in this application, we reach the end of method IncrementLetterGradeCounter's body, so control returns to line 55 in method InputGrades (the first line after the call to IncrementLetterGradeCounter). This line uses the ReadLine method to read the next line entered by the user and assign it to the variable input. Line 56 marks the end of the body of the while statement that inputs grades (lines 46–56), so control flows to the while's condition (line 46) to determine whether the loop should continue executing based on the value just assigned to the variable input.

The cases in our switch explicitly test for the values 10, 9, 8, 7 and 6. Note the case labels at lines 65–66 that test for the values 9 and 10 (both of which represent the grade A). Listing case labels consecutively in this manner with no statements between them enables the cases to perform the same set of statements—when the switch expression evaluates to 9 or 10, the statements in lines 67–68 execute. The switch statement does not provide a mechanism for testing ranges of values, so every value to be tested must be listed in a separate case label. Note that each case can have multiple statements. The switch statement differs from other control statements in that it does not require braces around multiple statements in each case.

In C, C++, and many other programming languages that use the switch statement, the break statement is not required at the end of a case. Without break statements, each time a match occurs in the switch, the statements for that case and subsequent cases execute until a break statement or the end of the switch is encountered. This is often referred to as "falling through" to the statements in subsequent cases. This frequently leads to logic errors when you forget the break statement. For this reason, C# has a "no fall through" rule for cases in a switch—after the statements in a case, you are required to include a statement that terminates the case, such as a break, a return or a throw. (We discuss the throw statement in Chapter 13, Exception Handling.)

Common Programming Error 6.7

Forgetting a break statement when one is needed in a switch is a compilation error.

If no match occurs between the switch expression's value and a case label, the statements after the default label (lines 79–80) execute. We use the default label in this example to process all switch-expression values that are less than 6—that is, all failing grades. If no match occurs and the switch does not contain a default label, program control simply continues with the first statement (if there is one) after the switch statement.

GradeBookTest *Class That Demonstrates Class* GradeBook
Class GradeBookTest (Fig. 6.10) creates a GradeBook object (lines 10–11). Line 13 invokes the object's DisplayMessage method to output a welcome message to the user. Line 14 invokes the object's InputGrades method to read a set of grades from the user and keep track of the sum of all the grades entered and the number of grades. Recall that method InputGrades also calls method IncrementLetterGradeCounter to keep track of the number of students who received each letter grade. Line 15 invokes method DisplayGradeReport of class GradeBook, which outputs a report based on the grades entered. Line 90 of class GradeBook (Fig. 6.9) determines whether the user entered at least one grade—this avoids dividing by zero. If so, line 93 calculates the average of the grades. Lines 96–105 then output the total of all the grades, the class average and the number of students who received each letter grade. If no grades were entered, line 108 outputs an appropriate message. The output in Fig. 6.10 shows a sample grade report based on 9 grades.

Note that class GradeBookTest (Fig. 6.10) does not directly call GradeBook method IncrementLetterGradeCounter (lines 60–82 of Fig. 6.9). This method is used exclusively by method InputGrades of class GradeBook to update the appropriate letter-grade counter as each new grade is entered by the user. Method IncrementLetterGradeCounter exists solely to support the operations of class GradeBook's other methods and thus is declared

```
 1   // Fig. 6.10: GradeBookTest.cs
 2   // Create GradeBook object, input grades and display grade report.
 3
 4   public class GradeBookTest
 5   {
 6      public static void Main( string[] args )
 7      {
 8         // create GradeBook object myGradeBook and
 9         // pass course name to constructor
10         GradeBook myGradeBook = new GradeBook(
11            "CS101 Introduction to C# Programming" );
12
13         myGradeBook.DisplayMessage(); // display welcome message
14         myGradeBook.InputGrades(); // read grades from user
15         myGradeBook.DisplayGradeReport(); // display report based on grades
16      } // end Main
17   } // end class GradeBookTest
```

```
Welcome to the grade book for
CS101 Introduction to C# Programming!

Enter the integer grades in the range 0-100.
Type <Ctrl> z and press Enter to terminate input:
99
92
45
100
57
63
76
14
92
^Z

Grade Report:
Total of the 9 grades entered is 638
Class average is 70.89
Number of students who received each grade:
A: 4
B: 0
C: 1
D: 1
F: 3
```

Fig. 6.10 | Create GradeBook object, input grades and display grade report.

private. Recall from Chapter 4 that methods declared with access modifier private can be called only by other methods of the class in which the private methods are declared. Such methods are commonly referred to as *utility methods* or *helper methods*, because they can be called only by other methods of that class and are used to support the operation of those methods.

switch Statement UML Activity Diagram

Figure 6.11 shows the UML activity diagram for the general switch statement. Every set of statements after a case label normally ends its execution with a break or return state-

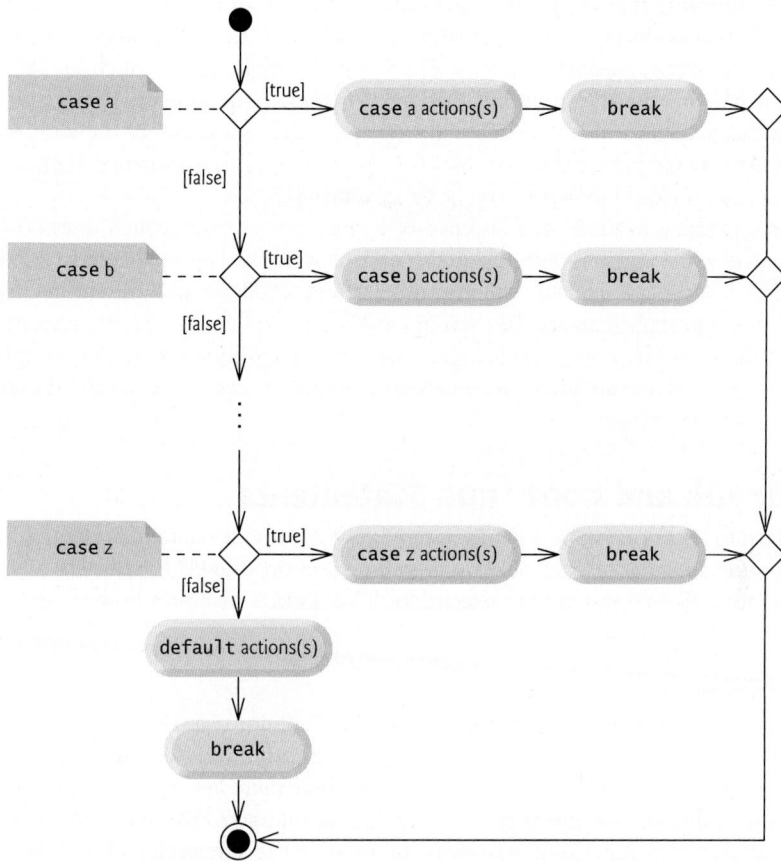

Fig. 6.11 | switch multiple-selection statement UML activity diagram with break statements.

ment to terminate the switch statement after processing the case. Typically, you'll use break statements. Figure 6.11 emphasizes this by including break statements in the activity diagram. The diagram makes it clear that the break statement at the end of a case causes control to exit the switch statement immediately.

Software Engineering Observation 6.2

Provide a default case in switch statements. Cases not explicitly tested in a switch that lacks a default case are ignored. Including a default case focuses you on the need to process exceptional conditions.

Good Programming Practice 6.7

Although each case and the default label in a switch can occur in any order, place the default label last for clarity.

When using the switch statement, remember that the expression after each case can be only a constant integral expression or a constant string expression—that is, any combination of constants that evaluates to a constant value of an integral or string type. An integer constant is simply an integer value (e.g., –7, 0 or 221). In addition, you can use null and *character constants*—specific characters in single quotes, such as 'A', '7' or '$'—which represent the integer values of characters. (Appendix F shows the integer values of the characters in the ASCII character set, which is a subset of the Unicode character set used by C#.) A string constant (or string literal) is a sequence of characters in double quotes, such as "Welcome to C# Programming!".

The expression in each case also can be a *constant*—a value which does not change for the entire application. Constants are is declared with the keyword const (discussed in Chapter 7). C# also has a feature called enumerations, which we also present in Chapter 7. Enumeration constants can also be used in case labels. In Chapter 12, we present a more elegant way to implement switch logic—we use a technique called polymorphism to create applications that are often clearer, easier to maintain and easier to extend than applications using switch logic.

6.7 break and continue Statements

In addition to selection and repetition statements, C# provides statements break and continue to alter the flow of control. The preceding section showed how break can be used to terminate a switch statement's execution. This section discusses how to use break to terminate any repetition statement.

break Statement

The break statement, when executed in a while, for, do...while, switch, or foreach, causes immediate exit from that statement. Execution typically continues with the first statement after the control statement—you'll see that there are other possibilities as you learn about additional statement types in C#. Common uses of the break statement are to escape early from a repetition statement or to skip the remainder of a switch (as in Fig. 6.9). Figure 6.12 demonstrates a break statement exiting a for.

```csharp
1   // Fig. 6.12: BreakTest.cs
2   // break statement exiting a for statement.
3   using System;
4
5   public class BreakTest
6   {
7      public static void Main( string[] args )
8      {
9         int count; // control variable also used after loop terminates
10
11         for ( count = 1; count <= 10; count++ ) // loop 10 times
12         {
13            if ( count == 5 ) // if count is 5,
14               break; // terminate loop
15
16            Console.Write( "{0} ", count );
17         } // end for
```

Fig. 6.12 | break statement exiting a for statement. (Part 1 of 2.)

```
18
19          Console.WriteLine( "\nBroke out of loop at count = {0}", count );
20      } // end Main
21  } // end class BreakTest
```

```
1 2 3 4
Broke out of loop at count = 5
```

Fig. 6.12 | break statement exiting a for statement. (Part 2 of 2.)

When the if nested at line 13 in the for statement (lines 11–17) determines that count is 5, the break statement at line 14 executes. This terminates the for statement, and the application proceeds to line 19 (immediately after the for statement), which displays a message indicating the value of the control variable when the loop terminated. The loop fully executes its body only four times instead of 10 because of the break.

continue *Statement*

The ***continue*** *statement*, when executed in a while, for, do...while, or foreach, skips the remaining statements in the loop body and proceeds with the next iteration of the loop. In while and do...while statements, the application evaluates the loop-continuation test immediately after the continue statement executes. In a for statement, the increment expression normally executes next, then the application evaluates the loop-continuation test.

Figure 6.13 uses the continue statement in a for to skip the statement at line 14 when the nested if (line 11) determines that the value of count is 5. When the continue

```
1   // Fig. 6.13: ContinueTest.cs
2   // continue statement terminating an iteration of a for statement.
3   using System;
4
5   public class ContinueTest
6   {
7      public static void Main( string[] args )
8      {
9         for ( int count = 1; count <= 10; count++ ) // loop 10 times
10        {
11           if ( count == 5 ) // if count is 5,
12              continue; // skip remaining code in loop
13
14           Console.Write( "{0} ", count );
15        } // end for
16
17        Console.WriteLine( "\nUsed continue to skip displaying 5" );
18     } // end Main
19  } // end class ContinueTest
```

```
1 2 3 4 6 7 8 9 10
Used continue to skip displaying 5
```

Fig. 6.13 | continue statement terminating an iteration of a for statement.

statement executes, program control continues with the increment of the control variable in the for statement (line 9).

In Section 6.3, we stated that a while can be used in most cases in place of for. One exception occurs when the increment expression in the while follows a continue statement. In this case, the increment doesn't execute before the repetition-continuation condition evaluates, so the while does not execute in the same manner as the for.

Software Engineering Observation 6.3

Some programmers feel that break and continue statements violate structured programming. Since the same effects are achievable with structured programming techniques, these programmers prefer not to use break or continue statements.

Software Engineering Observation 6.4

There is a tension between achieving quality software engineering and achieving the best-performing software. Often, one of these goals is achieved at the expense of the other. For all but the most performance-intensive situations, apply the following rule: First, make your code simple and correct; then make it fast, but only if necessary.

6.8 Logical Operators

The if, if...else, while, do...while and for statements each require a condition to determine how to continue an application's flow of control. So far, we have studied only *simple conditions*, such as count <= 10, number != sentinelValue and total > 1000. Simple conditions are expressed in terms of the relational operators >, <, >= and <=, and the equality operators == and !=. Each expression tests only one condition. To test multiple conditions in the process of making a decision, we performed these tests in separate statements or in nested if or if...else statements. Sometimes, control statements require more complex conditions to determine an application's flow of control.

C# provides *logical operators* to enable you to form more complex conditions by combining simple conditions. The logical operators are && (conditional AND), || (conditional OR), & (boolean logical AND), | (boolean logical inclusive OR), ^ (boolean logical exclusive OR) and ! (logical negation).

Conditional AND (&&) Operator

Suppose that we wish to ensure at some point in an application that two conditions are *both* true before we choose a certain path of execution. In this case, we can use the *&& (conditional AND)* operator, as follows:

```
if ( gender == "F" && age >= 65 )
    ++seniorFemales;
```

This if statement contains two simple conditions. The condition gender == "F" determines whether a person is female. This might be evaluated, for example, to determine whether a person is female. The condition age >= 65 might be evaluated to determine whether a person is a senior citizen. The if statement considers the combined condition

```
gender == "F" && age >= 65
```

which is true if and only if *both* simple conditions are true. If the combined condition is true, the if statement's body increments seniorFemales by 1. If either or both of the simple conditions are false, the application skips the increment. Some programmers find that the preceding combined condition is more readable when redundant parentheses are added, as in:

```
( gender == "F" ) && ( age >= 65 )
```

The table in Fig. 6.14 summarizes the **&&** operator. The table shows all four possible combinations of `false` and `true` values for *expression1* and *expression2*. Such tables are called *truth tables*. C# evaluates all expressions that include relational operators, equality operators or logical operators to `bool` values—which are either `true` or `false`.

expression1	expression2	expression1 && expression2
false	false	false
false	true	false
true	false	false
true	true	true

Fig. 6.14 | && (conditional AND) operator truth table.

Conditional OR (| |) Operator

Now suppose we wish to ensure that *either or both* of two conditions are true before we choose a certain path of execution. In this case, we use the **| |** (*conditional OR*) operator, as in the following application segment:

```
if ( ( semesterAverage >= 90 ) || ( finalExam >= 90 ) )
    Console.WriteLine ( "Student grade is A" );
```

This statement also contains two simple conditions. The condition `semesterAverage >= 90` is evaluated to determine whether the student deserves an A in the course because of a solid performance throughout the semester. The condition `finalExam >= 90` is evaluated to determine whether the student deserves an A in the course because of an outstanding performance on the final exam. The `if` statement then considers the combined condition

```
( semesterAverage >= 90 ) || ( finalExam >= 90 )
```

and awards the student an A if either or both of the simple conditions are true. The only time the message "Student grade is A" is *not* displayed is when both of the simple conditions are false. Figure 6.15 is a truth table for operator conditional OR (| |). Operator && has a higher precedence than operator | |. Both operators associate from left to right.

expression1	expression2	expression1 || expression2
false	false	false
false	true	true
true	false	true
true	true	true

Fig. 6.15 | | | (conditional OR) operator truth table.

Short-Circuit Evaluation of Complex Conditions

The parts of an expression containing && or || operators are evaluated only until it is known whether the condition is true or false. Thus, evaluation of the expression

```
( gender == "F" ) && ( age >= 65 )
```

stops immediately if gender is not equal to "F" (i.e., at that point, it is certain that the entire expression is false) and continues if gender *is* equal to "F" (i.e., the entire expression could still be true if the condition age >= 65 is true). This feature of conditional AND and conditional OR expressions is called *short-circuit evaluation*.

Common Programming Error 6.8

In expressions using operator &&, a condition—which we refer to as the dependent condition—may require another condition to be true for the evaluation of the dependent condition to be meaningful. In this case, the dependent condition should be placed after the other condition, or an error might occur. For example, in the expression (i != 0) && (10 / i == 2), the second condition must appear after the first condition, or a divide-by-zero error might occur.

Boolean Logical AND (&) and Boolean Logical OR (|) Operators

The *boolean logical AND (&)* and *boolean logical inclusive OR (|)* operators work identically to the && (conditional AND) and || (conditional OR) operators, with one exception—the boolean logical operators always evaluate both of their operands (i.e., they do not perform short-circuit evaluation). Therefore, the expression

```
( gender == "F" ) & ( age >= 65 )
```

evaluates age >= 65 regardless of whether gender is equal to "F". This is useful if the right operand of the boolean logical AND or boolean logical inclusive OR operator has a required *side effect*—a modification of a variable's value. For example, the expression

```
( birthday == true ) | ( ++age >= 65 )
```

guarantees that the condition ++age >= 65 will be evaluated. Thus, the variable age is incremented in the preceding expression, regardless of whether the overall expression is true or false.

Error-Prevention Tip 6.5

For clarity, avoid expressions with side effects in conditions. The side effects may look clever, but they can make it harder to understand code and can lead to subtle logic errors.

Boolean Logical Exclusive OR (^)

A complex condition containing the *boolean logical exclusive OR (^)* operator (also called the *logical XOR operator*) is true *if and only if one of its operands is true and the other is false*. If both operands are true or both are false, the entire condition is false. Figure 6.16 is a truth table for the boolean logical exclusive OR operator (^). This operator is also guaranteed to evaluate both of its operands.

Logical Negation (!) Operator

The *!* (*logical negation*) operator enables you to "reverse" the meaning of a condition. Unlike the logical operators &&, ||, &, | and ^, which are binary operators that combine

expression1	expression2	expression1 ∧ expression2
false	false	false
false	true	true
true	false	true
true	true	false

Fig. 6.16 | ∧ (boolean logical exclusive OR) operator truth table.

two conditions, the logical negation operator is a unary operator that has only a single condition as an operand. The logical negation operator is placed before a condition to choose a path of execution if the original condition (without the logical negation operator) is false, as in the code segment

```
if ( ! ( grade == sentinelValue ) )
    Console.WriteLine( "The next grade is {0}", grade );
```

which executes the WriteLine call only if grade is not equal to sentinelValue. The parentheses around the condition grade == sentinelValue are needed because the logical negation operator has a higher precedence than the equality operator.

In most cases, you can avoid using logical negation by expressing the condition differently with an appropriate relational or equality operator. For example, the previous statement may also be written as follows:

```
if ( grade != sentinelValue )
    Console.WriteLine( "The next grade is {0}", grade );
```

This flexibility can help you express a condition in a more convenient manner. Figure 6.17 is a truth table for the logical negation operator.

expression	!expression
false	true
true	false

Fig. 6.17 | ! (logical negation) operator truth table.

Logical Operators Example

Figure 6.18 demonstrates the logical operators and boolean logical operators by producing their truth tables. The output shows the expression that was evaluated and the bool result of that expression. Lines 10–14 produce the truth table for && (conditional AND). Lines 17–21 produce the truth table for || (conditional OR). Lines 24–28 produce the truth table for & (boolean logical AND). Lines 31–36 produce the truth table for | (boolean logical inclusive OR). Lines 39–44 produce the truth table for ∧ (boolean logical exclusive OR). Lines 47–49 produce the truth table for ! (logical negation).

```csharp
1   // Fig. 6.18: LogicalOperators.cs
2   // Logical operators.
3   using System;
4
5   public class LogicalOperators
6   {
7      public static void Main( string[] args )
8      {
9         // create truth table for && (conditional AND) operator
10        Console.WriteLine( "{0}\n{1}: {2}\n{3}: {4}\n{5}: {6}\n{7}: {8}\n",
11           "Conditional AND (&&)", "false && false", ( false && false ),
12           "false && true", ( false && true ),
13           "true && false", ( true && false ),
14           "true && true", ( true && true ) );
15
16        // create truth table for || (conditional OR) operator
17        Console.WriteLine( "{0}\n{1}: {2}\n{3}: {4}\n{5}: {6}\n{7}: {8}\n",
18           "Conditional OR (||)", "false || false", ( false || false ),
19           "false || true", ( false || true ),
20           "true || false", ( true || false ),
21           "true || true", ( true || true ) );
22
23        // create truth table for & (boolean logical AND) operator
24        Console.WriteLine( "{0}\n{1}: {2}\n{3}: {4}\n{5}: {6}\n{7}: {8}\n",
25           "Boolean logical AND (&)", "false & false", ( false & false ),
26           "false & true", ( false & true ),
27           "true & false", ( true & false ),
28           "true & true", ( true & true ) );
29
30        // create truth table for | (boolean logical inclusive OR) operator
31        Console.WriteLine( "{0}\n{1}: {2}\n{3}: {4}\n{5}: {6}\n{7}: {8}\n",
32           "Boolean logical inclusive OR (|)",
33           "false | false", ( false | false ),
34           "false | true", ( false | true ),
35           "true | false", ( true | false ),
36           "true | true", ( true | true ) );
37
38        // create truth table for ^ (boolean logical exclusive OR) operator
39        Console.WriteLine( "{0}\n{1}: {2}\n{3}: {4}\n{5}: {6}\n{7}: {8}\n",
40           "Boolean logical exclusive OR (^)",
41           "false ^ false", ( false ^ false ),
42           "false ^ true", ( false ^ true ),
43           "true ^ false", ( true ^ false ),
44           "true ^ true", ( true ^ true ) );
45
46        // create truth table for ! (logical negation) operator
47        Console.WriteLine( "{0}\n{1}: {2}\n{3}: {4}",
48           "Logical negation (!)", "!false", ( !false ),
49           "!true", ( !true ) );
50     } // end Main
51  } // end class LogicalOperators
```

Fig. 6.18 | Logical operators. (Part 1 of 2.)

```
Conditional AND (&&)
false && false: False
false && true: False
true && false: False
true && true: True

Conditional OR (||)
false || false: False
false || true: True
true || false: True
true || true: True

Boolean logical AND (&)
false & false: False
false & true: False
true & false: False
true & true: True

Boolean logical inclusive OR (|)
false | false: False
false | true: True
true | false: True
true | true: True

Boolean logical exclusive OR (^)
false ^ false: False
false ^ true: True
true ^ false: True
true ^ true: False

Logical negation (!)
!false: True
!true: False
```

Fig. 6.18 | Logical operators. (Part 2 of 2.)

Figure 6.19 shows the precedence and associativity of the C# operators introduced so far. The operators are shown from top to bottom in decreasing order of precedence.

Operators						Associativity	Type
.	new	++(postfix)	--(postfix)			left to right	highest precedence
++	--	+	-	!	(type)	right to left	unary prefix
*	/	%				left to right	multiplicative
+	-					left to right	additive
<	<=	>	>=			left to right	relational
==	!=					left to right	equality
&						left to right	boolean logical AND

Fig. 6.19 | Precedence/associativity of the operators discussed so far. (Part 1 of 2.)

Operators						Associativity	Type
∧						left to right	boolean logical exclusive OR
|						left to right	boolean logical inclusive OR
&&						left to right	conditional AND
||						left to right	conditional OR
?:						right to left	conditional
=	+=	-=	*=	/=	%=	right to left	assignment

Fig. 6.19 | Precedence/associativity of the operators discussed so far. (Part 2 of 2.)

6.9 (Optional) Software Engineering Case Study: Identifying Objects' States and Activities in the ATM System

In Section 5.12, we identified many of the class attributes needed to implement the ATM system and added them to the class diagram in Fig. 5.16. In this section, we show how these attributes represent an object's state. We identify some key states that our objects may occupy and discuss how objects change state in response to various events occurring in the system. We also discuss the workflow, or *activities*, that various objects perform in the ATM system. We present the activities of BalanceInquiry and Withdrawal transaction objects in this section.

State Machine Diagrams
Each object in a system goes through a series of discrete states. An object's state at a given point in time is indicated by the values of its attributes at that time. *State machine diagrams* model key states of an object and show under what circumstances the object changes state. Unlike the class diagrams presented in earlier case study sections, which focused primarily on the *structure* of the system, state machine diagrams model some of the *behavior* of the system.

Figure 6.20 is a simple state machine diagram that models two of the states of an object of class ATM. The UML represents each state in a state machine diagram as a *rounded rectangle* with the name of the state placed inside it. A *solid circle* with an attached stick arrowhead designates the *initial state*. Recall that we modeled this state information as the bool attribute userAuthenticated in the class diagram of Fig. 5.16. This attribute is initialized to false, or the "User not authenticated" state, according to the state machine diagram.

Fig. 6.20 | State machine diagram for some of the states of the ATM object.

The arrows with stick arrowheads indicate *transitions* between states. An object can transition from one state to another in response to various events that occur in the system. The name or description of the event that causes a transition is written near the line that corresponds to the transition. For example, the ATM object changes from the "User not authenticated" state to the "User authenticated" state after the bank database authenticates the user. Recall from the requirements document that the database authenticates a user by comparing the account number and PIN entered by the user with those of the corresponding account in the database. If the database indicates that the user has entered a valid account number and the correct PIN, the ATM object transitions to the "User authenticated" state and changes its userAuthenticated attribute to the value true. When the user exits the system by choosing the "exit" option from the main menu, the ATM object returns to the "User not authenticated" state in preparation for the next ATM user.

Software Engineering Observation 6.5

Software designers do not generally create state machine diagrams showing every possible state and state transition for all attributes—there are simply too many of them. State machine diagrams typically show only the most important or complex states and state transitions.

Activity Diagrams

Like a state machine diagram, an activity diagram models aspects of system behavior. Unlike a state machine diagram, an activity diagram models an object's workflow (sequence of tasks) during application execution. An activity diagram models the actions to perform and in what order the object will perform them. Recall that we used UML activity diagrams to illustrate the flow of control for the control statements presented in Chapter 5 and this chapter.

The activity diagram in Fig. 6.21 models the actions involved in executing a Balance-Inquiry transaction. We assume that a BalanceInquiry object has already been initialized and assigned a valid account number (that of the current user), so the object knows which balance to retrieve. The diagram includes the actions that occur after the user selects a balance inquiry from the main menu and before the ATM returns the user to the main

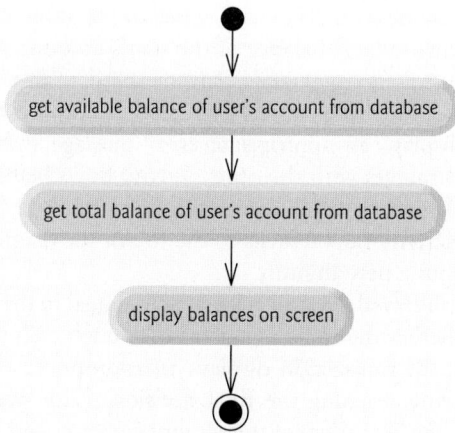

Fig. 6.21 | Activity diagram for a BalanceInquiry transaction.

menu—a BalanceInquiry object does not perform or initiate these actions, so we do not model them here. The diagram begins with the retrieval of the available balance of the user's account from the database. Next, the BalanceInquiry retrieves the total balance of the account. Finally, the transaction displays the balances on the screen.

The UML represents an action in an activity diagram as an action state, which is modeled by a rectangle with its left and right sides replaced by arcs curving outward. Each action state contains an action expression—for example, "get available balance of user's account from database"—that specifies an action to perform. An arrow with a stick arrowhead connects two action states, indicating the order in which the actions represented by the action states occur. The solid circle (at the top of Fig. 6.21) represents the activity's initial state—the beginning of the workflow before the object performs the modeled actions. In this case, the transaction first executes the "get available balance of user's account from database" action expression. Second, the transaction retrieves the total balance. Finally, the transaction displays both balances on the screen. The solid circle enclosed in an open circle (at the bottom of Fig. 6.21) represents the final state—the end of the workflow after the object performs the modeled actions.

Figure 6.22 shows an activity diagram for a Withdrawal transaction. We assume that a Withdrawal object has been assigned a valid account number. We do not model the user selecting a withdrawal from the main menu or the ATM returning the user to the main menu, because these are not actions performed by a Withdrawal object. The transaction first displays a menu of standard withdrawal amounts (Fig. 3.26) and an option to cancel the transaction. The transaction then inputs a menu selection from the user. The activity flow now arrives at a decision symbol. This point determines the next action based on the associated guard conditions. If the user cancels the transaction, the system displays an appropriate message. Next, the cancellation flow reaches a merge symbol, where this activity flow joins the transaction's other possible activity flows (which we discuss shortly). Note that a merge can have any number of incoming transition arrows, but only one outgoing transition arrow. The decision at the bottom of the diagram determines whether the transaction should repeat from the beginning. When the user has canceled the transaction, the guard condition "cash dispensed or user canceled transaction" is true, so control transitions to the activity's final state.

If the user selects a withdrawal amount from the menu, amount (an attribute of class Withdrawal originally modeled in Fig. 5.16) is set to the value chosen by the user. The transaction next gets the available balance of the user's account (i.e., the availableBalance attribute of the user's Account object) from the database. The activity flow then arrives at another decision. If the requested withdrawal amount exceeds the user's available balance, the system displays an appropriate error message informing the user of the problem. Control then merges with the other activity flows before reaching the decision at the bottom of the diagram. The guard condition "cash not dispensed and user did not cancel" is true, so the activity flow returns to the top of the diagram, and the transaction prompts the user to input a new amount.

If the requested withdrawal amount is less than or equal to the user's available balance, the transaction tests whether the cash dispenser has enough cash to satisfy the withdrawal request. If it does not, the transaction displays an appropriate error message and passes through the merge before reaching the final decision. Cash was not dispensed, so the activity flow returns to the beginning of the activity diagram, and the transaction prompts the user to choose a new amount. If sufficient cash is available, the transaction interacts

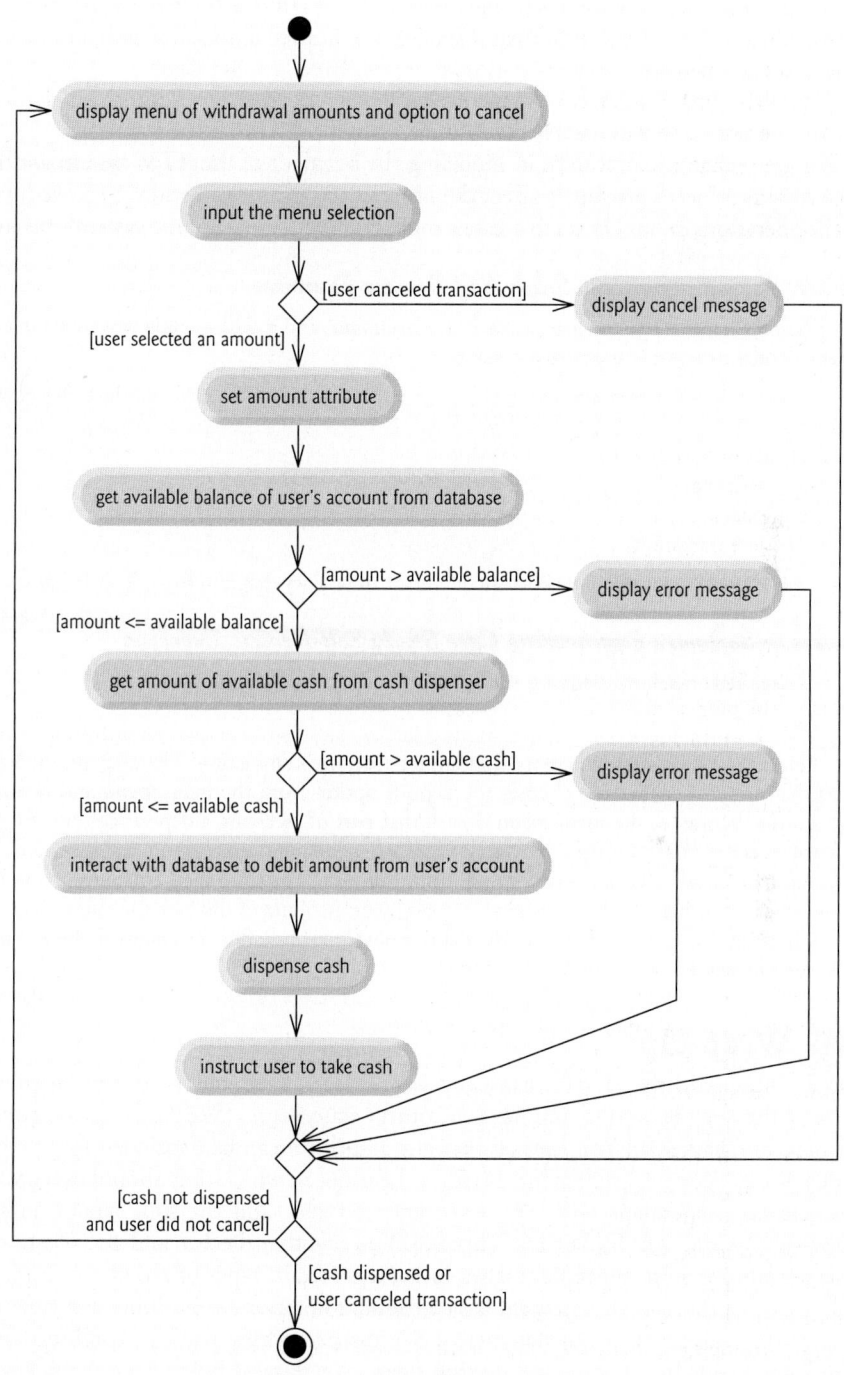

Fig. 6.22 | Activity diagram for a `Withdrawal` transaction.

with the database to debit the withdrawal amount from the user's account (i.e., subtract the amount from *both* the availableBalance and totalBalance attributes of the user's Account object). The transaction then dispenses the desired amount of cash and instructs the user to take the cash.

The main flow of activity next merges with the two error flows and the cancellation flow. In this case, cash was dispensed, so the activity flow reaches the final state.

We have taken the first steps in modeling the behavior of the ATM system and have shown how an object's attributes affect the object's activities. In Section 7.15, we investigate the operations of our classes to create a more complete model of the system's behavior.

Software Engineering Case Study Self-Review Exercises

6.1 State whether the following statement is *true* or *false*, and if *false*, explain why: State machine diagrams model structural aspects of a system.

6.2 An activity diagram models the _____ that an object performs and the order in which it performs them.
   a) actions
   b) attributes
   c) states
   d) state transitions

6.3 Based on the requirements document, create an activity diagram for a deposit transaction.

Answers to Software Engineering Case Study Self-Review Exercises

6.1 False. State machine diagrams model some of the behaviors of a system.

6.2 a.

6.3 Figure 6.23 presents an activity diagram for a deposit transaction. The diagram models the actions that occur after the user chooses the deposit option from the main menu and before the ATM returns the user to the main menu. Recall that part of receiving a deposit amount from the user involves converting an integer number of cents to a dollar amount. Also recall that crediting a deposit amount to an account involves increasing only the totalBalance attribute of the user's Account object. The bank updates the availableBalance attribute of the user's Account object only after confirming the amount of cash in the deposit envelope and after the enclosed checks clear—this occurs independently of the ATM system.

6.10 Wrap-Up

Chapter 5 discussed the if, if...else and while control statements. In this chapter, we discussed the for, do...while and switch control statements. (We'll discuss the foreach statement in Chapter 8.) You learned that any algorithm can be developed using combinations of sequence (i.e., statements listed in the order in which they should execute), the three selection statements—if, if...else and switch—and the four repetition statements—while, do...while, for and foreach. You saw that the for and do...while statements are simply more convenient ways to express certain types of repetition. Similarly, we showed that the switch statement is a convenient notation for multiple selection, rather than using nested if...else statements. We discussed how you can combine various control statements by stacking and nesting them. We showed how to use the break and continue statements to alter the flow of control in repetition statements. You also learned

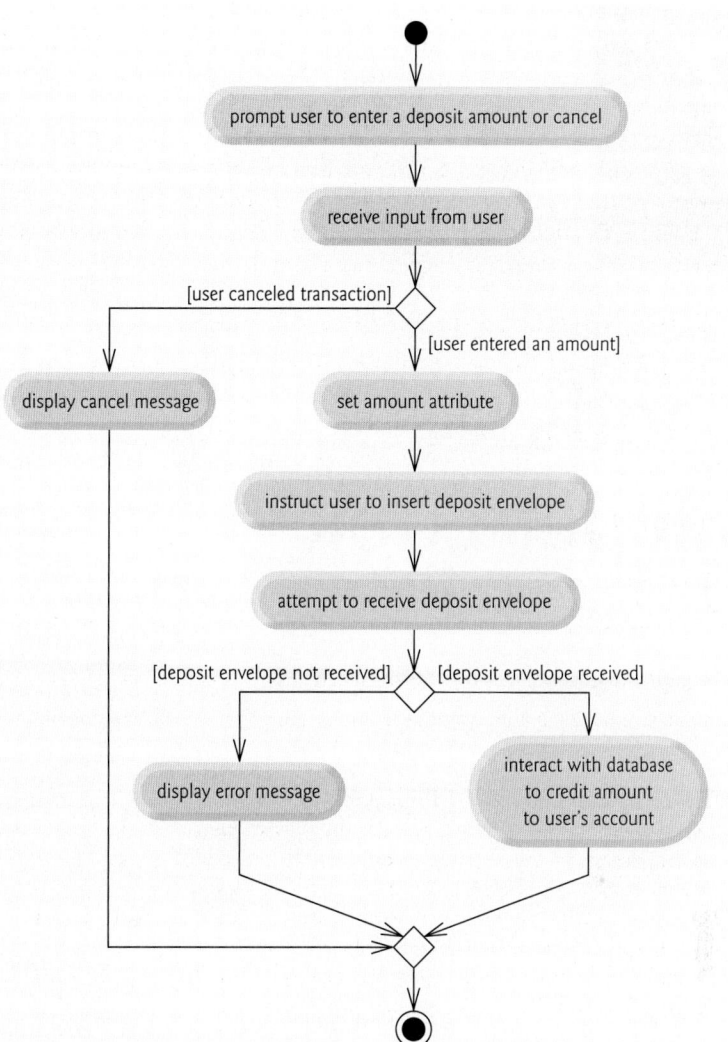

Fig. 6.23 | Activity diagram for a Deposit transaction.

about the logical operators, which enable you to use more complex conditional expressions in control statements.

In Chapter 4, we introduced the basic concepts of objects, classes and methods. Chapters 5 and 6 provided a thorough introduction to the control statements that you use to specify application logic in methods. In Chapter 7, we examine methods in greater depth.

7

Methods: A Deeper Look

Form ever follows function.
—Louis Henri Sullivan

E pluribus unum.
(One composed of many.)
—Virgil

O! call back yesterday, bid time return.
—William Shakespeare

Call me Ishmael.
—Herman Melville

When you call me that, smile!
—Owen Wister

Answer me in one word.
—William Shakespeare

There is a point at which methods devour themselves.
—Frantz Fanon

Life can only be understood backwards; but it must be lived forwards.
—Soren Kierkegaard

OBJECTIVES

In this chapter you'll learn:

- How static methods and variables are associated with a class rather than specific instances of the class.

- How the method call/return mechanism is supported by the method-call stack and activation records.

- How to use random-number generation to implement game-playing applications.

- How the visibility of declarations is limited to specific regions of applications.

- What method overloading is and how to create overloaded methods.

- What recursive methods are.

- The differences between passing method arguments by value and by reference.

Outline

7.1 Introduction
7.2 Packaging Code in C#
7.3 `static` Methods, `static` Variables and Class `Math`
7.4 Declaring Methods with Multiple Parameters
7.5 Notes on Declaring and Using Methods
7.6 Method-Call Stack and Activation Records
7.7 Argument Promotion and Casting
7.8 The .NET Framework Class Library
7.9 Case Study: Random-Number Generation
    7.9.1 Scaling and Shifting Random Numbers
    7.9.2 Random-Number Repeatability for Testing and Debugging
7.10 Case Study: A Game of Chance (Introducing Enumerations)
7.11 Scope of Declarations
7.12 Method Overloading
7.13 Recursion
7.14 Passing Arguments: Pass-by-Value vs. Pass-by-Reference
7.15 (Optional) Software Engineering Case Study: Identifying Class Operations in the ATM System
7.16 Wrap-Up

7.1 Introduction

We introduced methods in Chapter 4. In this chapter we study methods in more depth. We emphasize how to declare and use methods to facilitate the design, implementation, operation and maintenance of large applications.

You'll see that it is possible for certain methods, called `static` methods, to be called without the need for an object of the class to exist. You'll learn how to declare a method with more than one parameter. You'll also learn how C# is able to keep track of which method is currently executing, how value-type and reference-type arguments are passed to methods, how local variables of methods are maintained in memory and how a method knows where to return after it completes execution.

We discuss *simulation* techniques with random-number generation and develop a version of the casino dice game called craps that uses most of the programming techniques you've learned to this point in the book. In addition, you'll learn to declare values that cannot change (i.e., constants). You'll also learn to write methods that call themselves—this is called *recursion*.

Many of the classes you'll use or create while developing applications will have more than one method of the same name. This technique, called ***method overloading***, is used to implement methods that perform similar tasks but with different types and/or different numbers of arguments.

7.2 Packaging Code in C#

Common ways of packaging code are properties, methods, classes and namespaces. C# applications are written by combining new properties, methods and classes that you write with predefined properties, methods and classes available in the .NET Framework Class Library and in various other class libraries. Related classes are often grouped into namespaces and compiled into class libraries so that they can be reused in other applications. You'll learn how to create your own namespaces and class libraries in Chapter 10. The .NET Framework Class Library provides many predefined classes that contain methods for performing common mathematical calculations, string manipulations, character manipulations, input/output operations, database operations, networking operations, file processing, error checking, web-application development and more.

Good Programming Practice 7.1

Familiarize yourself with the classes and methods provided by the .NET Framework Class Library (msdn.microsoft.com/en-us/library/ms229335.aspx). In Section 7.8, we present an overview of several common namespaces.

Software Engineering Observation 7.1

Don't try to "reinvent the wheel." When possible, reuse .NET Framework Class Library classes and methods. This reduces application-development time, avoids introducing programming errors and contributes to good application performance.

Software Engineering Observation 7.2

To promote software reusability, every method should be limited to performing a single, well-defined task, and the name of the method should express that task effectively. Such methods make applications easier to write, debug, maintain and modify.

Error-Prevention Tip 7.1

A small method that performs one task is easier to test and debug than a larger method that performs many tasks.

Software Engineering Observation 7.3

If you cannot choose a concise name that expresses a method's task, your method might be attempting to perform too many diverse tasks. It is usually best to break such a method into several smaller methods.

7.3 static Methods, static Variables and Class Math

Although most methods execute on specific objects in response to method calls, this is not always the case. Sometimes a method performs a task that does not depend on the contents of any object. Such a method applies to the class in which it is declared as a whole and is known as a static method. It is not uncommon for a class to contain a group of static methods to perform common tasks. For example, recall that we used static method Pow of class Math to raise a value to a power in Fig. 6.6. To declare a method as static, place the keyword static before the return type in the method's declaration. You call any static method by specifying the name of the class in which the method is declared, followed by the member access (.) operator and the method name, as in

> *ClassName.MethodName(arguments)*

We use various methods of the Math class here to present the concept of static methods. Class Math (from the System namespace) provides a collection of methods that enable you to perform common mathematical calculations. For example, you can calculate the square root of 900.0 with the static method call

```
Math.Sqrt( 900.0 )
```

The preceding expression evaluates to 30.0. Method Sqrt takes an argument of type double and returns a result of type double. To output the value of the preceding method call in the console window, you might write the statement

```
Console.WriteLine( Math.Sqrt( 900.0 ) );
```

In this statement, the value that Sqrt returns becomes the argument to method WriteLine. Note that we did not create a Math object before calling method Sqrt. Also note that *all* of Math's methods are static—therefore, each is called by preceding the name of the method with the class name Math and the member access (.) operator. Similarly, Console method WriteLine is a static method of class Console, so we invoke the method by preceding its name with the class name Console and the member access (.) operator.

Method arguments may be constants, variables or expressions. If c = 13.0, d = 3.0 and f = 4.0, then the statement

```
Console.WriteLine( Math.Sqrt( c + d * f ) );
```

calculates and displays the square root of 13.0 + 3.0 * 4.0 = 25.0—namely, 5.0. Figure 7.1 summarizes several Math class methods. In the figure, x and y are of type double.

Method	Description	Example
Abs(x)	absolute value of x	Abs(23.7) is 23.7 Abs(0.0) is 0.0 Abs(-23.7) is 23.7
Ceiling(x)	rounds x to the smallest integer not less than x	Ceiling(9.2) is 10.0 Ceiling(-9.8) is -9.0
Cos(x)	trigonometric cosine of x (x in radians)	Cos(0.0) is 1.0
Exp(x)	exponential method e^x	Exp(1.0) is 2.71828 Exp(2.0) is 7.38906
Floor(x)	rounds x to the largest integer not greater than x	Floor(9.2) is 9.0 Floor(-9.8) is -10.0
Log(x)	natural logarithm of x (base e)	Log(Math.E) is 1.0 Log(Math.E * Math.E) is 2.0
Max(x, y)	larger value of x and y	Max(2.3, 12.7) is 12.7 Max(-2.3, -12.7) is -2.3
Min(x, y)	smaller value of x and y	Min(2.3, 12.7) is 2.3 Min(-2.3, -12.7) is -12.7

Fig. 7.1 | Math class methods. (Part 1 of 2.)

Method	Description	Example
Pow(x, y)	x raised to the power y (i.e., x^y)	Pow(**2.0, 7.0**) is 128.0 Pow(**9.0, 0.5**) is 3.0
Sin(x)	trigonometric sine of x (x in radians)	Sin(**0.0**) is 0.0
Sqrt(x)	square root of x	Sqrt(**900.0**) is 30.0
Tan(x)	trigonometric tangent of x (x in radians)	Tan(**0.0**) is 0.0

Fig. 7.1 | Math class methods. (Part 2 of 2.)

Math Class Constants PI and E

Class Math also declares two static constants that represent commonly used mathematical values: **Math.PI** and **Math.E**. The constant Math.PI (3.14159265358979323846) is the ratio of a circle's circumference to its diameter. The constant Math.E (2.7182818284590452354) is the base value for natural logarithms (calculated with static Math method Log). These constants are declared in class Math with the modifiers public and const. Making them public allows other programmers to use these variables in their own classes. A constant is declared with the keyword **const**—its value cannot be changed after the constant is declared. Both PI and E are declared const because their values never change.

 Common Programming Error 7.1

Every constant declared in a class, but not inside a method of the class is implicitly static, *so it is a syntax error to declare such a constant with keyword* static *explicitly.*

Because these constants are static, you can access them via the class name Math and the member access (.) operator, just like class Math's methods. Recall from Section 4.5 that when each object of a class maintains its own copy of an attribute, the variable that represents the attribute is also known as an instance variable—each object (instance) of the class has a separate instance of the variable. There are also variables for which each object of a class does *not* have a separate instance of the variable. That is the case with static variables. When objects of a class containing static variables are created, all the objects of that class share one copy of the class's static variables. Together the static variables and instance variables represent the *fields* of a class. You'll learn more about static variables in Section 10.10.

Why Is Method Main Declared static?

Why must Main be declared static? During application startup, when no objects of the class have been created, the Main method must be called to begin program execution. The Main method is sometimes called the application's *entry point*. Declaring Main as static allows the execution environment to invoke Main without creating an instance of the class. Method Main is often declared with the header:

```
public static void Main( string args[] )
```

When you execute your application from the command line, you type the application name, as in

    ApplicationName argument1 argument2 ...

where *argument1* and *argument2* are the **command-line arguments** to the application that specify a list of strings (separated by spaces) the execution environment will pass to the Main method of your application. Such arguments might be used to specify options (e.g., a file name) to run the application. As you'll learn in Chapter 8, Arrays, your application can access those command-line arguments and use them to customize the application.

Additional Comments about Method `Main`

The header of a Main method does not need to appear exactly as we've shown. Applications that do not take command-line arguments may omit the string[] args parameter. The public keyword may also be omitted. In addition, you can declare Main with return type int (instead of void) to enable Main to return an error code with the return statement. A Main method declared with any one of these headers can be used as the application's entry point—but you can declare only one such Main method in each class.

In earlier chapters, most applications had one class that contained only Main, and some examples had a second class that was used by Main to create and manipulate objects. Actually, any class can contain a Main method. In fact, each of our two-class examples could have been implemented as one class. For example, in the application in Figs. 6.9 and 6.10, method Main (lines 6–16 of Fig. 6.10) could have been taken as is and placed in class GradeBook (Fig. 6.9). The application results would have been identical to those of the two-class version. You can place a Main method in every class you declare. Some programmers take advantage of this to build a small test application into each class they declare. However, if you declare more than one Main method among the classes of your project, you'll need to indicate to the IDE which one you would like to be the application's entry point. You can do this by clicking the menu **Project > [ProjectName] Properties...** (where **[ProjectName]** is the name of your project) and selecting the class containing the Main method that should be the entry point from the **Startup object** list box.

7.4 Declaring Methods with Multiple Parameters

The application in Fig. 7.2 and Fig. 7.3 uses a user-defined method called Maximum to determine and return the largest of three double values that are input by the user. When the application begins execution, class MaximumFinderTest's Main method (lines 6–10 of Fig. 7.3) creates an object of class MaximumFinder (line 8) and calls the object's DetermineMaximum method (line 9) to produce the application's output. In class Maximum-Finder (Fig. 7.2), lines 11–15 of method DetermineMaximum prompt the user to enter three double values and read them from the user. Line 18 calls method Maximum (declared in lines 25–38) to determine the largest of the three double values passed as arguments to the method. When method Maximum returns the result to line 18, the application assigns Maximum's return value to local variable result. Then line 21 outputs the maximum value. At the end of this section, we'll discuss the use of operator + in line 21.

Consider the declaration of method Maximum (lines 25–38). Line 25 indicates that the method returns a double value, that the method's name is Maximum and that the method requires three double parameters (x, y and z) to accomplish its task. When a method has

```
 1   // Fig. 7.2: MaximumFinder.cs
 2   // User-defined method Maximum.
 3   using System;
 4
 5   public class MaximumFinder
 6   {
 7      // obtain three floating-point values and determine maximum value
 8      public void DetermineMaximum()
 9      {
10         // prompt for and input three floating-point values
11         Console.WriteLine( "Enter three floating-point values,\n"
12            + " pressing 'Enter' after each one: " );
13         double number1 = Convert.ToDouble( Console.ReadLine() );
14         double number2 = Convert.ToDouble( Console.ReadLine() );
15         double number3 = Convert.ToDouble( Console.ReadLine() );
16
17         // determine the maximum value
18         double result = Maximum( number1, number2, number3 );
19
20         // display maximum value
21         Console.WriteLine( "Maximum is: " + result );
22      } // end method DetermineMaximum
23
24      // returns the maximum of its three double parameters
25      public double Maximum( double x, double y, double z )
26      {
27         double maximumValue = x; // assume x is the largest to start
28
29         // determine whether y is greater than maximumValue
30         if ( y > maximumValue )
31            maximumValue = y;
32
33         // determine whether z is greater than maximumValue
34         if ( z > maximumValue )
35            maximumValue = z;
36
37         return maximumValue;
38      } // end method Maximum
39   } // end class MaximumFinder
```

Fig. 7.2 | User-defined method `Maximum`.

more than one parameter, the parameters are specified as a comma-separated list. When `Maximum` is called in line 18 of Fig. 7.2, the parameter x is initialized with the value of the argument `number1`, the parameter y is initialized with the value of the argument `number2` and the parameter z is initialized with the value of the argument `number3`. There must be one argument in the method call for each parameter (sometimes called a *formal parameter*) in the method declaration. Also, each argument must be consistent with the type of the corresponding parameter. For example, a parameter of type `double` can receive values like `7.35` (a `double`), `22` (an `int`) or `-0.03456` (a `double`), but not `strings` like `"hello"`. Section 7.7 discusses the argument types that can be provided in a method call for each parameter of a simple type.

```
 1    // Fig. 7.3: MaximumFinderTest.cs
 2    // Application to test class MaximumFinder.
 3    public class MaximumFinderTest
 4    {
 5       // application starting point
 6       public static void Main( string[] args )
 7       {
 8          MaximumFinder maximumFinder = new MaximumFinder();
 9          maximumFinder.DetermineMaximum();
10       } // end Main
11    } // end class MaximumFinderTest
```

```
Enter three floating-point values,
   pressing 'Enter' after each one:
3.33
2.22
1.11
Maximum is: 3.33
```

```
Enter three floating-point values,
   pressing 'Enter' after each one:
2.22
3.33
1.11
Maximum is: 3.33
```

```
Enter three floating-point values,
   pressing 'Enter' after each one:
1.11
2.22
867.5309
Maximum is: 867.5309
```

Fig. 7.3 | Application to test class MaximumFinder.

To determine the maximum value, we begin with the assumption that parameter x contains the largest value, so line 27 (Fig. 7.2) declares local variable maximumValue and initializes it with the value of parameter x. Of course, it is possible that parameter y or z contains the largest value, so we must compare each of these values with maximumValue. The if statement at lines 30–31 determines whether y is greater than maximumValue. If so, line 31 assigns y to maximumValue. The if statement at lines 34–35 determines whether z is greater than maximumValue. If so, line 35 assigns z to maximumValue. At this point, the largest of the three values resides in maximumValue, so line 37 returns that value to line 18. When program control returns to the point in the application where Maximum was called, Maximum's parameters x, y and z are no longer accessible. Note that methods can return at most one value; the returned value can be a value type that contains many values (implemented as a struct) or a reference to an object that contains many values.

Note that result is a local variable in method DetermineMaximum because it is declared in the block that represents the method's body. Variables should be declared as fields of a class (i.e., as either instance variables or static variables of the class) only if they are required for use in more than one method of the class or if the application should save their values between calls to the class's methods.

Common Programming Error 7.2

Declaring method parameters of the same type as float x, y *instead of* float x, float y *is a syntax error—a type is required for each parameter in the parameter list.*

Software Engineering Observation 7.4

A method that has many parameters may be performing too many tasks. Consider dividing the method into smaller methods that perform the separate tasks. As a guideline, try to fit the method header on one line if possible.

Implementing Method Maximum *by Reusing Method* Math.Max

Recall from Fig. 7.1 that class Math has a Max method that can determine the larger of two values. The entire body of our maximum method could also be implemented with nested calls to Math.Max, as follows:

```
return Math.Max( x, Math.Max( y, z ) );
```

The leftmost call to Math.Max specifies arguments x and Math.Max(y, z). Before any method can be called, all its arguments must be evaluated to determine their values. If an argument is a method call, the method call must be performed to determine its return value. So, in the preceding statement, Math.Max(y, z) is evaluated first to determine the maximum of y and z. Then the result is passed as the second argument to the other call to Math.Max, which returns the larger of its two arguments. Using Math.Max in this manner is a good example of software reuse—we find the largest of three values by reusing Math.Max, which finds the larger of two values. Note how concise this code is compared to lines 27–37 of Fig. 7.2.

Assembling Strings with String Concatenation

C# allows string objects to be created by assembling smaller strings into larger strings using operator + (or the compound assignment operator +=). This is known as ***string concatenation***. When both operands of operator + are string objects, operator + creates a new string object in which a copy of the characters of the right operand is placed at the end of a copy of the characters in the left operand. For example, the expression "hello " + "there" creates the string "hello there" without disturbing the original strings.

In line 21 of Fig. 7.2, the expression "Maximum is: " + result uses operator + with operands of types string and double. Every value of a simple type in C# has a string representation. When one of the + operator's operands is a string, the other is implicitly converted to a string, then the two are concatenated. In line 21, the double value is implicitly converted to its string representation and placed at the end of the string "Maximum is: ". If there are any trailing zeros in a double value, these will be discarded when the number is converted to a string. Thus, the number 9.3500 would be represented as 9.35 in the resulting string.

For values of simple types used in string concatenation, the values are converted to strings. If a bool is concatenated with a string, the bool is converted to the string

"True" or "False" (note that each is capitalized). All objects have a `ToString` method that returns a `string` representation of the object. When an object is concatenated with a `string`, the object's `ToString` method is implicitly called to obtain the `string` representation of the object. If the object is `null`, an empty string is written.

Line 21 of Fig. 7.2 could also be written using `string` formatting as

```
Console.WriteLine( "Maximum is: {0}", result );
```

As with `string` concatenation, using a format item to substitute an object into a `string` implicitly calls the object's `ToString` method to obtain the object's `string` representation. You'll learn more about method `ToString` in Chapter 8, Arrays.

When a large `string` literal is typed into an application's source code, you can break that `string` into several smaller `strings` and place them on multiple lines for readability. The `strings` can be reassembled using either string concatenation or string formatting. We discuss the details of `strings` in Chapter 18.

Common Programming Error 7.3

It is a syntax error to break a `string` literal across multiple lines in an application. If a `string` does not fit on one line, split the `string` into several smaller `strings` and use concatenation to form the desired `string`. C# also provides so-called verbatim `string` literals, which are preceded by the @ character. Such literals can be split over multiple lines and the characters in the literal are processed exactly as they appear in the literal.

Common Programming Error 7.4

Confusing the + operator used for string concatenation with the + operator used for addition can lead to strange results. The + operator is left-associative. For example, if integer variable y has the value 5, the expression "y + 2 = " + y + 2 results in the string "y + 2 = 52", not "y + 2 = 7", because first the value of y (5) is concatenated with the string "y + 2 = ", then the value 2 is concatenated with the new larger string "y + 2 = 5". The expression "y + 2 = " + (y + 2) produces the desired result "y + 2 = 7".

7.5 Notes on Declaring and Using Methods

You've seen three ways to call a method:

1. Using a method name by itself to call a method of the same class—such as `Maximum( number1, number2, number3 )` in line 18 of Fig. 7.2.

2. Using a variable that contains a reference to an object, followed by the member access (.) operator and the method name to call a non-`static` method of the referenced object—such as the method call in line 9 of Fig. 7.3, `maximumFinder.DetermineMaximum()`, which calls a method of class `MaximumFinder` from the `Main` method of `MaximumFinderTest`.

3. Using the class name and the member access (.) operator to call a `static` method of a class—such as `Convert.ToDouble( Console.ReadLine() )` in lines 13–15 of Fig. 7.2 or `Math.Sqrt( 900.0 )` in Section 7.3.

Note that a `static` method can call only other `static` methods of the same class directly (i.e., using the method name by itself) and can manipulate only `static` variables in the same class directly. To access the class's non-`static` members, a `static` method must use a reference to an object of the class. Recall that `static` methods relate to a class as a whole, whereas non-`static` methods are associated with a specific instance (object) of the class and may manipulate the instance variables of that object. Many objects of a class, each with its own copies of the instance variables, may exist at the same time. Suppose a `static` method were to invoke a non-`static` method directly. How would the method know which object's instance variables to manipulate? What would happen if no objects of the class existed at the time the non-`static` method was invoked? Thus, C# does not allow a `static` method to access non-`static` members of the same class directly.

There are three ways to return control to the statement that calls a method. If the method does not return a result, control returns when the program flow reaches the method-ending right brace or when the statement

> **return**;

is executed. If the method returns a result, the statement

> **return** *expression*;

evaluates the *expression*, then returns the result (and control) to the caller.

Common Programming Error 7.5

Declaring a method outside the body of a class declaration or inside the body of another method is a syntax error.

Common Programming Error 7.6

Omitting the return type in a method declaration is a syntax error.

Common Programming Error 7.7

Redeclaring a method parameter as a local variable in the method's body is a compilation error.

Common Programming Error 7.8

Forgetting to return a value from a method that should return one is a compilation error. If a return type other than void *is specified, the method must contain a* return *statement in each possible execution path through the method and each* return *statement must return a value consistent with the method's return type. Returning a value from a method whose return type has been declared* void *is a compilation error.*

7.6 Method-Call Stack and Activation Records

To understand how C# performs method calls, we first need to consider a data structure (i.e., collection of related data items) known as a *stack* (we discuss data structures in more detail in Chapters 25–27). You can think of a stack as analogous to a pile of dishes. When a dish is placed on the pile, it is normally placed at the top (referred to as *pushing* the dish onto the stack). Similarly, when a dish is removed from the pile, it is always removed from the top (referred to as *popping* the dish off the stack). Stacks are known as *last-in, first-out (LIFO) data structures*—the last item pushed (inserted) on the stack is the first item popped off (removed from) the stack.

When an application calls a method, the called method must know how to return to its caller, so the return address of the calling method is pushed onto the ***program-execution stack*** (sometimes referred to as the ***method-call stack***). If a series of method calls occurs, the successive return addresses are pushed onto the stack in last-in, first-out order so that each method can return to its caller.

The program-execution stack also contains the memory for the local variables used in each invocation of a method during an application's execution. This data, stored as a portion of the program-execution stack, is known as the ***activation record*** or ***stack frame*** of the method call. When a method call is made, the activation record for it is pushed onto the program-execution stack. When the method returns to its caller, the activation record for this method call is popped off the stack, and those local variables are no longer known to the application. If a local variable holding a reference to an object is the only variable in the application with a reference to that object, when the activation record containing that local variable is popped off the stack, the object can no longer be accessed by the application and will eventually be deleted from memory during "garbage collection." We'll discuss garbage collection in Section 10.9.

Of course, the amount of memory in a computer is finite, so only a certain amount of memory can be used to store activation records on the program-execution stack. If more method calls occur than can have their activation records stored on the program-execution stack, an error known as a ***stack overflow*** occurs.

7.7 Argument Promotion and Casting

Another important feature of method calls is ***argument promotion***—implicitly converting an argument's value to the type that the method expects to receive in its corresponding parameter. For example, an application can call Math method Sqrt with an integer argument even though the method expects to receive a double argument (but, as we'll soon see, not vice versa). The statement

```
Console.WriteLine( Math.Sqrt( 4 ) );
```

correctly evaluates Math.Sqrt(4) and displays the value 2.0. The method declaration's parameter list causes C# to convert the int value 4 to the double value 4.0 before passing the value to Sqrt. Attempting these conversions may lead to compilation errors if C#'s ***promotion rules*** are not satisfied. The promotion rules specify which conversions are allowed—that is, which conversions can be performed without losing data. In the Sqrt example above, an int is converted to a double without changing its value. However, converting a double to an int truncates the fractional part of the double value—thus, part of the value is lost. Also, double variables can hold values much larger (and much smaller) than int variables, so assigning a double to an int can cause a loss of information when the double value doesn't fit in the int. Converting large integer types to small integer types (e.g., long to int) can also result in changed values.

The promotion rules apply to expressions containing values of two or more simple types and to simple-type values passed as arguments to methods. Each value is promoted to the appropriate type in the expression. (Actually, the expression uses a temporary copy of each value—the types of the original values remain unchanged.) Figure 7.4 lists the simple types alphabetically and the types to which each can be promoted. Note that values of all simple types can also be implicitly converted to type object. We demonstrate such implicit conversions in Chapter 25, Data Structures.

By default, C# does not allow you to implicitly convert values between simple types if the target type cannot represent the value of the original type (e.g., the int value 2000000 cannot be represented as a short, and any floating-point number with digits after its decimal point cannot be represented in an integer type such as long, int or short). Therefore, to prevent a compilation error in cases where information may be lost due to an implicit conversion between simple types, the compiler requires you to use a cast operator (introduced in Section 5.7) to explicitly force the conversion. This enables you to "take control" from the compiler. You essentially say, "I know this conversion might cause loss of information, but for my purposes here, that's fine." Suppose you create a method Square that calculates the square of an integer and thus requires an int argument. To call Square with a double argument named doubleValue, you would write the method call as Square((int) doubleValue). This method call explicitly casts (converts) the value of doubleValue to an integer for use in method Square. Thus, if doubleValue's value is 4.5, the method receives the value 4 and returns 16, not 20.25 (which does, unfortunately, result in the loss of information).

 Common Programming Error 7.9

Converting a simple-type value to a value of another simple type may change the value if the promotion is not allowed. For example, converting a floating-point value to an integral value may introduce truncation errors (loss of the fractional part) in the result.

Type	Conversion types
bool	no possible implicit conversions to other simple types
byte	*ushort*, *short*, *uint*, *int*, *ulong*, *long*, *decimal*, *float* or *double*
char	*ushort*, *int*, *uint*, *long*, *ulong*, *decimal*, *float* or *double*
decimal	no possible implicit conversions to other simple types
double	no possible implicit conversions to other simple types
float	*double*
int	*long*, *decimal*, *float* or *double*
long	*decimal*, *float* or *double*
sbyte	*short*, *int*, *long*, *decimal*, *float* or *double*
short	*int*, *long*, *decimal*, *float* or *double*
uint	*ulong*, *long*, *decimal*, *float* or *double*
ulong	*decimal*, *float* or *double*
ushort	*uint*, *int*, *ulong*, *long*, *decimal*, *float* or *double*

Fig. 7.4 | Implicit conversions between simple types.

7.8 The .NET Framework Class Library

Many predefined classes are grouped into categories of related classes called namespaces. Together, these namespaces are referred to as the .NET Framework Class Library.

Throughout the text, *using* directives allow us to use library classes from the .NET Framework Class Library without specifying their fully qualified names. For example, an application includes the declaration

```
using System;
```

in order to use the class names from the System namespace without fully qualifying their names. This allows you to use the *unqualified class name* Console, rather than the fully qualified class name System.Console, in your code. A great strength of C# is the large number of classes in the namespaces of the .NET Framework Class Library. Some key .NET Framework Class Library namespaces are described in Fig. 7.5, which represents only a small portion of the reusable classes in the .NET Framework Class Library. When learning C#, spend some of your time browsing the namespaces and classes in the .NET documentation (msdn.microsoft.com/en-us/library/ms229335.aspx).

Namespace	Description
System.Windows.Forms	Contains the classes required to create and manipulate GUIs. (Various classes in this namespace are discussed in Chapter 14, Graphical User Interfaces with Windows Forms: Part 1, and Chapter 15, Graphical User Interfaces with Windows Forms: Part 2.)
System.Windows.Controls System.Windows.Input System.Windows.Media System.Windows.Shapes	Contain the classes of the Windows Presentation Foundation for GUIs, 2-D and 3-D graphics, multimedia and animation. (You'll learn more about these namespaces in Chapter 16, GUI with Windows Presentation Foundation, Chapter 17, WPF Graphics and Multimedia and Chapter 24, Silverlight, Rich Internet Applications and Multimedia.)
System.Linq	Contains the classes that support Language Integrated Query (LINQ). (You'll learn more about this namespace in Chapter 9, Introduction to LINQ and Generic Collections, and several other chapters throughout the book.)
System.Data System.Data.Linq	Contain the classes for manipulating data in databases (i.e., organized collections of data), including support for LINQ to SQL. (You'll learn more about these namespaces in Chapter 21, Databases and LINQ to SQL.)
System.IO	Contains the classes that enable programs to input and output data. (You'll learn more about this namespace in Chapter 19, Files and Streams.)

Fig. 7.5 | .NET Framework Class Library namespaces (a subset). (Part 1 of 2.)

Namespace	Description
System.Web	Contains the classes used for creating and maintaining web applications, which are accessible over the Internet. (You'll learn more about this namespace in Chapter 22, ASP.NET 3.5 and ASP.NET AJAX.)
System.Xml.Linq	Contains the classes that support Language Integrated Query (LINQ) for XML documents. (You'll learn more about this namespace in Chapter 20, XML and LINQ to XML, and several other chapters throughout the book.)
System.Xml	Contains the classes for creating and manipulating XML data. Data can be read from or written to XML files. (You'll learn more about this namespace in Chapter 20.)
System.Collections System.Collections.Generic	Contain the classes that define data structures for maintaining collections of data. (You'll learn more about these namespaces in Chapter 27, Collections.)
System.Text	Contains the classes that enable programs to manipulate characters and strings. (You'll learn more about this namespace in Chapter 18, Strings, Characters and Regular Expressions.)

Fig. 7.5 | .NET Framework Class Library namespaces (a subset). (Part 2 of 2.)

The set of namespaces available in the .NET Framework Class Library is quite large. Besides those summarized in Fig. 7.5, the .NET Framework Class Library contains namespaces for complex graphics, advanced graphical user interfaces, printing, advanced networking, security, database processing, multimedia, accessibility (for people with disabilities) and many other capabilities—over 100 namespaces in all.

You can locate additional information about a predefined C# class's methods in the *.NET Framework Class Library* reference (msdn.microsoft.com/en-us/library/ms229335.aspx). When you visit this site, you'll see an alphabetical listing of all the namespaces in the .NET Framework Class Library. Locate the namespace and click its link to see an alphabetical listing of all its classes, with a brief description of each. Click a class's link to see a more complete description of the class. Click the **Methods** link in the left-hand column to see a listing of the class's methods.

Good Programming Practice 7.2

The online .NET Framework documentation is easy to search and provides many details about each class. As you learn each class in this book, you should review the class in the online documentation for additional information.

7.9 Case Study: Random-Number Generation

In this and the next section, we develop a nicely structured game-playing application with multiple methods. The application uses most of the control statements presented thus far in the book and introduces several new C# programming concepts.

There is something in the air of a casino that invigorates people—from the high rollers at the plush mahogany-and-felt craps tables to the quarter poppers at the one-armed bandits. It is the ***element of chance***, the possibility that luck will convert a pocketful of money into a mountain of wealth. The element of chance can be introduced in an application via an object of class Random (of namespace System). Objects of class **Random** can produce random byte, int and double values. In the next several examples, we use objects of class Random to produce random numbers.

A new random-number generator object can be created as follows:

```
Random randomNumbers = new Random();
```

The random-number generator object can then be used to generate random byte, int and double values—we discuss only random int values here. For more information on the Random class, see msdn.microsoft.com/en-us/library/system.random.aspx.

Consider the following statement:

```
int randomValue = randomNumbers.Next();
```

Method Next of class Random generates a random int value in the range 0 to +2,147,483,646, inclusive. If the Next method truly produces values at random, then every value in that range should have an equal chance (or probability) of being chosen each time method Next is called. The values returned by Next are actually ***pseudorandom numbers***—a sequence of values produced by a complex mathematical calculation. The calculation uses the current time of day (which, of course, changes constantly) to *seed* the random-number generator such that each execution of an application yields a different sequence of random values.

The range of values produced directly by method Next often differs from the range of values required in a particular C# application. For example, an application that simulates coin tossing might require only 0 for "heads" and 1 for "tails." An application that simulates the rolling of a six-sided die might require random integers in the range 1–6. A video game that randomly predicts the next type of spaceship (out of four possibilities) that will fly across the horizon might require random integers in the range 1–4. For cases like these, class Random provides other versions of method Next. One receives an int argument and returns a value from 0 up to, but not including, the argument's value. For example, you might use the statement

```
int randomValue = randomNumbers.Next( 6 );
```

which returns 0, 1, 2, 3, 4 or 5. The argument 6—called the *scaling factor*—represents the number of unique values that Next should produce (in this case, six—0, 1, 2, 3, 4 and 5). This manipulation is called *scaling* the range of values produced by Random method Next.

Suppose we wanted to simulate a six-sided die that has the numbers 1–6 on its faces, not 0–5. Scaling the range of values alone is not enough. So we *shift* the range of numbers produced. We could do this by adding a *shifting value*—in this case 1—to the result of method Next, as in

```
face = 1 + randomNumbers.Next( 6 );
```

The shifting value (1) specifies the first value in the desired set of random integers. The preceding statement assigns to face a random integer in the range 1–6.

The third alternative of method Next provides a more intuitive way to express both shifting and scaling. This method receives two int arguments and returns a value from the first argument's value up to, but not including, the second argument's value. We could use this method to write a statement equivalent to our previous statement, as in

```
face = randomNumbers.Next( 1, 7 );
```

Rolling a Six-Sided Die

To demonstrate random numbers, let's develop an application that simulates 20 rolls of a six-sided die and displays each roll's value. Figure 7.6 shows two sample outputs, which confirm that the results of the preceding calculation are integers in the range 1–6 and that each run of the application can produce a different sequence of random numbers. The using directive in line 3 enables us to use class Random without fully qualifying its name. Line 9 creates the Random object randomNumbers to produce random values. Line 16 executes 20 times in a loop to roll the die. The if statement (lines 21–22) in the loop starts a new line of output after every five numbers, so the results can be presented on multiple lines.

```
 1   // Fig. 7.6: RandomIntegers.cs
 2   // Shifted and scaled random integers.
 3   using System;
 4
 5   public class RandomIntegers
 6   {
 7      public static void Main( string[] args )
 8      {
 9         Random randomNumbers = new Random(); // random-number generator
10         int face; // stores each random integer generated
11
12         // loop 20 times
13         for ( int counter = 1; counter <= 20; counter++ )
14         {
15            // pick random integer from 1 to 6
16            face = randomNumbers.Next( 1, 7 );
17
18            Console.Write( "{0}  ", face ); // display generated value
19
20            // if counter is divisible by 5, start a new line of output
21            if ( counter % 5 == 0 )
22               Console.WriteLine();
23         } // end for
24      } // end Main
25   } // end class RandomIntegers
```

```
3  3  3  1  1
2  1  2  4  2
2  3  6  2  5
3  4  6  6  1
```

Fig. 7.6 | Shifted and scaled random integers. (Part 1 of 2.)

```
6  2  5  1  3
5  2  1  6  5
4  1  6  1  3
3  1  4  3  4
```

Fig. 7.6 | Shifted and scaled random integers. (Part 2 of 2.)

Rolling a Six-Sided Die 6000 Times

To show that the numbers produced by Next occur with approximately equal likelihood, let us simulate 6000 rolls of a die (Fig. 7.7). Each integer from 1 to 6 should appear approximately 1000 times.

```csharp
 1  // Fig. 7.7: RollDie.cs
 2  // Roll a six-sided die 6000 times.
 3  using System;
 4
 5  public class RollDie
 6  {
 7     public static void Main( string[] args )
 8     {
 9        Random randomNumbers = new Random(); // random-number generator
10
11        int frequency1 = 0; // count of 1s rolled
12        int frequency2 = 0; // count of 2s rolled
13        int frequency3 = 0; // count of 3s rolled
14        int frequency4 = 0; // count of 4s rolled
15        int frequency5 = 0; // count of 5s rolled
16        int frequency6 = 0; // count of 6s rolled
17
18        int face; // stores most recently rolled value
19
20        // summarize results of 6000 rolls of a die
21        for ( int roll = 1; roll <= 6000; roll++ )
22        {
23           face = randomNumbers.Next( 1, 7 ); // number from 1 to 6
24
25           // determine roll value 1-6 and increment appropriate counter
26           switch ( face )
27           {
28              case 1:
29                 ++frequency1; // increment the 1s counter
30                 break;
31              case 2:
32                 ++frequency2; // increment the 2s counter
33                 break;
34              case 3:
35                 ++frequency3; // increment the 3s counter
36                 break;
37              case 4:
38                 ++frequency4; // increment the 4s counter
39                 break;
```

Fig. 7.7 | Roll a six-sided die 6000 times. (Part I of 2.)

```
40                  case 5:
41                      ++frequency5; // increment the 5s counter
42                      break;
43                  case 6:
44                      ++frequency6; // increment the 6s counter
45                      break;
46              } // end switch
47          } // end for
48
49          Console.WriteLine( "Face\tFrequency" ); // output headers
50          Console.WriteLine(
51              "1\t{0}\n2\t{1}\n3\t{2}\n4\t{3}\n5\t{4}\n6\t{5}", frequency1,
52              frequency2, frequency3, frequency4, frequency5, frequency6 );
53      } // end Main
54  } // end class RollDie
```

```
Face        Frequency
1           1039
2           994
3           991
4           970
5           978
6           1028
```

```
Face        Frequency
1           985
2           985
3           1001
4           1017
5           1002
6           1010
```

Fig. 7.7 | Roll a six-sided die 6000 times. (Part 2 of 2.)

As the two sample outputs show, the values produced by method Next enable the application to realistically simulate rolling a six-sided die. The application uses nested control statements (the switch is nested inside the for) to determine the number of times each side of the die occurred. The for statement (lines 21–47) iterates 6000 times. During each iteration, line 23 produces a random value from 1 to 6. This face value is then used as the switch expression (line 26) in the switch statement (lines 26–46). Based on the face value, the switch statement increments one of the six counter variables during each iteration of the loop. (In Chapter 8, we show an elegant way to replace the entire switch statement in this application with a single statement.) Note that the switch statement has no default label because we have a case label for every possible die value that the expression in line 23 can produce. Run the application several times and observe the results. You'll see that every time you execute this application, it produces different results.

7.9.1 Scaling and Shifting Random Numbers

Previously, we demonstrated the statement

```
face = randomNumbers.Next( 1, 7 );
```

which simulates the rolling of a six-sided die. This statement always assigns to variable `face` an integer in the range $1 \le$ `face` < 7. The width of this range (i.e., the number of consecutive integers in the range) is 6, and the starting number in the range is 1. Referring to the preceding statement, we see that the width of the range is determined by the difference between the two integers passed to `Random` method `Next`, and the starting number of the range is the value of the first argument. We can generalize this result as

```
number = randomNumbers.Next( shiftingValue, shiftingValue + scalingFactor );
```

where *shiftingValue* specifies the first number in the desired range of consecutive integers and *scalingFactor* specifies how many numbers are in the range.

It is also possible to choose integers at random from sets of values other than ranges of consecutive integers. For this purpose, it is simpler to use the version of the `Next` method that takes only one argument. For example, to obtain a random value from the sequence 2, 5, 8, 11 and 14, you could use the statement

```
number = 2 + 3 * randomNumbers.Next( 5 );
```

In this case, `randomNumberGenerator.Next( 5 )` produces values in the range 0–4. Each value produced is multiplied by 3 to produce a number in the sequence 0, 3, 6, 9 and 12. We then add 2 to that value to shift the range of values and obtain a value from the sequence 2, 5, 8, 11 and 14. We can generalize this result as

```
number = shiftingValue +
         differenceBetweenValues * randomNumbers.Next( scalingFactor );
```

where *shiftingValue* specifies the first number in the desired range of values, *differenceBetweenValues* represents the difference between consecutive numbers in the sequence and *scalingFactor* specifies how many numbers are in the range.

7.9.2 Random-Number Repeatability for Testing and Debugging

As we mentioned earlier in Section 7.9, the methods of class `Random` actually generate pseudorandom numbers based on complex mathematical calculations. Repeatedly calling any of `Random`'s methods produces a sequence of numbers that appears to be random. The calculation that produces the pseudorandom numbers uses the time of day as a *seed value* to change the sequence's starting point. Each new `Random` object seeds itself with a value based on the computer system's clock at the time the object is created, enabling each execution of an application to produce a different sequence of random numbers.

When debugging an application, it is sometimes useful to repeat the exact same sequence of pseudorandom numbers during each execution of the application. This repeatability enables you to prove that your application is working for a specific sequence of random numbers before you test the application with different sequences of random numbers. When repeatability is important, you can create a `Random` object as follows:

```
Random randomNumbers = new Random( seedValue );
```

The `seedValue` argument (type `int`) seeds the random-number calculation. If the same `seedValue` is used every time, the `Random` object produces the same sequence of random numbers.

Error-Prevention Tip 7.2

While an application is under development, create the Random object with a specific seed value to produce a repeatable sequence of random numbers each time the application executes. If a logic error occurs, fix the error and test the application again with the same seed value—this allows you to reconstruct the same sequence of random numbers that caused the error. Once the logic errors have been removed, create the Random object without using a seed value, causing the Random object to generate a new sequence of random numbers each time the application executes.

7.10 Case Study: A Game of Chance (Introducing Enumerations)

One popular game of chance is the dice game known as "craps," which is played in casinos and back alleys throughout the world. The rules of the game are straightforward:

> *You roll two dice. Each die has six faces, which contain one, two, three, four, five and six spots, respectively. After the dice have come to rest, the sum of the spots on the two upward faces is calculated. If the sum is 7 or 11 on the first throw, you win. If the sum is 2, 3 or 12 on the first throw (called "craps"), you lose (i.e., "the house" wins). If the sum is 4, 5, 6, 8, 9 or 10 on the first throw, that sum becomes your "point." To win, you must continue rolling the dice until you "make your point" (i.e., roll that same point value). You lose by rolling a 7 before making your point.*

The application in Fig. 7.8 and Fig. 7.9 simulates the game of craps, using methods to define the logic of the game. In the Main method of class CrapsTest (Fig. 7.9), line 7 creates an object of class Craps (Fig. 7.8), and line 8 calls its Play method to start the game. The Play method (Fig. 7.8, lines 24–70) calls the RollDice method (Fig. 7.8, lines 73–85) as needed to roll the two dice and compute their sum. The four sample outputs in Fig. 7.9 show winning on the first roll, losing on the first roll, winning on a subsequent roll and losing on a subsequent roll, respectively.

Let's discuss the declaration of class Craps in Fig. 7.8. In the rules of the game, the player must roll two dice on the first roll and must do the same on all subsequent rolls. We declare method RollDice (lines 73–85) to roll the dice and compute and display their sum. Method RollDice is declared once, but it is called from two places (lines 30 and 54) in method Play, which contains the logic for one complete game of craps. Method RollDice takes no arguments, so it has an empty parameter list. Each time it is called, RollDice returns the sum of the dice, so the return type int is indicated in the method header (line 73). Although lines 76 and 77 look the same (except for the die names), they do not necessarily produce the same result. Each of these statements produces a random value in the range 1–6. Note that randomNumbers (used in lines 76 and 77) is not declared in the method. Rather it is declared as a private instance variable of the class and initialized in line 8. This enables us to create one Random object that is reused in each call to RollDice.

```
1   // Fig. 7.8: Craps.cs
2   // Craps class simulates the dice game craps.
3   using System;
4
```

Fig. 7.8 | Craps class simulates the dice game craps. (Part 1 of 3.)

```
5    public class Craps
6    {
7        // create random-number generator for use in method RollDice
8        private Random randomNumbers = new Random();
9
10       // enumeration with constants that represent the game status
11       private enum Status { CONTINUE, WON, LOST }
12
13       // enumeration with constants that represent common rolls of the dice
14       private enum DiceNames
15       {
16           SNAKE_EYES = 2,
17           TREY = 3,
18           SEVEN = 7,
19           YO_LEVEN = 11,
20           BOX_CARS = 12
21       }
22
23       // plays one game of craps
24       public void Play()
25       {
26           // gameStatus can contain CONTINUE, WON or LOST
27           Status gameStatus = Status.CONTINUE;
28           int myPoint = 0; // point if no win or loss on first roll
29
30           int sumOfDice = RollDice(); // first roll of the dice
31
32           // determine game status and point based on first roll
33           switch ( ( DiceNames ) sumOfDice )
34           {
35               case DiceNames.SEVEN: // win with 7 on first roll
36               case DiceNames.YO_LEVEN: // win with 11 on first roll
37                   gameStatus = Status.WON;
38                   break;
39               case DiceNames.SNAKE_EYES: // lose with 2 on first roll
40               case DiceNames.TREY: // lose with 3 on first roll
41               case DiceNames.BOX_CARS: // lose with 12 on first roll
42                   gameStatus = Status.LOST;
43                   break;
44               default: // did not win or lose, so remember point
45                   gameStatus = Status.CONTINUE; // game is not over
46                   myPoint = sumOfDice; // remember the point
47                   Console.WriteLine( "Point is {0}", myPoint );
48                   break;
49           } // end switch
50
51           // while game is not complete
52           while ( gameStatus == Status.CONTINUE ) // game not WON or LOST
53           {
54               sumOfDice = RollDice(); // roll dice again
55
```

Fig. 7.8 | Craps class simulates the dice game craps. (Part 2 of 3.)

```
56          // determine game status
57          if ( sumOfDice == myPoint ) // win by making point
58              gameStatus = Status.WON;
59          else
60              // lose by rolling 7 before point
61              if ( sumOfDice == ( int ) DiceNames.SEVEN )
62                  gameStatus = Status.LOST;
63      } // end while
64
65      // display won or lost message
66      if ( gameStatus == Status.WON )
67          Console.WriteLine( "Player wins" );
68      else
69          Console.WriteLine( "Player loses" );
70  } // end method Play
71
72  // roll dice, calculate sum and display results
73  public int RollDice()
74  {
75      // pick random die values
76      int die1 = randomNumbers.Next( 1, 7 ); // first die roll
77      int die2 = randomNumbers.Next( 1, 7 ); // second die roll
78
79      int sum = die1 + die2; // sum of die values
80
81      // display results of this roll
82      Console.WriteLine( "Player rolled {0} + {1} = {2}",
83          die1, die2, sum );
84      return sum; // return sum of dice
85  } // end method RollDice
86  } // end class Craps
```

Fig. 7.8 | Craps class simulates the dice game craps. (Part 3 of 3.)

```
1   // Fig. 7.9: CrapsTest.cs
2   // Application to test class Craps.
3   public class CrapsTest
4   {
5       public static void Main( string[] args )
6       {
7           Craps game = new Craps();
8           game.Play(); // play one game of craps
9       } // end Main
10  } // end class CrapsTest
```

```
Player rolled 2 + 5 = 7
Player wins
```

```
Player rolled 2 + 1 = 3
Player loses
```

Fig. 7.9 | Application to test class Craps. (Part 1 of 2.)

```
Player rolled 4 + 6 = 10
Point is 10
Player rolled 1 + 3 = 4
Player rolled 1 + 3 = 4
Player rolled 2 + 3 = 5
Player rolled 4 + 4 = 8
Player rolled 6 + 6 = 12
Player rolled 4 + 4 = 8
Player rolled 4 + 5 = 9
Player rolled 2 + 6 = 8
Player rolled 6 + 6 = 12
Player rolled 6 + 4 = 10
Player wins
```

```
Player rolled 2 + 4 = 6
Point is 6
Player rolled 3 + 1 = 4
Player rolled 5 + 5 = 10
Player rolled 6 + 1 = 7
Player loses
```

Fig. 7.9 | Application to test class `Craps`. (Part 2 of 2.)

The game is reasonably involved. The player may win or lose on the first roll or may win or lose on any subsequent roll. Method `Play` (lines 24–70) uses local variable `gameStatus` (line 27) to keep track of the overall game status, local variable `myPoint` (line 28) to store the "point" if the player does not win or lose on the first roll and local variable `sumOfDice` (line 30) to maintain the sum of the dice for the most recent roll. Note that `myPoint` is initialized to 0 to ensure that the application will compile. If you do not initialize `myPoint`, the compiler issues an error, because `myPoint` is not assigned a value in every branch of the `switch` statement—thus, the application could try to use `myPoint` before it is definitely assigned a value. By contrast, `gameStatus` does not require initialization because it *is* assigned a value in every branch of the `switch` statement—thus, it is guaranteed to be initialized before it is used. However, as good programming practice, we initialize it anyway.

Note that local variable `gameStatus` is declared to be of a new type called `Status`, which we declared in line 11. Type `Status` is declared as a `private` member of class `Craps`, because `Status` will be used only in that class. `Status` is a user-defined type called an *enumeration*, which declares a set of constants represented by identifiers. An enumeration is introduced by the keyword *enum* and a type name (in this case, `Status`). As with a class, braces ({ and }) delimit the body of an `enum` declaration. Inside the braces is a comma-separated list of *enumeration constants*. The enum constant names must be unique, but the value associated with each constant need not be.

Good Programming Practice 7.3

Use only uppercase letters in the names of constants. This makes the constants stand out in an application and reminds you that enumeration constants are not variables.

Variables of type Status should be assigned only one of the three constants declared in the enumeration. When the game is won, the application sets local variable gameStatus to Status.WON (lines 37 and 58). When the game is lost, the application sets local variable gameStatus to Status.LOST (lines 42 and 62). Otherwise, the application sets local variable gameStatus to Status.CONTINUE (line 45) to indicate that the dice must be rolled again.

Good Programming Practice 7.4

Using enumeration constants (like Status.WON, Status.LOST and Status.CONTINUE) rather than literal integer values (such as 0, 1 and 2) can make code easier to read and maintain.

Line 30 in method Play calls RollDice, which picks two random values from 1 to 6, displays the value of the first die, the value of the second die and the sum of the dice, and returns the sum of the dice. Method Play next enters the switch statement at lines 33–49, which uses the sumOfDice value from line 30 to determine whether the game has been won or lost, or whether it should continue with another roll.

The sums of the dice that would result in a win or loss on the first roll are declared in the DiceNames enumeration in lines 14–21. These are used in the cases of the switch statement. The identifier names use casino parlance for these sums. Notice that in the DiceNames enumeration, a value is explicitly assigned to each identifier name. When the enum is declared, each constant in the enum declaration is a constant value of type int. If you do not assign a value to an identifier in the enum declaration, the compiler will do so. If the first enum constant is unassigned, the compiler gives it the value 0. If any other enum constant is unassigned, the compiler gives it a value equal to one more than the value of the preceding enum constant. For example, in the Status enumeration, the compiler implicitly assigns 0 to Status.WON, 1 to Status.CONTINUE and 2 to Status.LOST.

You could also declare an enum's underlying type to be byte, sbyte, short, ushort, int, uint, long or ulong by writing

```
private enum MyEnum : typeName { Constant1, Constant2, ... }
```

where *typeName* represents one of the integral simple types.

If you need to compare a simple integral type value to the underlying value of an enumeration constant, you must use a cast operator to make the two types match. In the switch statement at lines 33–49, we use the cast operator to convert the int value in sumOfDice to type DiceNames and compare it to each of the constants in DiceNames. Lines 35–36 determine whether the player won on the first roll with SEVEN (7) or YO_LEVEN (11). Lines 39–41 determine whether the player lost on the first roll with SNAKE_EYES (2), TREY (3) or BOX_CARS (12). After the first roll, if the game is not over, the default case (lines 44–48) saves sumOfDice in myPoint (line 46) and displays the point (line 47).

If we're still trying to "make our point" (i.e., the game is continuing from a prior roll), the loop in lines 52–63 executes. Line 54 rolls the dice again. If sumOfDice matches myPoint in line 57, line 58 sets gameStatus to Status.WON, and the loop terminates because the game is complete. In line 61, we use the cast operator (int) to obtain the underlying value of DiceNames.SEVEN so that we can compare it to sumOfDice. If sumOfDice is equal to SEVEN (7), line 62 sets gameStatus to Status.LOST, and the loop terminates because the game is over. When the game completes, lines 66–69 display a message indicating whether the player won or lost, and the application terminates.

Note the use of the various program-control mechanisms we have discussed. The Craps class uses two methods—Play (called from CrapsTest.Main) and RollDice (called twice from Play)—and the switch, while, if...else and nested if control statements. Note also the use of multiple case labels in the switch statement to execute the same statements for sums of SEVEN and YO_LEVEN (lines 35–36) and for sums of SNAKE_EYES, TREY and BOX_CARS (lines 39–41). To easily create a switch statement with all possible values for an enum type, you can use the switch code snippet. Type switch in the C# code then press *Tab* twice. If you enter an enum type into the switch statement's expression (the highlighted code of the snippet) and press *Enter*, a case for each enum constant will be generated automatically.

7.11 Scope of Declarations

You've seen declarations of C# entities, such as classes, methods, properties, variables and parameters. Declarations introduce names that can be used to refer to such C# entities. The *scope* of a declaration is the portion of the application that can refer to the declared entity by its unqualified name. Such an entity is said to be "in scope" for that portion of the application. This section introduces several important scope issues. For more information, see *Section 3.7, Scopes,* of the *C# Language Specification* (available at msdn.micro-soft.com/en-us/vcsharp/aa336809.aspx). The basic scope rules are as follows:

1. The scope of a parameter declaration is the body of the method in which the declaration appears.

2. The scope of a local-variable declaration is from the point at which the declaration appears to the end of the block containing the declaration.

3. The scope of a local-variable declaration that appears in the initialization section of a for statement's header is the body of the for statement and the other expressions in the header.

4. The scope of a method, property or field of a class is the entire body of the class. This enables non-static methods and properties of a class to use any of the class's fields, methods and properties, regardless of the order in which they are declared. Similarly, static methods and properties can use any of the static members of the class.

Any block may contain variable declarations. If a local variable or parameter in a method has the same name as a field, the field is hidden until the block terminates. In Chapter 10, we discuss how to access hidden fields.

Error-Prevention Tip 7.3

Use different names for fields and local variables to help prevent subtle logic errors that occur when a method is called and a local variable of the method hides a field of the same name in the class.

The application in Figs. 7.10 and 7.12 demonstrates scoping issues with fields and local variables. When the application begins execution, class ScopeTest's Main method (Fig. 7.11, lines 6–10) creates an object of class Scope (line 8) and calls the object's Begin method (line 9) to produce the application's output (shown in Fig. 7.11).

In class Scope (Fig. 7.11), line 8 declares and initializes the instance variable x to 1. This instance variable is hidden in any block (or method) that declares local variable named x. Method `Begin` (lines 12–31) declares local variable x (line 14) and initializes it to 5. This local variable's value is output to show that instance variable x (whose value is 1) is hidden in method `Begin`. The application declares two other methods—`UseLocal-Variable` (lines 34–43) and `UseInstanceVariable` (lines 46–53)—that each take no arguments and do not return results. Method `Begin` calls each method twice (lines 19–28). Method `UseLocalVariable` declares local variable x (line 36). When `UseLocalVariable` is first called (line 19), it creates local variable x and initializes it to 25 (line 36), outputs the value of x (lines 38–39), increments x (line 40) and outputs the value of x again (lines 41–42). When `UseLocalVariable` is called a second time (line 25), it re-creates local variable x and reinitializes it to 25, so the output of each `UseLocalVariable` call is identical.

```
 1   // Fig. 7.10: Scope.cs
 2   // Scope class demonstrates instance- and local-variable scopes.
 3   using System;
 4
 5   public class Scope
 6   {
 7      // instance variable that is accessible to all methods of this class
 8      private int x = 1;
 9
10      // method Begin creates and initializes local variable x
11      // and calls methods UseLocalVariable and UseInstanceVariable
12      public void Begin()
13      {
14         int x = 5; // method's local variable x hides instance variable x
15
16         Console.WriteLine( "local x in method Begin is {0}", x );
17
18         // UseLocalVariable has its own local x
19         UseLocalVariable();
20
21         // UseInstanceVariable uses class Scope's instance variable x
22         UseInstanceVariable();
23
24         // UseLocalVariable reinitializes its own local x
25         UseLocalVariable();
26
27         // class Scope's instance variable x retains its value
28         UseInstanceVariable();
29
30         Console.WriteLine( "\nlocal x in method Begin is {0}", x );
31      } // end method Begin
32
33      // create and initialize local variable x during each call
34      public void UseLocalVariable()
35      {
36         int x = 25; // initialized each time UseLocalVariable is called
37
38         Console.WriteLine(
39            "\nlocal x on entering method UseLocalVariable is {0}", x );
40         ++x; // modifies this method's local variable x
```

Fig. 7.10 | Scope class demonstrates instance- and local-variable scopes. (Part 1 of 2.)

```
41          Console.WriteLine(
42              "local x before exiting method UseLocalVariable is {0}", x );
43      } // end method UseLocalVariable
44
45      // modify class Scope's instance variable x during each call
46      public void UseInstanceVariable()
47      {
48          Console.WriteLine( "\ninstance variable x on entering {0} is {1}",
49              "method UseInstanceVariable", x );
50          x *= 10; // modifies class Scope's instance variable x
51          Console.WriteLine( "instance variable x before exiting {0} is {1}",
52              "method UseInstanceVariable", x );
53      } // end method UseInstanceVariable
54  } // end class Scope
```

Fig. 7.10 | Scope class demonstrates instance- and local-variable scopes. (Part 2 of 2.)

```
1   // Fig. 7.11: ScopeTest.cs
2   // Application to test class Scope.
3   public class ScopeTest
4   {
5       // application starting point
6       public static void Main( string[] args )
7       {
8           Scope testScope = new Scope();
9           testScope.Begin();
10      } // end Main
11  } // end class ScopeTest
```

```
local x in method Begin is 5

local x on entering method UseLocalVariable is 25
local x before exiting method UseLocalVariable is 26

instance variable x on entering method UseInstanceVariable is 1
instance variable x before exiting method UseInstanceVariable is 10

local x on entering method UseLocalVariable is 25
local x before exiting method UseLocalVariable is 26

instance variable x on entering method UseInstanceVariable is 10
instance variable x before exiting method UseInstanceVariable is 100

local x in method Begin is 5
```

Fig. 7.11 | Application to test class Scope.

Method UseInstanceVariable does not declare any local variables. Therefore, when it refers to x, instance variable x (line 8) of the class is used. When method UseInstance-Variable is first called (line 22), it outputs the value (1) of instance variable x (lines 48–49), multiplies the instance variable x by 10 (line 50) and outputs the value (10) of instance variable x again (lines 51–52) before returning. The next time method UseInstanceVariable is called (line 28), the instance variable has its modified value, 10, so the method outputs 10, then 100. Finally, in method Begin, the application outputs the value of local variable x again (line 30) to show that none of the method calls modified Begin's local variable x, because the methods all referred to variables named x in other scopes.

7.12 Method Overloading

Methods of the same name can be declared in the same class, as long as they have different sets of parameters (determined by the number, types and order of the parameters). This is called *method overloading*. When an *overloaded method* is called, the C# compiler selects the appropriate method by examining the number, types and order of the arguments in the call. Method overloading is commonly used to create several methods with the same name that perform the same or similar tasks, but on different types or different numbers of arguments. For example, Math methods Min and Max (summarized in Section 7.3) are overloaded with 11 versions. These find the minimum and maximum, respectively, of two values of each of the 11 numeric simple types. Our next example demonstrates declaring and invoking overloaded methods. You'll see examples of overloaded constructors in Chapter 10.

Declaring Overloaded Methods

In class MethodOverload (Fig. 7.12), we include two overloaded versions of a method called Square—one that calculates the square of an int (and returns an int) and one that calculates the square of a double (and returns a double). Although these methods have the same name and similar parameter lists and bodies, you can think of them simply as *different* methods. It may help to think of the method names as "Square of int" and "Square of double," respectively. When the application begins execution, class MethodOverload-Test's Main method (Fig. 7.13, lines 5–9) creates an object of class MethodOverload (line 7) and calls the object's TestOverloadedMethods method (line 8) to produce the application's output (Fig. 7.13).

In Fig. 7.12, line 10 invokes method Square with the argument 7. Literal integer values are treated as type int, so the method call in line 10 invokes the version of Square at lines 15–20 that specifies an int parameter. Similarly, line 11 invokes method Square with the argument 7.5. Literal real-number values are treated as type double, so the method call in line 11 invokes the version of Square at lines 23–28 that specifies a double parameter. Each method first outputs a line of text to prove that the proper method was called in each case.

Notice that the overloaded methods in Fig. 7.12 perform the same calculation, but with two different types. C#'s generics feature provides a mechanism for writing a single "generic method" that can perform the same tasks as an entire set of overloaded methods. We discuss generic methods in Chapter 26.

```
1   // Fig. 7.12: MethodOverload.cs
2   // Overloaded method declarations.
3   using System;
4
```

Fig. 7.12 | Overloaded method declarations. (Part 1 of 2.)

```
 5    public class MethodOverload
 6    {
 7        // test overloaded square methods
 8        public void TestOverloadedMethods()
 9        {
10            Console.WriteLine( "Square of integer 7 is {0}", Square( 7 ) );
11            Console.WriteLine( "Square of double 7.5 is {0}", Square( 7.5 ) );
12        } // end method TestOverloadedMethods
13
14        // square method with int argument
15        public int Square( int intValue )
16        {
17            Console.WriteLine( "Called square with int argument: {0}",
18                intValue );
19            return intValue * intValue;
20        } // end method Square with int argument
21
22        // square method with double argument
23        public double Square( double doubleValue )
24        {
25            Console.WriteLine( "Called square with double argument: {0}",
26                doubleValue );
27            return doubleValue * doubleValue;
28        } // end method Square with double argument
29    } // end class MethodOverload
```

Fig. 7.12 | Overloaded method declarations. (Part 2 of 2.)

```
 1    // Fig. 7.13: MethodOverloadTest.cs
 2    // Application to test class MethodOverload.
 3    public class MethodOverloadTest
 4    {
 5        public static void Main( string[] args )
 6        {
 7            MethodOverload methodOverload = new MethodOverload();
 8            methodOverload.TestOverloadedMethods();
 9        } // end Main
10    } // end class MethodOverloadTest
```

```
Called square with int argument: 7
Square of integer 7 is 49
Called square with double argument: 7.5
Square of double 7.5 is 56.25
```

Fig. 7.13 | Application to test class MethodOverload.

Distinguishing Between Overloaded Methods

The compiler distinguishes overloaded methods by their *signature*—a combination of the method's name and the number, types and order of its parameters. The signature also includes the way those parameters are passed, which can be modified by the ref and out keywords that we discuss in Section 7.14. If the compiler looked only at method names during compilation, the code in Fig. 7.12 would be ambiguous—the compiler would not know how to distinguish between the two Square methods (lines 15–20 and 23–28). Internally, the compiler uses signatures to determine whether the methods in a class are unique in that class.

For example, in Fig. 7.12, the compiler will use the method signatures to distinguish between the "Square of int" method (the Square method that specifies an int parameter) and the "Square of double" method (the Square method that specifies a double parameter). If Method1's declaration begins as

> *void* Method1(*int* a, *float* b)

then that method will have a different signature than the method declared beginning with

> *void* Method1(*float* a, *int* b)

The order of the parameter types is important—the compiler considers the preceding two Method1 headers to be distinct.

Return Types of Overloaded Methods

In discussing the logical names of methods used by the compiler, we did not mention the return types of the methods. This is because method *calls* cannot be distinguished by return type. The application in Fig. 7.14 illustrates the compiler errors generated when two methods have the same signature but different return types. Overloaded methods can have the same or different return types if the methods have different parameter lists. Also, overloaded methods need not have the same number of parameters.

Common Programming Error 7.10

Declaring overloaded methods with identical parameter lists is a compilation error regardless of whether the return types are different.

```
 1    // Fig. 7.14: MethodOverload.cs
 2    // Overloaded methods with identical signatures
 3    // cause compilation errors, even if return types are different.
 4    public class MethodOverloadError
 5    {
 6       // declaration of method Square with int argument
 7       public int Square( int x )
 8       {
 9          return x * x;
10       } // end method Square
11
12       // second declaration of method Square with int argument
13       // causes compilation error even though return types are different
14       public double Square( int y )
15       {
16          return y * y;
17       } // end method Square
18    } // end class MethodOverloadError
```

Fig. 7.14 | Overloaded methods with identical signatures cause compilation errors, even if return types are different. (Part 1 of 2.)

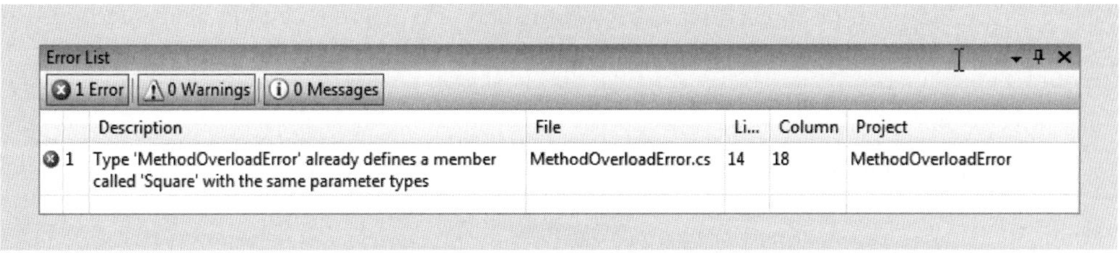

Fig. 7.14 | Overloaded methods with identical signatures cause compilation errors, even if return types are different. (Part 2 of 2.)

7.13 Recursion

The applications we have discussed thus far are generally structured as methods that call one another in a disciplined, hierarchical manner. For some problems, however, it is useful to have a method call itself. A *recursive method* is a method that calls itself, either directly or indirectly through another method.

We consider recursion conceptually first. Then we examine an application containing a recursive method. Recursive problem-solving approaches have a number of elements in common. When a recursive method is called to solve a problem, it actually is capable of solving only the simplest case(s), or *base case(s)*. If the method is called with a base case, it returns a result. If the method is called with a more complex problem, it divides the problem into two conceptual pieces: a piece that the method knows how to do and a piece that it does not know how to do. To make recursion feasible, the latter piece must resemble the original problem, but be a slightly simpler or slightly smaller version of it. Because this new problem looks like the original problem, the method calls a fresh copy of itself to work on the smaller problem; this is referred to as a *recursive call* and is also called the *recursion step*. The recursion step normally includes a return statement, because its result will be combined with the portion of the problem the method knew how to solve to form a result that will be passed back to the original caller.

The recursion step executes while the original call to the method is still active (i.e., while it has not finished executing). The recursion step can result in many more recursive calls, as the method divides each new subproblem into two conceptual pieces. For the recursion to terminate eventually, each time the method calls itself with a slightly simpler version of the original problem, the sequence of smaller and smaller problems must converge on the base case. At that point, the method recognizes the base case and returns a result to the previous copy of the method. A sequence of returns ensues until the original method call returns the result to the caller. This process sounds complex compared with the conventional problem solving we have performed to this point.

Recursive Factorial Calculations

As an example of recursion concepts at work, let us write a recursive application to perform a popular mathematical calculation. Consider the factorial of a nonnegative integer n, written $n!$ (and pronounced "n factorial"), which is the product

$$n \cdot (n-1) \cdot (n-2) \cdot \ldots \cdot 1$$

1! is equal to 1 and 0! is defined to be 1. For example, 5! is the product $5 \cdot 4 \cdot 3 \cdot 2 \cdot 1$, which is equal to 120.

The factorial of an integer, number, greater than or equal to 0 can be calculated iteratively (nonrecursively) using the for statement as follows:

```
factorial = 1;

for ( int counter = number; counter >= 1; counter-- )
    factorial *= counter;
```

A recursive declaration of the factorial method is arrived at by observing the following relationship:

$$n! = n \cdot (n - 1)!$$

For example, 5! is clearly equal to 5 · 4!, as is shown by the following equations:

$$5! = 5 \cdot 4 \cdot 3 \cdot 2 \cdot 1$$
$$5! = 5 \cdot (4 \cdot 3 \cdot 2 \cdot 1)$$
$$5! = 5 \cdot (4!)$$

The evaluation of 5! would proceed as shown in Fig. 7.15. Figure 7.15(a) shows how the succession of recursive calls proceeds until 1! is evaluated to be 1, which terminates the recursion. Figure 7.15(b) shows the values returned from each recursive call to its caller until the value is calculated and returned.

Figure 7.16 uses recursion to calculate and display the factorials of the integers from 0 to 10. The recursive method Factorial (lines 16–24) first tests to determine whether a terminating condition (line 19) is true. If number is less than or equal to 1 (the base case), Factorial returns 1, no further recursion is necessary and the method returns. If number is greater than 1, line 23 expresses the problem as the product of number and a recursive

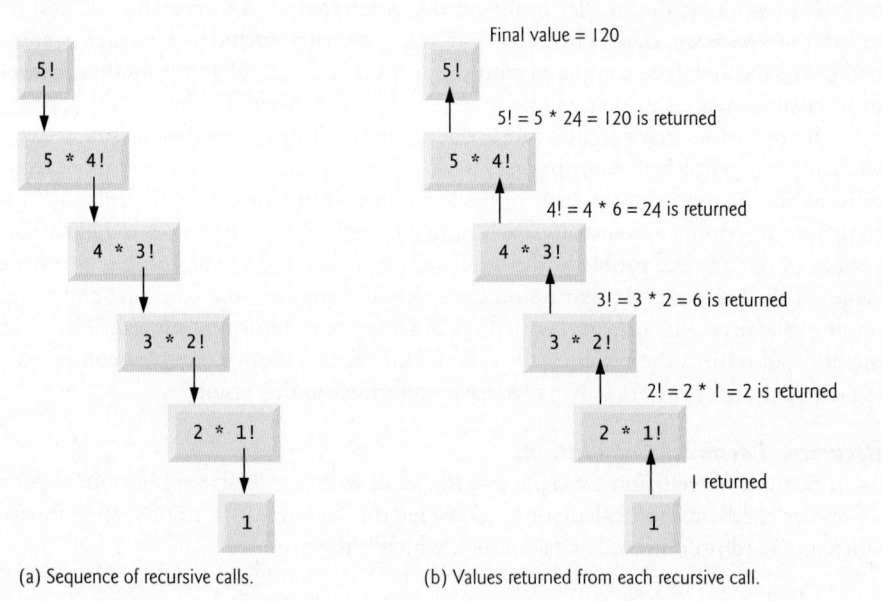

(a) Sequence of recursive calls.   (b) Values returned from each recursive call.

Fig. 7.15 | Recursive evaluation of 5!.

```
1    // Fig. 7.16: FactorialTest.cs
2    // Recursive Factorial method.
3    using System;
4
5    public class FactorialTest
6    {
7       public static void Main( string[] args )
8       {
9          // calculate the factorials of 0 through 10
10         for ( long counter = 0; counter <= 10; counter++ )
11            Console.WriteLine( "{0}! = {1}",
12               counter, Factorial( counter ) );
13      } // end Main
14
15      // recursive declaration of method Factorial
16      public static long Factorial( long number )
17      {
18         // base case
19         if ( number <= 1 )
20            return 1;
21         // recursion step
22         else
23            return number * Factorial( number - 1 );
24      } // end method Factorial
25   } // end class FactorialTest
```

```
0! = 1
1! = 1
2! = 2
3! = 6
4! = 24
5! = 120
6! = 720
7! = 5040
8! = 40320
9! = 362880
10! = 3628800
```

Fig. 7.16 | Recursive Factorial method.

call to Factorial evaluating the factorial of number - 1, which is a slightly simpler problem than the original calculation, Factorial(number).

Method Factorial (lines 16–24) receives a parameter of type long and returns a result of type long. As can be seen in Fig. 7.16, factorial values become large quickly. We chose type long (which can represent relatively large integers) so that the application could calculate factorials greater than 20!. Unfortunately, the Factorial method produces large values so quickly that factorial values soon exceed even the maximum value that can be stored in a long variable. Due to the restrictions on the integral types, variables of type float, double or decimal might ultimately be needed to calculate factorials of larger numbers. This situation points to a weakness in many programming languages—the languages are not easily extended to handle the unique requirements of various applications. As you know, C# allows you to create a type that supports arbitrarily large integers if you wish.

For example, you could create a `HugeInteger` class that would enable an application to calculate the factorials of arbitrarily large numbers.

Common Programming Error 7.11

*Either omitting the base case or writing the recursion step incorrectly so that it does not converge on the base case will cause **infinite recursion**, eventually exhausting memory. This error is analogous to the problem of an infinite loop in an iterative (nonrecursive) solution.*

7.14 Passing Arguments: Pass-by-Value vs. Pass-by-Reference

Two ways to pass arguments to functions in many programming languages are *pass-by-value* and *pass-by-reference*. When an argument is passed by value (the default in C#), a *copy* of its value is made and passed to the called function. Changes to the copy do not affect the original variable's value in the caller. This prevents the accidental side effects that so greatly hinder the development of correct and reliable software systems. Each argument that has been passed in the programs in this chapter so far has been passed by value. When an argument is passed by reference, the caller gives the method the ability to access and modify the caller's original variable.

Software Engineering Observation 7.5

Pass-by-reference can weaken security, because the called function can corrupt the caller's data.

To pass an object by reference into a method, simply provide as an argument in the method call the variable that refers to the object. Then, in the method body, reference the object using the parameter name. The parameter refers to the original object in memory, so the called method can access the original object directly.

Previously, we discussed the difference between value types and reference types. A major difference between them is that value-type variables store values, so specifying a value-type variable in a method call passes a copy of that variable's value to the method. Reference-type variables store references to objects, so specifying a reference-type variable as an argument passes the method a copy of the actual reference that refers to the object. Even though the reference itself is passed by value, the method can still use the reference it receives to interact with—and possibly modify—the original object. Similarly, when returning information from a method via a `return` statement, the method returns a copy of the value stored in a value-type variable or a copy of the reference stored in a reference-type variable. When a reference is returned, the calling method can use that reference to interact with the referenced object. So, in effect, objects are always passed by reference.

What if you would like to pass a variable by reference so the called method can modify the variable's value? To do this, C# provides keywords *ref* and *out*. Applying the ref keyword to a parameter declaration allows you to pass a variable to a method by reference—the called method will be able to modify the original variable in the caller. The ref keyword is used for variables that already have been initialized in the calling method. Normally, when a method call contains an uninitialized variable as an argument, the compiler generates an error. Preceding a parameter with keyword out creates an ***output parameter***. This indicates to the compiler that the argument will be passed into the called method by reference and that the called method will assign a value to the original variable in the caller. If the method does not assign a value to the output parameter in every possible path of execution, the compiler generates an error. This also prevents the compiler from generating an error message for an uninitialized variable that is passed as an argument to a method. A method can return only one value to its caller via a return statement, but can return many values by specifying multiple output (ref and/or out) parameters.

You can also pass a reference-type variable by reference, which allows you to modify reference-type variable so that it refers to a new object. Passing a reference by reference is a tricky but powerful technique that we discuss in Section 8.8.

The application in Figs. 7.17 and 7.18 uses the ref and out keywords to manipulate integer values. Class ReferenceAndOutputParameters (Fig. 7.17) contains three methods that calculate the square of an integer. Method SquareRef (lines 37–40) multiplies its parameter x by itself and assigns the new value to x. SquareRef's parameter x is declared as ref int, which indicates that the argument passed to this method must be an integer that is passed by reference. Because the argument is passed by reference, the assignment at line 39 modifies the original argument's value in the caller.

```
1   // Fig. 7.17: ReferenceAndOutputParameters.cs
2   // Reference, output and value parameters.
3   using System;
4
5   class ReferenceAndOutputParameters
6   {
7      // call methods with reference, output and value parameters
8      public void DemonstrateReferenceAndOutputParameters()
9      {
10        int y = 5; // initialize y to 5
11        int z; // declares z, but does not initialize it
12
13        // display original values of y and z
14        Console.WriteLine( "Original value of y: {0}", y );
15        Console.WriteLine( "Original value of z: uninitialized\n" );
16
17        // pass y and z by reference
18        SquareRef( ref y ); // must use keyword ref
19        SquareOut( out z ); // must use keyword out
20
21        // display values of y and z after they are modified by
22        // methods SquareRef and SquareOut, respectively
23        Console.WriteLine( "Value of y after SquareRef: {0}", y );
24        Console.WriteLine( "Value of z after SquareOut: {0}\n", z );
25
26        // pass y and z by value
27        Square( y );
28        Square( z );
29
30        // display values of y and z after they are passed to method Square
31        // to demonstrate that arguments passed by value are not modified
32        Console.WriteLine( "Value of y after Square: {0}", y );
```

Fig. 7.17 | Reference, output and value parameters. (Part 1 of 2.)

```
33          Console.WriteLine( "Value of z after Square: {0}", z );
34       } // end method DemonstrateReferenceAndOutputParameters
35
36       // uses reference parameter x to modify caller's variable
37       void SquareRef( ref int x )
38       {
39          x = x * x; // squares value of caller's variable
40       } // end method SquareRef
41
42       // uses output parameter x to assign a value
43       // to an uninitialized variable
44       void SquareOut( out int x )
45       {
46          x = 6; // assigns a value to caller's variable
47          x = x * x; // squares value of caller's variable
48       } // end method SquareOut
49
50       // parameter x receives a copy of the value passed as an argument,
51       // so this method cannot modify the caller's variable
52       void Square( int x )
53       {
54          x = x * x;
55       } // end method Square
56    } // end class ReferenceAndOutputParameters
```

Fig. 7.17 | Reference, output and value parameters. (Part 2 of 2.)

```
1    // Fig. 7.18: ReferenceAndOutputParamtersTest.cs
2    // Application to test class ReferenceAndOutputParameters.
3    class ReferenceAndOutputParamtersTest
4    {
5       public static void Main( string[] args )
6       {
7          ReferenceAndOutputParameters test =
8             new ReferenceAndOutputParameters();
9          test.DemonstrateReferenceAndOutputParameters();
10      } // end Main
11   } // end class ReferenceAndOutputParamtersTest
```

```
Original value of y: 5
Original value of z: uninitialized

Value of y after SquareRef: 25
Value of z after SquareOut: 36

Value of y after Square: 25
Value of z after Square: 36
```

Fig. 7.18 | Application to test class ReferenceAndOutputParameters.

Method SquareOut (lines 44–48) assigns its parameter the value 6 (line 46), then squares that value. SquareOut's parameter is declared as out int, which indicates that the argument passed to this method must be an integer that is passed by reference and that the argument does not need to be initialized in advance.

Method `Square` (lines 52–55) multiplies its parameter x by itself and assigns the new value to x. When this method is called, a copy of the argument is passed to the parameter x. Thus, even though parameter x is modified in the method, the original value in the caller is not modified.

Method `DemonstrateReferenceAndOutputParameters` (lines 8–34) invokes methods `SquareRef`, `SquareOut` and `Square`. This method begins by initializing variable y to 5 and declaring, but not initializing, variable z. Lines 18–19 call methods `SquareRef` and `SquareOut`. Notice that when you pass a variable to a method with a reference parameter, you must precede the argument with the same keyword (`ref` or `out`) that was used to declare the reference parameter. Lines 23–24 display the values of y and z after the calls to `SquareRef` and `SquareOut`. Notice that y has been changed to 25 and z has been set to 36.

Lines 27–28 call method `Square` with y and z as arguments. In this case, both variables are passed by value—only copies of their values are passed to `Square`. As a result, the values of y and z remain 25 and 36, respectively. Lines 32–33 output the values of y and z to show that they were not modified.

Common Programming Error 7.12

The ref and out arguments in a method call must match the parameters specified in the method declaration; otherwise, a compilation error occurs.

Software Engineering Observation 7.6

By default, C# does not allow you to choose whether to pass each argument by value or by reference. Value types are passed by value. Objects are not passed to methods; rather, references to objects are passed to methods. The references themselves are passed by value. When a method receives a reference to an object, the method can manipulate the object directly, but the reference value cannot be changed to refer to a new object. In Section 8.8, you'll see that references also can be passed by reference.

7.15 (Optional) Software Engineering Case Study: Identifying Class Operations in the ATM System

In the Software Engineering Case Study sections at the ends of Chapters 4–6, we performed the first few steps in the object-oriented design of our ATM system. In Chapter 4, we identified the classes that we'll likely need to implement, and we created our first class diagram. In Chapter 5, we described some attributes of our classes. In Chapter 6, we examined our objects' states and modeled their state transitions and activities. In this section, we determine some of the class operations (or behaviors) needed to implement the ATM system.

Identifying Operations

An operation is a service that objects of a class provide to clients of the class. Consider the operations of some real-world objects. A radio's operations include setting its station and volume (typically invoked by a person adjusting the radio's controls). A car's operations include accelerating (invoked by the driver pressing the accelerator pedal), decelerating (invoked by the driver pressing the brake pedal or releasing the gas pedal), turning, and shifting gears. Software objects can offer operations as well—for example, a software graphics object might offer operations for drawing a circle, drawing a line and drawing a square. A spreadsheet software object might offer operations like printing the spreadsheet, totaling the elements in a row or column and graphing information in the spreadsheet as a bar chart or pie chart.

We can derive many of the operations of the classes in our ATM system by examining the verbs and verb phrases in the requirements document. We then relate each of these to particular classes in our system (Fig. 7.19). The verbs and verb phrases in Fig. 7.19 help us determine the operations of our classes.

Class	Verbs and verb phrases
ATM	executes financial transactions
BalanceInquiry	[none in the requirements document]
Withdrawal	[none in the requirements document]
Deposit	[none in the requirements document]
BankDatabase	authenticates a user, retrieves an account balance, credits an account, debits an account
Account	retrieves an account balance, credits a deposit amount to an account, debits a withdrawal amount to an account
Screen	displays a message to the user
Keypad	receives numeric input from the user
CashDispenser	dispenses cash, indicates whether it contains enough cash to satisfy a withdrawal request
DepositSlot	receives a deposit envelope

Fig. 7.19 | Verbs and verb phrases for each class in the ATM system.

Modeling Operations

To identify operations, we examine the verb phrases listed for each class in Fig. 7.19. The "executes financial transactions" phrase associated with class ATM implies that class ATM instructs transactions to execute. Therefore, classes BalanceInquiry, Withdrawal and Deposit each need an operation to provide this service to the ATM. We place this operation (which we have named Execute) in the third compartment of the three transaction classes in the updated class diagram of Fig. 7.20. During an ATM session, the ATM object will invoke the Execute operation of each transaction object to tell it to execute.

The UML represents operations (which are implemented as methods in C#) by listing the operation name, followed by a comma-separated list of parameters in parentheses, a colon and the return type:

operationName(parameter1, parameter2, ..., parameterN) : returnType

Each parameter in the comma-separated parameter list consists of a parameter name, followed by a colon and the parameter type:

parameterName : parameterType

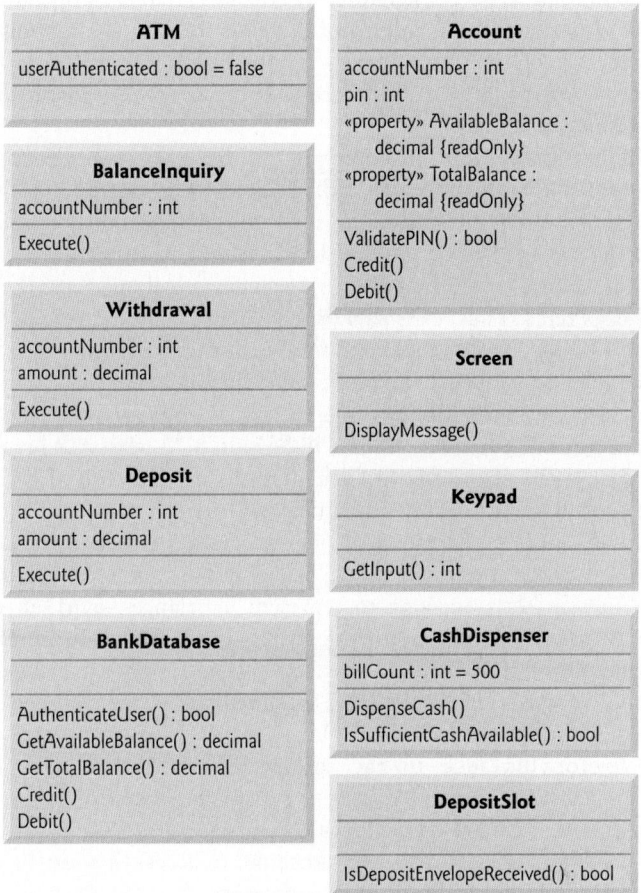

Fig. 7.20 | Classes in the ATM system with attributes and operations.

For the moment, we do not list the parameters of our operations—we'll identify and model the parameters of some of the operations shortly. For some of the operations, we do not yet know the return types, so we also omit them from the diagram. These omissions are perfectly normal at this point. As our design and implementation proceed, we'll add the remaining return types.

Operations of Class *BankDatabase* and Class *Account*

Figure 7.19 lists the phrase "authenticates a user" next to class BankDatabase—the database is the object that contains the account information necessary to determine whether the account number and PIN entered by a user match those of an account at the bank. Therefore, class BankDatabase needs an operation that provides an authentication service to the ATM. We place the operation AuthenticateUser in the third compartment of class BankDatabase (Fig. 7.20). However, an object of class Account, not class BankDatabase, stores the account number and PIN that must be accessed to authenticate a user, so class Account must provide a service to validate a PIN obtained through user input against a

PIN stored in an Account object. Therefore, we add a ValidatePIN operation to class Account. Note that we specify a return type of bool for the AuthenticateUser and ValidatePIN operations. Each operation returns a value indicating either that the operation was successful in performing its task (i.e., a return value of true) or that it was not successful (i.e., a return value of false).

Figure 7.19 lists several additional verb phrases for class BankDatabase: "retrieves an account balance," "credits an account" and "debits an account." Like "authenticates a user," these remaining phrases refer to services that the database must provide to the ATM, because the database holds all the account data used to authenticate a user and perform ATM transactions. However, objects of class Account actually perform the operations to which these phrases refer. Thus, class BankDatabase and class Account both need operations that correspond to each of these phrases. Recall from Section 4.12 that, because a bank account contains sensitive information, we do not allow the ATM to access accounts directly. The database acts as an intermediary between the ATM and the account data, preventing unauthorized access. As we'll see in Section 8.14, class ATM invokes the operations of class BankDatabase, each of which in turn invokes corresponding operations (which are get accessors of read-only properties) in class Account.

The phrase "retrieves an account balance" suggests that classes BankDatabase and Account each need an operation that gets the balance. However, recall that Fig. 5.16 specified two attributes in class Account to represent a balance—availableBalance and totalBalance. A balance inquiry requires access to both balance attributes so that it can display them to the user, but a withdrawal needs to check only the value of availableBalance. To allow objects in the system to obtain these balance attributes individually from a specific Account object in the BankDatabase, we add operations GetAvailableBalance and GetTotalBalance to the third compartment of class BankDatabase (Fig. 7.20). We specify a return type of decimal for each of these operations, because the balances that they retrieve are of type decimal.

Once the BankDatabase knows which Account to access, it must be able to obtain each balance attribute individually from that Account. For this purpose, we could add operations GetAvailableBalance and GetTotalBalance to the third compartment of class Account (Fig. 7.20). However, in C#, simple operations such as getting the value of an attribute are typically performed by a property's get accessor (at least when that particular class "owns" the underlying attribute). This design is for a C# application, so, rather than modeling operations GetAvailableBalance and GetTotalBalance, we model decimal properties AvailableBalance and TotalBalance in class Account. Properties are placed in the second compartment of a class diagram. These properties replace the availableBalance and totalBalance attributes that we modeled for class Account in Fig. 5.16. Recall from Chapter 4 that a property's accessors are implied—thus, they are not modeled in a class diagram. Figure 7.19 does not mention the need to set the balances, so Fig. 7.20 shows properties AvailableBalance and TotalBalance as read-only properties (i.e., they have only get accessors). To indicate a read-only property in the UML, we follow the property's type with "{readOnly}."

You may be wondering why we modeled AvailableBalance and TotalBalance *properties* in class Account, but modeled GetAvailableBalance and GetTotalBalance *operations* in class BankDatabase. Since there can be many Account objects in the BankDatabase, the ATM must specify which Account to access when invoking BankDatabase operations GetAvailableBalance and GetTotalBalance. The ATM does this by passing an account-number argument to each BankDatabase operation. The get accessors of the properties you've seen in C# code cannot receive arguments. Thus, we modeled GetAvailableBalance and GetTotalBalance as operations in class BankDatabase so that we could specify parameters to which the ATM can pass arguments. Also, the underlying balance attributes are not owned by the BankDatabase, so get accessors are not appropriate here. We discuss the parameters for the BankDatabase operations shortly.

The phrases "credits an account" and "debits from an account" indicate that classes BankDatabase and Account must perform operations to update an account during deposits and withdrawals, respectively. We therefore assign Credit and Debit operations to classes BankDatabase and Account. You may recall that crediting an account (as in a deposit) adds an amount only to the Account's total balance. Debiting an account (as in a withdrawal), on the other hand, subtracts the amount from both the total and available balances. We hide these implementation details inside class Account. This is a good example of encapsulation and information hiding.

If this were a real ATM system, classes BankDatabase and Account would also provide a set of operations to allow another banking system to update a user's account balance after either confirming or rejecting all or part of a deposit. Operation ConfirmDepositAmount, for example, would add an amount to the Account's available balance, thus making deposited funds available for withdrawal. Operation RejectDepositAmount would subtract an amount from the Account's total balance to indicate that a specified amount, which had recently been deposited through the ATM and added to the Account's total balance, was invalidated (or checks may have "bounced"). The bank would invoke operation Reject-DepositAmount after determining either that the user failed to include the correct amount of cash or that any checks did not clear (i.e., they "bounced"). While adding these operations would make our system more complete, we do not include them in our class diagrams or implementation because they are beyond the scope of the case study.

Operations of Class *Screen*

Class Screen "displays a message to the user" at various times in an ATM session. All visual output occurs through the screen of the ATM. The requirements document describes many types of messages (e.g., a welcome message, an error message, a thank-you message) that the screen displays to the user. The requirements document also indicates that the screen displays prompts and menus to the user. However, a prompt is really just a message describing what the user should input next, and a menu is essentially a type of prompt consisting of a series of messages (i.e., menu options) displayed consecutively. Therefore, rather than provide class Screen with an individual operation to display each type of message, prompt and menu, we simply create one operation that can display any message specified by a parameter. We place this operation (DisplayMessage) in the third compartment of class Screen in our class diagram (Fig. 7.20). Note that we do not worry about the parameter of this operation at this time—we model the parameter momentarily.

Operations of Class *Keypad*

From the phrase "receives numeric input from the user" listed by class Keypad in Fig. 7.19, we conclude that class Keypad should perform a GetInput operation. Because the ATM's keypad, unlike a computer keyboard, contains only the numbers 0–9, we specify that this operation returns an integer value. Recall from the requirements document that in different situations, the user may be required to enter a different type of number (e.g., an account number, a PIN, the number of a menu option, a deposit amount as a number of cents). Class Keypad simply obtains a numeric value for a client of the class—it does not determine whether the value meets any specific criteria. Any class that uses this operation must verify that the user entered appropriate numbers and, if not, display error messages via class Screen. [*Note:* When we implement the system, we simulate the ATM's keypad with a computer keyboard, and for simplicity, we assume that the user does not enter non-numeric input using keys on the computer keyboard that do not appear on the ATM's keypad. In Chapter 18, you'll see how to examine inputs to determine if they are of particular types.]

Operations of Class `CashDispenser` and Class `DepositSlot`

Figure 7.19 lists "dispenses cash" for class CashDispenser. Therefore, we create operation DispenseCash and list it under class CashDispenser in Fig. 7.20. Class CashDispenser also "indicates whether it contains enough cash to satisfy a withdrawal request." Thus, we include IsSufficientCashAvailable, an operation that returns a value of type bool, in class CashDispenser. Figure 7.19 also lists "receives a deposit envelope" for class Deposit-Slot. The deposit slot must indicate whether it received an envelope, so we place the operation IsDepositEnvelopeReceived, which returns a bool value, in the third compartment of class DepositSlot. [*Note:* A real hardware deposit slot would most likely send the ATM a signal to indicate that an envelope was received. We simulate this behavior, however, with an operation in class DepositSlot that class ATM can invoke to find out whether the deposit slot received an envelope.]

Operations of Class `ATM`

We do not list any operations for class ATM at this time. We're not yet aware of any services that class ATM provides to other classes in the system. When we implement the system in C# (Appendix D, ATM Case Study Code), however, operations of this class, and additional operations of the other classes in the system, may become apparent.

Identifying and Modeling Operation Parameters

So far, we have not been concerned with the parameters of our operations—we have attempted to gain only a basic understanding of the operations of each class. Let's now take a closer look at some operation parameters. We identify an operation's parameters by examining what data the operation requires to perform its assigned task.

Consider the AuthenticateUser operation of class BankDatabase. To authenticate a user, this operation must know the account number and PIN supplied by the user. Thus we specify that operation AuthenticateUser takes int parameters userAccountNumber and userPIN, which the operation must compare to the account number and PIN of an Account object in the database. We prefix these parameter names with user to avoid confusion between the operation's parameter names and the attribute names that belong to class Account. We list these parameters in the class diagram in Fig. 7.21, which models only class BankDatabase. [*Note:* It is perfectly normal to model only one class in a class diagram. In this case, we're most concerned with examining the parameters of this particular class, so we omit the other classes. In class diagrams later in the case study, parameters are no longer the focus of our attention, so we omit the parameters to save space. Remember, however, that the operations listed in these diagrams still have parameters.]

BankDatabase
AuthenticateUser(userAccountNumber : int, userPIN : int) : bool GetAvailableBalance(userAccountNumber : int) : decimal GetTotalBalance(userAccountNumber : int) : decimal Credit(userAccountNumber : int, amount : decimal) Debit(userAccountNumber : int, amount : decimal)

Fig. 7.21 | Class BankDatabase with operation parameters.

Recall that the UML models each parameter in an operation's comma-separated parameter list by listing the parameter name, followed by a colon and the parameter type. Figure 7.21 thus specifies, for example, that operation AuthenticateUser takes two parameters—userAccountNumber and userPIN, both of type int.

Class BankDatabase operations GetAvailableBalance, GetTotalBalance, Credit and Debit also each require a userAccountNumber parameter to identify the account to which the database must apply the operations, so we include these parameters in the class diagram. In addition, operations Credit and Debit each require a decimal parameter amount to specify the amount of money to be credited or debited, respectively.

The class diagram in Fig. 7.22 models the parameters of class Account's operations. Operation ValidatePIN requires only a userPIN parameter, which contains the user-specified PIN to be compared with the PIN associated with the account. Like their counterparts in class BankDatabase, operations Credit and Debit in class Account each require a decimal parameter amount that indicates the amount of money involved in the operation. Note that class Account's operations do not require an account-number parameter—each can be invoked only on the Account object in which they are executing, so including a parameter to specify an Account is unnecessary.

Figure 7.23 models class Screen with a parameter for operation DisplayMessage. This operation requires only string parameter message, which is the text to be displayed.

The class diagram in Fig. 7.24 specifies that operation DispenseCash of class CashDispenser takes decimal parameter amount to indicate the amount of cash (in dollars) to be dispensed. Operation IsSufficientCashAvailable also takes decimal parameter amount to indicate the amount of cash in question.

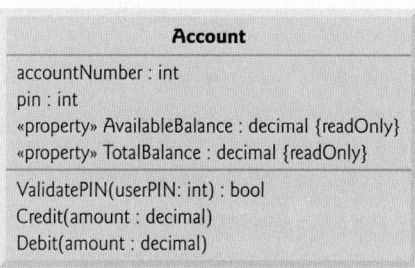

Fig. 7.22 | Class Account with operation parameters.

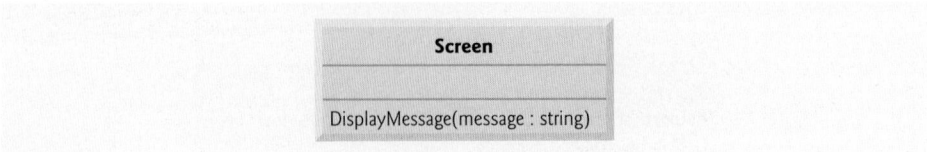

Fig. 7.23 | Class Screen with an operation parameter.

CashDispenser
billCount : int = 500
DispenseCash(amount : decimal) IsSufficientCashAvailable(amount : decimal) : bool

Fig. 7.24 | Class CashDispenser with operation parameters.

Note that we do not discuss parameters for operation Execute of classes Balance-Inquiry, Withdrawal and Deposit, operation GetInput of class Keypad and operation IsDepositEnvelopeReceived of class DepositSlot. At this point in our design process, we cannot determine whether these operations require additional data to perform their tasks, so we leave their parameter lists empty. As we progress through the case study, we may decide to add parameters to these operations.

In this section, we have determined many of the operations performed by the classes in the ATM system. We have identified the parameters and return types of some of the operations. As we continue our design process, the number of operations belonging to each class may vary—we might find that new operations are needed or that some current operations are unnecessary—and we might determine that some of our class operations need additional parameters and different return types. Again, all of this is perfectly normal.

Software Engineering Case Study Self-Review Exercises

7.1 Which of the following is not a behavior?
a) reading data from a file
b) displaying output
c) text output
d) obtaining input from the user

7.2 If you were to add to the ATM system an operation that returns the amount attribute of class Withdrawal, how and where would you specify this operation in the class diagram of Fig. 7.20?

7.3 Describe the meaning of the following operation listing that might appear in a class diagram for an object-oriented design of a calculator:

```
Add( x : int, y : int ) : int
```

Answers to Software Engineering Case Study Self-Review Exercises

7.1 c.

7.2   An operation that retrieves the amount attribute of class Withdrawal would typically be implemented as a get accessor of a property of class Withdrawal. The following would replace attribute amount in the attribute (i.e., second) compartment of class Withdrawal:

```
«property» Amount : decimal {readOnly}
```

7.3   This is an operation named Add that takes int parameters x and y and returns an int value. This operation would most likely sum its parameters x and y and return the result.

7.16 Wrap-Up

In this chapter, we discussed the difference between non-static and static methods, and we showed how to call static methods by preceding the method name with the name of the class in which it appears and the member access (.) operator. You saw that the Math class in the .NET Framework Class Library provides many static methods to perform mathematical calculations. We presented several commonly used .NET Framework Class Library namespaces. You learned how to use operator + to perform string concatenations. You also learned how to declare constant values in two ways—with the const keyword and with enum types. We demonstrated simulation techniques and used class Random to generate sets of random numbers. We discussed the scope of fields and local variables in a class. You saw how to overload methods in a class by providing methods with the same name but different signatures. We discussed how recursive methods call themselves, breaking larger problems into smaller subproblems until eventually the original problem is solved. You learned the differences between value types and reference types with respect to how they are passed to methods, and how to use the ref and out keywords to pass arguments by reference.

In Chapter 8, you'll learn how to maintain lists and tables of data in arrays. You'll see a more elegant implementation of the application that rolls a die 6000 times and two enhanced versions of our GradeBook case study. You'll also learn how to access an application's command-line arguments that are passed to method Main when a console application begins execution.

8

Arrays

OBJECTIVES

In this chapter you'll learn:

- To use arrays to store data in and retrieve data from lists and tables of values.

- To declare arrays, initialize arrays and refer to individual elements of arrays.

- To use the `foreach` statement to iterate through arrays.

- To use implicitly typed local variables.

- To pass arrays to methods.

- To declare and manipulate multidimensional arrays.

- To write methods that use variable-length argument lists.

- To read command-line arguments into an application.

Outline

8.1 Introduction
8.2 Arrays
8.3 Declaring and Creating Arrays
8.4 Examples Using Arrays
8.5 Case Study: Card Shuffling and Dealing Simulation
8.6 foreach Statement
8.7 Passing Arrays and Array Elements to Methods
8.8 Passing Arrays by Value and by Reference
8.9 Case Study: Class GradeBook Using an Array to Store Grades
8.10 Multidimensional Arrays
8.11 Case Study: Class GradeBook Using a Rectangular Array
8.12 Variable-Length Argument Lists
8.13 Using Command-Line Arguments
8.14 (Optional) Software Engineering Case Study: Collaboration Among Objects in the ATM System
8.15 Wrap-Up

8.1 Introduction

This chapter introduces the important topic of *data structures*—collections of related data items. *Arrays* are data structures consisting of related data items of the same type. Arrays are fixed-length entities—they remain the same length once they are created, although an array variable may be reassigned such that it refers to a new array of a different length.

After discussing how arrays are declared, created and initialized, we present a series of examples that demonstrate several common array manipulations. We also present a case study that uses arrays to simulate shuffling and dealing playing cards for use in card-game applications. The chapter demonstrates C#'s last structured control statement—the foreach repetition statement—which provides a concise notation for accessing the data in arrays (and other data structures, as you'll see in Chapter 9 and later in the book). Two sections of the chapter enhance the GradeBook case study from Chapters 4–6. In particular, we use arrays to enable the class to store a set of grades and analyze student grades from multiple exams.

8.2 Arrays

An array is a group of variables (called *elements*) containing values that all have the same type. Recall that types are divided into two categories—value types and reference types. Arrays are reference types. As you'll see, what we typically think of as an array is actually a reference to an array object. The elements of an array can be either value types or reference types (including other arrays, as we'll see in Section 8.10). To refer to a particular element in an array, we specify the name of the reference to the array and the position number of the element in the array. The position number of the element is called the element's *index*.

Figure 8.1 shows a logical representation of an integer array called c. This array contains 12 elements. An application refers to any one of these elements with an *array-access expression* that includes the name of the array, followed by the index of the particular ele-

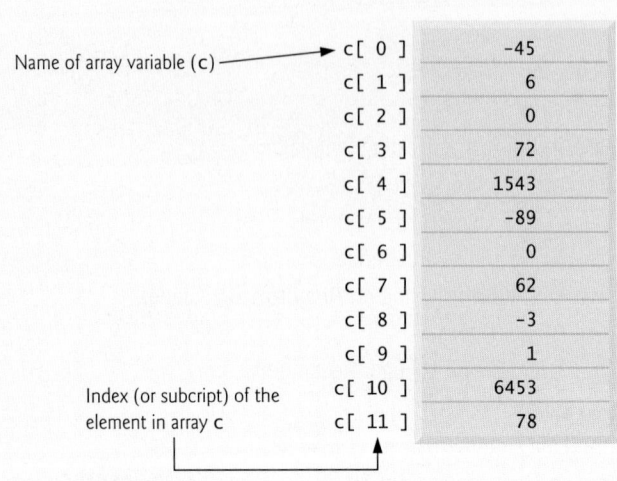

Name of array variable (c)

c[0]	-45
c[1]	6
c[2]	0
c[3]	72
c[4]	1543
c[5]	-89
c[6]	0
c[7]	62
c[8]	-3
c[9]	1
c[10]	6453
c[11]	78

Index (or subcript) of the
element in array c

Fig. 8.1 | A 12-element array.

ment in *square brackets* ([]). The first element in every array has *index zero* and is sometimes called the *zeroth element.* Thus, the elements of array c are c[0], c[1], c[2] and so on. The highest index in array c is 11, which is one less than the number of elements in the array, because indices begin at 0. Array names follow the same conventions as other variable names.

An index must be a nonnegative integer and can be an expression. For example, if we assume that variable a is 5 and variable b is 6, then the statement

```
c[ a + b ] += 2;
```

adds 2 to array element c[11]. Note that an indexed array name is an array-access expression. Such expressions can be used on the left side of an assignment to place a new value into an array element. The array index must be a value of type int, uint, long or ulong, or a value of a type that can be implicitly promoted to one of these types.

Let's examine array c in Fig. 8.1 more closely. The *name* of the variable that references the array is c. Every array instance knows its own length and provides access to this information with the Length property. For example, the expression c.Length uses array c's Length property to determine the length of the array. Note that the Length property of an array cannot be changed, because it does not provide a set accessor. The array's 12 elements are referred to as c[0], c[1], c[2], ..., c[11]. It is an error to refer to elements outside of this range, such as c[-1] or c[12]. The value of c[0] is -45, the value of c[1] is 6, the value of c[2] is 0, the value of c[7] is 62 and the value of c[11] is 78. To calculate the sum of the values contained in the first three elements of array c and store the result in variable sum, we would write

```
sum = c[ 0 ] + c[ 1 ] + c[ 2 ];
```

To divide the value of c[6] by 2 and assign the result to the variable x, we would write

```
x = c[ 6 ] / 2;
```

8.3 Declaring and Creating Arrays

Arrays occupy space in memory. Since they are objects, they are typically created with keyword new. To create an array object, you specify the type and the number of array elements as part of an *array-creation expression* that uses keyword new. Such an expression returns a reference that can be stored in an array variable. The following declaration and array-creation expression create an array object containing 12 int elements and store the array's reference in variable c:

```
int[] c = new int[ 12 ];
```

This expression can be used to create the array shown in Fig. 8.1 (but not the initial values in the array—we'll show how to initialize the elements of an array momentarily). This task also can be performed as follows:

```
int[] c; // declare the array variable
c = new int[ 12 ]; // create the array; assign to array variable
```

In the declaration, the square brackets following the type int indicate that c is a variable that will refer to an array of ints (i.e., c will store a reference to an array object). In the assignment statement, the array variable c receives the reference to a new array object of 12 int elements. Note that the number of elements can also be specified as an expression that is calculated at execution time. When an array is created, each element of the array receives a default value—0 for the numeric simple-type elements, false for bool elements and null for references. As we'll soon see, we can provide specific, nondefault initial element values when we create an array.

Common Programming Error 8.1

In the declaration of a variable that will refer to an array, specifying the number of elements in the square brackets (e.g., int[12] c;) is a syntax error.

An application can create several arrays in a single declaration. The following statement reserves 100 elements for string array b and 27 elements for string array x:

```
string[] b = new string[ 100 ], x = new string[ 27 ];
```

In this statement, string[] applies to each variable. For readability, we prefer to split the preceding statement into two statements, as in:

```
string[] b = new string[ 100 ]; // create string array b
string[] x = new string[ 27 ]; // create string array x
```

Good Programming Practice 8.1

For readability, declare only one variable per declaration. Keep each declaration on a separate line and include a comment describing the variable being declared.

An application can declare variables that will refer to arrays of value-type elements or reference-type elements. For example, every element of an int array is an int value, and every element of a string array is a reference to a string object.

Resizing an Array

Though arrays are fixed-length entities, you can resize an array using the static Array method Resize, which takes two arguments—the array to be resized and the new length.

This method creates a new array with the specified length, copies the contents of the old array into the new array and sets the variable it receives as its first argument to reference the new array. For example, consider the following statements:

```
int[] newArray = new int[ 5 ];
Array.Resize( ref newArray, 10 );
```

The variable newArray initially refers to a five-element array. The resize method sets newArray to refer to a new 10-element array. If the new array is smaller than the old array, any content that cannot fit into the new array is truncated.

8.4 Examples Using Arrays

This section presents several examples that demonstrate declaring arrays, creating arrays, initializing arrays and manipulating array elements.

Creating and Initializing an Array

The application of Fig. 8.2 uses keyword new to create an array of 10 int elements that are initially 0 (the default for int variables).

```
 1  // Fig. 8.2: InitArray.cs
 2  // Creating an array.
 3  using System;
 4
 5  public class InitArray
 6  {
 7     public static void Main( string[] args )
 8     {
 9        int[] array; // declare array named array
10
11        // create the space for array and initialize to default zeros
12        array = new int[ 10 ]; // 10 int elements
13
14        Console.WriteLine( "{0}{1,8}", "Index", "Value" ); // headings
15
16        // output each array element's value
17        for ( int counter = 0; counter < array.Length; counter++ )
18           Console.WriteLine( "{0,5}{1,8}", counter, array[ counter ] );
19     } // end Main
20  } // end class InitArray
```

```
Index   Value
    0       0
    1       0
    2       0
    3       0
    4       0
    5       0
    6       0
    7       0
    8       0
    9       0
```

Fig. 8.2 | Creating an array.

Line 9 declares array—a variable capable of referring to an array of int elements. Line 12 creates the 10-element array object and assigns its reference to variable array. Line 14 outputs the column headings. The first column contains the index (0–9) of each array element, and the second column contains the default value (0) of each array element and has a field width of 8.

The for statement in lines 17–18 outputs the index number (represented by counter) and the value (represented by array[counter]) of each array element. Note that the loop-control variable counter is initially 0—index values start at 0, so using zero-based counting allows the loop to access every element of the array. The for statement's loop-continuation condition uses the property array.Length (line 17) to obtain the length of the array. In this example, the length of the array is 10, so the loop continues executing as long as the value of control variable counter is less than 10. The highest index value of a 10-element array is 9, so using the less-than operator in the loop-continuation condition guarantees that the loop does not attempt to access an element beyond the end of the array (i.e., during the final iteration of the loop, counter is 9). We'll soon see what happens when such an out-of-range index is encountered at execution time.

Using an Array Initializer

An application can create an array and initialize its elements with an *array initializer*, which is a comma-separated list of expressions (called an *initializer list*) enclosed in braces. In this case, the array length is determined by the number of elements in the initializer list. For example, the declaration

```
int[] n = { 10, 20, 30, 40, 50 };
```

creates a five-element array with index values 0, 1, 2, 3 and 4. Element n[0] is initialized to 10, n[1] is initialized to 20 and so on. This statement does not require new to create the array object. When the compiler encounters an array initializer list, the compiler counts the number of initializers in the list to determine the size of the array, then sets up the appropriate new operation "behind the scenes."

The application in Fig. 8.3 initializes an integer array with 10 values (line 10) and displays the array in tabular format. The code for displaying the array elements (lines 15–16) is identical to that in Fig. 8.2 (lines 17–18).

```
1   // Fig. 8.3: InitArray.cs
2   // Initializing the elements of an array with an array initializer.
3   using System;
4
5   public class InitArray
6   {
7      public static void Main( string[] args )
8      {
9         // initializer list specifies the value for each element
10        int[] array = { 32, 27, 64, 18, 95, 14, 90, 70, 60, 37 };
11
12        Console.WriteLine( "{0}{1,8}", "Index", "Value" ); // headings
13
```

Fig. 8.3 | Initializing the elements of an array with an array initializer. (Part 1 of 2.)

```
14          // output each array element's value
15          for ( int counter = 0; counter < array.Length; counter++ )
16              Console.WriteLine( "{0,5}{1,8}", counter, array[ counter ] );
17      } // end Main
18  } // end class InitArray
```

```
Index   Value
   0      32
   1      27
   2      64
   3      18
   4      95
   5      14
   6      90
   7      70
   8      60
   9      37
```

Fig. 8.3 | Initializing the elements of an array with an array initializer. (Part 2 of 2.)

Calculating a Value to Store in Each Array Element

Some applications calculate the value to be stored in each array element. The application in Fig. 8.4 creates a 10-element array and assigns to each element one of the even integers from 2 to 20 (2, 4, 6, ..., 20). Then the application displays the array in tabular format. The for statement at lines 13–14 calculates an array element's value by multiplying the current value of the for loop's control variable counter by 2, then adding 2.

```
1   // Fig. 8.4: InitArray.cs
2   // Calculating values to be placed into the elements of an array.
3   using System;
4
5   public class InitArray
6   {
7       public static void Main( string[] args )
8       {
9           const int ARRAY_LENGTH = 10; // create a named constant
10          int[] array = new int[ ARRAY_LENGTH ]; // create array
11
12          // calculate value for each array element
13          for ( int counter = 0; counter < array.Length; counter++ )
14              array[ counter ] = 2 + 2 * counter;
15
16          Console.WriteLine( "{0}{1,8}", "Index", "Value" ); // headings
17
18          // output each array element's value
19          for ( int counter = 0; counter < array.Length; counter++ )
20              Console.WriteLine( "{0,5}{1,8}", counter, array[ counter ] );
21      } // end Main
22  } // end class InitArray
```

Fig. 8.4 | Calculating values to be placed into the elements of an array. (Part 1 of 2.)

```
Index   Value
    0       2
    1       4
    2       6
    3       8
    4      10
    5      12
    6      14
    7      16
    8      18
    9      20
```

Fig. 8.4 | Calculating values to be placed into the elements of an array. (Part 2 of 2.)

Line 9 uses the modifier const to declare the constant ARRAY_LENGTH, whose value is 10. Constants must be initialized when they are declared and cannot be modified thereafter. Note that we declare constants with all capital letters by convention to make them stand out in the code.

Good Programming Practice 8.2

*Constants also are called **named constants**. Applications using constants often are more readable than those that use literal values (e.g., 10)—a named constant such as ARRAY_LENGTH clearly indicates its purpose, whereas a literal value could have different meanings based on the context in which it is used. Another advantage to using named constants is that if the value of the constant must be changed, the change is necessary only in the declaration, thus reducing the cost of maintaining the code.*

Common Programming Error 8.2

Assigning a value to a named constant after it has been initialized is a compilation error.

Common Programming Error 8.3

Attempting to declare a named constant without initializing it is a compilation error.

Summing the Elements of an Array

Often, the elements of an array represent a series of values to be used in a calculation. For example, if the elements of an array represent exam grades, an instructor may wish to total the elements and use that total to calculate the class average for the exam. The GradeBook examples later in the chapter (Fig. 8.15 and Fig. 8.20) use this technique.

The application in Fig. 8.5 sums the values contained in a 10-element integer array. The application creates and initializes the array at line 9. The for statement performs the calculations. [*Note:* The values supplied as array initializers are often read into an application, rather than specified in an initializer list. For example, an application could input the values from a user or from a file on disk (as discussed in Chapter 19, Files and Streams). Reading the data into an application makes the application more reusable, because it can be used with different sets of data.]

```
 1   // Fig. 8.5: SumArray.cs
 2   // Computing the sum of the elements of an array.
 3   using System;
 4
 5   public class SumArray
 6   {
 7      public static void Main( string[] args )
 8      {
 9         int[] array = { 87, 68, 94, 100, 83, 78, 85, 91, 76, 87 };
10         int total = 0;
11
12         // add each element's value to total
13         for ( int counter = 0; counter < array.Length; counter++ )
14            total += array[ counter ];
15
16         Console.WriteLine( "Total of array elements: {0}", total );
17      } // end Main
18   } // end class SumArray
```

```
Total of array elements: 849
```

Fig. 8.5 | Computing the sum of the elements of an array.

Using Bar Charts to Display Array Data Graphically

Many applications present data to users in a graphical manner. For example, numeric values are often displayed as bars in a bar chart. In such a chart, longer bars represent proportionally larger numeric values. One simple way to display numeric data graphically is with a bar chart that shows each numeric value as a bar of asterisks (*).

Instructors often like to examine the distribution of grades on an exam. An instructor might graph the number of grades in each of several categories to visualize the grade distribution for the exam. Suppose the grades on an exam were 87, 68, 94, 100, 83, 78, 85, 91, 76 and 87. Note that there was one grade of 100, two grades in the 90s, four grades in the 80s, two grades in the 70s, one grade in the 60s and no grades below 60. Our next application (Fig. 8.6) stores this grade distribution data in an array of 11 elements, each corresponding to a category of grades. For example, array[0] indicates the number of grades in the range 0–9, array[7] the number of grades in the range 70–79 and array[10] the number of 100 grades. The two versions of class GradeBook later in the chapter (Figs. 8.15 and 8.20) contain code that calculates these grade frequencies based on a set of grades. For now, we manually create array by examining the set of grades and initializing the elements of array to the number of values in each range (line 9).

The application reads the numbers from the array and graphs the information as a bar chart. Each grade range is followed by a bar of asterisks indicating the number of grades in that range. To label each bar, lines 17–21 output a grade range (e.g., "70-79: ") based on the current value of counter. When counter is 10, line 18 outputs " 100: " to align the colon with the other bar labels. When counter is not 10, line 20 uses the format items {0:D2} and {1:D2} to output the label of the grade range. The format specifier D indicates that the value should be formatted as an integer, and the number after the D indicates how many digits this formatted integer must contain. The 2 indicates that values with fewer than two digits should begin with a leading 0.

```
1   // Fig. 8.6: BarChart.cs
2   // Bar chart displaying application.
3   using System;
4
5   public class BarChart
6   {
7      public static void Main( string[] args )
8      {
9         int[] array = { 0, 0, 0, 0, 0, 0, 1, 2, 4, 2, 1 };
10
11        Console.WriteLine( "Grade distribution:" );
12
13        // for each array element, output a bar of the chart
14        for ( int counter = 0; counter < array.Length; counter++ )
15        {
16           // output bar labels ( "00-09: ", ..., "90-99: ", "100: " )
17           if ( counter == 10 )
18              Console.Write( "  100: " );
19           else
20              Console.Write( "{0:D2}-{1:D2}: ",
21                 counter * 10, counter * 10 + 9 );
22
23           // display bar of asterisks
24           for ( int stars = 0; stars < array[ counter ]; stars++ )
25              Console.Write( "*" );
26
27           Console.WriteLine(); // start a new line of output
28        } // end outer for
29     } // end Main
30  } // end class BarChart
```

```
Grade distribution:
00-09:
10-19:
20-29:
30-39:
40-49:
50-59:
60-69: *
70-79: **
80-89: ****
90-99: **
  100: *
```

Fig. 8.6 | Bar chart displaying application.

The nested for statement (lines 24–25) outputs the bars. Note the loop-continuation condition at line 24 (stars < array[counter]). Each time the application reaches the inner for, the loop counts from 0 up to one less than array[counter], thus using a value in array to determine the number of asterisks to display. In this example, array[0]– array[5] contain 0s because no students received a grade below 60. Thus, the application displays no asterisks next to the first six grade ranges.

Using the Elements of an Array as Counters

Sometimes, applications use counter variables to summarize data, such as the results of a survey. In Fig. 7.7, we used separate counters in our die-rolling application to track the number of times each face of a six-sided die appeared as the application rolled the die 6000 times. An array version of the application in Fig. 7.7 is shown in Fig. 8.7.

Figure 8.7 uses array frequency (line 10) to count the occurrences of each side of the die. *The single statement in line 14 of this application replaces lines 23–46 of Fig. 7.7.* Line 14 uses the random value to determine which frequency element to increment during each iteration of the loop. The calculation in line 14 produces random numbers from 1 to 6, so array frequency must be large enough to store six counters. We use a seven-element array in which we ignore frequency[0]—it is more logical to have the face value 1 increment frequency[1] than frequency[0]. Thus, each face value is used as an index for array frequency. We also replaced lines 50–52 of Fig. 7.7 by looping through array frequency to output the results (Fig. 8.7, lines 19–20).

```
1   // Fig. 8.7: RollDie.cs
2   // Roll a six-sided die 6000 times.
3   using System;
4
5   public class RollDie
6   {
7      public static void Main( string[] args )
8      {
9         Random randomNumbers = new Random(); // random-number generator
10        int[] frequency = new int[ 7 ]; // array of frequency counters
11
12        // roll die 6000 times; use die value as frequency index
13        for ( int roll = 1; roll <= 6000; roll++ )
14           ++frequency[ randomNumbers.Next( 1, 7 ) ];
15
16        Console.WriteLine( "{0}{1,10}", "Face", "Frequency" );
17
18        // output each array element's value
19        for ( int face = 1; face < frequency.Length; face++ )
20           Console.WriteLine( "{0,4}{1,10}", face, frequency[ face ] );
21     } // end Main
22  } // end class RollDie
```

```
Face Frequency
   1      956
   2      981
   3     1001
   4     1030
   5     1035
   6      997
```

Fig. 8.7 | Roll a six-sided die 6000 times.

Using Arrays to Analyze Survey Results

Our next example uses arrays to summarize the results of data collected in a survey:

Forty students were asked to rate the quality of the food in the student cafeteria on a scale of 1 to 10 (where 1 means awful and 10 means excellent). Place the 40 responses in an integer array and summarize the results of the poll.

This is a typical array-processing application (see Fig. 8.8). We wish to summarize the number of responses of each type (i.e., 1 through 10). The array responses (lines 10–12) is a 40-element int array of the students' responses to the survey. We use 11-element array frequency (line 13) to count the number of occurrences of each response. Each element of the array is used as a counter for one of the survey responses and is initialized to 0 by default. As in Fig. 8.7, we ignore frequency[0].

The for loop at lines 17–18 takes the responses one at a time from array responses and increments one of the 10 counters in the frequency array (frequency[1] to

```
1   // Fig. 8.8: StudentPoll.cs
2   // Poll analysis application.
3   using System;
4
5   public class StudentPoll
6   {
7      public static void Main( string[] args )
8      {
9         // array of survey responses
10        int[] responses = { 1, 2, 6, 4, 8, 5, 9, 7, 8, 10, 1, 6, 3, 8, 6,
11           10, 3, 8, 2, 7, 6, 5, 7, 6, 8, 6, 7, 5, 6, 6, 5, 6, 7, 5, 6,
12           4, 8, 6, 8, 10 };
13        int[] frequency = new int[ 11 ]; // array of frequency counters
14
15        // for each answer, select responses element and use that value
16        // as frequency index to determine element to increment
17        for ( int answer = 0; answer < responses.Length; answer++ )
18           ++frequency[ responses[ answer ] ];
19
20        Console.WriteLine( "{0}{1,10}", "Rating", "Frequency" );
21
22        // output each array element's value
23        for ( int rating = 1; rating < frequency.Length; rating++ )
24           Console.WriteLine( "{0,6}{1,10}", rating, frequency[ rating ] );
25     } // end Main
26  } // end class StudentPoll
```

```
Rating Frequency
    1       2
    2       2
    3       2
    4       2
    5       5
    6      11
    7       5
    8       7
    9       1
   10       3
```

Fig. 8.8 | Poll analysis application.

frequency[10]). The key statement in the loop is line 18, which increments the appropriate frequency counter, depending on the value of responses[answer].

Let's consider several iterations of the for loop. When control variable answer is 0, the value of responses[answer] is the value of responses[0] (i.e., 1 in line 10), so the application interprets ++frequency[responses[answer]] as

```
++frequency[ 1 ]
```

which increments the value in frequency array element 1. To evaluate the expression, start with the value in the innermost set of square brackets, answer. Once you know answer's value (which is the value of the loop-control variable in line 17), plug it into the expression and evaluate the next outer set of square brackets—i.e., responses[answer], which is a value selected from the responses array in lines 10–12. Then use the resulting value as the index for the frequency array to specify which counter to increment (line 18).

When answer is 1, responses[answer] is the value of responses[1], which is 2, so the application interprets ++frequency[responses[answer]] as

```
++frequency[ 2 ]
```

which increments the frequency array element 2.

When answer is 2, responses[answer] is the value of responses[2], which is 6, so the application interprets ++frequency[responses[answer]] as

```
++frequency[ 6 ]
```

which increments frequency array element 6, and so on. Regardless of the number of responses processed in the survey, the application requires only an 11-element array (in which we ignore element 0) to summarize the results, because all the response values are between 1 and 10, inclusive, and the index values for an 11-element array are 0 through 10.

If the data in the responses array had contained invalid values, such as 13, the application would have attempted to add 1 to frequency[13], which is outside the bounds of the array. In many programming languages, like C and C++, writing outside the bounds of an array is actually allowed and would overwrite arbitrary information in memory, often causing disastrous results. C# does not allow this—accessing any array element forces a check on the array index to ensure that it is valid (i.e., it must be greater than or equal to 0 and less than the length of the array). This is called **_bounds checking_**. If an application uses an invalid index, the Common Language Runtime generates an exception (specifically, an **_IndexOutOfRangeException_**) to indicate that an error occurred in the application at execution time. The condition in a control statement could determine whether an index is valid before allowing it to be used in an *array-access expression*, thus avoiding the exception.

Error-Prevention Tip 8.1

An exception indicates that an error has occurred in an application. You often can write code to recover from an exception and continue application execution, rather than abnormally terminating the application. Exception handling is discussed in Chapter 13.

Error-Prevention Tip 8.2

When writing code to loop through an array, ensure that the array index remains greater than or equal to 0 and less than the length of the array. The loop-continuation condition should prevent the accessing of elements outside this range.

8.5 Case Study: Card Shuffling and Dealing Simulation

So far, this chapter's examples have used arrays of value-type elements. This section uses random-number generation and an array of reference-type elements—namely, objects representing playing cards—to develop a class that simulates card shuffling and dealing. This class can then be used to implement applications that play card games.

We first develop class Card (Fig. 8.9), which represents a playing card that has a face (e.g., "Ace", "Deuce", "Three", ..., "Jack", "Queen", "King") and a suit (e.g., "Hearts", "Diamonds", "Clubs", "Spades"). Next, we develop the DeckOfCards class (Fig. 8.10), which creates a deck of 52 playing cards in which each element is a Card object. Then we build a test application (Fig. 8.11) that demonstrates class DeckOfCards's card-shuffling-and-dealing capabilities.

Class Card

Class Card (Fig. 8.9) contains two string instance variables—face and suit—that are used to store references to the face value and suit name for a specific Card. The constructor for the class (lines 9–13) receives two strings that it uses to initialize face and suit. Method ToString (lines 16–19) creates a string consisting of the face of the card, the string " of " and the suit of the card. Recall from Chapter 7 that the + operator can be used to concatenate (i.e., combine) several strings to form one larger string. Card's ToString method can be invoked explicitly to obtain a string representation of a Card object (e.g., "Ace of Spades"). The ToString method of an object is called implicitly in many cases when the object is used where a string is expected (e.g., when WriteLine outputs the object with a format item or when the object is concatenated to a string using the + operator). For this behavior to occur, ToString must be declared with the header exactly as shown in line 16 of Fig. 8.9. We'll explain the purpose of the override keyword in more detail when we discuss inheritance in Chapter 11.

```
1   // Fig. 8.9: Card.cs
2   // Card class represents a playing card.
3   public class Card
4   {
5      private string face; // face of card ("Ace", "Deuce", ...)
6      private string suit; // suit of card ("Hearts", "Diamonds", ...)
7
8      // two-parameter constructor initializes card's face and suit
9      public Card( string cardFace, string cardSuit )
10     {
11        face = cardFace; // initialize face of card
12        suit = cardSuit; // initialize suit of card
13     } // end two-parameter Card constructor
14
15     // return string representation of Card
16     public override string ToString()
17     {
18        return face + " of " + suit;
19     } // end method ToString
20  } // end class Card
```

Fig. 8.9 | Card class represents a playing card.

Class DeckOfCards

Class DeckOfCards (Fig. 8.10) declares an instance-variable named deck that will refer to an array of Card objects (line 7). Like simple-type array variable declarations, the declaration of a variable for an array of objects includes the type of the elements in the array, followed by square brackets and the name of the array variable (e.g., Card[] deck). Class DeckOfCards also declares int instance variable currentCard (line 8), representing the next Card to be dealt from the deck array, and named constant NUMBER_OF_CARDS (line 9), indicating the number of Cards in the deck (52).

```
1   // Fig. 8.10: DeckOfCards.cs
2   // DeckOfCards class represents a deck of playing cards.
3   using System;
4
5   public class DeckOfCards
6   {
7      private Card[] deck; // array of Card objects
8      private int currentCard; // index of next Card to be dealt
9      private const int NUMBER_OF_CARDS = 52; // constant number of Cards
10     private Random randomNumbers; // random-number generator
11
12     // constructor fills deck of Cards
13     public DeckOfCards()
14     {
15        string[] faces = { "Ace", "Deuce", "Three", "Four", "Five", "Six",
16           "Seven", "Eight", "Nine", "Ten", "Jack", "Queen", "King" };
17        string[] suits = { "Hearts", "Diamonds", "Clubs", "Spades" };
18
19        deck = new Card[ NUMBER_OF_CARDS ]; // create array of Card objects
20        currentCard = 0; // set currentCard so deck[ 0 ] is dealt first
21        randomNumbers = new Random(); // create random-number generator
22
23        // populate deck with Card objects
24        for ( int count = 0; count < deck.Length; count++ )
25           deck[ count ] =
26              new Card( faces[ count % 13 ], suits[ count / 13 ] );
27     } // end DeckOfCards constructor
28
29     // shuffle deck of Cards with one-pass algorithm
30     public void Shuffle()
31     {
32        // after shuffling, dealing should start at deck[ 0 ] again
33        currentCard = 0; // reinitialize currentCard
34
35        // for each Card, pick another random Card and swap them
36        for ( int first = 0; first < deck.Length; first++ )
37        {
38           // select a random number between 0 and 51
39           int second = randomNumbers.Next( NUMBER_OF_CARDS );
40
41           // swap current Card with randomly selected Card
42           Card temp = deck[ first ];
```

Fig. 8.10 | DeckOfCards class represents a deck of playing cards. (Part 1 of 2.)

```
43              deck[ first ] = deck[ second ];
44              deck[ second ] = temp;
45          } // end for
46      } // end method Shuffle
47
48      // deal one Card
49      public Card DealCard()
50      {
51          // determine whether Cards remain to be dealt
52          if ( currentCard < deck.Length )
53              return deck[ currentCard++ ]; // return current Card in array
54          else
55              return null; // indicate that all Cards were dealt
56      } // end method DealCard
57  } // end class DeckOfCards
```

Fig. 8.10 | DeckOfCards class represents a deck of playing cards. (Part 2 of 2.)

The class's constructor instantiates the deck array (line 19) to be of size NUMBER_OF_CARDS. When first created, the elements of the deck array are null by default, so the constructor uses a for statement (lines 24–26) to fill the deck array with Cards. The for statement initializes control variable count to 0 and loops while count is less than deck.Length, causing count to take on each integer value from 0 to 51 (the indices of the deck array). Each Card is instantiated and initialized with two strings—one from the faces array (which contains the strings "Ace" through "King") and one from the suits array (which contains the strings "Hearts", "Diamonds", "Clubs" and "Spades"). The calculation count % 13 always results in a value from 0 to 12 (the 13 indices of the faces array in lines 15–16), and the calculation count / 13 always results in a value from 0 to 3 (the four indices of the suits array in line 17). When the deck array is initialized, it contains the Cards with faces "Ace" through "King" in order for each suit.

Method Shuffle (lines 30–46) shuffles the Cards in the deck. The method loops through all 52 Cards (array indices 0 to 51). For each Card, a number between 0 and 51 is picked randomly to select another Card. Next, the current Card object and the randomly selected Card object are swapped in the array. This exchange is performed by the three assignments in lines 42–44. The extra variable temp temporarily stores one of the two Card objects being swapped. The swap cannot be performed with only the two statements

```
deck[ first ] = deck[ second ];
deck[ second ] = deck[ first ];
```

If deck[first] is the "Ace" of "Spades" and deck[second] is the "Queen" of "Hearts", then after the first assignment, both array elements contain the "Queen" of "Hearts", and the "Ace" of "Spades" is lost—hence, the extra variable temp is needed. After the for loop terminates, the Card objects are randomly ordered. Only 52 swaps are made in a single pass of the entire array, and the array of Card objects is shuffled.

Method DealCard (lines 49–56) deals one Card in the array. Recall that currentCard indicates the index of the next Card to be dealt (i.e., the Card at the top of the deck). Thus, line 52 compares currentCard to the length of the deck array. If the deck is not empty (i.e., currentCard is less than 52), line 53 returns the top Card and increments currentCard to prepare for the next call to DealCard—otherwise, null is returned.

Shuffling and Dealing Cards

The application of Fig. 8.11 demonstrates the card dealing and shuffling capabilities of class DeckOfCards (Fig. 8.10). Line 10 creates a DeckOfCards object named myDeckOf-Cards. Recall that the DeckOfCards constructor creates the deck with the 52 Card objects in order by suit and face. Line 11 invokes myDeckOfCards's Shuffle method to rearrange the Card objects. The for statement in lines 14–20 deals all 52 Cards in the deck and displays them in four columns of 13 Cards each. Line 16 deals and displays a Card object by invoking myDeckOfCards's DealCard method. When Console.Write outputs a Card with string formatting, the Card's ToString method (declared in lines 16–19 of Fig. 8.9) is invoked implicitly. Because the field width is negative, the result is output *left* justified in a field of width 19.

```csharp
1   // Fig. 8.11: DeckOfCardsTest.cs
2   // Card shuffling and dealing application.
3   using System;
4
5   public class DeckOfCardsTest
6   {
7      // execute application
8      public static void Main( string[] args )
9      {
10        DeckOfCards myDeckOfCards = new DeckOfCards();
11        myDeckOfCards.Shuffle(); // place Cards in random order
12
13        // display all 52 Cards in the order in which they are dealt
14        for ( int i = 0; i < 52; i++ )
15        {
16           Console.Write( "{0,-19}", myDeckOfCards.DealCard() );
17
18           if ( ( i + 1 ) % 4 == 0 )
19              Console.WriteLine();
20        } // end for
21     } // end Main
22  } // end class DeckOfCardsTest
```

Eight of Clubs	Ten of Clubs	Ten of Spades	Four of Spades
Ace of Spades	Jack of Spades	Three of Spades	Seven of Spades
Three of Diamonds	Five of Clubs	Eight of Spades	Five of Hearts
Ace of Hearts	Ten of Hearts	Deuce of Hearts	Deuce of Clubs
Jack of Hearts	Nine of Spades	Four of Hearts	Seven of Clubs
Queen of Spades	Seven of Diamonds	Five of Diamonds	Ace of Clubs
Four of Clubs	Ten of Diamonds	Jack of Clubs	Six of Diamonds
Eight of Diamonds	King of Hearts	Three of Clubs	King of Spades
King of Diamonds	Six of Spades	Deuce of Spades	Five of Spades
Queen of Clubs	King of Clubs	Queen of Hearts	Seven of Hearts
Ace of Diamonds	Deuce of Diamonds	Four of Diamonds	Nine of Clubs
Queen of Diamonds	Jack of Diamonds	Six of Hearts	Nine of Diamonds
Nine of Hearts	Three of Hearts	Six of Clubs	Eight of Hearts

Fig. 8.11 | Card shuffling and dealing application.

8.6 foreach Statement

In previous examples, we demonstrated how to use counter-controlled for statements to iterate through the elements in an array. In this section, we introduce the ***foreach statement***, which iterates through the elements of an entire array or collection. This section discusses how to use the foreach statement to loop through an array. We show how to use it with collections in Chapter 27. The syntax of a foreach statement is:

> **foreach** (*type identifier* **in** *arrayName*)
> *statement*

where *type* and *identifier* are the type and name (e.g., int number) of the ***iteration variable***, and *arrayName* is the array through which to iterate. The type of the iteration variable must match the type of the elements in the array. As the next example illustrates, the iteration variable represents successive values in the array on successive iterations of the foreach statement.

Figure 8.12 uses the foreach statement (lines 13–14) to calculate the sum of the integers in an array of student grades. The type specified is int, because array contains int values—therefore, the loop will select one int value from the array during each iteration. The foreach statement iterates through successive values in the array one by one. The foreach header can be read concisely as "for each iteration, assign the next element of array to int variable number, then execute the following statement." Thus, for each iteration, identifier number represents the next int value in the array. Lines 13–14 are equivalent to the following counter-controlled repetition used in lines 13–14 of Fig. 8.5 to total the integers in array:

```
for ( int counter = 0; counter < array.Length; counter++ )
    total += array[ counter ];
```

```
1   // Fig. 8.12: ForEachTest.cs
2   // Using the foreach statement to total integers in an array.
3   using System;
4
5   public class ForEachTest
6   {
7      public static void Main( string[] args )
8      {
9         int[] array = { 87, 68, 94, 100, 83, 78, 85, 91, 76, 87 };
10        int total = 0;
11
12        // add each element's value to total
13        foreach ( int number in array )
14           total += number;
15
16        Console.WriteLine( "Total of array elements: {0}", total );
17     } // end Main
18  } // end class ForEachTest
```

```
Total of array elements: 849
```

Fig. 8.12 | Using the foreach statement to total integers in an array.

Common Programming Error 8.4

The foreach *statement can be used only to access array elements—it cannot be used to modify elements. Any attempt to change the value of the iteration variable in the body of a* foreach *statement will cause a compilation error.*

The foreach statement can be used in place of the for statement whenever code looping through an array does not require access to the counter indicating the index of the current array element. For example, totaling the integers in an array requires access only to the element values—the index of each element is irrelevant. However, if an application must use a counter for some reason other than simply to loop through an array (e.g., to display an index number next to each array element value, as in the examples earlier in this chapter), use the for statement.

Implicitly Typed Local Variables

In each for statement presented so far and in the foreach statement of Fig. 8.12, we declared the type of the control variable either in the for or foreach statement's header. C# provides a new feature—called *implicitly typed local variables*—that enables the compiler to infer a local variable's type based on the type of the variable's initializer. To distinguish such an initialization from a simple assignment statement, the **var** keyword is used in place of the variable's type. Recall that a local variable is any variable declared in the body of a method. In the declaration

```
var x = 7;
```

the compiler infers that the variable x should be of type int, because the compiler assumes that whole-number values, like 7, are of type int. Similarly, in the declaration

```
var y = -123.45;
```

the compiler infers that the variable y should be of type double, because the compiler assumes that floating-point number values, like -123.45, are of type double.

You can also use local type inference with control variables in the header of a for or foreach statement. For example, the for statement header

```
for ( int counter = 1; counter < 10; counter++ )
```

can be written as

```
for ( var counter = 1; counter  < 10; counter++ )
```

In this case, counter is of type int because it is initialized with a whole-number value (1). Similarly, assuming that myArray is an array of ints, the foreach statement header

```
foreach ( int number in myArray )
```

can be written as

```
foreach ( var number in myArray )
```

In this case, number is of type int because it is used to process elements of the int array myArray. The implicitly typed local-variable feature is one of several new Visual C# 2008 features that support Language Integrated Query (LINQ).

Implicitly typed local variables can be also used to initialize arrays without explicitly giving their type. For example, the following statement creates an array of int values:

```
var array = new[] { 32, 27, 64, 18, 95, 14, 90, 70, 60, 37 };
```

Note that there are no square brackets on the left side of the assignment operator, and that new[] is used to specify that the variable is an array. We'll use implicitly typed local variables when we present LINQ examples in Chapters 9 and 18–24.

8.7 Passing Arrays and Array Elements to Methods

To pass an array argument to a method, specify the name of the array without any brackets. For example, if hourlyTemperatures is declared as

```
double[] hourlyTemperatures = new double[ 24 ];
```

then the method call

```
ModifyArray( hourlyTemperatures );
```

passes the reference of array hourlyTemperatures to method ModifyArray. Every array object "knows" its own length (and makes it available via its Length property). Thus, when we pass an array object's reference to a method, we need not pass the array length as an additional argument.

For a method to receive an array reference through a method call, the method's parameter list must specify an array parameter. For example, the method header for method ModifyArray might be written as

```
void ModifyArray( double[] b )
```

indicating that ModifyArray receives the reference of an array of doubles in parameter b. The method call passes array hourlyTemperature's reference, so when the called method uses the array variable b, it refers to the same array object as hourlyTemperatures in the calling method.

When an argument to a method is an entire array or an individual array element of a reference type, the called method receives a copy of the reference. However, when an argument to a method is an individual array element of a value type, the called method receives a copy of the element's value. To pass an individual array element to a method, use the indexed name of the array as an argument in the method call. If you want to pass a value-type array element to a method by reference, you must use the ref keyword as shown in Section 7.14.

Figure 8.13 demonstrates the difference between passing an entire array and passing a value-type array element to a method. The foreach statement at lines 17–18 outputs the five elements of array (an array of int values). Line 20 invokes method ModifyArray,

```
1   // Fig. 8.13: PassArray.cs
2   // Passing arrays and individual array elements to methods.
3   using System;
4
```

Fig. 8.13 | Passing arrays and individual array elements to methods. (Part 1 of 3.)

```
5   public class PassArray
6   {
7      // Main creates array and calls ModifyArray and ModifyElement
8      public static void Main( string[] args )
9      {
10        int[] array = { 1, 2, 3, 4, 5 };
11
12        Console.WriteLine(
13           "Effects of passing reference to entire array:\n" +
14           "The values of the original array are:" );
15
16        // output original array elements
17        foreach ( int value in array )
18           Console.Write( "   {0}", value );
19
20        ModifyArray( array ); // pass array reference
21        Console.WriteLine( "\n\nThe values of the modified array are:" );
22
23        // output modified array elements
24        foreach ( int value in array )
25           Console.Write( "   {0}", value );
26
27        Console.WriteLine(
28           "\n\nEffects of passing array element value:\n" +
29           "array[3] before ModifyElement: {0}", array[ 3 ] );
30
31        ModifyElement( array[ 3 ] ); // attempt to modify array[ 3 ]
32        Console.WriteLine(
33           "array[3] after ModifyElement: {0}", array[ 3 ] );
34     } // end Main
35
36     // multiply each element of an array by 2
37     public static void ModifyArray( int[] array2 )
38     {
39        for ( int counter = 0; counter < array2.Length; counter++ )
40           array2[ counter ] *= 2;
41     } // end method ModifyArray
42
43     // multiply argument by 2
44     public static void ModifyElement( int element )
45     {
46        element *= 2;
47        Console.WriteLine(
48           "Value of element in ModifyElement: {0}", element );
49     } // end method ModifyElement
50  } // end class PassArray
```

```
Effects of passing reference to entire array:
The values of the original array are:
   1   2   3   4   5

The values of the modified array are:
   2   4   6   8   10
```

Fig. 8.13 | Passing arrays and individual array elements to methods. (Part 2 of 3.)

```
Effects of passing array element value:
array[3] before ModifyElement: 8
Value of element in ModifyElement: 16
array[3] after ModifyElement: 8
```

Fig. 8.13 | Passing arrays and individual array elements to methods. (Part 3 of 3.)

passing array as an argument. Method ModifyArray (lines 37–41) receives a copy of array's reference and uses the reference to multiply each of array's elements by 2. To prove that array's elements (in Main) were modified, the foreach statement at lines 24–25 outputs the five elements of array again. As the output shows, method ModifyArray doubled the value of each element.

Figure 8.13 next demonstrates that when a copy of an individual value-type array element is passed to a method, modifying the copy in the called method does not affect the original value of that element in the calling method's array. To show the value of array[3] before invoking method ModifyElement, lines 27–29 output the value of array[3], which is 8. Line 31 calls method ModifyElement and passes array[3] as an argument. Remember that array[3] is actually one int value (8) in array. Therefore, the application passes a copy of the value of array[3]. Method ModifyElement (lines 44–49) multiplies the value received as an argument by 2, stores the result in its parameter element, then outputs the value of element (16). Since method parameters, like local variables, cease to exist when the method in which they are declared completes execution, the method parameter element is destroyed when method ModifyElement terminates. Thus, when the application returns control to Main, lines 32–33 output the unmodified value of array[3] (i.e., 8).

8.8 Passing Arrays by Value and by Reference

In C#, a variable that "stores" an object, such as an array, does not actually store the object itself. Instead, such a variable stores a reference to the object. The distinction between reference-type variables and value-type variables raises some subtle issues that you must understand to create secure, stable programs.

As you know, when an application passes an argument to a method, the called method receives a copy of that argument's value. Changes to the local copy in the called method do not affect the original variable in the caller. If the argument is of a reference type, the method makes a copy of the reference, not a copy of the actual object that is referenced. The local copy of the reference also refers to the original object, which means that changes to the object in the called method affect the original object.

Performance Tip 8.1

Passing arrays and other objects by reference makes sense for performance reasons. If arrays were passed by value, a copy of each element would be passed. For large, frequently passed arrays, this would waste time and would consume considerable storage for the copies of the arrays—both of these problems cause poor performance.

In Section 7.14, you learned that C# allows variables to be passed by reference with keyword ref. You can also use keyword ref to pass a reference-type variable *by reference,* which allows the called method to modify the original variable in the caller and make that variable refer to a different object. This is a subtle capability, which, if misused, can lead to problems. For instance, when a reference-type object like an array is passed with ref, the called method actually gains control over the reference itself, allowing the called method to replace the original reference in the caller with a reference to a different object, or even with null. Such behavior can lead to unpredictable effects, which can be disastrous in mission-critical applications. The application in Fig. 8.14 demonstrates the subtle difference between passing a reference by value and passing a reference by reference with keyword ref.

```
 1   // Fig. 8.14: ArrayReferenceTest.cs
 2   // Testing the effects of passing array references
 3   // by value and by reference.
 4   using System;
 5
 6   public class ArrayReferenceTest
 7   {
 8      public static void Main( string[] args )
 9      {
10         // create and initialize firstArray
11         int[] firstArray = { 1, 2, 3 };
12
13         // copy the reference in variable firstArray
14         int[] firstArrayCopy = firstArray;
15
16         Console.WriteLine(
17            "Test passing firstArray reference by value" );
18
19         Console.Write( "\nContents of firstArray " +
20            "before calling FirstDouble:\n\t" );
21
22         // display contents of firstArray
23         for ( int i = 0; i < firstArray.Length; i++ )
24            Console.Write( "{0} ", firstArray[ i ] );
25
26         // pass variable firstArray by value to FirstDouble
27         FirstDouble( firstArray );
28
29         Console.Write( "\n\nContents of firstArray after " +
30            "calling FirstDouble\n\t" );
31
32         // display contents of firstArray
33         for ( int i = 0; i < firstArray.Length; i++ )
34            Console.Write( "{0} ", firstArray[ i ] );
35
36         // test whether reference was changed by FirstDouble
37         if ( firstArray == firstArrayCopy )
38            Console.WriteLine(
39               "\n\nThe references refer to the same array" );
40         else
41            Console.WriteLine(
42               "\n\nThe references refer to different arrays" );
```

Fig. 8.14 | Passing an array reference by value and by reference. (Part 1 of 3.)

```
43
44        // create and initialize secondArray
45        int[] secondArray = { 1, 2, 3 };
46
47        // copy the reference in variable secondArray
48        int[] secondArrayCopy = secondArray;
49
50        Console.WriteLine( "\nTest passing secondArray " +
51           "reference by reference" );
52
53        Console.Write( "\nContents of secondArray " +
54           "before calling SecondDouble:\n\t" );
55
56        // display contents of secondArray before method call
57        for ( int i = 0; i < secondArray.Length; i++ )
58           Console.Write( "{0} ", secondArray[ i ] );
59
60        // pass variable secondArray by reference to SecondDouble
61        SecondDouble( ref secondArray );
62
63        Console.Write( "\n\nContents of secondArray " +
64           "after calling SecondDouble:\n\t" );
65
66        // display contents of secondArray after method call
67        for ( int i = 0; i < secondArray.Length; i++ )
68           Console.Write( "{0} ", secondArray[ i ] );
69
70        // test whether reference was changed by SecondDouble
71        if ( secondArray == secondArrayCopy )
72           Console.WriteLine(
73              "\n\nThe references refer to the same array" );
74        else
75           Console.WriteLine(
76              "\n\nThe references refer to different arrays" );
77     } // end Main
78
79     // modify elements of array and attempt to modify reference
80     public static void FirstDouble( int[] array )
81     {
82        // double each element's value
83        for ( int i = 0; i < array.Length; i++ )
84           array[ i ] *= 2;
85
86        // create new object and assign its reference to array
87        array = new int[] { 11, 12, 13 };
88     } // end method FirstDouble
89
90     // modify elements of array and change reference array
91     // to refer to a new array
92     public static void SecondDouble( ref int[] array )
93     {
```

Fig. 8.14 | Passing an array reference by value and by reference. (Part 2 of 3.)

```
94              // double each element's value
95              for ( int i = 0; i < array.Length; i++ )
96                  array[ i ] *= 2;
97
98              // create new object and assign its reference to array
99              array = new int[] { 11, 12, 13 };
100          } // end method SecondDouble
101      } // end class ArrayReferenceTest
```

```
Test passing firstArray reference by value

Contents of firstArray before calling FirstDouble:
      1 2 3

Contents of firstArray after calling FirstDouble
      2 4 6

The references refer to the same array

Test passing secondArray reference by reference

Contents of secondArray before calling SecondDouble:
      1 2 3

Contents of secondArray after calling SecondDouble:
      11 12 13

The references refer to different arrays
```

Fig. 8.14 | Passing an array reference by value and by reference. (Part 3 of 3.)

Lines 11 and 14 declare two integer array variables, firstArray and firstArrayCopy. Line 11 initializes firstArray with the values 1, 2 and 3. The assignment statement at line 14 copies the reference stored in firstArray to variable firstArrayCopy, causing these variables to reference the same array object. We make the copy of the reference so that we can determine later whether reference firstArray gets overwritten. The for statement at lines 23–24 displays the contents of firstArray before it is passed to method First-Double (line 27) so that we can verify that the array is passed by reference (i.e., the called method indeed changes the array's contents).

The for statement in method FirstDouble (lines 83–84) multiplies the values of all the elements in the array by 2. Line 87 creates a new array containing the values 11, 12 and 13, and assigns the array's reference to parameter array in an attempt to overwrite reference firstArray in the caller—this, of course, does not happen, because the reference was passed by value. After method FirstDouble executes, the for statement at lines 33–34 displays the contents of firstArray, demonstrating that the values of the elements have been changed by the method. The if...else statement at lines 37–42 uses the == operator to compare references firstArray (which we just attempted to overwrite) and firstArray-Copy. The expression in line 37 evaluates to true if the operands of operator == reference the same object. In this case, the object represented by firstArray is the array created in line 11—not the array created in method FirstDouble (line 87)—so the original reference stored in firstArray was not modified.

Lines 45–76 perform similar tests, using array variables secondArray and second-ArrayCopy, and method SecondDouble (lines 92–100). Method SecondDouble performs the same operations as FirstDouble, but receives its array argument using keyword ref. In this case, the reference stored in secondArray after the method call is a reference to the array created in line 99 of SecondDouble, demonstrating that a variable passed with keyword ref can be modified by the called method so that the variable in the caller actually points to a different object—in this case, an array created in SecondDouble. The if...else statement in lines 71–76 confirms that secondArray and secondArrayCopy no longer refer to the same array.

Software Engineering Observation 8.1

When a method receives a reference-type parameter by value, a copy of the object's reference is passed. This prevents a method from overwriting references passed to that method. In the vast majority of cases, protecting the caller's reference from modification is the desired behavior. If you encounter a situation where you truly want the called procedure to modify the caller's reference, pass the reference-type parameter using keyword ref—but, again, such situations are rare.

Software Engineering Observation 8.2

In C#, objects (including arrays) are effectively passed by reference, because references to objects are passed to called methods. A called method receiving a reference to an object in a caller can interact with, and possibly change, the caller's object.

8.9 Case Study: Class GradeBook Using an Array to Store Grades

This section further evolves class GradeBook, introduced in Chapter 4 and expanded in Chapters 5–6. Recall that this class represents a grade book used by an instructor to store and analyze a set of student grades. Previous versions of the class process a set of grades entered by the user, but do not maintain the individual grade values in instance variables of the class. Thus, repeat calculations require the user to re-enter the same grades. One way to solve this problem would be to store each grade entered in an individual instance of the class. For example, we could create instance variables grade1, grade2, …, grade10 in class GradeBook to store 10 student grades. However, the code to total the grades and determine the class average would be cumbersome, and the class would not be able to process any more than 10 grades at a time. In this section, we solve this problem by storing grades in an array.

Storing Student Grades in an Array in Class GradeBook

The version of class GradeBook (Fig. 8.15) presented here uses an array of integers to store the grades of several students on a single exam. This eliminates the need to repeatedly input the same set of grades. Variable grades (which will refer to an array of ints) is declared as an instance variable in line 7—therefore, each GradeBook object maintains its own set of grades. The class's constructor (lines 14–18) has two parameters—the name of the course and an array of grades. When an application (e.g., class GradeBookTest in Fig. 8.16) creates a GradeBook object, the application passes an existing int array to the constructor, which assigns the array's reference to instance variable grades (line 17). The size of array grades is determined by the class that passes the array to the constructor.

```
1   // Fig. 8.15: GradeBook.cs
2   // Grade book using an array to store test grades.
3   using System;
4
5   public class GradeBook
6   {
7      private int[] grades; // array of student grades
8
9      // auto-implemented property CourseName
10     public string CourseName { get; set; }
11
12     // two-parameter constructor initializes
13     // auto-implemented property CourseName and grades array
14     public GradeBook( string name, int[] gradesArray )
15     {
16        CourseName = name; // set CourseName to name
17        grades = gradesArray; // initialize grades array
18     } // end two-parameter GradeBook constructor
19
20     // display a welcome message to the GradeBook user
21     public void DisplayMessage()
22     {
23        // auto-implemented property CourseName gets the name of course
24        Console.WriteLine( "Welcome to the grade book for\n{0}!\n",
25           CourseName );
26     } // end method DisplayMessage
27
28     // perform various operations on the data
29     public void ProcessGrades()
30     {
31        // output grades array
32        OutputGrades();
33
34        // call method GetAverage to calculate the average grade
35        Console.WriteLine( "\nClass average is {0:F}", GetAverage() );
36
37        // call methods GetMinimum and GetMaximum
38        Console.WriteLine( "Lowest grade is {0}\nHighest grade is {1}\n",
39           GetMinimum(), GetMaximum() );
40
41        // call OutputBarChart to display grade distribution chart
42        OutputBarChart();
43     } // end method ProcessGrades
44
45     // find minimum grade
46     public int GetMinimum()
47     {
48        int lowGrade = grades[ 0 ]; // assume grades[ 0 ] is smallest
49
50        // loop through grades array
51        foreach ( int grade in grades )
52        {
```

Fig. 8.15 | Grade book using an array to store test grades. (Part 1 of 3.)

```
53            // if grade lower than lowGrade, assign it to lowGrade
54            if ( grade < lowGrade )
55               lowGrade = grade; // new lowest grade
56         } // end for
57
58         return lowGrade; // return lowest grade
59      } // end method GetMinimum
60
61      // find maximum grade
62      public int GetMaximum()
63      {
64         int highGrade = grades[ 0 ]; // assume grades[ 0 ] is largest
65
66         // loop through grades array
67         foreach ( int grade in grades )
68         {
69            // if grade greater than highGrade, assign it to highGrade
70            if ( grade > highGrade )
71               highGrade = grade; // new highest grade
72         } // end for
73
74         return highGrade; // return highest grade
75      } // end method GetMaximum
76
77      // determine average grade for test
78      public double GetAverage()
79      {
80         int total = 0; // initialize total
81
82         // sum grades for one student
83         foreach ( int grade in grades )
84            total += grade;
85
86         // return average of grades
87         return ( double ) total / grades.Length;
88      } // end method GetAverage
89
90      // output bar chart displaying grade distribution
91      public void OutputBarChart()
92      {
93         Console.WriteLine( "Grade distribution:" );
94
95         // stores frequency of grades in each range of 10 grades
96         int[] frequency = new int[ 11 ];
97
98         // for each grade, increment the appropriate frequency
99         foreach ( int grade in grades )
100           ++frequency[ grade / 10 ];
101
102        // for each grade frequency, display bar in chart
103        for ( int count = 0; count < frequency.Length; count++ )
104        {
```

Fig. 8.15 | Grade book using an array to store test grades. (Part 2 of 3.)

```
105          // output bar label ( "00-09: ", ..., "90-99: ", "100: " )
106          if ( count == 10 )
107             Console.Write( "  100: " );
108          else
109             Console.Write( "{0:D2}-{1:D2}: ",
110                count * 10, count * 10 + 9 );
111
112          // display bar of asterisks
113          for ( int stars = 0; stars < frequency[ count ]; stars++ )
114             Console.Write( "*" );
115
116          Console.WriteLine(); // start a new line of output
117       } // end outer for
118    } // end method OutputBarChart
119
120    // output the contents of the grades array
121    public void OutputGrades()
122    {
123       Console.WriteLine( "The grades are:\n" );
124
125       // output each student's grade
126       for ( int student = 0; student < grades.Length; student++ )
127          Console.WriteLine( "Student {0,2}: {1,3}",
128             student + 1, grades[ student ] );
129    } // end method OutputGrades
130 } // end class GradeBook
```

Fig. 8.15 | Grade book using an array to store test grades. (Part 3 of 3.)

Thus, a GradeBook object can process a variable number of grades—as many as are in the array in the caller. The grade values in the passed array could have been input from a user at the keyboard or read from a file on disk (as discussed in Chapter 19). In our test application, we simply initialize an array with a set of grade values (Fig. 8.16, line 9). Once the grades are stored in instance variable grades of class GradeBook, all the class's methods can access the elements of grades as needed to perform various calculations.

Method ProcessGrades (lines 29–43) contains a series of method calls that result in the output of a report summarizing the grades. Line 32 calls method OutputGrades to display the contents of array grades. Lines 126–128 in method OutputGrades use a for statement to output the student grades. A for statement, rather than a foreach, must be used in this case, because lines 127–128 use counter variable student's value to output each grade next to a particular student number (see Fig. 8.16). Although array indices start at 0, an instructor would typically number students starting at 1. Thus, lines 127–128 output student + 1 as the student number to produce grade labels "Student 1: ", "Student 2: " and so on.

Method ProcessGrades next calls method GetAverage (line 35) to obtain the average of the grades in the array. Method GetAverage (lines 78–88) uses a foreach statement to total the values in array grades before calculating the average. The iteration variable in the foreach's header (e.g., int grade) indicates that for each iteration, int variable grade takes on a value in array grades. Note that the averaging calculation in line 87 uses grades.Length to determine the number of grades being averaged.

Lines 38–39 in method ProcessGrades call methods GetMinimum and GetMaximum to determine the lowest and highest grades of any student on the exam, respectively. Each of these methods uses a foreach statement to loop through array grades. Lines 51–56 in method GetMinimum loop through the array, and lines 54–55 compare each grade to lowGrade. If a grade is less than lowGrade, lowGrade is set to that grade. When line 58 executes, lowGrade contains the lowest grade in the array. Method GetMaximum (lines 62–75) works the same way as method GetMinimum.

Finally, line 42 in method ProcessGrades calls method OutputBarChart to display a distribution chart of the grade data, using a technique similar to that in Fig. 8.6. In that example, we manually calculated the number of grades in each category (i.e., 0–9, 10–19, ..., 90–99 and 100) by simply looking at a set of grades. In this example, lines 99–100 use a technique similar to that in Figs. 8.7 and 8.8 to calculate the frequency of grades in each category. Line 96 declares variable frequency and initializes it with an array of 11 ints to store the frequency of grades in each grade category. For each grade in array grades, lines 99–100 increment the appropriate element of the frequency array. To determine which element to increment, line 100 divides the current grade by 10, using integer division. For example, if grade is 85, line 100 increments frequency[8] to update the count of grades in the range 80–89. Lines 103–117 next display the bar chart (see Fig. 8.6) based on the values in array frequency. Like lines 24–25 of Fig. 8.6, lines 113–114 of Fig. 8.15 use a value in array frequency to determine the number of asterisks to display in each bar.

Class GradeBookTest That Demonstrates Class GradeBook
The application of Fig. 8.16 creates an object of class GradeBook (Fig. 8.15) using int array gradesArray (declared and initialized in line 9). Lines 11–12 pass a course name and gradesArray to the GradeBook constructor. Line 13 displays a welcome message, and line 14 invokes the GradeBook object's ProcessGrades method. The output reveals the summary of the 10 grades in myGradeBook.

Software Engineering Observation 8.3

A test harness (or test application) is responsible for creating an object of the class being tested and providing it with data. This data could come from any of several sources. Test data can be placed directly into an array with an array initializer, it can come from the user at the keyboard or it can come from a file (as you'll see in Chapter 19). After passing this data to the class's constructor to instantiate the object, the test harness should call the object to test its methods and manipulate its data. Gathering data in the test harness like this allows the class to manipulate data from several sources.

```
1   // Fig. 8.16: GradeBookTest.cs
2   // Create GradeBook object using an array of grades.
3   public class GradeBookTest
4   {
5      // Main method begins application execution
6      public static void Main( string[] args )
7      {
8         // one-dimensional array of student grades
9         int[] gradesArray = { 87, 68, 94, 100, 83, 78, 85, 91, 76, 87 };
```

Fig. 8.16 | Create a GradeBook object using an array of grades. (Part 1 of 2.)

```
10
11          GradeBook myGradeBook = new GradeBook(
12             "CS101 Introduction to C# Programming", gradesArray );
13          myGradeBook.DisplayMessage();
14          myGradeBook.ProcessGrades();
15      } // end Main
16   } // end class GradeBookTest
```

```
Welcome to the grade book for
CS101 Introduction to C# Programming!

The grades are:

Student  1:  87
Student  2:  68
Student  3:  94
Student  4: 100
Student  5:  83
Student  6:  78
Student  7:  85
Student  8:  91
Student  9:  76
Student 10:  87

Class average is 84.90
Lowest grade is 68
Highest grade is 100

Grade distribution:
00-09:
10-19:
20-29:
30-39:
40-49:
50-59:
60-69: *
70-79: **
80-89: ****
90-99: **
  100: *
```

Fig. 8.16 | Create a `GradeBook` object using an array of grades. (Part 2 of 2.)

8.10 Multidimensional Arrays

Multidimensional arrays with two dimensions are often used to represent *tables of values* consisting of information arranged in *rows* and *columns*. To identify a particular table element, we must specify two indices. By convention, the first identifies the element's row and the second its column. Arrays that require two indices to identify a particular element are called *two-dimensional arrays*. (Multidimensional arrays can have more than two dimensions, but such arrays are beyond the scope of this book.) C# supports two types of two-dimensional arrays—*rectangular arrays* and *jagged arrays*.

Rectangular Arrays
Rectangular arrays are used to represent tables of information in the form of rows and columns, where each row has the same number of columns. Figure 8.17 illustrates a rectan-

gular array named a containing three rows and four columns—a three-by-four array. In general, an array with *m* rows and *n* columns is called an *m-by-n array*.

Every element in array a is identified in Fig. 8.17 by an array-access expression of the form a[*row*, *column*]; a is the name of the array, and *row* and *column* are the indices that uniquely identify each element in array a by row and column number. Note that the names of the elements in row 0 all have a first index of 0, and the names of the elements in column 3 all have a second index of 3.

Like one-dimensional arrays, multidimensional arrays can be initialized with array initializers in declarations. A rectangular array b with two rows and two columns could be declared and initialized with *nested array initializers* as follows:

```
int[ , ] b = { { 1, 2 }, { 3, 4 } };
```

The initializer values are grouped by row in braces. So 1 and 2 initialize b[0, 0] and b[0, 1], respectively, and 3 and 4 initialize b[1, 0] and b[1, 1], respectively. The compiler counts the number of nested array initializers (represented by sets of two inner braces within the outer braces) in the initializer list to determine the number of rows in array b. The compiler counts the initializer values in the nested array initializer for a row to determine the number of columns (two) in that row. The compiler will generate an error if the number of initializers in each row is not the same, because every row of a rectangular array must have the same length.

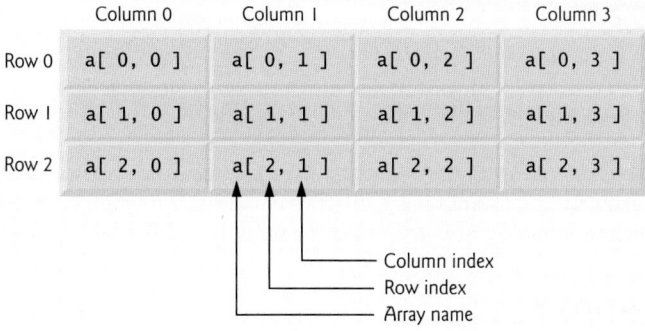

Fig. 8.17 | Rectangular array with three rows and four columns.

Jagged Arrays

A *jagged array* is maintained as a one-dimensional array in which each element refers to a one-dimensional array. The manner in which jagged arrays are represented makes them quite flexible, because the lengths of the rows in the array need not be the same. For example, jagged arrays could be used to store a single student's exam grades across multiple classes, where the number of exams may vary from class to class.

We can access the elements in a jagged array by an array-access expression of the form *arrayName*[*row*][*column*]—similar to the array-access expression for rectangular arrays, but with a separate set of square brackets for each dimension. A jagged array with three rows of different lengths could be declared and initialized as follows:

```
int[][] jagged = { new int[] { 1, 2 },
                   new int[] { 3 },
                   new int[] { 4, 5, 6 } };
```

In this statement, 1 and 2 initialize jagged[0][0] and jagged[0][1], respectively; 3 initializes jagged[1][0]; and 4, 5 and 6 initialize jagged[2][0], jagged[2][1] and jagged[2][2], respectively. Therefore, array jagged in the preceding declaration is actually composed of four separate one-dimensional arrays—one that represents the rows, one containing the values in the first row ({ 1, 2 }), one containing the value in the second row ({ 3 }) and one containing the values in the third row ({ 4, 5, 6 }). Thus, array jagged itself is an array of three elements, each a reference to a one-dimensional array of int values.

Observe the differences between the array-creation expressions for rectangular arrays and for jagged arrays. Two sets of square brackets follow the type of jagged, indicating that this is an array of int arrays. Furthermore, in the array initializer, C# requires the keyword new to create an array object for each row. Figure 8.18 illustrates the array reference jagged after it has been declared and initialized.

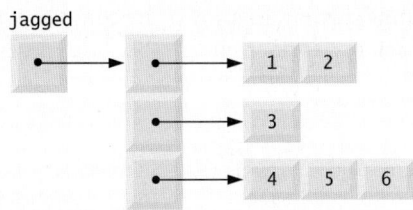

Fig. 8.18 | Jagged array with three rows of different lengths.

Creating Two-Dimensional Arrays with Array-Creation Expressions

A rectangular array can be created with an array-creation expression. For example, the following lines declare variable b and assign it a reference to a three-by-four rectangular array:

```
int[ , ] b;
b = new int[ 3, 4 ];
```

In this case, we use the literal values 3 and 4 to specify the number of rows and number of columns, respectively, but this is not required—applications can also use variables and expressions to specify array dimensions. As with one-dimensional arrays, the elements of a rectangular array are initialized when the array object is created.

A jagged array cannot be completely created with a single array-creation expression. The following statement is a syntax error:

```
int[][] c = new int[ 2 ][ 5 ]; // error
```

Instead, each one-dimensional array in the jagged array must be initialized separately. A jagged array can be created as follows:

```
int[][] c;
c = new int[ 2 ][ ]; // create 2 rows
c[ 0 ] = new int[ 5 ]; // create 5 columns for row 0
c[ 1 ] = new int[ 3 ]; // create 3 columns for row 1
```

The preceding statements create a jagged array with two rows. Row 0 has five columns, and row 1 has three columns.

Two-Dimensional Array Example: Displaying Element Values

Figure 8.19 demonstrates initializing rectangular and jagged arrays with array initializers and using nested for loops to *traverse* the arrays (i.e., visit every element of each array).

```csharp
 1   // Fig. 8.19: InitArray.cs
 2   // Initializing rectangular and jagged arrays.
 3   using System;
 4
 5   public class InitArray
 6   {
 7      // create and output rectangular and jagged arrays
 8      public static void Main( string[] args )
 9      {
10         // with rectangular arrays,
11         // every column must be the same length.
12         int[ , ] rectangular = { { 1, 2, 3 }, { 4, 5, 6 } };
13
14         // with jagged arrays,
15         // we need to use "new int[]" for every row,
16         // but every column does not need to be the same length.
17         int[][] jagged = { new int[] { 1, 2 },
18                            new int[] { 3 },
19                            new int[] { 4, 5, 6 } };
20
21         OutputArray( rectangular ); // displays array rectangular by row
22         Console.WriteLine(); // output a blank line
23         OutputArray( jagged ); // displays array jagged by row
24      } // end Main
25
26      // output rows and columns of a rectangular array
27      public static void OutputArray( int[ , ] array )
28      {
29         Console.WriteLine( "Values in the rectangular array by row are" );
30
31         // loop through array's rows
32         for ( int row = 0; row < array.GetLength( 0 ); row++ )
33         {
34            // loop through columns of current row
35            for ( int column = 0; column < array.GetLength( 1 ); column++ )
36               Console.Write( "{0}  ", array[ row, column ] );
37
38            Console.WriteLine(); // start new line of output
39         } // end outer for
40      } // end method OutputArray
41
42      // output rows and columns of a jagged array
43      public static void OutputArray( int[][] array )
44      {
```

Fig. 8.19 | Initializing jagged and rectangular arrays. (Part I of 2.)

```
45              Console.WriteLine( "Values in the jagged array by row are" );
46
47              // loop through each row
48              foreach ( var row in array )
49              {
50                  // loop through each element in current row
51                  foreach ( var element in row )
52                      Console.Write( "{0}  ", element );
53
54                  Console.WriteLine(); // start new line of output
55              } // end outer foreach
56          } // end method OutputArray
57      } // end class InitArray
```

```
Values in the rectangular array by row are
1  2  3
4  5  6

Values in the jagged array by row are
1  2
3
4  5  6
```

Fig. 8.19 | Initializing jagged and rectangular arrays. (Part 2 of 2.)

Class InitArray's Main method creates two arrays. Line 12 uses nested array initializers to initialize variable rectangular with an array in whic row 0 has the values 1, 2 and 3, and row 1 has the values 4, 5 and 6. Lines 17–19 uses nested initializers of different lengths to initialize variable jagged. In this case, the initializer uses the keyword new to create a one-dimensional array for each row. Row 0 is initialized to have two elements with values 1 and 2, respectively. Row 1 is initialized to have one element with value 3. Row 2 is initialized to have three elements with the values 4, 5 and 6, respectively.

Method OutputArray has been overloaded with two versions. The first version (lines 27–40) specifies the array parameter as int[,] array to indicate that it takes a rectangular array. The second version (lines 43–56) takes a jagged array, because its array parameter is listed as int[][] array.

Line 21 invokes method OutputArray with argument rectangular, so the version of OutputArray at lines 27–40 is called. The nested for statement (lines 32–39) outputs the rows of a rectangular array. The loop-continuation condition of each for statement (lines 32 and 35) uses the rectangular array's GetLength method to obtain the length of each dimension. Dimensions are numbered starting from 0, so the method call GetLength(0) on array returns the size of the first dimension of the array (the number of rows), and the call GetLength(1) returns the size of the second dimension (the number of columns).

Line 23 invokes method OutputArray with argument jagged, so the version of OutputArray at lines 43–56 is called. The nested foreach statement (lines 48–55) outputs the rows of a jagged array. The inner foreach statement (line 51) iterates through each element in the current row of the array. This allows the loop to determine the exact number of columns in each row. Since the jagged array is created as an array of arrays, we can use nested foreach statements to output the elements in the console window. When you use a foreach statement with a rectangular array, the foreach iterates through all the rows and columns starting from row 0, as if the elements were in a one-dimensional array.

Common Multidimensional-Array Manipulations Performed with for Statements
Many common array manipulations use for statements. As an example, the following for statement sets all the elements in row 2 of rectangular array a in Fig. 8.17 to 0:

```
for ( int column = 0; column < a.GetLength( 1 ); column++)
   a[ 2, column ] = 0;
```

We specified row 2; therefore, we know that the first index is always 2 (0 is the first row, and 1 is the second row). This for loop varies only the second index (i.e., the column index). The preceding for statement is equivalent to the assignment statements

```
a[ 2, 0 ] = 0;
a[ 2, 1 ] = 0;
a[ 2, 2 ] = 0;
a[ 2, 3 ] = 0;
```

The following nested for statement totals the values of all the elements in array a:

```
int total = 0;

for ( int row = 0; row < a.GetLength( 0 ); row++ )
{
   for ( int column = 0; column < a.GetLength( 1 ); column++ )
      total += a[ row, column ];
} // end outer for
```

These nested for statements total the array elements one row at a time. The outer for statement begins by setting the row index to 0 so that row 0's elements can be totaled by the inner for statement. The outer for then increments row to 1 so that row 1's elements can be totaled. Then the outer for increments row to 2 so that row 2's elements can be totaled. The variable total can be displayed when the outer for statement terminates. In the next example, we show how to process a rectangular array in a more concise manner using foreach statements.

8.11 Case Study: Class GradeBook Using a Rectangular Array

In Section 8.9, we presented class GradeBook (Fig. 8.15), which used a one-dimensional array to store student grades on a single exam. In most courses, students take several exams. Instructors are likely to want to analyze grades across the entire course, both for a single student and for the class as a whole.

Storing Student Grades in a Rectangular Array in Class GradeBook
Figure 8.20 contains a version of class GradeBook that uses a rectangular array grades to store the grades of a number of students on multiple exams. Each row of the array represents a single student's grades for the entire course, and each column represents the grades for the whole class on one of the exams the students took during the course. An application such as GradeBookTest (Fig. 8.21) passes the array as an argument to the GradeBook con-

structor. In this example, we use a 10-by-3 array containing 10 students' grades on three exams. Five methods perform array manipulations to process the grades. Each method is similar to its counterpart in the earlier one-dimensional-array version of class GradeBook (Fig. 8.15). Method GetMinimum (lines 44–58) determines the lowest grade of any student for the semester. Method GetMaximum (lines 61–75) determines the highest grade of any student for the semester. Method GetAverage (lines 78–90) determines a particular student's semester average. Method OutputBarChart (lines 93–122) outputs a bar chart of the distribution of all student grades for the semester. Method OutputGrades (lines 125–149) outputs the two-dimensional array in tabular format, along with each student's semester average.

```csharp
1   // Fig. 8.20: GradeBook.cs
2   // Grade book using rectangular array to store grades.
3   using System;
4
5   public class GradeBook
6   {
7      private int[ , ] grades; // rectangular array of student grades
8
9      // auto-implemented property CourseName
10     public string CourseName { get; set; }
11
12     // two-parameter constructor initializes
13     // auto-implemented property CourseName and grades array
14     public GradeBook( string name, int[ , ] gradesArray )
15     {
16        CourseName = name; // set CourseName to name
17        grades = gradesArray; // initialize grades array
18     } // end two-parameter GradeBook constructor
19
20     // display a welcome message to the GradeBook user
21     public void DisplayMessage()
22     {
23        // auto-implemented property CourseName gets the name of course
24        Console.WriteLine( "Welcome to the grade book for\n{0}!\n",
25           CourseName );
26     } // end method DisplayMessage
27
28     // perform various operations on the data
29     public void ProcessGrades()
30     {
31        // output grades array
32        OutputGrades();
33
34        // call methods GetMinimum and GetMaximum
35        Console.WriteLine( "\n{0} {1}\n{2} {3}\n",
36           "Lowest grade in the grade book is", GetMinimum(),
37           "Highest grade in the grade book is", GetMaximum() );
38
```

Fig. 8.20 | Grade book using rectangular array to store grades. (Part 1 of 4.)

```
39          // output grade distribution chart of all grades on all tests
40          OutputBarChart();
41       } // end method ProcessGrades
42
43       // find minimum grade
44       public int GetMinimum()
45       {
46          // assume first element of grades array is smallest
47          int lowGrade = grades[ 0, 0 ];
48
49          // loop through elements of rectangular grades array
50          foreach ( int grade in grades )
51          {
52             // if grade less than lowGrade, assign it to lowGrade
53             if ( grade < lowGrade )
54                lowGrade = grade;
55          } // end foreach
56
57          return lowGrade; // return lowest grade
58       } // end method GetMinimum
59
60       // find maximum grade
61       public int GetMaximum()
62       {
63          // assume first element of grades array is largest
64          int highGrade = grades[ 0, 0 ];
65
66          // loop through elements of rectangular grades array
67          foreach ( int grade in grades )
68          {
69             // if grade greater than highGrade, assign it to highGrade
70             if ( grade > highGrade )
71                highGrade = grade;
72          } // end foreach
73
74          return highGrade; // return highest grade
75       } // end method GetMaximum
76
77       // determine average grade for particular student
78       public double GetAverage( int student )
79       {
80          // get the number of grades per student
81          int amount = grades.GetLength( 1 );
82          int total = 0; // initialize total
83
84          // sum grades for one student
85          for ( int exam = 0; exam < amount; exam++ )
86             total += grades[ student, exam ];
87
88          // return average of grades
89          return ( double ) total / amount;
90       } // end method GetAverage
```

Fig. 8.20 | Grade book using rectangular array to store grades. (Part 2 of 4.)

```
91
92        // output bar chart displaying overall grade distribution
93        public void OutputBarChart()
94        {
95            Console.WriteLine( "Overall grade distribution:" );
96
97            // stores frequency of grades in each range of 10 grades
98            int[] frequency = new int[ 11 ];
99
100           // for each grade in GradeBook, increment the appropriate frequency
101           foreach ( int grade in grades )
102           {
103               ++frequency[ grade / 10 ];
104           } // end foreach
105
106           // for each grade frequency, display bar in chart
107           for ( int count = 0; count < frequency.Length; count++ )
108           {
109               // output bar label ( "00-09: ", ..., "90-99: ", "100: " )
110               if ( count == 10 )
111                   Console.Write( "  100: " );
112               else
113                   Console.Write( "{0:D2}-{1:D2}: ",
114                       count * 10, count * 10 + 9 );
115
116               // display bar of asterisks
117               for ( int stars = 0; stars < frequency[ count ]; stars++ )
118                   Console.Write( "*" );
119
120               Console.WriteLine(); // start a new line of output
121           } // end outer for
122       } // end method OutputBarChart
123
124       // output the contents of the grades array
125       public void OutputGrades()
126       {
127           Console.WriteLine( "The grades are:\n" );
128           Console.Write( "                " ); // align column heads
129
130           // create a column heading for each of the tests
131           for ( int test = 0; test < grades.GetLength( 1 ); test++ )
132               Console.Write( "Test {0}  ", test + 1 );
133
134           Console.WriteLine( "Average" ); // student average column heading
135
136           // create rows/columns of text representing array grades
137           for ( int student = 0; student < grades.GetLength( 0 ); student++ )
138           {
139               Console.Write( "Student {0,2}", student + 1 );
140
141               // output student's grades
142               for ( int grade = 0; grade < grades.GetLength( 1 ); grade++ )
143                   Console.Write( "{0,8}", grades[ student, grade ] );
```

Fig. 8.20 | Grade book using rectangular array to store grades. (Part 3 of 4.)

```
144
145            // call method GetAverage to calculate student's average grade;
146            // pass row number as the argument to GetAverage
147            Console.WriteLine( "{0,9:F}", GetAverage( student ) );
148         } // end outer for
149      } // end method OutputGrades
150   } // end class GradeBook
```

Fig. 8.20 | Grade book using rectangular array to store grades. (Part 4 of 4.)

Methods GetMinimum, GetMaximum and OutputBarChart each loop through array grades using the foreach statement—for example, the foreach statement from method GetMinimum (lines 50–55). To find the lowest overall grade, this foreach statement iterates through rectangular array grades and compares each element to variable lowGrade. If a grade is less than lowGrade, lowGrade is set to that grade.

When the foreach statement traverses the elements of array grades, it looks at each element of the first row in order by index, then each element of the second row in order by index and so on. The foreach statement in lines 50–55 traverses the elements of grade in the same order as the following equivalent code, expressed with nested for statements:

```
for ( int row = 0; row < grades.GetLength( 0 ); row++ )
   for ( int column = 0; column < grades.GetLength( 1 ); column++ )
   {
      if ( grades[ row, column ] < lowGrade )
         lowGrade = grades[ row, column ];
   }
```

When the foreach statement completes, lowGrade contains the lowest grade in the rectangular array. Method GetMaximum works similarly to method GetMinimum.

Method OutputBarChart in Fig. 8.20 displays the grade distribution as a bar chart. Note that the syntax of the foreach statement (lines 101–104) is identical for one-dimensional and two-dimensional arrays.

Method OutputGrades (lines 125–149) uses nested for statements to output values of the array grades, in addition to each student's semester average. The output in Fig. 8.21 shows the result, which resembles the tabular format of an instructor's physical grade book. Lines 131–132 display the column headings for each test. We use the for statement rather than the foreach statement here so that we can identify each test with a number. Similarly, the for statement in lines 137–148 first outputs a row label using a counter variable to identify each student (line 139). Although array indices start at 0, note that lines 132 and 139 output test + 1 and student + 1, respectively, to produce test and student numbers starting at 1 (see Fig. 8.21). The inner for statement in lines 142–143 uses the outer for statement's counter variable student to loop through a specific row of array grades and output each student's test grade. Finally, line 147 obtains each student's semester average by passing the row index of grades (i.e., student) to method Get-Average.

Method GetAverage (lines 78–90) takes one argument—the row index for a particular student. When line 147 calls GetAverage, the argument is int value student, which specifies the particular row of rectangular array grades. Method GetAverage calculates the

sum of the array elements on this row, divides the total by the number of test results and
returns the floating-point result as a `double` value (line 89).

Class GradeBookTest That Demonstrates Class GradeBook

The application in Fig. 8.21 creates an object of class GradeBook (Fig. 8.20) using the two-
dimensional array of ints that gradesArray references (lines 9–18). Lines 20–21 pass a
course name and gradesArray to the GradeBook constructor. Lines 22–23 then invoke
myGradeBook's DisplayMessage and ProcessGrades methods to display a welcome message and obtain a report summarizing the students' grades for the semester, respectively.

```
 1   // Fig. 8.21: GradeBookTest.cs
 2   // Create GradeBook object using a rectangular array of grades.
 3   public class GradeBookTest
 4   {
 5      // Main method begins application execution
 6      public static void Main( string[] args )
 7      {
 8         // rectangular array of student grades
 9         int[ , ] gradesArray = { { 87, 96, 70 },
10                                  { 68, 87, 90 },
11                                  { 94, 100, 90 },
12                                  { 100, 81, 82 },
13                                  { 83, 65, 85 },
14                                  { 78, 87, 65 },
15                                  { 85, 75, 83 },
16                                  { 91, 94, 100 },
17                                  { 76, 72, 84 },
18                                  { 87, 93, 73 } };
19
20         GradeBook myGradeBook = new GradeBook(
21            "CS101 Introduction to C# Programming", gradesArray );
22         myGradeBook.DisplayMessage();
23         myGradeBook.ProcessGrades();
24      } // end Main
25   } // end class GradeBookTest
```

```
Welcome to the grade book for
CS101 Introduction to C# Programming!

The grades are:

            Test 1  Test 2  Test 3  Average
Student  1     87      96      70    84.33
Student  2     68      87      90    81.67
Student  3     94     100      90    94.67
Student  4    100      81      82    87.67
Student  5     83      65      85    77.67
Student  6     78      87      65    76.67
Student  7     85      75      83    81.00
Student  8     91      94     100    95.00
Student  9     76      72      84    77.33
Student 10     87      93      73    84.33
```

Fig. 8.21 | Create GradeBook object using a rectangular array of grades. (Part 1 of 2.)

```
Lowest grade in the grade book is 65
Highest grade in the grade book is 100

Overall grade distribution:
00-09:
10-19:
20-29:
30-39:
40-49:
50-59:
60-69: ***
70-79: ******
80-89: ***********
90-99: *******
  100: ***
```

Fig. 8.21 | Create `GradeBook` object using a rectangular array of grades. (Part 2 of 2.)

8.12 Variable-Length Argument Lists

Variable-length argument lists allow you to create methods that receive an arbitrary number of arguments. A one-dimensional array-type argument preceded by the keyword *params* in a method's parameter list indicates that the method receives a variable number of arguments with the type of the array's elements. This use of a `params` modifier can occur only in the last entry of the parameter list. While you can use method overloading and array passing to accomplish much of what is accomplished with variable-length argument lists, using the `params` modifier is more concise.

Figure 8.22 demonstrates method `Average` (lines 8–17), which receives a variable-length sequence of `doubles` (line 8). C# treats the variable-length argument list as a one-dimensional array whose elements are all of the same type. Hence, the method body can manipulate the parameter `numbers` as an array of `doubles`. Lines 13–14 use the `foreach` loop to walk through the array and calculate the total of the `doubles` in the array. Line 16 accesses `numbers.Length` to obtain the size of the `numbers` array for use in the averaging calculation. Lines 31, 33 and 35 in `Main` call method `Average` with two, three and four arguments, respectively. Method `Average` has a variable-length argument list, so it can average as many `double` arguments as the caller passes. The output reveals that each call to method `Average` returns the correct value.

```
 1   // Fig. 8.22: ParamArrayTest.cs
 2   // Using variable-length argument lists.
 3   using System;
 4
 5   public class ParamArrayTest
 6   {
 7      // calculate average
 8      public static double Average( params double[] numbers )
 9      {
10         double total = 0.0; // initialize total
11
```

Fig. 8.22 | Using variable-length argument lists. (Part 1 of 2.)

```
12          // calculate total using the foreach statement
13          foreach ( double d in numbers )
14             total += d;
15
16          return total / numbers.Length;
17       } // end method Average
18
19       public static void Main( string[] args )
20       {
21          double d1 = 10.0;
22          double d2 = 20.0;
23          double d3 = 30.0;
24          double d4 = 40.0;
25
26          Console.WriteLine(
27             "d1 = {0:F1}\nd2 = {1:F1}\nd3 = {2:F1}\nd4 = {3:F1}\n",
28             d1, d2, d3, d4 );
29
30          Console.WriteLine( "Average of d1 and d2 is {0:F1}",
31             Average( d1, d2 ) );
32          Console.WriteLine( "Average of d1, d2 and d3 is {0:F1}",
33             Average( d1, d2, d3 ) );
34          Console.WriteLine( "Average of d1, d2, d3 and d4 is {0:F1}",
35             Average( d1, d2, d3, d4 ) );
36       } // end Main
37    } // end class ParamArrayTest
```

```
d1 = 10.0
d2 = 20.0
d3 = 30.0
d4 = 40.0

Average of d1 and d2 is 15.0
Average of d1, d2 and d3 is 20.0
Average of d1, d2, d3 and d4 is 25.0
```

Fig. 8.22 | Using variable-length argument lists. (Part 2 of 2.)

Common Programming Error 8.5

The params modifier may be used only with the last parameter of the parameter list.

8.13 Using Command-Line Arguments

On many systems, it is possible to pass arguments from the command line (these are known as *command-line arguments*) to an application by including a parameter of type string[] (i.e., an array of strings) in the parameter list of Main, exactly as we have done in every application in the book. By convention, this parameter is named args (Fig. 8.23, line 7). When an application is executed from the **Command Prompt**, the execution environment passes the command-line arguments that appear after the application name to the application's Main method as strings in the one-dimensional array args. The number of arguments passed from the command line is obtained by accessing the array's Length

```
 1   // Fig. 8.23: InitArray.cs
 2   // Using command-line arguments to initialize an array.
 3   using System;
 4
 5   public class InitArray
 6   {
 7      public static void Main( string[] args )
 8      {
 9         // check number of command-line arguments
10         if ( args.Length != 3 )
11            Console.WriteLine(
12               "Error: Please re-enter the entire command, including\n" +
13               "an array size, initial value and increment." );
14         else
15         {
16            // get array size from first command-line argument
17            int arrayLength = Convert.ToInt32( args[ 0 ] );
18            int[] array = new int[ arrayLength ]; // create array
19
20            // get initial value and increment from command-line argument
21            int initialValue = Convert.ToInt32( args[ 1 ] );
22            int increment = Convert.ToInt32( args[ 2 ] );
23
24            // calculate value for each array element
25            for ( int counter = 0; counter < array.Length; counter++ )
26               array[ counter ] = initialValue + increment * counter;
27
28            Console.WriteLine( "{0}{1,8}", "Index", "Value" );
29
30            // display array index and value
31            for ( int counter = 0; counter < array.Length; counter++ )
32               Console.WriteLine( "{0,5}{1,8}", counter, array[ counter ] );
33         } // end else
34      } // end Main
35   } // end class InitArray
```

```
C:\Examples\ch08\fig08_23>InitArray.exe
Error: Please re-enter the entire command, including
an array size, initial value and increment.
```

```
C:\Examples\ch08\fig08_23>InitArray.exe 10 1 2
Index   Value
    0       1
    1       3
    2       5
    3       7
    4       9
    5      11
    6      13
    7      15
    8      17
    9      19
```

Fig. 8.23 | Using command-line arguments to initialize an array. (Part 1 of 2.)

```
C:\Examples\ch08\fig08_23>InitArray.exe 5 0 4
Index    Value
    0        0
    1        4
    2        8
    3       12
    4       16
```

Fig. 8.23 | Using command-line arguments to initialize an array. (Part 2 of 2.)

property. For example, the command "MyApplication a b" passes two command-line arguments to application MyApplication. Note that command-line arguments are separated by white space, not commas. When the preceding command executes, the Main method entry point receives the two-element array args (i.e., args.Length is 2) in which args[0] contains the string "a" and args[1] contains the string "b". Common uses of command-line arguments include passing options and file names to applications.

Figure 8.23 uses three command-line arguments to initialize an array. When the application executes, if args.Length is not 3, the application displays an error message and terminates (lines 10–13). Otherwise, lines 16–32 initialize and display the array based on the values of the command-line arguments.

The command-line arguments become available to Main as strings in args. Line 17 gets args[0]—a string that specifies the array size—and converts it to an int value, which the application uses to create the array in line 18. The static method ToInt32 of class Convert converts its string argument to an int.

Lines 21–22 convert the args[1] and args[2] command-line arguments to int values and store them in initialValue and increment, respectively. Lines 25–26 calculate the value for each array element.

The output of the first sample execution indicates that the application received an insufficient number of command-line arguments. The second sample execution uses command-line arguments 5, 0 and 4 to specify the size of the array (5), the value of the first element (0) and the increment of each value in the array (4), respectively. The corresponding output indicates that these values create an array containing the integers 0, 4, 8, 12 and 16. The output from the third sample execution illustrates that the command-line arguments 10, 1 and 2 produce an array whose 10 elements are the nonnegative odd integers from 1 to 19.

8.14 (Optional) Software Engineering Case Study: Collaboration Among Objects in the ATM System

When two objects communicate with each other to accomplish a task, they are said to *collaborate*. A *collaboration* consists of an object of one class sending a *message* to an object of another class. Messages are sent in C# via method calls. In this section, we concentrate on the collaborations (interactions) among the objects in our ATM system.

In Section 7.15, we determined many of the operations of the classes in our system. In this section, we concentrate on the messages that invoke these operations. To identify the collaborations in the system, we return to the requirements document of Section 3.9. Recall that this document specifies the activities that occur during an ATM session (e.g., authenticating a user, performing transactions). The steps used to describe how the system must perform each of these tasks are our first indication of the collaborations in our system. As we proceed through this and the remaining Software Engineering Case Study sections, we may discover additional collaborations.

Identifying the Collaborations in a System

We begin to identify the collaborations in the system by carefully reading the sections of the requirements document that specify what the ATM should do to authenticate a user and to perform each transaction type. For each action or step described in the requirements document, we decide which objects in our system must interact to achieve the desired result. We identify one object as the sending object (i.e., the object that sends the message) and another as the receiving object (i.e., the object that offers that operation to clients of the class). We then select one of the receiving object's operations (identified in Section 7.15) that must be invoked by the sending object to produce the proper behavior. For example, the ATM displays a welcome message when idle. We know that an object of class Screen displays a message to the user via its DisplayMessage operation. Thus, we decide that the system can display a welcome message by employing a collaboration between the ATM and the Screen in which the ATM sends a DisplayMessage message to the Screen by invoking the DisplayMessage operation of class Screen. [*Note:* To avoid repeating the phrase "an object of class…," we refer to each object simply by using its class name preceded by an article (e.g., "a," "an" or "the")—for example, "the ATM" refers to an object of class ATM.]

Figure 8.24 lists the collaborations that can be derived from the requirements document. For each sending object, we list the collaborations in the order in which they are discussed in the requirements document. We list each collaboration involving a unique sender, message and recipient only once, even though the collaboration may occur several times during an ATM session. For example, the first row in Fig. 8.24 indicates that the ATM collaborates with the Screen whenever the ATM needs to display a message to the user.

Let's consider the collaborations in Fig. 8.24. Before allowing a user to perform any transactions, the ATM must prompt the user to enter an account number, then a PIN. It accomplishes each of these tasks by sending a DisplayMessage message to the Screen.

An object of class...	sends the message...	to an object of class...
ATM	DisplayMessage	Screen
	GetInput	Keypad
	AuthenticateUser	BankDatabase
	Execute	BalanceInquiry
	Execute	Withdrawal
	Execute	Deposit
BalanceInquiry	GetAvailableBalance	BankDatabase
	GetTotalBalance	BankDatabase
	DisplayMessage	Screen

Fig. 8.24 | Collaborations in the ATM system. (Part 1 of 2.)

An object of class...	sends the message...	to an object of class...
Withdrawal	DisplayMessage	Screen
	GetInput	Keypad
	GetAvailableBalance	BankDatabase
	IsSufficientCashAvailable	CashDispenser
	Debit	BankDatabase
	DispenseCash	CashDispenser
Deposit	DisplayMessage	Screen
	GetInput	Keypad
	IsDepositEnvelopeReceived	DepositSlot
	Credit	BankDatabase
BankDatabase	ValidatePIN	Account
	AvailableBalance (get)	Account
	TotalBalance (get)	Account
	Debit	Account
	Credit	Account

Fig. 8.24 | Collaborations in the ATM system. (Part 2 of 2.)

Both of these actions refer to the same collaboration between the ATM and the Screen, which is already listed in Fig. 8.24. The ATM obtains input in response to a prompt by sending a GetInput message to the Keypad. Next the ATM must determine whether the user-specified account number and PIN match those of an account in the database. It does so by sending an AuthenticateUser message to the BankDatabase. Recall that the Bank-Database cannot authenticate a user directly—only the user's Account (i.e., the Account that contains the account number specified by the user) can access the user's PIN to authenticate the user. Figure 8.24 therefore lists a collaboration in which the Bank-Database sends a ValidatePIN message to an Account.

After the user is authenticated, the ATM displays the main menu by sending a series of DisplayMessage messages to the Screen and obtains input containing a menu selection by sending a GetInput message to the Keypad. We have already accounted for these collaborations. After the user chooses a type of transaction to perform, the ATM executes the transaction by sending an Execute message to an object of the appropriate transaction class (i.e., a BalanceInquiry, a Withdrawal or a Deposit). For example, if the user chooses to perform a balance inquiry, the ATM sends an Execute message to a BalanceInquiry.

Further examination of the requirements document reveals the collaborations involved in executing each transaction type. A BalanceInquiry retrieves the amount of money available in the user's account by sending a GetAvailableBalance message to the BankDatabase, which sends a get message to an Account's AvailableBalance property to access the available balance. Similarly, the BalanceInquiry retrieves the amount of money on deposit by sending a GetTotalBalance message to the BankDatabase, which sends a get message to an Account's TotalBalance property to access the total balance on deposit. To display both measures of the user's balance at the same time, the BalanceInquiry sends DisplayMessage messages to the Screen.

A `Withdrawal` sends `DisplayMessage` messages to the `Screen` to display a menu of standard withdrawal amounts (i.e., $20, $40, $60, $100, $200). The `Withdrawal` sends a `GetInput` message to the `Keypad` to obtain the user's menu selection. Next, the `Withdrawal` determines whether the requested withdrawal amount is less than or equal to the user's account balance. The `Withdrawal` obtains the amount of money available in the user's account by sending a `GetAvailableBalance` message to the `BankDatabase`. The `Withdrawal` then tests whether the cash dispenser contains enough cash by sending an `IsSufficientCashAvailable` message to the `CashDispenser`. A `Withdrawal` sends a `Debit` message to the `BankDatabase` to decrease the user's account balance. The `BankDatabase` in turn sends the same message to the appropriate `Account`. Recall that debiting an `Account` decreases both the total balance and the available balance. To dispense the requested amount of cash, the `Withdrawal` sends a `DispenseCash` message to the `CashDispenser`. Finally, the `Withdrawal` sends a `DisplayMessage` message to the `Screen`, instructing the user to take the cash.

A `Deposit` responds to an `Execute` message first by sending a `DisplayMessage` message to the `Screen` to prompt the user for a deposit amount. The `Deposit` sends a `GetInput` message to the `Keypad` to obtain the user's input. The `Deposit` then sends a `DisplayMessage` message to the `Screen` to tell the user to insert a deposit envelope. To determine whether the deposit slot received an incoming deposit envelope, the `Deposit` sends an `IsDepositEnvelopeReceived` message to the `DepositSlot`. The `Deposit` updates the user's account by sending a `Credit` message to the `BankDatabase`, which subsequently sends a `Credit` message to the user's `Account`. Recall that crediting an `Account` increases the total balance but not the available balance.

Interaction Diagrams

Now that we have identified a set of possible collaborations between the objects in our ATM system, let us graphically model these interactions. The UML provides several types of *interaction diagrams* that model the behavior of a system by modeling how objects interact with one another. The *communication diagram* emphasizes *which objects* participate in collaborations. [*Note:* Communication diagrams were called *collaboration diagrams* in earlier versions of the UML.] Like the communication diagram, the *sequence diagram* shows collaborations among objects, but it emphasizes *when* messages are sent between objects.

Communication Diagrams

Figure 8.25 shows a communication diagram that models the ATM executing a `BalanceInquiry`. Objects are modeled in the UML as rectangles containing names in the form `objectName : ClassName`. In this example, which involves only one object of each type, we disregard the object name and list only a colon followed by the class name. Specifying the name of each object in a communication diagram is recommended when modeling multiple objects of the same type. Communicating objects are connected with solid lines, and messages are passed between objects along these lines in the direction shown by arrows with filled arrowheads. The name of the message, which appears next to the arrow, is the name of an operation (i.e., a method) belonging to the receiving object—think of the name as a service that the receiving object provides to sending objects (its "clients").

The filled arrow in Fig. 8.25 represents a message—or *synchronous call*—in the UML and a method call in C#. This arrow indicates that the flow of control is from the sending object (the ATM) to the receiving object (a BalanceInquiry). Since this is a synchronous call, the sending object cannot send another message, or do anything at all, until the receiving object processes the message and returns control (and possibly a return value) to the sending object. The sender just waits. For example, in Fig. 8.25, the ATM calls method Execute of a BalanceInquiry and cannot send another message until Execute finishes and returns control to the ATM. [*Note:* If this were an *asynchronous call*, represented by a stick arrowhead, the sending object would not have to wait for the receiving object to return control—it would continue sending additional messages immediately following the asynchronous call. Such calls are beyond the scope of this book.]

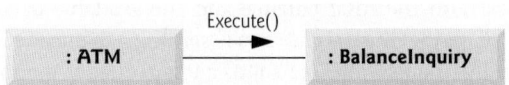

Fig. 8.25 | Communication diagram of the ATM executing a balance inquiry.

Sequence of Messages in a Communication Diagram

Figure 8.26 shows a communication diagram that models the interactions among objects in the system when an object of class BalanceInquiry executes. We assume that the object's accountNumber attribute contains the account number of the current user. The collaborations in Fig. 8.26 begin after the ATM sends an Execute message to a BalanceInquiry (i.e., the interaction modeled in Fig. 8.25). The number to the left of a message name indicates the order in which the message is passed. The *sequence of messages* in a communication diagram progresses in numerical order from least to greatest. In this diagram, the number-

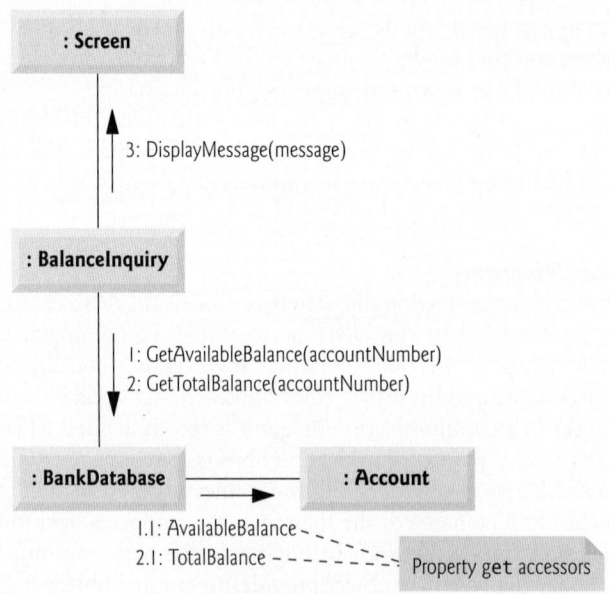

Fig. 8.26 | Communication diagram for executing a BalanceInquiry.

ing starts with message 1 and ends with message 3. The BalanceInquiry first sends a GetAvailableBalance message to the BankDatabase (message 1), then sends a GetTotal-Balance message to the BankDatabase (message 2). Within the parentheses following a message name, we can specify a comma-separated list of the names of the arguments sent with the message (i.e., arguments in a C# method call)—the BalanceInquiry passes attribute accountNumber with its messages to the BankDatabase to indicate which Account's balance information to retrieve. Recall from Fig. 7.21 that operations GetAvailableBalance and GetTotalBalance of class BankDatabase each require a parameter to identify an account. The BalanceInquiry next displays the available balance and the total balance to the user by passing a DisplayMessage message to the Screen (message 3) that includes a parameter indicating the message to be displayed.

Note that Fig. 8.26 models two additional messages passing from the BankDatabase to an Account (message 1.1 and message 2.1). To provide the ATM with the two balances of the user's Account (as requested by messages 1 and 2), the BankDatabase must send get messages to the Account's AvailableBalance and TotalBalance properties. A message passed within the handling of another message is called a ***nested message***. The UML recommends using a decimal numbering scheme to indicate nested messages. For example, message 1.1 is the first message nested in message 1—the BankDatabase sends the get message to the Account's AvailableBalance property during BankDatabase's processing of a GetAvailableBalance message. [*Note:* If the BankDatabase needed to pass a second nested message while processing message 1, it would be numbered 1.2.] A message may be passed only when all the nested messages from the previous message have been passed. For example, the BalanceInquiry passes message 3 to the Screen only after messages 2 and 2.1 have been passed, in that order.

The nested numbering scheme used in communication diagrams helps clarify precisely when and in what context each message is passed. For example, if we numbered the five messages in Fig. 8.26 using a flat numbering scheme (i.e., 1, 2, 3, 4, 5), someone looking at the diagram might not be able to determine that BankDatabase passes the get message to an Account's AvailableBalance property (message 1.1) *during* the BankDatabase's processing of message 1, as opposed to *after* completing the processing of message 1. The nested decimal numbers make it clear that the get message (message 1.1) is passed to an Account's AvailableBalance property within the handling of the GetAvailable-Balance message (message 1) by the BankDatabase.

Sequence Diagrams

Communication diagrams emphasize the participants in collaborations but model their timing a bit awkwardly. A sequence diagram helps model the timing of collaborations more clearly. Figure 8.27 shows a sequence diagram modeling the sequence of interactions that occur when a Withdrawal executes. The dotted line extending down from an object's rectangle is that object's ***lifeline***, which represents the progression of time. Actions typically occur along an object's lifeline in chronological order from top to bottom—an action near the top happens before one near the bottom.

Message passing in sequence diagrams is similar to message passing in communication diagrams. An arrow with a filled arrowhead extending from the sending object to the receiving object represents a message between two objects. The arrowhead points to an activation on the receiving object's lifeline. An ***activation***, shown as a thin vertical rect-

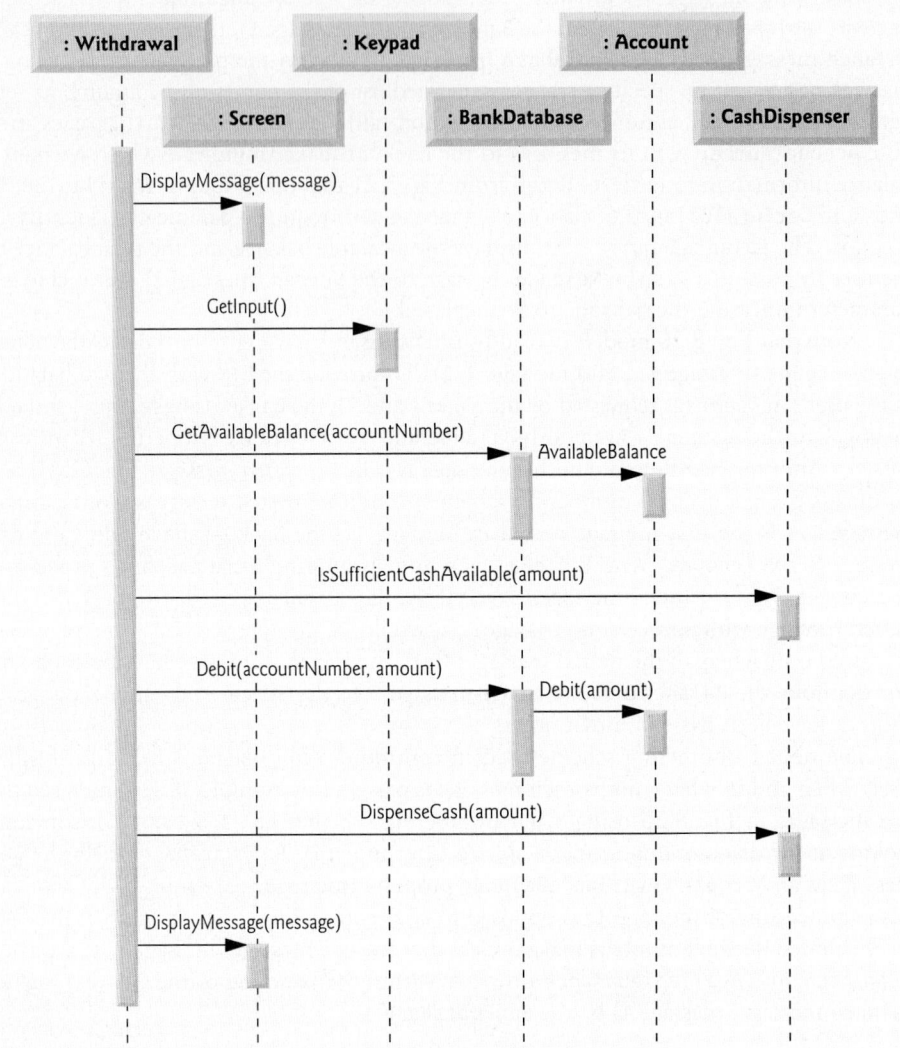

Fig. 8.27 | Sequence diagram that models a `Withdrawal` executing.

angle, indicates that an object is executing. When an object returns control, a return message, represented as a dashed line with a stick arrowhead, extends from the activation of the object returning control to the activation of the object that initially sent the message. To eliminate clutter, we omit the return-message arrows—the UML allows this practice to make diagrams more readable. Like communication diagrams, sequence diagrams can indicate message parameters between the parentheses following a message name.

The sequence of messages in Fig. 8.27 begins when a `Withdrawal` prompts the user to choose a withdrawal amount by sending a `DisplayMessage` message to the `Screen`. The `Withdrawal` then sends a `GetInput` message to the `Keypad`, which obtains input from the user. We have already modeled the control logic involved in a `Withdrawal` in the activity diagram of Fig. 6.22, so we do not show this logic in the sequence diagram of Fig. 8.27. Instead, we model the best-case scenario, in which the balance of the user's account is greater than or equal to the chosen withdrawal amount, and the cash dispenser contains a sufficient amount of cash to satisfy the request. For information on how to model control logic in a sequence diagram, please refer to the web resources and recommended readings listed at the end of Section 3.9.

After obtaining a withdrawal amount, the `Withdrawal` sends a `GetAvailableBalance` message to the `BankDatabase`, which in turn sends a `get` message to the `Account`'s `AvailableBalance` property. Assuming that the user's account has enough money available to permit the transaction, the `Withdrawal` next sends an `IsSufficientCashAvailable` message to the `CashDispenser`. Assuming that there is enough cash available, the `Withdrawal` decreases the balance of the user's account (both the total balance and the available balance) by sending a `Debit` message to the `BankDatabase`. The `BankDatabase` responds by sending a `Debit` message to the user's `Account`. Finally, the `Withdrawal` sends a `DispenseCash` message to the `CashDispenser` and a `DisplayMessage` message to the `Screen`, telling the user to remove the cash from the machine.

We have identified collaborations among objects in the ATM system and modeled some of these collaborations using UML interaction diagrams—communication diagrams and sequence diagrams. In the next Software Engineering Case Study section (Section 10.22), we enhance the structure of our model to complete a preliminary object-oriented design; then we begin implementing the ATM system in C#.

Software Engineering Case Study Self-Review Exercises

8.1   A(n) _____ consists of an object of one class sending a message to an object of another class.
- a) association
- b) aggregation
- c) collaboration
- d) composition

8.2   Which form of interaction diagram emphasizes *what* collaborations occur? Which form emphasizes *when* collaborations occur?

8.3   Create a sequence diagram that models the interactions among objects in the ATM system that occur when a `Deposit` executes successfully. Explain the sequence of messages modeled by the diagram.

Answers to Software Engineering Case Study Self-Review Exercises

8.1   c.

8.2   Communication diagrams emphasize *what* collaborations occur. Sequence diagrams emphasize *when* collaborations occur.

8.3   Figure 8.28 presents a sequence diagram that models the interactions between objects in the ATM system that occur when a `Deposit` executes successfully. It indicates that a `Deposit` first sends a `DisplayMessage` message to the `Screen` (to ask the user to enter a deposit amount). Next, the `Deposit` sends a `GetInput` message to the `Keypad` to receive the amount the user will be depositing. The `Deposit` then prompts the user (to insert a deposit envelope) by sending a `DisplayMessage` message to the `Screen`. The `Deposit` next sends an `IsDepositEnvelopeReceived` message to the `DepositSlot` to confirm that the deposit envelope has been received by the ATM. Finally, the `Deposit` increases the total balance (but not the available balance) of the user's Account by sending a Credit message to the BankDatabase. The BankDatabase responds by sending the same message to the user's Account.

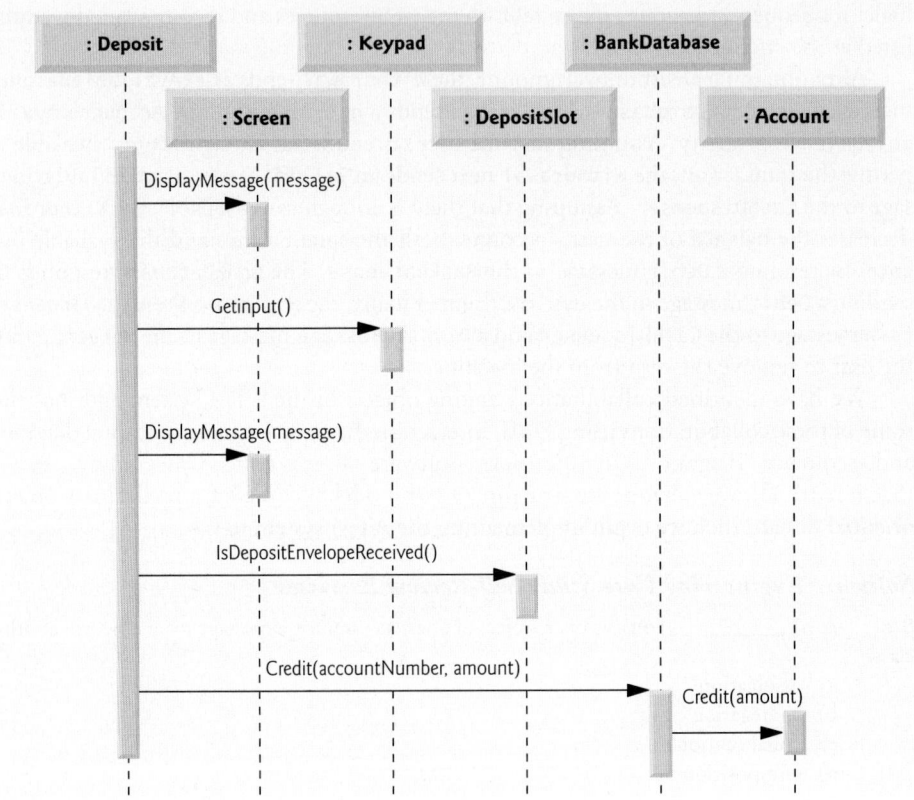

Fig. 8.28 | Sequence diagram that models a Deposit executing.

8.15 Wrap-Up

This chapter began our introduction to data structures, exploring the use of arrays to store data in and retrieve data from lists and tables of values. The chapter examples demonstrated how to declare array variables, initialize arrays and refer to individual elements of arrays. The chapter introduced the foreach statement as an additional means (besides the for statement) for iterating through arrays. We showed how to pass arrays to methods and how to declare and manipulate multidimensional arrays. Finally, the chapter showed how to write methods that use variable-length argument lists and how to read arguments passed to an application from the command line.

We continue our coverage of data structures in Chapter 9, Introduction to LINQ and Generic Collections, where we discuss List collections, which are dynamically resizable array-based collections. Chapter 25, Data Structures, introduces dynamic data structures, such as lists, queues, stacks and trees, that can grow and shrink as applications execute.

Chapter 26, Generics, presents one of C#'s new features—generics—which provides the means to create general models of methods and classes that can be declared once, but used with many different data types. Chapter 27, Collections, introduces the data structure classes provided by the .NET Framework Class Library, some of which use generics to allow you to specify the exact types of objects that a particular data structure will store. You can use these predefined data structures instead of building your own. Chapter 27 discusses many data-structure classes that can grow and shrink in response to an application's changing storage requirements. The .NET Framework Class Library also provides class `Array`, which contains utility methods for array manipulation. Chapter 27 uses several `static` methods of class `Array` to perform such manipulations as sorting and searching the data in an array.

We've now introduced the basic concepts of classes, objects, control statements, methods and arrays. In Chapter 9 we introduce one of Visual C# 2008's key new features—Language Integrated Query (LINQ)—which enables you to write expressions that can retrieve information from a wide variety of data sources, such as arrays and collections. You'll see how to search, sort and filter data using LINQ.

9

Introduction to LINQ and Generic Collections

To write it, it took three months; to conceive it three minutes; to collect the data in it—all my life.
—F. Scott Fitzgerald

Science is feasible when the variables are few and can be enumerated; when their combinations are distinct and clear.
—Paul Valéry

You shall listen to all sides and filter them from your self.
—Walt Whitman

The portraitist can select one tiny aspect of everything shown at a moment to incorporate into the final painting.
—Robert Nozick

List, list, O, list!
—William Shakespeare

Be wise to-day; 'tis madness to defer.
—Edward Young

OBJECTIVES

In this chapter you'll learn:

- Basic LINQ concepts.

- How to query an array using LINQ.

- Basic .NET collections concepts.

- How to create and use a generic List collection.

- How to write a generic method.

- How to query a generic List collection using LINQ.

Outline

9.1 Introduction
9.2 Querying an Array Using LINQ
9.3 Introduction to Collections
9.4 Querying a Generic Collection Using LINQ
9.5 Wrap-Up
9.6 Deitel LINQ Resource Center

9.1 Introduction

The preceding chapter introduced arrays—simple data structures used to store data items of a specific type. Although commonly used, arrays have limited capabilities. For instance, you must specify an array's size, and if at execution time, you wish to modify it, you must do so manually by creating a new array or by using the Array class's Resize method, which creates a new array and copies the existing elements into the new array for you. Here, we introduce a set of prepackaged data structures—the .NET Framework's collection classes—that offer greater capabilities than traditional arrays. They are reusable, reliable, powerful and efficient and have been carefully designed and tested to ensure quality and performance. This chapter focuses on the List collection. Lists are similar to arrays but provide additional functionality, such as *dynamic resizing*—they automatically increase their size at execution time to accommodate additional elements. We use the List collection to implement several examples similar to those used in the precedings chapter.

Large amounts of data are often stored in a database—an organized collection of data. (We discuss databases in detail in Chapter 21, Databases and LINQ to SQL.) A database management system (DBMS) provides mechanisms for storing, organizing, retrieving and modifying data in the database. A language called SQL—pronounced "sequel"—is the international standard used almost universally with relational databases to perform *queries* (i.e., to request information that satisfies given criteria) and to manipulate data. For years, programs accessing a relational database passed SQL queries, represented as strings, to the database management system, then processed the results. This chapter introduces C#'s new *LINQ* (*Language Integrated Query*) capabilities. LINQ allows you to write *query expressions* (similar to SQL queries) that retrieve information from a wide variety of data sources, not just databases. We use *LINQ to Objects* in this chapter to query arrays and Lists, selecting elements that satisfy a set of conditions—this is known as *filtering*. Figure 9.1 shows where and how we use LINQ throughout the book to retrieve information from many data sources.

Chapter	Used to
Chapter 9, Introduction to LINQ and Generic Collections	Query arrays and Lists.
Chapter 18, Strings, Characters and Regular Expressions	Select GUI controls in a Windows Forms application.

Fig. 9.1 | LINQ usage throughout the book. (Part 1 of 2.)

Chapter	Used to
Chapter 19, Files and Streams	Search a directory and manipulate text files.
Chapter 20, XML and LINQ to XML	Query an XML document.
Chapter 21, Databases and LINQ to SQL	Retrieve information from a database; insert data into a database.
Chapter 22, ASP.NET 3.5 and ASP.NET AJAX	Retrieve information from a database to be used in a web-based application.
Chapter 23, Windows Communication Foundation (WCF) Web Services	Query and update a database. Process XML returned by WCF services.
Chapter 24, Silverlight, Rich Internet Applications and Multimedia	Process XML returned by web services to a Silverlight application.

Fig. 9.1 | LINQ usage throughout the book. (Part 2 of 2.)

LINQ Providers

The syntax of LINQ is built into the language, but LINQ queries may be used in many different contexts because of libraries known as providers. A *LINQ provider* is a set of classes that implement LINQ operations and enable programs to interact with data sources to perform tasks such as projecting, sorting, grouping and filtering elements.

In this book, we discuss LINQ to SQL and LINQ to XML, which allow you to query databases and XML documents using LINQ. These providers, along with LINQ to Objects, mentioned above, are included with Visual Studio and the .NET Framework. There are many providers that are more specialized, allowing you to interact with a specific website or data format. An extensive list of available providers is located at:

```
blogs.msdn.com/charlie/archive/2006/10/05/Links-to-LINQ.aspx
```

9.2 Querying an Array Using LINQ

Figure 9.2 demonstrates querying an array of integers using LINQ. Repetition statements that filter arrays focus on the process of getting the results—iterating through the elements and checking whether they satisfy the desired criteria. LINQ specifies, not the steps necessary to get the results, but rather the conditions that selected elements must satisfy. This is known as *declarative programming*—as opposed to *imperative programming* (which we've been doing so far) in which you specify the actual steps to perform a task. Object-oriented programming is a subset of imperative. The query in lines 18–20 specifies that the results should consist of all the ints in the values array that are greater than 4. It does not specify *how* those results are obtained—the C# compiler generates all the necessary code automatically, which is one of the great strengths of LINQ.

Line 4 imports the System.Linq namespace, which contains the LINQ to Objects provider. Without importing it, the compiler cannot locate a provider for the LINQ queries and issues errors on LINQ queries.

A LINQ query begins with a ***from clause*** (line 18), which specifies a ***range variable*** (value) and the data source to query (values). The range variable represents each item in the data source, much like the control variable in a foreach statement. Introducing it in the from clause at the beginning of the query allows the IDE to provide *IntelliSense* while you write the rest of the query. The IDE knows the type of the range variable, so it can display the methods and properties of the object.

```csharp
 1    // Fig. 9.2: LINQWithSimpleTypeArray.cs
 2    // LINQ to Objects using an Integer array.
 3    using System;
 4    using System.Linq;
 5    using System.Collections.Generic;
 6
 7    class LINQWithSimpleTypeArray
 8    {
 9       public static void Main( string[] args )
10       {
11          // create an integer array
12          int[] values = { 2, 9, 5, 0, 3, 7, 1, 4, 8, 5 };
13
14          Display( values, "Original array:" ); // display original values
15
16          // LINQ query that obtains values greater than 4 from the array
17          var filtered =
18             from value in values
19             where value > 4
20             select value;
21
22          // display filtered results
23          Display( filtered, "Array values greater than 4:" );
24
25          // use orderby clause to sort original array in ascending order
26          var sorted =
27             from value in values
28             orderby value
29             select value;
30
31          // display sorted results
32          Display( sorted, "Original array, sorted:" );
33
34          // sort the filtered results into descending order
35          var sortFilteredResults =
36             from value in filtered
37             orderby value descending
38             select value;
39
40          // display the sorted results
41          Display( sortFilteredResults,
42             "Values greater than 4, descending order (separately):" );
43
```

Fig. 9.2 | LINQ to Objects using an int array. (Part I of 2.)

```
44          // filter original array and sort in descending order
45          var sortAndFilter =
46              from value in values
47              where value > 4
48              orderby value descending
49              select value;
50
51          // display the filtered and sorted results
52          Display( sortAndFilter,
53              "Values greater than 4, descending order (one query):" );
54      } // end Main
55
56      // display a sequence of integers with the specified header
57      public static void Display(
58          IEnumerable< int > results, string header )
59      {
60          Console.Write( "{0}", header ); // display header
61
62          // display each element, separated by spaces
63          foreach ( var element in results )
64              Console.Write( " {0}", element );
65
66          Console.WriteLine(); // add end of line
67      } // end method Display
68  } // end class LINQWithSimpleTypeArray
```

```
Original array: 2 9 5 0 3 7 1 4 8 5
Array values greater than 4: 9 5 7 8 5
Original array, sorted: 0 1 2 3 4 5 5 7 8 9
Values greater than 4, descending order (separately): 9 8 7 5 5
Values greater than 4, descending order (one query): 9 8 7 5 5
```

Fig. 9.2 | LINQ to Objects using an int array. (Part 2 of 2.)

If the condition in the *where clause* (line 19) evaluates to true, the element is selected—i.e., it's included in the results. Here, the ints in the array are included only if they are greater than 4. An expression that takes an element of a collection and returns true or false by testing a condition on that element is known as a *predicate.*

For each item in the data source, the *select clause* (line 20) determines what value appears in the results. In this case, it is the int that the range variable currently represents. A LINQ query typically ends with a select clause—queries using advanced features may end with other clauses. Later, you'll see that the select clause can transform the selected items—this is known as a *projection.*

Line 23 calls the Display method to show the query results in the console. Note that the Display method (lines 57–67) takes an IEnumerable<int> object as an argument. The type int enclosed in angle brackets after the type name indicates that this IEnumerable may only hold integers. Any type may be used as a *type argument* in this manner—types can be passed as arguments to *generic types* just as objects are passed as arguments to methods. Generic types are covered in more depth in the next section. When we speak of a generic type without using a specific type argument, we use the form IEnumerable<T>, where T represens a type.

IEnumerable<T> is an *interface.* Interfaces define and standardize the ways in which people and systems can interact with one another. For example, the controls on a radio serve as an interface between radio users and the radio's internal components. The controls allow users to perform a limited set of operations (e.g., changing the station, adjusting the volume, and choosing between AM and FM), and different radios may implement the controls in different ways (e.g., using push buttons, dials or voice commands). The interface specifies *what* operations a radio permits users to perform but does not specify *how* the operations are implemented. Similarly, the interface between a driver and a car with a manual transmission includes the steering wheel, the gear shift, the clutch, the gas pedal and the brake pedal. This same interface is found in nearly all manual-transmission cars, enabling someone who knows how to drive one manual-transmission car to drive another.

Software objects also communicate via interfaces. A C# interface describes a set of methods that can be called on an object—to tell the object, for example, to perform some task or return some piece of information. The IEnumerable<T> interface describes the functionality of any object that can be iterated over and thus offers methods to access each element. A class that implements an interface must define each method in the interface with a signature identical to the one in the interface definition. Implementing an interface is like signing a contract with the compiler that states, "I will declare all the methods specified by the interface." Chapter 12, Polymorphism, Interfaces and Operator Overloading covers use of interfaces in more detail, as well as how to define your own interfaces.

Arrays and collections already implement the IEnumerable<T> interface—they define the methods it describes. You can call any method defined by IEnumerable<T> on an array or collection to iterate through its elements. In fact, the foreach statement uses IEnumerable<T> methods to iterate over each element of a collection. A LINQ query returns an object that implements the IEnumerable<T> interface. Therefore, you can use a foreach statement to iterate over the results of any LINQ query. The foreach statement in lines 63–64 iterates over the query result, displaying each item in the console.

It would be simple to display the integers greater than 4 using a repetition statement that tests each value before displaying it. However, this would intertwine the code that selects elements and the code that displays them. With LINQ, these are kept separate, making the code easier to understand and maintain.

The **orderby clause** (line 28) sorts the query results in ascending order. Lines 37 and 48 use the **descending** modifier in the orderby clause to sort the results in descending order. An **ascending** modifier also exists but is not normally used, because ascending order is the default. Any value that can be compared with other values of the same type may be used with the orderby clause. A value of a simple type (e.g., int) can always be compared to another value of the same type; we'll say more about comparing values of reference types in Chapter 12.

The queries in lines 36–38 and 46–49 generate the same results, but in different ways. The first query uses LINQ to sort the results of the query from lines 18–20. The second query uses both the where and orderby clauses. Because queries can operate on the results of other queries, it is possible to build a query one step at a time, and pass the results of queries between methods for further processing.

Using LINQ to Query an Array of Employee Objects

LINQ is not limited to querying arrays of primitive types such as integers. It can be used with most data types, including strings and user-defined classes. It cannot be used when a query does not have a defined meaning—for example, you cannot use orderby on objects that are not comparable. Comparable types in .NET are those that implement the IComparable<T> interface, which is discussed in Section 26.4. All built-in types, such as string, int and double implement IComparable<T>. Figure 9.3 presents the Employee class. Figure 9.4 uses LINQ to query an array of Employee objects.

Line 26 of Fig. 9.4 shows a where clause that accesses the properties of the range variable. In this example, the compiler infers that the range variable is of type Employee based

```csharp
 1  // Fig. 9.3: Employee.cs
 2  // Employee class with FirstName, LastName and MonthlySalary properties.
 3  public class Employee
 4  {
 5     private decimal monthlySalaryValue; // monthly salary of employee
 6
 7     // auto-implemented property FirstName
 8     public string FirstName { get; set; }
 9
10     // auto-implemented property LastName
11     public string LastName { get; set; }
12
13     // constructor initializes first name, last name and monthly salary
14     public Employee( string first, string last, decimal salary )
15     {
16        FirstName = first;
17        LastName = last;
18        MonthlySalary = salary;
19     } // end constructor
20
21     // property that gets and sets the employee's monthly salary
22     public decimal MonthlySalary
23     {
24        get
25        {
26           return monthlySalaryValue;
27        } // end get
28        set
29        {
30           if ( value >= 0M ) // if salary is nonnegative
31           {
32              monthlySalaryValue = value;
33           } // end if
34        } // end set
35     } // end property MonthlySalary
36
37     // return a string containing the employee's information
38     public override string ToString()
39     {
40        return string.Format( "{0,-10} {1,-10} {2,10:C}",
41           FirstName, LastName, MonthlySalary );
42     } // end method ToString
43  } // end class Employee
```

Fig. 9.3 | Employee class with FirstName, LastName and MonthlySalary properties.

on its knowledge that employees was defined as an array of Employee objects (lines 12–19). Any Boolean expression can be used in a where clause. Line 26 uses the conditional AND (&&) operator to combine conditions. Here, only employees that have a salary between $4,000 and $6,000 per month, inclusive, are included in the query result.

```
1   // Fig. 9.4: LINQWithArrayOfObjects.cs
2   // LINQ to Objects using an array of Employee objects.
3   using System;
4   using System.Linq;
5   using System.Collections.Generic;
6
7   public class LINQWithArrayOfObjects
8   {
9      public static void Main( string[] args )
10     {
11        // initialize array of employees
12        Employee[] employees = {
13           new Employee( "Jason", "Red", 5000M ),
14           new Employee( "Ashley", "Green", 7600M ),
15           new Employee( "Matthew", "Indigo", 3587.5M ),
16           new Employee( "James", "Indigo", 4700.77M ),
17           new Employee( "Luke", "Indigo", 6200M ),
18           new Employee( "Jason", "Blue", 3200M ),
19           new Employee( "Wendy", "Brown", 4236.4M ) }; // end init list
20
21        Display( employees, "Original array" ); // display all employees
22
23        // filter a range of salaries using && in a LINQ query
24        var between4K6K =
25           from e in employees
26           where e.MonthlySalary >= 4000M && e.MonthlySalary <= 6000M
27           select e;
28
29        // display employees making between 4000 and 6000 per month
30        Display( between4K6K, string.Format(
31           "Employees earning in the range {0:C}-{1:C} per month",
32           4000, 6000 ) );
33
34        // order the employees by last name, then first name with LINQ
35        var nameSorted =
36           from e in employees
37           orderby e.LastName, e.FirstName
38           select e;
39
40        // header
41        Console.WriteLine( "First employee when sorted by name:" );
42
43        // attempt to display the first result of the above LINQ query
44        if ( nameSorted.Any() )
45           Console.WriteLine( nameSorted.First().ToString() + "\n" );
46        else
47           Console.WriteLine( "not found\n" );
```

Fig. 9.4 | LINQ to Objects using an array of Employee objects. (Part 1 of 3.)

```
48
49          // use LINQ to select employee last names
50          var lastNames =
51              from e in employees
52              select e.LastName;
53
54          // use method Distinct to select unique last names
55          Display( lastNames.Distinct(), "Unique employee last names" );
56
57          // use LINQ to select first and last names
58          var names =
59              from e in employees
60              select new { e.FirstName, Last = e.LastName };
61
62          Display( names, "Names only" ); // display full names
63       } // end Main
64
65       // display a sequence of any type, each on a separate line
66       public static void Display< T >(
67          IEnumerable< T > results, string header )
68       {
69          Console.WriteLine( "{0}:", header ); // display header
70
71          // display each element, separated by spaces
72          foreach ( T element in results )
73              Console.WriteLine( element );
74
75          Console.WriteLine(); // add a blank line
76       } // end method Display
77    } // end class LINQWithArrayOfObjects
```

```
Original array:
Jason       Red         $5,000.00
Ashley      Green       $7,600.00
Matthew     Indigo      $3,587.50
James       Indigo      $4,700.77
Luke        Indigo      $6,200.00
Jason       Blue        $3,200.00
Wendy       Brown       $4,236.40

Employees earning in the range $4,000.00-$6,000.00 per month
Jason       Red         $5,000.00
James       Indigo      $4,700.77
Wendy       Brown       $4,236.40

First employee when sorted by name:
Jason       Blue        $3,200.00

Unique employee last names:
Red
Green
Indigo
Blue
Brown
```

Fig. 9.4 | LINQ to Objects using an array of `Employee` objects. (Part 2 of 3.)

```
Names only:
{ FirstName = Jason, Last = Red }
{ FirstName = Ashley, Last = Green }
{ FirstName = Matthew, Last = Indigo }
{ FirstName = James, Last = Indigo }
{ FirstName = Luke, Last = Indigo }
{ FirstName = Jason, Last = Blue }
{ FirstName = Wendy, Last = Brown }
```

Fig. 9.4 | LINQ to Objects using an array of `Employee` objects. (Part 3 of 3.)

Line 37 uses an `orderby` clause to sort the results according to multiple properties—specified in a comma-separated list. In this query, the employees are sorted alphabetically by last name. Each group of `Employee`s that have the same last name is then sorted within the group by first name.

Line 44 introduces the query result's *Any* method, which returns `true` if there is at least one element, and `false` if there are no elements. The query result's *First* method (line 45) returns the first element in the result. You should check that the query result is not empty (line 44) before calling `First`.

Note that we have not specified the class that defines methods `First` and `Any`. Your intuition probably tells you they are methods declared in the `IEnumerable<T>` interface, but they aren't. They're actually extension methods, but they can be used as if they were methods of `IEnumerable<T>`. We explain the concept of extension methods in Chapter 10, Classes and Objects: A Deeper Look.

LINQ defines many more extension methods, such as *Count*, which returns the number of elements in the results. Rather than using `Any`, we could have checked that `Count` was nonzero, but it is more efficient to determine whether there is at least one element than to count all the elements. Note that the LINQ query syntax is actually transformed by the compiler into extension method calls, with the results of one method call used in the next. It is this design that allows queries to be run on the results of previous queries, as it simply involves passing the result of a method call to another method.

Line 52 uses the `select` clause to select the range variable's `LastName` property rather than the range variable itself. This causes the results of the query to consist of only the last names (as `string`s), instead of complete `Employee` objects. The *Distinct method* (line 55) removes duplicate elements, causing all elements in the result to be unique. In this case, `Distinct` eliminates duplicate last names.

The last LINQ query in the example (lines 59–60) selects the properties `FirstName` and `LastName`. The syntax

```
new { e.FirstName, Last = e.LastName }
```

creates a new object of an *anonymous type* (a type with no name), which the compiler generates for you based on the properties listed in the curly braces ({}). In this case, the anonymous type consists of properties for the first and last names of the selected `Employee`. Note that the `LastName` property is assigned to the property `Last` in the `select` clause. This shows how you can specify a new name for the selected property. If you don't specify a new name, the name of the property being selected is used as the property's name in the result—this is the case for `FirstName` in this example.

When creating a new anonymous type, you can select any number of properties by specifying them in a comma-separated list within the curly braces ({}) that delineate the anonymous type definition. In this case, the compiler automatically creates a new class having properties FirstName and Last, and the values are copied from the Employee objects. These selected properties can then be accessed when iterating over the results. Implicitly typed local variables allow you to use anonymous types because you do not have to explicitly state the type when declaring such variables.

When the compiler creates an anonymous type, it automatically generates a ToString method that returns a string representation of the object. You can see this in the program's output—it consists of the property names and their values, enclosed in braces. Anonymous types are discussed in depth in Chapter 10.

Using a Generic Method to Display LINQ Query Results

Figure 9.2 used LINQ to select integers from an array, then used method Display to output each query's results. Since each query returned an IEnumerable<int>, we used that type as the parameter of method Display. Figure 9.4 performs several LINQ queries that return different types—IEnumerable<Employee>, IEnumerable<string> and IEnumerable of an anonymous type. We'd like to output the string representations of the elements returned by each query. One way to perform the same operation on multiple types is to define overloaded methods. We could do this for the LINQ queries that return IEnumerable<Employee> and IEnumerable<string>, respectively. Unfortunately, we cannot do this for a query that returns an IEnumerable of an anonymous type—there is no type name that we can use to specify the method's parameter type.

If the operations you wish to perform for several types are identical (such as displaying string representations of the elements in query results), overloaded methods can be more compactly and conveniently coded using a *generic method*. This enables you to create a single method definition that can be called with arguments of many types. The compiler infers the type to process based on the generic method call. So, we can create a generic method that iterates through the results of any query (including an IEnumerable of an anonymous type) and outputs each element as a string.

To define a generic method, you must specify a *type-parameter list*—e.g., the < T > in line 66. A type-parameter list—which is placed in angle brackets following the method name—contains one or more type parameters separated by commas. A *type parameter* (T in this example) is a placeholder for a type argument. When you call a generic method, the compiler infers from the arguments in the call what each type parameter represents. Type parameters can be used to declare return types, parameter types (e.g., line 67) and local variable types (e.g., line 72) in generic method declarations.

Lines 66–76 define generic method Display. The parameter named results is of type IEnumerable<T>, indicating that an IEnumerable of any element type can be passed to this method. For example, the call to Display in line 21 passes the employees array as the first element. Since all arrays are also IEnumerables and the employees array contains Employee objects, the compiler infers for this call that the type parameter T should be replaced with the type Employee. In this case, Employee is known as the type argument for the type parameter T. Line 55 calls method Distinct on the results of the query at lines 51–52. In this case, method Distinct returns an IEnumerable<string> (containing the unique last names), which is then passed to method Display. In this case, the compiler infers that the type argument is string. The call in line 62 receives an IEnumerable of an anonymous type. In this case, the compiler infers from the call that the type argument is of the anonymous type that was created in response to the query in lines 59–60.

Notes About Type Parameters and Generic Methods

A type parameter can be declared only once in the type-parameter list but can appear more than once in the method's parameter list and body, and as the method's return type. The type-parameter names throughout the method declaration must match those declared in the type-parameter list. For example, line 72 declares element in the foreach statement as type T, which matches the type parameter (T) declared in line 66. Type-parameter names need not be unique among different generic methods.

Common Programming Error 9.1

If you forget to include the type-parameter list when declaring a generic method, the compiler will not recognize the type-parameter names when they're encountered in the method, causing compilation errors.

When compiling a generic method, the compiler also determines whether the operations in the method body can be performed on any type that a type parameter may represent. The only operation performed on the IEnumerable<T> elements in this example is to output their string representations. In .NET, all values and objects have string representations (see Section 10.2), so our Display method works for any type of element. When we discuss generic methods in more detail in Chapter 26, Generics, we'll introduce type constraints, which enable you to restrict the types of values and objects that can be used with a generic method.

9.3 Introduction to Collections

The .NET Framework Class Library provides several classes, called collections, used to store groups of related objects. These classes provide efficient methods that organize, store and retrieve your data without requiring knowledge of how the data is being stored. This reduces application-development time.

You've used arrays to store sequences of objects. Arrays do not automatically change their size at execution time to accommodate additional elements—you must do so manually by creating a new array or by using the Array class's Resize method.

The collection class *List<T>* (from namespace System.Collections.Generic) provides a convenient solution to this problem. The T is a placeholder—when declaring a new List, replace it with the type of elements that you want the List to hold. This is similar to specifying the type when declaring an array. For example,

        List< *int* > list1;

declares list1 as a List collection that can store only int values, and

        List< *string* > list2;

declares list2 as a List of strings. Classes with this kind of placeholder that can be used with any type are called *generic classes*. Generic classes and additional generic collection classes are discussed in Chapters 26 and 27, respectively. Figure 27.2 provides a table of collection classes. Figure 9.5 shows some common methods and properties of class List<T>.

Method or property	Description
Add	Adds an element to the end of the List.
Capacity	Property that gets or sets the number of elements a List can store.
Clear	Removes all the elements from the List.
Contains	Returns true if the List contains the specified element; otherwise, returns false.
Count	Property that returns the number of elements stored in the List.
IndexOf	Returns the index of the first occurrence of the specified value in the List.
Insert	Inserts an element at the specified index.
Remove	Removes the first occurrence of the specified value.
RemoveAt	Removes the element at the specified index.
RemoveRange	Removes a specified number of elements starting at a specified index.
Sort	Sorts the List.
TrimExcess	Sets the Capacity of the List to the number of elements the List currently contains (Count).

Fig. 9.5 | Some methods and properties of class List<T>.

Figure 9.6 demonstrates dynamically resizing a List object. The Add and Insert methods add elements to the List (lines 13–14). The **Add** method appends its argument to the end of the List. The **Insert** method inserts a new element at the specified position. The first argument is an index—as with arrays, collection indices start at zero. The second argument is the value that is to be inserted at the specified index. All elements at the specified index and above are shifted up by one position. This is usually slower than adding an element to the end of the List.

Lines 21–22 display the items in the List. The **Count** property returns the number of elements currently in the List—note that while they provide the same functionality, it is unrelated to the Count method provided by LINQ. Lists can be indexed like arrays by

```
1   // Fig. 9.6: ListCollection.cs
2   // Generic List collection demonstration.
3   using System;
4   using System.Collections.Generic;
5
6   public class ListCollection
7   {
8      public static void Main( string[] args )
9      {
10         // create a new List of strings
11         List< string > items = new List< string >();
```

Fig. 9.6 | Generic List<T> collection demonstration. (Part 1 of 3.)

```
12
13        items.Add( "red" ); // append an item to the List
14        items.Insert( 0, "yellow" ); // insert the value at index 0
15
16        // header
17        Console.Write(
18           "Display list contents with counter-controlled loop:" );
19
20        // display the colors in the list
21        for ( int i = 0; i < items.Count; i++ )
22           Console.Write( " {0}", items[ i ] );
23
24        // display colors using foreach in the Display method
25        Display( items,
26           "\nDisplay list contents with foreach statement:" );
27
28        items.Add( "green" ); // add "green" to the end of the List
29        items.Add( "yellow" ); // add "yellow" to the end of the List
30        // display the List
31        Display( items, "List with two new elements:" );
32
33        items.Remove( "yellow" ); // remove the first "yellow"
34        // display List
35        Display( items, "Remove first instance of yellow:" );
36
37        items.RemoveAt( 1 ); // remove item at index 1
38        // display List
39        Display( items, "Remove second list element (green):" );
40
41        // check if a value is in the List
42        Console.WriteLine( "\"red\" is {0}in the list",
43           items.Contains( "red" ) ? string.Empty : "not " );
44
45        // display number of elements in the List
46        Console.WriteLine( "Count: {0}", items.Count );
47
48        // display the capacity of the List
49        Console.WriteLine( "Capacity: {0}", items.Capacity );
50     } // end Main
51
52     // display the List's elements on the console
53     public static void Display( List< string > items, string header )
54     {
55        Console.Write( header ); // display header
56
57        // display each element in items
58        foreach ( var item in items )
59           Console.Write( " {0}", item );
60
61        Console.WriteLine(); // display end of line
62     } // end method Display
63  } // end class ListCollection
```

Fig. 9.6 | Generic List<T> collection demonstration. (Part 2 of 3.)

```
Display list contents with counter-controlled loop: yellow red
Display list contents with foreach statement: yellow red
List with two new elements: yellow red green yellow
Remove first instance of yellow: red green yellow
Remove second list element (green): red yellow
"red" is in the list
Count: 2
Capacity: 4
```

Fig. 9.6 | Generic List<T> collection demonstration. (Part 3 of 3.)

placing the index in square brackets after the List variable's name. The indexed List expression can be used to modify the element at the index. More elements are then added to the List, and it is displayed again (lines 28–31).

The **Remove** method is used to remove an element with a specific value (line 33). Note that it removes only the first such element. If no such element is in the List, Remove does nothing. A similar method, **RemoveAt**, removes the element at the specified index (line 37). When an element is removed through either of these methods, all elements above that index are shifted down by one—the opposite of the Insert method.

Line 43 uses the **Contains** method to check if an item is in the List. The Contains method returns true if the element is found in the List, and false otherwise. The method compares its argument to each element of the List in order, so using Contains on a large List is inefficient.

Lines 46 and 49 display the List's Count and Capacity. Recall that the Count property (line 46) indicates the number of items in the List. The **Capacity** property (line 49) indicates how many items the List can hold without growing. List is implemented using an array behind the scenes. When the List grows, it must create a larger internal array and copy each element to the new array. This is a time-consuming operation. It would be inefficient for the List to grow each time an element is added. Instead, the List grows only when an element is added *and* the Count and Capacity properties are equal—there is no space for the new element. The List doubles its Capacity each time it grows. This reduces the number of times the internal array must be recreated.

9.4 Querying a Generic Collection Using LINQ

You can use LINQ to Objects to query Lists just as arrays. In Fig. 9.7, a List of strings is converted to uppercase and searched for those that begin with "R".

```
1   // Fig. 9.7: LINQWithListCollection.cs
2   // LINQ to Objects using a List< string >.
3   using System;
4   using System.Linq;
5   using System.Collections.Generic;
6
7   public class LINQWithListCollection
8   {
```

Fig. 9.7 | LINQ to Objects using a List<string>. (Part 1 of 2.)

```
 9       public static void Main( string[] args )
10       {
11           // populate a List of strings with random case
12           List< string > items = new List< string >();
13           items.Add( "aQua" ); // add "aQua" to the end of the List
14           items.Add( "RusT" ); // add "RusT" to the end of the List
15           items.Add( "yElLow" ); // add "yElLow" to the end of the List
16           items.Add( "rEd" ); // add "rEd" to the end of the List
17
18           // convert all strings to uppercase; select those starting with "R"
19           var startsWithR =
20               from item in items
21               let uppercasedString = item.ToUpper()
22               where uppercasedString.StartsWith( "R" )
23               orderby uppercasedString
24               select uppercasedString;
25
26           // display query results
27           foreach ( var item in startsWithR )
28               Console.Write( "{0} ", item );
29
30           Console.WriteLine(); // output end of line
31
32           items.Add( "rUbY" ); // add "rUbY" to the end of the List
33           items.Add( "SaFfRon" ); // add "SaFfRon" to the end of the List
34
35           // display updated query results
36           foreach ( var item in startsWithR )
37               Console.Write( "{0} ", item );
38
39           Console.WriteLine(); // output end of line
40       } // end Main
41   } // end class LINQWithListCollection
```

```
RED RUST
RED RUBY RUST
```

Fig. 9.7 | LINQ to Objects using a List<string>. (Part 2 of 2.)

Line 21 uses LINQ's **let clause** to create a new range variable. This is useful if you need to store a temporary result for use later in the LINQ query. Typically, let declares a new range variable to which you assign the result of an expression that operates on the query's original range variable. In this case, we use string method **ToUpper** to convert each item to uppercase, then store the result in the new range variable uppercasedString. We then use the new range variable uppercasedString in the where, orderby and select clauses. The where clause (line 22) uses string method **StartsWith** to determine whether uppercasedString starts with the character "R". Method StartsWith performs a case sensitive comparison to determine whether a string starts with the string received as an argument. If uppercasedString starts with "R", method StartsWith returns true, and the element is included in the query results. More powerful string matching can be done using the regular-expression capabilities introduced in Chapter 18, Strings, Characters and Regular Expressions.

Note that the query is created only once (lines 20–24), yet iterating over the results (lines 27–28 and 36–37) gives two different lists of colors. This demonstrates LINQ's *deferred execution*—the query executes only when you access the results—such as iterating over them or using the Count method—not when you define the query. This allows you to create a query once and execute it many times. Any changes to the data source are reflected in the results each time the query executes.

There may be times when you do not want this behavior, and want to retrieve a collection of the results immediately. LINQ provides extension methods ToArray and ToList for this purpose. These methods execute the query on which they are called and give you the results as an array or List<T>, respectively. These methods can also improve efficiency if you will be iterating over the results multiple times, as you execute the query only once.

C# now has a feature called *collection initializers*, which provide a convenient syntax (similar to array initializers) for initializing a collection. For example, lines 12–16 of Fig. 9.7 could be replaced with the following statement:

```
List< string > items =
    new List< string > { "aQua", "RusT", "yElLow", "rEd" };
```

9.5 Wrap-Up

This chapter introduced LINQ (Language Integrated Query), a powerful new feature for querying data. We showed how to filter an array or collection using LINQ's where clause, and how to sort the query results using the orderby clause. We used the select clause to select specific properties of an object, and the let clause to introduce a new range variable to make writing queries more convenient. The StartsWith method of class string was used to filter strings starting with a specified character or series of characters. We used several extension methods provided by LINQ to perform operations not provided by the query syntax—the Distinct method to remove duplicates from the results, the Any method to determine if the results contain any items, and the First method to retrieve the first element in the results.

We introduced the List<T> generic collection, which provides all the functionality and performance of arrays, along with other useful capabilities such as dynamic resizing. We used the Add method to append new items to the end of the List. Then we used the Insert method to insert new items into specified locations in the List. The Remove method was used to remove the first occurrence of a specified item, and the RemoveAt method was used to remove an item at a specified index. The Count property returns the number of items in the List, and the Capacity property is the size the List can grow to without reallocating the internal array. In Chapter 10 we take a deeper look at classes and objects.

9.6 Deitel LINQ Resource Center

LINQ is a powerful new programming feature in C# 3.0—the version of C# in Visual C# 2008. We use more advanced features of LINQ in later chapters. We've also created an extensive LINQ Resource Center that contains many links to additional information, including blogs by Microsoft LINQ team members, sample chapters, tutorials and videos. We encourage you to browse the LINQ Resource Center (www.deitel.com/LINQ/) to learn more about this exciting technology.

10

Classes and Objects: A Deeper Look

Instead of this absurd division into sexes, they ought to class people as static and dynamic.
—Evelyn Waugh

Is it a world to hide virtues in?
—William Shakespeare

But what, to serve our private ends, Forbids the cheating of our friends?
—Charles Churchill

This above all: to thine own self be true.
—William Shakespeare

Don't be "consistent," but be simply true.
—Oliver WendellHolmes, Jr.

OBJECTIVES

In this chapter you'll learn:

- Encapsulation and data hiding.
- The concepts of data abstraction and abstract data types (ADTs).
- To use keyword `this`.
- To use indexers to access members of a class.
- To use `static` variables and methods.
- To use `readonly` fields.
- To take advantage of C#'s memory-management features.
- How to create a class library.
- When to use the `internal` access modifier.
- To use object initializers to set property values as you create a new object.
- To add functionality to existing classes with extension methods.
- To use delegates and lambda expressions to pass methods to other methods for execution at a later time.
- To create objects of anonymous types.

Outline

10.1 Introduction

10.2 Time Class Case Study

10.3 Controlling Access to Members

10.4 Referring to the Current Object's Members with the **this** Reference

10.5 Indexers

10.6 Time Class Case Study: Overloaded Constructors

10.7 Default and Parameterless Constructors

10.8 Composition

10.9 Garbage Collection and Destructors

10.10 **static** Class Members

10.11 **readonly** Instance Variables

10.12 Software Reusability

10.13 Data Abstraction and Encapsulation

10.14 Time Class Case Study: Creating Class Libraries

10.15 **internal** Access

10.16 **Class View** and **Object Browser**

10.17 Object Initializers

10.18 Time Class Case Study: Extension Methods

10.19 Delegates

10.20 Lambda Expressions

10.21 Anonymous Types

10.22 (Optional) Software Engineering Case Study: Starting to Program the Classes of the ATM System

10.23 Wrap-Up

10.1 Introduction

In our discussions of object-oriented applications in the preceding chapters, we introduced many basic concepts and terminology that relate to C# object-oriented programming (OOP). We also discussed our application-development methodology: We selected appropriate variables and methods for each application and specified the manner in which an object of our class collaborated with objects of classes in the .NET Framework Class Library to accomplish the application's overall goals.

In this chapter, we take a deeper look at building classes, controlling access to members of a class and creating constructors. We discuss composition—a capability that allows a class to have references to objects of other classes as members. We reexamine the use of properties and explore indexers as an alternative notation for accessing the members of a class. The chapter also discusses static class members and readonly instance variables in detail. We investigate issues such as software reusability, data abstraction and encapsulation. Finally, we explain how to organize classes in assemblies to help manage large applications and promote reuse, then show a special relationship between classes in the same assembly.

Chapter 11, Object-Oriented Programming: Inheritance, and Chapter 12, Polymorphism, Interfaces and Operator Overloading, introduce two additional key object-oriented programming technologies.

10.2 Time Class Case Study

Time1 *Class Declaration*
Our first example consists of two classes—Time1 (Fig. 10.1) and Time1Test (Fig. 10.2). Class Time1 represents the time of day. Class Time1Test is a testing class in which the Main method creates an object of class Time1 and invokes its methods. The output of this application appears in Fig. 10.2.

Class Time1 contains three private instance variables of type int (Fig. 10.1, lines 5–7)—hour, minute and second—that represent the time in universal-time format (24-hour clock format, in which hours are in the range 0–23). Class Time1 contains public methods SetTime (lines 11–16), ToUniversalString (lines 19–23) and ToString (lines 26–31). These are the ***public services*** or the ***public interface*** that the class provides to its clients.

```csharp
 1   // Fig. 10.1: Time1.cs
 2   // Time1 class declaration maintains the time in 24-hour format.
 3   public class Time1
 4   {
 5      private int hour;   // 0 - 23
 6      private int minute; // 0 - 59
 7      private int second; // 0 - 59
 8
 9      // set a new time value using universal time; ensure that
10      // the data remains consistent by setting invalid values to zero
11      public void SetTime( int h, int m, int s )
12      {
13         hour = ( ( h >= 0 && h < 24 ) ? h : 0 ); // validate hour
14         minute = ( ( m >= 0 && m < 60 ) ? m : 0 ); // validate minute
15         second = ( ( s >= 0 && s < 60 ) ? s : 0 ); // validate second
16      } // end method SetTime
17
18      // convert to string in universal-time format (HH:MM:SS)
19      public string ToUniversalString()
20      {
21         return string.Format( "{0:D2}:{1:D2}:{2:D2}",
22            hour, minute, second );
23      } // end method ToUniversalString
24
25      // convert to string in standard-time format (H:MM:SS AM or PM)
26      public override string ToString()
27      {
28         return string.Format( "{0}:{1:D2}:{2:D2} {3}",
29            ( ( hour == 0 || hour == 12 ) ? 12 : hour % 12 ),
30            minute, second, ( hour < 12 ? "AM" : "PM" ) );
31      } // end method ToString
32   } // end class Time1
```

Fig. 10.1 | Time1 class declaration maintains the time in 24-hour format.

In this example, class Time1 does not declare a constructor, so the class has a default constructor that is supplied by the compiler. Each instance variable implicitly receives the default value 0 for an int. Note that when instance variables are declared in the class body, they can be initialized using the same initialization syntax as a local variable.

Method SetTime (lines 11–16) is a public method that declares three int parameters and uses them to set the time. A conditional expression tests each argument to determine whether the value is in a specified range. For example, the hour value (line 13) must be greater than or equal to 0 and less than 24, because universal-time format represents hours as integers from 0 to 23 (e.g., 1 PM is hour 13 and 11 PM is hour 23; midnight is hour 0 and noon is hour 12). Similarly, both minute and second values (lines 14 and 15) must be greater than or equal to 0 and less than 60. Any out-of-range values are set to 0 to ensure that a Time1 object always contains consistent data—that is, the object's data values are always kept in range, even if the values provided as arguments to method SetTime are incorrect. In this example, 0 is a consistent value for hour, minute and second.

A value passed to SetTime is a correct value if that value is in the allowed range for the member it is initializing. So, any number in the range 0–23 would be a correct value for the hour. A correct value is always a consistent value. However, a consistent value is not necessarily a correct value. If SetTime sets hour to 0 because the argument received was out of range, then SetTime is taking an incorrect value and making it consistent, so the object remains in a consistent state at all times. In this case, the application might want to indicate that the object is incorrect. In Chapter 13, Exception Handling, you'll learn techniques that enable your classes to indicate when incorrect values are received.

Software Engineering Observation 10.1

Methods and properties that modify the values of private *variables should verify that the intended new values are valid. If they are not, they should place the* private *variables in an appropriate consistent state.*

Method ToUniversalString (lines 19–23) takes no arguments and returns a string in universal-time format, consisting of six digits—two for the hour, two for the minute and two for the second. For example, if the time were 1:30:07 PM, method ToUniversal-String would return 13:30:07. The return statement (lines 21–22) uses static method **Format** of class string to return a string containing the formatted hour, minute and second values, each with two digits and, where needed, a leading 0 (specified with the D2 format specifier—which pads the integer with 0s if it has less than two digits). Method Format is similar to the string formatting in method Console.Write, except that Format returns a formatted string rather than displaying it in a console window. The formatted string is returned by method ToUniversalString.

Method ToString (lines 26–31) takes no arguments and returns a string in standard-time format, consisting of the hour, minute and second values separated by colons and followed by an AM or PM indicator (e.g., 1:27:06 PM). Like method ToUniversal-String, method ToString uses static string method Format to format the minute and second as two-digit values with leading 0s, if necessary. Line 29 uses a conditional operator (?:) to determine the value for hour in the string—if the hour is 0 or 12 (AM or PM), it appears as 12—otherwise, it appears as a value from 1 to 11. The conditional operator in line 30 determines whether AM or PM will be returned as part of the string.

Recall from Section 7.4 that all objects in C# have a ToString method that returns a string representation of the object. We chose to return a string containing the time in standard-time format. Method ToString is called implicitly when an object's value is output with a format item in a call to Console.Write. Remember that to enable objects to be converted to their string representations, we need to declare method ToString with keyword override—the reason for this will become clear when we discuss inheritance in Chapter 11.

Using Class Time1

As you learned in Chapter 4, each class you declare represents a new type in C#. Therefore, after declaring class Time1, we can use it as a type in declarations such as

```
Time1 sunset; // sunset can hold a reference to a Time1 object
```

The Time1Test application class (Fig. 10.2) uses class Time1. Line 10 creates a Time1 object and assigns it to local variable time. Note that new invokes class Time1's default constructor, since Time1 does not declare any constructors. Lines 13–17 output the time, first in universal-time format (by invoking time's ToUniversalString method in line 14), then in standard-time format (by explicitly invoking time's ToString method in line 16) to confirm that the Time1 object was initialized properly.

```
 1   // Fig. 10.2: Time1Test.cs
 2   // Time1 object used in an application.
 3   using System;
 4
 5   public class Time1Test
 6   {
 7      public static void Main( string[] args )
 8      {
 9         // create and initialize a Time1 object
10         Time1 time = new Time1(); // invokes Time1 constructor
11
12         // output string representations of the time
13         Console.Write( "The initial universal time is: " );
14         Console.WriteLine( time.ToUniversalString() );
15         Console.Write( "The initial standard time is: " );
16         Console.WriteLine( time.ToString() );
17         Console.WriteLine(); // output a blank line
18
19         // change time and output updated time
20         time.SetTime( 13, 27, 6 );
21         Console.Write( "Universal time after SetTime is: " );
22         Console.WriteLine( time.ToUniversalString() );
23         Console.Write( "Standard time after SetTime is: " );
24         Console.WriteLine( time.ToString() );
25         Console.WriteLine(); // output a blank line
26
27         // set time with invalid values; output updated time
28         time.SetTime( 99, 99, 99 );
29         Console.WriteLine( "After attempting invalid settings:" );
```

Fig. 10.2 | Time1 object used in an application. (Part 1 of 2.)

```
30          Console.Write( "Universal time: " );
31          Console.WriteLine( time.ToUniversalString() );
32          Console.Write( "Standard time: " );
33          Console.WriteLine( time.ToString() );
34      } // end Main
35  } // end class Time1Test
```

```
The initial universal time is: 00:00:00
The initial standard time is: 12:00:00 AM

Universal time after SetTime is: 13:27:06
Standard time after SetTime is: 1:27:06 PM

After attempting invalid settings:
Universal time: 00:00:00
Standard time: 12:00:00 AM
```

Fig. 10.2 | Time1 object used in an application. (Part 2 of 2.)

Line 20 invokes method SetTime of the time object to change the time. Then lines 21–25 output the time again in both formats to confirm that the time was set correctly.

To illustrate that method SetTime maintains the object in a consistent state, line 28 calls method SetTime with invalid arguments of 99 for the hour, minute and second. Lines 29–33 output the time again in both formats to confirm that SetTime maintains the object's consistent state, then the application terminates. The last two lines of the application's output show that the time is reset to midnight—the initial value of a Time1 object—after an attempt to set the time with three out-of-range values.

Notes on the Time1 Class Declaration

Consider several issues of class design with respect to class Time1. The instance variables hour, minute and second are each declared private. The actual data representation used within the class is of no concern to the class's clients. For example, it would be perfectly reasonable for Time1 to represent the time internally as the number of seconds since midnight or the number of minutes and seconds since midnight. Clients could use the same public methods and properties to get the same results without being aware of this.

Software Engineering Observation 10.2

Classes simplify programming because the client can use only the public members exposed by the class. Such members are usually client oriented rather than implementation oriented. Clients are neither aware of, nor involved in, a class's implementation. Clients generally care about what the class does but not how the class does it. (Clients do, of course, care that the class operates correctly and efficiently.)

Software Engineering Observation 10.3

Interfaces change less frequently than implementations. When an implementation changes, implementation-dependent code must change accordingly. Hiding the implementation reduces the possibility that other application parts become dependent on class-implementation details.

10.3 Controlling Access to Members

The access modifiers public and private control access to a class's variables and methods. (In Section 10.15 and Chapter 11, we'll introduce the additional access modifiers internal and protected, respectively.) As we stated in Section 10.2, the primary purpose of public methods is to present to the class's clients a view of the services the class provides (that is, the class's public interface). Clients of the class need not be concerned with how the class accomplishes its tasks. For this reason, a class's private variables, properties and methods (i.e., the class's implementation details) are not directly accessible to the class's clients.

Figure 10.3 demonstrates that private class members are not directly accessible outside the class. Lines 9–11 attempt to access directly private instance variables hour, minute and second of Time1 object time. When this application is compiled, the compiler generates error messages stating that these private members are not accessible. [*Note:* This application assumes that the Time1 class from Fig. 10.1 is used.]

Common Programming Error 10.1

An attempt by a method that is not a member of a class to access a private member of that class is a compilation error.

Notice that members of a class—for instance, properties, methods and instance variables—do not need to be explicitly declared private. If a class member is not declared with an access modifier, it has private access by default. We always explicitly declare private members.

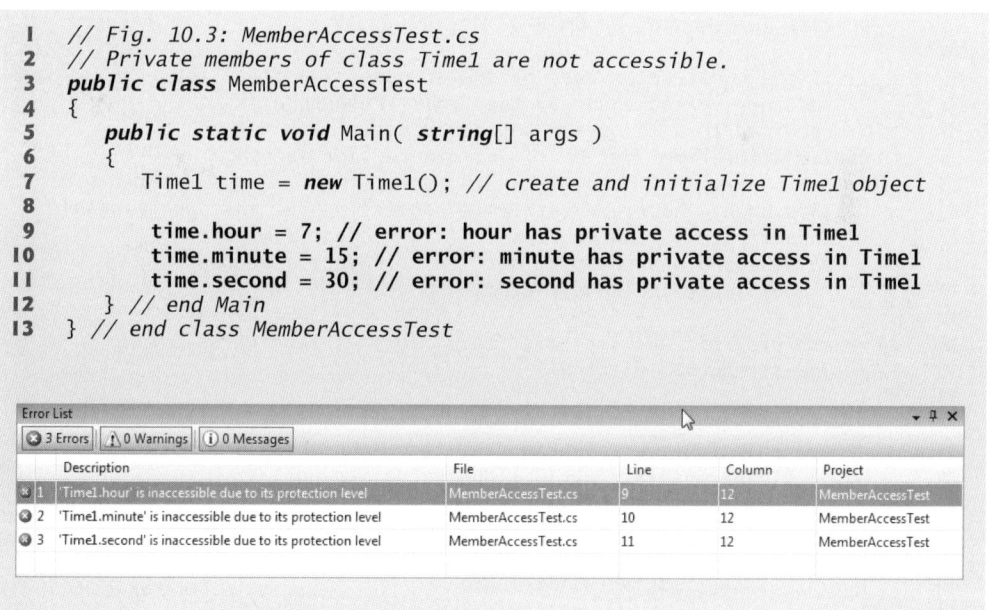

```
1   // Fig. 10.3: MemberAccessTest.cs
2   // Private members of class Time1 are not accessible.
3   public class MemberAccessTest
4   {
5      public static void Main( string[] args )
6      {
7         Time1 time = new Time1(); // create and initialize Time1 object
8
9         time.hour = 7; // error: hour has private access in Time1
10        time.minute = 15; // error: minute has private access in Time1
11        time.second = 30; // error: second has private access in Time1
12     } // end Main
13  } // end class MemberAccessTest
```

	Description	File	Line	Column	Project
1	'Time1.hour' is inaccessible due to its protection level	MemberAccessTest.cs	9	12	MemberAccessTest
2	'Time1.minute' is inaccessible due to its protection level	MemberAccessTest.cs	10	12	MemberAccessTest
3	'Time1.second' is inaccessible due to its protection level	MemberAccessTest.cs	11	12	MemberAccessTest

Fig. 10.3 | Private members of class Time1 are not accessible.

10.4 Referring to the Current Object's Members with the this Reference

Every object can access a reference to itself with keyword *this* (also called the *this reference*). When a non-static method is called for a particular object, the method's body implicitly uses keyword this to refer to the object's instance variables and other methods. As you'll see in Fig. 10.4, you can also use keyword this *explicitly* in a non-static method's body. Section 10.5 and Section 10.6 show two more interesting uses of keyword this. Section 10.10 explains why keyword this cannot be used in a static method.

```
 1  // Fig. 10.4: ThisTest.cs
 2  // this used implicitly and explicitly to refer to members of an object.
 3  using System;
 4
 5  public class ThisTest
 6  {
 7     public static void Main( string[] args )
 8     {
 9        SimpleTime time = new SimpleTime( 15, 30, 19 );
10        Console.WriteLine( time.BuildString() );
11     } // end Main
12  } // end class ThisTest
13
14  // class SimpleTime demonstrates the "this" reference
15  public class SimpleTime
16  {
17     private int hour;   // 0-23
18     private int minute; // 0-59
19     private int second; // 0-59
20
21     // if the constructor uses parameter names identical to
22     // instance-variable names, the "this" reference is
23     // required to distinguish between names
24     public SimpleTime( int hour, int minute, int second )
25     {
26        this.hour = hour; // set "this" object's hour instance variable
27        this.minute = minute; // set "this" object's minute
28        this.second = second; // set "this" object's second
29     } // end SimpleTime constructor
30
31     // use explicit and implicit "this" to call ToUniversalString
32     public string BuildString()
33     {
34        return string.Format( "{0,24}: {1}\n{2,24}: {3}",
35           "this.ToUniversalString()", this.ToUniversalString(),
36           "ToUniversalString()", ToUniversalString() );
37     } // end method BuildString
38
39     // convert to string in universal-time format (HH:MM:SS)
40     public string ToUniversalString()
41     {
```

Fig. 10.4 | this used implicitly and explicitly to refer to members of an object. (Part 1 of 2.)

```
42              // "this" is not required here to access instance variables,
43              // because method does not have local variables with same
44              // names as instance variables
45              return string.Format( "{0:D2}:{1:D2}:{2:D2}",
46                  this.hour, this.minute, this.second );
47          } // end method ToUniversalString
48      } // end class SimpleTime
```

```
this.ToUniversalString(): 15:30:19
    ToUniversalString(): 15:30:19
```

Fig. 10.4 | this used implicitly and explicitly to refer to members of an object. (Part 2 of 2.)

We now demonstrate implicit and explicit use of the this reference to enable class ThisTest's Main method to display the private data of a class SimpleTime object (Fig. 10.4). For the sake of brevity, we declare two classes in one file—class ThisTest is declared in lines 5–12, and class SimpleTime is declared in lines 15–48.

Class SimpleTime (lines 15–48) declares three private instance variables—hour, minute and second (lines 17–19). The constructor (lines 24–29) receives three int arguments to initialize a SimpleTime object. Note that for the constructor we used parameter names that are identical to the class's instance-variable names (lines 17–19). We don't recommend this practice, but we did it here to hide the corresponding instance variables so that we could illustrate explicit use of the this reference. Recall from Section 7.11 that if a method contains a local variable with the same name as a field, that method will refer to the local variable rather than the field. In this case, the parameter hides the field in the method's scope. However, the method can use the this reference to refer to the hidden instance variable explicitly, as shown in lines 26–28 for SimpleTime's hidden instance variables.

Method BuildString (lines 32–37) returns a string created by a statement that uses the this reference explicitly and implicitly. Line 35 uses the this reference explicitly to call method ToUniversalString. Line 36 uses the this reference implicitly to call the same method. Note that both lines perform the same task. Programmers typically do not use the this reference explicitly to reference other methods in the current object. Also, note that line 46 in method ToUniversalString explicitly uses the this reference to access each instance variable. This is not necessary here, because the method does not have any local variables that hide the instance variables of the class.

Common Programming Error 10.2

It is often a logic error when a method contains a parameter or local variable that has the same name as an instance variable of the class. In such a case, use reference this if you wish to access the instance variable of the class—otherwise, the method parameter or local variable will be referenced.

Error-Prevention Tip 10.1

Avoid method-parameter names or local-variable names that conflict with field names. This helps prevent subtle, hard-to-locate bugs.

Class ThisTest (Fig. 10.4, lines 5–12) demonstrates class SimpleTime. Line 9 creates an instance of class SimpleTime and invokes its constructor. Line 10 invokes the object's BuildString method, then displays the results.

Performance Tip 10.1

C# conserves memory by maintaining only one copy of each method per class—this method is invoked by every object of the class. Each object, on the other hand, has its own copy of the class's instance variables (i.e., non-static variables). Each method of the class implicitly uses the this reference to determine the specific object of the class to manipulate.

10.5 Indexers

Chapter 4 introduced properties as a way to access a class's private data in a controlled manner via the properties' get and set accessors. Sometimes a class encapsulates lists of data such as arrays. Such a class can use keyword this to define property-like class members called *indexers* that allow array-style indexed access to lists of elements. With "conventional" C# arrays, the index must be an integer value. A benefit of indexers is that you can define both integer indices and noninteger indices. For example, you could allow client code to manipulate data using strings as indices that represent the data items' names or descriptions. When manipulating "conventional" C# array elements, the array element-access operator always returns a value of the same type—i.e., the type of the array's elements. Indexers are more flexible—they can return any type, even one that is different from the type of the underlying data.

Although an indexer's element-access operator is used like an array element-access operator, indexers are defined like properties in a class. Unlike properties, for which you can choose an appropriate property name, indexers must be defined with keyword this. Indexers have the general form:

```
accessModifier returnType this[ IndexType1 name1, IndexType2 name2, ... ]
{
    get
    {
        // use name1, name2, ... here to get data
    }
    set
    {
        // use name1, name2, ... here to set data
    }
}
```

The *IndexType* parameters specified in the brackets ([]) are accessible to the get and set accessors. These accessors define how to use the index (or indices) to retrieve or modify the appropriate data member. As with properties, the indexer's get accessor must return a value of type *returnType*, and the set accessor can use the implicit parameter value to reference the value that should be assigned to the element.

Common Programming Error 10.3

Declaring indexers as static is a syntax error.

The application of Figs. 10.5 and 10.6 contains two classes—class Box represents a box with a length, a width and a height, and class BoxTest demonstrates class Box's indexers.

```
1   // Fig. 10.5: Box.cs
2   // Box class definition represents a box with length,
3   // width and height dimensions with indexers.
4   public class Box
5   {
6      private string[] names = { "length", "width", "height" };
7      private double[] dimensions = new double[ 3 ];
8
9      // constructor
10     public Box( double length, double width, double height )
11     {
12        dimensions[ 0 ] = length;
13        dimensions[ 1 ] = width;
14        dimensions[ 2 ] = height;
15     }
16
17     // indexer to access dimensions by integer index number
18     public double this[ int index ]
19     {
20        get
21        {
22           // validate index to get
23           if ( ( index < 0 ) || ( index >= dimensions.Length ) )
24              return -1;
25           else
26              return dimensions[ index ];
27        } // end get
28        set
29        {
30           if ( index >= 0 && index < dimensions.Length )
31              dimensions[ index ] = value;
32        } // end set
33     } // end numeric indexer
34
35     // indexer to access dimensions by their string names
36     public double this[ string name ]
37     {
38        get
39        {
40           // locate element to get
41           int i = 0;
42           while ( ( i < names.Length ) &&
43              ( name.ToLower() != names[ i ] ) )
44              ++i;
45
46           return ( i == names.Length ) ? -1 : dimensions[ i ];
47        } // end get
```

Fig. 10.5 | Box class definition represents a box with length, width and height dimensions with indexers. (Part 1 of 2.)

```
48        set
49        {
50            // locate element to set
51            int i = 0;
52            while ( ( i < names.Length ) &&
53                ( name.ToLower() != names[ i ] ) )
54                ++i;
55
56            if ( i != names.Length )
57                dimensions[ i ] = value;
58        } // end set
59    } // end string indexer
60 } // end class Box
```

Fig. 10.5 | Box class definition represents a box with length, width and height dimensions with indexers. (Part 2 of 2.)

The private data members of class Box are string array names (line 6), which contains the names (i.e., "length", "width" and "height") for the dimensions of a Box, and double array dimensions (line 7), which contains the size of each dimension. Each element in array names corresponds to an element in array dimensions (e.g., dimensions[2] contains the height of the Box).

Box defines two indexers (lines 18–33 and lines 36–59) that each return a double value representing the size of the dimension specified by the indexer's parameter. Indexers can be overloaded like methods. The first indexer uses an int index to manipulate an element in the dimensions array. The second indexer uses a string index representing the name of the dimension to manipulate an element in the dimensions array. Each indexer returns -1 if its get accessor encounters an invalid index. Each indexer's set accessor assigns value to the appropriate element of the array dimensions only if the index specified is valid. Normally, you would have an indexer throw an exception if it receives an invalid index. We discuss how to throw exceptions and process them in Chapter 13, Exception Handling.

Notice that the indexer that receives a string argument uses a while statement to search for a matching string in the names array (lines 42–44 and lines 52–54). If it finds a match, the indexer manipulates the corresponding element in array dimensions (lines 46 and 57).

Class BoxTest (Fig. 10.6) manipulates the private data members of class Box through Box's indexers. Local variable box is declared at line 10 and initialized to a new instance of class Box. We use the Box class's constructor to initialize box with dimensions of 30, 30, and 30. Lines 14–16 use the indexer declared with parameter int to obtain the three dimensions of box and display them with WriteLine. The expression box[0] (line 14) implicitly calls the get accessor of the indexer to obtain the value of box's private instance variable dimensions[0]. Similarly, the assignment to box[0] in line 20 implicitly calls the indexer's set accessor in lines 28–32 of Fig. 10.5. The set accessor implicitly sets its value parameter to 10, then sets dimensions[0] to value (10). Lines 24 and 28–30 in Fig. 10.6 take similar actions, using the overloaded indexer with a string parameter to manipulate the Box's properties.

```
 1   // Fig. 10.6: BoxTest.cs
 2   // Indexers provide access to a Box object's members.
 3   using System;
 4
 5   public class BoxTest
 6   {
 7      public static void Main( string[] args )
 8      {
 9         // create a box
10         Box box = new Box( 30, 30, 30 );
11
12         // show dimensions with numeric indexers
13         Console.WriteLine( "Created a box with the dimensions:" );
14         Console.WriteLine( "box[ 0 ] = {0}", box[ 0 ] );
15         Console.WriteLine( "box[ 1 ] = {0}", box[ 1 ] );
16         Console.WriteLine( "box[ 2 ] = {0}", box[ 2 ] );
17
18         // set a dimension with the numeric indexer
19         Console.WriteLine( "\nSetting box[ 0 ] to 10...\n" );
20         box[ 0 ] = 10;
21
22         // set a dimension with the string indexer
23         Console.WriteLine( "Setting box[ \"width\" ] to 20...\n" );
24         box[ "width" ] = 20;
25
26         // show dimensions with string indexers
27         Console.WriteLine( "Now the box has the dimensions:" );
28         Console.WriteLine( "box[ \"length\" ] = {0}", box[ "length" ] );
29         Console.WriteLine( "box[ \"width\" ] = {0}", box[ "width" ] );
30         Console.WriteLine( "box[ \"height\" ] = {0}", box[ "height" ] );
31      } // end Main
32   } // end class BoxTest
```

```
Created a box with the dimensions:
box[ 0 ] = 30
box[ 1 ] = 30
box[ 2 ] = 30

Setting box[ 0 ] to 10...

Setting box[ "width" ] to 20...

Now the box has the dimensions:
box[ "length" ] = 10
box[ "width" ] = 20
box[ "height" ] = 30
```

Fig. 10.6 | Indexers provide access to an object's members.

10.6 Time Class Case Study: Overloaded Constructors

As you know, you can declare your own constructor to specify how objects of a class should be initialized. Next, we demonstrate a class with several *overloaded constructors* that enable objects of that class to be initialized in different ways. To overload constructors, simply provide multiple constructor declarations with different signatures. Recall from Section 7.12 that the compiler differentiates signatures by the number, types and order of the parameters in each signature.

Class Time2 with Overloaded Constructors

By default, instance variables hour, minute and second of class Time1 (Fig. 10.1) are initialized to their default values of 0 (which is midnight in universal time). Class Time1 does not enable the class's clients to initialize the time with specific nonzero values. Class Time2 (Fig. 10.7) contains five overloaded constructors for conveniently initializing its objects in a variety of ways. The constructors ensure that each Time2 object begins in a consistent state. In this application, four of the constructors invoke a fifth constructor, which in turn calls method SetTime. Method SetTime invokes the set accessors of properties Hour, Minute and Second, which ensure that the value supplied for hour is in the range 0 to 23 and that the values for minute and second are each in the range 0 to 59. If a value is out of range, it is set to 0 by the corresponding property (once again ensuring that each instance variable remains in a consistent state). The compiler invokes the appropriate constructor by matching the number and types of the arguments specified in the constructor call with the number and types of the parameters specified in each constructor declaration. Note that class Time2 also provides properties for each instance variable.

```
1   // Fig. 10.7: Time2.cs
2   // Time2 class declaration with overloaded constructors.
3   public class Time2
4   {
5      private int hour; // 0 - 23
6      private int minute; // 0 - 59
7      private int second; // 0 - 59
8
9      // Time2 no-argument constructor: initializes each instance variable
10     // to zero; ensures that Time2 objects start in a consistent state
11     public Time2() : this( 0, 0, 0 ) { }
12
13     // Time2 constructor: hour supplied, minute and second defaulted to 0
14     public Time2( int h ) : this( h, 0, 0 ) { }
15
16     // Time2 constructor: hour and minute supplied, second defaulted to 0
17     public Time2( int h, int m ) : this( h, m, 0 ) { }
18
19     // Time2 constructor: hour, minute and second supplied
20     public Time2( int h, int m, int s )
21     {
22        SetTime( h, m, s ); // invoke SetTime to validate time
23     } // end Time2 three-argument constructor
24
25     // Time2 constructor: another Time2 object supplied
26     public Time2( Time2 time )
27        : this( time.Hour, time.Minute, time.Second ) { }
28
```

Fig. 10.7 | Time2 class declaration with overloaded constructors. (Part 1 of 3.)

```
29      // set a new time value using universal time; ensure that
30      // the data remains consistent by setting invalid values to zero
31      public void SetTime( int h, int m, int s )
32      {
33         Hour = h; // set the Hour property
34         Minute = m; // set the Minute property
35         Second = s; // set the Second property
36      } // end method SetTime
37
38      // Properties for getting and setting
39      // property that gets and sets the hour
40      public int Hour
41      {
42         get
43         {
44            return hour;
45         } // end get
46         // make writing inaccessible outside the class
47         private set
48         {
49            hour = ( ( value >= 0 && value < 24 ) ? value : 0 );
50         } // end set
51      } // end property Hour
52
53      // property that gets and sets the minute
54      public int Minute
55      {
56         get
57         {
58            return minute;
59         } // end get
60         // make writing inaccessible outside the class
61         private set
62         {
63            minute = ( ( value >= 0 && value < 60 ) ? value : 0 );
64         } // end set
65      } // end property Minute
66
67      // property that gets and sets the second
68      public int Second
69      {
70         get
71         {
72            return second;
73         } // end get
74         // make writing inaccessible outside the class
75         private set
76         {
77            second = ( ( value >= 0 && value < 60 ) ? value : 0 );
78         } // end set
79      } // end property Second
80
```

Fig. 10.7 | Time2 class declaration with overloaded constructors. (Part 2 of 3.)

```
81      // convert to string in universal-time format (HH:MM:SS)
82      public string ToUniversalString()
83      {
84          return string.Format(
85              "{0:D2}:{1:D2}:{2:D2}", Hour, Minute, Second );
86      } // end method ToUniversalString
87
88      // convert to string in standard-time format (H:MM:SS AM or PM)
89      public override string ToString()
90      {
91          return string.Format( "{0}:{1:D2}:{2:D2} {3}",
92              ( ( Hour == 0 || Hour == 12 ) ? 12 : Hour % 12 ),
93              Minute, Second, ( Hour < 12 ? "AM" : "PM" ) );
94      } // end method ToString
95  } // end class Time2
```

Fig. 10.7 | Time2 class declaration with overloaded constructors. (Part 3 of 3.)

Class Time2's Constructors

Line 11 declares a *parameterless constructor*—a constructor invoked without arguments. Note that this constructor has an empty body, as indicated by the empty set of curly braces after the constructor header. Instead, we introduce a use of the this reference that is allowed only in the constructor's header. In line 11, the usual constructor header is followed by a colon (:), then the keyword this. The this reference is used in method-call syntax (along with the three int arguments) to invoke the Time2 constructor that takes three int arguments (lines 20–23). The parameterless constructor passes values of 0 for the hour, minute and second to the constructor with three int parameters. The use of the this reference as shown here is called a *constructor initializer*. Constructor initializers are a popular way to reuse initialization code provided by one of the class's constructors rather than defining similar code in another constructor's body. We use this syntax in four of the five Time2 constructors to make the class easier to maintain. If we needed to change how objects of class Time2 are initialized, only the constructor that the class's other constructors call would need to be modified. Even that constructor might not need modification—it simply calls the SetTime method to perform the actual initialization, so it is possible that the changes the class might require would be localized to this method.

Line 14 declares a Time2 constructor with a single int parameter representing the hour, which is passed with 0 for the minute and second to the constructor at lines 20–23. Line 17 declares a Time2 constructor that receives two int parameters representing the hour and minute, which are passed with 0 for the second to the constructor at lines 20–23. Like the parameterless constructor, each of these constructors invokes the constructor at lines 20–23 to minimize code duplication. Lines 20–23 declare the Time2 constructor that receives three int parameters representing the hour, minute and second. This constructor calls SetTime to initialize the instance variables to consistent values. SetTime, in turn, invokes the set accessors of properties Hour, Minute and Second.

Common Programming Error 10.4

A constructor can call methods of the class. Be aware that the instance variables might not yet be in a consistent state, because the constructor is in the process of initializing the object. Using instance variables before they have been initialized properly is a logic error.

Lines 26–27 declare a Time2 constructor that receives a reference to another Time2 object. In this case, the values from the Time2 argument are passed to the three-parameter constructor at lines 20–23 to initialize the hour, minute and second. Note that line 27 could have directly accessed the hour, minute and second instance variables of the constructor's time argument with the expressions time.hour, time.minute and time.second—even though hour, minute and second are declared as private variables of class Time2.

Software Engineering Observation 10.4

When one object of a class has a reference to another object of the same class, the first object can access all the second object's data and methods (including those that are private).

Notes Regarding Class Time2's Methods, Properties and Constructors

Note that Time2's properties are accessed throughout the body of the class. In particular, method SetTime assigns values to properties Hour, Minute and Second in lines 33–35, and methods ToUniversalString and ToString use properties Hour, Minute and Second in line 85 and lines 92–93, respectively. In each case, these methods could have accessed the class's private data directly without using the properties. However, consider changing the representation of the time from three int values (requiring 12 bytes of memory) to a single int value representing the total number of seconds that have elapsed since midnight (requiring only 4 bytes of memory). If we make such a change, only the bodies of the methods that access the private data directly would need to change—in particular, the individual properties Hour, Minute and Second. There would be no need to modify the bodies of methods SetTime, ToUniversalString or ToString, because they do not access the private data directly. Designing the class in this manner reduces the likelihood of programming errors when altering the class's implementation.

Similarly, each Time2 constructor could be written to include a copy of the appropriate statements from method SetTime. Doing so may be slightly more efficient, because the extra constructor call and the call to SetTime are eliminated. However, duplicating statements in multiple methods or constructors makes changing the class's internal data representation more difficult and error-prone. Having the Time2 constructors call the three-parameter constructor (or even call SetTime directly) requires any changes to the implementation of SetTime to be made only once.

Software Engineering Observation 10.5

When implementing a method of a class, use the class's properties to access the class's private data. This simplifies code maintenance and reduces the likelihood of errors.

Also notice that class Time2 takes advantage of access modifiers to ensure that clients of the class must use the appropriate methods and properties to access private data. In particular, the properties Hour, Minute and Second declare private set accessors (lines 47, 61 and 75, respectively) to restrict the use of the set accessors to members of the class. We declare these private for the same reasons that we declare the instance variables private—to simplify code maintenance and ensure that the data remains in a consistent state. Although the methods in class Time2 still have all the advantages of using the set accessors to perform validation, clients of the class must use the SetTime method to modify this data. The get accessors of properties Hour, Minute and Second are implicitly declared `public` because their properties are declared `public`—when there is no access modifier before a `get` or `set` accessor, the accessor inherits the access modifier preceding the property name.

Using Class Time2's Overloaded Constructors

Class Time2Test (Fig. 10.8) creates six Time2 objects (lines 9–14) to invoke the overloaded Time2 constructors. Line 9 shows that the parameterless constructor (line 11 of Fig. 10.7) is invoked by placing an empty set of parentheses after the class name when allocating a Time2 object with new. Lines 10–14 of the application demonstrate passing arguments to the other Time2 constructors. C# invokes the appropriate overloaded constructor by matching the number and types of the arguments specified in the constructor call with the number and types of the parameters specified in each constructor declaration. Line 10 invokes the constructor at line 14 of Fig. 10.7. Line 11 invokes the constructor at line 17 of Fig. 10.7. Lines 12–13 invoke the constructor at lines 20–23 of Fig. 10.7. Line 14 invokes the constructor at lines 26–27 of Fig. 10.7. The application displays the string representation of each initialized Time2 object to confirm that each was initialized properly.

```
1    // Fig. 10.8: Time2Test.cs
2    // Overloaded constructors used to initialize Time2 objects.
3    using System;
4
5    public class Time2Test
6    {
7       public static void Main( string[] args )
8       {
9          Time2 t1 = new Time2(); // 00:00:00
10         Time2 t2 = new Time2( 2 ); // 02:00:00
11         Time2 t3 = new Time2( 21, 34 ); // 21:34:00
12         Time2 t4 = new Time2( 12, 25, 42 ); // 12:25:42
13         Time2 t5 = new Time2( 27, 74, 99 ); // 00:00:00
14         Time2 t6 = new Time2( t4 ); // 12:25:42
15
16         Console.WriteLine( "Constructed with:\n" );
17         Console.WriteLine( "t1: all arguments defaulted" );
18         Console.WriteLine( "   {0}", t1.ToUniversalString() ); // 00:00:00
19         Console.WriteLine( "   {0}\n", t1.ToString() ); // 12:00:00 AM
20
21         Console.WriteLine(
22            "t2: hour specified; minute and second defaulted" );
23         Console.WriteLine( "   {0}", t2.ToUniversalString() ); // 02:00:00
24         Console.WriteLine( "   {0}\n", t2.ToString() ); // 2:00:00 AM
25
26         Console.WriteLine(
27            "t3: hour and minute specified; second defaulted" );
28         Console.WriteLine( "   {0}", t3.ToUniversalString() ); // 21:34:00
29         Console.WriteLine( "   {0}\n", t3.ToString() ); // 9:34:00 PM
30
31         Console.WriteLine( "t4: hour, minute and second specified" );
32         Console.WriteLine( "   {0}", t4.ToUniversalString() ); // 12:25:42
33         Console.WriteLine( "   {0}\n", t4.ToString() ); // 12:25:42 PM
```

Fig. 10.8 | Overloaded constructors used to initialize Time2 objects. (Part 1 of 2.)

```
34
35           Console.WriteLine( "t5: all invalid values specified" );
36           Console.WriteLine( "   {0}", t5.ToUniversalString() ); // 00:00:00
37           Console.WriteLine( "   {0}\n", t5.ToString() ); // 12:00:00 AM
38
39           Console.WriteLine( "t6: Time2 object t4 specified" );
40           Console.WriteLine( "   {0}", t6.ToUniversalString() ); // 12:25:42
41           Console.WriteLine( "   {0}", t6.ToString() ); // 12:25:42 PM
42       } // end Main
43   } // end class Time2Test
```

```
Constructed with:

t1: all arguments defaulted
    00:00:00
    12:00:00 AM

t2: hour specified; minute and second defaulted
    02:00:00
    2:00:00 AM

t3: hour and minute specified; second defaulted
    21:34:00
    9:34:00 PM

t4: hour, minute and second specified
    12:25:42
    12:25:42 PM

t5: all invalid values specified
    00:00:00
    12:00:00 AM

t6: Time2 object t4 specified
    12:25:42
    12:25:42 PM
```

Fig. 10.8 | Overloaded constructors used to initialize `Time2` objects. (Part 2 of 2.)

10.7 Default and Parameterless Constructors

Every class must have at least one constructor. Recall from Section 4.10 that if you do not provide any constructors in a class's declaration, the compiler creates a default constructor that takes no arguments when it is invoked. In Section 11.4.2, you'll learn that the default constructor implicitly performs a special task.

The compiler will not create a default constructor for a class that explicitly declares at least one constructor. In this case, if you want to be able to invoke the constructor with no arguments, you must declare a parameterless constructor—as in line 11 of Fig. 10.7. Like a default constructor, a parameterless constructor is invoked with empty parentheses. Note that the `Time2` parameterless constructor explicitly initializes a `Time2` object by passing to the three-parameter constructor 0 for each parameter. Since 0 is the default value for `int` instance variables, the parameterless constructor in this example could actually omit the constructor initializer. In this case, each instance variable would receive its default value when the object is created. If we omit the parameterless constructor, clients of this class would not be able to create a `Time2` object with the expression `new Time2()`.

Common Programming Error 10.5

If a class has constructors, but none of the public constructors are parameterless constructors, and an application attempts to call a parameterless constructor to initialize an object of the class, a compilation error occurs. A constructor can be called with no arguments only if the class does not have any constructors (in which case the default constructor is called) or if the class has a public parameterless constructor.

Common Programming Error 10.6

Only constructors can have the same name as the class. Declaring a method, property or field with the same name as the class is a compilation error.

10.8 Composition

A class can have references to objects of other classes as members. Such a capability is called *composition* and is sometimes referred to as a *has-a relationship*. For example, an object of class AlarmClock needs to know the current time and the time when it is supposed to sound its alarm, so it is reasonable to include two references to Time objects as members of the AlarmClock object.

Software Engineering Observation 10.6

One form of software reuse is composition, in which a class has as members references to objects of other classes.

Our example of composition contains three classes—Date (Fig. 10.9), Employee (Fig. 10.10) and EmployeeTest (Fig. 10.11). Class Date (Fig. 10.9) declares instance variables month and day (lines 7–9) and auto-implemented property Year (line 11) to represent a date. The constructor receives three int parameters. Line 17 implicitly invokes the set accessor of property Month (lines 24–40) to validate the month—an out-of-range value is set to 1 to maintain a consistent state. Line 18 uses property Year to set the year. Since Year is an auto-implemented property, we're assuming in this example that the value for Year is correct. Line 19 uses property Day (lines 43–67), which validates and assigns the value for day based on the current month and Year (by using properties Month and Year in turn to obtain the values of month and Year). Note that the order of initialization is important, because the set accessor of property Day validates the value for day based on the assumption that month and Year are correct. Line 55 determines whether the day is correct based on the number of days in the particular Month. If the day is not correct, lines 58–59 determine whether the Month is February, the day is 29 and the Year is a leap year. Otherwise, if the parameter value does not contain a correct value for day, line 64 sets day to 1 to maintain the Date in a consistent state. Note that line 20 in the constructor outputs the this reference as a string. Since this is a reference to the current Date object, the object's ToString method (lines 70–73) is called implicitly to obtain the object's string representation.

```
1    // Fig. 10.9: Date.cs
2    // Date class declaration.
3    using System;
```

Fig. 10.9 | Date class declaration. (Part 1 of 3.)

```
 4
 5  public class Date
 6  {
 7     private int month; // 1-12
 8     private int day; // 1-31 based on month
 9
10     // auto-implemented property Year
11     public int Year { get; set; }
12
13     // constructor: use property Month to confirm proper value for month;
14     // use property Day to confirm proper value for day
15     public Date( int theMonth, int theDay, int theYear )
16     {
17        Month = theMonth; // validate month
18        Year = theYear; // could validate year
19        Day = theDay; // validate day
20        Console.WriteLine( "Date object constructor for date {0}", this );
21     } // end Date constructor
22
23     // property that gets and sets the month
24     public int Month
25     {
26        get
27        {
28           return month;
29        } // end get
30        private set // make writing inaccessible outside the class
31        {
32           if ( value > 0 && value <= 12 ) // validate month
33              month = value;
34           else // month is invalid
35           {
36              Console.WriteLine( "Invalid month ({0}) set to 1.", value );
37              month = 1; // maintain object in consistent state
38           } // end else
39        } // end set
40     } // end property Month
41
42     // property that gets and sets the day
43     public int Day
44     {
45        get
46        {
47           return day;
48        } // end get
49        private set // make writing inaccessible outside the class
50        {
51           int[] daysPerMonth = { 0, 31, 28, 31, 30, 31, 30,
52                                  31, 31, 30, 31, 30, 31 };
53
54           // check if day in range for month
55           if ( value > 0 && value <= daysPerMonth[ Month ] )
56              day = value;
```

Fig. 10.9 | Date class declaration. (Part 2 of 3.)

```
57              // check for leap year
58              else if ( Month == 2 && value == 29 &&
59                 ( Year % 400 == 0 || ( Year % 4 == 0 && Year % 100 != 0 ) ) )
60                 day = value;
61              else
62              {
63                 Console.WriteLine( "Invalid day ({0}) set to 1.", value );
64                 day = 1; // maintain object in consistent state
65              } // end else
66           } // end set
67        } // end property Day
68
69        // return a string of the form month/day/year
70        public override string ToString()
71        {
72           return string.Format( "{0}/{1}/{2}", Month, Day, Year );
73        } // end method ToString
74     } // end class Date
```

Fig. 10.9 | Date class declaration. (Part 3 of 3.)

Class Employee (Fig. 10.10) has instance variables firstName, lastName, birthDate and hireDate. Members birthDate and hireDate (lines 7–8) are references to Date objects, demonstrating that a class can have as instance variables references to objects of other classes. The Employee constructor (lines 11–18) takes four parameters—first, last, dateOfBirth and dateOfHire. The objects referenced by parameters dateOfBirth and dateOfHire are assigned to the Employee object's birthDate and hireDate instance variables, respectively. Note that when class Employee's ToString method is called, it returns a string containing the string representations of the two Date objects. Each of these strings is obtained with an implicit call to the Date class's ToString method.

```
1    // Fig. 10.10: Employee.cs
2    // Employee class with references to other objects.
3    public class Employee
4    {
5       private string firstName;
6       private string lastName;
7       private Date birthDate;
8       private Date hireDate;
9
10      // constructor to initialize name, birth date and hire date
11      public Employee( string first, string last,
12         Date dateOfBirth, Date dateOfHire )
13      {
14         firstName = first;
15         lastName = last;
16         birthDate = dateOfBirth;
17         hireDate = dateOfHire;
18      } // end Employee constructor
19
```

Fig. 10.10 | Employee class with references to other objects. (Part 1 of 2.)

```
20        // convert Employee to string format
21        public override string ToString()
22        {
23            return string.Format( "{0}, {1}  Hired: {2}  Birthday: {3}",
24                lastName, firstName, hireDate, birthDate );
25        } // end method ToString
26    } // end class Employee
```

Fig. 10.10 | Employee class with references to other objects. (Part 2 of 2.)

Class EmployeeTest (Fig. 10.11) creates two Date objects (lines 9–10) to represent an Employee's birthday and hire date, respectively. Line 11 creates an Employee and initializes its instance variables by passing to the constructor two strings (representing the Employee's first and last names) and two Date objects (representing the birthday and hire date). Line 13 implicitly invokes the Employee's ToString method to display the values of its instance variables and demonstrate that the object was initialized properly.

```
1    // Fig. 10.11: EmployeeTest.cs
2    // Composition demonstration.
3    using System;
4
5    public class EmployeeTest
6    {
7        public static void Main( string[] args )
8        {
9            Date birth = new Date( 7, 24, 1949 );
10           Date hire = new Date( 3, 12, 1988 );
11           Employee employee = new Employee( "Bob", "Blue", birth, hire );
12
13           Console.WriteLine( employee );
14       } // end Main
15   } // end class EmployeeTest
```

```
Date object constructor for date 7/24/1949
Date object constructor for date 3/12/1988
Blue, Bob  Hired: 3/12/1988  Birthday: 7/24/1949
```

Fig. 10.11 | Composition demonstration.

10.9 Garbage Collection and Destructors

Every object you create uses various system resources, such as memory. In many programming languages, these system resources are reserved for the object's use until they are explicitly released by the programmer. If all the references to the object that manages the resource are lost before the resource is explicitly released, the application can no longer access the resource to release it. This is known as a *resource leak*.

We need a disciplined way to give resources back to the system when they are no longer needed, thus avoiding resource leaks. The Common Language Runtime (CLR) performs automatic memory management by using a *garbage collector* to reclaim the memory occupied by objects that are no longer in use, so the memory can be used for other objects. When there are no more references to an object, the object becomes *eligible for destruction*. Every object has a special member, called a *destructor*, that is invoked by the garbage collector to perform *termination housekeeping* on an object just before the garbage collector reclaims the object's memory. A destructor is declared like a parameterless constructor, except that its name is the class name, preceded by a tilde (~), and it has no access modifier in its header. After the garbage collector calls the object's destructor, the object becomes *eligible for garbage collection*. The memory for such an object can be reclaimed by the garbage collector. *Memory leaks*, which are common in other languages such as C and C++ (because memory is not automatically reclaimed in those languages), are less likely in C# (but some can still happen in subtle ways). Other types of resource leaks can occur. For example, an application could open a file on disk to modify its contents. If the application does not close the file, no other application can modify (or possibly even use) the file until the application that opened it terminates.

A problem with the garbage collector is that it is not guaranteed to perform its tasks at a specified time. Therefore, the garbage collector may call the destructor any time after the object becomes eligible for destruction, and may reclaim the memory any time after the destructor executes. In fact, neither may happen before an application terminates. Thus, it is unclear whether, or when, the destructor will be called. For this reason, destructors are rarely used.

Software Engineering Observation 10.7

A class that uses system resources, such as files on disk, should provide a method to eventually release the resources. Many .NET Framework Class Library classes provide Close *or* Dispose *methods for this purpose.*

10.10 static Class Members

Every object has its own copy of all the instance variables of the class. In certain cases, only one copy of a particular variable should be shared by all objects of a class. A static *variable* is used in such cases. A static variable represents *classwide information*—all objects of the class share the same piece of data. The declaration of a static variable begins with the keyword static.

Let's motivate static data with an example. Suppose that we have a video game with Martians and other space creatures. Each Martian tends to be brave and willing to attack other space creatures when it is aware that there are at least four other Martians present. If fewer than five Martians are present, each Martian becomes cowardly. Thus each Martian needs to know the martianCount. We could endow class Martian with martianCount as an instance variable. If we do this, every Martian will have a separate copy of the instance variable, and every time we create a new Martian, we'll have to update the instance variable martianCount in every Martian. This wastes space on redundant copies, wastes time updating the separate copies and is error prone. Instead, we declare martianCount to be static, making martianCount classwide data. Every Martian can access the martianCount as if it were an instance variable of class Martian, but only one copy of the static martianCount is maintained. This saves space. We save time by having the Martian constructor increment the static martianCount—there is only one copy, so we do not have to increment separate copies of martianCount for each Martian object.

Software Engineering Observation 10.8

Use a static variable when all objects of a class must use the same copy of the variable.

The scope of a static variable is the body of its class. A class's public static members can be accessed by qualifying the member name with the class name and the member access (.) operator, as in Math.PI. A class's private static class members can be accessed only through the methods and properties of the class. Actually, static class members exist even when no objects of the class exist—they are available as soon as the class is loaded into memory at execution time. To access a private static member from outside its class, a public static method or property can be provided.

Common Programming Error 10.7

It is a compilation error to access or invoke a static member by referencing it through an instance of the class, like a non-static member.

Software Engineering Observation 10.9

Static variables and methods exist, and can be used, even if no objects of that class have been instantiated.

Our next application declares two classes—Employee (Fig. 10.12) and EmployeeTest (Fig. 10.13). Class Employee declares private static variable count (Fig. 10.12, line 8) and public static property Count (lines 38–44). We omit the set accessor of property Count to make the property read-only—we do not want clients of the class to be able to modify count. The static variable count is initialized to 0 in line 8. If a static variable is not initialized, the compiler assigns a default value to the variable—in this case 0, the default value for type int. Variable count maintains a count of the number of objects of class Employee that have been created.

When Employee objects exist, member count can be used in any method of an Employee object—this example increments count in the constructor (line 22). When no objects of class Employee exist, member count can still be referenced, but only through a call to public static property Count (lines 28–34), as in Employee.Count, which evaluates to the number of Employee objects currently in memory.

```
1   // Fig. 10.12: Employee.cs
2   // Static variable used to maintain a count of the number of
3   // Employee objects that have been created.
4   using System;
5
6   public class Employee
7   {
8      private static int count = 0; // number of objects in memory
9
10     // read-only auto-implemented property FirstName
11     public string FirstName { get; private set; }
12
```

Fig. 10.12 | static variable used to maintain a count of the number of Employee objects in memory. (Part 1 of 2.)

```
13      // read-only auto-implemented property LastName
14      public string LastName { get; private set; }
15
16      // initialize employee, add 1 to static count and
17      // output string indicating that constructor was called
18      public Employee( string first, string last )
19      {
20          FirstName = first;
21          LastName = last;
22          count++; // increment static count of employees
23          Console.WriteLine( "Employee constructor: {0} {1}; count = {2}",
24              FirstName, LastName, Count );
25      } // end Employee constructor
26
27      // read-only property that gets the employee count
28      public static int Count
29      {
30          get
31          {
32              return count;
33          } // end get
34      } // end property Count
35  } // end class Employee
```

Fig. 10.12 | static variable used to maintain a count of the number of Employee objects in memory. (Part 2 of 2.)

EmployeeTest method Main (Fig. 10.13) instantiates two Employee objects (lines 14–15). When each Employee object's constructor is invoked, lines 20–21 of Fig. 10.12 assign the Employee's first name and last name to properties FirstName and LastName. Note that these two statements do not make copies of the original string arguments. Actually, string objects in C# are immutable—they cannot be modified after they are created. Therefore, it is safe to have many references to one string object. This is not normally the case for objects of most other classes in C#. If string objects are immutable, you might wonder why we're able to use operators + and += to concatenate string objects. String-concatenation operations actually result in a new string object containing the concatenated values. The original string objects are not modified.

```
1   // Fig. 10.13: EmployeeTest.cs
2   // Static member demonstration.
3   using System;
4
5   public class EmployeeTest
6   {
7       public static void Main( string[] args )
8       {
9           // show that count is 0 before creating Employees
10          Console.WriteLine( "Employees before instantiation: {0}",
11              Employee.Count );
```

Fig. 10.13 | static member demonstration. (Part 1 of 2.)

```
12
13          // create two Employees; count should become 2
14          Employee e1 = new Employee( "Susan", "Baker" );
15          Employee e2 = new Employee( "Bob", "Blue" );
16
17          // show that count is 2 after creating two Employees
18          Console.WriteLine( "\nEmployees after instantiation: {0}",
19             Employee.Count );
20
21          // get names of Employees
22          Console.WriteLine( "\nEmployee 1: {0} {1}\nEmployee 2: {2} {3}\n",
23             e1.FirstName, e1.LastName,
24             e2.FirstName, e2.LastName );
25
26          // in this example, there is only one reference to each Employee,
27          // so the following statements cause the CLR to mark each
28          // Employee object as being eligible for garbage collection
29          e1 = null; // good practice: mark object e1 no longer needed
30          e2 = null; // good practice: mark object e2 no longer needed
31       } // end Main
32    } // end class EmployeeTest
```

```
Employees before instantiation: 0
Employee constructor: Susan Baker; count = 1
Employee constructor: Bob Blue; count = 2

Employees after instantiation: 2

Employee 1: Susan Baker
Employee 2: Bob Blue
```

Fig. 10.13 | static member demonstration. (Part 2 of 2.)

Lines 18–19 display the updated Count. When Main has finished using the two Employee objects, references e1 and e2 are set to null at lines 29–30, so they no longer refer to the objects that were instantiated in lines 14–15. The objects become "eligible for garbage collection" because there are no more references to them in the application.

Eventually, the garbage collector might reclaim the memory for these objects (or the operating system will reclaim the memory when the application terminates). C# does not guarantee when, or even whether, the garbage collector will execute. When the garbage collector does run, it is possible that no objects or only a subset of the eligible objects will be collected.

A method declared static cannot access non-static class members directly, because a static method can be called even when no objects of the class exist. For the same reason, the this reference cannot be used in a static method—the this reference must refer to a specific object of the class, and when a static method is called, there might not be any objects of its class in memory.

Common Programming Error 10.8

A compilation error occurs if a static method calls an instance (non-static) method in the same class by using only the method name. Similarly, a compilation error occurs if a static method attempts to access an instance variable in the same class by using only the variable name.

Common Programming Error 10.9

Referring to the `this` *reference in a* `static` *method is a syntax error.*

10.11 `readonly` Instance Variables

The *principle of least privilege* is fundamental to good software engineering. In the context of an application, the principle states that code should be granted only the amount of privilege and access needed to accomplish its designated task, but no more. Let us see how this principle applies to instance variables.

Some instance variables need to be modifiable, and some do not. In Section 8.4, we introduced keyword `const` for declaring constants. These constants must be initialized to a constant value when they are declared. Suppose, however, we want to initialize a constant belonging to an object in the object's constructor. C# provides keyword **`readonly`** to specify that an instance variable of an object is not modifiable and that any attempt to modify it after the object is constructed is an error. For example,

```
private readonly int INCREMENT;
```

declares `readonly` instance variable `INCREMENT` of type `int`. Like constants, `readonly` variables are declared with all capital letters by convention. Although `readonly` instance variables can be initialized when they are declared, this is not required. Readonly variables can be initialized by each of the class's constructors. The constructor can assign values to a `readonly` instance variable multiple times—the variable doesn't become unmodifiable until after the constructor completes execution.

Software Engineering Observation 10.10

Declaring an instance variable as `readonly` *helps enforce the principle of least privilege. If an instance variable should not be modified after the object is constructed, declare it to be* `readonly` *to prevent modification.*

Members that are declared as `const` must be assigned values at compile time. Therefore, `const` members can be initialized only with other constant values, such as integers, `string` literals, characters and other `const` members. Constant members with values that cannot be determined at compile time must be declared with keyword `readonly`, so they can be initialized at execution time. Variables that are `readonly` can be initialized with more complex expressions, such as an array initializer or a method call that returns a value or a reference to an object.

Our next example contains two classes—class `Increment` (Fig. 10.14) and class `IncrementTest` (Fig. 10.15). Class `Increment` contains a `readonly` instance variable of type `int` named `INCREMENT` (Fig. 10.14, line 6). Note that the `readonly` variable is not initialized in its declaration, so it should be initialized by the class's constructor (lines 10–13). If the class provides multiple constructors, every constructor should initialize the `readonly` variable. If a constructor does not initialize the `readonly` variable, the variable receives the same default value as any other instance variable (0 for numeric simple types, `false` for `bool` types and `null` for reference types), and the compiler generates a warning. In Fig. 10.14, the constructor receives `int` parameter `incrementValue` and assigns its value to `INCREMENT` (line 12). If class `Increment`'s constructor does not initialize `INCREMENT` (if line 12 were omitted), the compiler would give the warning:

```
 1   // Fig. 10.14: Increment.cs
 2   // readonly instance variable in a class.
 3   public class Increment
 4   {
 5      // readonly instance variable (uninitialized)
 6      private readonly int INCREMENT;
 7      private int total = 0; // total of all increments
 8
 9      // constructor initializes readonly instance variable INCREMENT
10      public Increment( int incrementValue )
11      {
12         INCREMENT = incrementValue; // initialize readonly variable (once)
13      } // end Increment constructor
14
15      // add INCREMENT to total
16      public void AddIncrementToTotal()
17      {
18         total += INCREMENT;
19      } // end method AddIncrementToTotal
20
21      // return string representation of an Increment object's data
22      public override string ToString()
23      {
24         return string.Format( "total = {0}", total );
25      } // end method ToString
26   } // end class Increment
```

Fig. 10.14 | readonly instance variable in a class.

```
Field 'Increment.INCREMENT' is never assigned to, and will always
have its default value 0
```

Application class IncrementTest creates an object of class Increment (Fig. 10.15, line 9) and provides as the argument to the constructor the value 5, which is assigned to the readonly variable INCREMENT. Lines 11 and 16 implicitly invoke class Increment's ToString method, which returns a formatted string describing the value of private instance variable total.

```
 1   // Fig. 10.15: IncrementTest.cs
 2   // readonly instance variable initialized with a constructor argument.
 3   using System;
 4
 5   public class IncrementTest
 6   {
 7      public static void Main( string[] args )
 8      {
 9         Increment incrementer = new Increment( 5 );
10
11         Console.WriteLine( "Before incrementing: {0}\n", incrementer );
12
```

Fig. 10.15 | readonly instance variable initialized with a constructor argument. (Part 1 of 2.)

```
13            for ( int i = 1; i <= 3; i++ )
14            {
15                incrementer.AddIncrementToTotal();
16                Console.WriteLine( "After increment {0}: {1}", i, incrementer );
17            } // end for
18        } // end Main
19    } // end class IncrementTest
```

```
Before incrementing: total = 0

After increment 1: total = 5
After increment 2: total = 10
After increment 3: total = 15
```

Fig. 10.15 | readonly instance variable initialized with a constructor argument. (Part 2 of 2.)

Common Programming Error 10.10

Attempting to modify a readonly instance variable anywhere but in its declaration or the object's constructors is a compilation error.

Error-Prevention Tip 10.2

Attempts to modify a readonly instance variable are caught at compilation time rather than causing execution-time errors. It is always preferable to get bugs out at compile time, if possible, rather than allowing them to slip through to execution time (where studies have found that repairing is often many times more costly).

Software Engineering Observation 10.11

If a readonly instance variable is initialized to a constant only in its declaration, it is not necessary to have a separate copy of the instance variable for every object of the class. The variable should be declared const instead. Constants declared with const are implicitly static, so there will only be one copy for the entire class.

10.12 Software Reusability

Programmers concentrate on crafting new classes and reusing existing classes. Many class libraries exist, and others are being developed worldwide. Software is then constructed from existing, well-defined, carefully tested, well-documented, portable, performance-tuned, widely available components. This kind of software reusability speeds the development of powerful, high-quality software. *Rapid application development (RAD)* is of great interest today.

Microsoft provides C# programmers with thousands of classes in the .NET Framework Class Library to help them implement C# applications. The .NET Framework enables C# developers to work to achieve true reusability and rapid application development. C# programmers can focus on the task at hand when developing their applications and leave the lower-level details to the classes of the .NET Framework Class Library. For example, to write an application that draws graphics, a programmer does not require knowledge of graphics on every computer platform where the application will execute. Instead, the programmer can concentrate on learning .NET's graphics capabilities (which are quite substantial and growing) and write a C# application that draws the graphics, using .NET Framework Class Library classes such as those in the System.Drawing namespace. When the application executes on a given computer, it is the job of the CLR to translate the MSIL commands compiled from the C# code into commands that the local computer can understand.

The .NET Framework Class Library classes enable C# programmers to bring new applications to market faster by using preexisting, tested components. Not only does this reduce development time, it also improves the programmer's ability to debug and maintain applications. To take advantage of C#'s many capabilities, it is essential that programmers familiarize themselves with the variety of classes in the .NET Framework. There are many web-based resources at msdn.microsoft.com/en-us/default.aspx to help you with this task. The primary resource for learning about the .NET Framework Class Library is the .NET Framework Reference in the MSDN library, which can be found at

msdn.microsoft.com/en-us/library/ms229335.aspx

In addition, msdn.microsoft.com/en-us/default.aspx provides many other resources, including tutorials, articles and sites specific to individual C# topics.

Good Programming Practice 10.1

Avoid reinventing the wheel. Study the capabilities of the .NET Framework Class Library. If the library contains a class that meets your application's requirements, use that class rather than create your own.

To realize the full potential of software reusability, we need to improve cataloging schemes, licensing schemes, protection mechanisms that prevent master copies of classes from being corrupted, description schemes that system designers use to determine whether existing classes meet their needs, browsing mechanisms that determine what classes are available and how closely they meet software-developer requirements, and the like. Many interesting research and development problems have been solved and many more need to be solved. These problems will likely be solved, because the potential value of increased software reuse is enormous.

10.13 Data Abstraction and Encapsulation

Classes normally hide the details of their implementation from their clients. This is called *information hiding*. As an example, let us consider the stack data structure introduced in Section 7.6. Recall that a stack is a last-in, first-out (LIFO) data structure—the last item pushed (inserted) on the stack is the first item popped (removed) off the stack.

Stacks can be implemented with arrays and with other data structures, such as linked lists. (We discuss stacks and linked lists in Chapter 25, Data Structures, and Chapter 27, Collections.) A client of a stack class need not be concerned with the stack's implementation. The client knows only that when data items are placed in the stack, they will be recalled in last-in, first-out order. The client cares about what functionality a stack offers, not about how that functionality is implemented. This concept is referred to as *data abstraction*. Although programmers might know the details of a class's implementation, they should not write code that depends on these details as the details may later change. This enables a particular class (such as one that implements a stack and its *push* and *pop* operations) to be replaced with another version without affecting the rest of the system. As long as the `public` services of the class do not change (i.e., every original method still has the same name, return type and parameter list in the new class declaration), the rest of the system is not affected.

Most programming languages emphasize actions. In these languages, data exists to support the actions that applications must take. Data is "less interesting" than actions. Data is "crude." Only a few simple types exist, and it is difficult for programmers to create their own types. C# and the object-oriented style of programming elevate the importance of data. The primary activities of object-oriented programming in C# are the creation of types (e.g., classes) and the expression of the interactions among objects of those types. To create languages that emphasize data, the programming-languages community needed to formalize some notions about data. The formalization we consider here is the notion of *abstract data types (ADTs)*, which improve the application-development process.

Consider simple type `int`, which most people would associate with an integer in mathematics. Actually, an `int` is an abstract representation of an integer. Unlike mathematical integers, computer `int`s are fixed in size. For example, simple type `int` in C# is limited to the range –2,147,483,648 to +2,147,483,647. If the result of a calculation falls outside this range, an error occurs, and the computer responds in some manner. It might, for example, "quietly" produce an incorrect result, such as a value too large to fit in an `int` variable—commonly called *arithmetic overflow*. It also might throw an exception, called an `OverflowException`. (We discuss the two ways of dealing with arithmetic overflow in Section 13.8.) Mathematical integers do not have this problem. Therefore, the computer `int` is only an approximation of the real-world integer. The same is true of `double` and other simple types.

We have taken the notion of `int` for granted until this point, but we now consider it from a new perspective. Types like `int`, `double`, and `char` are all examples of abstract data types. They are representations of real-world concepts to some satisfactory level of precision within a computer system.

An ADT actually captures two notions: a *data representation* and the *operations* that can be performed on that data. For example, in C#, an `int` contains an integer value (data) and provides addition, subtraction, multiplication, division and remainder operations—division by zero is undefined. C# programmers use classes to implement abstract data types.

Software Engineering Observation 10.12

Programmers create types through the class mechanism. New types can be designed to be as convenient to use as the simple types. Although the language is easy to extend via new types, the programmer cannot alter the base language itself.

Another ADT we discuss is a *queue*, which is similar to a "waiting line." Computer systems use many queues internally. A queue offers well-understood behavior to its clients: Clients place items in a queue one at a time via an *enqueue* operation, then get them back one at a time via a *dequeue* operation. A queue returns items in *first-in, first-out (FIFO)* order, which means that the first item inserted in a queue is the first item removed from the queue. Conceptually, a queue can become infinitely long, but real queues are finite.

The queue hides an internal data representation that keeps track of the items currently waiting in line, and it offers operations to its clients (*enqueue* and *dequeue*). The clients are not concerned about the implementation of the queue—they simply depend on the queue to operate "as advertised." When a client enqueues an item, the queue should accept that item and place it in some kind of internal FIFO data structure. Similarly, when the client wants the next item from the front of the queue, the queue should remove the item from its internal representation and deliver it in FIFO order (i.e., the item that has been in the queue the longest should be returned by the next dequeue operation).

The queue ADT guarantees the integrity of its internal data structure. Clients cannot manipulate this data structure directly—only the queue ADT has access to its internal data. Clients are able to perform only allowable operations on the data representation—the ADT rejects operations that its public interface does not provide. We'll discuss stacks and queues in greater depth in Chapter 25, Data Structures.

10.14 Time Class Case Study: Creating Class Libraries

In almost every example in the book, we have seen that classes from preexisting libraries, such as the .NET Framework Class Library, can be imported into a C# application. Each class belongs to a namespace that contains a group of related classes. As applications become more complex, namespaces help you manage the complexity of application components. Class libraries and namespaces also facilitate software reuse by enabling applications to add classes from other namespaces (as we have done in most examples). This section introduces how to create your own class libraries.

Steps for Declaring and Using a Reusable Class

Before a class can be used in multiple applications, it must be placed in a class library to make it reusable. Figure 10.16 shows how to specify the namespace in which a class should be placed in the library. Figure 10.19 shows how to use our class library in an application. The steps for creating a reusable class are:

1. Declare a `public` class. If the class is not `public`, it can be used only by other classes in the same assembly.

2. Choose a namespace name and add a ***namespace*** *declaration* to the source-code file for the reusable class declaration.

3. Compile the class into a class library.

4. Add a reference to the class library in an application.

5. Specify a `using` directive for the namespace of the reusable class and use the class.

Step 1: Creating a `public` Class

For *Step 1* in this discussion, we use the `public` class `Time1` declared in Fig. 10.1. No modifications have been made to the implementation of the class, so we'll not discuss its implementation details again here.

Step 2: Adding the `namespace` Declaration

For *Step 2*, we add a `namespace` declaration to Fig. 10.1. The new version is shown in Fig. 10.16. Line 3 declares a `namespace` named `Chapter10`. Placing the `Time1` class inside the `namespace` declaration indicates that the class is part of the specified namespace. The `namespace` name is part of the fully qualified class name, so the name of class `Time1` is actually `Chapter10.Time1`. You can use this fully qualified name in your applications, or you can write a `using` directive (as we'll see shortly) and use its ***simple name*** (the unqualified class name—`Time1`) in the application. If another namespace also contains a `Time1`

```
 1   // Fig. 10.16: Time1.cs
 2   // Time1 class declaration in a namespace.
 3   namespace Chapter10
 4   {
 5      public class Time1
 6      {
 7         private int hour; // 0 - 23
 8         private int minute; // 0 - 59
 9         private int second; // 0 - 59
10
11         // set a new time value using universal time; ensure that
12         // the data remains consistent by setting invalid values to zero
13         public void SetTime( int h, int m, int s )
14         {
15            hour = ( ( h >= 0 && h < 24 ) ? h : 0 ); // validate hour
16            minute = ( ( m >= 0 && m < 60 ) ? m : 0 ); // validate minute
17            second = ( ( s >= 0 && s < 60 ) ? s : 0 ); // validate second
18         } // end method SetTime
19
20         // convert to string in universal-time format (HH:MM:SS)
21         public string ToUniversalString()
22         {
23            return string.Format( "{0:D2}:{1:D2}:{2:D2}",
24               hour, minute, second );
25         } // end method ToUniversalString
26
27         // convert to string in standard-time format (H:MM:SS AM or PM)
28         public override string ToString()
29         {
30            return string.Format( "{0}:{1:D2}:{2:D2} {3}",
31               ( ( hour == 0 || hour == 12 ) ? 12 : hour % 12 ),
32               minute, second, ( hour < 12 ? "AM" : "PM" ) );
33         } // end method ToString
34      } // end class Time1
35   } // end namespace Chapter10
```

Fig. 10.16 | Time1 class declaration in a namespace.

class, the fully qualified class names can be used to distinguish between the classes in the application and prevent a *name conflict* (also called a *name collision*).

Most language elements must appear inside the braces of a type declaration (e.g., classes and enumerations). Some exceptions are namespace declarations, using directives, comments and C# attributes (first used in Chapter 19). Only class declarations declared public will be reusable by clients of the class library. Non-public classes are typically placed in a library to support the public reusable classes in that library.

Step 3: Compiling the Class Library
Step 3 is to compile the class into a class library. To create a class library in Visual C# Express, we must create a new project by clicking the **File** menu, selecting **New Project...** and choosing **Class Library** from the list of templates, as shown in Fig. 10.17. Then add the code from Fig. 10.16 into the new project (either by copying our code from the book's examples or by typing the code yourself). In the projects you've created so far, the C# com-

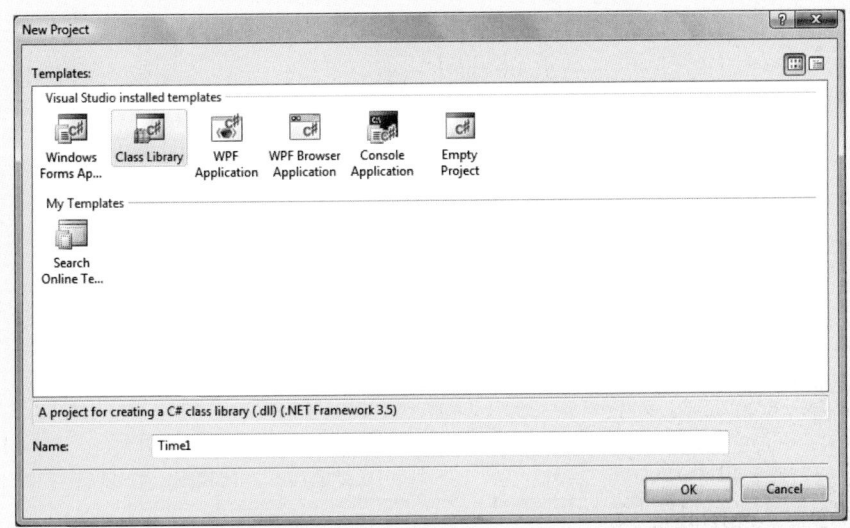

Fig. 10.17 | Creating a **Class Library** Project.

piler created an executable .exe containing the application. When you compile a **Class Library** project, the compiler creates a **.dll** *file*, known as a *dynamically linked library*—a type of assembly that you can reference from other applications.

Step 4: Adding a Reference to the Class Library

Once the class is compiled and stored in the class library file, the library can be referenced from any application by indicating to the Visual C# Express IDE where to find the class library file. Create a new (empty) project and right-click the project name in the **Solution Explorer** window. Select **Add Reference...** from the pop-up menu that appears. The dialog box that appears will contain a list of class libraries from the .NET Framework. Some class libraries, like the one containing the System namespace, are so common that they are added to your application by the IDE. The ones in this list are not.

In the **Add Reference...** dialog box, click the **Browse** tab. Recall from Section 3.3 that when you build an application, Visual C# 2008 places the .exe file in the bin\Release folder in the directory of your application. When you build a class library, Visual C# places the .dll file in the same place. In the **Browse** tab, you can navigate to the directory containing the class library file you created in *Step 3*, as shown in Fig. 10.18. Select the .dll file and click **OK**.

Step 5: Using the Class from an Application

Add a new code file to your application and enter the code for class Time1NamespaceTest (Fig. 10.19). Now that you've added a reference to your class library in this application, your Time1 class can be used by Time1NamespaceTest without adding the Time1.cs source-code file to the project.

In Fig. 10.19, the using directive in line 3 specifies that we'd like to use the class(es) of namespace Chapter10 in this file. Class Time1NamespaceTest is in the global namespace of this application, because the class's file does not contain a namespace declaration. Since

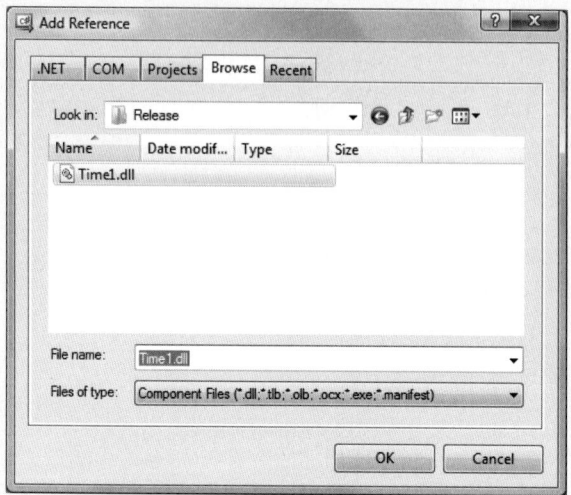

Fig. 10.18 | Adding a Reference.

```
1   // Fig. 10.19: Time1NamespaceTest.cs
2   // Time1 object used in an application.
3   using Chapter10;
4   using System;
5
6   public class Time1NamespaceTest
7   {
8      public static void Main( string[] args )
9      {
10        // create and initialize a Time1 object
11        Time1 time = new Time1(); // calls Time1 constructor
12
13        // output string representations of the time
14        Console.Write( "The initial universal time is: " );
15        Console.WriteLine( time.ToUniversalString() );
16        Console.Write( "The initial standard time is: " );
17        Console.WriteLine( time.ToString() );
18        Console.WriteLine(); // output a blank line
19
20        // change time and output updated time
21        time.SetTime( 13, 27, 6 );
22        Console.Write( "Universal time after SetTime is: " );
23        Console.WriteLine( time.ToUniversalString() );
24        Console.Write( "Standard time after SetTime is: " );
25        Console.WriteLine( time.ToString() );
26        Console.WriteLine(); // output a blank line
27
28        // set time with invalid values; output updated time
29        time.SetTime( 99, 99, 99 );
```

Fig. 10.19 | Time1 object used in an application. (Part 1 of 2.)

```
30          Console.WriteLine( "After attempting invalid settings:" );
31          Console.Write( "Universal time: " );
32          Console.WriteLine( time.ToUniversalString() );
33          Console.Write( "Standard time: " );
34          Console.WriteLine( time.ToString() );
35       } // end Main
36    } // end class Time1NamespaceTest
```

```
The initial universal time is: 00:00:00
The initial standard time is: 12:00:00 AM

Universal time after SetTime is: 13:27:06
Standard time after SetTime is: 1:27:06 PM

After attempting invalid settings:
Universal time: 00:00:00
Standard time: 12:00:00 AM
```

Fig. 10.19 | Time1 object used in an application. (Part 2 of 2.)

the two classes are in different namespaces, the using directive at line 3 allows class Time1NamespaceTest to use class Time1 as if it were in the same namespace.

Recall from Section 4.4 that we could omit the using directive in line 4 if we always referred to class Console by its fully qualified class name, System.Console. Similarly, we could omit the using directive in line 3 for namespace Chapter10 if we changed the Time1 declaration in line 11 of Fig. 10.19 to use class Time1's fully qualified name, as in:

```
Chapter10.Time1 time = new Chapter10.Time1();
```

10.15 internal Access

Classes like the ones we've defined so far can be declared with only two access modifiers—public and internal. Such classes are sometimes called top-level classes. C# also supports nested classes—classes defined inside other classes. In addition to public and internal, such classes can be declared private or protected. If there is no access modifier in the class declaration, the class defaults to *internal access*. This allows the class to be used by all code in the same assembly as the class, but not by code in other assemblies. Within the same assembly as the class, this is equivalent to public access. However, if a class library is referenced from an application, the library's internal classes will be inaccessible from the code of the application. Similarly, methods, instance variables and other members of a class declared internal are accessible to all code compiled in the same assembly, but not to code in other assemblies.

The application in Fig. 10.20 demonstrates internal access. The application contains two classes in one source-code file—the InternalAccessTest application class (lines 6–22) and the InternalData class (lines 25–43).

In the InternalData class declaration, lines 27–28 declare the instance variables number and message with the internal access modifier—class InternalData has access internal by default, so there is no need for an access modifier. The InternalAccessTest's static Main method creates an instance of the InternalData class (line 10) to demonstrate modifying the `InternalData` instance variables directly (as shown in lines 16–17). Within the same assembly, `internal` access is equivalent to `public` access. The results can be seen in the output window. If we compile this class into a `.dll` class library file and reference it from a new application, that application will have access to `public` class `InternalAccessTest`, but not to `internal` class `InternalData`, or its `internal` members.

```
1   // Fig. 10.20: InternalAccessTest.cs
2   // Members declared internal in a class are accessible by other classes
3   // in the same assembly.
4   using System;
5
6   public class InternalAccessTest
7   {
8      public static void Main( string[] args )
9      {
10         InternalData internalData = new InternalData();
11
12         // output string representation of internalData
13         Console.WriteLine( "After instantiation:\n{0}", internalData );
14
15         // change internal-access data in internalData
16         internalData.number = 77;
17         internalData.message = "Goodbye";
18
19         // output string representation of internalData
20         Console.WriteLine( "\nAfter changing values:\n{0}", internalData );
21      } // end Main
22   } // end class InternalAccessTest
23
24   // class with internal-access instance variables
25   class InternalData
26   {
27      internal int number; // internal-access instance variable
28      internal string message; // internal-access instance variable
29
30      // constructor
31      public InternalData()
32      {
33         number = 0;
34         message = "Hello";
35      } // end InternalData constructor
36
37      // return InternalData object string representation
38      public override string ToString()
39      {
40         return string.Format(
41            "number: {0}; message: {1}", number, message );
42      } // end method ToString
43   } // end class InternalData
```

Fig. 10.20 | Members declared `internal` in a class are accessible by other classes in the same assembly. (Part 1 of 2.)

```
After instantiation:
number: 0; message: Hello

After changing values:
number: 77; message: Goodbye
```

Fig. 10.20 | Members declared `internal` in a class are accessible by other classes in the same assembly. (Part 2 of 2.)

10.16 Class View and Object Browser

Now that we have introduced key concepts of object-oriented programming, we present two features that Visual Studio provides to facilitate the design of object-oriented applications—***Class View*** and ***Object Browser***.

Using the Class View *Window*

The **Class View** displays the fields and methods for all classes in a project. To access this feature, select **Class View** from the **View** menu. Figure 10.21 shows the **Class View** for the Time1 project of Fig. 10.1 (class Time1) and Fig. 10.2 (class TimeTest1). The view follows a hierarchical structure, positioning the project name (Time1) as the root and including a series of nodes that represent the classes, variables and methods in the project. If a plus sign (+) appears to the left of a node, that node can be expanded to show other nodes. If a minus sign (–) appears to the left of a node, that node can be collapsed. According to the **Class View**, project Time1 contains class Time1 and class TimeTest1 as children. When class Time1 is selected, the class's members appear in the lower half of the window. Class Time1 contains methods SetTime, ToString and ToUniversalString (indicated by purple boxes) and instance variables hour, minute and second (indicated by blue boxes). The lock icons, placed to the left of the blue box icons for the instance variables, specify that the variables are private. Class TimeTest1 contains method Main. Note that both class Time1

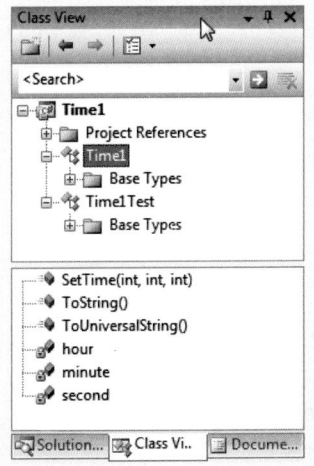

Fig. 10.21 | **Class View** of class Time1 (Fig. 10.1) and class TimeTest (Fig. 10.2).

and class `TimeTest1` contain the **Base Types** node. If you expand this node, you'll see class `object` in each case, because each class inherits from class `System.Object` (discussed in Chapter 11, Object-Oriented Programming: Inheritance).

Using the Object Browser

Visual C# Express's **Object Browser** lists all classes in the C# library. You can use the **Object Browser** to learn about the functionality provided by a specific class. To open the **Object Browser**, select **Other Windows** from the **View** menu and click **Object Browser**. Figure 10.22 depicts the **Object Browser** when the user navigates to the `Math` class in namespace `System` in the assembly `mscorlib.dll` (Microsoft Core Library). [*Note:* Be careful not to confuse the `System` namespace with the assembly named `System.dll`. The `System.dll` assembly describes other members of the `System` namespace, but class `System.Math` is in `mscorlib`.] The **Object Browser** lists all methods provided by class `Math` in the upper-right frame—this offers you "instant access" to information regarding the functionality of various objects. If you click the name of a member in the upper-right frame, a description of that member appears in the lower-right frame. Note also that the **Object Browser** lists all classes of the .NET Framework Class Library. The **Object Browser** can be a quick mechanism to learn about a class or a method of a class. Remember that you can also view the complete description of a class or a method in the online documentation available through the **Help** menu in Visual C# Express.

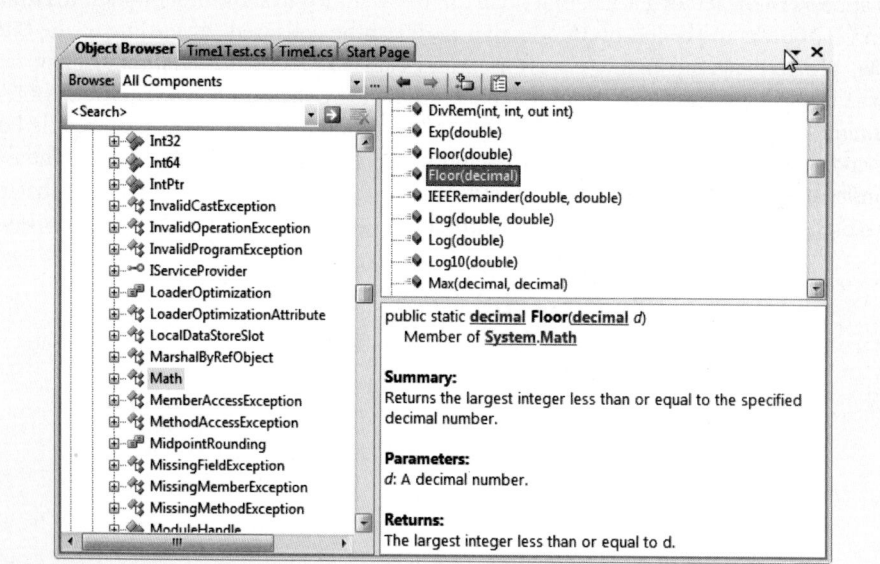

Fig. 10.22 | Object Browser for class `Math`.

10.17 Object Initializers

Visual C# 2008 provides a new feature—*object initializers*—that allow you to create an object and initialize its properties in the same statement. This is useful when a class does not provide an appropriate constructor to meet your needs. For this example, we created a version of the Time class (Fig. 10.23) in which we did not define any constructors—so this class's only constructor is the default one provided by the compiler, which does not allow client code to specify hour, minute and second values in the constructor call. Figure 10.24 demonstrates object initializers.

```
 1   // Fig. 10.23: Time.cs
 2   // Time class declaration maintains the time in 24-hour format.
 3   public class Time
 4   {
 5      private int hour; // 0 - 23
 6      private int minute; // 0 - 59
 7      private int second; // 0 - 59
 8
 9      // set a new time value using universal time; ensure that
10      // the data remains consistent by setting invalid values to zero
11      public void SetTime( int h, int m, int s )
12      {
13         Hour = h; // validate hour
14         Minute = m; // validate minute
15         Second = s; // validate second
16      } // end method SetTime
17
18      // convert to string in universal-time format (HH:MM:SS)
19      public string ToUniversalString()
20      {
21         return string.Format( "{0:D2}:{1:D2}:{2:D2}",
22            hour, minute, second );
23      } // end method ToUniversalString
24
25      // convert to string in standard-time format (H:MM:SS AM or PM)
26      public override string ToString()
27      {
28         return string.Format( "{0}:{1:D2}:{2:D2} {3}",
29            ( ( hour == 0 || hour == 12 ) ? 12 : hour % 12 ),
30            minute, second, ( hour < 12 ? "AM" : "PM" ) );
31      } // end method ToString
32
33      // Properties for getting and setting
34      // property that gets and sets the hour
35      public int Hour
36      {
37         get
38         {
39            return hour;
40         } // end get
41         set
42         {
43            hour = ( ( value >= 0 && value < 24 ) ? value : 0 );
44         } // end set
45      } // end property Hour
46
```

Fig. 10.23 | Time class declaration maintains the time in 24-hour format. (Part 1 of 2.)

```
47      // property that gets and sets the minute
48      public int Minute
49      {
50         get
51         {
52            return minute;
53         } // end get
54         set
55         {
56            minute = ( ( value >= 0 && value < 60 ) ? value : 0 );
57         } // end set
58      } // end property Minute
59
60      // property that gets and sets the second
61      public int Second
62      {
63         get
64         {
65            return second;
66         } // end get
67         set
68         {
69            second = ( ( value >= 0 && value < 60 ) ? value : 0 );
70         } // end set
71      } // end property Second
72   } // end class Time
```

Fig. 10.23 | Time class declaration maintains the time in 24-hour format. (Part 2 of 2.)

Line 12 (Fig. 10.24) creates a Time object and initializes it with class Time's parameterless constructor, then uses an object initializer to set its Hour, Minute and Second properties. Notice that new Time is immediately followed by an *object-initializer list*—a comma-separated list in curly braces ({ }) of properties and their values. Each property name can appear only once in the object-initializer list.

```
1   // Fig. 10.24: ObjectInitializerTest.cs
2   // Demonstrate object initializers using class Time.
3   using System;
4
5   class ObjectInitializerTest
6   {
7      static void Main( string[] args )
8      {
9         Console.WriteLine( "Time object created with object initializer" );
10
11         // create a Time object and initialize its properties
12         Time aTime = new Time { Hour = 14, Minute = 145, Second = 12 };
13
14         // display the time in both standard and universal format
15         Console.WriteLine( "Standard time: {0}", aTime.ToString() );
```

Fig. 10.24 | Demonstrate object initializers using class Time. (Part 1 of 2.)

```
16          Console.WriteLine( "Universal time: {0}\n",
17              aTime.ToUniversalString() );
18
19          Console.WriteLine( "Time object created with Minute property set" );
20
21          // create a Time object and initialize its Minute property only
22          Time anotherTime = new Time { Minute = 45 };
23
24          // display the time in both standard and universal format
25          Console.WriteLine( "Standard time: {0}", anotherTime.ToString() );
26          Console.WriteLine( "Universal time: {0}",
27              anotherTime.ToUniversalString() );
28      } // end Main
29  } // end class ObjectInitializerTest
```

```
Time object created with object initializer
Standard time: 2:00:12 PM
Universal time: 14:00:12

Time object created with Minute property set
Standard time: 12:45:00 AM
Universal time: 00:45:00
```

Fig. 10.24 | Demonstrate object initializers using class Time. (Part 2 of 2.)

The object initializer executes the property initializers in the order in which they appear. Lines 15–17 display the Time object in standard and universal time formats. Note that the Minute property's value is 0. The value supplied for the Minute property in the object initializer (145) is invalid. The Minute property's set accessor validates the supplied value, setting the Minute property to 0.

Line 22 uses an object initializer to create a new Time object (anotherTime) and set only its Minute property. Lines 25–27 display the Time object in both standard and universal time formats. Note that the time is set to 12:45:00 AM. Recall that an object initializer first calls the class's constructor. The Time constructor initializes the time to midnight (00:00:00). The object initializer then sets each specified property to the supplied value. In this case, the Minute property is set to 45. The Hour and Second properties retain their default values, because no values are specified for them in the object initializer.

10.18 Time Class Case Study: Extension Methods

Sometimes it is useful to add new functionality to an existing class. However, you cannot modify code for classes in the .NET Framework Class Library or other class libraries that you did not create. In Visual C# 2008, you can use *extension methods* to add functionality to an existing class without modifying the class's source code. Many LINQ capabilities are also available as extension methods.

Figure 10.25 uses extension methods to add functionality to class Time (from Section 10.17). The extension method DisplayTime (lines 35–38) displays the time in the console window using the Time object's ToString method. The key new feature of method DisplayTime is the this keyword that precedes the Time object parameter in the method header (line 35). The this keyword notifies the compiler that the DisplayTime method extends an existing class. The C# compiler uses this information to inject additional code into the compiled program that enables extension methods to work with existing types. The type of an extension method's first parameter specifies the class that is being extended—extension methods must define at least one parameter. Also, extension methods must be defined as static methods in a static top-level class such as TimeExtensions (lines 32–53). A static class can contain only static members and cannot be instantiated.

```csharp
1   // Fig. 10.25: TimeExtensionsTest.cs
2   // Demonstrating extension methods.
3   using System;
4
5   class TimeExtensionsTest
6   {
7      static void Main( string[] args )
8      {
9         Time myTime = new Time(); // call Time constructor
10        myTime.SetTime( 11, 34, 15 ); // set the time to 11:34:15
11
12        // test the DisplayTime extension method
13        Console.Write( "Use the DisplayTime method: " );
14        myTime.DisplayTime();
15
16        // test the AddHours extension method
17        Console.Write( "Add 5 hours to the Time object: " );
18        Time timeAdded = myTime.AddHours( 5 ); // add five hours
19        timeAdded.DisplayTime(); // display the new Time object
20
21        // add hours and display the time in one statement
22        Console.Write( "Add 15 hours to the Time object: " );
23        myTime.AddHours( 15 ).DisplayTime(); // add hours and display time
24
25        // use fully qualified extension-method name to display the time
26        Console.Write( "Use fully qualified extension-method name: " );
27        TimeExtensions.DisplayTime( myTime );
28     } // end Main
29  } // end class TimeExtensionsTest
30
31  // extension-methods class
32  static class TimeExtensions
33  {
34     // display the Time object in console
35     public static void DisplayTime( this Time aTime )
36     {
37        Console.WriteLine( aTime.ToString() );
38     } // end method DisplayTime
39
40     // add the specified number of hours to the time
41     // and return a new Time object
42     public static Time AddHours( this Time aTime, int hours )
43     {
44        Time newTime = new Time(); // create a new Time object
45        newTime.Minute = aTime.Minute; // set the minutes
```

Fig. 10.25 | Demonstrating extension methods. (Part 1 of 2.)

```
46          newTime.Second = aTime.Second; // set the seconds
47
48          // add the specified number of hours to the given time
49          newTime.Hour = ( aTime.Hour + hours ) % 24;
50
51          return newTime; // return the new Time object
52      } // end method AddHours
53  } // end class TimeExtensions
```

```
Use the DisplayTime method: 11:34:15 AM
Add 5 hours to the Time object: 4:34:15 PM
Add 15 hours to the Time object: 2:34:15 AM
Use fully qualified extension-method name: 11:34:15 AM
```

Fig. 10.25 | Demonstrating extension methods. (Part 2 of 2.)

The parameter list for the DisplayTime method (line 35) contains a single parameter of type Time, indicating that this method extends class Time. Line 14 of Fig. 10.25 uses Time object myTime to call the DisplayTime extension method. Note that line 14 does not provide an argument to the method call. The compiler implicitly passes the object that is used to call the method (myTime in this case) as the extension method's first argument. This allows you to call an extension method as if it were an instance method of the extended class. In fact, *IntelliSense* displays extension methods with the extended class's instance methods and identifies them with a distinct icon (Fig. 10.26). Note the blue down-arrow in the icon to the left of the method name in the *IntelliSense* window—this denotes an extension method. The tool tip shown to the right of the *IntelliSense* window includes the text **(extension)** to indicate that DisplayTime is an extension method. Also note in the tool tip that the method's signature shows an empty parameter list.

Lines 42–52 of Fig. 10.25 define the AddHours extension method. Again, the method parameter contains the this keyword (line 42). The first parameter of AddHours is a Time

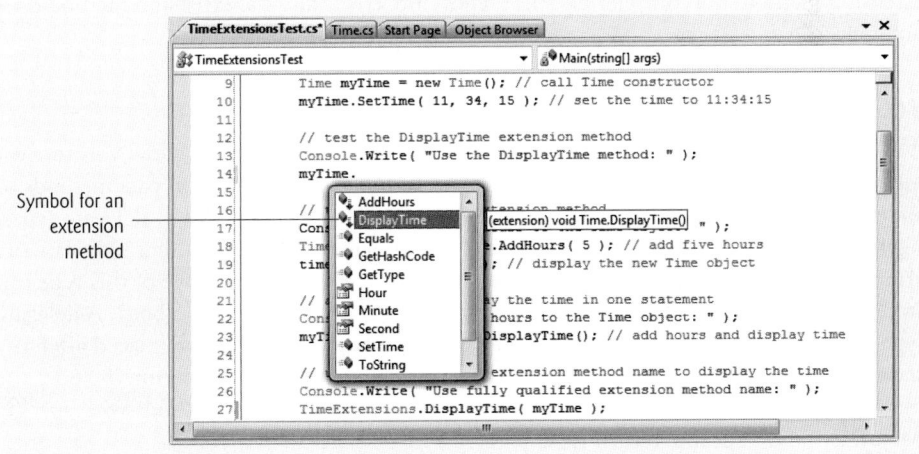

Fig. 10.26 | *IntelliSense* support for extension methods.

object, indicating that the method extends class Time. The second parameter is an int value specifying the number of hours to add to the time. The AddHours method returns a new Time object with the specified number of hours added. Line 44 creates the new Time object. Lines 45–46 set the new Time's Minute and Second properties using the values of the Time object received as an argument. Line 49 adds the specified number of hours to the value of the original Time object's Hour property, then uses the % operator to ensure the value is in the range 0–23. This value is assigned to the new Time object's Hour property. Line 51 returns the new Time object to the caller. Line 18 calls the AddHours extension method to add five hours to the myTime object's hour value. Note that the method call receives one argument—the number of hours to add. Again, the compiler implicitly passes the object that is used to call the method (myTime) as the extension method's first argument. The Time object returned by AddHours is assigned to a local variable (timeAdded) and displayed in the console using the DisplayTime extension method (line 19). Line 23 uses both extension methods (DisplayTime and AddHours) in a single statement to add 15 hours to myTime and display the result in the console. Extension methods, as well as instance methods, allow *cascaded method calls*—that is, invoking multiple methods in the same statement (line 23). The methods are called from left to right. In line 23, the DisplayTime method is called on the Time object returned by method AddHours.

Line 27 calls extension method DisplayTime using its fully qualified name—the name of the class in which the extension method is defined (TimeExtensions), followed by the method name (DisplayTime) and its argument list. Note in line 27 that the call to DisplayTime passes a Time object as an argument to the method. When using the fully qualified method name, you must specify an argument for extension method's first parameter. This use of the extension method resembles a call to a static method.

Extension Method Notes

Be careful when using extension methods to add functionality to preexisting classes. If the type being extended defines an instance method with the same name as your extension method and a compatible signature, the instance method will shadow the extension method. If a predefined class is later updated to include an instance method that shadows an extension method, the compiler does not report any errors and the extension method does not appear in *IntelliSense*.

10.19 Delegates

A *delegate* is an object that holds a reference to a method. Delegates allow you to treat methods as data—via delegates, you can assign methods to variables, and pass methods to and from other methods. You can also call methods through variables of delegate types. Figure 10.27 uses delegates to customize the functionality of a method that filters an int array. Line 9 defines a delegate type named NumberPredicate. A variable of this type can store a reference to any method that takes an int argument and returns a bool. A delegate type is declared by preceeding a method header with keyword *delegate* (placed after any access specifiers, such as public or private). The delegate type declaration includes the method header only—the delegate type simply describes a set of methods with specific parameters and a specific return type.

Line 16 declares evenPredicate as a variable of type NumberPredicate and assigns to it a reference to the IsEven method (defined in lines 61–64). Since method IsEven's signature matches the NumberPredicate delegate's signature, IsEven can be referenced by a variable of type NumberPredicate. Variable evenPredicate can now be used as an alias for method IsEven. A NumberPredicate variable can hold a reference to any method that receives an int and returns a bool. Lines 19–20 use variable evenPredicate to call method IsEven, then display the result. The method referenced by the delegate is called using the delegate variable's name in place of the method's name (i.e., evenPredicate(4)).

```csharp
1   // Fig. 10.27: Delegates.cs
2   // Using delegates to pass functions as arguments.
3   using System;
4   using System.Collections.Generic;
5
6   class Delegates
7   {
8      // delegate for a function that receives an int and returns a bool
9      public delegate bool NumberPredicate( int number );
10
11     static void Main( string[] args )
12     {
13        int[] numbers = { 1, 2, 3, 4, 5, 6, 7, 8, 9, 10 };
14
15        // create an instance of the NumberPredicate delegate type
16        NumberPredicate evenPredicate = IsEven;
17
18        // call IsEven using a delegate variable
19        Console.WriteLine( "Call IsEven using a delegate variable: {0}",
20           evenPredicate( 4 ) );
21
22        // filter the even numbers using method IsEven
23        List< int > evenNumbers = FilterArray( numbers, evenPredicate );
24
25        // display the result
26        DisplayList( "Use IsEven to filter even numbers: ", evenNumbers );
27
28        // filter the odd numbers using method IsOdd
29        List< int > oddNumbers = FilterArray( numbers, IsOdd );
30
31        // display the result
32        DisplayList( "Use IsOdd to filter odd numbers: ", oddNumbers );
33
34        // filter numbers greater than 5 using method IsOver5
35        List< int > numbersOver5 = FilterArray( numbers, IsOver5 );
36
37        // display the result
38        DisplayList( "Use IsOver5 to filter numbers over 5: ",
39           numbersOver5 );
40     } // end Main
41
42     // select an array's elements that satisfy the predicate
43     private static List< int > FilterArray( int[] intArray,
44        NumberPredicate predicate )
45     {
```

Fig. 10.27 | Using delegates to pass functions as arguments. (Part 1 of 2.)

```
46          // hold the selected elements
47          List< int > result = new List< int >();
48
49          // iterate over each element in the array
50          foreach ( int item in intArray )
51          {
52              // if the element satisfies the predicate
53              if ( predicate( item ) )
54                  result.Add( item ); // add the element to the result
55          } // end foreach
56
57          return result; // return the result
58      } // end method FilterArray
59
60      // determine whether an int is even
61      private static bool IsEven( int number )
62      {
63          return ( number % 2 == 0 );
64      } // end method IsEven
65
66      // determine whether an int is odd
67      private static bool IsOdd( int number )
68      {
69          return ( number % 2 == 1 );
70      } // end method IsOdd
71
72      // determine whether an int is positive
73      private static bool IsOver5( int number )
74      {
75          return ( number > 5 );
76      } // end method IsOver5
77
78      // display the elements of a List
79      private static void DisplayList( string description, List< int > list )
80      {
81          Console.Write( description ); // display the output's description
82
83          // iterate over each element in the List
84          foreach ( int item in list )
85              Console.Write( "{0} ", item ); // print item followed by a space
86
87          Console.WriteLine(); // add a new line
88      } // end method DisplayList
89  } // end class Delegates
```

```
Call IsEven using a delegate variable: True
Use IsEven to filter even numbers: 2 4 6 8 10
Use IsOdd to filter odd numbers: 1 3 5 7 9
Use IsOver5 to filter numbers over 5: 6 7 8 9 10
```

Fig. 10.27 | Using delegates to pass functions as arguments. (Part 2 of 2.)

The real power of delegates is the ability to pass a method reference as an argument to another method, as shown by method FilterArray (lines 43–58). FilterArray takes as arguments an int array and a NumberPredicate that references a method used to filter the array elements. The foreach statement (lines 50–55) calls the method referenced by the NumberPredicate delegate (line 53) on each element of the array. If the method call returns true, the element is included in the result. The NumberPredicate is guaranteed to return either true or false, because any method referenced by a NumberPredicate must return a bool—as specified by the definition of the NumberPredicate delegate type. Line 23 passes FilterArray the int array (numbers) and the NumberPredicate that references the IsEven method (evenPredicate). FilterArray calls the NumberPredicate delegate on each array element. FilterArray returns a List of ints, because we don't know in advance how many elements will be selected. Line 23 assigns the List returned by FilterArray to variable evenNumbers and line 26 calls method DisplayList to display the results.

Line 29 calls method FilterArray to select the odd numbers in the array. We reference method IsOdd (defined in lines 67–70) in FilterArray's second argument, rather than creating a NumberPredicate variable. Line 32 displays the results. Line 35 calls method FilterArray to select the numbers greater than five in the array. Method IsOver5 is referenced by a NumberPredicate delegate and passed to method FilterArray (line 35). The filtered list is then displayed in lines 38–39.

10.20 Lambda Expressions

Lambda expressions (new in Visual C# 2008) allow you to define simple, *anonymous functions*. Figure 10.28 uses lambda expressions to reimplement the previous example that introduced delegates. A lambda expression (line 17) begins with a parameter list. The parameter list is followed by the => *lambda operator* (read as "goes to") and an expression that represents the body of the function. The lambda expression in line 17 uses the % operator to determine whether the parameter's number value is an even int. The value produced by the expression—true if the int is even, false otherwise—is implicitly returned by the lambda expression. Note that we do not specify a return type for the lambda expression—the return type is inferred from the return value or, in some cases, from the delegate's return type. The lambda expression in line 17 produces the same results as the IsEven method in Fig. 10.27. In fact, the expression used in the body of the IsEven method is the same one used in the lambda expression.

```
 1   // Fig. 10.28: Lambdas.cs
 2   // Using lambda expressions.
 3   using System;
 4   using System.Collections.Generic;
 5
 6   class Lambdas
 7   {
 8      // delegate for a function that receives an int and returns a bool
 9      public delegate bool NumberPredicate( int number );
10
11      static void Main( string[] args )
12      {
13         int[] numbers = { 1, 2, 3, 4, 5, 6, 7, 8, 9, 10 };
14
```

Fig. 10.28 | Using lambda expressions. (Part 1 of 3.)

```
15      // create an instance of the NumberPredicate delegate type using an
16      // implicit lambda expression
17      NumberPredicate evenPredicate = number => ( number % 2 == 0 );
18
19      // call a lambda expression through a variable
20      Console.WriteLine( "Use a lambda-expression variable: {0}",
21         evenPredicate( 4 ) );
22
23      // filter the even numbers using a lambda expression
24      List< int > evenNumbers = FilterArray( numbers, evenPredicate );
25
26      // display the result
27      DisplayList( "Use a lambda expression to filter even numbers: ",
28         evenNumbers );
29
30      // filter the odd numbers using an explicitly typed lambda
31      // expression
32      List< int > oddNumbers = FilterArray( numbers,
33         ( int number ) => ( number % 2 == 1 ) );
34
35      // display the result
36      DisplayList( "Use a lambda expression to filter odd numbers: ",
37         oddNumbers );
38
39      // filter numbers greater than 5 using an implicit lambda statement
40      List< int > numbersOver5 = FilterArray( numbers,
41         number => { return number > 5; } );
42
43      // display the result
44      DisplayList( "Use a lambda expression to filter numbers over 5: ",
45         numbersOver5 );
46   } // end Main
47
48   // select an array's elements that satisfy the predicate
49   private static List< int > FilterArray( int[] intArray,
50      NumberPredicate predicate )
51   {
52      // hold the selected elements
53      List< int > result = new List< int >();
54
55      // iterate over each element in the array
56      foreach ( int item in intArray )
57      {
58         // if the element satisfies the predicate
59         if ( predicate( item ) )
60            result.Add( item ); // add the element to the result
61      } // end foreach
62
63      return result; // return the result
64   } // end method FilterArray
65
```

Fig. 10.28 | Using lambda expressions. (Part 2 of 3.)

```
66        // display the elements of a List
67        private static void DisplayList( string description, List< int > list )
68        {
69            Console.Write( description ); // display the output's description
70
71            // iterate over each element in the List
72            foreach ( int item in list )
73                Console.Write( "{0} ", item ); // print item followed by a space
74
75            Console.WriteLine(); // add a new line
76        } // end method DisplayList
77   } // end class Lambdas
```

```
Use a lambda expression variable: True
Use a lambda expression to filter even numbers: 2 4 6 8 10
Use a lambda expression to filter odd numbers: 1 3 5 7 9
Use a lambda expression to filter numbers over 5: 6 7 8 9 10
```

Fig. 10.28 | Using lambda expressions. (Part 3 of 3.)

In line 17, the lambda expression is assigned to a variable of type NumberPredicate (defined in line 9). Recall that NumberPredicate is the delegate type used in the previous example. A delegate can hold a reference to a lambda expression. As with traditional methods, a method defined by a lambda expression must have a signature that is compatible with the delegate type. The NumberPredicate delegate can hold a reference to any method that takes an int as an argument and returns a bool. Based on this, the compiler is able to infer that the lambda expression in line 17 defines a method that implicitly takes an int as an argument and returns the bool result of the expression in its body. Lambda expressions are often used as arguments to methods with parameters of delegate types, rather than defining and referencing a separate method.

Lines 20–21 display the result of calling the lambda expression defined in line 17. The lambda expression is called via the variable that references it (evenPredicate). Line 24 passes evenPredicate to method FilterArray (lines 49–64), which is identical to the method used in Fig. 10.27—it uses the NumberPredicate delegate to determine whether an array element should be included in the result. Lines 27–28 display the filtered results.

Lines 32–33 select the odd array elements and store the results. The lambda expression's input parameter number is explicitly typed as an int, rather than implicitly typed like the lambda expression in line 17. The lambda expressions in lines 17 and 33 are called *expression lambdas* because they have an expression to the right of the lambda operator. In this case, the lambda expression is passed directly to method FilterArray and is implicitly converted to a NumberPredicate delegate. The lambda expression in line 33 is equivalent to the IsOdd method defined in Fig. 10.27. Lines 36–37 display the filtered results.

Lines 40–41 filter ints greater than 5 from the array and store the results. The lambda expression in line 41 is equivalent to the IsOver5 method in Fig. 10.27. This lambda expression is called a *statement lambda*, because it contains a statement block—a set of statements enclosed in braces ({})—to the right of the lambda operator. The statement block of a statement lambda can contain multiple statements. The lambda expression's sig-

nature is compatible with the NumberPredicate delegate, because the parameter's type is
inferred to be int and the statement in the lambda returns a bool.

Lambda expressions can help reduce the size of your code and the complexity of
working with delegates—the program in Fig. 10.28 performs the same actions as the one
in Fig. 10.27 but is 12 lines shorter. Lambda expressions are particularly powerful when
combined with the where clause in LINQ queries.

10.21 Anonymous Types

Anonymous types (new in Visual C# 2008) allow you to create simple classes used to store
data without writing a class definition. An anonymous type declaration (line 10 of
Fig. 10.29)—known formally as an *anonymous object-creation expression*—is similar to
an object initializer (discussed in Section 10.17). The anonymous type declaration begins
with the keyword new followed by a member-initializer list in braces ({}). Notice that no
class name is specified after the new keyword. The compiler generates a new class definition
based on the anonymous object-creation expression. The new class contains the properties
specified in the member-initializer list—Name and Age. All properties of an anonymous
type are public and immutable. Anonymous type properties are read-only—you cannot
modify a property's value once the object is created. Each property's type is inferred from
the values assigned to it. The class definition is generated automatically by the compiler,
so you don't know the class's type name (hence the term anonymous type). Thus, you
must use implicitly typed local variables to store references to objects of anonymous types
(e.g., line 10). Line 13 uses the anonymous type's ToString method to display the object's
information on the console. The compiler defines the ToString method when creating the
anonymous type's class definition. The method returns a string in curly braces containing a comma-separated list of *PropertyName* = *value* pairs.

```csharp
1    // Fig. 10.29: AnonymousTypes.cs
2    // Using anonymous types.
3    using System;
4
5    class AnonymousTypes
6    {
7       static void Main( string[] args )
8       {
9          // create a "person" object using an anonymous type
10         var bob = new { Name = "Bob Smith", Age = 37 };
11
12         // display Bob's information
13         Console.WriteLine( "Bob: " + bob.ToString() );
14
15         // create another "person" object using the same anonymous type
16         var steve = new { Name = "Steve Jones", Age = 26 };
17
18         // display Steve's information
19         Console.WriteLine( "Steve: " + steve.ToString() );
20
```

Fig. 10.29 | Using anonymous types. (Part 1 of 2.)

```
21          // determine if objects of the same anonymous type are equal
22          Console.WriteLine( "\nBob and Steve are {0}",
23             ( bob.Equals( steve ) ? "equal" : "not equal" ) );
24
25          // create a "person" object using an anonymous type
26          var bob2 = new { Name = "Bob Smith", Age = 37 };
27
28          // display Bob's information
29          Console.WriteLine( "\nBob2: " + bob2.ToString() );
30
31          // determine whether objects of the same anonymous type are equal
32          Console.WriteLine( "\nBob and Bob2 are {0}\n",
33             ( bob.Equals( bob2 ) ? "equal" : "not equal" ) );
34       } // end Main
35   } // end class AnonymousTypes
```

```
Bob: { Name = Bob Smith, Age = 37 }
Steve: { Name = Steve Jones, Age = 26 }

Bob and Steve are not equal

Bob2: { Name = Bob Smith, Age = 37 }

Bob and Bob2 are equal
```

Fig. 10.29 | Using anonymous types. (Part 2 of 2.)

Line 16 creates another anonymous object and assigns it to variable steve. The anonymous object-creation expression uses the same property names (Name and Age) and types in the member-initializer list as the anonymous type defined in line 10. Two anonymous objects that specify the same property names and types, in the same order, use the same anonymous class definition and are considered to be of the same type.

Lines 22–23 determine if the two anonymous objects, bob and steve, are equal and display the results. When anonymous objects are compared for equality, all properties are considered. Line 23 uses the anonymous type's Equals method (also defined by the compiler), which compares the properties of the anonymous object that calls the method and the anonymous object that it receives as an argument. Since bob's Name and Age properties are not equal to steve's Name and Age properties, the two objects are not equal.

Line 26 creates an object of the same anonymous type as bob and steve and assigns it to variable bob2. This object specifies the same property values as bob. Line 33 uses the anonymous type's Equals method to determine that bob and bob2 are equal—both have the same Name and Age property values and the properties are declared in the same order.

Anonymous Types in LINQ
Anonymous types are frequently used in LINQ queries to select specific properties from the items being queried. Recall the Employee class used in Section 9.2. The class defines three properties—FirstName, LastName and MonthlySalary. The statement

```
var names =
    from e in employees
    select new { e.FirstName, Last = e.LastName };
```

from lines 58–60 of Fig. 9.4 uses a LINQ query to select properties FirstName and LastName of each Employee object (e) in an array of Employees (employees). The select clause creates an anonymous type with properties `FirstName` and `Last` to store the selected property values. The syntax used in the `select` clause to create the anonymous type is different than what you've seen in this section. The member-initializer list doesn't specify a name for the `FirstName` property. As explained in Chapter 9, the compiler implicitly uses the name of the selected property unless you specify otherwise.

10.22 (Optional) Software Engineering Case Study: Starting to Program the Classes of the ATM System

In the Software Engineering Case Study sections in Chapters 1 and 3–8, we introduced the fundamentals of object orientation and developed an object-oriented design for our ATM system. In Chapters 4–7, we introduced object-oriented programming in C#. In Chapter 8, we took a deeper look at the details of programming with classes. We now begin implementing our object-oriented design by converting class diagrams to C# code. In the final Software Engineering Case Study section (Section 12.9), we modify the code to incorporate the object-oriented concepts of inheritance and polymorphism. We present the full C# code implementation in Appendix D.

Visibility

We now apply access modifiers to the members of our classes. In Chapter 4, we introduced access modifiers `public` and `private`. Access modifiers determine the *visibility*, or accessibility, of an object's attributes and operations to other objects. Before we can begin implementing our design, we must consider which attributes and methods of our classes should be `public` and which should be `private`.

In Chapter 4, we observed that attributes normally should be `private` and that methods invoked by clients of a class should be `public`. Methods that are called only by other methods of the class as "utility functions," however, should be `private`. The UML employs *visibility markers* for modeling the visibility of attributes and operations. Public visibility is indicated by placing a plus sign (+) before an operation or an attribute; a minus sign (–) indicates private visibility. Figure 10.30 shows our updated class diagram with visibility markers included. [*Note:* We do not include any operation parameters in Fig. 10.30. This is perfectly normal. Adding visibility markers does not affect the parameters already modeled in the class diagrams of Figs. 7.20–7.24.]

Navigability

Before we begin implementing our design in C#, we introduce an additional UML notation. The class diagram in Fig. 10.31 further refines the relationships among classes in the ATM system by adding navigability arrows to the association lines. *Navigability arrows* (represented as arrows with stick arrowheads in the class diagram) indicate in which direction an association can be traversed and are based on the collaborations modeled in communication and sequence diagrams (see Section 8.14). When implementing a system designed using the UML, programmers use navigability arrows to help determine which objects need references to other objects. For example, the navigability arrow pointing from class `ATM` to class `BankDatabase` indicates that we can navigate from the former to the latter, thereby enabling the `ATM` to invoke the `BankDatabase`'s operations. However, since Fig. 10.31 does not contain a navigability arrow pointing from class `BankDatabase` to class `ATM`, the `BankDatabase` cannot

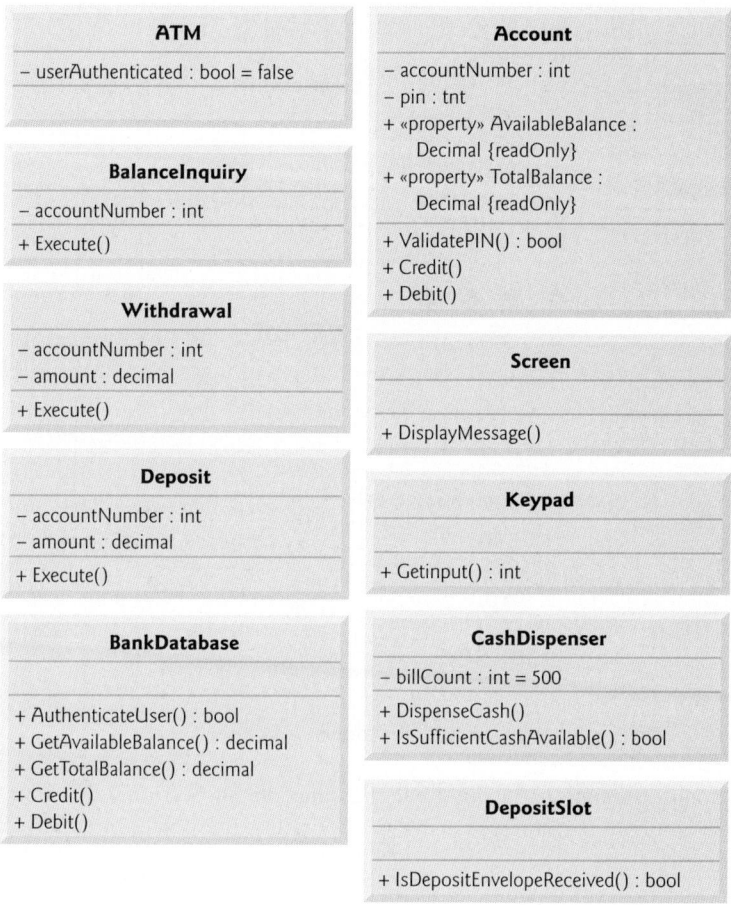

Fig. 10.30 | Class diagram with visibility markers.

access the ATM's operations. Note that associations in a class diagram that have navigability arrows at both ends or do not have navigability arrows at all indicate *bidirectional naviga-bility*—navigation can proceed in either direction across the association.

Like the class diagram of Fig. 4.26, the class diagram of Fig. 10.31 omits classes BalanceInquiry and Deposit to keep the diagram simple. The navigability of the associations in which these classes participate closely parallels the navigability of class With-drawal's associations. Recall from Section 4.12 that BalanceInquiry has an association with class Screen. We can navigate from class BalanceInquiry to class Screen along this association, but we cannot navigate from class Screen to class BalanceInquiry. Thus, if we were to model class BalanceInquiry in Fig. 10.31, we would place a navigability arrow at class Screen's end of this association. Also recall that class Deposit associates with classes Screen, Keypad and DepositSlot. We can navigate from class Deposit to each of these classes, but not vice versa. We therefore would place navigability arrows at the Screen, Keypad and DepositSlot ends of these associations. [*Note:* We model these addi-

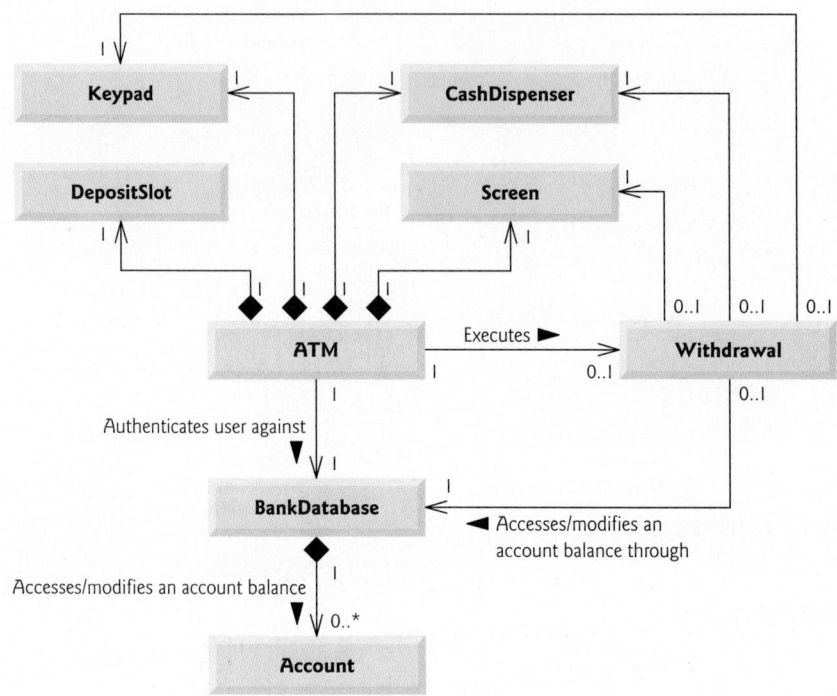

Fig. 10.31 | Class diagram with navigability arrows.

tional classes and associations in our final class diagram in Section 12.9, after we have simplified the structure of our system by incorporating the object-oriented concept of inheritance.]

Implementing the ATM System from Its UML Design

We're now ready to begin implementing the ATM system. We first convert the classes in the diagrams of Fig. 10.30 and Fig. 10.31 into C# code. This code will represent the "skeleton" of the system. In Chapter 12, we modify the code to incorporate the object-oriented concept of inheritance. In Appendix D, we present the complete working C# code that implements our object-oriented design.

As an example, we begin to develop the code for class Withdrawal from our design of class Withdrawal in Fig. 10.30. We use this figure to determine the attributes and operations of the class. We use the UML model in Fig. 10.31 to determine the associations among classes. We follow these four guidelines for each class:

1. Use the name located in the first compartment of a class in a class diagram to declare the class as a public class with an empty parameterless constructor—we include this constructor simply as a placeholder to remind us that most classes will need one or more constructors. In Appendix D, when we complete a working version of this class, we add any necessary arguments and code to the body of the constructor. Class Withdrawal initially yields the code in Fig. 10.32.

```
 1   // Fig. 10.32: Withdrawal.cs
 2   // Class Withdrawal represents an ATM withdrawal transaction
 3   public class Withdrawal
 4   {
 5       // parameterless constructor
 6       public Withdrawal()
 7       {
 8           // constructor body code
 9       } // end constructor
10   } // end class Withdrawal
```

Fig. 10.32 | Initial C# code for class Withdrawal based on Figs. 10.30 and 10.31.

  2. Use the attributes located in the class's second compartment to declare the instance variables. The private attributes accountNumber and amount of class Withdrawal yield the code in Fig. 10.33.

```
 1   // Fig. 10.33: Withdrawal.cs
 2   // Class Withdrawal represents an ATM withdrawal transaction
 3   public class Withdrawal
 4   {
 5       // attributes
 6       private int accountNumber; // account to withdraw funds from
 7       private decimal amount; // amount to withdraw from account
 8
 9       // parameterless constructor
10       public Withdrawal()
11       {
12           // constructor body code
13       } // end constructor
14   } // end class Withdrawal
```

Fig. 10.33 | Incorporating private variables for class Withdrawal based on Figs. 10.30–10.31.

  3. Use the associations described in the class diagram to declare references to other objects. According to Fig. 10.31, Withdrawal can access one object of class Screen, one object of class Keypad, one object of class CashDispenser and one object of class BankDatabase. Class Withdrawal must maintain references to these objects to send messages to them, so lines 10–13 of Fig. 10.34 declare the appropriate references as private instance variables. In the implementation of class Withdrawal in Appendix D, a constructor initializes these instance variables with references to the actual objects.

```
 1   // Fig. 10.34: Withdrawal.cs
 2   // Class Withdrawal represents an ATM withdrawal transaction
 3   public class Withdrawal
 4   {
```

Fig. 10.34 | Incorporating private reference handles for the associations of class Withdrawal based on Figs. 10.30 and 10.31. (Part 1 of 2.)

```
5        // attributes
6        private int accountNumber; // account to withdraw funds from
7        private decimal amount;  // amount to withdraw
8
9        // references to associated objects
10       private Screen screen; // ATM's screen
11       private Keypad keypad; // ATM's keypad
12       private CashDispenser cashDispenser; // ATM's cash dispenser
13       private BankDatabase bankDatabase; // account-information database
14
15       // parameterless constructor
16       public Withdrawal()
17       {
18           // constructor body code
19       } // end constructor
20   } // end class Withdrawal
```

Fig. 10.34 | Incorporating `private` reference handles for the associations of class `Withdrawal` based on Figs. 10.30 and 10.31. (Part 2 of 2.)

   4. Use the operations located in the third compartment of Fig. 10.30 to declare the shells of the methods. If we have not yet specified a return type for an operation, we declare the method with return type `void`. Refer to the class diagrams of Figs. 7.20–7.24 to declare any necessary parameters. Adding the `public` operation `Execute` (which has an empty parameter list) in class `Withdrawal` yields the code in lines 23–26 of Fig. 10.35. [*Note:* We code the bodies of the methods when we implement the complete ATM system in Appendix D.]

```
1    // Fig. 10.35: Withdrawal.cs
2    // Class Withdrawal represents an ATM withdrawal transaction
3    public class Withdrawal
4    {
5        // attributes
6        private int accountNumber; // account to withdraw funds from
7        private decimal amount;  // amount to withdraw
8
9        // references to associated objects
10       private Screen screen; // ATM's screen
11       private Keypad keypad; // ATM's keypad
12       private CashDispenser cashDispenser; // ATM's cash dispenser
13       private BankDatabase bankDatabase; // account-information database
14
15       // parameterless constructor
16       public Withdrawal()
17       {
18           // constructor body code
19       } // end constructor
20
```

Fig. 10.35 | C# code incorporating method `Execute` in class `Withdrawal` based on Figs. 10.30 and 10.31. (Part 1 of 2.)

```
21      // operations
22      // perform transaction
23      public void Execute()
24      {
25          // Execute method body code
26      } // end method Execute
27  } // end class Withdrawal
```

Fig. 10.35 | C# code incorporating method Execute in class Withdrawal based on Figs. 10.30 and 10.31. (Part 2 of 2.)

 Software Engineering Observation 10.13

Many UML modeling tools can convert UML-based designs into C# code, considerably speeding up the implementation process. For more information on these "automatic" code generators, refer to the web resources listed at the end of Section 3.9.

This concludes our discussion of the basics of generating class files from UML diagrams. In the final Software Engineering Case Study section (Section 12.9), we demonstrate how to modify the code in Fig. 10.35 to incorporate the object-oriented concepts of inheritance and polymorphism, which we present in Chapters 11 and 12, respectively.

Software Engineering Case Study Self-Review Exercises

10.1   State whether the following statement is *true* or *false*, and if *false*, explain why: If an attribute of a class is marked with a minus sign (-) in a class diagram, the attribute is not directly accessible outside of the class.

10.2   In Fig. 10.31, the association between the ATM and the Screen indicates:
a) that we can navigate from the Screen to the ATM.
b) that we can navigate from the ATM to the Screen.
c) Both a and b; the association is bidirectional.
d) None of the above.

10.3   Write C# code to begin implementing the design for class Account.

Answers to Software Engineering Case Study Self-Review Exercises

10.1   True. The minus sign (-) indicates private visibility.

10.2   b.

10.3   The design for class Account yields the code in Fig. 10.36. Note that we public auto-implemented properties AvailableBalance and TotalBalance to store the data that methods Credit and Debit, will manipulate.

```
1   // Fig. 10.36: Account.cs
2   // Class Account represents a bank account.
3   public class Account
4   {
5       private int accountNumber; // account number
6       private int pin; // PIN for authentication
7
```

Fig. 10.36 | C# code for class Account based on Figs. 10.30 and 10.31. (Part 1 of 2.)

```
 8        // automatic read-only property AvailableBalance
 9        public decimal AvailableBalance { get; private set; }
10
11        // automatic read-only property TotalBalance
12        public decimal TotalBalance { get; private set; }
13
14        // parameterless constructor
15        public Account()
16        {
17           // constructor body code
18        } // end constructor
19
20        // validates user PIN
21        public bool ValidatePIN()
22        {
23           // ValidatePIN method body code
24        } // end method ValidatePIN
25
26        // credits the account
27        public void Credit()
28        {
29           // Credit method body code
30        } // end method Credit
31
32        // debits the account
33        public void Debit()
34        {
35           // Debit method body code
36        } // end method Debit
37     } // end class Account
```

Fig. 10.36 | C# code for class Account based on Figs. 10.30 and 10.31. (Part 2 of 2.)

10.23 Wrap-Up

In this chapter, we discussed additional class concepts. The Time class case study presented a complete class declaration consisting of private data, overloaded public constructors for initialization flexibility, properties for manipulating the class's data and methods that returned string representations of a Time object in two different formats. You learned that every class can declare a ToString method that returns a string representation of an object of the class and that this method is invoked implicitly when an object of a class is output as a string or concatenated with a string.

You learned that the this reference is used implicitly in a class's non-static methods to access the class's instance variables and other non-static methods. You saw explicit uses of the this reference to access the class's members (including hidden fields) and learned how to use keyword this in a constructor to call another constructor of the class. You also learned how to declare indexers with the this keyword, allowing you to access the data of an object in much the same manner as you access the elements of an array.

You saw that composition enables a class to have references to objects of other classes as members. You learned about C#'s garbage-collection capability and how it reclaims the memory of objects that are no longer used. We explained the motivation for static variables in a class and demonstrated how to declare and use `static` variables and methods in your own classes. You also learned how to declare and initialize `readonly` variables.

We showed how to create a class library for reuse and how to use the classes of the library in an application. You learned that classes declared without an access modifier are given `internal` access by default. You saw that classes in an assembly can access the `internal`-access members of the other classes in the same assembly. We also showed how to use Visual Studio's **Class View** and **Object Browser** windows to navigate the classes of the .NET Framework Class Library and your own applications to discover information about those classes.

You learned how to initialize an object's properties as you create it with an object-initializer list. We used extension methods to add functionality to a class without modifying the class's source code. You then learned that a delegate is an object that holds a method reference. We showed you how to use delegates to assign methods to variables and pass methods to other methods. Next we demonstrated lambda expressions for defining simple, anonymous methods that can also be used with delegates. Finally, you learned how to use anonymous types to create simple classes that store data without writing a class definition.

In the next chapter, you'll learn another key object-oriented programming technology—inheritance. You'll see that all classes in C# are related directly or indirectly to the `object` class. You'll also begin to understand how inheritance enables you to build more powerful applications faster.

11

Object-Oriented Programming: Inheritance

OBJECTIVES

In this chapter you'll learn:

- How inheritance promotes software reusability.

- The concepts of base classes and derived classes.

- To create a derived class that inherits attributes and behaviors from a base class.

- To use access modifier **protected** to give derived-class methods access to base-class members.

- To access base-class members with **base**.

- How constructors are used in inheritance hierarchies.

- The methods of class **object**, the direct or indirect base class of all classes.

*Say not you know
another entirely,
till you have divided an
inheritance with him.*
—Johann Kasper Lavater

*This method is to define as
the number of a class the
class of all classes similar to
the given class.*
—Bertrand Russell

*Good as it is to inherit
a library, it is better to
collect one.*
—Augustine Birrell

*Save base authority from
others' books.*
—William Shakespeare

Outline

11.1 Introduction

11.2 Base Classes and Derived Classes

11.3 `protected` Members

11.4 Relationship between Base Classes and Derived Classes

    11.4.1 Creating and Using a `CommissionEmployee` Class

    11.4.2 Creating a `BasePlusCommissionEmployee` Class without Using Inheritance

    11.4.3 Creating a `CommissionEmployee`–`BasePlusCommissionEmployee` Inheritance Hierarchy

    11.4.4 `CommissionEmployee`–`BasePlusCommissionEmployee` Inheritance Hierarchy Using `protected` Instance Variables

    11.4.5 `CommissionEmployee`–`BasePlusCommissionEmployee` Inheritance Hierarchy Using `private` Instance Variables

11.5 Constructors in Derived Classes

11.6 Software Engineering with Inheritance

11.7 Class `object`

11.8 Wrap-Up

11.1 Introduction

This chapter continues our discussion of object-oriented programming (OOP) by introducing one of its primary features—*inheritance*, a form of software reuse in which a new class is created by absorbing an existing class's members and enhancing them with new or modified capabilities. Inheritance lets programmers save time during application development by reusing proven and debugged high-quality software. This also increases the likelihood that a system will be implemented effectively.

The existing class from which a new class inherits members is called the *base class*, and the new class is the *derived class.* Each derived class can become the base class for future derived classes.

A derived class normally adds its own fields and methods. Therefore, it is more specific than its base class and represents a more specialized group of objects. Typically, the derived class exhibits the behaviors of its base class and additional behaviors that are specific to itself.

The *direct base class* is the base class from which the derived class explicitly inherits. An *indirect base class* is any class above the direct base class in the *class hierarchy*, which defines the inheritance relationships among classes. The class hierarchy begins with class `object` (which is the C# alias for `System.Object` in the .NET Framework Class Library), which *every* class directly or indirectly *extends* (or "inherits from"). Section 11.7 lists the methods of class `object`, which every other class inherits. In the case of *single inheritance,* a class is derived from one direct base class. C#, unlike C++, does not support multiple inheritance (which occurs when a class is derived from more than one direct base class). In Chapter 12, Polymorphism, Interfaces and Operator Overloading, we explain how you can use interfaces to realize many of the benefits of multiple inheritance while avoiding the associated problems.

Experience in building software systems indicates that significant amounts of code deal with closely related special cases. When you are preoccupied with special cases, the details can obscure the big picture. With object-oriented programming, you can, when appropriate, focus on the commonalities among objects in the system rather than the special cases.

We distinguish between the *is-a relationship* and the *has-a relationship*. *Is-a* represents inheritance. In an *is-a* relationship, an object of a derived class can also be treated as an object of its base class. For example, a car *is a* vehicle, and a truck *is a* vehicle. By contrast, *has-a* represents composition (see Chapter 10). In a *has-a* relationship, an object contains as members references to other objects. For example, a car *has a* steering wheel, and a car object *has a* reference to a steering-wheel object.

New classes can inherit from classes in *class libraries*. Organizations develop their own class libraries and can take advantage of others available worldwide. Some day, most new software likely will be constructed from *standardized reusable components*, just as automobiles and most computer hardware are constructed today. This will facilitate the development of more powerful, abundant and economical software.

11.2 Base Classes and Derived Classes

Often, an object of one class *is an* object of another class as well. For example, in geometry, a rectangle *is a* quadrilateral (as are squares, parallelograms and trapezoids). Thus, class Rectangle can be said to inherit from class Quadrilateral. In this context, class Quadrilateral is a base class and class Rectangle is a derived class. A rectangle *is a* specific type of quadrilateral, but it is incorrect to claim that every quadrilateral *is a* rectangle—the quadrilateral could be a parallelogram or some other shape. Figure 11.1 lists several simple examples of base classes and derived classes—note that base classes tend to be "more general," and derived classes tend to be "more specific."

Because every derived-class object *is an* object of its base class, and one base class can have many derived classes, the set of objects represented by a base class is typically larger than the set of objects represented by any of its derived classes. For example, the base class Vehicle represents all vehicles—cars, trucks, boats, bicycles and so on. By contrast, derived class Car represents a smaller, more specific subset of vehicles.

Base class	Derived classes
Student	GraduateStudent, UndergraduateStudent
Shape	Circle, Triangle, Rectangle
Loan	CarLoan, HomeImprovementLoan, MortgageLoan
Employee	Faculty, Staff, HourlyWorker, CommissionWorker
BankAccount	CheckingAccount, SavingsAccount

Fig. 11.1 | Inheritance examples.

Inheritance relationships form treelike hierarchical structures (Figs. 11.2 and 11.3). A base class exists in a hierarchical relationship with its derived classes. When classes participate in inheritance relationships, they become "affiliated" with other classes. A class becomes either a base class, supplying members to other classes, or a derived class, inheriting its members from another class. Sometimes, a class is both a base and a derived class.

Let us develop a sample class hierarchy, also called an *inheritance hierarchy* (Fig. 11.2). The UML class diagram of Fig. 11.2 shows a university community that has many types of members, including employees, students and alumni. Employees are either faculty members or staff members. Faculty members are either administrators (such as deans and department chairpersons) or teachers. Note that the hierarchy could contain many other classes. For example, students can be graduate or undergraduate students. Undergraduate students can be freshmen, sophomores, juniors or seniors.

Each arrow with a hollow triangular arrowhead in the hierarchy diagram represents an *is-a* relationship. As we follow the arrows, we can state, for instance, that "an Employee *is a* CommunityMember" and "a Teacher *is a* Faculty member." CommunityMember is the direct base class of Employee, Student and Alumnus and is an indirect base class of all the other classes in the diagram. Starting from the bottom, you can follow the arrows and apply the *is-a* relationship up to the topmost base class. For example, an Administrator *is a* Faculty member, *is an* Employee and *is a* CommunityMember.

Now consider the Shape inheritance hierarchy in Fig. 11.3. This hierarchy begins with base class Shape, which is extended by derived classes TwoDimensionalShape and ThreeDimensionalShape—a Shape is either a TwoDimensionalShape or a ThreeDimensionalShape. The third level of this hierarchy contains some specific TwoDimensionalShapes and ThreeDimensionalShapes. As in Fig. 11.2, we can follow the arrows from the bottom to the topmost base class in this class hierarchy to identify several *is-a* relationships. For instance, a Triangle *is a* TwoDimensionalShape and *is a* Shape, while a Sphere *is a* ThreeDimensionalShape and *is a* Shape. Note that this hierarchy could contain many other classes. For example, ellipses and trapezoids are TwoDimensionalShapes.

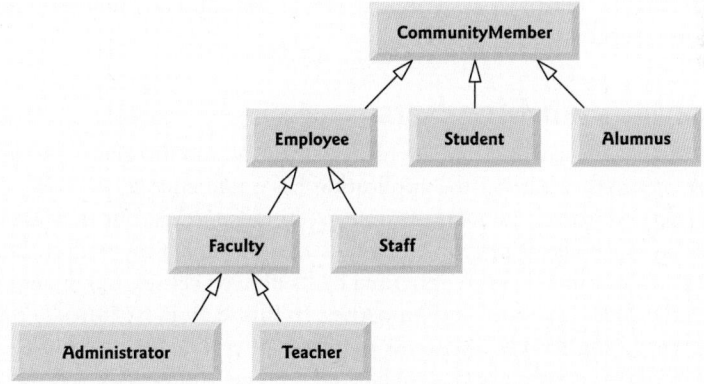

Fig. 11.2 | UML class diagram showing an inheritance hierarchy for university CommunityMembers.

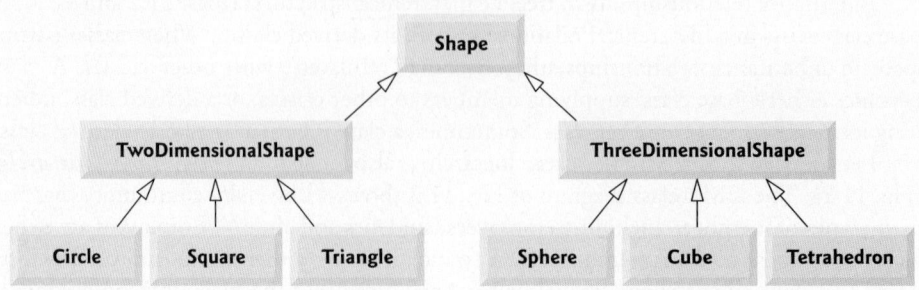

Fig. 11.3 | UML class diagram showing an inheritance hierarchy for Shapes.

Not every class relationship is an inheritance relationship. In Chapter 10 we discussed the *has-a* relationship, in which classes have members that are references to objects of other classes. Such relationships create classes by composition of existing classes. For example, given the classes Employee, BirthDate and TelephoneNumber, it is improper to say that an Employee *is a* BirthDate or that an Employee *is a* TelephoneNumber. However, an Employee *has a* BirthDate, and an Employee *has a* TelephoneNumber.

It is possible to treat base-class objects and derived-class objects similarly—their commonalities are expressed in the members of the base class. Objects of all classes that extend a common base class can be treated as objects of that base class (i.e., such objects have an *is-a* relationship with the base class). However, base-class objects cannot be treated as objects of their derived classes. For example, all cars are vehicles, but not all vehicles are cars (the other vehicles could be trucks, planes or bicycles, for example). In this chapter and in Chapter 12, Polymorphism, Interfaces and Operator Overloading, we consider many examples of *is-a* relationships.

One problem with inheritance is that a derived class can inherit methods that it does not need or should not have. Even when a base-class method is appropriate for a derived class, that derived class often needs a customized version. In such cases, the derived class can *override* (redefine) the base-class method with an appropriate implementation, as we'll see often in the chapter's code examples.

11.3 protected Members

Chapter 10 discussed access modifiers public, private and internal. A class's public members are accessible wherever the application has a reference to an object of that class or one of its derived classes. (There are some exceptions to this, but they are beyond the scope of this book.) A class's private members are accessible only within the class itself. A base class's private members are inherited by its derived classes, but are not directly accessible by derived-class methods and properties. In this section, we introduce access modifier protected. Using protected access offers an intermediate level of access between public and private. A base class's protected members can be accessed by members of that base class *and* by members of its derived classes. (Members of a class can also be declared ***protected internal***. A base class's protected internal members can be accessed by members of that base class, by members of its derived classes *and* by any class in the same assembly.)

All non-`private` base-class members retain their original access modifier when they become members of the derived class (i.e., `public` members of the base class become `public` members of the derived class, and `protected` members of the base class become `protected` members of the derived class).

Derived-class methods can refer to `public` and `protected` members inherited from the base class simply by using the member names. When a derived-class method overrides a base-class method, the base-class version can be accessed from the derived class by preceding the base-class method name with the keyword `base` and the member access (.) operator. We discuss accessing overridden members of the base class in Section 11.4.

Software Engineering Observation 11.1

Properties and methods of a derived class cannot directly access `private` members of the base class. A derived class can change the state of `private` base-class fields only through non-`private` methods and properties provided in the base class.

Software Engineering Observation 11.2

Declaring `private` fields in a base class helps you test, debug and correctly modify systems. If a derived class could access its base class's `private` fields, classes that inherit from that base class could access the fields as well. This would propagate access to what should be `private` fields, and the benefits of information hiding would be lost.

11.4 Relationship between Base Classes and Derived Classes

In this section, we use an inheritance hierarchy containing types of employees in a company's payroll application to discuss the relationship between a base class and its derived classes. In this company, commission employees (who will be represented as objects of a base class) are paid a percentage of their sales, while base-salaried commission employees (who will be represented as objects of a derived class) receive a base salary plus a percentage of their sales.

We divide our discussion of the relationship between commission employees and base-salaried commission employees into a series of five examples:

1. The first example creates class `CommissionEmployee`, which directly inherits from class `object` and declares as `private` instance variables a first name, last name, social security number, commission rate and gross (i.e., total) sales amount.

2. The second example declares class `BasePlusCommissionEmployee`, which also directly inherits from class `object` and declares as `private` instance variables a first name, last name, social security number, commission rate, gross sales amount and base salary. We create the latter class by writing every line of code the class requires—we'll soon see that it is much more efficient to create this class by inheriting from class `CommissionEmployee`.

3. The third example declares a separate `BasePlusCommissionEmployee` class that extends class `CommissionEmployee` (i.e., a `BasePlusCommissionEmployee` *is a* `CommissionEmployee` who also has a base salary). We show that base-class methods must be explicitly declared `virtual` if they are to be overridden by methods in derived classes. `BasePlusCommissionEmployee` attempts to access class `Com-`

missionEmployee's private members—this results in compilation errors, because a derived class cannot access its base class's private instance variables.

4. The fourth example shows that if base class CommissionEmployee's instance variables are declared as protected, a BasePlusCommissionEmployee class that inherits from class CommissionEmployee can access that data directly. For this purpose, we declare class CommissionEmployee with protected instance variables.

5. After we discuss the convenience of using protected instance variables, we create the fifth example, which sets the CommissionEmployee instance variables back to private in class CommissionEmployee to enforce good software engineering. Then we show how a separate BasePlusCommissionEmployee class, which inherits from class CommissionEmployee, can use CommissionEmployee's public methods to manipulate CommissionEmployee's private instance variables.

11.4.1 Creating and Using a CommissionEmployee Class

We begin by declaring class CommissionEmployee (Fig. 11.4). Line 3 begins the class declaration. The colon (:) followed by class name object at the end of the declaration header indicates that class CommissionEmployee extends (i.e., inherits from) class object (System.Object in the .NET Framework Class Library). C# programmers use inheritance to create classes from existing classes. In fact, every class in C# (except object) extends an existing class. Because class CommissionEmployee extends class object, class CommissionEmployee inherits the methods of class object—class object has no fields. Every C# class directly or indirectly inherits object's methods. If a class does not specify that it inherits from another class, the new class implicitly inherits from object. For this reason, you typically do not include ": object" in your code—we do so in this example for demonstration purposes.

```
1   // Fig. 11.4: CommissionEmployee.cs
2   // CommissionEmployee class represents a commission employee.
3   public class CommissionEmployee : object
4   {
5      private string firstName;
6      private string lastName;
7      private string socialSecurityNumber;
8      private decimal grossSales; // gross weekly sales
9      private decimal commissionRate; // commission percentage
10
11     // five-parameter constructor
12     public CommissionEmployee( string first, string last, string ssn,
13        decimal sales, decimal rate )
14     {
15        // implicit call to object constructor occurs here
16        firstName = first;
17        lastName = last;
18        socialSecurityNumber = ssn;
19        GrossSales = sales; // validate gross sales via property
20        CommissionRate = rate; // validate commission rate via property
21     } // end five-parameter CommissionEmployee constructor
22
```

Fig. 11.4 | CommissionEmployee class represents a commission employee. (Part 1 of 3.)

```
23        // read-only property that gets commission employee's first name
24        public string FirstName
25        {
26           get
27           {
28              return firstName;
29           } // end get
30        } // end property FirstName
31
32        // read-only property that gets commission employee's last name
33        public string LastName
34        {
35           get
36           {
37              return lastName;
38           } // end get
39        } // end property LastName
40
41        // read-only property that gets
42        // commission employee's social security number
43        public string SocialSecurityNumber
44        {
45           get
46           {
47              return socialSecurityNumber;
48           } // end get
49        } // end property SocialSecurityNumber
50
51        // property that gets and sets commission employee's gross sales
52        public decimal GrossSales
53        {
54           get
55           {
56              return grossSales;
57           } // end get
58           set
59           {
60              grossSales = ( value < 0 ) ? 0 : value;
61           } // end set
62        } // end property GrossSales
63
64        // property that gets and sets commission employee's commission rate
65        public decimal CommissionRate
66        {
67           get
68           {
69              return commissionRate;
70           } // end get
71           set
72           {
73              commissionRate = ( value > 0 && value < 1 ) ? value : 0;
74           } // end set
75        } // end property CommissionRate
```

Fig. 11.4 | `CommissionEmployee` class represents a commission employee. (Part 2 of 3.)

```
76
77       // calculate commission employee's pay
78       public decimal Earnings()
79       {
80          return commissionRate * grossSales;
81       } // end method Earnings
82
83       // return string representation of CommissionEmployee object
84       public override string ToString()
85       {
86          return string.Format(
87             "{0}: {1} {2}\n{3}: {4}\n{5}: {6:C}\n{7}: {8:F2}",
88             "commission employee", FirstName, LastName,
89             "social security number", SocialSecurityNumber,
90             "gross sales", GrossSales, "commission rate", CommissionRate );
91       } // end method ToString
92    } // end class CommissionEmployee
```

Fig. 11.4 | CommissionEmployee class represents a commission employee. (Part 3 of 3.)

Software Engineering Observation 11.3

The compiler sets the base class of a class to object *when the class declaration does not explicitly extend a base class.*

The public services of class CommissionEmployee include a constructor (lines 12–21) and methods Earnings (lines 78–81) and ToString (lines 84–91). Lines 24–75 declare public properties for manipulating the class's instance variables firstName, lastName, socialSecurityNumber, grossSales and commissionRate (declared in lines 5–9). Class CommissionEmployee declares each of its instance variables as private, so objects of other classes cannot directly access these variables. Declaring instance variables as private and providing public properties to manipulate and validate them helps enforce good software engineering. The set accessors of properties GrossSales and CommissionRate, for example, validate their arguments before assigning the values to instance variables grossSales and commissionRate, respectively.

Constructors are not inherited, so class CommissionEmployee does not inherit class object's constructor. However, class CommissionEmployee's constructor calls class object's constructor implicitly. In fact, before executing the code in its own body, the derived class's constructor calls its direct base class's constructor, either explicitly or implicitly (if no constructor call is specified), to ensure that the instance variables inherited from the base class are initialized properly. The syntax for calling a base-class constructor explicitly is discussed in Section 11.4.3. If the code does not include an explicit call to the base-class constructor, the compiler generates an implicit call to the base class's default or parameterless constructor. The comment in line 15 of Fig. 11.4 indicates where the implicit call to the base class object's default constructor is made (you do not write the code for this call). Class object's default (empty) constructor does nothing. Note that even if a class does not have constructors, the default constructor that the compiler implicitly declares for the class will call the base class's default or parameterless constructor. Class object is the only class that does not have a base class.

After the implicit call to object's constructor occurs, lines 16–20 of CommissionEmployee's constructor assign values to the class's instance variables. Note that we do not validate the values of arguments first, last and ssn before assigning them to the corresponding instance variables. We certainly could validate the first and last names—perhaps by ensuring that they are of a reasonable length. Similarly, a social security number could be validated to ensure that it contains nine digits, with or without dashes (e.g., 123-45-6789 or 123456789).

Method Earnings (lines 78–81) calculates a CommissionEmployee's earnings. Line 80 multiplies the commissionRate by the grossSales and returns the result.

Method ToString (lines 84–91) is special—it is one of the methods that every class inherits directly or indirectly from class object, which is the root of the C# class hierarchy. Section 11.7 summarizes class object's methods. Method ToString returns a string representing an object. It's called implicitly by an application whenever an object must be converted to a string representation, such as in Console's Write method or string method Format using a format item. Class object's ToString method returns a string that includes the name of the object's class. It is primarily a placeholder that can be (and typically should be) overridden by a derived class to specify an appropriate string representation of the data in a derived class object. Method ToString of class CommissionEmployee overrides (redefines) class object's ToString method. When invoked, CommissionEmployee's ToString method uses string method Format to return a string containing information about the CommissionEmployee. We use format specifier C to format grossSales as currency and the format specifier F2 to format the commissionRate with two digits of precision to the right of the decimal point. To override a base-class method, a derived class must declare a method with keyword **override** and with the same signature (method name, number of parameters and parameter types) and return type as the base-class method—object's ToString method takes no parameters and returns type string, so CommissionEmployee declares ToString with no parameters and returns type string.

Common Programming Error 11.1

It is a compilation error to override a method with a different access modifier. Notice that overriding a method with a more restrictive access modifier would break the is-a relationship. If a public method could be overridden as a protected or private method, the derived-class objects would not be able to respond to the same method calls as base-class objects. Once a method is declared in a base class, the method must have the same access modifier for all that class's direct and indirect derived classes.

Figure 11.5 tests class CommissionEmployee. Lines 10–11 instantiate a CommissionEmployee object and invoke CommissionEmployee's constructor (lines 12–21 of Fig. 11.4) to initialize it with "Sue" as the first name, "Jones" as the last name, "222-22-2222" as the social security number, 10000.00M as the gross sales amount and .06M as the commission rate. We append the M suffix to the gross sales amount and the commission rate to indicate that these should be interpreted as decimal literals, rather than doubles. Lines 16–22 use CommissionEmployee's properties to retrieve the object's instance-variable values for output. Line 23 outputs the amount calculated by the Earnings method. Lines 25–26 invoke the set accessors of the object's GrossSales and CommissionRate properties to change the values of instance variables grossSales and commissionRate. Lines 28–29 output the string representation of the updated CommissionEmployee. Note that when an object is output using a format item, the object's ToString method is invoked implicitly to obtain the object's string representation. Line 30 outputs the earnings again.

```csharp
1    // Fig. 11.5: CommissionEmployeeTest.cs
2    // Testing class CommissionEmployee.
3    using System;
4
5    public class CommissionEmployeeTest
6    {
7       public static void Main( string[] args )
8       {
9          // instantiate CommissionEmployee object
10         CommissionEmployee employee = new CommissionEmployee( "Sue",
11            "Jones", "222-22-2222", 10000.00M, .06M );
12
13         // display commission-employee data
14         Console.WriteLine(
15            "Employee information obtained by properties and methods: \n" );
16         Console.WriteLine( "First name is {0}", employee.FirstName );
17         Console.WriteLine( "Last name is {0}", employee.LastName );
18         Console.WriteLine( "Social security number is {0}",
19            employee.SocialSecurityNumber );
20         Console.WriteLine( "Gross sales are {0:C}", employee.GrossSales );
21         Console.WriteLine( "Commission rate is {0:F2}",
22            employee.CommissionRate );
23         Console.WriteLine( "Earnings are {0:C}", employee.Earnings() );
24
25         employee.GrossSales = 5000.00M; // set gross sales
26         employee.CommissionRate = .1M; // set commission rate
27
28         Console.WriteLine( "\n{0}:\n\n{1}",
29            "Updated employee information obtained by ToString", employee );
30         Console.WriteLine( "earnings: {0:C}", employee.Earnings() );
31      } // end Main
32   } // end class CommissionEmployeeTest
```

```
Employee information obtained by properties and methods:

First name is Sue
Last name is Jones
Social security number is 222-22-2222
Gross sales are $10,000.00
Commission rate is 0.06
Earnings are $600.00

Updated employee information obtained by ToString:

commission employee: Sue Jones
social security number: 222-22-2222
gross sales: $5,000.00
commission rate: 0.10
earnings: $500.00
```

Fig. 11.5 | Testing class CommissionEmployee.

11.4.2 Creating a BasePlusCommissionEmployee Class without Using Inheritance

We now discuss the second part of our introduction to inheritance by declaring and testing (completely new and independent) class BasePlusCommissionEmployee (Fig. 11.6),

```csharp
 1   // Fig. 11.6: BasePlusCommissionEmployee.cs
 2   // BasePlusCommissionEmployee class represents an employee that receives
 3   // a base salary in addition to a commission.
 4   public class BasePlusCommissionEmployee
 5   {
 6      private string firstName;
 7      private string lastName;
 8      private string socialSecurityNumber;
 9      private decimal grossSales; // gross weekly sales
10      private decimal commissionRate; // commission percentage
11      private decimal baseSalary; // base salary per week
12
13      // six-parameter constructor
14      public BasePlusCommissionEmployee( string first, string last,
15         string ssn, decimal sales, decimal rate, decimal salary )
16      {
17         // implicit call to object constructor occurs here
18         firstName = first;
19         lastName = last;
20         socialSecurityNumber = ssn;
21         GrossSales = sales; // validate gross sales via property
22         CommissionRate = rate; // validate commission rate via property
23         BaseSalary = salary; // validate base salary via property
24      } // end six-parameter BasePlusCommissionEmployee constructor
25
26      // read-only property that gets
27      // base-salaried commission employee's first name
28      public string FirstName
29      {
30         get
31         {
32            return firstName;
33         } // end get
34      } // end property FirstName
35
36      // read-only property that gets
37      // base-salaried commission employee's last name
38      public string LastName
39      {
40         get
41         {
42            return lastName;
43         } // end get
44      } // end property LastName
45
```

Fig. 11.6 | BasePlusCommissionEmployee class represents an employee that receives a base salary in addition to a commission. (Part 1 of 3.)

```
46          // read-only property that gets
47          // base-salaried commission employee's social security number
48          public string SocialSecurityNumber
49          {
50             get
51             {
52                return socialSecurityNumber;
53             } // end get
54          } // end property SocialSecurityNumber
55
56          // property that gets and sets
57          // base-salaried commission employee's gross sales
58          public decimal GrossSales
59          {
60             get
61             {
62                return grossSales;
63             } // end get
64             set
65             {
66                grossSales = ( value < 0 ) ? 0 : value;
67             } // end set
68          } // end property GrossSales
69
70          // property that gets and sets
71          // base-salaried commission employee's commission rate
72          public decimal CommissionRate
73          {
74             get
75             {
76                return commissionRate;
77             } // end get
78             set
79             {
80                commissionRate = ( value > 0 && value < 1 ) ? value : 0;
81             } // end set
82          } // end property CommissionRate
83
84          // property that gets and sets
85          // base-salaried commission employee's base salary
86          public decimal BaseSalary
87          {
88             get
89             {
90                return baseSalary;
91             } // end get
92             set
93             {
94                baseSalary = ( value < 0 ) ? 0 : value;
95             } // end set
96          } // end property BaseSalary
```

Fig. 11.6 | BasePlusCommissionEmployee class represents an employee that receives a base salary in addition to a commission. (Part 2 of 3.)

```
97
98        // calculate earnings
99        public decimal Earnings()
100       {
101          return BaseSalary + ( CommissionRate * GrossSales );
102       } // end method earnings
103
104       // return string representation of BasePlusCommissionEmployee
105       public override string ToString()
106       {
107          return string.Format(
108             "{0}: {1} {2}\n{3}: {4}\n{5}: {6:C}\n{7}: {8:F2}\n{9}: {10:C}",
109             "base-salaried commission employee", FirstName, LastName,
110             "social security number", SocialSecurityNumber,
111             "gross sales", GrossSales, "commission rate", CommissionRate,
112             "base salary", BaseSalary );
113       } // end method ToString
114 } // end class BasePlusCommissionEmployee
```

Fig. 11.6 | `BasePlusCommissionEmployee` class represents an employee that receives a base salary in addition to a commission. (Part 3 of 3.)

which contains a first name, last name, social security number, gross sales amount, commission rate and base salary. Class `BasePlusCommissionEmployee`'s public services include a `BasePlusCommissionEmployee` constructor (lines 14–24) and methods `Earnings` (lines 99–102) and `ToString` (lines 105–113). Lines 28–96 declare public properties for the class's private instance variables `firstName`, `lastName`, `socialSecurityNumber`, `grossSales`, `commissionRate` and `baseSalary` (declared in lines 6–11). These variables, properties and methods encapsulate all the necessary features of a base-salaried commission employee. Note the similarity between this class and class `CommissionEmployee` (Fig. 11.4)—in this example, we do not yet exploit that similarity.

Note that class `BasePlusCommissionEmployee` does not specify that it extends `object` with the syntax ": `object`" in line 4, so the class implicitly extends `object`. Also note that, like class `CommissionEmployee`'s constructor (lines 12–21 of Fig. 11.4), class `BasePlusCommissionEmployee`'s constructor invokes class `object`'s default constructor implicitly, as noted in the comment in line 17 of Fig. 11.6.

Class `BasePlusCommissionEmployee`'s `Earnings` method (lines 99–102) computes the earnings of a base-salaried commission employee. Line 101 adds the employee's base salary to the product of the commission rate and the gross sales, and returns the result.

Class `BasePlusCommissionEmployee` overrides `object` method `ToString` to return a string containing the `BasePlusCommissionEmployee`'s information (lines 105–113). Once again, we use format specifier `C` to format the gross sales and base salary as currency and format specifier `F2` to format the commission rate with two digits of precision to the right of the decimal point (line 108).

Figure 11.7 tests class `BasePlusCommissionEmployee`. Lines 10–12 instantiate a `BasePlusCommissionEmployee` object and pass "Bob", "Lewis", "333-33-3333", 5000.00M, .04M and 300.00M to the constructor as the first name, last name, social security number, gross sales, commission rate and base salary, respectively. Lines 17–25 use `BasePlusCommissionEmployee`'s properties and methods to retrieve the values of the object's

```csharp
 1   // Fig. 11.7: BasePlusCommissionEmployeeTest.cs
 2   // Testing class BasePlusCommissionEmployee.
 3   using System;
 4
 5   public class BasePlusCommissionEmployeeTest
 6   {
 7      public static void Main( string[] args )
 8      {
 9         // instantiate BasePlusCommissionEmployee object
10         BasePlusCommissionEmployee employee =
11            new BasePlusCommissionEmployee( "Bob", "Lewis",
12            "333-33-3333", 5000.00M, .04M, 300.00M );
13
14         // display base-salaried commission-employee data
15         Console.WriteLine(
16            "Employee information obtained by properties and methods: \n" );
17         Console.WriteLine( "First name is {0}", employee.FirstName );
18         Console.WriteLine( "Last name is {0}", employee.LastName );
19         Console.WriteLine( "Social security number is {0}",
20            employee.SocialSecurityNumber );
21         Console.WriteLine( "Gross sales are {0:C}", employee.GrossSales );
22         Console.WriteLine( "Commission rate is {0:F2}",
23            employee.CommissionRate );
24         Console.WriteLine( "Earnings are {0:C}", employee.Earnings() );
25         Console.WriteLine( "Base salary is {0:C}", employee.BaseSalary );
26
27         employee.BaseSalary = 1000.00M; // set base salary
28
29         Console.WriteLine( "\n{0}:\n\n{1}",
30            "Updated employee information obtained by ToString", employee );
31         Console.WriteLine( "earnings: {0:C}", employee.Earnings() );
32      } // end Main
33   } // end class BasePlusCommissionEmployeeTest
```

```
Employee information obtained by properties and methods:

First name is Bob
Last name is Lewis
Social security number is 333-33-3333
Gross sales are $5,000.00
Commission rate is 0.04
Earnings are $500.00
Base salary is $300.00

Updated employee information obtained by ToString:

base-salaried commission employee: Bob Lewis
social security number: 333-33-3333
gross sales: $5,000.00
commission rate: 0.04
base salary: $1,000.00
earnings: $1,200.00
```

Fig. 11.7 | Testing class BasePlusCommissionEmployee.

instance variables and calculate the earnings for output. Line 27 invokes the object's Base-Salary property to change the base salary. Property BaseSalary's set accessor (Fig. 11.6, lines 92–95) ensures that instance variable baseSalary is not assigned a negative value, because an employee's base salary cannot be negative. Lines 29–30 of Fig. 11.7 invoke the object's ToString method implicitly to get the object's string representation.

Note that much of the code for class BasePlusCommissionEmployee (Fig. 11.6) is similar, if not identical, to the code for class CommissionEmployee (Fig. 11.4). For example, in class BasePlusCommissionEmployee, private instance variables firstName and lastName and properties FirstName and LastName are identical to those of class CommissionEmployee. Classes CommissionEmployee and BasePlusCommissionEmployee also both contain private instance variables socialSecurityNumber, commissionRate and grossSales, as well as properties to manipulate these variables. In addition, the BasePlusCommissionEmployee constructor is almost identical to that of class CommissionEmployee, except that BasePlusCommissionEmployee's constructor also sets the baseSalary. The other additions to class BasePlusCommissionEmployee are private instance variable baseSalary and property BaseSalary. Class BasePlusCommissionEmployee's ToString method is nearly identical to that of class CommissionEmployee, except that BasePlusCommissionEmployee's ToString also formats the value of instance variable baseSalary as currency.

We literally copied the code from class CommissionEmployee and pasted it into class BasePlusCommissionEmployee, then modified class BasePlusCommissionEmployee to include a base salary and methods and properties that manipulate the base salary. This "copy-and-paste" approach is often error prone and time consuming. Worse yet, it can spread many physical copies of the same code throughout a system, creating a code-maintenance nightmare. Is there a way to "absorb" the members of one class in a way that makes them part of other classes without copying code? In the next several examples we answer this question, using a more elegant approach to building classes—namely, inheritance.

Error-Prevention Tip 11.1

Copying and pasting code from one class to another can spread errors across multiple source-code files. To avoid duplicating code (and possibly errors) in situations where you want one class to "absorb" the members of another class, use inheritance rather than the "copy-and-paste" approach.

Software Engineering Observation 11.4

With inheritance, the common members of all the classes in the hierarchy are declared in a base class. When changes are required for these common features, you need to make the changes only in the base class—derived classes then inherit the changes. Without inheritance, changes would need to be made to all the source-code files that contain a copy of the code in question.

11.4.3 Creating a CommissionEmployee– BasePlusCommissionEmployee Inheritance Hierarchy

Now we declare class BasePlusCommissionEmployee (Fig. 11.8), which extends class CommissionEmployee (Fig. 11.4). A BasePlusCommissionEmployee object *is a* CommissionEmployee (because inheritance passes on the capabilities of class CommissionEmployee), but class BasePlusCommissionEmployee also has instance variable baseSalary (Fig. 11.8, line

5). The colon (:) in line 3 of the class declaration indicates inheritance. As a derived class, BasePlusCommissionEmployee inherits the members of class CommissionEmployee and can

```
1   // Fig. 11.8: BasePlusCommissionEmployee.cs
2   // BasePlusCommissionEmployee inherits from class CommissionEmployee.
3   public class BasePlusCommissionEmployee : CommissionEmployee
4   {
5      private decimal baseSalary; // base salary per week
6
7      // six-parameter derived-class constructor
8      // with call to base class CommissionEmployee constructor
9      public BasePlusCommissionEmployee( string first, string last,
10        string ssn, decimal sales, decimal rate, decimal salary )
11        : base( first, last, ssn, sales, rate )
12     {
13        BaseSalary = salary; // validate base salary via property
14     } // end six-parameter BasePlusCommissionEmployee constructor
15
16     // property that gets and sets
17     // base-salaried commission employee's base salary
18     public decimal BaseSalary
19     {
20        get
21        {
22           return baseSalary;
23        } // end get
24        set
25        {
26           baseSalary = ( value < 0 ) ? 0 : value;
27        } // end set
28     } // end property BaseSalary
29
30     // calculate earnings
31     public override decimal Earnings()
32     {
33        // not allowed: commissionRate and grossSales private in base class
34        return baseSalary + ( commissionRate * grossSales );
35     } // end method Earnings
36
37     // return string representation of BasePlusCommissionEmployee
38     public override string ToString()
39     {
40        // not allowed: attempts to access private base-class members
41        return string.Format(
42           "{0}: {1} {2}\n{3}: {4}\n{5}: {6:C}\n{7}: {8:F2}\n{9}: {10:C}",
43           "base-salaried commission employee", firstName, lastName,
44           "social security number", socialSecurityNumber,
45           "gross sales", grossSales, "commission rate", commissionRate,
46           "base salary", baseSalary );
47     } // end method ToString
48  } // end class BasePlusCommissionEmployee
```

Fig. 11.8 | BasePlusCommissionEmployee inherits from class CommissionEmployee. (Part 1 of 2.)

Error List					
⊗ 1 Error ⚠ 0 Warnings ⓘ 0 Messages					
Description	File	Line	Column	Project	
⊗ 1 'BasePlusCommissionEmployee.Earnings()': cannot override inherited member 'CommissionEmployee.Earnings()' because it is not marked virtual, abstract, or override	BasePlusCommissionl	31	28	BasePlusCommission Employee	

Fig. 11.8 | `BasePlusCommissionEmployee` inherits from class `CommissionEmployee`. (Part 2 of 2.)

access those members that are non-`private`. The constructor of class `CommissionEmployee` is not inherited. Thus, the `public` services of `BasePlusCommissionEmployee` include its constructor (lines 9–14), `public` methods and properties inherited from class `Commission-Employee`, property `BaseSalary` (lines 18–28), method `Earnings` (lines 31–35) and method `ToString` (lines 38–47).

Each derived-class constructor must implicitly or explicitly call its base-class constructor to ensure that the instance variables inherited from the base class are initialized properly. `BasePlusCommissionEmployee`'s six-parameter constructor explicitly calls class `CommissionEmployee`'s five-parameter constructor to initialize the base-class portion of a `BasePlusCommissionEmployee` object (i.e., variables `firstName`, `lastName`, `social-SecurityNumber`, `grossSales` and `commissionRate`). Line 11 in the header of `Base-PlusCommissionEmployee`'s six-parameter constructor invokes the `CommissionEmployee`'s five-parameter constructor (declared at lines 12–21 of Fig. 11.4) by using a constructor initializer. In Section 10.6, we used constructor initializers with keyword `this` to call over-loaded constructors in the same class. In line 11 of Fig. 11.8, we use a constructor initial-izer with keyword `base` to invoke the base-class constructor. The arguments `first`, `last`, `ssn`, `sales` and `rate` are used to initialize base-class members `firstName`, `lastName`, `socialSecurityNumber`, `grossSales` and `commissionRate`, respectively. If `BasePlus-CommissionEmployee`'s constructor did not invoke `CommissionEmployee`'s constructor explicitly, C# would attempt to invoke class `CommissionEmployee`'s parameterless or default constructor—but the class does not have such a constructor, so the compiler would issue an error. When a base class contains a parameterless constructor, you can use `base()` in the constructor initializer to call that constructor explicitly, but this is rarely done.

Common Programming Error 11.2

A compilation error occurs if a derived-class constructor calls one of its base-class constructors with arguments that do not match the number and types of parameters specified in one of the base-class constructor declarations.

Lines 31–35 of Fig. 11.8 declare method `Earnings` using keyword `override` to over-ride the `CommissionEmployee`'s `Earnings` method, as we did with method `ToString` in previous examples. Line 31 causes a compilation error indicating that we cannot override the base class's `Earnings` method because it was not explicitly "marked virtual, abstract, or override." The ***virtual*** and `abstract` keywords indicate that a base-class method can be overridden in derived classes. (As you'll learn in Section 12.4, `abstract` methods are implicitly `virtual`.) The `override` modifier declares that a derived-class method overrides a virtual or abstract base-class method. This modifier also implicitly declares the derived-class method `virtual` and allows it to be overridden in derived classes further down the inheritance hierarchy.

If we add the keyword `virtual` to the declaration of method `Earnings` in Fig. 11.4 and recompile, other compilation errors appear. As shown in Fig. 11.9, the compiler generates additional errors for line 34 of Fig. 11.8 because base class `CommissionEmployee`'s instance variables `commissionRate` and `grossSales` are `private`—derived class `BasePlusCommissionEmployee`'s methods are not allowed to access base class `CommissionEmployee`'s `private` instance variables. Note that we used bold black text in Fig. 11.8 to indicate erroneous code. The compiler issues additional errors at lines 43–45 of `BasePlusCommissionEmployee`'s `ToString` method for the same reason. The errors in `BasePlusCommissionEmployee` could have been prevented by using the `public` properties inherited from class `CommissionEmployee`. For example, line 34 could have invoked the `get` accessors of properties `CommissionRate` and `GrossSales` to access `CommissionEmployee`'s `private` instance variables `commissionRate` and `grossSales`, respectively. Lines 43–45 also could have used appropriate properties to retrieve the values of the base class's instance variables.

	Description	File	Line	Column	Project
⊗ 1	'CommissionEmployee.commissionRate' is inaccessible due to its protection level	BasePlusCommissionl	34	29	BasePlusCommission Employee
⊗ 2	'CommissionEmployee.grossSales' is inaccessible due to its protection level	BasePlusCommissionl	34	46	BasePlusCommission Employee
⊗ 3	'CommissionEmployee.firstName' is inaccessible due to its protection level	BasePlusCommissionl	43	47	BasePlusCommission Employee
⊗ 4	'CommissionEmployee.lastName' is inaccessible due to its protection level	BasePlusCommissionl	43	58	BasePlusCommission Employee
⊗ 5	'CommissionEmployee.socialSecurityNumber' is inaccessible due to its protection level	BasePlusCommissionl	44	36	BasePlusCommission Employee
⊗ 6	'CommissionEmployee.grossSales' is inaccessible due to its protection level	BasePlusCommissionl	45	25	BasePlusCommission Employee
⊗ 7	'CommissionEmployee.commissionRate' is inaccessible due to its protection level	BasePlusCommissionl	45	56	BasePlusCommission Employee

Error List — 7 Errors · 0 Warnings · 0 Messages

Fig. 11.9 | Compilation errors generated by `BasePlusCommissionEmployee` (Fig. 11.8) after declaring the `Earnings` method in Fig. 11.4 with keyword `virtual`.

11.4.4 CommissionEmployee–BasePlusCommissionEmployee Inheritance Hierarchy Using protected Instance Variables

To enable class `BasePlusCommissionEmployee` to directly access base-class instance variables `firstName`, `lastName`, `socialSecurityNumber`, `grossSales` and `commissionRate`, we can declare those members as `protected` in the base class. As we discussed in Section 11.3, a base class's `protected` members *are* inherited by all derived classes of that base class. Class `CommissionEmployee` (Fig. 11.10) is a modification of class `CommissionEmployee` (Fig. 11.4) that declares instance variables `firstName`, `lastName`, `socialSecurityNumber`, `grossSales` and `commissionRate` as `protected` rather than `private` (Fig. 11.10, lines 5–9). As discussed in Section 11.4.3, we also declare the `Earnings` method `virtual` in line 78 so that `BasePlusCommissionEmployee` can override the method. Other than the change in the class name (and thus the change in the constructor name) to

CommissionEmployee, the rest of the class declaration in Fig. 11.10 is identical to that of Fig. 11.4.

```
 1   // Fig. 11.10: CommissionEmployee.cs
 2   // CommissionEmployee with protected instance variables.
 3   public class CommissionEmployee
 4   {
 5      protected string firstName;
 6      protected string lastName;
 7      protected string socialSecurityNumber;
 8      protected decimal grossSales; // gross weekly sales
 9      protected decimal commissionRate; // commission percentage
10
11      // five-parameter constructor
12      public CommissionEmployee( string first, string last, string ssn,
13         decimal sales, decimal rate )
14      {
15         // implicit call to object constructor occurs here
16         firstName = first;
17         lastName = last;
18         socialSecurityNumber = ssn;
19         GrossSales = sales; // validate gross sales via property
20         CommissionRate = rate; // validate commission rate via property
21      } // end five-parameter CommissionEmployee constructor
22
23      // read-only property that gets commission employee's first name
24      public string FirstName
25      {
26         get
27         {
28            return firstName;
29         } // end get
30      } // end property FirstName
31
32      // read-only property that gets commission employee's last name
33      public string LastName
34      {
35         get
36         {
37            return lastName;
38         } // end get
39      } // end property LastName
40
41      // read-only property that gets
42      // commission employee's social security number
43      public string SocialSecurityNumber
44      {
45         get
46         {
47            return socialSecurityNumber;
48         } // end get
49      } // end property SocialSecurityNumber
```

Fig. 11.10 | CommissionEmployee with protected instance variables. (Part 1 of 2.)

```
50
51      // property that gets and sets commission employee's gross sales
52      public decimal GrossSales
53      {
54         get
55         {
56            return grossSales;
57         } // end get
58         set
59         {
60            grossSales = ( value < 0 ) ? 0 : value;
61         } // end set
62      } // end property GrossSales
63
64      // property that gets and sets commission employee's commission rate
65      public decimal CommissionRate
66      {
67         get
68         {
69            return commissionRate;
70         } // end get
71         set
72         {
73            commissionRate = ( value > 0 && value < 1 ) ? value : 0;
74         } // end set
75      } // end property CommissionRate
76
77      // calculate commission employee's pay
78      public virtual decimal Earnings()
79      {
80         return commissionRate * grossSales;
81      } // end method Earnings
82
83      // return string representation of CommissionEmployee object
84      public override string ToString()
85      {
86         return string.Format(
87            "{0}: {1} {2}\n{3}: {4}\n{5}: {6:C}\n{7}: {8:F2}",
88            "commission employee", firstName, lastName,
89            "social security number", socialSecurityNumber,
90            "gross sales", grossSales, "commission rate", commissionRate );
91      } // end method ToString
92   } // end class CommissionEmployee
```

Fig. 11.10 | CommissionEmployee with protected instance variables. (Part 2 of 2.)

We could have declared base class CommissionEmployee's instance variables first-Name, lastName, socialSecurityNumber, grossSales and commissionRate as public to enable derived class BasePlusCommissionEmployee to access the base-class instance variables. However, declaring public instance variables is poor software engineering, because it allows unrestricted access to the instance variables, greatly increasing the chance of errors. With protected instance variables, the derived class gets access to the instance variables, but classes that are not derived from the base class cannot access its variables directly.

Class `BasePlusCommissionEmployee` (Fig. 11.11) is a modification of class `Base-PlusCommissionEmployee` (Fig. 11.8) that extends `CommissionEmployee` (line 4) rather than class `CommissionEmployee`. Objects of class `BasePlusCommissionEmployee` inherit `CommissionEmployee`'s protected instance variables `firstName`, `lastName`, `social-SecurityNumber`, `grossSales` and `commissionRate`—all these variables are now protected members of `BasePlusCommissionEmployee`. As a result, the compiler does not generate errors when compiling line 34 of method `Earnings` and lines 42–44 of method `ToString`. If another class extends `BasePlusCommissionEmployee`, the new derived class also inherits the protected members.

```
1   // Fig. 11.11: BasePlusCommissionEmployee.cs
2   // BasePlusCommissionEmployee inherits from CommissionEmployee and has
3   // access to CommissionEmployee's protected members.
4   public class BasePlusCommissionEmployee : CommissionEmployee2
5   {
6       private decimal baseSalary; // base salary per week
7
8       // six-parameter derived-class constructor
9       // with call to base class CommissionEmployee constructor
10      public BasePlusCommissionEmployee( string first, string last,
11          string ssn, decimal sales, decimal rate, decimal salary )
12          : base( first, last, ssn, sales, rate )
13      {
14          BaseSalary = salary; // validate base salary via property
15      } // end six-parameter BasePlusCommissionEmployee constructor
16
17      // property that gets and sets
18      // base-salaried commission employee's base salary
19      public decimal BaseSalary
20      {
21          get
22          {
23              return baseSalary;
24          } // end get
25          set
26          {
27              baseSalary = ( value < 0 ) ? 0 : value;
28          } // end set
29      } // end property BaseSalary
30
31      // calculate earnings
32      public override decimal Earnings()
33      {
34          return baseSalary + ( commissionRate * grossSales );
35      } // end method Earnings
36
37      // return string representation of BasePlusCommissionEmployee
38      public override string ToString()
39      {
```

Fig. 11.11 | `BasePlusCommissionEmployee` inherits from `CommissionEmployee` and has access to `CommissionEmployee`'s protected members. (Part 1 of 2.)

```
40         return string.Format(
41             "{0}: {1} {2}\n{3}: {4}\n{5}: {6:C}\n{7}: {8:F2}\n{9}: {10:C}",
42             "base-salaried commission employee", firstName, lastName,
43             "social security number", socialSecurityNumber,
44             "gross sales", grossSales, "commission rate", commissionRate,
45             "base salary", baseSalary );
46      } // end method ToString
47 } // end class BasePlusCommissionEmployee
```

Fig. 11.11 | BasePlusCommissionEmployee inherits from CommissionEmployee and has access to CommissionEmployee's protected members. (Part 2 of 2.)

Class BasePlusCommissionEmployee does not inherit class CommissionEmployee's constructor. However, class BasePlusCommissionEmployee's six-parameter constructor (lines 10–15) calls class CommissionEmployee's five-parameter constructor with a constructor initializer. BasePlusCommissionEmployee's six-parameter constructor must explicitly call the five-parameter constructor of class CommissionEmployee, because CommissionEmployee does not provide a parameterless constructor that could be invoked implicitly.

Figure 11.12 uses a BasePlusCommissionEmployee object to perform the same tasks that Fig. 11.7 performed on the version of the class from Fig. 11.6. Note that the outputs of the two applications are identical. Although we declared the version of the class in Fig. 11.6 without using inheritance and declared the version in Fig. 11.11 using inheritance, both classes provide the same functionality. The source code in Fig. 11.6 (which is 47 lines) is considerably shorter than version in Fig. 11.11 (which is 114 lines), because the new class inherits most of its functionality from CommissionEmployee, whereas the version in Fig. 11.6 inherits only class object's functionality. Also, there is now only one copy of the commission-employee functionality declared in class CommissionEmployee. This makes the code easier to maintain, modify and debug, because the code related to a commission employee exists only in class CommissionEmployee.

```
1  // Fig. 11.12: BasePlusCommissionEmployee.cs
2  // Testing class BasePlusCommissionEmployee.
3  using System;
4
5  public class BasePlusCommissionEmployee
6  {
7     public static void Main( string[] args )
8     {
9        // instantiate BasePlusCommissionEmployee object
10       BasePlusCommissionEmployee basePlusCommissionEmployee =
11          new BasePlusCommissionEmployee( "Bob", "Lewis",
12          "333-33-3333", 5000.00M, .04M, 300.00M );
13
14       // display base-salaried commission-employee data
15       Console.WriteLine(
16          "Employee information obtained by properties and methods: \n" );
```

Fig. 11.12 | Testing class BasePlusCommissionEmployee. (Part 1 of 2.)

```
17        Console.WriteLine( "First name is {0}",
18            basePlusCommissionEmployee.FirstName );
19        Console.WriteLine( "Last name is {0}",
20            basePlusCommissionEmployee.LastName );
21        Console.WriteLine( "Social security number is {0}",
22            basePlusCommissionEmployee.SocialSecurityNumber );
23        Console.WriteLine( "Gross sales are {0:C}",
24            basePlusCommissionEmployee.GrossSales );
25        Console.WriteLine( "Commission rate is {0:F2}",
26            basePlusCommissionEmployee.CommissionRate );
27        Console.WriteLine( "Earnings are {0:C}",
28            basePlusCommissionEmployee.Earnings() );
29        Console.WriteLine( "Base salary is {0:C}",
30            basePlusCommissionEmployee.BaseSalary );
31
32        basePlusCommissionEmployee.BaseSalary = 1000.00M; // set base salary
33
34        Console.WriteLine( "\n{0}:\n\n{1}",
35            "Updated employee information obtained by ToString",
36            basePlusCommissionEmployee );
37        Console.WriteLine( "earnings: {0:C}",
38            basePlusCommissionEmployee.Earnings() );
39    } // end Main
40 } // end class BasePlusCommissionEmployee
```

```
Employee information obtained by properties and methods:

First name is Bob
Last name is Lewis
Social security number is 333-33-3333
Gross sales are $5,000.00
Commission rate is 0.04
Earnings are $500.00
Base salary is $300.00

Updated employee information obtained by ToString:

base-salaried commission employee: Bob Lewis
social security number: 333-33-3333
gross sales: $5,000.00
commission rate: 0.04
base salary: $1,000.00
earnings: $1,200.00
```

Fig. 11.12 | Testing class `BasePlusCommissionEmployee`. (Part 2 of 2.)

In this example, we declared base-class instance variables as `protected` so that derived classes could access them. Inheriting `protected` instance variables enables you to directly access the variables in the derived class without invoking the `set` or `get` accessors of the corresponding property. In most cases, however, it is better to use `private` instance variables to encourage proper software engineering. Your code will be easier to maintain, modify and debug.

Using protected instance variables creates several potential problems. First, the derived-class object can set an inherited variable's value directly without using the property's set accessor. Therefore, a derived-class object can assign an invalid value to the variable, thus leaving the object in an inconsistent state. For example, if we were to declare CommissionEmployee's instance variable grossSales as protected, a derived-class object (e.g., BasePlusCommissionEmployee) could then assign a negative value to grossSales. The second problem with using protected instance variables is that derived-class methods are more likely to be written to depend on the base class's data implementation. In practice, derived classes should depend only on the base-class services (i.e., non-private methods and properties) and not on the base-class data implementation. With protected instance variables in the base class, we may need to modify all the derived classes of the base class if the base-class implementation changes. For example, if for some reason we were to change the names of instance variables firstName and lastName to first and last, then we would have to do so for all occurrences in which a derived class directly references base-class instance variables firstName and lastName. In such a case, the software is said to be *fragile* or *brittle*, because a small change in the base class can "break" derived-class implementation. You should be able to change the base-class implementation while still providing the same services to the derived classes. Of course, if the base-class services change, we must reimplement our derived classes.

Software Engineering Observation 11.5

Declaring base-class instance variables private (as opposed to protected) enables the base-class implementation of these instance variables to change without affecting derived-class implementations.

11.4.5 CommissionEmployee–BasePlusCommissionEmployee Inheritance Hierarchy Using private Instance Variables

We now reexamine our hierarchy once more, this time using the best software engineering practices. Class CommissionEmployee (Fig. 11.13) declares instance variables firstName, lastName, socialSecurityNumber, grossSales and commissionRate as private (lines 5–9) and provides public properties FirstName, LastName, SocialSecurityNumber, GrossSales and GrossSales for manipulating these values. Note that methods Earnings (lines 78–81) and ToString (lines 84–91) use the class's properties to obtain the values of its instance variables. If we decide to change the instance-variable names, the Earnings and ToString declarations will not require modification—only the bodies of the properties that directly manipulate the instance variables will need to change. Note that these changes occur solely within the base class—no changes to the derived class are needed. Localizing the effects of changes like this is a good software engineering practice. Derived class BasePlusCommissionEmployee (Fig. 11.14) inherits from CommissionEmployee's and can access the private base-class members via the inherited public properties.

```
1   // Fig. 11.13: CommissionEmployee.cs
2   // CommissionEmployee class represents a commission employee.
3   public class CommissionEmployee
4   {
5      private string firstName;
6      private string lastName;
```

Fig. 11.13 | CommissionEmployee class represents a commission employee. (Part 1 of 3.)

```
 7       private string socialSecurityNumber;
 8       private decimal grossSales; // gross weekly sales
 9       private decimal commissionRate; // commission percentage
10
11       // five-parameter constructor
12       public CommissionEmployee( string first, string last, string ssn,
13          decimal sales, decimal rate )
14       {
15          // implicit call to object constructor occurs here
16          firstName = first;
17          lastName = last;
18          socialSecurityNumber = ssn;
19          GrossSales = sales; // validate gross sales via property
20          CommissionRate = rate; // validate commission rate via property
21       } // end five-parameter CommissionEmployee constructor
22
23       // read-only property that gets commission employee's first name
24       public string FirstName
25       {
26          get
27          {
28             return firstName;
29          } // end get
30       } // end property FirstName
31
32       // read-only property that gets commission employee's last name
33       public string LastName
34       {
35          get
36          {
37             return lastName;
38          } // end get
39       } // end property LastName
40
41       // read-only property that gets
42       // commission employee's social security number
43       public string SocialSecurityNumber
44       {
45          get
46          {
47             return socialSecurityNumber;
48          } // end get
49       } // end property SocialSecurityNumber
50
51       // property that gets and sets commission employee's gross sales
52       public decimal GrossSales
53       {
54          get
55          {
56             return grossSales;
57          } // end get
58          set
59          {
```

Fig. 11.13 | CommissionEmployee class represents a commission employee. (Part 2 of 3.)

```
60          grossSales = ( value < 0 ) ? 0 : value;
61       } // end set
62    } // end property GrossSales
63
64    // property that gets and sets commission employee's commission rate
65    public decimal CommissionRate
66    {
67       get
68       {
69          return commissionRate;
70       } // end get
71       set
72       {
73          commissionRate = ( value > 0 && value < 1 ) ? value : 0;
74       } // end set
75    } // end property CommissionRate
76
77    // calculate commission employee's pay
78    public virtual decimal Earnings()
79    {
80       return CommissionRate * GrossSales;
81    } // end method Earnings
82
83    // return string representation of CommissionEmployee object
84    public override string ToString()
85    {
86       return string.Format(
87          "{0}: {1} {2}\n{3}: {4}\n{5}: {6:C}\n{7}: {8:F2}",
88          "commission employee", FirstName, LastName,
89          "social security number", SocialSecurityNumber,
90          "gross sales", GrossSales, "commission rate", CommissionRate );
91    } // end method ToString
92 } // end class CommissionEmployee
```

Fig. 11.13 | CommissionEmployee class represents a commission employee. (Part 3 of 3.)

Class BasePlusCommissionEmployee (Fig. 11.14) has several changes to its method implementations that distinguish it from the version in Fig. 11.11. Methods Earnings (Fig. 11.14, lines 33–36) and ToString (lines 39–43) each invoke property BaseSalary's get accessor to obtain the base-salary value, rather than accessing baseSalary directly. If we decide to rename instance variable baseSalary, only the body of property BaseSalary will need to change.

```
1  // Fig. 11.14: BasePlusCommissionEmployee.cs
2  // BasePlusCommissionEmployee inherits from CommissionEmployee and has
3  // access to CommissionEmployee's private data via
4  // its public properties.
5  public class BasePlusCommissionEmployee : CommissionEmployee
6  {
```

Fig. 11.14 | BasePlusCommissionEmployee inherits from CommissionEmployee and has access to CommissionEmployee's private data via its public properties. (Part 1 of 2.)

```
 7        private decimal baseSalary; // base salary per week
 8
 9        // six-parameter derived class constructor
10        // with call to base class CommissionEmployee constructor
11        public BasePlusCommissionEmployee( string first, string last,
12           string ssn, decimal sales, decimal rate, decimal salary )
13           : base( first, last, ssn, sales, rate )
14        {
15           BaseSalary = salary; // validate base salary via property
16        } // end six-parameter BasePlusCommissionEmployee constructor
17
18        // property that gets and sets
19        // base-salaried commission employee's base salary
20        public decimal BaseSalary
21        {
22           get
23           {
24              return baseSalary;
25           } // end get
26           set
27           {
28              baseSalary = ( value < 0 ) ? 0 : value;
29           } // end set
30        } // end property BaseSalary
31
32        // calculate earnings
33        public override decimal Earnings()
34        {
35           return BaseSalary + base.Earnings();
36        } // end method Earnings
37
38        // return string representation of BasePlusCommissionEmployee
39        public override string ToString()
40        {
41           return string.Format( "base-salaried {0}\nbase salary: {1:C}",
42              base.ToString(), BaseSalary );
43        } // end method ToString
44     } // end class BasePlusCommissionEmployee
```

Fig. 11.14 | BasePlusCommissionEmployee inherits from CommissionEmployee and has access to CommissionEmployee's private data via its public properties. (Part 2 of 2.)

Class BasePlusCommissionEmployee's Earnings method (Fig. 11.14, lines 33–36) overrides class CommissionEmployee's Earnings method (Fig. 11.13, lines 78–81) to calculate the earnings of a base-salaried commission employee. The new version obtains the portion of the employee's earnings based on commission alone by calling CommissionEmployee's Earnings method with the expression base.Earnings() (Fig. 11.14, line 35). BasePlusCommissionEmployee's Earnings method then adds the base salary to this value to calculate the total earnings of the employee. Note the syntax used to invoke an overridden base-class method from a derived class—place the keyword base and the member access (.) operator before the base-class method name. This method invocation is a good software engineering practice—by having BasePlusCommissionEmployee's Earnings method invoke CommissionEmployee's Earnings method to calculate part of a Base-PlusCommissionEmployee object's earnings, we avoid duplicating the code and reduce code-maintenance problems.

Common Programming Error 11.3

When a base-class method is overridden in a derived class, the derived-class version often calls the base-class version to do a portion of the work. Failure to prefix the base-class method name with the keyword base and the member access (.) operator when referencing the base class's method causes the derived-class method to call itself, creating an error called infinite recursion. Recursion, used correctly, is a powerful capability, as you learned in Section 7.13.

Common Programming Error 11.4

The use of "chained" base references to refer to a member (a method, property or variable) several levels up the hierarchy—as in base.base.Earnings()—is a compilation error.

Similarly, BasePlusCommissionEmployee's ToString method (Fig. 11.14, lines 39–43) overrides class CommissionEmployee's ToString method (Fig. 11.13, lines 84–91) to return a string representation that is appropriate for a base-salaried commission employee. The new version creates part of a BasePlusCommissionEmployee object's string representation (i.e., the string "commission employee" and the values of class CommissionEmployee's private instance variables) by calling CommissionEmployee's ToString method with the expression base.ToString() (Fig. 11.14, line 42). The derived class's ToString method then outputs the remainder of the object's string representation (i.e., the value of class BasePlusCommissionEmployee's base salary).

Figure 11.15 performs the same manipulations on a BasePlusCommissionEmployee object as did Figures 11.7 and 11.12, respectively. Although each "base-salaried commis-

```
1   // Fig. 11.15: BasePlusCommissionEmployeeTest.cs
2   // Testing class BasePlusCommissionEmployee.
3   using System;
4
5   public class BasePlusCommissionEmployeeTest
6   {
7      public static void Main( string[] args )
8      {
9         // instantiate BasePlusCommissionEmployee4 object
10        BasePlusCommissionEmployee employee =
11           new BasePlusCommissionEmployee( "Bob", "Lewis",
12           "333-33-3333", 5000.00M, .04M, 300.00M );
13
14        // display base-salaried commission-employee data
15        Console.WriteLine(
16           "Employee information obtained by properties and methods: \n" );
17        Console.WriteLine( "First name is {0}", employee.FirstName );
18        Console.WriteLine( "Last name is {0}", employee.LastName );
19        Console.WriteLine( "Social security number is {0}",
20           employee.SocialSecurityNumber );
21        Console.WriteLine( "Gross sales are {0:C}", employee.GrossSales );
```

Fig. 11.15 | Testing class BasePlusCommissionEmployee4. (Part 1 of 2.)

```
22              Console.WriteLine( "Commission rate is {0:F2}",
23                  employee.CommissionRate );
24              Console.WriteLine( "Earnings are {0:C}", employee.Earnings() );
25              Console.WriteLine( "Base salary is {0:C}", employee.BaseSalary );
26
27              employee.BaseSalary = 1000.00M; // set base salary
28
29              Console.WriteLine( "\n{0}:\n\n{1}",
30                  "Updated employee information obtained by ToString", employee );
31              Console.WriteLine( "earnings: {0:C}", employee.Earnings() );
32          } // end Main
33      } // end class BasePlusCommissionEmployeeTest
```

```
Employee information obtained by properties and methods:

First name is Bob
Last name is Lewis
Social security number is 333-33-3333
Gross sales are $5,000.00
Commission rate is 0.04
Earnings are $500.00
Base salary is $300.00

Updated employee information obtained by ToString:

base-salaried commission employee: Bob Lewis
social security number: 333-33-3333
gross sales: $5,000.00
commission rate: 0.04
base salary: $1,000.00
earnings: $1,200.00
```

Fig. 11.15 | Testing class `BasePlusCommissionEmployee4`. (Part 2 of 2.)

sion employee" class behaves identically, the `BasePlusCommissionEmployee` in this example is the best engineered. By using inheritance and by using properties that hide the data and ensure consistency, we have efficiently and effectively constructed a well-engineered class.

In this section, you saw an evolutionary set of examples that was carefully designed to teach key capabilities for good software engineering with inheritance. You learned how to create a derived class using inheritance, how to use `protected` base-class members to enable a derived class to access inherited base-class instance variables and how to override base-class methods to provide versions that are more appropriate for derived-class objects. In addition, you applied software engineering techniques from Chapter 4, Chapter 10 and this chapter to create classes that are easy to maintain, modify and debug.

11.5 Constructors in Derived Classes

As we explained in the preceding section, instantiating a derived-class object begins a chain of constructor calls. The derived-class constructor, before performing its own tasks, invokes its direct base class's constructor either explicitly (via a constructor initializer with the base reference) or implicitly (calling the base class's default constructor or parameter-less constructor). Similarly, if the base class is derived from another class (as every class except object is), the base-class constructor invokes the constructor of the next class up in the hierarchy, and so on. The last constructor called in the chain is always the constructor for class object. The original derived-class constructor's body finishes executing last. Each base class's constructor manipulates the base-class instance variables that the derived-class object inherits. For example, consider again the CommissionEmployee–BasePlusCommissionEmployee hierarchy from Figures 11.13 and 11.14. When an application creates a BasePlusCommissionEmployee object, the BasePlusCommissionEmployee constructor is called. That constructor calls CommissionEmployee's constructor, which in turn implicitly calls object's constructor. Class object's constructor has an empty body, so it immediately returns control to CommissionEmployee's constructor, which then initializes the private instance variables of CommissionEmployee that are part of the BasePlusCommissionEmployee object. When CommissionEmployee's constructor completes execution, it returns control to BasePlusCommissionEmployee's constructor, which initializes the BasePlusCommissionEmployee object's baseSalary.

Software Engineering Observation 11.6

When an application creates a derived-class object, the derived-class constructor calls the base-class constructor (explicitly, via base, or implicitly). The base-class constructor's body executes to initialize the base class's instance variables that are part of the derived-class object, then the derived class constructor's body executes to initialize the derived-class-only instance variables. Even if a constructor does not assign a value to an instance variable, the variable is still initialized to its default value (i.e., 0 for simple numeric types, false for bools and null for references).

Our next example revisits the commission-employee hierarchy by declaring a CommissionEmployee class (Fig. 11.16) and a BasePlusCommissionEmployee class (Fig. 11.17). Each class's constructor prints a message when invoked, enabling us to observe the order in which the constructors in the hierarchy execute.

Class CommissionEmployee (Fig. 11.16) contains the same features as the version of the class shown in Fig. 11.13. We modified the constructor (lines 14–25) to output text when it is invoked. Note that concatenating this with a string literal (line 24) implicitly invokes the ToString method of the object being constructed to obtain the object's string representation.

```
1   // Fig. 11.16: CommissionEmployee.cs
2   // CommissionEmployee class represents a commission employee.
3   using System;
4
5   public class CommissionEmployee
6   {
7      private string firstName;
8      private string lastName;
9      private string socialSecurityNumber;
10     private decimal grossSales; // gross weekly sales
11     private decimal commissionRate; // commission percentage
```

Fig. 11.16 | CommissionEmployee class represents a commission employee. (Part 1 of 3.)

```
12
13      // five-parameter constructor
14      public CommissionEmployee( string first, string last, string ssn,
15         decimal sales, decimal rate )
16      {
17         // implicit call to object constructor occurs here
18         firstName = first;
19         lastName = last;
20         socialSecurityNumber = ssn;
21         GrossSales = sales; // validate gross sales via property
22         CommissionRate = rate; // validate commission rate via property
23
24         Console.WriteLine( "\nCommissionEmployee constructor:\n" + this );
25      } // end five-parameter CommissionEmployee constructor
26
27      // read-only property that gets commission employee's first name
28      public string FirstName
29      {
30         get
31         {
32            return firstName;
33         } // end get
34      } // end property FirstName
35
36      // read-only property that gets commission employee's last name
37      public string LastName
38      {
39         get
40         {
41            return lastName;
42         } // end get
43      } // end property LastName
44
45      // read-only property that gets
46      // commission employee's social security number
47      public string SocialSecurityNumber
48      {
49         get
50         {
51            return socialSecurityNumber;
52         } // end get
53      } // end property SocialSecurityNumber
54
55      // property that gets and sets commission employee's gross sales
56      public decimal GrossSales
57      {
58         get
59         {
60            return grossSales;
61         } // end get
62         set
63         {
```

Fig. 11.16 | CommissionEmployee class represents a commission employee. (Part 2 of 3.)

```
64          grossSales = ( value < 0 ) ? 0 : value;
65       } // end set
66    } // end property GrossSales
67
68    // property that gets and sets commission employee's commission rate
69    public decimal CommissionRate
70    {
71       get
72       {
73          return commissionRate;
74       } // end get
75       set
76       {
77          commissionRate = ( value > 0 && value < 1 ) ? value : 0;
78       } // end set
79    } // end property CommissionRate
80
81    // calculate commission employee's pay
82    public virtual decimal Earnings()
83    {
84       return CommissionRate * GrossSales;
85    } // end method Earnings
86
87    // return string representation of CommissionEmployee object
88    public override string ToString()
89    {
90       return string.Format(
91          "{0}: {1} {2}\n{3}: {4}\n{5}: {6:C}\n{7}: {8:F2}",
92          "commission employee", FirstName, LastName,
93          "social security number", SocialSecurityNumber,
94          "gross sales", GrossSales, "commission rate", CommissionRate );
95    } // end method ToString
96 } // end class CommissionEmployee
```

Fig. 11.16 | CommissionEmployee class represents a commission employee. (Part 3 of 3.)

Class BasePlusCommissionEmployee (Fig. 11.17) is almost identical to the version in Fig. 11.14, except that this BasePlusCommissionEmployee's constructor outputs text when invoked. As in CommissionEmployee (Fig. 11.16), we concatenate this with a string literal to implicitly obtain the object's string representation.

```
1  // Fig. 11.17: BasePlusCommissionEmployee.cs
2  // BasePlusCommissionEmployee class declaration.
3  using System;
4
5  public class BasePlusCommissionEmployee : CommissionEmployee
6  {
7     private decimal baseSalary; // base salary per week
8
9     // six-parameter derived-class constructor
10    // with call to base class CommissionEmployee constructor
```

Fig. 11.17 | BasePlusCommissionEmployee class declaration. (Part 1 of 2.)

```
11    public BasePlusCommissionEmployee( string first, string last,
12       string ssn, decimal sales, decimal rate, decimal salary )
13       : base( first, last, ssn, sales, rate )
14    {
15       BaseSalary = salary; // validate base salary via property
16
17       Console.WriteLine(
18          "\nBasePlusCommissionEmployee5 constructor:\n" + this );
19    } // end six-parameter BasePlusCommissionEmployee constructor
20
21    // property that gets and sets
22    // base-salaried commission employee's base salary
23    public decimal BaseSalary
24    {
25       get
26       {
27          return baseSalary;
28       } // end get
29       set
30       {
31          baseSalary = ( value < 0 ) ? 0 : value;
32       } // end set
33    } // end property BaseSalary
34
35    // calculate earnings
36    public override decimal Earnings()
37    {
38       return BaseSalary + base.Earnings();
39    } // end method Earnings
40
41    // return string representation of BasePlusCommissionEmployee
42    public override string ToString()
43    {
44       return string.Format( "base-salaried {0}\nbase salary: {1:C}",
45          base.ToString(), BaseSalary );
46    } // end method ToString
47 } // end class BasePlusCommissionEmployee
```

Fig. 11.17 | BasePlusCommissionEmployee class declaration. (Part 2 of 2.)

Figure 11.18 demonstrates the order in which constructors are called for objects of classes that are part of an inheritance hierarchy. Method Main begins by instantiating CommissionEmployee object employee1 (lines 10–11). Next, lines 14–16 instantiate BasePlusCommissionEmployee object employee2. This invokes the constructor for class CommissionEmployee, which displays the values passed from the BasePlusCommissionEmployee constructor, then performs the output specified in the BasePlusCommissionEmployee constructor. Note in the output from the CommissionEmployee constructor displays baseSalary as $0.00. This is because the BasePlusCommissionEmployee constructor has not yet set baseSalary's value. Lines 19–21 then instantiate BasePlusCommissionEmployee object employee3. Again, the CommissionEmployee and BasePlusCommissionEmployee constructors are both called. In each case, the body of the CommissionEmployee constructor

```
1   // Fig. 10.18: ConstructorTest.cs
2   // Display order in which base-class and derived-class constructors
3   // are called.
4   using System;
5
6   public class ConstructorTest
7   {
8      public static void Main( string[] args )
9      {
10        CommissionEmployee employee1 = new CommissionEmployee( "Bob",
11           "Lewis", "333-33-3333", 5000.00M, .04M );
12
13        Console.WriteLine();
14        BasePlusCommissionEmployee employee2 =
15           new BasePlusCommissionEmployee( "Lisa", "Jones",
16           "555-55-5555", 2000.00M, .06M, 800.00M );
17
18        Console.WriteLine();
19        BasePlusCommissionEmployee employee3 =
20           new BasePlusCommissionEmployee( "Mark", "Sands",
21           "888-88-8888", 8000.00M, .15M, 2000.00M );
22     } // end Main
23  } // end class ConstructorTest
```

```
CommissionEmployee constructor:
commission employee: Bob Lewis
social security number: 333-33-3333
gross sales: $5,000.00
commission rate: 0.04


CommissionEmployee constructor:
base-salaried commission employee: Lisa Jones
social security number: 555-55-5555
gross sales: $2,000.00
commission rate: 0.06
base salary: $0.00

BasePlusCommissionEmployee constructor:
base-salaried commission employee: Lisa Jones
social security number: 555-55-5555
gross sales: $2,000.00
commission rate: 0.06
base salary: $800.00


CommissionEmployee constructor:
base-salaried commission employee: Mark Sands
social security number: 888-88-8888
gross sales: $8,000.00
commission rate: 0.15
base salary: $0.00
```

Fig. 11.18 | Display order in which base-class and derived-class constructors are called. (Part 1 of 2.)

```
BasePlusCommissionEmployee constructor:
base-salaried commission employee: Mark Sands
social security number: 888-88-8888
gross sales: $8,000.00
commission rate: 0.15
base salary: $2,000.00
```

Fig. 11.18 | Display order in which base-class and derived-class constructors are called. (Part 2 of 2.)

executes before the body of the BasePlusCommissionEmployee constructor. Note that employee2 is constructed completely before construction of employee3 begins.

11.6 Software Engineering with Inheritance

This section discusses customizing existing software with inheritance. When a new class extends an existing class, the new class inherits the members of the existing class. We can customize the new class to meet our needs by including additional members and by overriding base-class members. Doing this does not require the derived-class programmer to change the base class's source code. C# simply requires access to the compiled base-class code, so it can compile and execute any application that uses or extends the base class. This powerful capability is attractive to independent software vendors (ISVs), who can develop proprietary classes for sale or license and make them available to users in class libraries. Users then can derive new classes from these library classes rapidly, without accessing the ISVs' proprietary source code.

Software Engineering Observation 11.7

Although inheriting from a class does not require access to the class's source code, developers often insist on seeing the source code to understand how the class is implemented. They may, for example, want to ensure that they are extending a class that performs well and is implemented securely.

People experienced with large-scale software projects in industry say that effective software reuse improves the software-development process. Object-oriented programming facilitates software reuse, potentially shortening development time. The availability of substantial and useful class libraries delivers the maximum benefits of software reuse through inheritance. The .NET Framework Class Library that is used by C# tends to be rather general purpose. Many special-purpose class libraries exist, and more are being created.

Software Engineering Observation 11.8

At the design stage in an object-oriented system, the designer often finds that certain classes are closely related. The designer should "factor out" common members and place them in a base class. Then the designer should use inheritance to develop derived classes, specializing them with capabilities beyond those inherited from the base class.

Software Engineering Observation 11.9

Declaring a derived class does not affect its base class's source code. Inheritance preserves the integrity of the base class.

Software Engineering Observation 11.10

Just as designers of non-object-oriented systems should avoid method proliferation, designers of object-oriented systems should avoid class proliferation. Such proliferation creates management problems and can hinder software reusability, because in a huge class library it becomes difficult for a client to locate the most appropriate classes. The alternative is to create fewer classes that provide more substantial functionality, but such classes might prove cumbersome.

Performance Tip 11.1

If derived classes are larger than they need to be (i.e., contain too much functionality), memory and processing resources might be wasted. Extend the base class containing the functionality that is closest to what is needed.

Reading derived-class declarations can be confusing, because inherited members are not declared explicitly in the derived classes, but are nevertheless present in them. A similar problem exists in documenting derived-class members.

11.7 Class object

As we discussed earlier in this chapter, all classes inherit directly or indirectly from the object class (System.Object in the .NET Framework Class Library), so its seven methods are inherited by all other classes. Figure 11.19 summarizes object's methods.

We discuss several of object's methods throughout this book (as indicated in the table). You can learn more about object's methods in object's online documentation in the .NET Framework Class Library Reference at:

msdn.microsoft.com/en-us/library/system.object_members.aspx

Method	Description
Equals	This method compares two objects for equality and returns true if they are equal and false otherwise. It takes any object as an argument. When objects of a particular class must be compared for equality, the class should override method Equals to compare the contents of the two objects. The method's implementation should meet the following requirements: • It should return false if the argument is null. • It should return true if an object is compared to itself, as in object1.Equals(object1). • It should return true only if both object1.Equals(object2) and object2.Equals(object1) would return true. • For three objects, if object1.Equals(object2) returns true and object2.Equals(object3) returns true, then object1.Equals(object3) should also return true. • A class that overrides the method Equals should also override the method GetHashCode to ensure that equal objects have identical hashcodes. The default Equals implementation determines only whether two references *refer to the same object.*

Fig. 11.19 | object methods that are inherited directly or indirectly by all classes. (Part 1 of 2.)

Method	Description
Finalize	This method cannot be explicitly declared or called. When a class contains a destructor, the compiler implicitly overrides protected method Finalize, which is called only by the garbage collector before it reclaims an object's memory. The garbage collector is not guaranteed to reclaim an object, thus it is not guaranteed that Finalize will execute. When a derived class's Finalize method executes, it performs its task, then invokes the base class's Finalize method. In general, you should avoid using Finalize.
GetHashCode	A hashtable is a data structure that relates one object, called the key, to another object, called the value. We discuss Hashtable in Chapter 27. When a value is inserted into a hashtable, the key's GetHashCode method is called. The hashcode value returned is used by the hashtable to determine the location at which to insert the corresponding value. The key's hashcode is also used by the hashtable to locate the key's corresponding value.
GetType	Every object knows its own type at execution time. Method GetType (used in Section 12.5) returns an object of class Type (namespace System) that contains information about the object's type, such as its class name.
Memberwise-Clone	This protected method, which takes no arguments and returns an object reference, makes a copy of the object on which it is called. The implementation of this method performs a *shallow copy*—instance-variable values in one object are copied into another object of the same type. For reference types, only the references are copied.
Reference-Equals	This static method returns true if its two object arguments are the same instance or if they are null references. Otherwise, it returns false.
ToString	This method (introduced in Section 7.4) returns a string representation of an object. The default implementation of this method returns the namespace followed by a dot and the class name of the object's class.

Fig. 11.19 | object methods that are inherited directly or indirectly by all classes. (Part 2 of 2.)

11.8 Wrap-Up

This chapter introduced inheritance—the ability to create classes by absorbing an existing class's members and enhancing them with new capabilities. You learned the notions of base classes and derived classes and created a derived class that inherits members from a base class. The chapter introduced access modifier protected; derived-class methods can access protected base-class members. You learned how to access base-class members with base. You also saw how constructors are used in inheritance hierarchies. Finally, you learned about the methods of class object, the direct or indirect base class of all classes.

In Chapter 12, Polymorphism, Interfaces and Operator Overloading, we build on our discussion of inheritance by introducing polymorphism—an object-oriented concept that enables us to write applications that handle, in a more general manner, objects of a wide variety of classes related by inheritance. After studying Chapter 12, you'll be familiar with classes, objects, encapsulation, inheritance and polymorphism—the most essential aspects of object-oriented programming.

12

Polymorphism, Interfaces and Operator Overloading

OBJECTIVES

In this chapter you'll learn:

- The concept of polymorphism and how it enables you to "program in the general."

- To use overridden methods to effect polymorphism.

- To distinguish between abstract and concrete classes.

- To declare abstract methods and to create abstract classes.

- How polymorphism makes systems extensible and maintainable.

- To determine an object's type at execution time.

- To create `sealed` methods and classes.

- To declare and implement interfaces.

- To overload operators to enable them to manipulate objects.

Outline

12.1 Introduction

12.2 Polymorphism Examples

12.3 Demonstrating Polymorphic Behavior

12.4 Abstract Classes and Methods

12.5 Case Study: Payroll System Using Polymorphism

    12.5.1 Creating Abstract Base Class `Employee`

    12.5.2 Creating Concrete Derived Class `SalariedEmployee`

    12.5.3 Creating Concrete Derived Class `HourlyEmployee`

    12.5.4 Creating Concrete Derived Class `CommissionEmployee`

    12.5.5 Creating Indirect Concrete Derived Class `BasePlusCommissionEmployee`

    12.5.6 Polymorphic Processing, Operator `is` and Downcasting

    12.5.7 Summary of the Allowed Assignments Between Base-Class and Derived-Class Variables

12.6 `sealed` Methods and Classes

12.7 Case Study: Creating and Using Interfaces

    12.7.1 Developing an `IPayable` Hierarchy

    12.7.2 Declaring Interface `IPayable`

    12.7.3 Creating Class `Invoice`

    12.7.4 Modifying Class `Employee` to Implement Interface `IPayable`

    12.7.5 Modifying Class `SalariedEmployee` for Use wth `IPayable`

    12.7.6 Using Interface `IPayable` to Process `Invoice`s and `Employee`s Polymorphically

    12.7.7 Common Interfaces of the .NET Framework Class Library

12.8 Operator Overloading

12.9 (Optional) Software Engineering Case Study: Incorporating Inheritance and Polymorphism into the ATM System

12.10 Wrap-Up

12.1 Introduction

We now continue our study of object-oriented programming by explaining and demonstrating *polymorphism* with inheritance hierarchies. Polymorphism enables us to "program in the general" rather than "program in the specific." In particular, polymorphism enables us to write applications that process objects that share the same base class in a class hierarchy as if they were all objects of the base class.

Consider the following example of polymorphism. Suppose we create an application that simulates the movement of several types of animals for a biological study. Classes Fish, Frog and Bird represent the three types of animals under investigation. Imagine that each of these classes extends base class Animal, which contains a method Move and maintains an animal's current location as *x–y–z* coordinates. Each derived class implements method Move. Our application maintains an array of references to objects of the various Animal-derived classes. To simulate an animals' movements, the application sends each object the same message once per second—namely, Move. However, each specific type of Animal responds to a Move message in a unique way—a Fish might swim three feet, a Frog might jump five feet and a Bird might fly 10 feet. The application issues the Move message to each animal object generically, but each object knows how to modify its *x–y* coordinates appropriately for its specific type of movement. Relying on each object to know how to "do the right thing" (i.e., do what is appropriate for that type of object) in response to the same method call is the key concept of polymorphism. The same message (in this case, Move) sent to a variety of objects has "many forms" of results—hence the term polymorphism.

With polymorphism, we can design and implement systems that are easily extensible—new classes can be added with little or no modification to the general portions of the application, as long as the new classes are part of the inheritance hierarchy that the application processes generically. The only parts of an application that must be altered to accommodate new classes are those that require direct knowledge of the new classes that the programmer adds to the hierarchy. For example, if we extend class Animal to create class Tortoise (which might respond to a Move message by crawling one inch), we need to write only the Tortoise class and the part of the simulation that instantiates a Tortoise object. The portions of the simulation that process each Animal generically can remain the same.

This chapter has several parts. First, we discuss common examples of polymorphism. We then provide a live-code example demonstrating polymorphic behavior. As you'll soon see, you'll use base-class references to manipulate both base-class objects and derived-class objects polymorphically.

We then present a case study that revisits the employee hierarchy of Section 11.4.5. We develop a simple payroll application that polymorphically calculates the weekly pay of several different types of employees using each employee's Earnings method. Though the earnings of each type of employee are calculated in a specific way, polymorphism allows us to process the employees "in the general." In the case study, we enlarge the hierarchy to include two new classes—SalariedEmployee (for people paid a fixed weekly salary) and HourlyEmployee (for people paid an hourly salary and "time-and-a-half" for overtime). We declare a common set of functionality for all the classes in the updated hierarchy in an "abstract" class, Employee, from which classes SalariedEmployee, HourlyEmployee and CommissionEmployee inherit directly and class BasePlusCommissionEmployee inherits indirectly. As you'll soon see, when we invoke each employee's Earnings method off a base-class Employee reference, the correct earnings calculation is performed due to C#'s polymorphic capabilities.

Occasionally, when performing polymorphic processing, we need to program "in the specific." Our Employee case study demonstrates that an application can determine the type of an object at execution time and act on that object accordingly. In the case study, we use these capabilities to determine whether a particular employee object *is a* BasePlusCommissionEmployee. If so, we increase that employee's base salary by 10%.

The chapter continues with an introduction to C# interfaces. An interface describes a set of methods and properties that can be called on an object, but does not provide concrete implementations for them. Programmers can declare classes that *implement* (i.e., provide concrete implementations for the methods and properties of) one or more interfaces. Each interface member must be defined for all the classes that implement the interface. Once a class implements an interface, all objects of that class have an *is-a* relationship with the interface type, and all objects of the class are guaranteed to provide the functionality described by the interface. This is true of all derived classes of that class as well.

Interfaces are particularly useful for assigning common functionality to possibly unrelated classes. This allows objects of unrelated classes to be processed polymorphically—objects of classes that implement the same interface can respond to the same method calls. To demonstrate creating and using interfaces, we modify our payroll application to create a general accounts-payable application that can calculate payments due for the earnings of company employees and for invoice amounts to be billed for purchased goods. As you'll see, interfaces enable polymorphic capabilities similar to those enabled by inheritance.

This chapter ends with an introduction to operator overloading. In previous chapters, we declared our own classes and used methods to perform tasks on objects of those classes. Operator overloading allows us to define the behavior of the built-in operators, such as +, - and <, when used on objects of our own classes. This provides a much more convenient notation than calling methods for performing tasks on objects.

12.2 Polymorphism Examples

We now consider several additional examples of polymorphism. If class Rectangle is derived from class Quadrilateral (a four-sided shape), then a Rectangle is a more specific version of a Quadrilateral. Any operation (e.g., calculating the perimeter or the area) that can be performed on a Quadrilateral object can also be performed on a Rectangle object. These operations also can be performed on other Quadrilaterals, such as Squares, Parallelograms and Trapezoids. The polymorphism occurs when an application invokes a method through a base-class variable—at execution time, the correct derived-class version of the method is called, based on the type of the referenced object. You'll see a simple code example that illustrates this process in Section 12.3.

As another example, suppose we design a video game that manipulates objects of many different types, including objects of classes Martian, Venusian, Plutonian, SpaceShip and LaserBeam. Imagine that each class inherits from the common base class SpaceObject, which contains method Draw. Each derived class implements this method. A screen-manager application maintains a collection (e.g., a SpaceObject array) of references to objects of the various classes. To refresh the screen, the screen manager periodically sends each object the same message—namely, Draw. However, each object responds in a unique way. For example, a Martian object might draw itself in red with the appropriate number of antennae. A SpaceShip object might draw itself as a bright silver flying saucer. A LaserBeam object might draw itself as a bright red beam across the screen. Again, the same message (in this case, Draw) sent to a variety of objects has "many forms" of results.

A polymorphic screen manager might use polymorphism to facilitate adding new classes to a system with minimal modifications to the system's code. Suppose we want to add Mercurian objects to our video game. To do so, we must build a Mercurian class that extends SpaceObject and provides its own Draw method implementation. When objects of class Mercurian appear in the SpaceObject collection, the screen-manager code invokes method Draw, exactly as it does for every other object in the collection, regardless of its type, so the new Mercurian objects simply "plug right in" without any modification of the screen-manager code by the programmer. Thus, without modifying the system (other than to build new classes and modify the code that creates new objects), programmers can use polymorphism to include additional types that might not have been envisioned when the system was created.

> **Software Engineering Observation 12.1**
>
> *Polymorphism promotes extensibility: Software that invokes polymorphic behavior is independent of the object types to which messages are sent. New object types that can respond to existing method calls can be incorporated into a system without requiring modification of the base system. Only client code that instantiates new objects must be modified to accommodate new types.*

12.3 Demonstrating Polymorphic Behavior

Section 11.4 created a commission-employee class hierarchy, in which class BasePlusCommissionEmployee inherited from class CommissionEmployee. The examples in that section manipulated CommissionEmployee and BasePlusCommissionEmployee objects by using references to them to invoke their methods. We aimed base-class references at base-class objects and derived-class references at derived-class objects. These assignments are natural and straightforward—base-class references are intended to refer to base-class objects, and derived-class references are intended to refer to derived-class objects. However, other assignments are possible.

In the next example, we aim a base-class reference at a derived-class object. We then show how invoking a method on a derived-class object via a base-class reference invokes the derived-class functionality—the type of the *actual referenced object*, not the type of the *reference*, determines which method is called. This example demonstrates the key concept that an object of a derived class can be treated as an object of its base class. This enables various interesting manipulations. An application can create an array of base-class references that refer to objects of many derived-class types. This is allowed because each derived-class object *is an* object of its base class. For instance, we can assign the reference of a BasePlusCommissionEmployee object to a base-class CommissionEmployee variable because a BasePlusCommissionEmployee *is a* CommissionEmployee—so we can treat a BasePlusCommissionEmployee as a CommissionEmployee.

A base-class object is not an object of any of its derived classes. For example, we cannot directly assign the reference of a CommissionEmployee object to a derived-class BasePlusCommissionEmployee variable, because a CommissionEmployee is not a BasePlusCommissionEmployee—a CommissionEmployee does not, for example, have a baseSalary instance variable and does not have a BaseSalary property. The *is-a* relationship applies from a derived class to its direct and indirect base classes, but not vice versa.

The compiler allows the assignment of a base-class reference to a derived-class variable *if* we explicitly cast the base-class reference to the derived-class type—a technique we discuss in greater detail in Section 12.5.6. Why would we ever want to perform such an assignment? A base-class reference can be used to invoke only the methods declared in the base class—attempting to invoke derived-class-only methods through a base-class reference results in compilation errors. If an application needs to perform a derived-class-specific operation on a derived-class object referenced by a base-class variable, the application must first cast the base-class reference to a derived-class reference through a technique known as ***downcasting***. This enables the application to invoke derived-class methods that are not in the base class. We present an example of downcasting in Section 12.5.6.

The example in Fig. 12.1 demonstrates three ways to use base-class and derived-class variables to store references to base-class and derived-class objects. The first two are straightforward—as in Section 11.4, we assign a base-class reference to a base-class variable, and we assign a derived class reference to a derived class variable. Then we demonstrate the relationship between derived classes and base classes (i.e., the *is-a* relationship) by assigning a derived-class reference to a base-class variable. [*Note:* This application uses classes CommissionEmployee and BasePlusCommissionEmployee from Fig. 11.13 and Fig. 11.14, respectively.]

```csharp
1   // Fig. 12.1: PolymorphismTest.cs
2   // Assigning base-class and derived-class references to base-class and
3   // derived-class variables.
4   using System;
5
6   public class PolymorphismTest
7   {
8      public static void Main( string[] args )
9      {
10        // assign base-class reference to base-class variable
11        CommissionEmployee commissionEmployee = new CommissionEmployee(
12           "Sue", "Jones", "222-22-2222", 10000.00M, .06M );
13
14        // assign derived-class reference to derived-class variable
15        BasePlusCommissionEmployee basePlusCommissionEmployee =
16           new BasePlusCommissionEmployee( "Bob", "Lewis",
17           "333-33-3333", 5000.00M, .04M, 300.00M );
18
19        // invoke ToString and Earnings on base-class object
20        // using base-class variable
21        Console.WriteLine( "{0} {1}:\n\n{2}\n{3}: {4:C}\n",
22           "Call CommissionEmployee's ToString with base-class reference",
23           "to base class object", commissionEmployee.ToString(),
24           "earnings", commissionEmployee.Earnings() );
25
26        // invoke ToString and Earnings on derived-class object
27        // using derived-class variable
28        Console.WriteLine( "{0} {1}:\n\n{2}\n{3}: {4:C}\n",
29           "Call BasePlusCommissionEmployee's ToString with derived class",
30           "reference to derived-class object",
31           basePlusCommissionEmployee.ToString(),
32           "earnings", basePlusCommissionEmployee.Earnings() );
33
34        // invoke ToString and Earnings on derived-class object
35        // using base-class variable
36        CommissionEmployee commissionEmployee2 =
37           basePlusCommissionEmployee;
38        Console.WriteLine( "{0} {1}:\n\n{2}\n{3}: {4:C}",
39           "Call BasePlusCommissionEmployee's ToString with base class",
40           "reference to derived-class object",
41           commissionEmployee2.ToString(), "earnings",
42           commissionEmployee2.Earnings() );
43     } // end Main
44  } // end class PolymorphismTest
```

Fig. 12.1 | Assigning base-class and derived-class references to base-class and derived-class variables. (Part 1 of 2.)

```
Call CommissionEmployee's ToString with base-class reference to base-class
object:

commission employee: Sue Jones
social security number: 222-22-2222
gross sales: $10,000.00
commission rate: 0.06
earnings: $600.00

Call BasePlusCommissionEmployee's ToString with derived-class reference to
derived-class object:

base-salaried commission employee: Bob Lewis
social security number: 333-33-3333
gross sales: $5,000.00
commission rate: 0.04
base salary: $300.00
earnings: $500.00

Call BasePlusCommissionEmployee's ToString with base-class reference to de-
rived-class object:

base-salaried commission employee: Bob Lewis
social security number: 333-33-3333
gross sales: $5,000.00
commission rate: 0.04
base salary: $300.00
earnings: $500.00
```

Fig. 12.1 | Assigning base-class and derived-class references to base-class and derived-class variables. (Part 2 of 2.)

In Fig. 12.1, lines 11–12 create a new CommissionEmployee object and assign its reference to a CommissionEmployee variable. Lines 15–17 create a new BasePlus-CommissionEmployee object and assign its reference to a BasePlusCommissionEmployee variable. These assignments are natural—for example, a CommissionEmployee variable's primary purpose is to hold a reference to a CommissionEmployee object. Lines 21–24 use the reference commissionEmployee to invoke methods ToString and Earnings. Because commissionEmployee refers to a CommissionEmployee object, base class Commission-Employee's version of the methods are called. Similarly, lines 28–32 use basePlusCommissionEmployee to invoke the methods ToString and Earnings on the BasePlusCommissionEmployee object. This invokes derived class BasePlusCommission-Employee's version of the methods.

Lines 36–37 then assign the reference to derived-class object basePlusCommission-Employee to a base-class CommissionEmployee variable, which lines 38–42 use to invoke methods ToString and Earnings. A base-class variable that contains a reference to a derived-class object and is used to call a virtual method actually calls the overriding derived-class version of the method. Hence, commissionEmployee2.ToString() in line 41 actually calls class BasePlusCommissionEmployee's ToString method. The compiler allows this "crossover" because an object of a derived class *is an* object of its base class (but not vice versa). When the compiler encounters a method call made through a variable, the compiler determines if the method can be called by checking the *variable's* class type. If that class contains the proper method declaration (or inherits one), the compiler allows the call to be compiled. At execution time, *the type of the object to which the variable refers* determines the actual method to use.

12.4 Abstract Classes and Methods

When we think of a class type, we assume that applications will create objects of that type. In some cases, however, it is useful to declare classes for which the programmer never intends to instantiate objects. Such classes are called ***abstract classes***. Because they are used only as base classes in inheritance hierarchies, we refer to them as ***abstract base classes***. These classes cannot be used to instantiate objects, because, as you'll soon see, abstract classes are incomplete—derived classes must define the "missing pieces." We demonstrate abstract classes in Section 12.5.1.

The purpose of an abstract class is primarily to provide an appropriate base class from which other classes can inherit, and thus share a common design. In the Shape hierarchy of Fig. 11.3, for example, derived classes inherit the notion of what it means to be a Shape—common attributes such as location, color and borderThickness, and behaviors such as Draw, Move, Resize and ChangeColor. Classes that can be used to instantiate objects are called ***concrete classes***. Such classes provide implementations of *every* method they declare (some of the implementations can be inherited). For example, we could derive concrete classes Circle, Square and Triangle from abstract base class TwoDimensionalShape. Similarly, we could derive concrete classes Sphere, Cube and Tetrahedron from abstract base class ThreeDimensionalShape. Abstract base classes are too general to create real objects—they specify only what is common among derived classes. We need to be more specific before we can create objects. For example, if you send the Draw message to abstract class TwoDimensionalShape, the class knows that two-dimensional shapes should be drawable, but it does not know what specific shape to draw, so it cannot implement a real Draw method. Concrete classes provide the specifics that make it reasonable to instantiate objects.

Not all inheritance hierarchies contain abstract classes. However, programmers often write client code that uses only abstract base-class types to reduce client code's dependencies on a range of specific derived-class types. For example, a programmer can write a method with a parameter of an abstract base-class type. When called, such a method can be passed an object of any concrete class that directly or indirectly extends the base class specified as the parameter's type.

Abstract classes sometimes constitute several levels of the hierarchy. For example, the Shape hierarchy of Fig. 11.3 begins with abstract class Shape. On the next level of the hierarchy are two more abstract classes, TwoDimensionalShape and ThreeDimensionalShape. The next level of the hierarchy declares concrete classes for TwoDimensionalShapes (Circle, Square and Triangle) and for ThreeDimensionalShapes (Sphere, Cube and Tetrahedron).

You make a class abstract by declaring it with keyword abstract. An abstract class normally contains one or more ***abstract methods***. An abstract method is one with keyword abstract in its declaration, as in

```
public abstract void Draw(); // abstract method
```

Abstract methods do not provide implementations. A class that contains abstract methods must be declared as an abstract class even if it contains concrete (nonabstract) methods.

Each concrete derived class of an abstract base class also must provide concrete implementations of the base class's abstract methods. We show an example of an abstract class with an abstract method in Fig. 12.4.

Properties can also be declared abstract or virtual, then overridden in derived classes with the override keyword, just like methods. This allows an abstract base class to specify common properties of its derived classes. Abstract property declarations have the form:

```
public abstract PropertyType MyProperty
{
   get;
   set;
} // end abstract property
```

The semicolons after the get and set keywords indicate that we provide no implementation for these accessors. An abstract property may omit implementations for the get accessor, the set accessor or both. Concrete derived classes must provide implementations for *every* accessor declared in the abstract property. When both get and set accessors are specified (as above), every concrete derived class must implement both. If one accessor is omitted, the derived class is not allowed to implement that accessor. Doing so causes a compilation error.

Constructors and static methods cannot be declared abstract. Constructors are not inherited, so an abstract constructor could never be implemented. Similarly, derived classes cannot override static methods, so an abstract static method could never be implemented.

Software Engineering Observation 12.2

An abstract class declares common attributes and behaviors of the various classes that inherit from it, either directly or indirectly, in a class hierarchy. An abstract class typically contains one or more abstract methods or properties that concrete derived classes must override. The instance variables, concrete methods and concrete properties of an abstract class are subject to the normal rules of inheritance.

Common Programming Error 12.1

Attempting to instantiate an object of an abstract class is a compilation error.

Common Programming Error 12.2

Failure to implement a base class's abstract methods and properties in a derived class is a compilation error unless the derived class is also declared abstract.

Although we cannot instantiate objects of abstract base classes, you'll soon see that we *can* use abstract base classes to declare variables that can hold references to objects of any concrete classes derived from those abstract classes. Applications typically use such variables to manipulate derived-class objects polymorphically. Also, you can use abstract base-class names to invoke static methods declared in those abstract base classes.

Polymorphism is particularly effective for implementing so-called layered software systems. In operating systems, for example, each type of physical device could operate quite differently from the others. Even so, common commands can read or write data from and to the devices. For each device, the operating system uses a piece of software called a device driver to control all communication between the system and the device. The write message sent to a device driver object needs to be interpreted specifically in the context of that driver and how it manipulates a specific device. However, the write call itself really is no different from the write to any other device in the system: Place some number of bytes from memory onto that device. An object-oriented operating system might use an abstract base class to provide an "interface" appropriate for all device drivers. Then, through inheritance from that abstract base class, derived classes are formed that all behave similarly. The device-driver methods are declared as abstract methods in the abstract base class. The implementations of these abstract methods are provided in the derived classes that correspond to the specific types of device drivers. New devices are always being developed, often long after the operating system has been released. When you buy a new device, it comes with a device driver provided by the device vendor. The device is immediately operational after you connect it to your computer and install the device driver. This is another elegant example of how polymorphism makes systems extensible.

It is common in object-oriented programming to declare an *iterator class* that can traverse all the objects in a collection, such as an array (Chapter 8) or a List (Chapter 9). For example, an application can print a List of objects by creating an iterator object and using it to obtain the next list element each time the iterator is called. Iterators often are used in polymorphic programming to traverse a collection that contains references to objects of various classes in an inheritance hierarchy. (Chapters 26–27 present a thorough treatment of C#'s "generics" capabilities and iterators.) A List of references to objects of class TwoDimensionalShape, for example, could contain references to objects from derived classes Square, Circle, Triangle and so on. Calling method Draw for each TwoDimensionalShape object off a TwoDimensionalShape variable would polymorphically draw each object correctly on the screen.

12.5 Case Study: Payroll System Using Polymorphism

This section reexamines the CommissionEmployee-BasePlusCommissionEmployee hierarchy that we explored throughout Section 11.4. Now we use an abstract method and polymorphism to perform payroll calculations based on the type of employee. We create an enhanced employee hierarchy to solve the following problem:

> *A company pays its employees on a weekly basis. The employees are of four types: Salaried employees are paid a fixed weekly salary regardless of the number of hours worked, hourly employees are paid by the hour and receive overtime pay for all hours worked in excess of 40 hours, commission employees are paid a percentage of their sales, and salaried-commission employees receive a base salary plus a percentage of their sales. For the current pay period, the company has decided to reward salaried-commission employees by adding 10% to their base salaries. The company wants to implement a C# application that performs its payroll calculations polymorphically.*

We use abstract class Employee to represent the general concept of an employee. The classes that extend Employee are SalariedEmployee, CommissionEmployee and HourlyEmployee. Class BasePlusCommissionEmployee—which extends CommissionEmployee—represents the last employee type. The UML class diagram in Fig. 12.2 shows the inheritance hierarchy for our polymorphic employee payroll application. Note that abstract class Employee is italicized, as per the convention of the UML.

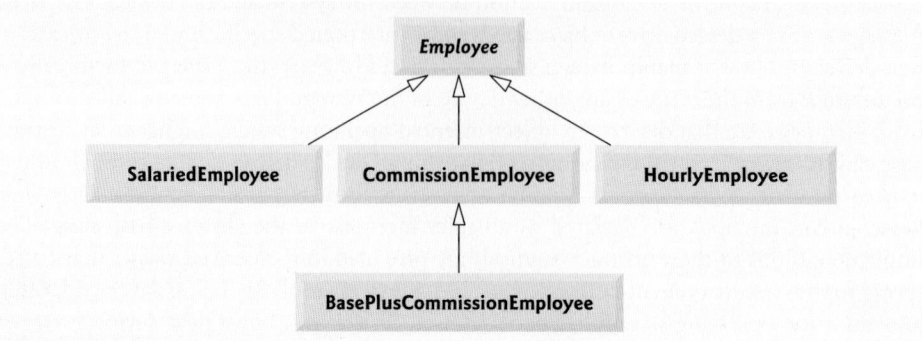

Fig. 12.2 | `Employee` hierarchy UML class diagram.

Abstract base class `Employee` declares the "interface" to the hierarchy—that is, the set of methods that an application can invoke on all `Employee` objects. We use the term "interface" here in a general sense to refer to the various ways applications can communicate with objects of any `Employee` derived class. Be careful not to confuse the general notion of an "interface" with the formal notion of a C# interface, the subject of Section 12.7. Each employee, regardless of the way his or her earnings are calculated, has a first name, a last name and a social security number, so `private` instance variables `firstName`, `lastName` and `socialSecurityNumber` appear in abstract base class `Employee`.

> ### Software Engineering Observation 12.3
> *A derived class can inherit "interface" or "implementation" from a base class. Hierarchies designed for **implementation inheritance** tend to have their functionality high in the hierarchy—each new derived class inherits one or more methods that were implemented in a base class, and the derived class uses the base-class implementations. Hierarchies designed for **interface inheritance** tend to have their functionality lower in the hierarchy—a base class specifies one or more abstract methods that must be declared for each concrete class in the hierarchy, and the individual derived classes override these methods to provide derived-class-specific implementations.*

The following sections implement the `Employee` class hierarchy. The first section implements `abstract` base class `Employee`. The next four sections each implement one of the concrete classes. The sixth section implements a test application that builds objects of all these classes and processes those objects polymorphically.

12.5.1 Creating Abstract Base Class `Employee`

Class `Employee` (Fig. 12.4) provides methods `Earnings` and `ToString`, in addition to the properties that manipulate `Employee`'s instance variables. An `Earnings` method certainly applies generically to all employees. But each earnings calculation depends on the employee's class. So we declare `Earnings` as `abstract` in base class `Employee`, because a default implementation does not make sense for that method—there is not enough information to determine what amount `Earnings` should return. Each derived class overrides `Earnings` with an appropriate implementation. To calculate an employee's earnings, the application assigns a reference to the employee's object to a base class `Employee` variable, then invokes the `Earnings` method on that variable. We maintain an array of `Employee` variables, each of which holds a reference to an `Employee` object (of course, there cannot be `Employee` objects because Employee is an abstract class—because of inheritance, however, all objects of all derived classes of Employee may nevertheless be thought of as Employee objects). The application iterates through the array and calls method Earnings for each Employee object. C# processes these method calls polymorphically. Including Earnings as an abstract method in Employee forces every directly derived concrete class of Employee to override Earnings with a method that performs an appropriate pay calculation.

Method ToString in class Employee returns a string containing the first name, last name and social security number of the employee. Each derived class of Employee overrides method ToString to create a string representation of an object of that class containing the employee's type (e.g., "salaried employee:"), followed by the rest of the employee's information.

The diagram in Fig. 12.3 shows each of the five classes in the hierarchy down the left side and methods Earnings and ToString across the top. For each class, the diagram shows the desired results of each method. [*Note:* We do not list base class Employee's properties because they are not overridden in any of the derived classes—each of these properties is inherited and used "as is" by each of the derived classes.]

Let us consider class Employee's declaration (Fig. 12.4). The class includes a constructor that takes the first name, last name and social security number as arguments (lines 15–20); read-only properties for obtaining the first name, last name and social security

	Earnings	ToString
Employee	abstract	*firstName lastName* social security number: *SSN*
Salaried-Employee	weeklySalary	salaried employee: *firstName lastName* social security number: *SSN* weekly salary: *weeklysalary*

Hourly-Employee	*If hours <= 40*
	    wage * hours
	If hours > 40
	    40 * wage +
	    (hours - 40) *
	    wage * 1.5
		hourly employee: *firstName lastName*
		social security number: *SSN*
		hourly wage: *wage*
		hours worked: *hours*

Commission-Employee	commissionRate * grossSales	commission employee: *firstName lastName* social security number: *SSN* gross sales: *grossSales* commission rate: *commissionRate*
BasePlus-Commission-Employee	(commissionRate * grossSales) + baseSalary	base salaried commission employee: *firstName lastName* social security number: *SSN* gross sales: *grossSales* commission rate: *commissionRate* base salary: *baseSalary*

Fig. 12.3 | Polymorphic interface for the Employee hierarchy classes.

number (lines 6, 9 and 12, respectively); method `ToString` (lines 23–27), which uses properties to return the string representation of `Employee`; and abstract method `Earnings` (line 30), which must be implemented by concrete derived classes. Note that the `Employee` constructor does not validate the social security number in this example. Normally, such validation should be provided.

Why did we declare `Earnings` as an abstract method? As explained earlier, it simply does not make sense to provide an implementation of this method in class `Employee`. We cannot calculate the earnings for a general `Employee`—we first must know the specific `Employee` type to determine the appropriate earnings calculation. By declaring this method abstract, we indicate that each concrete derived class *must* provide an appropriate `Earnings` implementation and that an application will be able to use base-class `Employee` variables to invoke method `Earnings` polymorphically for any type of `Employee`.

```csharp
1   // Fig. 12.4: Employee.cs
2   // Employee abstract base class.
3   public abstract class Employee
4   {
5       // read-only property that gets employee's first name
6       public string FirstName { get; private set; }
7
8       // read-only property that gets employee's last name
9       public string LastName { get; private set; }
10
11      // read-only property that gets employee's social security number
12      public string SocialSecurityNumber { get; private set; }
13
14      // three-parameter constructor
15      public Employee( string first, string last, string ssn )
16      {
17          FirstName = first;
18          LastName = last;
19          SocialSecurityNumber = ssn;
20      } // end three-parameter Employee constructor
21
22      // return string representation of Employee object, using properties
23      public override string ToString()
24      {
25          return string.Format( "{0} {1}\nsocial security number: {2}",
26              FirstName, LastName, SocialSecurityNumber );
27      } // end method ToString
28
29      // abstract method overridden by derived classes
30      public abstract decimal Earnings(); // no implementation here
31  } // end abstract class Employee
```

Fig. 12.4 | Employee abstract base class.

12.5.2 Creating Concrete Derived Class `SalariedEmployee`

Class `SalariedEmployee` (Fig. 12.5) extends class `Employee` (line 3) and overrides `Earnings` (lines 28–31), which makes `SalariedEmployee` a concrete class. The class includes a constructor (lines 8–12) that takes a first name, a last name, a social security number and

```
 1   // Fig. 12.5: SalariedEmployee.cs
 2   // SalariedEmployee class that extends Employee.
 3   public class SalariedEmployee : Employee
 4   {
 5      private decimal weeklySalary;
 6
 7      // four-parameter constructor
 8      public SalariedEmployee( string first, string last, string ssn,
 9         decimal salary ) : base( first, last, ssn )
10      {
11         WeeklySalary = salary; // validate salary via property
12      } // end four-parameter SalariedEmployee constructor
13
14      // property that gets and sets salaried employee's salary
15      public decimal WeeklySalary
16      {
17         get
18         {
19            return weeklySalary;
20         } // end get
21         set
22         {
23            weeklySalary = ( ( value >= 0 ) ? value : 0 ); // validation
24         } // end set
25      } // end property WeeklySalary
26
27      // calculate earnings; override abstract method Earnings in Employee
28      public override decimal Earnings()
29      {
30         return WeeklySalary;
31      } // end method Earnings
32
33      // return string representation of SalariedEmployee object
34      public override string ToString()
35      {
36         return string.Format( "salaried employee: {0}\n{1}: {2:C}",
37            base.ToString(), "weekly salary", WeeklySalary );
38      } // end method ToString
39   } // end class SalariedEmployee
```

Fig. 12.5 | SalariedEmployee class that extends Employee.

a weekly salary as arguments; property WeeklySalary to manipulate instance variable weeklySalary, including a set accessor that ensures we assign only nonnegative values to weeklySalary (lines 15–25); method Earnings (lines 28–31) to calculate a SalariedEmployee's earnings; and method ToString (lines 34–38), which returns a string including the employee's type, namely, "salaried employee: ", followed by employee-specific information produced by base class Employee's ToString method and SalariedEmployee's WeeklySalary property. Class SalariedEmployee's constructor passes the first name, last name and social security number to the Employee constructor (line 9) via a constructor initializer to initialize the private instance variables not inherited from the base class. Method Earnings overrides Employee's abstract method Earnings to provide a concrete implementation that returns the SalariedEmployee's weekly salary. If we do not implement Earnings, class SalariedEmployee must be declared abstract—otherwise, a compilation error occurs (and, of course, we want SalariedEmployee to be a concrete class).

Method ToString (lines 34–38) of class SalariedEmployee overrides Employee method ToString. If class SalariedEmployee did not override ToString, Salaried-Employee would have inherited the Employee version of ToString. In that case, Salaried-Employee's ToString method would simply return the employee's full name and social security number, which does not adequately represent a SalariedEmployee. To produce a complete string representation of a SalariedEmployee, the derived class's ToString method returns "salaried employee: ", followed by the base-class Employee-specific information (i.e., first name, last name and social security number) obtained by invoking the base class's ToString (line 37)—this is a nice example of code reuse. The string representation of a SalariedEmployee also contains the employee's weekly salary, obtained by using the class's WeeklySalary property.

12.5.3 Creating Concrete Derived Class HourlyEmployee

Class HourlyEmployee (Fig. 12.6) also extends class Employee (line 3). The class includes a constructor (lines 9–15) that takes as arguments a first name, a last name, a social security number, an hourly wage and the number of hours worked. Lines 18–28 and 31–42 declare properties Wage and Hours for instance variables wage and hours, respectively. The set accessor in property Wage (lines 24–27) ensures that wage is nonnegative, and the set accessor in property Hours (lines 37–41) ensures that hours is in the range 0–168 (the total number of hours in a week) inclusive. Class HourlyEmployee also includes method Earnings (lines 45–51) to calculate an HourlyEmployee's earnings; and method ToString (lines 54–59), which returns the employee's type, namely, "hourly employee: ", and employee-specific information. Note that the HourlyEmployee constructor, like the SalariedEmployee constructor, passes the first name, last name and social security number to the base-class Employee constructor (line 11) to initialize the base class's private instance variables. Also, method ToString calls base-class method ToString (line 58) to obtain the Employee-specific information (i.e., first name, last name and social security number)—this is another nice example of code reuse.

```csharp
1   // Fig. 12.6: HourlyEmployee.cs
2   // HourlyEmployee class that extends Employee.
3   public class HourlyEmployee : Employee
4   {
5      private decimal wage; // wage per hour
6      private decimal hours; // hours worked for the week
7
8      // five-parameter constructor
9      public HourlyEmployee( string first, string last, string ssn,
10        decimal hourlyWage, decimal hoursWorked )
11        : base( first, last, ssn )
12     {
13        Wage = hourlyWage; // validate hourly wage via property
```

Fig. 12.6 | HourlyEmployee class that extends Employee. (Part 1 of 2.)

```
14              Hours = hoursWorked; // validate hours worked via property
15        } // end five-parameter HourlyEmployee constructor
16
17        // property that gets and sets hourly employee's wage
18        public decimal Wage
19        {
20           get
21           {
22              return wage;
23           } // end get
24           set
25           {
26              wage = ( value >= 0 ) ? value : 0; // validation
27           } // end set
28        } // end property Wage
29
30        // property that gets and sets hourly employee's hours
31        public decimal Hours
32        {
33           get
34           {
35              return hours;
36           } // end get
37           set
38           {
39              hours = ( ( value >= 0 ) && ( value <= 168 ) ) ?
40                      value : 0; // validation
41           } // end set
42        } // end property Hours
43
44        // calculate earnings; override Employee's abstract method Earnings
45        public override decimal Earnings()
46        {
47           if ( Hours <= 40 ) // no overtime
48              return Wage * Hours;
49           else
50              return ( 40 * Wage ) + ( ( Hours - 40 ) * Wage * 1.5M );
51        } // end method Earnings
52
53        // return string representation of HourlyEmployee object
54        public override string ToString()
55        {
56           return string.Format(
57              "hourly employee: {0}\n{1}: {2:C}; {3}: {4:F2}",
58              base.ToString(), "hourly wage", Wage, "hours worked", Hours );
59        } // end method ToString
60     } // end class HourlyEmployee
```

Fig. 12.6 | HourlyEmployee class that extends Employee. (Part 2 of 2.)

12.5.4 Creating Concrete Derived Class CommissionEmployee

Class CommissionEmployee (Fig. 12.7) extends class Employee (line 3). The class includes a constructor (lines 9–14) that takes a first name, a last name, a social security number, a sales

amount and a commission rate; properties (lines 17–28 and 31–41) for instance variables
commissionRate and grossSales, respectively; method Earnings (lines 44–47) to calculate
a CommissionEmployee's earnings; and method ToString (lines 50–55), which returns the
employee's type, namely, "commission employee: ", and employee-specific information.
The CommissionEmployee's constructor also passes the first name, last name and social security number to the Employee constructor (line 10) to initialize Employee's private instance variables. Method ToString calls base-class method ToString (line 53) to obtain the
Employee-specific information (i.e., first name, last name and social security number).

```csharp
1   // Fig. 12.7: CommissionEmployee.cs
2   // CommissionEmployee class that extends Employee.
3   public class CommissionEmployee : Employee
4   {
5      private decimal grossSales; // gross weekly sales
6      private decimal commissionRate; // commission percentage
7
8      // five-parameter constructor
9      public CommissionEmployee( string first, string last, string ssn,
10        decimal sales, decimal rate ) : base( first, last, ssn )
11     {
12        GrossSales = sales; // validate gross sales via property
13        CommissionRate = rate; // validate commission rate via property
14     } // end five-parameter CommissionEmployee constructor
15
16     // property that gets and sets commission employee's commission rate
17     public decimal CommissionRate
18     {
19        get
20        {
21           return commissionRate;
22        } // end get
23        set
24        {
25           commissionRate = ( value > 0 && value < 1 ) ?
26                            value : 0; // validation
27        } // end set
28     } // end property CommissionRate
29
30     // property that gets and sets commission employee's gross sales
31     public decimal GrossSales
32     {
33        get
34        {
35           return grossSales;
36        } // end get
37        set
38        {
39           grossSales = ( value >= 0 ) ? value : 0; // validation
40        } // end set
41     } // end property GrossSales
42
```

Fig. 12.7 | CommissionEmployee class that extends Employee. (Part 1 of 2.)

```
43        // calculate earnings; override abstract method Earnings in Employee
44        public override decimal Earnings()
45        {
46           return CommissionRate * GrossSales;
47        } // end method Earnings
48
49        // return string representation of CommissionEmployee object
50        public override string ToString()
51        {
52           return string.Format( "{0}: {1}\n{2}: {3:C}\n{4}: {5:F2}",
53              "commission employee", base.ToString(),
54              "gross sales", GrossSales, "commission rate", CommissionRate );
55        } // end method ToString
56   } // end class CommissionEmployee
```

Fig. 12.7 | CommissionEmployee class that extends Employee. (Part 2 of 2.)

12.5.5 Creating Indirect Concrete Derived Class BasePlusCommissionEmployee

Class BasePlusCommissionEmployee (Fig. 12.8) extends class CommissionEmployee (line 3) and therefore is an indirect derived class of class Employee. Class BasePlusCommissionEmployee has a constructor (lines 8–13) that takes as arguments a first name, a last name, a social security number, a sales amount, a commission rate and a base salary. It then passes the first name, last name, social security number, sales amount and commission rate to the CommissionEmployee constructor (line 10) to initialize the base class's private data members. BasePlusCommissionEmployee also contains property BaseSalary (lines 17–27) to manipulate instance variable baseSalary. Method Earnings (lines 30–33) calculates a BasePlusCommissionEmployee's earnings. Note that line 32 in method Earnings calls base class CommissionEmployee's Earnings method to calculate the commission-based portion of the employee's earnings. Again, this shows the benefits of code reuse. BasePlusCommissionEmployee's ToString method (lines 36–40) creates a string representation of a BasePlusCommissionEmployee that contains "base-salaried", followed by the string obtained by invoking base class CommissionEmployee's ToString method (another example of code reuse), then the base salary. The result is a string beginning with "base-salaried commission employee", followed by the rest of the BasePlusCommissionEmployee's information. Recall that CommissionEmployee's ToString method obtains the employee's first name, last name and social security number by invoking the ToString method of its base class (i.e., Employee)—a further demonstration of code reuse. Note that BasePlusCommissionEmployee's ToString initiates a chain of method calls that span all three levels of the Employee hierarchy.

```
1   // Fig. 12.8: BasePlusCommissionEmployee.cs
2   // BasePlusCommissionEmployee class that extends CommissionEmployee.
3   public class BasePlusCommissionEmployee : CommissionEmployee
4   {
```

Fig. 12.8 | BasePlusCommissionEmployee class that extends CommissionEmployee. (Part 1 of 2.)

```
 5      private decimal baseSalary; // base salary per week
 6
 7      // six-parameter constructor
 8      public BasePlusCommissionEmployee( string first, string last,
 9          string ssn, decimal sales, decimal rate, decimal salary )
10          : base( first, last, ssn, sales, rate )
11      {
12          BaseSalary = salary; // validate base salary via property
13      } // end six-parameter BasePlusCommissionEmployee constructor
14
15      // property that gets and sets
16      // base-salaried commission employee's base salary
17      public decimal BaseSalary
18      {
19          get
20          {
21              return baseSalary;
22          } // end get
23          set
24          {
25              baseSalary = ( value >= 0 ) ? value : 0; // validation
26          } // end set
27      } // end property BaseSalary
28
29      // calculate earnings; override method Earnings in CommissionEmployee
30      public override decimal Earnings()
31      {
32          return BaseSalary + base.Earnings();
33      } // end method Earnings
34
35      // return string representation of BasePlusCommissionEmployee object
36      public override string ToString()
37      {
38          return string.Format( "base-salaried {0}; base salary: {1:C}",
39              base.ToString(), BaseSalary );
40      } // end method ToString
41  } // end class BasePlusCommissionEmployee
```

Fig. 12.8 | BasePlusCommissionEmployee class that extends CommissionEmployee. (Part 2 of 2.)

12.5.6 Polymorphic Processing, Operator is and Downcasting

To test our Employee hierarchy, the application in Fig. 12.9 creates an object of each of the four concrete classes SalariedEmployee, HourlyEmployee, CommissionEmployee and BasePlusCommissionEmployee. The application manipulates these objects, first via variables of each object's own type, then polymorphically, using an array of Employee variables. While processing the objects polymorphically, the application increases the base salary of each BasePlusCommissionEmployee by 10% (this, of course, requires determining the object's type at execution time). Finally, the application polymorphically determines and outputs the type of each object in the Employee array. Lines 10–20 create objects of each of the four concrete Employee derived classes. Lines 24–32 output the string representation and earnings of each of these objects. Note that each object's ToString method is called implicitly by Write when the object is output as a string with format items.

```csharp
1   // Fig. 12.9: PayrollSystemTest.cs
2   // Employee hierarchy test application.
3   using System;
4
5   public class PayrollSystemTest
6   {
7      public static void Main( string[] args )
8      {
9         // create derived-class objects
10        SalariedEmployee salariedEmployee =
11           new SalariedEmployee( "John", "Smith", "111-11-1111", 800.00M );
12        HourlyEmployee hourlyEmployee =
13           new HourlyEmployee( "Karen", "Price",
14           "222-22-2222", 16.75M, 40.0M );
15        CommissionEmployee commissionEmployee =
16           new CommissionEmployee( "Sue", "Jones",
17           "333-33-3333", 10000.00M, .06M );
18        BasePlusCommissionEmployee basePlusCommissionEmployee =
19           new BasePlusCommissionEmployee( "Bob", "Lewis",
20           "444-44-4444", 5000.00M, .04M, 300.00M );
21
22        Console.WriteLine( "Employees processed individually:\n" );
23
24        Console.WriteLine( "{0}\nearned: {1:C}\n",
25           salariedEmployee, salariedEmployee.Earnings() );
26        Console.WriteLine( "{0}\nearned: {1:C}\n",
27           hourlyEmployee, hourlyEmployee.Earnings() );
28        Console.WriteLine( "{0}\nearned: {1:C}\n",
29           commissionEmployee, commissionEmployee.Earnings() );
30        Console.WriteLine( "{0}\nearned: {1:C}\n",
31           basePlusCommissionEmployee,
32           basePlusCommissionEmployee.Earnings() );
33
34        // create four-element Employee array
35        Employee[] employees = new Employee[ 4 ];
36
37        // initialize array with Employees of derived types
38        employees[ 0 ] = salariedEmployee;
39        employees[ 1 ] = hourlyEmployee;
40        employees[ 2 ] = commissionEmployee;
41        employees[ 3 ] = basePlusCommissionEmployee;
42
43        Console.WriteLine( "Employees processed polymorphically:\n" );
44
45        // generically process each element in array employees
46        foreach ( var currentEmployee in employees )
47        {
48           Console.WriteLine( currentEmployee ); // invokes ToString
49
```

Fig. 12.9 | Employee hierarchy test application. (Part 1 of 3.)

```
50              // determine whether element is a BasePlusCommissionEmployee
51              if ( currentEmployee is BasePlusCommissionEmployee )
52              {
53                 // downcast Employee reference to
54                 // BasePlusCommissionEmployee reference
55                 BasePlusCommissionEmployee employee =
56                     ( BasePlusCommissionEmployee ) currentEmployee;
57
58                 employee.BaseSalary *= 1.10M;
59                 Console.WriteLine(
60                     "new base salary with 10% increase is: {0:C}",
61                     employee.BaseSalary );
62              } // end if
63
64              Console.WriteLine(
65                  "earned {0:C}\n", currentEmployee.Earnings() );
66          } // end foreach
67
68          // get type name of each object in employees array
69          for ( int j = 0; j < employees.Length; j++ )
70              Console.WriteLine( "Employee {0} is a {1}", j,
71                  employees[ j ].GetType() );
72      } // end Main
73  } // end class PayrollSystemTest
```

```
Employees processed individually:

salaried employee: John Smith
social security number: 111-11-1111
weekly salary: $800.00
earned: $800.00

hourly employee: Karen Price
social security number: 222-22-2222
hourly wage: $16.75; hours worked: 40.00
earned: $670.00

commission employee: Sue Jones
social security number: 333-33-3333
gross sales: $10,000.00
commission rate: 0.06
earned: $600.00

base-salaried commission employee: Bob Lewis
social security number: 444-44-4444
gross sales: $5,000.00
commission rate: 0.04; base salary: $300.00
earned: $500.00


Employees processed polymorphically:

salaried employee: John Smith
social security number: 111-11-1111
```

Fig. 12.9 | Employee hierarchy test application. (Part 2 of 3.)

```
weekly salary: $800.00
earned $800.00

hourly employee: Karen Price
social security number: 222-22-2222
hourly wage: $16.75; hours worked: 40.00
earned $670.00

commission employee: Sue Jones
social security number: 333-33-3333
gross sales: $10,000.00
commission rate: 0.06
earned $600.00

base-salaried commission employee: Bob Lewis
social security number: 444-44-4444
gross sales: $5,000.00
commission rate: 0.04; base salary: $300.00
new base salary with 10% increase is: $330.00
earned $530.00

Employee 0 is a SalariedEmployee
Employee 1 is a HourlyEmployee
Employee 2 is a CommissionEmployee
Employee 3 is a BasePlusCommissionEmployee
```

Fig. 12.9 | Employee hierarchy test application. (Part 3 of 3.)

Line 35 declares employees and assigns it an array of four Employee variables. Lines 38–41 assign a SalariedEmployee object, an HourlyEmployee object, a Commission-Employee object and a BasePlusCommissionEmployee object to employees[0], employees[1], employees[2] and employees[3], respectively. Each assignment is allowed, because a SalariedEmployee *is an* Employee, an HourlyEmployee *is an* Employee, a CommissionEmployee *is an* Employee and a BasePlusCommissionEmployee *is an* Employee. Therefore, we can assign the references of SalariedEmployee, HourlyEmployee, CommissionEmployee and BasePlusCommissionEmployee objects to base-class Employee variables, even though Employee is an abstract class.

Lines 46–66 iterate through array employees and invoke methods ToString and Earnings with Employee variable currentEmployee, which is assigned the reference to a different Employee during each iteration. The output illustrates that the appropriate methods for each class are indeed invoked. All calls to virtual method's ToString and Earnings are resolved at execution time, based on the type of the object to which currentEmployee refers. This process is known as *dynamic binding* or *late binding*. For example, line 48 implicitly invokes method ToString of the object to which current-Employee refers. Note that only the methods of class Employee can be called via an Employee variable—and Employee includes class object's methods, such as ToString. (Section 11.7 discussed the methods that all classes inherit from class object.) A base-class reference can be used to invoke only methods of the base class.

We perform special processing on BasePlusCommissionEmployee objects—as we encounter them, we increase their base salary by 10%. When processing objects polymorphically, we typically do not need to worry about the "specifics," but to adjust the base salary, we do have to determine the specific type of each Employee object at execution time. Line 51 uses the `is` operator to determine whether a particular `Employee` object's type is `BasePlusCommissionEmployee`. The condition in line 51 is true if the object referenced by `currentEmployee` *is a* `BasePlusCommissionEmployee`. This would also be true for any object of a `BasePlusCommissionEmployee` derived class (if there were any), because of the *is-a* relationship a derived class has with its base class. Lines 55–56 downcast `currentEmployee` from type `Employee` to type `BasePlusCommissionEmployee`—this cast is allowed only if the object has an *is-a* relationship with `BasePlusCommissionEmployee`. The condition at line 51 ensures that this is the case. This cast is required if we are to use derived class `BasePlusCommissionEmployee`'s `BaseSalary` property on the current `Employee` object—attempting to invoke a derived-class-only method directly on a base class reference is a compilation error.

Common Programming Error 12.3

Assigning a base-class variable to a derived-class variable (without an explicit downcast) is a compilation error.

Software Engineering Observation 12.4

If at execution time the reference to a derived-class object has been assigned to a variable of one of its direct or indirect base classes, it is acceptable to cast the reference stored in that base-class variable back to a reference of the derived-class type. Before performing such a cast, use the `is` operator to ensure that the object is indeed an object of an appropriate derived-class type.

Common Programming Error 12.4

When downcasting an object, an `InvalidCastException` (of namespace `System`) occurs if at execution time the object does not have an is-a *relationship with the type specified in the cast operator. An object can be cast only to its own type or to the type of one of its base classes.*

You can avoid a potential `InvalidCastException` by using the **as** operator to perform a downcast rather than a cast operator. For example, in the statement

```
var employee = currentEmployee as BasePlusCommissionEmployee;
```

`employee` is assigned a reference to an object that *is a* `BasePlusCommissionEmployee`, or the value `null` if `currentEmployee` is not a `BasePlusCommissionEmployee`. You can then compare `employee` with `null` to determine whether the cast succeeded.

If the `is` expression in line 51 is `true`, the `if` statement (lines 51–62) performs the special processing required for the `BasePlusCommissionEmployee` object. Using `BasePlusCommissionEmployee` variable `employee`, line 58 accesses the derived-class-only property `BaseSalary` to retrieve and update the employee's base salary with the 10% raise.

Lines 64–65 invoke method `Earnings` on `currentEmployee`, which calls the appropriate derived-class object's `Earnings` method polymorphically. Note that obtaining the earnings of the `SalariedEmployee`, `HourlyEmployee` and `CommissionEmployee` polymorphically in lines 64–65 produces the same result as obtaining these employees' earnings individually in lines 24–32. However, the earnings amount obtained for the `BasePlusCommissionEmployee` in lines 64–65 is higher than that obtained in lines 30–32, due to the 10% increase in its base salary.

Lines 69–71 display each employee's type as a string. Every object in C# knows its own type and can access this information through method ***GetType***, which all classes inherit from class `object`. Method `GetType` returns an object of class `Type` (of namespace

System), which contains information about the object's type, including its class name, the names of its methods, and the name of its base class. Line 71 invokes method GetType on the object to get its runtime class (i.e., a Type object that represents the object's type). Then method ToString is implicitly invoked on the object returned by GetType. The Type class's ToString method returns the class name.

In the previous example, we avoid several compilation errors by downcasting an Employee variable to a BasePlusCommissionEmployee variable in lines 55–56. If we remove the cast operator (BasePlusCommissionEmployee) from line 56 and attempt to assign Employee variable currentEmployee directly to BasePlusCommissionEmployee variable employee, we receive a "Cannot implicitly convert type" compilation error. This error indicates that the attempt to assign the reference of base-class object commissionEmployee to derived-class variable basePlusCommissionEmployee is not allowed without an appropriate cast operator. The compiler prevents this assignment, because a CommissionEmployee is not a BasePlusCommissionEmployee—again, the *is-a* relationship applies only between the derived class and its base classes, not vice versa.

Similarly, if lines 58 and 61 use base-class variable currentEmployee, rather than derived-class variable employee, to use derived-class-only property BaseSalary, we receive an "'Employee' does not contain a definition for 'BaseSalary'" compilation error on each of these lines. Attempting to invoke derived-class-only methods on a base-class reference is not allowed. While lines 58 and 61 execute only if is in line 51 returns true to indicate that currentEmployee has been assigned a reference to a BasePlusCommission-Employee object, we cannot attempt to use derived-class BasePlusCommissionEmployee property BaseSalary with base-class Employee reference currentEmployee. The compiler would generate errors in lines 58 and 61, because BaseSalary is not a base-class member and cannot be used with a base-class variable. Although the actual method that is called depends on the object's type at execution time, a variable can be used to invoke only those methods that are members of that variable's type, which the compiler verifies. Using a base-class Employee variable, we can invoke only methods and properties found in class Employee—methods Earnings and ToString, and properties FirstName, LastName and SocialSecurityNumber.

12.5.7 Summary of the Allowed Assignments Between Base-Class and Derived-Class Variables

Now that you have seen a complete application that processes diverse derived-class objects polymorphically, we summarize what you can and cannot do with base-class and derived-class objects and variables. Although a derived-class object also *is a* base-class object, the two are nevertheless different. As discussed previously, derived-class objects can be treated as if they were base-class objects. However, the derived class can have additional derived-class-only members. For this reason, assigning a base-class reference to a derived-class variable is not allowed without an explicit cast—such an assignment would leave the derived-class members undefined for a base-class object.

We have discussed four ways to assign base-class and derived-class references to variables of base-class and derived-class types:

1. Assigning a base-class reference to a base-class variable is straightforward.

2. Assigning a derived-class reference to a derived-class variable is straightforward.

3. Assigning a derived-class reference to a base-class variable is safe, because the derived-class object *is an* object of its base class. However, this reference can be used to refer only to base-class members. If this code refers to derived-class-only members through the base-class variable, the compiler reports errors.

4. Attempting to assign a base-class reference to a derived-class variable is a compilation error. To avoid this error, the base-class reference must be cast to a derived-class type explicitly or must be converted using the as operator. At execution time, if the object to which the reference refers is not a derived-class object, an exception will occur. (For more on exception handling, see Chapter 13, Exception Handling.) The is operator can be used to ensure that such a cast is performed only if the object is a derived-class object.

12.6 sealed Methods and Classes

We saw in Section 11.4 that only methods declared virtual, override or abstract can be overridden in derived classes. A method declared **sealed** in a base class cannot be overridden in a derived class. Methods that are declared private are implicitly sealed, because it is impossible to override them in a derived class (though the derived class can declare a new method with the same signature as the private method in the base class). Methods that are declared static also are implicitly sealed, because static methods cannot be overridden either. A derived-class method declared both override and sealed can override a base-class method, but cannot be overridden in derived classes further down the inheritance hierarchy.

A sealed method's declaration can never change, so all derived classes use the same method implementation, and calls to sealed methods are resolved at compile time—this is known as *static binding*. Since the compiler knows that sealed methods cannot be overridden, it can often optimize code by removing calls to sealed methods and replacing them with the expanded code of their declarations at each method-call location—a technique known as *inlining the code*.

Performance Tip 12.1

The compiler can decide to inline a sealed method call and will do so for small, simple sealed methods. Inlining does not violate encapsulation or information hiding, but does improve performance, because it eliminates the overhead of making a method call.

A class that is declared sealed cannot be a base class (i.e., a class cannot extend a sealed class). All methods in a sealed class are implicitly sealed. Class string is a sealed class. This class cannot be extended, so applications that use strings can rely on the functionality of string objects as specified in the .NET Framework Class Library.

Common Programming Error 12.5

Attempting to declare a derived class of a sealed class is a compilation error.

Software Engineering Observation 12.5

In the .NET Framework Class Library, the vast majority of classes are not declared sealed. This enables inheritance and polymorphism—the fundamental capabilities of object-oriented programming.

12.7 Case Study: Creating and Using Interfaces

Our next example (Figs. 12.11–12.15) reexamines the payroll system of Section 12.5. Suppose that the company involved wishes to perform several accounting operations in a single accounts-payable application—in addition to calculating the payroll earnings that must be paid to each employee, the company must also calculate the payment due on each of several invoices (i.e., bills for goods purchased). Though applied to unrelated things (i.e., employees and invoices), both operations have to do with calculating some kind of payment amount. For an employee, the payment refers to the employee's earnings. For an invoice, the payment refers to the total cost of the goods listed on the invoice. Can we calculate such different things as the payments due for employees and invoices polymorphically in a single application? Does C# offer a capability that requires that unrelated classes implement a set of common methods (e.g., a method that calculates a payment amount)? C# interfaces offer exactly this capability.

Interfaces define and standardize the ways in which people and systems can interact with one another. For example, the controls on a radio serve as an interface between a radio's users and its internal components. The controls allow users to perform a limited set of operations (e.g., changing the station, adjusting the volume, choosing between AM and FM), and different radios may implement the controls in different ways (e.g., using push buttons, dials, voice commands). The interface specifies *what* operations a radio must permit users to perform but does not specify *how* they are performed. Similarly, the interface between a driver and a car with a manual transmission includes the steering wheel, the gear shift, the clutch pedal, the gas pedal and the brake pedal. This same interface is found in nearly all manual-transmission cars, enabling someone who knows how to drive one particular manual-transmission car to drive just about any other. The components of each car may look a bit different, but the general purpose is the same—to allow people to drive the car.

Software objects also communicate via interfaces. A C# interface describes a set of methods that can be called on an object—to tell it, for example, to perform some task or return some piece of information. The next example introduces an interface named `IPayable` that describes the functionality of any object that must be capable of being paid and thus must offer a method to determine the proper payment amount due. An *interface declaration* begins with the keyword `interface` and can contain only abstract methods, properties, indexers and events (events are discussed in Chapter 14, Graphical User Interfaces with Windows Forms: Part 1.) All interface members are implicitly declared both `public` and `abstract`. In addition, each interface can extend one or more other interfaces to create a more elaborate interface that other classes can implement.

Common Programming Error 12.6

It is a compilation error to declare an interface member `public` or `abstract` explicitly, because they are redundant in interface-member declarations. It is also a compilation error to specify any implementation details, such as concrete method declarations, in an interface.

To use an interface, a class must specify that it *implements* the interface by listing the interface after the colon (`:`) in the class declaration. Note that this is the same syntax used to indicate inheritance from a base class. A concrete class implementing the interface must declare each member of the interface with the signature specified in the interface declaration. A class that implements an interface but does not implement all its members is an abstract class—it must be declared `abstract` and must contain an `abstract` declaration for each unimplemented member of the interface. Implementing an interface is like signing a contract with the compiler that states, "I will provide an implementation for all the members specified by the interface, or I will declare them `abstract`."

Common Programming Error 12.7

Failing to define or declare any member of an interface in a class that implements the interface results in a compilation error.

An interface is typically used when disparate (i.e., unrelated) classes need to share common methods. This allows objects of unrelated classes to be processed polymorphically—objects of classes that implement the same interface can respond to the same method calls. Programmers can create an interface that describes the desired functionality, then implement this interface in any classes requiring that functionality. For example, in the accounts-payable application developed in this section, we implement interface `IPayable` in any class that must be able to calculate a payment amount (e.g., `Employee`, `Invoice`).

An interface often is used in place of an `abstract` class when there is no default implementation to inherit—that is, no fields and no default method implementations. Like `abstract` classes, interfaces are typically `public` types, so they are normally declared in files by themselves with the same name as the interface and the `.cs` file-name extension.

12.7.1 Developing an `IPayable` Hierarchy

To build an application that can determine payments for employees and invoices alike, we first create an interface named `IPayable`. Interface `IPayable` contains method `Get-PaymentAmount` that returns a `decimal` amount to be paid for an object of any class that implements the interface. Method `GetPaymentAmount` is a general-purpose version of method `Earnings` of the `Employee` hierarchy—method `Earnings` calculates a payment amount specifically for an `Employee`, while `GetPaymentAmount` can be applied to a broad range of unrelated objects. After declaring interface `IPayable`, we introduce class `Invoice`, which implements interface `IPayable`. We then modify class `Employee` such that it also implements interface `IPayable`. Finally, we update `Employee` derived class `SalariedEmployee` to "fit" into the `IPayable` hierarchy (i.e., rename `SalariedEmployee` method `Earnings` as `GetPaymentAmount`).

Good Programming Practice 12.1

By convention, the name of an interface begins with "I". This helps distinguish interfaces from classes, improving code readability.

Good Programming Practice 12.2

When declaring a method in an interface, choose a name that describes the method's purpose in a general manner, because the method may be implemented by a broad range of unrelated classes.

Classes `Invoice` and `Employee` both represent things for which the company must be able to calculate a payment amount. Both classes implement `IPayable`, so an application can invoke method `GetPaymentAmount` on `Invoice` objects and `Employee` objects alike. This enables the polymorphic processing of `Invoice`s and `Employee`s required for our company's accounts-payable application.

The UML class diagram in Fig. 12.10 shows the interface and class hierarchy used in our accounts-payable application. The hierarchy begins with interface IPayable. The UML distinguishes an interface from a class by placing the word "interface" in guillemets (« and ») above the interface name. The UML expresses the relationship between a class and an interface through a ***realization***. A class is said to "realize," or implement, an interface. A class diagram models a realization as a dashed arrow with a hollow arrowhead pointing from the implementing class to the interface. The diagram in Fig. 12.10 indicates that classes Invoice and Employee each realize (i.e., implement) interface IPayable. Note that, as in the class diagram of Fig. 12.2, class Employee appears in italics, indicating that it is an abstract class. Concrete class SalariedEmployee extends Employee and inherits its base class's realization relationship with interface IPayable.

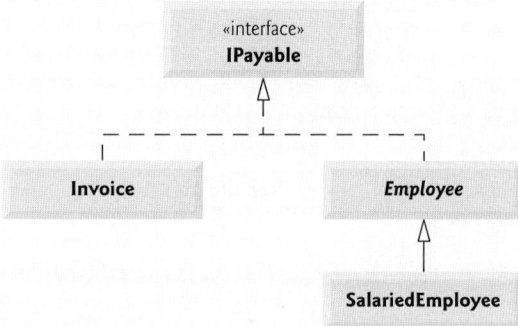

Fig. 12.10 | IPayable interface and class hierarchy UML class diagram.

12.7.2 Declaring Interface IPayable

The declaration of interface IPayable begins in Fig. 12.11 at line 3. Interface IPayable contains public abstract method GetPaymentAmount (line 5). Note that the method cannot be explicitly declared public or abstract. Interface IPayable has only one method, but interfaces can have any number of members. In addition, method GetPaymentAmount has no parameters, but interface methods can have parameters.

```
1   // Fig. 12.11: IPayable.cs
2   // IPayable interface declaration.
3   public interface IPayable
4   {
5      decimal GetPaymentAmount(); // calculate payment; no implementation
6   } // end interface IPayable
```

Fig. 12.11 | IPayable interface declaration.

12.7.3 Creating Class Invoice

We now create class Invoice (Fig. 12.12) to represent a simple invoice that contains billing information for one kind of part. The class contains properties PartNumber (line 9), PartDescription (line 12), Quantity (lines 25–35) and PricePerItem (lines 38–48) that indicate the part number, the description of the part, the quantity of the part ordered and the price per item. Class `Invoice` also contains a constructor (lines 15–22) and a `ToString` method (lines 51–57) that returns a string representation of an `Invoice` object. Note that the `set` accessors of properties `Quantity` (lines 25–35) and `PricePerItem` (lines 38–48) ensure that `quantity` and `pricePerItem` are assigned only nonnegative values.

```csharp
1   // Fig. 12.12: Invoice.cs
2   // Invoice class implements IPayable.
3   public class Invoice : IPayable
4   {
5       private int quantity;
6       private decimal pricePerItem;
7
8       // property that gets and sets the part number on the invoice
9       public string PartNumber { get; set; }
10
11      // property that gets and sets the part description on the invoice
12      public string PartDescription { get; set; }
13
14      // four-parameter constructor
15      public Invoice( string part, string description, int count,
16          decimal price )
17      {
18          PartNumber = part;
19          PartDescription = description;
20          Quantity = count; // validate quantity via property
21          PricePerItem = price; // validate price per item via property
22      } // end four-parameter Invoice constructor
23
24      // property that gets and sets the quantity on the invoice
25      public int Quantity
26      {
27          get
28          {
29              return quantity;
30          } // end get
31          set
32          {
33              quantity = ( value < 0 ) ? 0 : value; // validate quantity
34          } // end set
35      } // end property Quantity
36
37      // property that gets and sets the price per item
38      public decimal PricePerItem
39      {
40          get
41          {
42              return pricePerItem;
43          } // end get
44          set
45          {
```

Fig. 12.12 | `Invoice` class implements `IPayable`. (Part 1 of 2.)

```
46          pricePerItem = ( value < 0 ) ? 0 : value; // validate price
47        } // end set
48      } // end property PricePerItem
49
50      // return string representation of Invoice object
51      public override string ToString()
52      {
53        return string.Format(
54          "{0}: \n{1}: {2} ({3}) \n{4}: {5} \n{6}: {7:C}",
55          "invoice", "part number", PartNumber, PartDescription,
56          "quantity", Quantity, "price per item", PricePerItem );
57      } // end method ToString
58
59      // method required to carry out contract with interface IPayable
60      public decimal GetPaymentAmount()
61      {
62        return Quantity * PricePerItem; // calculate total cost
63      } // end method GetPaymentAmount
64    } // end class Invoice
```

Fig. 12.12 | `Invoice` class implements `IPayable`. (Part 2 of 2.)

Line 3 of Fig. 12.12 indicates that class `Invoice` implements interface `IPayable`. Like all classes, class `Invoice` also implicitly inherits from class `object`. C# does not allow derived classes to inherit from more than one base class, but it does allow a class to inherit from a base class and implement any number of interfaces. All objects of a class that implement multiple interfaces have the *is-a* relationship with each implemented interface type. To implement more than one interface, use a comma-separated list of interface names after the colon (:) in the class declaration, as in:

> **public class** *ClassName* : *BaseClassName*, *FirstInterface*, *SecondInterface*, …

When a class inherits from a base class and implements one or more interfaces, the class declaration must list the base-class name before any interface names.

Class `Invoice` implements the one method in interface `IPayable`—method `GetPaymentAmount` is declared in lines 60–63. The method calculates the amount required to pay the invoice. The method multiplies the values of `quantity` and `pricePerItem` (obtained through the appropriate properties) and returns the result (line 62). This method satisfies the implementation requirement for the method in interface `IPayable`— we have fulfilled the interface contract with the compiler.

12.7.4 Modifying Class `Employee` to Implement Interface `IPayable`

We now modify class `Employee` to implement interface `IPayable`. Figure 12.13 contains the modified `Employee` class. This class declaration is identical to that of Fig. 12.4 with two exceptions. First, line 3 of Fig. 12.13 indicates that class `Employee` now implements interface `IPayable`. Second, since `Employee` now implements interface `IPayable`, we must rename `Earnings` to `GetPaymentAmount` throughout the `Employee` hierarchy. As with method `Earnings` in the version of class `Employee` in Fig. 12.4, however, it does not make sense to implement method `GetPaymentAmount` in class `Employee`, because we cannot calculate the earnings payment owed to a general `Employee`—first, we must know the specific type of Employee. In Fig. 12.4, we declared method `Earnings` as `abstract` for this reason, and as a result, class `Employee` had to be declared `abstract`. This forced each `Employee` derived class to override `Earnings` with a concrete implementation.

In Fig. 12.13, we handle this situation the same way. Recall that when a class implements an interface, the class makes a contract with the compiler stating that the class either will implement each of the methods in the interface or will declare them `abstract`. If the latter option is chosen, we must also declare the class `abstract`. As we discussed in Section 12.4, any concrete derived class of the abstract class must implement the `abstract` methods of the base class. If the derived class does not do so, it too must be declared `abstract`. As indicated by the comments in lines 29–30, class `Employee` of Fig. 12.13 does not implement method `GetPaymentAmount`, so the class is declared `abstract`.

```
1   // Fig. 12.13: Employee.cs
2   // Employee abstract base class.
3   public abstract class Employee : IPayable
4   {
5      // read-only property that gets employee's first name
6      public string FirstName { get; private set; }
7
8      // read-only property that gets employee's last name
9      public string LastName { get; private set; }
10
11     // read-only property that gets employee's social security number
12     public string SocialSecurityNumber { get; private set; }
13
14     // three-parameter constructor
15     public Employee( string first, string last, string ssn )
16     {
17        FirstName = first;
18        LastName = last;
19        SocialSecurityNumber = ssn;
20     } // end three-parameter Employee constructor
21
22     // return string representation of Employee object
23     public override string ToString()
24     {
25        return string.Format( "{0} {1}\nsocial security number: {2}",
26           FirstName, LastName, SocialSecurityNumber );
27     } // end method ToString
28
29     // Note: We do not implement IPayable method GetPaymentAmount here, s
30     // this class must be declared abstract to avoid a compilation error.
31     public abstract decimal GetPaymentAmount();
32  } // end abstract class Employee
```

Fig. 12.13 | `Employee` abstract base class.

12.7.5 Modifying Class `SalariedEmployee` for Use with `IPayable`

Figure 12.14 contains a modified version of class `SalariedEmployee` that extends `Employee` and implements method `GetPaymentAmount`. This version of `SalariedEmployee` is identical to that of Fig. 12.5 with the exception that the version here implements method GetPaymentAmount (lines 29–32) instead of method Earnings. The two methods contain the same functionality but have different names. Recall that the IPayable version of the method has a more general name to be applicable to possibly disparate classes. The remaining Employee derived classes (e.g., HourlyEmployee, CommissionEmployee and BasePlusCommissionEmployee) also must be modified to contain method GetPaymentAmount in place of Earnings to reflect the fact that Employee now implements IPayable. We leave these modifications as an exercise and use only SalariedEmployee in our test application in this section.

When a class implements an interface, the same *is-a* relationship provided by inheritance applies. For example, class Employee implements IPayable, so we can say that an

```
1   // Fig. 12.14: SalariedEmployee.cs
2   // SalariedEmployee class that extends Employee.
3   public class SalariedEmployee : Employee
4   {
5      private decimal weeklySalary;
6
7      // four-parameter constructor
8      public SalariedEmployee( string first, string last, string ssn,
9         decimal salary ) : base( first, last, ssn )
10     {
11        WeeklySalary = salary; // validate salary via property
12     } // end four-parameter SalariedEmployee constructor
13
14     // property that gets and sets salaried employee's salary
15     public decimal WeeklySalary
16     {
17        get
18        {
19           return weeklySalary;
20        } // end get
21        set
22        {
23           weeklySalary = value < 0 ? 0 : value; // validation
24        } // end set
25     } // end property WeeklySalary
26
27     // calculate earnings; implement interface IPayable method
28     // that was abstract in base class Employee
29     public override decimal GetPaymentAmount()
30     {
31        return WeeklySalary;
32     } // end method GetPaymentAmount
33
34     // return string representation of SalariedEmployee object
35     public override string ToString()
36     {
37        return string.Format( "salaried employee: {0}\n{1}: {2:C}",
38           base.ToString(), "weekly salary", WeeklySalary );
39     } // end method ToString
40  } // end class SalariedEmployee
```

Fig. 12.14 | SalariedEmployee class that extends Employee.

Employee *is an* IPayable, as are any classes that extend Employee. SalariedEmployee objects, for instance, are IPayable objects. As with inheritance relationships, an object of a class that implements an interface may be thought of as an object of the interface type. Objects of any classes derived from the class that implements the interface can also be thought of as objects of the interface type. Thus, just as we can assign the reference of a SalariedEmployee object to a base-class Employee variable, we can assign the reference of a SalariedEmployee object to an interface IPayable variable. Invoice implements IPayable, so an Invoice object also *is an* IPayable object, and we can assign the reference of an Invoice object to an IPayable variable.

Software Engineering Observation 12.6

Inheritance and interfaces are similar in their implementation of the is-a *relationship. An object of a class that implements an interface may be thought of as an object of that interface type. An object of any derived classes of a class that implements an interface also can be thought of as an object of the interface type.*

Software Engineering Observation 12.7

The is-a *relationship that exists between base classes and derived classes, and between interfaces and the classes that implement them, holds when passing an object to a method. When a method parameter receives an argument of a base class or interface type, the method polymorphically processes the object received as an argument.*

12.7.6 Using Interface IPayable to Process Invoices and Employees Polymorphically

PayableInterfaceTest (Fig. 12.15) illustrates that interface IPayable can be used to process a set of Invoices and Employees polymorphically in a single application. Line 10 declares payableObjects and assigns it an array of four IPayable variables. Lines 13–14 assign the references of Invoice objects to the first two elements of payableObjects. Lines 15–18 assign the references of SalariedEmployee objects to the remaining two elements of payableObjects. These assignments are allowed because an Invoice *is an* IPayable, a SalariedEmployee *is an* Employee and an Employee *is an* IPayable. Lines 24–29 use a foreach statement to process each IPayable object in payableObjects polymorphically, printing the object as a string, along with the payment due. Note that line 27 implicitly invokes method ToString off an IPayable interface reference, even though ToString is not declared in interface IPayable—all references (including those of interface types) refer to objects that extend object and therefore have a ToString method. Line 28 invokes IPayable method GetPaymentAmount to obtain the payment amount for each object in payableObjects, regardless of the actual type of the object. The output reveals that the method calls in lines 27–28 invoke the appropriate class's implementation of methods ToString and GetPaymentAmount. For instance, when currentEmployee refers to an Invoice during the first iteration of the foreach loop, class Invoice's ToString and GetPaymentAmount methods execute.

Software Engineering Observation 12.8

All methods of class object can be called by using a reference of an interface type—the reference refers to an object, and all objects inherit the methods of class object.

```
1    // Fig. 12.15: PayableInterfaceTest.cs
2    // Tests interface IPayable with disparate classes.
3    using System;
4
5    public class PayableInterfaceTest
6    {
7       public static void Main( string[] args )
8       {
9          // create four-element IPayable array
10         IPayable[] payableObjects = new IPayable[ 4 ];
11
12         // populate array with objects that implement IPayable
13         payableObjects[ 0 ] = new Invoice( "01234", "seat", 2, 375.00M );
14         payableObjects[ 1 ] = new Invoice( "56789", "tire", 4, 79.95M );
15         payableObjects[ 2 ] = new SalariedEmployee( "John", "Smith",
16            "111-11-1111", 800.00M );
17         payableObjects[ 3 ] = new SalariedEmployee( "Lisa", "Barnes",
18            "888-88-8888", 1200.00M );
19
20         Console.WriteLine(
21            "Invoices and Employees processed polymorphically:\n" );
22
23         // generically process each element in array payableObjects
24         foreach ( var currentPayable in payableObjects )
25         {
26            // output currentPayable and its appropriate payment amount
27            Console.WriteLine( "payment due \n{0}: {1:C}\n",
28               currentPayable, currentPayable.GetPaymentAmount() );
29         } // end foreach
30      } // end Main
31   } // end class PayableInterfaceTest
```

```
Invoices and Employees processed polymorphically:

invoice:
part number: 01234 (seat)
quantity: 2
price per item: $375.00
payment due: $750.00

invoice:
part number: 56789 (tire)
quantity: 4
price per item: $79.95
payment due: $319.80

salaried employee: John Smith
social security number: 111-11-1111
weekly salary: $800.00
payment due: $800.00

salaried employee: Lisa Barnes
social security number: 888-88-8888
weekly salary: $1,200.00
payment due: $1,200.00
```

Fig. 12.15 | Tests interface IPayable with disparate classes.

12.7.7 Common Interfaces of the .NET Framework Class Library

In this section, we overview several common interfaces in the .NET Framework Class Library. These interfaces are implemented and used in the same manner as those you create (e.g., interface IPayable in Section 12.7.2). The .NET Framework Class Library's interfaces enable you to extend many important aspects of C# with your own classes. Figure 12.16 overviews several commonly used .NET Framework Class Library interfaces.

Interface	Description
IComparable	C# contains several comparison operators (e.g., <, <=, >, >=, ==, !=) that allow you to compare simple-type values. In Section 12.8 you'll see that these operators can be defined to compare two objects. Interface IComparable can also be used to allow objects of a class that implements the interface to be compared to one another. The interface contains one method, CompareTo, that compares the object that calls the method to the object passed as an argument to the method. Classes must implement CompareTo to return a value indicating whether the object on which it is invoked is less than (negative integer return value), equal to (0 return value) or greater than (positive integer return value) the object passed as an argument, using any criteria specified by the programmer. For example, if class Employee implements IComparable, its CompareTo method could compare Employee objects by their earnings amounts. Interface IComparable is commonly used for ordering objects in a collection such as an array. We use IComparable in Chapter 26, Generics, and Chapter 27, Collections.
IComponent	Implemented by any class that represents a component, including Graphical User Interface (GUI) controls (such as buttons or labels). Interface IComponent defines the behaviors that components must implement. We discuss IComponent and many GUI controls that implement this interface in Chapter 14, Graphical User Interfaces with Windows Forms: Part 1, and Chapter 15, Graphical User Interfaces with Windows Forms: Part 2.
IDisposable	Implemented by classes that must provide an explicit mechanism for releasing resources. Some resources can be used by only one program at a time. In addition, some resources, such as files on disk, are unmanaged resources that, unlike memory, cannot be released by the garbage collector. Classes that implement interface IDisposable provide a Dispose method that can be called to explicitly release resources. We discuss IDisposable briefly in Chapter 13, Exception Handling. You can learn more about this interface at msdn.microsoft.com/en-us/library/system.idisposable.aspx. The MSDN article *Implementing a Dispose Method* at msdn.microsoft.com/en-us/library/fs2xkftw.aspx discusses the proper implementation of this interface in your classes.

Fig. 12.16 | Common interfaces of the .NET Framework Class Library. (Part 1 of 2.)

Interface	Description
IEnumerator	Used for iterating through the elements of a collection (such as an array) one element at a time. Interface IEnumerator contains method MoveNext to move to the next element in a collection, method Reset to move to the position before the first element and property Current to return the object at the current location. We use IEnumerator in Chapter 27, Collections.

Fig. 12.16 | Common interfaces of the .NET Framework Class Library. (Part 2 of 2.)

12.8 Operator Overloading

Manipulations of class objects are accomplished by sending messages (in the form of method calls) to the objects. This method-call notation is cumbersome for certain kinds of classes, especially mathematical classes. For these classes, it would be convenient to use C#'s rich set of built-in operators to specify object manipulations. In this section, we show how to enable these operators to work with class objects—via a process called *operator overloading*.

Software Engineering Observation 12.9

Use operator overloading when it makes an application clearer than accomplishing the same operations with explicit method calls.

C# enables you to overload most operators to make them sensitive to the context in which they are used. Some operators are overloaded more frequently than others, especially the various arithmetic operators, such as + and -, where operator notation often is more natural. Figures 12.17 and 12.18 provide an example of using operator overloading with a ComplexNumber class.

Class ComplexNumber (Fig. 12.17) overloads the plus (+), minus (-) and multiplication (*) operators to enable programs to add, subtract and multiply instances of class ComplexNumber using common mathematical notation. Lines 9 and 12 define properties for the Real and Imaginary components of the complex number.

```
1   // Fig. 12.17: ComplexNumber.cs
2   // Class that overloads operators for adding, subtracting
3   // and multiplying complex numbers.
4   using System;
5
6   public class ComplexNumber
7   {
8      // read-only property that gets the real component
9      public double Real { get; private set; }
10
```

Fig. 12.17 | Class that overloads operators for adding, subtracting and multiplying complex numbers. (Part 1 of 2.)

```
11      // read-only property that gets the imaginary component
12      public double Imaginary { get; private set; }
13
14      // constructor
15      public ComplexNumber( double a, double b )
16      {
17         Real = a;
18         Imaginary = b;
19      } // end constructor
20
21      // return string representation of ComplexNumber
22      public override string ToString()
23      {
24         return string.Format( "({0} {1} {2}i)",
25            Real, ( Imaginary < 0 ? "-" : "+" ), Math.Abs( Imaginary ) );
26      } // end method ToString
27
28      // overload the addition operator
29      public static ComplexNumber operator +(
30         ComplexNumber x, ComplexNumber y )
31      {
32         return new ComplexNumber( x.Real + y.Real,
33            x.Imaginary + y.Imaginary );
34      } // end operator +
35
36      // overload the subtraction operator
37      public static ComplexNumber operator -(
38         ComplexNumber x, ComplexNumber y )
39      {
40         return new ComplexNumber( x.Real - y.Real,
41            x.Imaginary - y.Imaginary );
42      } // end operator -
43
44      // overload the multiplication operator
45      public static ComplexNumber operator *(
46         ComplexNumber x, ComplexNumber y )
47      {
48         return new ComplexNumber(
49            x.Real * y.Real - x.Imaginary * y.Imaginary,
50            x.Real * y.Imaginary + y.Real * x.Imaginary );
51      } // end operator *
52   } // end class ComplexNumber
```

Fig. 12.17 | Class that overloads operators for adding, subtracting and multiplying complex numbers. (Part 2 of 2.)

Lines 29–34 overload the plus operator (+) to perform addition of ComplexNumbers. Keyword **operator**, followed by an operator symbol, indicates that a method overloads the specified operator. Methods that overload binary operators must take two arguments. The first argument is the left operand, and the second argument is the right operand. Class ComplexNumber's overloaded plus operator takes two ComplexNumber references as arguments and returns a ComplexNumber that represents the sum of the arguments. Note that this method is marked public and static, which is required for overloaded operators. The body of the method (lines 32–33) performs the addition and returns the result as a new Complex-Number. Notice that we do not modify the contents of either of the original operands passed as arguments x and y. This matches our intuitive sense of how this operator should behave—adding two numbers does not modify either of the original numbers. Lines 37–51 provide similar overloaded operators for subtracting and multiplying ComplexNumbers.

Software Engineering Observation 12.10

Overload operators to perform the same function or similar functions on class objects as the operators perform on objects of simple types. Avoid nonintuitive use of operators.

Software Engineering Observation 12.11

At least one parameter of an overloaded operator method must be a reference to an object of the class in which the operator is overloaded. This prevents programmers from changing how operators work on simple types.

Class ComplexTest (Fig. 12.18) demonstrates the overloaded operators for adding, subtracting and multiplying ComplexNumbers. Lines 14–27 prompt the user to enter two complex numbers, then use this input to create two ComplexNumbers and assign them to variables x and y.

```
1   // Fig. 12.18: OperatorOverloading.cs
2   // Overloading operators for complex numbers.
3   using System;
4
5   public class ComplexTest
6   {
7      public static void Main( string[] args )
8      {
9         // declare two variables to store complex numbers
10        // to be entered by user
11        ComplexNumber x, y;
12
13        // prompt the user to enter the first complex number
14        Console.Write( "Enter the real part of complex number x: " );
15        double realPart = Convert.ToDouble( Console.ReadLine() );
16        Console.Write(
17           "Enter the imaginary part of complex number x: " );
18        double imaginaryPart = Convert.ToDouble( Console.ReadLine() );
19        x = new ComplexNumber( realPart, imaginaryPart );
20
21        // prompt the user to enter the second complex number
22        Console.Write( "\nEnter the real part of complex number y: " );
23        realPart = Convert.ToDouble( Console.ReadLine() );
24        Console.Write(
25           "Enter the imaginary part of complex number y: " );
26        imaginaryPart = Convert.ToDouble( Console.ReadLine() );
27        y = new ComplexNumber( realPart, imaginaryPart );
28
29        // display the results of calculations with x and y
30        Console.WriteLine();
```

Fig. 12.18 | Overloading operators for complex numbers. (Part 1 of 2.)

```
31          Console.WriteLine( "{0} + {1} = {2}", x, y, x + y );
32          Console.WriteLine( "{0} - {1} = {2}", x, y, x - y );
33          Console.WriteLine( "{0} * {1} = {2}", x, y, x * y );
34       } // end method Main
35    } // end class ComplexTest
```

```
Enter the real part of complex number x: 2
Enter the imaginary part of complex number x: 4

Enter the real part of complex number y: 4
Enter the imaginary part of complex number y: -2

(2 + 4i) + (4 - 2i) = (6 + 2i)
(2 + 4i) - (4 - 2i) = (-2 + 6i)
(2 + 4i) * (4 - 2i) = (16 + 12i)
```

Fig. 12.18 | Overloading operators for complex numbers. (Part 2 of 2.)

Lines 31–33 add, subtract and multiply x and y with the overloaded operators, then output the results. In line 31, we perform the addition by using the plus operator with ComplexNumber operands x and y. Without operator overloading, the expression x + y would not make sense—the compiler would not know how two objects should be added. This expression makes sense here because we've defined the plus operator for two ComplexNumbers in lines 29–34 of Fig. 12.17. When the two ComplexNumbers are "added" in line 31 of Fig. 12.18, this invokes the operator+ declaration, passing the left operand as the first argument and the right operand as the second argument. When we use the subtraction and multiplication operators in lines 32–33, their respective overloaded operator declarations are invoked similarly.

Notice that the result of each calculation is a reference to a new ComplexNumber object. When this new object is passed to the Console class's WriteLine method, its ToString method (lines 22–26 of Fig. 12.17) is implicitly invoked. We do not need to assign an object to a reference-type variable to invoke its ToString method. Line 31 of Fig. 12.18 could be rewritten to explicitly invoke the ToString method of the object created by the overloaded plus operator, as in:

```
Console.WriteLine( "{0} + {1} = {2}", x, y, ( x + y ).ToString() );
```

12.9 (Optional) Software Engineering Case Study: Incorporating Inheritance and Polymorphism into the ATM System

We now revisit our ATM system design to see how it might benefit from inheritance and polymorphism. To apply inheritance, we first look for commonality among classes in the system. We create an inheritance hierarchy to model similar classes in an elegant and efficient manner that enables us to process objects of these classes polymorphically. We then modify our class diagram to incorporate the new inheritance relationships. Finally, we demonstrate how the inheritance aspects of our updated design are translated into C# code.

In Section 4.12, we encountered the problem of representing a financial transaction in the system. Rather than create one class to represent all transaction types, we created three distinct transaction classes—BalanceInquiry, Withdrawal and Deposit—to represent the transactions that the ATM system can perform. The class diagram of Fig. 12.19 shows the attributes and operations of these classes. Note that they have one private attribute (accountNumber) and one public operation (Execute) in common. Each class requires attribute accountNumber to specify the account to which the transaction applies. Each class contains operation Execute, which the ATM invokes to perform the transaction. Clearly, BalanceInquiry, Withdrawal and Deposit represent *types of* transactions. Figure 12.19 reveals commonality among the transaction classes, so using inheritance to factor out the common features seems appropriate for designing these classes. We place the common functionality in base class Transaction and derive classes BalanceInquiry, Withdrawal and Deposit from Transaction (Fig. 12.20).

The UML specifies a relationship called a *generalization* to model inheritance. Figure 12.20 is the class diagram that models the inheritance relationship between base class Transaction and its three derived classes. The arrows with triangular hollow arrowheads indicate that classes BalanceInquiry, Withdrawal and Deposit are derived from class Transaction by inheritance. Class Transaction is said to be a generalization of its derived classes. The derived classes are said to be *specializations* of class Transaction.

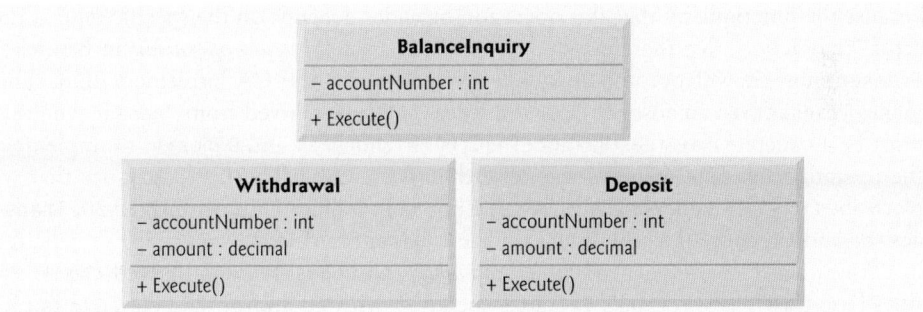

Fig. 12.19 | Attributes and operations of classes BalanceInquiry, Withdrawal and Deposit.

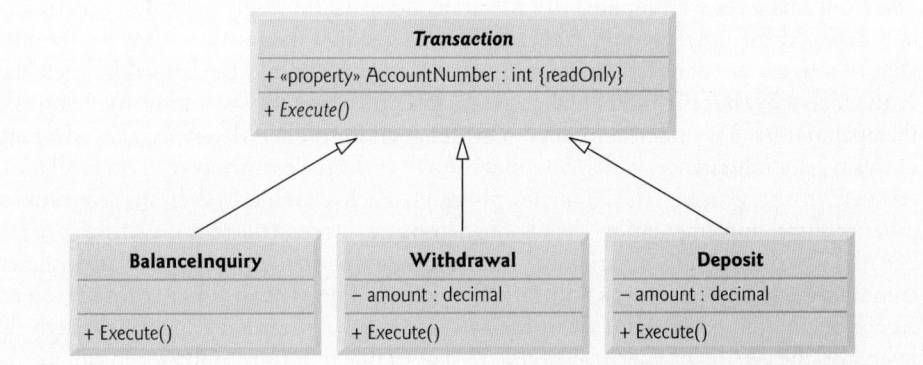

Fig. 12.20 | Class diagram modeling the generalization (i.e., inheritance) relationship between the base class Transaction and its derived classes BalanceInquiry, Withdrawal and Deposit.

As Fig. 12.19 shows, classes BalanceInquiry, Withdrawal and Deposit share private int attribute accountNumber. We'd like to factor out this common attribute and place it in the base class Transaction. However, recall that a base class's private attributes are not accessible in derived classes. The derived classes of Transaction require access to attribute accountNumber so that they can specify which Account to process in the BankDatabase. As you learned in Chapter 11, a derived class can access only the public, protected and protected internal members of its base class. However, the derived classes in this case do not need to modify attribute accountNumber—they need only to access its value. For this reason, we have chosen to replace private attribute accountNumber in our model with the public read-only property AccountNumber. Since this is a read-only property, it provides only a get accessor to access the account number. Each derived class inherits this property, enabling the derived class to access its account number as needed to execute a transaction. We no longer list accountNumber in the second compartment of each derived class, because the three derived classes inherit property AccountNumber from Transaction.

According to Fig. 12.19, classes BalanceInquiry, Withdrawal and Deposit also share operation Execute, so base class Transaction should contain public operation Execute. However, it does not make sense to implement Execute in class Transaction, because the functionality that this operation provides depends on the specific type of the actual transaction. We therefore declare Execute as an *abstract operation* in base class Transaction—it will become an abstract method in the C# implementation. This makes Transaction an abstract class and forces any class derived from Transaction that must be a concrete class (i.e., BalanceInquiry, Withdrawal and Deposit) to implement the operation Execute to make the derived class concrete. The UML requires that we place abstract class names and abstract operations in italics. Thus, in Fig. 12.20, Transaction and Execute appear in italics for the Transaction class; Execute is not italicized in derived classes BalanceInquiry, Withdrawal and Deposit. Each derived class overrides base class Transaction's Execute operation with an appropriate concrete implementation. Note that Fig. 12.20 includes operation Execute in the third compartment of classes BalanceInquiry, Withdrawal and Deposit, because each class has a different concrete implementation of the overridden operation.

As you learned in this chapter, a derived class can inherit interface and implementation from a base class. Compared to a hierarchy designed for implementation inheritance, one designed for interface inheritance tends to have its functionality lower in the hierarchy—a base class signifies one or more operations that should be defined by each class in the hierarchy, but the individual derived classes provide their own implementations of the operation(s). The inheritance hierarchy designed for the ATM system takes advantage of this type of inheritance, which provides the ATM with an elegant way to execute all transactions "in the general" (i.e., polymorphically). Each class derived from Transaction inherits some implementation details (e.g., property AccountNumber), but the primary benefit of incorporating inheritance into our system is that the derived classes share a common interface (e.g., abstract operation Execute). The ATM can aim a Transaction reference at any transaction, and when the ATM invokes the operation Execute through this reference, the version of Execute specific to that transaction runs (polymorphically) automatically (due to polymorphism). For example, suppose a user chooses to perform a balance inquiry. The ATM aims a Transaction reference at a new object of class BalanceInquiry, which the C# compiler allows because a BalanceInquiry *is a* Transaction. When the ATM uses this reference to invoke Execute, BalanceInquiry's version of Execute is called (polymorphically).

This polymorphic approach also makes the system easily extensible. Should we wish to create a new transaction type (e.g., funds transfer or bill payment), we would simply create an additional Transaction derived class that overrides the Execute operation with a version appropriate for the new transaction type. We would need to make only minimal changes to the system code to allow users to choose the new transaction type from the main menu and for the ATM to instantiate and execute objects of the new derived class. The ATM could execute transactions of the new type using the current code, because it executes all transactions identically (through polymorphism).

As you learned earlier in the chapter, an abstract class like Transaction is one for which the programmer never intends to (and, in fact, cannot) instantiate objects. An abstract class simply declares common attributes and behaviors for its derived classes in an inheritance hierarchy. Class Transaction defines the concept of what it means to be a transaction that has an account number and can be executed. You may wonder why we bother to include abstract operation Execute in class Transaction if Execute lacks a concrete implementation. Conceptually, we include this operation because it is the defining behavior of all transactions—executing. Technically, we must include operation Execute in base class Transaction so that the ATM (or any other class) can invoke each derived class's overridden version of this operation polymorphically via a Transaction reference.

Derived classes BalanceInquiry, Withdrawal and Deposit inherit property Account-Number from base class Transaction, but classes Withdrawal and Deposit contain the additional attribute amount that distinguishes them from class BalanceInquiry. Classes Withdrawal and Deposit require this additional attribute to store the amount of money that the user wishes to withdraw or deposit. Class BalanceInquiry has no need for such an attribute and requires only an account number to execute. Even though two of the three Transaction derived classes share the attribute amount, we do not place it in base class Transaction—we place only features common to *all* the derived classes in the base class, so derived classes do not inherit unnecessary attributes (and operations).

Figure 12.21 presents an updated class diagram of our model that incorporates inheritance and introduces abstract base class Transaction. We model an association between class ATM and class Transaction to show that the ATM, at any given moment, either is executing a transaction or is not (i.e., zero or one objects of type Transaction exist in the system at a time). Because a Withdrawal is a type of Transaction, we no longer draw an association line directly between class ATM and class Withdrawal—derived class Withdrawal inherits base class Transaction's association with class ATM. Derived classes BalanceInquiry and Deposit also inherit this association, which replaces the previously omitted associations between classes BalanceInquiry and Deposit, and class ATM. Note again the use of triangular hollow arrowheads to indicate the specializations (i.e., derived classes) of class Transaction, as indicated in Fig. 12.20.

We also add an association between Transaction and BankDatabase (Fig. 12.21). All Transactions require a reference to the BankDatabase so that they can access and modify account information. Each Transaction derived class inherits this reference, so we no longer model the association between Withdrawal and BankDatabase. Note that the association between class Transaction and the BankDatabase replaces the previously omitted associations between classes BalanceInquiry and Deposit, and the BankDatabase.

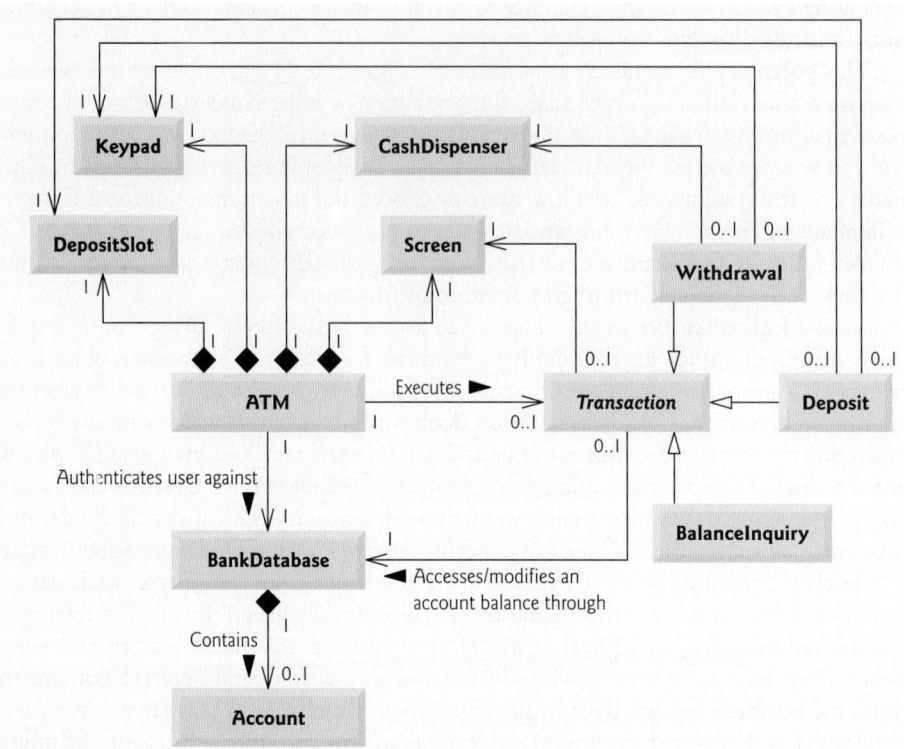

Fig. 12.21 | Class diagram of the ATM system (incorporating inheritance). Note that abstract class name `Transaction` appears in italics.

We include an association between class `Transaction` and the `Screen` because all `Transaction`s display output to the user via the `Screen`. Each derived class inherits this association. Therefore, we no longer include the association previously modeled between `Withdrawal` and the `Screen`. Class `Withdrawal` still participates in associations with the `CashDispenser` and the `Keypad`, however—these associations apply to derived class `Withdrawal` but not to derived classes `BalanceInquiry` and `Deposit`, so we do not move these associations to base class `Transaction`.

Our class diagram incorporating inheritance (Fig. 12.21) also models classes `Deposit` and `BalanceInquiry`. We show associations between `Deposit` and both the `DepositSlot` and the `Keypad`. Note that class `BalanceInquiry` takes part in only those associations inherited from class `Transaction`—a `BalanceInquiry` interacts only with the `BankDatabase` and the `Screen`.

The class diagram of Fig. 10.30 showed attributes, properties and operations with visibility markers. Now we present a modified class diagram in Fig. 12.22 that includes abstract base class `Transaction`. This abbreviated diagram does not show inheritance relationships (these appear in Fig. 12.21), but instead shows the attributes and operations after we have employed inheritance in our system. Note that abstract class name `Transaction` and abstract operation name `Execute` in class `Transaction` appear in italics. To save space, as we did in Fig. 5.16, we do not include those attributes shown by associations

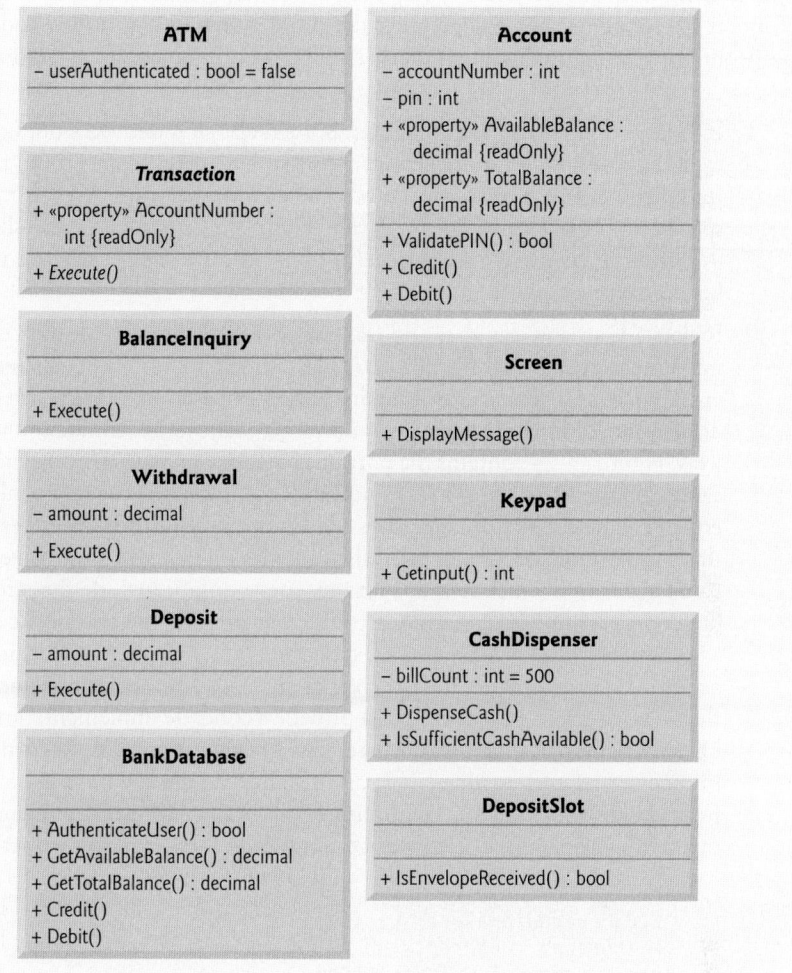

Fig. 12.22 | Class diagram after incorporating inheritance into the system.

in Fig. 12.21—we do, however, include them in the C# implementation in Appendix D. We also omit all operation parameters, as we did in Fig. 10.30—incorporating inheritance does not affect the parameters already modeled in Figs. 7.21–7.24.

Software Engineering Observation 12.12

A complete class diagram shows all the associations among classes, and all the attributes and operations for each class. When the number of class attributes, operations and associations is substantial (as in Figs. 12.21 and 12.22), a good practice that promotes readability is to divide this information between two class diagrams—one focusing on associations and the other on attributes and operations. When examining classes modeled in this fashion, it is crucial to consider both *class diagrams to get a complete picture of the classes. For example, one must refer to Fig. 12.21 to observe the inheritance relationship between* Transaction *and its derived classes; that relationship is omitted from Fig. 12.22.*

Implementing the ATM System Design Incorporating Inheritance

In Section 10.22, we began implementing the ATM system design in C# code. We now modify our implementation to incorporate inheritance, using class Withdrawal as an example.

1. If a class A is a generalization of class B, then class B is derived from (and is a specialization of) class A. For example, abstract base class Transaction is a generalization of class Withdrawal. Thus, class Withdrawal is derived from (and is a specialization of) class Transaction. Figure 12.23 contains the shell of class Withdrawal, in which the class definition indicates the inheritance relationship between Withdrawal and Transaction (line 3).

2. If class A is an abstract class and class B is derived from class A, then class B must implement the abstract operations of class A if class B is to be a concrete class. For example, class Transaction contains abstract operation Execute, so class Withdrawal must implement this operation if we want to instantiate Withdrawal objects. Figure 12.24 contains the portions of the C# code for class Withdrawal that can be inferred from Fig. 12.21 and Fig. 12.22. Class Withdrawal inherits property AccountNumber from base class Transaction, so Withdrawal does not declare this property. Class Withdrawal also inherits references to the Screen and the BankDatabase from class Transaction, so we do not include these references in our code. Figure 12.22 specifies attribute amount and operation Execute for class Withdrawal. Line 6 of Fig. 12.24 declares an instance variable for attribute amount. Lines 17–20 declare the shell of a method for operation Execute. Recall that derived class Withdrawal must provide a concrete implementation of the abstract method Execute from base class Transaction. The keypad and cashDispenser references (lines 7–8) are instance variables whose need is apparent from class Withdrawal's associations in Fig. 12.21—in the C# implementation of this class in Appendix D, a constructor initializes these references to actual objects.

```
1   // Fig. 12.23: Withdrawal.cs
2   // Class Withdrawal represents an ATM withdrawal transaction.
3   public class Withdrawal : Transaction
4   {
5      // code for members of class Withdrawal
6   } // end class Withdrawal
```

Fig. 12.23 | C# code for shell of class Withdrawal.

```
1   // Fig. 12.24: Withdrawal.cs
2   // Class Withdrawal represents an ATM withdrawal transaction.
3   public class Withdrawal : Transaction
4   {
5      // attributes
6      private decimal amount; // amount to withdraw
7      private Keypad keypad; // reference to keypad
8      private CashDispenser cashDispenser; // reference to cash dispenser
```

Fig. 12.24 | C# code for class Withdrawal based on Figures 12.21 and 12.22. (Part 1 of 2.)

```
 9
10        // parameterless constructor
11        public Withdrawal()
12        {
13           // constructor body code
14        } // end constructor
15
16        // method that overrides Execute
17        public override void Execute()
18        {
19           // Execute method body code
20        } // end method Execute
21     } // end class Withdrawal
```

Fig. 12.24 | C# code for class Withdrawal based on Figures 12.21 and 12.22. (Part 2 of 2.)

We discuss the polymorphic processing of Transactions in Section D.2 of the ATM implementation. Class ATM performs the actual polymorphic call to method Execute at line 99 of Fig. D.1.

ATM Case Study Wrap-Up

This concludes our object-oriented design of the ATM system. A complete C# implementation of the ATM system in 655 lines of code appears in Appendix D. This working implementation uses most of the key object-oriented programming concepts that we have covered to this point in the book, including classes, objects, encapsulation, visibility, composition, inheritance and polymorphism. The code is abundantly commented and conforms to the coding practices you've learned so far. Mastering this code is a wonderful capstone experience for you after studying the nine Software Engineering Case Study sections in Chapters 1, 3–10 and 12.

Software Engineering Case Study Self-Review Exercises

12.1 The UML uses an arrow with a _____ to indicate a generalization relationship.
   a)   solid filled arrowhead
   b)   triangular hollow arrowhead
   c)   diamond-shaped hollow arrowhead
   d)   stick arrowhead

12.2 State whether the following statement is *true* or *false*, and if *false*, explain why: The UML requires that we underline abstract class names and abstract operation names.

12.3 Write C# code to begin implementing the design for class Transaction specified in Figures 12.21 and 12.22. Be sure to include private references based on class Transaction's associations. Also, be sure to include properties with public get accessors for any of the private instance variables that the derived classes must access to perform their tasks.

Answers to Software Engineering Case Study Self-Review Exercises

12.1 b.

12.2 False. The UML requires that we italicize abstract class names and operation names.

12.3 The design for class `Transaction` yields the code in Fig. 12.25. In the implementation in Appendix D, a constructor initializes `private` instance variables `userScreen` and `database` to actual objects, and read-only properties `UserScreen` and `Database` access these instance variables. These properties allow classes derived from `Transaction` to access the ATM's screen and interact with the bank's database. Note that we chose the names of the `UserScreen` and `Database` properties for clarity—we wanted to avoid property names that are the same as the class names `Screen` and `BankDatabase`, which can be confusing.

```csharp
1   // Fig. 12.25: Transaction.cs
2   // Abstract base class Transaction represents an ATM transaction.
3   public abstract class Transaction
4   {
5      private int accountNumber; // indicates account involved
6      private Screen userScreen; // ATM's screen
7      private BankDatabase database; // account info database
8
9      // parameterless constructor
10     public Transaction()
11     {
12        // constructor body code
13     } // end constructor
14
15     // read-only property that gets the account number
16     public int AccountNumber
17     {
18        get
19        {
20           return accountNumber;
21        } // end get
22     } // end property AccountNumber
23
24     // read-only property that gets the screen reference
25     public Screen UserScreen
26     {
27        get
28        {
29           return userScreen;
30        } // end get
31     } // end property UserScreen
32
33     // read-only property that gets the bank database reference
34     public BankDatabase Database
35     {
36        get
37        {
38           return database;
39        } // end get
40     } // end property Database
41
42     // perform the transaction (overridden by each derived class)
43     public abstract void Execute();
44  } // end class Transaction
```

Fig. 12.25 | C# code for class `Transaction` based on Figures 12.21 and 12.22.

12.10 Wrap-Up

This chapter introduced polymorphism—the ability to process objects that share the same base class in a class hierarchy as if they were all objects of the base class. The chapter discussed how polymorphism makes systems extensible and maintainable, then demonstrated how to use overridden methods to effect polymorphic behavior. We introduced the notion of an abstract class, which allows you to provide an appropriate base class from which other classes can inherit. You learned that an abstract class can declare abstract methods that each derived class must implement to become a concrete class, and that an application can use variables of an abstract class to invoke derived class implementations of abstract methods polymorphically. You also learned how to determine an object's type at execution time. We showed how to create `sealed` methods and classes. The chapter discussed declaring and implementing an interface as another way to achieve polymorphic behavior, often among objects of different classes. Finally, you learned how to define the behavior of the built-in operators on objects of your own classes with operator overloading.

You should now be familiar with classes, objects, encapsulation, inheritance, interfaces and polymorphism—the most essential aspects of object-oriented programming. In the next chapter, we take a deeper look at how to use exception handling to deal with errors during execution time.

13

Exception Handling

OBJECTIVES

In this chapter you'll learn:

- What exceptions are and how they are handled.

- When to use exception handling.

- To use **try** blocks to delimit code in which exceptions might occur.

- To **throw** exceptions to indicate a problem.

- To use **catch** blocks to specify exception handlers.

- To use the **finally** block to release resources.

- The .NET exception class hierarchy.

- **Exception** properties.

- To create user-defined exceptions.

It is common sense to take a method and try it. If it fails, admit it frankly and try another. But above all, try something.
—Franklin Delano Roosevelt

O! throw away the worser part of it, And live the purer with the other half.
—William Shakespeare

If they're running and they don't look where they're going I have to come out from somewhere and catch them.
—J. D. Salinger

And oftentimes excusing of a fault Doth make the fault the worse by the excuse.
—William Shakespeare

O infinite virtue! com'st thou smiling from the world's great snare uncaught?
—William Shakespeare

Outline

13.1 Introduction

13.2 Exception-Handling Overview

13.3 Example: Divide by Zero without Exception Handling

13.4 Example: Handling `DivideByZeroExceptions` and `FormatExceptions`

    13.4.1 Enclosing Code in a `try` Block

    13.4.2 Catching Exceptions

    13.4.3 Uncaught Exceptions

    13.4.4 Termination Model of Exception Handling

    13.4.5 Flow of Control When Exceptions Occur

13.5 .NET `Exception` Hierarchy

    13.5.1 Class `SystemException`

    13.5.2 Determining Which Exceptions a Method Throws

13.6 `finally` Block

13.7 `Exception` Properties

13.8 User-Defined Exception Classes

13.9 Wrap-Up

13.1 **Introduction**

In this chapter, we introduce *exception handling*. An *exception* is an indication of a problem that occurs during a program's execution. The name "exception" comes from the fact that, although the problem can occur, it occurs infrequently. If the "rule" is that a statement normally executes correctly, then the occurrence of a problem represents the "exception to the rule." Exception handling enables programmers to create applications that can resolve (or handle) exceptions. In many cases, handling an exception allows a program to continue executing as if no problems were encountered. However, more severe problems may prevent a program from continuing normal execution, instead requiring the program to notify the user of the problem, then terminate in a controlled manner. The features presented in this chapter enable programmers to write clear, *robust* and more *fault-tolerant programs* (i.e., programs that are able to deal with problems that may arise and continue executing). The style and details of C# exception handling are based in part on the work of Andrew Koenig and Bjarne Stroustrup. "Best practices" for exception handling in Visual C# 2008 are specified in the Visual Studio documentation.[1]

 Error-Prevention Tip 13.1

Exception handling helps improve a program's fault tolerance.

This chapter begins with an overview of exception-handling concepts and demonstrations of basic exception-handling techniques. The chapter also overviews .NET's exception-handling class hierarchy. Programs typically request and release resources (such as files on disk) during program execution. Often, the supply of these resources is limited, or the resources can be used by only one program at a time. We demonstrate a part of the

---

1. "Best Practices for Handling Exceptions [C#]," *.NET Framework Developer's Guide*, Visual Studio .NET Online Help. Available at msdn.microsoft.com/en-us/library/seyhszts(vs.80).aspx.

exception-handling mechanism that enables a program to use a resource, then guarantee that the resource will be released for use by other programs, even if an exception occurs. The chapter demonstrates several properties of class System.Exception (the base class of all exception classes) and discusses how you can create and use your own exception classes.

13.2 Exception-Handling Overview

Programs frequently test conditions to determine how program execution should proceed. Consider the following pseudocode:

> *Perform a task*
>
> *If the preceding task did not execute correctly*
>   *Perform error processing*
>
> *Perform next task*
>
> *If the preceding task did not execute correctly*
>   *Perform error processing*
>
> *…*

In this pseudocode, we begin by performing a task; then we test whether that task executed correctly. If not, we perform error processing. Otherwise, we continue with the next task. Although this form of error handling works, intermixing program logic with error-handling logic can make programs difficult to read, modify, maintain and debug—especially in large applications.

Exception handling enables programmers to remove error-handling code from the "main line" of the program's execution, improving program clarity and enhancing modifiability. Programmers can decide to handle any exceptions they choose—all exceptions, all exceptions of a certain type or all exceptions of a group of related types (i.e., exception types that are related through an inheritance hierarchy). Such flexibility reduces the likelihood that errors will be overlooked, thus making programs more robust.

With programming languages that do not support exception handling, programmers often delay writing *error-processing code* and sometimes forget to include it. This results in less robust software products. C# enables programmers to deal with exception handling easily from the beginning of a project.

13.3 Example: Divide by Zero without Exception Handling

First we demonstrate what happens when errors arise in a console application that does not use exception handling. Figure 13.1 inputs two integers from the user, then divides the first integer by the second using integer division to obtain an int result. In this example, we'll see that an exception is *thrown* (i.e., an exception occurs) when a method detects a problem and is unable to handle it.

Running the Application

In most of our examples, the application appears to run the same with or without debugging. As we discuss shortly, the example in Fig. 13.1 might cause errors, depending on the user's input. If you run this application using the **Debug > Start Debugging** menu option,

```
 1   // Fig. 13.1: DivideByZeroNoExceptionHandling.cs
 2   // Integer division without exception handling.
 3   using System;
 4
 5   class DivideByZeroNoExceptionHandling
 6   {
 7      static void Main()
 8      {
 9         // get numerator and denominator
10         Console.Write( "Please enter an integer numerator: " );
11         int numerator = Convert.ToInt32( Console.ReadLine() );
12         Console.Write( "Please enter an integer denominator: " );
13         int denominator = Convert.ToInt32( Console.ReadLine() );
14
15         // divide the two integers, then display the result
16         int result = numerator / denominator;
17         Console.WriteLine( "\nResult: {0:D} / {1:D} = {2:D}",
18            numerator, denominator, result );
19      } // end Main
20   } // end class DivideByZeroNoExceptionHandling
```

```
Please enter an integer numerator: 100
Please enter an integer denominator: 7

Result: 100 / 7 = 14
```

```
Please enter an integer numerator: 100
Please enter an integer denominator: 0

Unhandled Exception: System.DivideByZeroException:
   Attempted to divide by zero.
   at DivideByZeroNoExceptionHandling.Main()
      in C:\examples\ch13\Fig13_01\DivideByZeroNoExceptionHandling\
      DivideByZeroNoExceptionHandling\
      DivideByZeroNoExceptionHandling.cs:line 16
```

```
Please enter an integer numerator: 100
Please enter an integer denominator: hello

Unhandled Exception: System.FormatException:
   Input string was not in a correct format.
   at System.Number.StringToNumber(String str, NumberStyles options,
      NumberBuffer& number, NumberFormatInfo info, Boolean parseDecimal)
   at System.Number.ParseInt32(String s, NumberStyles style,
      NumberFormatInfo info)
   at System.Convert.ToInt32(String value)
   at DivideByZeroNoExceptionHandling.Main()
      in C:\examples\ch13\Fig13_01\DivideByZeroNoExceptionHandling\
      DivideByZeroNoExceptionHandling\
      DivideByZeroNoExceptionHandling.cs:line 13
```

Fig. 13.1 | Integer division without exception handling.

the program pauses at the line where an exception occurs, displays the Exception Assistant and allows you to analyze the current state of the program and debug it. We discuss the Exception Assistant in Section 13.4.3. We discuss debugging in detail in Appendix H.

In this example, we do not wish to debug the application; we simply want to see what happens when errors arise. For this reason, we execute this application from a **Command Prompt** window. Select **Start > All Programs > Accessories > Command Prompt** to open a **Command Prompt** window, then use the cd command to change to the application's Debug directory. For example, if this application resides in the directory C:\examples\ ch13\Fig13_01\DivideByZeroNoExceptionHandling on your system, you will type

```
cd /d C:\examples\ch13\Fig13_01\DivideByZeroNoExceptionHandling\
DivideByZeroNoExceptionHandling\bin\Debug
```

in the **Command Prompt**, then press *Enter* to change to the application's Debug directory. To execute the application, type

```
DivideByZeroNoExceptionHandling.exe
```

in the **Command Prompt**, then press *Enter*. If an error arises during execution, a dialog is displayed indicating that the application has encountered a problem and needs to close. In Windows XP, the dialog also asks whether you'd like to send information about this error to Microsoft. Since we're creating this error for demonstration purposes, click **Don't Send**. In Windows Vista, the system tries to find a solution to the problem, then asks you to choose between closing the program or debugging it. [*Note:* On some systems a **Just-In-Time Debugging** dialog is displayed instead. If this occurs, simply click the **No** button to dismiss the dialog.] At this point, an error message describing the problem is displayed in the **Command Prompt**. We formatted the error messages in Fig. 13.1 for readability. [*Note:* Selecting **Debug > Start Without Debugging** (or *<Ctrl> F5*) to run the application from Visual Studio executes the application's so-called release version. The error messages produced by this version of the application may differ from those shown in Fig. 13.1, owing to optimizations that the compiler performs to create an application's release version.]

Analyzing the Results
The first sample execution in Fig. 13.1 shows a successful division. In the second, the user enters 0 as the denominator. Note that several lines of information are displayed in response to the invalid input. This information—known as a *stack trace*—includes the exception name (System.DivideByZeroException) in a message indicating the problem that occurred and the path of execution that led to the exception, method by method. This information helps you debug a program. The first line of the error message specifies that a DivideByZeroException has occurred. When *division by zero* in integer arithmetic occurs, the CLR throws a *DivideByZeroException* (namespace System). The text after the name of the exception, "Attempted to divide by zero," indicates that this exception occurred as a result of an attempt to divide by zero. Division by zero is not allowed in integer arithmetic. [*Note:* Division by zero with floating-point values is allowed. Such a calculation results in the value infinity, which is represented by either constant *Double.PositiveInfinity* or constant *Double.NegativeInfinity*, depending on whether the numerator is positive or negative. These values are displayed as Infinity or -Infinity. If both the numerator and denominator are zero, the result of the calculation is the constant *Double.NaN* ("not a number"), which is returned when a calculation's result is undefined.]

Each "at" line in the stack trace indicates a line of code in the particular method that was executing when the exception occurred. The "at" line contains the namespace, class name and method name in which the exception occurred (DivideByZeroNoException-Handling.Main), the location and name of the file in which the code resides (C:\examples\ch13\Fig13_01\DivideByZeroNoExceptionHandling\DivideByZeroNoException Handling\DivideByZeroNoExceptionHandling.cs) and the line number (:line 16) where the exception occurred. In this case, the stack trace indicates that the DivideByZeroException occurred when the program was executing line 16 of method Main. The first "at" line in the stack trace indicates the exception's *throw point*—the initial point at which the exception occurred (i.e., line 16 in Main). This information makes it easy for the programmer to see where the exception originated, and what method calls were made to get to that point in the program.

Now, let's look at a more detailed stack trace. In the third sample execution, the user enters the string "hello" as the denominator. This causes a FormatException, and another stack trace is displayed. Our earlier examples that read numeric values from the user assumed that the user would input an integer value. However, a user could erroneously input a noninteger value. A *FormatException* (namespace System) occurs, for example, when Convert method ToInt32 receives a string that does not represent a valid integer. Starting from the last "at" line in the stack trace, we see that the exception was detected in line 13 of method Main. The stack trace also shows the other methods that led to the exception being thrown—Convert.ToInt32, Number.ParseInt32 and Number.StringToNumber. To perform its task, Convert.ToInt32 calls method Number.ParseInt32, which in turn calls Number.StringToNumber. The throw point occurs in Number.StringToNumber, as indicated by the first "at" line in the stack trace.

Note that in the sample executions in Fig. 13.1, the program also terminates when exceptions occur and stack traces are displayed. This does not always happen—sometimes a program may continue executing even though an exception has occurred and a stack trace has been printed. In such cases, the application may produce incorrect results. The next section demonstrates how to handle exceptions to enable the program to run to normal completion.

13.4 Example: Handling DivideByZeroExceptions and FormatExceptions

Let us consider a simple example of exception handling. The application in Fig. 13.2 uses exception handling to process any DivideByZeroExceptions and FormatExceptions that might arise. The application displays two TextBoxes in which the user can type integers. When the user presses **Click To Divide**, the program invokes event handler DivideButton_Click (lines 17–48), which obtains the user's input, converts the input values to type int and divides the first number (numerator) by the second number (denominator). Assuming that the user provides integers as input and does not specify 0 as the denominator for the division, DivideButton_Click displays the division result in Output-Label. However, if the user inputs a noninteger value or supplies 0 as the denominator, an exception occurs. This program demonstrates how to *catch* and *handle* (i.e., deal with) such exceptions—in this case, displaying an error message and allowing the user to enter another set of values.

Before we discuss the details of the program, let's consider the sample output windows in Fig. 13.2. The window in Fig. 13.2(a) shows a successful calculation, in which the user enters the numerator 100 and the denominator 7. Note that the result (14) is an int, because integer division always yields an int result. The next two windows, Figs. 13.2(b) and 13.2(c), demonstrate the result of an attempt to divide by zero. In integer arithmetic, the CLR tests for division by zero and generates a DivideByZeroException if the denominator is zero. The program detects the exception and displays the error message dialog in Fig. 13.2(c) indicating the attempt to divide by zero. The last two output windows, Figs. 13.2(d) and 13.2(e), depict the result of inputting a non-int value—in this case, the

```
 1    // Fig. 13.2: DivideByZeroTest.cs
 2    // FormatException and DivideByZeroException handlers.
 3    using System;
 4    using System.Windows.Forms;
 5
 6    namespace DivideByZeroTest
 7    {
 8       public partial class DivideByZeroTestForm : Form
 9       {
10          public DivideByZeroTestForm()
11          {
12             InitializeComponent();
13          } // end constructor
14
15          // obtain 2 integers from the user
16          // and divide numerator by denominator
17          private void divideButton_Click( object sender, EventArgs e )
18          {
19             outputLabel.Text = ""; // clear Label OutputLabel
20
21             // retrieve user input and calculate quotient
22             try
23             {
24                // Convert.ToInt32 generates FormatException
25                // if argument cannot be converted to an integer
26                int numerator = Convert.ToInt32( numeratorTextBox.Text );
27                int denominator = Convert.ToInt32( denominatorTextBox.Text );
28
29                // division generates DivideByZeroException
30                // if denominator is 0
31                int result = numerator / denominator;
32
33                // display result in OutputLabel
34                outputLabel.Text = result.ToString();
35             } // end try
36             catch ( FormatException )
37             {
38                MessageBox.Show( "You must enter two integers.",
39                   "Invalid Number Format", MessageBoxButtons.OK,
40                   MessageBoxIcon.Error );
41             } // end catch
```

Fig. 13.2 | FormatException and DivideByZeroException handlers. (Part 1 of 2.)

```
42                catch ( DivideByZeroException divideByZeroExceptionParameter )
43                {
44                   MessageBox.Show( divideByZeroExceptionParameter.Message,
45                      "Attempted to Divide by Zero", MessageBoxButtons.OK,
46                      MessageBoxIcon.Error );
47                } // end catch
48             } // end method divideButton_Click
49          } // end class DivideByZeroTestForm
50       } // end namespace DivideByZeroTest
```

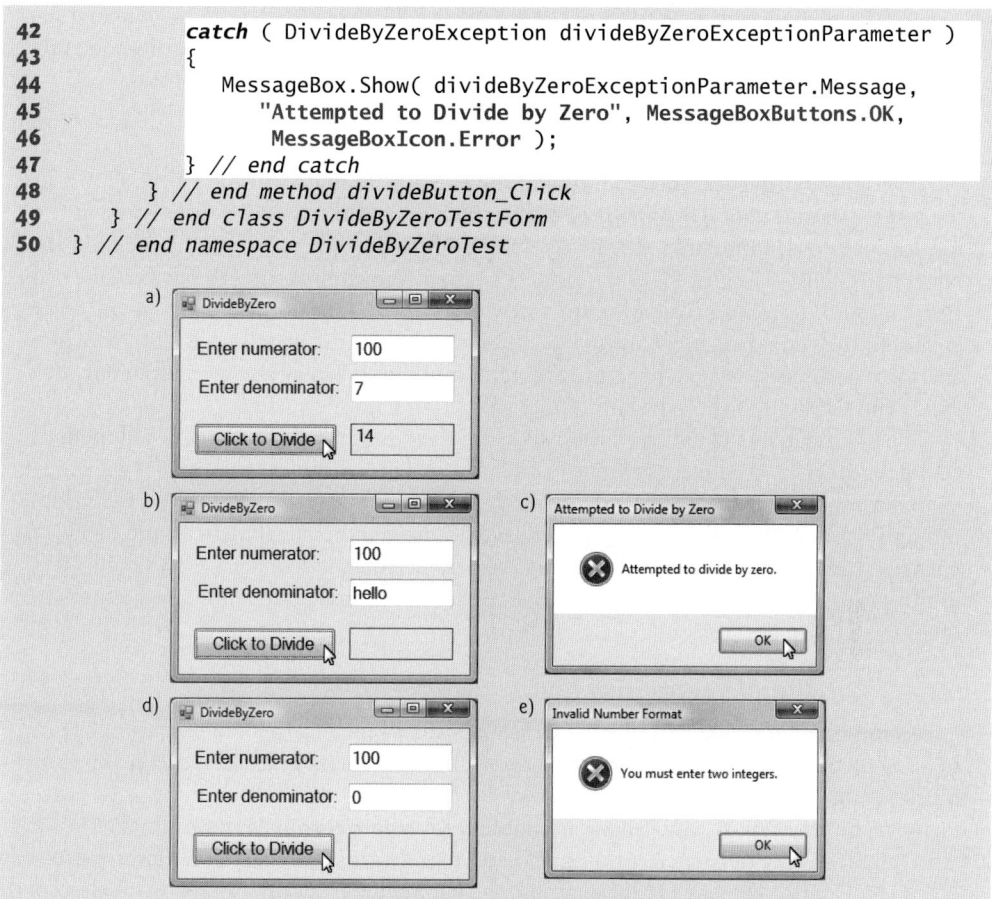

Fig. 13.2 | FormatException and DivideByZeroException handlers. (Part 2 of 2.)

user enters "hello" in the second TextBox, as shown in Fig. 13.2(d). When the user clicks **Click To Divide**, the program attempts to convert the input strings to ints using method Convert.ToInt32 (lines 26–27). If an argument cannot be converted to an int, the method throws a FormatException. The program catches the exception and displays the error-message dialog in Fig. 13.2(e), indicating that the user must enter two ints. Notice that we did not include a parameter name for the catch at line 36. In the catch's block, we do not use any information from the FormatException object. Omitting the parameter name prevents the compiler from issuing a warning which indicates that we declared a variable but did not use it in the catch block.

Another way to validate the input is to use the *Int32.TryParse* method, which converts a string to an int value if possible. All of the numeric types have TryParse methods. The method requires two arguments—one is the string to parse and the other is the variable in which the converted value is to be stored. The method returns a bool value that is true only if the string was parsed successfully. If the string could not be converted, the value 0 is assigned to the second argument, which is passed by reference so its value can be modified in the calling method. Method TryParse can be used to validate input in code rather than allowing the code to throw an exception. For errors such as these that are predictable and occur relatively frequently, it is considered a better practice to use in-code validation. We used exceptions in this example strictly for demonstration purposes.

13.4.1 Enclosing Code in a `try` Block

Now we consider the user interactions and flow of control that yield the results shown in the sample output windows. The user inputs values into the TextBoxes that represent the numerator and denominator, then presses **Click To Divide**. At this point, the program invokes method DivideButton_Click. Line 19 assigns the empty string to OutputLabel to clear any prior result in preparation for a new calculation. Lines 22–35 define a *try block* enclosing the code that might throw exceptions, as well as the code that is skipped when an exception occurs. For example, the program should not display a new result in OutputLabel (line 34) unless the calculation in line 31 completes successfully.

The two statements that read the ints from the TextBoxes (lines 26–27) call method Convert.ToInt32 to convert strings to int values. This method throws a FormatException if it cannot convert its string argument to an int. If lines 26–27 convert the values properly (i.e., no exceptions occur), then line 31 divides the numerator by the denominator and assigns the result to variable result. If denominator is 0, line 31 causes the CLR to throw a DivideByZeroException. If line 31 does not cause an exception to be thrown, then line 34 displays the result of the division.

13.4.2 Catching Exceptions

Exception-handling code appears in a *catch block*. In general, when an exception occurs in a try block, a corresponding catch block catches the exception and handles it. The try block in this example is followed by two catch blocks—one that handles a FormatException (lines 36–41) and one that handles a DivideByZeroException (lines 42–47). A catch block specifies an exception parameter representing the exception that the catch block can handle. The catch block can use the parameter's identifier (which you choose) to interact with a caught exception object. If there is no need to use the exception object in the catch block, the exception parameter's identifier can be omitted. The type of the catch's parameter is the type of the exception that the catch block handles. Optionally, you can include a catch block that does not specify an exception type—such a catch block (known as a *general catch clause*) catches all exception types. At least one catch block and/or a *finally block* (discussed in Section 13.6) must immediately follow a try block.

In Fig. 13.2, the first catch block catches FormatExceptions (thrown by method Convert.ToInt32), and the second catch block catches DivideByZeroExceptions (thrown by the CLR). If an exception occurs, the program executes only the first matching catch block. Both exception handlers in this example display an error-message dialog. After either catch block terminates, program control continues with the first statement after the last catch block (the end of the method, in this example). We'll soon take a deeper look at how this flow of control works in exception handling.

13.4.3 Uncaught Exceptions

An *uncaught exception* (or *unhandled exception*) is an exception for which there is no matching catch block. You saw the results of uncaught exceptions in the second and third outputs of Fig. 13.1. Recall that when exceptions occur in that example, the application terminates early (after displaying the exception's stack trace). The result of an uncaught exception depends on how you execute the program—Fig. 13.1 demonstrated the results of an uncaught exception when an application is executed in a **Command Prompt**. If you run the application from Visual Studio with debugging, and the runtime environment detects an uncaught exception, the application pauses, and a window called the *Exception Assistant* appears indicating where the exception occurred, the type of the exception and links to helpful information on handling the exception. Figure 13.3 shows the Exception Assistant that is displayed if the user attempts to divide by zero in the application of Fig. 13.1.

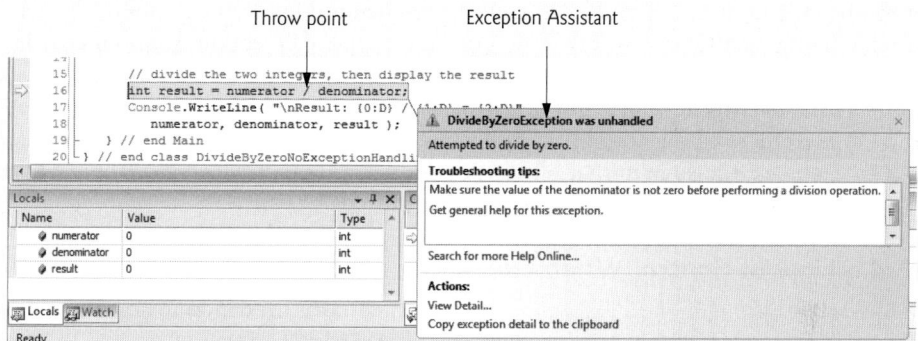

Fig. 13.3 | Exception Assistant.

13.4.4 Termination Model of Exception Handling

When a method called in a program or the CLR detects a problem, the method or the CLR throws an exception. Recall that the point in the program at which an exception occurs is called the throw point—this is an important location for debugging purposes (as we demonstrate in Section 13.7). If an exception occurs in a try block (such as a FormatException being thrown as a result of the code in line 27 in Fig. 13.2), the try block terminates immediately, and program control transfers to the first of the following catch blocks in which the exception parameter's type matches the type of the thrown exception. In Fig. 13.2, the first catch block catches FormatExceptions (which occur if input of an invalid type is entered); the second catch block catches DivideByZeroExceptions (which occur if an attempt is made to divide by zero). After the exception is handled, program control does not return to the throw point because the try block has expired (which also causes any of its local variables to go out of scope). Rather, control resumes after the last catch block. This is known as the *termination model of exception handling*. [*Note:* Some languages use the *resumption model of exception handling*, in which, after an exception is handled, control resumes just after the throw point.]

 Common Programming Error 13.1

Logic errors can occur if you assume that after an exception is handled, control will return to the first statement after the throw point.

If no exceptions occur in the try block, the program of Fig. 13.2 successfully completes the try block by ignoring the catch blocks in lines 36–41 and 42–47, and passing line 47. Then the program executes the first statement following the try and catch blocks.

In this example, the program reaches the end of event handler DivideButton_Click (line 48), so the method terminates, and the program awaits the next user interaction.

The try block and its corresponding catch and finally blocks together form a ***try statement***. It is important not to confuse the terms "try block" and "try statement"—the term "try block" refers to the block of code following the keyword try (but before any catch or finally blocks), while the term "try statement" includes all the code from the opening try keyword to the end of the last catch or finally block. This includes the try block, as well as any associated catch blocks and finally block.

As with any other block of code, when a try block terminates, local variables defined in the block go out of scope. If a try block terminates due to an exception, the CLR searches for the first catch block that can process the type of exception that occurred. The CLR locates the matching catch by comparing the type of the thrown exception to each catch's parameter type. A match occurs if the types are identical or if the thrown exception's type is a derived class of the catch's parameter type. Once an exception is matched to a catch block, the code in that block executes and the other catch blocks in the try statement are ignored.

13.4.5 Flow of Control When Exceptions Occur

In the sample output of Fig. 13.2(b), the user inputs hello as the denominator. When line 27 executes, Convert.ToInt32 cannot convert this string to an int, so Convert.ToInt32 throws a FormatException object to indicate that the method was unable to convert the string to an int. When the exception occurs, the try block expires (terminates). Next, the CLR attempts to locate a matching catch block. A match occurs with the catch block in line 36, so the exception handler executes and the program ignores all other exception handlers following the try block.

Common Programming Error 13.2

Specifying a comma-separated list of parameters in a catch *block is a syntax error. A* catch *block can have at most one parameter.*

In the sample output of Fig. 13.2(d), the user inputs 0 as the denominator. When the division in line 31 executes, a DivideByZeroException occurs. Once again, the try block terminates, and the program attempts to locate a matching catch block. In this case, the first catch block does not match—the exception type in the catch-handler declaration is not the same as the type of the thrown exception, and FormatException is not a base class of DivideByZeroException. Therefore the program continues to search for a matching catch block, which it finds in line 42. Line 44 displays the value of property ***Message*** of class Exception, which contains the error message. Note that our program never "sets" this error-message attribute. This is done by the CLR when it creates the exception object.

13.5 .NET Exception Hierarchy

In C#, the exception-handling mechanism allows only objects of class ***Exception*** (namespace System) and its derived classes to be thrown and caught. Note, however, that C# programs may interact with software components written in other .NET languages (such as C++) that do not restrict exception types. The general catch clause can be used to catch such exceptions.

This section overviews several of the .NET Framework's exception classes and focuses exclusively on exceptions that derive from class `Exception`. In addition, we discuss how to determine whether a particular method throws exceptions.

13.5.1 Class SystemException

Class **Exception** (namespace `System`) is the base class of .NET's exception class hierarchy. An important class derived from `Exception` is **SystemException**. The CLR generates `SystemException`s, which can occur at any point during program execution. Many of these exceptions can be avoided if applications are coded properly. For example, if a program attempts to access an *out-of-range array index*, the CLR throws an exception of type **IndexOutOfRangeException** (a derived class of `SystemException`). Similarly, an exception occurs when a program uses an object reference to manipulate an object that does not yet exist (i.e., the reference has a value of `null`). Attempting to use a `null` reference causes a **NullReferenceException** (another derived class of `SystemException`). You saw earlier in this chapter that a `DivideByZeroException` occurs in integer division when a program attempts to divide by zero.

Other `SystemException` types thrown by the CLR include **OutOfMemoryException**, **StackOverflowException** and **ExecutionEngineException**. These are thrown when the something goes wrong that causes the CLR to become unstable. In some cases, such exceptions cannot even be caught. In general, it is best to simply log such exceptions, then terminate your application.

A benefit of the exception class hierarchy is that a `catch` block can catch exceptions of a particular type or—because of the *is-a* relationship of inheritance—can use a base-class type to catch exceptions in a hierarchy of related exception types. For example, Section 13.4.2 discussed the `catch` block with no parameter, which catches exceptions of all types (including those that are not derived from `Exception`). A `catch` block that specifies a parameter of type `Exception` can catch all exceptions that derive from `Exception`, because `Exception` is the base class of all exception classes. The advantage of this approach is that the exception handler can access the caught exception's information via the parameter in the `catch`. We demonstrated accessing the information in an exception in line 44 of Fig. 13.2. We'll say more about accessing exception information in Section 13.7.

Using inheritance with exceptions enables an `catch` block to catch related exceptions using a concise notation. A set of exception handlers could catch each derived-class exception type individually, but catching the base-class exception type is more concise. However, this technique makes sense only if the handling behavior is the same for a base class and all derived classes. Otherwise, catch each derived-class exception individually.

Common Programming Error 13.3

The compiler issues an error if a `catch` block that catches a base-class exception is placed before a `catch` block for any of that class's derived-class types. In this case, the base-class `catch` block would catch all base-class and derived-class exceptions, so the derived-class exception handler would never execute—a possible logic error.

13.5.2 Determining Which Exceptions a Method Throws

How do we determine that an exception might occur in a program? For methods contained in the .NET Framework classes, read the detailed descriptions of the methods in the online documentation. If a method throws an exception, its description contains a section called **Exceptions** that specifies the types of exceptions the method throws and briefly describes possible causes them. For example, search for "Convert.ToInt32 method" in the **Index** of the Visual Studio online documentation (use the **.NET Framework** filter). Select the document entitled **Convert.ToInt32 Method (System)**. In the document that describes the method, click the link **ToInt32(String)**. In the document that appears, the **Exceptions** section (near the top of the document) indicates that method Convert.ToInt32 throws two exception types—FormatException and OverflowException—and describes the reason why each might occur. [*Note:* You can also find this information in the **Object Browser** described in Section 10.16.]

Software Engineering Observation 13.1

If a method throws exceptions, statements that invoke the method directly or indirectly should be placed in try blocks, and those exceptions should be caught and handled.

It is more difficult to determine when the CLR throws exceptions. Such information appears in the *C# Language Specification* (available from msdn.microsoft.com/en-us/vcsharp/aa336809.aspx). This document defines C#'s syntax and specifies cases in which exceptions are thrown. Figure 13.2 demonstrated that the CLR throws a DivideByZeroException in integer arithmetic when a program attempts to divide by zero. Section 7.7.2 of the language specification (14.7.2 in the ECMA version) discusses the division operator and when DivideByZeroExceptions occur.

13.6 finally Block

Programs frequently request and release resources dynamically (i.e., at execution time). For example, a program that reads a file from disk first makes a file-open request (as we'll see in Chapter 19, Files and Streams). If that request succeeds, the program reads the contents of the file. Operating systems typically prevent more than one program from manipulating a file at once. Therefore, when a program finishes processing a file, the program should close the file (i.e., release the resource) so other programs can use it. If the file is not closed, a *resource leak* occurs. In such a case, the file resource is not available to other programs, possibly because a program using the file has not closed it.

In programming languages such as C and C++, in which the programmer is responsible for dynamic memory management, the most common type of resource leak is a *memory leak*. A memory leak occurs when a program allocates memory (as C# programmers do via keyword new), but does not deallocate the memory when it is no longer needed. Normally, this is not an issue in C#, because the CLR performs garbage collection of memory that is no longer needed by an executing program (Section 10.9). However, other kinds of resource leaks (such as unclosed files) can occur.

Error-Prevention Tip 13.2

The CLR does not completely eliminate memory leaks. The CLR will not garbage collect an object until the program contains no more references to that object, and even then there may be a delay until the memory is required. Thus, memory leaks can occur if programmers inadvertently keep references to unwanted objects.

Moving Resource-Release Code to a finally Block

Typically, exceptions occur when processing resources that require explicit release. For example, a program that processes a file might receive IOExceptions during the processing. For this reason, file-processing code normally appears in a try block. Regardless of whether a program experiences exceptions while processing a file, the program should close the file when it is no longer needed. Suppose a program places all resource-request and resource-release code in a try block. If no exceptions occur, the try block executes normally and releases the resources after using them. However, if an exception occurs, the try block may expire before the resource-release code can execute. We could duplicate all the resource-release code in each of the catch blocks, but this would make the code more difficult to modify and maintain. We could also place the resource-release code after the try statement; however, if the try block terminated due to a return statement, code following the try statement would never execute.

To address these problems, C#'s exception-handling mechanism provides the finally block, which is guaranteed to execute regardless of whether the try block executes successfully or an exception occurs. This makes the finally block an ideal location in which to place resource-release code for resources that are acquired and manipulated in the corresponding try block. If the try block executes successfully, the finally block executes immediately after the try block terminates. If an exception occurs in the try block, the finally block executes immediately after a catch block completes. If the exception is not caught by a catch block associated with the try block, or if a catch block associated with the try block throws an exception itself, the finally block executes before the exception is processed by the next enclosing try block, which could be in the calling method. By placing the resource-release code in a finally block, we ensure that even if the program terminates due to an uncaught exception, the resource will be deallocated. Note that local variables in a try block cannot be accessed in the corresponding finally block. For this reason, variables that must be accessed in both a try block, and its corresponding finally block should be declared before the try block.

Error-Prevention Tip 13.3

A finally block typically contains code to release resources acquired in the corresponding try block, which makes the finally block an effective mechanism for eliminating resource leaks.

Performance Tip 13.1

As a rule, resources should be released as soon as they are no longer needed in a program. This makes them available for reuse promptly.

If one or more catch blocks follow a try block, the finally block is optional. However, if no catch blocks follow a try block, a finally block must appear immediately after the try block. If any catch blocks follow a try block, the finally block (if there is one) appears after the last catch block. Only whitespace and comments can separate the blocks in a try statement.

Common Programming Error 13.4

Placing the finally block before a catch block is a syntax error.

Demonstrating the `finally` Block

The application in Fig. 13.4 demonstrates that the `finally` block always executes, regardless of whether an exception occurs in the corresponding try block. The program consists of method Main (lines 8–47) and four other methods that Main invokes to demonstrate finally. These methods are DoesNotThrowException (lines 50–67), ThrowException-WithCatch (lines 70–89), ThrowExceptionWithoutCatch (lines 92–108) and ThrowExceptionCatchRethrow (lines 111–136).

```csharp
1   // Fig. 13.4: UsingExceptions.cs
2   // Using finally blocks.
3   // finally blocks always execute, even when no exception occurs.
4   using System;
5
6   class UsingExceptions
7   {
8      static void Main()
9      {
10         // Case 1: No exceptions occur in called method
11         Console.WriteLine( "Calling DoesNotThrowException" );
12         DoesNotThrowException();
13
14         // Case 2: Exception occurs and is caught in called method
15         Console.WriteLine( "\nCalling ThrowExceptionWithCatch" );
16         ThrowExceptionWithCatch();
17
18         // Case 3: Exception occurs, but is not caught in called method
19         // because there is no catch block.
20         Console.WriteLine( "\nCalling ThrowExceptionWithoutCatch" );
21
22         // call ThrowExceptionWithoutCatch
23         try
24         {
25            ThrowExceptionWithoutCatch();
26         } // end try
27         catch
28         {
29            Console.WriteLine( "Caught exception from " +
30               "ThrowExceptionWithoutCatch in Main" );
31         } // end catch
32
33         // Case 4: Exception occurs and is caught in called method,
34         // then rethrown to caller.
35         Console.WriteLine( "\nCalling ThrowExceptionCatchRethrow" );
36
37         // call ThrowExceptionCatchRethrow
38         try
39         {
40            ThrowExceptionCatchRethrow();
41         } // end try
42         catch
43         {
```

Fig. 13.4 | `finally` blocks always execute, even when no exception occurs. (Part 1 of 4.)

```
44                Console.WriteLine( "Caught exception from " +
45                   "ThrowExceptionCatchRethrow in Main" );
46          } // end catch
47       } // end method Main
48
49       // no exceptions thrown
50       static void DoesNotThrowException()
51       {
52          // try block does not throw any exceptions
53          try
54          {
55             Console.WriteLine( "In DoesNotThrowException" );
56          } // end try
57          catch
58          {
59             Console.WriteLine( "This catch never executes" );
60          } // end catch
61          finally
62          {
63             Console.WriteLine( "finally executed in DoesNotThrowException" );
64          } // end finally
65
66          Console.WriteLine( "End of DoesNotThrowException" );
67       } // end method DoesNotThrowException
68
69       // throws exception and catches it locally
70       static void ThrowExceptionWithCatch()
71       {
72          // try block throws exception
73          try
74          {
75             Console.WriteLine( "In ThrowExceptionWithCatch" );
76             throw new Exception( "Exception in ThrowExceptionWithCatch" );
77          } // end try
78          catch ( Exception exceptionParameter )
79          {
80             Console.WriteLine( "Message: " + exceptionParameter.Message );
81          } // end catch
82          finally
83          {
84             Console.WriteLine(
85                "finally executed in ThrowExceptionWithCatch" );
86          } // end finally
87
88          Console.WriteLine( "End of ThrowExceptionWithCatch" );
89       } // end method ThrowExceptionWithCatch
90
91       // throws exception and does not catch it locally
92       static void ThrowExceptionWithoutCatch()
93       {
94          // throw exception, but do not catch it
95          try
96          {
```

Fig. 13.4 | finally blocks always execute, even when no exception occurs. (Part 2 of 4.)

```
 97            Console.WriteLine( "In ThrowExceptionWithoutCatch" );
 98            throw new Exception( "Exception in ThrowExceptionWithoutCatch" );
 99        } // end try
100        finally
101        {
102            Console.WriteLine( "finally executed in " +
103                "ThrowExceptionWithoutCatch" );
104        } // end finally
105
106        // unreachable code; logic error
107        Console.WriteLine( "End of ThrowExceptionWithoutCatch" );
108    } // end method ThrowExceptionWithoutCatch
109
110    // throws exception, catches it and rethrows it
111    static void ThrowExceptionCatchRethrow()
112    {
113        // try block throws exception
114        try
115        {
116            Console.WriteLine( "In ThrowExceptionCatchRethrow" );
117            throw new Exception( "Exception in ThrowExceptionCatchRethrow" );
118        } // end try
119        catch ( Exception exceptionParameter )
120        {
121            Console.WriteLine( "Message: " + exceptionParameter.Message );
122
123            // rethrow exception for further processing
124            throw;
125
126            // unreachable code; logic error
127        } // end catch
128        finally
129        {
130            Console.WriteLine( "finally executed in " +
131                "ThrowExceptionCatchRethrow" );
132        } // end finally
133
134        // any code placed here is never reached
135        Console.WriteLine( "End of ThrowExceptionCatchRethrow" );
136    } // end method ThrowExceptionCatchRethrow
137 } // end class UsingExceptions
```

```
Calling DoesNotThrowException
In DoesNotThrowException
finally executed in DoesNotThrowException
End of DoesNotThrowException

Calling ThrowExceptionWithCatch
In ThrowExceptionWithCatch
Message: Exception in ThrowExceptionWithCatch
finally executed in ThrowExceptionWithCatch
End of ThrowExceptionWithCatch
```

Fig. 13.4 | `finally` blocks always execute, even when no exception occurs. (Part 3 of 4.)

```
Calling ThrowExceptionWithoutCatch
In ThrowExceptionWithoutCatch
finally executed in ThrowExceptionWithoutCatch
Caught exception from ThrowExceptionWithoutCatch in Main

Calling ThrowExceptionCatchRethrow
In ThrowExceptionCatchRethrow
Message: Exception in ThrowExceptionCatchRethrow
finally executed in ThrowExceptionCatchRethrow
Caught exception from ThrowExceptionCatchRethrow in Main
```

Fig. 13.4 | finally blocks always execute, even when no exception occurs. (Part 4 of 4.)

Line 12 of Main invokes method DoesNotThrowException. This method's try block outputs a message (line 55). Because the try block does not throw any exceptions, program control ignores the catch block (lines 57–60) and executes the finally block (lines 61–64), which outputs a message. At this point, program control continues with the first statement after the close of the finally block (line 66), which outputs a message indicating that the end of the method has been reached. Then, program control returns to Main.

Throwing Exceptions Using the throw Statement

Line 16 of Main invokes method ThrowExceptionWithCatch (lines 70–89), which begins in its try block (lines 73–77) by outputting a message. Next, the try block creates an Exception object and uses a ***throw statement*** to throw it (line 76). Executing the throw statement indicates that a problem has occurred in the code. So far you have only caught exceptions thrown by called methods. You can throw exceptions by using the throw statement. Just as with exceptions thrown by the .NET Framework Class Library's methods and the CLR, this indicates to client applications that an error has occurred. A throw statement specifies an object to be thrown. The operand of a throw statement can be of type Exception or of any type derived from class Exception.

Common Programming Error 13.5

It is a compilation error if the argument of a throw—an exception object—is not of class Exception or one of its derived classes.

The string passed to the constructor becomes the exception object's error message. When a throw statement in a try block executes, the try block expires immediately, and program control continues with the first matching catch block (lines 78–81) following the try block. In this example, the type thrown (Exception) matches the type specified in the catch, so line 80 outputs a message indicating the exception that occurred. Then, the finally block (lines 82–86) executes and outputs a message. At this point, program control continues with the first statement after the close of the finally block (line 88), which outputs a message indicating that the end of the method has been reached. Program control then returns to Main. In line 80, note that we use the exception object's Message property to retrieve the error message associated with the exception (i.e., the message passed to the Exception constructor). Section 13.7 discusses several properties of class Exception.

Lines 23–31 of Main define a try statement in which Main invokes method Throw-ExceptionWithoutCatch (lines 92–108). The try block enables Main to catch any exceptions thrown by ThrowExceptionWithoutCatch. The try block in lines 95–99 of ThrowExceptionWithoutCatch begins by outputting a message. Next, the try block throws an Exception (line 98) and expires immediately.

Normally, program control would continue at the first catch following this try block. However, this try block does not have any catch blocks. Therefore, the exception is not caught in the method ThrowExceptionWithoutCatch. Program control proceeds to the finally block (lines 100–104), which outputs a message. At this point, program control returns to the Main method—any statements appearing after the finally block (e.g., line 107) do not execute. In this example, such statements could cause logic errors, because the exception thrown in line 98 is not caught. In Main, the catch block in lines 27–31 catches the exception and displays a message indicating that the exception was caught in Main.

Rethrowing Exceptions

Lines 38–46 of Main define a try statement in which Main invokes method Throw-ExceptionCatchRethrow (lines 111–136). The try statement enables Main to catch any exceptions thrown by ThrowExceptionCatchRethrow. The try statement in lines 114–132 of ThrowExceptionCatchRethrow begins by outputting a message. Next, the try block throws an Exception (line 117). The try block expires immediately, and program control continues at the first catch (lines 119–127) following the try block. In this example, the type thrown (Exception) matches the type specified in the catch, so line 121 outputs a message indicating where the exception occurred. Line 124 uses the throw statement to *rethrow* the exception. This indicates that the catch block performed partial processing of the exception and now is throwing the exception again (in this case, back to the method Main) for further processing. In general, it is considered better practice to throw a new exception and pass the original one to the new exception's constructor. This maintains all of the stack-trace information from the original exception. Rethrowing an exception loses the original exception's stack-trace information.

You can also rethrow an exception with a version of the throw statement which takes an operand that is the reference to the exception that was caught. It is important to note, however, that this form of throw statement resets the throw point, so the original throw point's stack-trace information is lost. Section 13.7 demonstrates using a throw statement with an operand from a catch block. In that section, you'll see that after an exception is caught, you can create and throw a different type of exception object from the catch block and you can include the original exception as part of the new exception object. Class library designers often do this to customize the exception types thrown from methods in their class libraries or to provide additional debugging information.

The exception handling in method ThrowExceptionCatchRethrow does not complete, because the program cannot run code in the catch block placed after the invocation of the throw statement in line 124. Therefore, method ThrowExceptionCatchRethrow terminates and returns control to Main. Once again, the finally block (lines 128–132) executes and outputs a message before control returns to Main. When control returns to Main, the catch block in lines 42–46 catches the exception and displays a message indicating that the exception was caught. Then the program terminates.

Returning After a *finally* Block

Note that the next statement to execute after a finally block terminates depends on the exception-handling state. If the try block successfully completes, or if a catch block catches and handles an exception, the program continues its execution with the next statement after the finally block. However, if an exception is not caught, or if a catch block rethrows an exception, program control continues in the next enclosing try block. The enclosing try could be in the calling method or in one of its callers. It also is possible to nest a try statement in a try block; in such a case, the outer try statement's catch blocks would process any exceptions that were not caught in the inner try statement. If a try block executes and has a corresponding finally block, the finally block executes even if the try block terminates due to a return statement. The return occurs after the execution of the finally block.

Common Programming Error 13.6

Throwing an exception from a finally block can be dangerous. If an uncaught exception is awaiting processing when the finally block executes, and the finally block throws a new exception that is not caught in the finally block, the first exception is lost, and the new exception is passed to the next enclosing try block.

Error-Prevention Tip 13.4

When placing code that can throw an exception in a finally block, always enclose the code in a try statement that catches the appropriate exception types. This prevents the loss of any uncaught and rethrown exceptions that occur before the finally block executes.

Software Engineering Observation 13.2

Do not place try blocks around every statement that might throw an exception—this can make programs difficult to read. It's better to place one try block around a significant portion of code, and follow this try block with catch blocks that handle each possible exception. Then follow the catch blocks with a single finally block. Separate try blocks should be used when it is important to distinguish between multiple statements that can throw the same exception type.

The *using* Statement

Recall from earlier in this section that resource-release code should be placed in a finally block to ensure that a resource is released, regardless of whether there were exceptions when the resource was used in the corresponding try block. An alternative notation—the *using* statement (not to be confused with the using directive for using namespaces)—simplifies writing code in which you obtain a resource, use the resource in a try block and release the resource in a corresponding finally block. For example, a file-processing application (Chapter 19) could process a file with a using statement to ensure that the file is closed properly when it is no longer needed. The resource must be an object that implements the IDisposable interface and therefore has a Dispose method. The general form of a using statement would be

```
using ( ExampleObject exampleObject = new ExampleObject() )
{
    exampleObject.SomeMethod();
}
```

where ExampleObject is a class that implements the IDisposable interface. This code creates an object of type ExampleObject and uses it in a statement, then calls its Dispose method to release any resources used by the object. The using statement implicitly places the code in its body in a try block with a corresponding finally block that calls the object's Dispose method. For instance, the preceding code is equivalent to

```
{
    ExampleObject exampleObject = new ExampleObject();

    try
    {
        exampleObject.SomeMethod();
    }
    finally
    {
        if ( exampleObject != null )
            ( ( IDisposable ) exampleObject ).Dispose();
    }
}
```

Note that the if statement ensures that exampleObject still references an object; otherwise, a NullReferenceException might occur. You can read more about the using statement in the *C# Language Specification* Section 8.13 (Section 15.13 in the ECMA version).

13.7 Exception Properties

As we discussed in Section 13.5, exception types derive from class Exception, which has several properties. These frequently are used to formulate error messages indicating a caught exception. Two important properties are Message and *StackTrace*. Property Message stores the error message associated with an Exception object. This message can be a default message associated with the exception type or a customized message passed to an Exception object's constructor when the Exception object is thrown. Property Stack-Trace contains a string that represents the *method-call stack*. Recall that the runtime environment at all times keeps a list of open method calls that have been made but have not yet returned. The StackTrace represents the series of methods that have not finished processing at the time the exception occurs.

Error-Prevention Tip 13.5

A stack trace shows the complete method-call stack at the time an exception occurred. This enables the programmer to view the series of method calls that led to the exception. Information in the stack trace includes the names of the methods on the call stack at the time of the exception, the names of the classes in which the methods are defined and the names of the namespaces in which the classes are defined. If the program database (PDB) file that contains the debugging information for the method is accessible to the IDE, the stack trace also includes line numbers; the first line number indicates the throw point, and subsequent line numbers indicate the locations from which the methods in the stack trace were called. PDB files are created by the IDE to maintain the debugging information for your projects.

Property InnerException

Another property used frequently by class-library programmers is *InnerException*. Typically, class library programmers "wrap" exception objects caught in their code so that they then can throw new exception types that are specific to their libraries. For example, a programmer implementing an accounting system might have some account-number processing code in which account numbers are input as strings but represented as ints in the code. Recall that a program can convert strings to int values with Convert.ToInt32, which throws a FormatException when it encounters an invalid number format. When an invalid account-number format occurs, the accounting-system programmer might wish to employ a different error message than the default message supplied by FormatException or might wish to indicate a new exception type, such as InvalidAccountNumberFormat-Exception. In such cases, the programmer would provide code to catch the FormatException, then create an appropriate type of Exception object in the catch block and pass the original exception as one of the constructor arguments. The original exception object becomes the InnerException of the new exception object. When an InvalidAccount-NumberFormatException occurs in code that uses the accounting system library, the catch block that catches the exception can obtain a reference to the original exception via property InnerException. Thus the exception indicates both that the user specified an invalid account number and that the problem was an invalid number format. If the InnerException property is null, this indicates that the exception was not caused by another exception.

Other Exception Properties

Class Exception provides other properties, including **HelpLink**, **Source** and **TargetSite**. Property HelpLink specifies the location of the help file that describes the problem that occurred. This property is null if no such file exists. Property Source specifies the name of the application or object that caused the exception. Property TargetSite specifies the method where the exception originated.

Demonstrating Exception Properties and Stack Unwinding

Our next example (Fig. 13.5) demonstrates properties Message, StackTrace and Inner-Exception of class Exception. In addition, the example introduces *stack unwinding*—when an exception is thrown but not caught in a particular scope, the method-call stack is "unwound," and an attempt is made to catch the exception in the next outer try block. We keep track of the methods on the call stack as we discuss property StackTrace and the stack-unwinding mechanism. To see the proper stack trace, you should execute this program using steps similar to those presented in Section 13.3.

Program execution begins with Main, which becomes the first method on the method-call stack. Line 14 of the try block in Main invokes Method1 (declared in lines 32–35), which becomes the second method on the stack. If Method1 throws an exception, the catch block in lines 16–28 handles the exception and outputs information about the exception that occurred. Line 34 of Method1 invokes Method2 (lines 38–41), which becomes the third method on the stack. Then line 40 of Method2 invokes Method3 (lines 44–57), which becomes the fourth method on the stack.

```
1   // Fig. 13.5: Properties.cs
2   // Stack unwinding and Exception class properties.
3   // Demonstrates using properties Message, StackTrace and InnerException.
4   using System;
5
6   class Properties
7   {
```

Fig. 13.5 | Stack unwinding and Exception class properties. (Part 1 of 3.)

```
 8      static void Main()
 9      {
10          // call Method1; any Exception generated is caught
11          // in the catch block that follows
12          try
13          {
14              Method1();
15          } // end try
16          catch ( Exception exceptionParameter )
17          {
18              // output the string representation of the Exception, then output
19              // properties InnerException, Message and StackTrace
20              Console.WriteLine( "exceptionParameter.ToString: \n{0}\n",
21                  exceptionParameter );
22              Console.WriteLine( "exceptionParameter.Message: \n{0}\n",
23                  exceptionParameter.Message );
24              Console.WriteLine( "exceptionParameter.StackTrace: \n{0}\n",
25                  exceptionParameter.StackTrace );
26              Console.WriteLine( "exceptionParameter.InnerException: \n{0}\n",
27                  exceptionParameter.InnerException );
28          } // end catch
29      } // end method Main
30
31      // calls Method2
32      static void Method1()
33      {
34          Method2();
35      } // end method Method1
36
37      // calls Method3
38      static void Method2()
39      {
40          Method3();
41      } // end method Method2
42
43      // throws an Exception containing an InnerException
44      static void Method3()
45      {
46          // attempt to convert string to int
47          try
48          {
49              Convert.ToInt32( "Not an integer" );
50          } // end try
51          catch ( FormatException formatExceptionParameter )
52          {
53              // wrap FormatException in new Exception
54              throw new Exception( "Exception occurred in Method3",
55                  formatExceptionParameter );
56          } // end catch
57      } // end method Method3
58  } // end class Properties
```

Fig. 13.5 | Stack unwinding and Exception class properties. (Part 2 of 3.)

```
exceptionParameter.ToString:
System.Exception: Exception occurred in Method3 --->
   System.FormatException: Input string was not in a correct format.
   at System.Number.StringToNumber(String str, NumberStyles options,
      NumberBuffer& number, NumberFormatInfo info, Boolean parseDecimal)
   at System.Number.ParseInt32(String s, NumberStyles style,
      NumberFormatInfo info)
   at System.Convert.ToInt32(String value)
   at Properties.Method3() in C:\examples\ch13\Fig13_05\Properties\
      Properties\Properties.cs:line 49
   --- End of inner exception stack trace ---
   at Properties.Method3() in C:\examples\ch13\Fig13_05\Properties\
      Properties\Properties.cs:line 54
   at Properties.Method2() in C:\examples\ch13\Fig13_05\Properties\
      Properties\Properties.cs:line 40
   at Properties.Method1() in C:\examples\ch13\Fig13_05\Properties\
      Properties\Properties.cs:line 34
   at Properties.Main() in C:\examples\ch13\Fig13_05\Properties\
      Properties\Properties.cs:line 14

exceptionParameter.Message:
Exception occurred in Method3

exceptionParameter.StackTrace:
   at Properties.Method3() in C:\examples\ch13\Fig13_05\Properties\
      Properties\Properties.cs:line 54
   at Properties.Method2() in C:\examples\ch13\Fig13_05\Properties\
      Properties\Properties.cs:line 40
   at Properties.Method1() in C:\examples\ch13\Fig13_05\Properties\
      Properties\Properties.cs:line 34
   at Properties.Main() in C:\examples\ch13\Fig13_05\Properties\
      Properties\Properties.cs:line 14

exceptionParameter.InnerException:
System.FormatException: Input string was not in a correct format.
   at System.Number.StringToNumber(String str, NumberStyles options,
      NumberBuffer& number, NumberFormatInfo info, Boolean parseDecimal)
   at System.Number.ParseInt32(String s, NumberStyles style,
      NumberFormatInfo info)
   at System.Convert.ToInt32(String value)
   at Properties.Method3() in C:\examples\ch13\Fig13_05\Properties\
      Properties\Properties.cs:line 49
```

Fig. 13.5 | Stack unwinding and Exception class properties. (Part 3 of 3.)

At this point, the method-call stack (from top to bottom) for the program is:

```
Method3
Method2
Method1
Main
```

The method called most recently (Method3) appears at the top of the stack; the first method called (Main) appears at the bottom. The try statement (lines 47–56) in Method3 invokes method Convert.ToInt32 (line 49), which attempts to convert a string to an int. At this point, Convert.ToInt32 becomes the fifth and final method on the call stack.

Throwing an Exception with an InnerException

Because the argument to Convert.ToInt32 is not in int format, line 49 throws a Format-Exception that is caught in line 51 of Method3. The exception terminates the call to Convert.ToInt32, so the method is removed (or unwound) from the method-call stack. The catch block in Method3 then creates and throws an Exception object. The first argument to the Exception constructor is the custom error message for our example, "Exception occurred in Method3." The second argument is the InnerException—the Format-Exception that was caught. The StackTrace for this new exception object reflects the point at which the exception was thrown (lines 54–55). Now Method3 terminates, because the exception thrown in the catch block is not caught in the method body. Thus, control returns to the statement that invoked Method3 in the prior method in the call stack (Method2). This removes, or *unwinds,* Method3 from the method-call stack.

When control returns to line 40 in Method2, the CLR determines that line 40 is not in a try block. Therefore the exception cannot be caught in Method2, and Method2 terminates. This unwinds Method2 from the call stack and returns control to line 34 in Method1.

Here again, line 34 is not in a try block, so Method1 cannot catch the exception. The method terminates and is unwound from the call stack, returning control to line 14 in Main, which *is* located in a try block. The try block in Main expires and the catch block (lines 16–28) catches the exception. The catch block uses properties Message, Stack-Trace and InnerException to create the output. Note that stack unwinding continues until a catch block catches the exception or the program terminates.

Displaying Information About the Exception

The first block of output (which we reformatted for readability) in Fig. 13.5 contains the exception's string representation, which is returned from an implicit call to method To-String. The string begins with the name of the exception class followed by the Message property value. The next four items present the stack trace of the InnerException object. The remainder of the block of output shows the StackTrace for the exception thrown in Method3. Note that the StackTrace represents the state of the method-call stack at the throw point of the exception, rather than at the point where the exception eventually is caught. Each StackTrace line that begins with "at" represents a method on the call stack. These lines indicate the method in which the exception occurred, the file in which the method resides and the line number of the throw point in the file. Note that the inner-exception information includes the inner-exception stack trace.

Error-Prevention Tip 13.6

When catching and rethrowing an exception, provide additional debugging information in the rethrown exception. To do so, create an Exception object containing more specific debugging information, then pass the original caught exception to the new exception object's constructor to initialize the InnerException property.

The next block of output (two lines) simply displays the Message property's value (Exception occurred in Method3) of the exception thrown in Method3.

The third block of output displays the StackTrace property of the exception thrown in Method3. Note that this StackTrace property contains the stack trace starting from line 54 in Method3, because that is the point at which the Exception object was created and thrown. The stack trace always begins from the exception's throw point.

Finally, the last block of output displays the `string` representation of the `Inner-Exception` property, which includes the namespace and class name of the exception object, as well as its `Message` and `StackTrace` properties.

13.8 User-Defined Exception Classes

In many cases, you can use existing exception classes from the .NET Framework Class Library to indicate exceptions that occur in your programs. In some cases, however, you might wish to create new exception classes specific to the problems that occur in your programs. *User-defined exception classes* should derive directly or indirectly from class `Exception` of namespace `System`. When you create code that throws exceptions, they should be well documented, so that other developers who use your code will know how to handle them.

Good Programming Practice 13.1

Associating each type of malfunction with an appropriately named exception class improves program clarity.

Software Engineering Observation 13.3

Before creating a user-defined exception class, investigate the existing exceptions in the .NET Framework Class Library to determine whether an appropriate exception type already exists.

Figures 13.6 and 13.7 demonstrate a user-defined exception class. Class `Negative-NumberException` (Fig. 13.6) is a user-defined exception class representing exceptions that occur when a program performs an illegal operation on a negative number, such as attempting to calculate its square root. Note that this class was created only for demonstration purposes. In real-world applications, it would be better to anticipate and handle this frequent error in your code with argument validation rather than with thrown exceptions.

```
1    // Fig. 13.6: NegativeNumberException.cs
2    // NegativeNumberException represents exceptions caused by
3    // illegal operations performed on negative numbers.
4    using System;
5
6    namespace SquareRootTest
7    {
8       class NegativeNumberException : Exception
9       {
10          // default constructor
11          public NegativeNumberException()
12             : base( "Illegal operation for a negative number" )
13          {
14             // empty body
15          } // end default constructor
16
```

Fig. 13.6 | `NegativeNumberException` represents exceptions caused by illegal operations performed on negative numbers. (Part 1 of 2.)

```
17      // constructor for customizing error message
18      public NegativeNumberException( string messageValue )
19         : base( messageValue )
20      {
21         // empty body
22      } // end one-argument constructor
23
24      // constructor for customizing the exception's error
25      // message and specifying the InnerException object
26      public NegativeNumberException( string messageValue,
27         Exception inner )
28         : base( messageValue, inner )
29      {
30         // empty body
31      } // end two-argument constructor
32   } // end class NegativeNumberException
33 } // end namespace SquareRootTest
```

Fig. 13.6 | NegativeNumberException represents exceptions caused by illegal operations performed on negative numbers. (Part 2 of 2.)

According to Microsoft's "Best Practices for Handling Exceptions" (msdn.microsoft.com/en-us/library/seyhszts.aspx), user-defined exceptions should typically extend class Exception, have a class name that ends with "Exception" and define three constructors: a parameterless constructor; a constructor that receives a string argument (the error message); and a constructor that receives a string argument and an Exception argument (the error message and the inner-exception object). Defining these three constructors makes your exception class more flexible, allowing other programmers to easily use and extend it.

NegativeNumberExceptions most frequently occur during arithmetic operations, so it seems logical to derive class NegativeNumberException from class ArithmeticException. However, class ArithmeticException derives from class SystemException—the category of exceptions thrown by the CLR. Per Microsoft's best practices for exception handling, user-defined exception classes should inherit from Exception rather than SystemException. In this case, we could have used the built-in ArgumentException class, which is recommended in the best practices for invalid argument values. We create our own exception type here simply for demonstration purposes.

Class SquareRootForm (Fig. 13.7) demonstrates our user-defined exception class. The application enables the user to input a numeric value, then invokes method SquareRoot (lines 17–25) to calculate the square root of that value. To perform this calculation, SquareRoot invokes class Math's Sqrt method, which receives a double value as its argument. Normally, if the argument is negative, method Sqrt returns NaN. In this program, we would like to prevent the user from calculating the square root of a negative number. If the numeric value that the user enters is negative, method SquareRoot throws a NegativeNumberException (lines 21–22). Otherwise, SquareRoot invokes class Math's method Sqrt to compute the square root (line 24).

When the user inputs a value and clicks the **Square Root** button, the program invokes event handler SquareRootButton_Click (lines 28–53). The try statement (lines 33–52) attempts to invoke SquareRoot using the value input by the user. If the user input is not a valid number, a FormatException occurs, and the catch block in lines 40–45 processes the exception. If the user inputs a negative number, method SquareRoot throws a NegativeNumberException (lines 21–22); the catch block in lines 46–52 catches and handles this type of exception.

```csharp
1   // Fig. 13.7: SquareRootTest.cs
2   // Demonstrating a user-defined exception class.
3   using System;
4   using System.Windows.Forms;
5
6   namespace SquareRootTest
7   {
8      public partial class SquareRootForm : Form
9      {
10        public SquareRootForm()
11        {
12           InitializeComponent();
13        } // end constructor
14
15        // computes square root of parameter; throws
16        // NegativeNumberException if parameter is negative
17        public double SquareRoot( double value )
18        {
19           // if negative operand, throw NegativeNumberException
20           if ( value < 0 )
21              throw new NegativeNumberException(
22                 "Square root of negative number not permitted" );
23           else
24              return Math.Sqrt( value ); // compute square root
25        } // end method SquareRoot
26
27        // obtain user input, convert to double, calculate square root
28        private void squareRootButton_Click( object sender, EventArgs e )
29        {
30           outputLabel.Text = ""; // clear OutputLabel
31
32           // catch any NegativeNumberException thrown
33           try
34           {
35              double result =
36                 SquareRoot( Convert.ToDouble( inputTextBox.Text ) );
37
38              outputLabel.Text = result.ToString();
39           } // end try
40           catch ( FormatException formatExceptionParameter )
41           {
42              MessageBox.Show( formatExceptionParameter.Message,
43                 "Invalid Number Format", MessageBoxButtons.OK,
44                 MessageBoxIcon.Error );
45           } // end catch
```

Fig. 13.7 | Demonstrating a user-defined exception class. (Part 1 of 2.)

```
46                   catch ( NegativeNumberException
47                      negativeNumberExceptionParameter )
48                   {
49                      MessageBox.Show( negativeNumberExceptionParameter.Message,
50                         "Invalid Operation", MessageBoxButtons.OK,
51                         MessageBoxIcon.Error );
52                   } // end catch
53               } // end method squareRootButton_Click
54           } // end class SquareRootForm
55       } // end namespace SquareRootTest
```

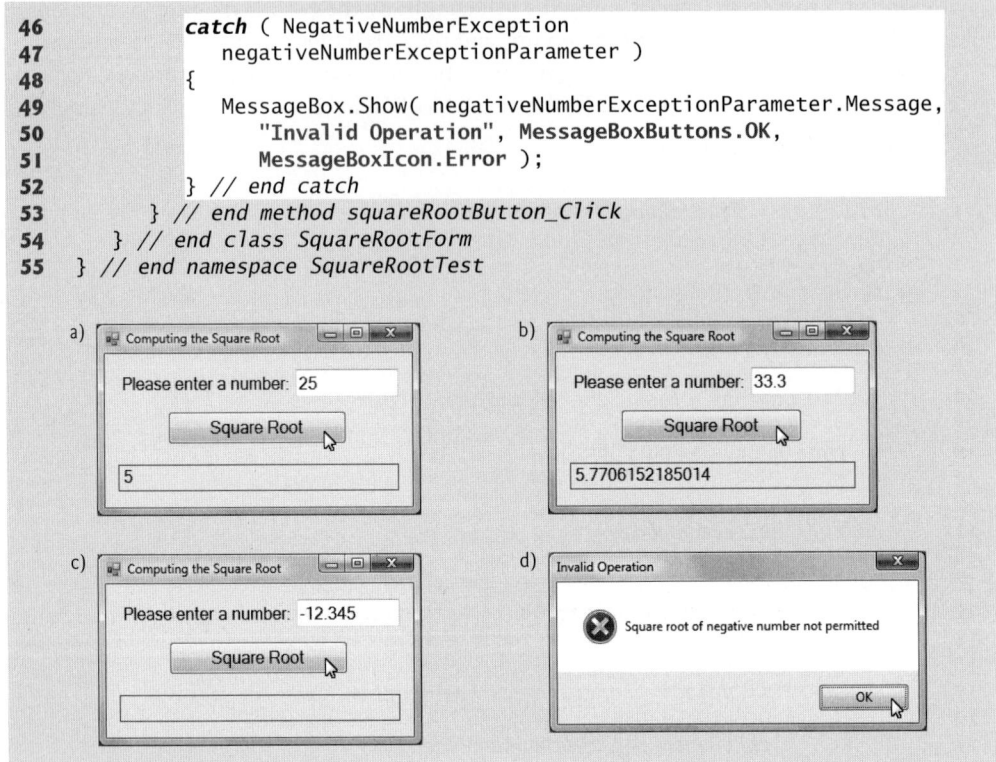

Fig. 13.7 | Demonstrating a user-defined exception class. (Part 2 of 2.)

13.9 Wrap-Up

In this chapter, you learned how to use exception handling to deal with errors in an application. We demonstrated that exception handling enables you to remove error-handling code from the "main line" of the program's execution. You saw exception handling in the context of a divide-by-zero example. You learned how to use `try` blocks to enclose code that may throw an exception, and how to use `catch` blocks to deal with exceptions that may arise. We discussed the termination model of exception handling, in which, after an exception is handled, program control does not return to the throw point. We also discussed several important classes of the .NET `Exception` hierarchy, including `Exception` (from which user-defined exception classes are derived) and `SystemException`. Next you learned how to use the `finally` block to release resources whether or not an exception occurs, and how to throw and rethrow exceptions with the `throw` statement. We also discussed how the `using` statement can be used to automate the process of releasing a resource. You then learned how to obtain information about an exception using `Exception` properties `Message`, `StackTrace` and `InnerException`, and method `ToString`. You learned how to create your own exception classes. In the next two chapters, we present an in-depth treatment of graphical user interfaces. In these chapters and throughout the rest of the book, we use exception handling to make our examples more robust, while still demonstrating new features of the language.

14

Graphical User Interfaces with Windows Forms: Part 1

... the wisest prophets make
sure of the event first.
—Horace Walpole

...The user should feel in
control of the computer; not
the other way around. This
is achieved in applications
that embody three qualities:
responsiveness,
permissiveness, and
consistency.
—*Inside Macintosh, Volume 1*
Apple Computer, Inc. 1985

All the better to see you with
my dear.
—The Big Bad Wolf to Little
Red Riding Hood

OBJECTIVES

In this chapter you'll learn:

■ Design principles of graphical user interfaces (GUIs).

■ How to create graphical user interfaces.

■ How to process events that are generated by user interactions with GUI controls.

■ The namespaces that contain the classes for graphical user interface controls and event handling.

■ How to create and manipulate Button, Label, RadioButton, CheckBox, TextBox, Panel and NumericUpDown controls.

■ How to add descriptive ToolTips to GUI controls.

■ How to process mouse and keyboard events.

Outline

14.1 Introduction
14.2 Windows Forms
14.3 Event Handling
    14.3.1 A Simple Event-Driven GUI
    14.3.2 Another Look at the Visual Studio Generated Code
    14.3.3 Delegates and the Event-Handling Mechanism
    14.3.4 Other Ways to Create Event Handlers
    14.3.5 Locating Event Information
14.4 Control Properties and Layout
14.5 Labels, TextBoxes and Buttons
14.6 GroupBoxes and Panels
14.7 CheckBoxes and RadioButtons
14.8 PictureBoxes
14.9 ToolTips
14.10 NumericUpDown Control
14.11 Mouse-Event Handling
14.12 Keyboard-Event Handling
14.13 Wrap-Up

14.1 Introduction

A graphical user interface (GUI) allows a user to interact visually with a program. A GUI (pronounced "GOO-ee") gives a program a distinctive "look" and "feel." Providing different applications with a consistent set of intuitive user-interface components enables users to become productive with each application faster.

Look-and-Feel Observation 14.1

Consistent user interfaces enable a user to learn new applications more quickly because the applications have the same "look" and "feel."

As an example of a GUI, consider Fig. 14.1, which shows a Visual C# 2008 Express Edition window containing various GUI controls. Near the top of the window, there is a menu bar containing the menus **File**, **Edit**, **View**, **Tools**, **Window**, and **Help**. Below the menu bar is a tool bar of buttons, each with a defined task, such as creating a new project or opening an existing project. Scrollbars are located at the right side and bottom of the **Start Page** section. Usually, scrollbars appear when an object contains more information than can be displayed in its viewable area. Scrollbars enable a user to view different portions of an object's contents, in this case the **Start Page**. In the bottom right corner are two tabs, which present information in a tabbed view and allow users to switch between them. These controls form a user-friendly interface through which you have been interacting with the Visual C# 2008 Express Edition IDE.

GUIs are built from GUI controls (which are sometimes called *components* or *widgets*—short for *window gadgets*). GUI controls are objects that can display information

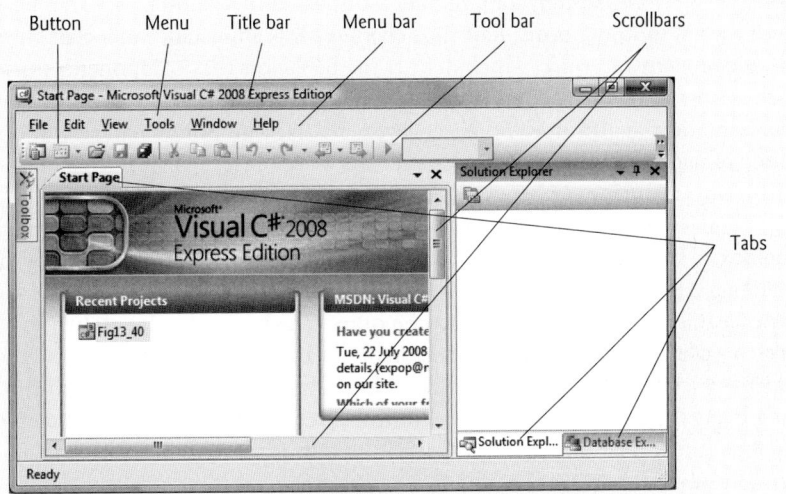

Fig. 14.1 | GUI controls in a Visual C# 2008 Express Edition window.

on the screen or enable users to interact with an application via the mouse, keyboard or some other form of input (such as voice commands). Several common GUI controls are listed in Fig. 14.2—in the sections that follow and in Chapter 15, we discuss each of these in detail. Chapter 15 also explores the features and properties of additional GUI controls.

Control	Description
Label	Displays images or uneditable text.
TextBox	Enables the user to enter data via the keyboard. It can also be used to display editable or uneditable text.
Button	Triggers an event when clicked with the mouse.
CheckBox	Specifies an option that can be selected (checked) or unselected (not checked).
ComboBox	Provides a drop-down list of items from which the user can make a selection either by clicking an item in the list or by typing in a box.
ListBox	Provides a list of items from which the user can make a selection by clicking an item in the list.
Panel	A container in which controls can be placed and organized.
NumericUpDown	Enables the user to select from a range of input values.

Fig. 14.2 | Some basic GUI controls.

14.2 Windows Forms

Windows Forms are used to create the GUIs for programs. A Form is a graphical element that appears on your computer's desktop; it can be a dialog, a window or an *MDI window* (*multiple document interface window*)—discussed in Chapter 15, Graphical User Interfaces with Windows Forms: Part 2. A *component* is an instance of a class that implements the *IComponent interface*, which defines the behaviors that components must implement, such as how the component is loaded. A control, such as a Button or Label, has a graphical representation at runtime. Some components lack graphical representations (e.g., class Timer of namespace System.Windows.Forms—see Chapter 15). Such components are not visible at run time.

Figure 14.3 displays the Windows Forms controls and components from the C# **Toolbox**. The controls and components are organized into categories by functionality. Selecting the category **All Windows Forms** at the top of the **Toolbox** allows you to view all the controls and components from the other tabs in one list (as shown in Fig. 14.3). In this chapter and the next, we discuss many of these controls and components. To add a control or component to a Form, select that control component or from the **Toolbox** and drag it on the Form. To deselect a control or component, select the **Pointer** item in the **Toolbox** (the icon at the top of the list). When the **Pointer** item is selected, you cannot accidentally add a new control to the Form.

When there are several windows on the screen, the *active window* is the frontmost and has a highlighted title bar. A window becomes the active window when the user clicks somewhere inside it. The active window is said to "have the *focus*." For example, in Visual

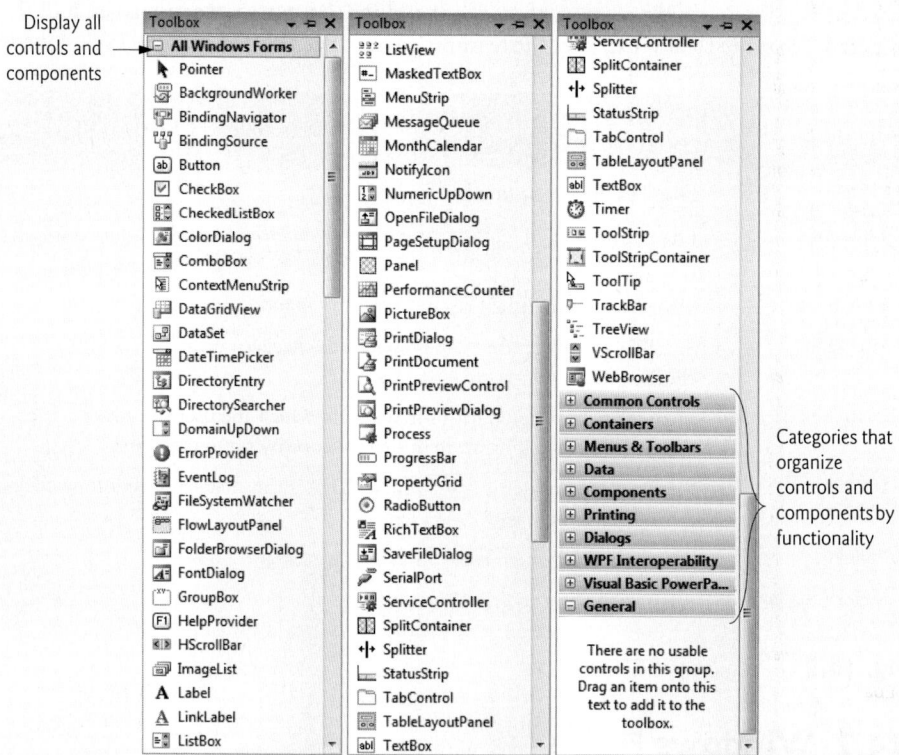

Fig. 14.3 | Components and controls for Windows Forms.

Studio the active window is the **Toolbox** when you are selecting an item from it, or the **Properties** window when you are editing a control's properties.

A Form is a *container* for controls and components. When you drag a control or component from the **Toolbox** on the Form, Visual Studio generates code that instantiates the object and sets its basic properties. This code is updated when the control or component's properties are modified in the IDE. If a control or component is removed from the Form, the generated code for that control is deleted. The generated code is placed by the IDE in a separate file using partial classes—classes that are split. Although we could write this code ourselves, it is much easier to create and modify controls and components using the **Toolbox** and **Properties** windows and allow Visual Studio to handle the details. We introduced visual programming concepts in Chapter 2. In this chapter and the next, we use visual programming to build more substantial GUIs.

Each control or component we present in this chapter is located in namespace System.Windows.Forms. To create a Windows application, you generally create a Windows Form, set its properties, add controls to the Form, set their properties and implement event handlers (methods) that respond to events generated by the controls. Figure 14.4 lists common Form properties, methods and a common event.

Form properties, methods and an event	Description
Common Properties	
AcceptButton	Button that is clicked when *Enter* is pressed.
AutoScroll	bool value that allows or disallows scrollbars when needed.
CancelButton	Button that is clicked when the *Escape* key is pressed.
FormBorderStyle	Border style for the Form (e.g., none, single, three-dimensional).
Font	Font of text displayed on the Form, and the default font for controls added to the Form.
Text	Text in the Form's title bar.
Common Methods	
Close	Closes a Form and releases all resources, such as the memory used for the Form's controls and components. A closed Form cannot be reopened.
Hide	Hides a Form, but does not destroy the Form or release its resources.
Show	Displays a hidden Form.
Common Event	
Load	Occurs before a Form is displayed to the user. The handler for this event is displayed in the Visual Studio editor when you double click the Form in the Visual Studio designer.

Fig. 14.4 | Common Form properties, methods and an event.

When we create controls and event handlers, Visual Studio generates much of the GUI-related code. In visual programming, the IDE maintains GUI-related code and you write the bodies of the event handlers to indicate what actions the program should take when particular events occur.

14.3 Event Handling

Normally, a user interacts with an application's GUI to indicate the tasks that the application should perform. For example, when you write an e-mail in an e-mail application, clicking the **Send** button tells the application to send the e-mail to the specified e-mail addresses. GUIs are *event driven*. When the user interacts with a GUI component, the interaction—known as an *event*—drives the program to perform a task. Common events (user interactions) that might cause an application to perform a task include clicking a Button, typing in a TextBox, selecting an item from a menu, closing a window and moving the mouse. All GUI controls have events associated with them. Objects of other types can also have associated events as well. A method that performs a task in response to an event is called an *event handler*, and the overall process of responding to events is known as *event handling*.

14.3.1 A Simple Event-Driven GUI

The Form in the application of Fig. 14.5 contains a Button that a user can click to display a MessageBox. You have already created several GUI examples that execute an event handler in response to clicking a Button. In this example, we discuss Visual Studio's auto-generated code in more depth.

```
1   // Fig. 14.5: SimpleEventExampleForm.cs
2   // Using Visual Studio to create event handlers.
3   using System;
4   using System.Windows.Forms;
5
6   namespace SimpleEventExample
7   {
8      // Form that shows a simple event handler
9      public partial class SimpleEventExampleForm : Form
10     {
11        // default constructor
12        public SimpleEventExampleForm()
13        {
14           InitializeComponent();
15        } // end constructor
16
17        // handles click event of Button clickButton
18        private void clickButton_Click( object sender, EventArgs e )
19        {
20           MessageBox.Show( "Button was clicked." );
21        } // end method clickButton_Click
22     } // end class SimpleEventExampleForm
23  } // end namespace SimpleEventExample
```

Fig. 14.5 | Simple event-handling example using visual programming. (Part 1 of 2.)

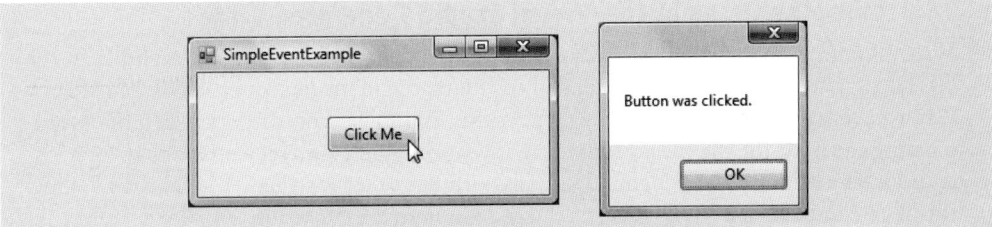

Fig. 14.5 | Simple event-handling example using visual programming. (Part 2 of 2.)

Using the techniques presented earlier in the book, create a Form containing a Button. First, create a new Windows application and add a Button to the Form. In the **Properties** window for the Button, set the (Name) property to clickButton and the Text property to Click Me. You'll notice that we use a convention in which each variable name we create for a control ends with the control's type. For example, in the variable name clickButton, "Button" is the control's type.

When the user clicks the Button in this example, we want the application to respond by displaying a MessageBox. To do this, you must create an event handler for the Button's Click event. You can create this event handler by double clicking the Button on the Form, which declares the following empty event handler in the program code:

```
private void clickButton_Click( object sender, EventArgs e )
{
} // end method clickButton_Click
```

By convention, C# names the event-handler method as *objectName_eventName* (e.g., clickButton_Click). The clickButton_Click event handler executes when the user clicks the clickButton control.

Each event handler receives two parameters when it is called. The first—an object reference named sender—is a reference to the object that generated the event. The second is a reference to an event arguments object of type EventArgs (or one of its derived classes), which is typically named e. This object contains additional information about the event that occurred. EventArgs is the base class of all classes that represent event information.

Software Engineering Observation 14.1

You should not expect return values from event handlers—event handlers are designed to execute code based on an action and return control to the main program.

Good Programming Practice 14.1

Use the event-handler naming convention controlName_eventName, *so method names are meaningful. Such names tell users what event a method handles for what control. This convention is not required, but it makes your code easier to read, understand, modify and maintain.*

To display a MessageBox in response to the event, insert the statement

```
MessageBox.Show( "Button was clicked." );
```

in the event handler's body. The resulting event handler appears in lines 18–21 of Fig. 14.5. When you execute the application and click the Button, a MessageBox appears displaying the text "Button was clicked".

14.3.2 Another Look at the Visual Studio Generated Code

Visual Studio generates the code that creates and initializes the GUI that you build in the GUI design window. This auto-generated code is placed in the Designer.cs file of the Form (SimpleEventExampleForm.Designer.cs in this example). You can open this file by expanding the node for the file you are currently working in (SimpleEventExampleForm.cs) and double clicking the file name that ends with Designer.cs. Figs. 14.6 and 14.7 show this file's contents. The IDE collapses the code in lines 23–56 of Fig. 14.7 by default.

Now that you have studied classes and objects in detail, this code will be easier to understand. Since this code is created and maintained by Visual Studio, you generally don't need to look at it. In fact, you do not need to understand most of the code shown here to build GUI applications. However, we now take a closer look to help you understand how GUI applications work.

The auto-generated code that defines the GUI is actually part of the Form's class—in this case, SimpleEventExampleForm. Line 3 of Fig. 14.6 uses the partial modifier, which allows this class to be split among multiple files, including the files that contain auto-generated code and those in which you write your own code. Line 58 contains the declaration of the Button control clickButton that we created in **Design** mode. Note that the control is declared as an instance variable of class SimpleEventExampleForm. By default, all variable declarations for controls created through C#'s design window have a private access modifier. The code also includes the Dispose method for releasing resources (lines 14–21) and method InitializeComponent (lines 29–54), which contains the code that creates the Button, then sets some of the Button's and the Form's properties. The property values correspond to the values set in the **Properties** window for each control. Note that Visual Studio adds comments to the code that it generates, as in lines 33–35. Line 41 was generated when we created the event handler for the Button's Click event.

Method InitializeComponent is called when the Form is created, and establishes such properties as the Form title, the Form size, control sizes and text. Visual Studio also uses the code in this method to create the GUI you see in design view. Changing the code in InitializeComponent may prevent Visual Studio from displaying the GUI properly.

```
     SimpleEventExampleForm.Designer.cs                                    ▾ ✕

   ⚙ SimpleEventExample.SimpleEventExampleForm        ▾  ⚙ components           ▾
    1  namespace SimpleEventExample
    2  {
    3      partial class SimpleEventExampleForm
    4      {
    5          /// <summary>
    6          /// Required designer variable.
    7          /// </summary>
    8          private System.ComponentModel.IContainer components = null;
    9
   10          /// <summary>
   11          /// Clean up any resources being used.
   12          /// </summary>
   13          /// <param name="disposing">true if managed resources should be disposed; otherwise,
   14          protected override void Dispose( bool disposing )
   15          {
   16              if ( disposing && ( components != null ) )
   17              {
   18                  components.Dispose();
   19              }
   20              base.Dispose( disposing );
   21          }
   22
```

Fig. 14.6 | First half of the Visual Studio generated code file.

```
SimpleEventExampleForm.Designer.cs                                    ▼ ×
📄 SimpleEventExample.SimpleEventExampleForm        ▼  🔧 components                ▼
23    #region Windows Form Designer generated code
24
25    /// <summary>
26    /// Required method for Designer support - do not modify
27    /// the contents of this method with the code editor.
28    /// </summary>
29    private void InitializeComponent()
30    {
31        this.clickButton = new System.Windows.Forms.Button();
32        this.SuspendLayout();
33        //
34        // clickButton
35        //
36        this.clickButton.Location = new System.Drawing.Point( 98, 32 );
37        this.clickButton.Name = "clickButton";
38        this.clickButton.Size = new System.Drawing.Size( 87, 33 );
39        this.clickButton.TabIndex = 0;
40        this.clickButton.Text = "Click Me";
41        this.clickButton.Click += new System.EventHandler( this.clickButton_Click );
42        //
43        // SimpleEventExampleForm
44        //
45        this.AutoScaleDimensions = new System.Drawing.SizeF( 7F, 15F );
46        this.AutoScaleMode = System.Windows.Forms.AutoScaleMode.Font;
47        this.ClientSize = new System.Drawing.Size( 282, 97 );
48        this.Controls.Add( this.clickButton );
49        this.Font = new System.Drawing.Font( "Segoe UI", 9F, System.Drawing.FontStyle.Regu
50        this.Name = "SimpleEventExampleForm";
51        this.Text = "Simple Event Example";
52        this.ResumeLayout( false );
53
54    }
55
56    #endregion
57
58    private System.Windows.Forms.Button clickButton;
59  }
60 }
```

Fig. 14.7 | Second half of the Visual Studio generated code file.

Error-Prevention Tip 14.1

*The code generated by building a GUI in **Design** mode is not meant to be modified directly, and doing so can result in an application that functions incorrectly. You should modify control properties through the **Properties** window.*

14.3.3 Delegates and the Event-Handling Mechanism

The control that generates an event is known as the ***event sender***. An event-handling method—known as the ***event receiver***—responds to a particular event that a control generates. When the event occurs, the event sender calls its event receiver to perform a task (i.e., to "handle the event").

The .NET event-handling mechanism allows you to choose your own names for event-handling methods. However, each event-handling method must declare the proper parameters to receive information about the event that it handles. Since you can choose your own method names, an event sender such as a Button cannot know in advance which method will respond to its events. So, we need a mechanism to indicate which method is the event receiver for an event.

Delegates

Event handlers are connected to a control's events via special objects called ***delegates***. A delegate object holds a reference to a method with a signature that is specified by the delegate type's declaration. GUI controls have predefined delegates that correspond to every event they can generate. For example, the delegate for a Button's Click event is of type EventHandler (namespace System). If you look at this type in the online help documentation, you'll see that it is declared as follows:

```
public delegate void EventHandler( object sender, EventArgs e );
```

This uses the *delegate* keyword to declare a delegate type named EventHandler, which can hold references to methods that return void and receive two parameters—one of type object (the event sender) and one of type EventArgs. If you compare the delegate declaration with clickButton_Click's header (Fig. 14.5, line 18), you'll see that this event handler indeed meets the requirements of the EventHandler delegate. Note that the preceding declaration actually creates an entire class for you. The details of this special class's declaration are handled by the compiler.

Indicating the Method that a Delegate Should Call
An event sender calls a delegate object like a method. Since each event handler is declared as a delegate, the event sender can simply call the appropriate delegate when an event occurs—a Button calls its EventHandler delegate in response to a click. The delegate's job is to invoke the appropriate method. To enable the clickButton_Click method to be called, Visual Studio assigns clickButton_Click to the delegate, as shown in line 41 of Fig. 14.7. This code is added by Visual Studio when you double click the Button control in **Design** mode. The expression

```
new System.EventHandler(this.clickButton_Click);
```

creates an EventHandler delegate object and initializes it with the clickButton_Click method. Line 41 uses the += operator to add the delegate to the Button's Click event. This indicates that clickButton_Click will respond when a user clicks the Button. Note that the += operator is overloaded by the delegate class that is created by the compiler.

You can actually specify that several different methods should be invoked in response to an event by adding other delegates to the Button's Click event with statements similar to line 41 of Fig. 14.7. Event delegates are *multicast*—they represent a set of delegate objects that all have the same signature. Multicast delegates enable several methods to be called in response to a single event. When an event occurs, the event sender calls every method referenced by the multicast delegate. This is known as *event multicasting*. Event delegates derive from class *MulticastDelegate*, which derives from class *Delegate* (both from namespace System).

14.3.4 Other Ways to Create Event Handlers
In all the GUI applications you have created so far, you double clicked a control on the Form to create an event handler for that control. This technique creates an event handler for a control's *default event*—the event that is most frequently used with that control. Typically, controls can generate many different types of events, and each type can have its own event handler. For instance, you already created Click event handlers for Buttons by double clicking a Button in design view (Click is the default event for a Button). However, your application can also provide an event handler for a Button's MouseHover event,

which occurs when the mouse pointer remains positioned over the Button. We now discuss how to create an event handler for an event that is not a control's default event.

Using the Properties *Window to Create Event Handlers*

You can create additional event handlers through the **Properties** window. If you select a control on the **Form**, then click the **Events** icon (the lightning bolt icon in Fig. 14.8) in the **Properties** window, all the events for that control are listed in the window. You can double click an event's name to display the event handler in the editor, if the event handler already exists, or to create the event handler. You can also select an event, then use the drop-down list to its right to choose an existing method that should be used as the event handler for that event. The methods that appear in this drop-down list are the class's methods that have the proper signature to be an event handler for the selected event. You can return to viewing the properties of a control by selecting the **Properties** icon (Fig. 14.8).

A single method can handle multiple events from multiple controls. For example, the Click events of three Buttons could all be handled by the same method. You can specify an event handler for multiple events by selecting multiple controls and selecting a single method in the Properties window. If you create a new event handler this way, you should rename it appropriately. You could also select each control individually and specify the same method for each one's event.

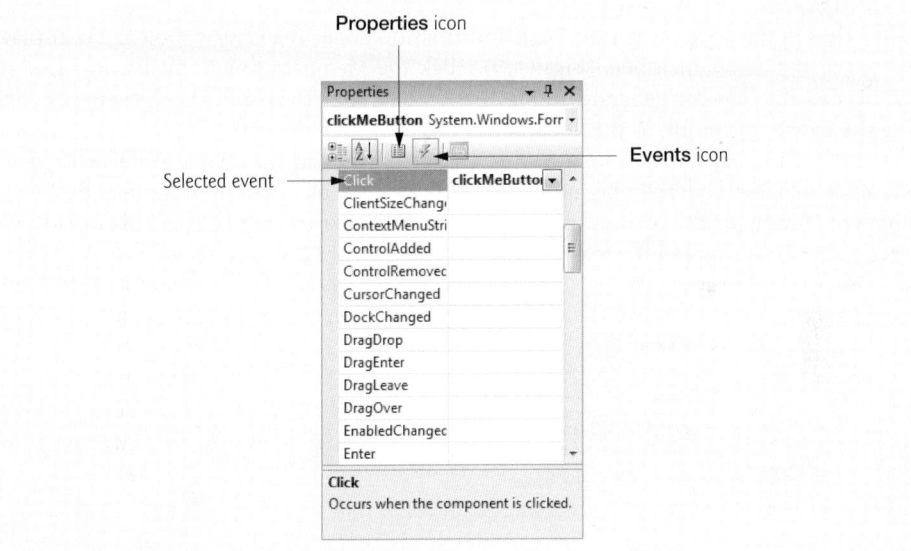

Fig. 14.8 | Viewing events for a Button control in the **Properties** window.

14.3.5 Locating Event Information

Read the Visual Studio documentation to learn about the different events raised by a control. To do this, select **Help > Index**. In the window that appears, select **.NET Framework** in the **Filtered by** drop-down list and enter the name of the control's class in the **Index** window. To ensure that you are selecting the proper class, enter the fully qualified class name as shown in Fig. 14.9 for class System.Windows.Forms.Button. Once you select a con-

Class name   List of events

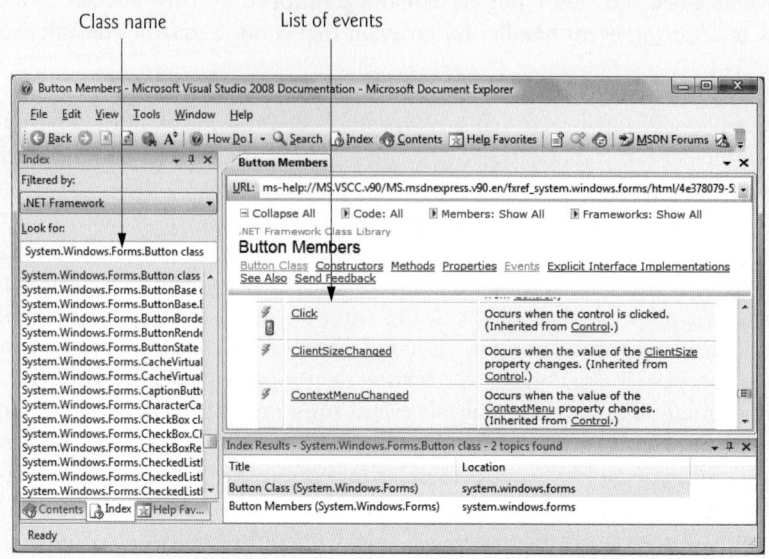

Fig. 14.9 | List of Button events.

trol's class in the documentation, basic information about the class is shown. To display a list of all the class's members (Fig. 14.9), click the **Members** link. This list includes the events that the class can generate. In Fig. 14.9, we scrolled to class Button's events by clicking the **Events** hyperlink in the document's header. Click the name of an event to view its description and examples of its use (Fig. 14.10). Note that the Click event is listed as a member of class Control, because class Button's Click event is inherited from class Control. Alternatively, you could use the **Object Browser** to look up this information. See Section 10.16 for more information regarding the **Object Browser**.

Event name
Event type
Event argument
class

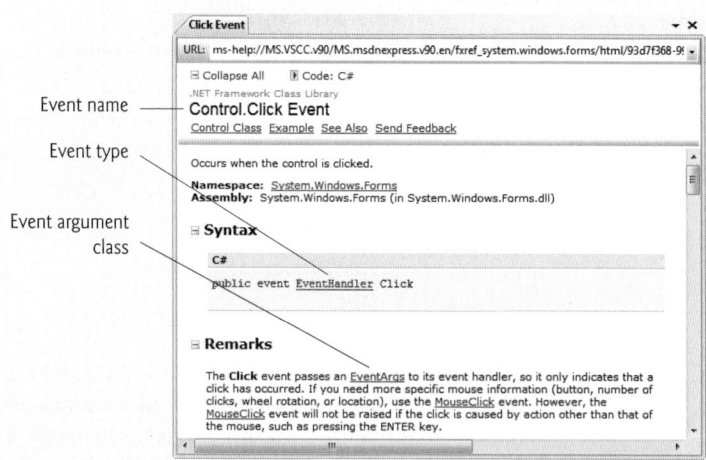

Fig. 14.10 | Click event details.

14.4 Control Properties and Layout

This section overviews properties that are common to many controls. Controls derive from class *Control* (namespace System.Windows.Forms). Figure 14.11 lists some of class Control's properties and methods. The properties shown here can be set for many controls. For example, the Text property specifies the text that appears on a control. The location of this text varies depending on the control. In a Form, the text appears in the title bar, but the text of a Button appears on its face.

The *Select* method transfers the focus to a control and makes it the *active control*. When you press the *Tab* key in an executing Windows application, controls receive the focus in the order specified by their *TabIndex* property. This property is set by Visual Studio based on the order in which controls are added to a Form, but you can change the tabbing order. TabIndex is helpful for users who enter information in many controls, such as a set of TextBoxes that represent a user's name, address and telephone number. The user can enter information, then quickly select the next control by pressing the *Tab* key.

Class Control properties and methods	Description
Common Properties	
BackColor	The control's background color.
BackgroundImage	The control's background image.
Enabled	Specifies whether the control is enabled (i.e., if the user can interact with it). Typically, portions of a disabled control appear "grayed out" as a visual indication to the user that the control is disabled.
Focused	Indicates whether the control has the focus.
Font	The Font used to display the control's text.
ForeColor	The control's foreground color. This usually determines the color of the text in the Text property.
TabIndex	The tab order of the control. When the *Tab* key is pressed, the focus transfers between controls based on the tab order. You can set this order.
TabStop	If true, then a user can give focus to this control via the *Tab* key.
Text	The text associated with the control. The location and appearance of the text vary depending on the type of control.
Visible	Indicates whether the control is visible.
Common Methods	
Hide	Hides the control (sets the Visible property to false).
Select	Acquires the focus.
Show	Shows the control (sets the Visible property to true).

Fig. 14.11 | Class Control properties and methods.

The ***Enabled*** property indicates whether the user can interact with a control to generate an event. Often, if a control is disabled, it is because an option is unavailable to the user at that time. For example, text editor applications often disable the "paste" command until the user copies some text. In most cases, a disabled control's text appears in gray (rather than in black). You can also hide a control from the user without disabling the control by setting the Visible property to false or by calling method Hide. In each case, the control still exists but is not visible on the Form.

You can use anchoring and docking to specify the layout of controls inside a container (such as a Form). *Anchoring* causes controls to remain at a fixed distance from the sides of the container even when the container is resized. Anchoring enhances the user experience. For example, if the user expects a control to appear in a particular corner of the application, anchoring ensures that the control will always be in that corner—even if the user resizes the Form. *Docking* attaches a control to a container such that the control stretches across an entire side or fills an entire area. For example, a button docked to the top of a container stretches across the entire top of that container, regardless of the width of the container.

When parent containers are resized, anchored controls are moved (and possibly resized) so that the distance from the sides to which they are anchored does not vary. By default, most controls are anchored to the top-left corner of the Form. To see the effects of anchoring a control, create a simple Windows application that contains two Buttons. Anchor one control to the right and bottom sides by setting the **Anchor** property as shown in Fig. 14.12. Leave the other control unanchored. Execute the application and enlarge the Form. Notice that the Button anchored to the bottom-right corner is always the same distance from the Form's bottom-right corner (Fig. 14.13), but that the other control stays its original distance from the top-left corner of the Form.

Sometimes, it is desirable for a control to span an entire side of the Form, even when the Form is resized. For example, a control such as a status bar typically should remain at the bottom of the Form. Docking allows a control to span an entire side (left, right, top or bottom) of its parent container or to fill the entire container. When the parent control is resized, the docked control resizes as well. In Fig. 14.14, a Button is docked at the top of the Form (spanning the top portion). When the Form is resized, the Button is resized to the Form's new width. Forms have a ***Padding*** property that specifies the distance between the

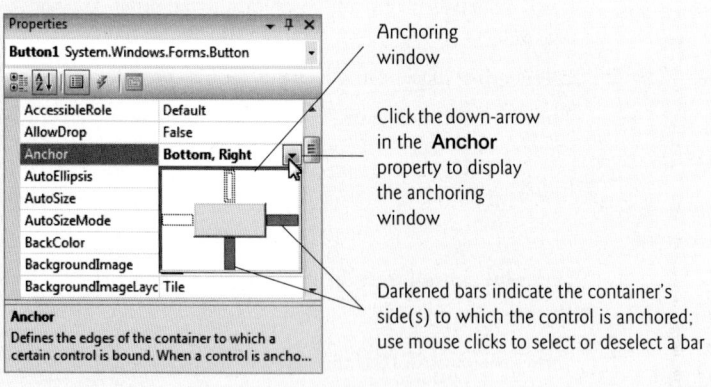

Fig. 14.12 | Manipulating the **Anchor** property of a control.

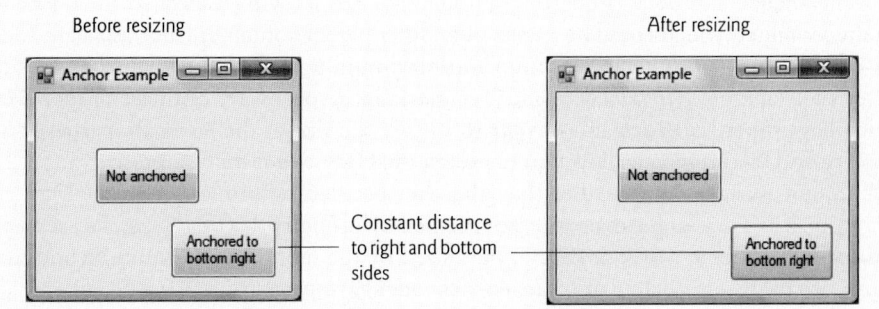

Fig. 14.13 | Anchoring demonstration.

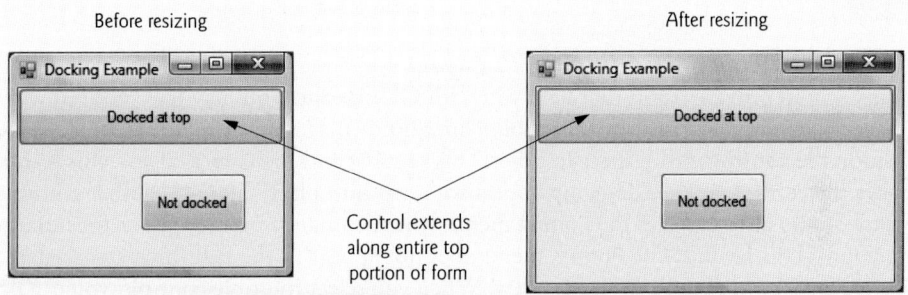

Fig. 14.14 | Docking a `Button` to the top of a `Form`.

docked controls and the `Form` edges. This property specifies four values (one for each side), and each value is set to 0 by default. Some common control layout properties are summarized in Fig. 14.15.

Control layout properties	Description
`Anchor`	Causes a control to remain at a fixed distance from the side(s) of the container even when the container is resized.
`Dock`	Allows a control to span one side of its container or to fill the remaining space in the container.
`Padding`	Sets the space between a container's edges and docked controls. The default is 0, causing the control to appear flush with the container's sides.
`Location`	Specifies the location (as a set of coordinates) of the upper-left corner of the control, in relation to its container.
`Size`	Specifies the size of the control in pixels as a `Size` object, which has properties `Width` and `Height`.
`MinimumSize`, `MaximumSize`	Indicates the minimum and maximum size of a `Control`, respectively.

Fig. 14.15 | `Control` layout properties.

The Anchor and Dock properties of a Control are set with respect to the Control's parent container, which could be a Form or another parent container (such as a Panel; discussed in Section 14.6). The minimum and maximum Form (or other Control) sizes can be set via properties *MinimumSize* and *MaximumSize*, respectively. Both are of type *Size*, which has properties *Width* and *Height* to specify the size of the Form. Properties MinimumSize and MaximumSize allow you to design the GUI layout for a given size range. The user cannot make a Form smaller than the size specified by property MinimumSize and cannot make a Form larger than the size specified by property MaximumSize. To set a Form to a fixed size (where the Form cannot be resized by the user), set its minimum and maximum size to the same value or set its FormBorderStyle property to FixedSingle.

Look-and-Feel Observation 14.2

For resizable Forms, ensure that the GUI layout appears consistent across various Form sizes.

Using Visual Studio To Edit a GUI's Layout

Visual Studio provides tools that help you with GUI layout. You may have noticed when dragging a control across a Form, that blue lines (known as *snap lines*) appear to help you position the control with respect to others (Fig. 14.16) and the Form's edges. This feature makes the control you are dragging appear to "snap into place" alongside other controls. Visual Studio also provides the **Format** menu, which contains several options for modifying your GUI's layout. The **Format** menu does not appear in the IDE unless you select a control (or set of controls) in design view. When you select multiple controls, you can use the **Format** menu's **Align** submenu to align the controls. The **Format** menu also enables you to modify the amount of space between controls or to center a control on the Form.

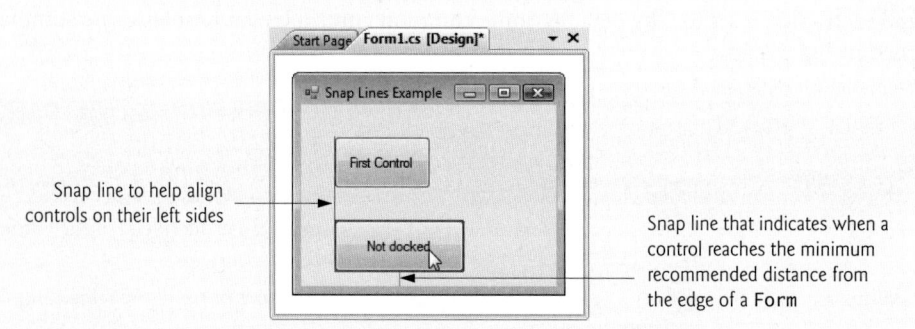

Fig. 14.16 | Snap lines in Visual Studio 2008.

14.5 Labels, TextBoxes and Buttons

Labels provide text information (as well as optional images) and are defined with class Label (a derived class of Control). A Label displays text that the user cannot directly modify. A Label's text can be changed programmatically by modifying the Label's Text property. Figure 14.17 lists common Label properties.

A textbox (class TextBox) is an area in which either text can be displayed by a program or the user can type text via the keyboard. A *password TextBox* is a TextBox that hides the information entered by the user. As the user types characters, the password TextBox masks the user input by displaying a password character. If you set the property ***UseSystemPass-wordChar*** to true, the TextBox becomes a password TextBox. Users often encounter both types of TextBoxes, when logging into a computer or website—the username TextBox allows users to input their usernames; the password TextBox allows users to enter their passwords. Figure 14.18 lists the common properties and a common event of TextBoxes.

Common Label properties	Description
Font	The font of the text on the Label.
Text	The text on the Label.
TextAlign	The alignment of the Label's text on the control—horizontally (left, center or right) and vertically (top, middle or bottom).

Fig. 14.17 | Common Label properties.

TextBox properties and an event	Description
Common Properties	
AcceptsReturn	If true in a multiline TextBox, pressing *Enter* in the TextBox creates a new line. If false, pressing *Enter* is the same as pressing the default Button on the Form. The default Button is the one assigned to a Form's AcceptButton property.
Multiline	If true, the TextBox can span multiple lines. The default value is false.
ReadOnly	If true, the TextBox has a gray background, and its text cannot be edited. The default value is false.
ScrollBars	For multiline textboxes, this property indicates which scrollbars appear (None, Horizontal, Vertical or Both).
Text	The TextBox's text content.
UseSystem-PasswordChar	When this property is set to true, the TextBox becomes a password TextBox, and the system-specified character masks each character the user types.
Common Event	
TextChanged	Generated when the text changes in a TextBox (i.e., when the user adds or deletes characters). When you double click the TextBox control in **Design** mode, an empty event handler for this event is generated.

Fig. 14.18 | TextBox properties and an event.

A button is a control that the user clicks to trigger a specific action or to select an option in a program. As you'll see, a program can use several types of buttons, such as *checkboxes* and *radio buttons*. All the button classes derive from class ***ButtonBase*** (namespace System.Windows.Forms), which defines common button features. In this section, we discuss class Button, which typically enables a user to issue a command to an application. Figure 14.19 lists common properties and a common event of class Button.

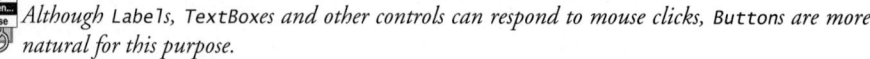

Look-and-Feel Observation 14.3

Although Labels, TextBoxes and other controls can respond to mouse clicks, Buttons are more natural for this purpose.

Figure 14.20 uses a TextBox, a Button and a Label. The user enters text into a password box and clicks the Button, causing the text input to be displayed in the Label. Normally, we would not display this text—the purpose of password TextBoxes is to hide the text being entered by the user. When the user clicks the **Show Me** Button, this application retrieves the text that the user typed in the password TextBox and displays it in a Label.

Button properties and events	Description
Common Properties	
Text	Specifies the text displayed on the Button face.
FlatStyle	Modifies a Button's appearance—attribute Flat (for the Button to display without a three-dimensional appearance), Popup (for the Button to appear flat until the user moves the mouse pointer over the Button), Standard (three-dimensional) and System, where the Button's appearance is controlled by the operating system. The default value is Standard.
Common Event	
Click	Generated when the user clicks the Button. When you double click a Button in design view, an empty event handler for this event is created.

Fig. 14.19 | Button properties and event.

```
1   // Fig. 14.20: LabelTextBoxButtonTestForm.cs
2   // Using a TextBox, Label and Button to display
3   // the hidden text in a password TextBox.
4   using System;
5   using System.Windows.Forms;
6
7   namespace LabelTextBoxButtonTest
8   {
9      // Form that creates a password TextBox and
10     // a Label to display TextBox contents
11     public partial class LabelTextBoxButtonTestForm : Form
12     {
```

Fig. 14.20 | Program to display hidden text in a password box. (Part 1 of 2.)

```
13          // default constructor
14          public LabelTextBoxButtonTestForm()
15          {
16              InitializeComponent();
17          } // end constructor
18
19          // display user input in Label
20          private void displayPasswordButton_Click(
21              object sender, EventArgs e )
22          {
23              // display the text that the user typed
24              displayPasswordLabel.Text = inputPasswordTextBox.Text;
25          } // end method displayPasswordButton_Click
26      } // end class LabelTextBoxButtonTestForm
27  } // end namespace LabelTextBoxButtonTest
```

Fig. 14.20 | Program to display hidden text in a password box. (Part 2 of 2.)

First, create the GUI by dragging the controls (a TextBox, a Button and a Label) on the Form. Once the controls are positioned, change their names in the **Properties** window from the default values—textBox1, button1 and label1—to the more descriptive displayPasswordLabel, displayPasswordButton and inputPasswordTextBox. The (Name) property in the **Properties** window enables us to change the variable name for a control. Visual Studio creates the necessary code and places it in method InitializeComponent of the partial class in the file LabelTextBoxButtonTestForm.Designer.cs.

We then set displayPasswordButton's Text property to "Show Me" and clear the Text of displayPasswordLabel and inputPasswordTextBox so that they are blank when the program begins executing. The BorderStyle property of displayPasswordLabel is set to Fixed3D, giving our Label a three-dimensional appearance. The BorderStyle property of all TextBoxes is set to Fixed3D by default. The password character for inputPasswordTextBox is determined by the user's system settings when you set UseSystemPasswordChar to true. This property accepts only one character.

We create an event handler for displayPasswordButton by double clicking this control in **Design** mode. We add line 24 to the event handler's body. When the user clicks the **Show Me** Button in the executing application, line 24 obtains the text entered by the user in inputPasswordTextBox and displays the text in displayPasswordLabel.

14.6 GroupBoxes and Panels

GroupBoxes and *Panels* arrange controls on a GUI. GroupBoxes and Panels are typically used to group several controls of similar functionality or several controls that are related in a GUI. All of the controls in a GroupBox or Panel move together when the GroupBox or

Panel is moved. Furthermore, a GroupBoxes and Panels can also be used to show or hide a set of controls at once. When you modify a container's Visible property, it toggles the visibility of all the controls within it.

The primary difference between these two controls is that GroupBoxes can display a caption (i.e., text) and do not include scrollbars, whereas Panels can include scrollbars and do not include a caption. GroupBoxes have thin borders by default; Panels can be set so that they also have borders by changing their BorderStyle property. Figures 14.21–14.22 list the common properties of GroupBoxes and Panels, respectively.

Look-and-Feel Observation 14.4

Panels and GroupBoxes can contain other Panels and GroupBoxes for more complex layouts.

Look-and-Feel Observation 14.5

You can organize a GUI by anchoring and docking controls inside a GroupBox or Panel. The GroupBox or Panel then can be anchored or docked inside a Form. This divides controls into functional "groups" that can be arranged easily.

To create a GroupBox, drag its icon from the **Toolbox** onto a Form. Then, drag new controls from the **Toolbox** into the GroupBox. These controls are added to the GroupBox's **Controls** property and become part of the GroupBox. The GroupBox's Text property specifies the caption.

To create a Panel, drag its icon from the **Toolbox** onto the Form. You can then add controls directly to the Panel by dragging them from the **Toolbox** onto the Panel. To enable the scrollbars, set the Panel's AutoScroll property to true. If the Panel is resized and cannot display all of its controls, scrollbars appear (Fig. 14.23). The scrollbars can be used to view all the controls in the Panel—both at design time and at execution time. In Fig. 14.23, we set the Panel's BorderStyle property to FixedSingle so that you can see the Panel in the Form.

GroupBox properties	Description
Controls	The set of controls that the GroupBox contains.
Text	Specifies the caption text displayed at the top of the GroupBox.

Fig. 14.21 | GroupBox properties.

Panel properties	Description
AutoScroll	Indicates whether scrollbars appear when the Panel is too small to display all of its controls. The default value is false.
BorderStyle	Sets the border of the Panel. The default value is None; other options are Fixed3D and FixedSingle.
Controls	The set of controls that the Panel contains.

Fig. 14.22 | Panel properties.

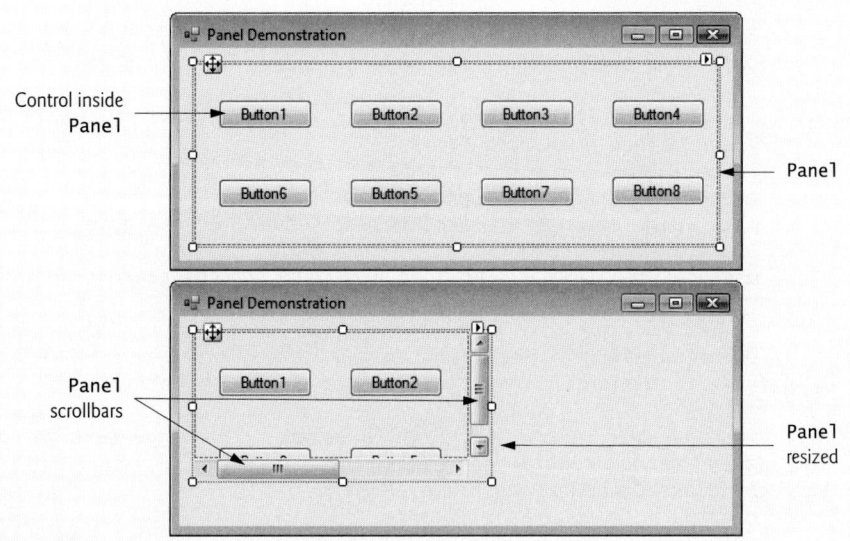

Fig. 14.23 | Creating a Panel with scrollbars.

Look-and-Feel Observation 14.6

Use Panels with scrollbars to avoid cluttering a GUI and to reduce the GUI's size.

The program in Fig. 14.24 uses a GroupBox and a Panel to arrange Buttons. When these Buttons are clicked, their event handlers change the text on a Label.

```
1   // Fig. 14.24: GroupboxPanelExampleForm.cs
2   // Using GroupBoxes and Panels to hold Buttons.
3   using System;
4   using System.Windows.Forms;
5
6   namespace GroupBoxPanelExample
7   {
8      // Form that displays a GroupBox and a Panel
9      public partial class GroupBoxPanelExampleForm : Form
10     {
11        // default constructor
12        public GroupBoxPanelExampleForm()
13        {
14           InitializeComponent();
15        } // end constructor
16
17        // event handler for Hi Button
18        private void hiButton_Click( object sender, EventArgs e )
19        {
20           messageLabel.Text = "Hi pressed"; // change text in Label
21        } // end method hiButton_Click
```

Fig. 14.24 | Using GroupBoxes and Panels to arrange Buttons. (Part 1 of 2.)

```
22
23        // event handler for Bye Button
24        private void byeButton_Click( object sender, EventArgs e )
25        {
26           messageLabel.Text = "Bye pressed"; // change text in Label
27        } // end method byeButton_Click
28
29        // event handler for Far Left Button
30        private void leftButton_Click( object sender, EventArgs e )
31        {
32           messageLabel.Text = "Far left pressed"; // change text in Label
33        } // end method leftButton_Click
34
35        // event handler for Far Right Button
36        private void rightButton_Click( object sender, EventArgs e )
37        {
38           messageLabel.Text = "Far right pressed"; // change text in Label
39        } // end method rightButton_Click
40     } // end class GroupBoxPanelExampleForm
41  } // end namespace GroupBoxPanelExample
```

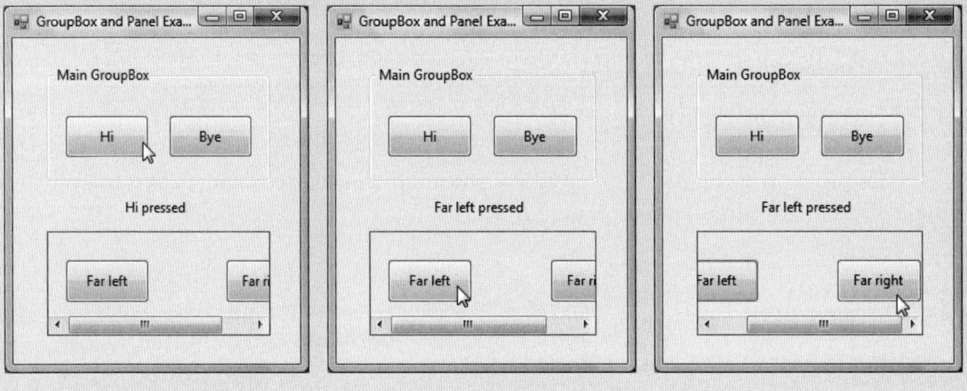

Fig. 14.24 | Using GroupBoxes and Panels to arrange Buttons. (Part 2 of 2.)

The GroupBox (named mainGroupBox) has two Buttons—hiButton (which displays the text **Hi**) and byeButton (which displays the text **Bye**). The Panel (named mainPanel) also has two Buttons, leftButton (which displays the text **Far Left**) and rightButton (which displays the text **Far Right**). The mainPanel has its AutoScroll property set to true, allowing scrollbars to appear when the contents of the Panel require more space than the Panel's visible area. The Label (named messageLabel) is initially blank. To add controls to mainGroupBox or mainPanel, Visual Studio calls method Add of each container's Controls property. This code is placed in the partial class located in the file Group-BoxPanelExampleForm.Designer.cs.

The event handlers for the four Buttons are located in lines 18–39. We added a line in each event handler (lines 20, 26, 32 and 38) to change the text of messageLabel to indicate which Button the user pressed.

14.7 CheckBoxes and RadioButtons

C# has two types of *state buttons* that can be in the on/off or true/false states—***CheckBoxes*** and ***RadioButtons***. Like class Button, classes CheckBox and RadioButton are derived from class ButtonBase.

CheckBoxes

A CheckBox is a small square that either is blank or contains a check mark. When the user clicks a CheckBox to select it, a check mark appears in the box. If the user clicks CheckBox again to deselect it, the check mark is removed. You can also configure a CheckBox to toggle between three states (checked, unchecked and indeterminate) by setting its ***ThreeState*** property to true. Any number of CheckBoxes can be selected at a time. A list of common CheckBox properties and events appears in Fig. 14.25.

The program in Fig. 14.26 allows the user to select CheckBoxes to change a Label's font style. The event handler for one CheckBox applies bold and the event handler for the other applies italic. If both CheckBoxes are selected, the font style is set to bold and italic. Initially, neither CheckBox is checked.

CheckBox properties and events	Description
Common Properties	
Appearance	By default, this property is set to Normal, and the CheckBox displays as a traditional checkbox. If it is set to Button, the CheckBox displays as a Button that looks pressed when the CheckBox is checked.
Checked	Indicates whether the CheckBox is checked (contains a check mark) or unchecked (blank). This property returns a bool value.
CheckState	Indicates whether the CheckBox is checked or unchecked with a value from the CheckState enumeration (Checked, Unchecked or Indeterminate). Indeterminate is used when it is unclear whether the state should be Checked or Unchecked. When CheckState is set to Indeterminate, the CheckBox is usually shaded.
Text	Specifies the text displayed to the right of the CheckBox.
ThreeState	When this property is true, the CheckBox has three states—checked, unchecked and indeterminate. The indeterminate state can only be set programmatically. By default, this property is false and the CheckBox has only two states—checked and unchecked.
Common Events	
CheckedChanged	Generated when the Checked property changes. This is a CheckBox's default event. When a user double clicks the CheckBox control in design view, an empty event handler for this event is generated.
CheckStateChanged	Generated when the CheckState property changes.

Fig. 14.25 | CheckBox properties and events.

```
 1   // Fig. 14.26: CheckBoxTestForm.cs
 2   // Using CheckBoxes to toggle italic and bold styles.
 3   using System;
 4   using System.Drawing;
 5   using System.Windows.Forms;
 6
 7   namespace CheckBoxTest
 8   {
 9      // Form contains CheckBoxes to allow the user to modify sample text
10      public partial class CheckBoxTestForm : Form
11      {
12         // default constructor
13         public CheckBoxTestForm()
14         {
15            InitializeComponent();
16         } // end constructor
17
18         // toggle the font style between bold and
19         // not bold based on the  current setting
20         private void boldCheckBox_CheckedChanged(
21            object sender, EventArgs e )
22         {
23            outputLabel.Font = new Font( outputLabel.Font,
24               outputLabel.Font.Style ^ FontStyle.Bold );
25         } // end metod boldCheckBox_CheckedChanged
26
27         // toggle the font style between italic and
28         // not italic based on the current setting
29         private void italicCheckBox_CheckedChanged(
30            object sender, EventArgs e )
31         {
32            outputLabel.Font = new Font( outputLabel.Font,
33               outputLabel.Font.Style ^ FontStyle.Italic );
34         } // end method italicCheckBox_CheckedChanged
35      } // end class CheckBoxTestForm
36   } // end namespace CheckBoxTest
```

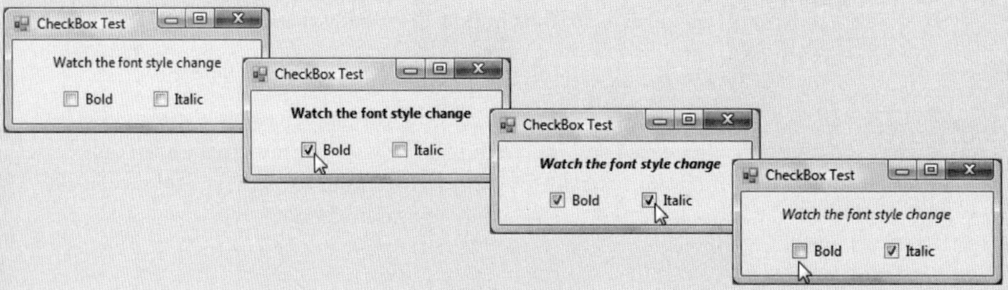

Fig. 14.26 | Using CheckBoxes to change font styles.

The boldCheckBox has its Text property set to Bold. The italicCheckBox has its Text property set to Italic. The Text property of outputLabel is set to Watch the font style change. After creating the controls, we define their event handlers. Double clicking the CheckBoxes at design time creates empty CheckedChanged event handlers.

To change the font style on a Label, you must set its Font property to a new **Font object** (lines 23–24 and 32–33). The Font constructor that we use here takes the current font and new style as arguments. The first two argument—outputLabel.Font—uses out-putLabel's original font name and size. The style is specified with a member of the **Font-Style enumeration**, which contains Regular, Bold, Italic, Strikeout and Underline. (The Strikeout style displays text with a line through it.) A Font object's **Style** property is read-only, so it can be set only when the Font object is created.

Styles can be combined via *bitwise operators*—operators that perform manipulation on bits of information. All data is represented in the computer as combinations of 0s and 1s. Each 0 or 1 represents a bit. FontStyle has a System.FlagsAttribute, meaning that the Font-Style bit values are selected in a way that allows us to combine different FontStyle elements to create compound styles, using bitwise operators. These styles are not mutually exclusive, so we can combine different styles and remove them without affecting the combination of previous FontStyle elements. We can combine these various font styles, using either the logical OR (|) operator or the logical exclusive OR (^) operator. When the logical OR operator is applied to two bits, if at least one bit of the two has the value 1, then the result is 1. Combining styles using the logical OR operator works as follows. Assume that FontStyle.Bold is represented by bits 01 and that FontStyle.Italic is represented by bits 10. When we use the logical OR (|) to combine the styles, we obtain the bits 11.

```
01  =  Bold
10  =  Italic
--
11  =  Bold and Italic
```

The logical OR operator helps create style combinations. However, what happens if we want to undo a style combination, as we did in Fig. 14.26?

The logical exclusive OR operator enables us to combine styles and to undo existing style settings. When logical exclusive OR is applied to two bits, if both bits have the same value, then the result is 0. If both bits are different, then the result is 1.

Combining styles using logical exclusive OR works as follows. Assume, again, that FontStyle.Bold is represented by bits 01 and that FontStyle.Italic is represented by bits 10. When we use logical exclusive OR (^) on both styles, we obtain the bits 11.

```
01  =  Bold
10  =  Italic
--
11  =  Bold and Italic
```

Now, suppose that we would like to remove the FontStyle.Bold style from the previous combination of FontStyle.Bold and FontStyle.Italic. The easiest way to do so is to reapply the logical exclusive OR (^) operator to the compound style and Font-Style.Bold.

```
11  =  Bold and Italic
01  =  Bold
--
10  =  Italic
```

This is a simple example. The advantages of using bitwise operators to combine FontStyle values become more evident when we consider that there are five different FontStyle values (Bold, Italic, Regular, Strikeout and Underline), resulting in 16 different Font-Style combinations. Using bitwise operators to combine font styles greatly reduces the amount of code required to check all possible font combinations.

In Fig. 14.26, we need to set the FontStyle so that the text appears in bold if it was not bold originally, and vice versa. Notice that line 24 uses the bitwise logical exclusive OR operator to do this. If outputLabel.Font.Style is bold, then the resulting style is not bold. If the text is originally italic, the resulting style is bold and italic, rather than just bold. The same applies for FontStyle.Italic in line 33.

If we did not use bitwise operators to compound FontStyle elements, we would have to test for the current style and change it accordingly. For example, in event handler boldCheckBox_CheckChanged, we could test for the regular style and make it bold; test for the bold style and make it regular; test for the italic style and make it bold italic; and test for the italic bold style and make it italic. This is cumbersome because, for every new style we add, we double the number of combinations. Adding a CheckBox for underline would require testing eight additional styles. Adding a CheckBox for strikeout would require testing 16 additional styles.

RadioButtons

Radio buttons (defined with class RadioButton) are similar to CheckBoxes in that they also have two states—*selected* and *not selected* (also called *deselected*). However, RadioButtons normally appear as a *group*, in which only one RadioButton can be selected at a time. Selecting one RadioButton in the group forces all the others to be deselected. Therefore, RadioButtons are used to represent a set of *mutually exclusive* options (i.e., a set in which multiple options cannot be selected at the same time).

Look-and-Feel Observation 14.7

Use RadioButtons when the user should choose only one option in a group.

Look-and-Feel Observation 14.8

Use CheckBoxes when the user should be able to choose multiple options in a group.

All RadioButtons added to a container become part of the same group. To divide RadioButtons into several groups, they must be added to separate containers, such as GroupBoxes or Panels. The common properties and a common event of class RadioButton are listed in Fig. 14.27.

RadioButton properties and an event	Description
Common Properties	
Checked	Indicates whether the RadioButton is checked.
Text	Specifies the RadioButton's text.

Fig. 14.27 | RadioButton properties and an event. (Part I of 2.)

RadioButton properties and an event	Description
Common Event	
CheckedChanged	Generated every time the RadioButton is checked or unchecked. When you double click a RadioButton control in design view, an empty event handler for this event is generated.

Fig. 14.27 | RadioButton properties and an event. (Part 2 of 2.)

Software Engineering Observation 14.2

Forms, GroupBoxes, and Panels can act as logical groups for RadioButtons. The RadioButtons within each group are mutually exclusive to each other, but not to RadioButtons in different logical groups.

The program in Fig. 14.28 uses RadioButtons to enable users to select options for a MessageBox. After selecting the desired attributes, the user presses the **Display** Button to display the MessageBox. A Label in the lower-left corner shows the result of the MessageBox (i.e., which Button the user clicked—**Yes, No, Cancel**, etc.).

To store the user's choices, we create and initialize the iconType and buttonType objects (lines 13–14). Object iconType is of type MessageBoxIcon, and can have values Asterisk, Error, Exclamation, Hand, Information, None, Question, Stop and Warning. The sample output shows only Error, Exclamation, Information and Question icons.

Object buttonType is of type MessageBoxButtons, and can have values AbortRetryIgnore, OK, OKCancel, RetryCancel, YesNo and YesNoCancel. The name indicates the options that are presented to the user in the MessageBox. The sample output windows show MessageBoxes for all of the MessageBoxButtons enumeration values.

```csharp
1   // Fig. 14.28: RadioButtonsTestForm.cs
2   // Using RadioButtons to set message window options.
3   using System;
4   using System.Windows.Forms;
5
6   namespace RadioButtonsTest
7   {
8      // Form contains several RadioButtons--user chooses one
9      // from each group to create a custom MessageBox
10     public partial class RadioButtonsTestForm : Form
11     {
12        // create variables that store the user's choice of options
13        private MessageBoxIcon iconType;
14        private MessageBoxButtons buttonType;
15
16        // default constructor
17        public RadioButtonsTestForm()
18        {
```

Fig. 14.28 | Using RadioButtons to set message-window options. (Part 1 of 4.)

```
19              InitializeComponent();
20        } // end constructor
21
22        // change Buttons based on option chosen by sender
23        private void buttonType_CheckedChanged(
24            object sender, EventArgs e )
25        {
26            if ( sender == okRadioButton ) // display OK Button
27                buttonType = MessageBoxButtons.OK;
28
29            // display OK and Cancel Buttons
30            else if ( sender == okCancelRadioButton )
31                buttonType = MessageBoxButtons.OKCancel;
32
33            // display Abort, Retry and Ignore Buttons
34            else if ( sender == abortRetryIgnoreRadioButton )
35                buttonType = MessageBoxButtons.AbortRetryIgnore;
36
37            // display Yes, No and Cancel Buttons
38            else if ( sender == yesNoCancelRadioButton )
39                buttonType = MessageBoxButtons.YesNoCancel;
40
41            // display Yes and No Buttons
42            else if ( sender == yesNoRadioButton )
43                buttonType = MessageBoxButtons.YesNo;
44
45            // only on option left--display Retry and Cancel Buttons
46            else
47                buttonType = MessageBoxButtons.RetryCancel;
48        } // end method buttonType_Changed
49
50        // change Icon based on option chosen by sender
51        private void iconType_CheckedChanged( object sender, EventArgs e )
52        {
53            if ( sender == asteriskRadioButton ) // display asterisk Icon
54                iconType = MessageBoxIcon.Asterisk;
55
56            // display error Icon
57            else if ( sender == errorRadioButton )
58                iconType = MessageBoxIcon.Error;
59
60            // display exclamation point Icon
61            else if ( sender == exclamationRadioButton )
62                iconType = MessageBoxIcon.Exclamation;
63
64            // display hand Icon
65            else if ( sender == handRadioButton )
66                iconType = MessageBoxIcon.Hand;
67
68            // display information Icon
69            else if ( sender == informationRadioButton )
70                iconType = MessageBoxIcon.Information;
```

Fig. 14.28 | Using RadioButtons to set message-window options. (Part 2 of 4.)

```
71
72              // display question mark Icon
73              else if ( sender == questionRadioButton )
74                  iconType = MessageBoxIcon.Question;
75
76              // display stop Icon
77              else if ( sender == stopRAdioButton )
78                  iconType = MessageBoxIcon.Stop;
79
80              // only one option left--display warning Icon
81              else
82                  iconType = MessageBoxIcon.Warning;
83          } // end method iconType_CheckChanged
84
85          // display MessageBox and Button user pressed
86          private void displayButton_Click( object sender, EventArgs e )
87          {
88              // display MessageBox and store
89              // the value of the Button that was pressed
90              DialogResult result = MessageBox.Show(
91                  "This is your Custom MessageBox.", "Custon MessageBox",
92                  buttonType, iconType, 0, 0 );
93
94              // check to see which Button was pressed in the MessageBox
95              // change text displayed accordingly
96              switch (result)
97              {
98                  case DialogResult.OK:
99                      displayLabel.Text = "OK was pressed.";
100                     break;
101                 case DialogResult.Cancel:
102                     displayLabel.Text = "Cancel was pressed.";
103                     break;
104                 case DialogResult.Abort:
105                     displayLabel.Text = "Abort was pressed.";
106                     break;
107                 case DialogResult.Retry:
108                     displayLabel.Text = "Retry was pressed.";
109                     break;
110                 case DialogResult.Ignore:
111                     displayLabel.Text = "Ignore was pressed.";
112                     break;
113                 case DialogResult.Yes:
114                     displayLabel.Text = "Yes was pressed.";
115                     break;
116                 case DialogResult.No:
117                     displayLabel.Text = "No was pressed.";
118                     break;
119             } // end switch
120         } // end method displayButton_Click
121     } // end class RadioButtonsTestForm
122 } // end namespace RadioButtonsTest
```

Fig. 14.28 | Using RadioButtons to set message-window options. (Part 3 of 4.)

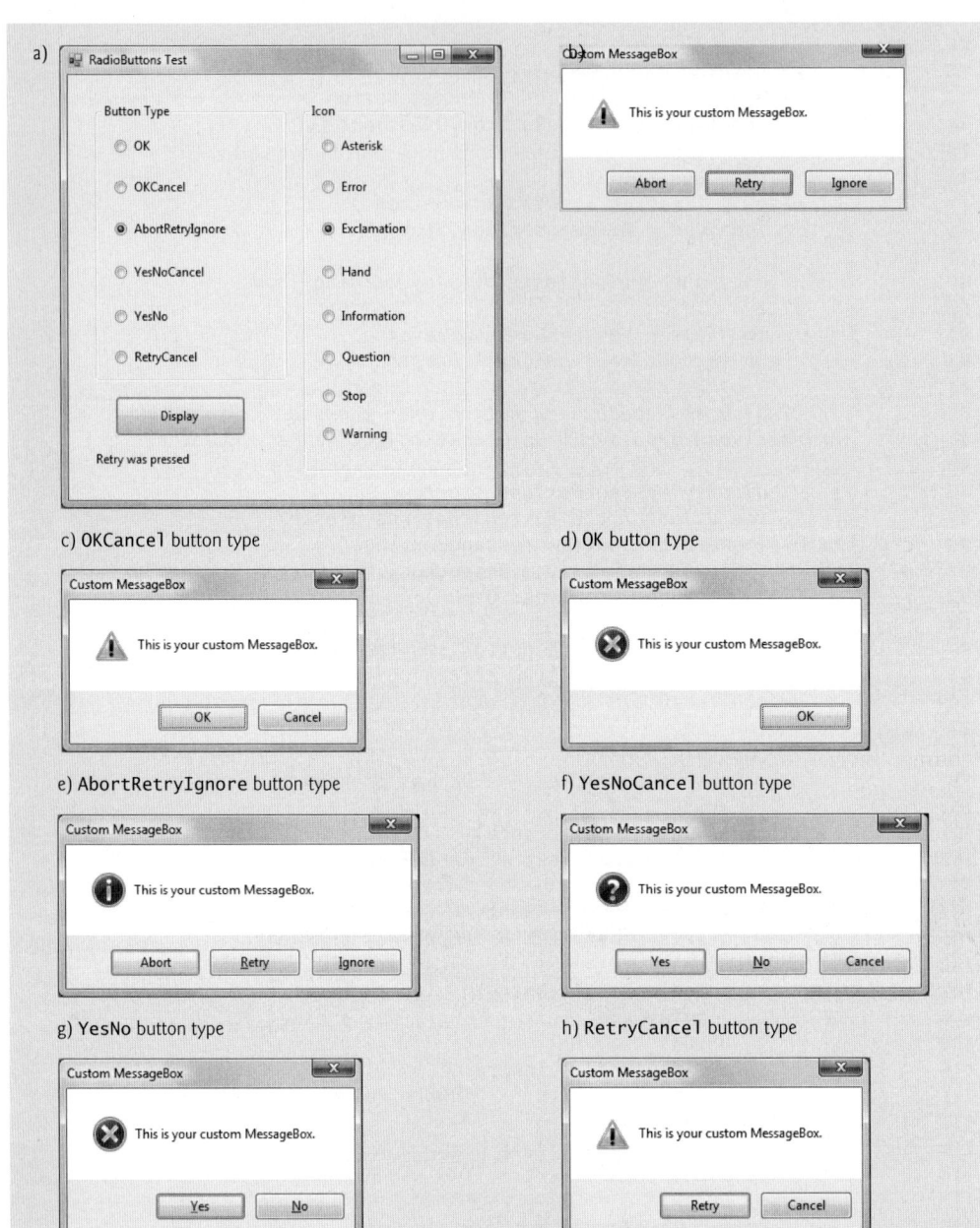

Fig. 14.28 | Using RadioButtons to set message-window options. (Part 4 of 4.)

We created two GroupBoxes, one for each set of enumeration values. The GroupBox captions are **Button Type** and **Icon**. The GroupBoxes contain RadioButtons for the corresponding enumeration options, and the RadioButtons' Text properties are set appropriately. Because the RadioButtons are grouped, only one RadioButton can be selected from each GroupBox. There is also a Button (displayButton) labeled **Display**. When a user clicks this `Button`, a customized `MessageBox` is displayed. A `Label` (`displayLabel`) displays which `Button` the user pressed within the `MessageBox`.

The event handler for the `RadioButtons` handles the `CheckedChanged` event of each `RadioButton`. When a `RadioButton` contained in the **Button Type** `GroupBox` is checked, the checked `RadioButton`'s corresponding event handler sets `buttonType` to the appropriate value. Lines 23–48 contain the event handling for these `RadioButtons`. Similarly, when the user checks the `RadioButtons` belonging to the **Icon** `GroupBox`, the event handlers associated with these events (lines 51–83) set `iconType` to its corresponding value.

The `Click` event handler for `displayButton` (lines 86–120) creates a `MessageBox` (lines 90–93). The `MessageBox` options are specified with the values stored in `iconType` and `buttonType`. When the user clicks one of the `MessageBox`'s buttons, the result of the message box is returned to the application. This result is a value from the ***DialogResult enumeration*** that contains `Abort`, `Cancel`, `Ignore`, `No`, `None`, `OK`, `Retry` or `Yes`. The `switch` statement in lines 96–119 tests for the result and sets `displayLabel.Text` appropriately.

14.8 PictureBoxes

A `PictureBox` displays an image. The image can be one of several formats, such as bitmap, GIF (Graphics Interchange Format) and JPEG. (Images are discussed in Chapter 17, WPF Graphics and Multimedia.) A `PictureBox`'s `Image` property specifies the image that is displayed, and the `SizeMode` property indicates how the image is displayed (`Normal`, `StretchImage`, `Autosize`, `CenterImage` or `Zoom`). Figure 14.29 describes common `PictureBox` properties and a common event.

Figure 14.30 uses a `PictureBox` named `imagePictureBox` to display one of three bitmap images—`image0.bmp`, `image1.bmp` or `image2.bmp`. These images are provided in the `images` subdirectory of this chapter's examples directory. Whenever a user clicks the **Next Image** `Button`, the image changes to the next image in sequence. When the last image is displayed and the user clicks the **Next Image** `Button`, the first image is displayed again.

PictureBox properties and an event	Description
Common Properties	
`Image`	Sets the image to display in the `PictureBox`.
`SizeMode`	Enumeration that controls image sizing and positioning. Values are `Normal` (default), `StretchImage`, `AutoSize`, `CenterImage`, and `Zoom`. `Normal` places the image in the `PictureBox`'s top-left corner, and `CenterImage` puts the image in the middle. These two options truncate the image if it is too large. `StretchImage` resizes the image to fit in the `PictureBox`. `AutoSize` resizes the `PictureBox` to hold the image.
Common Event	
`Click`	Occurs when the user clicks a control. When you double click this control in the designer, an event handler is generated for this event.

Fig. 14.29 | `PictureBox` properties and event.

```
1   // Fig. 14.30: PictureBoxTestForm.cs
2   // Using a PictureBox to display images.
3   using System;
4   using System.Drawing;
5   using System.Windows.Forms;
6
7   namespace PictureBoxTest
8   {
9      // Form to display different images when PictureBox is clicked
10     public partial class PictureBoxTestForm : Form
11     {
12        private int imageNum = -1; // determines which image is displayed
13
14        // default constructor
15        public PictureBoxTestForm()
16        {
17           InitializeComponent();
18        } // end constructor
19
20        // change image whenever Next Button is clicked
21        private void nextButton_Click( object sender, EventArgs e )
22        {
23           imageNum = ( imageNum + 1 ) % 3; // imageNum cycles from 0 to 2
24
25           // retrieve image from resources and load into PictureBox
26           imagePictureBox.Image = ( Image )
27              ( Properties.Resources.ResourceManager.GetObject(
28              string.Format( "image{0}", imageNum ) ) );
29        } // end method nextButton_Click
30     } // end class PictureBoxTestForm
31  } // end namespace PictureBoxTest
```

a)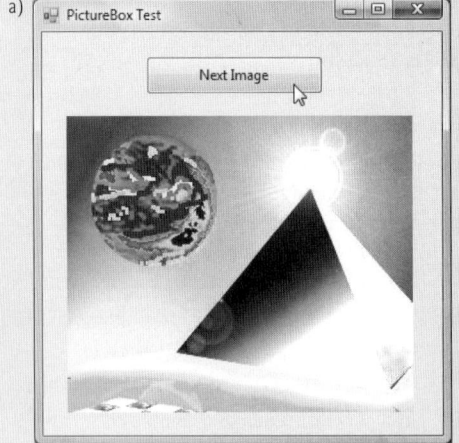

b)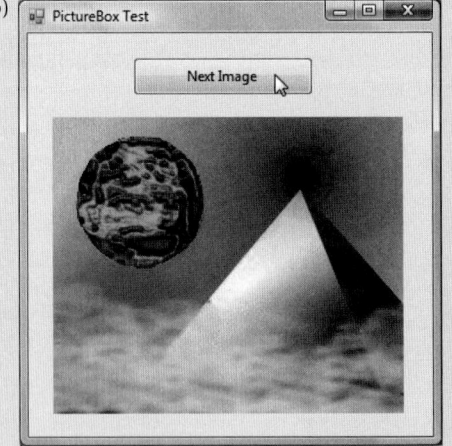

Fig. 14.30 | Using a PictureBox to display images. (Part 1 of 2.)

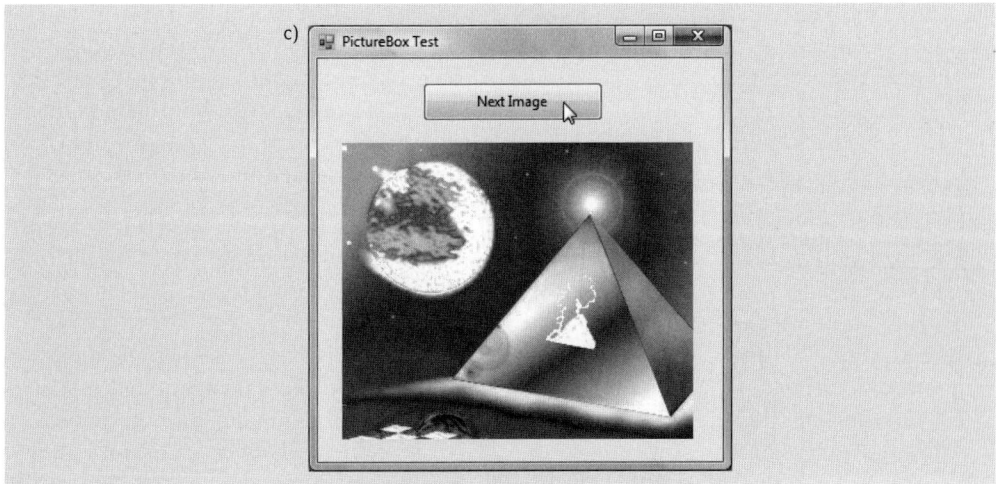

Fig. 14.30 | Using a `PictureBox` to display images. (Part 2 of 2.)

Using Resources Programmatically

In this example, we embedded the images into the project as *resources*. This causes the compiler to embed the images in the application's executable file and enables the application to access the images through the project's `Properties` namespace. By embedding the images in the application, you don't need to worry about wrapping the images with the application when you move it to another location or computer.

If you are creating a new project, use the following steps to add images to the project as resources:

1. After creating your project, double click the project's **Properties** node in the **Solution Explorer** to display the project's properties.

2. Click the **Resources** tab.

3. At the top of the **Resources** tab click the down arrow next to the **Add Resource** button and select **Add Existing File...** to display the **Add** existing file to resources dialog.

4. Locate the image files you wish to add as resources and click the **Open** button.

5. Save your project.

The files now appear in a folder named **Resources** in the **Solution Explorer**. We'll use this technique in most examples that use images going forward.

A project's resources are stored in its ***Resources*** class (of the project's properties namespace). In addition to the project's resources, the `Resources` class contains a ***ResourceManager*** object for interacting with the resources programmatically. To access an image, you can use the method ***GetObject***, which takes as an argument the resource name as it appears in the **Resources** tab (e.g., "image0") and returns the resource as an `Object`. Lines 27–28 invoke `GetObject` with the result of the expression

```
string.Format( "image{0}", imageNum )
```

which builds the name of the resource by placing the index of the next picture (imageNum, which was obtained earlier in line 23) at the end of the word "image". You must convert this Object to type Image to assign it to the PictureBox's Image property (line 26).

The Resources class also provides direct access to the resources you define with expressions of the form Resources.*resourceName*, where *resourceName* is the name you provided to the resource when you created it. When using such an expression, the resource returned already has the appropriate type. For example, Properties.Resources.image0 is an Image object representing the first image.

14.9 ToolTips

In Chapter 2, we demonstrated tool tips—the helpful text that appears when the mouse hovers over an item in a GUI. Recall that the tool tips displayed in Visual Studio help you become familiar with the IDE's features and serve as useful reminders for each toolbar icon's functionality. Many programs use tool tips to remind users of each control's purpose. For example, Microsoft Word has tool tips that help users determine the purpose of the application's icons. This section demonstrates how to use the ***ToolTip component*** to add tool tips to your applications. Figure 14.31 describes common properties and a common event of class ToolTip.

When you add a ToolTip component from the **Toolbox**, it appears in the ***component tray***—the gray region below the Form in **Design** mode. Once a ToolTip is added to a Form, a new property appears in the **Properties** window for the Form's other controls. This property appears in the **Properties** window as **ToolTip on**, followed by the name of the ToolTip component. For instance, if our Form's ToolTip were named helpfulToolTip, you would set a control's **ToolTip on helpfulToolTip** property value to specify the control's tool tip text. Figure 14.32 demonstrates the ToolTip component. For this example, we create a GUI containing two Labels, so we can demonstrate different tool tip text for each Label. To make the sample outputs clearer, we set the BorderStyle property of each Label to

ToolTip properties and an event	Description
Common Properties	
AutoPopDelay	The amount of time (in milliseconds) that the tool tip appears while the mouse is over a control.
InitialDelay	The amount of time (in milliseconds) that a mouse must hover over a control before a tool tip appears.
ReshowDelay	The amount of time (in milliseconds) between which two different tool tips appear (when the mouse is moved from one control to another).
Common Event	
Draw	Raised when the tool tip is displayed. This event allows programmers to modify the appearance of the tool tip.

Fig. 14.31 | ToolTip properties and an event.

```
 I    // Fig. 14.32: ToolTipDemonstrationForm.cs
 2    // Demonstrating the ToolTip component.
 3    using System;
 4    using System.Windows.Forms;
 5
 6    namespace ToolTipDemonstration
 7    {
 8       public partial class ToolTipDemonstrationForm : Form
 9       {
10          // default constructor
11          public ToolTipDemonstrationForm()
12          {
13             InitializeComponent();
14          } // end constructor
15
16          // no event handlers needed for this example
17
18       } // end class ToolTipDemonstrationForm
19    } // end namespace ToolTipDemonstration
```

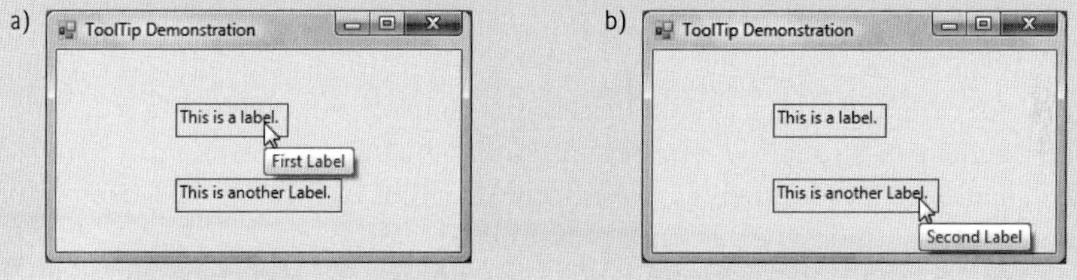

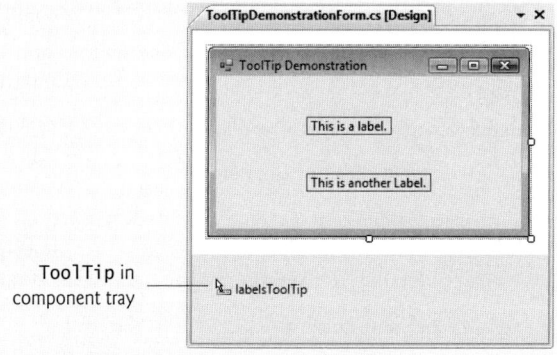

Fig. 14.32 | Demonstrating the ToolTip component.

FixedSingle, which displays a solid border. Since there is no event-handling code in this example, the class in Fig. 14.32 contains only a constructor.

In this example, we named the ToolTip component labelsToolTip. Figure 14.33 shows the ToolTip in the component tray. We set the tool tip text for the first Label to "First Label" and the tool tip text for the second Label to "Second Label". Figure 14.34 demonstrates setting the tool tip text for the first Label.

Fig. 14.33 | Demonstrating the component tray.

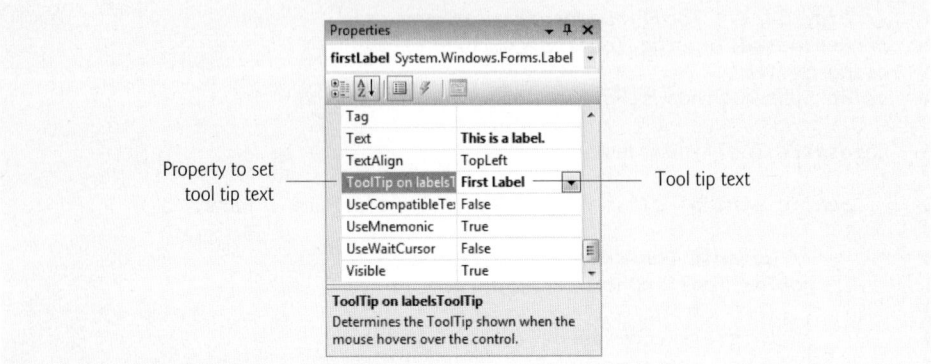

Fig. 14.34 | Setting a control's tool tip text.

14.10 NumericUpDown Control

At times, we'll want to restrict a user's input choices to a specific range of numeric values. This is the purpose of the **NumericUpDown control**. This control appears as a TextBox, with two small Buttons on the right side—one with an up arrow and one with a down arrow. By default, a user can type numeric values into this control as if it were a TextBox or click the up and down arrows to increase or decrease the value in the control, respectively. The largest and smallest values in the range are specified with the **Maximum** and **Minimum** properties, respectively (both of type decimal). The **Increment** property (also of type decimal) specifies by how much the current number in the control changes when the user clicks the control's up and down arrows. The **DecimalPlaces** property specifies the number of decimal places that the control should display as an integer. Figure 14.35 describes common properties and a common event of class NumericUpDown.

NumericUpDown properties and an event	Description
Common Properties	
DecimalPlaces	Specifies how many decimal places to display in the control.
Increment	Specifies by how much the current number in the control changes when the user clicks the control's up and down arrows.
Maximum	Largest value in the control's range.
Minimum	Smallest value in the control's range.
UpDownAlign	Modifies the alignment of the up and down Buttons on the NumericUpDown control. This property can be used to display these Buttons either to the left or to the right of the control.
Value	The numeric value currently displayed in the control.

Fig. 14.35 | NumericUpDown properties and an event. (Part 1 of 2.)

NumericUpDown properties and an event	Description
Common Event	
ValueChanged	This event is raised when the value in the control is changed. This is the default event for the NumericUpDown control.

Fig. 14.35 | NumericUpDown properties and an event. (Part 2 of 2.)

Figure 14.36 demonstrates a NumericUpDown control in a GUI that calculates interest rate. The calculations performed in this application are similar to those in Fig. 6.6. Text-Boxes are used to input the principal and interest rate amounts, and a NumericUpDown control is used to input the number of years for which we want to calculate interest.

```
1   // Fig. 14.36: interestCalculatorForm.cs
2   // Demonstrating the NumericUpDown control.
3   using System;
4   using System.Windows.Forms;
5
6   namespace NumericUpDownTest
7   {
8      public partial class interestCalculatorForm : Form
9      {
10        // default constructor
11        public interestCalculatorForm()
12        {
13           InitializeComponent();
14        } // end constructor
15
16        private void calculateButton_Click(
17           object sender, EventArgs e )
18        {
19           // declare variables to store user input
20           decimal principal; // store principal
21           double rate; // store interest rate
22           int year; // store number of years
23           decimal amount; // store amount
24           string output; // store output
25
26           // retrieve user input
27           principal = Convert.ToDecimal( principalTextBox.Text );
28           rate = Convert.ToDouble( interestTextBox.Text );
29           year = Convert.ToInt32( yearUpDown.Value );
30
31           // set output header
32           output = "Year\tAmount on Deposit\r\n";
33
```

Fig. 14.36 | Demonstrating the NumericUpDown control. (Part 1 of 2.)

```
34              // calculate amount after each year and append to output
35              for ( int yearCounter = 1; yearCounter <= year;  yearCounter++ )
36              {
37                  amount =  principal * ( ( decimal )
38                      Math.Pow( ( 1 + rate / 100 ), yearCounter ) );
39                  output += ( yearCounter + "\t" +
40                      string.Format( "{0:C}", amount ) + "\r\n" );
41              } // end for
42
43              displayTextBox.Text = output; // display result
44          } // end method calculateButton_Click
45      } // end class interestCalculatorForm
46  } // end namespace NumericUpDownTest
```

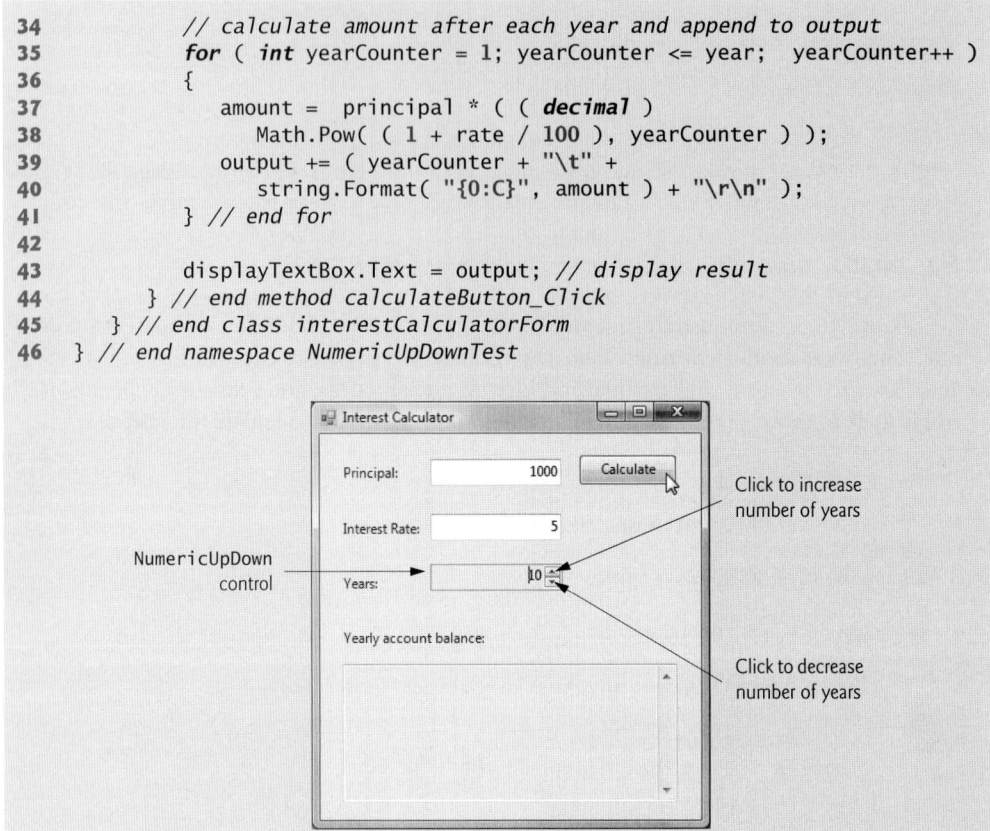

Fig. 14.36 | Demonstrating the NumericUpDown control. (Part 2 of 2.)

For the NumericUpDown control named yearUpDown, we set the Minimum property to 1 and the Maximum property to 10. We left the Increment property set to 1, its default value. These settings specify that users can enter a number of years in the range 1 to 10 in increments of 1. If we had set the Increment to 0.5, we could also input values such as 1.5 or 2.5. Note that if you don't modify the DecimalPlaces property (0 by default), 1.5 and 2.5 display as 2 and 3, respectively. We set the NumericUpDown's **ReadOnly property** to true to indicate that the user cannot type a number into the control to make a selection. Thus, the user must click the up and down arrows to modify the value in the control. By default, the ReadOnly property is set to false. The output for this application is displayed in a multiline read-only TextBox with a vertical scrollbar, so the user can scroll through the entire output.

14.11 Mouse-Event Handling

This section explains how to handle *mouse events*, such as *clicks* and *moves*, which are generated when the user interacts with a control via the mouse. Mouse events can be handled for any control that derives from class System.Windows.Forms.Control. For most mouse events, information about the event is passed to the event-handling method through an object of class *MouseEventArgs*, and the delegate used to create the mouse-event handlers is *MouseEventHandler*. Each mouse-event-handling method for these events requires an object and a MouseEventArgs object as arguments.

Class MouseEventArgs contains information related to the mouse event, such as the mouse pointer's *x*- and *y*-coordinates, the mouse button pressed (Right, Left or Middle) and the number of times the mouse was clicked. Note that the *x*- and *y*-coordinates of the MouseEventArgs object are relative to the control that generated the event—i.e., point *(0,0)* represents the upper-left corner of the control where the mouse event occurred. Several common mouse events are described in Fig. 14.37.

Figure 14.38 uses mouse events to draw on a Form. Whenever the user drags the mouse (i.e., moves the mouse while a mouse button is pressed), small circles appear on the Form at the position where each mouse event occurs during the drag operation.

Mouse events and event arguments	
Mouse Events with Event Argument of Type EventArgs	
MouseEnter	Occurs when the mouse cursor enters the control's boundaries.
MouseLeave	Occurs when the mouse cursor leaves the control's boundaries.
Mouse Events with Event Argument of Type MouseEventArgs	
MouseDown	Occurs when a mouse button is pressed while the mouse cursor is within a control's boundaries.
MouseHover	Occurs when the mouse cursor hovers within the control's boundaries.
MouseMove	Occurs when the mouse cursor is moved while in the control's boundaries.
MouseUp	Occurs when a mouse button is released when the cursor is over the control's boundaries.
Class MouseEventArgs Properties	
Button	Specifies which mouse button was pressed (Left, Right, Middle or none).
Clicks	The number of times that the mouse button was clicked.
X	The *x*-coordinate within the control where the event occurred.
Y	The *y*-coordinate within the control where the event occurred.

Fig. 14.37 | Mouse events and event arguments.

```
1    // Fig. 14.38: PainterForm.cs
2    // Using the mouse to draw on a Form.
3    using System;
4    using System.Drawing;
5    using System.Windows.Forms;
6
7    namespace Painter
8    {
```

Fig. 14.38 | Using the mouse to draw on a Form. (Part 1 of 2.)

```
 9     // creates a Form that is a drawing surface
10     public partial class PainterForm : Form
11     {
12        bool shouldPaint = false; // determines whether to paint
13
14        // default constructor
15        public PainterForm()
16        {
17           InitializeComponent();
18        } // end constructor
19
20        // should paint when mouse button is pressed down
21        private void PainterForm_MouseDown(
22           object sender, MouseEventArgs e )
23        {
24           // indicate that user is dragging the mouse
25           shouldPaint = true;
26        } // end method PainterForm_MouseDown
27
28        // stop painting when mouse button is released
29        private void PainterForm_MouseUp( object sender, MouseEventArgs e )
30        {
31           // indicate that user released the mouse button
32           shouldPaint = false;
33        } // end method PainterForm_MouseUp
34
35        // draw circle whenever mouse moves with its button held down
36        private void PainterForm_MouseMove(
37           object sender, MouseEventArgs e )
38        {
39           if ( shouldPaint ) // check if mouse button is being pressed
40           {
41              // draw a circle where the mouse pointer is present
42              Graphics graphics = CreateGraphics();
43              graphics.FillEllipse(
44                 new SolidBrush( Color.BlueViolet ), e.X, e.Y, 4, 4 );
45              graphics.Dispose();
46           } // end if
47        } // end method PainterForm_MouseMove
48     } // end class PainterForm
49  } // end namespace Painter
```

Fig. 14.38 | Using the mouse to draw on a Form. (Part 2 of 2.)

In line 12, the program declares variable shouldPaint, which determines whether to draw on the Form. We want the program to draw only while the mouse button is pressed (i.e., held down). Thus, when the user clicks or holds down a mouse button, the system generates a MouseDown event, and the event handler (lines 21–26) sets shouldPaint to true. When the user releases the mouse button, the system generates a MouseUp event, shouldPaint is set to false in the PainterForm_MouseUp event handler (lines 29–33) and the program stops drawing. Unlike MouseMove events, which occur continuously as the user moves the mouse, the system generates a MouseDown event only when a mouse button is first pressed and generates a MouseUp event only when a mouse button is released.

Whenever the mouse moves over a control, the MouseMove event for that control occurs. Inside the PainterForm_MouseMove event handler (lines 36–47), the program draws only if shouldPaint is true (i.e., a mouse button is pressed). Line 42 calls inherited Form method CreateGraphics to create a *Graphics* object that allows the program to draw on the Form. Class Graphics provides methods that draw various shapes. For example, lines 43–44 use method *FillEllipse* to draw a circle. The first parameter to method FillEllipse in this case is an object of class *SolidBrush*, which specifies the solid color that will fill the shape. The color is provided as an argument to class SolidBrush's constructor. Type *Color* contains numerous predefined color constants—we selected Color.BlueViolet. FillEllipse draws an oval in a bounding rectangle that is specified by the *x*- and *y*-coordinates of its upper-left corner, its width and its height—the final four arguments to the method. The *x*- and *y*-coordinates represent the location of the mouse event and can be taken from the mouse-event arguments (e.X and e.Y). To draw a circle, we set the width and height of the bounding rectangle so that they are equal—in this example, both are 4 pixels. Graphics, SolidBrush and Color are all part of the namespace System.Drawing. Instead of having to manually dispose of resources, lines 42–45 could have been written as follows to use the using statement from Section 13.6.

```
using ( Graphics graphics = CreateGraphics() )
{
   graphics.FillEllipse(
      new SolidBrush( Color.BlueViolet ), e.X, e.Y, 4, 4 );
}
```

14.12 Keyboard-Event Handling

Key events occur when keyboard keys are pressed and released. Such events can be handled for any control that inherits from System.Windows.Forms.Control. There are three key events—KeyPress, KeyUp and KeyDown. The *KeyPress* event occurs when the user presses a key that represents an ASCII character. The specific key can be determined with property *KeyChar* of the event handler's *KeyPressEventArgs* argument. ASCII is a 128-character set of alphanumeric symbols, a full listing of which can be found in Appendix F.

The KeyPress event does not indicate whether *modifier keys* (e.g., *Shift*, *Alt* and *Ctrl*) were pressed when a key event occurred. If this information is important, the *KeyUp* or *Key-Down* events can be used. The *KeyEventArgs* argument for each of these events contains information about modifier keys. Often, modifier keys are used in conjunction with the mouse to select or highlight information. Figure 14.39 lists important key event information. Several properties return values from the *Keys enumeration*, which provides constants that specify the various keys on a keyboard. Like the FontStyle enumeration (Section 14.7),

Keyboard events and event arguments	
Key Events with Event Arguments of Type `KeyEventArgs`	
KeyDown	Generated when a key is initially pressed.
KeyUp	Generated when a key is released.
Key Event with Event Argument of Type `KeyPressEventArgs`	
KeyPress	Generated when a key is pressed. Raised after `KeyDown` and before `KeyUp`.
Class `KeyPressEventArgs` Properties	
KeyChar	Returns the ASCII character for the key pressed.
Handled	Indicates whether the `KeyPress` event was handled.
Class `KeyEventArgs` Properties	
Alt	Indicates whether the *Alt* key was pressed.
Control	Indicates whether the *Ctrl* key was pressed.
Shift	Indicates whether the *Shift* key was pressed.
Handled	Indicates whether the event was handled.
KeyCode	Returns the key code for the key as a value from the `Keys` enumeration. This does not include modifier-key information. It is used to test for a specific key.
KeyData	Returns the key code for a key combined with modifier information as a `Keys` value. This property contains all information about the pressed key.
KeyValue	Returns the key code as an `int`, rather than as a value from the `Keys` enumeration. This property is used to obtain a numeric representation of the pressed key. The `int` value is known as a Windows virtual key code.
Modifiers	Returns a `Keys` value indicating any pressed modifier keys (*Alt*, *Ctrl* and *Shift*). This property is used to determine modifier-key information only.

Fig. 14.39 | Keyboard events and event arguments.

the `Keys` enumeration is a `System.FlagsAttribute`, so the enumeration's constants can be combined to indicate multiple keys pressed at the same time.

Figure 14.40 demonstrates the use of the key-event handlers to display a key pressed by a user. The program is a `Form` with two `Label`s that displays the pressed key on one `Label` and modifier key information on the other.

```
1    // Fig. 14.40: KeyDemoForm.cs
2    // Displaying information about the key the user pressed.
3    using System;
4    using System.Windows.Forms;
5
6    namespace KeyDemo
7    {
```

Fig. 14.40 | Demonstrating keyboard events. (Part 1 of 2.)

```
 8        // Form to display key information when key is pressed
 9        public partial class KeyDemoForm : Form
10        {
11           // default constructor
12           public KeyDemoForm()
13           {
14              InitializeComponent();
15           } // end constructor
16
17           // display the character pressed using KeyChar
18           private void KeyDemoForm_KeyPress(
19              object sender, KeyPressEventArgs e )
20           {
21              charLabel.Text = "Key pressed: " + e.KeyChar;
22           } // end method KeyDemoForm_KeyPress
23
24           // display modifier keys, key code, key data and key value
25           private void KeyDemoForm_KeyDown( object sender, KeyEventArgs e )
26           {
27              keyInfoLabel.Text =
28                 "Alt: " + ( e.Alt ? "Yes" : "No" ) + '\n' +
29                 "Shift: " + ( e.Shift ? "Yes" : "No" ) + '\n' +
30                 "Ctrl: " + ( e.Control ? "Yes" : "No" ) + '\n' +
31                 "KeyCode: " + e.KeyCode + '\n' +
32                 "KeyData: " + e.KeyData + '\n' +
33                 "KeyValue: " + e.KeyValue;
34           } // end method KeyDemoForm_KeyDown
35
36           // clear Labels when key released
37           private void KeyDemoForm_KeyUp( object sender, KeyEventArgs e )
38           {
39              charLabel.Text = "";
40              keyInfoLabel.Text = "";
41           } // end method KeyDemoForm_KeyUp
42        } // end class KeyDemoForm
43     } // end namespace KeyDemo
```

a) *H* pressed   b) *F12* pressed   c) *$* pressed   d) *Insert* pressed

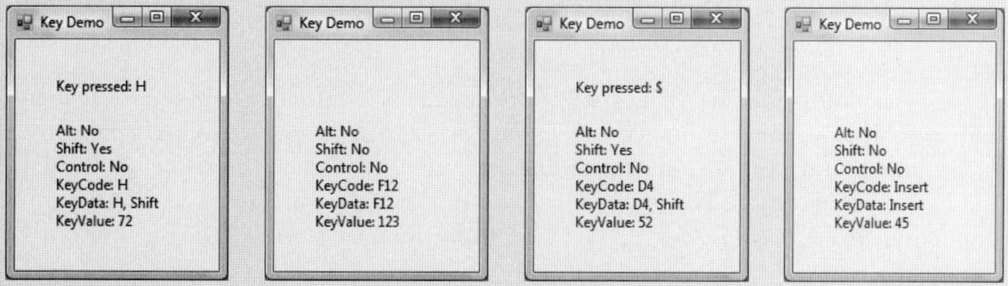

Key Demo	Key Demo	Key Demo	Key Demo
Key pressed: H		Key pressed: $	
Alt: No	Alt: No	Alt: No	Alt: No
Shift: Yes	Shift: No	Shift: Yes	Shift: No
Control: No	Control: No	Control: No	Control: No
KeyCode: H	KeyCode: F12	KeyCode: D4	KeyCode: Insert
KeyData: H, Shift	KeyData: F12	KeyData: D4, Shift	KeyData: Insert
KeyValue: 72	KeyValue: 123	KeyValue: 52	KeyValue: 45

Fig. 14.40 | Demonstrating keyboard events. (Part 2 of 2.)

Initially, the two Labels (charLabel and keyInfoLabel) are empty. Control char-Label displays the character value of the key pressed, whereas keyInfoLabel displays information relating to the pressed key. Because the KeyDown and KeyPress events convey different information, the Form (KeyDemoForm) handles both.

The KeyPress event handler (lines 18–22) accesses the KeyChar property of the Key-PressEventArgs object. This returns the pressed key as a char, which we then display in charLabel (line 21). If the pressed key is not an ASCII character, then the KeyPress event will not occur, and charLabel will not display any text. ASCII is a common encoding format for letters, numbers, punctuation marks and other characters. It does not support keys such as the *function keys* (like *F1*) or the modifier keys (*Alt*, *Ctrl* and *Shift*).

The KeyDown event handler (lines 25–34) displays information from its KeyEventArgs object. The event handler tests for the *Alt*, *Shift* and *Ctrl* keys by using the Alt, Shift and Control properties, each of which returns a bool value—true if the corresponding key is pressed and false otherwise. The event handler then displays the KeyCode, KeyData and KeyValue properties.

The KeyCode property returns a Keys enumeration value (line 31). The KeyCode property returns the pressed key, but does not provide any information about modifier keys. Thus, both a capital and a lowercase "a" are represented as the *A* key.

The KeyData property (line 32) also returns a Keys enumeration value, but this property includes data about modifier keys. Thus, if "A" is input, the KeyData shows that both the *A* key and the *Shift* key were pressed. Lastly, KeyValue (line 33) returns the key code of the pressed key as an int. This int is the *key code*, which provides an int value for a wide range of keys and for mouse buttons. The Windows virtual key code is useful when one is testing for non-ASCII keys (such as *F12*).

The KeyUp event handler (lines 37–41) clears both Labels when the key is released. As we can see from the output, non-ASCII keys are not displayed in charLabel, because the KeyPress event is not generated. For example, charLabel does not display any text when you press the *F12* or *Insert* keys, as shown in Fig. 14.40(b) and (d). However, the KeyDown event still is generated, and keyInfoLabel displays information about the key that is pressed. The Keys enumeration can be used to test for specific keys by comparing the key pressed to a specific KeyCode.

Software Engineering Observation 14.3

To cause a control to react when a particular key is pressed (such as Enter*), handle a key event and test for the pressed key. To cause a* Button *to be clicked when the* Enter *key is pressed on a* Form*, set the* Form's AcceptButton *property.*

By default, a keyboard event is handled by the control that currently has the focus. However, it is often appropriate to have the Form handle keyboard events. This can be accomplished by setting the Form's KeyPreview property to true, which makes the Form receive keyboard events before they are passed to another control. For example, a key press would raise the Form's KeyPress, even if a control within the Form has the focus instead of the Form itself.

14.13 Wrap-Up

This chapter introduced several common GUI controls. We discussed event handling in detail, and showed how to create event handlers. We also discussed how delegates are used to connect event handlers to the events of specific controls. You learned how to use a control's properties and Visual Studio to specify the layout of your GUI. We then demonstrated several controls, beginning with Labels, Buttons and TextBoxes. You learned how to use GroupBoxes and Panels to organize other controls. We then demonstrated CheckBoxes and RadioButtons, which are state buttons that allow users to select among several options. We displayed images in PictureBox controls, displayed helpful text on a GUI with ToolTip components and specified a range of input values for users with a NumericUpDown control. We then demonstrated how to handle mouse and keyboard events. The next chapter introduces additional GUI controls. You'll learn how to add menus to your GUIs and create Windows applications that display multiple Forms.

15

Graphical User Interfaces with Windows Forms: Part 2

OBJECTIVES

In this chapter you'll learn:

- To create menus, tabbed windows and multiple document interface (MDI) programs.

- To use the `ListView` and `TreeView` controls for displaying information.

- To create hyperlinks using the `LinkLabel` control.

- To display lists of information in `ListBox` and `ComboBox` controls.

- To input date and time data with the `DateTimePicker`.

- To create custom controls.

I claim not to have controlled events, but confess plainly that events have controlled me.
—Abraham Lincoln

Capture its reality in paint!
—Paul Cézanne

An actor entering through the door, you've got nothing. But if he enters through the window, you've got a situation.
—Billy Wilder

But, soft! what light through yonder window breaks? It is the east, and Juliet is the sun!
—William Shakespeare

Outline

15.1 Introduction

15.2 Menus

15.3 MonthCalendar Control

15.4 DateTimePicker Control

15.5 LinkLabel Control

15.6 ListBox Control

15.7 CheckedListBox Control

15.8 ComboBox Control

15.9 TreeView Control

15.10 ListView Control

15.11 TabControl Control

15.12 Multiple Document Interface (MDI) Windows

15.13 Visual Inheritance

15.14 User-Defined Controls

15.15 Wrap-Up

15.1 Introduction

This chapter continues our study of GUIs. We start with menus, which present users with logically organized commands (or options). Next, we discuss how to input and display dates and times using the MonthCalendar and DateTimePicker controls. We show how to develop menus with the tools provided by Visual Studio. We also introduce LinkLabels— powerful GUI components that enable the user to visit one of several destinations, such as a file on the current machine or a web page, by simply clicking the mouse.

We demonstrate how to manipulate a list of values via a ListBox and how to combine several checkboxes in a CheckedListBox. We also create drop-down lists using ComboBoxes and display data hierarchically with a TreeView control. You'll learn two other important GUI elements—tab controls and multiple document interface (MDI) windows. These components enable you to create real-world programs with sophisticated GUIs.

Visual Studio provides a large set of GUI components, several of which are discussed in this (and the previous) chapter. Visual Studio also enables you to design custom controls and add them to the **ToolBox**, as we demonstrate in the last example of this chapter. The techniques presented here form the groundwork for creating more substantial GUIs and custom controls.

15.2 Menus

Menus provide groups of related commands for Windows applications. Although these commands depend on the program, some—such as **Open** and **Save**—are common to many applications. Menus are an integral part of GUIs, because they organize commands without "cluttering" the GUI.

In Fig. 15.1, an expanded menu from Visual C# 2008 Express Edition lists various commands (called *menu items*), plus *submenus* (menus within a menu). Notice that the

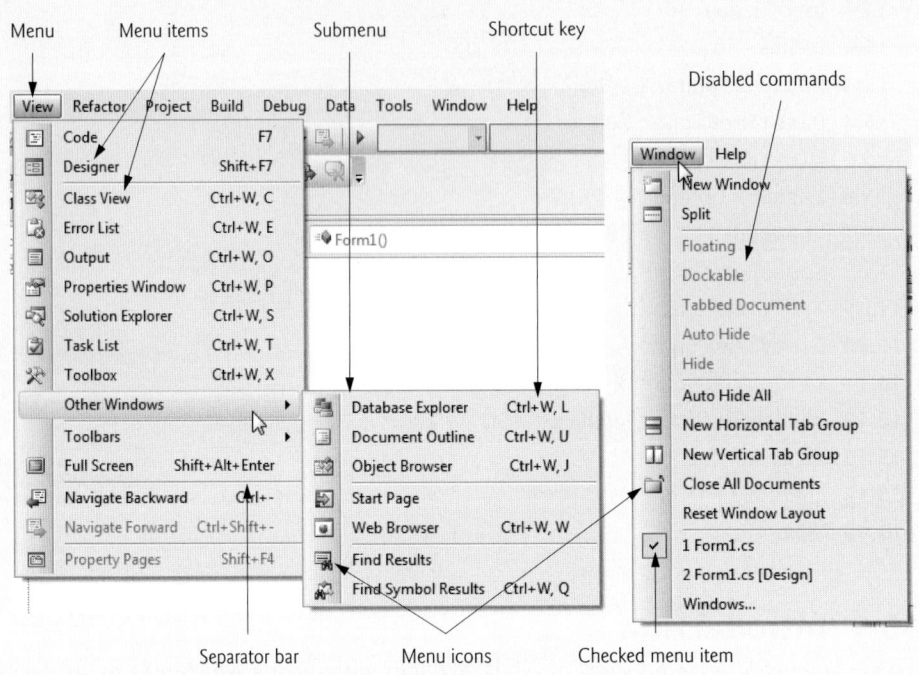

Fig. 15.1 | Menus, submenus and menu items.

top-level menus appear in the left portion of the figure, whereas any submenus or menu items are displayed to the right. The menu that contains a menu item is called that menu item's *parent menu*. A menu item that contains a submenu is considered to be the parent of that submenu.

Menus can have *Alt* key shortcuts (also called *access shortcuts* or *hotkeys*), which are accessed by pressing *Alt* and the underlined letter (for example, *Alt F* typically expands the **File** menu). Menu items can have shortcut keys as well (combinations of *Ctrl, Shift, Alt, F1, F2,* letter keys, and so on). Some menu items display checkmarks, usually indicating that multiple options on the menu can be selected at once.

To create a menu, open the **Toolbox** and drag a *MenuStrip* control onto the Form. This creates a menu bar across the top of the Form (below the title bar) and places a MenuStrip icon in the component tray. To select the MenuStrip, click this icon. You can now use **Design** mode to create and edit menus for your application. Menus, like other controls, have properties and events, which can be accessed through the **Properties** window.

To add menu items to the menu, click the **Type Here** TextBox (Fig. 15.2) and type the menu item's name. This action adds an entry to the menu of type *ToolStripMenuItem*. After you press the *Enter* key, the menu item name is added to the menu. Then more **Type Here** TextBoxes appear, allowing you to add items underneath or to the side of the original menu item (Fig. 15.3).

To create an *access shortcut* (or *keyboard shortcut*), type an ampersand (&) before the character to be underlined. For example, to create the **File** menu item with the letter **F** underlined, type &File. To display an ampersand, type &&. To add other shortcut keys

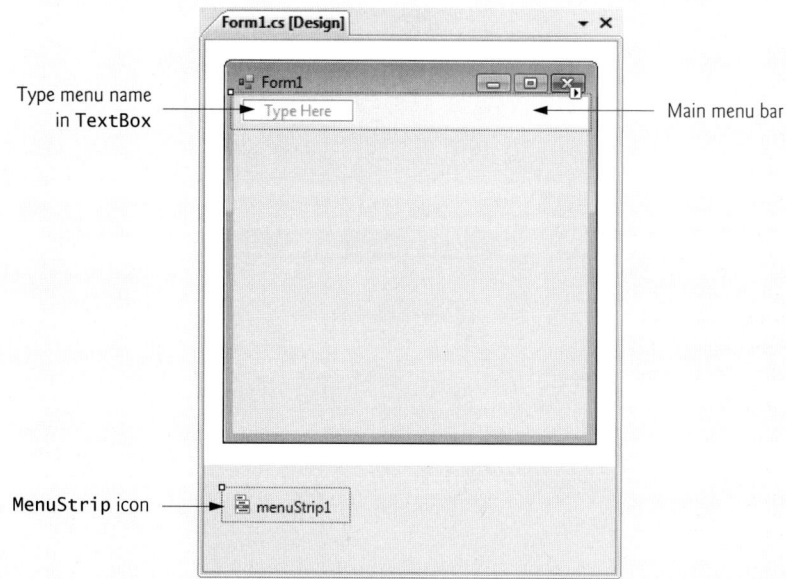

Type menu name in TextBox

Main menu bar

MenuStrip icon

Fig. 15.2 | Editing menus in Visual Studio.

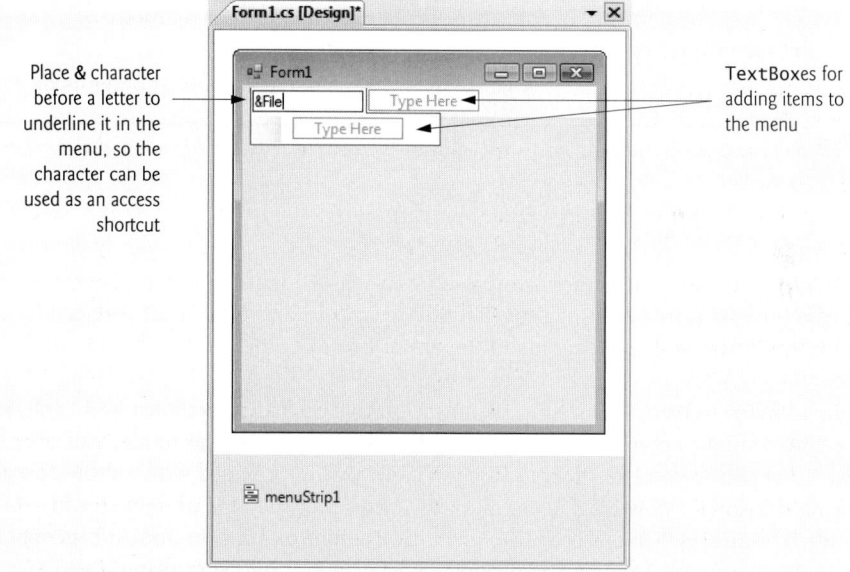

Place & character before a letter to underline it in the menu, so the character can be used as an access shortcut

TextBoxes for adding items to the menu

Fig. 15.3 | Adding ToolStripMenuItems to a MenuStrip.

(e.g., *<Ctrl>-F9*) for menu items, set the ***ShortcutKeys*** property of the appropriate Tool-StripMenuItems. To do this, select the down arrow to the right of this property in the **Properties** window. In the window that appears (Fig. 15.4), use the CheckBoxes and drop-

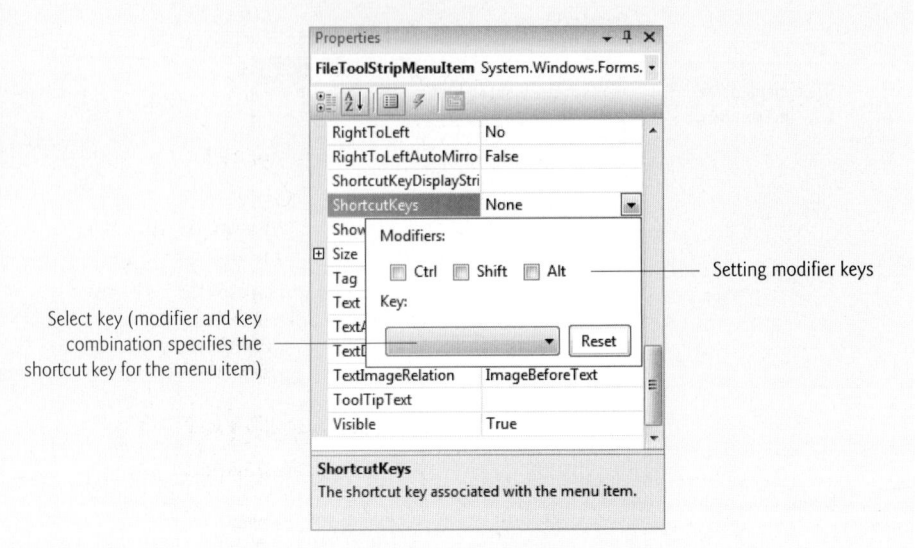

Fig. 15.4 | Setting a menu item's shortcut keys.

down list to select the shortcut keys. When you are finished, click elsewhere on the screen. You can hide the shortcut keys by setting property *ShowShortcutKeys* to false, and you can modify how the control keys are displayed in the menu item by modifying property *ShortcutKeyDisplayString*.

Look-and-Feel Observation 15.1

Buttons can have access shortcuts. Place the & symbol immediately before the desired character in the Button's text. To press the button by using its access key in the running application, the user presses Alt and the underlined character. If the underline is not visible when the application runs, press the Alt key to display the underlines.

You can remove a menu item by selecting it with the mouse and pressing the *Delete* key. Menu items can be grouped logically by *separator bars*, which are inserted by right clicking the menu and selecting **Insert Separator** or by typing "-" for the text of a menu item.

In addition to text, Visual Studio allows you to easily add TextBoxes and ComboBoxes (drop-down lists) as menu items. When adding an item in **Design** mode, you may have noticed that before you enter text for a new item, you are provided with a drop-down list. Clicking the down arrow (Fig. 15.5) allows you to select the type of item to add—**Menu-Item** (of type ToolStripMenuItem, the default), **ComboBox** (of type ToolStripComboBox) and **TextBox** (of type ToolStripTextBox). We focus on ToolStripMenuItems. [*Note:* If you view this drop-down list for menu items that are not on the top level, a fourth option appears, allowing you to insert a separator bar.]

ToolStripMenuItems generate a *Click* event when selected. To create an empty Click event handler, double click the menu item in **Design** mode. Common actions in response to these events include displaying dialogs and setting properties. Common menu properties and a common event are summarized in Fig. 15.6.

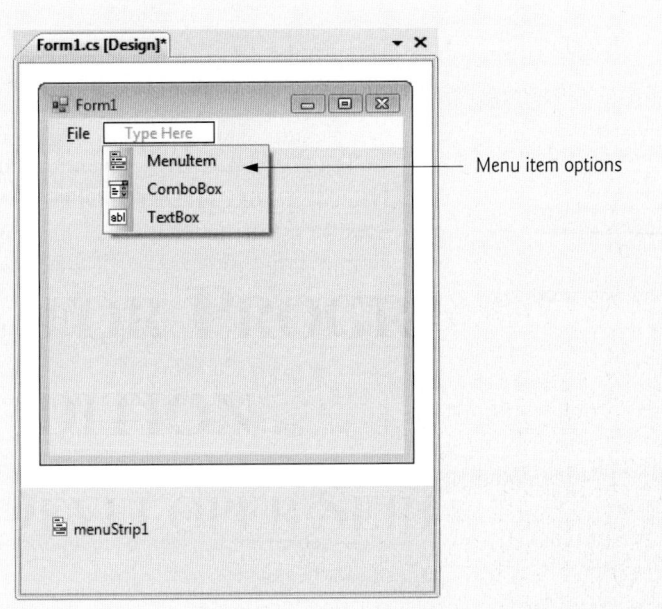

Fig. 15.5 | Menu-item options.

MenuStrip and ToolStripMenuItem properties and an event	Description
MenuStrip Properties	
MenuItems	Contains the top-level menu items for this MenuStrip.
HasChildren	Indicates whether MenuStrip has any child controls (menu items).
RightToLeft	Causes text to display from right to left. This is useful for languages that are read from right to left.
ToolStripMenuItem Properties	
Checked	Indicates whether a menu item is checked. The default value is false, meaning that the menu item is unchecked.
CheckOnClick	Indicates that a menu item should appear checked or unchecked as it is clicked.
Index	Specifies an item's position in its parent menu. A value of 0 places the MenuItem at the beginning of the menu.
MenuItems	Lists the submenu items for a particular menu item.

Fig. 15.6 | MenuStrip and ToolStripMenuItem properties and an event. (Part 1 of 2.)

MenuStrip and ToolStripMenuItem properties and an event	Description
ShortcutKey-DisplayString	Specifies text that should appear beside a menu item for a shortcut key. If left blank, the key names are displayed. Otherwise, the text in this property is displayed for the shortcut key.
ShortcutKeys	Specifies the shortcut key for the menu item (e.g., *<Ctrl>-F9* is equivalent to clicking a specific item).
ShowShortcutKeys	Indicates whether a shortcut key is shown beside menu item text. The default is true, which displays the shortcut key.
Text	Specifies the menu item's text. To create an *Alt* access shortcut, precede a character with **&** (e.g., &File to specify a menu named **File** with the letter **F** underlined).
Common ToolStripMenuItem Event	
Click	Generated when an item is clicked or a shortcut key is used. This is the default event when the menu is double clicked in the designer.

Fig. 15.6 | MenuStrip and ToolStripMenuItem properties and an event. (Part 2 of 2.)

Look-and-Feel Observation 15.2

*It is a convention to place an ellipsis (...) after the name of a menu item (e.g., **Save As...**) that requires the user to provide more information—typically through a dialog. A menu item that produces an immediate action without prompting the user for more information (e.g., **Save**) should not have an ellipsis following its name.*

Class MenuTestForm (Fig. 15.7) creates a simple menu on a Form. The Form has a top-level **File** menu with menu items **About** (which displays a MessageBox) and **Exit** (which terminates the program). The program also includes a **Format** menu, which contains menu items that change the format of the text on a Label. The **Format** menu has submenus **Color** and **Font**, which change the color and font of the text on a Label.

To create this GUI, begin by dragging the MenuStrip from the **ToolBox** onto the Form. Then use **Design** mode to create the menu structure shown in the sample outputs. The **File** menu (fileToolStripMenuItem) has menu items **About** (aboutToolStripMenuItem) and **Exit** (exitToolStripMenuItem); the **Format** menu (formatToolStripMenuItem) has two submenus. The first submenu, **Color** (colorToolStripMenuItem), contains menu items **Black** (blackToolStripMenuItem), **Blue** (blueToolStripMenuItem), **Red** (redToolStripMenuItem) and **Green** (greenToolStripMenuItem). The second submenu, **Font** (fontToolStripMenuItem), contains menu items **Times New Roman** (timesToolStripMenuItem), **Courier** (courierToolStripMenuItem), **Comic Sans** (comicToolStripMenuItem), a separator bar (dashToolStripMenuItem), **Bold** (boldToolStripMenuItem) and **Italic** (italicToolStripMenuItem).

The **About** menu item in the **File** menu displays a MessageBox when clicked (lines 20–25). The **Exit** menu item closes the application through static method *Exit* of class

Application (line 31). Class Application's static methods control program execution. Method Exit causes our application to terminate.

```
 1   // Fig. 15.7: MenuTestForm.cs
 2   // Using Menus to change font colors and styles.
 3   using System;
 4   using System.Drawing;
 5   using System.Windows.Forms;
 6
 7   namespace MenuTest
 8   {
 9      // our Form contains a Menu that changes the font color
10      // and style of the text displayed in Label
11      public partial class MenuTestForm : Form
12      {
13         // constructor
14         public MenuTestForm()
15         {
16            InitializeComponent();
17         } // end constructor
18
19         // display MessageBox when About ToolStripMenuItem is selected
20         private void aboutToolStripMenuItem_Click(
21            object sender, EventArgs e )
22         {
23            MessageBox.Show( "This is an example\nof using menus.", "About",
24               MessageBoxButtons.OK, MessageBoxIcon.Information );
25         } // end method aboutToolStripMenuItem_Click
26
27         // exit program when Exit ToolStripMenuItem is selected
28         private void exitToolStripMenuItem_Click(
29            object sender, EventArgs e )
30         {
31            Application.Exit();
32         } // end method exitToolStripMenuItem_Click
33
34         // reset checkmarks for Color ToolStripMenuItems
35         private void ClearColor()
36         {
37            // clear all checkmarks
38            blackToolStripMenuItem.Checked = false;
39            blueToolStripMenuItem.Checked = false;
40            redToolStripMenuItem.Checked = false;
41            greenToolStripMenuItem.Checked = false;
42         } // end method ClearColor
43
44         // update Menu state and color display black
45         private void blackToolStripMenuItem_Click(
46            object sender, EventArgs e )
47         {
48            // reset checkmarks for Color ToolStripMenuItems
49            ClearColor();
```

Fig. 15.7 | Menus for changing text font and color. (Part 1 of 4.)

```
50
51              // set Color to Black
52              displayLabel.ForeColor = Color.Black;
53              blackToolStripMenuItem.Checked = true;
54          } // end method blackToolStripMenuItem_Click
55
56          // update Menu state and color display blue
57          private void blueToolStripMenuItem_Click(
58              object sender, EventArgs e )
59          {
60              // reset checkmarks for Color ToolStripMenuItems
61              ClearColor();
62
63              // set Color to Blue
64              displayLabel.ForeColor = Color.Blue;
65              blueToolStripMenuItem.Checked = true;
66          } // end method blueToolStripMenuItem_Click
67
68          // update Menu state and color display red
69          private void redToolStripMenuItem_Click(
70              object sender, EventArgs e )
71          {
72              // reset checkmarks for Color ToolStripMenuItems
73              ClearColor();
74
75              // set Color to Red
76              displayLabel.ForeColor = Color.Red;
77              redToolStripMenuItem.Checked = true;
78          } // end method redToolStripMenuItem_Click
79
80          // update Menu state and color display green
81          private void greenToolStripMenuItem_Click(
82              object sender, EventArgs e )
83          {
84              // reset checkmarks for Color ToolStripMenuItems
85              ClearColor();
86
87              // set Color to Green
88              displayLabel.ForeColor = Color.Green;
89              greenToolStripMenuItem.Checked = true;
90          } // end method greenToolStripMenuItem_Click
91
92          // reset checkmarks for Font ToolStripMenuItems
93          private void ClearFont()
94          {
95              // clear all checkmarks
96              timesToolStripMenuItem.Checked = false;
97              courierToolStripMenuItem.Checked = false;
98              comicToolStripMenuItem.Checked = false;
99          } // end method ClearFont
100
```

Fig. 15.7 | Menus for changing text font and color. (Part 2 of 4.)

```
101    // update Menu state and set Font to Times New Roman
102    private void timesToolStripMenuItem_Click(
103        object sender, EventArgs e )
104    {
105        // reset checkmarks for Font ToolStripMenuItems
106        ClearFont();
107
108        // set Times New Roman font
109        timesToolStripMenuItem.Checked = true;
110        displayLabel.Font = new Font( "Times New Roman", 14,
111            displayLabel.Font.Style );
112    } // end method timesToolStripMenuItem_Click
113
114    // update Menu state and set Font to Courier
115    private void courierToolStripMenuItem_Click(
116        object sender, EventArgs e )
117    {
118        // reset checkmarks for Font ToolStripMenuItems
119        ClearFont();
120
121        // set Courier font
122        courierToolStripMenuItem.Checked = true;
123        displayLabel.Font = new Font( "Courier", 14,
124            displayLabel.Font.Style );
125    } // end method courierToolStripMenuItem_Click
126
127    // update Menu state and set Font to Comic Sans MS
128    private void comicToolStripMenuItem_Click(
129        object sender, EventArgs e )
130    {
131        // reset checkmarks for Font ToolStripMenuItems
132        ClearFont();
133
134        // set Comic Sans font
135        comicToolStripMenuItem.Checked = true;
136        displayLabel.Font = new Font( "Comic Sans MS", 14,
137            displayLabel.Font.Style );
138    } // end method comicToolStripMenuItem_Click
139
140    // toggle checkmark and toggle bold style
141    private void boldToolStripMenuItem_Click(
142        object sender, EventArgs e )
143    {
144        // toggle checkmark
145        boldToolStripMenuItem.Checked = !boldToolStripMenuItem.Checked;
146
147        // use Xor to toggle italic, keep all other styles
148        displayLabel.Font = new Font( displayLabel.Font
149            displayLabel.Font.Style ^ FontStyle.Bold );
150    } // end method boldToolStripMenuItem_Click
151
```

Fig. 15.7 | Menus for changing text font and color. (Part 3 of 4.)

```
152        // toggle checkmark and toggle italic style
153        private void italicToolStripMenuItem_Click(
154           object sender, EventArgs e )
155        {
156           // toggle checkmark
157           italicToolStripMenuItem.Checked =
158              !italicToolStripMenuItem.Checked;
159
160           // use Xor to toggle italic, keep all other styles
161           displayLabel.Font = new Font( displayLabel.Font
162              displayLabel.Font.Style ^ FontStyle.Italic );
163        } // end method italicToolStripMenuItem_Click
164     } // end class MenuTestForm
165  } // end namespace MenuTest
```

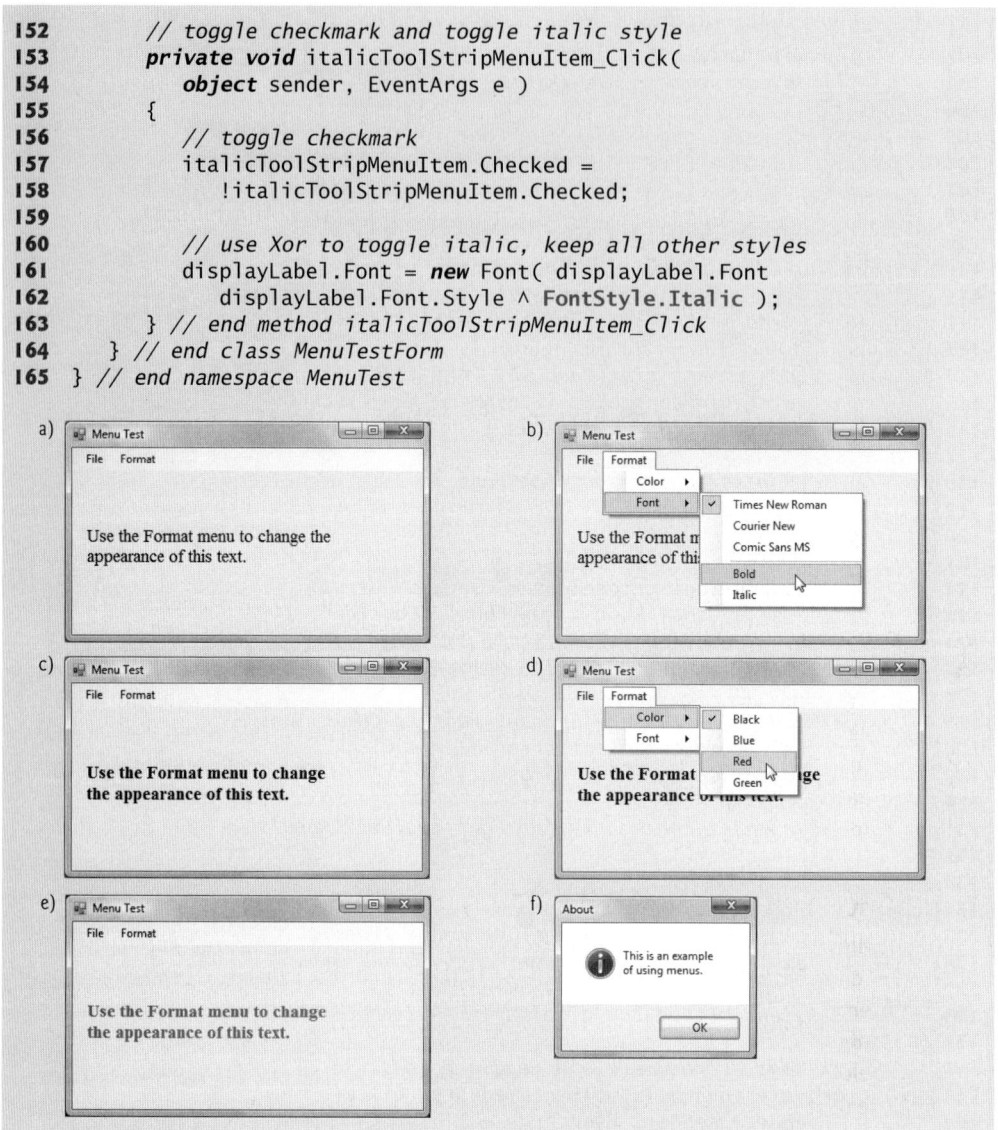

Fig. 15.7 | Menus for changing text font and color. (Part 4 of 4.)

We made the items in the **Color** submenu (**Black**, **Blue**, **Red** and **Green**) mutually exclusive—the user can select only one at a time (we explain how we did this shortly). To indicate that a menu item is selected, we will set each **Color** menu item's *Checked* property to true. This causes a check to appear to the left of a menu item.

Each **Color** menu item has its own Click event handler. The method handler for color **Black** is blackToolStripMenuItem_Click (lines 45–54). Similarly, the event handlers for colors **Blue**, **Red** and **Green** are blueToolStripMenuItem_Click (lines 57–66), redTool-StripMenuItem_Click (lines 69–78) and greenToolStripMenuItem_Click (lines 81–90), respectively. Each **Color** menu item must be mutually exclusive, so each event handler calls method ClearColor (lines 35–42) before setting its corresponding Checked property to true. Method ClearColor sets the Checked property of each color MenuItem to false, effectively preventing more than one menu item from being selected at a time. In the designer, we initially set the **Black** menu item's Checked property to true, because at the start of the program, the text on the Form is black.

Software Engineering Observation 15.1

The mutual exclusion of menu items is not enforced by the MenuStrip, even when the Checked property is true. You must program this behavior.

The **Font** menu contains three menu items for fonts (**Courier**, **Times New Roman** and **Comic Sans**) and two menu items for font styles (**Bold** and **Italic**). We added a separator bar between the font and font-style menu items to indicate that these are separate options. A Font object can specify only one font at a time but can set multiple styles at once (e.g., a font can be both bold and italic). We set the font menu items to display checks. As with the **Color** menu, we must enforce mutual exclusion of these items in our event handlers.

Event handlers for font menu items **TimesRoman**, **Courier** and **ComicSans** are timesToolStripMenuItem_Click (lines 102–112), courierToolStripMenuItem_Click (lines 115–125) and comicToolStripMenuItem_Click (lines 128–138), respectively. These event handlers behave in a manner similar to that of the event handlers for the **Color** menu items. Each event handler clears the Checked properties for all font menu items by calling method ClearFont (lines 93–99), then sets the Checked property of the menu item that raised the event to true. This enforces the mutual exclusion of the font menu items. In the designer, we initially set the **Times New Roman** menu item's Checked property to true, because this is the original font for the text on the Form. The event handlers for the **Bold** and **Italic** menu items (lines 141–163) use the bitwise logical exclusive OR (^) operator to combine font styles, as we discussed in Chapter 14.

15.3 MonthCalendar Control

Many applications must perform date and time calculations. The .NET Framework provides two controls that allow an application to retrieve date and time information—the MonthCalendar and DateTimePicker (Section 15.4) controls.

The **MonthCalendar** (Fig. 15.8) control displays a monthly calendar on the Form. The user can select a date from the currently displayed month or can use the provided arrows to navigate to another month. When a date is selected, it is highlighted. Multiple dates can

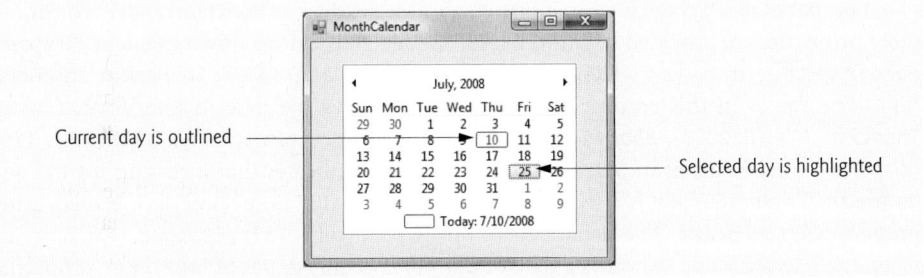

Fig. 15.8 | MonthCalendar control.

be selected by clicking dates on the calendar while holding down the *Shift* key. The default event for this control is **DateChanged**, which is generated when a new date is selected. Properties are provided that allow you to modify the appearance of the calendar, how many dates can be selected at once, and the minimum and maximum dates that may be selected. MonthCalendar properties and a common event are summarized in Fig. 15.9.

MonthCalendar properties and an event	Description
MonthCalendar Properties	
FirstDayOfWeek	Sets which day of the week is the first displayed for each week in the calendar.
MaxDate	The last date that can be selected.
MaxSelectionCount	The maximum number of dates that can be selected at once.
MinDate	The first date that can be selected.
MonthlyBoldedDates	An array of dates that will displayed in bold in the calendar.
SelectionEnd	The last of the dates selected by the user.
SelectionRange	The dates selected by the user.
SelectionStart	The first of the dates selected by the user.
Common MonthCalendar Event	
DateChanged	Generated when a date is selected in the calendar.

Fig. 15.9 | MonthCalendar properties and an event.

15.4 DateTimePicker Control

The **DateTimePicker** control (see output of Fig. 15.11) is similar to the MonthCalendar control but displays the calendar when a down arrow is selected. The DateTimePicker can be used to retrieve date and time information from the user. A DateTimePicker's **Value** property stores a DateTime object, which always contains both date and time information. You can retrieve the date information alone by using property **Date**, and you can retrieve only the time information by using the **TimeOfDay** property.

The DateTimePicker is also more customizable than a MonthCalendar control—more properties are provided to edit the look and feel of the drop-down calendar. Property **Format** specifies the user's selection options using the **DateTimePickerFormat** enumeration. The values in this enumeration are **Long** (displays the date in long format, as in Thursday, July 10, 2008), **Short** (displays the date in short format, as in 7/10/2008), **Time** (displays a time value, as in 5:31:02 PM) and **Custom** (indicates that a custom format will be used). If value Custom is used, the display in the DateTimePicker is specified using property **CustomFormat**. The default event for this control is **ValueChanged**, which occurs when the selected value (whether a date or a time) is changed. DateTimePicker properties and a common event are summarized in Fig. 15.10.

DateTimePicker properties and an event	Description
DateTimePicker *Properties*	
CalendarForeColor	Sets the text color for the calendar.
CalendarMonth-Background	Sets the calendar's background color.
CustomFormat	Sets the custom format string for the user's options.
Date	The date.
Format	Sets the format of the date and/or time used for the user's options.
MaxDate	The maximum date and time that can be selected.
MinDate	The minimum date and time that can be selected.
ShowCheckBox	Indicates if a CheckBox should be displayed to the left of the selected date and time.
ShowUpDown	Indicates whether the control displays up and down Buttons. Helpful when the DateTimePicker is used to select a time—the Buttons can be used to increase or decrease hour, minute and second.
TimeOfDay	The time.
Value	The data selected by the user.
Common DateTimePicker Event	
ValueChanged	Generated when the Value property changes, including when the user selects a new date or time.

Fig. 15.10 | DateTimePicker properties and an event.

Figure 15.11 demonstrates using the DateTimePicker control to select an item's drop-off time. Many companies use such functionality. For instance, several online DVD rental companies specify the day a movie is sent out and the estimated time that it will arrive at your home. In this application, the user selects a drop-off day, and then an estimated arrival date is displayed. The date is always two days after drop-off, three days if a Sunday is reached (mail is not delivered on Sunday).

```
1   // Fig. 15.11: DateTimePickerForm.cs
2   // Using a DateTimePicker to select a drop-off time.
3   using System;
4   using System.Windows.Forms;
5
6   namespace DateTimePickerTest
7   {
8      // Form lets user select a drop-off date using a DateTimePicker
9      // and displays an estimated delivery date
```

Fig. 15.11 | Demonstrating DateTimePicker. (Part 1 of 3.)

```
10   public partial class DateTimePickerForm : Form
11   {
12      // constructor
13      public DateTimePickerForm()
14      {
15         InitializeComponent();
16      } // end constructor
17
18      private void dateTimePickerDropOff_ValueChanged(
19         object sender, EventArgs e )
20      {
21         DateTime dropOffDate = dateTimePickerDropOff.Value;
22
23         // add extra time when items are dropped off around Sunday
24         if ( dropOffDate.DayOfWeek == DayOfWeek.Friday ||
25            dropOffDate.DayOfWeek == DayOfWeek.Saturday ||
26            dropOffDate.DayOfWeek == DayOfWeek.Sunday )
27
28            //estimate three days for delivery
29            outputLabel.Text =
30               dropOffDate.AddDays( 3 ).ToLongDateString();
31         else
32            // otherwise estimate only two days for delivery
33            outputLabel.Text =
34               dropOffDate.AddDays( 2 ).ToLongDateString();
35      } // end method dateTimePickerDropOff_ValueChanged
36
37      private void DateTimePickerForm_Load( object sender, EventArgs e )
38      {
39         // user cannot select days before today
40         dateTimePickerDropOff.MinDate = DateTime.Today;
41
42         // user can only select days of this year
43         dateTimePickerDropOff.MaxDate = DateTime.Today.AddYears( 1 );
44      } // end method DateTimePickerForm_Load
45   } // end class DateTimePickerForm
46 } // end namespace DateTimePickerTest
```

a)

DateTimePickerTest

Drop Off Date:

Thursday , July 10, 2008 ▾

Estimated Delivery Date:

b)

DateTimePickerTest

Drop Off Date:

Thursday , July   10, 2008 ▾

◄   July, 2008   ►
Sun Mon Tue Wed Thu Fri Sat
                      10   11   12
13 14 15 16 17   18   19
20 21 22 23 24   25   26
27 28 29 30 31   1   2
 3   4   5   6   7   8   9
        Today: 7/10/2008

Fig. 15.11 | Demonstrating DateTimePicker. (Part 2 of 3.)

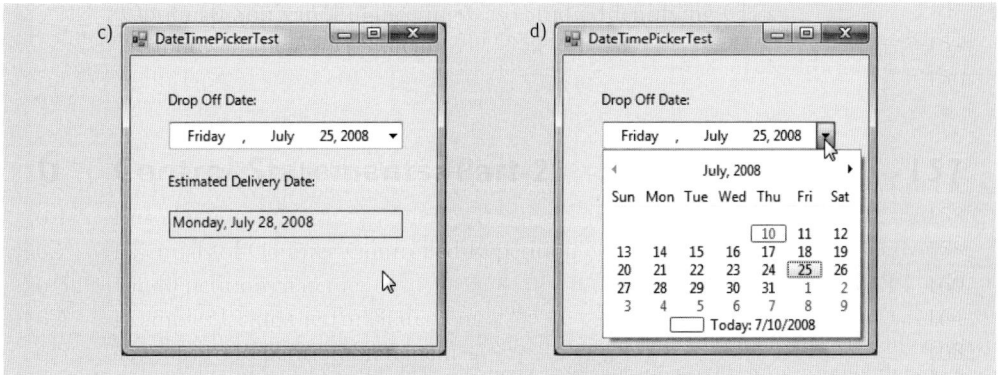

Fig. 15.11 | Demonstrating DateTimePicker. (Part 3 of 3.)

The DateTimePicker (dateTimePickerDropOff) has its Format property set to Long, so the user can select a date and not a time in this application. When the user selects a date, the ValueChanged event occurs. The event handler for this event (lines 18–35) first retrieves the selected date from the DateTimePicker's *Value* property (line 21). Lines 24–26 use the DateTime structure's *DayOfWeek* property to determine the day of the week on which the selected date falls. The day values are represented using the *DayOfWeek* enumeration. Lines 29–30 and 33–34 use DateTime's *AddDays* method to increase the date by two days or three days, respectively. The resulting date is then displayed in Long format using method *ToLongDateString*.

In this application, we do not want the user to be able to select a drop-off day before the current day, or one that is more than a year into the future. To enforce this, we set the DateTimePicker's *MinDate* and *MaxDate* properties when the Form is loaded (lines 39 and 42). Property Today returns the current day, and method *AddYears* (with an argument of 1) is used to specify a date one year in the future.

Let's take a closer look at the output. This application begins by displaying the current date (Fig. 15.11(a)). In Fig. 15.11(b), we selected the 12th of July. In Fig. 15.11(c), the estimated arrival date is displayed as the 14th. Figure 15.11(d) shows that the 12th, after it is selected, is highlighted in the calendar.

15.5 LinkLabel Control

The *LinkLabel* control displays links to other resources, such as files or web pages (Fig. 15.12). A LinkLabel appears as underlined text (colored blue by default). When the mouse moves over the link, the pointer changes to a hand; this is similar to the behavior of a hyperlink in a web page. The link can change color to indicate whether it is not yet visited, previously visited or active. When clicked, the LinkLabel generates a *LinkClicked* event (see Fig. 15.13). Class LinkLabel is derived from class Label and therefore inherits all of class Label's functionality.

Look-and-Feel Observation 15.3

A LinkLabel is the preferred control for indicating that the user can click a link to jump to a resource such as a web page, though other controls can perform similar tasks.

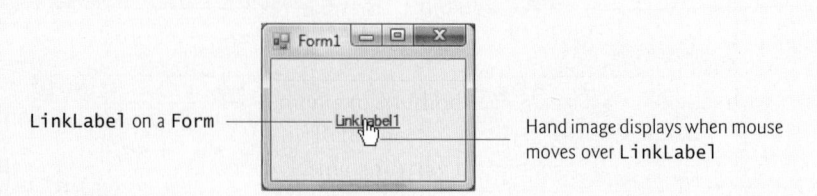

LinkLabel on a Form

Hand image displays when mouse moves over LinkLabel

Fig. 15.12 | LinkLabel control in running program.

LinkLabel properties and an event	Description
Common Properties	
ActiveLinkColor	Specifies the color of the active link when clicked.
LinkArea	Specifies which portion of text in the LinkLabel is part of the link.
LinkBehavior	Specifies the link's behavior, such as how the link appears when the mouse is placed over it.
LinkColor	Specifies the original color of all links before they have been visited. The default color is set by the system, and is usually blue.
LinkVisited	If true, the link appears as though it has been visited (its color is changed to that specified by property VisitedLinkColor). The default value is false.
Text	Specifies the control's text.
UseMnemonic	If true, the & character in the Text property acts as a shortcut (similar to the *Alt* shortcut in menus).
VisitedLinkColor	Specifies the color of visited links. The default color is set by the system, and is usually purple.
Common Event	*(Event arguments LinkLabelLinkClickedEventArgs)*
LinkClicked	Generated when the link is clicked. This is the default event when the control is double clicked in **Design** mode.

Fig. 15.13 | LinkLabel properties and an event.

Class LinkLabelTestForm (Fig. 15.14) uses three LinkLabels to link to the C: drive, the Deitel website (www.deitel.com) and the Notepad application, respectively. The Text properties of the LinkLabel's driveLinkLabel, deitelLinkLabel and notepadLinkLabel describe each link's purpose.

The event handlers for the LinkLabels call method *Start* of class *Process* (namespace *System.Diagnostics*), which allows you to execute other programs, or load documents or web sites from an application. Method Start can take one argument, the file to open, or two arguments, the application to run and its command-line arguments. Method Start's arguments can be in the same form as if they were provided for input to the Windows **Run** command (**Start > Run...**). For applications that are known to Windows, full path names are not needed, and the file extension often can be omitted. To open a file of a type that Windows recognizes (and knows how to handle), simply use the file's full path name. For example, if you a pass the method a .doc file, Windows will open it in Micrsoft Word. The Windows operating system must be able to use the application associated with the given file's extension to open the file.

```
 1   // Fig. 15.14: LinkLabelTestForm.cs
 2   // Using LinkLabels to create hyperlinks.
 3   using System;
 4   using System.Windows.Forms;
 5
 6   namespace LinkLabelTest
 7   {
 8      // Form using LinkLabels to browse the C:\ drive,
 9      // load a web page and run Notepad
10      public partial class LinkLabelTestForm : Form
11      {
12         // constructor
13         public LinkLabelTestForm()
14         {
15            InitializeComponent();
16         } // end constructor
17
18         // browse C:\ drive
19         private void cDriveLinkLabel_LinkClicked( object sender,
20            LinkLabelLinkClickedEventArgs e )
21         {
22            // change LinkColor after it has been clicked
23            driveLinkLabel.LinkVisited = true;
24
25            System.Diagnostics.Process.Start( @"C:\" );
26         } // end method driveLinkLabel_LinkClicked
27
28         // load www.deitel.com in web browser
29         private void deitelLinkLabel_LinkClicked( object sender,
30            LinkLabelLinkClickedEventArgs e )
31         {
32            // change LinkColor after it has been clicked
33            deitelLinkLabel.LinkVisited = true;
34
35            System.Diagnostics.Process.Start( "http://www.deitel.com" );
36         } // end method deitelLinkLabel_LinkClicked
37
38         // run application Notepad
39         private void notepadLinkLabel_LinkClicked( object sender,
40            LinkLabelLinkClickedEventArgs e )
41         {
42            // change LinkColor after it has been clicked
43            notepadLinkLabel.LinkVisited = true;
44
45            // program called as if in run
46            // menu and full path not needed
```

Fig. 15.14 | LinkLabels used to link to a drive, a web page and an application. (Part 1 of 2.)

```
47              System.Diagnostics.Process.Start( "notepad" );
48          } // end method driveLinkLabel_LinkClicked
49      } // end class LinkLabelTestForm
50  } // end namespace LinkLabelTest
```

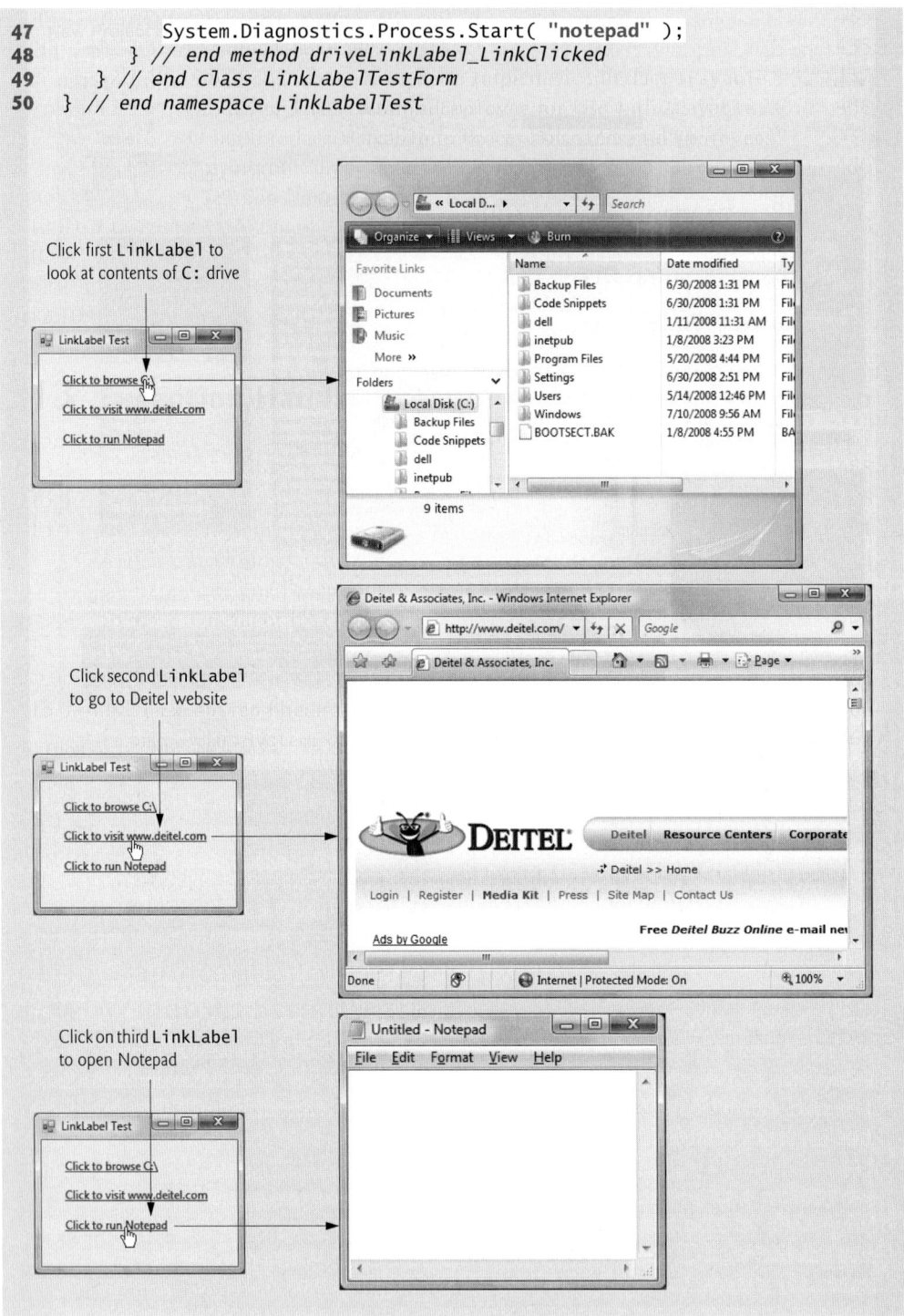

Fig. 15.14 | LinkLabels used to link to a drive, a web page and an application. (Part 2 of 2.)

The event handler for driveLinkLabel's LinkClicked event browses the C: drive (lines 19–26). Line 23 sets the LinkVisited property to true, which changes the link's color from blue to purple (the LinkVisited colors can be configured through the **Properties** window in Visual Studio). The event handler then passes @"C:\" to method Start (line 25), which opens a **Windows Explorer** window. The @ symbol that we placed before "C:\" indicates that all characters in the string should be interpreted literally—this is known as a *verbatim string*. Thus, the backslash within the string is not considered to be the first character of an escape sequence. This simplifies strings that represent directory paths, since you do not need to use \\ for each \ character in the path.

The event handler for deitelLinkLabel's LinkClicked event (lines 29–36) opens the web page www.deitel.com in the user's default web browser. We achieve this by passing the web-page address as a string (line 35), which opens the web page in a new web browser window or tab. Line 33 sets the LinkVisited property to true.

The event handler for notepadLinkLabel's LinkClicked event (lines 39–48) opens the Notepad application. Line 43 sets the LinkVisited property to true so that the link appears as a visited link. Line 47 passes the argument "notepad" to method Start, which runs notepad.exe. Note that in line 47, neither the full path nor the .exe extension is required—Windows automatically recognizes the argument given to method Start as an executable file.

15.6 ListBox **Control**

The *ListBox* control allows the user to view and select from multiple items in a list. List-Boxes are static GUI entities, which means that users cannot directly edit the list of items. The user can be provided with TextBoxes and Buttons with which to specify items to be added to the list, but the actual additions must be performed in code. The *CheckedListBox* control (Section 15.7) extends a ListBox by including CheckBoxes next to each item in the list. This allows users to place checks on multiple items at once, as is possible with CheckBox controls. (Users also can select multiple items from a ListBox by setting the ListBox's *SelectionMode* property, which is discussed shortly.) Figure 15.15 displays a ListBox and a CheckedListBox. In both controls, scrollbars appear if the number of items exceeds the ListBox's viewable area.

Figure 15.16 lists common ListBox properties and methods and a common event. The SelectionMode property determines the number of items that can be selected. This

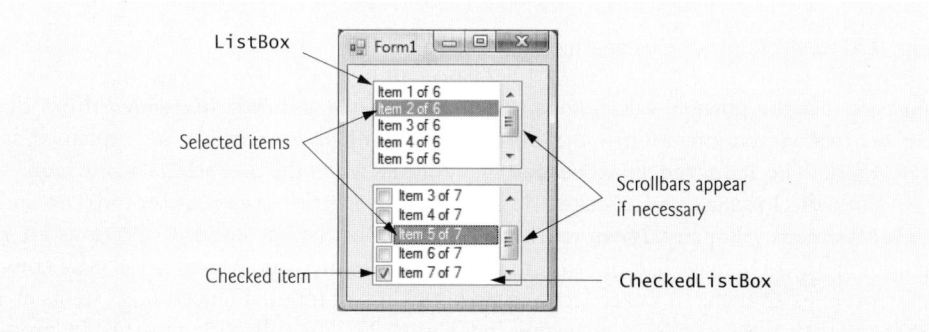

Fig. 15.15 | ListBox and CheckedListBox on a Form.

ListBox properties, methods and an event	Description
Common Properties	
Items	The collection of items in the ListBox.
MultiColumn	Indicates whether the ListBox can display multiple columns. Multiple columns eliminate vertical scrollbars from the display.
SelectedIndex	Returns the index of the selected item. If no items have been selected, the property returns -1. If the user selects multiple items, this property returns only one of the selected indices. For this reason, if multiple items are selected, you should use property SelectedIndices.
SelectedIndices	Returns a collection containing the indices for all selected items.
SelectedItem	Returns a reference to the selected item. If multiple items are selected, it returns the item with the lowest index number.
SelectedItems	Returns a collection of the selected item(s).
SelectionMode	Determines the number of items that can be selected and the means through which multiple items can be selected. Values None, One, MultiSimple (multiple selection allowed) or MultiExtended (multiple selection allowed using a combination of arrow keys or mouse clicks and *Shift* and *Ctrl* keys).
Sorted	Indicates whether items are sorted alphabetically. Setting this property's value to true sorts the items. The default value is false.
Common Methods	
ClearSelected	Deselects every item.
GetSelected	Takes an index as an argument and returns true if the corresponding item is selected.
Common Event	
SelectedIndexChanged	Generated when the selected index changes. This is the default event when the control is double clicked in the designer.

Fig. 15.16 | ListBox properties, methods and an event.

property has the possible values *None*, *One*, *MultiSimple* and *MultiExtended* (from the *SelectionMode* enumeration)—the differences among these settings are explained in Fig. 15.16. The *SelectedIndexChanged* event occurs when the user selects a new item.

Both the ListBox and CheckedListBox have properties Items, SelectedItem and SelectedIndex. Property *Items* returns a collaction of the list items. Collections are a common way to manage lists of objects in the .NET framework. Many .NET GUI components (e.g., ListBoxes) use collections to expose lists of internal objects (e.g., items in a ListBox). We discuss collections further in Chapter 27. The collection returned by property Items is represented as an object of type *ObjectCollection*. Property *SelectedItem* returns the ListBox's currently selected item. If the user can select multiple items, use collection ***SelectedItems*** to return all the selected items as a collection. Property ***Selected-Index*** returns the index of the selected item—if there could be more than one, use property ***SelectedIndices***. If no items are selected, property SelectedIndex returns -1. Method ***GetSelected*** takes an index and returns true if the corresponding item is selected.

To add items to a ListBox or to a CheckedListBox, we must add objects to its Items collection. This can be accomplished by calling method Add to add a string to the ListBox's or CheckedListBox's Items collection. For example, we could write

> *myListBox*.Items.Add(*myListItem*);

to add string *myListItem* to ListBox *myListBox*. To add multiple objects, you can either call method Add multiple times or call method AddRange to add an array of objects. Classes ListBox and CheckedListBox each call the submitted object's ToString method to determine the Label for the corresponding object's entry in the list. This allows you to add different objects to a ListBox or a CheckedListBox that later can be returned through properties SelectedItem and SelectedItems.

Alternatively, you can add items to ListBoxes and CheckedListBoxes visually by examining the Items property in the **Properties** window. Clicking the ellipsis button opens the **String Collection Editor**, which contains a text area for adding items; each item appears on a separate line (Fig. 15.17). Visual Studio then writes code to add these strings to the Items collection inside method InitializeComponent.

Figure 15.18 uses class ListBoxTestForm to add, remove and clear items from ListBox displayListBox. Class ListBoxTestForm uses TextBox inputTextBox to allow the user to type in a new item. When the user clicks the **Add** Button, the new item appears in displayListBox. Similarly, if the user selects an item and clicks **Remove**, the item is deleted. When clicked, **Clear** deletes all entries in displayListBox. The user terminates the application by clicking **Exit**.

The addButton_Click event handler (lines 20–24) calls method ***Add*** of the Items collection in the ListBox. This method takes a string as the item to add to displayListBox. In this case, the string used is the user input from the inputTextBox (line 22). After the item is added, inputTextBox.Text is cleared (line 23).

The removeButton_Click event handler (lines 27–33) uses method ***RemoveAt*** to remove an item from the ListBox. Event handler removeButton_Click first uses property SelectedIndex to determine which index is selected. If SelectedIndex is not -1 (i.e., an item is selected), lines 31–32 remove the item that corresponds to the selected index.

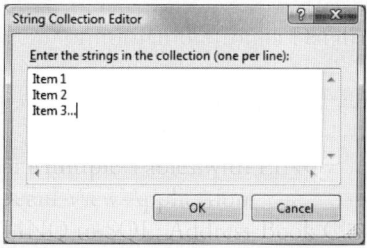

Fig. 15.17 | String Collection Editor.

The clearButton_Click event handler (lines 36–39) calls method *Clear* of the Items collection (line 38). This removes all the entries in displayListBox. Finally, event handler exitButton_Click (lines 32–45) terminates the application by calling method Application.Exit (line 44).

```csharp
1    // Fig. 15.18: ListBoxTestForm.cs
2    // Program to add, remove and clear ListBox items
3    using System;
4    using System.Windows.Forms;
5
6    namespace ListBoxTest
7    {
8       // Form uses a TextBox and Buttons to add,
9       // remove, and clear ListBox items
10      public partial class ListBoxTestForm : Form
11      {
12         // constructor
13         public ListBoxTestForm()
14         {
15            InitializeComponent();
16         } // end constructor
17
18         // add new item to ListBox (text from input TextBox)
19         // and clear input TextBox
20         private void addButton_Click( object sender, EventArgs e )
21         {
22            displayListBox.Items.Add( inputTextBox.Text );
23            inputTextBox.Clear();
24         } // end method addButton_Click
25
26         // remove item if one is selected
27         private void removeButton_Click( object sender, EventArgs e )
28         {
29            // check whether item is selected, remove if
30            if ( displayListBox.SelectedIndex != -1 )
31               displayListBox.Items.RemoveAt(
32                  displayListBox.SelectedIndex );
33         } // end method removeButton_Click
34
35         // clear all items in ListBox
36         private void clearButton_Click( object sender, EventArgs e )
37         {
38            displayListBox.Items.Clear();
39         } // end method clearButton_Click
40
41         // exit application
42         private void exitButton_Click( object sender, EventArgs e )
43         {
44            Application.Exit();
45         } // end method exitButton_Click
46      } // end class ListBoxTestForm
47   } // end namespace ListBoxTest
```

Fig. 15.18 | Program that adds, removes and clears ListBox items. (Part 1 of 2.)

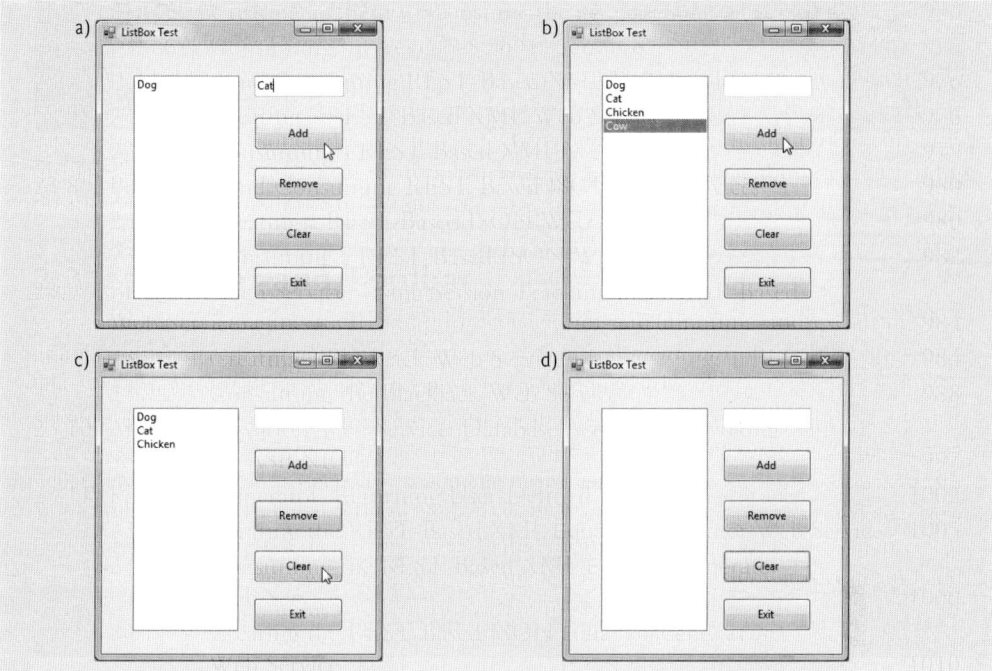

Fig. 15.18 | Program that adds, removes and clears ListBox items. (Part 2 of 2.)

15.7 CheckedListBox Control

The CheckedListBox control derives from ListBox and displays a CheckBox with each item. Items can be added via methods Add and AddRange or through the **String Collection Editor**. CheckedListBoxes allow multiple items to be checked, but item selection is more restrictive. The only values for the SelectionMode property are None and One. One allows a single selection, whereas None allows no selections. Note that because an item must by selected to be checked, you must set the SelectionMode to be One if you wish to allow users to check items. Thus, toggling property SelectionMode between One and None effectively switches between enabling and disabling the user's ability to check list items. Common properties, events and methods of CheckedListBoxes appear in Fig. 15.19.

 Common Programming Error 15.1

*The IDE displays an error message if you attempt to set the SelectionMode property to Multi-Simple or MultiExtended in the **Properties** window of a CheckedListBox. If this value is set programmatically, a runtime error occurs.*

Event ***ItemCheck*** occurs whenever a user checks or unchecks a CheckedListBox item. Event-argument properties CurrentValue and NewValue return CheckState values for the current and new state of the item, respectively. A comparison of these values allows you to determine whether the CheckedListBox item was checked or unchecked. The Checked-ListBox control retains the SelectedItems and SelectedIndices properties (it inherits them from class ListBox). However, it also includes properties CheckedItems and CheckedIndices, which return information about the checked items and indices.

CheckedListBox properties, a method and an event	Description
Common Properties	*(All the ListBox properties, methods and events are inherited by CheckedListBox.)*
CheckedItems	Contains the collection of items that are checked. This is distinct from the selected item, which is highlighted (but not necessarily checked). [*Note:* There can be at most one selected item at any given time.]
CheckedIndices	Returns indices for all checked items.
CheckOnClick	When true and the user clicks an item, the item is both selected and checked or unchecked. By default, this property is false, which menas that the user must select an item, then click it again to check or uncheck it.
SelectionMode	Determines whether items can be checked. The possible values are One (allows multiple checks to be placed) or None (does not allow any checks to be placed).
Common Method	
GetItemChecked	Takes an index and returns true if the corresponding item is checked.
Common Event	*(Event arguments ItemCheckEventArgs)*
ItemCheck	Generated when an item is checked or unchecked.
ItemCheckEventArgs Properties	
CurrentValue	Indicates whether the current item is checked or unchecked. Possible values are Checked, Unchecked and Indeterminate.
Index	Returns the zero-based index of the item that changed.
NewValue	Specifies the new state of the item.

Fig. 15.19 | CheckedListBox properties, a method and an event.

In Fig. 15.20, class CheckedListBoxTestForm uses a CheckedListBox and a ListBox to display a user's selection of books. The CheckedListBox allows the user to select multiple titles. In the **String Collection Editor**, items were added for some Deitel books: C++, Java™, Visual Basic, Internet & WWW, Perl, Python, Wireless Internet and Advanced Java (the acronym HTP stands for "How to Program"). The ListBox (named displayListBox) displays the user's selection. In the screenshots accompanying this example, the CheckedListBox appears to the left, the ListBox on the right.

When the user checks or unchecks an item in inputCheckedListBox, an ItemCheck event occurs and event handler inputCheckedListBox_ItemCheck (lines 19–31) executes. An if...else statement (lines 27–30) determines whether the user checked or unchecked an item in the CheckedListBox. Line 27 uses the NewValue property to determine whether the item is being checked (CheckState.Checked). If the user checks an item, line 28 adds

```
 1    // Fig. 15.20: CheckedListBoxTestForm.cs
 2    // Using the checked ListBox to add items to a display ListBox
 3    using System;
 4    using System.Windows.Forms;
 5
 6    namespace CheckedListBoxTest
 7    {
 8       // Form uses a checked ListBox to add items to a display ListBox
 9       public partial class CheckedListBoxTestForm : Form
10       {
11          // constructor
12          public CheckedListBoxTestForm()
13          {
14             InitializeComponent();
15          } // end constructor
16
17          // item about to change
18          // add or remove from display ListBox
19          private void itemCheckedListBox_ItemCheck(
20             object sender, ItemCheckEventArgs e )
21          {
22             // obtain reference of selected item
23             string item = itemCheckedListBox.SelectedItem.ToString();
24
25             // if item checked, add to ListBox
26             // otherwise remove from ListBox
27             if ( e.NewValue == CheckState.Checked )
28                displayListBox.Items.Add( item );
29             else
30                displayListBox.Items.Remove( item );
31          } // end method inputCheckedListBox_ItemCheck
32       } // end class CheckedListBoxTestForm
33    } // end namespace CheckedListBoxTest
```

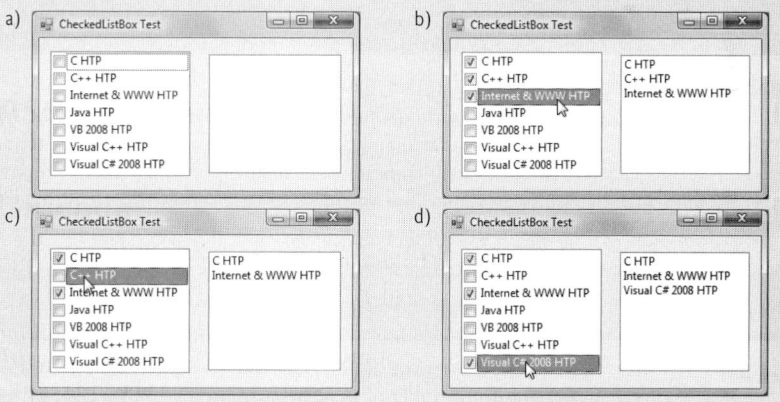

Fig. 15.20 | CheckedListBox and ListBox used in a program to display a user selection.

the checked entry to the ListBox displayListBox. If the user unchecks an item, line 30 removes the corresponding item from displayListBox. This event handler was created by selecting the CheckedListBox in **Design** mode, viewing the control's events in the **Proper-ties** window and double clicking the ItemCheck event.

15.8 ComboBox Control

The *ComboBox* control combines TextBox features with a ***drop-down list***—a GUI compo-nent that contains a list from which a value can be selected. A ComboBox usually appears as a TextBox with a down arrow to its right. By default, the user can enter text into the Text-Box or click the down arrow to display a list of predefined items. If a user chooses an ele-ment from this list, that element is displayed in the TextBox. If the list contains more elements than can be displayed in the drop-down list, a scrollbar appears. The maximum number of items that a drop-down list can display at one time is set by property *MaxDrop-DownItems*. Figure 15.21 shows a sample ComboBox in three different states.

As with the ListBox control, you can add objects to collection Items programmati-cally, using methods Add and AddRange, or visually, with the **String Collection Editor**. Figure 15.22 lists common properties and a common event of class ComboBox.

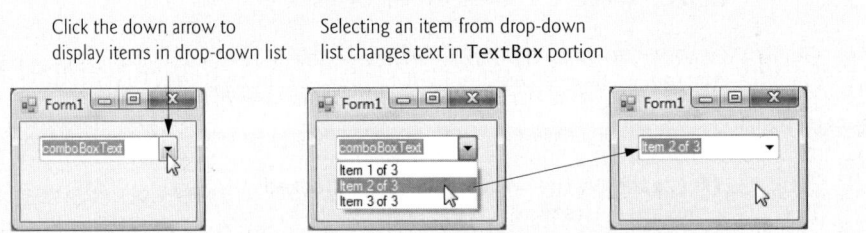

Fig. 15.21 | ComboBox demonstration.

ComboBox properties and an event	Description
Common Properties	
DropDownStyle	Determines the type of ComboBox. Value Simple means that the text portion is editable and the list portion is always visible. Value Drop-Down (the default) means that the text portion is editable but the user must click an arrow button to see the list portion. Value DropDown-List means that the text portion is not editable and the user must click the arrow button to see the list portion.
Items	The collection of items in the ComboBox control.
MaxDropDownItems	Specifies the maximum number of items (between 1 and 100) that the drop-down list can display. If the number of items exceeds the maximum number of items to display, a scrollbar appears.
SelectedIndex	Returns the index of the selected item. If there is no selected item, -1 is returned.

Fig. 15.22 | ComboBox properties and an event. (Part 1 of 2.)

ComboBox properties and an event	Description
SelectedItem	Returns a reference to the selected item.
Sorted	Indicates whether items are sorted alphabetically. Setting this property's value to true sorts the items. The default is false.
Common Event	
SelectedIndexChanged	Generated when the selected index changes (such as when a different item is selected). This is the default event when control is double clicked in the designer.

Fig. 15.22 | ComboBox properties and an event. (Part 2 of 2.)

Look-and-Feel Observation 15.4

Use a ComboBox to save space on a GUI. A disadvantage is that, unlike with a ListBox, the user cannot see available items without expanding the drop-down list.

Property **DropDownStyle** determines the type of ComboBox and is represented as a value of the **ComboBoxStyle** enumeration, which contains values Simple, DropDown and DropDownList. Option **Simple** does not display a drop-down arrow. Instead, a scrollbar appears next to the control, allowing the user to select a choice from the list. The user also can type in a selection. Style **DropDown** (the default) displays a drop-down list when the down arrow is clicked (or the down arrow key is pressed). The user can type a new item in the ComboBox. The last style is **DropDownList**, which displays a drop-down list but does not allow the user to type in the TextBox.

The ComboBox control has properties **Items** (a collection), **SelectedItem** and **SelectedIndex**, which are similar to the corresponding properties in ListBox. There can be at most one selected item in a ComboBox. If no items are selected, then SelectedIndex is -1. When the selected item changes, a **SelectedIndexChanged** event occurs.

Class ComboBoxTestForm (Fig. 15.23) allows users to select a shape to draw—circle, ellipse, square or pie (in both filled and unfilled versions)—by using a ComboBox. The ComboBox in this example is uneditable, so the user cannot type in the TextBox.

Look-and-Feel Observation 15.5

Make lists (such as ComboBoxes) editable only if the program is designed to accept user-submitted elements. Otherwise, the user might try to enter a custom item that is improper for the purposes of your application.

```
1   // Fig. 15.23: ComboBoxTestForm.cs
2   // Using ComboBox to select a shape to draw.
3   using System;
4   using System.Drawing;
5   using System.Windows.Forms;
6
```

Fig. 15.23 | ComboBox used to draw a selected shape. (Part 1 of 3.)

```
7    namespace ComboBoxTest
8    {
9       // Form uses a ComboBox to select different shapes to draw
10      public partial class ComboBoxTestForm : Form
11      {
12         // constructor
13         public ComboBoxTestForm()
14         {
15            InitializeComponent();
16         } // end constructor
17
18         // get index of selected shape, draw shape
19         private void imageComboBox_SelectedIndexChanged(
20            object sender, EventArgs e )
21         {
22            // create graphics object, Pen and SolidBrush
23            Graphics myGraphics = base.CreateGraphics();
24
25            // create Pen using color DarkRed
26            Pen myPen = new Pen( Color.DarkRed );
27
28            // create SolidBrush using color DarkRed
29            SolidBrush mySolidBrush = new SolidBrush( Color.DarkRed );
30
31            // clear drawing area, setting it to color white
32            myGraphics.Clear( Color.White );
33
34            // find index, draw proper shape
35            switch ( imageComboBox.SelectedIndex )
36            {
37               case 0: // case Circle is selected
38                  myGraphics.DrawEllipse( myPen, 50, 50, 150, 150 );
39                  break;
40               case 1: // case Rectangle is selected
41                  myGraphics.DrawRectangle( myPen, 50, 50, 150, 150 );
42                  break;
43               case 2: // case Ellipse is selected
44                  myGraphics.DrawEllipse( myPen, 50, 85, 150, 115 );
45                  break;
46               case 3: // case Pie is selected
47                  myGraphics.DrawPie( myPen, 50, 50, 150, 150, 0, 45 );
48                  break;
49               case 4: // case Filled Circle is selected
50                  myGraphics.FillEllipse( mySolidBrush, 50, 50, 150, 150 );
51                  break;
52               case 5: // case Filled Rectangle is selected
53                  myGraphics.FillRectangle( mySolidBrush, 50, 50, 150,
54                     150 );
55                  break;
56               case 6: // case Filled Ellipse is selected
57                  myGraphics.FillEllipse( mySolidBrush, 50, 85, 150, 115 );
58                  break;
```

Fig. 15.23 | ComboBox used to draw a selected shape. (Part 2 of 3.)

```
59                   case 7: // case Filled Pie is selected
60                      myGraphics.FillPie( mySolidBrush, 50, 50, 150, 150, 0,
61                         45 );
62                      break;
63                } // end switch
64
65                myGraphics.Dispose(); // release the Graphics object
66             } // end method imageComboBox_SelectedIndexChanged
67          } // end class ComboBoxTestForm
68       } // end namespace ComboBoxTest
```

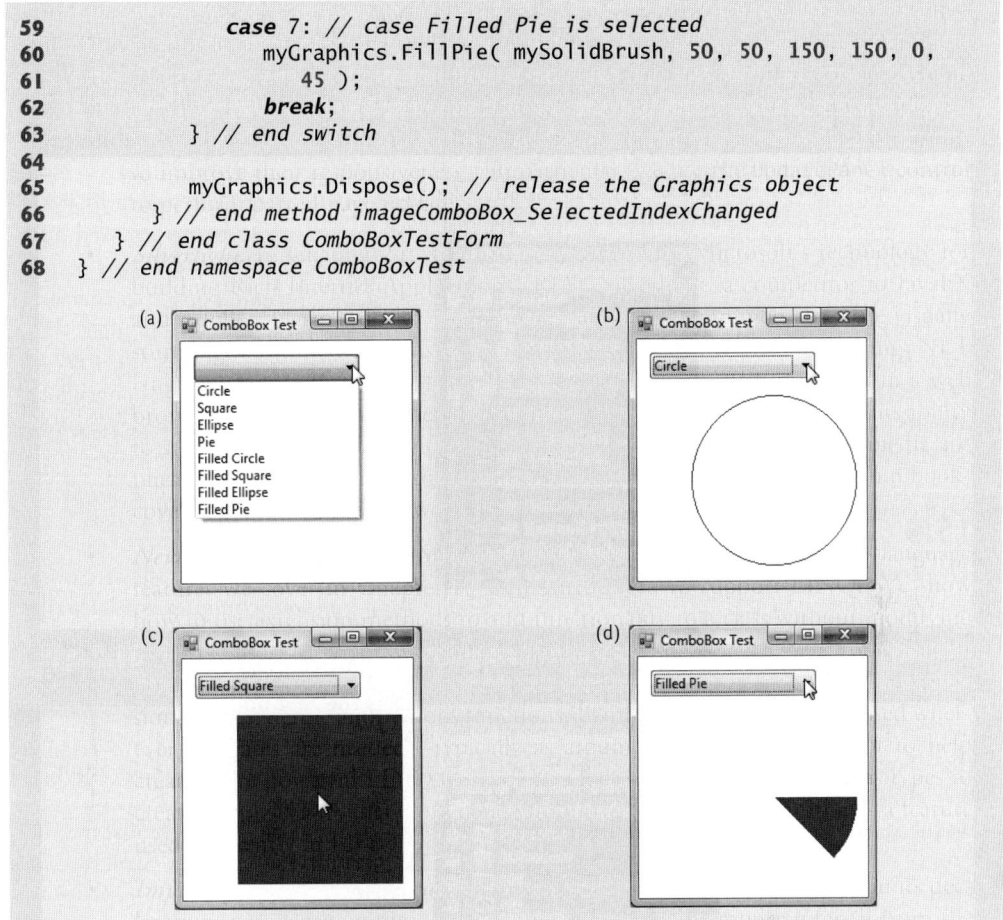

Fig. 15.23 │ ComboBox used to draw a selected shape. (Part 3 of 3.)

After creating ComboBox imageComboBox, make it uneditable by setting its DropDown-Style to DropDownList in the **Properties** window. Next, add items Circle, Square, Ellipse, Pie, Filled Circle, Filled Square, Filled Ellipse and Filled Pie to the Items collection using the **String Collection Editor**. Whenever the user selects an item from imageComboBox, a SelectedIndexChanged event occurs and event handler imageCombo-Box_SelectedIndexChanged (lines 19–66) executes. Lines 23–29 create a Graphics object, a Pen and a SolidBrush, which are used to draw on the Form. The Graphics object (line 23) allows a pen or brush to draw on a component, using one of several Graphics methods. The Pen object (line 26) is used by methods DrawEllipse, DrawRectangle and DrawPie (lines 38, 41, 44 and 47) to draw the outlines of their corresponding shapes. The SolidBrush object (line 29) is used by methods FillEllipse, FillRectangle and FillPie (lines 50, 53–54, 57 and 60–61) to fill their corresponding solid shapes. Line 32 colors the entire Form White, using Graphics method ***Clear***.

The application draws a shape based on the selected item's index. The switch statement (lines 35–63) uses imageComboBox.SelectedIndex to determine which item the user selected. `Graphics` method **DrawEllipse** (line 38) takes a `Pen`, the *x*- and *y*-coordinates of the center and the width and height of the ellipse to draw. The origin of the coordinate system is in the upper-left corner of the `Form`; the *x*-coordinate increases to the right, and the *y*-coordinate increases downward. A circle is a special case of an ellipse (with the width and height equal). Line 38 draws a circle. Line 44 draws an ellipse that has different values for width and height.

Class `Graphics` method **DrawRectangle** (line 41) takes a `Pen`, the *x*- and *y*-coordinates of the upper-left corner and the width and height of the rectangle to draw. Method **DrawPie** (line 47) draws a pie as a portion of an ellipse. The ellipse is bounded by a rectangle. Method `DrawPie` takes a `Pen`, the *x*- and *y*-coordinates of the upper-left corner of the rectangle, its width and height, the start angle (in degrees) and the sweep angle (in degrees) of the pie. Angles increase clockwise. The **FillEllipse** (lines 50 and 57), **FillRectangle** (line 53–54) and **FillPie** (line 60–61) methods are similar to their unfilled counterparts, except that they take a `Brush` (e.g., `SolidBrush`) instead of a `Pen`. Some of the drawn shapes are illustrated in the screenshots of Fig. 15.23.

15.9 TreeView Control

The **TreeView** control displays *nodes* hierarchically in a *tree*. Traditionally, nodes are objects that contain values and can refer to other nodes. A *parent node* contains *child nodes*, and the child nodes can be parents to other nodes. Two child nodes that have the same parent node are considered *sibling nodes*. A tree is a collection of nodes, usually organized in a hierarchical manner. The first parent node of a tree is the *root* node (a `TreeView` can have multiple roots). For example, the file system of a computer can be represented as a tree. The top-level directory (perhaps `C:`) would be the root, each subfolder of `C:` would be a child node and each child folder could have its own children. `TreeView` controls are useful for displaying hierarchical information, such as the file structure that we just mentioned. We cover nodes and trees in greater detail in Chapter 25, Data Structures. Figure 15.24 displays a sample `TreeView` control on a `Form`.

A parent node can be expanded or collapsed by clicking the plus box or minus box to its left. Nodes without children do not have these boxes.

The nodes in a `TreeView` are instances of class **TreeNode**. Each `TreeNode` has a **Nodes** *collection* (type **TreeNodeCollection**), which contains a list of other `TreeNodes`—known as its children. The `Parent` property returns a reference to the parent node (or `null` if the node is a root node). Figure 15.25 and Fig. 15.26 list the common properties of `TreeViews` and `TreeNodes`, common `TreeNode` methods and a common `TreeView` event.

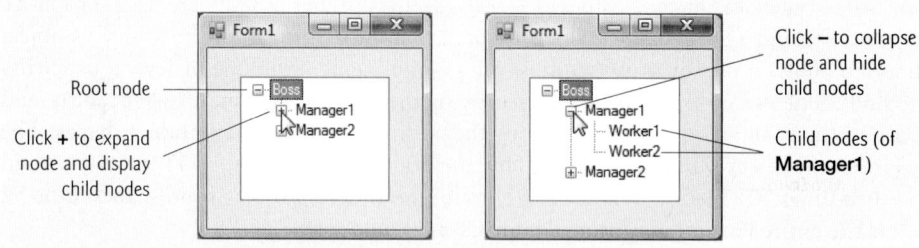

Fig. 15.24 | `TreeView` displaying a sample tree.

TreeView properties and an event	Description
Common Properties	
CheckBoxes	Indicates whether CheckBoxes appear next to nodes. A value of true displays CheckBoxes. The default value is false.
ImageList	Specifies an ImageList object containing the node icons. An *ImageList* object is a collection that contains Image objects.
Nodes	Lists the collection of TreeNodes in the control. It contains methods Add (adds a TreeNode object), Clear (deletes the entire collection) and Remove (deletes a specific node). Removing a parent node deletes all of its children.
SelectedNode	The selected node.
Common Event (Event arguments TreeViewEventArgs)	
AfterSelect	Generated after selected node changes. This is the default event when the control is double clicked in the designer.

Fig. 15.25 | TreeView properties and an event.

TreeNode properties and methods	Description
Common Properties	
Checked	Indicates whether the TreeNode is checked (CheckBoxes property must be set to true in the parent TreeView).
FirstNode	Specifies the first node in the Nodes collection (i.e., the first child in the tree).
FullPath	Indicates the path of the node, starting at the root of the tree.
ImageIndex	Specifies the index of the image shown when the node is deselected.
LastNode	Specifies the last node in the Nodes collection (i.e., the last child in the tree).
NextNode	Next sibling node.
Nodes	Collection of TreeNodes contained in the current node (i.e., all the children of the current node). It contains methods Add (adds a TreeNode object), Clear (deletes the entire collection) and Remove (deletes a specific node). Removing a parent node deletes all of its children.
PrevNode	Previous sibling node.
SelectedImageIndex	Specifies the index of the image to use when the node is selected.
Text	Specifies the TreeNode's text.

Fig. 15.26 | TreeNode properties and methods. (Part 1 of 2.)

TreeNode properties and methods	Description
Common Methods	
Collapse	Collapses a node.
Expand	Expands a node.
ExpandAll	Expands all the children of a node.
GetNodeCount	Returns the number of child nodes.

Fig. 15.26 | TreeNode properties and methods. (Part 2 of 2.)

To add nodes to the TreeView visually, click the ellipsis next to the Nodes property in the **Properties** window. This opens the **TreeNode Editor** (Fig. 15.27), which displays an empty tree representing the TreeView. There are Buttons to create a root and to add or delete a node. To the right are the properties of current node. Here you can rename the node.

To add nodes programmatically, first create a root node. Create a new TreeNode object and pass it a string to display. Then call method Add to add this new TreeNode to the TreeView's Nodes collection. Thus, to add a root node to TreeView *myTreeView*, write

   myTreeView.Nodes.Add(**new** TreeNode(*rootLabel*));

where *myTreeView* is the TreeView to which we are adding nodes, and *rootLabel* is the text to display in *myTreeView*. To add children to a root node, add new TreeNodes to its Nodes collection. We select the appropriate root node from the TreeView by writing

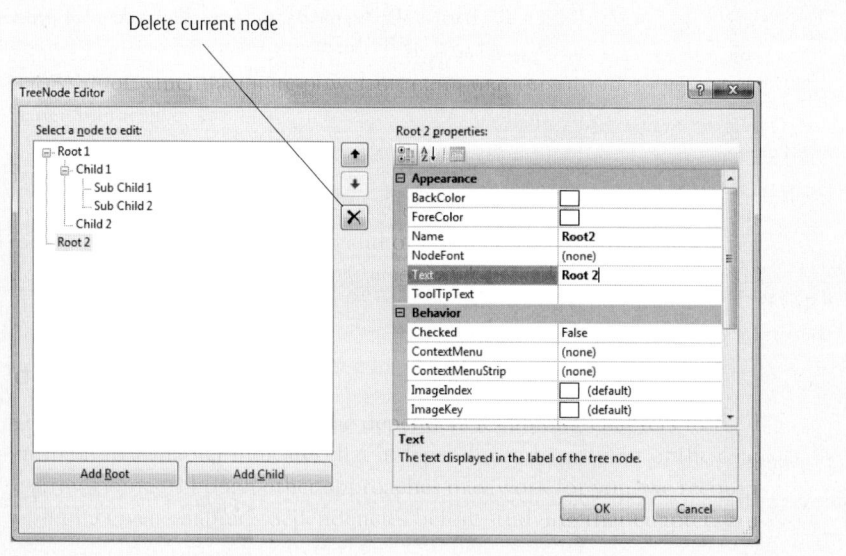

Fig. 15.27 | TreeNode Editor.

myTreeView.Nodes[myIndex]

where *myIndex* is the root node's index in *myTreeView*'s Nodes collection. We add nodes to child nodes through the same process by which we added root nodes to *myTreeView*. To add a child to the root node at index *myIndex*, write

myTreeView.Nodes[myIndex].Nodes.Add(**new** TreeNode(*ChildLabel*));

Class TreeViewDirectoryStructureForm (Fig. 15.28) uses a TreeView to display the contents of a directory chosen by the user. A TextBox and a Button are used to specify the directory. First, enter the full path of the directory you want to display. Then click the Button to set the specified directory as the root node in the TreeView. Each subdirectory of this directory becomes a child node. This layout is similar to that used in **Windows Explorer.** Folders can be expanded or collapsed by clicking the plus or minus boxes that appear to their left.

```
1    // Fig. 15.28: TreeViewDirectoryStructureForm.cs
2    // Using TreeView to display directory structure.
3    using System;
4    using System.Windows.Forms;
5    using System.IO;
6
7    namespace TreeViewDirectoryStructure
8    {
9       // Form uses TreeView to display directory structure
10      public partial class TreeViewDirectoryStructureForm : Form
11      {
12         string substringDirectory; // store last part of full path name
13
14         // constructor
15         public TreeViewDirectoryStructureForm()
16         {
17            InitializeComponent();
18         } // end constructor
19
20         // populate current node with subdirectories
21         public void PopulateTreeView(
22            string directoryValue, TreeNode parentNode )
23         {
24            // array stores all subdirectories in the directory
25            string[] directoryArray =
26               Directory.GetDirectories( directoryValue );
27
28            // populate current node with subdirectories
29            try
30            {
31               // check to see if any subdirectories are present
32               if ( directoryArray.Length != 0 )
33               {
34                  // for every subdirectory, create new TreeNode,
35                  // add as a child of current node and recursively
36                  // populate child nodes with subdirectories
```

Fig. 15.28 | TreeView used to display directories. (Part 1 of 3.)

```
37                      foreach ( string directory in directoryArray )
38                      {
39                          // obtain last part of path name from the full path
40                          // name by calling the GetFileNameWithoutExtension
41                          // method of class Path
42                          substringDirectory =
43                              Path.GetFileNameWithoutExtension( directory );
44
45                          // create TreeNode for current directory
46                          TreeNode myNode = new TreeNode( substringDirectory );
47
48                          // add current directory node to parent node
49                          parentNode.Nodes.Add( myNode );
50
51                          // recursively populate every subdirectory
52                          PopulateTreeView( directory, myNode );
53                      } // end foreach
54                  } // end if
55              } //end try
56
57              // catch exception
58              catch ( UnauthorizedAccessException )
59              {
60                  parentNode.Nodes.Add( "Access denied" );
61              } // end catch
62          } // end method PopulateTreeView
63
64          // handles enterButton click event
65          private void enterButton_Click( object sender, EventArgs e )
66          {
67              // clear all nodes
68              directoryTreeView.Nodes.Clear();
69
70              // check if the directory entered by user exists
71              // if it does, then fill in the TreeView,
72              // if not, display error MessageBox
73              if ( Directory.Exists( inputTextBox.Text ) )
74              {
75                  // add full path name to directoryTreeView
76                  directoryTreeView.Nodes.Add( inputTextBox.Text );
77
78                  // insert subfolders
79                  PopulateTreeView(
80                      inputTextBox.Text, directoryTreeView.Nodes[ 0 ] );
81              }
82              // display error MessageBox if directory not found
83              else
84                  MessageBox.Show( inputTextBox.Text + " could not be found.",
85                      "Directory Not Found", MessageBoxButtons.OK,
86                      MessageBoxIcon.Error );
87          } // end method enterButton_Click
88      } // end class TreeViewDirectoryStructureForm
89  } // end namespace TreeViewDirectoryStructure
```

Fig. 15.28 | TreeView used to display directories. (Part 2 of 3.)

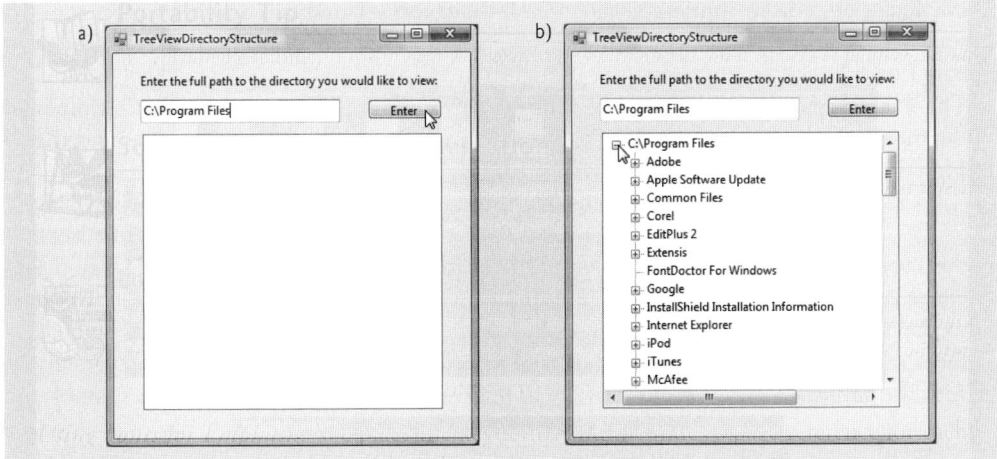

Fig. 15.28 | TreeView used to display directories. (Part 3 of 3.)

When the user clicks the enterButton, all the nodes in directoryTreeView are cleared (line 68). Then the path entered in inputTextBox is used to create the root node. Line 76 adds the directory to directoryTreeView as the root node, and lines 79–80 call method PopulateTreeView (lines 21–62), which takes a directory (a string) and a parent node. Method PopulateTreeView then creates child nodes corresponding to the subdirectories of the directory it receives as an argument.

Method PopulateTreeView (lines 21–62) obtains a list of subdirectories, using method **GetDirectories** of class Directory (namespace System.IO) in lines 25–26. Method GetDirectories takes a string (the current directory) and returns an array of strings (the subdirectories). If a directory is not accessible for security reasons, an UnauthorizedAccessException is thrown. Lines 58–61 catch this exception and add a node containing "Access Denied" instead of displaying the subdirectories.

If there are accessible subdirectories, lines 42–43 use method GetFileNameWithoutExtension of class Path to increase readability by shortening the full path name to just the directory name. The **Path** class provides functionality for working with strings that are file or directory paths. Next, each string in the directoryArray is used to create a new child node (line 46). We use method Add (line 49) to add each child node to the parent. Then method PopulateTreeView is called recursively on every subdirectory (line 52), which eventually populates the TreeView with the entire directory structure. Note that our recursive algorithm may cause a delay when the program loads large directories. However, once the folder names are added to the appropriate Nodes collection, they can be expanded and collapsed without delay. In the next section, we present an alternate algorithm to solve this problem.

15.10 ListView Control

The **ListView** control is similar to a ListBox in that both display lists from which the user can select one or more items (an example of a ListView can be found in Fig. 15.31). ListView is more versatile and can display items in different formats. For example, a ListView can display icons next to the list items (controlled by its ImageList property) and show the details of items in columns. Property ***MultiSelect*** (a bool) determines whether multiple items can be selected. CheckBoxes can be included by setting property ***CheckBoxes*** (a bool) to true, making the ListView's appearance similar to that of a CheckedListBox. The ***View*** property specifies the layout of the ListBox. Property ***Activation*** determines the method by which the user selects a list item. The details of these properties and the ItemActivate event are explained in Fig. 15.29.

ListView allows you to define the images used as icons for ListView items. To display images, an ImageList component is required. Create one by dragging it to a Form from the **ToolBox**. Then, select the ***Images*** property in the **Properties** window to display the **Image Collection Editor** (Fig. 15.30). Here you can browse for images that you wish to add to the ImageList, which contains an array of Images. Adding images this way embeds them into the application (like resources), so they do not need to be included separately with the published application. They are not however part of the project. In this example,

ListView properties and an event	Description
Common Properties	
Activation	Determines how the user activates an item. This property takes a value in the ItemActivation enumeration. Possible values are OneClick (single-click activation), TwoClick (double-click activation, item changes color when selected) and Standard (double-click activation, item does not change color).
CheckBoxes	Indicates whether items appear with CheckBoxes. true displays CheckBoxes. The default is false.
LargeImageList	Specifies the ImageList containing large icons for display.
Items	Returns the collection of ListViewItems in the control.
MultiSelect	Determines whether multiple selection is allowed. The default is true, which enables multiple selection.
SelectedItems	Gets the collection of selected items.
SmallImageList	Specifies the ImageList containing small icons for display.
View	Determines appearance of ListViewItems. Possible values are LargeIcon (large icon displayed, items can be in multiple columns), SmallIcon (small icon displayed, items can be in multiple columns), List (small icons displayed, items appear in a single column), Details (like List, but multiple columns of information can be displayed per item) and Tile (large icons displayed, information provided to right of icon; valid only in Windows XP or later).
Common Event	
ItemActivate	Generated when an item in the ListView is activated. Does not contain the specifics of which item is activated.

Fig. 15.29 | ListView properties and an event.

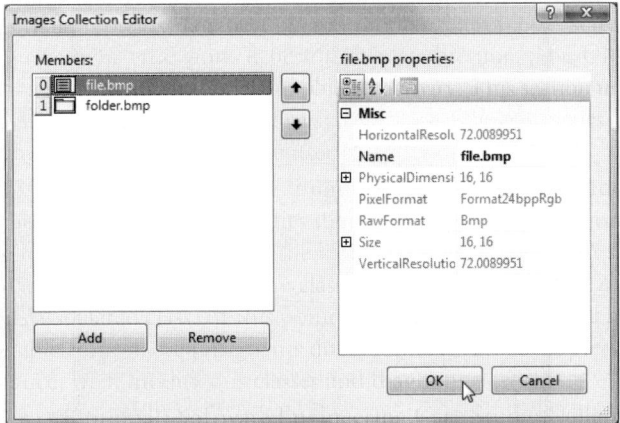

Fig. 15.30 | Image Collection Editor window for an ImageList component.

we added images to the ImageList programmatically rather than using the **Image Collection Editor** so that we could use image resources. After creating an empty ImageList, add the file and folder icon images to the project as resources. Next, set property SmallImage-List of the ListView to the new ImageList object. Property *SmallImageList* specifies the image list for the small icons. Property *LargeImageList* sets the ImageList for large icons. The items in a ListView are each of type *ListViewItem*. Icons for the ListView items are selected by setting the item's *ImageIndex* property to the appropriate index.

Class ListViewTestForm (Fig. 15.31) displays files and folders in a ListView, along with small icons representing each file or folder. If a file or folder is inaccessible because of permission settings, a MessageBox appears. The program scans the contents of the directory as it browses, rather than indexing the entire drive at once.

Method ListViewTestForm_Load (lines 114–123) handles the Form's Load event. When the application loads, the folder and file icon images are added to the Images collection of fileFolderImageList (lines 117–118). Since the ListView's SmallImageList property is set to this ImageList, the ListView can display these images as icons for each item. Because the folder icon was added first, it has array index 0, and the file icon has array index 1. The application also loads its home directory into the ListView when it first loads (line 121) and displays the directory path (line 122).

```
1   // Fig. 15.31: ListViewTestForm.cs
2   // Displaying directories and their contents in ListView.
3   using System;
4   using System.Windows.Forms;
5   using System.IO;
6
7   namespace ListViewTest
8   {
9      // Form contains a ListView which displays
10     // folders and files in a directory
```

Fig. 15.31 | ListView displaying files and folders. (Part 1 of 4.)

```
11    public partial class ListViewTestForm : Form
12    {
13        // store current directory
14        string currentDirectory = Directory.GetCurrentDirectory();
15
16        // constructor
17        public ListViewTestForm()
18        {
19            InitializeComponent();
20        } // end constructor
21
22        // browse directory user clicked or go up one level
23        private void browserListView_Click( object sender, EventArgs e )
24        {
25            // ensure an item is selected
26            if ( browserListView.SelectedItems.Count != 0 )
27            {
28                // if first item selected, go up one level
29                if ( browserListView.Items[ 0 ].Selected )
30                {
31                    // create DirectoryInfo object for directory
32                    DirectoryInfo directoryObject =
33                        new DirectoryInfo( currentDirectory );
34
35                    // if directory has parent, load it
36                    if ( directoryObject.Parent != null )
37                    {
38                        LoadFilesInDirectory(
39                            directoryObject.Parent.FullName );
40                    } // end if
41                } // end if
42
43                // selected directory or file
44                else
45                {
46                    // directory or file chosen
47                    string chosen = browserListView.SelectedItems[ 0 ].Text;
48
49                    // if item selected is directory, load selected directory
50                    if ( Directory.Exists(
51                        Path.Combine( currentDirectory, chosen ) ) )
52                    {
53                        LoadFilesInDirectory(
54                            Path.Combine( currentDirectory, chosen ) );
55                    } // end if
56                } // end else
57
58                // update displayLabel
59                displayLabel.Text = currentDirectory;
60            } // end if
61        } // end method browserListView_Click
62
```

Fig. 15.31 | ListView displaying files and folders. (Part 2 of 4.)

```
63         // display files/subdirectories of current directory
64         public void LoadFilesInDirectory( string currentDirectoryValue )
65         {
66            // load directory information and display
67            try
68            {
69               // clear ListView and set first item
70               browserListView.Items.Clear();
71               browserListView.Items.Add( "Go Up One Level" );
72
73               // update current directory
74               currentDirectory = currentDirectoryValue;
75               DirectoryInfo newCurrentDirectory =
76                  new DirectoryInfo( currentDirectory );
77
78               // put files and directories into arrays
79               DirectoryInfo[] directoryArray =
80                  newCurrentDirectory.GetDirectories();
81               FileInfo[] fileArray = newCurrentDirectory.GetFiles();
82
83               // add directory names to ListView
84               foreach ( DirectoryInfo dir in directoryArray )
85               {
86                  // add directory to ListView
87                  ListViewItem newDirectoryItem =
88                     browserListView.Items.Add( dir.Name );
89
90                  newDirectoryItem.ImageIndex = 0;   // set directory image
91               } // end foreach
92
93               // add file names to ListView
94               foreach ( FileInfo file in fileArray )
95               {
96                  // add file to ListView
97                  ListViewItem newFileItem =
98                     browserListView.Items.Add( file.Name );
99
100                 newFileItem.ImageIndex = 1;   // set file image
101              } // end foreach
102           } // end try
103
104           // access denied
105           catch ( UnauthorizedAccessException )
106           {
107              MessageBox.Show( "Warning: Some fields may not be " +
108                 "visible due to permission settings",
109                 "Attention", 0, MessageBoxIcon.Warning );
110           } // end catch
111        } // end method LoadFilesInDirectory
112
113        // handle load event when Form displayed for first time
114        private void ListViewTestForm_Load( object sender, EventArgs e )
115        {
```

Fig. 15.31 | ListView displaying files and folders. (Part 3 of 4.)

```
116            // add icon images to ImageList
117            fileFolderImageList.Images.Add( Properties.Resources.folder );
118            fileFolderImageList.Images.Add( Properties.Resources.file );
119
120            // load current directory into browserListView
121            LoadFilesInDirectory( currentDirectory );
122            displayLabel.Text = currentDirectory;
123         } // end method ListViewTestForm_Load
124      } // end class ListViewTestForm
125   } // end namespace ListViewTest
```

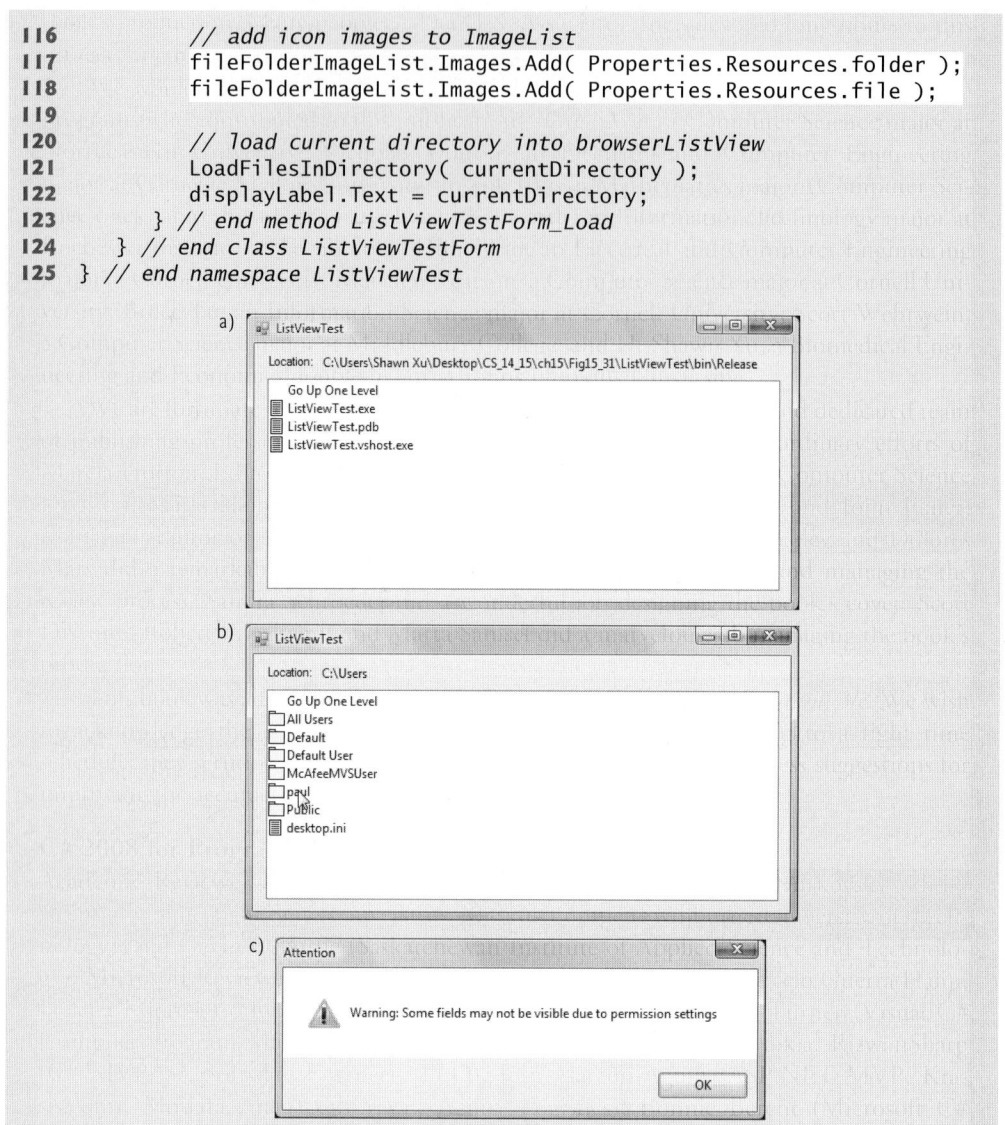

Fig. 15.31 | ListView displaying files and folders. (Part 4 of 4.)

TheLoadFilesInDirectory method (lines 64–111) populates browserListView with the directory passed to it (currentDirectoryValue). It clears browserListView and adds the element "Go Up One Level". When the user clicks this element, the program attempts to move up one level (we see how shortly). The method then creates a DirectoryInfo object initialized with the string currentDirectory (lines 75–76). If permission is not given to browse the directory, an exception is thrown (and caught in line 105). Method LoadFilesInDirectory works differently from method PopulateTreeView in the previous program (Fig. 15.28). Instead of loading all the folders on the hard drive, method LoadFilesInDirectory loads only the folders in the current directory.

Class *DirectoryInfo* (namespace System.IO) enables us to browse or manipulate the directory structure easily. Method *GetDirectories* (line 80) returns an array of DirectoryInfo objects containing the subdirectories of the current directory. Similarly, method *GetFiles* (line 80) returns an array of class *FileInfo* objects containing the files in the current directory. Property *Name* (of both class DirectoryInfo and class FileInfo) contains only the directory or file name, such as temp instead of C:\myfolder\temp. To access the full name, use property *FullName*.

Lines 84–91 and lines 94–101 iterate through the subdirectories and files of the current directory and add them to browserListView. Lines 90 and 100 set the ImageIndex properties of the newly created items. If an item is a directory, we set its icon to a directory icon (index 0); if an item is a file, we set its icon to a file icon (index 1).

Method browserListView_Click (lines 23–61) responds when the user clicks control browserListView. Line 26 checks whether anything is selected. If a selection has been made, line 29 determines whether the user chose the first item in browserListView. The first item in browserListView is always **Go up one level**; if it is selected, the program attempts to go up a level. Lines 32–33 create a DirectoryInfo object for the current directory. Line 36 tests property Parent to ensure that the user is not at the root of the directory tree. Property *Parent* indicates the parent directory as a DirectoryInfo object; if no parent directory exists, Parent returns the value null. If a parent directory does exist, lines 38–39 pass the parent directory's full name to LoadFilesInDirectory.

If the user did not select the first item in browserListView, lines 44–56 allow the user to continue navigating through the directory structure. Line 47 creates string chosen and assigns it the text of the selected item (the first item in collection SelectedItems). Lines 50–51 determine whether the user selected a valid directory (rather than a file). Using the Combine method of class Path, the program combines strings currentDirectory and chosen to form the new directory path. Note that the Combine method automatically adds a backslash (\), if necessary, between the two pieces. This value is passed to the *Exists* method of class Directory. Method Exists returns true if its string parameter is a valid directory. If so, the program passes the string to method LoadFilesInDirectory (lines 53–54). Finally, displayLabel is updated with the new directory (line 59).

This program loads quickly, because it indexes only the files in the current directory. This means that a small delay may occur when a new directory is loaded. In addition, changes in the directory structure can be shown by reloading a directory. The previous program (Fig. 15.28) may have a large initial delay, as it loads an entire directory structure. This type of trade-off is typical in the software world.

Software Engineering Observation 15.2

When designing applications that run for long periods of time, you might choose a large initial delay to improve performance throughout the rest of the program. However, in applications that run for only short periods, developers often prefer fast initial loading times and small delays after each action.

15.11 TabControl Control

The *TabControl* creates tabbed windows, such as those we have seen in Visual Studio (Fig. 15.32). This allows you to specify more information in the same space on a Form and enables you to group displayed data logically.

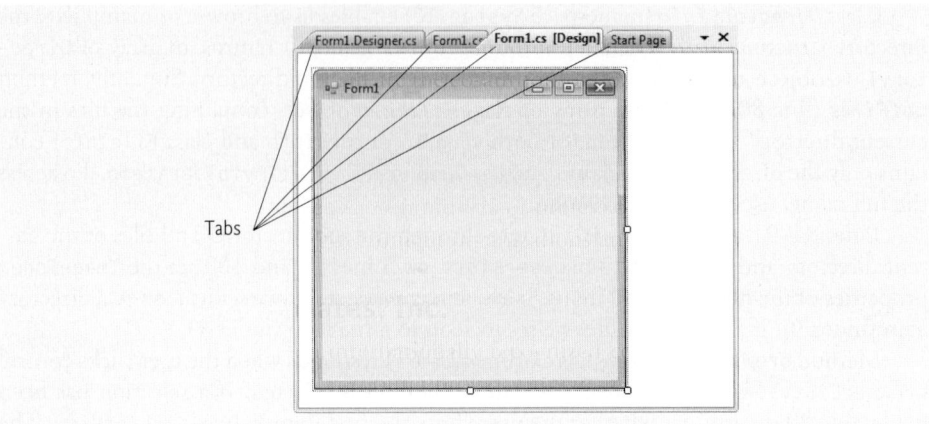

Fig. 15.32 | Tabbed windows in Visual Studio.

TabControls contain *TabPage* objects, which are similar to Panels and GroupBoxes in that TabPages also can contain controls. You first add controls to the TabPage objects, then add the TabPages to the TabControl. Only one TabPage is displayed at a time. To add objects to the TabPage and the TabControl, write

> *myTabPage*.Controls.Add(*myControl*);
> *myTabControl*.TabPages.Add(*myTabPage*);

These statements call method Add of the Controls collection and method Add of the Tab-Pages collection. The example adds TabControl *myControl* to TabPage *myTabPage*, then adds *myTabPage* to *myTabControl*. Alternatively, we can use method AddRange to add an array of TabPages or controls to a TabControl or TabPage, respectively. Figure 15.33 depicts a sample TabControl.

You can add TabControls visually by dragging and dropping them onto a Form in **Design** mode. To add TabPages in **Design** mode, right click the TabControl and select **Add Tab** (Fig. 15.34). Alternatively, click the *TabPages* property in the **Properties** window and add tabs in the dialog that appears. To change a tab label, set the *Text* property of the TabPage. Note that clicking the tabs selects the TabControl—to select the TabPage, click the control area underneath the tabs. You can add controls to the TabPage by dragging and dropping

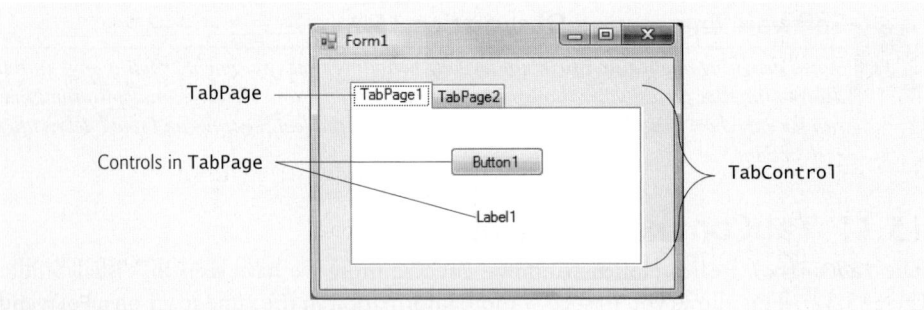

Fig. 15.33 | TabControl with TabPages example.

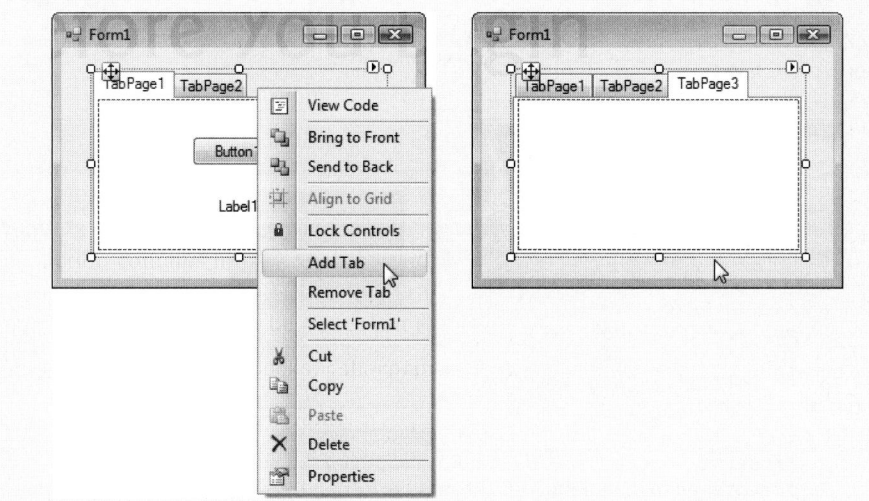

Fig. 15.34 | TabPages added to a TabControl.

items from the **ToolBox**. To view different TabPages, click the appropriate tab (in either design or run mode). Common properties and a common event of TabControls are described in Fig. 15.35.

Each TabPage generates a Click event when its tab is clicked. Event handlers for this event can be created by double clicking the body of the TabPage.

Class UsingTabsForm (Fig. 15.36) uses a TabControl to display various options relating to the text on a label (**Color**, **Size** and **Message**). The last TabPage displays an **About** message, which describes the use of TabControls.

TabControl properties and an event	Description
Common Properties	
ImageList	Specifies images to be displayed on tabs.
ItemSize	Specifies the tab size.
Multiline	Indicates whether multiple rows of tabs can be displayed.
SelectedIndex	Index of the selected TabPage.
SelectedTab	The selected TabPage.
TabCount	Returns the number of tab pages.
TabPages	Collection of TabPages within the TabControl.
Common Event	
SelectedIndexChanged	Generated when SelectedIndex changes (i.e., another TabPage is selected).

Fig. 15.35 | TabControl properties and an event.

```
1   // Fig. 15.36: UsingTabsForm.cs
2   // Using TabControl to display various font settings.
3   using System;
4   using System.Drawing;
5   using System.Windows.Forms;
6
7   namespace UsingTabs
8   {
9      // Form uses Tabs and RadioButtons to display various font settings
10     public partial class UsingTabsForm : Form
11     {
12        // constructor
13        public UsingTabsForm()
14        {
15           InitializeComponent();
16        } // end constructor
17
18        // event handler for Black RadioButton
19        private void blackRadioButton_CheckedChanged(
20           object sender, EventArgs e )
21        {
22           displayLabel.ForeColor = Color.Black; // change color to black
23        } // end method blackRadioButton_CheckedChanged
24
25        // event handler for Red RadioButton
26        private void redRadioButton_CheckedChanged(
27           object sender, EventArgs e )
28        {
29           displayLabel.ForeColor = Color.Red; // change color to red
30        } // end method redRadioButton_CheckedChanged
31
32        // event handler for Green RadioButton
33        private void greenRadioButton_CheckedChanged(
34           object sender, EventArgs e )
35        {
36           displayLabel.ForeColor = Color.Green; // change color to green
37        } // end method greenRadioButton_CheckedChanged
38
39        // event handler for 12-point RadioButton
40        private void size12RadioButton_CheckedChanged(
41           object sender, EventArgs e )
42        {
43           // change font size to 12
44           displayLabel.Font = new Font( displayLabel.Font.Name, 12 );
45        } // end method size12RadioButton_CheckedChanged
46
47        // event handler for 16-point RadioButton
48        private void size16RadioButton_CheckedChanged(
49           object sender, EventArgs e )
50        {
51           // change font size to 16
52           displayLabel.Font = new Font( displayLabel.Font.Name, 16 );
53        } // end method size16RadioButton_CheckedChanged
```

Fig. 15.36 | TabControl used to display various font settings. (Part 1 of 2.)

```
54
55        // event handler for 20-point RadioButton
56        private void size20RadioButton_CheckedChanged(
57           object sender, EventArgs e )
58        {
59           // change font size to 20
60           displayLabel.Font = new Font( displayLabel.Font.Name, 20 );
61        } // end method size20RadioButton_CheckedChanged
62
63        // event handler for  Hello! RadioButton
64        private void helloRadioButton_CheckedChanged(
65           object sender, EventArgs e )
66        {
67           displayLabel.Text = "Hello!"; // change text to Hello!
68        } // end method helloRadioButton_CheckedChanged
69
70        // event handler for Goodbye! RadioButton
71        private void goodbyeRadioButton_CheckedChanged(
72           object sender, EventArgs e )
73        {
74           displayLabel.Text = "Goodbye!"; // change text to Goodbye!
75        } // end method goodbyeRadioButton_CheckedChanged
76     } // end class UsingTabsForm
77  } // end namespace UsingTabs
```

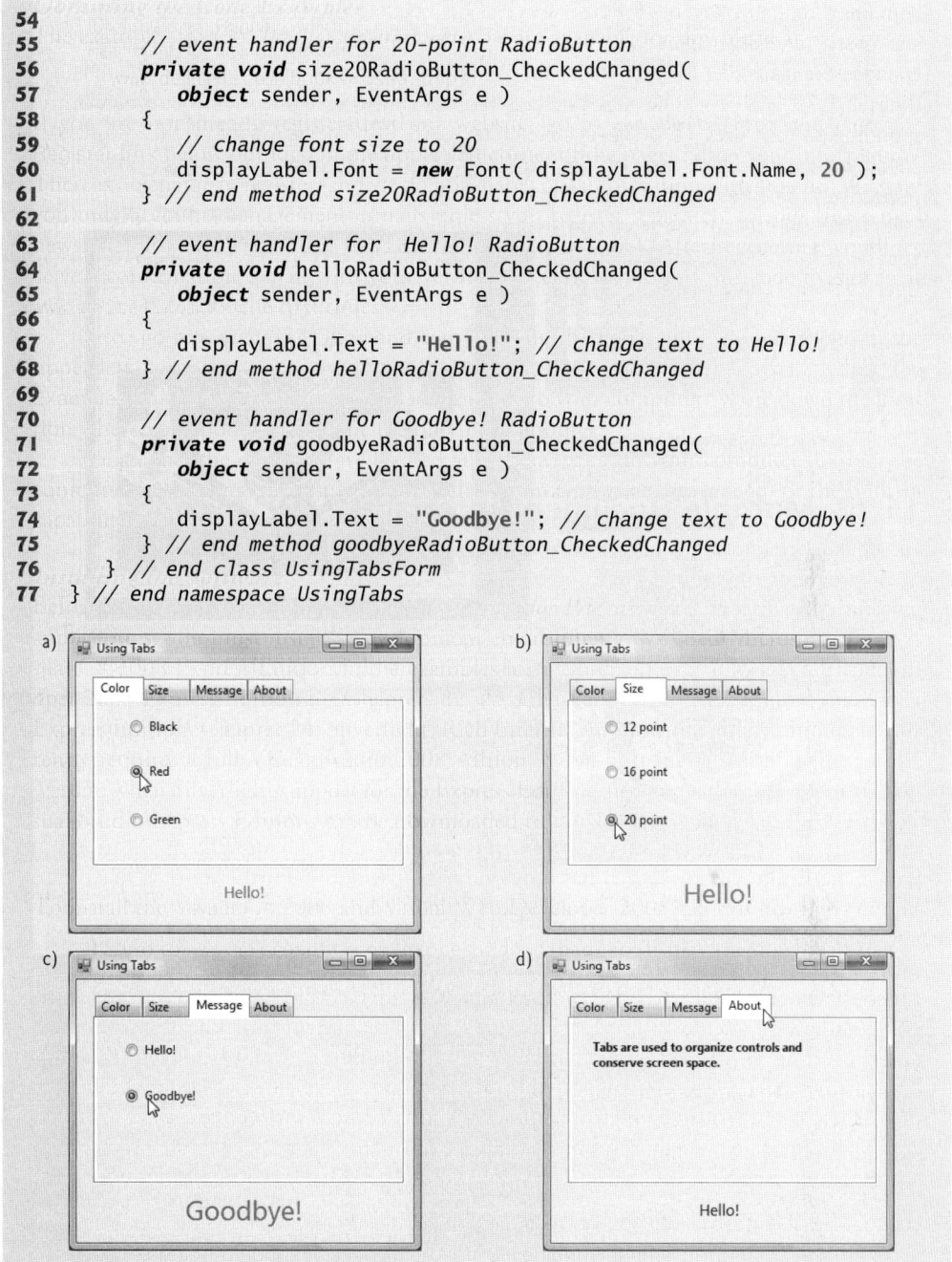

Fig. 15.36 | TabControl used to display various font settings. (Part 2 of 2.)

The textOptionsTabControl and the colorTabPage, sizeTabPage, messageTabPage and aboutTabPage are created in the designer (as described previously). The colorTabPage contains three RadioButtons for the colors black (blackRadioButton), red (redRadioButton) and green (greenRadioButton). This TabPage is displayed in Fig. 15.36(a). The Check-Changed event handler for each RadioButton updates the color of the text in displayLabel (lines 22, 29 and 36). The sizeTabPage (Fig. 15.36(b)) has three RadioButtons, corresponding to font sizes 12 (size12RadioButton), 16 (size16RadioButton) and 20 (size-20RadioButton), which change the font size of displayLabel—lines 44, 52 and 60, respectively. The messageTabPage (Fig. 15.36(c)) contains two RadioButtons for the messages **Hello!** (helloRadioButton) and **Goodbye!** (goodbyeRadioButton). The two RadioButtons determine the text on displayLabel (lines 67 and 74, respectively). The aboutTabPage (Fig. 15.36(d)) contains a Label (messageLabel) describing the purpose of TabControls.

> **Software Engineering Observation 15.3**
>
> *A TabPage can act as a container for a single logical group of RadioButtons, enforcing their mutual exclusivity. To place multiple RadioButton groups inside a single TabPage, you should group RadioButtons within Panels or GroupBoxes contained within the TabPage.*

15.12 Multiple Document Interface (MDI) Windows

In previous chapters, we have built only *single document interface (SDI)* applications. Such programs (including Microsoft's Notepad and Paint) can support only one open window or document at a time. SDI applications usually have limited abilities—Paint and Notepad, for example, have limited image- and text-editing features. To edit multiple documents, the user must execute another instance of the SDI application.

Many complex applications are *multiple document interface (MDI)* programs, which allow users to edit multiple documents at once (e.g., Microsoft Office products). MDI programs also tend to be more complex—Paint Shop Pro and Photoshop have a greater number of image-editing features than does Paint.

An MDI program's main window is called the *parent window*, and each window inside the application is referred to as a *child window*. Although an MDI application can have many child windows, each has only one parent window. Furthermore, a maximum of one child window can be active at once. Child windows cannot be parents themselves and cannot be moved outside their parent. Otherwise, a child window behaves like any other window (with regard to closing, minimizing, resizing, and so on). A child window's functionality can differ from that of other child windows of the parent. For example, one child window might allow the user to edit images, another might allow the user to edit text and a third might display network traffic graphically, but all could belong to the same MDI parent. Figure 15.37 depicts a sample MDI application with two child windows.

To create an MDI Form, create a new Form and set its **IsMdiContainer** property to true. The Form changes appearance, as in Fig. 15.38.

Next, create a child Form class to be added to the Form. To do this, right click the project in the **Solution Explorer**, select **Project > Add Windows Form...** and name the file. Edit the Form as you like. To add the child Form to the parent, we must create a new child Form object, set its **MdiParent** property to the parent Form and call the child Form's Show method. In general, to add a child Form to a parent, write

```
ChildFormClass childForm = New ChildFormClass();
childForm.MdiParent = parentForm;
childForm.Show();
```

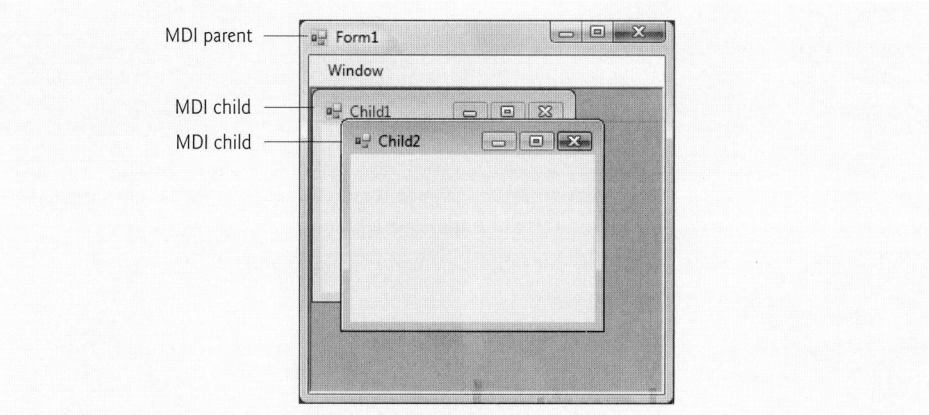

Fig. 15.37 | MDI parent window and MDI child windows.

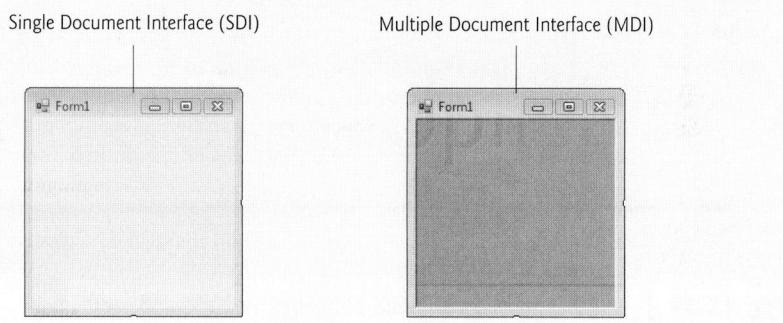

Fig. 15.38 | SDI and MDI forms.

In most cases, the parent Form creates the child, so the *parentForm* reference is this. The code to create a child usually lies inside an event handler, which creates a new window in response to a user action. Menu selections (such as **File**, followed by a submenu option of **New**, followed by a submenu option of **Window**) are common techniques for creating new child windows.

Class Form property ***MdiChildren*** returns an array of child Form references. This is useful if the parent window wants to check the status of all its children (for example, ensuring that all are saved before the parent closes). Property ***ActiveMdiChild*** returns a reference to the active child window; it returns null if there are no active child windows. Other features of MDI windows are described in Fig. 15.39.

Child windows can be minimized, maximized and closed independently of the parent window. Figure 15.40 shows two images: one containing two minimized child windows and a second containing a maximized child window. When the parent is minimized or closed, the child windows are minimized or closed as well. Notice that the title bar in Fig. 15.40(b) is **Form1 - [Child1]**. When a child window is maximized, its title-bar text is inserted into the parent window's title bar. When a child window is minimized or maximized, its title bar displays a restore icon, which can be used to return the child window to its previous size (its size before it was minimized or maximized).

MDI Form properties, a method and an event	Description
Common MDI Child Properties	
IsMdiChild	Indicates whether the Form is an MDI child. If true, Form is an MDI child (read-only property).
MdiParent	Specifies the MDI parent Form of the child.
Common MDI Parent Properties	
ActiveMdiChild	Returns the Form that is the currently active MDI child (returns null if no children are active).
IsMdiContainer	Indicates whether a Form can be an MDI parent. If true, the Form can be an MDI parent. The default value is false.
MdiChildren	Returns the MDI children as an array of Forms.
Common Method	
LayoutMdi	Determines the display of child forms on an MDI parent. The method takes as a parameter an MdiLayout enumeration with possible values ArrangeIcons, Cascade, TileHorizontal and TileVertical. Figure 15.42 depicts the effects of these values.
Common Event	
MdiChildActivate	Generated when an MDI child is closed or activated.

Fig. 15.39 | MDI parent and MDI child properties, method and event.

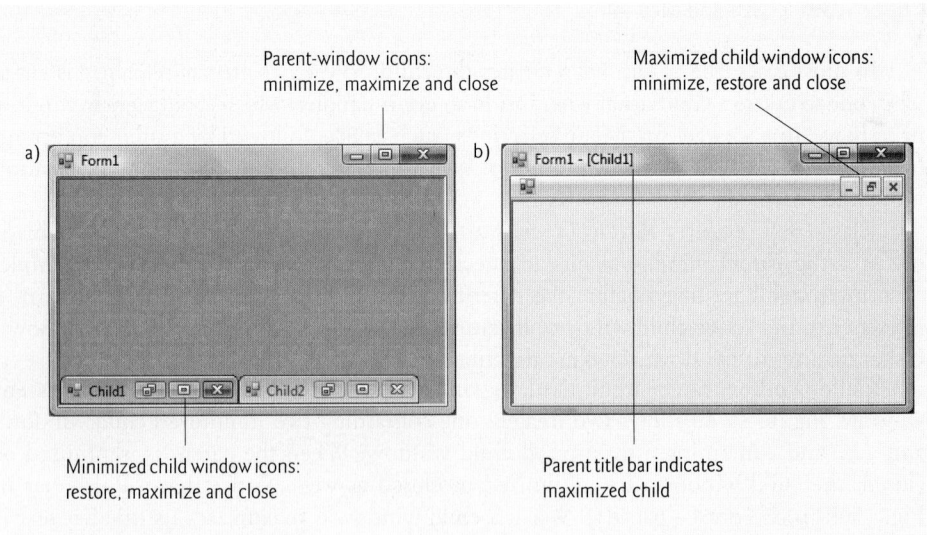

Fig. 15.40 | Minimized and maximized child windows.

C# provides a property that helps track which child windows are open in an MDI container. Property *MdiWindowListItem* of class MenuStrip specifies which menu, if any, displays a list of open child windows. When a new child window is opened, an entry is added to the list (as in the first screen of Figure 15.41). If nine or more child windows are open, the list includes the option **More Windows...**, which allows the user to select a window from a list in a dialog.

Good Programming Practice 15.1

When creating MDI applications, include a menu that displays a list of the open child windows. This helps the user select a child window quickly, rather than having to search for it in the parent window.

MDI containers allow you to organize the placement of its child windows. The child windows in an MDI application can be arranged by calling method *LayoutMdi* of the parent Form. Method LayoutMdi takes a *MdiLayout* enumeration, which can have values *ArrangeIcons*, *Cascade*, *TileHorizontal* and *TileVertical*. *Tiled windows* completely fill the parent and do not overlap; such windows can be arranged horizontally (value Tile-Horizontal) or vertically (value TileVertical). *Cascaded windows* (value Cascade)

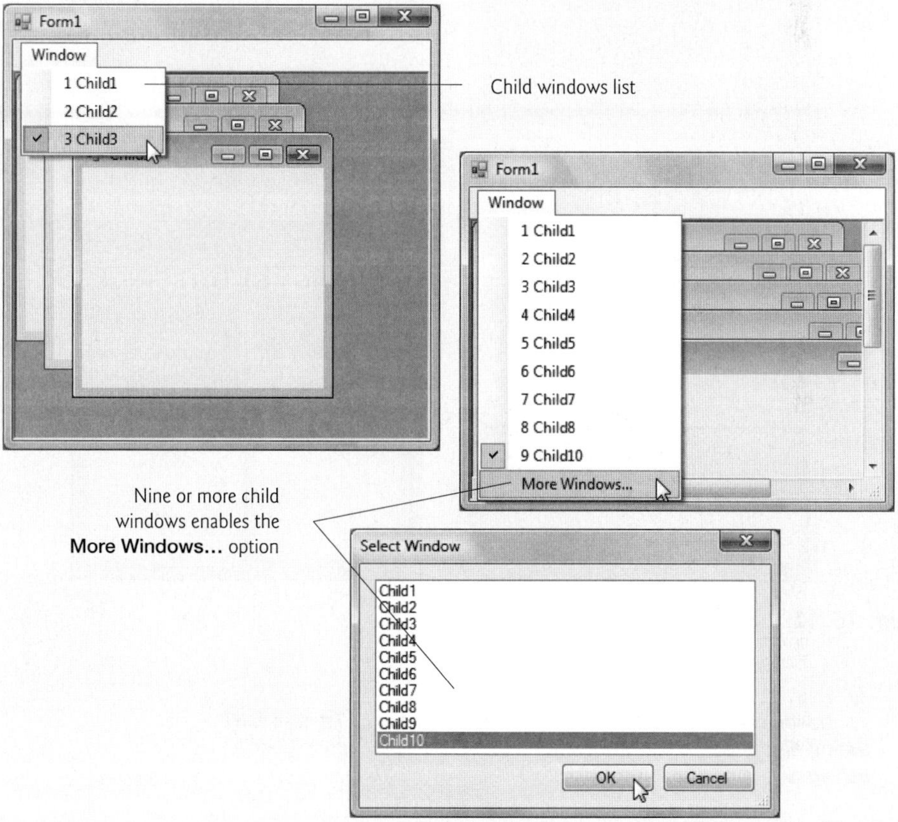

Child windows list

Nine or more child
windows enables the
More Windows... option

Fig. 15.41 | MenuItem property MdiList example.

overlap—each is the same size and displays a visible title bar, if possible. Value Arrange-Icons arranges the icons for any minimized child windows. If minimized windows are scattered around the parent window, value ArrangeIcons orders them neatly at the bottom-left corner of the parent window. Figure 15.42 illustrates the values of the MdiLayout enumeration.

Class UsingMDIForm (Fig. 15.43) demonstrates MDI windows. Class UsingMDIForm uses three instances of child Form ChildForm (Fig. 15.44), each containing a PictureBox that displays an image. The parent MDI Form contains a menu enabling users to create and arrange child Forms.

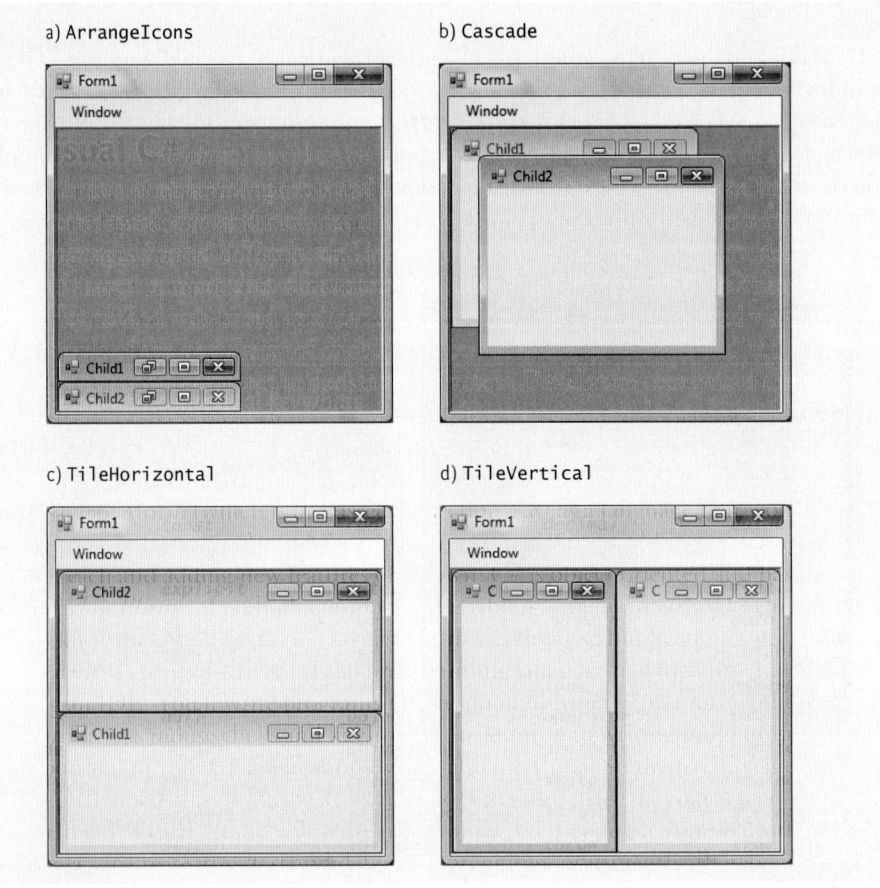

Fig. 15.42 | MdiLayout enumeration values.

```
1   // Fig. 15.43: UsingMDIForm.cs
2   // Demonstrating use of MDI parent and child windows.
3   using System;
4   using System.Windows.Forms;
```

Fig. 15.43 | MDI parent-window class. (Part 1 of 3.)

```
 5
 6    namespace UsingMDI
 7    {
 8       // Form demonstrates the use of MDI parent and child windows
 9       public partial class UsingMDIForm : Form
10       {
11          // constructor
12          public UsingMDIForm()
13          {
14             InitializeComponent();
15          } // end constructor
16
17          // create Visual C# image window
18          private void csToolStripMenuItem_Click(
19             object sender, EventArgs e )
20          {
21             // create new child
22             ChildForm child = new ChildForm(
23                "Visual C# 2008 How to Program", "vcs2008htp" );
24             child.MdiParent = this; // set parent
25             child.Show(); // display child
26          } // end method child1ToolStripMenuItem_Click
27
28          // create Visual C++ image window
29          private void cppToolStripMenuItem_Click(
30             object sender, EventArgs e )
31          {
32             // create new child
33             ChildForm child = new ChildForm(
34                "Visual C++ 2008 How to Program", "vcpp2008htp" );
35             child.MdiParent = this; // set parent
36             child.Show(); // display child
37          } // end method child2ToolStripMenuItem_Click
38
39          // create Visual Basic image window
40          private void vbToolStripMenuItem_Click(
41             object sender, EventArgs e )
42          {
43             // create new child
44             Child child = new ChildForm(
45                "Visual Basic 2008 How to Program", "vb2008htp" );
46             child.MdiParent = this; // set parent
47             child.Show(); // display child
48          } // end method child3ToolStripMenuItem_Click
49
50          // exit application
51          private void exitToolStripMenuItem_Click(
52             object sender, EventArgs e )
53          {
54             Application.Exit();
55          } // end method exitToolStripMenuItem_Click
56
```

Fig. 15.43 | MDI parent-window class. (Part 2 of 3.)

```
57        // set Cascade layout
58        private void cascadeToolStripMenuItem_Click(
59           object sender, EventArgs e )
60        {
61           this.LayoutMdi( MdiLayout.Cascade );
62        } // end method cascadeToolStripMenuItem_Click
63
64        // set TileHorizontal layout
65        private void tileHorizontalToolStripMenuItem_Click(
66           object sender, EventArgs e )
67        {
68           this.LayoutMdi( MdiLayout.TileHorizontal );
69        } // end method tileHorizontalToolStripMenuItem
70
71        // set TileVertical layout
72        private void tileVerticalToolStripMenuItem_Click(
73           object sender, EventArgs e )
74        {
75           this.LayoutMdi( MdiLayout.TileVertical );
76        } // end method tileVerticalToolStripMenuItem_Click
77     } // end class UsingMDIForm
78  } // end namespace UsingMDI
```

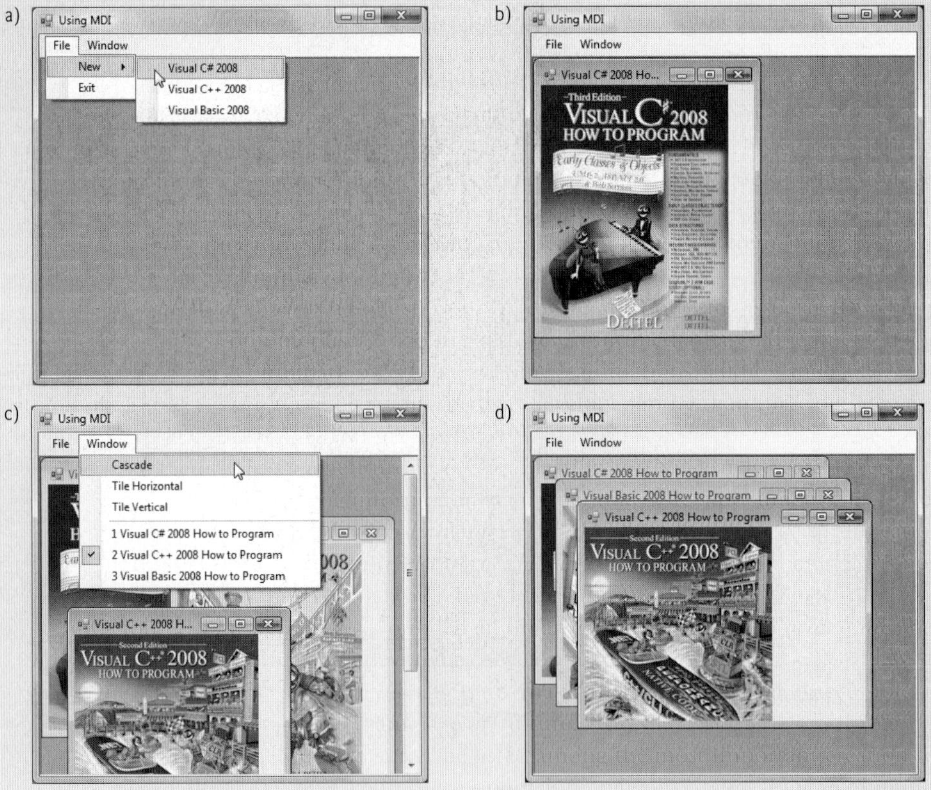

Fig. 15.43 | MDI parent-window class. (Part 3 of 3.)

MDI *Parent* Form

Figure 15.43 presents class UsingMDIForm—the application's MDI parent Form. This Form, which is created first, contains two top-level menus. The first of these menus, **File** (fileToolStripMenuItem), contains both an **Exit** item (exitToolStripMenuItem) and a **New** submenu (newToolStripMenuItem) consisting of items for each child window. The second menu, **Window** (windowToolStripMenuItem), provides options for laying out the MDI children, plus a list of the active MDI children.

In the **Properties** window, we set the Form's IsMdiContainer property to true, making the Form an MDI parent. In addition, we set the MenuStrip's MdiWindowListItem property to windowToolStripMenuItem. This enables the **Window** menu to contain the list of child MDI windows.

The **Cascade** menu item (cascadeToolStripMenuItem) has an event handler (cascadeToolStripMenuItem_Click, lines 58–62) that arranges the child windows in a cascading manner. The event handler calls method LayoutMdi with the argument Cascade from the MdiLayout enumeration (line 61).

The **Tile Horizontal** menu item (tileHorizontalToolStripMenuItem) has an event handler (tileHorizontalToolStripMenuItem_Click, lines 65–69) that arranges the child windows in a horizontal manner. The event handler calls method LayoutMdi with the argument TileHorizontal from the MdiLayout enumeration (line 68).

Finally, the **Tile Vertical** menu item (tileVerticalToolStripMenuItem) has an event handler (tileVerticalToolStripMenuItem_Click, lines 72–76) that arranges the child windows in a vertical manner. The event handler calls method LayoutMdi with the argument TileVertical from the MdiLayout enumeration (line 75).

MDI *Child* Form

At this point, the application is still incomplete—we must define the MDI child class. To do this, right click the project in the **Solution Explorer** and select **Add > Windows Form....** Then name the new class in the dialog as ChildForm (Fig. 15.44). Next, we add a PictureBox (displayPictureBox) to ChildForm. In ChildForm's constructor, line 17 sets the title-bar text. Lines 20–22 retrieve the appropriate image resource, cast it to an Image and set displayPictureBox's Image property. The images that are used can be found in the Images subfolder of this chapter's examples directory.

```
1   // Fig. 15.44: ChildForm.cs
2   // Child window of MDI parent.
3   using System;
4   using System.Drawing;
5   using System.Windows.Forms;
6   using System.IO;
7
8   namespace UsingMDI
9   {
10     public partial class ChildForm : Form
11     {
12        public ChildForm( string title, string resourceName )
13        {
```

Fig. 15.44 | MDI child ChildForm. (Part 1 of 2.)

```
14                // Required for Windows Form Designer support
15                InitializeComponent();
16
17                Text = title; // set title text
18
19                // set image to display in pictureBox
20                displayPictureBox.Image =
21                    ( Image ) ( Properties.Resources.ResourceManager.GetObject(
22                        resourceName );
23            } // end constructor
24        } // end class ChildForm
25    } // end namespace UsingMDI
```

Fig. 15.44 | MDI child `ChildForm`. (Part 2 of 2.)

After the MDI child class is defined, the parent MDI Form (Fig. 15.43) can create new child windows. The event handlers in lines 16–46 create a new child Form corresponding to the menu item clicked. Lines 22–23, 33–34 and 44–45 create new instances of Child-Form. Lines 24, 35 and 46 set each Child's MdiParent property to the parent Form. Lines 25, 36 and 46 call method Show to display each child Form.

15.13 Visual Inheritance

Chapter 11 discussed how to create classes by inheriting from other classes. We have also used inheritance to create Forms that display a GUI, by deriving our new Form classes from class System.Windows.Forms.Form. This is an example of *visual inheritance*. The derived Form class contains the functionality of its Form base class, including any base-class properties, methods, variables and controls. The derived class also inherits all visual aspects—such as sizing, component layout, spacing between GUI components, colors and fonts—from its base class.

Visual inheritance enables you to achieve visual consistency across applications. For example, you could define a base Form that contains a product's logo, a specific background color, a predefined menu bar and other elements. You then could use the base Form throughout an application for uniformity and branding. You can also create controls that inherit from other controls. For example, you might create a custom UserControl (discussed in Section 15.14) that is derived from an existing control.

Creating a Base Form

Class VisualInheritanceBaseForm (Fig. 15.45) derives from Form. The output depicts the workings of the program. The GUI contains two Labels with text **Bugs, Bugs, Bugs** and **Copyright 2008, by Deitel & Associates, Inc.**, as well as one Button displaying the text **Learn More**. When a user presses the **Learn More** Button, method learnMoreButton_Click (lines 16–22) is invoked. This method displays a MessageBox that provides some informative text.

To allow other Forms to inherit from VisualInheritanceForm, we must package VisualInheritanceForm as a .dll (class library). Right click the project name in the **Solution Explorer** and select **Properties**, then choose the **Application** tab. In the **Output type** drop-down list, change **Windows Application** to **Class Library**. Building the project pro-

```
 1   // Fig. 15.45: VisualInheritanceBaseForm.cs
 2   // Base Form for use with visual inheritance.
 3   using System;
 4   using System.Windows.Forms;
 5
 6   // base Form used to demonstrate visual inheritance
 7   public partial class VisualInheritanceBaseForm : Form
 8   {
 9      // constructor
10      public VisualInheritanceForm()
11      {
12         InitializeComponent();
13      } // end constructor
14
15      // display MessageBox when Button is clicked
16      private void learnMoreButton_Click( object sender, EventArgs e )
17      {
18         MessageBox.Show(
19            "Bugs, Bugs, Bugs is a product of deitel.com",
20            "Learn More", MessageBoxButtons.OK,
21            MessageBoxIcon.Information );
22      } // end method learnMoreButton_Click
23   } // end class VisualInheritanceBaseForm
```

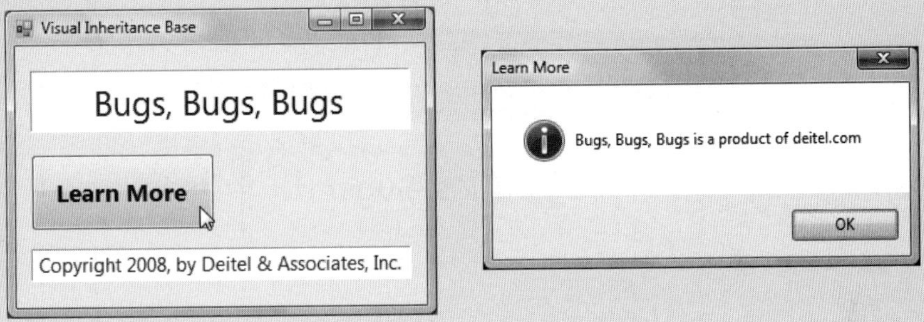

Fig. 15.45 | Class `VisualInheritanceBaseForm`, which inherits from class `Form`, contains a Button (**Learn More**).

duces the .dll. You can configure a project to be a class library when you first create it by selecting the **Class Library** template in the **New Project** dialog. [*Note:* A class library cannot be executed as a stand-alone application. The screen captures in Fig. 15.45 were taken before changing the project to be a class library.]

Deriving From a Base Form
To visually inherit from `VisualInheritanceBaseForm`, first create a new Windows application. In this application, add a reference to the .dll you just created (located in the bin\Debug or bin\Release folder of the solution containing Fig. 15.45). Then open the file that defines the new application's GUI and modify the line that defines the class to indicate that the application's Form should inherit from class `VisualInheritanceBaseForm`. The class-declaration line should now appear as follows:

```
public partial class VisualInheritanceTestForm :
    VisualInheritanceBase.VisualInheritanceBaseForm
```

Note that unless you have specified namespace VisualInheritanceBase in a using directive, you must use the fully qualified name VisualInheritanceBase.VisualInheritanceBaseForm. In **Design** view, the new application's Form should now display the controls inherited from the base Form (Fig. 15.46). We can now add more components to the Form.

Class VisualInheritanceTestForm (Fig. 15.47) is a derived class of VisualInheritanceBaseForm. The output illustrates the functionality of the program. The components, their layouts and the functionality of base class VisualInheritanceBaseForm (Fig. 15.45) are inherited by VisualInheritanceTestForm. We added an additional Button with text **About this Program**. When a user presses this Button, method aboutButton_Click (lines 19–25) is invoked. This method displays another MessageBox providing different informative text (lines 21–24).

If a user clicks the **Learn More** button, the event is handled by the base-class event handler learnMoreButton_Click. Because VisualInheritanceBaseForm uses a private access modifier to declare its controls, VisualInheritanceTestForm cannot modify the controls inherited from class VisualInheritanceBaseForm in any way. Note that the IDE displays a small icon at the top left of the visually inherited controls to indicate that they are inherited and cannot be altered.

Fig. 15.46 | Form demonstrating visual inheritance.

```
1   // Fig. 15.47: VisualInheritanceTestForm.cs
2   // Derived Form using visual inheritance.
3   using System;
4   using System.Windows.Forms;
5
6   namespace VisualInheritanceTest
7   {
```

Fig. 15.47 | Class VisualInheritanceTestForm, which inherits from class VisualInheritanceBaseForm, contains an additional Button. (Part 1 of 2.)

```
8       // derived form using visual inheritance
9       public partial class VisualInheritanceTestForm :
10         VisualInheritanceBase.VisualInheritanceBaseForm
11      {
12         // constructor
13         public VisualInheritanceTestForm()
14         {
15            InitializeComponent();
16         } // end constructor
17
18         // display MessageBox when Button is clicked
19         private void aboutButton_Click(object sender, EventArgs e)
20         {
21            MessageBox.Show(
22               "This program was created by Deitel & Associates.",
23               "About This Program", MessageBoxButtons.OK,
24               MessageBoxIcon.Information );
25         } // end method aboutButton_Click
26      } // end class VisualInheritanceTestForm
27   } // end namespace VisualInheritanceTest
```

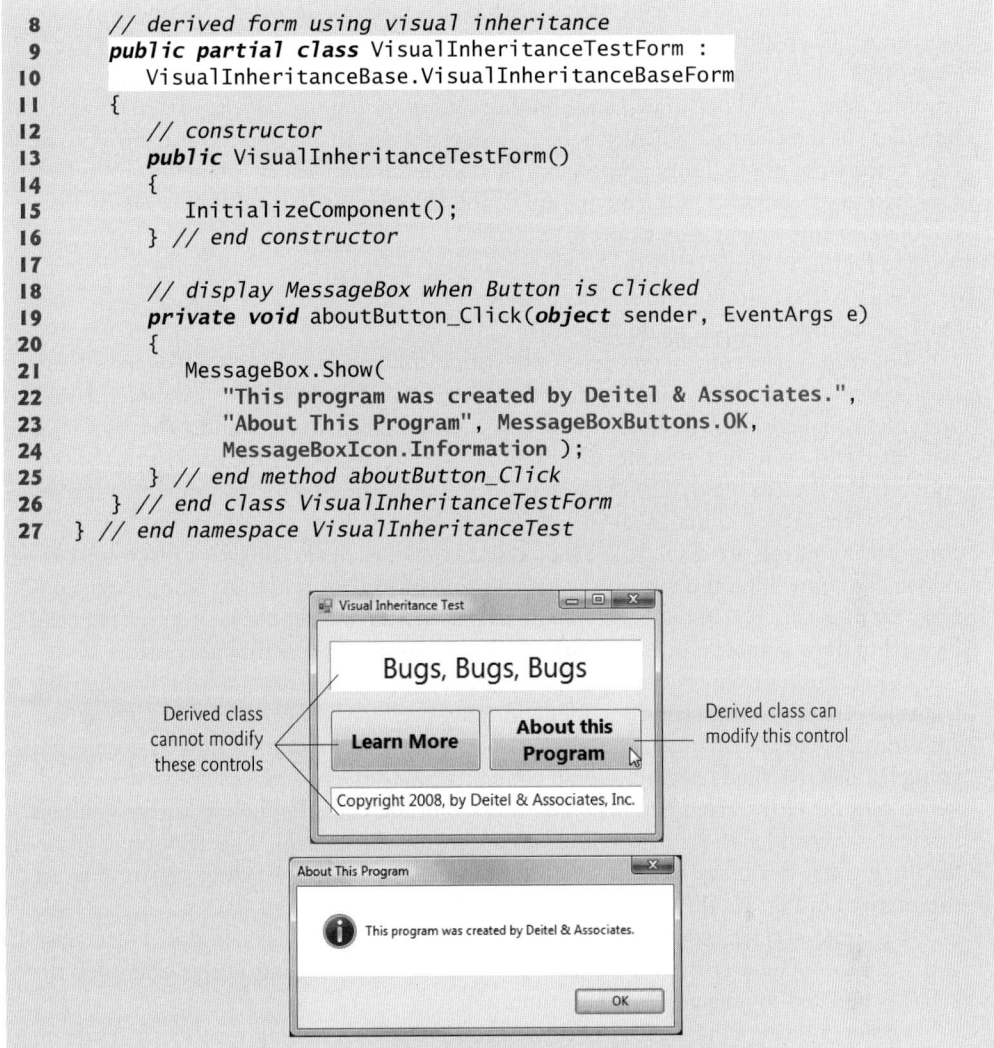

Fig. 15.47 | Class VisualInheritanceTestForm, which inherits from class VisualInheritanceBaseForm, contains an additional Button. (Part 2 of 2.)

15.14 User-Defined Controls

The .NET Framework allows you to create *custom controls*. These custom controls appear in the user's **Toolbox** and can be added to Forms, Panels or GroupBoxes in the same way that we add Buttons, Labels and other predefined controls. The simplest way to create a custom control is to derive a class from an existing control, such as a Label. This is useful if you want to add functionality to an existing control, rather than replacing it with one that provides the desired functionality. For example, you can create a new type of Label that behaves like a normal Label but has a different appearance. You accomplish this by inheriting from class Label and overriding method OnPaint.

All controls have an ***OnPaint*** method, which the system calls when a component must be redrawn (such as when the component is resized). Method OnPaint is passed a ***Paint-EventArgs*** object, which contains graphics information—property ***Graphics*** is the graphics object used to draw, and property ***ClipRectangle*** defines the rectangular boundary of the control. Whenever the system raises the Paint event, our control's base class catches the event. Through polymorphism, our control's OnPaint method is called. Our base class's OnPaint implementation is not called, so we must call it explicitly from our OnPaint implementation before we execute our custom-paint code. In most cases, you want to do this to ensure that the original painting code executes in addition to the code you define in the custom control's class. Alternately, if we do not wish to let the base-class OnPaint method execute, we do not call it.

To create a new control composed of existing controls, use class ***UserControl***. Controls added to a custom control are called ***constituent controls***. For example, a programmer could create a UserControl composed of a Button, a Label and a TextBox, each associated with some functionality (for example, the Button setting the Label's text to that contained in the TextBox). The UserControl acts as a container for the controls added to it. The UserControl contains constituent controls, so it does not determine how these constituent controls are displayed. Method OnPaint of the UserControl cannot be overridden. To control the appearance of each constituent control, you must handle each control's Paint event. The Paint event handler is passed a PaintEventArgs object, which can be used to draw graphics (lines, rectangles, and so on) on the constituent controls.

Using another technique, a programmer can create a brand-new control by inheriting from class Control. This class does not define any specific behavior; that task is left to you. Instead, class Control handles the items associated with all controls, such as events and sizing handles. Method OnPaint should contain a call to the base class's OnPaint method, which calls the Paint event handlers. You must then add code that draws custom graphics inside the overridden OnPaint method when drawing the control. This technique allows for the greatest flexibility but also requires the most planning. All three approaches are summarized in Fig. 15.48.

We create a "clock" control in Fig. 15.49. This is a UserControl composed of a Label and a Timer—whenever the Timer raises an event (once per second in this example), the Label is updated to reflect the current time.

Timers (System.Windows.Forms namespace) are invisible components that reside on a Form, generating ***Tick*** events at a set interval. This interval is set by the Timer's ***Interval***

Custom-control techniques and PaintEventArgs properties	Description
Custom-Control Techniques	
Inherit from Windows Forms control	You can do this to add functionality to a preexisting control. If you override method OnPaint, call the base class's OnPaint method. Note that you only can add to the original control's appearance, not redesign it.

Fig. 15.48 | Custom-control creation. (Part 1 of 2.)

Custom-control techniques and PaintEventArgs properties	Description
Create a UserControl	You can create a UserControl composed of multiple preexisting controls (e.g., to combine their functionality). Note that you cannot override the OnPaint methods of custom controls. Instead, you must place drawing code in a Paint event handler. Again, note that you only can add to the original control's appearance, not redesign it
Inherit from class Control	Define a brand new control. Override method OnPaint, then call base-class method OnPaint and include methods to draw the control. With this method you can customize control appearance and functionality.
PaintEventArgs Properties	
Graphics	The control's graphics object. It is used to draw on the control.
ClipRectangle	Specifies the rectangle indicating the boundary of the control.

Fig. 15.48 | Custom-control creation. (Part 2 of 2.)

property, which defines the number of milliseconds (thousandths of a second) between events. By default, timers are disabled and do not generate events.

```
1   // Fig. 15.49: ClockUserControl.cs
2   // User-defined control with a timer and a Label.
3   using System;
4   using System.Windows.Forms;
5
6   namespace ClockExample
7   {
8      // UserControl that displays the time on a Label
9      public partial class ClockUserControl : UserControl
10     {
11        // constructor
12        public ClockUserControl()
13        {
14           InitializeComponent();
15        } // end constructor
16
17        // update Label at every tick
18        private void clockTimer_Tick(object sender, EventArgs e)
19        {
20           // get current time (Now), convert to string
21           displayLabel.Text = DateTime.Now.ToLongTimeString();
22        } // end method clockTimer_Tick
23     } // end class ClockUserControl
24  } // end namespace ClockExample
```

Fig. 15.49 | UserControl-defined clock. (Part 1 of 2.)

Fig. 15.49 | UserControl-defined clock. (Part 2 of 2.)

This application contains a user control (ClockUserControl) and a Form that displays the user control. We begin by creating a Windows application. Next, we create a User-Control class for the project by selecting **Project > Add User Control…**. This displays a dialog from which we can select the type of control to add—user controls are already selected. We then name the file (and the class) ClockUserControl. Our empty Clock-UserControl is displayed as a grey rectangle.

You can treat this control like a Windows Form, meaning that you can add controls using the **ToolBox** and set properties using the **Properties** window. However, instead of creating an application, you are simply creating a new control composed of other controls. Add a Label (displayLabel) and a Timer (clockTimer) to the UserControl. Set the Timer interval to 1000 milliseconds and set displayLabel's text with each Tick event (lines 18–22). To generate events, clockTimer must be enabled by setting property Enabled to true in the **Properties** window.

Structure *DateTime* (namespace System) contains property *Now*, which is the current time. Method *ToLongTimeString* converts Now to a string containing the current hour, minute and second (along with AM or PM). We use this to set the time in displayLabel in line 21.

Once created, our clock control appears as an item on the **ToolBox**. You may need to switch to the application's Form before the item appears in the **ToolBox**. To use the control, simply drag it to the Form and run the Windows application. We gave the ClockUserControl object a white background to make it stand out in the Form. Figure 15.49 shows the output of ClockForm, which contains our ClockUserControl. There are no event handlers in ClockForm, so we show only the code for ClockUserControl.

Sharing Custom Controls with Other Developers
Visual Studio allows you to share custom controls with other developers. To create a User-Control that can be exported to other solutions, do the following:

1. Create a new **Class Library** project.
2. Delete Class1.cs, initially provided with the application.
3. Right click the project in the **Solution Explorer** and select **Add > User Control…**. In the dialog that appears, name the user-control file and click **Add**.
4. Inside the project, add controls and functionality to the UserControl (Fig. 15.50).
5. Build the project. Visual Studio creates a .dll file for the UserControl in the output directory (bin/Release). The file is not executable; class libraries are used to define classes that are reused in other executable applications.

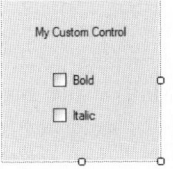

Fig. 15.50 | Custom-control creation.

6. Create a new Windows application.

7. In the new Windows application, right click the **ToolBox** and select **Choose Items....** In the **Choose Toolbox Items** dialog that appears, click **Browse....** Browse for the .dll file from the class library created in *Steps 1–5*. The item will then appear in the **Choose Toolbox Items** dialog (Fig. 15.51). If it is not already checked, check this item. Click **OK** to add the item to the **Toolbox**. This control can now be added to the Form as if it were any other control (Fig. 15.52).

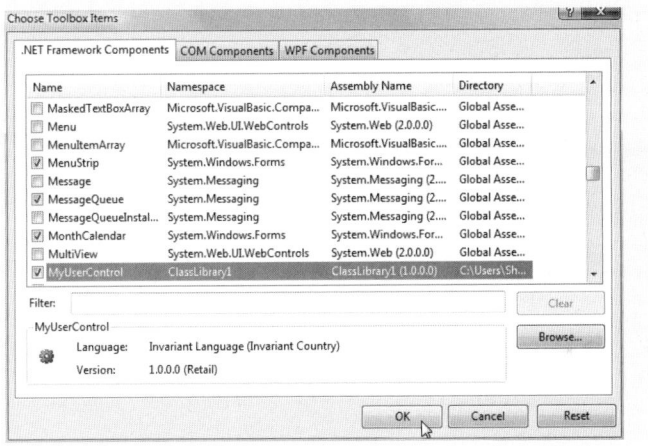

Fig. 15.51 | Custom control added to the **ToolBox**.

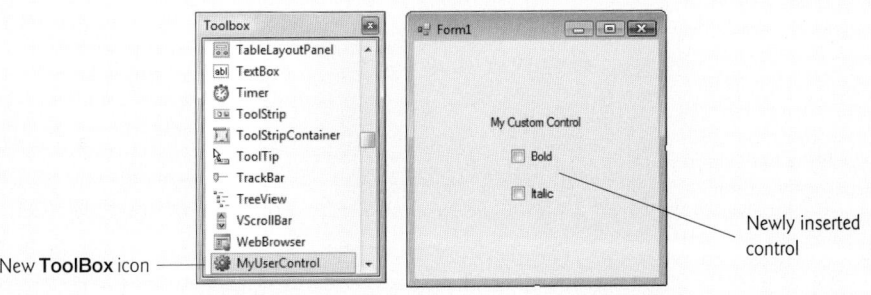

Fig. 15.52 | Custom control added to a Form.

15.15 Wrap-Up

Many of today's commercial applications provide GUIs that are easy to use and manipulate. Because of this demand for user-friendly GUIs, the ability to design sophisticated GUIs is an essential programming skill. Visual Studio's IDE makes GUI development quick and easy. In Chapters 14 and 15, we presented basic Windows Forms GUI development techniques. In Chapter 15, we demonstrated how to create menus, which provide users easy access to an application's functionality. You learned the DateTimePicker and MonthCalendar controls, which allow users to input date and time values. We demonstrated LinkLabels, which are used to link the user to an application or a web page. You used several controls that provide lists of data to the user—ListBoxes, CheckedListBoxes and ListViews. We used the ComboBox control to create drop-down lists, and the TreeView control to display data in hierarchical form. We then introduced complex GUIs that use tabbed windows and multiple document interfaces. The chapter concluded with demonstrations of visual inheritance and creating custom controls. The next chapter explores GUIs using Windows Presentation Foundation (WPF).

16

GUI with Windows Presentation Foundation

My function is to present old masterpieces in modern frames.
—Rudolf Bing

Instead of being a static one-time event, bonding is a process, a dynamic and continuous one.
—Julius Segal

…they do not declare but only hint.
—Friedrich Nietzsche

Science is the knowledge of consequences, and dependence of one fact upon another.
—Thomas Hobbes

Here form is content, content is form.
—Samuel Beckett

OBJECTIVES

In this chapter you'll learn:

- What Windows Presentation Foundation (WPF) is.
- Differences between WPF and Windows Forms.
- To mark up data using XML.
- How XML namespaces help provide unique XML element and attribute names.
- To define a WPF GUI with Extensible Application Markup Language (XAML).
- To handle WPF user-interface events.
- To use WPF's commands feature to handle common application tasks such as cut, copy and paste.
- To customize the look-and-feel of WPF GUIs using styles and control templates.
- To use data binding to display data in WPF controls.

Outline

16.1 Introduction

16.2 Windows Presentation Foundation (WPF)

16.3 XML Basics

16.4 Structuring Data

16.5 XML Namespaces

16.6 Declarative GUI Programming Using XAML

16.7 Creating a WPF Application in Visual C# Express

16.8 Laying Out Controls

    16.8.1 General Layout Principles

    16.8.2 Layout in Action

16.9 Event Handling

16.10 Commands and Common Application Tasks

16.11 WPF GUI Customization

16.12 Using Styles to Change a Control's Appearance

16.13 Customizing `Windows`

16.14 Defining a Control's Appearance with Control Templates

16.15 Data-Driven GUIs with Data Binding

16.16 Wrap-Up

16.17 Web Resources

16.1 Introduction

In Chapters 14–15, you built GUIs using Windows Forms. In this chapter, you'll build GUIs using *Windows Presentation Foundation* (*WPF*)—Microsoft's new framework for GUI, graphics, animation and multimedia. In Chapter 17, WPF Graphics and Multimedia, you'll learn how to incorporate 2D graphics, 3D graphics, animation, audio and video in WPF applications. In Chapter 24, Silverlight, Rich Internet Applications and Multimedia, we'll demonstrate how to use Silverlight (a subset of WPF and a new platform for web applications) to create Rich Internet Applications (RIA).

We begin with an introduction to WPF. Next, we discuss an important tool for creating WPF applications called *XAML* (pronounced "zammel")—*Extensible Application Markup Language*. XAML is a descriptive markup language that can be used to define and arrange GUI controls without any C# code. Its syntax is XML (Extensible Markup Language), a widely supported standard for describing data that is commonly used to exchange that data between applications over the Internet. We present an introduction to XML in Sections 16.3–16.5. Section 16.6 demonstrates how to define a WPF GUI with XAML. Sections 16.7–16.10 demonstrate the basics of creating a WPF GUI—layout, controls and events. You'll also learn new capabilities that are available in WPF controls and event handling.

WPF allows you to easily customize the look-and-feel of a GUI beyond what is possible in Windows Forms. Sections 16.11–16.14 demonstrate several techniques for manipulating the appearance of your GUIs. WPF also allows you to create data-driven GUIs that interact with many types of data. We demonstrate how to do this in Section 16.15.

16.2 Windows Presentation Foundation (WPF)

Previously, you often had to use multiple technologies to build client applications. If a Windows Forms application required video and audio capabilities, you needed to incorporate an additional technology such as Windows Media Player. Likewise, if your application required 3D graphics capabilities, you had to incorporate a separate technology such as Direct3D. WPF provides a single platform capable of handling both of these requirements, and more. It enables you to use one technology to build applications containing GUI, images, animation, 2D or 3D graphics, audio and video capabilities. In this chapter and Chapters 17 and 24, we demonstrate each of these capabilities.

WPF can interoperate with existing technologies. For example, you can include WPF controls in Windows Forms applications to incorporate multimedia content (such as audio or video) without converting the entire application to WPF, which could be a costly and time-consuming process. You can also use Windows Forms controls in WPF applications.

WPF's ability to use the acceleration capabilities of your computer's graphics hardware increases your applications' performance. In addition, WPF generates *vector-based graphics* and is *resolution independent*. Vector-based graphics are defined, not by a grid of pixels as *raster-based graphics* (also known as *bitmap graphics*) are, but rather by mathematical models. An advantage of vector-based graphics is that when you change the resolution, there is no loss of quality. Hence, the graphics become portable to a great variety of devices. Moreover, your applications won't appear smaller on higher-resolution screens. Instead, they'll remain the same size and display sharper. Chapter 17 presents more information about vector-based graphics and resolution independence.

Building a GUI with WPF is similar to building a GUI with Windows Forms—you drag-and-drop predefined controls from the **Toolbox** onto the design area. Many WPF controls correspond directly to those in Windows Forms. Just as in a Windows Forms application, the functionality is event driven. Many of the Windows Forms events you're familiar with are also in WPF. A WPF `Button`, for example, is similar to a Windows Forms `Button`, and both raise `Click` events.

There are several important differences between the two technologies. The WPF layout scheme is different. WPF properties and events have more capabilities. Most notably, WPF allows designers to define the appearance and content of a GUI without any C# code by defining it in XAML, a descriptive *markup* language (i.e., a text-based notation for describing something).

Introduction to XAML
In Windows Forms, when you use the designer to create a GUI, the IDE generates code statements that create and configure the controls. In WPF, it generates XAML markup. Because markup is designed to be readable by both humans and computers, you can also manually write XAML markup to define GUI controls. When you compile your WPF application, a XAML compiler generates code to create and configure controls based on your XAML markup. This technique of defining *what* the GUI should contain without specifying *how* to generate it is an example of *declarative programming*. LINQ is another example of a declarative programming language—a query describes *what* data to obtain but not *how* to obtain it.

XAML allows designers and programmers to work together more efficiently. Without writing any code, a graphic designer can edit the look-and-feel of an application using a

XAML graphic design program, such as Microsoft's *Expression Blend*. A programmer can import the XAML markup into Visual Studio and focus on coding the logic that gives an application its functionality. Even if you are working alone, however, this separation of front-end appearance from back-end logic improves your program's organization and makes it easier to maintain. XAML is an essential component of WPF programming.

Because XAML is implemented with XML, it is important that you understand the basics of XML before we continue our discussion of XAML and WPF GUIs.

16.3 XML Basics

The Extensible Markup Language was developed in 1996 by the *World Wide Web Consortium's* (*W3C's*) XML Working Group. XML is a widely supported standard for describing data that is commonly used to exchange that data between applications over the Internet. It permits document authors to create markup for virtually any type of information. This enables them to create entirely new markup languages for describing any type of data, such as mathematical formulas, software-configuration instructions, chemical molecular structures, music, news, recipes and financial reports. XML describes data in a way that both human beings and computers can understand.

Figure 16.1 is a simple XML document that describes information for a baseball player. We focus on lines 5–11 to introduce basic XML syntax. You'll learn about the other elements of this document in Section 16.4.

XML documents contain *elements* that specify the document's structure, such as firstName (line 6), and text that represents content (i.e., data), such as John (line 6). XML documents delimit elements with *start tags* and *end tags*. A start tag consists of the element name in *angle brackets* (e.g., <player> and <firstName> in lines 5 and 6, respectively). An end tag consists of the element name preceded by a *forward slash* (/) in angle brackets (e.g., </firstName> and </player> in lines 6 and 11, respectively). An element's start and end tags enclose text that represents a piece of data (e.g., the firstName of the player—John—in line 6, which is enclosed by the <firstName> start tag and and </firstName> end tag) or other elements (e.g., the firstName, lastName, and battingAverage elements in the player element. Every XML document must have exactly one *root element* that contains all the other elements. In Fig. 16.1, player (lines 5–11) is the root element.

Examples of XML-based markup languages include XHTML (Extensible HyperText Markup Language—HTML's replacement for marking up web content), MathML (for

```
1   <?xml version = "1.0"?>
2   <!-- Fig. 16.1: player.xml -->
3   <!-- Baseball player structured with XML -->
4
5   <player>
6       <firstName>John</firstName>
7
8       <lastName>Doe</lastName>
9
10      <battingAverage>0.375</battingAverage>
11  </player>
```

Fig. 16.1 | XML that describes a baseball player's information.

mathematics), VoiceXML™ (for speech), CML (Chemical Markup Language—for chemistry) and XBRL (Extensible Business Reporting Language—for financial data exchange). ODF (Open Document Format—developed by Sun Microsystems) and OOXML (Office Open XML—developed by Microsoft as a replacement for the old proprietary Microsoft Office formats) are two competing standards for electronic office documents such as spreadsheets, presentations, and word processing documents. These markup languages are called XML *vocabularies* and provide a means for describing particular types of data in standardized, structured ways.

Massive amounts of data are currently stored on the Internet in a variety of formats (e.g., databases, web pages, text files). Based on current trends, it is likely that much of this data, especially that which is passed between systems, will soon take the form of XML. Organizations see XML as the future of data encoding. Information-technology groups are planning ways to integrate XML into their systems. Industry groups are developing custom XML vocabularies for most major industries that will allow computer-based business applications to communicate in common languages. For example, web services, which we discuss in Chapter 23, allow web-based applications to exchange data seamlessly through standard protocols based on XML. Web services are described by an XML vocabulary called WSDL (Web Services Description Language).

The next generation of the Internet and World Wide Web is being built on a foundation of XML, which enables the development of more sophisticated web-based applications. XML allows you to assign meaning to what would otherwise be random pieces of data. As a result, programs can "understand" the data they manipulate. For example, a web browser might view a street address listed on a simple HTML web page as a string of characters without any real meaning. In an XML document, however, this data can be clearly identified (i.e., marked up) as an address. A program that uses the document can recognize this data as an address and provide links to a map of that location, driving directions from that location or other location-specific information. Likewise, an application can recognize names of people, dates, ISBN numbers and any other type of XML-encoded data. Based on this data, the application can present users with other related information, providing a richer, more meaningful user experience.

Viewing and Modifying XML Documents

XML documents are portable. Viewing or modifying an XML document—a text file, usually with the **.xml** file-name extension—does not require special software, although many software tools exist. New ones are frequently released that make it more convenient to develop XML-based applications. Most text editors can open XML documents for viewing and editing. Visual C# Express includes an XML editor that provides *IntelliSense* for tag and attribute names. The editor also checks that the document is well formed and is valid if a schema (discussed shortly) is present. Also, most web browsers can display an XML document in a formatted manner that shows its structure. We demonstrate this using Internet Explorer in Section 16.4. One important characteristic of XML is that it is both human readable and machine readable.

Processing XML Documents

Processing an XML document requires software called an ***XML parser*** (or ***XML processor***). A parser makes the document's data available to applications. While reading the contents of an XML document, a parser checks that the document follows the syntax rules specified by the W3C's XML Recommendation (www.w3.org/XML). XML syntax requires a single root element, a start tag and end tag for each element, and properly nested tags (i.e., the end tag for a nested element must appear before the end tag of the enclosing element). Furthermore, XML is case sensitive, so the proper capitalization must be used in elements. A document that conforms to this syntax is a *well-formed XML document*, and is syntactically correct. We present fundamental XML syntax in Section 16.4. If an XML parser can process an XML document successfully, that XML document is well formed. Parsers can provide access to XML-encoded data in well-formed documents only—if a document is not well-formed, the parser will report an error to the user or calling application.

Often, XML parsers are built into software such as Visual Studio or available for download over the Internet. Popular parsers include *Microsoft XML Core Services* (*MSXML*), the .NET Framework's *XmlReader class*, XDocument and LINQ to XML (Chapter 20, XML and LINQ to XML), the Apache Software Foundation's *Xerces* (available from xerces.apache.org) and the open-source *Expat XML Parser* (available from expat.sourceforge.net).

Validating XML Documents

An XML document can optionally reference a *Document Type Definition* (*DTD*) or a *W3C XML Schema* (referred to simply as a "schema" for the rest of this book) that defines the XML document's proper structure. When an XML document references a DTD or a schema, some parsers (called *validating parsers*) can use the DTD/schema to check that it has the appropriate structure. If the XML document conforms to the DTD/schema (i.e., the document has the appropriate structure), the XML document is *valid*. For example, if in Fig. 16.1 we were referencing a DTD that specifies that a player element must have firstName, lastName and battingAverage elements, then omitting the lastName element (line 8) would cause the XML document player.xml to be invalid. The XML document would still be well formed, however, because it follows proper XML syntax (i.e., it has one root element, and each element has a start and an end tag). By definition, a valid XML document is well formed. Parsers that cannot check for document conformity against DTDs/schemas are *nonvalidating parsers*—they determine only whether an XML document is well formed.

For more information about validation, DTDs and schemas, as well as the key differences between these two types of structural specifications, see Chapter 20. For now, note that schemas are XML documents themselves, whereas DTDs are not. As you'll learn in Chapter 20, this difference presents several advantages in using schemas over DTDs.

Software Engineering Observation 16.1

DTDs and schemas are essential for business-to-business (B2B) transactions and mission-critical systems. Validating XML documents ensures that disparate systems can manipulate data structured in standardized ways and prevents errors caused by missing or malformed data.

Formatting and Manipulating XML Documents

XML documents contain only data, not formatting instructions, so applications that process XML documents must decide how to manipulate or display each document's data. For example, a PDA (personal digital assistant) may render an XML document differently than a wireless phone or a desktop computer. You can use *Extensible Stylesheet Language* (*XSL*) to specify rendering instructions for different platforms. We discuss XSL in Chapter 20.

XML-processing programs can also search, sort and manipulate XML data using technologies such as XSL. Some other XML-related technologies are XPath (XML Path Language—a language for accessing parts of an XML document), XSL-FO (XSL Formatting Objects—an XML vocabulary used to describe document formatting) and XSLT (XSL Transformations—a language for transforming XML documents into other documents). We present XSLT and XPath in Chapter 20. We'll also present new LINQ features that simplify working with XML in your code.

16.4 Structuring Data

In Fig. 16.2, we present an XML document that marks up a simple article using XML. The line numbers shown are for reference only and are not part of the XML document.

This document begins with an *XML declaration* (line 1), which identifies the document as an XML document. The *version attribute* specifies the XML version to which the document conforms. The current XML standard is version 1.0. Though the W3C released a version 1.1 specification in February 2004, this newer version is not yet widely supported. The W3C may continue to release new versions as XML evolves to meet the requirements of different fields.

Some XML documents also specify an *encoding attribute* in the XML declaration. An encoding specifies how characters are stored in memory and on disk—historically, the way an uppercase "A" was stored on one computer architecture was different than the way it was stored on a different computer architecture. Appendix G describes Unicode, which specifies encodings that can describe characters in any written language. An introduction to different encodings in XML can be found at the website msdn.microsoft.com/en-us/library/aa468560.aspx.

```
1   <?xml version = "1.0"?>
2   <!-- Fig. 16.2: article.xml -->
3   <!-- Article structured with XML -->
4
5   <article>
6      <title>Simple XML</title>
7
8      <date>July 24, 2008</date>
9
10     <author>
11        <firstName>John</firstName>
12        <lastName>Doe</lastName>
13     </author>
14
15     <summary>XML is pretty easy.</summary>
16
17     <content>
18        In this chapter, we present a wide variety of examples that use XML.
19     </content>
20  </article>
```

Fig. 16.2 | XML used to mark up an article.

Portability Tip 16.1

Documents should include the XML declaration to identify the version of XML used. A document that lacks an XML declaration might be assumed erroneously to conform to the latest version of XML—in which case, errors could result.

Common Programming Error 16.1

Placing whitespace characters before the XML declaration is an error.

XML comments (lines 2–3), which begin with <!-- and end with -->, can be placed almost anywhere in an XML document. XML comments can span multiple lines—an end marker on each line is not needed; the end marker can appear on a subsequent line, as long as there is exactly one end marker (-->) for each begin marker (<!--). Comments are used in XML for documentation purposes. Line 4 is a blank line. As in a C# program, blank lines, whitespaces and indentation are used in XML to improve readability. Later you'll see that the blank lines are normally ignored by XML parsers.

Common Programming Error 16.2

In an XML document, each start tag must have a matching end tag; omitting either tag is an error. Soon, you'll learn how such errors are detected.

Common Programming Error 16.3

XML is case sensitive. Using different cases for the start-tag and end-tag names for the same element is a syntax error.

In Fig. 16.2, article (lines 5–20) is the root element. The lines that precede the root element (lines 1–4) are the XML *prolog*. In an XML prolog, the XML declaration must appear before the comments and any other markup.

The elements we used in the example do not come from any specific markup language. Instead, we chose the element names and markup structure that best describe our particular data. You can invent whatever elements make sense for the particular data you are dealing with. For example, element title (line 6) contains text that describes the article's title (e.g., Simple XML). Similarly, date (line 8), author (lines 10–13), firstName (line 11), lastName (line 12), summary (line 15) and content (lines 17–19) contain text that describes the date, author, the author's first name, the author's last name, a summary and the content of the document, respectively. XML element and attribute names can be of any length and may contain letters, digits, underscores, hyphens and periods. However, they must begin with either a letter or an underscore, and they should not begin with "xml" in any combination of uppercase and lowercase letters (e.g., XML, Xml, xMl), as this is reserved for use in the XML standards.

Common Programming Error 16.4

Using a whitespace character in an XML element name is an error.

Good Programming Practice 16.1

XML element names should be meaningful to humans and should not use abbreviations.

XML elements are *nested* to form hierarchies—with the root element at the top of the hierarchy. This allows document authors to create parent/child relationships between data. For example, elements `title`, `date`, `author`, `summary` and `content` are nested within `article`. Elements `firstName` and `lastName` are nested within `author`.

Common Programming Error 16.5

Nesting XML tags improperly is a syntax error—it causes an XML document to not be well-formed. For example, `<x><y>hello</x></y>` is an error, because the `</y>` tag must precede the `</x>` tag.

Any element that contains other elements (e.g., `article` or `author`) is a *container element*. Container elements also are called *parent elements*. Elements nested inside a container element are *child elements* (or children) of that container element.

Viewing an XML Document in Internet Explorer

The XML document in Fig. 16.2 is simply a text file named `article.xml`. This document does not contain formatting information for the article. The reason is that XML is a technology for describing the structure of data. Formatting and displaying data from an XML document are application-specific issues. For example, when the user loads `article.xml` in Internet Explorer (IE), MSXML (Microsoft XML Core Services) parses and displays the document's data. Internet Explorer uses a built-in *style sheet* to format the data. Note that the resulting format of the data (Fig. 16.3) is similar to the format of the listing in Fig. 16.2. In Chapter 20, we show how to create style sheets to transform your XML data into various formats suitable for display.

Note the minus sign (–) and plus sign (+) in the screenshots of Fig. 16.3. Although these symbols are not part of the XML document, Internet Explorer places them next to every container element. A minus sign indicates that Internet Explorer is displaying the container element's child elements. Clicking the minus sign next to an element collapses that element (i.e., causes Internet Explorer to hide the container element's children and

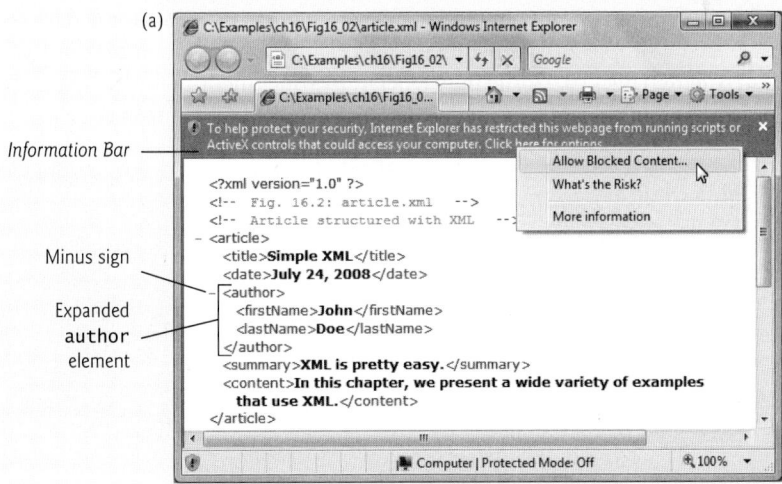

Fig. 16.3 | `article.xml` displayed by Internet Explorer. (Part 1 of 2.)

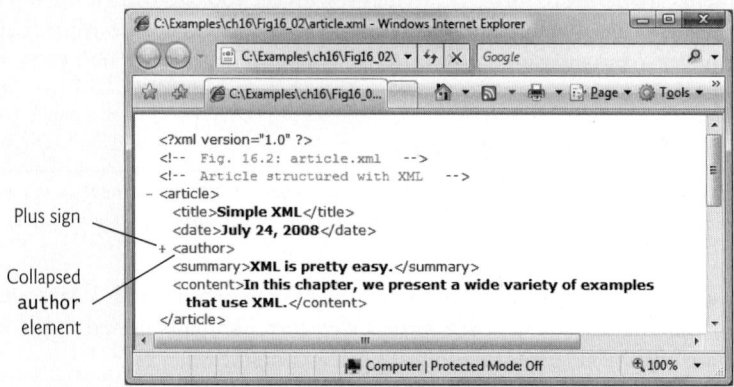

Plus sign

Collapsed author element

Fig. 16.3 | `article.xml` displayed by Internet Explorer. (Part 2 of 2.)

replace the minus sign with a plus sign). Conversely, clicking the plus sign next to an element expands that element (i.e., causes Internet Explorer to display the container element's children and replace the plus sign with a minus sign). This behavior is similar to viewing the directory structure using Windows Explorer. In fact, a directory structure often is modeled as a series of tree structures, in which the *root* of a tree represents a drive letter (e.g., C:), and *nodes* in the tree represent directories. Parsers often store XML data as tree structures to facilitate efficient manipulation.

[*Note:* In Windows XP Service Pack 2 and Windows Vista, by default Internet Explorer displays all the XML elements in expanded view, and clicking the minus sign (Fig. 16.3(a)) does not do anything. So, by default, Windows will not be able to collapse the element. To enable this functionality, right click the *Information Bar* just below the **Address** field and select **Allow Blocked Content....** Then click **Yes** in the popup window that appears.]

XML Markup for a Business Letter

Now that we have seen a simple XML document, let's examine a more complex one that marks up a business letter (Fig. 16.4). Again, we begin the document with the XML declaration (line 1) that states the XML version to which the document conforms.

```
1   <?xml version = "1.0"?>
2   <!-- Fig. 16.4: letter.xml -->
3   <!-- Business letter marked up as XML -->
4
5   <!DOCTYPE letter SYSTEM "letter.dtd">
6
7   <letter>
8      <contact type = "sender">
9         <name>Jane Doe</name>
10        <address1>Box 12345</address1>
11        <address2>15 Any Ave.</address2>
12        <city>Othertown</city>
```

Fig. 16.4 | Business letter marked up as XML. (Part 1 of 2.)

```
13          <state>Otherstate</state>
14          <zip>67890</zip>
15          <phone>555-4321</phone>
16          <flag gender = "F" />
17      </contact>
18
19      <contact type = "receiver">
20          <name>John Doe</name>
21          <address1>123 Main St.</address1>
22          <address2></address2>
23          <city>Anytown</city>
24          <state>Anystate</state>
25          <zip>12345</zip>
26          <phone>555-1234</phone>
27          <flag gender = "M" />
28      </contact>
29
30      <salutation>Dear Sir:</salutation>
31
32      <paragraph>It is our privilege to inform you about our new database
33          managed with XML. This new system allows you to reduce the
34          load on your inventory list server by having the client machine
35          perform the work of sorting and filtering the data.
36      </paragraph>
37
38      <paragraph>Please visit our website for availability
39          and pricing.
40      </paragraph>
41
42      <closing>Sincerely,</closing>
43      <signature>Ms. Jane Doe</signature>
44  </letter>
```

Fig. 16.4 | Business letter marked up as XML. (Part 2 of 2.)

Line 5 specifies that this XML document references a DTD. Recall from Section 16.3 that DTDs define the structure of the data for an XML document. For example, a DTD specifies the elements and parent/child relationships between elements permitted in an XML document.

Error-Prevention Tip 16.1

An XML document is not required to reference a DTD, but validating XML parsers can use a DTD to ensure that the document has the proper structure.

Portability Tip 16.2

Validating an XML document helps guarantee that independent developers will exchange data in a standardized form that conforms to the DTD.

The DTD reference (line 5) contains three items: the name of the root element that the DTD specifies (letter); the keyword **SYSTEM** (which denotes an *external DTD*—a DTD declared in a separate file, as opposed to a DTD declared locally in the same file);

and the DTD's name and location (i.e., letter.dtd in the same directory as the XML document). DTD document file names typically end with the *.dtd* extension. We discuss DTDs and letter.dtd in detail in Chapter 20.

Root element letter (lines 7–44 of Fig. 16.4) contains the child elements contact, contact, salutation, paragraph, paragraph, closing and signature. Besides being placed between tags, data also can be placed in *attributes*—name/value pairs that appear within the angle brackets of start tags. Elements can have any number of attributes (separated by spaces) in their start tags, provided all the attribute names are unique. The first contact element (lines 8–17) has an attribute named type with *attribute value* "sender", which indicates that this contact element identifies the letter's sender. The second contact element (lines 19–28) has attribute type with value "receiver", which indicates that this contact element identifies the letter's recipient. Like element names, attribute names are case sensitive, can be of any length, may contain letters, digits, underscores, hyphens and periods, and must begin with either a letter or an underscore character. A contact element stores various items of information about a contact, such as the contact's name (represented by element name), address (represented by elements address1, address2, city, state and zip), phone number (represented by element phone) and gender (represented by attribute gender of element flag). Element salutation (line 30) marks up the letter's salutation. Lines 32–40 mark up the letter's body using two paragraph elements. Elements closing (line 42) and signature (line 43) mark up the closing sentence and the author's "signature," respectively.

Common Programming Error 16.6

Failure to enclose attribute values in double ("") or single (' ') quotes is a syntax error.

Line 16 introduces the *empty element* flag. An empty element contains no content. However, it may sometimes contain data in the form of attributes. Empty element flag contains an attribute that indicates the gender of the contact (represented by the parent contact element). Document authors can close an empty element either by placing a slash immediately preceding the right angle bracket, as shown in line 16, or by explicitly writing an end tag, as in line 22

> *<address2></address2>*

Line 22 can also be written as:

> *<address2/>*

Note that the address2 element in line 22 is empty, because there is no second part to this contact's address. However, we must include this element to conform to the structural rules specified in the XML document's DTD—letter.dtd (which we present in Chapter 20). This DTD specifies that each contact element must have an address2 child element (even if it is empty). In Chapter 20, you'll learn how DTDs indicate that certain elements are required while others are optional.

16.5 XML Namespaces

XML allows document authors to create custom elements. This extensibility can result in *naming collisions*—elements with identical names that represent different things—when combining content from multiple sources. For example, we may use the element book to mark up data about a Deitel publication. A stamp collector may use the element book to mark up data about a book of stamps. Using both of these elements in the same document could create a naming collision, making it difficult to determine which kind of data each element contains.

An XML *namespace* is a collection of element and attribute names. Like C# namespaces, XML namespaces provide a means for document authors to unambiguously refer to elements that have the same name (i.e., prevent collisions). For example,

> *<subject>*Math*</subject>*

and

> *<subject>*Cardiology*</subject>*

use element subject to mark up data. In the first case, the subject is something one studies in school, whereas in the second case, the subject is a field of medicine. Namespaces can differentiate these two subject elements. For example,

> *<school:subject>*Math*</school:subject>*

and

> *<medical:subject>*Cardiology*</medical:subject>*

Both school and medical are *namespace prefixes*. A document author places a namespace prefix and colon (:) before an element name to specify the namespace to which that element belongs. Document authors can create their own namespace prefixes using virtually any name except the reserved namespace prefixes xml and xmlns. In the subsections that follow, we demonstrate how document authors ensure that namespaces are unique.

Common Programming Error 16.7

Attempting to create a namespace prefix named xml in any mixture of uppercase and lowercase letters is a syntax error—the xml namespace prefix is reserved for internal use by XML itself.

Differentiating Elements with Namespaces

Figure 16.5 demonstrates namespaces. In this document, namespaces differentiate two distinct elements—the file element related to a text file and the file document related to an image file.

```
 1   <?xml version = "1.0"?>
 2   <!-- Fig. 16.5: namespace.xml -->
 3   <!-- Demonstrating namespaces -->
 4
 5   <text:directory
 6      xmlns:text = "urn:deitel:textInfo"
 7      xmlns:image = "urn:deitel:imageInfo">
 8
 9      <text:file filename = "book.xml">
10         <text:description>A book list</text:description>
11      </text:file>
```

Fig. 16.5 | XML namespaces demonstration. (Part 1 of 2.)

```
12
13     <image:file filename = "funny.jpg">
14        <image:description>A funny picture</image:description>
15        <image:size width = "200" height = "100" />
16     </image:file>
17  </text:directory>
```

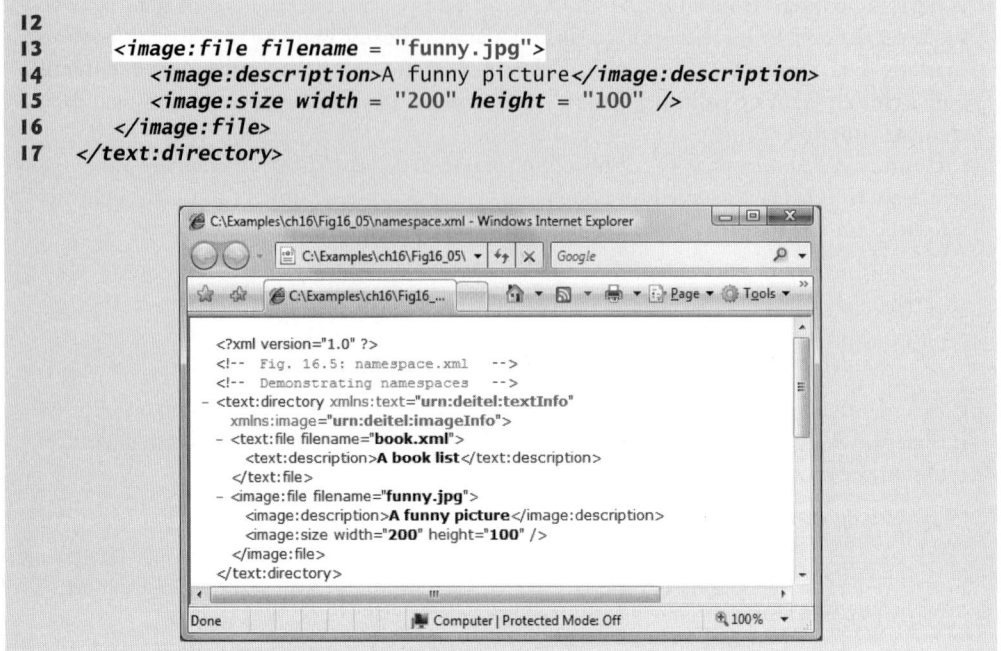

Fig. 16.5 | XML namespaces demonstration. (Part 2 of 2.)

Lines 6–7 use the XML-namespace reserved attribute *xmlns* to create two namespace prefixes—text and image. Creating a namespace prefix is similar to defining a using directive in C#—it allows you to access XML elements from a given namespace. Each namespace prefix is bound to a series of characters called a *Uniform Resource Identifier* (*URI*) that uniquely identifies the namespace. Document authors create their own namespace prefixes and URIs. A URI is a way to identify a resource, typically on the Internet. Two popular types of URI are *Uniform Resource Name* (*URN*) and *Uniform Resource Locator* (*URL*).

To ensure that namespaces are unique, document authors must provide unique URIs. In this example, we use the text urn:deitel:textInfo and urn:deitel:imageInfo as URIs. These URIs employ the URN scheme frequently used to identify namespaces. Under this naming scheme, a URI begins with "urn:", followed by a unique series of additional names separated by colons. Note that these URIs are not guaranteed to be unique— the idea is simply that creating a long URI in this way makes it unlikely that two authors will use the same namespace.

Another common practice is to use URLs, which specify the location of a file or a resource on the Internet. For example, http://www.deitel.com is the URL that identifies the home page of the Deitel & Associates website. Using URLs guarantees that the namespaces are unique, because the domain names (e.g., www.deitel.com) are guaranteed to be unique. For example, lines 5–7 could be rewritten as

```
<text:directory
    xmlns:text = "http://www.deitel.com/xmlns-text"
    xmlns:image = "http://www.deitel.com/xmlns-image">
```

where URLs related to the Deitel & Associates, Inc. domain name serve as URIs to identify the `text` and `image` namespaces. The parser does not visit these URLs, nor do these URLs need to refer to actual web pages. Each simply represents a unique series of characters used to differentiate URI names. In fact, any string can represent a namespace. For example, our `image` namespace URI could be `hgjfkdlsa4556`, in which case our prefix assignment would be

    xmlns:image = "hgjfkdlsa4556"

Lines 9–11 use the `text` namespace prefix for elements `file` and `description`. Note that the end tags must also specify the namespace prefix `text`. Lines 13–16 apply namespace prefix `image` to the elements `file`, `description` and `size`. Note that attributes do not require namespace prefixes (although they can have them), because each attribute is already part of an element that specifies the namespace prefix. For example, attribute `filename` (line 9) is already uniquely identified by being in the context of the `filename` start tag, which is prefixed with `text`.

Specifying a Default Namespace

To eliminate the need to place namespace prefixes in each element, document authors may specify a *default namespace* for an element and its children. Figure 16.6 demonstrates using a default namespace (`urn:deitel:textInfo`) for element `directory`.

Line 5 defines a default namespace using attribute `xmlns` with a URI as its value. Once we define this default namespace, child elements which do not specify a prefix belong to the default namespace. Thus, element `file` (lines 8–10) is in the default namespace `urn:deitel:textInfo`. Compare this to lines 9–11 of Fig. 16.5, where we had to prefix the `file` and `description` element names with the namespace prefix `text`.

Common Programming Error 16.8

The default namespace can be overridden at any point in the document with another xmlns attribute. All direct and indirect children of the element with the xmlns attribute use the new default namespace.

```
 1   <?xml version = "1.0"?>
 2   <!-- Fig. 16.6: defaultnamespace.xml -->
 3   <!-- Using default namespaces -->
 4
 5   <directory xmlns = "urn:deitel:textInfo"
 6      xmlns:image = "urn:deitel:imageInfo">
 7
 8      <file filename = "book.xml">
 9         <description>A book list</description>
10      </file>
11
12      <image:file filename = "funny.jpg">
13         <image:description>A funny picture</image:description>
14         <image:size width = "200" height = "100" />
15      </image:file>
16   </directory>
```

Fig. 16.6 | Default namespace demonstration. (Part 1 of 2.)

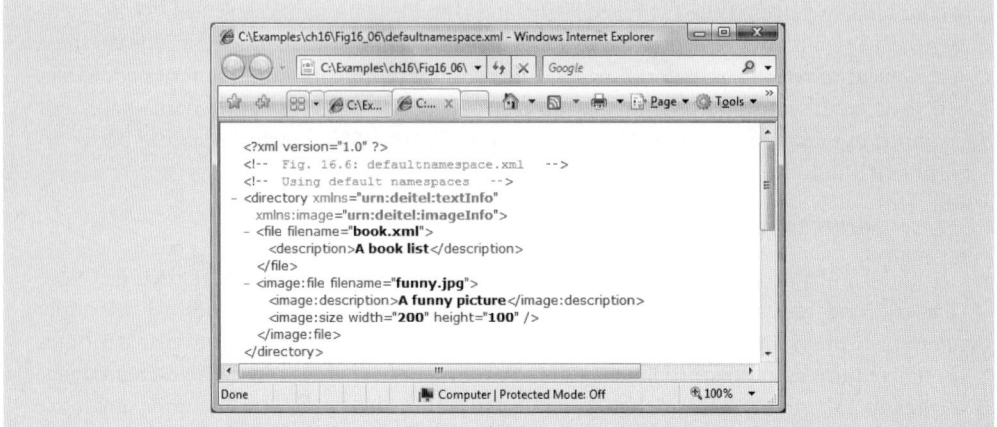

Fig. 16.6 | Default namespace demonstration. (Part 2 of 2.)

The default namespace applies to the `directory` element and all elements that are not qualified with a namespace prefix. However, we can use a namespace prefix to specify a different namespace for particular elements. For example, the `file` element in lines 12–15 includes the `image` namespace prefix, indicating that this element is in the `urn:deitel:imageInfo` namespace, not the default namespace.

Namespaces in XML Vocabularies

XML-based languages, such as XML Schema, Extensible Stylesheet Language (XSL) and BizTalk (`www.microsoft.com/biztalk`), often use namespaces to identify their elements. Each of these vocabularies defines special-purpose elements that are grouped in namespaces. These namespaces help prevent naming collisions between predefined elements and user-defined elements.

16.6 Declarative GUI Programming Using XAML

A XAML document defines the appearance of a WPF application. Figure 16.7 is a simple XAML document that defines a window that displays `Welcome to WPF!`

Since XAML documents are XML documents, a XAML document consists of many nested elements, delimited by start tags and end tags. As with any other XML document, each XAML document must contain a single root element. Just as in XML, data is placed as nested content or in attributes.

```
1   <!-- Fig. 16.7: XAMLIntroduction.xaml -->
2   <!-- A simple XAML document. -->
3
4   <!-- the Window control is the root element of the GUI -->
5   <Window x:Class="XAMLIntroduction.XAMLIntroductionWindow"
6       xmlns="http://schemas.microsoft.com/winfx/2006/xaml/presentation"
7       xmlns:x="http://schemas.microsoft.com/winfx/2006/xaml"
8       Title="A Simple Window" Height="150" Width="250">
```

Fig. 16.7 | A simple XAML document. (Part 1 of 2.)

```
 9
10       <!-- a layout container -->
11       <Grid Background="Gold">
12
13           <!-- a Label control -->
14           <Label HorizontalAlignment="Center" VerticalAlignment="Center">
15               Welcome to WPF!
16           </Label>
17       </Grid>
18   </Window>
```

A Simple Window

Welcome to WPF!

Fig. 16.7 | A simple XAML document. (Part 2 of 2.)

Two standard namespaces must be defined in every XAML document so that the XAML compiler can interpret your markup—the *presentation XAML namespace*, which defines WPF-specific elements and attributes, and the *standard XAML namespace*, which defines elements and attributes that are standard to all types of XAML documents. Usually, the presentation XAML namespace (`http://schemas.microsoft.com/winfx/2006/xaml/presentation`) is defined as the default namespace (line 6), and the standard XAML namespace (`http://schemas.microsoft.com/winfx/2006/xaml`) is mapped to the prefix x (line 7). These are both automatically included in the `Window` element's start tag when you create a WPF application in Visual Studio.

WPF *controls* are represented by elements in XAML markup. The root element of the XAML document in Fig. 16.7 is a *Window* control (lines 5–18), which defines the application's window—this corresponds to the `Form` control in Windows `Forms`.

The `Window` start tag (line 5) also defines another important attribute, *x:Class*, which specifies the class name of the associated code-behind class that provides the GUI's functionality. The x: signifies that the `Class` attribute is located in the standard XAML namespace. A XAML document typically has an associated code-behind file to handle events.

Using attributes, you can define a control's properties in XAML. For example, the `Window`'s `Title`, `Width` and `Height` properties are set in line 8. A `Window`'s `Title` specifies the text that is displayed in the `Window`'s title bar. The `Width` and `Height` properties apply to a control of any type and specify the control's width and height, respectively, using system-independent pixels.

`Window` is a *content control* (a control derived from class *ContentControl*), meaning it can have exactly one child element or text content. You'll almost always set a *layout container* (a control derived from the *Panel* class) as the child element so that you can host multiple controls in a `Window`. A layout container such as a `Grid` (lines 11–17) can have many child elements, allowing it to contain many controls. In Section 16.8, you'll use content controls and layout containers to arrange a GUI.

Like Window, a *Label*—corresponding to the Label control in Windows Forms—is also a ContentControl. It is generally used to display a small amount of information.

16.7 Creating a WPF Application in Visual C# Express

To create a new WPF application, open the **New Project** dialog (Fig. 16.8) and select **WPF Application** from the list of template types. The IDE for a WPF application looks nearly identical to that of a Windows Forms application. You'll recognize the familiar **Toolbox**, **Design** view, **Solution Explorer** and **Properties** window.

There are differences, however. One is the new *XAML view* (Fig. 16.9) that appears when you open a XAML document. This view is linked to the **Design** view and the **Properties** window. When you edit content in the **Design** view, the **XAML** view automatically updates, and vice versa. Likewise, when you edit properties in the **Properties** window, the **XAML** view automatically updates, and vice versa.

When you create a WPF application, four files are generated and can be viewed in the **Solution Explorer**. *App.xaml* defines the Application object and its settings. The most noteworthy setting is the *StartupUri* attribute, which defines the XAML document that executes first when the Application loads (Window1.xaml by default). *App.xaml.cs* is its code-behind class and handles application-level events. Window1.xaml defines an applica-

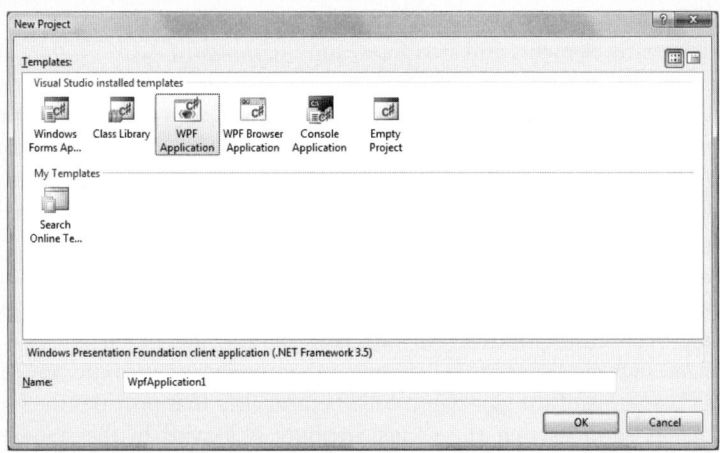

Fig. 16.8 | **New Project** dialog.

```
1 <Window x:Class="Window1"
2     xmlns="http://schemas.microsoft.com/winfx/2006/xaml/presentation"
3     xmlns:x="http://schemas.microsoft.com/winfx/2006/xaml"
4     Title="Window1" Height="300" Width="300">
5     <Grid>
6
7     </Grid>
8 </Window>
9
```

Fig. 16.9 | XAML view.

tion window, and `Window1.xaml.cs` is its code-behind class, which handles the window's events. The file name of the code-behind class is always the file name of the associated XAML document appended by the `.cs` file-name extension.

Error-Prevention Tip 16.2

Before you begin designing and coding your WPF application, make sure that the `StartupUri` attribute of `App.xaml` points to the correct XAML document. You can do this either by editing the XAML markup. In addition, ensure that every XAML document references the correct class name (not file name) of its associated code-behind class.

We use three-space indents in our code. To ensure that your code appears the same as the book's examples, change the tab spacing for XAML documents to three spaces (the default is four). Select **Tools > Options** and ensure that the **Show all settings** checkbox is checked. In **Text Editor > XAML > Tabs** change both the **Tab size** and **Indent size** properties to 3 (Fig. 16.10). In addition, you should configure the **XAML** editor to display line numbers by checking the **Line numbers** checkbox in **Text Editor > XAML > General**. You are now ready to create your first WPF application.

Creating a WPF application in Visual C# Express is similar to creating a Windows `Forms` application. Just as you did in the last chapter to create a Windows `Forms` application, you can drag-and-drop controls onto the **Design** view of your WPF GUI. A control's properties can be edited in the **Properties** window. As of Visual Studio 2008 Service Pack 1 and Visual C# 2008 Service Pack 1, you are able to create event handlers from the **Properties** window for WPF applications.

Because XAML is easy to understand and edit, it is often less difficult to manually edit your GUI's XAML markup than to do everything through the visual programming tools of the IDE. In some cases, you must manually write XAML markup in order to take full advantage of the features that are offered in WPF. Nevertheless, the visual programming tools in Visual Studio are often handy, and we'll point out the situations in which they might be useful as they occur.

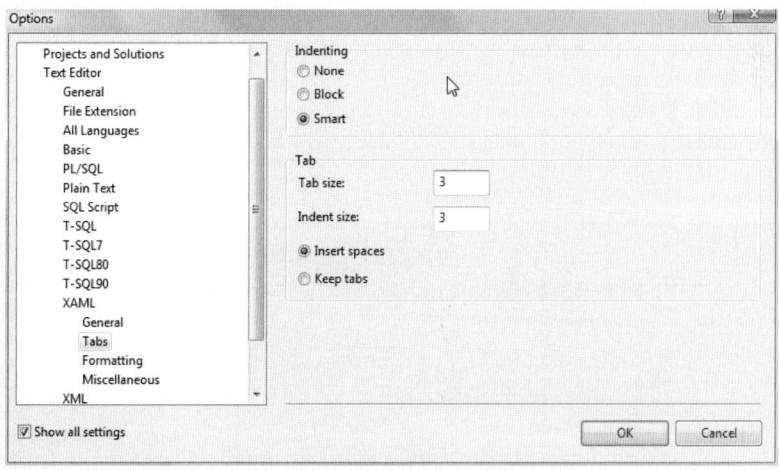

Fig. 16.10 | Changing the tab spacing.

16.8 Laying Out Controls

In Windows Forms, a control's size and location are specified explicitly. In WPF, a control's size should be specified as a range of possible values rather than fixed values, and its location specified relative to those of other controls. This type of layout scheme, in which you specify how controls share the available space, is called *flow-based layout*. Its advantage is that it enables your GUIs, if designed properly, to be aesthetically pleasing, no matter how a user might resize the application. Likewise, it enables your GUIs to be resolution independent.

16.8.1 General Layout Principles

Layout refers to the size and positioning of controls. The WPF layout scheme addresses both of these in a flow-based fashion and can be summarized by two fundamental principles.

Generally, a control's size should not be defined explicitly. Doing so often creates a design that looks pleasing when it first loads, but deteriorates when the window is resized or the content updates. Thus, in addition to the Width and Height properties associated with every control, all WPF controls have the *MinWidth*, *MinHeight*, *MaxWidth* and *MaxHeight* properties. If the Width and Height properties are both Auto (which is the default), you can use these minimum and maximum properties to specify a range of acceptable sizes for a control. Its size will automatically adjust as the size of its container changes.

A control's position should not be defined in absolute terms. Instead, it should be specified based on its position relative to the layout container in which it is included and the other controls in the same container. All controls have three properties for doing this—*Margin*, *HorizontalAlignment* and *VerticalAlignment*. Margin specifies how much space to put around a control's edges. The parameters of Margin are a comma-separated list of four integers, representing the left, top, right and bottom margins. Additionally, you can pass it two integers, which it interprets as the left–right and top–bottom margins. If you pass it just one integer, it uses the same margin on all four sides.

HorizontalAlignment and VerticalAlignment specify how to align a control within its layout container. Valid options of HorizontalAlignment are Left, Center, Right and Stretch. Valid options of VerticalAlignment are Top, Center, Bottom and Stretch. Stretch means that the object will occupy as much space as possible.

A control can have other layout properties specific to the layout container in which it is contained. We'll discuss these as we examine the specific layout containers. WPF provides many controls for laying out a GUI. Figure 16.11 lists some of the common controls used for layout.

Control	Description
Layout containers (derived from Panel)	
Grid	Layout is defined by a grid of rows and columns, depending on the RowDefinitions and ColumnDefinitions properties. Elements are placed into cells.
Canvas	Layout is coordinate based. Element positions are defined explicitly by their distance from the top and left edges of the Canvas.

Fig. 16.11 | Common controls used for layout. (Part 1 of 2.)

Control	Description
StackPanel	Elements are arranged in a single row or column, depending on the Orientation property.
DockPanel	Elements are positioned based on which edge they are docked to. If the LastChildFill property is true, the last element gets the remaining space in the middle.
WrapPanel	A wrapping StackPanel. Elements are arranged sequentially in rows or columns (depending on the Orientation), each row or column wrapping to start a new one when it reaches the WrapPanel's right or bottom edge, respectively.
Content controls (derived from ContentControl)	
Border	Adds a background or a border to the child element.
GroupBox	Surrounds the child element with a titled box.
Window	The application window. Also the root element.
Expander	Puts the child element in a titled area that collapses to display just the header and expands to display the header and the content.

Fig. 16.11 | Common controls used for layout. (Part 2 of 2.)

16.8.2 Layout in Action

Figure 16.12 shows the XAML document and the GUI display of a painter application. Note the use of Margin, HorizontalAlignment and VerticalAlignment throughout the markup. This example introduces several WPF controls that are commonly used for layout, as well as a few other basic ones.

Note that the controls in this application look similar to Windows Forms controls. WPF *RadioButton*s function as mutually exclusive options, just like their Windows Forms counterparts. However, a WPF RadioButton does not have a Text property. Instead, it is a ContentControl, meaning it can have exactly one direct child (which may be a layout container) or text content. This makes the control more versatile, enabling it to be labeled by an image or other item. In this example, each RadioButton is labeled by plain text (e.g., lines 33–34). A WPF *Button* behaves like a Windows Forms Button but is a ContentControl. As such, a WPF Button can display any single element as its content, not just text. Lines 59–63 define the two buttons seen in the Painter application. You can drag and drop controls onto the WPF designer and create their event handlers, just as you do in the Windows Forms designer.

```
1   <!-- Fig. 16.12: Painter.xaml -->
2   <!-- XAML of a painter application. -->
3   <Window x:Class="Painter.PainterWindow"
4       xmlns="http://schemas.microsoft.com/winfx/2006/xaml/presentation"
5       xmlns:x="http://schemas.microsoft.com/winfx/2006/xaml"
6       Title="Painter" Height="340" Width="350" Background="Beige">
```

Fig. 16.12 | XAML of a painter application. (Part 1 of 3.)

```
 7
 8      <!-- creates a Grid -->
 9      <Grid>
10         <!-- defines columns -->
11         <Grid.ColumnDefinitions>
12            <ColumnDefinition Width="Auto" />
13            <ColumnDefinition Width="*" />
14         </Grid.ColumnDefinitions>
15
16         <!-- creates a Canvas -->
17         <Canvas Grid.Column="1" Margin="0" Name="paintCanvas"
18            Background="White" MouseMove="paintCanvas_MouseMove"
19            MouseLeftButtonDown="paintCanvas_MouseLeftButtonDown"
20            MouseLeftButtonUp="paintCanvas_MouseLeftButtonUp"
21            MouseRightButtonDown="paintCanvas_MouseRightButtonDown"
22            MouseRightButtonUp="paintCanvas_MouseRightButtonUp"/>
23
24         <!-- creates a StackPanel-->
25         <StackPanel Margin="3">
26            <!-- creates a GroupBox for color options -->
27            <GroupBox Grid.ColumnSpan="1" Header="Color" Margin="3"
28               HorizontalAlignment="Stretch" VerticalAlignment="Top">
29               <StackPanel Margin="3" HorizontalAlignment="Left"
30                  VerticalAlignment="Top">
31
32                  <!-- creates RadioButtons for selecting color -->
33                  <RadioButton Name="redRadioButton" Margin="3"
34                     Checked="redRadioButton_Checked">Red</RadioButton>
35                  <RadioButton Name="blueRadioButton" Margin="3"
36                     Checked="blueRadioButton_Checked">Blue</RadioButton>
37                  <RadioButton Name="greenRadioButton" Margin="3"
38                     Checked="greenRadioButton_Checked">Green</RadioButton>
39                  <RadioButton Name="blackRadioButton" IsChecked="True"
40                     Checked="blackRadioButton_Checked" Margin="3">Black
41                  </RadioButton>
42               </StackPanel>
43            </GroupBox>
44
45            <!-- creates GroupBox for size options -->
46            <GroupBox Header="Size" Margin="3">
47               <StackPanel Margin="3">
48                  <RadioButton Name="smallRadioButton" Margin="3"
49                     Checked="smallRadioButton_Checked">Small</RadioButton>
50                  <RadioButton Name="mediumRadioButton" IsChecked="True"
51                     Checked="mediumRadioButton_Checked" Margin="3">Medium
52                  </RadioButton>
53                  <RadioButton Name="largeRadioButton" Margin="3"
54                     Checked="largeRadioButton_Checked">Large</RadioButton>
55               </StackPanel>
56            </GroupBox>
57
```

Fig. 16.12 | XAML of a painter application. (Part 2 of 3.)

```
58                 <!-- creates a Button-->
59                 <Button Height="23" Name="undoButton" Width="75"
60                    Margin="3,10,3,3" Click="undoButton_Click">Undo</Button>
61
62                 <Button Height="23" Name="clearButton" Width="75"
63                    Margin="3" Click="clearButton_Click">Clear</Button>
64           </StackPanel>
65        </Grid>
66   </Window>
```

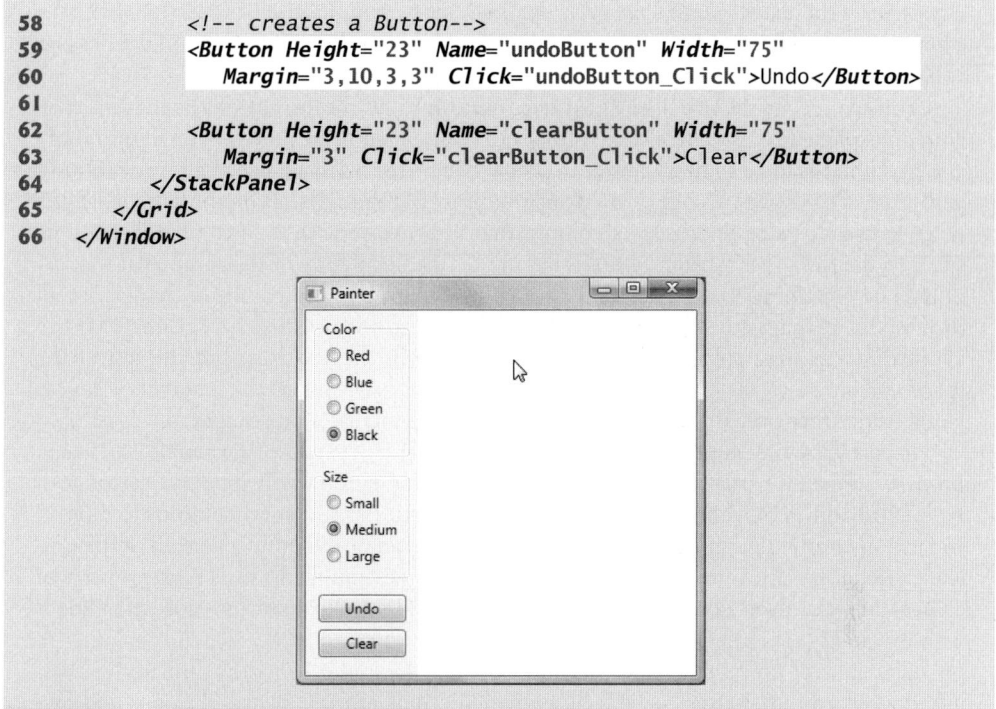

Fig. 16.12 | XAML of a painter application. (Part 3 of 3.)

GroupBox Control

A WPF *GroupBox* arranges controls and displays just as a Windows Forms GroupBox would, but using one is slightly different. The *Header* property replaces the Windows Forms version's Text property. The major difference is that a GroupBox is a ContentControl, which can only have one direct child element. Thus, to place multiple controls in it, you must place them in a layout container (e.g., lines 27–43).

StackPanel Control

In the Painter application, we organized each GroupBox's RadioButtons by placing them in *StackPanel*s (e.g., lines 25–64). A StackPanel is the simplest of layout containers. It arranges its content either horizontally or verticallly, depending on the *Orientation* property's setting. The default Orientation is Vertical, which is used by every StackPanel in the Painter example.

Grid Control

The Painter Window's contents are contained within a *Grid*—a flexible, all-purpose layout container. A Grid organizes controls into a user-defined number of rows and columns (one row and one column by default). You can define a Grid's rows and columns by setting its *Grid.RowDefinitions* and *Grid.ColumnDefinitions* properties, whose values are a collection of *RowDefinition* and *ColumnDefinition* objects, respectively. Because these properties do not take string values, they cannot be specified as attributes in the Grid tag. Another syntax is used instead. A class's property can be defined in XAML as a nested element with the name *ClassName.PropertyName*. For example, the Grid.ColumnDefinitions element in lines 11–14 sets the Grid's ColumnDefinitions property and defines two columns, which separate the options from the painting area, as shown in Fig. 16.12.

You can specify the Width of a ColumnDefinition and the Height of a RowDefinition with an explicit size, a relative size (using *) or Auto. Auto makes the row or column only as big as it needs to be to fit its contents. The setting * specifies the size of a row or column with respect to the Grid's other rows and columns. For example, a column with a Height of 2* would be twice the size of a column that is 1* (or just *). A Grid first allocates its space to the rows and columns whose sizes are defined explicitly or determined automatically. The remaining space is divided among the other rows and columns. By default, all Widths and Heights are set to *, so every cell in the grid is of equal size. In the Painter application, the first column is just wide enough to fit the controls, and the rest of the space is allotted to the painting area (lines 12–13). If you resize the Painter window, you'll notice that only the width of the paintable area increases or decreases.

If you click the ellipsis button next to the RowDefinitions or ColumnDefinitions property in the **Properties** window, the **Collection Editor** window will appear. This tool can be used to add, remove, reorder, and edit the properties of rows and columns in a Grid. In fact, any property that takes a collection as a value can be edited in a version of the **Collection Editor** specific to that collection. For example, you could edit the Items property of a ComboBox (i.e., drop-down list) in such a way. The ColumnDefinitions **Collection Editor** is shown in Fig. 16.13.

The control properties we've introduced so far look and function similarly to their Windows Forms counterparts. To indicate which cell of a Grid a control belongs in, however, you use the **Grid.Row** and **Grid.Column** properties. These are known as *attached properties*—they are defined by a different control than that to which they are applied. In this case, Row and Column are defined by the Grid itself but applied to the controls contained in the Grid (e.g., line 17). To specify the number of rows or columns that a control spans, you can use the **Grid.RowSpan** or **Grid.ColumnSpan** attached properties, respectively (e.g., line 27). By default, a control is placed in the top left cell of the Grid (row 0, column 0) and spans a single row and column.

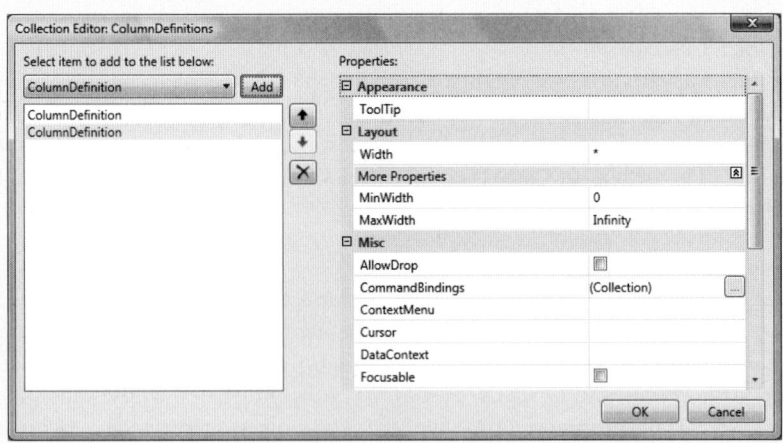

Fig. 16.13 | Using the **Collection Editor**.

Canvas Control

The painting area of the Painter application is a ***Canvas*** (lines 17–22), another layout container. A Canvas allows users to position controls by defining explicit coordinates. Controls in a Canvas have the attached properties, ***Canvas.Left*** and ***Canvas.Top***, which specify the control's coordinate position based on its distance from the Canvas's left and top borders, respectively. If two controls overlap, the one with the greater ***Canvas.ZIndex*** displays in the foreground. If this property is not defined for the controls, then the last control added to the canvas displays in the foreground.

DockPanel Control

The DockPanel container (which is not used in this chapter) allows you to make a child element stretch across an entire edge. In this example, we could have used a DockPanel to replace the Grid, and docked the StackPanel of controls to the DockPanel's left edge. To specify the edge a contained control should dock to, use the DockPanel.Dock attached property. If you set a DockPanel's LastChildFill property to True, the last element fills up the remaining space not occupied by other controls.

Layout in Design *Mode*

As you are creating your GUI in **Design** mode, you'll notice many helpful layout features. For example, as you resize a control, its width and height are displayed. In addition, red snaplines appear as necessary to help you align the edges of elements. These lines will also appear when you move controls around the design area.

   When you select a control, margin lines that extend from the control to the edges of its container appear, as shown in Fig. 16.14. If a line extends to the edge of the container, then the distance between the control and that edge is fixed. If it displays as a little circular stub, then the distance between the control and that edge is dynamic and changes as its surroundings change. You can toggle between the two by clicking on the margin line or the stub.

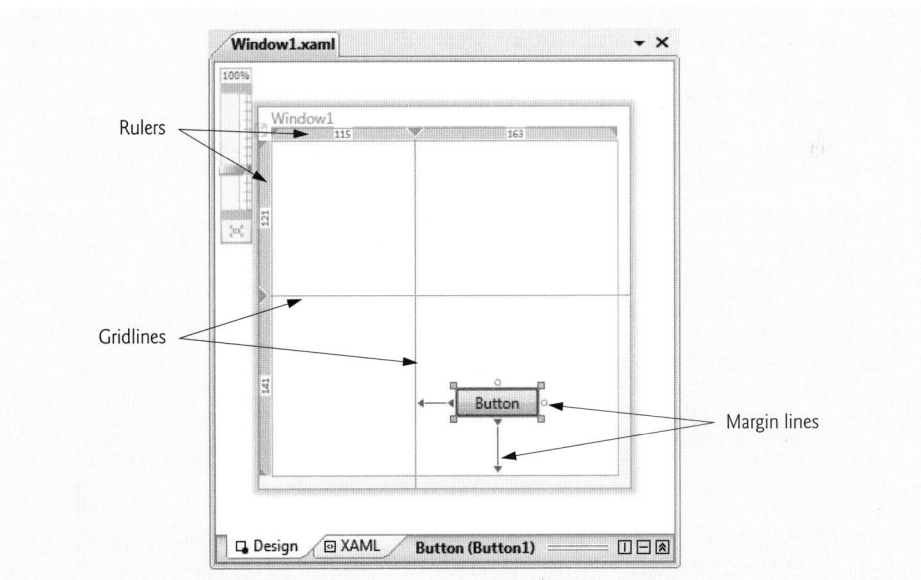

Fig. 16.14 | Margin lines and gridlines in **Design** view.

Furthermore, the **Design** view also helps you use a Grid. As shown in Fig. 16.14, when you select a control in a Grid, the Grid's rulers appear to the left and on top of it. The widths and heights of each column and row, respectively, appear on the rulers. Gridlines that outline the Grid's rows and columns also appear, helping you align and position the Grid's elements. You can also create more rows and columns by clicking where you want to separate them on the ruler.

16.9 Event Handling

Basic event handling in WPF is almost identical to Windows Forms event handling, but there is a fundamental difference, which we'll explain later in this section. We'll use the Painter example to introduce WPF event handling. Figure 16.15 provides the code-behind class for the Painter Window.

The Painter application "draws" by placing colored circles on the Canvas at the mouse pointer's position as you drag the mouse. The PaintCircle method (lines 32–45 in Fig. 16.15) creates the circle by defining an Ellipse object (lines 34–38), and positions it using the **Canvas.SetLeft** and **Canvas.SetTop** methods (lines 41–42), which change the circle's Canvas.Left and Canvas.Top attached properties, respectively.

```csharp
1   // Fig. 16.15: Painter.xaml.cs
2   // Code-behind class for Painter.
3   using System.Windows;
4   using System.Windows.Controls;
5   using System.Windows.Input;
6   using System.Windows.Media;
7   using System.Windows.Shapes;
8
9   namespace Painter
10  {
11     public partial class PainterWindow : Window
12     {
13        private int diameter = 8; // set diameter of circle
14        private Brush brushColor = Brushes.Black; // set the drawing color
15        private bool shouldErase = false; // specify whether to erase
16        private bool shouldPaint = false; // specify whether to paint
17
18        private enum Sizes // size constants for diameter of the circle
19        {
20           SMALL = 4,
21           MEDIUM = 8,
22           LARGE = 10
23        } // end enum Sizes
24
25        // constructor
26        public PainterWindow()
27        {
28           InitializeComponent();
29        } // end constructor
30
```

Fig. 16.15 | Code-behind class for Painter. (Part 1 of 4.)

```
31      // paints a circle on the Canvas
32      private void PaintCircle( Brush circleColor, Point position )
33      {
34          Ellipse newEllipse = new Ellipse(); // create an Ellipse
35
36          newEllipse.Fill = circleColor; // set Ellipse's color
37          newEllipse.Width = diameter; // set its horizontal diameter
38          newEllipse.Height = diameter; // set its vertical diameter
39
40          // set the Ellipse's position
41          Canvas.SetTop( newEllipse, position.Y );
42          Canvas.SetLeft( newEllipse, position.X );
43
44          paintCanvas.Children.Add( newEllipse );
45      } // end method PaintCircle
46
47      // handles paintCanvas's MouseLeftButtonDown event
48      private void paintCanvas_MouseLeftButtonDown( object sender,
49          MouseButtonEventArgs e )
50      {
51          shouldPaint = true; // OK to draw on the Canvas
52      } // end method paintCanvas_MouseLeftButtonDown
53
54      // handles paintCanvas's MouseLeftButtonUp event
55      private void paintCanvas_MouseLeftButtonUp( object sender,
56          MouseButtonEventArgs e )
57      {
58          shouldPaint = false; // do not draw on the Canvas
59      } // end method paintCanvas_MouseLeftButtonUp
60
61      // handles paintCanvas's MouseRightButtonDown event
62      private void paintCanvas_MouseRightButtonDown( object sender,
63          MouseButtonEventArgs e )
64      {
65          shouldErase = true; // OK to erase the Canvas
66      } // end method paintCanvas_MouseRightButtonDown
67
68      // handles paintCanvas's MouseRightButtonUp event
69      private void paintCanvas_MouseRightButtonUp( object sender,
70          MouseButtonEventArgs e )
71      {
72          shouldErase = false; // do not erase the Canvas
73      } // end method paintCanvas_MouseRightButtonUp
74
75      // handles paintCanvas's MouseMove event
76      private void paintCanvas_MouseMove( object sender,
77          MouseEventArgs e )
78      {
79          if ( shouldPaint )
80          {
81              // draw a circle of selected color at current mouse position
82              Point mousePosition = e.GetPosition( paintCanvas );
```

Fig. 16.15 | Code-behind class for Painter. (Part 2 of 4.)

```
83              PaintCircle( brushColor, mousePosition );
84          } // end if
85          else if ( shouldErase )
86          {
87              // erase by drawing circles of the Canvas's background color
88              Point mousePosition = e.GetPosition( paintCanvas );
89              PaintCircle( paintCanvas.Background, mousePosition );
90          } // end else if
91      } // end method paintCanvas_MouseMove
92
93      // handles Red RadioButton's Checked event
94      private void redRadioButton_Checked( object sender,
95          RoutedEventArgs e )
96      {
97          brushColor = Brushes.Red;
98      } // end method redRadioButton_Checked
99
100     // handles Blue RadioButton's Checked event
101     private void blueRadioButton_Checked( object sender,
102         RoutedEventArgs e )
103     {
104         brushColor = Brushes.Blue;
105     } // end method blueRadioButton_Checked
106
107     // handles Green RadioButton's Checked event
108     private void greenRadioButton_Checked( object sender,
109         RoutedEventArgs e )
110     {
111         brushColor = Brushes.Green;
112     } // end method greenRadioButton_Checked
113
114     // handles Black RadioButton's Checked event
115     private void blackRadioButton_Checked( object sender,
116         RoutedEventArgs e )
117     {
118         brushColor = Brushes.Black;
119     } // end method blackRadioButton_Checked
120
121     // handles Small RadioButton's Checked event
122     private void smallRadioButton_Checked( object sender,
123         RoutedEventArgs e )
124     {
125         diameter = ( int ) Sizes.SMALL;
126     } // end method smallRadioButton_Checked
127
128     // handles Medium RadioButton's Checked event
129     private void mediumRadioButton_Checked( object sender,
130         RoutedEventArgs e )
131     {
132         diameter = ( int ) Sizes.MEDIUM;
133     } // end method mediumRadioButton_Checked
134
```

Fig. 16.15 | Code-behind class for Painter. (Part 3 of 4.)

```
135            // handles Large RadioButton's Checked event
136            private void largeRadioButton_Checked( object sender,
137               RoutedEventArgs e )
138            {
139               diameter = ( int ) Sizes.LARGE;
140            } // end method largeRadioButton_Checked
141
142            // handles Undo Button's Click event
143            private void undoButton_Click( object sender, RoutedEventArgs e )
144            {
145               int count = paintCanvas.Children.Count;
146
147               // if there are any shapes on Canvas remove the last one added
148               if ( count > 0 )
149                  paintCanvas.Children.RemoveAt( count - 1 );
150            } // end method undoButton_Click
151
152            // handles Clear Button's Click event
153            private void clearButton_Click( object sender, RoutedEventArgs e )
154            {
155               paintCanvas.Children.Clear(); // clear the canvas
156            } // end method clearButton_Click
157         } // end class PainterWindow
158      } // end namespace Painter
```

Fig. 16.15 | Code-behind class for `Painter`. (Part 4 of 4.)

The **Children** property stores a list (of type **UIElementCollection**) of a layout container's child elements. This allows you to edit the layout container's child elements with C# code as you would the elements of any other collection. For example, you can add an element to the container by calling the **Add** method of the Children list (e.g., line 44). The **Undo** and **Clear** buttons work by invoking the **RemoveAt** and **Clear** methods of the Children list (lines 149 and 155), respectively.

A WPF RadioButton has a Checked event. Lines 94–140 handle the **Checked** event for each of the RadioButtons in this example, which change the color and the size of the circles painted on the Canvas. The Button control's **Click** event functions the same in WPF as it did in Windows Forms. Lines 143–156 handle the **Undo** and **Clear** Buttons. The event-handler declarations look almost identical to how they would look in a Windows Forms application, except that the event-arguments object (e) is a RoutedEventArgs object instead of an EventArgs object. We'll explain why later in this section.

Mouse and Keyboard Events

WPF has built-in support for keyboard and mouse events that is nearly identical to the support in Windows Forms. Painter uses the **MouseMove** event of the paintable Canvas to paint and erase (lines 76–91). A control's MouseMove event is triggered whenever the mouse moves while within the boundaries of the control. Information for the event is passed to the event handler using **MouseEventArgs**, which contains mouse-specific information. The **GetPosition** method of MouseEventArgs, for example, returns the current position of the mouse relative to the control passed as the argument to the method (e.g., lines 82 and 88). MouseMove works exactly the same as it does in Windows Forms. [*Note:* Much of the functionality in our sample Painter application is already provided by the WPF InkCanvas control. We chose not to use this control so we could demonstrate various other WPF features.]

WPF has additional mouse events. Painter also uses the **MouseLeftButtonDown** and **MouseLeftButtonUp** events to toggle painting on and off (lines 48–59), and the **MouseRightButtonDown** and **MouseRightButtonUp** events to toggle erasing on and off (lines 62–73). All of these events pass information to the event handler using the **MouseButtonEventArgs** object, which has properties specific to a mouse button (e.g., ButtonState or ClickCount) in addition to mouse-specific ones. These events are new to WPF and are more specific versions of MouseUp and MouseDown (which are still available in WPF). A summary of commonly used mouse and keyboard events is provided in Fig. 16.16.

Common mouse and keyboard events	
Mouse Events with an Event Argument of Type MouseEventArgs	
MouseMove	Raised when the mouse cursor is moved while within the control's boundaries.
Mouse Events with an Event Argument of Type MouseButtonEventArgs	
MouseLeftButtonDown	Raised when the left mouse button is pressed.
MouseLeftButtonUp	Raised when the left mouse button is released.
MouseRightButtonDown	Raised when the right mouse button is pressed.
MouseRightButtonUp	Raised when the right mouse button is released.
Mouse Events with an Event Argument of Type MouseWheelEventArgs	
MouseWheel	Raised when the mouse wheel is rotated.
Keyboard Events with an Event Argument of Type KeyEventArgs	
KeyDown	Raised when a key is pressed.
KeyUp	Raised when a key is released.

Fig. 16.16 | Common mouse and keyboard events.

Routed Events

WPF events have a significant distinction from their Windows Forms counterparts—they can travel either up (from child to parent) or down (from parent to child) the containment hierarchy—the hierarchy of nested elements defined within a control. This is called *event routing*, and all WPF events are *routed events*.

This explains why the event-arguments object that is passed to the event handler of a Button's Click event or a RadioButton's Check event is of the type ***RoutedEventArgs***. In fact, all event-argument objects in WPF are of type RoutedEventArgs or one of its subclasses. As an event travels up or down the hierarchy, it may be useful to stop it before it reaches the end. When the ***Handled*** property of the RoutedEventArgs parameter is set to true, event handlers ignore the event. It may also be useful to know the source where the event was first triggered. The ***Source*** property stores this information.

Figures 16.17 and 16.18 show the XAML and code-behind for a program that demonstrates event routing. The program contains two GroupBoxes, each with a Label inside (lines 15–28 in Fig. 16.17). One group handles a left-mouse-button press with MouseLeftButtonUp, and the other with ***PreviewMouseLeftButtonUp***. As the event travels up or down the containment hierarchy, a log of where the event has traveled is displayed in a ***TextBox*** (line 30). The WPF TextBox functions just like its Windows Forms counterpart.

```
1    <!-- Fig. 16.17: RoutedEvents.xaml -->
2    <!-- Routed-events example (XAML). -->
3    <Window x:Class="RoutedEvents.RoutedEventsWindow"
4       xmlns="http://schemas.microsoft.com/winfx/2006/xaml/presentation"
5       xmlns:x="http://schemas.microsoft.com/winfx/2006/xaml"
6       Title="Routed Events" Height="300" Width="300"
7       Name="routedEventsWindow">
8       <Grid>
9          <Grid.RowDefinitions>
10            <RowDefinition Height="Auto" />
11            <RowDefinition Height="Auto" />
12            <RowDefinition Height="*" />
13         </Grid.RowDefinitions>
14
15         <GroupBox Name="tunnelingGroupBox" Grid.Row="0" Header="Tunneling"
16            Margin="5" PreviewMouseLeftButtonUp="Tunneling">
17            <Label Margin="5" HorizontalAlignment="Center"
18               Name="tunnelingLabel" PreviewMouseLeftButtonUp="Tunneling">
19               Click Here
20            </Label>
21         </GroupBox>
22
23         <GroupBox Name="bubblingGroupBox" Grid.Row="1" Header="Bubbling"
24            Margin="5" MouseLeftButtonUp="Bubbling">
25            <Label Margin="5" MouseLeftButtonUp="Bubbling"
26               Name="bubblingLabel" HorizontalAlignment="Center">Click Here
27            </Label>
28         </GroupBox>
29
```

Fig. 16.17 | Routed-events example (XAML). (Part 1 of 2.)

```
30              <TextBox Name="logTextBox" Grid.Row="2" Margin="5" />
31      </Grid>
32  </Window>
```

Fig. 16.17 | Routed-events example (XAML). (Part 2 of 2.)

```
1   // Fig. 16.18: RoutedEvents.xaml.cs
2   // Routed-events example (code-behind).
3   using System.Windows;
4   using System.Windows.Controls;
5   using System.Windows.Input;
6
7   namespace RoutedEvents
8   {
9      public partial class RoutedEventsWindow : Window
10     {
11        int bubblingEventStep = 1; // step counter for Bubbling
12        int tunnelingEventStep = 1; // step counter for Tunneling
13        string tunnelingLogText = string.Empty; // temporary Tunneling log
14
15        public RoutedEventsWindow()
16        {
17           InitializeComponent();
18        } // end constructor
19
20        // PreviewMouseUp is a tunneling event
21        private void Tunneling( object sender, MouseButtonEventArgs e )
22        {
23           // append step number and sender
24           tunnelingLogText = string.Format( "{0}({1}): {2}\n",
25              tunnelingLogText, tunnelingEventStep,
26              ( ( Control ) sender ).Name );
27           ++tunnelingEventStep; // increment counter
28
29           // execution goes from parent to child, ending with the source
30           if ( e.Source.Equals( sender ) )
31           {
32              tunnelingLogText = string.Format(
33                 "This is a tunneling event:\n{0}", tunnelingLogText );
34              logTextBox.Text = tunnelingLogText; // set LogTextBox text
35              tunnelingLogText = string.Empty; // clear temporary log
36              tunnelingEventStep = 1; // reset counter
37           } // end if
38        } // end method Tunneling
39
40        // MouseUp is a bubbling event
41        private void Bubbling( object sender, MouseButtonEventArgs e )
42        {
43           // execution goes from child to parent, starting at the source
44           if ( e.Source.Equals( sender ) )
45           {
```

Fig. 16.18 | Routed-events example (code-behind). (Part 1 of 2.)

```
46              logTextBox.Clear(); // clear the logTextBox
47              bubblingEventStep = 1; // reset counter
48              logTextBox.Text = "This is a bubbling event:\n";
49          } // end if
50
51          // append step number and sender
52          logTextBox.Text = string.Format( "{0}({1}): {2}\n",
53              logTextBox.Text, bubblingEventStep,
54              ( ( Control ) sender ).Name );
55          ++bubblingEventStep;
56       } // end method Bubbling
57    } // end class RoutedEventsWindow
58 } // end namespace RoutedEvents
```

Fig. 16.18 | Routed-events example (code-behind). (Part 2 of 2.)

There are three types of routed events—*direct events*, *bubbling events* and *tunneling events*. Direct events are similar to Windows Forms events—they do not travel up or down the containment hierarchy. Bubbling events start at the Source and travel up the hierarchy ending at the Window or until you set Handled to true. Tunneling events start at the top of the containment hierarchy and travel down the hierarchy until they reach the Source or Handled is true. To help you distinguish tunneling events from bubbling events, WPF prefixes the names of tunneling events with Preview. For example, *PreviewMouseLeftButtonDown* is the tunneling version of MouseLeftButtonDown, which is a bubbling event.

If you click the **Click Here** Label in the **Tunneling** GroupBox, the click is handled first by the GroupBox, then by the contained Label. The event handler that responds to the click handles the *PreviewMouseLeftButtonUp* event—a tunneling event. Note that the Tunneling method handles the events of both the GroupBox and the Label (lines 16 and 18 in Fig. 16.17). An event handler can handle events for many controls. You can specify, in the XAML, which method handles a particular event of a control. For example, you can define a Button's Click handler by setting the Click attribute of the Button element, as in <Button Click="*EventHandlerName*">. If you click the other Label, the click is handled first by the Label, then by the containing GroupBox. The event that is handled in this case is MouseLeftButtonUp—the bubbling event (lines 24–25 in Fig. 16.17).

16.10 Commands and Common Application Tasks

In Windows Forms, event handling is the only way to respond to user actions. WPF provides an alternate technique called a *command*—an action or a task that may be triggered by many different user interactions. In Visual Studio, for example, you can cut, copy and paste code. You can execute these tasks through the **Edit** menu, a toolbar or keyboard shortcuts. To program this functionality in WPF, you can define a single command for each task. In Windows Forms, you must code and maintain the handling of an event for each menu item, one for each toolbar item and one to handle the key presses.

Commands also enable you to synchronize a task's availability to the state of its corresponding controls. For example, users should be able to copy something only if they have content selected. When you define the copy command, you can specify this as a requirement. As a result, if the user has no content selected, then the menu item, toolbar item and keyboard shortcut for copying are all automatically disabled.

Commands are *RoutedCommand* objects. Every RoutedCommand has a Name and a collection of *InputGestures* (i.e., keyboard shortcuts) associated with it. Class RoutedCommand is the standard implementation of the *ICommand* interface. When a command is executed, the *Execute* method is called. However, the command's execution logic (i.e., how it should execute) is not defined in its Execute method. You must specify this logic when implementing the command. A RoutedCommand's *CanExecute* method works in the same way. The logic that specifies when a command is enabled and disabled is not determined by the CanExecute method and must instead be specified at implementation. RoutedUICommand is an extension of RoutedCommand with a Text property, which specifies the default text to display on a GUI element that triggers the command.

WPF provides a command library of built-in commands. These commands have their standard keyboard shortcuts already associated with them. For example, Copy is a built-in command and has *Ctrl-C* associated with it. Figure 16.19 provides a list of some common built-in commands, listed by the class in which they are defined. Like any command, none of these commands contains any built-in application logic.

Figures 16.20 and 16.21 are the XAML markup and code-behind for a simple text-editor application that allows users to format text into bold and italics, and also to cut, copy and paste text. The example uses the *RichTextBox* control (line 58), which allows users to enter, edit and format text. We use this application to demonstrate several built-in commands from the command library.

A command is executed when it is triggered by a command source. For example, the Close command is triggered by a MenuItem (line 25 in Fig. 16.20). The Cut command has

---

Common built-in commands from the WPF command library

ApplicationCommands properties

New	Open	Save	Close
Cut	Copy	Paste	

EditingCommands properties

ToggleBold	ToggleItalic	ToggleUnderline

MediaCommands properties

Play	Stop	Rewind	FastForward
IncreaseVolume	DecreaseVolume	NextTrack	PreviousTrack

Fig. 16.19 | Common built-in commands from the WPF command library.

```xml
1    <!-- Fig. 16.20: TextEditor.xaml -->
2    <!-- Creating menus and toolbars, and using commands (XAML). -->
3    <Window x:Class="TextEditor.TextEditorWindow"
4       xmlns="http://schemas.microsoft.com/winfx/2006/xaml/presentation"
5       xmlns:x="http://schemas.microsoft.com/winfx/2006/xaml"
6       Title="Text Editor" Height="300" Width="300">
7
8       <!-- define command bindings -->
9       <Window.CommandBindings>
10         <!-- bind the Close command to handler -->
11         <CommandBinding Command="Close" Executed="closeCommand_Executed" />
12      </Window.CommandBindings>
13
14      <Grid>
15         <Grid.RowDefinitions>
16            <RowDefinition Height="Auto" />
17            <RowDefinition Height="Auto" />
18            <RowDefinition Height="*" />
19         </Grid.RowDefinitions>
20
21         <!-- create the menu -->
22         <Menu Grid.Row="0">
23            <!-- map each menu item to corresponding command -->
24            <MenuItem Header="File">
25               <MenuItem Header="Exit" Command="Close" />
26            </MenuItem>
27            <MenuItem Header="Edit">
28               <MenuItem Header="Cut" Command="Cut" />
29               <MenuItem Header="Copy" Command="Copy" />
30               <MenuItem Header="Paste" Command="Paste" />
31
32               <!-- separates groups of menu items -->
33               <Separator />
34
35               <MenuItem Header="Bold" Command="ToggleBold"
36                  FontWeight="Bold" />
37               <MenuItem Header="Italic" Command="ToggleItalic"
38                  FontStyle="Italic" />
39            </MenuItem>
40         </Menu>
41
42         <!-- create the toolbar -->
43         <ToolBar Grid.Row="1">
44            <!-- map each toolbar item to corresponding command -->
45            <Button Command="Cut">Cut</Button>
46            <Button Command="Copy">Copy</Button>
47            <Button Command="Paste">Paste</Button>
48
49            <!-- separates groups of toolbar items -->
50            <Separator />
51
52            <Button FontWeight="Bold" Command="ToggleBold">Bold</Button>
```

Fig. 16.20 | Creating menus and toolbars, and using commands (XAML). (Part 1 of 2.)

```
53              <Button FontStyle="Italic" Command="ToggleItalic">
54                 Italic</Button>
55           </ToolBar>
56
57           <!-- display editable, formattable text -->
58           <RichTextBox Grid.Row="2" Margin="5" />
59        </Grid>
60     </Window>
```

Fig. 16.20 | Creating menus and toolbars, and using commands (XAML). (Part 2 of 2.)

two sources, a MenuItem and a ToolBar Button (lines 28 and 45, respectively). A command can have many sources.

To make use of a command, you must create a *command binding*—a link between a command and the methods containing its application logic. You can declare a command binding by creating a *CommandBinding* object in XAML and setting its Command property to the name of the associated command (line 11). A command binding raises the *Executed* and *PreviewExecuted* events (bubbling and tunneling versions of the same event) when its associated command is executed. You program the command's functionality into an event handler for one of these events. In line 11, we set the Executed attribute to a method name, telling the program that the specified method (closeCommand_Executed) handles the command binding's Executed event.

In this example, we demonstrate the use of a command binding by implementing the Close command. When it executes, it shuts down the application. The method that executes this task is *Application.Current.Shutdown*, as shown in line 19 of Fig. 16.21.

You can also use a command binding to specify the application logic for determining when a command should be enabled or disabled. You can do so by handling either the *CanExecute* or *PreviewCanExecute* (bubbling and tunneling versions of the same events) events in the same way that you handle the Executed or PreviewExecuted events. Because we do not define such a handler for the Close command in its command binding, it is always enabled. Command bindings should be defined within the *Window.Command-Bindings* element (e.g., lines 9–12 of Fig. 16.20).

```
 1    // Fig. 16.21: TextEditor.xaml.cs
 2    // Code-behind class for a simple text editor.
 3    using System.Windows;
 4    using System.Windows.Input;
 5
 6    namespace TextEditor
 7    {
 8       public partial class TextEditorWindow : Window
 9       {
10          public TextEditorWindow()
11          {
12             InitializeComponent();
13          } // end constructor
14
```

Fig. 16.21 | Code-behind class for a simple text editor. (Part 1 of 2.)

```
15          // exit the application
16          private void closeCommand_Executed( object sender,
17             ExecutedRoutedEventArgs e )
18          {
19             Application.Current.Shutdown();
20          } // end method closeCommand_Executed
21       } // end class TextEditorWindow
22    } // end namespace TextEditor
```

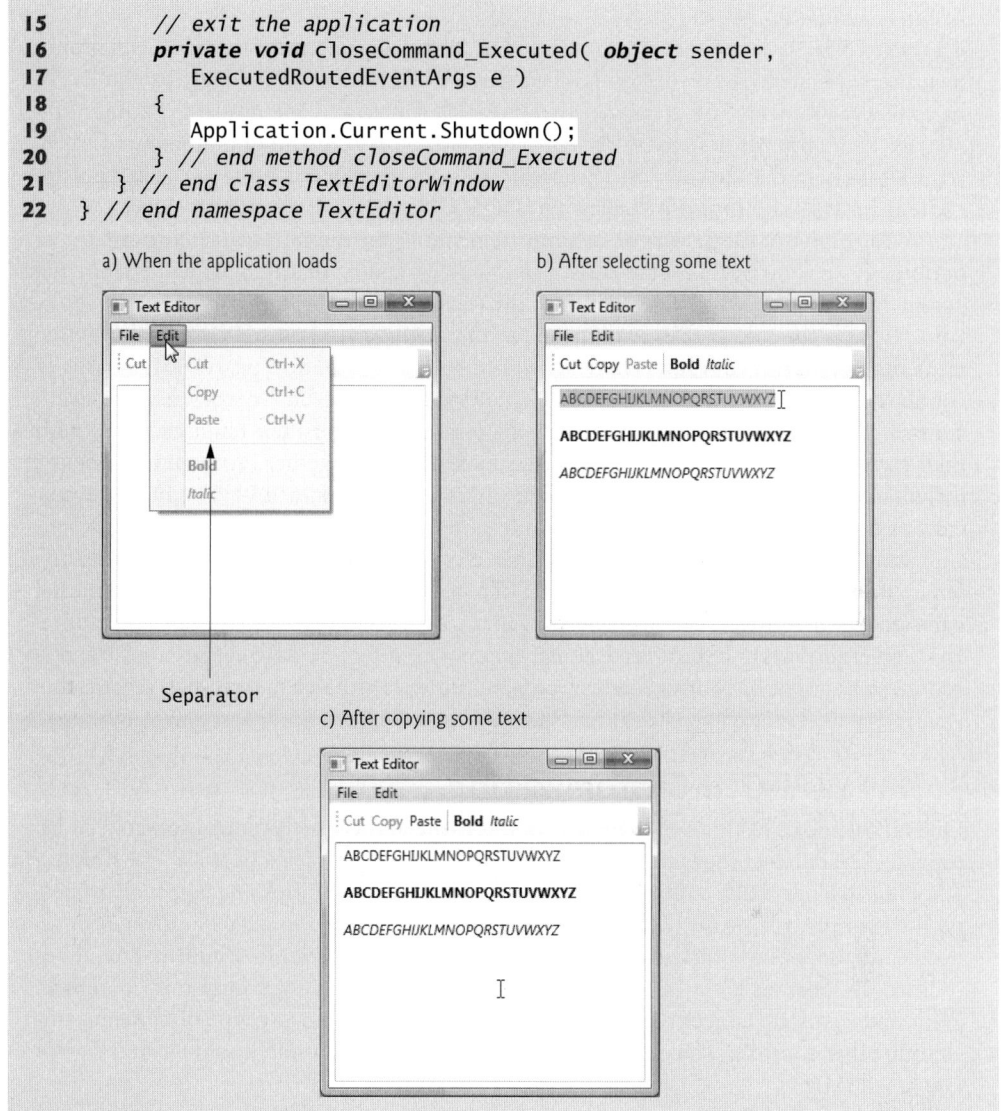

a) When the application loads

b) After selecting some text

Separator

c) After copying some text

Fig. 16.21 | Code-behind class for a simple text editor. (Part 2 of 2.)

The only time a command binding is not necessary is when a control has built-in functionality for dealing with a command. A Button or MenuItem linked to the Cut, Copy, or Paste commands is an example (e.g., lines 28–30 and lines 45–47). As Fig. 16.21(a) shows, all three commands are disabled when the application loads. If you select some text, the Cut and Copy commands are enabled, as shown in Fig. 16.21(b). Once you have copied some text, the Paste command is enabled, as evidenced by Fig. 16.21(c). Note that we did not have to define any associated command bindings or event handlers to implement these commands. The ToggleBold and ToggleItalic commands are also implemented without any command bindings.

Menus and Toolbars

The text editor uses menus and toolbars. The **Menu** control creates a menu containing **MenuItem**s. MenuItems can be top-level menus such as **File** or **Edit** (lines 24 and 27 in Fig. 16.20), submenus, or items in a menu, which function like Buttons (e.g., lines 28–30). If a MenuItem has nested MenuItems, then it's a top-level menu or a submenu. Otherwise, it's an item that executes an action via either an event or a command. MenuItems are content controls and thus can display any single GUI element as content.

A **ToolBar** is a single row or column (depending on the Orientation property) of options. A ToolBar's Orientation is a read-only property that gets its value from the parent **ToolBarTray**, which can host multiple ToolBars. If a ToolBar has no parent Tool-BarTray, as is the case in this example, its Orientation is Horizontal by default. Unlike elements in a Menu, a ToolBar's child elements are not of a specific type. A ToolBar usually contains Buttons, CheckBoxes, ComboBoxes, RadioButtons and Separators, but any WPF control can be used. ToolBars overwrite the look-and-feel of their child elements with their own specifications, so that the controls look seamless together. You can override the default specifications to create your own look-and-feel. Lines 43–55 define the text editor's ToolBar.

Both Menus and ToolBars can incorporate **Separators** (e.g., lines 33 and 50) that differentiate groups of MenuItems or controls. In a Menu, a Separator displays as a horizontal bar—as shown between the **Paste** and **Bold** menu options in Fig. 16.21(a). In a horizontal ToolBar, it displays as a short vertical bar—as shown in Fig. 16.21(b). You can use Separators in any type of control that can contain multiple child elements, such as a Stack-Panel.

16.11 WPF GUI Customization

One advantage of WPF over Windows Forms is the ability to customize controls. WPF provides several techniques to customize the look and behavior of controls. The simplest takes full advantage of a control's properties. The value of a control's **Background** property, for example, is a brush (i.e, Brush object). This allows you to create a gradient or an image and use it as the background rather than a solid color. For more information about brushes, see Section 17.5. In addition, many controls that allowed only text content in Windows Forms are ContentControls in WPF, which can host any type of content—including other controls. The caption of a WPF Button, for example, could be an image or even a video.

In Section 16.12, we demonstrate how to use styles in WPF to achieve a uniform look-and-feel. In Windows Forms, if you want to make all your Buttons look the same, you have to manually set properties for every Button, or copy and paste. To achieve the same result in WPF, you can define the properties once as a style and apply the style to each Button. This is similar to the CSS/XHTML implementation of styles. XHTML specifies the content and structure of a website, and CSS defines styles that specify the presentation of elements in a website. For more information on CSS and XHTML, see Chapter 22, ASP.NET 3.5 and ASP.NET AJAX, or visit our XHTML and CSS Resource Centers at www.deitel.com/xhtml/ and www.deitel.com/css21/, respectively.

Styles are limited to modifying a control's look-and-feel through its properties. In Section 16.14, we introduce control templates, which offer you the freedom to define a control's appearance by modifying its visual structure. With a custom control template, you can completely strip a control of all its visual settings and rebuild it to look exactly the way you like, while maintaining its existing functionality. A Button with a custom control template might look structurally different from a default Button, but it still functions the same as any other Button.

If you want to change only the appearance of an element, a style or control template should suffice. However, you can also create entirely new custom controls that have their own functionality, properties, methods and events. We demonstrate how to create a custom control in Section 24.4.3.

16.12 Using Styles to Change a Control's Appearance

Once defined, a *WPF style* is a collection of property-value and event-handler definitions that can be reused. Styles allow you to avoid writing repetitive code or markup. For example, if you want to change the look-and-feel of the standard Button throughout a section of your application, you can define a style and apply it to all the Buttons in that section. Without styles, you have to set the properties for each individual Button. Furthermore, if you later decided that you wanted to tweak the appearance of these Buttons, you would have to modify your markup or code several times. By using a style, you would need to make the change only once in the style and it would automatically be applied to any control which used that style.

Styles are *WPF resources*. A resource is an object that is defined for an entire section of your application and can be reused multiple times. A resource can be as simple as a property or as complex as a control template. Every WPF control can hold a collection of resources that can be accessed by any element down the containment hierarchy. In a way, this is similar in approach to the concept of variable scope that you learned about in Chapter 7. For example, if you define a style as a resource of a Window, then the contents of the Window can apply that style. If you define a style as a resource of a layout container, then only the elements of the layout container can apply that style. You can also define application-level resources for an Application object in the App.xaml file. These resources can be accessed in any file in the application.

Figure 16.22 provides the XAML markup and Fig. 16.23 provides the code-behind for a color-chooser application. This example demonstrates the use of styles and introduces the Slider user input control.

```
1   <!-- Fig. 16.22: ColorChooser.xaml -->
2   <!-- Color-chooser application showing the use of styles (XAML). -->
3   <Window x:Class="ColorChooser.ColorChooserWindow"
4       xmlns="http://schemas.microsoft.com/winfx/2006/xaml/presentation"
5       xmlns:x="http://schemas.microsoft.com/winfx/2006/xaml"
6       Title="Color Chooser" Height="150" Width="450">
7
8       <!-- define Window's resources -->
9       <Window.Resources>
10          <Style x:Key="SliderStyle">
11              <!-- set properties for Sliders -->
12              <Setter Property="Slider.Width" Value="256" />
13              <Setter Property="Slider.Minimum" Value="0" />
```

Fig. 16.22 | Color-chooser application showing the use of styles (XAML). (Part 1 of 2.)

```
14          <Setter Property="Slider.Maximum" Value="255" />
15          <Setter Property="Slider.IsSnapToTickEnabled" Value="True" />
16          <Setter Property="Slider.VerticalAlignment" Value="Center" />
17          <Setter Property="Slider.HorizontalAlignment" Value="Center" />
18          <Setter Property="Slider.Value" Value="0" />
19          <Setter Property="Slider.AutoToolTipPlacement"
20              Value="TopLeft" />
21
22          <!-- set event handler for ValueChanged event -->
23          <EventSetter Event="Slider.ValueChanged"
24              Handler="slider_ValueChanged" />
25        </Style>
26     </Window.Resources>
27
28     <Grid Margin="5">
29        <Grid.RowDefinitions>
30           <RowDefinition />
31           <RowDefinition />
32           <RowDefinition />
33           <RowDefinition />
34        </Grid.RowDefinitions>
35
36        <Grid.ColumnDefinitions>
37           <ColumnDefinition Width="Auto" />
38           <ColumnDefinition Width="Auto" />
39           <ColumnDefinition />
40        </Grid.ColumnDefinitions>
41
42        <!-- define Labels for Sliders -->
43        <Label Grid.Row="0" Grid.Column="0" HorizontalAlignment="Right"
44           VerticalAlignment="Center">Red:</Label>
45        <Label Grid.Row="1" Grid.Column="0" HorizontalAlignment="Right"
46           VerticalAlignment="Center">Green:</Label>
47        <Label Grid.Row="2" Grid.Column="0" HorizontalAlignment="Right"
48           VerticalAlignment="Center">Blue:</Label>
49        <Label Grid.Row="3" Grid.Column="0" HorizontalAlignment="Right"
50           VerticalAlignment="Center">Alpha:</Label>
51
52        <!-- define Label that displays the color -->
53        <Label Name="colorLabel" Grid.RowSpan="4" Grid.Column="2"
54           Margin="10" />
55
56        <!-- define Sliders and apply style to them -->
57        <Slider Name="redSlider" Grid.Row="0" Grid.Column="1"
58           Style="{StaticResource SliderStyle}" />
59        <Slider Name="greenSlider" Grid.Row="1" Grid.Column="1"
60           Style="{StaticResource SliderStyle}" />
61        <Slider Name="blueSlider" Grid.Row="2" Grid.Column="1"
62           Style="{StaticResource SliderStyle}" />
63        <Slider Name="alphaSlider" Grid.Row="3" Grid.Column="1"
64           Style="{StaticResource SliderStyle}" Value="255" />
65     </Grid>
66  </Window>
```

Fig. 16.22 | Color-chooser application showing the use of styles (XAML). (Part 2 of 2.)

```
1    // Fig. 16.23: ColorChooser.xaml.cs
2    // Color-chooser application showing the use of styles (code-behind).
3    using System.Windows;
4    using System.Windows.Media;
5
6    namespace ColorChooser
7    {
8       public partial class ColorChooserWindow : Window
9       {
10          public ColorChooserWindow()
11          {
12             InitializeComponent();
13          } // constructor
14
15          // handles the ValueChanged event for the Sliders
16          private void slider_ValueChanged( object sender,
17             RoutedPropertyChangedEventArgs< double > e )
18          {
19             // generates new color
20             SolidColorBrush backgroundColor = new SolidColorBrush();
21             backgroundColor.Color = Color.FromArgb(
22                ( byte ) alphaSlider.Value, ( byte ) redSlider.Value,
23                ( byte ) greenSlider.Value, ( byte ) blueSlider.Value );
24
25             // set colorLabel's background to new color
26             colorLabel.Background = backgroundColor;
27          } // end method slider_ValueChanged
28       } // end class ColorChooserWindow
29    } // end namespace ColorChooser
```

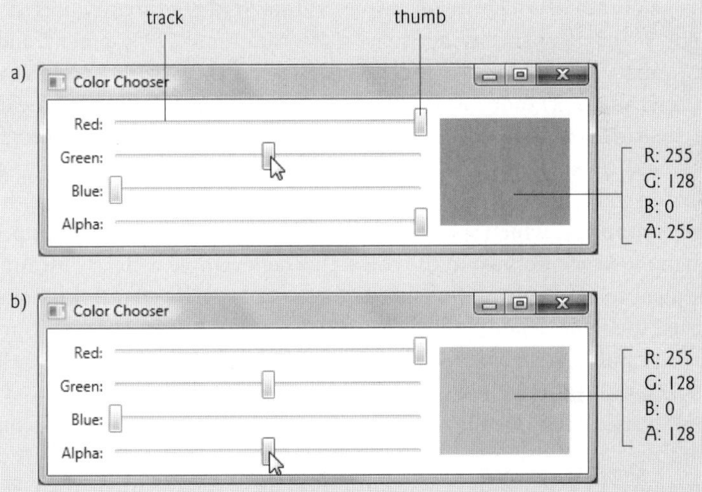

Fig. 16.23 | Color-chooser application showing the use of styles (code-behind).

The color-chooser application uses the RGBA system of color selection. Every color is represented by its red, green and blue color values, each ranging from 0 to 255, where 0 denotes no color and 255 full color. For example, a color with a red value of 0 would contain no red component. The alpha value (A)—which also ranges from 0 to 255—represents a color's opacity, with 0 being completely transparent and 255 completely opaque. For example, the two colors in Fig. 16.23 have the same base color, but the color displayed in Fig. 16.23(b) is semitransparent.

The color-chooser GUI is composed of four *Slider* controls that change the RGBA values of a color displayed by a Label. A Slider, as shown in Fig. 16.23(a), is a numeric user input control that allows users to drag a "thumb" along a track to select the value. Whenever the user moves a Slider, the application generates a new color, and the Label displays the new color as its background. The new color is generated by using class Color's FromArgb method, which returns a color based on the four RGBA byte values you pass it (lines 21–23). The color is then applied as the background of the Label using a Solid-ColorBrush. For more information about brushes, please see Chapter 17.

Styles can be defined as a resource of any control. In the color-chooser application, we defined the style as a resource of the entire Window. We also could have defined it as a resource of the Grid. To define resources for a control, you set a control's *Resources* property. Thus, to define a resource for a Window, as we did in this example, you would use Window.Resources (lines 9–26 in Fig. 16.22). To define a resource for a Grid, you would use Grid.Resources.

Style objects can be defined in XAML using the *Style* element. The x:Key attribute (i.e., attribute Key from the standard XAML namespace) must be set in every style (or other resource) so that it can be referenced later by other controls (line 10). The children of a Style element set properties and define event handlers. A *Setter* sets a property to a specific value (e.g., line 12, which sets the styled Slider's Width property to 256). An *EventSetter* specifies the method that responds to an event (e.g., lines 23–24, which specifies that method slider_ValueChanged handles the Slider's ValueChanged event).

The Style in the color-chooser example (SliderStyle) primarily uses Setters. It lays out the color Sliders by specifying their Width, HorizontalAlignment and Vertical-Alignment properties (lines 12, 16 and 17). It also sets the Minimum and Maximum properties, which determine a Slider's range of values (lines 13–14). In line 18, the default Value is set to 0. IsSnapToTickEnabled is set to true, meaning that only values that fall on a "tick" are allowed (line 15). By default, each tick is separated by a value of 1, so this setting makes the styled Slider accept only integer values. Lastly, the style also sets the AutoTool-TipPlacement property, which specifies where a Slider's tooltip should appear, if at all.

Although the Style defined in the color-chooser example is clearly meant for Sliders, it can be applied to any control. Styles are not control specific. You can make all controls of one type use the same default style by setting the style's *TargetType* attribute to the control type. For example, if we wanted all of the Window's Sliders to use a Style, we would add TargetType="Slider" to the its start tag.

To apply a style to a control, you create a *resource binding* between a control's Style property and the Style resource. You can create a resource binding in XAML by specifying the resource in a *markup extension*—an expression enclosed in curly braces ({}). The form of a markup extension calling a resource is {*ResourceType ResourceKey*} (e.g., {StaticResource SliderStyle} in line 58).

There are two types of resources. *Static resources* are applied at initialization time only. *Dynamic resources* are applied every time the resource is modified by the application, and are therefore less efficient than static resources. Dynamic resources should not be used where static resources will suffice. To use a style as a static resource, use `StaticRe-source` as the type in the markup extension. To use a style as a dynamic resource, use `DynamicResource` as the type. Because styles don't normally change during runtime, they are usually used as static resources. However, using one as a dynamic resource is sometimes necessary, such as when you wish to enable users to customize a style at runtime.

In the color-chooser application, we apply `SliderStyle` as a static resource to each of the four `Sliders` (lines 58, 60, 62 and 64). Note that once you apply a style to a control, the **Design** view and **Properties** window update to display the control's new appearance settings. If you then modify the control through the **Properties** window, the control itself is updated, not the style. We changed the alpha value `Slider`'s `Value` to 255 in line 64 of Fig. 16.22.

Dependency Properties

Most WPF properties, though they might look and behave exactly like ordinary ones, are in fact *dependency properties*. They are coded differently than ordinary properties and are more advanced. They have built-in support for change notification—that is, an application knows and can be made to respond when a property has been modified. In addition, they support inheritance down the control-containment hierarchy. For example, when you specify `FontSize` in a `Window`, every control in the `Window` inherits it as the default `FontSize`. You can also specify a control's property in one of its child elements. This is how attached properties work.

A control's properties may be set at many different levels in WPF, so instead of holding a fixed value, a dependency property's value is determined during execution by a value-determination system. If a property is defined at several levels at once, then the current value is the one defined at the level with the highest precedence. A style, for example, overrides the default appearance of a control, because it takes higher precedence. A summary of the levels, in order from highest to lowest precedence, is shown in Fig. 16.24.

As shown in Fig. 16.25, the `Slider` that adjusts the alpha value in the color-chooser example starts with a value of 255, whereas the R, G and B `Sliders`' values start at 0. The `Value` property is defined by a `Setter` in the style to be 0 (line 18 in Fig. 16.22). This is why the R, G and B values are 0. The `Value` property of the alpha `Slider` is locally defined

Levels of value-determination system	
Animation	The value is defined by an active animation. For more information about animation, see Chapter 17.
Local declaration	The value is defined as an attribute in XAML or set in code. This is how ordinary properties are set.
Trigger	The value is defined by an active trigger. For more information about triggers, see Section 16.14.
Style	The value is defined by a setter in a style.
Inherited value	The value is inherited from a definition in a containing element.
Default value	The value is not explicitly defined.

Fig. 16.24 | Levels of property-value determination from highest to lowest precedence.

Fig. 16.25 | GUI of the color-chooser application at initialization.

to be 255 (line 64). Because a local declaration takes precedence over a style setter, the alpha Slider's value starts at 255 when the application loads.

16.13 Customizing Windows

For over a decade, the standard design of an application window has remained practically the same—a framed rectangular box with a header in the top left and a set of buttons in the top right for minimizing, maximizing and closing the window. Cutting-edge applications, however, have begun to use custom windows that diverge from this standard to create a more interesting look.

WPF lets you do this more easily. To create a custom window, set the *WindowStyle* property to None. This removes the standard frame around your Window. To make your Window irregularly shaped, you set the *AllowsTransparency* property to true and the Background property to Transparent. If you then add controls, only the space within the boundaries of those controls behaves as part of the window. This works because a user cannot interact with any part of a Window that is transparent. You still define your Window as a rectangle with a width and a height, but when a user clicks in a transparent part of the Window, it behaves as if the user clicked outside the Window's boundaries—that is, the window does not respond to the click.

Figure 16.26 is the XAML markup that defines a GUI for a circular digital clock. Note that the Window's WindowStyle is set to None and AllowsTransparency is set to true (line 7). In this example, we set the background to be an image using an ImageBrush (lines 11–13). The background image is a circle with a drop shadow surrounded by transparency. Thus, the Window appears circular.

```xaml
1    <!-- Fig. 16.26: BasicClock.xaml -->
2    <!-- Creating custom windows and using timers (XAML). -->
3    <Window x:Class="BasicClock.BasicClockWindow"
4        xmlns="http://schemas.microsoft.com/winfx/2006/xaml/presentation"
5        xmlns:x="http://schemas.microsoft.com/winfx/2006/xaml"
6        Title="Clock" Name="clockWindow" Height="118" Width="118"
7        WindowStyle="None" AllowsTransparency="True"
8        MouseLeftButtonDown="clockWindow_MouseLeftButtonDown">
9
10       <!-- set background image -->
11       <Window.Background>
12           <ImageBrush ImageSource="images/circle.png" />
13       </Window.Background>
```

Fig. 16.26 | Creating custom windows and using timers (XAML). (Part 1 of 2.)

```
14
15     <Grid>
16         <TextBox Name="timeTextBox" Margin="0,42,0,0"
17             Background="Transparent" TextAlignment="Center"
18             FontWeight="Bold" Foreground="White" FontSize="16"
19             BorderThickness="0" Cursor="Arrow" Focusable="False" />
20     </Grid>
21 </Window>
```

Fig. 16.26 | Creating custom windows and using timers (XAML). (Part 2 of 2.)

The time is displayed in the center of the window in a TextBox (lines 16–19). Its Background is set to Transparent so that the text displays directly on the circular background (line 17). We configured the text to be size 16, bold, and white by setting the FontSize, FontWeight, and Foreground properties. The Cursor property is set to Arrow, so that the mouse cursor doesn't change when it moves over the time (line 19). Setting Focusable to false disables the user's ability to select the text (line 19).

When you create a custom window, there is no built-in functionality for doing the simple tasks that normal windows do. For example, there is no way for the user to move, resize, minimize, maximize, or close a window unless you write the code to enable these features. You can move the clock around, because we implemented this functionality in the Window's code-behind class (Fig. 16.27). Whenever the left mouse button is held down on the clock (handled by the MouseLeftButtonDown event), the Window is dragged around using the **DragMove** method (e.g., line 30). Because we did not define how to close or minimize the Window, there is no way of doing so (one way to shut down the clock is to press *Alt-F4*—this is a feature built into Windows).

```
1  // Fig. 16.27: BasicClock.xaml.cs
2  // Creating custom windows and using timers (code-behind).
3  using System;
4  using System.Windows;
5  using System.Windows.Input;
6
7  namespace BasicClock
8  {
9     public partial class BasicClockWindow : Window
10    {
11       // create a timer to control clock
12       private System.Windows.Threading.DispatcherTimer timer =
13          new System.Windows.Threading.DispatcherTimer();
```

Fig. 16.27 | Creating custom windows and using timers (code-behind). (Part 1 of 2.)

```
14
15          // constructor
16          public BasicClockWindow()
17          {
18              InitializeComponent();
19
20              timer.Interval = TimeSpan.FromSeconds( 1 ); // tick every second
21              timer.IsEnabled = true; // enable timer
22
23              timer.Tick += timer_Tick;
24          } // end constructor
25
26          // drag Window when the left mouse button is held down
27          private void clockWindow_MouseLeftButtonDown( object sender,
28              MouseButtonEventArgs e )
29          {
30              this.DragMove(); // moves the window
31          } // end method clockWindow_MouseLeftButtonDown
32
33          // update the time when the timer ticks
34          private void timer_Tick( object sender, EventArgs e )
35          {
36              DateTime currentTime = DateTime.Now; // get the current time
37
38              // display the time as hh:mm:ss
39              timeTextBox.Text = currentTime.ToLongTimeString();
40          } // end method timer_Tick
41      } // end class BasicClockWindow
42  } // end namespace BasicClock
```

Fig. 16.27 | Creating custom windows and using timers (code-behind). (Part 2 of 2.)

The clock works by getting the current time every second and displaying it in the TextBox. To do this, the clock uses a **DispatcherTimer** object (of the System.Windows.Threading namespace), which raises the **Tick** event repeatedly at a prespecified time interval. Since the DispatcherTimer is defined in the C# code rather than the XAML, we need to specify the method to handle the Tick event in the C# code. Line 23 assigns method timer_Tick to the Tick event's delegate. This adds a new EventHandler—which takes a method name as an argument—to the specified event. After it is declared, you must specify the interval between Ticks by setting the **Interval** property, which takes a TimeSpan as its value. The **TimeSpan** class has several class methods for instantiating a TimeSpan object, including FromSeconds, which defines a TimeSpan lasting the number of seconds you pass the method. Line 20 creates a one-second TimeSpan and sets it as the DispatcherTimer's Interval. A DispatcherTimer is disabled by default. Until you enable it by setting the **IsEnabled** property to true (line 21), it will not Tick. In this example, the Tick event handler gets the current time and displays it in the TextBox.

You may recall that the Timer component provided the same capabilities in Windows Forms. A similar object that you can drag-and-drop onto your GUI doesn't exist in WPF. Instead, you must create a DispatcherTimer object, as illustrated in this example.

16.14 Defining a Control's Appearance with Control Templates

We now update the clock example to include buttons for minimizing and closing the application. We also introduce *control templates*—a powerful tool for customizing the look-and-feel of your GUIs. As previously mentioned, a custom control template can redefine the appearance of any control without changing its functionality. In Windows Forms, if you want to create a round button, you have to create a new control and simulate the functionality of a Button. With control templates, you can simply redefine the visual elements that compose the Button control and still use the preexisting functionality.

All WPF controls are *lookless*—that is, a control's properties, methods and events are coded into the control's class, but its appearance is not. Instead, the appearance of a control is determined by a control template, which is a hierarchy of visual elements. Every control has a built-in default control template. All of the GUIs discussed so far have used these default templates.

The hierarchy of visual elements defined by a control template can be represented as a tree, called a control's *visual tree*. Figure 16.28(b) shows the visual tree of a default Button (Fig. 16.29). This is a more detailed version of the same Button's *logical tree*, which is shown in Fig. 16.28(a). A logical tree depicts how a control is a defined, whereas a visual tree depicts how a control is graphically rendered.

A control's logical tree always mirrors its definition in XAML. For example, you'll notice that the Button's logical tree, which comprises only the Button and its string caption, exactly represents the hierarchy outlined by its XAML definition, which is

```
<Button>
   Click Me
</Button>
```

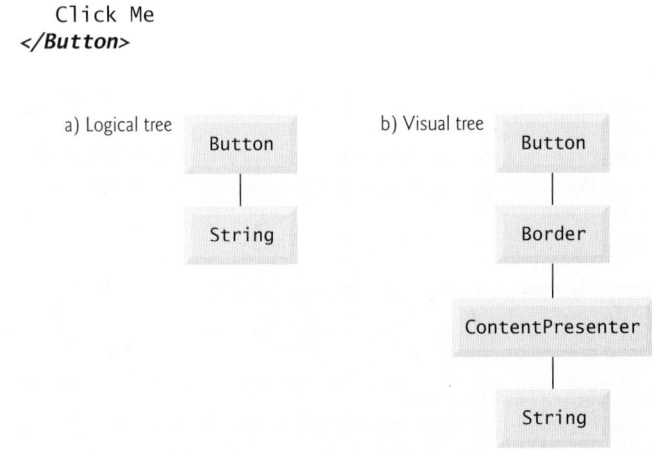

Fig. 16.28 | The logical and visual trees for a default Button.

Fig. 16.29 | The default Button.

To actually render the Button, WPF displays a ContentPresenter with a Border around it. These elements are included in the Button's visual tree. A **ContentPresenter** is an object used to display a single element of content on the screen. It is often used in a template to specify where to display content.

In the updated clock example, we create a custom control template (named Button-Template) for rendering Buttons and apply it to the two Buttons in the application. The XAML markup is shown in Fig. 16.30. Like a style, a control template is usually defined as a resource, and applied by binding a control's **Template** property to the control template using a resource binding (e.g., lines 48 and 53). After you apply a control template to a control, the **Design** view will update to display the new appearance of the control. Note that the **Properties** window remains unchanged, since a control template does not modify a control's properties.

To define a control template in XAML, you create a **ControlTemplate** element. Just as with a style, you must specify the control template's x:Key attribute so you can reference it later (e.g., line 12). You must also set the **TargetType** attribute to the type of control for which the template is designed (e.g., line 12). Inside the ControlTemplate element, you can build the control using any WPF visual element (e.g., lines 13–19). In this example, we replace the default Border and ContentPresenter with our own custom ones.

```
1   <!-- Fig. 16.30: Clock.xaml -->
2   <!-- Using control templates (XAML). -->
3   <Window x:Class="Clock.ClockWindow"
4      xmlns="http://schemas.microsoft.com/winfx/2006/xaml/presentation"
5      xmlns:x="http://schemas.microsoft.com/winfx/2006/xaml"
6      Title="Clock" Name="clockWindow" Height="118" Width="118"
7      WindowStyle="None" AllowsTransparency="True"
8      MouseLeftButtonDown="clockWindow_MouseLeftButtonDown">
9
10     <Window.Resources>
11        <!-- control template for Buttons -->
12        <ControlTemplate x:Key="ButtonTemplate" TargetType="Button">
13           <Border Name="Border" BorderThickness="2" CornerRadius="2"
14              BorderBrush="RoyalBlue">
15
16              <!-- TemplateBinding to Button.Content -->
17              <ContentPresenter Margin="0" Width="8"
18                 Content="{TemplateBinding Content}" />
19           </Border>
20
21           <ControlTemplate.Triggers>
22              <!-- if mouse is over the button -->
23              <Trigger Property="IsMouseOver" Value="True">
24                 <!-- make the background blue -->
25                 <Setter TargetName="Border" Property="Background"
26                    Value="LightBlue" />
27              </Trigger>
28           </ControlTemplate.Triggers>
29        </ControlTemplate>
30     </Window.Resources>
```

Fig. 16.30 | Using control templates (XAML). (Part 1 of 2.)

```
31
32        <!-- set background image -->
33        <Window.Background>
34           <ImageBrush ImageSource="images/circle.png" />
35        </Window.Background>
36
37        <Grid>
38           <Grid.RowDefinitions>
39              <RowDefinition Height="Auto" />
40              <RowDefinition />
41           </Grid.RowDefinitions>
42
43           <StackPanel Grid.Row="0" Orientation="Horizontal"
44              HorizontalAlignment="Right">
45
46              <!-- these buttons use the control template -->
47              <Button Name="minimizeButton" Margin="0" Focusable="False"
48                 IsTabStop="False" Template="{StaticResource ButtonTemplate}"
49                 Click="minimizeButton_Click">
50                 <Image Source="images/minimize.png" Margin="0" />
51              </Button>
52              <Button Name="closeButton" Margin="1,0,0,0" Focusable="False"
53                 IsTabStop="False" Template="{StaticResource ButtonTemplate}"
54                 Click="closeButton_Click">
55                 <Image Source="images/close.png" Margin="0"/>
56              </Button>
57           </StackPanel>
58
59           <TextBox Name="timeTextBox" Grid.Row="1" Margin="0,30,0,0"
60              Background="Transparent" TextAlignment="Center"
61              FontWeight="Bold" Foreground="White" FontSize="16"
62              BorderThickness="0" Cursor="Arrow" Focusable="False" />
63        </Grid>
64     </Window>
```

Fig. 16.30 | Using control templates (XAML). (Part 2 of 2.)

Sometimes, when defining a control template, it may be beneficial to use the value of one of the templated control's properties. For example, if you want several controls of different sizes to use the same control template, you may need to use the values of their Width and Height properties in the template. WPF allows you to do this with a *template binding*, which can be created in XAML with the markup extension, {TemplateBinding *PropertyName*}. To bind a property of an element in a control template to one of the properties of the templated control (i.e., the control that the template is applied to), you need to set the appropriate markup extension as the value of that property. In ButtonTemplate, we bind the **Content** property of a ContentPresenter to the Content property of the templated Button (line 18). Note that the nested element of a ContentControl is the value of its Content property. Thus, the images defined in lines 50 and 55 are the Content of the Buttons and are displayed by the ContentPresenters in their respective control templates. You can also create template bindings to a control's events.

Often you'll use a combination of control templates, styles and local declarations to define the appearance of your application. Recall that a control template defines the default appearance of a control and thus has a lower precedence than a style in dependency property-value determination.

Triggers

The control template for Buttons used in the updated clock example defines a *trigger*, which changes a control's appearance when that control enters a certain state. For example, when your mouse is over the clock's minimize or close Buttons, the Button is highlighted with a light blue background, as shown in Fig. 16.30(b). This simple change in appearance is caused by a trigger that fires whenever the IsMouseOver property becomes true.

A trigger must be defined in the ***Style.Triggers*** or ***ControlTemplate.Triggers*** element of a style or a control template, respectively (e.g., lines 21–28). You can create a trigger by defining a ***Trigger*** object. The ***Property*** and ***Value*** attributes define the state when a trigger is active. Setters nested in the Trigger element are carried out when the trigger is fired. When the trigger no longer applies, the changes are removed. A Setter's ***TargetName*** property specifies the name of the element that the Setter applies to (e.g., line 25).

Lines 23–27 define the IsMouseOver trigger for the minimize and close Buttons. When the mouse is over the Button, ***IsMouseOver*** becomes true, and the trigger becomes active. The trigger's Setter makes the background of the Border in the control template temporarily light blue. When the mouse exits the boundaries of the Button, IsMouseOver becomes false. Thus, the Border's background returns to its default setting, which in this case is transparent.

Functionality

Figure 16.31 shows the code-behind class for the clock application. Although the custom control template makes the Buttons in this application look different, it doesn't change how they behave. Lines 1–40 remain unchanged from the code in the first clock example (Fig. 16.27). The functionality for the close and minimize Buttons is implemented in the same way as any other button—by handling the Click event (lines 43–47 and 50–53 of Fig. 16.31, respectively). To minimize the window, we set the ***WindowState*** of the Window to ***WindowState.Minimized*** (line 46).

```
1   // Fig. 16.31: Clock.xaml.cs
2   // Using control templates (code-behind).
3   using System;
```

Fig. 16.31 | Using control templates (code-behind). (Part 1 of 2.)

```csharp
 4   using System.Windows;
 5   using System.Windows.Input;
 6
 7   namespace Clock
 8   {
 9      public partial class ClockWindow : Window
10      {
11         // creates a timer to control clock
12         private System.Windows.Threading.DispatcherTimer timer =
13            new System.Windows.Threading.DispatcherTimer();
14
15         // constructor
16         public ClockWindow()
17         {
18            InitializeComponent();
19
20            timer.Interval = TimeSpan.FromSeconds( 1 ); // tick every second
21            timer.IsEnabled = true; // enable timer
22
23            timer.Tick += timer_Tick;
24         } // end constructor
25
26         // update the time when the timer ticks
27         private void timer_Tick( object sender, EventArgs e )
28         {
29            DateTime currentTime = DateTime.Now; // get the current time
30
31            // display the time as hh:mm:ss
32            timeTextBox.Text = currentTime.ToLongTimeString();
33         } // end method timer_Tick
34
35         // drag Window when the left mouse button is held down
36         private void clockWindow_MouseLeftButtonDown( object sender,
37            MouseButtonEventArgs e )
38         {
39            this.DragMove();
40         } // end method clockWindow_MouseLeftButtonDown
41
42         // minimize the application
43         private void minimizeButton_Click( object sender,
44            RoutedEventArgs e )
45         {
46            this.WindowState = WindowState.Minimized; // minimize window
47         } // end method minimizeButton_Click
48
49         // close the application
50         private void closeButton_Click( object sender, RoutedEventArgs e )
51         {
52            Application.Current.Shutdown(); // shut down application
53         } // end method closeButton_Click
54      } // end class ClockWindow
55   } // end namespace Clock
```

Fig. 16.31 | Using control templates (code-behind). (Part 2 of 2.)

16.15 Data-Driven GUIs with Data Binding

Often, an application needs to edit and display data. WPF provides a comprehensive model for allowing GUIs to interact with data.

Bindings

A *data binding* is a pointer to data, represented by a *Binding* object. WPF allows you to create a binding to a broad range of data types. At the simplest level, you could create a binding to a single property. Often, however, it is useful to create a binding to a data object—an object of a class with properties that describe the data. You can also create a binding to objects like arrays, collections and data in an XML document. The versatility of the WPF data model even allows you to bind to data represented by LINQ statements.

Like other binding types, a data binding can be created declaratively in XAML markup with a markup extension. To declare a data binding, you must specify the data's source. If it's another element in the XAML markup, use property *ElementName*. Otherwise, use *Source*. Then, if you are binding to a specific data point of the source, such as a property of a control, you must specify the *Path* to that piece of information. Use a comma to separate the binding's property declarations. For example, to create a binding to a control's property, you would use {Binding ElementName=*ControlName*, Path=*PropertyName*}.

Figure 16.32 presents the XAML markup of a book-cover viewer that lets the user select from a list of books, and displays the cover of the currently selected book. The list of books is presented in a *ListView* control (lines 14–23), which displays a set of data as items in a selectable list. Its current selection can be retrieved from the *SelectedItem* property. A large image of the currently selected book's cover is displayed in an Image control (lines 26–27), which automatically updates when the user makes a new selection. Each book is represented by a Book object, which stores four properties:

1. Title (string)—the title of the book.

2. ISBN (string)—the 10-digit ISBN of the book.

3. ThumbImage (string)—the full path to the small cover image of the book.

4. LargeImage (string)—the full path to the large cover image of the book.

```
 1    <!-- Fig. 16.32: BookViewer.xaml -->
 2    <!-- Using data binding (XAML). -->
 3    <Window x:Class="BookViewer.BookViewerWindow"
 4       xmlns="http://schemas.microsoft.com/winfx/2006/xaml/presentation"
 5       xmlns:x="http://schemas.microsoft.com/winfx/2006/xaml"
 6       Title="Book Viewer" Height="400" Width="600">
 7       <Grid>
 8          <Grid.ColumnDefinitions>
 9             <ColumnDefinition Width="Auto" />
10             <ColumnDefinition />
11          </Grid.ColumnDefinitions>
12
13          <!-- use ListView and GridView to display data -->
14          <ListView Grid.Column="0" Name="booksListView" MaxWidth="250">
15             <ListView.View>
```

Fig. 16.32 | Using data binding (XAML). (Part 1 of 2.)

```
16          <GridView>
17              <GridViewColumn Header="Title" Width="100"
18                  DisplayMemberBinding="{Binding Path=Title}" />
19              <GridViewColumn Header="ISBN" Width="80"
20                  DisplayMemberBinding="{Binding Path=ISBN}" />
21          </GridView>
22        </ListView.View>
23      </ListView>
24
25      <!-- bind to selected item's full-size image -->
26      <Image Grid.Column="1" Source="{Binding ElementName=booksListView,
27          Path=SelectedItem.LargeImage}" Margin="5" />
28    </Grid>
29  </Window>
```

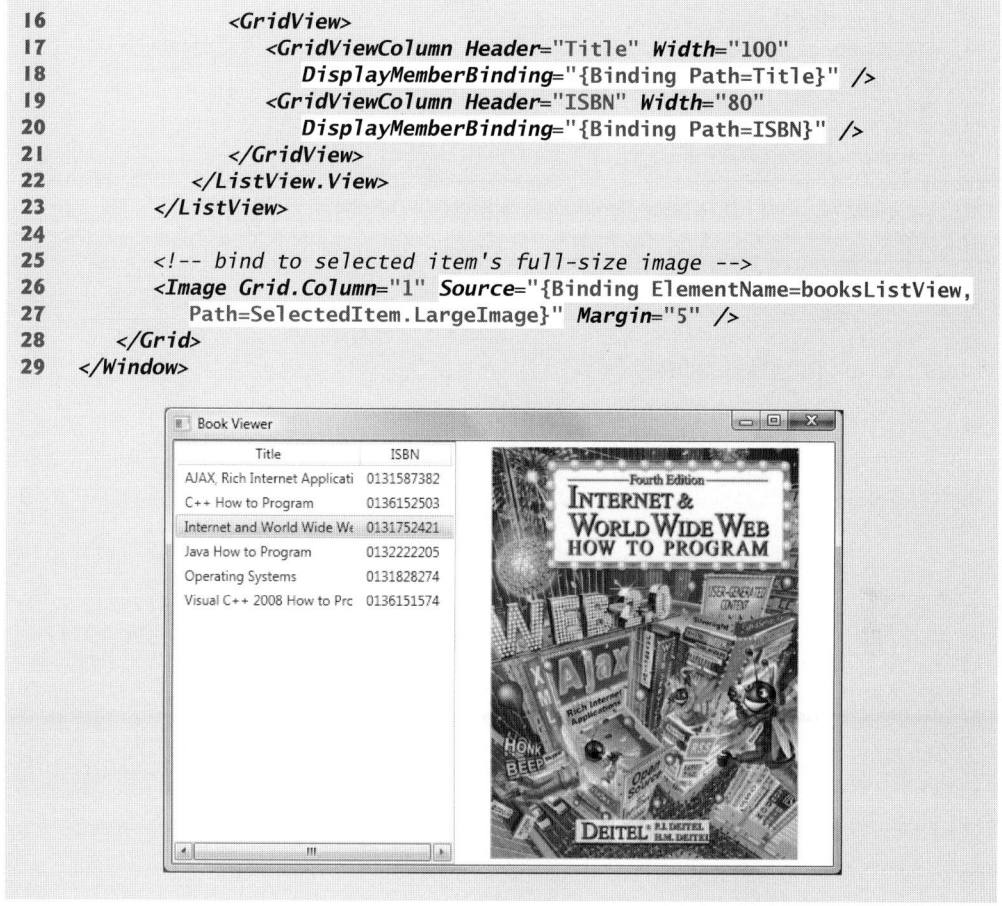

Fig. 16.32 | Using data binding (XAML). (Part 2 of 2.)

Class Book also contains a constructor that initializes a Book and sets each of its properties. The full source code of the Book class is not presented here but is included in the directory containing this chapter's examples.

To synchronize the book cover that is being displayed with the currently selected book, we bind the Image's Source property to the file location of the currently selected book's large cover image (lines 26–27). The Binding's ElementName property is the name of the selector control, booksListView. The Path property is SelectedItem.LargeImage. This indicates that the binding should be linked to the LargeImage property of the Book object that is currently booksListView's SelectedItem.

Some controls have built-in support for data binding, and a separate Binding object doesn't need to be created. A ListView, for example, has a built-in *ItemsSource* property that specifies the data source from which the items of the list are determined. There is no need to create a binding—instead, you can just set the ItemsSource property as you would any other property. When you set ItemsSource to a collection of data, the objects in the collection automatically become the items in the list. Figure 16.33 presents the code-behind class for the book-cover viewer. When the Window loads, a list of six Book objects

```
 I    // Fig. 16.33: BookViewer.xaml.cs
 2    // Using data binding (code-behind).
 3    using System.Collections.Generic;
 4    using System.Windows;
 5
 6    namespace BookViewer
 7    {
 8       public partial class BookViewerWindow : Window
 9       {
10          private List< Book > books = new List< Book >();
11
12          public BookViewerWindow()
13          {
14             InitializeComponent();
15
16             // add Book objects to the List
17             books.Add( new Book( "AJAX, Rich Internet Applications, " +
18                "and Web Development for Programmers", "0131587382",
19                "images/small/ajax.jpg", "images/large/ajax.jpg" ) );
20             books.Add( new Book( "C++ How to Program", "0136152503",
21                "images/small/cppHTP6e.jpg", "images/large/cppHTP6e.jpg" ) );
22             books.Add( new Book(
23                "Internet and World Wide Web How to Program", "0131752421",
24                "images/small/iw3htp4.jpg", "images/large/iw3htp4.jpg" ) );
25             books.Add( new Book( "Java How to Program", "0132222205",
26                "images/small/jhtp7.jpg", "images/large/jhtp7.jpg" ) );
27             books.Add( new Book( "Operating Systems", "0131828274",
28                "images/small/os3e.jpg", "images/large/os3e.jpg" ) );
29             books.Add( new Book( "Visual C++ 2008 How to Program",
30                "0136151574", "images/small/vcpp2008htp2e.jpg",
31                "images/large/vcpp2008htp2e.jpg" ) );
32
33             booksListView.ItemsSource = books; // bind data to the list
34          } // end constructor
35       } // end class BookViewerWindow
36    } // end namespace BookViewer
```

Fig. 16.33 | Using data binding (code-behind).

is initialized (lines 17–31) and set as the ItemsSource of the booksListView, meaning that each item displayed in the selector is one of the Books.

Data Templates

For a ListView to display objects in a useful manner, you must specify how. For example, if you don't specify how to display each Book, the ListView simply displays the result of the item's ToString method, as shown in Fig. 16.34.

There are many ways to format the display of a ListView. One such method is to display each item as a row in a tabular grid, as shown in Fig. 16.32. This can be achieved by setting a *GridView* as the View property of a ListView (lines 16–21). A GridView consists of many *GridViewColumns*, each representing a property. In this example, we define two columns, one for Title and one for ISBN (lines 17–18 and 19–20, respectively). A Grid-ViewColumn's Header property specifies what to display as its header. The values displayed

Fig. 16.34 | `ListView` display with no data template.

in each column are determined by its ***DisplayMemberBinding*** property. We set the **Title** column's `DisplayMemberBinding` to a `Binding` object that points to the `Title` property (line 18), and the **ISBN** column's to one that points to the `ISBN` property (line 20). Note that neither of the `Binding`s has a specified `ElementName` or `Source`. Because the `ListView` already has a data source (specified in line 33 of Fig. 16.33), the two data bindings inherit this source, and we do not need to specify it again.

A much more powerful technique for formatting a `ListView` is to specify a template for displaying each item in the list. This template defines how to display bound data and is called a ***data template***. Figure 16.35 is the XAML markup that describes a modified version of the book-cover viewer GUI. Each book, instead of being displayed as a row in a table, is represented by a small thumbnail of its cover image with its title and ISBN. Lines 11–32 define the data template (i.e., ***DataTemplate*** object) that specifies how to display a `Book` object. Note the similarity between the structure of a data template and that of a control template. If you define a data template as a resource, you apply it by using a resource binding, just as you would a style or control template. To apply a data template to items in a `ListView`, use the ***ItemTemplate*** property (e.g., line 43).

A data template uses data bindings to specify how to display data. Once again, we can omit the data binding's `ElementName` and `Source` properties, because its source has already been specified by the `ListView` (line 33 of Fig. 16.33). The same principle can be applied in other scenarios as well. If you bind an element's ***DataContext*** property to a data source, then its child elements can access data within that source without your having to specify it again. In other words, if a binding already has a context (i.e, a `DataContext` has already been defined by a parent), it automatically inherits the data source. For example, if you bind a data source to the `DataContext` property of a `Grid`, then any data binding created in the `Grid` uses that source by default. You can, however, override this source by explicitly defining a new one when you define a binding.

In the `Book` data template, lines 19–20 of Fig. 16.35 define an `Image` whose `Source` is bound to the `Book`'s `ThumbImage` property, which stores the relative file path to the thumbnail cover image. The `Book`'s `Title` and `ISBN` are displayed to the right of the book using ***TextBlocks***—lightweight controls for displaying text. The `TextBlock` in lines 24–25 displays the `Book`'s `Title` because the `Text` property is bound to it. Because some of the books' titles are long, we set the `TextWrapping` property to `Wrap` (line 25) so that, if the title is too long, it will wrap to multiple lines. We also set the `FontWeight` property to `Bold`. Lines 27–28 displays two additional `TextBlock`s, one that displays `ISBN:`, and another that is bound to the `Book`'s `ISBN` property.

Figure 16.35(a) shows the book-viewer application when it first loads. Each item in the `ListView` is represented by a thumbnail of its cover image, its title and its ISBN, as specified in the data template. As illustrated by Fig. 16.35(b), when you select an item in

the ListView, the large cover image on the right automatically updates, because it is bound
to the SelectedItem property of the list.

```
 1   <!-- Fig. 16.35: BookViewer.xaml -->
 2   <!-- Using data templates (XAML). -->
 3   <Window x:Class="BookViewer.BookViewerWindow"
 4      xmlns="http://schemas.microsoft.com/winfx/2006/xaml/presentation"
 5      xmlns:x="http://schemas.microsoft.com/winfx/2006/xaml"
 6      Title="Book Viewer" Height="400" Width="600" Name="bookViewerWindow">
 7
 8      <!-- define Window's resources -->
 9      <Window.Resources>
10         <!-- define data template -->
11         <DataTemplate x:Key="BookTemplate">
12            <Grid MaxWidth="250" Margin="3">
13               <Grid.ColumnDefinitions>
14                  <ColumnDefinition Width="Auto" />
15                  <ColumnDefinition />
16               </Grid.ColumnDefinitions>
17
18               <!-- bind image source -->
19               <Image Grid.Column="0" Source="{Binding Path=ThumbImage}"
20                  Width="50" />
21
22               <!-- bind Title and ISBN -->
23               <StackPanel Grid.Column="1">
24                  <TextBlock Margin="3,0" Text="{Binding Path=Title}"
25                     FontWeight="Bold" TextWrapping="Wrap" />
26                  <StackPanel Margin="3,0" Orientation="Horizontal">
27                     <TextBlock Text="ISBN: " />
28                     <TextBlock Text="{Binding Path=ISBN}" />
29                  </StackPanel>
30               </StackPanel>
31            </Grid>
32         </DataTemplate>
33      </Window.Resources>
34
35      <Grid>
36         <Grid.ColumnDefinitions>
37            <ColumnDefinition Width="Auto" />
38            <ColumnDefinition />
39         </Grid.ColumnDefinitions>
40
41         <!-- use ListView and template to display data -->
42         <ListView Grid.Column="0" Name="booksListView"
43            ItemTemplate="{StaticResource BookTemplate}" />
44
45         <!-- bind to selected item's full-size image -->
46         <Image Grid.Column="1" Source="{Binding ElementName=booksListView,
47            Path=SelectedItem.LargeImage}" Margin="5" />
48      </Grid>
49   </Window>
```

Fig. 16.35 | Using data templates (XAML). (Part 1 of 2.)

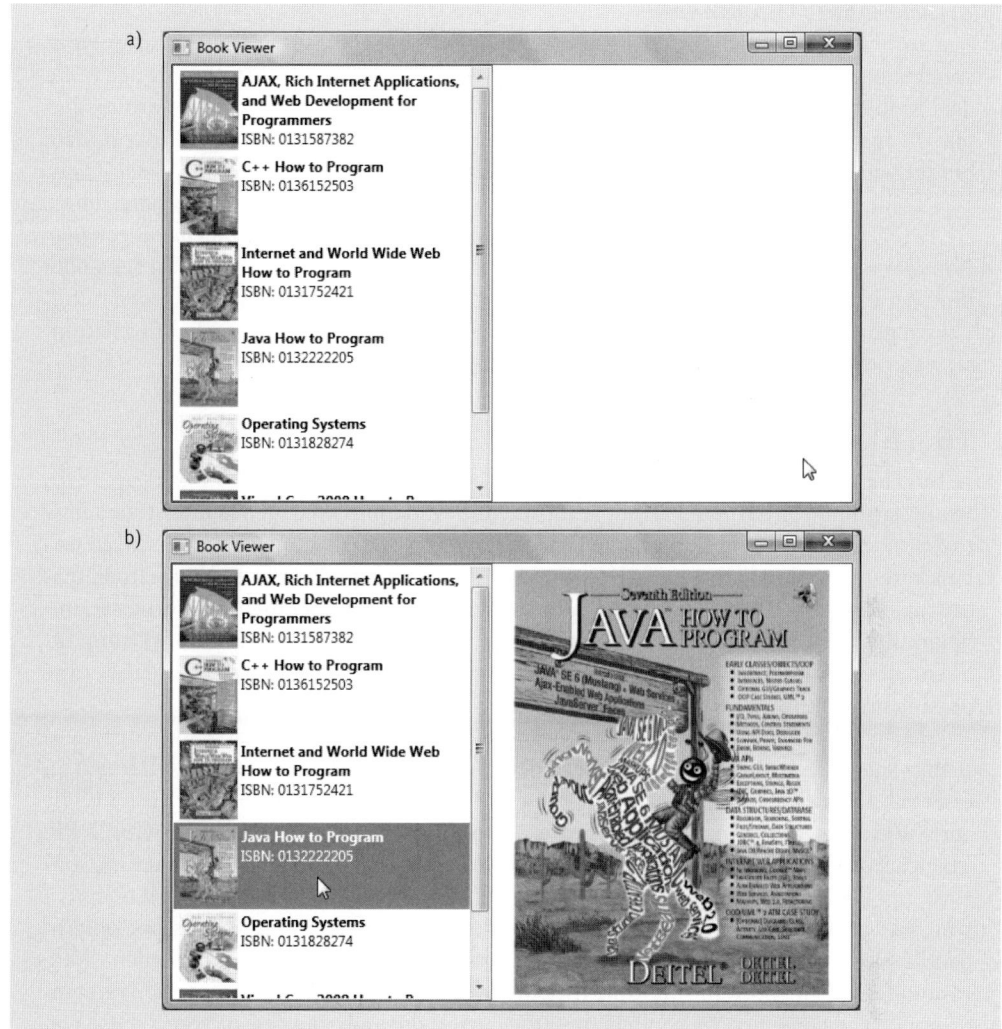

Fig. 16.35 | Using data templates (XAML). (Part 2 of 2.)

Data Views

A *data view* (of class type **CollectionView**) is a wrapper around a collection of data that can provide us with multiple "views" of the same data based on how we filter, sort and group the data. A default view is automatically created in the background every time a data binding is created. To retrieve the data view, use the **CollectionViewSource.GetDefaultView** method and pass it the source of your data binding. For example, to retrieve the default view of bookListView in the book-viewer application, you would use CollectionViewSource.GetDefaultView(bookListView.ItemsSource).

You can then modify the view to create the exact view of the data that you want to display. The methods of filtering, sorting and grouping data are beyond the scope of this book. For more information, see msdn.microsoft.com/en-us/library/ms752347.aspx# what_are_collection_views.

Asynchronous Data Binding

Sometimes you may wish to create asynchronous data bindings that don't hold up your application while data is being transmitted. To do this, you set the *IsAsync* property of a data binding to `true` (it is `false` by default). Often, however, it is not the transmission but the instantiation of data that is the most expensive operation. An asynchronous data binding does not provide a solution for instantiating data asynchronously.

To do so, you must use a *data provider*, a class that can create or retrieve data. There are two types of data providers, *XmlDataProvider* (for XML) and *ObjectDataProvider* (for data objects). Both can be declared as a resource in XAML markup. If you set a data provider's *IsAsynchronous* property to `true`, the provider will run in the background. Creating and using data providers is beyond the scope of this book. For more information, see msdn.microsoft.com/en-us/library/aa480224.aspx.

16.16 Wrap-Up

In this chapter, we discussed basic XML terminology and introduced XML markup, XML vocabularies and XML parsers (validating and nonvalidating). We then demonstrated how to describe and structure data in XML with examples that marked up an article and a business letter. Next, we discussed XML namespaces and namespace prefixes. You learned that each namespace has a unique name that provides a means for document authors to unambiguously refer to elements with the same name (i.e., prevent naming collisions) from different namespaces. We presented examples of defining two namespaces in the same document, as well as setting the default namespace for a document.

Many of today's commercial applications provide GUIs that are easy to use and manipulate. The demand for sophisticated and user-friendly GUIs makes GUI design an essential programming skill. In Chapter 14 and 15, we showed you how to create GUIs with Windows Forms. In this chapter, we demonstrated how to create GUIs with WPF. You learned how to design a WPF GUI with XAML markup and how to give it functionality in a C# code-behind class. We presented WPF's new flow-based layout scheme, in which a control's size and position are both defined relatively. You learned not only to handle events just as you did in a Windows Forms application, but also to implement WPF commands when you want multiple user interactions to execute the same task. We demonstrated the flexibility WPF offers for customizing the look-and-feel of your GUIs. You learned how to use styles, control templates and triggers to define a control's appearance. The chapter concluded with a demonstration of how to create data-driven GUIs with data bindings and data templates.

But WPF is not merely a GUI-building platform. Chapter 17 explores some of the many other capabilities of WPF, showing you how to incorporate 2D and 3D graphics, animation and multimedia into your WPF applications. Chapter 24 demonstrates how to create Internet applications using a subset of WPF's features that are available in the Silverlight runtime, which executes as a plug-in for several popular browsers and platforms.

16.17 Web Resources

There is a tremendous amount of material on the web to help you learn more about WPF. Check out our Windows Presentation Foundation Resource Center www.deitel.com/wpf/ for the latest WPF articles, books, sample chapters, tutorials, webcasts, blogs and more.

WPF Graphics and Multimedia

Nowadays people's visual imagination is so much more sophisticated, so much more developed, particularly in young people, that now you can make an image which just slightly suggests something, they can make of it what they will.

—Robert Doisneau

In shape, it is perfectly elliptical. In texture, it is smooth and lustrous. In color, it ranges from pale alabaster to warm terra cotta.

—Sydney J Harris, "Tribute to an Egg"

There are painters who transform the sun into a yellow spot, but there are others who, thanks to their art and intelligence, transform a yellow spot into the sun.

—Pablo Picasso

OBJECTIVES

In this chapter you'll learn:

- To manipulate fonts.

- To draw basic shapes like `Line`s, `Rectangle`s, `Ellipse`s and `Polygon`s.

- To use brushes to customize the `Fill` or `Background` of a GUI object.

- To use transforms to reposition or reorient GUI elements.

- To completely customize the look of a control while maintaining its functionality.

- To animate the properties of a GUI element.

- To transform and animate 3-D objects.

Outline

17.1 Introduction

17.2 Controlling Fonts

17.3 Basic Shapes

17.4 Polygons and Polylines

17.5 Brushes

17.6 Transforms

17.7 WPF Customization: A Television GUI

17.8 Animations

17.9 (Optional) 3-D Objects and Transforms

17.10 Wrap-Up

17.1 Introduction

Chapter 16 began our introduction to WPF. This chapter overviews WPF's graphics and multimedia capabilities, including two-dimensional and three-dimensional shapes, fonts, transformations, animations, audio and video. WPF integrates drawing and animation features that were previously available only in special libraries (such as Microsoft's GDI+ and DirectX). The graphics system in WPF is designed to use your computer's graphics hardware to reduce the load on the CPU and in many cases speed up graphics rendering.

WPF graphics use resolution-independent measurement units to make applications more uniform and portable across devices. The size properties of elements in WPF are measured in *resolution-independent pixels*, where one pixel typically represents 1/96 of an inch—but, this depends on the computer's DPI (dots per inch) setting. The graphics engine determines the correct pixel count so that all users see elements of the same size on all devices. Graphic elements are rendered on screen using a *vector-based* system in which calculations determine how to size and scale each element. This produces smoother graphics than the so called *raster-based* systems, in which the precise pixels are specified for each graphical element. Raster-based graphics tend to degrade in appearance as they are scaled larger. Vector-based graphics appear smooth at any scale. Graphic elements other than images and video are drawn using WPF's vector-based system.

The basic 2-D shapes are Lines, Rectangles and Ellipses. WPF also has controls that can be used to create custom shapes or curves. Brushes can be used to fill an element with solid colors, complex patterns, gradients, images or videos, allowing for unique and interesting visual experiences. WPF's robust animation and transform capabilities allow you to further customize GUIs. Transforms reposition and reorient graphic elements.

WPF also includes 3-D modeling and rendering capabilities. In addition, 2-D manipulations can be applied to 3-D objects as well. You can find more information on WPF in our WPF Resource Center at www.deitel.com/wpf/.

17.2 Controlling Fonts

This section introduces how to control fonts by modifying the font properties of a *Text-Block* control in the XAML code. Figure 17.1 shows how to use TextBlocks and how to change the properties to control the appearance of the displayed text. The manipulations discussed in this section can also be applied to other text-based controls such as a TextBox.

```
 1   <!-- Fig. 17.1: UsingFonts.xaml -->
 2   <!-- Formatting fonts in XAML code. -->
 3   <Window x:Class="UsingFonts.UsingFontsWindow"
 4      xmlns="http://schemas.microsoft.com/winfx/2006/xaml/presentation"
 5      xmlns:x="http://schemas.microsoft.com/winfx/2006/xaml"
 6      Title="UsingFonts" Height="120" Width="400">
 7
 8      <StackPanel>
 9         <!-- make a font bold using the FontWeight -->
10         <TextBlock FontFamily="Arial" FontSize="12" FontWeight="Bold">
11            Arial 12 point bold.</TextBlock>
12
13         <!-- if no font size is specified, default size is used -->
14         <TextBlock FontFamily="Times New Roman">
15            Times New Roman plain, default size.</TextBlock>
16
17         <!-- specifying a different font size and using FontStyle -->
18         <TextBlock FontFamily="Courier New" FontSize="16"
19            FontStyle="Italic" FontWeight="Bold">
20            Courier New 16 point bold and italic.
21         </TextBlock>
22
23         <!-- using Overline and Baseline TextDecorations -->
24         <TextBlock>
25            <TextBlock.TextDecorations>
26               <TextDecoration Location="OverLine" />
27               <TextDecoration Location="Baseline" />
28            </TextBlock.TextDecorations>
29            Default font with overline and baseline.
30         </TextBlock>
31
32         <!-- using Strikethrough and Underline TextDecorations -->
33         <TextBlock>
34            <TextBlock.TextDecorations>
35               <TextDecoration Location="Strikethrough" />
36               <TextDecoration Location="Underline" />
37            </TextBlock.TextDecorations>
38            Default font with strikethrough and underline.
39         </TextBlock>
40      </StackPanel>
41   </Window>
```

Fig. 17.1 | Formatting fonts in XAML code.

The text that you want to display in the TextBlock is placed between the TextBlock tags. The **FontFamily** property defines the font of the displayed text. This property can be set to any font. Lines 10, 14 and 18 define the separate TextBlock fonts to be Arial, Times

New Roman and Courier New, respectively. If the font is not specified, the default font—Segoe UI for Windows Vista and Tahoma for Windows XP—is used (lines 24 and 33). The default font is also used if the font is specified but is not available on the machine.

The *FontSize* property defines the text size measured in points. When no FontSize is specified, the property is set to the system's default value. The font sizes are defined in lines 10 and 18. Notice in lines 14, 24 and 33 that the FontSize is not defined, assigning the default value to each corresponding block of text.

TextBlocks have various properties that can further modify the font. Lines 10 and 19 set the *FontWeight* property to Bold to make the font thicker. This property can be set either to a numeric value (1–999) or to a predefined descriptive value—such as Light or UltraBold—to define the thickness of the text. You can use the *FontStyle* property to make the text either Italic or Oblique—which is simply a more emphasized italic. Line 19 sets the FontStyle property to Italic.

You can also define *TextDecorations* for a TextBlock to draw a horizontal line through the text. *Overline* and *Baseline*—shown in the fourth TextBlock of Fig. 17.1—create lines above the text and at the base of the text, respectively (lines 26–27). *Strikethrough* and *Underline*—shown in the fifth TextBlock—create lines through the middle of the text and under the text, respectively (lines 35–36). The Underline option leaves a small amount of space between the text and the line, unlike the Baseline. The *Location* property of the *TextDecoration* class defines which decoration you want to apply.

Default values for these properties can be set by parent elements of the TextBlock. The properties assigned by a parent will be inherited by all children with the corresponding property.

17.3 Basic Shapes

WPF has several built-in shapes. The BasicShapes example (Fig. 17.2) shows you how to display Lines, Rectangles and Ellipses.

Lines 9–10 use the *Rectangle* element to create a filled rectangle in the window. Notice that the layout control is a Canvas allowing us to use coordinates to position the shapes. To specify the upper-left corner of the Rectangle, we set the attached properties Canvas.Left and Canvas.Top to 90 and 30, respectively. We then set the Width and Height properties to 150 and 90, respectively, to specify the size. To define the Rectangle's color, we use the *Fill* property (line 10). You can assign any Color or Brush to this property. Rectangles also have a *Stroke* property, which defines the color of the outline of the shape (line 20). If either the Fill or the Stroke is not specified, that property will be rendered transparently. For this reason, the blue Rectangle in the window has no outline, while the second Rectangle drawn has only an outline (with a transparent center). Notice you can see the blue Rectangle even though it is rendered behind the Rectangle with no Fill, because the latter is transparent. Shape objects have a *StrokeThickness* property which defines the thickness of the outline. The default value for StrokeThickness is 1 pixel.

```
1   <!-- Fig. 17.2: BasicShapes.xaml -->
2   <!-- Drawing basic shapes in XAML. -->
```

Fig. 17.2 | Drawing basic shapes in XAML. (Part 1 of 2.)

```
3   <Window x:Class="BasicShapes.BasicShapesWindow"
4      xmlns="http://schemas.microsoft.com/winfx/2006/xaml/presentation"
5      xmlns:x="http://schemas.microsoft.com/winfx/2006/xaml"
6      Title="BasicShapes" Height="200" Width="500">
7      <Canvas>
8         <!-- Rectangle with fill but no stroke -->
9         <Rectangle Canvas.Left="90" Canvas.Top="30" Width="150" Height="90"
10           Fill="Blue" />
11
12        <!-- Lines defined by starting points and ending points-->
13        <Line X1="90" Y1="30" X2="110" Y2="40" Stroke="Black" />
14        <Line X1="90" Y1="120" X2="110" Y2="130" Stroke="Black" />
15        <Line X1="240" Y1="30" X2="260" Y2="40" Stroke="Black" />
16        <Line X1="240" Y1="120" X2="260" Y2="130" Stroke="Black" />
17
18        <!-- Rectangle with stroke but no fill -->
19        <Rectangle Canvas.Left="110" Canvas.Top="40" Width="150"
20           Height="90" Stroke="Black" />
21
22        <!-- Ellipse with fill and no stroke -->
23        <Ellipse Canvas.Left="280" Canvas.Top="75" Width="100" Height="50"
24           Fill="Red" />
25        <Line X1="380" Y1="55" X2="380" Y2="100" Stroke="Black" />
26        <Line X1="280" Y1="55" X2="280" Y2="100" Stroke="Black" />
27
28        <!-- Ellipse with stroke and no fill -->
29        <Ellipse Canvas.Left="280" Canvas.Top="30" Width="100" Height="50"
30           Stroke="Black" />
31     </Canvas>
32  </Window>
```

Fig. 17.2 | Drawing basic shapes in XAML. (Part 2 of 2.)

A **Line** is defined by its endpoints—X1, Y1 and X2, Y2. Lines have a Stroke property that defines the line's color. In this example, the lines all have black Strokes (lines 13–16 or lines 25–26).

To draw a circle or oval, you can use the **Ellipse** element. An Ellipse's location and size are defined like a Rectangle—with the Canvas.Left and Canvas.Top properties for the upper-left corner, and the Width and Height properties for the size (line 23). Together, the Canvas.Left, Canvas.Top, Width and Height of an Ellipse define a "bounding rectangle" in which the Ellipse touches the center of each side. To draw a circle, provide the same value for the Width and Height properties. As with Rectangles, having an unspecified Fill property for an Ellipse makes the shape transparent (lines 29–30).

17.4 Polygons and Polylines

There are two elements for drawing multisided shapes—*Polyline* and *Polygon*. Polyline draws a series of connected lines defined by a set of points, while Polygon does the same but connects the start and end points to make a closed figure. The application DrawPolygons (Fig. 17.3) allows you to click anywhere on the Canvas to define points for one of three shapes. You select which shape you want to display by selecting one of the RadioButtons in the second column. The difference between the **Filled Polygon** and the **Polygon** options is that the former has a Fill property specified while the latter does not.

```
 1   <!-- Fig. 17.3: DrawPolygons.xaml -->
 2   <!-- Defining Polylines and Polygons in XAML. -->
 3   <Window x:Class="DrawPolygons.DrawPolygonsWindow"
 4      xmlns="http://schemas.microsoft.com/winfx/2006/xaml/presentation"
 5      xmlns:x="http://schemas.microsoft.com/winfx/2006/xaml"
 6      Title="DrawPolygons" Height="400" Width="450" Name="mainWindow">
 7      <Grid>
 8         <Grid.ColumnDefinitions>
 9            <ColumnDefinition />
10            <ColumnDefinition Width="Auto" />
11         </Grid.ColumnDefinitions>
12
13         <!-- Canvas contains two polygons and a polyline -->
14         <!-- only the shape selected by the radio button is visible -->
15         <Canvas Name="drawCanvas" Grid.Column="0" Background="White"
16            MouseDown="drawCanvas_MouseDown">
17            <Polyline Name="polyLine" Stroke="Black"
18               Visibility="Collapsed" />
19            <Polygon Name="polygon" Stroke="Black" Visibility="Collapsed" />
20            <Polygon Name="filledPolygon" Fill="DarkBlue"
21               Visibility="Collapsed" />
22         </Canvas>
23
24         <!-- StackPanel containing the RadioButton options -->
25         <StackPanel Grid.Column="1" Orientation="Vertical"
26            Background="WhiteSmoke">
27            <GroupBox Header="Select Type" Margin="10">
28               <StackPanel>
29                  <!-- Polyline option -->
30                  <RadioButton Name="lineRadio" Margin="5"
31                     Checked="lineRadio_Checked">Polyline</RadioButton>
32
33                  <!-- unfilled Polygon option -->
34                  <RadioButton Name="polygonRadio" Margin="5"
35                     Checked="polygonRadio_Checked">Polygon</RadioButton>
36
37                  <!-- filled Polygon option -->
38                  <RadioButton Name="filledPolygonRadio" Margin="5"
39                     Checked="filledPolygonRadio_Checked">
40                     Filled Polygon</RadioButton>
41               </StackPanel>
42            </GroupBox>
```

Fig. 17.3 | Defining Polylines and Polygons in XAML. (Part 1 of 2.)

```
43
44            <!-- Button clears the shape from the canvas -->
45            <Button Name="clearButton" Click="clearButton_Click"
46               Margin="5">Clear</Button>
47         </StackPanel>
48      </Grid>
49   </Window>
```

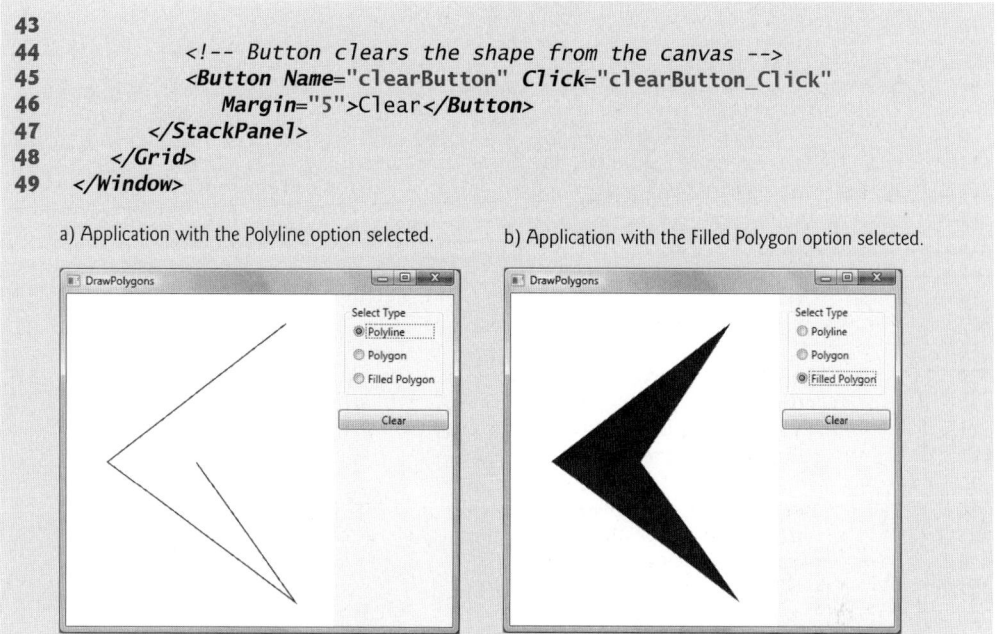

a) Application with the Polyline option selected.

b) Application with the Filled Polygon option selected.

Fig. 17.3 | Defining Polylines and Polygons in XAML. (Part 2 of 2.)

The code defines a two-column GUI (lines 9–10). The first column contains a Canvas (lines 15–22) that the user interacts with to create the points of the selected shape. Nested in the Canvas are a Polyline (lines 17–18) and two Polygons—one with a Fill (lines 20–21) and one without (line 19). The *Visibility* of a GUI element can be set to *Visible*, *Collapsed* or *Hidden*. This property is initially set to Collapsed for all three shapes (lines 18, 19 and 21), because we'll display only the shape that corresponds to the selected RadioButton. The difference between Hidden and Collapsed is that a Hidden object occupies space in the GUI but is not visible, while a Collapsed object has a Width and Height of 0. As you can see, Polyline and Polygon objects have Fill and Stroke properties like the simple shapes we discussed earlier.

The RadioButtons (lines 30–40) allow you to select which shape appears in the Canvas. There is also a Button (lines 45–46) that clears the shape's points to allow you to start over. Notice the column that contains these RadioButtons is set with the Width value "Auto" (line 10). This enables you to effectively create a "docked" area in the window, since this column is always attached to the right side of the window and has a constant Width. The code-behind file for this application is shown in Fig. 17.4.

```
1   // Fig. 17.4: DrawPolygons.xaml.cs
2   // Drawing Polylines and Polygons.
3   using System.Windows;
4   using System.Windows.Input;
5   using System.Windows.Media;
```

Fig. 17.4 | Drawing Polylines and Polygons. (Part 1 of 3.)

```
 6
 7   namespace DrawPolygons
 8   {
 9      public partial class DrawPolygonsWindow : Window
10      {
11         // stores the collection of points for the multisided shapes
12         private PointCollection points = new PointCollection();
13
14         // initialize the points of the shapes
15         public DrawPolygonsWindow()
16         {
17            InitializeComponent();
18
19            polyLine.Points = points; // assign Polyline points
20            polygon.Points = points; // assign Polygon points
21            filledPolygon.Points = points; // assign filled Polygon points
22         } // end constructor
23
24         // adds a new point when the user clicks on the canvas
25         private void drawCanvas_MouseDown( object sender,
26            MouseButtonEventArgs e )
27         {
28            // add point to collection
29            points.Add( e.GetPosition( drawCanvas ) );
30         } // end method drawCanvas_MouseDown
31
32         // when the clear Button is clicked
33         private void clearButton_Click( object sender, RoutedEventArgs e )
34         {
35            points.Clear(); // clear the points from the collection
36         } // end method clearButton_Click
37
38         // when the user selects the Polyline
39         private void lineRadio_Checked( object sender, RoutedEventArgs e )
40         {
41            // Polyline is visible, the other two are not
42            polyLine.Visibility = Visibility.Visible;
43            polygon.Visibility = Visibility.Collapsed;
44            filledPolygon.Visibility = Visibility.Collapsed;
45         } // end method lineRadio_Checked
46
47         //  when the user selects the Polygon
48         private void polygonRadio_Checked( object sender,
49            RoutedEventArgs e )
50         {
51            // Polygon is visible, the other two are not
52            polyLine.Visibility = Visibility.Collapsed;
53            polygon.Visibility = Visibility.Visible;
54            filledPolygon.Visibility = Visibility.Collapsed;
55         } // end method polygonRadio_Checked
56
```

Fig. 17.4 | Drawing Polylines and Polygons. (Part 2 of 3.)

```
57        // when the user selects the filled Polygon
58        private void filledPolygonRadio_Checked( object sender,
59           RoutedEventArgs e )
60        {
61           // filled Polygon is visible, the other two are not
62           polyLine.Visibility = Visibility.Collapsed;
63           polygon.Visibility = Visibility.Collapsed;
64           filledPolygon.Visibility = Visibility.Visible;
65        } // end method filledPolygonRadio_Checked
66     } // end class DrawPolygonsWindow
67  } // end namespace DrawPolygons
```

Fig. 17.4 | Drawing `Polylines` and `Polygons`. (Part 3 of 3.)

To allow the user to specify a variable number of points, line 12 declares a ***PointCollection***, which is a collection that stores `Point` objects. This keeps track of each mouse-click location. The collection's ***Add*** method adds new points to the end of the collection. When the window is loaded, we set the ***Points*** property (lines 19–21) of each shape to reference the `PointCollection` instance variable.

We created a `MouseDown` event handler to capture mouse clicks on the `Canvas` (lines 25–30). When the user clicks the mouse on the `Canvas`, the mouse coordinates are recorded and the `points` collection is updated (line 28). Since the `Points` property of each of the three shapes has a reference to our `PointCollection` object, the shapes are automatically updated with the new `Point`. WPF handles redrawing the shape when it detects a change to the `PointCollection` instance. The `Polyline` and `Polygon` shapes connect the `Points` based on the ordering in the collection.

Each `RadioButton`'s `Checked` event handler sets the corresponding shape's `Visibility` property to `Visible` and sets the other two to `Collapsed` to display the correct shape in the `Canvas`. For example, the `lineRadio_Checked` event handler (lines 39–45) makes `polyLine` `Visible` (line 42) and makes `polygon` and `filledPolygon` `Collapsed` (lines 43–44). The other two `RadioButton` event handlers are defined similarly in lines 48–55 and lines 58–65.

The `clearButton_Click` event handler erases the `Points` stored in the `PointCollection` (line 33–36). The ***Clear*** method of `points` erases its elements.

17.5 Brushes

Brushes change an element's graphic properties, such as the `Fill`, `Stroke` or `Background`. WPF provides various types of brushes to customize the graphic properties of an element. A `SolidColorBrush` fills the element with the specified color. To customize elements further, you can use `ImageBrushes`, `VisualBrushes` and gradient brushes. Run the `UsingBrushes` application (Fig. 17.5) to see `Brushes` applied to `TextBlocks` and `Ellipses`.

```
1  <!-- Fig. 17.5: UsingBrushes.xaml -->
2  <!-- Applying brushes to various XAML elements. -->
3  <Window x:Class="UsingBrushes.UsingBrushesWindow"
4     xmlns="http://schemas.microsoft.com/winfx/2006/xaml/presentation"
```

Fig. 17.5 | Applying brushes to various XAML elements. (Part 1 of 3.)

```xaml
 5        xmlns:x="http://schemas.microsoft.com/winfx/2006/xaml"
 6        Title="UsingBrushes" Height="450" Width="700">
 7        <Grid>
 8           <Grid.RowDefinitions>
 9              <RowDefinition />
10              <RowDefinition />
11              <RowDefinition />
12           </Grid.RowDefinitions>
13
14           <Grid.ColumnDefinitions>
15              <ColumnDefinition />
16              <ColumnDefinition />
17           </Grid.ColumnDefinitions>
18
19           <!-- TextBlock with a SolidColorBrush -->
20           <TextBlock FontSize="100" FontWeight="999">
21              <TextBlock.Foreground>
22                 <SolidColorBrush Color="#5F2CAE" />
23              </TextBlock.Foreground>
24              Color
25           </TextBlock>
26
27           <!-- Ellipse with a SolidColorBrush (just a Fill) -->
28           <Ellipse Grid.Column="1" Height="100" Width="300" Fill="#5F2CAE" />
29
30           <!-- TextBlock with an ImageBrush -->
31           <TextBlock Grid.Row="1" FontSize="100" FontWeight="999">
32              <TextBlock.Foreground>
33                 <!-- Flower image as an ImageBrush -->
34                 <ImageBrush ImageSource="flowers.jpg" />
35              </TextBlock.Foreground>
36              Image
37           </TextBlock>
38
39           <!-- Ellipse with an ImageBrush -->
40           <Ellipse Grid.Row="1" Grid.Column="1" Height="100" Width="300">
41              <Ellipse.Fill>
42                 <ImageBrush ImageSource="flowers.jpg" />
43              </Ellipse.Fill>
44           </Ellipse>
45
46           <!-- TextBlock with a MediaElement as a VisualBrush -->
47           <TextBlock Grid.Row="2" FontSize="100" FontWeight="999">
48              <TextBlock.Foreground>
49                 <!-- VisualBrush with an embedded MediaElement-->
50                 <VisualBrush>
51                    <VisualBrush.Visual>
52                       <MediaElement Source="nasa.wmv" />
53                    </VisualBrush.Visual>
54                 </VisualBrush>
55              </TextBlock.Foreground>
56              Video
57           </TextBlock>
```

Fig. 17.5 | Applying brushes to various XAML elements. (Part 2 of 3.)

```
58
59          <!-- Ellipse with a MediaElement as a VisualBrush -->
60          <Ellipse Grid.Row="2" Grid.Column="1" Height="100" Width="300">
61             <Ellipse.Fill>
62                <VisualBrush>
63                   <VisualBrush.Visual>
64                      <MediaElement Source="nasa.wmv" />
65                   </VisualBrush.Visual>
66                </VisualBrush>
67             </Ellipse.Fill>
68          </Ellipse>
69       </Grid>
70    </Window>
```

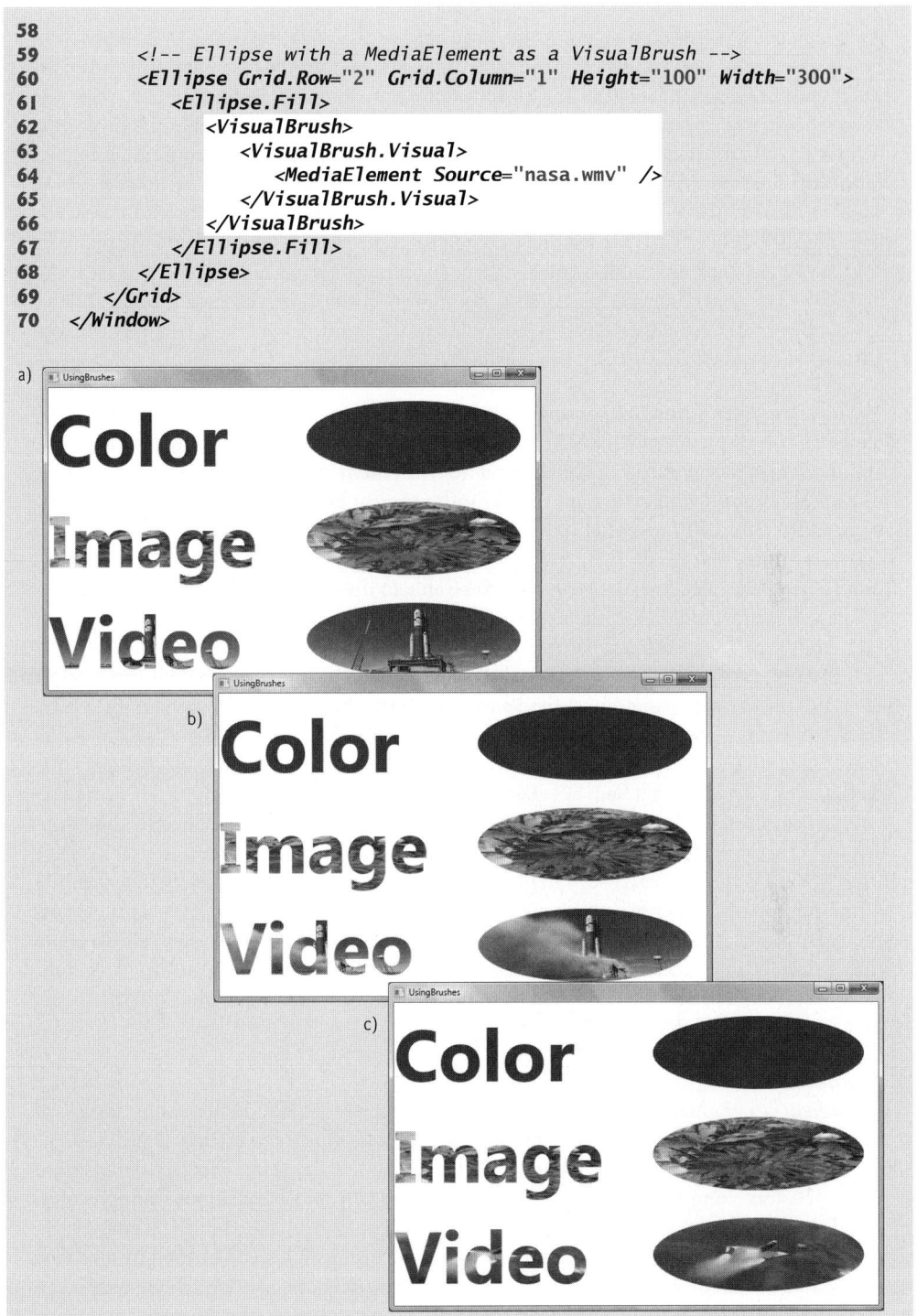

Fig. 17.5 | Applying brushes to various XAML elements. (Part 3 of 3.)

ImageBrush

An *ImageBrush* paints an image into the property it is assigned to (such as a Background). For instance, the TextBlock with the text "Image" and the Ellipse next to it are both filled with the same flower picture. To fill the text, we can assign the ImageBrush to the Foreground property of the TextBlock. The *Foreground* property specifies the fill for the text itself while the *Background* property specifies the fill for the area surrounding the text. Notice in lines 32–35 we apply the ImageBrush with its *ImageSource* set to the file we want to display (the image file must be included in the project). We can also assign the brush to the Fill of the Ellipse (lines 41–43) to display the image inside the shape. Note that the Ellipse in this application does not have a top-left corner specified. We cannot define the attached Canvas property in this application since the Ellipse is not a child of a Canvas control, so the top-left corner of the shape's bounding rectangle is simply the top-left corner of the enclosing cell of the Grid.

VisualBrush and MediaElement

This example displays a video in a TextBlock's Foreground and an Ellipse's Fill. To use audio or video in a WPF application, use a *MediaElement* object. Before using a video file in your application, add it to your Visual Studio project by first selecting the **Add Existing Item...** option in the **Project** menu. In the file dialog that appears, find and select the video you want to use. Note that in the drop-down menu next to the **File Name** TextBox, you must change the selection to **All Files (*.*)** to be able to find your file. Once you have selected your file, click **Add**. Select the newly added video in the **Solution Explorer**. Then, in the **Properties** window, change the **Copy to Output Directory** property to **Copy if newer**. This tells the project to copy your video to the project's output directory where it can directly reference the file. You can now set the *Source* property of your MediaElement to the video. In the UsingBrushes application, we use nasa.wmv (line 52 and 64).

We use the *VisualBrush* element to display a video in the desired objects. Lines 50–54 define the Brush with a MediaElement assigned to its *Visual* property. In this property you can completely customize the look of the brush. By assigning the video to this property, we can apply the brush to the Foreground of the TextBlock (lines 48–55) and the Fill of the Ellipse (lines 61–67) to play the video inside the objects. Notice that the Fill of the third Row's elements is different in each screen capture in Fig. 17.5. This is because the video is playing inside the two elements. Although we have only a MediaElement in the VisualBrush, you can add other GUI elements to display a more customized graphic. A VisualBrush can have only one child, so if you want more than one object in the brush, they must be nested in a layout control.

Gradients

A *gradient* is a gradual transition through two or more colors. Gradients can be applied as the background or fill for various elements. There are two types of gradients in WPF—LinearGradientBrush and RadialGradientBrush. The *LinearGradientBrush* transitions through colors along a straight path. The *RadialGradientBrush* transitions through colors radially outward from a specified point. Linear gradients are discussed in the UsingGradients example, which displays a gradient across the window. This was created by applying a LinearGradientBrush to a Rectangle's Fill. The gradient starts white and transitions linearly to black from left to right. You can set the start and end colors to change the look of the gradient. Note that the values entered in the TextBoxes must be in the range 0–255 for the application to run properly. If you set either color's Alpha value to less than 255, you'll see the text "Transparency test" in the background, showing that the Rectangle is semitransparent. The XAML code for this application is shown in Fig. 17.6.

```xaml
1   <!-- Fig. 17.6: UsingGradients.xaml -->
2   <!-- Defining gradients in XAML. -->
3   <Window x:Class="UsingGradients.UsingGradientsWindow"
4      xmlns="http://schemas.microsoft.com/winfx/2006/xaml/presentation"
5      xmlns:x="http://schemas.microsoft.com/winfx/2006/xaml"
6      Title="UsingGradients" Height="200" Width="450">
7      <Grid>
8         <Grid.RowDefinitions>
9            <RowDefinition />
10           <RowDefinition Height="Auto" />
11           <RowDefinition Height="Auto" />
12           <RowDefinition Height="Auto" />
13        </Grid.RowDefinitions>
14
15        <!-- TextBlock in the background to show transparency -->
16        <TextBlock FontSize="30" HorizontalAlignment="Center"
17           VerticalAlignment="Center">Transparency test</TextBlock>
18
19        <!-- sample rectangle with linear gradient fill -->
20        <Rectangle>
21           <Rectangle.Fill>
22              <LinearGradientBrush StartPoint="0,0" EndPoint="1,0">
23                 <!-- gradient stop can define a color at any offset -->
24                 <GradientStop x:Name="startGradient" Offset="0.0"
25                    Color="White" />
26                 <GradientStop x:Name="stopGradient" Offset="1.0"
27                    Color="Black" />
28              </LinearGradientBrush>
29           </Rectangle.Fill>
30        </Rectangle>
31
32        <!-- shows which TextBox corresponds with which ARGB value-->
33        <StackPanel Grid.Row="1" Orientation="Horizontal">
34           <TextBlock Width="75" Margin="5">Alpha:</TextBlock>
35           <TextBlock Width="75" Margin="5">Red:</TextBlock>
36           <TextBlock Width="75" Margin="5">Green:</TextBlock>
37           <TextBlock Width="75" Margin="5">Blue:</TextBlock>
38        </StackPanel>
39
40        <!-- GUI to select the color of the first GradientStop -->
41        <StackPanel Grid.Row="2" Orientation="Horizontal">
42           <TextBox Name="fromAlpha" Width="75" Margin="5">255</TextBox>
43           <TextBox Name="fromRed" Width="75" Margin="5">255</TextBox>
44           <TextBox Name="fromGreen" Width="75" Margin="5">255</TextBox>
45           <TextBox Name="fromBlue" Width="75" Margin="5">255</TextBox>
46           <Button Name="fromButton" Width="75" Margin="5"
47              Click="fromButton_Click">Start Color</Button>
48        </StackPanel>
```

Fig. 17.6 | Defining gradients in XAML. (Part 1 of 2.)

```
49
50        <!-- GUI to select the color of second GradientStop -->
51        <StackPanel Grid.Row="3" Orientation="Horizontal">
52           <TextBox Name="toAlpha" Width="75" Margin="5">255</TextBox>
53           <TextBox Name="toRed" Width="75" Margin="5">0</TextBox>
54           <TextBox Name="toGreen" Width="75" Margin="5">0</TextBox>
55           <TextBox Name="toBlue" Width="75" Margin="5">0</TextBox>
56           <Button Name="toButton" Width="75" Margin="5"
57              Click="toButton_Click">End Color</Button>
58        </StackPanel>
59     </Grid>
60  </Window>
```

a) The application immediately after it is loaded.   b) The application after changing the start and end colors.

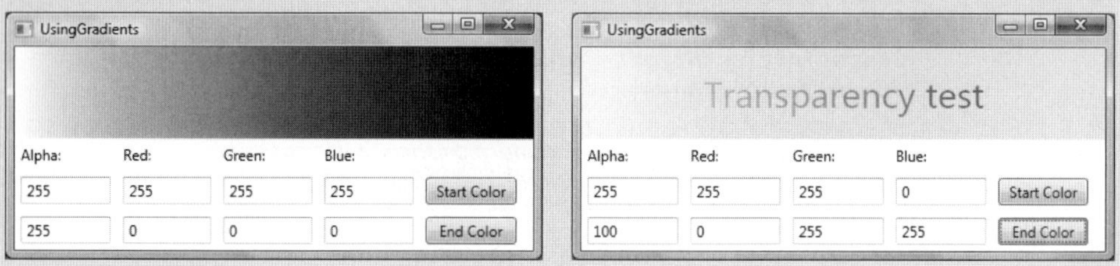

Fig. 17.6 | Defining gradients in XAML. (Part 2 of 2.)

The GUI for this application contains a single Rectangle with a LinearGradient-Brush applied to its Fill (lines 21–29). We define the **StartPoint** and **EndPoint** of the gradient in line 22. You must assign *logical points* to these properties, meaning the x- and y-coordinates take values between 0 and 1, inclusive. Logical points are used to reference locations in the GUI element independent of the actual size. The point (0,0) represents the top-left corner, the point (1,1) the bottom-right corner. The gradient transitions linearly from the start to the end—for RadialGradientBrush, the StartPoint represents the center of the gradient.

A gradient's colors are defined using GradientStop child elements. A **GradientStop** defines a single color along the gradient. You can define as many stops as you want by nesting them in the brush element. A GradientStop is defined by its Offset and Color properties. The **Color** property defines the color you want the gradient to transition to—lines 25 and 27 indicate that it transitions through white and black. The **Offset** property defines where the color appears along the transition. You can assign any double value between 0 and 1, inclusive, which represent the start and end of the gradient. In the example we use 0.0 and 1.0 offsets (lines 24 and 26), indicating that these colors appear at the start and end of the gradient (which were defined in line 22), respectively. The code in Fig. 17.7 allows the user to change the Colors of the two stops.

```
1   // Fig. 17.7: UsingGradients.xaml.cs
2   // Customizing gradients.
3   using System;
4   using System.Windows;
```

Fig. 17.7 | Customizing gradients. (Part 1 of 2.)

```
 5  using System.Windows.Media;
 6
 7  namespace UsingGradients
 8  {
 9     public partial class UsingGradientsWindow : Window
10     {
11        // constructor
12        public UsingGradientsWindow()
13        {
14           InitializeComponent();
15        } // end constructor
16
17        // change the starting color of the gradient when the user clicks
18        private void fromButton_Click( object sender, RoutedEventArgs e )
19        {
20           // change the color to use the ARGB values specified by user
21           startGradient.Color = Color.FromArgb(
22              Convert.ToByte( fromAlpha.Text ),
23              Convert.ToByte( fromRed.Text ),
24              Convert.ToByte( fromGreen.Text ),
25              Convert.ToByte( fromBlue.Text ) );
26        } // end method fromButton_Click
27
28        // change the ending color of the gradient when the user clicks
29        private void toButton_Click( object sender, RoutedEventArgs e )
30        {
31           // change the color to use the ARGB values specified by user
32           stopGradient.Color = Color.FromArgb(
33              Convert.ToByte( toAlpha.Text ),
34              Convert.ToByte( toRed.Text ),
35              Convert.ToByte( toGreen.Text ),
36              Convert.ToByte( toBlue.Text ) );
37        } // end method toButton_Click
38     } // end class UsingGradientsWindow
39  } // end namespace UsingGradients
```

Fig. 17.7 | Customizing gradients. (Part 2 of 2.)

When fromButton is clicked, we use the Text properties of the corresponding Text-Boxes to obtain the input values and create a new color. We then assign it to the Color property of startGradient (lines 21–25). When the toButton is clicked, we do the same for stopGradient's Color (lines 32–36).

17.6 Transforms

A *transform* can be applied to any UI element to reposition or reorient the graphic. There are four types of transforms—***TranslateTransform***, ***RotateTransform***, ***SkewTransform*** and ***ScaleTransform***. A TranslateTransform moves an object to a new location. A RotateTransform rotates the object around a point and by a specified RotationAngle. A SkewTransform skews (or shears) the object. A ScaleTransform scales the object's x- and y-coordinate points by different specified amounts. See Section 17.7 for an example using a SkewTransform and a ScaleTransform.

In the `DrawStars` example (Fig. 17.9), we draw a star using the `Polygon` element and use `RotateTransforms` to create a circle of randomly colored stars. Figure 17.8 shows the XAML code and a screen capture of the example. Lines 10–11 define a `Polygon` in the shape of a star. The `Points` property of the `Polygon` in this example is defined here in a new syntax. Each `Point` in the collection is defined with a comma separating the *x*- and *y*-coordinates. A single space separates each `Point`. Note that we defined ten `Points` in the collection. The code-behind file is shown in Fig. 17.9.

```
 1    <!-- Fig. 17.8: DrawStars.xaml -->
 2    <!-- Defining a Polygon representing a star in XAML. -->
 3    <Window x:Class="DrawStars.DrawStarsWindow"
 4        xmlns="http://schemas.microsoft.com/winfx/2006/xaml/presentation"
 5        xmlns:x="http://schemas.microsoft.com/winfx/2006/xaml"
 6        Title="DrawStars" Height="330" Width="330" Name="DrawStars">
 7        <Canvas Name="mainCanvas">
 8
 9            <!-- Polygon with points that make up a star -->
10            <Polygon Name="star" Fill="Green" Points="205,150 217,186 259,186
11                223,204 233,246 205,222 177,246 187,204 151,186 193,186" />
12        </Canvas>
13    </Window>
```

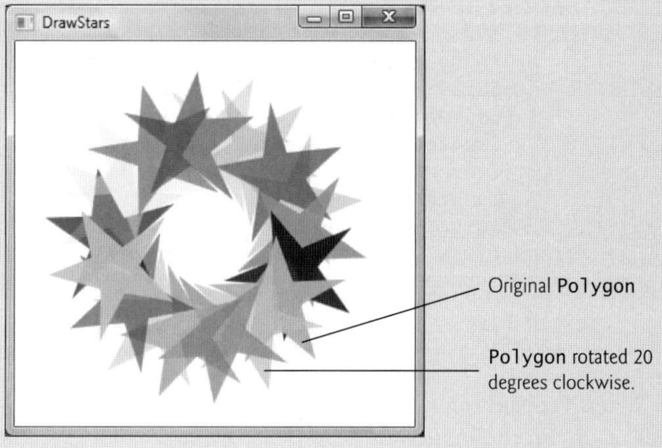

Original **Polygon**

Polygon rotated 20 degrees clockwise.

Fig. 17.8 | Defining a `Polygon` representing a star in XAML.

```
 1    // Fig. 17.9: DrawStars.xaml.cs
 2    // Applying transforms to a Polygon.
 3    using System;
 4    using System.Windows;
 5    using System.Windows.Media;
 6    using System.Windows.Shapes;
 7
```

Fig. 17.9 | Applying transforms to a `Polygon`. (Part 1 of 2.)

```
 8    namespace DrawStars
 9    {
10       public partial class DrawStarsWindow : Window
11       {
12          // constructor
13          public DrawStarsWindow()
14          {
15             InitializeComponent();
16
17             Random random = new Random(); // get random values for colors
18
19             // create 18 more stars
20             for ( int count = 0; count < 18; count++ )
21             {
22                Polygon newStar = new Polygon(); // create a polygon object
23                newStar.Points = star.Points; // copy the points collection
24
25                byte[] colorValues = new byte[ 4 ]; // create a Byte array
26                random.NextBytes( colorValues ); // create four random values
27                newStar.Fill = new SolidColorBrush( Color.FromArgb(
28                   colorValues[ 0 ], colorValues[ 1 ], colorValues[ 2 ],
29                   colorValues[ 3 ] ) ); // creates a random color brush
30
31                // apply a rotation to the shape
32                RotateTransform rotate =
33                   new RotateTransform( count * 20, 150, 150 );
34                newStar.RenderTransform = rotate;
35                mainCanvas.Children.Add( newStar );
36             } // end for
37          } // end constructor
38       } // end class DrawStarsWindow
39    } // end namespace DrawSttars
```

Fig. 17.9 | Applying transforms to a `Polygon`. (Part 2 of 2.)

In the code-behind, we replicate star 18 times and apply a different RotateTransform to each to get the circle of Polygons shown in the screen capture of Fig. 17.8. Each iteration of the for statement duplicates star by creating a new Polygon with the same set of points (lines 22–23). To generate the random colors for each star, we use the Random class's **NextBytes** method, which assigns a random value in the range 0–255 to each element in its byte array argument. Lines 25–26 define a four-element byte array and supply the array to the NextBytes method. We then create a new Brush with a color that uses the four randomly generated values as its ARGB values (lines 27–29).

To apply a rotation to the new Polygon, we set the **RenderTransform** property to a new RotateTransform object (lines 32–33). Each iteration of the for statement assigns a new rotation-angle value by using the count variable multiplied by 20 as the RotationAngle argument. The first argument in the RotateTransform's constructor is the angle by which to rotate the object. The next two arguments are the x- and y-coordinates of the point of rotation. The center of the circle of stars is the point (150,150), because all 18 stars were rotated about that point. Each new shape is added as a new Child element to mainCanvas (line 35) so it can be rendered on screen.

17.7 WPF Customization: A Television GUI

In Chapter 16, we introduced several techniques for customizing the appearance of WPF controls. We revisit them in this section, now that we have a basic understanding of how to create and manipulate 2-D graphics in WPF. You'll learn to apply combinations of shapes, brushes and transforms to define every aspect of a control's appearance and to create graphically sophisticated GUIs.

This case study presents a WPF application that models a television. The GUI depicts a 3-D-looking environment featuring a TV that can be turned on and off. When it is on, the user can play, pause and stop the TV's video. When the video plays, a semitransparent reflection plays simultaneously on what appears to be a flat surface in front of the screen (Fig. 17.10).

The TV GUI may appear overwhelmingly complex, but it's actually just a basic WPF GUI built using controls with modified appearances. This example demonstrates the use of *WPF bitmap effects* to apply simple visual effects to some of the GUI elements. In addition, it introduces *opacity masks*, which can be used to hide parts of an element. Other than these two new concepts, the TV application is created using only the WPF elements and concepts that you've already learned. Figure 17.11 presents the XAML markup and a screen capture of the application when it first loads. The video used in this case study is a public-domain NASA video entitled *Animation: To the Moon* and can be downloaded from the NASA website (www.nasa.gov/multimedia/hd/index.html).

Fig. 17.10 | GUI representing a television.

```
1    <!-- Fig. 17.11: TV.xaml -->
2    <!-- TV GUI showing the versatility of WPF customization. -->
3    <Window x:Class="TV.TVWindow"
4       xmlns="http://schemas.microsoft.com/winfx/2006/xaml/presentation"
5       xmlns:x="http://schemas.microsoft.com/winfx/2006/xaml"
6       Title="TV" Height="720" Width="720">
7       <Window.Resources>
8          <!-- define template for play, pause and stop buttons -->
9          <ControlTemplate x:Key="RadioButtonTemplate"
10            TargetType="RadioButton">
11            <Grid>
12               <!-- create a circular border -->
13               <Ellipse Width="25" Height="25" Fill="Silver" />
14
15               <!-- create an "illuminated" background -->
16               <Ellipse Name="backgroundEllipse" Width="22" Height="22">
17                  <Ellipse.Fill>
18                     <!-- enabled and unchecked state -->
19                     <RadialGradientBrush>
20                        <!-- red "light" -->
21                        <GradientStop Offset="0" Color="Red" />
22                        <GradientStop Offset="1.25" Color="Black" />
23                     </RadialGradientBrush>
24                  </Ellipse.Fill>
25               </Ellipse>
26
27               <!-- display button image -->
28               <ContentPresenter Content="{TemplateBinding Content}" />
29            </Grid>
30
31            <!-- change appearance when state changes -->
32            <ControlTemplate.Triggers>
33               <!-- disabled state -->
34               <Trigger Property="RadioButton.IsEnabled" Value="False">
35                  <Setter TargetName="backgroundEllipse" Property="Fill">
36                     <Setter.Value>
37                        <RadialGradientBrush>
38                           <!-- dim "light" -->
39                           <GradientStop Offset="0" Color="LightGray" />
40                           <GradientStop Offset="1.25" Color="Black" />
41                        </RadialGradientBrush>
42                     </Setter.Value>
43                  </Setter>
44               </Trigger>
45
46               <!-- checked state -->
47               <Trigger Property="RadioButton.IsChecked" Value="True">
48                  <Setter TargetName="backgroundEllipse" Property="Fill">
49                     <Setter.Value>
50                        <RadialGradientBrush>
51                           <!-- green "light" -->
52                           <GradientStop Offset="0" Color="LimeGreen" />
53                           <GradientStop Offset="1.25" Color="Black" />
```

Fig. 17.11 | TV GUI showing the versatility of WPF customization (XAML). (Part 1 of 5.)

```
54              </RadialGradientBrush>
55            </Setter.Value>
56          </Setter>
57        </Trigger>
58      </ControlTemplate.Triggers>
59    </ControlTemplate>
60  </Window.Resources>
61
62  <!-- define the GUI -->
63  <Canvas>
64    <!-- define the "TV" -->
65    <Border Canvas.Left="150" Height="370" Width="490"
66        Canvas.Top="20" Background="DimGray">
67      <Grid>
68        <Grid.RowDefinitions>
69          <RowDefinition />
70          <RowDefinition Height="Auto" />
71        </Grid.RowDefinitions>
72
73        <!-- define the screen -->
74        <Border Margin="0,20,0,10" Background="Black"
75            HorizontalAlignment="Center" VerticalAlignment="Center"
76            BorderThickness="2" BorderBrush="Silver" CornerRadius="2">
77          <MediaElement Height="300" Width="400"
78              Name="videoMediaElement" Source="Video/future_nasa.wmv"
79              LoadedBehavior="Manual" Stretch="Fill" />
80        </Border>
81
82        <!-- define the play, pause, and stop buttons -->
83        <StackPanel Grid.Row="1" HorizontalAlignment="Right"
84            Orientation="Horizontal">
85          <RadioButton Name="playRadioButton" IsEnabled="False"
86              Margin="0,0,5,15" Checked="playRadioButton_Checked"
87              Template="{StaticResource RadioButtonTemplate}">
88            <Image Height="20" Width="20"
89                Source="Images/play.png" Stretch="Uniform" />
90          </RadioButton>
91          <RadioButton Name="pauseRadioButton" IsEnabled="False"
92              Margin="0,0,5,15" Checked="pauseRadioButton_Checked"
93              Template="{StaticResource RadioButtonTemplate}">
94            <Image Height="20" Width="20"
95                Source="Images/pause.png" Stretch="Uniform" />
96          </RadioButton>
97          <RadioButton Name="stopRadioButton" IsEnabled="False"
98              Margin="0,0,15,15" Checked="stopRadioButton_Checked"
99              Template="{StaticResource RadioButtonTemplate}">
100           <Image Height="20" Width="20"
101               Source="Images/stop.png" Stretch="Uniform" />
102         </RadioButton>
103       </StackPanel>
104
```

Fig. 17.11 | TV GUI showing the versatility of WPF customization (XAML). (Part 2 of 5.)

```
105         <!-- define the power button -->
106         <CheckBox Name="powerCheckBox" Grid.Row="1" Width="25"
107            Height="25" HorizontalAlignment="Left"
108            Margin="15,0,0,15" Checked="powerCheckBox_Checked"
109            Unchecked="powerCheckBox_Unchecked">
110            <!-- set the template -->
111            <CheckBox.Template>
112               <ControlTemplate TargetType="CheckBox">
113                  <Grid>
114                     <!-- create a circular border -->
115                     <Ellipse Width="25" Height="25"
116                        Fill="Silver" />
117
118                     <!-- create an "illuminated" background -->
119                     <Ellipse Name="backgroundEllipse" Width="22"
120                        Height="22">
121                        <Ellipse.Fill>
122                           <!-- unchecked state -->
123                           <RadialGradientBrush>
124                              <!-- dim "light" -->
125                              <GradientStop Offset="0"
126                                 Color="LightGray" />
127                              <GradientStop Offset="1.25"
128                                 Color="Black" />
129                           </RadialGradientBrush>
130                        </Ellipse.Fill>
131                     </Ellipse>
132
133                     <!-- display power button image-->
134                     <Image Source="Images/power.png" Width="20"
135                        Height="20" />
136                  </Grid>
137
138                  <!-- change appearance when state changes -->
139                  <ControlTemplate.Triggers>
140                     <!-- checked state -->
141                     <Trigger Property="CheckBox.IsChecked"
142                        Value="True">
143                        <Setter TargetName="backgroundEllipse"
144                           Property="Fill">
145                           <Setter.Value>
146                              <!-- green "light" -->
147                              <RadialGradientBrush>
148                                 <GradientStop Offset="0"
149                                    Color="LimeGreen" />
150                                 <GradientStop Offset="1.25"
151                                    Color="Black" />
152                              </RadialGradientBrush>
153                           </Setter.Value>
154                        </Setter>
155                     </Trigger>
156                  </ControlTemplate.Triggers>
157               </ControlTemplate>
```

Fig. 17.11 | TV GUI showing the versatility of WPF customization (XAML). (Part 3 of 5.)

```
158                 </CheckBox.Template>
159               </CheckBox>
160           </Grid>
161
162           <!-- skew "TV" to give a 3D appearance -->
163           <Border.RenderTransform>
164               <SkewTransform AngleY="15" />
165           </Border.RenderTransform>
166
167           <!-- apply bitmap effects to "TV" -->
168           <Border.BitmapEffect>
169               <BitmapEffectGroup>
170                   <!-- make "TV" panel look "raised" -->
171                   <BevelBitmapEffect BevelWidth="10" />
172
173                   <!-- create a drop shadow -->
174                   <DropShadowBitmapEffect Color="Gray" ShadowDepth="15"
175                       Softness="1"/>
176               </BitmapEffectGroup>
177           </Border.BitmapEffect>
178       </Border>
179
180       <!-- define reflection -->
181       <Border Canvas.Left="185" Canvas.Top="410" Height="300"
182           Width="400">
183           <Rectangle Name="reflectionRectangle">
184               <Rectangle.Fill>
185                   <!-- create a reflection of the video -->
186                   <VisualBrush
187                       Visual="{Binding ElementName=videoMediaElement}">
188                       <VisualBrush.RelativeTransform>
189                           <ScaleTransform ScaleY="-1" CenterY="0.5" />
190                       </VisualBrush.RelativeTransform>
191                   </VisualBrush>
192               </Rectangle.Fill>
193
194               <!-- make reflection more transparent the further it gets
195                   from the screen -->
196               <Rectangle.OpacityMask>
197                   <LinearGradientBrush StartPoint="0,0" EndPoint="0,1">
198                       <GradientStop Color="Black" Offset="-0.25" />
199                       <GradientStop Color="Transparent" Offset="0.5" />
200                   </LinearGradientBrush>
201               </Rectangle.OpacityMask>
202           </Rectangle>
203
204           <!-- skew reflection to look 3D -->
205           <Border.RenderTransform>
206               <SkewTransform AngleY="15" AngleX="-45"/>
207           </Border.RenderTransform>
208       </Border>
209   </Canvas>
210 </Window>
```

Fig. 17.11 | TV GUI showing the versatility of WPF customization (XAML). (Part 4 of 5.)

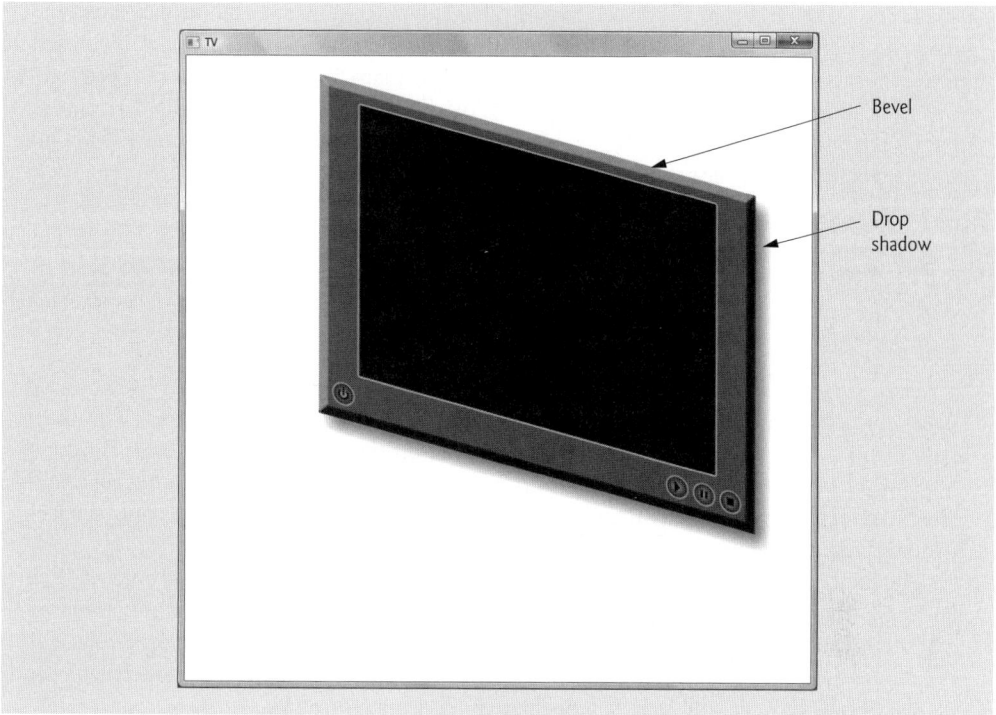

Fig. 17.11 | TV GUI showing the versatility of WPF customization (XAML). (Part 5 of 5.)

WPF Bitmap Effects

Five bitmap effects can be applied to any WPF graphic element. Figure 17.12 summarizes the effects of each. The TV GUI uses two of these effects—the ***BevelBitmapEffect*** and the ***DropShadowBitmapEffect***. As shown in Fig. 17.11, the BevelBitmapEffect appears to raise an element's edges to give it a three-dimensional look. The DropShadowBitmap-Effect gives an element a shadow as if a light were shining at it.

You can apply a single bitmap effect to any element by setting its ***BitmapEffect*** property. To apply more than one effect, you must define the effects in a ***BitmapEffectGroup***,

WPF bitmap effects	
BevelBitmapEffect	"Raises" the edges of an element.
BlurBitmapEffect	Blurs an element.
DropShadowBitmapEffect	Gives an element a shadow.
EmbossBitmapEffect	Uses changes in color to make an element appear raised out of the screen or lowered into the screen.
OuterGlowBitmapEffect	Surrounds an element with a small amount of color to make it look like it's glowing.

Fig. 17.12 | Summary of WPF bitmap effects.

then set it as the BitmapEffect property's value (lines 168–177). Each bitmap effect has its own set of unique properties. The ***BevelWidth*** property of a BevelBitmapEffect sets the size of its raised edge (line 171). A DropShadowBitmapEffect's ***ShadowDepth*** property sets the distance from the element to the shadow (line 174). The DropShadowBitmapEffect's ***Softness*** property defines how sharp the outline of the shadow is (line 175). This property takes values between 0 (sharp) and 1 (blurry), inclusive.

Performance Tip 17.1

The bitmap effects presented here should be used sparingly in your applications as they can degrade your machine's performance. The .NET Framework 3.5 Service Pack 1 includes new Blur and DropShadow bitmap effects are hardware accelerated.

Creating Buttons on the TV

The representations of TV buttons in this example are not Button controls. The play, pause, and stop buttons are RadioButtons, and the power button is a CheckBox. Lines 9–59 and 112–157 define the ControlTemplates used to render the RadioButtons and CheckBox, respectively. The two templates are defined similarly, so we discuss only the RadioButton template in detail.

In the background of each button are two circles, defined by Ellipse objects. The larger Ellipse acts as a border (line 13). The smaller Ellipse (lines 16–25) is colored by a RadialGradientBrush. The gradient is a light color in the center and becomes black as it extends farther out. This makes it appear to be a source of light. The content of the RadioButton is then applied on top of the two Ellipses (line 28).

The images used in this example are black play, pause and stop symbols on a transparent background. When the button is applied over the RadialGradientBrush, it appears to be illuminated. In its default state (enabled and unchecked), each playback button glows red. This represents the TV being on, with the playback option not active. When the application first loads, the TV is off, so the playback buttons are disabled. In this state, the background gradient is gray. When a playback option is active (i.e. RadioButton is checked), it glows green. The latter two deviations in appearance when the control changes states are defined by triggers (lines 32–58).

The power button, represented by a CheckBox, behaves similarly. When the TV is off (i.e., CheckBox is unchecked), the control is gray. When the user presses the power button and turns the TV on (i.e., CheckBox becomes checked), the control turns green. The power button is never disabled.

Creating the TV Interface

The TV panel is represented by a beveled Border with a gray background (lines 65–178). Recall that a Border is a ContentControl and can host only one direct child element. Thus, all of the Border's elements are contained in a Grid layout container. Nested within the TV panel is another Border with a black background containing a MediaElement object (lines 74–80). This portrays the TV's screen. The power button is placed in the bottom-left corner (106–159), and the playback buttons are nested in a StackPanel in the bottom-right corner (lines 83–103). The HorizontalAlignment properties set in lines 83 and 107 ensure that the buttons stay in the appropriate positions on the TV—on the left for the power button and on the right for the playback buttons.

Creating the Reflection of the TV Screen

Lines 181–208 define the GUI's video reflection using a Rectangle element nested in a Border. The Rectangle's Fill is a VisualBrush that is bound to the MediaElement (lines 186–191). To invert the video, we define a ScaleTransform and specify it as the RelativeTransform property, which is common to all brushes (lines 188–190). You can invert an element by setting the **ScaleX** or **ScaleY**—the amounts by which to scale the respective coordinates—property of a ScaleTransform to a negative number. In this example, we set ScaleY to -1 and CenterY to 0.5, inverting the VisualBrush vertically centered around the midpoint. The **CenterX** and **CenterY** properties specify the point from which the image expands or contracts. When you scale an image, most of the points move as a result of the altered size. When ScaleX and ScaleY are set to values other than 1, the center point is the only point that stays at its original location.

To achieve the semitransparent look, we applied an opacity mask to the Rectangle by setting the **OpacityMask** property (lines 196–201). The mask uses a LinearGradientBrush that changes from black near the top to transparent near the bottom. When the gradient is applied as an opacity mask, the gradient translates to a range from completely opaque, where it is black, to completely transparent. In this example, we set the Offset of the black GradientStop to -0.25, so that even the opaque edge of the mask is slightly transparent. We also set the Offset of the transparent GradientStop to 0.5, indicating that only the top half of the Rectangle (or bottom half of the movie) should display.

Skewing the GUI Components to Create a 3-D Look

When you draw a three-dimensional object on a two-dimensional plane, you are creating a 2-D projection of that 3-D environment. For example, to represent a simple box, you draw three adjoining parallelograms. Each face of the box is actually a flat, skewed rectangle rather than a 2-D view of a 3-D object. You can apply the same concept to create simple 3-D-looking GUIs without using a 3-D engine.

In this case study, we applied a SkewTransform to the TV representation, skewing it vertically by 15 degrees clockwise from the x-axis (lines 163–165). The reflection is then skewed vertically by 15 degrees clockwise from the x-axis and horizontally by 45 degrees clockwise from the y-axis (lines 205–207). Thus the GUI becomes a 2-D *orthographic projection* of a 3-D space with the axes 105, 120, and 135 degrees from each other, as shown in Fig. 17.13. Unlike a *perspective projection*, an orthographic projection does not show depth. Thus, the TV GUI does not present a realistic 3-D view, but rather a graphical representation. In Section 17.9, we present a 3-D object in perspective.

Examining the Code-Behind Class

Figure 17.14 presents the code-behind class that provides the functionality for the TV application. When the user turns on the TV (i.e. checks the powerCheckBox), the reflection is made visible and the playback options are enabled (lines 20–25). When the user turns off the TV, the MediaElement's Close method is called to close the media. In addition, the reflection is made invisible and the playback options are disabled (lines 36–44).

Whenever one of the RadioButtons that represent each playback option is checked, the MediaElement executes the corresponding task (lines 48–66). The methods that execute these tasks are built into the MediaElement class. Playback can be modified programmatically only if the LoadedBehavior is Manual (line 79 in Fig. 17.11).

Fig. 17.13 | The effect of skewing the TV application's GUI components.

```
1   // Fig. 17.14: TV.xaml.cs
2   // TV GUI showing the versatility of WPF customization (code-behind).
3   using System.Windows;
4
5   namespace TV
6   {
7      public partial class TVWindow : Window
8      {
9         // constructor
10        public TVWindow()
11        {
12           InitializeComponent();
13        } // end constructor
14
15        // turns "on" the TV
16        private void powerCheckBox_Checked( object sender,
17           RoutedEventArgs e )
18        {
19           // render the reflection visible
20           reflectionRectangle.Visibility = Visibility.Visible;
21
22           // enable play, pause, and stop buttons
23           playRadioButton.IsEnabled = true;
24           pauseRadioButton.IsEnabled = true;
25           stopRadioButton.IsEnabled = true;
26        } // end method powerCheckBox_Checked
```

Fig. 17.14 | TV GUI showing the versatility of WPF customization (code-behind). (Part 1 of 2.)

```
27
28          // turns "off" the TV
29          private void powerCheckBox_Unchecked( object sender,
30             RoutedEventArgs e )
31          {
32             // shut down the screen
33             videoMediaElement.Close();
34
35             // hide the reflection
36             reflectionRectangle.Visibility = Visibility.Hidden;
37
38             // disable the play, pause, and stop buttons
39             playRadioButton.IsChecked = false;
40             pauseRadioButton.IsChecked = false;
41             stopRadioButton.IsChecked = false;
42             playRadioButton.IsEnabled = false;
43             pauseRadioButton.IsEnabled = false;
44             stopRadioButton.IsEnabled = false;
45          } // end method powerCheckBox_Unchecked
46
47          // plays the video
48          private void playRadioButton_Checked( object sender,
49             RoutedEventArgs e )
50          {
51             videoMediaElement.Play();
52          } // end method playRadioButton_Checked
53
54          // pauses the video
55          private void pauseRadioButton_Checked( object sender,
56             RoutedEventArgs e )
57          {
58             videoMediaElement.Pause();
59          } // end method pauseRadioButton_Checked
60
61          // stops the video
62          private void stopRadioButton_Checked( object sender,
63             RoutedEventArgs e )
64          {
65             videoMediaElement.Stop();
66          } // end method stopRadioButton_Checked
67       } // end class TVWindow
68    } // end namespace TV
```

Fig. 17.14 | TV GUI showing the versatility of WPF customization (code-behind). (Part 2 of 2.)

17.8 Animations

An animation in WPF applications simply means a transition of a property from one value to another in a specified amount of time. Most graphic properties of a GUI element can be animated. The UsingAnimations example (Fig. 17.15) shows a video's size being animated. A MediaElement along with two input TextBoxes—one for Width and one for Height—and an animate Button are created in the GUI. When you click the animate Button, the video's Width and Height properties animate to the values typed in the corresponding TextBoxes by the user.

```
 1    <!-- Fig. 17.15: UsingAnimations.xaml -->
 2    <!-- Animating graphic elements with Storyboards. -->
 3    <Window x:Class="UsingAnimations.UsingAnimationsWindow"
 4       xmlns="http://schemas.microsoft.com/winfx/2006/xaml/presentation"
 5       xmlns:x="http://schemas.microsoft.com/winfx/2006/xaml"
 6       Title="UsingAnimations" Height="400" Width="500">
 7       <Grid>
 8          <Grid.ColumnDefinitions>
 9             <ColumnDefinition />
10             <ColumnDefinition Width="Auto" />
11          </Grid.ColumnDefinitions>
12
13          <!-- Animated video -->
14          <MediaElement Name="video" Height="100" Width="100" Stretch="Fill"
15             Source="newfractal.wmv" />
16
17          <StackPanel Grid.Column="1">
18             <!-- TextBox will contain the new Width for the video -->
19             <TextBlock Margin="5,0,0,0">Width:</TextBlock>
20             <TextBox Name="widthValue" Width="75" Margin="5">100</TextBox>
21
22             <!-- TextBox will contain the new Height for the video -->
23             <TextBlock Margin="5,0,0,0">Height:</TextBlock>
24             <TextBox Name="heightValue" Width="75" Margin="5">100</TextBox>
25
26             <!-- When clicked, rectangle animates to the input values -->
27             <Button Width="75" Margin="5">Animate
28                <Button.Triggers>
29                   <!-- When button is clicked -->
30                   <EventTrigger RoutedEvent="Button.Click">
31                      <BeginStoryboard>
32                         <Storyboard Storyboard.TargetName="video">
33                            <!-- Animates the Width -->
34                            <DoubleAnimation Duration="0:0:2"
35                               Storyboard.TargetProperty="Width"
36                               To="{Binding ElementName=widthValue,
37                               Path=Text}" />
38
39                            <!-- Animates the Height -->
40                            <DoubleAnimation Duration="0:0:2"
41                               Storyboard.TargetProperty="Height"
42                               To="{Binding ElementName=heightValue,
43                               Path=Text}" />
44                         </Storyboard>
45                      </BeginStoryboard>
46                   </EventTrigger>
47                </Button.Triggers>
48             </Button>
49          </StackPanel>
50       </Grid>
51    </Window>
```

Fig. 17.15 | Animating the width and height of a video. (Part 1 of 2.)

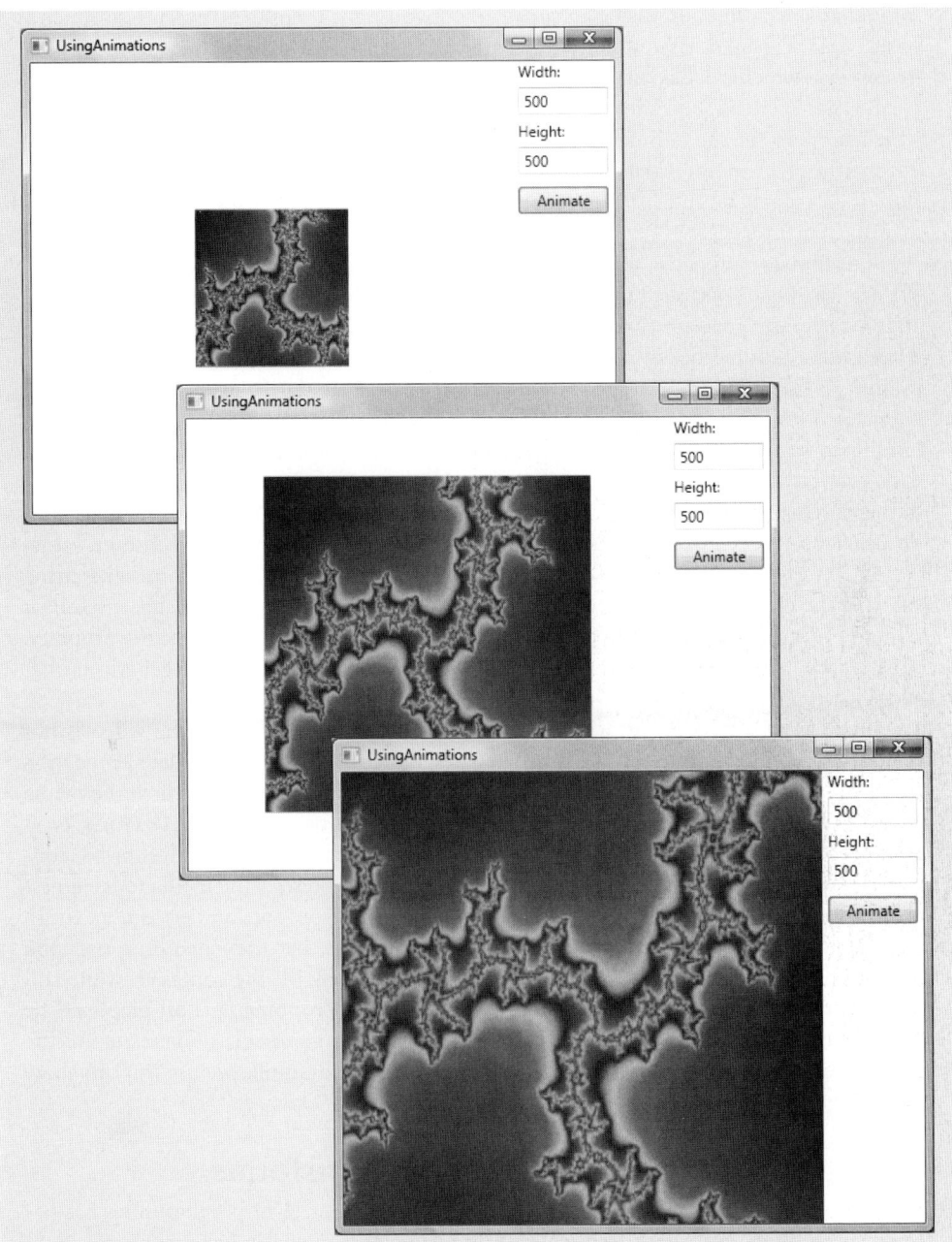

Fig. 17.15 | Animating the width and height of a video. (Part 2 of 2.)

As you can see, the animations create a smooth transition from the original `Height` and `Width` to the new values. Lines 32–44 define a **Storyboard** element nested in the `Button`'s click event `Trigger`. A `Storyboard` contains nested animation elements. When the `Storyboard` begins executing (line 31), all child animations execute. You can define more than one animation inside a `Storyboard` if you want them to all execute simultaneously. A `Storyboard` has two important attached properties—*TargetName* and *TargetProperty*—which can be defined in either the `Storyboard` or the animation element. The `TargetName` (line 32) specifies which element to animate. The `TargetProperty` specifies which property of the animated object to change. In this case, the `Width` (line 35) and `Height` (line 41) are the `TargetProperties`, because we're changing the size of the video. Both the `TargetName` and `TargetProperty` can be defined in the `Storyboard` or in the animation element itself.

To animate a property, you can use one of several animation classes available in WPF. We use the `DoubleAnimation` for the `Width` and `Height` properties—`PointAnimations` and `ColorAnimations` are two other commonly used animation classes. A *DoubleAnimation* animates properties of type `double`. The `Width` and `Height` animations are defined in lines 34–37 and 40–43, respectively. Lines 36–37 define the *To* property of the `Width` animation, which specifies the value of the `Width` at the end of the animation. We use data binding to set this to the value in the `widthValue` `TextBox`. The animation also has a *Duration* property that specifies how long it takes. Notice in line 34 that we set the `Duration` of the `Width` animation to 0:0:2, meaning that it takes 0 hours, 0 minutes and 2 seconds. You can specify fractions of a second by using a decimal point. Hour and minute values must be integers. Animations also have a *From* property which defines a constant starting value of the animated property. Animations also have a *By* property which is useful for numeric animations. This property specifies an amount by which to change the property. This can be used in place of the `From` and `To` properties for creating more generic animations.

Since we're animating its `Width` and `Height` properties separately, the video is not always displayed at its original width and height. In line 14, we define the `MediaElement`'s *Stretch* property. This is a property for graphic elements and determines how the media stretches to fit the size of its enclosure. This property can be set to *None*, *Uniform*, *UniformToFill* or *Fill*. None allows the media to stay at its native size regardless of the container's size. `Uniform`—the default value for this property—resizes the media to its largest possible size while maintaining its native *aspect ratio*—the proportion between its width and height. Keeping this ratio at its original value ensures that the video does not look "stretched." `UniformToFill` resizes the media to completely fill the container while still keeping its aspect ratio—as a result, it could be *cropped*. Cropping cuts off pieces of the media's edges to fit the shape of the container. `Fill` forces the media to be resized to the size of the container (aspect ratio is not preserved). In the example, we use `Fill` to show the changing size of the container.

17.9 (Optional) 3-D Objects and Transforms

WPF has substantial three-dimensional graphics capabilities. 3-D programming has become increasingly important, especially in the game and movie industries. Once a 3-D shape is created, it can be manipulated using 3-D transforms and animations. This section requires an understanding of 3-D analytical geometry. Readers without a strong background in these geometric concepts can still enjoy this section. We overview several advanced WPF 3-D capabilities.

The next example creates a rotating pyramid. The user can change the axis of rotation to see all sides of the object. The XAML code for this application is shown in Fig. 17.16.

```
 1   <!-- Fig. 17.16: Application3D.xaml -->
 2   <!-- Animating a 3-D object. -->
 3   <Window x:Class="Application3D.Application3DWindow"
 4      xmlns="http://schemas.microsoft.com/winfx/2006/xaml/presentation"
 5      xmlns:x="http://schemas.microsoft.com/winfx/2006/xaml"
 6      Title="Application3D" Height="300" Width="300">
 7      <Grid>
 8         <Grid.RowDefinitions>
 9            <RowDefinition />
10            <RowDefinition Height="Auto" />
11         </Grid.RowDefinitions>
12
13         <Grid.Triggers>
14            <!-- when the window has loaded, begin the animation -->
15            <EventTrigger RoutedEvent="Grid.Loaded">
16               <BeginStoryboard>
17                  <Storyboard Storyboard.TargetName="rotation"
18                     RepeatBehavior="Forever">
19
20                     <!-- rotate the object 360 degrees -->
21                     <DoubleAnimation Storyboard.TargetProperty="Angle"
22                        To="360" Duration="0:0:3" />
23                  </Storyboard>
24               </BeginStoryboard>
25            </EventTrigger>
26         </Grid.Triggers>
27
28         <!-- viewport window for viewing the 3D object -->
29         <Viewport3D>
30            <Viewport3D.Camera>
31               <!-- camera represents what user sees -->
32               <PerspectiveCamera x:Name="camera" Position="6,0,1"
33                  LookDirection="-1,0,0" UpDirection="0,0,1" />
34            </Viewport3D.Camera>
35
36            <!-- defines the 3-D content in the viewport -->
37            <ModelVisual3D>
38               <ModelVisual3D.Content>
39                  <Model3DGroup>
40
41                     <!-- two light sources to illuminate the objects-->
42                     <DirectionalLight Color="White" Direction="-1,0,0" />
43                     <DirectionalLight Color="White" Direction="0,0,-1" />
44
45                     <GeometryModel3D>
46                        <!-- rotate the geometry about the z-axis -->
47                        <GeometryModel3D.Transform>
48                           <RotateTransform3D>
49                              <RotateTransform3D.Rotation>
50                                 <AxisAngleRotation3D x:Name="rotation"
51                                    Angle="0" Axis="0,0,1" />
52                              </RotateTransform3D.Rotation>
53                           </RotateTransform3D>
```

Fig. 17.16 | Animating a 3-D object. (Part 1 of 2.)

```
54                      </GeometryModel3D.Transform>
55
56                      <!-- defines the pyramid -->
57                      <GeometryModel3D.Geometry>
58                          <MeshGeometry3D Positions="1,1,0 1,-1,0 -1,1,0
59                              -1,-1,0 0,0,2" TriangleIndices="0,4,1 2,4,0
60                              3,4,2 3,1,4 2,0,1 3,2,1"
61                              TextureCoordinates="0,0 1,0 0,1 1,1 0,0" />
62                      </GeometryModel3D.Geometry>
63
64                      <!-- defines the surface of the object -->
65                      <GeometryModel3D.Material>
66                          <DiffuseMaterial>
67                              <DiffuseMaterial.Brush>
68                                  <ImageBrush ImageSource="cover.png" />
69                              </DiffuseMaterial.Brush>
70                          </DiffuseMaterial>
71                      </GeometryModel3D.Material>
72                  </GeometryModel3D>
73              </Model3DGroup>
74          </ModelVisual3D.Content>
75        </ModelVisual3D>
76      </Viewport3D>
77
78      <!-- RadioButtons to change the axis of rotation -->
79      <GroupBox Grid.Row="1" Header="Axis of rotation">
80          <StackPanel Orientation="Horizontal"
81              HorizontalAlignment="Center">
82              <RadioButton Name="xRadio" Margin="5"
83                  Checked="xRadio_Checked">x-axis</RadioButton>
84              <RadioButton Name="yRadio" Margin="5"
85                  Checked="yRadio_Checked">y-axis</RadioButton>
86              <RadioButton Name="zRadio" Margin="5"
87                  Checked="zRadio_Checked">z-axis</RadioButton>
88          </StackPanel>
89      </GroupBox>
90    </Grid>
91 </Window>
```

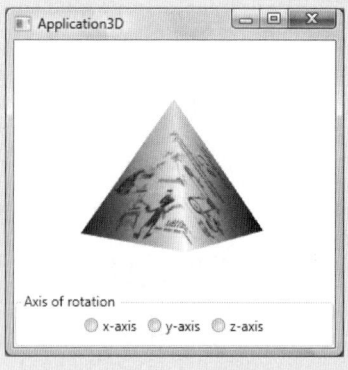

Fig. 17.16 | Animating a 3-D object. (Part 2 of 2.)

The first step in creating a 3-D object is to create a *Viewport3D* object (lines 29–76). The viewport represents the 2-D view the user sees when the application executes. This object defines a rendering surface for the content and contains content that represents the 3-D objects to render.

Create a *ModelVisual3D* object (lines 37–75) to define a 3-D object in a parent Viewport 3D element. ModelVisual3D's **Content** property contains the shapes you wish to define in your space. To add multiple objects to the Content, nest them in a *Model3DGroup*.

Creating the 3-D Object

3-D objects are modeled as sets of triangles, because you need a minimum of three points to make a flat surface. Every surface must be created or approximated with triangles. For this reason, shapes with flat surfaces (like cubes) are relatively simple to create, while curved surfaces (like spheres) are extremely complex. To make more complicated 3-D elements, you can use 3-D application-development tools such as Electric Rain's ZAM 3D (erain.com/products/zam3d/DefaultPDC.asp), which generates the XAML markup.

Use the *GeometryModel3D* element to define a shape (lines 45–72). This class creates and textures your 3-D model. First we discuss this object's *Geometry* property (lines 57–62). Use a *MeshGeometry3D* object (lines 58–61) to specify the exact shape of the object you want to create in the Geometry property. To create the object, you need two collections— one is a set of points to represent the vertices, and the other uses those vertices to specify the triangles that define the shape. These collections are assigned to the *Positions* and *TriangleIndices* properties of MeshGeometry3D, respectively. The points that we assigned to the Positions attribute (lines 58–59) are shown in a 3-D space in Fig. 17.17. The view in the figure does not directly correspond to the view of the pyramid shown in the application. In the screen capture of Fig. 17.16, the z-axis of the displayed space is pointing upward. The original view of the pyramid is what you would see if you were located at the positive x-axis, looking toward the origin. The view of the 3-D space can be changed using the Camera property of the Viewport3D, which is described later in this section.

The points are labeled in the order they are defined in the Positions collection. For instance, the text 0. (1,1,0) in the diagram refers to the first defined point, which has an index of 0 in the collection. Points in 3-D are defined with the notation "(x-coordinate, y-coordinate, z-coordinate)." With these points, we can define the triangles that we use to

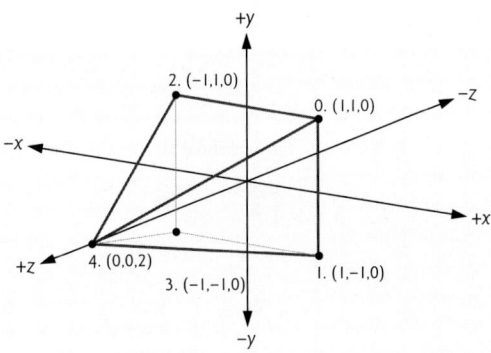

Fig. 17.17 | 3-D points making up a pyramid with a square base.

model the 3-D shape. The `TriangleIndices` property specifies the three corners of each individual triangle in the collection. Note that the first element in the collection defined in line 59 is (0,4,1). This indicates that we want to create a triangle with corners at points 0, 4 and 1 defined in the `Positions` collection. You can see this triangle in Fig. 17.17 (the frontmost triangle in the picture). We can define all the sides of the pyramid by defining the rest of the triangles. Note also that while the pyramid has five flat surfaces, six triangles are defined, because we need two triangles to create the pyramid's square base.

The order in which you define the triangle's corners dictates which side is considered the "front" versus the "back." Suppose you want to create a flat square in your viewport. This can be done using two triangles, as shown in Fig. 17.18. If you want the surface facing toward you to be the "front," you must define the corners in counterclockwise order. So, to define the lower-left triangle, you need to define the triangle as "0,1,3". The upper-right triangle needs to be "1,2,3". By default, the "front" of the triangle is drawn with your defined `Material` (described in the next section) while the "back" is made transparent. Therefore, the order in which you define the triangle's vertices is significant.

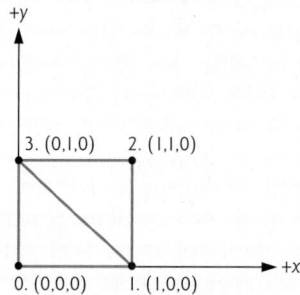

Fig. 17.18 | Defining two triangles to create a square in 3-D space.

Using a Brush on the Surface of a 3-D Object

By defining the *Material* property of the `GeometryModel3D`, we can specify what type of brush to use when painting each surface of the 3-D object. You can use several different classes to set the `Material` property. Each material gives a different "look" to the surface. Figure 17.19 describes the available materials.

3-D materials	
DiffuseMaterial	Creates a "flat" surface that reflects light evenly in all directions.
SpecularMaterial	Creates a glossy-looking material. It creates a surface similar to that of metal or glass.
EmissiveMaterial	Creates a glowing surface that generates its own light (this light does not act as a light source for other objects).
MaterialGroup	Allows you to combine multiple materials, which are layered in the order they are added to the group.

Fig. 17.19 | 3-D materials.

In the example, we use the ***DiffuseMaterial***. We can assign the brushes described in Section 17.5 to the material's ***Brush*** property to define how to paint the 3-D object's surface. We use an ImageBrush with cover.png as its source (line 68) to draw an image on the pyramid.

Notice in line 61 of Fig. 17.16 that we define the ***TextureCoordinates*** of the 3-D object. This property takes a PointCollection and determines how the Material is mapped onto the object's surfaces. If this property is not defined, the brush may not render correctly on the surface. The TextureCoordinates property defines which point on the image is mapped onto which vertex—an intersection of two or more edges—of the object. Notice we assigned the string "0,0 1,0 0,1 1,1 0,0" to the TextureCoordinates property. This string is translated into a PointCollection containing Points (0,0), (1,0), (0,1), (1,1) and (0,0). These points are logical points—as described in Section 17.5—on the image. The five points defined here correspond directly to the five points defined in the Positions collection. The image's top-left corner (0,0)—defined first in Texture-Coordinates—is mapped onto the first point in the Positions collection (1,1,0). The bottom-right corner (1,1) of the image—defined fourth in TextureCoordinates—is mapped onto the fourth point in the Positions collection (-1,-1,0). The other two corners are also mapped accordingly to the second and third points. This makes the image fully appear on the bottom surface of the pyramid, since that face is rectangular.

If a point is shared by two adjacent sides, you may not want to map the same point of the image to that particular vertex for the two different sides. To have complete control over how the brush is mapped onto the surfaces of the object, you may need to define a vertex more than once in the Positions collection.

Defining a Camera and a Light Source

The ***Camera*** property of Viewport3D (lines 30–34) defines a virtual camera for viewing the defined 3-D space. In this example, we use a ***PerspectiveCamera*** to define what the user sees. We must set the camera's ***Position***, ***LookDirection*** and ***UpDirection*** (lines 32–33). The Position property requires a ***Point3D*** object which defines a 3-D point, while the LookDirection and UpDirection require ***Vector3D*** objects which define vectors in 3-D space. 3-D vectors are defined by an *x*-, a *y*- and a *z*-component (defined in that order in the XAML markup). For instance, the vector applied to the UpDirection is written as "0,0,1" (line 33) and represents a vector with an *x*- and *y*-component of 0 and a *z*-component of 1. This vector points in the positive direction of the *z*-axis.

The Position defines the location of the camera in the 3-D space. The LookDirection defines the direction in which the camera is pointed. The UpDirection defines the orientation of the camera by specifying the upward direction in the viewport. Note that if the UpDirection in this example were set to "0,0,-1", then the pyramid would appear "upside-down" in the viewport.

Unlike 2-D objects, a 3-D object needs a virtual light source so the camera can actually "see" the 3-D scene. In the Model3DGroup, which groups all of the ModelVisual3D's objects, we define two ***DirectionalLight*** objects (lines 42–43) to illuminate the pyramid. This element creates uniform rays of light pointing in the direction specified by the ***Direction*** property. This property receives a vector that points in the direction of the light. You can also define the ***Color*** property to change the light's color.

Animating the 3-D Object

As with 2-D animations, a set of 3-D animations can be applied to 3-D objects. Lines 47–54 define the **Transform** property of the GeometryModel3D element that models a pyramid. We use the **RotateTransform3D** class to implement a rotation of the pyramid. We then use the **AxisAngleRotation3D** to strictly define the transform's rotation (lines 50–51). The **Angle** and **Axis** properties can be modified to customize the transform. The Angle is initially set to 0 (i.e., not rotated) and the Axis of rotation to the *z*-axis, represented by the vector defined as "0,0,1" (line 51).

To animate the rotation, we created a Storyboard that modifies the Angle property of the AxisAngleRotation3D (lines 17–23). Notice we set the **RepeatBehavior** of the Storyboard to **Forever** (line 18), indicating that the animation repeats continuously while the window is open. This Storyboard is set to begin when the page loads (line 15).

The application contains RadioButtons at the bottom of the window that change the axis of rotation. The code-behind for this functionality appears in Fig. 17.20.

With each RadioButton's Checked event, we change the Axis of rotation to the appropriate Vector3D. We also change the Position of the PerspectiveCamera to give a better view of the rotating object. For instance, when xButton is clicked, we change the axis of rotation to the *x*-axis (line 19) and the camera's position to give a better view (line 20).

```
1  // Fig. 17.20: Application3D.xaml.cs
2  // Changing the axis of rotation for a 3-D animation.
3  using System.Windows;
4  using System.Windows.Media.Media3D;
5
6  namespace Application3D
7  {
8     public partial class Application3DWindow : Window
9     {
10        // constructor
11        public Application3DWindow()
12        {
13           InitializeComponent();
14        } // end constructor
15
16        // when user selects xRadio, set axis of rotation
17        private void xRadio_Checked( object sender, RoutedEventArgs e )
18        {
19           rotation.Axis = new Vector3D( 1, 0, 0 ); // set rotation axis
20           camera.Position = new Point3D( 6, 0, 0 ); // set camera position
21        } // end method xRadio_Checked
22
23        // when user selects yRadio, set axis of rotation
24        private void yRadio_Checked( object sender, RoutedEventArgs e )
25        {
26           rotation.Axis = new Vector3D( 0, 1, 0 ); // set rotation axis
27           camera.Position = new Point3D( 6, 0, 0 ); // set camera position
28        } // end method yRadio_Checked
29
```

Fig. 17.20 | Changing the axis of rotation for a 3-D animation. (Part 1 of 2.)

```
30        // when user selects zRadio, set axis of rotation
31        private void zRadio_Checked( object sender, RoutedEventArgs e )
32        {
33           rotation.Axis = new Vector3D( 0, 0, 1 ); // set rotation axis
34           camera.Position = new Point3D( 6, 0, 1 ); // set camera position
35        } // end method zRadio_Checked
36     } // end class Application3DWindow
37  } // end namespace Application3D
```

Fig. 17.20 | Changing the axis of rotation for a 3-D animation. (Part 2 of 2.)

17.10 Wrap-Up

In this chapter you learned how to manipulate graphic elements in your WPF application. We introduced how to control fonts using the properties of TextBlocks. You learned to change the TextBlock's FontFamily, FontSize, FontWeight and FontStyle in XAML. We also demonstrated the TextDecorations Underline, Overline, Baseline and Strikethrough.

Next, you learned how to create basic shapes such as Lines, Rectangles and Ellipses. You set the Fill and Stroke of these shapes. We then discussed an application that created a Polyline and two Polygons. These shapes allow you to create multisided objects using a set of Points in a PointCollection.

You learned that there are several types of brushes for customizing an object's Fill. We demonstrated the SolidColorBrush, the ImageBrush, the VisualBrush and the LinearGradientBrush. Though the VisualBrush was used only with a MediaElement, this brush has a wide range of capabilities.

We explained how to apply transforms to an object to reposition or reorient any graphic element. You used transforms such as the TranslateTransform, the Rotate-Transform, the SkewTransform and the ScaleTransform to manipulate various GUI elements.

The television GUI application used ControlTemplates and BitmapEffects to create a completely customized 3-D-looking television set. You saw how to use Control-Templates to customize the look of RadioButtons and CheckBoxes. The application also included an opacity mask, which can be used on any shape to define the opaque or transparent regions of the GUI element. Opacity masks are particularly useful with images and video where you cannot change the Fill to directly control transparency.

We showed how animations can be applied to transition properties from one value to another. Common 2-D animation types include DoubleAnimations, PointAnimations and ColorAnimations.

Finally, you learned how to create a 3-D space using a Viewport3D object. You saw how to model 3-D objects as sets of triangles using the MeshGeometry3D element. The ImageBrush, which was previously applied to a 2-D object, was used to display a book-cover image on the surface of the 3-D pyramid using GeometryModel3D's mapping techniques. We discussed how to include lighting and camera objects in your Viewport3D to modify the view shown in the application. We showed how similar transforms and animations are in 2-D and 3-D. In Chapter 18, we introduce string and character processing.

18

Strings, Characters and Regular Expressions

The chief defect of Henry King
Was chewing little bits of string.
—Hilaire Belloc

Vigorous writing is concise. A
sentence should contain no
unnecessary words, a paragraph
no unnecessary sentences.
—William Strunk, Jr.

I have made this letter longer
than usual, because I lack the
time to make it short.
—Blaise Pascal

The difference between the
almost-right word and the right
word is really a large matter—it's
the difference between the
lightning bug and the lightning.
—Mark Twain

Mum's the word.
—Miguel de Cervantes

OBJECTIVES

In this chapter you'll learn:

- To create and manipulate immutable character-string objects of class `string`.

- To create and manipulate mutable character-string objects of class `StringBuilder`.

- To manipulate character objects of struct `Char`.

- To use regular-expression classes `Regex` and `Match`.

- To iterate through matches to a regular expression.

- To use character classes to match any character from a set of characters.

- To use quantifiers to match a pattern multiple times.

- To search for complex patterns in text using regular expressions.

- To validate data using regular expressions and LINQ.

- To modify `string`s using regular expressions and class Regex.

Outline

18.1 Introduction

18.2 Fundamentals of Characters and Strings

18.3 `string` Constructors

18.4 `string` Indexer, `Length` Property and `CopyTo` Method

18.5 Comparing `strings`

18.6 Locating Characters and Substrings in `strings`

18.7 Extracting Substrings from `strings`

18.8 Concatenating `strings`

18.9 Miscellaneous `string` Methods

18.10 Class `StringBuilder`

18.11 `Length` and `Capacity` Properties, `EnsureCapacity` Method and Indexer of Class `StringBuilder`

18.12 Append and `AppendFormat` Methods of Class `StringBuilder`

18.13 `Insert`, `Remove` and `Replace` Methods of Class `StringBuilder`

18.14 Char Methods

18.15 Card Shuffling and Dealing Simulation

18.16 Introduction to Regular-Expression Processing

    18.16.1 Simple Regular Expressions and Class **Regex**

    18.16.2 Complex Regular Expressions

    18.16.3 Validating User Input with Regular Expressions and LINQ

    18.16.4 Regex Methods `Replace` and `Split`

18.17 Wrap-Up

18.1 Introduction

This chapter introduces the .NET Framework Class Library's string- and character-processing capabilities and demonstrates how to use regular expressions to search for patterns in text. The techniques it presents can be employed in text editors, word processors, page-layout software, computerized typesetting systems and other kinds of text-processing software. Previous chapters presented some basic string-processing capabilities. Now we discuss in detail the text-processing capabilities of class `string` and type `char` from the System namespace and class `StringBuilder` from the System.Text namespace.

We begin with an overview of the fundamentals of characters and strings in which we discuss character constants and string literals. We then provide examples of class `string`'s many constructors and methods. The examples demonstrate how to determine the length of strings, copy strings, access individual characters in strings, search strings, obtain substrings from larger strings, compare strings, concatenate strings, replace characters in strings and convert strings to uppercase or lowercase letters.

Next, we introduce class `StringBuilder`, which is used to build strings dynamically. We demonstrate `StringBuilder` capabilities for determining and specifying the size of a `StringBuilder`, as well as appending, inserting, removing and replacing characters in a `StringBuilder` object. We then introduce the character-testing methods of struct `Char` letter, an uppercase letter, a punctuation mark or a symbol other than a punctuation mark. Such methods are useful for validating individual characters in user input. In addition, type Char provides methods for converting a character to uppercase or lowercase.

The chapter concludes with a discussion of regular expressions. We discuss classes Regex and Match from the System.Text.RegularExpressions namespace as well as the symbols that are used to form regular expressions. We then demonstrate how to find patterns in a string, match entire strings to patterns, replace characters in a string that match a pattern and split strings at delimiters specified as a pattern in a regular expression.

18.2 Fundamentals of Characters and Strings

Characters are the fundamental building blocks of C# source code. Every program is composed of characters that, when grouped together meaningfully, create a sequence that the compiler interprets as instructions describing how to accomplish a task. In addition to normal characters, a program also can contain *character constants*. A character constant is a character that is represented as an integer value, called a *character code*. For example, the integer value 122 corresponds to the character constant 'z'. The integer value 10 corresponds to the newline character '\n'. Character constants are established according to the *Unicode character set*, an international character set that contains many more symbols and letters than does the ASCII character set (listed in Appendix F). To learn more about Unicode, see Appendix G.

A string is a series of characters treated as a unit. These characters can be uppercase letters, lowercase letters, digits and various *special characters*: +, -, *, /, $ and others. A string is an object of class string in the System namespace.[1] We write *string literals*, also called *string constants*, as sequences of characters in double quotation marks, as follows:

```
"John Q. Doe"
"9999 Main Street"
"Waltham, Massachusetts"
"(201) 555-1212"
```

A declaration can assign a string literal to a string reference. The declaration

```
string color = "blue";
```

initializes string reference color to refer to the string literal object "blue".

Performance Tip 18.1

If there are multiple occurrences of the same string literal object in an application, a single copy of it will be referenced from each location in the program that uses that string literal. It is possible to share the object in this manner, because string literal objects are implicitly constant. Such sharing conserves memory.

On occasion, a string will contain multiple backslash characters (this often occurs in the name of a file). To avoid excessive backslash characters, it is possible to exclude escape sequences and interpret all the characters in a string literally, using the @ character. Backslashes within the double quotation marks following the @ character are not considered

---

1. C# provides the string keyword as an alias for class String. In this book, we use the term string.

escape sequences, but rather regular backslash characters. Often this simplifies programming and makes the code easier to read. For example, consider the string "C:\MyFolder\MySubFolder\MyFile.txt" with the following assignment:

```
string file = "C:\\MyFolder\\MySubFolder\\MyFile.txt";
```

Using the verbatim string syntax, the assignment can be altered to

```
string file = @"C:\MyFolder\MySubFolder\MyFile.txt";
```

This approach also has the advantage of allowing strings to span multiple lines by preserving all newlines, spaces and tabs.

18.3 string Constructors

Class string provides eight constructors for initializing strings in various ways. Figure 18.1 demonstrates the use of three of the constructors.

Lines 10–11 allocate the char array characterArray, which contains nine characters. Lines 12–16 declare the strings originalString, string1, string2, string3 and

```
1   // Fig. 18.1: StringConstructor.cs
2   // Demonstrating string class constructors.
3   using System;
4
5   class StringConstructor
6   {
7      public static void Main( string[] args )
8      {
9         // string initialization
10        char[] characterArray =
11           { 'b', 'i', 'r', 't', 'h', ' ', 'd', 'a', 'y' };
12        string originalString = "Welcome to C# programming!";
13        string string1 = originalString;
14        string string2 = new string( characterArray );
15        string string3 = new string( characterArray, 6, 3 );
16        string string4 = new string( 'C', 5 );
17
18        Console.WriteLine( "string1 = " + "\"" + string1 + "\"\n" +
19           "string2 = " + "\"" + string2 + "\"\n" +
20           "string3 = " + "\"" + string3 + "\"\n" +
21           "string4 = " + "\"" + string4 + "\"\n" );
22     } // end Main
23  } // end class StringConstructor
```

```
string1 = "Welcome to C# programming!"
string2 = "birth day"
string3 = "day"
string4 = "CCCCC"
```

Fig. 18.1 | string constructors.

string4. Line 12 assigns string literal "Welcome to C# programming!" to string reference originalString. Line 13 sets string1 to reference the same string literal.

Line 14 assigns to string2 a new string, using the string constructor that takes a character array as an argument. The new string contains a copy of the characters in array characterArray.

Software Engineering Observation 18.1

In most cases, it is not necessary to make a copy of an existing string. All strings are immutable—their character contents cannot be changed after they are created. Also, if there are one or more references to a string (or any object for that matter), the object cannot be reclaimed by the garbage collector.

Line 15 assigns to string3 a new string, using the string constructor that takes a char array and two int arguments. The second argument specifies the starting index position (the *offset*) from which characters in the array are to be copied. The third argument specifies the number of characters (the *count*) to be copied from the specified starting position in the array. The new string contains a copy of the specified characters in the array. If the specified offset or count indicates that the program should access an element outside the bounds of the character array, an ArgumentOutOfRangeException is thrown.

Line 16 assigns to string4 a new string, using the string constructor that takes as arguments a character and an int specifying the number of times to repeat that character in the string.

18.4 string Indexer, Length Property and CopyTo Method

The application in Fig. 18.2 presents the string indexer, which facilitates the retrieval of any character in the string, and the string property Length, which returns the length of the string. The string method CopyTo copies a specified number of characters from a string into a char array.

```
1   // Fig. 18.2: StringMethods.cs
2   // Using the indexer, property Length and method CopyTo
3   // of class string.
4   using System;
5
6   class StringMethods
7   {
8      public static void Main( string[] args )
9      {
10        string string1 = "hello there";
11        char[] characterArray = new char[ 5 ];
12
13        // output string1
14        Console.WriteLine( "string1: \"" + string1 + "\"" );
15
16        // test Length property
17        Console.WriteLine( "Length of string1: " + string1.Length );
```

Fig. 18.2 | string indexer, Length property and CopyTo method. (Part 1 of 2.)

```
18
19          // loop through characters in string1 and display reversed
20          Console.Write( "The string reversed is: " );
21
22          for ( int i = string1.Length - 1; i >= 0; i-- )
23             Console.Write( string1[ i ] );
24
25          // copy characters from string1 into characterArray
26          string1.CopyTo( 0, characterArray, 0, characterArray.Length );
27          Console.Write( "\nThe character array is: " );
28
29          for ( int i = 0; i < characterArray.Length; i++ )
30             Console.Write( characterArray[ i ] );
31
32          Console.WriteLine( "\n" );
33       } // end Main
34    } // end class StringMethods
```

```
string1: "hello there"
Length of string1: 11
The string reversed is: ereht olleh
The character array is: hello
```

Fig. 18.2 | string indexer, Length property and CopyTo method. (Part 2 of 2.)

This application determines the length of a string, displays its characters in reverse order and copies a series of characters from the string to a character array. Line 17 uses string property Length to determine the number of characters in string1. Like arrays, strings always know their own size.

Lines 22–23 write the characters of string1 in reverse order using the string indexer. The string indexer treats a string as an array of chars and returns each character at a specific position in the string. The indexer receives an integer argument as the *position number* and returns the character at that position. As with arrays, the first element of a string is considered to be at position 0.

Common Programming Error 18.1

Attempting to access a character that is outside a string's bounds (i.e., an index less than 0 or an index greater than or equal to the string's length) results in an IndexOutOfRangeException.

Line 26 uses string method CopyTo to copy the characters of string1 into a character array (characterArray). The first argument given to method CopyTo is the index from which the method begins copying characters in the string. The second argument is the character array into which the characters are copied. The third argument is the index specifying the starting location at which the method begins placing the copied characters into the character array. The last argument is the number of characters that the method will copy from the string. Lines 29–30 output the char array contents one character at a time.

18.5 Comparing strings

The next two examples demonstrate various methods for comparing strings. To understand how one string can be "greater than" or "less than" another, consider the process of alphabetizing a series of last names. You would, no doubt, place "Jones" before "Smith", because the first letter of "Jones" comes before the first letter of "Smith" in the alphabet. The alphabet is more than just a set of 26 letters—it is an ordered list of characters in which each letter occurs in a specific position. For example, Z is more than just a letter of the alphabet; it is specifically the twenty-sixth letter of the alphabet.

Computers can order characters alphabetically because they are represented internally as Unicode numeric codes. When comparing two strings, C# simply compares the numeric codes of the characters in the strings.

Class string provides several ways to compare strings. The application in Fig. 18.3 demonstrates the use of method Equals, method CompareTo and the equality operator (==).

The condition in the if statement (line 21) uses string method Equals to compare string1 and literal string "hello" to determine whether they are equal. Method Equals (inherited from object and overridden in string) tests any two objects for equality (i.e., checks whether the objects contain identical contents). The method returns true if the objects are equal and false otherwise. In this instance, the preceding condition returns true, because string1 references string literal object "hello". Method Equals uses a *lexicographical comparison*—comparing the integer Unicode values that represent each character in each string. A comparison of the string "hello" with the string "HELLO" would return false, because the numeric representations of lowercase letters are different from the those of corresponding uppercase letters.

```
1   // Fig. 18.3: StringCompare.cs
2   // Comparing strings
3   using System;
4
5   class StringCompare
6   {
7      public static void Main( string[] args )
8      {
9         string string1 = "hello";
10        string string2 = "good bye";
11        string string3 = "Happy Birthday";
12        string string4 = "happy birthday";
13
14        // output values of four strings
15        Console.WriteLine( "string1 = \"" + string1 + "\"" +
16           "\nstring2 = \"" + string2 + "\"" +
17           "\nstring3 = \"" + string3 + "\"" +
18           "\nstring4 = \"" + string4 + "\"\n" );
19
20        // test for equality using Equals method
21        if ( string1.Equals( "hello" ) )
22           Console.WriteLine( "string1 equals \"hello\"" );
23        else
24           Console.WriteLine( "string1 does not equal \"hello\"" );
25
26        // test for equality with ==
27        if ( string1 == "hello" )
28           Console.WriteLine( "string1 equals \"hello\"" );
```

Fig. 18.3 | string test to determine equality. (Part 1 of 2.)

```
29            else
30               Console.WriteLine( "string1 does not equal \"hello\"" );
31
32            // test for equality comparing case
33            if ( string.Equals( string3, string4 ) ) // static method
34               Console.WriteLine( "string3 equals string4" );
35            else
36               Console.WriteLine( "string3 does not equal string4" );
37
38            // test CompareTo
39            Console.WriteLine( "\nstring1.CompareTo( string2 ) is " +
40               string1.CompareTo( string2 ) + "\n" +
41               "string2.CompareTo( string1 ) is " +
42               string2.CompareTo( string1 ) + "\n" +
43               "string1.CompareTo( string1 ) is " +
44               string1.CompareTo( string1 ) + "\n" +
45               "string3.CompareTo( string4 ) is " +
46               string3.CompareTo( string4 ) + "\n" +
47               "string4.CompareTo( string3 ) is " +
48               string4.CompareTo( string3 ) + "\n\n" );
49         } // end Main
50      } // end class StringCompare
```

```
string1 = "hello"
string2 = "good bye"
string3 = "Happy Birthday"
string4 = "happy birthday"

string1 equals "hello"
string1 equals "hello"
string3 does not equal string4

string1.CompareTo( string2 ) is 1
string2.CompareTo( string1 ) is -1
string1.CompareTo( string1 ) is 0
string3.CompareTo( string4 ) is 1
string4.CompareTo( string3 ) is -1
```

Fig. 18.3 | string test to determine equality. (Part 2 of 2.)

The condition in line 27 uses the overloaded equality operator (==) to compare string string1 with the literal string "hello" for equality. In C#, the equality operator also uses a lexicographical comparison to compare two strings. Thus, the condition in the if statement evaluates to true, because the values of string1 and "hello" are equal.

We present the test for string equality between string3 and string4 (line 33) to illustrate that comparisons are indeed case sensitive. Here, static method Equals is used to compare the values of two strings. "Happy Birthday" does not equal "happy birthday", so the condition of the if statement fails, and the message "string3 does not equal string4" is output (line 36).

Lines 40–48 use string method CompareTo to compare strings. Method CompareTo returns 0 if the strings are equal, a negative value if the string that invokes CompareTo is less than the string that is passed as an argument and a positive value if the string that invokes CompareTo is greater than the string that is passed as an argument. Method CompareTo uses a lexicographical comparison.

Notice that CompareTo considers string3 to be larger than string4. The only difference between these two strings is that string3 contains two uppercase letters in positions where string4 contains lowercase letters.

Figure 18.4 shows how to test whether a string instance begins or ends with a given string. Method StartsWith determines whether a string instance starts with the string text passed to it as an argument. Method EndsWith determines whether a string instance ends with the string text passed to it as an argument. Class stringStartEnd's Main method defines an array of strings (called strings), which contains "started", "starting", "ended" and "ending". The remainder of method Main tests the elements of the array to determine whether they start or end with a particular set of characters.

Line 13 uses method StartsWith, which takes a string argument. The condition in the if statement determines whether the string at index i of the array starts with the characters "st". If so, the method returns true, and strings[i] is output along with a message.

```csharp
1   // Fig. 18.4: StringStartEnd.cs
2   // Demonstrating StartsWith and EndsWith methods.
3   using System;
4
5   class StringStartEnd
6   {
7      public static void Main( string[] args )
8      {
9         string[] strings = { "started", "starting", "ended", "ending" };
10
11         // test every string to see if it starts with "st"
12         for ( int i = 0; i < strings.Length; i++ )
13            if ( strings[ i ].StartsWith( "st" ) )
14               Console.WriteLine( "\"" + strings[ i ] + "\"" +
15                  " starts with \"st\"" );
16
17         Console.WriteLine();
18
19         // test every string to see if it ends with "ed"
20         for ( int i = 0; i < strings.Length; i++ )
21            if ( strings[ i ].EndsWith( "ed" ) )
22               Console.WriteLine( "\"" + strings[ i ] + "\"" +
23                  " ends with \"ed\"" );
24
25         Console.WriteLine();
26      } // end Main
27   } // end class StringStartEnd
```

```
"started" starts with "st"
"starting" starts with "st"

"started" ends with "ed"
"ended" ends with "ed"
```

Fig. 18.4 | StartsWith and EndsWith methods.

Line 21 uses method EndsWith, which also takes a string argument. The condition in the if statement determines whether the string at index i of the array ends with the characters "ed". If so, the method returns true, and strings[i] is displayed along with a message.

18.6 Locating Characters and Substrings in strings

In many applications, it is necessary to search for a character or set of characters in a string. For example, a programmer creating a word processor would want to provide capabilities for searching through documents. The application in Fig. 18.5 demonstrates some of the many versions of string methods IndexOf, IndexOfAny, LastIndexOf and LastIndexOfAny, which search for a specified character or substring in a string. We perform all searches in this example on the string letters (initialized with "abcdefghijklmabcdefghijklm") located in method Main of class StringIndexMethods.

```csharp
1   // Fig. 18.5: StringIndexMethods.cs
2   // Using string-searching methods.
3   using System;
4
5   class StringIndexMethods
6   {
7      public static void Main( string[] args )
8      {
9         string letters = "abcdefghijklmabcdefghijklm";
10        char[] searchLetters = { 'c', 'a', '$' };
11
12        // test IndexOf to locate a character in a string
13        Console.WriteLine( "First 'c' is located at index " +
14           letters.IndexOf( 'c' ) );
15        Console.WriteLine( "First 'a' starting at 1 is located at index " +
16           letters.IndexOf( 'a', 1 ) );
17        Console.WriteLine( "First '$' in the 5 positions starting at 3 " +
18           "is located at index " + letters.IndexOf( '$', 3, 5 ) );
19
20        // test LastIndexOf to find a character in a string
21        Console.WriteLine( "\nLast 'c' is located at index " +
22           letters.LastIndexOf( 'c' ) );
23        Console.WriteLine( "Last 'a' up to position 25 is located at " +
24           "index " + letters.LastIndexOf( 'a', 25 ) );
25        Console.WriteLine( "Last '$' in the 5 positions starting at 15 " +
26           "is located at index " + letters.LastIndexOf( '$', 15, 5 ) );
27
28        // test IndexOf to locate a substring in a string
29        Console.WriteLine( "\nFirst \"def\" is located at index " +
30           letters.IndexOf( "def" ) );
31        Console.WriteLine( "First \"def\" starting at 7 is located at " +
32           "index " + letters.IndexOf( "def", 7 ) );
33        Console.WriteLine( "First \"hello\" in the 15 positions " +
34           "starting at 5 is located at index " +
35           letters.IndexOf( "hello", 5, 15 ) );
```

Fig. 18.5 | Searching for characters and substrings in strings. (Part 1 of 2.)

```
36
37          // test LastIndexOf to find a substring in a string
38          Console.WriteLine( "\nLast \"def\" is located at index " +
39             letters.LastIndexOf( "def" ) );
40          Console.WriteLine( "Last \"def\" up to position 25 is located " +
41             "at index " + letters.LastIndexOf( "def", 25 ) );
42          Console.WriteLine( "Last \"hello\" in the 15 positions " +
43             "ending at 20 is located at index " +
44             letters.LastIndexOf( "hello", 20, 15 ) );
45
46          // test IndexOfAny to find first occurrence of character in array
47          Console.WriteLine( "\nFirst 'c', 'a' or '$' is " +
48             "located at index " + letters.IndexOfAny( searchLetters ) );
49          Console.WriteLine("First 'c', 'a' or '$' starting at 7 is " +
50             "located at index " + letters.IndexOfAny( searchLetters, 7 ) );
51          Console.WriteLine( "First 'c', 'a' or '$' in the 5 positions " +
52             "starting at 7 is located at index " +
53             letters.IndexOfAny( searchLetters, 7, 5 ) );
54
55          // test LastIndexOfAny to find last occurrence of character
56          // in array
57          Console.WriteLine( "\nLast 'c', 'a' or '$' is " +
58             "located at index " + letters.LastIndexOfAny( searchLetters ) );
59          Console.WriteLine( "Last 'c', 'a' or '$' up to position 1 is " +
60             "located at index " +
61             letters.LastIndexOfAny( searchLetters, 1 ) );
62          Console.WriteLine( "Last 'c', 'a' or '$' in the 5 positions " +
63             "ending at 25 is located at index " +
64             letters.LastIndexOfAny( searchLetters, 25, 5 ) );
65       } // end Main
66    } // end class StringIndexMethods
```

```
First 'c' is located at index 2
First 'a' starting at 1 is located at index 13
First '$' in the 5 positions starting at 3 is located at index -1

Last 'c' is located at index 15
Last 'a' up to position 25 is located at index 13
Last '$' in the 5 positions starting at 15 is located at index -1

First "def" is located at index 3
First "def" starting at 7 is located at index 16
First "hello" in the 15 positions starting at 5 is located at index -1

Last "def" is located at index 16
Last "def" up to position 25 is located at index 16
Last "hello" in the 15 positions ending at 20 is located at index -1

First 'c', 'a' or '$' is located at index 0
First 'c', 'a' or '$' starting at 7 is located at index 13
First 'c', 'a' or '$' in the 5 positions starting at 7 is located at index -1

Last 'c', 'a' or '$' is located at index 15
Last 'c', 'a' or '$' up to position 1 is located at index 0
Last 'c', 'a' or '$' in the 5 positions ending at 25 is located at index -1
```

Fig. 18.5 | Searching for characters and substrings in strings. (Part 2 of 2.)

Lines 14, 16 and 18 use method IndexOf to locate the first occurrence of a character or substring in a string. If it finds a character, IndexOf returns the index of the specified character in the string; otherwise, IndexOf returns -1. The expression in line 16 uses a version of method IndexOf that takes two arguments—the character to search for and the starting index at which the search of the string should begin. The method does not examine any characters that occur prior to the starting index (in this case, 1). The expression in line 18 uses another version of method IndexOf that takes three arguments—the character to search for, the index at which to start searching and the number of characters to search.

Lines 22, 24 and 26 use method LastIndexOf to locate the last occurrence of a character in a string. Method LastIndexOf performs the search from the end of the string to the beginning of the string. If it finds the character, LastIndexOf returns the index of the specified character in the string; otherwise, LastIndexOf returns -1. There are three versions of method LastIndexOf. The expression in line 22 uses the version that takes as an argument the character for which to search. The expression in line 24 uses the version that takes two arguments—the character for which to search and the highest index from which to begin searching backward for the character. The expression in line 26 uses a third version of method LastIndexOf that takes three arguments—the character for which to search, the starting index from which to start searching backward and the number of characters (the portion of the string) to search.

Lines 30–44 use versions of IndexOf and LastIndexOf that take a string instead of a character as the first argument. These versions of the methods perform identically to those described above except that they search for sequences of characters (or substrings) that are specified by their string arguments.

Lines 48–64 use methods IndexOfAny and LastIndexOfAny, which take an array of characters as the first argument. These versions of the methods also perform identically to those described above, except that they return the index of the first occurrence of any of the characters in the character-array argument.

Common Programming Error 18.2

In the overloaded methods LastIndexOf and LastIndexOfAny that take three parameters, the second argument must be greater than or equal to the third. This might seem counterintuitive, but remember that the search moves from the end of the string toward the start of the string.

18.7 Extracting Substrings from strings

Class string provides two Substring methods, which create a new string by copying part of an existing string. Each method returns a new string. The application in Fig. 18.6 demonstrates the use of both methods.

```
 1   // Fig. 18.6: SubString.cs
 2   // Demonstrating the string Substring method.
 3   using System;
 4
 5   class SubString
 6   {
```

Fig. 18.6 | Substrings generated from strings. (Part 1 of 2.)

```
7       public static void Main( string[] args )
8       {
9          string letters = "abcdefghijklmabcdefghijklm";
10
11         // invoke Substring method and pass it one parameter
12         Console.WriteLine( "Substring from index 20 to end is \"" +
13            letters.Substring( 20 ) + "\"" );
14
15         // invoke Substring method and pass it two parameters
16         Console.WriteLine( "Substring from index 0 of length 6 is \"" +
17            letters.Substring( 0, 6 ) + "\"" );
18      } // end method Main
19   } // end class SubString
```

```
Substring from index 20 to end is "hijklm"
Substring from index 0 of length 6 is "abcdef"
```

Fig. 18.6 | Substrings generated from `strings`. (Part 2 of 2.)

The statement in line 13 uses the `Substring` method that takes one `int` argument. The argument specifies the starting index from which the method copies characters in the original `string`. The substring returned contains a copy of the characters from the starting index to the end of the `string`. If the index specified in the argument is outside the bounds of the `string`, the program throws an `ArgumentOutOfRangeException`.

The second version of method `Substring` (line 17) takes two `int` arguments. The first argument specifies the starting index from which the method copies characters from the original `string`. The second argument specifies the length of the substring to copy. The substring returned contains a copy of the specified characters from the original `string`. If the supplied length of the substring is too large (i.e., the substring tries to retrieve characters past the end of the original `string`), an `ArgumentOutOfRangeException` is thrown.

18.8 Concatenating `strings`

The + operator is not the only way to perform `string` concatenation. The `static` method `Concat` of class `string` (Fig. 18.7) concatenates two `strings` and returns a new `string` containing the combined characters from both original `strings`. Line 16 appends the characters from `string2` to the end of a copy of `string1`, using method `Concat`. The statement in line 16 does not modify the original `strings`.

```
1    // Fig. 18.7: SubConcatenation.cs
2    // Demonstrating string class Concat method.
3    using System;
4
5    class StringConcatenation
6    {
7       public static void Main( string[] args )
8       {
```

Fig. 18.7 | `Concat` static method. (Part 1 of 2.)

```
 9          string string1 = "Happy ";
10          string string2 = "Birthday";
11
12          Console.WriteLine( "string1 = \"" + string1 + "\"\n" +
13             "string2 = \"" + string2 + "\"" );
14          Console.WriteLine(
15             "\nResult of string.Concat( string1, string2 ) = " +
16             string.Concat( string1, string2 ) );
17          Console.WriteLine( "string1 after concatenation = " + string1 );
18       } // end Main
19    } // end class StringConcatenation
```

```
string1 = "Happy "
string2 = "Birthday"

Result of string.Concat( string1, string2 ) = Happy Birthday
string1 after concatenation = Happy
```

Fig. 18.7 | Concat static method. (Part 2 of 2.)

18.9 Miscellaneous `string` Methods

Class string provides several methods that return modified copies of strings. The application in Fig. 18.8 demonstrates the use of these methods, which include string methods Replace, ToLower, ToUpper and Trim.

```
 1    // Fig. 18.8: StringMethods2.cs
 2    // Demonstrating string methods Replace, ToLower, ToUpper, Trim,
 3    // and ToString.
 4    using System;
 5
 6    class StringMethods2
 7    {
 8       public static void Main( string[] args )
 9       {
10          string string1 = "cheers!";
11          string string2 = "GOOD BYE ";
12          string string3 = "   spaces   ";
13
14          Console.WriteLine( "string1 = \"" + string1 + "\"\n" +
15             "string2 = \"" + string2 + "\"\n" +
16             "string3 = \"" + string3 + "\"" );
17
18          // call method Replace
19          Console.WriteLine(
20             "\nReplacing \"e\" with \"E\" in string1: \"" +
21             string1.Replace( 'e', 'E' ) + "\"" );
22
23          // call ToLower and ToUpper
24          Console.WriteLine( "\nstring1.ToUpper() = \"" +
25             string1.ToUpper() + "\"\nstring2.ToLower() = \"" +
26             string2.ToLower() + "\"" );
```

Fig. 18.8 | string methods Replace, ToLower, ToUpper and Trim. (Part 1 of 2.)

```
27
28          // call Trim method
29          Console.WriteLine( "\nstring3 after trim = \"" +
30              string3.Trim() + "\"" );
31
32          Console.WriteLine( "\nstring1 = \"" + string1 + "\"" );
33      } // end Main
34  } // end class StringMethods2
```

```
string1 = "cheers!"
string2 = "GOOD BYE "
string3 = "   spaces   "

Replacing "e" with "E" in string1: "chEErs!"

string1.ToUpper() = "CHEERS!"
string2.ToLower() = "good bye "

string3 after trim = "spaces"

string1 = "cheers!"
```

Fig. 18.8 | string methods Replace, ToLower, ToUpper and Trim. (Part 2 of 2.)

Line 21 uses string method Replace to return a new string, replacing every occurrence in string1 of character 'e' with 'E'. Method Replace takes two arguments—a string for which to search and another string with which to replace all matching occurrences of the first argument. The original string remains unchanged. If there are no occurrences of the first argument in the string, the method returns the original string.

string method ToUpper generates a new string (line 25) that replaces any lowercase letters in string1 with their uppercase equivalents. The method returns a new string containing the converted string; the original string remains unchanged. If there are no characters to convert, the original string is returned. Line 26 uses string method ToLower to return a new string in which any uppercase letters in string2 are replaced by their lowercase equivalents. The original string is unchanged. As with ToUpper, if there are no characters to convert to lowercase, method ToLower returns the original string.

Line 30 uses string method Trim to remove all whitespace characters that appear at the beginning and end of a string. Without otherwise altering the original string, the method returns a new string that contains the string, but omits leading or trailing whitespace characters. This method is particularly useful for retrieving user input (i.e., via a TextBox). Another version of method Trim takes a character array and returns a copy of the string that does not begin or end with the characters in the array argument.

18.10 Class StringBuilder

The string class provides many capabilities for processing strings. However a string's contents can never change. Operations that seem to concatenate strings are in fact assigning string references to newly created strings (e.g., the += operator creates a new string and assigns the initial string reference to the newly created string).

The next several sections discuss the features of class StringBuilder (namespace System.Text), used to create and manipulate dynamic string information—i.e., mutable strings. Every StringBuilder can store a certain number of characters that is specified by its capacity. Exceeding the capacity of a StringBuilder causes the capacity to expand to accommodate the additional characters. As we will see, members of class StringBuilder, such as methods Append and AppendFormat, can be used for concatenation like the operators + and += for class string. StringBuilder is particularly useful for manipulating a large number of strings, as it is much more efficient than creating individual immutable strings.

Performance Tip 18.2

Objects of class string *are immutable (i.e., constant strings), whereas objects of class* String- Builder *are mutable. C# can perform certain optimizations involving* strings *(such as the sharing of one string among multiple references), because it knows these objects will not change.*

Class StringBuilder provides six overloaded constructors. Class StringBuilderConstructor (Fig. 18.9) demonstrates three of these overloaded constructors.

Line 10 employs the no-parameter StringBuilder constructor to create a String- Builder that contains no characters and has a default initial capacity of 16 characters. Line 11 uses the StringBuilder constructor that takes an int argument to create a String- Builder that contains no characters and has the initial capacity specified in the int argument (i.e., 10). Line 12 uses the StringBuilder constructor that takes a string argument to create a StringBuilder containing the characters of the string argument. The initial capacity is the smallest power of two greater than or equal to the number of characters in the argument string, with a minimum of 16. Lines 14–16 implicitly use StringBuilder method ToString to obtain string representations of the StringBuilders' contents.

```
1   // Fig. 18.9: StringBuilderConstructor.cs
2   // Demonstrating StringBuilder class constructors.
3   using System;
4   using System.Text;
5
6   class StringBuilderConstructor
7   {
8      public static void Main( string[] args )
9      {
10         StringBuilder buffer1 = new StringBuilder();
11         StringBuilder buffer2 = new StringBuilder( 10 );
12         StringBuilder buffer3 = new StringBuilder( "hello" );
13
14         Console.WriteLine( "buffer1 = \"" + buffer1 + "\"" );
15         Console.WriteLine( "buffer2 = \"" + buffer2 + "\"" );
16         Console.WriteLine( "buffer3 = \"" + buffer3 + "\"" );
17      } // end Main
18   } // end class StringBuilderConstructor
```

```
buffer1 = ""
buffer2 = ""
buffer3 = "hello"
```

Fig. 18.9 | StringBuilder class constructors.

18.11 Length and Capacity Properties, EnsureCapacity Method and Indexer of Class StringBuilder

Class `StringBuilder` provides the `Length` and `Capacity` properties to return the number of characters currently in a `StringBuilder` and the number of characters that a `String-Builder` can store without allocating more memory, respectively. These properties also can increase or decrease the length or the capacity of the `StringBuilder`.

Method `EnsureCapacity` allows you to reduce the number of times that a `String-Builder`'s capacity must be increased. The method doubles the `StringBuilder` instance's current capacity. If this doubled value is greater than the value that the programmer wishes to ensure, that value becomes the new capacity. Otherwise, `EnsureCapacity` alters the capacity to make it equal to the requested number. For example, if the current capacity is 17 and we wish to make it 40, 17 multiplied by 2 is not greater than 40, so the call will result in a new capacity of 40. If the current capacity is 23 and we wish to make it 40, 23 will be multiplied by 2 to result in a new capacity of 46. Both 40 and 46 are greater than or equal to 40, so a capacity of 40 is indeed ensured by method `EnsureCapacity`. The program in Fig. 18.10 demonstrates the use of these methods and properties.

```csharp
1   // Fig. 18.10: StringBuilderFeatures.cs
2   // Demonstrating some features of class StringBuilder.
3   using System;
4   using System.Text;
5
6   class StringBuilderFeatures
7   {
8      public static void Main( string[] args )
9      {
10        StringBuilder buffer =
11           new StringBuilder( "Hello, how are you?" );
12
13        // use Length and Capacity properties
14        Console.WriteLine( "buffer = " + buffer +
15           "\nLength = " + buffer.Length +
16           "\nCapacity = " + buffer.Capacity );
17
18        buffer.EnsureCapacity( 75 ); // ensure a capacity of at least 75
19        Console.WriteLine( "\nNew capacity = " +
20           buffer.Capacity );
21
22        // truncate StringBuilder by setting Length property
23        buffer.Length = 10;
24        Console.Write( "\nNew length = " +
25           buffer.Length + "\nbuffer = " );
26
27        // use StringBuilder indexer
28        for ( int i = 0; i < buffer.Length; i++ )
29           Console.Write( buffer[ i ] );
30
```

Fig. 18.10 | StringBuilder size manipulation. (Part 1 of 2.)

```
31          Console.WriteLine( "\n" );
32       } // end Main
33    } // end class StringBuilderFeatures
```

```
buffer = Hello, how are you?
Length = 19
Capacity = 32

New capacity = 75

New length = 10
buffer = Hello, how
```

Fig. 18.10 | StringBuilder size manipulation. (Part 2 of 2.)

The program contains one StringBuilder, called buffer. Lines 10–11 of the program use the StringBuilder constructor that takes a string argument to instantiate the StringBuilder and initialize its value to "Hello, how are you?". Lines 14–16 output the content, length and capacity of the StringBuilder. In the output window, notice that the capacity of the StringBuilder is initially 32. Remember, the StringBuilder constructor that takes a string argument creates a StringBuilder object with an initial capacity that is the smallest power of two greater than or equal to the number of characters in the string passed as an argument.

Line 18 expands the capacity of the StringBuilder to a minimum of 75 characters. The current capacity (32) multiplied by two is less than 75, so method EnsureCapacity increases the capacity to 75. If new characters are added to a StringBuilder so that its length exceeds its capacity, the capacity grows to accommodate the additional characters in the same manner as if method EnsureCapacity had been called.

Line 23 uses property Length to set the length of the StringBuilder to 10. If the specified length is less than the current number of characters in the StringBuilder, the contents of the StringBuilder are truncated to the specified length. If the specified length is greater than the number of characters currently in the StringBuilder, space characters are appended to the StringBuilder until the total number of characters in the String-Builder is equal to the specified length.

Common Programming Error 18.3

Assigning null to a string reference can lead to logic errors if you attempt to compare null to an empty string. The keyword null represents a null reference (i.e., a reference that does not refer to an object), not an empty string (which is a string object that is of length 0 and contains no characters). The string.Empty should be used if you need a string with no characters.

18.12 Append and AppendFormat Methods of Class StringBuilder

Class StringBuilder provides 19 overloaded Append methods that allow various types of values to be added to the end of a StringBuilder. The .NET Framework Class Library provides versions for each of the simple types and for character arrays, `strings` and objects. (Remember that method `ToString` produces a `string` representation of any object.) Each method takes an argument, converts it to a `string` and appends it to the `StringBuilder`. Figure 18.11 demonstrates the use of several `Append` methods.

```
1   // Fig. 18.11: StringBuilderAppend.cs
2   // Demonstrating StringBuilder Append methods.
3   using System;
4   using System.Text;
5
6   class StringBuilderAppend
7   {
8      public static void Main( string[] args )
9      {
10        object objectValue = "hello";
11        string stringValue = "good bye";
12        char[] characterArray = { 'a', 'b', 'c', 'd', 'e', 'f' };
13        bool booleanValue = true;
14        char characterValue = 'Z';
15        int integerValue = 7;
16        long longValue = 1000000;
17        float floatValue = 2.5F; // F suffix indicates that 2.5 is a float
18        double doubleValue = 33.333;
19        StringBuilder buffer = new StringBuilder();
20
21        // use method Append to append values to buffer
22        buffer.Append( objectValue );
23        buffer.Append( "   " );
24        buffer.Append( stringValue );
25        buffer.Append( "   " );
26        buffer.Append( characterArray );
27        buffer.Append( "  ");
28        buffer.Append( characterArray, 0, 3 );
29        buffer.Append( "   " );
30        buffer.Append( booleanValue );
31        buffer.Append( "   " );
32        buffer.Append( characterValue );
33        buffer.Append( "   " );
34        buffer.Append( integerValue );
35        buffer.Append( "   " );
36        buffer.Append( longValue );
37        buffer.Append( "   " );
38        buffer.Append( floatValue );
39        buffer.Append( "   " );
40        buffer.Append( doubleValue );
41
42        Console.WriteLine( "buffer = " + buffer.ToString() + "\n" );
43     } // end Main
44  } // end class StringBuilderAppend
```

```
buffer = hello   good bye   abcdef   abc   True   Z   7   1000000   2.5   33.333
```

Fig. 18.11 | Append methods of `StringBuilder`.

Lines 22–40 use 10 different overloaded Append methods to attach the string representations of objects created in lines 10–18 to the end of the StringBuilder. Append behaves similarly to the + operator, which is used to concatenate strings.

Class StringBuilder also provides method AppendFormat, which converts a string to a specified format, then appends it to the StringBuilder. The example in Fig. 18.12 demonstrates the use of this method.

Line 13 creates a string that contains formatting information. The information enclosed in braces specifies how to format a specific piece of data. Formats have the form {X[,Y][:FormatString]}, where X is the number of the argument to be formatted,

```csharp
1   // Fig. 18.12: StringBuilderAppendFormat.cs
2   // Demonstrating method AppendFormat.
3   using System;
4   using System.Text;
5
6   class StringBuilderAppendFormat
7   {
8      public static void Main( string[] args )
9      {
10         StringBuilder buffer = new StringBuilder();
11
12         // formatted string
13         string string1 = "This {0} costs: {1:C}.\n";
14
15         // string1 argument array
16         object[] objectArray = new object[ 2 ];
17
18         objectArray[ 0 ] = "car";
19         objectArray[ 1 ] = 1234.56;
20
21         // append to buffer formatted string with argument
22         buffer.AppendFormat( string1, objectArray );
23
24         // formatted string
25         string string2 = "Number:{0:d3}.\n" +
26            "Number right aligned with spaces:{0, 4}.\n" +
27            "Number left aligned with spaces:{0, -4}.";
28
29         // append to buffer formatted string with argument
30         buffer.AppendFormat( string2, 5 );
31
32         // display formatted strings
33         Console.WriteLine( buffer.ToString() );
34      } // end Main
35   } // end class StringBuilderAppendFormat
```

```
This car costs: $1,234.56.
Number:005.
Number right aligned with spaces:    5.
Number left aligned with spaces:5    .
```

Fig. 18.12 | StringBuilder's AppendFormat method.

counting from zero. Y is an optional argument, which can be positive or negative, indicating how many characters should be in the result. If the resulting string is less than the number Y, it will be padded with spaces to make up for the difference. A positive integer aligns the string to the right; a negative integer aligns it to the left. The optional Format-String applies a particular format to the argument—currency, decimal or scientific, among others. In this case, "{0}" means the first argument will be printed out. "{1:C}" specifies that the second argument will be formatted as a currency value.

Line 22 shows a version of AppendFormat that takes two parameters—a string specifying the format and an array of objects to serve as the arguments to the format string. The argument referred to by "{0}" is in the object array at index 0.

Lines 25–27 define another string used for formatting. The first format "{0:d3}", specifies that the first argument will be formatted as a three-digit decimal, meaning that any number having fewer than three digits will have leading zeros placed in front to make up the difference. The next format, "{0, 4}", specifies that the formatted string should have four characters and be right aligned. The third format, "{0, -4}", specifies that the strings should be aligned to the left. For more formatting options, please refer to the online help documentation.

Line 30 uses a version of AppendFormat that takes two parameters—a string containing a format and an object to which the format is applied. In this case, the object is the number 5. The output of Fig. 18.12 displays the result of applying these two versions of AppendFormat with their respective arguments.

18.13 Insert, Remove and Replace Methods of Class StringBuilder

Class StringBuilder provides 18 overloaded Insert methods to allow various types of data to be inserted at any position in a StringBuilder. The class provides versions for each of the simple types and for character arrays, strings and objects. Each method takes its second argument, converts it to a string and inserts the string into the StringBuilder in front of the character in the position specified by the first argument. The index specified by the first argument must be greater than or equal to 0 and less than the length of the StringBuilder; otherwise, the program throws an ArgumentOutOfRangeException.

Class StringBuilder also provides method Remove for deleting any portion of a StringBuilder. Method Remove takes two arguments—the index at which to begin deletion and the number of characters to delete. The sum of the starting index and the number of characters to be deleted must always be less than the length of the StringBuilder; otherwise, the program throws an ArgumentOutOfRangeException. The Insert and Remove methods are demonstrated in Fig. 18.13.

```
1   // Fig. 18.13: StringBuilderInsertRemove.cs
2   // Demonstrating methods Insert and Remove of the
3   // StringBuilder class.
4   using System;
5   using System.Text;
6
```

Fig. 18.13 | StringBuilder text insertion and removal. (Part 1 of 2.)

```
7    class StringBuilderInsertRemove
8    {
9       public static void Main( string[] args )
10      {
11         object objectValue = "hello";
12         string stringValue = "good bye";
13         char[] characterArray = { 'a', 'b', 'c', 'd', 'e', 'f' };
14         bool booleanValue = true;
15         char characterValue = 'K';
16         int integerValue = 7;
17         long longValue = 10000000;
18         float floatValue = 2.5F; // F suffix indicates that 2.5 is a float
19         double doubleValue = 33.333;
20         StringBuilder buffer = new StringBuilder();
21
22         // insert values into buffer
23         buffer.Insert( 0, objectValue );
24         buffer.Insert( 0, "  " );
25         buffer.Insert( 0, stringValue );
26         buffer.Insert( 0, "  " );
27         buffer.Insert( 0, characterArray );
28         buffer.Insert( 0, "  " );
29         buffer.Insert( 0, booleanValue );
30         buffer.Insert( 0, "  " );
31         buffer.Insert( 0, characterValue );
32         buffer.Insert( 0, "  " );
33         buffer.Insert( 0, integerValue );
34         buffer.Insert( 0, "  " );
35         buffer.Insert( 0, longValue );
36         buffer.Insert( 0, "  " );
37         buffer.Insert( 0, floatValue );
38         buffer.Insert( 0, "  " );
39         buffer.Insert( 0, doubleValue );
40         buffer.Insert( 0, "  " );
41
42         Console.WriteLine( "buffer after Inserts: \n" + buffer + "\n" );
43
44         buffer.Remove( 10, 1 ); // delete 2 in 2.5
45         buffer.Remove( 4, 4 );  // delete .333 in 33.333
46
47         Console.WriteLine( "buffer after Removes:\n" + buffer );
48      } // end Main
49   } // end class StringBuilderInsertRemove
```

```
buffer after Inserts:
  33.333  2.5  10000000  7  K  True  abcdef  good bye  hello

buffer after Removes:
  33  .5  10000000  7  K  True  abcdef  good bye  hello
```

Fig. 18.13 | StringBuilder text insertion and removal. (Part 2 of 2.)

Another useful method included with StringBuilder is Replace. Replace searches for a specified string or character and substitutes another string or character in its place. Figure 18.14 demonstrates this method.

```
 1    // Fig. 18.14: StringBuilderReplace.cs
 2    // Demonstrating method Replace.
 3    using System;
 4    using System.Text;
 5
 6    class StringBuilderReplace
 7    {
 8       public static void Main( string[] args )
 9       {
10          StringBuilder builder1 =
11             new StringBuilder( "Happy Birthday Jane" );
12          StringBuilder builder2 =
13             new StringBuilder( "good bye greg" );
14
15          Console.WriteLine( "Before replacements:\n" +
16             builder1.ToString() + "\n" + builder2.ToString() );
17
18          builder1.Replace( "Jane", "Greg" );
19          builder2.Replace( 'g', 'G', 0, 5 );
20
21          Console.WriteLine( "\nAfter replacements:\n" +
22             builder1.ToString() + "\n" + builder2.ToString() );
23       } // end Main
24    } // end class StringBuilderReplace
```

```
Before Replacements:
Happy Birthday Jane
good bye greg

After replacements:
Happy Birthday Greg
Good bye greg
```

Fig. 18.14 | StringBuilder text replacement.

Line 18 uses method Replace to replace all instances of the string "Jane" with the string "Greg" in builder1. Another overload of this method takes two characters as parameters and replaces each occurrence of the first character with the second character. Line 19 uses an overload of Replace that takes four parameters, of which the first two are characters and the second two are ints. The method replaces all instances of the first character with the second character, beginning at the index specified by the first int and continuing for a count specified by the second int. Thus, in this case, Replace looks through only five characters, starting with the character at index 0. As the output illustrates, this version of Replace replaces g with G in the word "good", but not in "greg". This is because the gs in "greg" are not in the range indicated by the int arguments (i.e., between indexes 0 and 4).

18.14 Char Methods

C# provides a concept called a *struct* (short for structure) that is similar to a class. Although structs and classes are comparable in many ways, structs represent value types.

Like classes, structs can have methods and properties, and can use the access modifiers public and private. Also, struct members are accessed via the member access operator (.).

The simple types are actually aliases for struct types. For instance, an int is defined by struct System.Int32, a long by System.Int64 and so on. All struct types derive from class *ValueType*, which in turn derives from object. Also, all struct types are implicitly sealed, so they do not support virtual or abstract methods, and their members cannot be declared protected or protected internal.

In the struct *Char*,[2] which is the struct for characters, most methods are static, take at least one character argument and perform either a test or a manipulation on the character. We present several of these methods in the next example. Figure 18.15 demonstrates static methods that test characters to determine whether they are of a specific character type and static methods that perform case conversions on characters.

```
1   // Fig. 18.15: StaticCharMethods.cs
2   // Demonstrates static character-testing methods
3   // from Char struct
4   using System;
5   using System.Windows.Forms;
6
7   namespace StaticCharMethods
8   {
9      public partial class StaticCharMethodsForm : Form
10     {
11        // default constructor
12        public StaticCharMethodsForm()
13        {
14           InitializeComponent();
15        } // end constructor
16
17        // handle analyzeButton_Click
18        private void analyzeButton_Click( object sender, EventArgs e )
19        {
20           // convert string entered to type char
21           char character = Convert.ToChar( inputTextBox.Text );
22           string output;
23
24           output = "is digit: " +
25              Char.IsDigit( character ) + "\r\n";
26           output += "is letter: " +
27              Char.IsLetter( character ) + "\r\n";
28           output += "is letter or digit: " +
29              Char.IsLetterOrDigit( character ) + "\r\n";
30           output += "is lower case: " +
31              Char.IsLower( character ) + "\r\n";
32           output += "is upper case: " +
33              Char.IsUpper( character ) + "\r\n";
```

Fig. 18.15 | Char's static character-testing and case-conversion methods. (Part 1 of 2.)

---

2. Just as keyword string is an alias for class String, keyword char is an alias for struct Char. In this book, we use the term Char when calling a static method of struct Char and the term char elsewhere.

```
34              output += "to upper case: " +
35                  Char.ToUpper( character ) + "\r\n";
36              output += "to lower case: " +
37                  Char.ToLower( character ) + "\r\n";
38              output += "is punctuation: " +
39                  Char.IsPunctuation( character ) + "\r\n";
40              output += "is symbol: " + Char.IsSymbol( character );
41              outputTextBox.Text = output;
42          } // end method analyzeButton_Click
43      } // end class StaticCharMethodsForm
44  } // end namespace StaticCharMethods
```

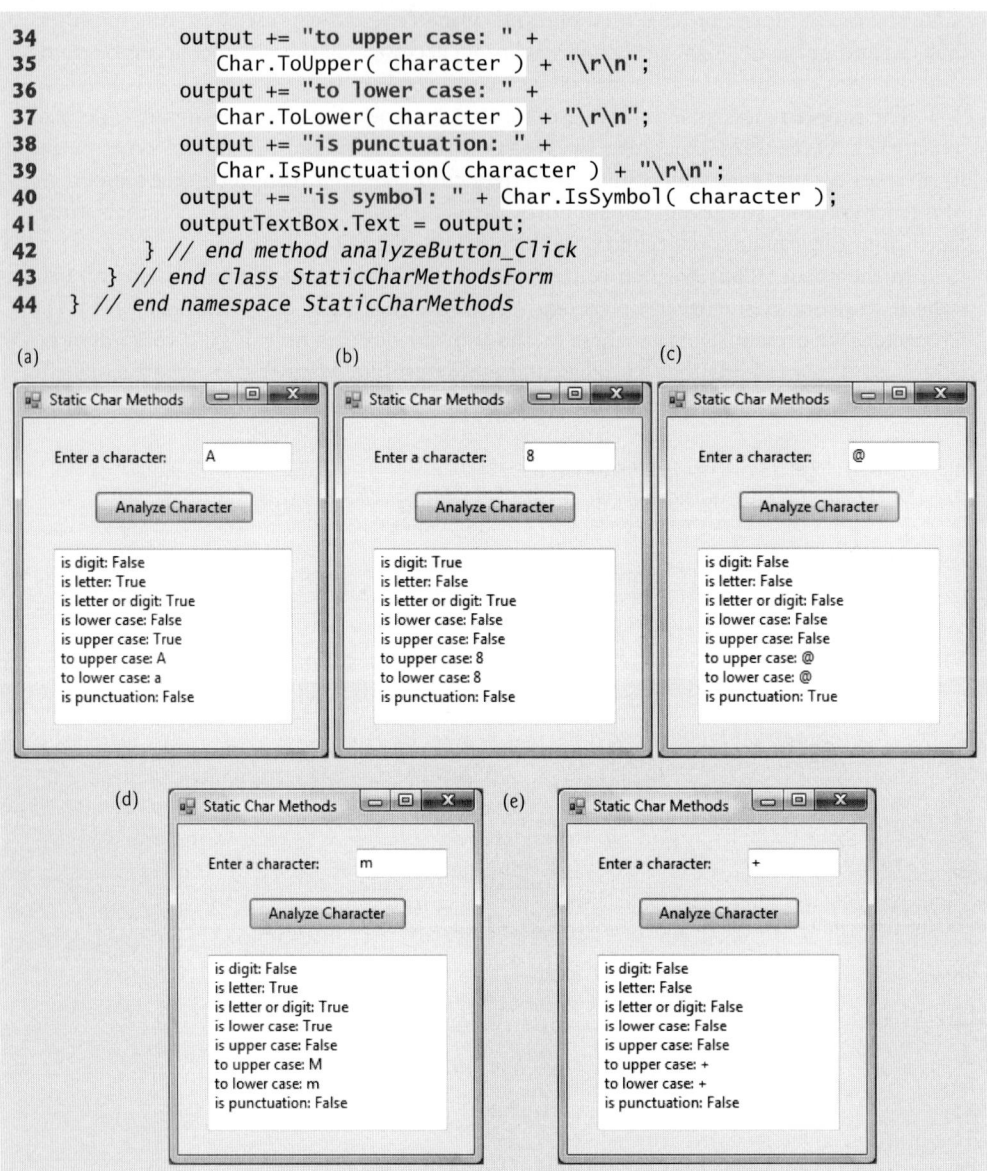

Fig. 18.15 | Char's static character-testing and case-conversion methods. (Part 2 of 2.)

This Windows Forms application contains a prompt, a TextBox in which the user can input a character, a button that the user can press after entering a character and a second TextBox that displays the output of our analysis. When the user clicks the **Analyze Character** button, event handler analyzeButton_Click (lines 18–42) is invoked. This event handler converts the input from a string to a char, using method Convert.ToChar (line 21).

Line 25 uses Char method IsDigit to determine whether character is defined as a digit. If so, the method returns true; otherwise, it returns false (note again that bool values are output capitalized). Line 27 uses Char method IsLetter to determine whether character character is a letter. Line 29 uses Char method IsLetterOrDigit to determine whether character character is a letter or a digit.

Line 31 uses Char method IsLower to determine whether character character is a lowercase letter. Line 33 uses Char method IsUpper to determine whether character character is an uppercase letter. Line 35 uses Char method ToUpper to convert character character to its uppercase equivalent. The method returns the converted character if the character has an uppercase equivalent; otherwise, the method returns its original argument. Line 37 uses Char method ToLower to convert character character to its lowercase equivalent. The method returns the converted character if the character has a lowercase equivalent; otherwise, the method returns its original argument.

Line 39 uses Char method IsPunctuation to determine whether character is a punctuation mark, such as "!", ":" or ")". Line 40 uses Char method IsSymbol to determine whether character character is a symbol, such as "+", "=" or "^".

Structure type Char also contains other methods not shown in this example. Many of the static methods are similar—for instance, IsWhiteSpace is used to determine whether a certain character is a whitespace character (e.g., newline, tab or space). The struct also contains several public instance methods; many of these, such as methods ToString and Equals, are methods that we have seen before in other classes. This group includes method CompareTo, which is used to compare two character values with one another.

18.15 Card Shuffling and Dealing Simulation

In this section, we use random-number generation to develop a program that simulates card shuffling and dealing. These techniques can form the basis of programs that implement specific card games.

Class Card (Fig. 18.16) contains two string instance variables—face and suit— that store references to the face value and suit name of a specific card. The constructor for the class receives two strings that it uses to initialize face and suit. Method ToString (lines 18–21) creates a string consisting of the card's face and suit to identify the card when it is dealt.

```
1   // Fig. 18.16: Card.cs
2   // Stores suit and face information on each card.
3   using System;
4
5   namespace DeckOfCards
6   {
7      public class Card
8      {
9         private string face;
10        private string suit;
11
12        public Card( string faceValue, string suitValue )
13        {
14           face = faceValue;
```

Fig. 18.16 | Card class. (Part 1 of 2.)

```
15              suit = suitValue;
16          } // end constructor
17
18          public override string ToString()
19          {
20              return face + " of " + suit;
21          } // end method ToString
22      } // end class Card
23  } // end namespace DeckOfCards
```

Fig. 18.16 | Card class. (Part 2 of 2.)

We develop the DeckForm application (Fig. 18.17), which creates a deck of 52 playing cards, using Card objects. Users can deal each card by clicking the **Deal Card** button. Each dealt card is displayed in a Label. Users can also shuffle the deck at any time by clicking the **Shuffle Cards** button.

```
1   // Fig. 18.17: DeckForm.cs
2   // Simulating card shuffling and dealing.
3   using System;
4   using System.Windows.Forms;
5
6   namespace DeckOfCards
7   {
8       public partial class DeckOfCardsForm : Form
9       {
10          private Card[] deck = new Card[ 52 ]; // deck of 52 cards
11          private int currentCard; // count which card was just dealt
12
13          // default constructor
14          public DeckOfCardsForm()
15          {
16              // Required for Windows Form Designer support
17              InitializeComponent();
18          } // end constructor
19
20          // handles form at load time
21          private void DeckForm_Load( object sender, EventArgs e )
22          {
23              string[] faces = { "Ace", "Deuce", "Three", "Four", "Five",
24                  "Six", "Seven", "Eight", "Nine", "Ten", "Jack", "Queen",
25                  "King" };
26              string[] suits = { "Hearts", "Diamonds", "Clubs", "Spades" };
27
28              currentCard = -1; // no cards have been dealt
29
30              // initialize deck
31              for ( int i = 0; i < deck.Length; i++ )
32                  deck[ i ] = new Card( faces[ i % 13 ], suits[ i / 13 ] );
33          } // end method DeckForm_Load
34
```

Fig. 18.17 | Card shuffling and dealing simulation. (Part 1 of 4.)

```
35        // handles dealButton Click
36        private void dealButton_Click( object sender, EventArgs e )
37        {
38            Card dealt = DealCard();
39
40            // if dealt card is null, then no cards left
41            // player must shuffle cards
42            if ( dealt != null )
43            {
44                displayLabel.Text = dealt.ToString();
45                statusLabel.Text = "Card #: " + currentCard;
46            } // end if
47            else
48            {
49                displayLabel.Text = "NO MORE CARDS TO DEAL";
50                statusLabel.Text = "Shuffle cards to continue";
51            } // end else
52        } // end method dealButton_Click
53
54        // shuffle cards
55        private void Shuffle()
56        {
57            Random randomNumber = new Random();
58            Card temporaryValue;
59
60            currentCard = -1;
61
62            // swap each card with randomly selected card (0-51)
63            for ( int i = 0; i < deck.Length; i++ )
64            {
65                int j = randomNumber.Next( 52 );
66
67                // swap cards
68                temporaryValue = deck[ i ];
69                deck[ i ] = deck[ j ];
70                deck[ j ] = temporaryValue;
71            } // end for
72
73            dealButton.Enabled = true; // shuffled deck can now deal cards
74        } // end method Shuffle
75
76        // deal a card if the deck is not empty
77        private Card DealCard()
78        {
79            // if there is a card to deal, then deal it
80            // otherwise signal that cards need to be shuffled by
81            // disabling dealButton and returning null
82            if ( currentCard + 1 < deck.Length )
83            {
84                currentCard++; // increment count
85                return deck[ currentCard ]; // return new card
86            } // end if
```

Fig. 18.17 | Card shuffling and dealing simulation. (Part 2 of 4.)

```
87                else
88                {
89                    dealButton.Enabled = false; // empty deck cannot deal cards
90                    return null; // do not return a card
91                } // end else
92            } // end method DealCard
93
94            // handles shuffleButton Click
95            private void shuffleButton_Click(object sender, EventArgs e)
96            {
97                displayLabel.Text = "SHUFFLING...";
98                Shuffle();
99                displayLabel.Text = "DECK IS SHUFFLED";
100           } // end method shuffleButton_Click
101       } // end class DeckForm
102   } // end namespace DeckOfCards
```

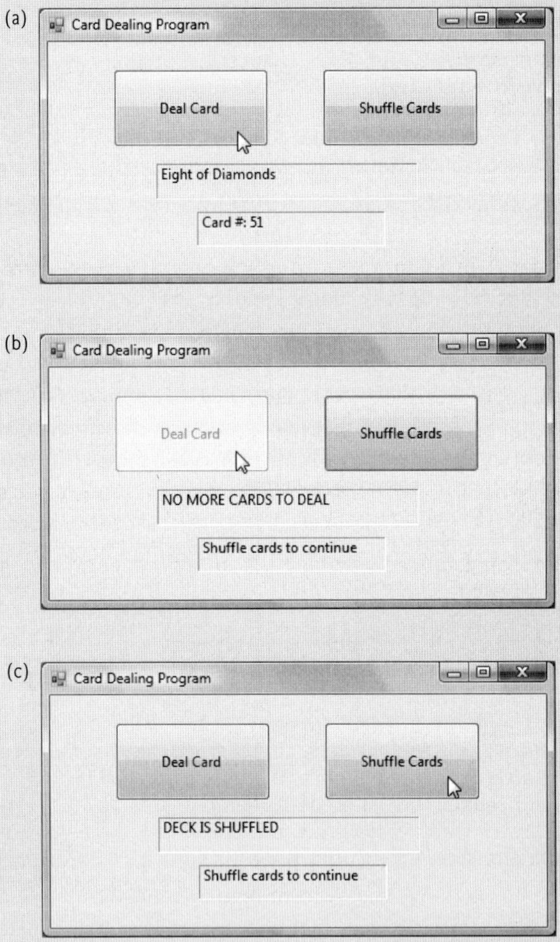

Fig. 18.17 | Card shuffling and dealing simulation. (Part 3 of 4.)

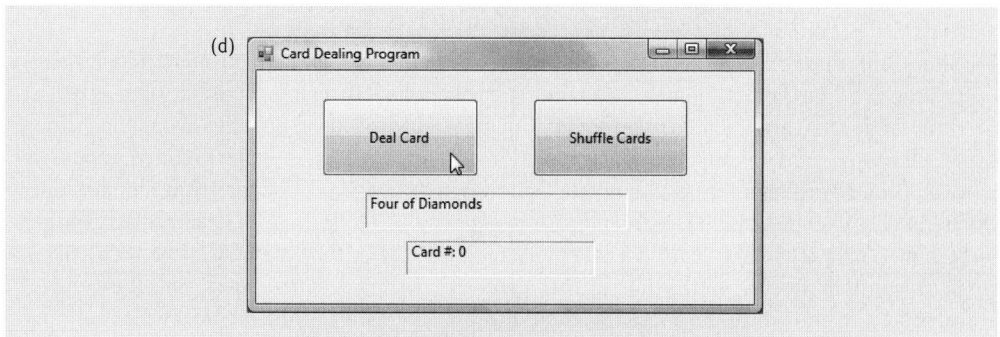

Fig. 18.17 | Card shuffling and dealing simulation. (Part 4 of 4.)

Method DeckForm_Load (lines 21–33 of Fig. 18.17) uses a for statement (lines 31–32) to fill the deck array with Cards. Note that each Card is instantiated and initialized with two strings—one from the faces array (strings "Ace" through "King") and one from the suits array ("Hearts", "Diamonds", "Clubs" or "Spades"). The calculation i % 13 always results in a value from 0 to 12 (the thirteen indices of the faces array), and the calculation i / 13 always results in a value from 0 to 3 (the four indices in the suits array). The initialized deck array contains the cards with faces Ace through King for each suit.

When the user clicks the **Deal Card** button, event handler dealButton_Click (lines 36–52) invokes method DealCard (defined in lines 77–92) to get the next card in the deck array. If the deck is not empty, the method returns a Card object reference; otherwise, it returns null. If the reference is not null, lines 44–45 display the Card in displayLabel and display the card number in statusLabel.

If DealCard returns null, the string "NO MORE CARDS TO DEAL" is displayed in displayLabel, and the string "Shuffle cards to continue" is displayed in statusLabel.

When the user clicks the **Shuffle Cards** button, event handler shuffleButton_Click (lines 95–100) invokes method Shuffle (defined in lines 55–74) to shuffle the cards. The method loops through all 52 cards (array indices 0–51). For each card, the method randomly picks a number in the range 0–51. Then the current Card object and the randomly selected Card object are swapped in the array. To shuffle the cards, method Shuffle makes a total of only 52 swaps during a single pass of the entire array. When the shuffling is complete, displayLabel displays the string "DECK IS SHUFFLED".

18.16 Introduction to Regular-Expression Processing

This section introduces *regular expressions*—specially formatted strings used to find patterns in text. They can be used to ensure that data is in a particular format. For example, a U.S. zip code must consist of five digits, or five digits followed by a dash followed by four more digits. Compilers use regular expressions to validate program syntax. If the program code does not match the regular expression, the compiler indicates that there is a syntax error. We discuss classes Regex and Match from the System.Text.RegularExpressions namespace as well as the symbols used to form regular expressions. We then demonstrate how to find patterns in a string, match entire strings to patterns, replace characters in a string that match a pattern and split strings at delimiters specified as a pattern in a regular expression.

18.16.1 Simple Regular Expressions and Class Regex

The .NET Framework provides several classes to help developers manipulate regular expressions. Figure 18.18 demonstrates the basic regular-expression classes. To use these classes, add a using statement for the namespace System.Text.RegularExpressions (line 4). Class *Regex* represents a regular expression. We create a Regex object named expression (line 16) to represent the regular expression "e". This regular expression matches the literal character "e" anywhere in an arbitrary string. Regex *method Match* returns an object of *class Match* that represents a single regular-expression match. Class Match's ToString method returns the substring that matched the regular expression. The call to method Match (line 17) matches the leftmost occurrence of the character "e" in testString. Class Regex also provides method *Matches* (line 21), which finds all matches of the regular expression in an arbitrary string and returns a MatchCollection object containing all the Matches. A *MatchCollection* is a collection, similar to an array, and can be used with a foreach statement to iterate through the collection's elements. We introduced collections in Chapter 9 and discuss them in more detail in Chapter 27, Collections. We use a foreach statement (lines 21–22) to display all the matches to expression in testString. The elements in the MatchCollection are Match objects, so the foreach statement infers variable myMatch to be of type Match. For each Match, line 22 outputs the text that matched the regular expression.

```
1   // Fig. 18.18: BasicRegex.cs
2   // Demonstrate basic regular expressions.
3   using System;
4   using System.Text.RegularExpressions;
5
6   class BasicRegex
7   {
8      static void Main( string[] args )
9      {
10        string testString =
11           "regular expressions are sometimes called regex or regexp";
12        Console.WriteLine( "The test string is\n   \"{0}\"", testString );
13        Console.Write( "Match 'e' in the test string: " );
14
15        // match 'e' in the test string
16        Regex expression = new Regex( "e" );
17        Console.WriteLine( expression.Match( testString ) );
18        Console.Write( "Match every 'e' in the test string: " );
19
20        // match 'e' multiple times in the test string
21        foreach ( var myMatch in expression.Matches( testString ) )
22           Console.Write( "{0} ", myMatch );
23
24        Console.Write( "\nMatch \"regex\" in the test string: " );
25
26        // match 'regex' in the test string
27        foreach ( var myMatch in Regex.Matches( testString, "regex" ) )
28           Console.Write( "{0} ", myMatch );
```

Fig. 18.18 | Demonstrating basic regular expressions. (Part 1 of 2.)

```
29
30        Console.Write(
31           "\nMatch \"regex\" or \"regexp\" using an optional 'p': " );
32
33        // use the ? quantifier to include an optional 'p'
34        foreach ( var myMatch in Regex.Matches( testString, "regexp?" ) )
35           Console.Write( "{0} ", myMatch );
36
37        // use alternation to match either 'cat' or 'hat'
38        expression = new Regex( "(c|h)at" );
39        Console.WriteLine(
40           "\n\"hat cat\" matches {0}, but \"cat hat\" matches {1}",
41           expression.Match( "hat cat" ), expression.Match( "cat hat" ) );
42     } // end Main
43  } // end class BasicRegex
```

```
The test string is
   "regular expressions are sometimes called regex or regexp"
Match 'e' in the test string: e
Match every 'e' in the test string: e e e e e e e e e e
Match "regex" in the test string: regex regex
Match "regex" or "regexp" using an optional 'p': regex regexp
"hat cat" matches hat, but "cat hat" matches cat
```

Fig. 18.18 | Demonstrating basic regular expressions. (Part 2 of 2.)

Regular expressions can also be used to match a sequence of literal characters anywhere in a string. Lines 27–28 display all the occurrences of the character sequence "regex" in testString. Here we use the Regex static method Matches. Class Regex provides static versions of both methods Match and Matches. The static versions take a regular expression as an argument in addition to the string to be searched. This is useful when you want to use a regular expression only once. The call to method Matches (line 27) returns two matches to the regular expression "regex". Notice that "regexp" in the teststring matches the regular expression "regex", but the "p" is excluded. We use the regular expression "regexp?" (line 34) to match occurrences of both "regex" and "regexp". The question mark (?) is a *metacharacter*—a character with special meaning in a regular expression. More specifically, the question mark is a *quantifier*—a metacharacter that describes how many times a part of the pattern may occur in a match. The *? quantifier* matches zero or one occurrence of the pattern to its left. In line 34, we apply the ? quantifier to the character "p". This means that a match to the regular expression contains the sequence of characters "regex" and may be followed by a "p". Notice that the foreach statement (lines 34–35) displays both "regex" and "regexp".

Metacharacters allow you to create more complex patterns. The *"|"* (*alternation*) metacharacter matches the expression to its left or to its right. We use alternation in the regular expression "(c|h)at" (line 38) to match either "cat" or "hat". Parentheses are used to group parts of a regular expression, much as you group parts of a mathematical expression. The "|" causes the pattern to match a sequence of characters starting with either "c" or "h", followed by "at". Note that the "|" character attempts to match the entire expression to its left or to its right. If we didn't use the parentheses around "c|h", the regular expression would match either the single character "c" or the sequence of characters "hat". Line 41 uses the regular expression (line 38) to search the strings "hat cat" and "cat hat". Notice in the output that the first match in "hat cat" is "hat", while the first match in "cat hat" is "cat". Alternation chooses the leftmost match in the string for either of the alternating expressions—the order of the expressions doesn't matter.

Regular-Expression Character Classes and Quantifiers

The table in Fig. 18.19 lists some character classes that can be used with regular expressions. A *character class* represents a group of characters that might appear in a string. For example, a *word character* (\w) is any alphanumeric character (a-z, A-Z and 0-9) or underscore. A *whitespace character* (\s) is a space, a tab, a carriage return, a newline or a form feed. A *digit* (\d) is any numeric character.

Figure 18.20 uses character classes in regular expressions. For this example, we use method DisplayMatches (lines 53–59) to display all matches to a regular expression. Method DisplayMatches takes two strings representing the string to search and the regular expression to match. The method uses a foreach statement to display each Match in the MatchCollection object returned by the static method Matches of class Regex.

Character class	Matches	Character class	Matches
\d	any digit	\D	any nondigit
\w	any word character	\W	any nonword character
\s	any whitespace	\S	any nonwhitespace

Fig. 18.19 | Character classes.

```
1   // Fig. 18.20: CharacterClasses.cs
2   // Demonstrate using character classes and quantifiers.
3   using System;
4   using System.Text.RegularExpressions;
5
6   class CharacterClasses
7   {
8      static void Main( string[] args )
9      {
10        string testString = "abc, DEF, 123";
11        Console.WriteLine( "The test string is: \"{0}\"", testString );
12
13        // find the digits in the test string
14        Console.WriteLine( "Match any digit" );
15        DisplayMatches( testString, @"\d" );
16
17        // find anything that isn't a digit
18        Console.WriteLine( "\nMatch any nondigit" );
19        DisplayMatches( testString, @"\D" );
20
```

Fig. 18.20 | Demonstrating using character classes and quantifiers. (Part 1 of 3.)

```
21            // find the word characters in the test string
22            Console.WriteLine( "\nMatch any word character" );
23            DisplayMatches( testString, @"\w" );
24
25            // find sequences of word characters
26            Console.WriteLine(
27               "\nMatch a group of at least one word character" );
28            DisplayMatches( testString, @"\w+" );
29
30            // use a lazy quantifier
31            Console.WriteLine(
32               "\nMatch a group of at least one word character (lazy)" );
33            DisplayMatches( testString, @"\w+?" );
34
35            // match characters from 'a' to 'f'
36            Console.WriteLine( "\nMatch anything from 'a' - 'f'" );
37            DisplayMatches( testString, "[a-f]" );
38
39            // match anything that isn't in the range 'a' to 'f'
40            Console.WriteLine( "\nMatch anything not from 'a' - 'f'" );
41            DisplayMatches( testString, "[^a-f]" );
42
43            // match any sequence of letters in any case
44            Console.WriteLine( "\nMatch a group of at least one letter" );
45            DisplayMatches( testString, "[a-zA-Z]+" );
46
47            // use the . (dot) metacharacter to match any character
48            Console.WriteLine( "\nMatch a group of any characters" );
49            DisplayMatches( testString, ".*" );
50      } // end Main
51
52      // display the matches to a regular expression
53      private static void DisplayMatches( string input, string expression )
54      {
55         foreach ( var regexMatch in Regex.Matches( input, expression ) )
56            Console.Write( "{0} ", regexMatch );
57
58         Console.WriteLine(); // move to the next line
59      } // end method DisplayMatches
60   } // end class CharacterClasses
```

```
The test string is: "abc, DEF, 123"
Match any digit
1 2 3

Match any nondigit
a b c ,     D E F ,

Match any word character
a b c D E F 1 2 3

Match a group of at least one word character
abc DEF 123
```

Fig. 18.20 | Demonstrating using character classes and quantifiers. (Part 2 of 3.)

```
Match a group of at least one word character (lazy)
a b c D E F 1 2 3

Match anything from 'a' - 'f'
a b c

Match anything not from 'a' - 'f'
,   D E F ,   1 2 3

Match a group of at least one letter
abc DEF

Match a group of any characters
abc, DEF, 123
```

Fig. 18.20 | Demonstrating using character classes and quantifiers. (Part 3 of 3.)

The first regular expression (line 15) matches digits in the testString. We use the digit character class (\d) to match any digit (0–9). Note that we precede the regular expression string with @. Recall that backslashes within the double quotation marks following the @ character are regular backslash characters, not the beginning of escape sequences. To define the regular expression without prefixing @ to the string, you would need to escape every backslash character, as in

```
"\\d"
```

which makes the regular expression more difficult to read.

The output shows that the regular expression matches 1, 2, and 3 in the testString. You can also match anything that *isn't* a member of a particular character class using an uppercase instead of a lowercase letter. For example, the regular expression "\D" (line 19) matches any character that isn't a digit. Notice in the output that this includes punctuation and whitespace. Negating a character class matches *everything* that *isn't* a member of the character class.

The next regular expression (line 23) uses the character class \w to match any word character in the testString. Notice that each match consists of a single character. It would be useful to match a sequence of word characters rather than a single character. The regular expression in line 28 uses the + quantifier to match a sequence of word characters. The *+ quantifier* matches one or more occurrences of the pattern to its left. There are three matches for this expression, each three characters long. Quantifiers are *greedy*—they match the *longest* possible occurrence of the pattern. You can follow a quantifier with a question mark (?) to make it *lazy*—it matches the *shortest* possible occurrence of the pattern. The regular expression "\w+?" (line 33) uses a lazy + quantifier to match the shortest sequence of word characters possible. This produces nine matches of length one instead of three matches of length three. Figure 18.21 lists other quantifiers that you can place after a pattern in a regular expression, and the purpose of each.

Regular expressions are not limited to the character classes in Fig. 18.19. You can create your own character class by listing the members of the character class between square brackets, [and]. [*Note:* Metacharacters in square brackets are treated as literal characters.] You can include a range of characters using the "-" character. The regular expression in line 37 of Fig. 18.20 creates a character class to match any lowercase letter

Quantifier	Matches
*	Matches zero or more occurrences of the preceding pattern.
+	Matches one or more occurrences of the preceding pattern.
?	Matches zero or one occurrences of the preceding pattern.
.	Matches any single character.
{n}	Matches exactly n occurrences of the preceding pattern.
{n,}	Matches at least n occurrences of the preceding pattern.
{n,m}	Matches between n and m (inclusive) occurrences of the preceding pattern.

Fig. 18.21 | Quantifiers used in regular expressions.

from a to f. These custom character classes match a single character that is a member of the class. The output shows three matches, a, b and c. Notice that D, E and F don't match the character class [a-f] because they are uppercase. You can negate a custom character class by placing a "^" character after the opening square bracket. The regular expression in line 41 matches any character that *isn't* in the range a-f. As with the predefined character classes, negating a custom character class matches *everything* that isn't a member, including punctuation and whitespace. You can also use quantifiers with custom character classes. The regular expression in line 45 uses a character class with two ranges of characters, a-z and A-Z, and the + quantifier to match a sequence of lowercase or uppercase letters. You can also use the "." (dot) character to match any character other than a newline. The regular expression ".*" (line 49) matches any sequence of characters. The * quantifier matches zero or more occurrences of the pattern to its left. Unlike the + quantifier, the * quantifier can be used to match an empty string.

18.16.2 Complex Regular Expressions

The program of Fig. 18.22 tries to match birthdays to a regular expression. For demonstration purposes, the expression matches only birthdays that do not occur in April and that belong to people whose names begin with "J". We can do this by combining the basic regular-expression techniques we've already discussed.

```
1   // Fig. 18.22: RegexMatches.cs
2   // A more complex regular expression.
3   using System;
4   using System.Text.RegularExpressions;
5
6   class RegexMatches
7   {
8      static void Main( string[] args )
9      {
10         // create a regular expression
11         Regex expression = new Regex( @"J.*\d[\d-[4]]-\d\d-\d\d" );
```

Fig. 18.22 | A more complex regular expression. (Part 1 of 2.)

```
12
13          string testString =
14             "Jane's Birthday is 05-12-75\n" +
15             "Dave's Birthday is 11-04-68\n" +
16             "John's Birthday is 04-28-73\n" +
17             "Joe's Birthday is 12-17-77";
18
19          // display all matches to the regular expression
20          foreach ( var regexMatch in expression.Matches( testString ) )
21             Console.WriteLine( regexMatch );
22      } // end Main
23   } // end class RegexMatches
```

```
Jane's Birthday is 05-12-75
Joe's Birthday is 12-17-77
```

Fig. 18.22 | A more complex regular expression. (Part 2 of 2.)

Line 11 creates a `Regex` object and passes a regular-expression pattern `string` to its constructor. The first character in the regular expression, `"J"`, is a literal character. Any `string` matching this regular expression must start with `"J"`. The next part of the regular expression (`".*"`) matches any number of unspecified characters except newlines. The pattern `"J.*"` matches a person's name that starts with J and any characters that may come after that.

Next we match the person's birthday. We use the `\d` character class to match the first digit of the month. Since the birthday must not occur in April, the second digit in the month can't be 4. We could use the character class `"[0-35-9]"` to match any digit other than 4. However, .NET regular expressions allow you to subtract members from a character class, called *character-class subtraction*. In line 11, we use the pattern `"[\d-[4]]"` to match any digit other than 4. When the `"-"` character in a character class is followed by a character class instead of a literal character, the `"-"` is interpreted as subtraction instead of a range of characters. The members of the character class following the `"-"` are removed from the character class preceding the `"-"`. When using character-class subtraction, the class being subtracted (`[4]`) must be the last item in the enclosing brackets (`[\d-[4]]`). This notation allows you to write shorter, easier-to-read regular expressions.

Although the `"-"` character indicates a range or character-class subtraction when it is enclosed in square brackets, instances of the `"-"` character outside a character class are treated as literal characters. Thus, the regular expression in line 11 searches for a `string` that starts with the letter `"J"`, followed by any number of characters, followed by a two-digit number (of which the second digit cannot be 4), followed by a dash, another two-digit number, a dash and another two-digit number.

Lines 20–21 use a `foreach` statement to iterate through the `MatchCollection` object returned by method `Matches`, which received `testString` as an argument. For each `Match`, line 21 outputs the text that matched the regular expression. The output in Fig. 18.22 displays the two matches that were found in `testString`. Notice that both matches conform to the pattern specified by the regular expression.

18.16.3 Validating User Input with Regular Expressions and LINQ

The application in Fig. 18.23 presents a more involved example that uses regular expressions to validate name, address and telephone-number information input by a user.

When a user clicks **OK**, the program uses a LINQ query to select any empty TextBoxes (lines 22–27) from the Controls collection. Notice that we explicitly declare the type of the range variable in the from clause (line 22). When working with nongeneric collections, such as Controls, you must explicitly type the range variable. The first where clause (line

```
 1   // Fig. 18.23: Validate.cs
 2   // Validate user information using regular expressions.
 3   using System;
 4   using System.Linq;
 5   using System.Text.RegularExpressions;
 6   using System.Windows.Forms;
 7
 8   namespace Validate
 9   {
10      public partial class ValidateForm : Form
11      {
12         public ValidateForm()
13         {
14            InitializeComponent();
15         } // end constructor
16
17         // handles OK Button's Click event
18         private void okButton_Click( object sender, EventArgs e )
19         {
20            // find blank TextBoxes and order by TabIndex
21            var emptyBoxes =
22               from Control currentControl in Controls
23               where currentControl is TextBox
24               let box = currentControl as TextBox
25               where string.IsNullOrEmpty( box.Text )
26               orderby box.TabIndex
27               select box;
28
29            // if there are any empty TextBoxes
30            if ( emptyBoxes.Count() > 0 )
31            {
32               // display message box indicating missing information
33               MessageBox.Show( "Please fill in all fields",
34                  "Missing Information", MessageBoxButtons.OK,
35                  MessageBoxIcon.Error );
36
37               emptyBoxes.First().Select(); // select first empty TextBox
38            } // end if
39            else
40            {
41               // check for invalid input
42               if ( !ValidateInput( lastNameTextBox.Text,
43                  "^[A-Z][a-zA-Z]*$", "Invalid last name" ) )
44
45                  lastNameTextBox.Select(); // select invalid TextBox
46               else if ( !ValidateInput( firstNameTextBox.Text,
47                  "^[A-Z][a-zA-Z]*$", "Invalid first name" ) )
```

Fig. 18.23 | Validating user information using regular expressions. (Part 1 of 4.)

```
48
49              firstNameTextBox.Select(); // select invalid TextBox
50          else if ( !ValidateInput( addressTextBox.Text,
51              @"^[0-9]+\s+([a-zA-Z]+|[a-zA-Z]+\s[a-zA-Z]+)$",
52              "Invalid address" ) )
53
54              addressTextBox.Select(); // select invalid TextBox
55          else if ( !ValidateInput( cityTextBox.Text,
56              @"^([a-zA-Z]+|[a-zA-Z]+\s[a-zA-Z]+)$", "Invalid city" ) )
57
58              cityTextBox.Select(); // select invalid TextBox
59          else if ( !ValidateInput( stateTextBox.Text,
60              @"^([a-zA-Z]+|[a-zA-Z]+\s[a-zA-Z]+)$", "Invalid state" ) )
61
62              stateTextBox.Select(); // select invalid TextBox
63          else if ( !ValidateInput( zipCodeTextBox.Text,
64              @"^\d{5}$", "Invalid zip code" ) )
65
66              zipCodeTextBox.Select(); // select invalid TextBox
67          else if ( !ValidateInput( phoneTextBox.Text,
68              @"^[1-9]\d{2}-[1-9]\d{2}-\d{4}$",
69              "Invalid phone number" ) )
70
71              phoneTextBox.Select(); // select invalid TextBox
72          else // if all input is valid
73          {
74              this.Hide(); // hide main window
75              MessageBox.Show( "Thank You!", "Information Correct",
76                  MessageBoxButtons.OK, MessageBoxIcon.Information );
77              Application.Exit(); // exit the application
78          } // end else
79      } // end else
80  } // end method okButton_Click
81
82  // use regular expressions to validate user input
83  private bool ValidateInput(
84      string input, string expression, string message )
85  {
86      // store whether the input is valid
87      bool valid = Regex.Match( input, expression ).Success;
88
89      // if the input doesn't match the regular expression
90      if ( !valid )
91      {
92          // signal the user that input was invalid
93          MessageBox.Show( message, "Invalid Input",
94              MessageBoxButtons.OK, MessageBoxIcon.Error );
95      } // end if
96
97      return valid; // return whether the input is valid
98  } // end method ValidateInput
99  } // end class ValidateForm
100 } // end namespace Validate
```

Fig. 18.23 | Validating user information using regular expressions. (Part 2 of 4.)

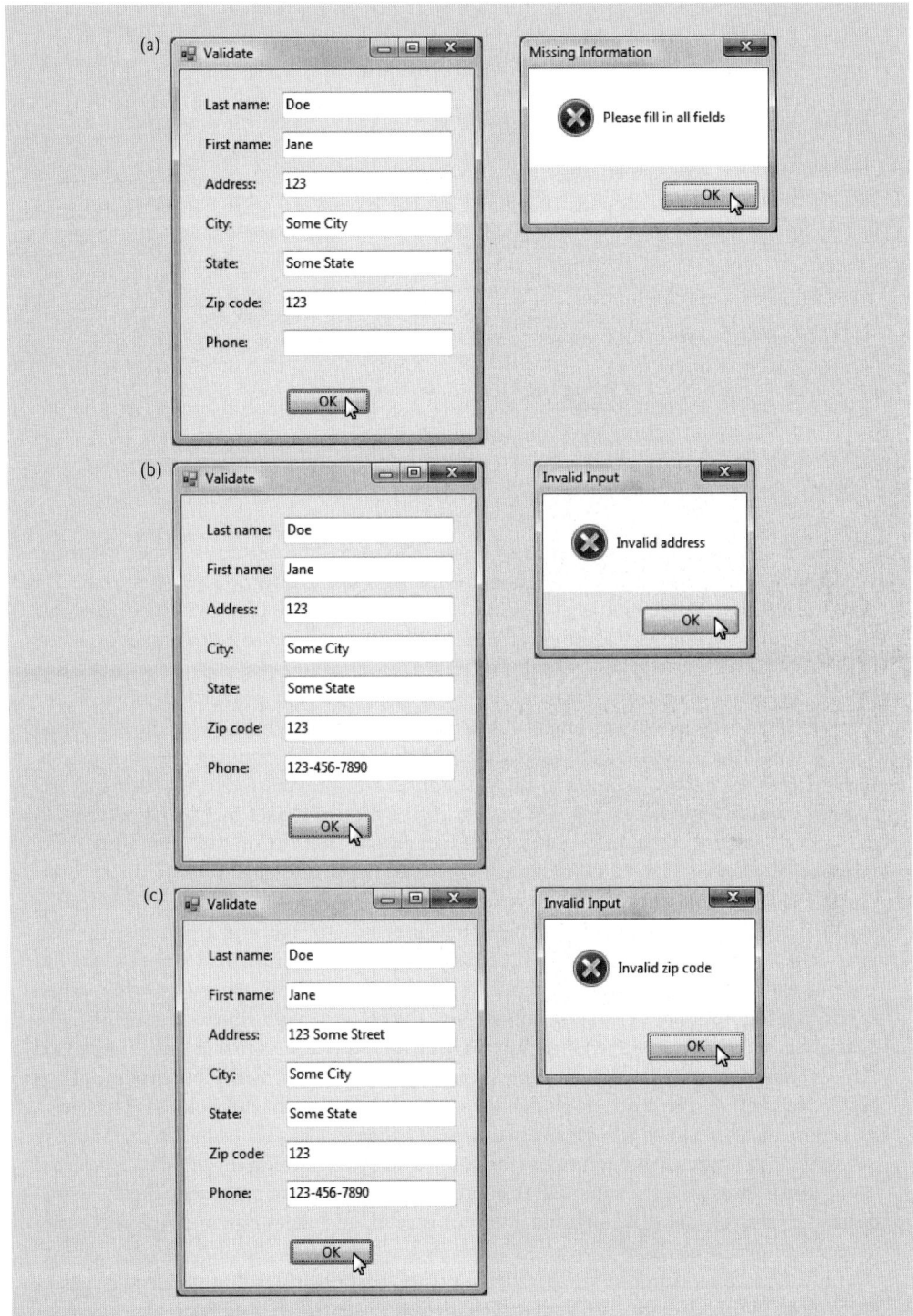

Fig. 18.23 | Validating user information using regular expressions. (Part 3 of 4.)

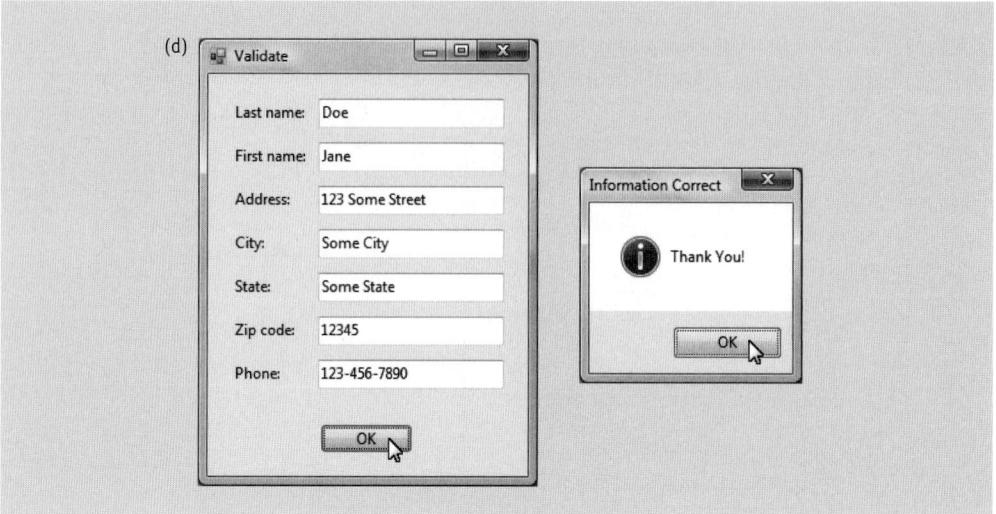

Fig. 18.23 | Validating user information using regular expressions. (Part 4 of 4.)

23) determines whether the currentControl is a TextBox. The *let* clause (line 24) creates and initializes a variable in a LINQ query for use later in the query. Here, we use the let clause to define variable box as a TextBox, which contains the Control object cast to a TextBox. This allows us to use the control in the LINQ query as a TextBox, enabling access to its properties (such as Text). You may include a second where clause after the let clause. The second where clause determines whether the TextBox's Text property is empty. If one or more TextBoxes are empty (line 30), the program displays a message to the user (lines 33–35) that all fields must be filled in before the program can validate the information. Line 37 calls the Select method of the first TextBox in the query result so that the user can begin typing in that TextBox. The query sorted the TextBoxes by TabIndex (line 26) so the first TextBox in the query result is the first empty TextBox on the Form. If there are no empty fields, lines 39–71 validate the user input.

We call method ValidateInput to determine whether the user input matches the specified regular expressions. ValidateInput (lines 83–98) takes as arguments the text input by the user (input), the regular expression the input must match (expression) and a message to display if the input is invalid (message). Line 87 calls Regex static method Match, passing both the string to validate and the regular expression as arguments. The *Success* property of class Match indicates whether method Match's first argument matched the pattern specified by the regular expression in the second argument. If the value of Success is false (i.e., there was no match), lines 93–94 display the error message passed as an argument to method ValidateInput. Line 97 then returns the value of the Success property. If ValidateInput returns false, the TextBox containing invalid data is selected so the user can correct the input. If all input is valid—the else statement (lines 72–78) displays a message dialog stating that all input is valid, and the program terminates when the user dismisses the dialog.

In the previous example, we searched a string for substrings that matched a regular expression. In this example, we want to ensure that the entire string for each input conforms to a particular regular expression. For example, we want to accept "Smith" as a last name, but not "9@Smith#". In a regular expression that begins with a "^" character and ends with a "$" character (e.g., line 43), the characters "^" and "$" represent the beginning and end of a string, respectively. These characters force a regular expression to return a match only if the entire string being processed matches the regular expression.

The regular expressions in lines 43 and 47 use a character class to match an uppercase first letter followed by letters of any case—a-z matches any lowercase letter, and A-Z matches any uppercase letter. The * quantifier signifies that the second range of characters may occur zero or more times in the string. Thus, this expression matches any string consisting of one uppercase letter, followed by zero or more additional letters.

The \s character class matches a single whitespace character (lines 51, 56 and 60). In the expression "\d{5}", used for the zipCode string (line 64), {5} is a quantifier (see Fig. 18.21). The pattern to the left of {n} must occur exactly n times. Thus "\d{5}" matches any five digits. Recall that the character "|" (lines 51, 56 and 60) matches the expression to its left *or* the expression to its right. In line 51, we use the character "|" to indicate that the address can contain a word of one or more characters *or* a word of one or more characters followed by a space and another word of one or more characters. Note the use of parentheses to group parts of the regular expression. This ensures that "|" is applied to the correct parts of the pattern.

The **Last Name:** and **First Name:** TextBoxes each accept strings that begin with an uppercase letter (lines 43 and 47). The regular expression for the **Address:** TextBox (line 51) matches a number of at least one digit, followed by a space and then either one or more letters or else one or more letters followed by a space and another series of one or more letters. Therefore, "10 Broadway" and "10 Main Street" are both valid addresses. As currently formed, the regular expression in line 51 doesn't match an address that does not start with a number, or that has more than two words. The regular expressions for the **City:** (line 56) and **State:** (line 60) TextBoxes match any word of at least one character or, alternatively, any two words of at least one character if the words are separated by a single space. This means both Waltham and West Newton would match. Again, these regular expressions would not accept names that have more than two words. The regular expression for the **Zip code:** TextBox (line 64) ensures that the zip code is a five-digit number. The regular expression for the **Phone:** TextBox (line 68) indicates that the phone number must be of the form xxx-yyy-yyyy, where the xs represent the area code and the ys the number. The first x and the first y cannot be zero, as specified by the range [1-9] in each case.

18.16.4 Regex Methods `Replace` and `Split`

Sometimes it's useful to replace parts of one string with another or to split a string according to a regular expression. For this purpose, class Regex provides static and instance versions of methods Replace and Split, which are demonstrated in Fig. 18.24.

```
1   // Fig. 18.24: RegexSubstitution.cs
2   // Using Regex methods Replace and Split.
3   using System;
4   using System.Text.RegularExpressions;
5
```

Fig. 18.24 | Using Regex methods `Replace` and `Split`. (Part 1 of 2.)

```
 6   class RegexSubstitution
 7   {
 8      static void Main( string[] args )
 9      {
10         string testString1 = "This sentence ends in 5 stars *****";
11         string testString2 = "1, 2, 3, 4, 5, 6, 7, 8";
12         Regex testRegex1 = new Regex( @"\d" );
13         string output = string.Empty;
14
15         Console.WriteLine( "First test string: {0}", testString1 );
16
17         // replace every '*' with a '^' and display the result
18         testString1 = Regex.Replace( testString1, @"\*", "^" );
19         Console.WriteLine( "^ substituted for *: {0}", testString1 );
20
21         // replace the word "stars" with "carets" and display the result
22         testString1 = Regex.Replace( testString1, "stars", "carets" );
23         Console.WriteLine( "\"carets\" substituted for \"stars\": {0}",
24            testString1 );
25
26         // replace every word with "word" and display the result
27         Console.WriteLine( "Every word replaced by \"word\": {0}",
28            Regex.Replace( testString1, @"\w+", "word" ) );
29
30         Console.WriteLine( "\nSecond test string: {0}", testString2 );
31
32         // replace the first three digits with the word "digit"
33         Console.WriteLine( "Replace first 3 digits by \"digit\": {0}",
34            testRegex1.Replace( testString2, "digit", 3 ) );
35
36         Console.Write( "string split at commas [" );
37
38         // split the string into individual strings, each containing a digit
39         string[] result = Regex.Split( testString2, @",\s" );
40
41         // add each digit to the output string
42         foreach( var resultString in result )
43            output += "\"" + resultString + "\", ";
44
45         // delete ", " at the end of output string
46         Console.WriteLine( output.Substring( 0, output.Length - 2 ) + "]" );
47      } // end Main
48   } // end class RegexSubstitution
```

Fig. 18.24 | Using Regex methods Replace and Split. (Part 2 of 2.)

Regex method **Replace** replaces text in a string with new text wherever the original string matches a regular expression. We use two versions of this method in Fig. 18.24. The first version (line 18) is a static method and takes three parameters—the string to modify, the string containing the regular expression to match and the replacement string. Here, Replace replaces every instance of "*" in testString1 with "^". Notice that the regular expression ("*") precedes character * with a backslash (\). Normally, * is a quantifier indicating that a regular expression should match any number of occurrences of a preceding pattern. However, in line 18, we want to find all occurrences of the literal character *; to do this, we must escape character * with character \. By escaping a special regular-expression character, we tell the regular-expression matching engine to find the actual character * rather than use it as a quantifier.

The second version of method `Replace` (line 34) is an instance method that uses the regular expression passed to the constructor for `testRegex1` (line 12) to perform the replacement operation. Line 12 instantiates `testRegex1` with argument @"\d". The call to instance method `Replace` in line 34 takes three arguments—a `string` to modify, a `string` containing the replacement text and an integer specifying the number of replacements to make. In this case, line 34 replaces the first three instances of a digit ("\d") in `testString2` with the text "digit".

Method *Split* divides a `string` into several substrings. The original `string` is broken at delimiters that match a specified regular expression. Method `Split` returns an `array` containing the substrings. In line 39, we use `static` method `Split` to separate a `string` of comma-separated integers. The first argument is the `string` to split; the second argument is the regular expression that represents the delimiter. The regular expression ",\s" separates the substrings at each comma. By matching a whitespace character (\s in the regular expression), we eliminate the extra spaces from the resulting substrings.

18.17 Wrap-Up

In this chapter, you learned about the .NET Framework Class Library's string- and character-processing capabilities. We overviewed the fundamentals of characters and strings. You saw how to determine the length of strings, copy strings, access the individual characters in strings, search strings, obtain substrings from larger strings, compare strings, concatenate strings, replace characters in strings and convert strings to uppercase or lowercase letters.

We showed how to use class `StringBuilder` to build strings dynamically. You learned how to determine and specify the size of a `StringBuilder` object, and how to append, insert, remove and replace characters in a `StringBuilder` object. We then introduced the character-testing methods of type `Char` that enable a program to determine whether a character is a digit, a letter, a lowercase letter, an uppercase letter, a punctuation mark or a symbol other than a punctuation mark, and the methods for converting a character to uppercase or lowercase.

Finally, we discussed classes `Regex`, `Match` and `MatchCollection` from namespace `System.Text.RegularExpressions` and the symbols that are used to form regular expressions. You learned how to find patterns in a `string` and match entire `strings` to patterns with `Regex` methods `Match` and `Matches`, how to replace characters in a `string` with `Regex` method `Replace` and how to split `strings` at delimiters with `Regex` method `Split`. In the next chapter, you'll learn how to read data from and write data to files.

19

Files and Streams

OBJECTIVES

In this chapter you'll learn:

- To create, read, write and update files.

- The C# streams class hierarchy.

- To use classes `File` and `Directory` to obtain information about files and directories on your computer.

- To use LINQ to search through directories.

- To become familiar with sequential-access file processing.

- To use classes `FileStream`, `StreamReader` and `StreamWriter` to read text from and write text to files.

- To use LINQ and `yield return` to iterate through the records in a file and locate records that match specified criteria.

- To use classes `FileStream` and `BinaryFormatter` to read objects from and write objects to files.

Outline

19.1 Introduction
19.2 Data Hierarchy
19.3 Files and Streams
19.4 Classes `File` and `Directory`
19.5 Creating a Sequential-Access Text File
19.6 Reading Data from a Sequential-Access Text File
19.7 Case Study: Credit Inquiry Program Using LINQ
19.8 Serialization
19.9 Creating a Sequential-Access File Using Object Serialization
19.10 Reading and Deserializing Data from a Binary File
19.11 Wrap-Up

19.1 Introduction

Variables and arrays offer only temporary storage of data—the data is lost when a local variable "goes out of scope" or when the program terminates. By contrast, files (and databases, which we cover in Chapter 21) are used for long-term retention of large amounts of data, even after the program that created the data terminates. Data maintained in files often is called *persistent data*. Computers store files on *secondary storage devices*, such as magnetic disks, optical disks, flash memory and magnetic tapes. In this chapter, we explain how to create, update and process data files in C# programs.

We begin with an overview of the data hierarchy from bits to files. Next, we overview some of the .NET Framework Class Library's file-processing classes. We then present two examples that show how you can determine information about the files and directories on your computer. The remainder of the chapter shows how to write to and read from text files that are human readable and binary files that store entire objects in binary format.

19.2 Data Hierarchy

Ultimately, all data items that computers process are reduced to combinations of 0s and 1s. This occurs because it is simple and economical to build electronic devices that can assume two stable states—one state represents 0 and the other represents 1. It is remarkable that the impressive functions performed by computers involve only the most fundamental manipulations of 0s and 1s.

The smallest data item that computers support is called a *bit* (short for "*binary digit*"—a digit that can assume one of two values). Each data item, or bit, can assume either the value 0 or the value 1. Computer circuitry performs various simple bit manipulations, such as examining the value of a bit, setting the value of a bit and reversing a bit (from 1 to 0 or from 0 to 1).

Programming with data in the low-level form of bits is cumbersome. It is preferable to program with data in forms such as *decimal digits* (i.e., 0, 1, 2, 3, 4, 5, 6, 7, 8 and 9), *letters* (i.e., A–Z and a–z) and *special symbols* (i.e., $, @, %, &, *, (,), -, +, ", :, ?, / and many others). Digits, letters and special symbols are referred to as *characters*. The set of all characters used to write programs and represent data items on a particular computer is called that computer's *character set*. Because computers can process only 0s and 1s, every character in a computer's character set is represented as a pattern of 0s and 1s. **Bytes** are composed of eight bits. C# uses the **Unicode® character set** (www.unicode.org) in which characters are composed of 2 bytes. Programmers create programs and data items with characters; computers manipulate and process these characters as patterns of bits.

Just as characters are composed of bits, fields are composed of characters. A *field* is a group of characters that conveys meaning. For example, a field consisting of uppercase and lowercase letters can represent a person's name.

Data items processed by computers form a ***data hierarchy*** (Fig. 19.1), in which data items become larger and more complex in structure as we progress from bits to characters to fields to larger data aggregates.

Typically, a *record* (which can be represented as a class) is composed of several related fields. In a payroll system, for example, a record for a particular employee might include the following fields:

1. Employee identification number

2. Name

3. Address

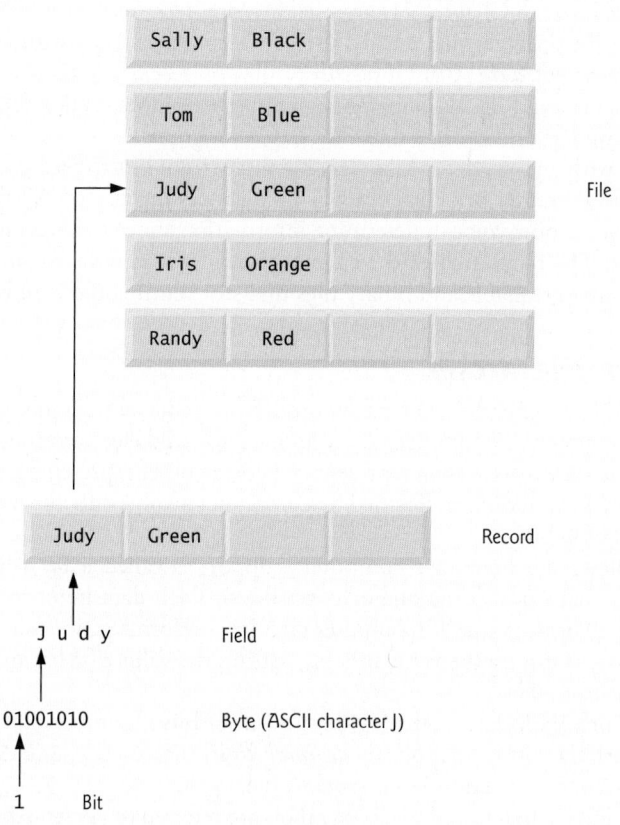

Fig. 19.1 | Data hierarchy.

4. Hourly pay rate

5. Number of exemptions claimed

6. Year-to-date earnings

7. Amount of taxes withheld

In the preceding example, each field is associated with the same employee. A file is a group of related records.[1] A company's payroll file normally contains one record for each employee. A payroll file for a small company might contain only 22 records, whereas one for a large company might contain 100,000. It is not unusual for a company to have many files, some containing millions, billions or even trillions of characters of information.

To facilitate the retrieval of specific records from a file, at least one field in each record is chosen as a *record key*, which identifies a record as belonging to a particular person or entity and distinguishes that record from all others. For example, in a payroll record, the employee identification number normally would be the record key.

There are many ways to organize records in a file. A common organization is called a *sequential file,* in which records typically are stored in order by a record-key field. In a payroll file, records usually are placed in order by employee identification number. The first employee record in the file contains the lowest employee identification number, and subsequent records contain increasingly higher ones.

Most businesses use many different files to store data. For example, a company might have payroll files, accounts-receivable files (listing money due from clients), accounts-payable files (listing money due to suppliers), inventory files (listing facts about all the items handled by the business) and many other files. A group of related files often are stored in a *database*. A collection of programs designed to create and manage databases is called a *database management system (DBMS)*. We discuss databases in Chapter 21.

19.3 Files and Streams

C# views each file as a sequential *stream* of bytes (Fig. 19.2). Each file ends either with an *end-of-file marker* or at a specific byte number that is recorded in a system-maintained administrative data structure. When a file is opened, an object is created and a stream is associated with the object. When a console application executes, the runtime environment creates three stream objects that are accessible via properties **Console.Out**, **Console.In** and **Console.Error**, respectively. These objects facilitate communication between a program and a particular file or device. Console.In refers to the *standard input stream object*,

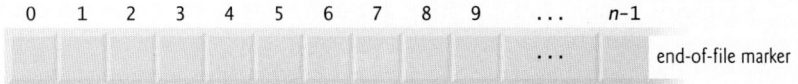

Fig. 19.2 | C#'s view of an *n*-byte file.

---

1. Generally, a file can contain arbitrary data in arbitrary formats. In some operating systems, a file is viewed as nothing more than a collection of bytes, and any organization of the bytes in a file (such as organizing the data into records) is a view created by the application programmer.

which enables a program to input data from the keyboard. `Console.Out` refers to the *standard output stream object*, which enables a program to output data to the screen. `Console.Error` refers to the *standard error stream object*, which enables a program to output error messages to the screen. We have been using `Console.Out` and `Console.In` in our console applications, `Console` methods `Write` and `WriteLine` use `Console.Out` to perform output, and `Console` methods `Read` and `ReadLine` use `Console.In` to perform input.

There are many file-processing classes in the .NET Framework Class Library. The `System.IO` namespace includes stream classes such as ***StreamReader*** (for text input from a file), ***StreamWriter*** (for text output to a file) and ***FileStream*** (for both input from and output to a file). These stream classes inherit from abstract classes ***TextReader***, ***TextWriter*** and `Stream`, respectively. Actually, properties `Console.In` and `Console.Out` are of type `TextReader` and `TextWriter`, respectively. The system creates objects of `TextReader` and `TextWriter` derived classes to initialize `Console` properties `Console.In` and `Console.Out`.

Abstract class ***Stream*** provides functionality for representing streams as bytes. Classes `FileStream`, ***MemoryStream*** and ***BufferedStream*** (all from namespace `System.IO`) inherit from class `Stream`. Class `FileStream` can be used to write data to and read data from files. Class `MemoryStream` enables the transfer of data directly to and from memory—this is much faster than reading from and writing to external devices. Class `BufferedStream` uses *buffering* to transfer data to or from a stream. Buffering is an I/O performance-enhancement technique, in which each output operation is directed to a region in memory, called a *buffer*, that is large enough to hold the data from many output operations. Then actual transfer to the output device is performed in one large *physical output operation* each time the buffer fills. The output operations directed to the output buffer in memory often are called *logical output operations*. Buffering can also be used to speed input operations by initially reading more data than is required into a buffer, so subsequent reads get data from memory rather than an external device.

In this chapter, we use key stream classes to implement file-processing programs that create and manipulate sequential-access files. In Chapter 24, Silverlight, Rich Internet Applications and Multimedia, we use stream classes to implement networking applications.

19.4 Classes `File` and `Directory`

Information is stored in files, which are organized in directories (also called folders). Classes `File` and `Directory` enable programs to manipulate files and directories on disk. Class ***File*** can determine information about files and can be used to open files for reading or writing. We discuss techniques for writing to and reading from files in subsequent sections.

Figure 19.3 lists several of class `File`'s `static` methods for manipulating and determining information about files. We demonstrate several of these methods in Fig. 19.5.

Class ***Directory*** provides capabilities for manipulating directories. Figure 19.4 lists some of class `Directory`'s `static` methods for directory manipulation. Figure 19.5 demonstrates several of these methods, as well. The ***DirectoryInfo*** object returned by method ***CreateDirectory*** contains information about a directory. Much of the information contained in class `DirectoryInfo` also can be accessed via the methods of class `Directory`.

static Method	Description
AppendText	Returns a StreamWriter that appends text to an existing file or creates a file if one does not exist.
Copy	Copies a file to a new file.
Create	Creates a file and returns its associated FileStream.
CreateText	Creates a text file and returns its associated StreamWriter.
Delete	Deletes the specified file.
Exists	Returns true if the specified file exists and false otherwise.
GetCreationTime	Returns a DateTime object representing when the file was created.
GetLastAccessTime	Returns a DateTime object representing when the file was last accessed.
GetLastWriteTime	Returns a DateTime object representing when the file was last modified.
Move	Moves the specified file to a specified location.
Open	Returns a FileStream associated with the specified file and equipped with the specified read/write permissions.
OpenRead	Returns a read-only FileStream associated with the specified file.
OpenText	Returns a StreamReader associated with the specified file.
OpenWrite	Returns a read/write FileStream associated with the specified file.

Fig. 19.3 | File class static methods (partial list).

static Method	Description
CreateDirectory	Creates a directory and returns its associated DirectoryInfo object.
Delete	Deletes the specified directory.
Exists	Returns true if the specified directory exists and false otherwise.
GetDirectories	Returns a string array containing the names of the subdirectories in the specified directory.
GetFiles	Returns a string array containing the names of the files in the specified directory.
GetCreationTime	Returns a DateTime object representing when the directory was created.
GetLastAccessTime	Returns a DateTime object representing when the directory was last accessed.
GetLastWriteTime	Returns a DateTime object representing when items were last written to the directory.
Move	Moves the specified directory to a specified location.

Fig. 19.4 | Directory class static methods.

Demonstrating Classes `File` and `Directory`

Class `FileTestForm` (Fig. 19.5) uses `File` and `Directory` methods to access file and directory information. This `Form` contains the control `inputTextBox`, in which the user enters a file or directory name. For each key that the user presses while typing in the `TextBox`, the program calls event handler `inputTextBox_KeyDown` (lines 19–75). If the user presses the *Enter* key (line 22), this method displays either the file's or directory's contents, depending on the text the user input. (If the user does not press the *Enter* key, this method returns without displaying any content.) Line 28 uses `File` method `Exists` to determine whether the user-specified text is the name of an existing file. If so, line 31 invokes `private` method `GetInformation` (lines 79–97), which calls `File` methods `GetCreationTime` (line 88), `GetLastWriteTime` (line 92) and `GetLastAccessTime` (line 96) to access file information. When method `GetInformation` returns, line 38 instantiates a `StreamReader` for reading text from the file. The `StreamReader` constructor takes as an argument a `string` containing the name of the file to open. Line 40 calls `StreamReader` method `ReadToEnd` to read the entire contents of the file as a `string`, then appends the `string` to `outputTextBox`. Once the file has been read, the `using` block terminates and closes the file.

```
1    // Fig 19.5: FileTestForm.cs
2    // Using classes File and Directory.
3    using System;
4    using System.Windows.Forms;
5    using System.IO;
6
7    namespace FileTest
8    {
9       // displays contents of files and directories
10      public partial class FileTestForm : Form
11      {
12         // parameterless constructor
13         public FileTestForm()
14         {
15            InitializeComponent();
16         } // end constructor
17
18         // invoked when user presses key
19         private void inputTextBox_KeyDown( object sender, KeyEventArgs e )
20         {
21            // determine whether user pressed Enter key
22            if ( e.KeyCode == Keys.Enter )
23            {
24               // get user-specified file or directory
25               string fileName = inputTextBox.Text;
26
27               // determine whether fileName is a file
28               if ( File.Exists( fileName ) )
29               {
30                  // get file's creation date, modification date, etc.
31                  GetInformation( fileName );
32                  StreamReader stream = null; // declare StreamReader
```

Fig. 19.5 | Testing classes `File` and `Directory`. (Part 1 of 3.)

```
33
34                    // display file contents through StreamReader
35                    try
36                    {
37                       // obtain reader and file contents
38                       using ( stream = new StreamReader( fileName ) )
39                       {
40                          outputTextBox.AppendText( stream.ReadToEnd() );
41                       } // end using
42                    } // end try
43                    catch ( IOException )
44                    {
45                       MessageBox.Show( "Error reading from file",
46                          "File Error", MessageBoxButtons.OK,
47                          MessageBoxIcon.Error );
48                    } // end catch
49                 } // end if
50                 // determine whether fileName is a directory
51                 else if ( Directory.Exists( fileName ) )
52                 {
53                    // get directory's creation date,
54                    // modification date, etc.
55                    GetInformation( fileName );
56
57                    // obtain file/directory list of specified directory
58                    string[] directoryList =
59                       Directory.GetDirectories( fileName );
60
61                    outputTextBox.AppendText( "Directory contents:\n" );
62
63                    // output directoryList contents
64                    foreach ( var directory in directoryList )
65                       outputTextBox.AppendText( directory + "\n" );
66                 } // end else if
67                 else
68                 {
69                    // notify user that neither file nor directory exists
70                    MessageBox.Show( inputTextBox.Text +
71                       " does not exist", "File Error",
72                       MessageBoxButtons.OK, MessageBoxIcon.Error );
73                 } // end else
74              } // end if
75           } // end method inputTextBox_KeyDown
76
77           // get information on file or directory,
78           // and output it to outputTextBox
79           private void GetInformation( string fileName )
80           {
81              outputTextBox.Clear();
82
83              // output that file or directory exists
84              outputTextBox.AppendText( fileName + " exists\n" );
```

Fig. 19.5 | Testing classes File and Directory. (Part 2 of 3.)

```
85
86                // output when file or directory was created
87                outputTextBox.AppendText( "Created: " +
88                    File.GetCreationTime( fileName ) + "\n" );
89
90                // output when file or directory was last modified
91                outputTextBox.AppendText( "Last modified: " +
92                    File.GetLastWriteTime( fileName ) + "\n" );
93
94                // output when file or directory was last accessed
95                outputTextBox.AppendText( "Last accessed: " +
96                    File.GetLastAccessTime( fileName ) + "\n" );
97            } // end method GetInformation
98        } // end class FileTestForm
99    } // end namespace FileTest
```

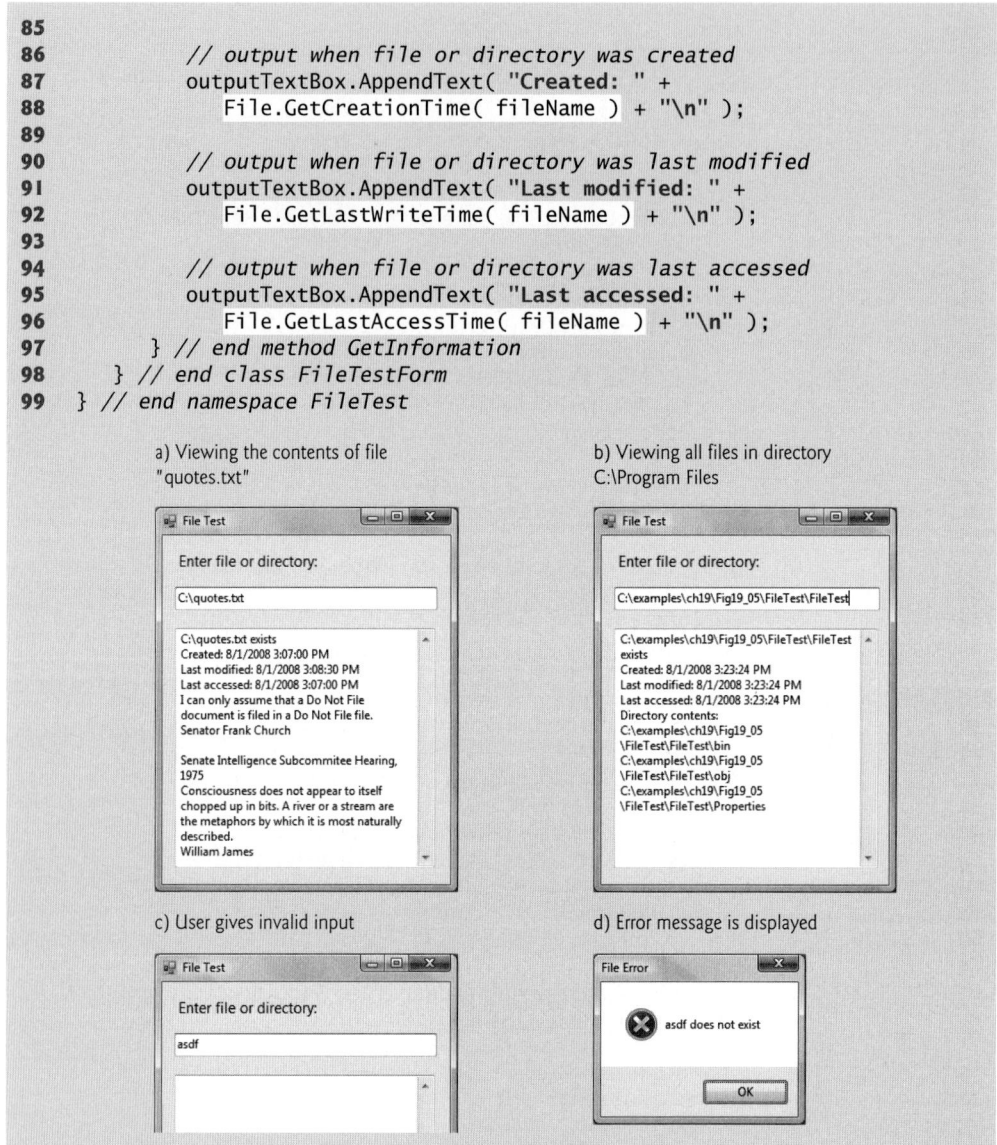

a) Viewing the contents of file "quotes.txt"

b) Viewing all files in directory C:\Program Files

c) User gives invalid input

d) Error message is displayed

Fig. 19.5 | Testing classes `File` and `Directory`. (Part 3 of 3.)

If line 28 determines that the user-specified text is not a file, line 51 determines whether it is a directory using `Directory` method ***Exists***. If the user specified an existing directory, line 55 invokes method `GetInformation` to access the directory information. Line 59 calls `Directory` method ***GetDirectories*** to obtain a `string` array containing the names of subdirectories in the specified directory. Lines 64–65 display each element in the `string` array. Note that, if line 51 determines that the user-specified text is not a directory name, lines 70–72 notify the user (via a `MessageBox`) that the name the user entered does not exist as a file or directory.

Searching Directories with LINQ

We now consider another example that uses file- and directory-manipulation capabilities. Class LINQToFileDirectoryForm (Fig. 19.6) uses LINQ with classes File, Path and Directory to report the number of files of each file type that exist in the specified directory path. The program also serves as a "clean-up" utility—when it finds a file that has the .bak file-name extension (i.e., a backup file), the program displays a MessageBox asking the user whether that file should be removed, then responds appropriately to the user's input. This example also uses LINQ to Objects to help delete the backup files.

When the user clicks **Search Directory**, the program invokes searchButton_Click (lines 25–65), which searches recursively through the directory path specified by the user. If the user inputs text in the TextBox, line 29 calls Directory method Exists to determine whether that text is a valid directory. If it is not, lines 32–33 notify the user of the error.

Lines 38–41 get the current directory (if the user did not specify a path) or the specified directory. Line 49 passes the directory name to recursive method SearchDirectory (lines 68–102). Line 71 calls Directory method **GetFiles** to get a string array containing file names in the specified directory. Line 74 calls Directory method Get-Directories to get a string array containing the subdirectory names in the specified directory.

```
1   // Fig. 19.6: LINQToFileDirectoryForm.cs
2   // Using LINQ to search directories and determine file types.
3   using System;
4   using System.Collections.Generic;
5   using System.Linq;
6   using System.Windows.Forms;
7   using System.IO;
8
9   namespace LINQToFileDirectory
10  {
11     public partial class LINQToFileDirectoryForm : Form
12     {
13        string currentDirectory; // directory to search
14
15        // store extensions found, and number of each extension found
16        Dictionary<string, int> found = new Dictionary<string, int>();
17
18        // parameterless constructor
19        public LINQToFileDirectoryForm()
20        {
21           InitializeComponent();
22        } // end constructor
23
24        // handles the Search Directory Button's Click event
25        private void searchButton_Click( object sender, EventArgs e )
26        {
27           // check whether user specified path exists
28           if ( pathTextBox.Text != string.Empty &&
29              !Directory.Exists( pathTextBox.Text ) )
30           {
```

Fig. 19.6 | Using LINQ to search directories and determine file types. (Part 1 of 4.)

```
31          // show error if user does not specify valid directory
32          MessageBox.Show( "Invalid Directory", "Error",
33             MessageBoxButtons.OK, MessageBoxIcon.Error );
34       } // end if
35       else
36       {
37          // use current directory if no directory is specified
38          if ( pathTextBox.Text == string.Empty )
39             currentDirectory = Directory.GetCurrentDirectory();
40          else
41             currentDirectory = pathTextBox.Text;
42
43          directoryTextBox.Text = currentDirectory; // show directory
44
45          // clear TextBoxes
46          pathTextBox.Clear();
47          resultsTextBox.Clear();
48
49          SearchDirectory( currentDirectory ); // search the directory
50
51          // allow user to delete .bak files
52          CleanDirectory( currentDirectory );
53
54          // summarize and display the results
55          foreach ( var current in found.Keys )
56          {
57             // display the number of files with current extension
58             resultsTextBox.AppendText( string.Format(
59                "* Found {0} {1} files.\r\n",
60                found[ current ], current ) );
61          } // end foreach
62
63          found.Clear(); // clear results for new search
64       } // end else
65    } // end method searchButton_Click
66
67    // search directory using LINQ
68    private void SearchDirectory( string folder )
69    {
70       // files contained in the directory
71       string[] files = Directory.GetFiles( folder );
72
73       // subdirectories in the directory
74       string[] directories = Directory.GetDirectories( folder );
75
76       // find all file extensions in this directory
77       var extensions =
78          ( from file in files
79            select Path.GetExtension( file ) ).Distinct();
80
81       // count the number of files using each extension
82       foreach ( var extension in extensions )
83       {
```

Fig. 19.6 | Using LINQ to search directories and determine file types. (Part 2 of 4.)

```
84                var temp = extension;
85
86                // count the number of files with the extension
87                var extensionCount =
88                    ( from file in files
89                       where Path.GetExtension( file ) == temp
90                       select file ).Count();
91
92                // if the Dictionary already contains a key for the extension
93                if ( found.ContainsKey( extension ) )
94                    found[ extension ] += extensionCount; // update the count
95                else
96                    found.Add( extension, extensionCount ); // add new count
97            } // end foreach
98
99            // recursive call to search subdirectories
100           foreach ( var subdirectory in directories )
101               SearchDirectory( subdirectory );
102       } // end method SearchDirectory
103
104       // allow user to delete backup files (.bak)
105       private void CleanDirectory( string folder )
106       {
107           // files contained in the directory
108           string[] files = Directory.GetFiles( folder );
109
110           // subdirectories in the directory
111           string[] directories = Directory.GetDirectories( folder );
112
113           // select all the backup files in this directory
114           var backupFiles =
115               from file in files
116               where Path.GetExtension( file ) == ".bak"
117               select file;
118
119           // iterate over all backup files (.bak)
120           foreach ( var backup in backupFiles )
121           {
122               DialogResult result = MessageBox.Show( "Found backup file " +
123                   Path.GetFileName( backup ) + ". Delete?", "Delete Backup",
124                   MessageBoxButtons.YesNo, MessageBoxIcon.Question );
125
126               // delete file if user clicked 'yes'
127               if ( result == DialogResult.Yes )
128               {
129                   File.Delete( backup ); // delete backup file
130                   --found[ ".bak" ]; // decrement count in Dictionary
131
132                   // if there are no .bak files, delete key from Dictionary
133                   if ( found[ ".bak" ] == 0 )
134                       found.Remove( ".bak" );
135               } // end if
136           } // end foreach
```

Fig. 19.6 | Using LINQ to search directories and determine file types. (Part 3 of 4.)

```
137
138          // recursive call to clean subdirectories
139          foreach ( var subdirectory in directories )
140              CleanDirectory( subdirectory );
141      } // end method CleanDirectory
142   } // end class LINQToFileDirectoryForm
143 } // end namespace LINQToFileDirectory
```

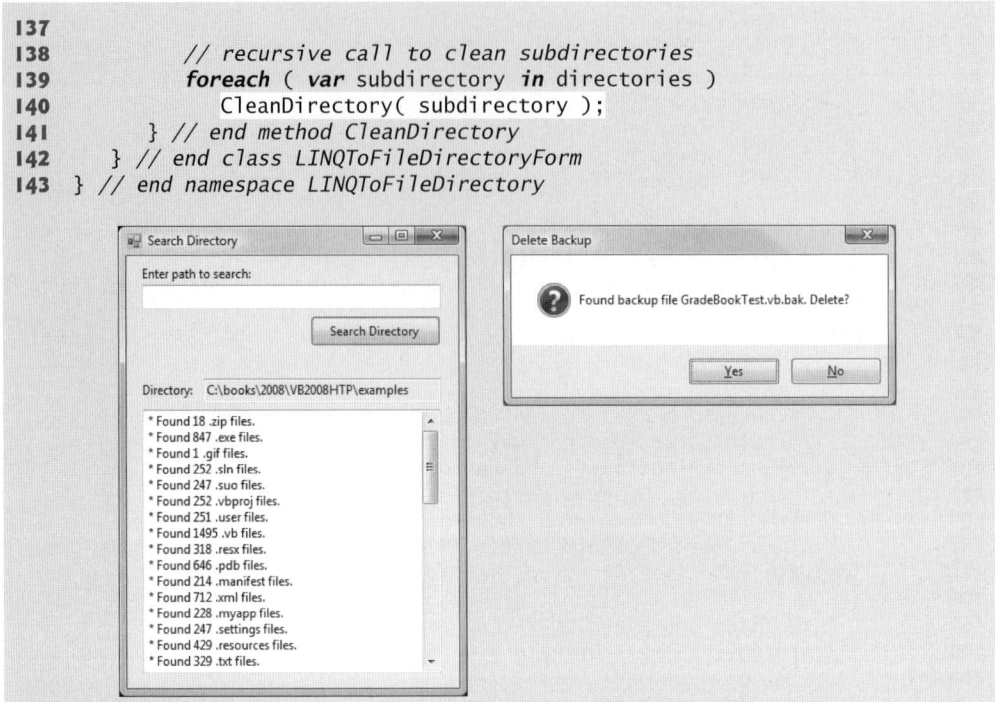

Fig. 19.6 | Using LINQ to search directories and determine file types. (Part 4 of 4.)

Lines 78–79 use LINQ to get the Distinct file-name extensions in the files array. *Path* method *GetExtension* obtains the extension for the specified file name. For each file-name extension returned by the LINQ query, lines 82–97 determine the number of occurrences of that extension in the files array. The LINQ query at lines 88–90 compares each file-name extension in the files array with the current extension being processed (line 89). All matches are included in the result. We then use LINQ method Count to determine the total number of files that matched the current extension.

Class LINQToFileDirectoryForm uses a Dictionary (declared in line 16) to store each file-name extension and the corresponding number of file names with that extension. A *Dictionary* (namespace System.Collections.Generic) is a collection of key/value pairs, in which each key has a corresponding value. Class Dictionary is a generic class like class List (presented in Section 9.3). Line 16 indicates that the Dictionary found contains pairs of strings and ints, which represent the file-name extensions and the number of files with those extensions, respectively. Line 93 uses Dictionary method *ContainsKey* to determine whether the specified file-name extension has been placed in the Dictionary previously. If this method returns true, line 94 adds the extensionCount determined in lines 88–90 to the current total for that extension that is stored in the Dictionary. Otherwise, line 96 uses Dictionary method *Add* to insert a new key/value pair into the Dictionary for the new file-name extension and its extensionCount. Lines 100–101 recursively call SearchDirectory for each subdirectory in the current directory.

When method SearchDirectory returns, line 52 calls CleanDirectory (defined at lines 105–141) to search for all files with extension .bak. Lines 108 and 111 obtain the list of file names and list of directory names in the current directory, respectively. The LINQ query in lines 115–117 locates all file names in the current directory that have the .bak extension. Lines 120–136 iterate through the query's results and prompt the user to determine whether each file should be deleted. If the user clicks **Yes** in the dialog, line 129 uses File method *Delete* to remove the file from disk, and line 130 subtracts 1 from the total number of .bak files. If the number of .bak files remaining is 0, line 134 uses Dictionary method *Remove* to delete the key/value pair for .bak files from the Dictionary. Lines 139–140 recursively call CleanDirectory for each subdirectory in the current directory. After each subdirectory has been checked for .bak files, method CleanDirectory returns, and lines 55–61 display the summary of file-name extensions and the number of files with each extension. Line 55 uses Dictionary property *Keys* to get all the keys in the Dictionary. Line 60 uses the Dictionary's indexer to get the value for the current key. Finally, line 63 uses Dictionary method *Clear* to delete the contents of the Dictionary.

19.5 Creating a Sequential-Access Text File

C# imposes no structure on files. Thus, the concept of a "record" does not exist in C# files. This means that you must structure files to meet the requirements of your applications. In the next few examples, we use text and special characters to organize our own concept of a "record."

Class BankUIForm
The following examples demonstrate file processing in a bank-account maintenance application. These programs have similar user interfaces, so we created reusable class BankUI-Form (Fig. 19.7) to encapsulate a base-class GUI (see the screen capture in Fig. 19.7). Class BankUIForm contains four Labels and four TextBoxes. Methods ClearTextBoxes (lines 28–40), SetTextBoxValues (lines 43–64) and GetTextBoxValues (lines 67–78) clear, set the values of and get the values of the text in the TextBoxes, respectively.

```
1   // Fig. 19.7: BankUIForm.cs
2   // A reusable Windows Form for the examples in this chapter.
3   using System;
4   using System.Windows.Forms;
5
6   namespace BankLibrary
7   {
8      public partial class BankUIForm : Form
9      {
10        protected int TextBoxCount = 4; // number of TextBoxes on Form
11
12        // enumeration constants specify TextBox indices
13        public enum TextBoxIndices
14        {
15           ACCOUNT,
16           FIRST,
17           LAST,
18           BALANCE
19        } // end enum
```

Fig. 19.7 | Base class for GUIs in our file-processing applications. (Part 1 of 3.)

```
20
21        // parameterless constructor
22        public BankUIForm()
23        {
24            InitializeComponent();
25        } // end constructor
26
27        // clear all TextBoxes
28        public void ClearTextBoxes()
29        {
30            // iterate through every Control on form
31            foreach ( Control guiControl in Controls )
32            {
33                // determine whether Control is TextBox
34                if ( guiControl is TextBox )
35                {
36                    // clear TextBox
37                    ( ( TextBox ) guiControl ).Clear();
38                } // end if
39            } // end for
40        } // end method ClearTextBoxes
41
42        // set text box values to string-array values
43        public void SetTextBoxValues( string[] values )
44        {
45            // determine whether string array has correct length
46            if ( values.Length != TextBoxCount )
47            {
48                // throw exception if not correct length
49                throw ( new ArgumentException( "There must be " +
50                    ( TextBoxCount + 1 ) + " strings in the array" ) );
51            } // end if
52            // set array values if array has correct length
53            else
54            {
55                // set array values to textbox values
56                accountTextBox.Text = values[ ( int )
57                    TextBoxIndices.ACCOUNT ];
58                firstNameTextBox.Text = values[ ( int )
59                    TextBoxIndices.FIRST ];
60                lastNameTextBox.Text = values[ ( int ) TextBoxIndices.LAST ];
61                balanceTextBox.Text = values[ ( int )
62                    TextBoxIndices.BALANCE ];
63            } // end else
64        } // end method SetTextBoxValues
65
66        // return textbox values as string array
67        public string[] GetTextBoxValues()
68        {
69            string[] values = new string[ TextBoxCount ];
70
71            // copy textbox fields to string array
72            values[ ( int ) TextBoxIndices.ACCOUNT ] = accountTextBox.Text;
```

Fig. 19.7 | Base class for GUIs in our file-processing applications. (Part 2 of 3.)

```
73              values[ ( int ) TextBoxIndices.FIRST ] = firstNameTextBox.Text;
74              values[ ( int ) TextBoxIndices.LAST ] = lastNameTextBox.Text;
75              values[ ( int ) TextBoxIndices.BALANCE ] = balanceTextBox.Text;
76
77              return values;
78          } // end method GetTextBoxValues
79      } // end class BankUIForm
80  } // end namespace BankLibrary
```

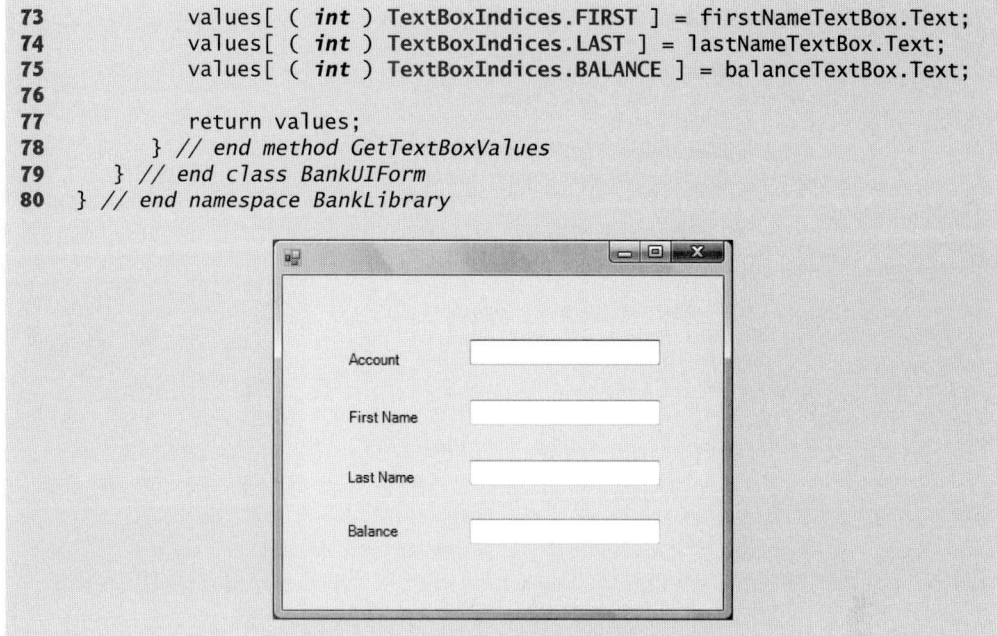

Fig. 19.7 | Base class for GUIs in our file-processing applications. (Part 3 of 3.)

To reuse class BankUIForm, you must compile the GUI into a DLL by creating a project of type **Windows Control Library** (we named it BankLibrary) and add a reference to in your project. This library is provided with the code for this chapter. You might need to change references to this library in our examples when you copy them to your system, since the library most likely will reside in a different location on your system.

Class Record

Figure 19.8 contains class Record that Figs. 19.9, 19.11 and 19.12 use for maintaining the information in each record that is written to or read from a file. This class also belongs to the BankLibrary DLL, so it is located in the same project as class BankUIForm.

Class Record contains auto-implemented properties for instance variables Account, FirstName, LastName and Balance (lines 11–20), which collectively represent all the information for a record. The parameterless constructor (lines 23–26) sets these members by calling the four-argument constructor with 0 for the account number, string.Empty for the first and last name and 0.0M for the balance. The four-argument constructor (lines 29–36) sets these members to the specified parameter values.

```
1   // Fig. 19.8: Record.cs
2   // Class that represents a data record.
3
4   namespace BankLibrary
5   {
```

Fig. 19.8 | Record for sequential-access file-processing applications. (Part 1 of 2.)

```
 6    public class Record
 7    {
 8        // auto-implemented Account property
 9        public int Account { get; set; }
10
11        // auto-implemented FirstName property
12        public string FirstName { get; set; }
13
14        // auto-implemented LastName property
15        public string LastName { get; set; }
16
17        // auto-implemented Balance property
18        public decimal Balance { get; set; }
19
20        // parameterless constructor sets members to default values
21        public Record()
22            : this( 0, string.Empty, string.Empty, 0M )
23        {
24        } // end constructor
25
26        // overloaded constructor sets members to parameter values
27        public RecordSerializable( int accountValue, string firstNameValue,
28            string lastNameValue, decimal balanceValue )
29        {
30            Account = accountValue;
31            FirstName = firstNameValue;
32            LastName = lastNameValue;
33            Balance = balanceValue;
34        } // end constructor
35    } // end class Record
36 } // end namespace BankLibrary
```

Fig. 19.8 | Record for sequential-access file-processing applications. (Part 2 of 2.)

Using a Character Stream to Create an Output File

Class CreateFileForm (Fig. 19.9) uses instances of class Record to create a sequential-access file that might be used in an accounts-receivable system—i.e., a program that organizes data regarding money owed by a company's credit clients. For each client, the program obtains an account number and the client's first name, last name and balance (i.e., the amount of money that the client owes to the company for previously received goods and services). The data obtained for each client constitutes a record for that client. In this application, the account number is used as the record key—files are created and maintained in account-number order. This program assumes that the user enters records in account-number order. However, a comprehensive accounts-receivable system would provide a sorting capability, so the user could enter the records in any order.

Class CreateFileForm either creates or opens a file (depending on whether one exists), then allows the user to write records to it. The using directive in line 6 enables us to use the classes of the BankLibrary namespace; this namespace contains class BankUI-Form, from which class CreateFileForm inherits (line 10). Class CreateFileForm's GUI enhances that of class BankUIForm with buttons **Save As**, **Enter** and **Exit**.

When the user clicks the **Save As** button, the program invokes the event handler saveButton_Click (lines 21–66). Line 27 instantiates an object of class *SaveFileDialog* (namespace System.Windows.Forms). By placing this object in a using statement (lines 27–32), we can ensure that the dialog's Dispose method is called to release its resources as soon as the program has retrieved user input from it. SaveFileDialog objects are used for

```
 1   // Fig. 19.9: CreateFileForm.cs
 2   // Creating a sequential-access file.
 3   using System;
 4   using System.Windows.Forms;
 5   using System.IO;
 6   using BankLibrary;
 7
 8   namespace CreateFile
 9   {
10      public partial class CreateFileForm : BankUIForm
11      {
12         private StreamWriter fileWriter; // writes data to text file
13
14         // parameterless constructor
15         public CreateFileForm()
16         {
17            InitializeComponent();
18         } // end constructor
19
20         // event handler for Save Button
21         private void saveButton_Click( object sender, EventArgs e )
22         {
23            // create and show dialog box enabling user to save file
24            DialogResult result; // result of SaveFileDialog
25            string fileName; // name of file containing data
26
27            using ( SaveFileDialog fileChooser = new SaveFileDialog() )
28            {
29               fileChooser.CheckFileExists = false; // let user create file
30               result = fileChooser.ShowDialog();
31               fileName = fileChooser.FileName; // name of file to save data
32            } // end using
33
34            // ensure that user clicked "OK"
35            if ( result == DialogResult.OK )
36            {
37               // show error if user specified invalid file
38               if ( fileName == string.Empty )
39                  MessageBox.Show( "Invalid File Name", "Error",
40                     MessageBoxButtons.OK, MessageBoxIcon.Error );
41               else
42               {
43                  // save file via FileStream if user specified valid file
44                  try
45                  {
```

Fig. 19.9 | Creating and writing to a sequential-access file. (Part 1 of 5.)

```
46                   // open file with write access
47                   FileStream output = new FileStream( fileName,
48                      FileMode.OpenOrCreate, FileAccess.Write );
49
50                   // sets file to where data is written
51                   fileWriter = new StreamWriter( output );
52
53                   // disable Save button and enable Enter button
54                   saveButton.Enabled = false;
55                   enterButton.Enabled = true;
56                } // end try
57                // handle exception if there is a problem opening the file
58                catch ( IOException )
59                {
60                   // notify user if file does not exist
61                   MessageBox.Show( "Error opening file", "Error",
62                      MessageBoxButtons.OK, MessageBoxIcon.Error );
63                } // end catch
64             } // end else
65          } // end if
66       } // end method saveButton_Click
67
68       // handler for enterButton Click
69       private void enterButton_Click( object sender, EventArgs e )
70       {
71          // store TextBox values string array
72          string[] values = GetTextBoxValues();
73
74          // Record containing TextBox values to serialize
75          Record record = new Record();
76
77          // determine whether TextBox account field is empty
78          if ( values[ ( int ) TextBoxIndices.ACCOUNT ] != string.Empty )
79          {
80             // store TextBox values in Record and serialize Record
81             try
82             {
83                // get account-number value from TextBox
84                int accountNumber = Int32.Parse(
85                   values[ ( int ) TextBoxIndices.ACCOUNT ] );
86
87                // determine whether accountNumber is valid
88                if ( accountNumber > 0 )
89                {
90                   // store TextBox fields in Record
91                   record.Account = accountNumber;
92                   record.FirstName = values[ ( int )
93                      TextBoxIndices.FIRST ];
94                   record.LastName = values[ ( int )
95                      TextBoxIndices.LAST ];
96                   record.Balance = Decimal.Parse(
97                      values[ ( int ) TextBoxIndices.BALANCE ] );
```

Fig. 19.9 | Creating and writing to a sequential-access file. (Part 2 of 5.)

```
98
99                      // write Record to file, fields separated by commas
100                     fileWriter.WriteLine(
101                        record.Account + "," + record.FirstName + "," +
102                        record.LastName + "," + record.Balance );
103                  } // end if
104                  else
105                  {
106                     // notify user if invalid account number
107                     MessageBox.Show( "Invalid Account Number", "Error",
108                        MessageBoxButtons.OK, MessageBoxIcon.Error );
109                  } // end else
110               } // end try
111               // notify user if error occurs in serialization
112               catch ( IOException )
113               {
114                  MessageBox.Show( "Error Writing to File", "Error",
115                     MessageBoxButtons.OK, MessageBoxIcon.Error );
116               } // end catch
117               // notify user if error occurs regarding parameter format
118               catch ( FormatException )
119               {
120                  MessageBox.Show( "Invalid Format", "Error",
121                     MessageBoxButtons.OK, MessageBoxIcon.Error );
122               } // end catch
123            } // end if
124
125            ClearTextBoxes(); // clear TextBox values
126         } // end method enterButton_Click
127
128         // handler for exitButton Click
129         private void exitButton_Click( object sender, EventArgs e )
130         {
131            // determine whether file exists
132            if ( fileWriter != null )
133            {
134               try
135               {
136                  // close StreamWriter and underlying file
137                  fileWriter.Close();
138               } // end try
139               // notify user of error closing file
140               catch ( IOException )
141               {
142                  MessageBox.Show( "Cannot close file", "Error",
143                     MessageBoxButtons.OK, MessageBoxIcon.Error );
144               } // end catch
145            } // end if
146
147            Application.Exit();
148         } // end method exitButton_Click
149      } // end class CreateFileForm
150   } // end namespace CreateFile
```

Fig. 19.9 | Creating and writing to a sequential-access file. (Part 3 of 5.)

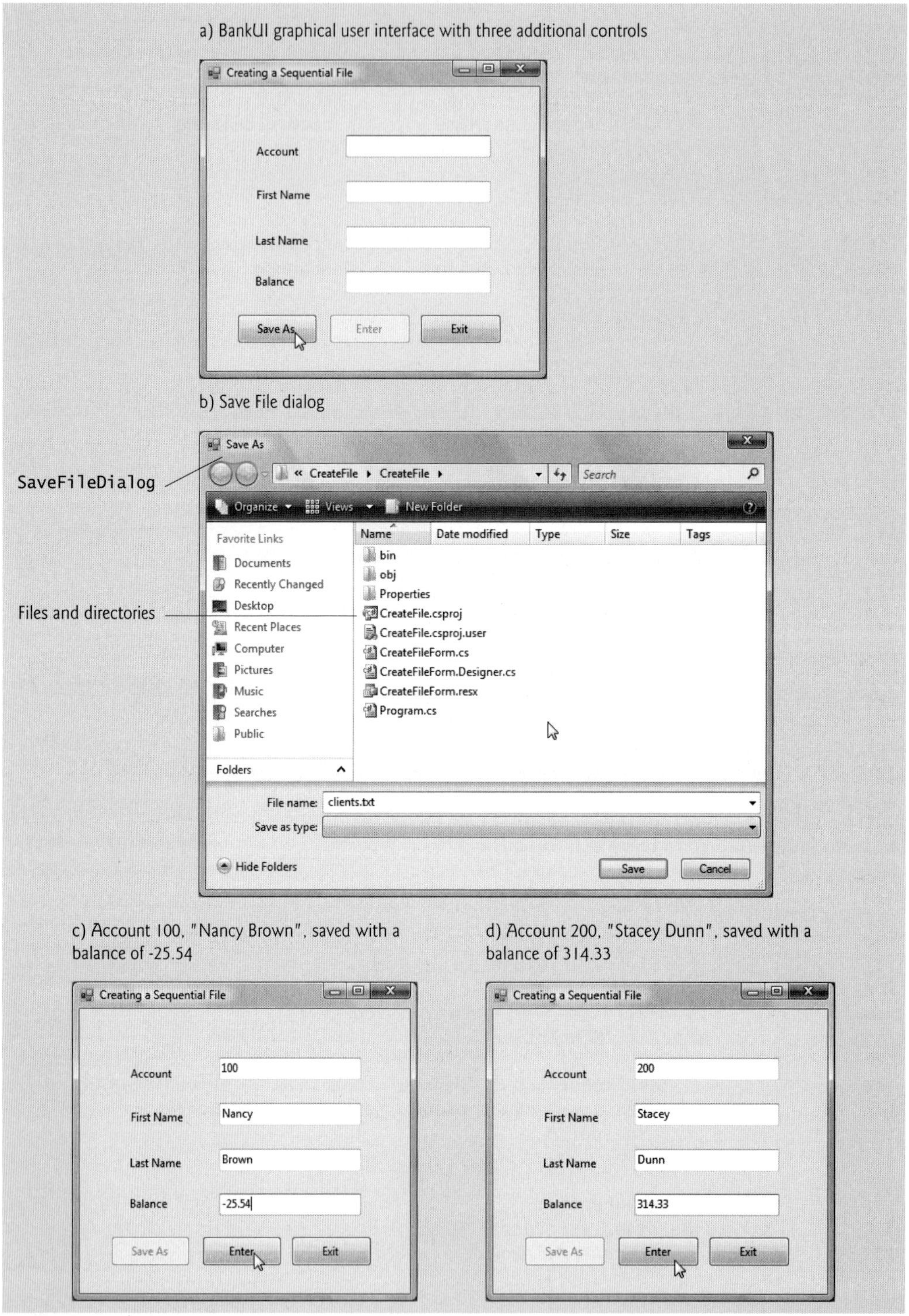

a) BankUI graphical user interface with three additional controls

d) Account 200, "Stacey Dunn", saved with a balance of 314.33

b) Save File dialog

SaveFileDialog

Files and directories

c) Account 100, "Nancy Brown", saved with a balance of -25.54

Fig. 19.9 | Creating and writing to a sequential-access file. (Part 4 of 5.)

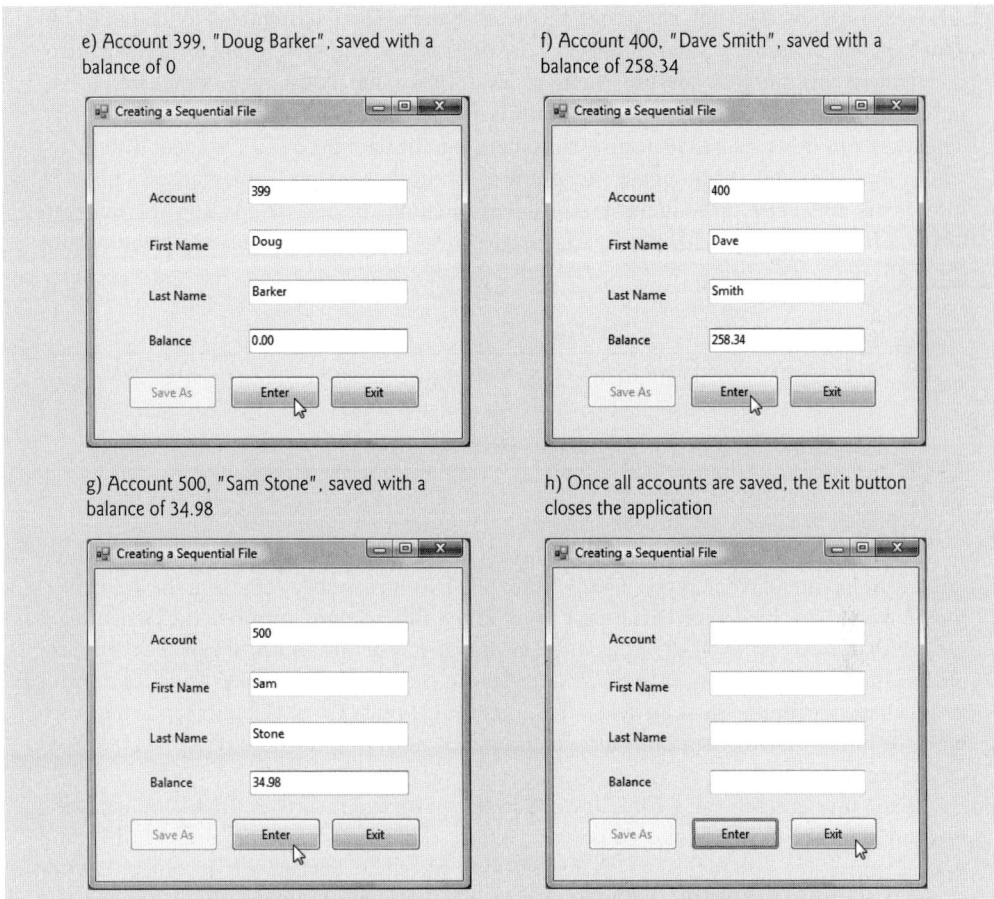

e) Account 399, "Doug Barker", saved with a balance of 0

f) Account 400, "Dave Smith", saved with a balance of 258.34

g) Account 500, "Sam Stone", saved with a balance of 34.98

h) Once all accounts are saved, the Exit button closes the application

Fig. 19.9 | Creating and writing to a sequential-access file. (Part 5 of 5.)

selecting files (see the second screen in Fig. 19.9). Line 30 calls SaveFileDialog method ShowDialog to display the dialog. When displayed, a SaveFileDialog prevents the user from interacting with any other window in the program until the user closes the Save-FileDialog by clicking either **Save** or **Cancel**. Dialogs that behave in this manner are called *modal dialogs*. The user selects the appropriate drive, directory and file name, then clicks **Save**. Method *ShowDialog* returns a DialogResult specifying which button (**Save** or **Cancel**) the user clicked to close the dialog. This is assigned to DialogResult variable result (line 30). Line 35 tests whether the user clicked **OK** by comparing this value to DialogResult.OK. If the values are equal, method saveButton_Click continues.

You can open files to perform text manipulation by creating objects of class FileStream. In this example, we want the file to be opened for output, so lines 47–48 create a FileStream object. The FileStream constructor that we use receives three arguments—a string containing the path and name of the file to open, a constant describing how to open the file and a constant describing the file permissions. The constant FileMode.OpenOrCreate (line 48) indicates that the FileStream object should open the file if it exists or create the file if it does not exist. Note that the contents of an existing file are overwritten by the StreamWriter. To preserve the original contents of a file, use File-Mode.Append. There are other FileMode constants describing how to open files; we introduce these constants as we use them in examples. The constant FileAccess.Write indicates that the program can perform only write operations with the FileStream object. There are two other constants for the third constructor parameter—FileAccess.Read for read-only access and FileAccess.ReadWrite for both read and write access. Line 58 catches an *IOException* if there is a problem opening the file or creating the Stream-Writer. If so, the program displays an error message (lines 61–62). If no exception occurs, the file is open for writing.

Good Programming Practice 19.1

When opening files, use the FileAccess enumeration to control user access to these files.

Common Programming Error 19.1

Failure to open a file before attempting to use it in a program is a logic error.

After typing information into each TextBox, the user clicks the **Enter** button, which calls event handler enterButton_Click (lines 69–126) to save the data from the TextBoxes into the user-specified file. If the user entered a valid account number (i.e., an integer greater than zero), lines 91–97 store the TextBox values in an object of type Record (created at line 75). If the user entered invalid data in one of the TextBoxes (such as nonnumeric characters in the **Balance** field), the program throws a FormatException. The catch block in lines 112–116 handles such exceptions by notifying the user (via a MessageBox) of the improper format.

If the user entered valid data, lines 100–102 write the record to the file by invoking method WriteLine of the StreamWriter object that was created at line 51. Method WriteLine writes a sequence of characters to a file. The StreamWriter object is constructed with a FileStream argument that specifies the file to which the StreamWriter will output text. Class StreamWriter belongs to the System.IO namespace.

When the user clicks **Exit**, exitButton_Click (lines 129–148) executes. Line 137 closes the StreamWriter, which automatically closes the FileStream. Then, line 147 terminates the program. Note that method Close is called in a try block. Method Close throws an IOException if the file or stream cannot be closed properly. In this case, it is important to notify the user that the information in the file or stream might be corrupted.

Performance Tip 19.1

Close each file explicitly when the program no longer needs to reference it. This can reduce resource usage in programs that continue executing long after they finish using a specific file. The practice of explicitly closing files also improves program clarity.

Performance Tip 19.2

Releasing resources explicitly when they are no longer needed makes them immediately available for reuse by other programs, thus improving resource utilization.

In the sample execution for the program in Fig. 19.9, we entered information for the five accounts shown in Fig. 19.10. The program does not depict how the data records are rendered in the file. To verify that the file has been created successfully, we create a program in the next section to read and display the file. Since this is a text file, you can actually open it in any text editor to see its contents.

Account number	First name	Last name	Balance
100	Nancy	Brown	-25.54
200	Stacey	Dunn	314.33
300	Doug	Barker	0.00
400	Dave	Smith	258.34
500	Sam	Stone	34.98

Fig. 19.10 | Sample data for the program of Fig. 19.9.

19.6 Reading Data from a Sequential-Access Text File

The previous section demonstrated how to create a file for use in sequential-access applications. In this section, we discuss how to read (or retrieve) data sequentially from a file.

Class `ReadSequentialAccessFileForm` (Fig. 19.11) reads records from the file created by the program in Fig. 19.9, then displays the contents of each record. Much of the code in this example is similar to that of Fig. 19.9, so we discuss only the unique aspects of the application.

```csharp
1   // Fig. 19.11: ReadSequentialAccessFileForm.cs
2   // Reading a sequential-access file.
3   using System;
4   using System.Windows.Forms;
5   using System.IO;
6   using BankLibrary;
7
8   namespace ReadSequentialAccessFile
9   {
10     public partial class ReadSequentialAccessFileForm : BankUIForm
11     {
12        private StreamReader fileReader; // reads data from a text file
13
14        // parameterless constructor
15        public ReadSequentialAccessFileForm()
16        {
17           InitializeComponent();
18        } // end constructor
19
20        // invoked when user clicks the Open button
21        private void openButton_Click( object sender, EventArgs e )
22        {
23           // create and show dialog box enabling user to open file
24           DialogResult result; // result of OpenFileDialog
25           string fileName; // name of file containing data
```

Fig. 19.11 | Reading sequential-access files. (Part 1 of 5.)

```
26
27        using ( OpenFileDialog fileChooser = new OpenFileDialog() )
28        {
29            result = fileChooser.ShowDialog();
30            fileName = fileChooser.FileName; // get specified name
31        } // end using
32
33        // ensure that user clicked "OK"
34        if ( result == DialogResult.OK )
35        {
36            ClearTextBoxes();
37
38            // show error if user specified invalid file
39            if ( fileName == string.Empty )
40                MessageBox.Show( "Invalid File Name", "Error",
41                    MessageBoxButtons.OK, MessageBoxIcon.Error );
42            else
43            {
44                try
45                {
46                    // create FileStream to obtain read access to file
47                    FileStream input = new FileStream(
48                        fileName, FileMode.Open, FileAccess.Read );
49
50                    // set file from where data is read
51                    fileReader = new StreamReader( input );
52
53                    openButton.Enabled = false; // disable Open File button
54                    nextButton.Enabled = true; // enable Next Record button
55                } // end try
56                catch ( IOException )
57                {
58                    MessageBox.Show( "Error reading from file",
59                        "File Error", MessageBoxButtons.OK,
60                        MessageBoxIcon.Error );
61                } // end catch
62            } // end else
63        } // end if
64    } // end method openButton_Click
65
66    // invoked when user clicks Next button
67    private void nextButton_Click( object sender, EventArgs e )
68    {
69        try
70        {
71            // get next record available in file
72            string inputRecord = fileReader.ReadLine();
73            string[] inputFields; // will store individual pieces of data
74
75            if ( inputRecord != null )
76            {
77                inputFields = inputRecord.Split( ',' );
78
```

Fig. 19.11 | Reading sequential-access files. (Part 2 of 5.)

```
79              Record record = new Record(
80                 Convert.ToInt32( inputFields[ 0 ] ), inputFields[ 1 ],
81                 inputFields[ 2 ], Convert.ToDecimal(
82                 inputFields[ 3 ] ) );
83
84              // copy string-array values to TextBox values
85              SetTextBoxValues( inputFields );
86           } // end if
87           else
88           {
89              // close StreamReader and underlying file
90              fileReader.Close();
91              openButton.Enabled = true; // enable Open File button
92              nextButton.Enabled = false; // disable Next Record button
93              ClearTextBoxes();
94
95              // notify user if no Records in file
96              MessageBox.Show( "No more records in file", string.Empty,
97                 MessageBoxButtons.OK, MessageBoxIcon.Information );
98           } // end else
99        } // end try
100       catch ( IOException )
101       {
102          MessageBox.Show( "Error Reading from File", "Error",
103             MessageBoxButtons.OK, MessageBoxIcon.Error );
104       } // end catch
105    } // end method nextButton_Click
106 } // end class ReadSequentialAccessFileForm
107 } // end namespace ReadSequentialAccessFile
```

a) BankUI graphical user interface with an Open File button

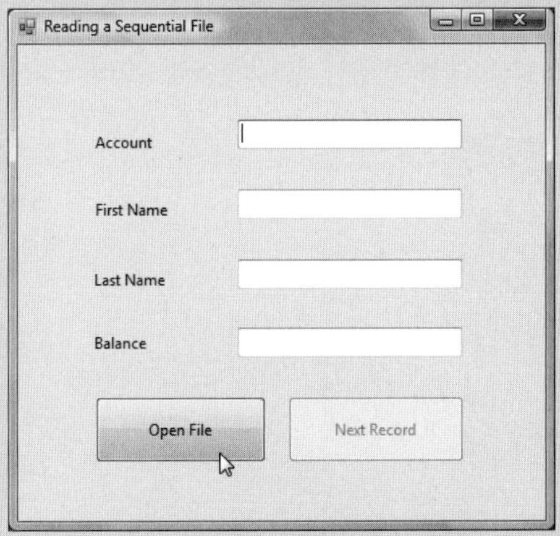

Fig. 19.11 | Reading sequential-access files. (Part 3 of 5.)

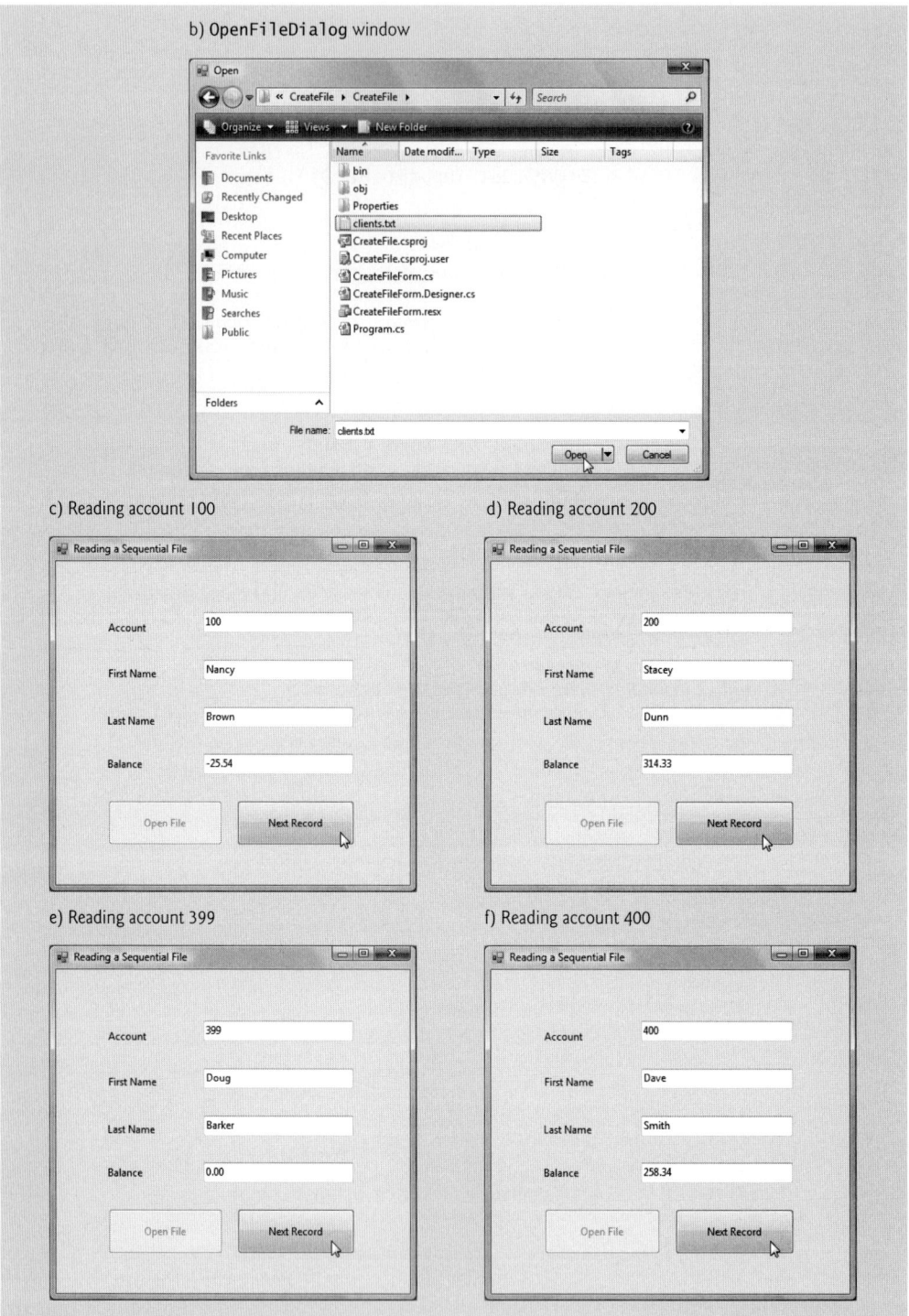

Fig. 19.11 | Reading sequential-access files. (Part 4 of 5.)

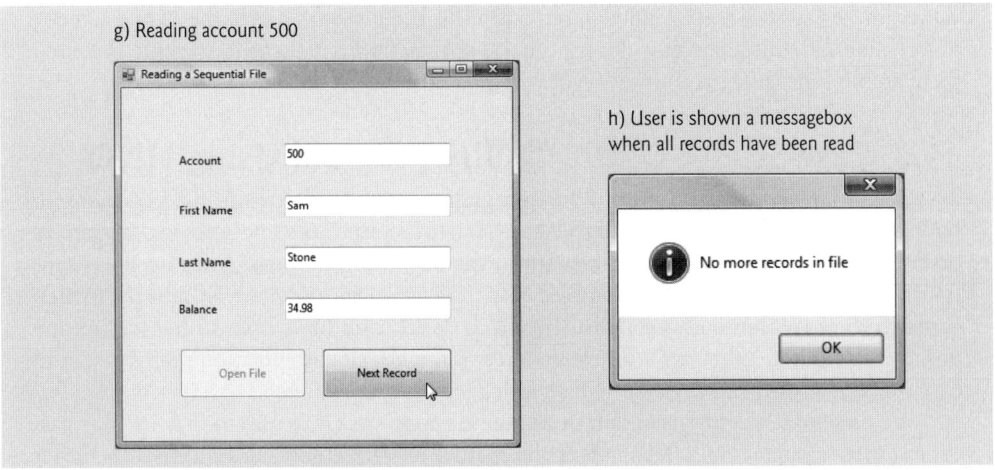

g) Reading account 500

h) User is shown a messagebox when all records have been read

Fig. 19.11 | Reading sequential-access files. (Part 5 of 5.)

When the user clicks the **Open File** button, the program calls event handler open-Button_Click (lines 21–64). Line 27 creates an ***OpenFileDialog***, and line 29 calls its ***ShowDialog*** method to display the **Open** dialog (see the second screenshot in Fig. 19.11). The behavior and GUI for the **Save** and **Open** dialog types are identical, except that **Save** is replaced by **Open**. If the user selects a valid file name, lines 47–48 create a FileStream object and assign it to reference input. We pass constant FileMode.Open as the second argument to the FileStream constructor to indicate that the FileStream should open the file if it exists or throw a FileNotFoundException if it does not. (In this example, the FileStream constructor will not throw a FileNotFoundException, because the Open-FileDialog requires the user to enter a name of a file that exists.) In the last example (Fig. 19.9), we wrote text to the file using a FileStream object with write-only access. In this example (Fig. 19.11), we specify read-only access to the file by passing constant File-Access.Read as the third argument to the FileStream constructor. This FileStream object is used to create a StreamReader object in line 51. The FileStream object specifies the file from which the StreamReader object will read text.

Error-Prevention Tip 19.1

Open a file with the FileAccess.Read file-open mode if its contents should not be modified. This prevents unintentional modification of the contents.

When the user clicks the **Next Record** button, the program calls event handler nextButton_Click (lines 67–104), which reads the next record from the user-specified file. (The user must click **Next Record** after opening the file to view the first record.) Line 72 calls StreamReader method ReadLine to read the next record. If an error occurs while reading the file, an IOException is thrown (caught at line 99), and the user is notified (lines 101–102). Otherwise, line 75 determines whether StreamReader method ReadLine returned null (i.e., there is no more text in the file). If not, line 77 uses method Split of class string to separate the stream of characters that was read from the file into strings that represent the Record's properties. These properties are then stored by constructing a Record object using the properties as arguments (lines 79–81). Line 84 displays the Record values in the TextBoxes. If ReadLine returns null, the program closes the StreamReader object (line 89), automatically closing the FileStream object, then notifies the user that there are no more records (lines 95–96).

19.7 Case Study: Credit Inquiry Program Using LINQ

To retrieve data sequentially from a file, programs normally start from the beginning of the file, reading consecutively until the desired data is found. It sometimes is necessary to process a file sequentially several times (from the beginning of the file) during the execution of a program. A FileStream object can reposition its *file-position pointer* (which contains the byte number of the next byte to be read from or written to the file) to any position in the file. When a FileStream object is opened, its file-position pointer is set to byte position 0 (i.e., the beginning of the file)

We now present a program that builds on the concepts employed in Fig. 19.11. Class CreditInquiryForm (Fig. 19.12) is a credit-inquiry program that enables a credit manager to search for and display account information for those customers with credit balances (i.e., customers to whom the company owes money), zero balances (i.e., customers who do not owe the company money) and debit balances (i.e., customers who owe the company money for previously received goods and services). We use a RichTextBox in the program to display the account information. RichTextBoxes provide more functionality than regular TextBoxes—for example, RichTextBoxes offer method Find for searching individual strings and method LoadFile for displaying file contents. Classes RichTextBox and TextBox both inherit from abstract class System.Windows.Forms.TextBoxBase. In this example, we chose a RichTextBox, because it displays multiple lines of text by default, whereas a regular TextBox displays only one. Alternatively, we could have specified that a TextBox object display multiple lines of text by setting its Multiline property to true.

The program displays buttons that enable a credit manager to obtain credit information. The **Open File** button opens a file for gathering data. The **Credit Balances** button displays a list of accounts that have credit balances, the **Debit Balances** button displays a list of accounts that have debit balances and the **Zero Balances** button displays a list of accounts that have zero balances. The **Done** button exits the application.

When the user clicks the **Open File** button, the program calls the event handler openButton_Click (lines 27–61). Line 32 creates an OpenFileDialog, and line 34 calls its ShowDialog method to display the **Open** dialog, in which the user selects the file to open. Lines 48–49 create a FileStream object with read-only file access and assign it to reference input. Line 52 creates a StreamReader object that we use to read text from the FileStream.

```
1   // Fig. 19.12: CreditInquiryForm.cs
2   // Read a file sequentially and display contents based on
3   // account type specified by user ( credit, debit or zero balances ).
4   using System;
5   using System.Windows.Forms;
6   using System.IO;
7   using System.Linq;
8   using System.Collections.Generic;
```

Fig. 19.12 | Credit-inquiry program. (Part 1 of 6.)

```
 9
10   namespace CreditInquiry
11   {
12      public partial class CreditInquiryForm : Form
13      {
14         private FileStream input; // maintains the connection to the file
15         private StreamReader fileReader; // reads data from text file
16
17         // name of file that stores credit, debit and zero balances
18         private string fileName;
19
20         // parameterless constructor
21         public CreditInquiryForm()
22         {
23            InitializeComponent();
24         } // end constructor
25
26         // invoked when user clicks Open File button
27         private void openButton_Click( object sender, EventArgs e )
28         {
29            // create dialog box enabling user to open file
30            DialogResult result;
31
32            using ( OpenFileDialog fileChooser = new OpenFileDialog() )
33            {
34               result = fileChooser.ShowDialog();
35               fileName = fileChooser.FileName;
36            } // end using
37
38            // exit event handler if user clicked Cancel
39            if ( result == DialogResult.OK )
40            {
41               // show error if user specified invalid file
42               if ( fileName == string.Empty )
43                  MessageBox.Show( "Invalid File Name", "Error",
44                     MessageBoxButtons.OK, MessageBoxIcon.Error );
45               else
46               {
47                  // create FileStream to obtain read access to file
48                  input = new FileStream( fileName,
49                     FileMode.Open, FileAccess.Read );
50
51                  // set file from where data is read
52                  fileReader = new StreamReader( input );
53
54                  // enable all GUI buttons, except for Open File button
55                  openButton.Enabled = false;
56                  creditButton.Enabled = true;
57                  debitButton.Enabled = true;
58                  zeroButton.Enabled = true;
59               } // end else
60            } // end if
61         } // end method openButton_Click
```

Fig. 19.12 | Credit-inquiry program. (Part 2 of 6.)

```
62
63      // invoked when user clicks credit balances,
64      // debit balances or zero balances button
65      private void getBalances_Click( object sender, System.EventArgs e )
66      {
67          // delegate used to check a balance against a certain condition
68          Func< decimal, bool > balanceChooser;
69
70          // convert sender explicitly to object of type button
71          Button senderButton = ( Button ) sender;
72
73          // determine the condition the account balances must satisfy
74          switch ( senderButton.Text )
75          {
76              case "Credit Balances":  // positive balances
77                  balanceChooser = balance => balance > 0M;
78                  break;
79              case "Debit Balances": // negative balances
80                  balanceChooser = balance => balance < 0M;
81                  break;
82              default: // zero balances
83                  balanceChooser = balance => balance == 0;
84                  break;
85          } // end switch
86
87          // read and display file information
88          try
89          {
90              displayTextBox.Text = "The accounts are:\n";
91
92              // select records that match account type
93              var balanceQuery =
94                  from line in fileReader.Lines()
95                  let record = line.Split( ',' ) as string[]
96                  where balanceChooser( Convert.ToDecimal( record[ 3 ] ) )
97                  select new Record
98                  {
99                      Account = Convert.ToInt32( record[ 0 ] ),
100                     FirstName = record[ 1 ],
101                     LastName = record[ 2 ],
102                     Balance = Convert.ToDecimal( record[ 3 ] )
103                 };
104
105             // display each selected Record
106             foreach ( var creditRecord in balanceQuery )
107             {
108                 // display the Record's information in the RichTextBox
109                 displayTextBox.AppendText(
110                     string.Format( "{0}\t{1}\t{2}\n", creditRecord.Account,
111                     creditRecord.FirstName, creditRecord.LastName ) );
112             } // end foreach
113         } // end try
```

Fig. 19.12 | Credit-inquiry program. (Part 3 of 6.)

```
114            // handle exception when file cannot be read
115            catch ( IOException )
116            {
117               MessageBox.Show( "Cannot Read File", "Error",
118                  MessageBoxButtons.OK, MessageBoxIcon.Error );
119            } // end catch
120         } // end method getBalances_Click
121
122         // invoked when user clicks Done button
123         private void doneButton_Click( object sender, EventArgs e )
124         {
125            if ( input != null )
126            {
127               // close file and StreamReader
128               try
129               {
130                  // close StreamReader and underlying file
131                  fileReader.Close();
132               } // end try
133               // handle exception if FileStream does not exist
134               catch ( IOException )
135               {
136                  // notify user of error closing file
137                  MessageBox.Show( "Cannot close file", "Error",
138                     MessageBoxButtons.OK, MessageBoxIcon.Error );
139               } // end catch
140            } // end if
141
142            Application.Exit();
143         } // end method doneButton_Click
144      } // end class CreditInquiryForm
145
146      // static class containing extension methods for class StreamReader
147      public static class StreamReaderExtensions
148      {
149         // iterate over each line in a file
150         public static IEnumerable<string> Lines( this StreamReader source )
151         {
152            // check for null reference
153            if ( source == null )
154               throw new ArgumentNullException( "StreamReader is null" );
155
156            // start at the beginning of the file
157            source.BaseStream.Seek( 0, SeekOrigin.Begin );
158
159            string line; // a line of text
160
161            // while there are lines left in the file
162            while ( ( line = source.ReadLine() ) != null )
163            {
164               yield return line; // return one line of the file as a string
165            } // end while
166         } // end extension method Lines
```

Fig. 19.12 | Credit-inquiry program. (Part 4 of 6.)

```
167     } // end static class StreamReaderExtensions
168 } // end namespace CreditInquiry
```

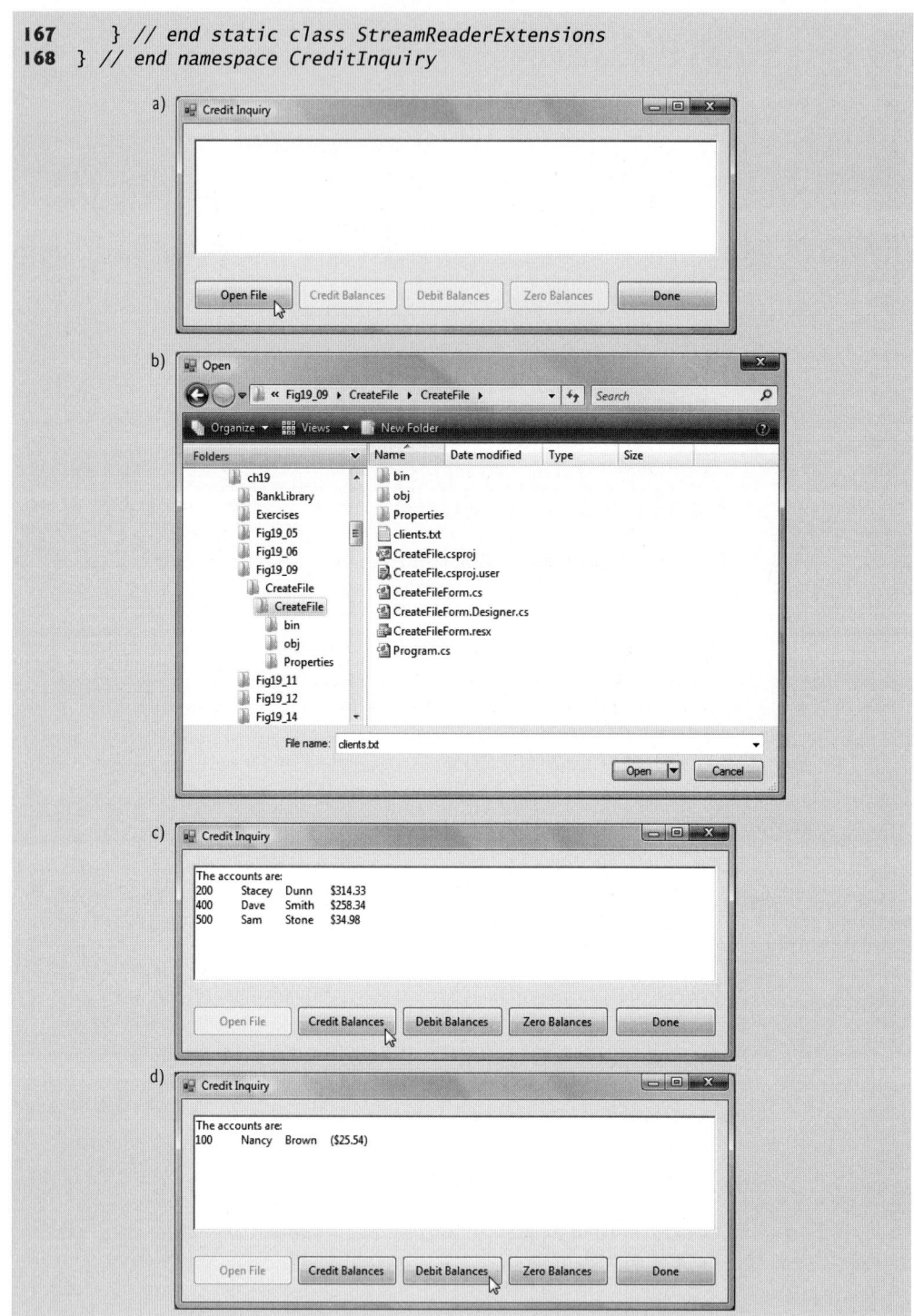

Fig. 19.12 | Credit-inquiry program. (Part 5 of 6.)

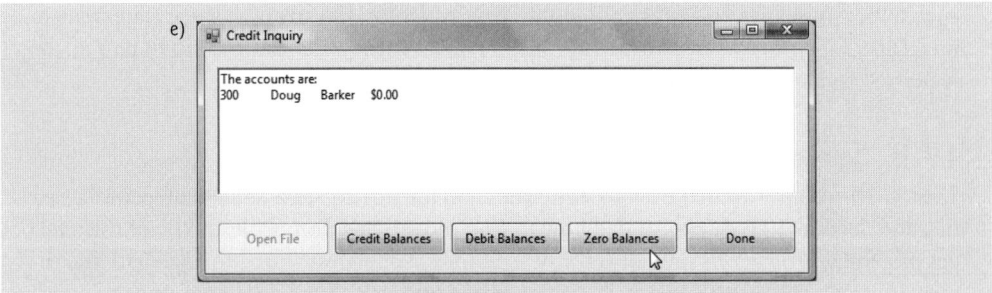

Fig. 19.12 | Credit-inquiry program. (Part 6 of 6.)

When the user clicks **Credit Balances, Debit Balances** or **Zero Balances**, the program invokes method getBalances_Click (lines 65–120). Line 68 uses class *Func* (namespace System) to declare variable balanceChooser as a delegate to a function that receives a decimal and returns a bool. The value for this variable is set in lines 47–57 and used in the LINQ query in lines 74–85 to determine which accounts are selected. Line 71 converts the sender parameter's type to Button. This parameter represents the control that generated the event. This conversion allows the event handler to use the properties and methods of the Button the user pressed. Line 74 obtains the Button object's text, which the program uses to determine which type of accounts to display.

Depending on the Button that was pressed, lines 74–85 create lambda expressions (Section 10.20) that determine the appropriate balances to select. For credit balances, line 77 assigns balanceChooser a lambda expression that determines whether a value is greater than 0. For debit balances, line 80 assigns balanceChooser a lambda expression that determines whether a value is less than 0. For zero balances, line 83 assigns balanceChooser a lambda expression that determines whether a value is equal to 0.

The LINQ query in lines 94–103 begins by calling the StreamReader extension method Lines, which we define in the static class StreamReaderExtensions (lines 147–167). Method Lines returns an IEnumerable<string> in which each string is a line of text from the specified StreamReader. We discuss this method in detail momentarily. Line 95 splits the current record into an array of strings and assigns the array to variable record. Line 96 uses the balanceChooser delegate to determine which records should be selected by the LINQ query. Then, lines 97–103 create new Record objects for each selected record. Lines 106–112 iterate through the query results and display the selected records in the displayTextBox.

Class StreamReaderExtensions (lines 147–167) defines the StreamReader extension method Lines (lines 150–166). This method acts as an iterator for the lines of text being read from a StreamReader—that is, method Lines returns only one line of text at a time and maintains state information indicating which line will be read next. Line 157 uses StreamReader property BaseStream to invoke the *Seek* method of the underlying FileStream to reset the file-position pointer back to the beginning of the file. To move the file-position pointer, you specify the number of bytes it should be offset from the file's beginning, end or current position. The part of the file you want to be offset from is chosen using constants from the *SeekOrigin* enumeration. In this case, our stream is offset by 0 bytes from the file's beginning (SeekOrigin.Begin). Lines 162–165 read one line at a time from the file until the end of file is reached. The state information details that enable method Lines to act as an iterator are handled by the ***yield return*** statement in line 164. This statement returns one line of text, then waits for the next item to be requested from the client code using method Lines.

19.8 Serialization

Section 19.5 demonstrated how to write the individual fields of a Record object to a text file, and Section 19.6 demonstrated how to read those fields from a file and place their values in a Record object in memory. In the examples, Record was used to aggregate the information for one record. When the instance variables for a Record were output to a disk file, certain information was lost, such as the type of each value. For instance, if the value "3" is read from a file, there is no way to tell if the value came from an int, a string or a decimal. We have only data, not type information, on disk. If the program that is going to read this data "knows" what object type the data corresponds to, then the data can be read directly into objects of that type. For example, in Fig. 19.9, we know that we are inputting an int (the account number), followed by two strings (the first and last name) and a decimal (the balance). We also know that these values are separated by commas, with only one record on each line. So, we are able to parse the strings and convert the account number to an int and the balance to a decimal. Sometimes it would be easier to read or write entire objects. C# provides such a mechanism, called ***object serialization***. A *serialized object* is an object represented as a sequence of bytes that includes the object's data, as well as information about the object's type and the types of data stored in the object. After a serialized object has been written to a file, it can be read from the file and *deserialized*—that is, the type information and bytes that represent the object and its data can be used to recreate the object in memory.

Class ***BinaryFormatter*** (namespace ***System.Runtime.Serialization.Formatters. Binary***) enables entire objects to be written to or read from a stream. BinaryFormatter method ***Serialize*** writes an object's representation to a file. BinaryFormatter method ***Deserialize*** reads this representation from a file and reconstructs the original object. Both methods throw a ***SerializationException*** if an error occurs during serialization or deserialization. Both methods require a Stream object (e.g., the FileStream) as a parameter so that the BinaryFormatter can access the correct stream.

In Sections 19.9–19.10, we create and manipulate sequential-access files using object serialization. Object serialization is performed with byte-based streams, so the sequential files created and manipulated will be binary files. Binary files are not human readable. For this reason, we write a separate application that reads and displays serialized objects.

19.9 Creating a Sequential-Access File Using Object Serialization

We begin by creating and writing serialized objects to a sequential-access file. In this section, we reuse much of the code from Section 19.5, so we focus only on the new features.

Defining the RecordSerializable Class
Let's begin by modifying our Record class (Fig. 19.8) so that objects of this class can be serialized. Class RecordSerializable (Fig. 19.13) is marked with the ***[Serializable]*** attribute (line 7), which indicates to the CLR that objects of class RecordSerializable can

be serialized. The classes for objects that we wish to write to or read from a stream must include this attribute in their declarations or must implement interface ***ISerializable***. Class RecordSerializable contains private data members account, firstName, last-Name and balance. This class also provides public properties for accessing the private fields.

In a class that is marked with the [Serializable] attribute or that implements interface ISerializable, you must ensure that every instance variable of the class is also serializable. All simple-type variables and strings are serializable. For variables of reference types, you must check the class declaration (and possibly its base classes) to ensure that the type is serializable. By default, array objects are serializable. However, if the array contains references to other objects, those objects may or may not be serializable.

```
 1   // Fig. 19.13: RecordSerializable.cs
 2   // Serializable class that represents a data record.
 3   using System;
 4
 5   namespace BankLibrary
 6   {
 7      [Serializable]
 8      public class RecordSerializable
 9      {
10         // automatic Account property
11         public int Account { get; set; }
12
13         // automatic FirstName property
14         public string FirstName { get; set; }
15
16         // automatic LastName property
17         public string LastName { get; set; }
18
19         // automatic Balance property
20         public decimal Balance { get; set; }
21
22         // default constructor sets members to default values
23         public RecordSerializable()
24            : this( 0, string.Empty, string.Empty, 0M )
25         {
26         } // end constructor
27
28         // overloaded constructor sets members to parameter values
29         public RecordSerializable( int accountValue, string firstNameValue,
30            string lastNameValue, decimal balanceValue )
31         {
32            Account = accountValue;
33            FirstName = firstNameValue;
34            LastName = lastNameValue;
35            Balance = balanceValue;
36         } // end constructor
37      } // end class RecordSerializable
38   } // end namespace BankLibrary
```

Fig. 19.13 | RecordSerializable class for serializable objects.

Using a Serialization Stream to Create an Output File

Now let's create a sequential-access file with serialization (Fig. 19.14). Line 15 creates a BinaryFormatter for writing serialized objects. Lines 54–55 open the FileStream to which this program writes the serialized objects. The string argument that is passed to the FileStream's constructor represents the name and path of the file to be opened. This specifies the file to which the serialized objects will be written.

Common Programming Error 19.2

It is a logic error to open an existing file for output when the user wishes to preserve the file. The original file's contents will be lost.

```
1   // Fig 19.14: CreateFileForm.cs
2   // Creating a sequential-access file using serialization.
3   using System;
4   using System.Windows.Forms;
5   using System.IO;
6   using System.Runtime.Serialization.Formatters.Binary;
7   using System.Runtime.Serialization;
8   using BankLibrary;
9
10  namespace CreateFile
11  {
12     public partial class CreateFileForm : BankUIForm
13     {
14        // object for serializing Records in binary format
15        private BinaryFormatter formatter = new BinaryFormatter();
16        private FileStream output; // stream for writing to a file
17
18        // parameterless constructor
19        public CreateFileForm()
20        {
21           InitializeComponent();
22        } // end constructor
23
24        // handler for saveButton_Click
25        private void saveButton_Click( object sender, EventArgs e )
26        {
27           // create and show dialog box enabling user to save file
28           DialogResult result;
29           string fileName; // name of file to save data
30
31           using ( SaveFileDialog fileChooser = new SaveFileDialog() )
32           {
33              fileChooser.CheckFileExists = false; // let user create file
34
35              // retrieve the result of the dialog box
36              result = fileChooser.ShowDialog();
37              fileName = fileChooser.FileName; // get specified file name
38           } // end using
39
```

Fig. 19.14 | Sequential file created using serialization. (Part 1 of 5.)

```
40              // ensure that user clicked "OK"
41              if ( result == DialogResult.OK )
42              {
43
44                 // show error if user specified invalid file
45                 if ( fileName == string.Empty )
46                    MessageBox.Show( "Invalid File Name", "Error",
47                       MessageBoxButtons.OK, MessageBoxIcon.Error );
48                 else
49                 {
50                    // save file via FileStream if user specified valid file
51                    try
52                    {
53                       // open file with write access
54                       output = new FileStream( fileName,
55                          FileMode.OpenOrCreate, FileAccess.Write );
56
57                       // disable Save button and enable Enter button
58                       saveButton.Enabled = false;
59                       enterButton.Enabled = true;
60                    } // end try
61                    // handle exception if there is a problem opening the file
62                    catch ( IOException )
63                    {
64                       // notify user if file could not be opened
65                       MessageBox.Show( "Error opening file", "Error",
66                          MessageBoxButtons.OK, MessageBoxIcon.Error );
67                    } // end catch
68                 } // end else
69              } // end if
70           } // end method saveButton_Click
71
72           // handler for enterButton Click
73           private void enterButton_Click( object sender, EventArgs e )
74           {
75              // store TextBox values string array
76              string[] values = GetTextBoxValues();
77
78              // Record containing TextBox values to serialize
79              RecordSerializable record = new RecordSerializable();
80
81              // determine whether TextBox account field is empty
82              if ( values[ ( int ) TextBoxIndices.ACCOUNT ] != string.Empty )
83              {
84                 // store TextBox values in Record and serialize Record
85                 try
86                 {
87                    // get account-number value from TextBox
88                    int accountNumber = Int32.Parse(
89                       values[ ( int ) TextBoxIndices.ACCOUNT ] );
90
```

Fig. 19.14 | Sequential file created using serialization. (Part 2 of 5.)

```
 91                      // determine whether accountNumber is valid
 92                      if ( accountNumber > 0 )
 93                      {
 94                          // store TextBox fields in Record
 95                          record.Account = accountNumber;
 96                          record.FirstName = values[ ( int )
 97                              TextBoxIndices.FIRST ];
 98                          record.LastName = values[ ( int )
 99                              TextBoxIndices.LAST ];
100                          record.Balance = Decimal.Parse( values[
101                              ( int ) TextBoxIndices.BALANCE ] );
102
103                          // write Record to FileStream ( serialize object )
104                          formatter.Serialize( output, record );
105                      } // end if
106                      else
107                      {
108                          // notify user if invalid account number
109                          MessageBox.Show( "Invalid Account Number", "Error",
110                              MessageBoxButtons.OK, MessageBoxIcon.Error );
111                      } // end else
112                  } // end try
113                  // notify user if error occurs in serialization
114                  catch ( SerializationException )
115                  {
116                      MessageBox.Show( "Error Writing to File", "Error",
117                          MessageBoxButtons.OK, MessageBoxIcon.Error );
118                  } // end catch
119                  // notify user if error occurs regarding parameter format
120                  catch ( FormatException )
121                  {
122                      MessageBox.Show( "Invalid Format", "Error",
123                          MessageBoxButtons.OK, MessageBoxIcon.Error );
124                  } // end catch
125              } // end if
126
127              ClearTextBoxes(); // clear TextBox values
128          } // end method enterButton_Click
129
130          // handler for exitButton Click
131          private void exitButton_Click( object sender, EventArgs e )
132          {
133              // determine whether file exists
134              if ( output != null )
135              {
136                  // close file
137                  try
138                  {
139                      output.Close(); // close FileStream
140                  } // end try
141                  // notify user of error closing file
142                  catch ( IOException )
143                  {
```

Fig. 19.14 | Sequential file created using serialization. (Part 3 of 5.)

```
144                    MessageBox.Show( "Cannot close file", "Error",
145                       MessageBoxButtons.OK, MessageBoxIcon.Error );
146             } // end catch
147          } // end if
148
149          Application.Exit();
150       } // end method exitButton_Click
151    } // end class CreateFileForm
152 } // end namespace CreateFile
```

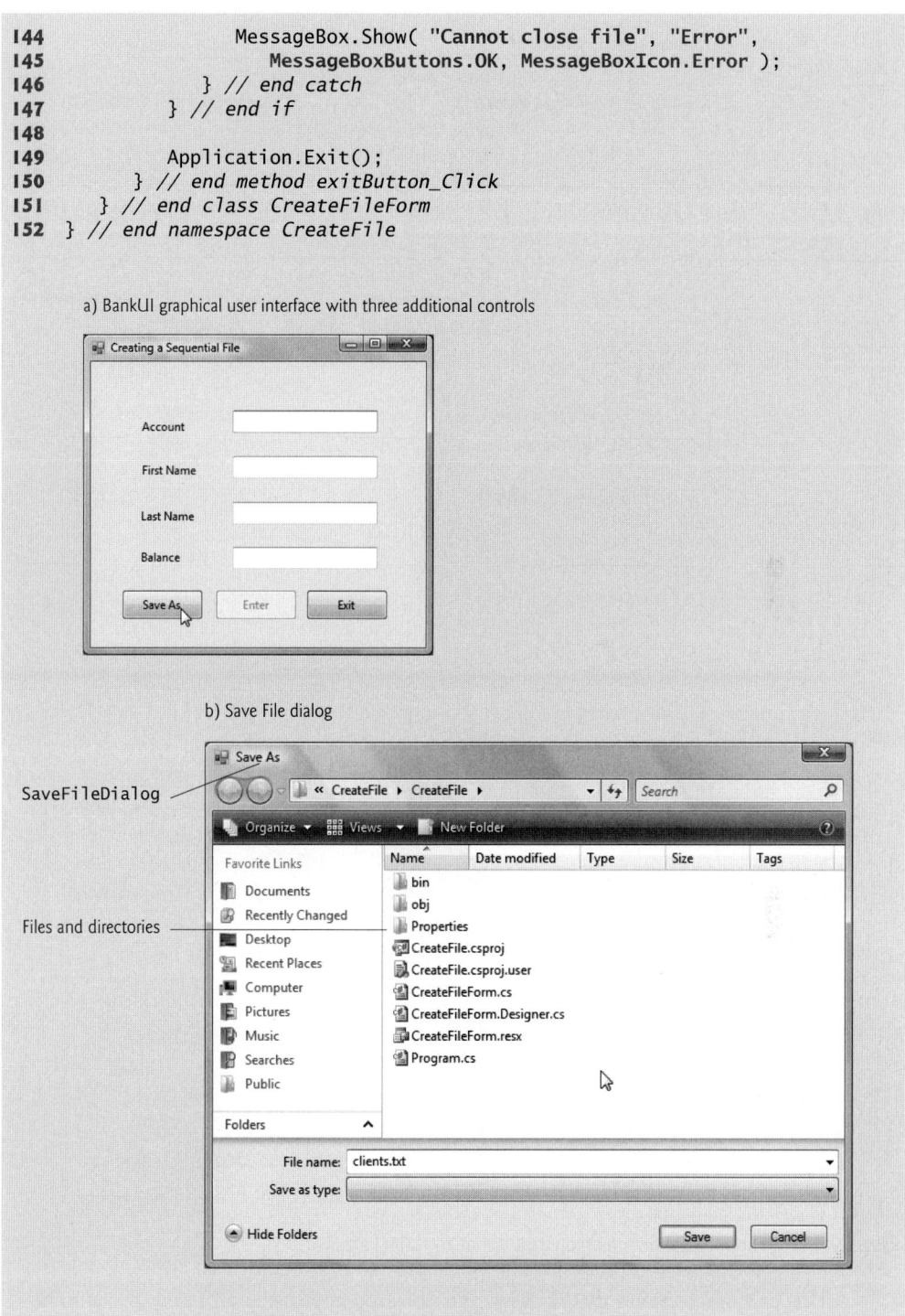

a) BankUI graphical user interface with three additional controls

b) Save File dialog

Fig. 19.14 | Sequential file created using serialization. (Part 4 of 5.)

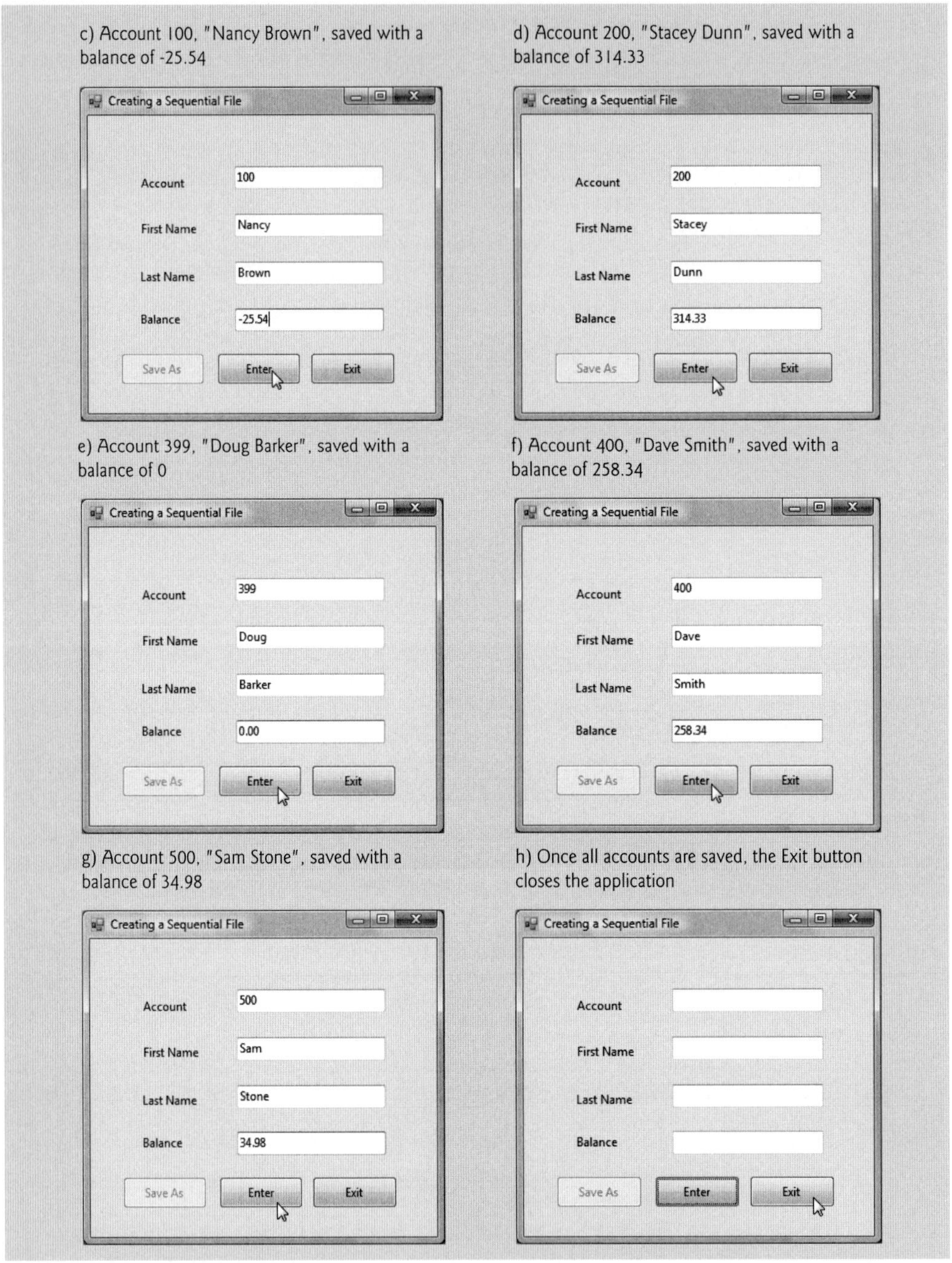
c) Account 100, "Nancy Brown", saved with a balance of -25.54
Creating a Sequential File
Account
100
First Name
Nancy
Last Name
Brown
Balance
-25.54
Save As
Enter
Exit
d) Account 200, "Stacey Dunn", saved with a balance of 314.33
Creating a Sequential File
Account
200
First Name
Stacey
Last Name
Dunn
Balance
314.33
Save As
Enter
Exit
e) Account 399, "Doug Barker", saved with a balance of 0
Creating a Sequential File
Account
399
First Name
Doug
Last Name
Barker
Balance
0.00
Save As
Enter
Exit
f) Account 400, "Dave Smith", saved with a balance of 258.34
Creating a Sequential File
Account
400
First Name
Dave
Last Name
Smith
Balance
258.34
Save As
Enter
Exit
g) Account 500, "Sam Stone", saved with a balance of 34.98
Creating a Sequential File
Account
500
First Name
Sam
Last Name
Stone
Balance
34.98
Save As
Enter
Exit
h) Once all accounts are saved, the Exit button closes the application
Creating a Sequential File
Account
First Name
Last Name
Balance
Save As
Enter
Exit

Fig. 19.14 | Sequential file created using serialization. (Part 5 of 5.)

This program assumes that data is input correctly and in the proper record-number order. Event handler `enterButton_Click` (lines 73–128) performs the write operation.

Line 79 creates a `RecordSerializable` object, which is assigned values in lines 95–101. Line 104 calls method `Serialize` to write the `RecordSerializable` object to the output file. Method `Serialize` takes the `FileStream` object as the first argument so that the `BinaryFormatter` can write its second argument to the correct file. Note that only one statement is required to write the entire object.

In the sample execution for the program in Fig. 19.14, we entered information for five accounts—the same information shown in Fig. 19.10. The program does not show how the data records actually appear in the file. Remember that we are now using binary files, which are not human readable. To verify that the file was created successfully, the next section presents a program to read the file's contents.

19.10 Reading and Deserializing Data from a Binary File

The preceding section showed how to create a sequential-access file using object serialization. In this section, we discuss how to read serialized objects sequentially from a file.

Figure 19.15 reads and displays the contents of the file created by the program in Fig. 19.14. Line 15 creates the `BinaryFormatter` that will be used to read objects. The program opens the file for input by creating a `FileStream` object (lines 49–50). The name of the file to open is specified as the first argument to the `FileStream` constructor.

```csharp
1   // Fig. 19.15: ReadSequentialAccessFileForm.cs
2   // Reading a sequential-access file using deserialization.
3   using System;
4   using System.Windows.Forms;
5   using System.IO;
6   using System.Runtime.Serialization.Formatters.Binary;
7   using System.Runtime.Serialization;
8   using BankLibrary;
9
10  namespace ReadSequentialAccessFile
11  {
12     public partial class ReadSequentialAccessFileForm : BankUIForm
13     {
14        // object for deserializing Record in binary format
15        private BinaryFormatter reader = new BinaryFormatter();
16        private FileStream input; // stream for reading from a file
17
18        // parameterless constructor
19        public ReadSequentialAccessFileForm()
20        {
21           InitializeComponent();
22        } // end constructor
23
24        // invoked when user clicks the Open button
25        private void openButton_Click( object sender, EventArgs e )
26        {
27           // create and show dialog box enabling user to open file
28           DialogResult result; // result of OpenFileDialog
29           string fileName; // name of file containing data
```

Fig. 19.15 | Sequential file read using deserialization. (Part 1 of 4.)

```
30
31         using ( OpenFileDialog fileChooser = new OpenFileDialog() )
32         {
33            result = fileChooser.ShowDialog();
34            fileName = fileChooser.FileName; // get specified name
35         } // end using
36
37         // ensure that user clicked "OK"
38         if ( result == DialogResult.OK )
39         {
40            ClearTextBoxes();
41
42            // show error if user specified invalid file
43            if ( fileName == string.Empty )
44               MessageBox.Show( "Invalid File Name", "Error",
45                  MessageBoxButtons.OK, MessageBoxIcon.Error );
46            else
47            {
48               // create FileStream to obtain read access to file
49               input = new FileStream(
50                  fileName, FileMode.Open, FileAccess.Read );
51
52               openButton.Enabled = false; // disable Open File button
53               nextButton.Enabled = true;  // enable Next Record button
54            } // end else
55         } // end if
56      } // end method openButton_Click
57
58      // invoked when user clicks Next button
59      private void nextButton_Click( object sender, EventArgs e )
60      {
61         // deserialize Record and store data in TextBoxes
62         try
63         {
64            // get next RecordSerializable available in file
65            RecordSerializable record =
66               ( RecordSerializable ) reader.Deserialize( input );
67
68            // store Record values in temporary string array
69            string[] values = new string[] {
70               record.Account.ToString(),
71               record.FirstName.ToString(),
72               record.LastName.ToString(),
73               record.Balance.ToString()
74            };
75
76            // copy string-array values to TextBox values
77            SetTextBoxValues( values );
78         } // end try
79         // handle exception when there are no Records in file
80         catch ( SerializationException )
81         {
82            input.Close(); // close FileStream if no Records in file
```

Fig. 19.15 | Sequential file read using deserialization. (Part 2 of 4.)

```
83            openButton.Enabled = true; // enable Open File button
84            nextButton.Enabled = false; // disable Next Record button
85
86            ClearTextBoxes();
87
88            // notify user if no Records in file
89            MessageBox.Show( "No more records in file", string.Empty,
90               MessageBoxButtons.OK, MessageBoxIcon.Information );
91         } // end catch
92      } // end method nextButton_Click
93   } // end class ReadSequentialAccessFileForm
94 } // end namespace ReadSequentialAccessFile
```

a) BankUI graphical user interface with an Open File button

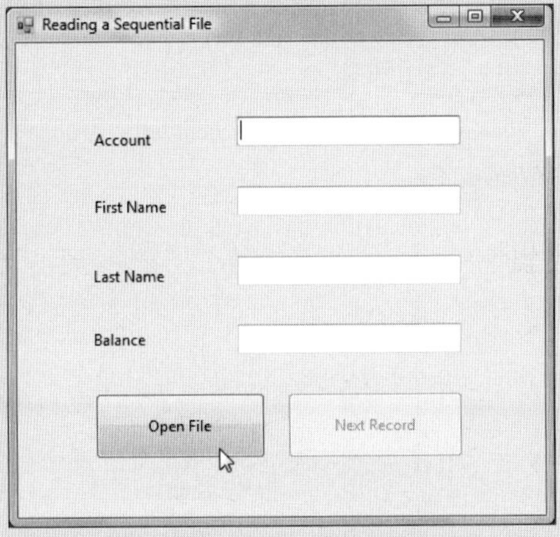

b) OpenFileDialog window

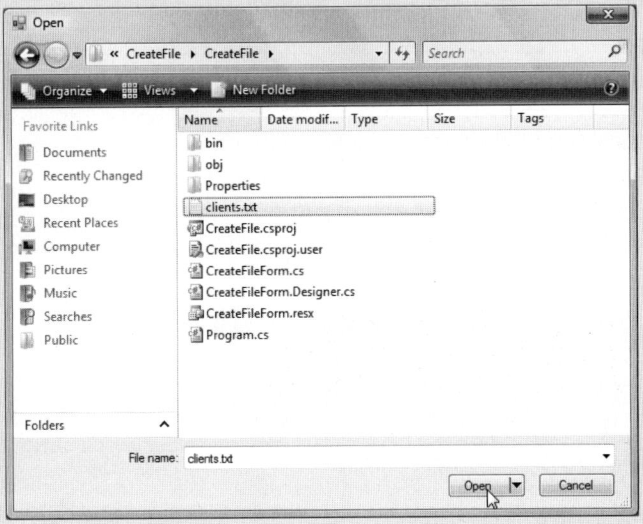

Fig. 19.15 | Sequential file read using deserialization. (Part 3 of 4.)

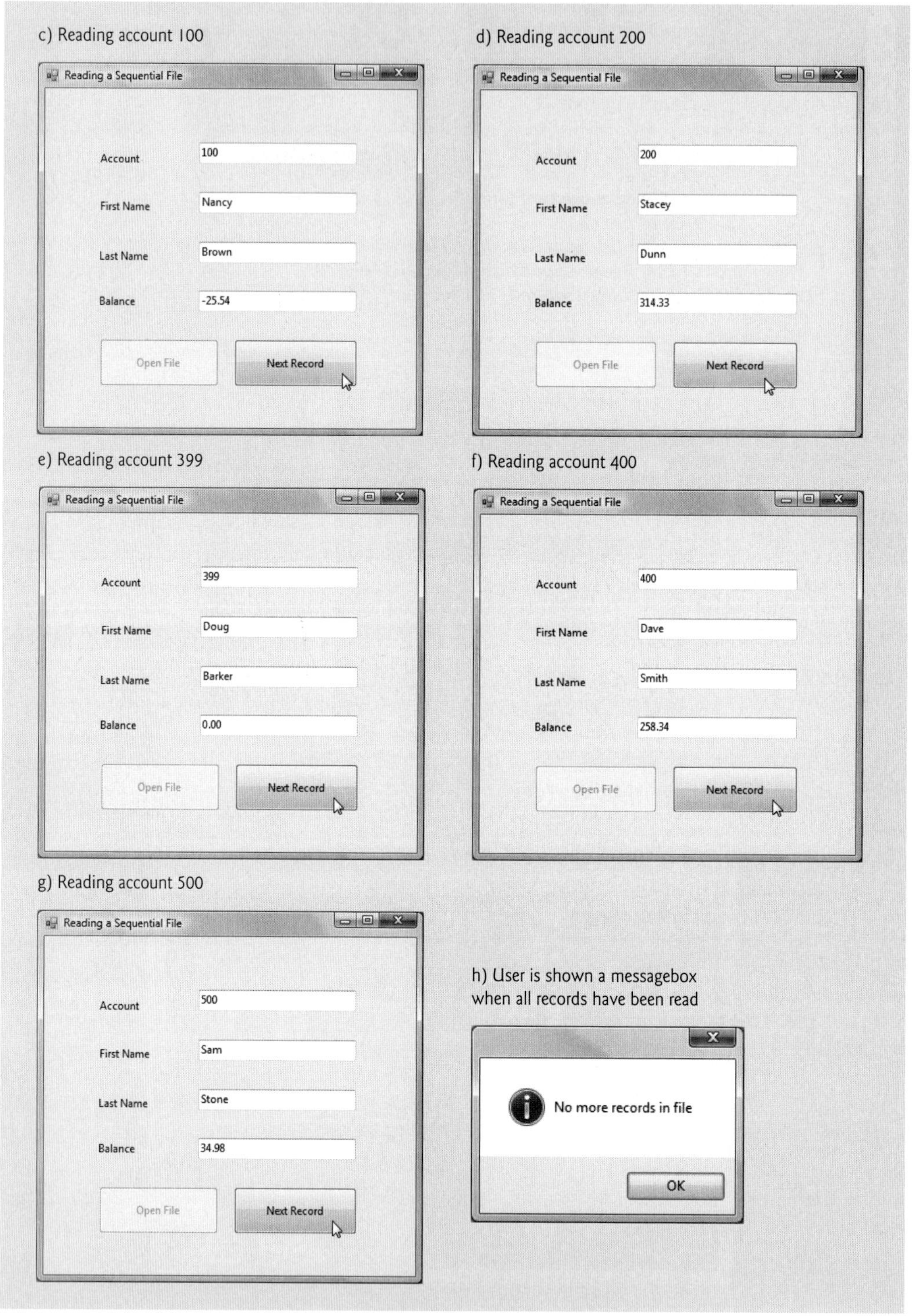
c) Reading account 100
Reading a Sequential File
Account
100
First Name
Nancy
Last Name
Brown
Balance
-25.54
Open File
Next Record
d) Reading account 200
Reading a Sequential File
Account
200
First Name
Stacey
Last Name
Dunn
Balance
314.33
Open File
Next Record
e) Reading account 399
Reading a Sequential File
Account
399
First Name
Doug
Last Name
Barker
Balance
0.00
Open File
Next Record
f) Reading account 400
Reading a Sequential File
Account
400
First Name
Dave
Last Name
Smith
Balance
258.34
Open File
Next Record
g) Reading account 500
Reading a Sequential File
Account
500
First Name
Sam
Last Name
Stone
Balance
34.98
Open File
Next Record
h) User is shown a messagebox when all records have been read
No more records in file
OK

Fig. 19.15 | Sequential file read using deserialization. (Part 4 of 4.)

The program reads objects from a file in event handler nextButton_Click (lines 59–92). We use method Deserialize (of the BinaryFormatter created in line 15) to read the data (lines 65–66). Note that we cast the result of Deserialize to type RecordSerializable (line 66)—this cast is necessary, because Deserialize returns a reference of type object and we need to access properties that belong to class RecordSerializable. If an error occurs during deserialization, a SerializationException is thrown, and the FileStream object is closed (line 82).

19.11 Wrap-Up

In this chapter, you learned how to use file processing to manipulate persistent data. You learned that data is stored in computers as 0s and 1s, and that combinations of these values are used to form bytes, fields, records and eventually files. We overviewed the differences between character-based and byte-based streams, as well as several file-processing classes from the System.IO namespace. You used class File to manipulate files, and classes Directory and DirectoryInfo to manipulate directories. Next, you learned how to use sequential-access file processing to manipulate records in text files. You also learned how to use the yield return statement to create an iterator that could then be used in a LINQ query to read lines of text from a text file. We then discussed the differences between text-file processing and object serialization, and used serialization to store entire objects in and retrieve entire objects from files.

In the next chapter, we present Extensible Markup Language (XML)—a widely supported technology for describing data. Using XML, we can describe any type of data, such as mathematical formulas, music and financial reports. We'll demonstrate how to describe data with XML and how to write programs that can process XML encoded data.

20

XML and LINQ to XML

OBJECTIVES

In this chapter you'll learn:

- To create DTDs and schemas for specifying and validating the structure of an XML document.

- To create and use simple XSL style sheets to render XML document data.

- To use the Document Object Model (DOM) to manipulate XML in C# programs.

- To use LINQ to XML to extract and manipulate data from XML documents.

- To create new XML documents using the classes provided by the .NET Framework.

- To work with XML namespaces in your C# code.

- To transform XML documents into XHTML using class `XslCompiledTransform`.

Outline

20.1 Introduction
20.2 Document Type Definitions (DTDs)
20.3 W3C XML Schema Documents
20.4 Extensible Stylesheet Language and XSL Transformations
20.5 LINQ to XML: Document Object Model (DOM)
20.6 LINQ to XML Class Hierarchy
20.7 LINQ to XML: Namespaces and Creating Documents
20.8 XSLT with Class `XslCompiledTransform`
20.9 Wrap-Up
20.10 Web Resources

20.1 Introduction

In Chapter 16, we began our introduction to XML to help explain the syntax of XAML (eXtensible Application Markup Language). You learned the syntax of XML, how to use XML namespaces and were introduced to the concept of DTDs and schemas. In this chapter, you learn how to create your own DTDs (Section 20.2) and schemas (Section 20.3) to validate your XML documents.

The .NET Framework uses XML extensively. Many of the configuration files that Visual Studio creates—such as those that represent project settings—use XML format. XML is also used heavily in serialization, as you'll see in Chapter 23, Windows Communication Foundation (WCF) Web Services. You've already used XAML—an XML vocabulary used for creating user interfaces—in Chapters 16–17. XAML is also used in Chapter 24, Silverlight, Rich Internet Applications and Multimedia.

Sections 20.4–20.8 demonstrate techniques for working with XML documents in C# applications. Visual C# 2008 introduces new language features and .NET Framework classes for working with XML. *LINQ to XML* provides a convenient way to manipulate data in XML documents using the same LINQ syntax you used on arrays and collections in Chapter 9. LINQ to XML also provides a set of classes for easily navigating and creating XML documents in your code.

20.2 Document Type Definitions (DTDs)

Document Type Definitions (DTDs) are one of two techniques you can use to specify XML document structure. Section 20.3 presents W3C XML Schema documents, which provide an improved method of specifying XML document structure.

Software Engineering Observation 20.1

XML documents can have many different structures, and for this reason an application cannot be certain whether a particular document it receives is complete, ordered properly, and not missing data. DTDs and schemas (Section 20.3) solve this problem by providing an extensible way to describe XML document structure. Applications should use DTDs or schemas to confirm whether XML documents are valid.

Software Engineering Observation 20.2

Many organizations and individuals are creating DTDs and schemas for a broad range of applications. These collections—called **repositories**—*are available free for download from the web (e.g., www.xml.org, www.oasis-open.org).*

Creating a Document Type Definition

Figure 16.4 presented a simple business letter marked up with XML. Recall that line 5 of letter.xml references a DTD—letter.dtd (Fig. 20.1). This DTD specifies the business letter's element types and attributes and their relationships to one another.

A DTD describes the structure of an XML document and enables an XML parser to verify whether an XML document is valid (i.e., whether its elements contain the proper attributes and appear in the proper sequence). DTDs allow users to check document structure and to exchange data in a standardized format. A DTD expresses the set of rules for document structure by specifying what attributes and other elements may appear inside a given element.

Common Programming Error 20.1

For documents validated with DTDs, any document that uses elements, attributes or relationships not explicitly defined by a DTD is an invalid document.

```
1   <!-- Fig. 20.1: letter.dtd        -->
2   <!-- DTD document for letter.xml -->
3
4   <!ELEMENT letter ( contact+, salutation, paragraph+,
5     closing, signature )>
6
7   <!ELEMENT contact ( name, address1, address2, city, state,
8     zip, phone, flag )>
9   <!ATTLIST contact type CDATA #IMPLIED>
10
11  <!ELEMENT name ( #PCDATA )>
12  <!ELEMENT address1 ( #PCDATA )>
13  <!ELEMENT address2 ( #PCDATA )>
14  <!ELEMENT city ( #PCDATA )>
15  <!ELEMENT state ( #PCDATA )>
16  <!ELEMENT zip ( #PCDATA )>
17  <!ELEMENT phone ( #PCDATA )>
18  <!ELEMENT flag EMPTY>
19  <!ATTLIST flag gender (M | F) "M">
20
21  <!ELEMENT salutation ( #PCDATA )>
22  <!ELEMENT closing ( #PCDATA )>
23  <!ELEMENT paragraph ( #PCDATA )>
24  <!ELEMENT signature ( #PCDATA )>
```

Fig. 20.1 | Document Type Definition (DTD) for a business letter.

Defining Elements in a DTD

The **ELEMENT** *element type declaration* in lines 4–5 defines the rules for element letter. In this case, letter contains one or more contact elements, one salutation element, one or more paragraph elements, one closing element and one signature element, in that sequence. The *plus sign* (+) *occurrence indicator* specifies that the DTD allows one or more occurrences of an element. Other occurrence indicators include the *asterisk* (*), which indicates an optional element that can occur zero or more times, and the *question mark* (?), which indicates an optional element that can occur at most once (i.e., zero or one occurrence). If an element does not have an occurrence indicator, the DTD allows exactly one occurrence.

The contact element type declaration (lines 7–8) specifies that a contact element contains child elements name, address1, address2, city, state, zip, phone and flag—in that order. The DTD requires exactly one occurrence of each of these elements.

Defining Attributes in a DTD

Line 9 uses the *ATTLIST attribute-list declaration* to define an attribute named type for the contact element. Keyword *#IMPLIED* specifies that the type attribute of the contact element is optional—a missing type attribute will not invalidate the document. Other keywords that can be used in place of #IMPLIED in an ATTLIST declaration include #RE-QUIRED and #FIXED. Keyword *#REQUIRED* specifies that the attribute must be present in the element, and keyword *#FIXED* specifies that the attribute (if present) must have the given fixed value. For example,

```
<!ATTLIST address zip CDATA #FIXED "01757">
```

indicates that attribute zip (if present in element address) must have the value 01757 for the document to be valid. If the attribute is not present, then the parser, by default, uses the fixed value that the ATTLIST declaration specifies. You can supply a default value instead of one of these keywords. Doing so makes the attribute optional, but the default value will be used if the attribute's value is not specified.

Character Data vs. Parsed Character Data

Keyword *CDATA* (line 9) specifies that attribute type contains *character data* (i.e., a string). A parser will pass such data to an application without modification.

 Software Engineering Observation 20.3

DTD syntax cannot describe an element's (or attribute's) type. For example, a DTD cannot specify that a particular element or attribute can contain only integer data.

Keyword *#PCDATA* (line 11) specifies that an element (e.g., name) may contain *parsed character data* (i.e., data that is processed by an XML parser). Elements with parsed character data cannot contain markup characters, such as less than (<), greater than (>) or ampersand (&). The document author should replace any markup character in a #PCDATA element with the character's corresponding *character entity reference*. For example, the character entity reference < should be used in place of the less-than symbol (<), and the character entity reference > should be used in place of the greater-than symbol (>). A document author who wishes to use a literal ampersand should use the entity reference & instead—parsed character data can contain ampersands (&) only for inserting entities. The final two entities defined by XML are ' and ", representing the single (') and double (") quote characters, respectively.

Common Programming Error 20.2

Using markup characters (e.g., <, > and &) in parsed character data is an error. Use character entity references (e.g., <, > and & instead).

Defining Empty Elements in a DTD

Line 18 defines an empty element named `flag`. Keyword *EMPTY* specifies that the element does not contain any data between its start and end tags. Empty elements commonly describe data via attributes. For example, `flag`'s data appears in its `gender` attribute (line 19). Line 19 specifies that the `gender` attribute's value must be one of the enumerated values (M or F) enclosed in parentheses and delimited by a vertical bar (|) meaning "or." Note that line 19 also indicates that `gender` has a default value of M.

Well-Formed Documents vs. Valid Documents

Recall that a well-formed document is syntactically correct (i.e., each start tag has a corresponding end tag, the document contains only one root element, and so on), and a valid document contains the proper elements with the proper attributes in the proper sequence. An XML document cannot be valid unless it is well formed.

Visual Studio 2008 can validate XML documents against both DTDs and schemas. You do not have to create a project to use this facility—simply open the XML file in Visual Studio as in Fig. 20.2. If the DTD or schema referenced in the XML document can be retrieved, Visual Studio will automatically validate the XML. If the XML file does not validate, Visual Studio will display a warning just as it does with errors in your C# code. Visit www.w3.org/XML/Schema for a list of additional validation tools.

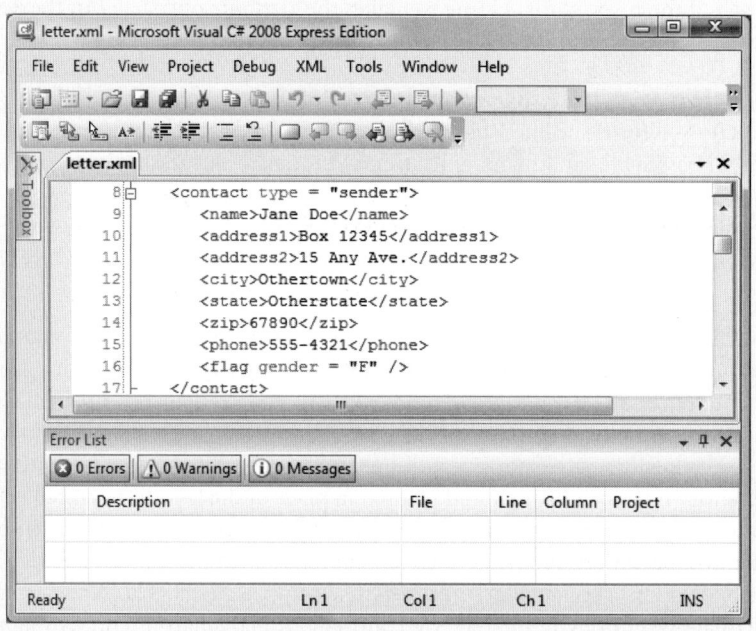

Fig. 20.2 | An XML file open in Visual C# 2008 Express Edition. (Part 1 of 2.)

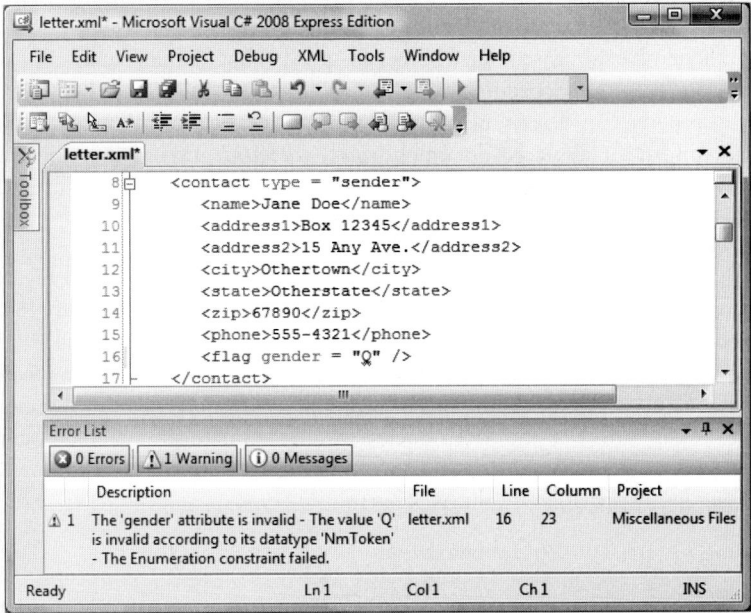

Fig. 20.2 | An XML file open in Visual C# 2008 Express Edition. (Part 2 of 2.)

20.3 W3C XML Schema Documents

In this section, we introduce schemas for specifying XML document structure and validating XML documents. Many developers in the XML community believe that DTDs are not flexible enough to meet today's programming needs. For example, DTDs lack a way of indicating what specific type of data (e.g., numeric, text) an element can contain, and DTDs are not themselves XML documents, making it difficult to manipulate them programmatically. These and other limitations have led to the development of schemas.

Unlike DTDs, schemas use XML syntax and are actually XML documents that programs can manipulate. Like DTDs, schemas are used by validating parsers to validate documents.

In this section, we focus on the W3C's *XML Schema* vocabulary. For the latest information on XML Schema, visit www.w3.org/XML/Schema. For tutorials on XML Schema concepts beyond what we present here, visit www.w3schools.com/schema/default.asp.

A DTD describes an XML document's structure, not the content of its elements. For example,

    *<quantity>*5*</quantity>*

contains character data. If the document that contains element `quantity` references a DTD, an XML parser can validate the document to confirm that this element indeed does contain PCDATA content. However, the parser cannot validate that the content is numeric; DTDs do not provide this capability. So, unfortunately, the parser also considers

    *<quantity>*hello*</quantity>*

to be valid. An application that uses the XML document containing this markup should test that the data in element `quantity` is numeric and take appropriate action if it is not.

XML Schema enables schema authors to specify that element `quantity`'s data must be numeric or, even more specifically, an integer. A parser validating the XML document against this schema can determine that 5 conforms and `hello` does not. An XML document that conforms to a schema document is *schema valid*, and one that does not conform is *schema invalid*. Schemas are XML documents and therefore must themselves be valid.

Validating Against an XML Schema Document

Figure 20.3 shows a schema-valid XML document named `book.xml`, and Fig. 20.4 shows the pertinent XML Schema document (`book.xsd`) that defines the structure for `book.xml`. By convention, schemas use the *.xsd* extension. Recall that Visual Studio can perform schema validation if it can locate the schema document. Visual Studio can locate a schema if it is specified in the XML document, is in the same solution or is simply open in Visual Studio at the same time as the XML document. To validate the schema document itself (i.e., `book.xsd`) and produce the output shown in Fig. 20.4, we used an online XSV (XML Schema Validator) provided by the W3C at

www.w3.org/2001/03/webdata/xsv

These tools are free and enforce the W3C's specifications regarding XML Schemas and schema validation. Figure 20.3 contains markup describing several books. The `books` element (line 5) has the namespace prefix `deitel`, indicating that the `books` element is a part

```
 1   <?xml version = "1.0"?>
 2   <!-- Fig. 20.3: book.xml -->
 3   <!-- Book list marked up as XML -->
 4
 5   <deitel:books xmlns:deitel = "http://www.deitel.com/booklist">
 6       <book>
 7           <title>Visual Basic 2008 How to Program</title>
 8       </book>
 9
10       <book>
11           <title>Visual C# 2008 How to Program, 3/e</title>
12       </book>
13
14       <book>
15           <title>Java How to Program, 7/e</title>
16       </book>
17
18       <book>
19           <title>C++ How to Program, 6/e</title>
20       </book>
21
22       <book>
23           <title>Internet and World Wide Web How to Program, 4/e</title>
24       </book>
25   </deitel:books>
```

Fig. 20.3 | Schema-valid XML document describing a list of books.

of the namespace `http://www.deitel.com/booklist`. We declare the namespace prefix `deitel` in line 5.

Creating an XML Schema Document

Figure 20.4 presents the XML Schema document that specifies the structure of `book.xml` (Fig. 20.3). This document defines an XML-based language (i.e., a vocabulary) for writing XML documents about collections of books. The schema defines the elements, attributes and parent-child relationships that such a document can (or must) include. The schema also specifies the type of data that these elements and attributes may contain.

Root element **schema** (Fig. 20.4, lines 5–23) contains elements that define the structure of an XML document such as `book.xml`. Line 5 specifies as the default namespace the standard W3C XML Schema namespace URI—***http://www.w3.org/2001/XMLSchema***. This namespace contains predefined elements (e.g., root element schema) that comprise the XML Schema vocabulary—the language used to write an XML Schema document.

```
 1  <?xml version = "1.0"?>
 2  <!-- Fig. 20.4: book.xsd            -->
 3  <!-- Simple W3C XML Schema document -->
 4
 5  <schema xmlns = "http://www.w3.org/2001/XMLSchema"
 6     xmlns:deitel = "http://www.deitel.com/booklist"
 7     targetNamespace = "http://www.deitel.com/booklist">
 8
 9     <element name = "books" type = "deitel:BooksType"/>
10
11     <complexType name = "BooksType">
12        <sequence>
13           <element name = "book" type = "deitel:SingleBookType"
14              minOccurs = "1" maxOccurs = "unbounded"/>
15        </sequence>
16     </complexType>
17
18     <complexType name = "SingleBookType">
19        <sequence>
20           <element name = "title" type = "string"/>
21        </sequence>
22     </complexType>
23  </schema>
```

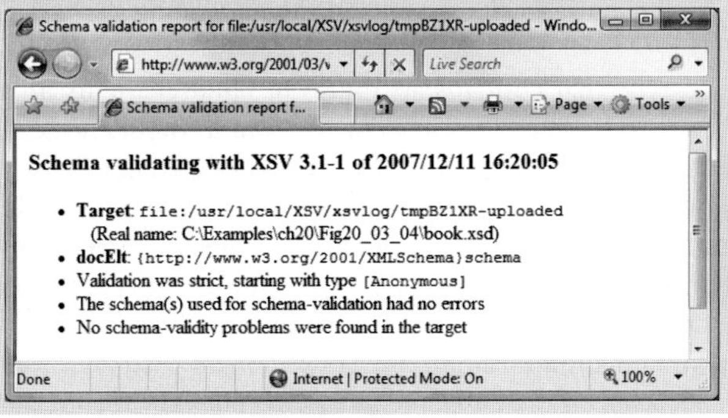

Schema validation report for file:/usr/local/XSV/xsvlog/tmpBZ1XR-uploaded - Windo...

http://www.w3.org/2001/03/ | Live Search

Schema validation report f... | Page ▾ | Tools ▾

Schema validating with XSV 3.1-1 of 2007/12/11 16:20:05

- **Target**: file:/usr/local/XSV/xsvlog/tmpBZ1XR-uploaded
  (Real name: C:\Examples\ch20\Fig20_03_04\book.xsd)
- **docElt**: {http://www.w3.org/2001/XMLSchema}schema
- Validation was strict, starting with type [Anonymous]
- The schema(s) used for schema-validation had no errors
- No schema-validity problems were found in the target

Done | Internet | Protected Mode: On | 100%

Fig. 20.4 | XML Schema document for `book.xml`.

Portability Tip 20.1

W3C XML Schema authors specify URI http://www.w3.org/2001/XMLSchema *when referring to the XML Schema namespace. This namespace contains predefined elements that comprise the XML Schema vocabulary. Specifying this URI ensures that validation tools correctly identify XML Schema elements and do not confuse them with those defined by document authors.*

Line 6 binds the URI http://www.deitel.com/booklist to namespace prefix deitel. As we discuss momentarily, the schema uses this namespace to differentiate names created by us from names that are part of the XML Schema namespace. Line 7 also specifies http://www.deitel.com/booklist as the ***targetNamespace*** of the schema. This attribute identifies the namespace of the XML vocabulary that this schema defines. Note that the targetNamespace of book.xsd is the same as the namespace referenced in line 5 of book.xml (Fig. 20.3). This is what "connects" the XML document with the schema that defines its structure. When an XML schema validator examines book.xml and book.xsd, it will recognize that book.xml uses elements and attributes from the http://www.deitel.com/booklist namespace. The validator also will recognize that this namespace is the one defined in book.xsd (i.e., the schema's targetNamespace). Thus the validator knows where to look for the structural rules for the elements and attributes used in book.xml.

Defining an Element in XML Schema

In XML Schema, the ***element*** tag (line 9) defines an element to be included in an XML document that conforms to the schema. In other words, element specifies the actual *elements* that can be used to mark up data. Line 9 defines the books element, which we use as the root element in book.xml (Fig. 20.3). Attributes ***name*** and ***type*** specify the element's name and type, respectively. An element's type attribute indicates the data type that the element may contain. Possible types include XML Schema–defined types (e.g., string, double) and user-defined types (e.g., BooksType, which is defined in lines 11–16). Figure 20.5 lists several of XML Schema's many built-in types. For a complete list of built-in types, see Section 3 of the specification found at www.w3.org/TR/xmlschema-2.

In this example, books is defined as an element of type deitel:BooksType (line 9). BooksType is a user-defined type (lines 11–16) in the http://www.deitel.com/booklist namespace and therefore must have the namespace prefix deitel. It is not an existing XML Schema type.

Two categories of types exist in XML Schema—*simple types* and *complex types*. They differ only in that simple types cannot contain attributes or child elements and complex types can.

A user-defined type that contains attributes or child elements must be defined as a complex type. Lines 11–16 use element ***complexType*** to define BooksType as a complex type that has a child element named book. The sequence element (lines 12–15) allows you to specify the sequential order in which child elements must appear. The element (lines 13–14) nested within the complexType element indicates that a BooksType element (e.g., books) can contain child elements named book of type deitel:SingleBookType (defined in lines 18–22). Attribute ***minOccurs*** (line 14), with value 1, specifies that elements of type BooksType must contain a minimum of one book element. Attribute ***maxOccurs*** (line 14), with value ***unbounded***, specifies that elements of type BooksType may have any number of book child elements. Both of these attributes have default values of 1.

Lines 18–22 define the complex type `SingleBookType`. An element of this type contains a child element named `title`. Line 20 defines element `title` to be of simple type `string`. Recall that elements of a simple type cannot contain attributes or child elements. The `schema` end tag (`</schema>`, line 23) declares the end of the XML Schema document.

A Closer Look at Types in XML Schema

Every element in XML Schema has a type. Types include the built-in types provided by XML Schema (Fig. 20.5) or user-defined types (e.g., `SingleBookType` in Fig. 20.4).

Type	Description	Range\s or structures	Examples
string	A character string.		"hello"
boolean	True or false.	true, false	true
decimal	A decimal numeral.	$i * (10^n)$, where i is an integer and n is an integer that is less than or equal to zero.	5, -12, -45.78
float	A floating-point number.	$m * (2^e)$, where m is an integer whose absolute value is less than 2^{24} and e is an integer in the range -149 to 104. Plus three additional numbers: positive infinity (INF), negative infinity (-INF) and not-a-number (NaN).	0, 12, -109.375, NaN
double	A floating-point number.	$m * (2^e)$, where m is an integer whose absolute value is less than 2^{53} and e is an integer in the range -1075 to 970. Plus three additional numbers: positive infinity, negative infinity and not-a-number (NaN).	0, 12, -109.375, NaN
long	A whole number.	-9223372036854775808 to 9223372036854775807, inclusive.	1234567890, -1234567890
int	A whole number.	-2147483648 to 2147483647, inclusive.	1234567890, -1234567890
short	A whole number.	-32768 to 32767, inclusive.	12, -345
date	A date consisting of a year, month and day.	yyyy-mm with an optional dd and an optional time zone, where yyyy is four digits long and mm and dd are two digits long. The time zone is specified as +hh:mm or -hh:mm, giving an offset in hours and minutes.	2008-07-25+01:00
time	A time consisting of hours, minutes and seconds.	hh:mm:ss with an optional time zone, where hh, mm and ss are two digits long.	16:30:25-05:00

Fig. 20.5 | Some XML Schema types.

Every simple type defines a *restriction* on an XML Schema-defined type or a restriction on a user-defined type. Restrictions limit the possible values that an element can hold.

Complex types are divided into two groups—those with *simple content* and those with *complex content*. Both can contain attributes, but only complex content can contain child elements. Complex types with simple content must extend or restrict some other existing type. Complex types with complex content do not have this limitation. We demonstrate complex types with each kind of content in the next example.

The schema document in Fig. 20.6 creates both simple types and complex types. The XML document in Fig. 20.7 (laptop.xml) follows the structure defined in Fig. 20.6 to describe parts of a laptop computer. A document such as laptop.xml that conforms to a schema is known as an *XML instance document*—the document is an instance (i.e., example) of the schema.

Line 5 (Fig. 20.6) declares the default namespace as the standard XML Schema namespace—any elements without a prefix are assumed to be in the XML Schema

```xml
 1   <?xml version = "1.0"?>
 2   <!-- Fig. 20.6: computer.xsd -->
 3   <!-- W3C XML Schema document -->
 4
 5   <schema xmlns = "http://www.w3.org/2001/XMLSchema"
 6      xmlns:computer = "http://www.deitel.com/computer"
 7      targetNamespace = "http://www.deitel.com/computer">
 8
 9      <simpleType name = "gigahertz">
10         <restriction base = "decimal">
11            <minInclusive value = "2.1"/>
12         </restriction>
13      </simpleType>
14
15      <complexType name = "CPU">
16         <simpleContent>
17            <extension base = "string">
18               <attribute name = "model" type = "string"/>
19            </extension>
20         </simpleContent>
21      </complexType>
22
23      <complexType name = "portable">
24         <all>
25            <element name = "processor" type = "computer:CPU"/>
26            <element name = "monitor" type = "int"/>
27            <element name = "CPUSpeed" type = "computer:gigahertz"/>
28            <element name = "RAM" type = "int"/>
29         </all>
30         <attribute name = "manufacturer" type = "string"/>
31      </complexType>
32
33      <element name = "laptop" type = "computer:portable"/>
34   </schema>
```

Fig. 20.6 | XML Schema document defining simple and complex types.

namespace. Line 6 binds the namespace prefix computer to the namespace http://
www.deitel.com/computer. Line 7 identifies this namespace as the targetNamespace—
the namespace being defined by the current XML Schema document.

To design the XML elements for describing laptop computers, we first create a simple
type in lines 9–13 using the *simpleType* element. We name this simpleType gigahertz
because it will be used to describe the clock speed of the processor in gigahertz. Simple
types are restrictions of a type typically called a *base type*. For this simpleType, line 10
declares the base type as decimal, and we restrict the value to be at least 2.1 by using the
minInclusive element in line 11.

Next, we declare a complexType named CPU that has *simpleContent* (lines 16–20).
Remember that a complex type with simple content can have attributes but not child elements. Also recall that complex types with simple content must extend or restrict some
XML Schema type or user-defined type. The *extension* element with attribute *base* (line
17) sets the base type to string. In this complexType, we extend the base type string with
an attribute. The *attribute* element (line 18) gives the complexType an attribute of type
string named model. Thus an element of type CPU must contain string text (because the
base type is string) and may contain a model attribute that is also of type string.

Last, we define type portable, which is a complexType with complex content (lines
23–31). Such types are allowed to have child elements and attributes. The element *all*
(lines 24–29) encloses elements that must each be included once in the corresponding
XML instance document. These elements can be included in any order. This complex type
holds four elements—processor, monitor, CPUSpeed and RAM. They are given types CPU,
int, gigahertz and int, respectively. When using types CPU and gigahertz, we must
include the namespace prefix computer, because these user-defined types are part of the
computer namespace (http://www.deitel.com/computer)—the namespace defined in
the current document (line 7). Also, portable contains an attribute defined in line 30.
The attribute element indicates that elements of type portable contain an attribute of
type string named manufacturer.

Line 33 declares the actual element that uses the three types defined in the schema.
The element is called laptop and is of type portable. We must use the namespace prefix
computer in front of portable.

We have now created an element named laptop that contains child elements processor, monitor, CPUSpeed and RAM, and an attribute manufacturer. Figure 20.7 uses the

```
1   <?xml version = "1.0"?>
2   <!-- Fig. 20.7: laptop.xml              -->
3   <!-- Laptop components marked up as XML -->
4
5   <computer:laptop xmlns:computer = "http://www.deitel.com/computer"
6      manufacturer = "IBM">
7
8      <processor model = "Centrino">Intel</processor>
9      <monitor>17</monitor>
10     <CPUSpeed>2.4</CPUSpeed>
11     <RAM>256</RAM>
12  </computer:laptop>
```

Fig. 20.7 | XML document using the laptop element defined in computer.xsd.

laptop element defined in the computer.xsd schema. We used Visual Studio's built-in schema validation to ensure that this XML instance document adheres to the schema's structural rules.

Line 5 declares namespace prefix computer. The laptop element requires this prefix because it is part of the http://www.deitel.com/computer namespace. Line 6 sets the laptop's manufacturer attribute, and lines 8–11 use the elements defined in the schema to describe the laptop's characteristics.

Automatically Creating Schemas using Visual Studio
Visual Studio includes a tool that allows you to create a schema from an existing XML document, using the document as a template. With an XML document open, select **XML > Create Schema** to use this feature. A new schema file opens that conforms to the standards of the XML document. You can now save it and add it to the project.

Good Programming Practice 20.1

The schema generated by Visual Studio is a good starting point, but you should refine the restrictions and types it specifies so they are appropriate for your XML documents.

20.4 Extensible Stylesheet Language and XSL Transformations

Extensible Stylesheet Language (*XSL*) documents specify how programs are to render XML document data. XSL is a group of three technologies—*XSL-FO* (*XSL Formatting Objects*), *XPath* (*XML Path Language*) and *XSLT* (*XSL Transformations*). XSL-FO is a vocabulary for specifying formatting, and XPath is a string-based language of expressions used by XML and many of its related technologies for effectively and efficiently locating structures and data (such as specific elements and attributes) in XML documents.

The third portion of XSL—XSL Transformations (XSLT)—is a technology for transforming XML documents into other documents—i.e., transforming the structure of the XML document data to another structure. XSLT provides elements that define rules for transforming one XML document to produce a different XML document. This is useful when you want to use data in multiple applications or on multiple platforms, each of which may be designed to work with documents written in a particular vocabulary. For example, XSLT allows you to convert a simple XML document to an *XHTML* (*Extensible HyperText Markup Language*) document that presents the XML document's data (or a subset of the data) formatted for display in a web browser. (See Fig. 20.8 for a sample "before" and "after" view of such a transformation.) XHTML is the W3C technical recommendation that replaces HTML for marking up web content. For more information on XHTML, visit www.deitel.com/xhtml/.

Transforming an XML document using XSLT involves two tree structures—the *source tree* (i.e., the XML document to be transformed) and the *result tree* (i.e., the XML document to be created). XPath is used to locate parts of the source-tree document that match *templates* defined in an *XSL style sheet*. When a match occurs (i.e., a node matches a template), the matching template executes and adds its result to the result tree. When there are no more matches, XSLT has transformed the source tree into the result tree. The XSLT does not analyze every node of the source tree; it selectively navigates the source tree using XSLT's select and match attributes. For XSLT to function, the source tree must be properly structured. Schemas, DTDs and validating parsers can validate document structure before using XPath and XSLTs.

A Simple XSL Example

Figure 20.8 lists an XML document that describes various sports. The output shows the result of the transformation (specified in the XSLT template of Fig. 20.9) rendered by Internet Explorer 7. Right click with the page open in Internet Explorer and select **View Source** to view the generated XHTML.

To perform transformations, an XSLT processor is required. Popular XSLT processors include Microsoft's MSXML, the Apache Software Foundation's *Xalan* (xalan.apache.org) and the XslCompiledTransform class from the .NET Framework that we use in Section 20.8. The XML document shown in Fig. 20.8 is transformed into an XHTML document by MSXML when the document is loaded in Internet Explorer. MSXML is both an XML parser and an XSLT processor.

Line 2 (Fig. 20.8) is a *processing instruction* (*PI*) that references the XSL style sheet sports.xsl (Fig. 20.9). A processing instruction is embedded in an XML document and provides application-specific information to whichever XML processor the application

```
 1   <?xml version = "1.0"?>
 2   <?xml-stylesheet type = "text/xsl" href = "sports.xsl"?>
 3
 4   <!-- Fig. 20.8: sports.xml -->
 5   <!-- Sports Database -->
 6
 7   <sports>
 8      <game id = "783">
 9         <name>Cricket</name>
10
11         <paragraph>
12            More popular among Commonwealth nations.
13         </paragraph>
14      </game>
15
16      <game id = "239">
17         <name>Baseball</name>
18
19         <paragraph>
20            More popular in America.
21         </paragraph>
22      </game>
23
24      <game id = "418">
25         <name>Soccer (Futbol)</name>
26
27         <paragraph>
28            Most popular sport in the world.
29         </paragraph>
30      </game>
31   </sports>
```

Fig. 20.8 | XML document that describes various sports. (Part 1 of 2.)

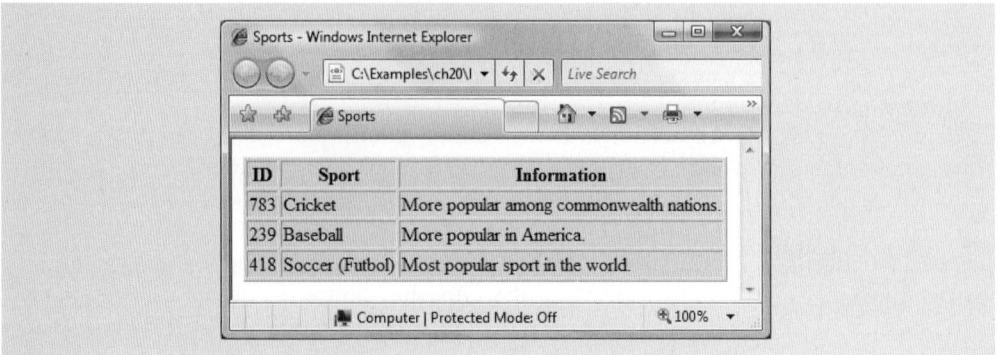

Fig. 20.8 | XML document that describes various sports. (Part 2 of 2.)

```
 1  <?xml version = "1.0"?>
 2  <!-- Fig. 20.9: sports.xsl -->
 3  <!-- A simple XSLT transformation -->
 4
 5  <!-- reference XSL style sheet URI -->
 6  <xsl:stylesheet version = "1.0"
 7     xmlns:xsl = "http://www.w3.org/1999/XSL/Transform">
 8
 9     <xsl:output method = "xml" omit-xml-declaration = "no"
10        doctype-system =
11           "http://www.w3.org/TR/xhtml1/DTD/xhtml1-strict.dtd"
12        doctype-public = "-//W3C//DTD XHTML 1.0 Strict//EN"/>
13
14     <xsl:template match = "/"> <!-- match root element -->
15
16     <html xmlns = "http://www.w3.org/1999/xhtml">
17        <head>
18           <title>Sports</title>
19        </head>
20
21        <body>
22           <table border = "1" style = "background-color: wheat">
23              <thead>
24                 <tr>
25                    <th>ID</th>
26                    <th>Sport</th>
27                    <th>Information</th>
28                 </tr>
29              </thead>
30
31              <!-- insert each name and paragraph element value -->
32              <!-- into a table row. -->
33              <xsl:for-each select = "/sports/game">
34                 <tr>
35                    <td><xsl:value-of select = "@id"/></td>
36                    <td><xsl:value-of select = "name"/></td>
```

Fig. 20.9 | XSLT that creates elements and attributes in an XHTML document. (Part 1 of 2.)

```
37                    <td><xsl:value-of select = "paragraph"/></td>
38                 </tr>
39              </xsl:for-each>
40           </table>
41        </body>
42     </html>
43
44     </xsl:template>
45  </xsl:stylesheet>
```

Fig. 20.9 | XSLT that creates elements and attributes in an XHTML document. (Part 2 of 2.)

uses. In this particular case, the processing instruction specifies the location of an XSLT document with which to transform the XML document. The characters **<?** and **?>** (line 2, Fig. 20.8) delimit a processing instruction, which consists of a *PI target* (e.g., xml-stylesheet) and a *PI value* (e.g., type = "text/xsl" href = "sports.xsl"). The PI value's type attribute specifies that sports.xsl is a text/xsl file (i.e., a text file containing XSL content). The href attribute specifies the name and location of the style sheet to apply—in this case, sports.xsl in the current directory.

Software Engineering Observation 20.4

XSL enables document authors to separate data presentation (specified in XSL documents) from data description (specified in XML documents).

Figure 20.9 shows the XSL document for transforming the structured data of the XML document of Fig. 20.8 into an XHTML document for presentation. By convention, XSL documents have the file-name extension **.xsl**.

Lines 6–7 begin the XSL style sheet with the **stylesheet** start tag. Attribute **version** specifies the XSLT version to which this document conforms. Line 7 binds namespace prefix **xsl** to the W3C's XSLT URI (i.e., http://www.w3.org/1999/XSL/Transform).

Lines 9–12 use element **xsl:output** to write an XHTML document type declaration (DOCTYPE) to the result tree (i.e., the XML document to be created). The DOCTYPE identifies XHTML as the type of the resulting document. Attribute method is assigned "xml", which indicates that XML is being output to the result tree. (Recall that XHTML is a type of XML.) Attribute **omit-xml-declaration** specifies whether the transformation should write the XML declaration to the result tree. In this case, we do not want to omit the XML declaration, so we assign to this attribute the value "no". Attributes doctype-system and doctype-public write the DOCTYPE DTD information to the result tree.

XSLT uses *templates* (i.e., **xsl:template** elements) to describe how to transform particular nodes from the source tree to the result tree. A template is applied to nodes that are specified in the match attribute. Line 14 uses the **match** attribute to select the *document root* (i.e., the conceptual part of the document that contains the root element and everything below it) of the XML source document (i.e., sports.xml). The XPath character / (a forward slash) is used as a separator between element names. Recall that XPath is a string-based language used to locate parts of an XML document easily. In XPath, a leading forward slash specifies that we are using *absolute addressing* (i.e., we are starting from the root and defining paths down the source tree). In the XML document of Fig. 20.8, the child nodes of the document root are the two processing-instruction nodes (lines 1–2), the two comment nodes (lines 4–5) and the sports element node (lines 7–31). The template in Fig. 20.9, line 14, matches a node (i.e., the document root), so the contents of the template are now added to the result tree.

The XSLT processor writes the XHTML in lines 16–29 (Fig. 20.9) to the result tree exactly as it appears in the XSL document. Now the result tree consists of the DOCTYPE definition and the XHTML code from lines 16–29. Lines 33–39 use element *xsl:for-each* to iterate through the source XML document, searching for game elements. The xsl:for-each element is similar to C#'s foreach statement. Attribute *select* is an XPath expression that specifies the nodes (called the *node set*) on which the xsl:for-each operates. Again, the first forward slash means that we are using absolute addressing. The forward slash between sports and game indicates that game is a child node of sports. Thus, the xsl:for-each finds game nodes that are children of the sports node. The XML document sports.xml contains only one sports node, which is also the document root element. After finding the elements that match the selection criteria, the xsl:for-each processes each element with the code in lines 34–38 (these lines produce one row in an XHTML table each time they execute) and places the result of lines 34–38 in the result tree.

Line 35 uses element *value-of* to retrieve attribute id's value and place it in a td element in the result tree. The XPath symbol @ specifies that id is an attribute node of the game context node (i.e., the current node being processed). Lines 36–37 place the name and paragraph element values in td elements and insert them in the result tree. When an XPath expression has no beginning forward slash, the expression uses *relative addressing*. Omitting the beginning forward slash tells the *xsl:value-of select* statements to search for name and paragraph elements that are children of the context node, not the root node. Owing to the last XPath expression selection, the current context node is game, which indeed has an id attribute, a name child element and a paragraph child element.

Using XSLT to Sort and Format Data

Figure 20.10 presents an XML document (sorting.xml) that marks up information about a book. Note that several elements of the markup describing the book appear out of order (e.g., the element describing Chapter 3 appears before the element describing Chapter 2). We arranged them this way purposely to demonstrate that the XSL style sheet referenced in line 5 (sorting.xsl) can sort the XML file's data for presentation purposes.

```
1   <?xml version = "1.0"?>
2   <!-- Fig. 20.10: sorting.xml -->
3   <!-- XML document containing book information -->
4
5   <?xml-stylesheet type = "text/xsl" href = "sorting.xsl"?>
6
7   <book isbn = "999-99999-9-X">
8      <title>Deitel&apos;s XML Primer</title>
9
10     <author>
11        <firstName>Jane</firstName>
12        <lastName>Blue</lastName>
13     </author>
```

Fig. 20.10 | XML document containing book information. (Part 1 of 2.)

```
14
15      <chapters>
16        <frontMatter>
17          <preface pages = "2" />
18          <contents pages = "5" />
19          <illustrations pages = "4" />
20        </frontMatter>
21
22        <chapter number = "3" pages = "44">Advanced XML</chapter>
23        <chapter number = "2" pages = "35">Intermediate XML</chapter>
24        <appendix number = "B" pages = "26">Parsers and Tools</appendix>
25        <appendix number = "A" pages = "7">Entities</appendix>
26        <chapter number = "1" pages = "28">XML Fundamentals</chapter>
27      </chapters>
28
29      <media type = "CD" />
30    </book>
```

Fig. 20.10 | XML document containing book information. (Part 2 of 2.)

Figure 20.11 presents an XSL document (sorting.xsl) for transforming sorting.xml (Fig. 20.10) to XHTML. Recall that an XSL document navigates a source tree and builds a result tree. In this example, the source tree is XML, and the output tree is XHTML. Line 14 of Fig. 20.11 matches the root element of the document in Fig. 20.10. Line 15 outputs an html start tag to the result tree. The <xsl:apply-templates/> element (line 16) specifies that the XSLT processor is to apply the xsl:templates defined in this XSL document to the current node's (i.e., the document root's) children. The content from the applied templates is output in the html element that ends at line 17. Lines 21–86 specify a template that matches element book. The template indicates how to format the information contained in book elements of sorting.xml (Fig. 20.10) as XHTML.

```
1     <?xml version = "1.0"?>
2     <!-- Fig. 20.11: sorting.xsl -->
3     <!-- Transformation of book information into XHTML -->
4
5     <xsl:stylesheet version = "1.0" xmlns = "http://www.w3.org/1999/xhtml"
6        xmlns:xsl = "http://www.w3.org/1999/XSL/Transform">
7
8        <!-- write XML declaration and DOCTYPE DTD information -->
9        <xsl:output method = "xml" omit-xml-declaration = "no"
10          doctype-system = "http://www.w3.org/TR/xhtml11/DTD/xhtml11.dtd"
11          doctype-public = "-//W3C//DTD XHTML 1.1//EN"/>
12
13       <!-- match document root -->
14       <xsl:template match = "/">
15          <html>
16             <xsl:apply-templates/>
17          </html>
18       </xsl:template>
```

Fig. 20.11 | XSL document that transforms sorting.xml into XHTML. (Part 1 of 3.)

```
19
20      <!-- match book -->
21      <xsl:template match = "book">
22         <head>
23            <title>ISBN <xsl:value-of select = "@isbn"/> -
24               <xsl:value-of select = "title"/></title>
25         </head>
26
27         <body>
28            <h1 style = "color: blue"><xsl:value-of select = "title"/></h1>
29            <h2 style = "color: blue">by
30               <xsl:value-of select = "author/firstName"/>
31               <xsl:text> </xsl:text>
32               <xsl:value-of select = "author/lastName"/>
33            </h2>
34
35            <table style = "border-style: groove; background-color: wheat">
36
37               <xsl:for-each select = "chapters/frontMatter/*">
38                  <tr>
39                     <td style = "text-align: right">
40                        <xsl:value-of select = "name()"/>
41                     </td>
42
43                     <td>
44                        ( <xsl:value-of select = "@pages"/> pages )
45                     </td>
46                  </tr>
47               </xsl:for-each>
48
49               <xsl:for-each select = "chapters/chapter">
50                  <xsl:sort select = "@number" data-type = "number"
51                     order = "ascending"/>
52                  <tr>
53                     <td style = "text-align: right">
54                        Chapter <xsl:value-of select = "@number"/>
55                     </td>
56
57                     <td>
58                        <xsl:value-of select = "text()"/>
59                        ( <xsl:value-of select = "@pages"/> pages )
60                     </td>
61                  </tr>
62               </xsl:for-each>
63
64               <xsl:for-each select = "chapters/appendix">
65                  <xsl:sort select = "@number" data-type = "text"
66                     order = "ascending"/>
67                  <tr>
68                     <td style = "text-align: right">
69                        Appendix <xsl:value-of select = "@number"/>
70                     </td>
71
```

Fig. 20.11 | XSL document that transforms sorting.xml into XHTML. (Part 2 of 3.)

```
72                      <td>
73                          <xsl:value-of select = "text()"/>
74                          ( <xsl:value-of select = "@pages"/> pages )
75                      </td>
76                  </tr>
77              </xsl:for-each>
78          </table>
79
80          <p style = "color: blue">Pages:
81              <xsl:variable name = "pagecount"
82                  select = "sum(chapters//*/@pages)"/>
83              <xsl:value-of select = "$pagecount"/>
84          <br />Media Type: <xsl:value-of select = "media/@type"/></p>
85      </body>
86  </xsl:template>
87 </xsl:stylesheet>
```

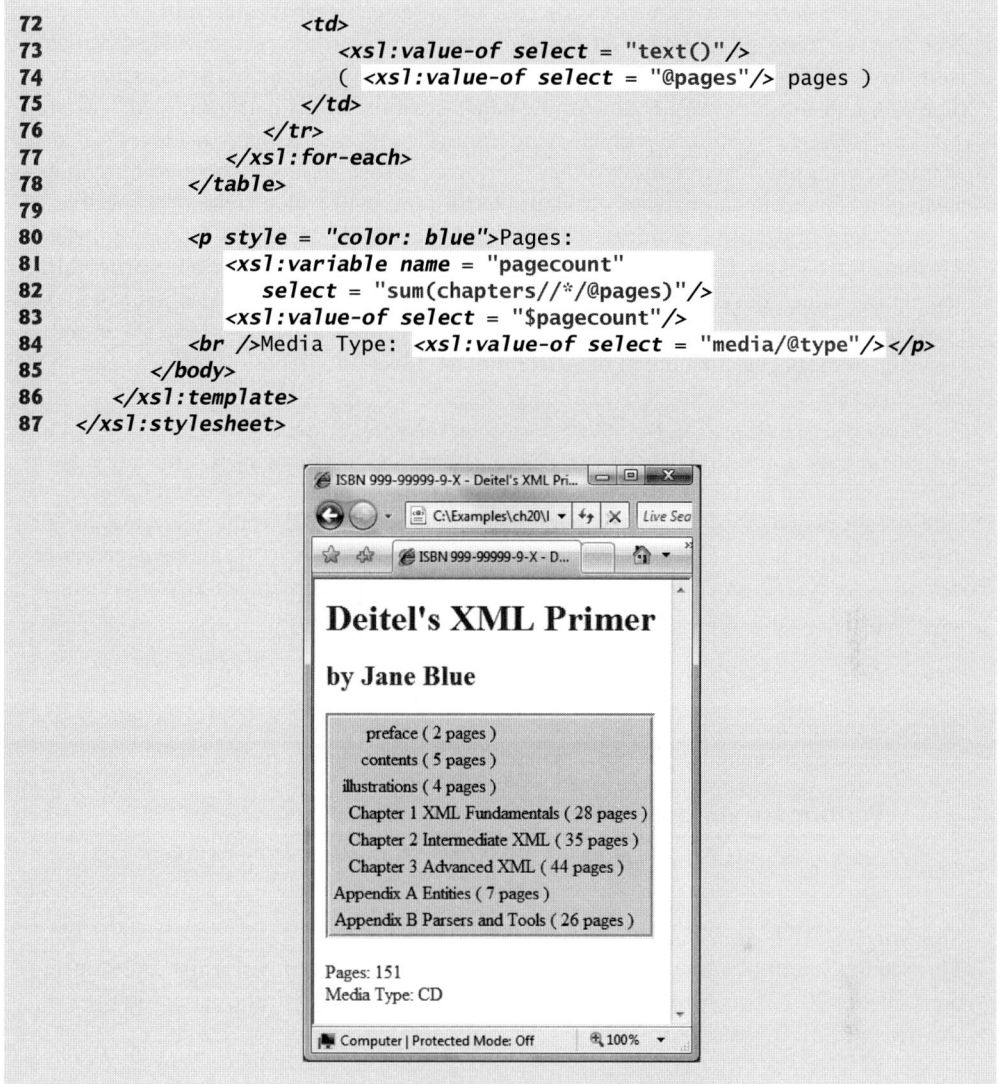

Fig. 20.11 | XSL document that transforms `sorting.xml` into XHTML. (Part 3 of 3.)

Lines 23–24 create the title for the XHTML document. We use the book's ISBN (from attribute `isbn`) and the contents of element `title` to create the string that appears in the browser window's title bar (**ISBN 999-99999-9-X - Deitel's XML Primer**).

Line 28 creates a header element that contains the book's title. Lines 29–33 create a header element that contains the book's author. Because the context node (i.e., the current node being processed) is `book`, the XPath expression `author/lastName` selects the author's last name, and the expression `author/firstName` selects the author's first name. The **xsl:text** element (line 31) is used to insert literal text. Because XML (and therefore XSLT) ignores whitespace, the author's name would appear as **JaneBlue** without inserting the explicit space.

Line 37 selects each element (indicated by an asterisk) that is a child of element
frontMatter. Line 40 calls *node-set function **name*** to retrieve the current node's element
name (e.g., preface). The current node is the context node specified in the xsl:for-each
(line 37). Line 44 retrieves the value of the pages attribute of the current node.

Line 49 selects each chapter element. Lines 50–51 use element ***xsl:sort*** to sort
chapters by number in ascending order. Attribute ***select*** selects the value of attribute
number in context node chapter. Attribute ***data-type***, with value "number", specifies a
numeric sort, and attribute ***order***, with value "ascending", specifies ascending order.
Attribute data-type also accepts the value "text" (line 65), and attribute order also
accepts the value "descending". Line 58 uses *node-set function **text*** to obtain the text
between the chapter start and end tags (i.e., the name of the chapter). Line 59 retrieves
the value of the pages attribute of the current node. Lines 64–77 perform similar tasks for
each appendix.

Lines 81–82 use an *XSL variable* to store the value of the book's total page count and
output the page count to the result tree. Note that such variables cannot be modified after
they are initialized. Attribute ***name*** specifies the variable's name (i.e., pagecount), and attribute select assigns a value to the variable. Function ***sum*** (line 82) totals the values for all
page attribute values. The two slashes between chapters and * indicate a *recursive
descent*—the XSLT processor will search for elements that contain an attribute named
pages in all descendant nodes of chapters. The XPath expression

    //*

selects all the nodes in an XML document. Line 83 retrieves the value of the newly created
XSL variable pagecount by placing a dollar sign in front of its name.

Performance Tip 20.1

Selecting all nodes in a document when it is not necessary slows XSLT processing.

Summary of XSL Style-Sheet Elements
This section's examples used several predefined XSL elements to perform various operations. Figure 20.12 lists commonly used XSL elements. For more information on these elements and XSL in general, see www.w3.org/Style/XSL.

Element	Description
<xsl:apply-templates>	Applies the templates of the XSL document to the children of the current node.
<xsl:apply-templates match = "*expression*">	Applies the templates of the XSL document to the children of the nodes matching *expression*. The value of the attribute match (i.e., *expression*) must be an XPath expression that specifies elements.
<xsl:template>	Contains rules to apply when a specified node is matched.

Fig. 20.12 | XSL style-sheet elements. (Part 1 of 2.)

Element	Description
`<xsl:value-of select = "expression">`	Selects the value of an XML element and adds it to the output tree of the transformation. The required `select` attribute contains an XPath expression.
`<xsl:for-each select = "expression">`	Applies a template to every node selected by the XPath specified by the `select` attribute.
`<xsl:sort select = "expression">`	Used as a child element of an `<xsl:apply-templates>` or `<xsl:for-each>` element. Sorts the nodes selected by the `<xsl:apply-template>` or `<xsl:for-each>` element so that the nodes are processed in sorted order.
`<xsl:output>`	Has various attributes to define the format (e.g., XML, XHTML), version (e.g., 1.0, 2.0), document type and MIME type of the output document. MIME types are discussed in Section 22.2. This tag is a top-level element—it can be used only as a child element of an `xsl:stylesheet`.
`<xsl:copy>`	Adds the current node to the output tree.

Fig. 20.12 | XSL style-sheet elements. (Part 2 of 2.)

This section introduced Extensible Stylesheet Language (XSL) and showed how to create XSL transformations to convert XML documents from one format to another. We showed how to transform XML documents to XHTML documents for display in a web browser. In most business applications, XML documents are transferred between business partners and are transformed to other XML vocabularies programmatically. In Section 20.8, we demonstrate how to perform XSL transformations using the `XslCompiledTransform` class provided by the .NET Framework.

20.5 LINQ to XML: Document Object Model (DOM)

Although an XML document is a text file, retrieving data from the document using traditional sequential file-processing techniques is not practical, especially for adding and removing elements dynamically.

On successfully parsing a document, some XML parsers store document data as trees in memory. Figure 20.13 illustrates the tree structure for the document `article.xml` discussed in Fig. 16.2. This hierarchical tree structure is called a *Document Object Model* (*DOM*) *tree*, and an XML parser that creates such a tree is known as a *DOM parser*. DOM gets its name from the conversion of an XML document's tree structure into a tree of objects that are then manipulated using an object-oriented programming language such as C#. Each element name (e.g., `article`, `date`, `firstName`) is represented by a node. A node that contains other nodes (called *child nodes* or children) is called a *parent node* (e.g., `author`). A parent node can have many children, but a child node can have only one parent node. Nodes that are peers (e.g., `firstName` and `lastName`) are called *sibling nodes*. A node's *descendant nodes* include its children, its children's children and so on. A node's *ancestor nodes* include its parent, its parent's parent and so on.

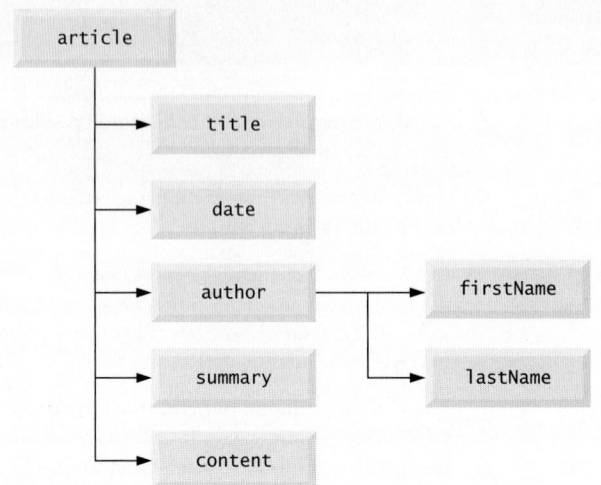

Fig. 20.13 | Tree structure for the document `article.xml`.

The DOM tree has a single *root node*, which contains all the other nodes in the document. For example, the root node of the DOM tree that represents `article.xml` (Fig. 16.2) contains a node for the XML declaration (line 1), two nodes for the comments (lines 2–3) and a node for the XML document's root element `article` (line 5).

Classes for creating, reading and manipulating XML documents are located in the *System.Xml* namespace, which also contains additional namespaces that provide other XML-related operations.

Reading an XML Document with an XDocument

Namespace *System.Xml.Linq* contains the classes used to manipulate a DOM in .NET. Though LINQ query expressions are not required to use them, the technologies used are collectively referred to as LINQ to XML. Previous versions of the .NET Framework used a different DOM implementation in the System.Xml namespace. These classes (such as XmlDocument) were made obsolete by LINQ to XML. The *XElement* class represents a DOM element node—an XML document is represented by a tree of XElement objects. The *XDocument* class represents an entire XML document. Unlike XElements, XDocuments cannot be nested. Figure 20.14 uses these classes to load the article.xml document (Fig. 16.2) and display its data in a TextBox. The program displays a formatted version of its input XML file. If article.xml were poorly formatted, such as being all on one line, this application would allow you to convert it into a form that is much easier to understand.

```
1   // Fig. 20.14: XDocumentTestForm.cs
2   // Reading an XML document and displaying it in a TextBox.
3   using System;
4   using System.Xml.Linq;
```

Fig. 20.14 | Reading an XML document and displaying it in a TextBox. (Part 1 of 3.)

```
 5    using System.Windows.Forms;
 6
 7    namespace XDocumentTest
 8    {
 9       public partial class XDocumentTestForm : Form
10       {
11          public XDocumentTestForm()
12          {
13             InitializeComponent();
14          } // end constructor
15
16          // read XML document and display its content
17          private void XDocumentTestForm_Load( object sender, EventArgs e )
18          {
19             // load the XML file into an XDocument
20             XDocument xmlFile = XDocument.Load( "article.xml" );
21             int indentLevel = 0; // no indentation for root element
22
23             // print elements recursively
24             PrintElement( xmlFile.Root, indentLevel );
25          } // end method XDocumentTestForm_Load
26
27          // display an element (and its children, if any) in the TextBox
28          private void PrintElement( XElement element, int indentLevel )
29          {
30             // get element name without namespace
31             string name = element.Name.LocalName;
32
33             // display the element's name within its tag
34             IndentOutput( indentLevel ); // indent correct amount
35             outputTextBox.AppendText( '<' + name + ">\n" );
36
37             // check for child elements and print value if none contained
38             if ( element.HasElements )
39             {
40                // print all child elements at the next indentation level
41                foreach ( var child in element.Elements() )
42                   PrintElement( child, indentLevel + 1 );
43             } // end if
44             else
45             {
46                // increase the indentation amount for text elements
47                IndentOutput( indentLevel + 1 );
48
49                // display the text inside this element
50                outputTextBox.AppendText( element.Value.Trim() + '\n' );
51             } // end else
52
53             // display end tag
54             IndentOutput( indentLevel );
55             outputTextBox.AppendText( "</" + name + ">\n" );
56          } // end method PrintElement
```

Fig. 20.14 | Reading an XML document and displaying it in a TextBox. (Part 2 of 3.)

```
57
58          // add the specified amount of indentation to the current line
59          private void IndentOutput( int number )
60          {
61             for ( int i = 0; i < number; i++ )
62                outputTextBox.AppendText( "   " );
63          } // end method IndentOutput
64       } // end class XDocumentTestForm
65    } // end namespace XDocumentTest
```

```
<article>
   <title>
      Simple XML
   </title>
   <date>
      July 24, 2008
   </date>
   <author>
      <firstName>
         John
      </firstName>
      <lastName>
         Doe
      </lastName>
   </author>
   <summary>
      XML is pretty easy.
   </summary>
   <content>
      In this chapter, we present a wide variety of examples t
   </content>
</article>
```

Fig. 20.14 | Reading an XML document and displaying it in a TextBox. (Part 3 of 3.)

To create an XDocument from an existing XML document, we use XDocument's static **Load** *method*, giving the location of the document as an argument (line 20). The returned XDocument contains a tree representation of the loaded XML file, which is used to navigate the file's contents. The XDocument's **Root** *property* (line 24) returns an XElement representing the root element of the XML file.

Method PrintElement (lines 28–56) displays an XElement in outputTextBox. Because nested elements should be at different indentation levels, PrintElement takes an int specifying the amount of indentation to use in addition to the XElement it is displaying. Variable indentLevel is passed as an argument to the IndentOutput method (lines 59–63) to add the correct amount of spacing before the begin (line 35) and end (line 50) tags are displayed.

As you've seen in previous sections, tag and attribute names often have a namespace prefix. Because the full names consist of two parts (the prefix and name), tag and attribute names are stored not simply as strings, but as objects of class **XName**. The **Name** *property* of an XElement (line 31) returns an XName object containing the tag name and namespace—we are not interested in the namespace for this example, so we retrieve the unqualified name using the XName's **LocalName** *property*.

XElements with and without children are treated differently in the program—this test is performed using the ***HasElements** property* (line 38). For XElements with children, we use the ***Elements** method* (line 41) to obtain the children, then iterate through them and recursively print their children by calling PrintElement (line 42). For XElements that do not have children, the text they contain is displayed using the ***Value** property* (line 50). If used on an element with children, the Value property returns all of the text contained within its descendants, with the tags removed. For simplicity, elements with attributes and those with both elements and text as children are not handled. The indentation is increased by one in both cases to allow for proper formatting.

20.6 LINQ to XML Class Hierarchy

As you saw in the previous section, XElement objects provide several methods for quickly traversing the DOM tree they represent. LINQ to XML provides many other classes for representing different parts of the tree. Figure 20.15 demonstrates the use of these additional classes to navigate the structure of an XML document and display it in a TreeView control. It also shows how to use these classes to get functionality equivalent to the XPath strings introduced in Section 20.4. The file used as a data source (sports.xml) is shown in Fig. 20.8.

```
 1    // Fig. 20.15: PathNavigatorForm.cs
 2    // Document navigation using XNode.
 3    using System;
 4    using System.Collections.Generic;
 5    using System.Linq;
 6    using System.Xml; // for XmlNodeType enumeration
 7    using System.Xml.Linq; // for XNode and others
 8    using System.Xml.XPath; // for XPathSelectElement
 9    using System.Windows.Forms;
10
11    namespace PathNavigator
12    {
13       public partial class PathNavigatorForm : Form
14       {
15          private XNode current; // currently selected node
16          private XDocument document; // the document to navigate
17          private TreeNode tree; // TreeNode used by TreeView control
18
19          public PathNavigatorForm()
20          {
21             InitializeComponent();
22          } // end PathNavigatorForm
23
24          // initialize variables and TreeView control
25          private void PathNavigatorForm_Load( object sender, EventArgs e )
26          {
27             document = XDocument.Load( "sports.xml" ); // load sports.xml
28
```

Fig. 20.15 | Document navigation using XNode. (Part I of 6.)

```
29          // current node is the entire document
30          current = document;
31
32          // create root TreeNode and add to TreeView
33          tree = new TreeNode( NodeText( current ) );
34          pathTreeView.Nodes.Add( tree ); // add TreeNode to TreeView
35          TreeRefresh(); // reset the tree display
36       } // end method PathNavigatorForm_Load
37
38       // print the elements of the selected path
39       private void locateComboBox_SelectedIndexChanged(
40          object sender, EventArgs e )
41       {
42          // retrieve the set of elements to output
43          switch ( locateComboBox.SelectedIndex )
44          {
45             case 0: // print all sports elements
46                PrintElements( document.Elements( "sports" ) );
47                break;
48             case 1: // print all game elements
49                PrintElements( document.Descendants( "game" ) );
50                break;
51             case 2: // print all name elements
52                PrintElements( document.XPathSelectElements( "//name" ) );
53                break;
54             case 3: // print all paragraph elements
55                PrintElements( document.Descendants( "game" )
56                   .Elements( "paragraph" ) );
57                break;
58             case 4: // print game elements with name element of "Cricket"
59                // use LINQ to XML to retrieve the correct node
60                var cricket =
61                   from game in document.Descendants( "game" )
62                   where game.Element( "name" ).Value == "Cricket"
63                   select game;
64                PrintElements( cricket );
65                break;
66             case 5: // print all id attributes of game
67                PrintIDs( document.Descendants( "game" ) );
68                break;
69          } // end switch
70       } // end method locateComboBox_SelectedIndexChanged
71
72       // traverse to first child
73       private void firstChildButton_Click( object sender, EventArgs e )
74       {
75          // try to convert to an XContainer
76          var container = current as XContainer;
77
78          // if container has children, move to first child
79          if ( container != null && container.Nodes().Any() )
80          {
81             current = container.Nodes().First(); // first child
```

Fig. 20.15 | Document navigation using XNode. (Part 2 of 6.)

```
 82
 83                          // create new TreeNode for this node with correct label
 84                          var newNode = new TreeNode( NodeText( current ) );
 85                          tree.Nodes.Add( newNode ); // add node to TreeNode Nodes list
 86                          tree = newNode; // move current selection to newNode
 87                          TreeRefresh(); // reset the tree display
 88                       } // end if
 89                       else
 90                       {
 91                          // current node is not a container or has no children
 92                          MessageBox.Show( "Current node has no children.", "Warning",
 93                             MessageBoxButtons.OK, MessageBoxIcon.Information );
 94                       } // end else
 95                    } // end method firstChildButton_Click
 96
 97                    // traverse to node's parent
 98                    private void parentButton_Click( object sender, EventArgs e )
 99                    {
100                       // if current node is not the root, move to parent
101                       if ( current.Parent != null )
102                          current = current.Parent; // get parent node
103                       else // node is at top level: move to document itself
104                          current = current.Document;
105
106                       // move TreeView if it is not already at the root
107                       if ( tree.Parent != null )
108                       {
109                          tree = tree.Parent; // get parent in tree structure
110                          tree.Nodes.Clear(); // remove all children
111                          TreeRefresh(); // reset the tree display
112                       } // end if
113                    } // end method parentButton_Click
114
115                    // traverse to previous node
116                    private void previousButton_Click( object sender, EventArgs e )
117                    {
118                       // if current node is not first, move to previous node
119                       if ( current.PreviousNode != null )
120                       {
121                          current = current.PreviousNode; // move to previous node
122                          var treeParent = tree.Parent; // get parent node
123                          treeParent.Nodes.Remove( tree ); // delete current node
124                          tree = treeParent.LastNode; // set current display position
125                          TreeRefresh(); // reset the tree display
126                       } // end if
127                       else // current element is first among its siblings
128                       {
129                          MessageBox.Show( "Current node is first sibling.", "Warning",
130                             MessageBoxButtons.OK, MessageBoxIcon.Information );
131                       } // end else
132                    } // end method previousButton_Click
133
```

Fig. 20.15 | Document navigation using XNode. (Part 3 of 6.)

```
134        // traverse to next node
135        private void nextButton_Click( object sender, EventArgs e )
136        {
137           // if current node is not last, move to next node
138           if ( current.NextNode != null )
139           {
140              current = current.NextNode; // move to next node
141
142              // create new TreeNode to display next node
143              var newNode = new TreeNode( NodeText( current ) );
144              var treeParent = tree.Parent; // get parent TreeNode
145              treeParent.Nodes.Add( newNode ); // add to parent node
146              tree = newNode; // set current position for display
147              TreeRefresh(); // reset the tree display
148           } // end if
149           else // current node is last among its siblings
150           {
151              MessageBox.Show( "Current node is last sibling.", "Warning",
152                 MessageBoxButtons.OK, MessageBoxIcon.Information );
153           } // end else
154        } // end method nextButton_Click
155
156        // update TreeView control
157        private void TreeRefresh()
158        {
159           pathTreeView.ExpandAll(); // expand tree node in TreeView
160           pathTreeView.Refresh(); // force TreeView update
161           pathTreeView.SelectedNode = tree; // highlight current node
162        } // end method TreeRefresh
163
164        // print values in the given collection
165        private void PrintElements( IEnumerable< XElement > elements )
166        {
167           locateTextBox.Clear(); // clear the text area
168
169           // display text inside all elements
170           foreach ( var element in elements )
171              locateTextBox.AppendText( element.Value.Trim() + '\n' );
172        } // end method PrintElements
173
174        // print the ID numbers of all games in elements
175        private void PrintIDs( IEnumerable< XElement > elements )
176        {
177           locateTextBox.Clear(); // clear the text area
178
179           // display "id" attribute of all elements
180           foreach ( var element in elements )
181              locateTextBox.AppendText(
182                 element.Attribute( "id" ).Value.Trim() + '\n' );
183        } // end method PrintIDs
184
```

Fig. 20.15 | Document navigation using XNode. (Part 4 of 6.)

```
185        // returns text used to represent an element in the tree
186        private string NodeText( XNode node )
187        {
188           // different node types are displayed in different ways
189           switch ( node.NodeType )
190           {
191              case XmlNodeType.Document:
192                 // display the document root
193                 return "Document root";
194              case XmlNodeType.Element:
195                 // represent node by tag name
196                 return '<' + ( node as XElement ).Name.LocalName + '>';
197              case XmlNodeType.Text:
198                 // represent node by text stored in Value property
199                 return ( node as XText ).Value;
200              case XmlNodeType.Comment:
201                 // represent node by comment text
202                 return ( node as XComment ).ToString();
203              case XmlNodeType.ProcessingInstruction:
204                 // represent node by processing-instruction text
205                 return ( node as XProcessingInstruction ).ToString();
206              default:
207                 // all nodes in this example are already covered;
208                 // return a reasonable default value for other nodes
209                 return node.NodeType.ToString();
210           } // end switch
211        } // end method NodeText
212     } // end class PathNavigatorForm
213  } // end namespace PathNavigator
```

a) **Path Navigator** form upon loading.   b) The **//name** path is selected.

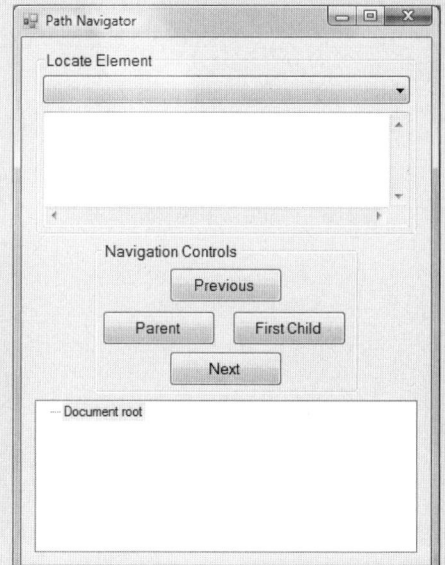

Fig. 20.15 | Document navigation using **XNode**. (Part 5 of 6.)

c) The **//name** path displays all **name** elements in the document.

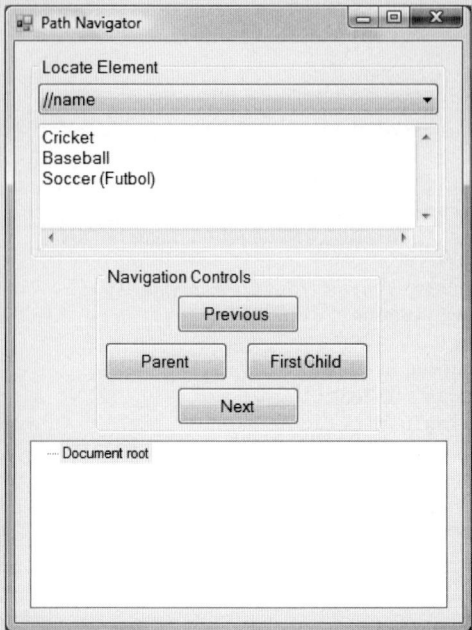

d) The **//game[name='Cricket']** path displays game elements with a **name** element containing "Cricket."

e) The **First Child** button expands the tree to show the first element in that group.

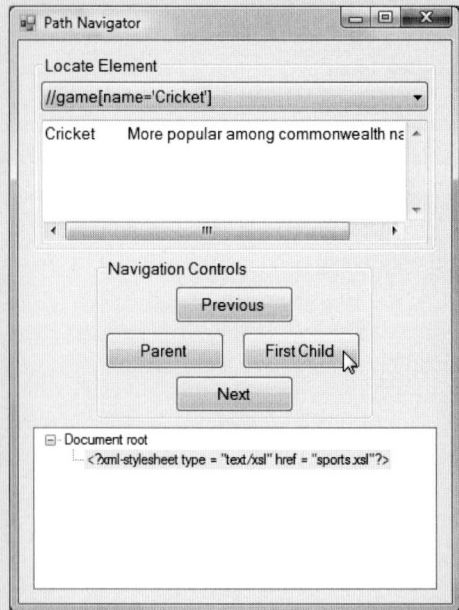

f) The **Next** button lets you view siblings of the current element

Fig. 20.15 | Document navigation using **XNode**. (Part 6 of 6.)

The interface for this example allows the user to display selected elements in the TextBox, or to navigate through the DOM tree in the lower TreeView. Initially, the TextBox is blank, and the TreeView is initialized to show the sports element—the root of the tree. The ComboBox at the top of the Form contains XPath expressions. These are not used directly—instead, the example uses the LINQ to XML DOM classes and a LINQ query to retrieve the same results. As in the previous example, the XDocument's Load method (line 27) is used to load the contents of the XML file into memory. Instance variable current, which points to the current position in the DOM, is initialized to the document itself (line 30). Line 33 creates a TreeNode for the XElement with the correct text, which is then inserted into the TreeView (lines 34–35). The TreeRefresh method (lines 157–162) refreshes the pathTreeView control so that the user interface updates correctly.

The SelectedIndexChanged event handler of locateComboBox (lines 39–70) fills the TextBox with the elements corresponding to the path the user selected. The first case (lines 45–47) uses the Elements method of the XDocument object document. The Elements method is overloaded—one version has no parameter and returns all child elements. The second version returns only elements with the given tag name. Recall from the previous example that XElement also has an Elements method. This is because the method is actually defined in the *XContainer class*, the base class of XDocument and XElement. XContainer represents nodes in the DOM tree that can contain other nodes. The results of the call to the method Elements are passed to the PrintElements method (lines 165–172). The PrintElements method uses the XElement's Value property (line 171) introduced in the previous example. Note that the Value property returns all text in the current node and its descendants. The text is displayed in locateTextBox.

The second case (lines 48–50) uses the *Descendants method*—another XContainer method common to XElement and XDocument—to get the same results as the XPath double slash (//) operator. In other words, the Descendants method returns all descendant elements with the given tag name, not just direct children. Like Elements, it is overloaded and has a version with no parameter that returns all descendants.

The third case (lines 51–53) uses extension method *XPathSelectElements* from namespace *System.Xml.XPath* (imported at line 8). This method allows you to use an XPath expression to navigate XDocument and XElement objects. It returns an IEnumerable<XElement>. There is also an XPathSelectElement method that returns a single XElement.

The fourth case (lines 54–57) also uses the Descendants method to retrieve all game elements, but it then calls the Elements method to retrieve the child paragraph elements. Note that because the Descendants method returns an IEnumerable<XElement>, the Elements method is not being called on the XContainer class that we previously stated contains the Elements method. Calling the Elements method in this way is allowed because there is an extension method in the System.Xml.Linq namespace that returns an IEnumerable<XElement> containing the children of all elements in the original collection. To match the interface of the XContainer class, there is also a Descendants extension method, and both have versions that do not take an argument.

In a document where a specific element appears at multiple nesting levels, you may need to use chained calls of the Elements method explicitly to return only the elements in which you are interested. Using the Descendants method in these cases can be a source of subtle bugs—if the XML document's structure changes, your code could silently accept input that the program should not treat as valid. The Descendants method is best used for tags that can appear at any nesting level within the document, such as formatting tags in XHTML, which can occur in many distinct parts of the text.

The fifth case (lines 58–65) retrieves only the game elements with a name element containing "Cricket". To do this, we use a LINQ query (lines 61–63). The Descendants and Elements methods return an IEnumerable<XElement>, so they can be used as the subject of a LINQ query. The where clause (line 62) uses the Element method to retrieve all name elements that are children of the game element the range variable represents. The **Element method**, a member of the XContainer class, returns the first child element with the given tag name or null if no such element exists. The where clause uses the Value property to retrieve the text contained in the element. We do not check for Element returning null because we know that all game elements in sports.xml contain name elements.

The PrintIDs method (lines 175–183) displays the id attributes of the XElement objects passed to it—specifically, the game elements in the document (line 67). To do this, it uses the **Attribute method** of the XElement class (line 182). The Attribute method returns an XAttribute object matching the given attribute name or null if no such object exists. The **XAttribute class** represents an XML attribute—it holds the attribute's name and value. Here, we access its Value property to get a string that contains the attribute's value—it can also be used as an *lvalue* to modify the value.

The Click event handlers for the Buttons in the example are used to update the data displayed in the TreeView. These methods introduce many other classes from the namespace System.Xml.Linq. The entire LINQ to XML class hierarchy is shown in the UML class diagram of Fig. 20.16. XNamespace will be covered in the next section, and **XDocumentType** holds a DTD, which may be defined directly in an XML file rather than externally referenced (as we did in Fig. 15.4, letter.xml).

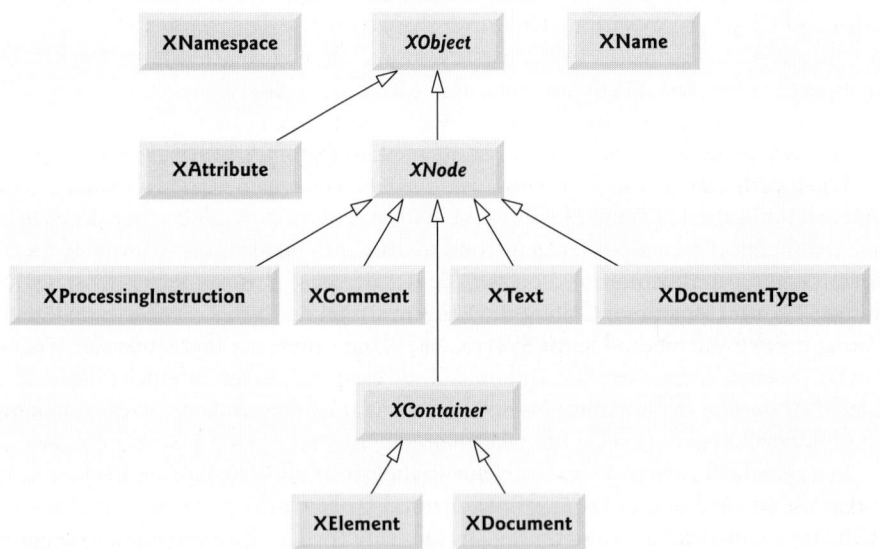

Fig. 20.16 | LINQ to XML class hierarchy diagram.

As you can see from the diagram, the ***XNode class*** is a common abstract base class of all the node types in an XML document—including elements, text and processing instructions. Because all DOM node classes inherit from XNode, an XNode object can be used to keep track of our current location as we navigate the DOM tree.

The firstChildButton_Click event handler (lines 73–95) uses the as operator to determine whether the current node is an XContainer (line 76). Recall that the as operator attempts to cast the reference to another type, and returns null if it cannot. If current is an XContainer and has children (line 79), we move current to its first child (line 81). These operations use the ***Nodes method*** of class XContainer, which returns an refernce to an object of type IEnumerable<XNode> containing all children of the given XContainer. Line 79 uses the Any extension method introduced in Chapter 9—all of the standard LINQ to Objects methods may be used with the LINQ to XML classes. The event handler then inserts a TreeNode into the TreeView to display the child element that current now references (lines 84–87).

Line 84 uses the NodeText method (lines 186–211) to determine what text to display in the TreeNode. It uses the ***NodeType property***, which returns a value of the ***XmlNodeType enumeration*** from the System.Xml namespace (imported at line 6) indicating the object's node type. Although we call it on an XNode, the NodeType property is actually defined in the ***XObject class***. XObject is an abstract base class for all nodes and attributes. The NodeType property is overridden in the concrete subclasses to return the correct value.

After the node's type has been determined, it is converted to the appropriate type using the as operator, then the correct text is retrieved. For the entire document, it returns the text **Document root** (line 193). For elements, NodeText returns the tag name enclosed in angle brackets (line 196). For text nodes, it uses the contained text. It retrieves this by converting the XNode to an XText object—the ***XText class*** holds the contents of a text node. XText's ***Value property*** returns the contained text (line 166)—we could also have used its ToString method, but, because Value is a property, it can be used as an *lvalue*. Comments, represented by the ***XComment class***, are displayed just as they are written in the XML file using the ToString method of XComment (line 202). The ToString methods of all subclasses of XNode return the XML they and their children (if any) represent with proper indentation. The last type handled is processing instructions, stored in the ***XProcessingInstruction class*** (line 205)—in this example, the only processing instruction is the XML declaration at the beginning of the file. A default case returning the name of the node type is included for other node types that do not appear in sports.xml (line 209).

The event handlers for the other Buttons are structured similarly to firstChildButton_Click—each moves current and updates the TreeView accordingly. The parentButton_Click method (lines 98–113) ensures that the current node has a parent—that is, it is not at the root of the XDocument—before it tries to move current to the parent (line 81). It uses the ***Parent property*** of XObject, which returns the parent of the given XObject or null if the parent does not exist. For nodes at the root of the document, including the root element, XML declaration, header comments and the document itself, Parent with return null. We want to move up to the document root in this case, so we use the ***Document property*** (also defined in XObject) to retrieve the XDocument representing the document root (line 104). Note that the Document property of an XDocument returns itself. This is consistent with most file systems—attempting to move up a directory from the root will succeed, but not move.

The event handlers for the **Previous** (lines 116–132) and **Next** (lines 135–154) Buttons use the *PreviousNode* (lines 119 and 121) and *NextNode* (lines 138 and 140) properties of XNode, respectively. As their names imply, they return the previous or next sibling node in the tree. If there is no previous or next node, the properties return null.

20.7 LINQ to XML: Namespaces and Creating Documents

As you learned in Chapter 16, XML namespaces provide a technique for preventing collisions between tag names used for different purposes. LINQ to XML provides the *XNamespace class* to enable creation and manipulation of XML namespaces.

Using LINQ to XML to navigate data already stored in an XML document is a common operation, but sometimes it is necessary to create an XML document from scratch. Figure 20.17 uses these features to update an XML document to a new format and combine the data in it with data from a document already in the new format. Figures 20.18 and 20.19 contain the XML files in the old and new formats, respectively. Figure 20.20 displays the file output by the program.

```
1   // Fig. 20.17: XMLCombine.cs
2   // Transforming an XML document and splicing its contents with another.
3   using System;
4   using System.Linq;
5   using System.Xml.Linq;
6
7   class XMLCombine
8   {
9      // namespaces used in XML files
10     private static readonly XNamespace employeesOld =
11        "http://www.deitel.com/employeesold";
12     private static readonly XNamespace employeesNew =
13        "http://www.deitel.com/employeesnew";
14
15     static void Main( string[] args )
16     {
17        // load files from disk
18        XDocument newDocument = XDocument.Load( "employeesNew.xml" );
19        XDocument oldDocument = XDocument.Load( "employeesOld.xml" );
20
21        // convert from old to new format
22        oldDocument = TransformDocument( oldDocument );
23
24        // combine documents and write to output file
25        SaveFinalDocument( newDocument, oldDocument );
26
27        // tell user we have finished
28        Console.WriteLine( "Documents successfully combined." );
29     } // end Main
30
31     // convert the given XDocument in the old format to the new format
32     private static XDocument TransformDocument( XDocument document )
33     {
```

Fig. 20.17 | Transforming an XML document and splicing its contents with another. (Part 1 of 2.)

```
34          // use a LINQ query to fill the new XML root with the correct data
35          var newDocumentRoot = new XElement( employeesNew + "employeelist",
36             from employee in document.Root.Elements()
37             select TransformEmployee( employee ) );
38
39          return new XDocument( newDocumentRoot ); // return new document
40       } // end method TransformDocument
41
42       // transform a single employee's data from old to new format
43       private static XElement TransformEmployee( XElement employee )
44       {
45          // retrieve values from old-format XML document
46          XNamespace old = employeesOld; // shorter name
47          string firstName = employee.Element( old + "firstname" ).Value;
48          string lastName = employee.Element( old + "lastname" ).Value;
49          string salary = employee.Element( old + "salary" ).Value;
50
51          // return new-format element with the correct data
52          return new XElement( employeesNew + "employee",
53             new XAttribute( "name", firstName + " " + lastName ),
54             new XAttribute( "salary", salary ) );
55       } // end method TransformEmployee
56
57       // take two new-format XDocuments and combine
58       // them into one, then save to output.xml
59       private static void SaveFinalDocument( XDocument document1,
60          XDocument document2 )
61       {
62          // create new root element
63          var root = new XElement( employeesNew + "employeelist" );
64
65          // fill with the elements contained in the roots of both documents
66          root.Add( document1.Root.Elements() );
67          root.Add( document2.Root.Elements() );
68
69          var finalDocument = new XDocument( root ); // create new document
70          finalDocument.Save( "output.xml" ); // save document to file
71       } // end method SaveFinalDocument
72    } // end class XMLCombine
```

Fig. 20.17 | Transforming an XML document and splicing its contents with another. (Part 2 of 2.)

```
1    <?xml version="1.0"?>
2    <!-- Fig. 20.18: employeesOld.xml -->
3    <!-- Sample old-format input for the XMLCombine application. -->
4    <employees xmlns="http://www.deitel.com/employeesold">
5       <employeelisting>
6          <firstname>Christopher</firstname>
7          <lastname>Green</lastname>
8          <salary>1460</salary>
9       </employeelisting>
```

Fig. 20.18 | Sample old-format input for the XMLCombine application. (Part 1 of 2.)

```
10      <employeelisting>
11         <firstname>Michael</firstname>
12         <lastname>Red</lastname>
13         <salary>1420</salary>
14      </employeelisting>
15   </employees>
```

Fig. 20.18 | Sample old-format input for the XMLCombine application. (Part 2 of 2.)

```
1    <?xml version="1.0"?>
2    <!-- Fig. 20.19: employeesNew.xml -->
3    <!-- Sample new-format input for the XMLCombine application. -->
4    <employeelist xmlns="http://www.deitel.com/employeesnew">
5       <employee name="Jenn Brown" salary="2300"/>
6       <employee name="Percy Indigo" salary="1415"/>
7    </employeelist>
```

Fig. 20.19 | Sample new-format input for the XMLCombine application.

```
1    <?xml version="1.0" encoding="utf-8"?>
2    <employeelist xmlns="http://www.deitel.com/employeesnew">
3      <employee name="Jenn Brown" salary="2300" />
4      <employee name="Percy Indigo" salary="1415" />
5      <employee name="Christopher Green" salary="1460" />
6      <employee name="Michael Red" salary="1420" />
7    </employeelist>
```

Fig. 20.20 | XML file generated by XMLCombine(Fig. 20.17).

Lines 10–13 of Fig. 20.17 define XNamespace objects for the two namespaces used in the input XML documents. There is an implicit conversion from string to XNamespace.

The TransformDocument method (lines 32–40) converts an XML document from the old format to the new format. It creates a new XElement newDocumentRoot, passing the desired name and child elements as arguments. It then creates and returns a new XDocument, with newDocumentRoot as its root element.

The first argument (line 35) creates an XName object for the tag name using the XNamespace's overloaded + operator—the XName contains the XNamespace from the left operand and the local name given by the string in the right operand. Recall that you can use XName's LocalName property to access the element's unqualified name. The *Namespace property* gives you access to the contained XNamespace object. The second argument is the result of a LINQ query (lines 36–37), which uses the TransformEmployee method to transform each employeelisting entry in the old format (returned by calling the Elements method on the root of the old document) into an employee entry in the new format. When passed a collection of XElements, the XElement constructor adds all members of the collection as children.

The TransformEmployee method (lines 43–55) reformats the data for one employee. It does this by retrieving the text contained in the child elements of each of the employeelisting entries, then creating a new employee element and returning it. Note that the expressions passed to the `Element` method use `XNamespaces`—this is necessary because the elements they are retrieving are in the old namespace. Passing just the tag's local name would cause the `Element` method to return `null`, creating a `NullReferenceException` when the `Value` property was accessed.

Once we've retrieved the values from the original XML document, we add them as attributes to an `employee` element. This is done by creating new `XAttribute` objects with the attribute's name and value, and passing these to the `XElement` constructor (lines 53–54).

The `SaveFinalDocument` method (lines 59–71) merges the two documents and saves them to disk. It first creates a new root element in the correct namespace (line 63). Then it adds the `employee` elements from both documents as children using the **Add** *method* defined in the `XContainer` class (lines 66–67). The `Add` method, like `XElement`'s constructor, will add all elements if passed a collection. After creating and filling the new root, it creates a new `XDocument` (line 69) and saves it to disk (line 70).

20.8 XSLT with Class `XslCompiledTransform`

Recall from Section 20.4 that XSL elements define rules for transforming one type of XML document to another type of XML document. We showed how to transform XML documents into XHTML documents and displayed the results in Internet Explorer. MSXML, the XSLT processor used by Internet Explorer, performed the transformations. We now perform a similar task in a C# program.

Performing an XSL Transformation in C# Using the .NET Framework
Figure 20.21 applies the style sheet `sports.xsl` (Fig. 20.9) to the XML document `sports.xml` (Fig. 20.8) programmatically. The result of the transformation is written to an XHTML file on disk and displayed in a text box. Figure 20.21(c) shows the resulting XHTML document (`sports.html`) when you view it in Internet Explorer.

```
 1   // Fig. 20.21: TransformTestForm.cs
 2   // Applying an XSLT style sheet to an XML Document.
 3   using System;
 4   using System.IO;
 5   using System.Windows.Forms;
 6   using System.Xml.Xsl; // contains class XslCompiledTransform
 7
 8   namespace TransformTest
 9   {
10      public partial class TransformTestForm : Form
11      {
12         public TransformTestForm()
13         {
14            InitializeComponent();
15         } // end constructor
16
17         // applies the transformation
18         private XslCompiledTransform transformer;
19
```

Fig. 20.21 | Applying an XSLT style sheet to an XML document. (Part 1 of 2.)

```
20          // initialize variables
21          private void TransformTestForm_Load( object sender, EventArgs e )
22          {
23             transformer = new XslCompiledTransform(); // create transformer
24
25             // load and compile the style sheet
26             transformer.Load( "sports.xsl" );
27          } // end TransformTestForm_Load
28
29          // transform data on transformButton_Click event
30          private void transformButton_Click( object sender, EventArgs e )
31          {
32             // perform the transformation and store the result in new file
33             transformer.Transform( "sports.xml", "sports.html" );
34
35             // read and display the XHTML document's text in a TextBox
36             consoleTextBox.Text = File.ReadAllText( "sports.html" );
37          } // end method transformButton_Click
38       } // end class TransformTestForm
39    } // end namespace TransformTest
```

a) Initial GUI

b) GUI showing transformed raw XHTML

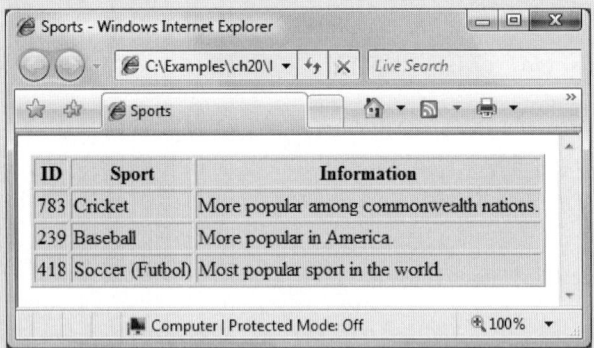

c) Transformed XHTML rendered in Internet Explorer.

Fig. 20.21 | Applying an XSLT style sheet to an XML document. (Part 2 of 2.)

Line 6 imports the *System.Xml.Xsl* namespace, which contains class *XslCompiledTransform* for applying XSL style sheets to XML documents. Line 18 declares XslCompiledTransform object transformer, which serves as an XSLT processor to transform XML data from one format to another.

In event handler TransformTestForm_Load (lines 21–27), line 23 creates and initializes transformer. Line 26 calls the XslCompiledTransform object's *Load* method, which loads and parses the style sheet that this application uses. This method takes an argument specifying the name and location of the style sheet—sports.xsl (Fig. 20.9) located in the current directory.

The event handler transformButton_Click (lines 30–37) calls the *Transform* method of class XslCompiledTransform to apply the style sheet (sports.xsl) to sports.xml (line 33). This method takes two string arguments—the first specifies the XML file to which the style sheet should be applied, and the second specifies the file in which the result of the transformation should be stored on disk. Thus the Transform method call in line 33 transforms sports.xml to XHTML and writes the result to disk as the file sports.html. Figure 20.21(c) shows the new XHTML document rendered in Internet Explorer. Note that the output is identical to that of Fig. 20.8—in the current example, though, the XHTML is stored on disk rather than generated dynamically by MSXML.

After applying the transformation, the program displays the content of the new file sports.html in consoleTextBox, as shown in Fig. 20.21(b). Line 36 obtains the text of the file by passing its name to method ReadAllText of the System.IO.File class, which simplifies file-processing tasks on the local system.

20.9 Wrap-Up

In this chapter, we continued our XML introduction that began in Chapter 16 by demonstrating several technologies related to XML. We discussed how to create DTDs and schemas for specifying and validating the structure of an XML document. We showed how to use various tools to confirm whether XML documents are valid (i.e., conform to a DTD or schema).

You learned how to create and use XSL documents to specify rules for converting XML documents between formats. Specifically, you learned how to format and sort XML data and output it as XHTML for display in a web browser.

The final sections of the chapter presented more advanced uses of XML in C# applications. We demonstrated how to retrieve and display data from an XML document using various .NET classes. We illustrated how a DOM tree represents each element of an XML document as a node in the tree. The chapter also demonstrated loading data from an XML document using the Load method of the XDocument class. We demonstrated the tools LINQ to XML provides for working with namespaces. Finally, we showed how to use the XslCompiledTransform class to perform XSL transformations.

In Chapter 21, we begin our discussion of databases, which organize data in such a way that the data can be selected and updated quickly. We introduce Structured Query Language (SQL) for writing simple database queries. We then introduce LINQ to SQL, which allows you to write LINQ queries that are automatically converted into SQL queries. These SQL queries are then used to query the database.

20.10 Web Resources

www.deitel.com/XML/

The Deitel XML Resource Center focuses on the vast amount of free XML content available online, plus some for-sale items. Start your search here for tools, downloads, tutorials, podcasts, wikis, documentation, conferences, FAQs, books, e-books, sample chapters, articles, newsgroups, forums, downloads from CNET's download.com, jobs and contract opportunities, and more that will help you develop XML applications.

Databases and LINQ to SQL

It is a capital mistake to theorize before one has data.
—Arthur Conan Doyle

Now go, write it before them in a table, and note it in a book, that it may be for the time to come for ever and ever.
—Isaiah 30:8

Get your facts first, and then you can distort them as much as you please.
—Mark Twain

I like two kinds of men: domestic and foreign.
—Mae West

OBJECTIVES

In this chapter you'll learn:

- The relational database model.
- To write basic database queries in SQL.
- To use LINQ to SQL to retrieve and manipulate data from a database.
- To add data sources to projects.
- To use the Object Relational Designer to create LINQ to SQL classes.
- To use the IDE's drag-and-drop capabilities to display database tables in applications.
- To use data binding to move data seamlessly between GUI controls and databases.
- To create Master/Detail views.

Outline

21.1 Introduction

21.2 Relational Databases

21.3 Relational Database Overview: **Books** Database

21.4 SQL

    21.4.1 Basic SELECT Query

    21.4.2 WHERE Clause

    21.4.3 ORDER BY Clause

    21.4.4 Retrieving Data from Multiple Tables: INNER JOIN

    21.4.5 INSERT Statement

    21.4.6 UPDATE Statement

    21.4.7 DELETE Statement

21.5 LINQ to SQL

21.6 LINQ to SQL: Extracting Information from a Database

    21.6.1 Creating LINQ to SQL Classes

    21.6.2 Creating Data Bindings

21.7 More Complex LINQ Queries and Data Binding

21.8 Retrieving Data from Multiple Tables with LINQ

21.9 Creating a Master/Detail View Application

21.10 Programming with LINQ to SQL: Address-Book Case Study

21.11 Wrap-Up

21.12 Tools and Web Resources

21.1 Introduction

A *database* is an organized collection of data. Many strategies exist for organizing data to facilitate easy access and manipulation. A ***database management system*** (***DBMS***) provides mechanisms for efficiently storing, organizing, retrieving and modifying data for many users. Database management systems allow access to and storage of data independently of its internal representation—this allows the internal representation to be structured to maximize efficiency while the external representation maximizes ease of use.

Today's most popular DBMSs manage ***relational databases***, which organize data simply as tables with rows and columns. A language called ***Structured Query Language*** (***SQL***)—pronounced "sequel," or as its individual letters—is the international standard language used almost universally with relational databases to perform queries (i.e., to request information that satisfies given criteria) and to manipulate data in a database. In this book, we pronounce SQL as "sequel."

Some popular proprietary database management systems are Microsoft SQL Server, Oracle, Sybase and IBM DB2. PostgreSQL and MySQL are open-source DBMSs that can be downloaded and used freely by anyone. You may also be familiar with Microsoft Access—a relational database system that is part of Microsoft Office. In this chapter, we use ***Microsoft SQL Server 2005 Express***. The latest version can be downloaded from www.microsoft.com/express/sql. As this book was sent to publication, SQL Server

2008 Express was released. You can use either the 2005 or the 2008 version with this chapter.

Chapter 9 introduced LINQ to Objects, which allows you to manipulate data stored in arrays and collections using a syntax similar to SQL. *LINQ to SQL* allows you to manipulate relational data stored in a SQL Server database. LINQ to SQL provides the expressiveness of SQL with the additional benefits of the C# compiler's type checking and the IDE's *IntelliSense*.

This chapter introduces general concepts of relational databases and SQL, then explores LINQ to SQL and the IDE's tools for working with databases. In the next two chapters, you'll see other practical database and LINQ to SQL applications. Chapter 22, ASP.NET 3.5 and ASP.NET AJAX, presents a web-based bookstore case study that retrieves user and book information from a database. Chapter 23, Windows Communication Foundation (WCF) Web Services, uses a database to store airline reservation data for a web service (i.e., a class that allows its methods to be called by methods on other machines via common data formats and protocols).

21.2 Relational Databases

A *relational database* is based on a logical representation of data that allows the data to be accessed independently of its physical structure. A relational database organizes data in *tables*. Figure 21.1 illustrates a sample Employees table that might be used in a personnel system. The table stores the attributes of employees. Tables are composed of *rows* and *columns* in which values are stored. This table consists of six rows and five columns. The ID column of each row is the table's *primary key*—a column (or group of columns) requiring a unique value that cannot be duplicated in other rows. This guarantees that a primary-key value can be used to uniquely identify a row. A primary key composed of two or more columns is known as a *composite key*. Good examples of primary-key columns in other applications are an employee ID number in a payroll system and a part number in an inventory system—values in each of these columns are guaranteed to be unique. The rows in Fig. 21.1 are displayed in order by primary key. In this case, the rows are listed in increasing (ascending) order, but they could also be listed in decreasing (descending) order or in no particular order at all. As we will demonstrate in an upcoming example, programs can specify ordering criteria when requesting data from a database.

Table Employees

	ID	Name	Department	Salary	Location
	23603	Jones	413	1100	New Jersey
	24568	Kerwin	413	2000	New Jersey
Row	34589	Larson	642	1800	Los Angeles
	35761	Myers	611	1400	Orlando
	47132	Neumann	413	9000	New Jersey
	78321	Stephens	611	8500	Orlando

Primary key   Column

Fig. 21.1 | Employees table sample data.

Each column represents a different data attribute. Rows are normally unique (by primary key) within a table, but some column values may be duplicated between rows. For example, three different rows in the Employees table's Department column contain the number 413, indicating that these employees work in the same department.

Different database users are often interested in different data and different relationships among the data. Most users require only subsets of the rows and columns. To obtain these subsets, programs use SQL to define queries that select subsets of the data from a table. For example, a program might select data from the Employees table to create a query result that shows where each department is located, in increasing order by Department number (Fig. 21.2). SQL queries are discussed in Section 21.4.

Department	Location
413	New Jersey
611	Orlando
642	Los Angeles

Fig. 21.2 | Distinct Department and Location data from the Employees table.

21.3 Relational Database Overview: Books Database

We now overview relational databases in the context of a simple Books database. The database stores information about some recent Deitel publications. First, we overview the Books database's tables. A database's tables, their fields and the relationships between them are collectively known as a *database schema*. After overviewing the database, we introduce database concepts, such as how to use SQL to retrieve information from the Books database and to manipulate the data. We provide the database file—Books.mdf—with the examples for this chapter (downloadable from www.deitel.com/books/csharpfp3/). SQL Server database files typically end with the .mdf ("master data file") file-name extension. Sections 21.6–21.9 explain how to use this file in an application.

Authors *Table of the* Books *Database*
The database consists of three tables: Authors, AuthorISBN and Titles. The Authors table (described in Fig. 21.3) consists of three columns that maintain each author's unique ID number, first name and last name, respectively. Figure 21.4 contains the data from the Authors table. We list the rows in order by the table's primary key—AuthorID. You'll learn how to sort data by other criteria (e.g., in alphabetical order by last name) using SQL's ORDER BY clause in Section 21.4.3.

Column	Description
AuthorID	Author's ID number in the database. In the Books database, this integer column is defined as an *identity* column, also known as an *autoincremented* column—for each row inserted in the table, the AuthorID value is increased by 1 automatically to ensure that each row has a unique AuthorID. This is the primary key.

Fig. 21.3 | Authors table of the Books database. (Part 1 of 2.)

Column	Description
FirstName	Author's first name (a string).
LastName	Author's last name (a string).

Fig. 21.3 | Authors table of the Books database. (Part 2 of 2.)

AuthorID	FirstName	LastName
1	Harvey	Deitel
2	Paul	Deitel
3	Greg	Ayer
4	Dan	Quirk

Fig. 21.4 | Data from the Authors table of the Books database.

Titles *Table of the Books Database*

The Titles table (described in Fig. 21.5) consists of four columns that maintain information about each book in the database, including the ISBN, title, edition number and copyright year. Figure 21.6 contains the data from the Titles table.

Column	Description
ISBN	ISBN of the book (a string). The table's primary key. ISBN is an abbreviation for "International Standard Book Number"—a numbering scheme that publishers worldwide use to give every book a unique identification number.
BookTitle	Title of the book (a string).
EditionNumber	Edition number of the book (an integer).
Copyright	Copyright year of the book (a string).

Fig. 21.5 | Titles table of the Books database.

ISBN	BookTitle	Edition-Number	Copy-right
0131752421	Internet & World Wide Web How to Program	4	2008
0132222205	Java How to Program	7	2007
0132404168	C How to Program	5	2007

Fig. 21.6 | Data from the Titles table of the Books database. (Part 1 of 2.)

ISBN	BookTitle	Edition-Number	Copy-right
0136053033	Simply Visual Basic 2008	3	2009
013605305X	Visual Basic 2008 How to Program	4	2009
013605322X	Visual C# 2008 How to Program	3	2009
0136151574	Visual C++ 2008 How to Program	2	2008
0136152503	C++ How to Program	6	2008

Fig. 21.6 | Data from the Titles table of the Books database. (Part 2 of 2.)

AuthorISBN *Table of the Books Database*

The AuthorISBN table (described in Fig. 21.7) consists of two columns that maintain ISBNs for each book and their corresponding authors' ID numbers. This table associates authors with their books. The AuthorID column is a *foreign key*—a column in this table that matches the primary-key column in another table (i.e., AuthorID in the Authors table). The ISBN column is also a foreign key—it matches the primary-key column (i.e., ISBN) in the Titles table. Together the AuthorID and ISBN columns in this table form a composite primary key. Every row in this table uniquely matches one author to one book's ISBN. Figure 21.8 contains the data from the AuthorISBN table of the Books database.

Column	Description
AuthorID	The author's ID number, a foreign key to the Authors table.
ISBN	The ISBN for a book, a foreign key to the Titles table.

Fig. 21.7 | AuthorISBN table of the Books database.

AuthorID	ISBN	AuthorID	ISBN
1	0131752421	2	0132222205
1	0132222205	2	0132404168
1	0132404168	2	0136053033
1	0136053033	2	013605305X
1	013605305X	2	013605322X
1	013605322X	2	0136151574
1	0136151574	2	0136152503
1	0136152503	3	0136053033
2	0131752421	4	0136151574

Fig. 21.8 | Data from the AuthorISBN table of Books.

Foreign Keys

Foreign keys can be specified when creating a table. A foreign key helps maintain the *Rule of Referential Integrity*—every foreign-key value must appear as another table's primary-key value. This enables the DBMS to determine whether the AuthorID value for a particular row of the AuthorISBN table is valid. Foreign keys also allow related data in multiple tables to be selected from those tables—this is known as *joining* the data. (You'll learn how to join data using SQL's INNER JOIN operator in Section 21.4.4.) There is a *one-to-many relationship* between a primary key and a corresponding foreign key (e.g., one author can write many books). This means that a foreign key can appear many times in its own table but only once (as the primary key) in another table. For example, the ISBN 0136151574 can appear in several rows of AuthorISBN (because this book has several authors) but only once in Titles, where ISBN is the primary key.

Entity-Relationship Diagram for the Books Database

Figure 21.9 is an *entity-relationship* (*ER*) *diagram* for the Books database. This diagram shows the tables in the database and the relationships among them. The first compartment in each box contains the table's name. The names in italic font are primary keys (e.g., AuthorID in the Authors table). A table's primary key uniquely identifies each row in the table. Every row must have a value in the primary-key column, and the value of the key must be unique in the table. This is known as the *Rule of Entity Integrity*. Note that the names AuthorID and ISBN in the AuthorISBN table are both italic—together these form a composite primary key for the AuthorISBN table.

 Common Programming Error 21.1

Not providing a value for every column in a primary key breaks the Rule of Entity Integrity *and causes the DBMS to report an error.*

 Common Programming Error 21.2

Providing the same value for the primary key in multiple rows breaks the Rule of Entity Integrity *and causes the DBMS to report an error.*

The lines connecting the tables in Fig. 21.9 represent the relationships among the tables. Consider the line between the Authors and AuthorISBN tables. On the Authors end of the line, there is a 1, and on the AuthorISBN end, an infinity symbol (∞). This indicates a one-to-many relationship—for each author in the Authors table, there can be an arbitrary number of ISBNs for books written by that author in the AuthorISBN table (i.e., an author can write any number of books). Note that the relationship line links the AuthorID

Fig. 21.9 | Entity-relationship diagram for the Books database.

column in the Authors table (where AuthorID is the primary key) to the AuthorID column in the AuthorISBN table (where AuthorID is a foreign key)—the line between the tables links the primary key to the matching foreign key.

Common Programming Error 21.3

Providing a foreign-key value that does not appear as a primary-key value in another table breaks the Rule of Referential Integrity *and causes the DBMS to report an error.*

The line between the Titles and AuthorISBN tables illustrates a one-to-many relationship—a book can be written by many authors. Note that the line between the tables links the primary key ISBN in table Titles to the corresponding foreign key in table AuthorISBN. The relationships in Fig. 21.9 illustrate that the sole purpose of the Author-ISBN table is to provide a many-to-many relationship between the Authors and Titles tables—an author can write many books, and a book can have many authors.

21.4 SQL

We now overview SQL in the context of the Books database. Though LINQ to SQL and the Visual C# IDE hide the SQL used to manipulate databases, it is nevertheless important to understand SQL basics. Knowing the types of operations you can perform will help you develop more advanced database-intensive applications.

Figure 21.10 lists some common *SQL keywords* used to form complete *SQL statements*—we discuss these keywords in the next several subsections. Other SQL keywords exist, but they are beyond the scope of this text.

SQL keyword	Description
SELECT	Retrieves data from one or more tables.
FROM	Specifies the tables involved in a query. Required in every query.
WHERE	Specifies optional criteria for selection that determine the rows to be retrieved, deleted or updated.
ORDER BY	Specifies optional criteria for ordering rows (e.g., ascending, descending).
INNER JOIN	Specifies optional operator for merging rows from multiple tables.
INSERT	Inserts rows in a specified table.
UPDATE	Updates rows in a specified table.
DELETE	Deletes rows from a specified table.

Fig. 21.10 | Common SQL keywords.

21.4.1 Basic SELECT Query

Let us consider several SQL queries that retrieve information from database Books. A SQL *query* "selects" rows and columns from one or more tables in a database. Such selections are performed by queries with the *SELECT* keyword. The basic form of a *SELECT query* is

```
SELECT * FROM tableName
```

in which the asterisk (*) indicates that all the columns from the *tableName* table should be retrieved. For example, to retrieve all the data in the Authors table, use

```
SELECT * FROM Authors
```

Note that the rows of the Authors table are not guaranteed to be returned in any particular order. You'll learn how to specify criteria for sorting rows in Section 21.4.3.

Most programs do not require all the data in a table—in fact, selecting all the data from a large table is discouraged, as it can cause performance problems. To retrieve only specific columns from a table, replace the asterisk (*) with a comma-separated list of the column names. For example, to retrieve only the columns AuthorID and LastName for all the rows in the Authors table, use the query

```
SELECT AuthorID, LastName FROM Authors
```

This query returns only the data listed in Fig. 21.11.

AuthorID	LastName
1	Deitel
2	Deitel
3	Ayer
4	Quirk

Fig. 21.11 | AuthorID and LastName data from the Authors table.

21.4.2 WHERE Clause

When users search a database for rows that satisfy certain *selection criteria* (formally called *predicates*), only rows that satisfy the selection criteria are selected. SQL uses the optional *WHERE clause* in a query to specify the selection criteria for the query. The basic form of a query with selection criteria is

```
SELECT columnName1, columnName2, ... FROM tableName WHERE criteria
```

For example, to select the BookTitle, EditionNumber and Copyright columns from table Titles for which the Copyright date is more recent than 2007, use the query

```
SELECT BookTitle, EditionNumber, Copyright
FROM Titles
WHERE Copyright > '2007'
```

Note that string literals in SQL are delimited by single quotes instead of double quotes as in C#. In SQL, double quotes are used around table and column names that would otherwise be invalid—names containing SQL keywords, spaces, or other punctuation characters. Figure 21.12 shows the result of the preceding query.

BookTitle	EditionNumber	Copyright
Internet & World Wide Web How to Program	4	2008
Simply Visual Basic 2008	3	2009
Visual Basic 2008 How to Program	4	2009
Visual C# 2008 How to Program	3	2009
Visual C++ 2008 How to Program	2	2008
C++ How to Program	6	2008

Fig. 21.12 | Books with copyright dates after 2007 from table `Titles`.

The WHERE-clause criteria can contain the comparison operators <, >, <=, >=, = (equality), <> (inequality) and LIKE, as well as the logical operators AND, OR and NOT (discussed in Section 21.4.6). Operator **LIKE** is used for *pattern matching* with wildcard characters *percent* (**%**) and *underscore* (**_**). Pattern matching allows SQL to search for strings that match a given pattern.

A pattern that contains a percent character (%) searches for strings that have zero or more characters at the percent character's position in the pattern. For example, the following query locates the rows of all the authors whose last names start with the letter D:

```
SELECT AuthorID, FirstName, LastName
FROM Authors
WHERE LastName LIKE 'D%'
```

The preceding query selects the two rows shown in Fig. 21.13, because two of the four authors in our database have a last name starting with the letter D (followed by zero or more characters). The % in the WHERE clause's LIKE pattern indicates that any number of characters can appear after the letter D in the LastName column. Note that the pattern string is surrounded by single-quote characters.

An underscore (_) in the pattern string indicates a single wildcard character at that position in the pattern. For example, the following query locates the rows of all the authors whose last names start with any character (specified by _), followed by the letter y, followed by any number of additional characters (specified by %):

```
SELECT AuthorID, FirstName, LastName
FROM Authors
WHERE LastName LIKE '_y%'
```

The preceding query produces the row shown in Fig. 21.14, because only one author in our database has a last name that contains the letter y as its second letter.

AuthorID	FirstName	LastName
1	Harvey	Deitel
2	Paul	Deitel

Fig. 21.13 | Authors from the `Authors` table whose last names start with D.

AuthorID	FirstName	LastName
3	Greg	Ayer

Fig. 21.14 | The only author from the Authors table whose last name contains y as the second letter.

21.4.3 ORDER BY Clause

The rows in the result of a query can be sorted into ascending or descending order by using the optional *ORDER BY clause*. The basic form of a query with an ORDER BY clause is

SELECT columnName1, columnName2, … *FROM* tableName *ORDER BY* column *ASC*
SELECT columnName1, columnName2, … *FROM* tableName *ORDER BY* column *DESC*

where *ASC* specifies ascending order (lowest to highest), *DESC* specifies descending order (highest to lowest) and *column* specifies the column on which the sort is based. For example, to obtain the list of authors in ascending order by last name (Fig. 21.15), use the query

```
SELECT AuthorID, FirstName, LastName
FROM Authors
ORDER BY LastName ASC
```

The default sorting order is ascending, so ASC is optional in the preceding query. To obtain the same list of authors in descending order by last name (Fig. 21.16), use

```
SELECT AuthorID, FirstName, LastName
FROM Authors
ORDER BY LastName DESC
```

AuthorID	FirstName	LastName
3	Greg	Ayer
1	Harvey	Deitel
2	Paul	Deitel
4	Dan	Quirk

Fig. 21.15 | Authors from table Authors in ascending order by LastName.

AuthorID	FirstName	LastName
4	Dan	Quirk
1	Harvey	Deitel
2	Paul	Deitel
3	Greg	Ayer

Fig. 21.16 | Authors from table Authors in descending order by LastName.

Multiple columns can be used for sorting with an ORDER BY clause of the form

> *ORDER BY* *column1 sortingOrder*, *column2 sortingOrder*, …

where *sortingOrder* is either ASC or DESC. Note that the *sortingOrder* does not have to be identical for each column. For example, the query

```
SELECT BookTitle, EditionNumber, Copyright
FROM Titles
ORDER BY Copyright DESC, BookTitle ASC
```

returns the rows of the Titles table sorted first in descending order by copyright date, then in ascending order by title (Fig. 21.17). This means that rows with higher Copyright values are returned before rows with lower Copyright values, and any rows that have the same Copyright values are sorted in ascending order by title.

The WHERE and ORDER BY clauses can be combined. If used, ORDER BY must be the last clause in the query. For example, the query

```
SELECT ISBN, BookTitle, EditionNumber, Copyright
FROM Titles
WHERE BookTitle LIKE '%How to Program'
ORDER BY BookTitle ASC
```

returns the ISBN, BookTitle, EditionNumber and Copyright of each book in the Titles table that has a BookTitle ending with "How to Program" and sorts them in ascending order by BookTitle. The query results are shown in Fig. 21.18.

BookTitle	EditionNumber	Copyright
Simply Visual Basic 2008	3	2009
Visual Basic 2008 How to Program	4	2009
Visual C# 2008 How to Program	3	2009
C++ How to Program	6	2008
Internet & World Wide Web How to Program	4	2008
Visual C++ 2008 How to Program	2	2008
C How to Program	5	2007
Java How to Program	7	2007

Fig. 21.17 | Data from Titles in descending order by Copyright and ascending order by BookTitle.

ISBN	BookTitle	EditionNumber	Copyright
0132404168	C How to Program	5	2007
0136152503	C++ How to Program	6	2008
0131752421	Internet & World Wide Web How to Program	4	2008

Fig. 21.18 | Books from table Titles whose BookTitles end with How to Program in ascending order by BookTitle. (Part 1 of 2.)

ISBN	BookTitle	EditionNumber	Copyright
0132222205	Java How to Program	7	2007
013605305X	Visual Basic 2008 How to Program	4	2009
013605322X	Visual C# 2008 How to Program	3	2009
0136151574	Visual C++ 2008 How to Program	2	2008

Fig. 21.18 | Books from table `Titles` whose `BookTitles` end with `How to Program` in ascending order by `BookTitle`. (Part 2 of 2.)

21.4.4 Retrieving Data from Multiple Tables: INNER JOIN

Database designers typically *normalize* databases—i.e., split related data into separate tables to ensure that a database does not store redundant data. For example, the `Books` database has tables `Authors` and `Titles`. We use an `AuthorISBN` table to store "links" between authors and titles. If we did not separate this information into individual tables, we would need to include author information with each entry in the `Titles` table. This would result in the database storing duplicate author information for authors who have written more than one book.

Redundant data in a database increases the likelihood of errors when manpulating the data. Figure 21.1 contains redundant information between the `Department` and `Location` columns—for each department number, there is a single location and vice versa. This relationship is not enforced by the table's structure. Normalization eliminates redundant data and allows the DBMS to prevent problems that could arise if queries depend on the one-to-one mapping between `Department` and `Location`.

Often, it is desirable to merge data from multiple tables into a single result—this is referred to as joining the tables. There are several kinds of joins, but the most common one is specified by an ***INNER JOIN** operator* in the query. An `INNER JOIN` merges rows from two tables by testing for matching values in a column that is common to the tables (though the column names can differ among the tables). The basic form of an `INNER JOIN` is:

```
SELECT columnName1, columnName2, ...
FROM table1 INNER JOIN table2
    ON table1.columnName = table2.columnName
```

The ***ON** clause* of the `INNER JOIN` specifies the columns from each table that are compared to determine which rows are merged. For example, the following query produces a list of authors accompanied by the ISBNs for books written by each author:

```
SELECT FirstName, LastName, ISBN
FROM Authors INNER JOIN AuthorISBN
    ON Authors.AuthorID = AuthorISBN.AuthorID
ORDER BY LastName, FirstName
```

The query combines the `FirstName` and `LastName` columns from table `Authors` and the `ISBN` column from table `AuthorISBN`, sorting the results in ascending order by `LastName` and `FirstName`. Note the use of the syntax *tableName.columnName* in the `ON` clause. This syntax (called a *qualified name*) specifies the columns from each table that should be compared to join the tables. The "*tableName.*" syntax is required if the columns have the same name in both tables. The same syntax can be used in any query to distinguish columns that have the same name in different tables.

Common Programming Error 21.4

In a SQL query, failure to qualify names for columns that have the same name in two or more tables is an error.

As always, the query can contain an ORDER BY clause. Figure 21.19 depicts the results of the preceding query, ordered by LastName and FirstName.

FirstName	LastName	ISBN
Greg	Ayer	0136053033
Harvey	Deitel	0131752421
Harvey	Deitel	0132222205
Harvey	Deitel	0132404168
Harvey	Deitel	0136053033
Harvey	Deitel	013605305X
Harvey	Deitel	013605322X
Harvey	Deitel	0136151574
Harvey	Deitel	0136152503
Paul	Deitel	0131752421
Paul	Deitel	0132222205
Paul	Deitel	0132404168
Paul	Deitel	0136053033
Paul	Deitel	013605305X
Paul	Deitel	013605322X
Paul	Deitel	0136151574
Paul	Deitel	0136152503
Dan	Quirk	0136151574

Fig. 21.19 | Authors and ISBNs for their books in ascending order by LastName and FirstName.

21.4.5 INSERT Statement

The *INSERT statement* inserts a row into a table. The basic form of this statement is

> **INSERT INTO** *tableName* (*columnName1*, *columnName2*, …, *columnNameN*)
> **VALUES** (*value1*, *value2*, …, *valueN*)

where *tableName* is the table in which to insert the row. The *tableName* is followed by a comma-separated list of column names in parentheses. The list of column names is followed by the SQL keyword **VALUES** and a comma-separated list of values in parentheses. The values specified here must match up with the columns specified after the table name in both order and type (e.g., if *columnName1* is supposed to be the FirstName column, then *value1* should be a string in single quotes representing the first name). Although the list of column names is not required if the INSERT operation specifies a value for every table column in the correct order, you should always explicitly list the columns when inserting rows—if the order of the columns in the table changes, using only VALUES may cause an error. The INSERT statement

```
INSERT INTO Authors ( FirstName, LastName )
VALUES ( 'Sue', 'Smith' )
```

inserts a row into the Authors table. The statement indicates that the values 'Sue' and 'Smith' are provided for the FirstName and LastName columns, respectively.

Some database tables allow NULL columns—that is, columns without values. Though the capitalization is different, NULL in SQL is similar to the idea of null in C#. All of the columns in the Books database are required, so they must be given values in an INSERT statement.

We do not specify an AuthorID in this example, because AuthorID is an identity column in the Authors table (see Fig. 21.3). For every row added to this table, SQL Server assigns a unique AuthorID value that is the next value in an autoincremented sequence (i.e., 1, 2, 3 and so on). In this case, Sue Smith would be assigned AuthorID number 5. Figure 21.20 shows the Authors table after the INSERT operation.

Common Programming Error 21.5

It is an error to specify a value for an identity column in an INSERT statement.

Common Programming Error 21.6

SQL uses the single-quote (') character to delimit strings. To specify a string containing a single quote (e.g., O'Malley) in a SQL statement, there must be two single quotes in the position where the single-quote character appears in the string (e.g., 'O''Malley'). The first of the two single-quote characters acts as an escape character for the second. Not escaping single-quote characters in a string that is part of a SQL statement is a syntax error.

AuthorID	FirstName	LastName
1	Harvey	Deitel
2	Paul	Deitel
3	Greg	Ayer
4	Dan	Quirk
5	Sue	Smith

Fig. 21.20 | Table Authors after an INSERT operation.

21.4.6 UPDATE Statement

An ***UPDATE statement*** modifies data in a table. The basic form of the UPDATE statement is

```
UPDATE tableName
SET columnName1 = value1, columnName2 = value2, ..., columnNameN = valueN
WHERE criteria
```

where *tableName* is the table to update. The *tableName* is followed by keyword **SET** and a comma-separated list of column name/value pairs in the format *columnName* = *value*. The optional WHERE clause provides criteria that determine which rows to update. While it is not required, the WHERE clause is almost always used, in an UPDATE statement because omitting it updates all rows in the table—an uncommon operation. The UPDATE statement

```
UPDATE Authors
SET LastName = 'Jones'
WHERE LastName = 'Smith' AND FirstName = 'Sue'
```

updates a row in the Authors table. Keyword **AND** is a logical operator that, like the C# **&&** operator, returns true *if and only if* both of its operands are true. Thus, the preceding statement assigns to LastName the value Jones for the row in which LastName is equal to Smith *and* FirstName is equal to Sue. [*Note:* If there are multiple rows with the first name "Sue" and the last name "Smith," this statement modifies all such rows to have the last name "Jones."] Figure 21.21 shows the Authors table after the UPDATE operation has taken place. SQL also provides other logical operators, such as **OR** and **NOT**, which behave like their C# counterparts || and !.

AuthorID	FirstName	LastName
1	Harvey	Deitel
2	Paul	Deitel
3	Greg	Ayer
4	Dan	Quirk
5	Sue	Jones

Fig. 21.21 | Table Authors after an UPDATE operation.

21.4.7 DELETE Statement

A **DELETE statement** removes rows from a table. Its basic form is

```
DELETE FROM tableName WHERE criteria
```

where *tableName* is the table from which to delete. The optional WHERE clause specifies the criteria used to determine which rows to delete. As with the UPDATE statement, the DELETE applies to all rows of the table if the WHERE clause is omitted. The DELETE statement

```
DELETE FROM Authors
WHERE LastName = 'Jones' AND FirstName = 'Sue'
```

deletes the row for Sue Jones in the Authors table. DELETE statements can delete multiple rows if the rows all meet the criteria in the WHERE clause. Figure 21.22 shows the Authors table after the DELETE operation has taken place.

SQL Wrap-Up

This concludes our SQL introduction. We demonstrated several commonly used SQL keywords, formed SQL queries that retrieved data from databases and formed other SQL statements that manipulated data in a database. Next, we introduce LINQ to SQL, which allows

AuthorID	FirstName	LastName
1	Harvey	Deitel
2	Paul	Deitel
3	Greg	Ayer
4	Dan	Quirk

Fig. 21.22 | Table `Authors` after a `DELETE` operation.

C# applications to interact with databases. As you will see, LINQ to SQL translates LINQ queries like the ones you wrote in Chapter 9 into SQL statements like those presented here.

21.5 LINQ to SQL

LINQ to SQL provides an API for accessing data in SQL Server databases using the same LINQ syntax used to query arrays and collections. For many applications, the LINQ to SQL API can entirely replace .NET's older ADO.NET API, though ADO.NET is still used internally by LINQ to SQL.

You interact with LINQ to SQL via classes that are automatically generated by the IDE's LINQ to SQL Designer based on the database schema. The IDE creates a class for each table, with a property for each column in the table. Objects of these classes hold the data from individual rows in the database's tables. Foreign-key relationships are taken into account in both directions. For each foreign key, a property is created that returns the row object that the foreign key references. Every object also contains a property that returns a collection of the rows that reference it. Once generated, these classes are normal C# classes with full *IntelliSense* support in the IDE.

A *cache* is a temporary store created for fast access to data that would otherwise be costly to retrieve or regenerate. LINQ to SQL caches all row objects that it creates, making interacting with the database more efficient in two significant ways. First, it does not have to recreate row objects each time data is retrieved from the database—it can simply reuse the ones it already has in memory. To do this, LINQ to SQL needs a way to determine if a row returned from the database already exists in the cache—therefore, LINQ to SQL requires every table to have a primary key. Second, having these row objects in memory allows you to manipulate them as much as necessary, then submit the changes you make all at once. This can reduce round trips to the database—a slow operation compared to manipulating objects that are already in memory.

LINQ to SQL works through the *IQueryable<T> interface*, which inherits from the `IEnumerable<T>` interface introduced in Chapter 9. With LINQ to Objects, LINQ iterates through the entire collection and applies the query operators one at a time—each operator uses the results of applying the previous operator. In contrast, LINQ queries on an `IQueryable` object are processed together—LINQ to SQL converts the entire query into a single SQL statement to execute against the database. If each query operator were handled separately, multiple round trips to the database would be needed, and the database management system would not be able to use its intimate knowledge of its data structures to optimize the query. When the results are returned from the database, they are loaded into the corresponding classes generated by LINQ to SQL for convenient access in your code.

All LINQ to SQL queries occur via a *DataContext class*, which controls the flow of data between the program and the database. A specific DataContext class, which inherits from the class System.Data.Linq.DataContext, is created when the classes representing each row of the table are generated. When instantiated, the DataContext has properties for each table in the database—these can be used as subjects of a LINQ query. When cached objects have been changed, these changes are saved back to the database, using the DataContext's *SubmitChanges method*.

21.6 LINQ to SQL: Extracting Information from a Database

In this section, we demonstrate how to connect to a database, query it and display the result of the query. There is little code in this section—the IDE provides visual programming tools and wizards that simplify accessing data in your projects. These tools establish database connections and create the *data-binding* objects necessary to view and manipulate the data through Windows Forms GUI controls.

The next example performs a simple query on the Books database from Section 21.3. The program retrieves the entire Authors table and uses data binding to display its data in a *DataGridView*—a control from namespace System.Windows.Forms that can display a data source in a GUI. First, we connect to the Books database and create the LINQ to SQL classes required to use it. Then, we add the Authors table as a data source. Finally, we drag the Authors table data source onto the **Design** view to create a GUI for displaying the table's data.

21.6.1 Creating LINQ to SQL Classes

This section presents the steps required to create LINQ to SQL classes for a database. Though we create a Windows Forms Application here, *Steps 2–3* apply to any type of application that manipulates a database via LINQ to SQL.

Step 1: Creating the Project
Create a new Windows Forms Application named DisplayTable. Change the name of the source file to DisplayTableForm.cs. When the IDE asks if you wish to update the Form's class name to match the source file, select **Yes**. Set the Form's **Text** property to Display Table.

Step 2: Adding a Database to the Project
To interact with a database, you must first add it to the project. Select **Tools > Connect to Database...**. If the **Choose Data Source** *dialog* appears, select **Microsoft SQL Server Database File** from the **Data source:** ListBox. If you check the **Always use this selection** CheckBox, Visual C# will use this type of database file by default when you add databases to your projects in the future. Click **Continue** to open the **Add Connection** *dialog*. Notice that the **Data source:** TextBox reflects your selection in the **Choose Data Source** dialog. You can click the **Change...** Button to select a different type of database. Next, click **Browse...** and locate the Books.mdf file in the Databases directory included with this chapter's examples. You can click **Test Connection** to verify that the IDE can connect to the database through SQL Server Express. Click **OK** to create the connection.

Error-Prevention Tip 21.1

SQL Server Express allows only one application at a time to access a database file. Ensure that no other program is using the database file before you attempt to add it to the project.

Step 3: Generating the LINQ to SQL classes

After the database has been added, you must create the classes based on the database schema. To do this, right click the project name in the **Solution Explorer** and select **Add > New Item...** to display the **Add New Item** dialog. Select **LINQ to SQL classes**, name the new item `Books.dbml` and click the **Add** button. After a few moments, the ***Object Relational Designer* window** appears. You can also double click the `Books.dbml` file in the **Solution Explorer** to open the **Object Relational Designer**.

The ***Database Explorer* window**, which lets you navigate the structure of databases, should have appeared on the left side of the IDE when you added the database to the project. If not, open it by selecting **View > Other Windows > Database Explorer**. Expand the `Books.mdf` database node, then expand the **Tables** node. Drag the `Authors`, `Titles` and `AuthorISBN` tables onto the **Object Relational Designer**. The IDE prompts whether you want to copy the database to the project directory. Select **Yes**. Then save the `Books.dbml` file. At this point, the IDE generates the LINQ to SQL classes—the next steps will not work if you do not save the `.dbml` file.

Error-Prevention Tip 21.2

*Be sure to save the file in the **Object Relational Designer** before trying to use the LINQ to SQL classes in code. The IDE does not generate the classes until you save the file.*

21.6.2 Creating Data Bindings

While they are not a part of LINQ to SQL, the automatic data bindings that the IDE provides greatly simplify the creation of applications to view and modify the data stored in the database's tables. You must write a small amount of code to bridge the gap between the autogenerated data-binding classes and the autogenerated LINQ to SQL classes.

Step 1: Adding a Data Source

To use the LINQ to SQL classes in our bindings, we must first add them as a data source. Select **Data > Add New Data Source...** to display the ***Data Source Configuration Wizard***. Since the LINQ to SQL classes can be used to create objects representing the tables in the database, we'll use an object data source. In the dialog, select **Object** and click **Next >**. Expand the tree view in the next screen and select **DisplayTable > DisplayTable > Author**. The first **DisplayTable** is the project's name, the second is the `DisplayTable` namespace where the automatically generated classes are located, and the last is the `Author` class—an object of this class will be used as the data source. Click **Next >** then **Finish**. The `Authors` table in the database is now a data source that can be used by the bindings.

Step 2: Create GUI Elements

Open the ***Data Sources* window** by selecting **Data > Show Data Sources**. The `Author` class that you added in the previous step should appear. The columns of the `Authors` table should appear below it, as well as an `AuthorISBNs` entry showing the relationship between the two tables.

Open the `DisplayTableForm` in **Design** view. Click the **Author** node in the **Data Sources** window—it should change to a drop-down list. Open the drop-down and ensure that the `DataGridView` option is selected—this is the GUI control that will be used to display and interact with the data.

Drag the **Author** node from the **Data Sources** window to the `DisplayTableForm`. The IDE creates a `DataGridView` with the correct column names and a `BindingNavigator`. The *BindingNavigator* contains `Buttons` for moving between entries, adding entries, deleting entries and saving changes to the database. The IDE also generates a *BindingSource*, which transfers data between the data source and the data-bound controls on the Form. Nonvisual components such as the `BindingSource` and the nonvisual aspects of the `BindingNavigator` appear in the *component tray*—the gray region below the Form in **Design** view (Fig. 21.23). We use the default names for automatically generated components throughout this chapter to show exactly what the IDE creates, but we have made small modifications to the layout such as setting the `DataGridView`'s `Dock` property to `Fill` so it fills the Form. These modifications have no effect on the behavior of the program, and are simply cosmetic—you may also want to tweak the GUI to suit your tastes.

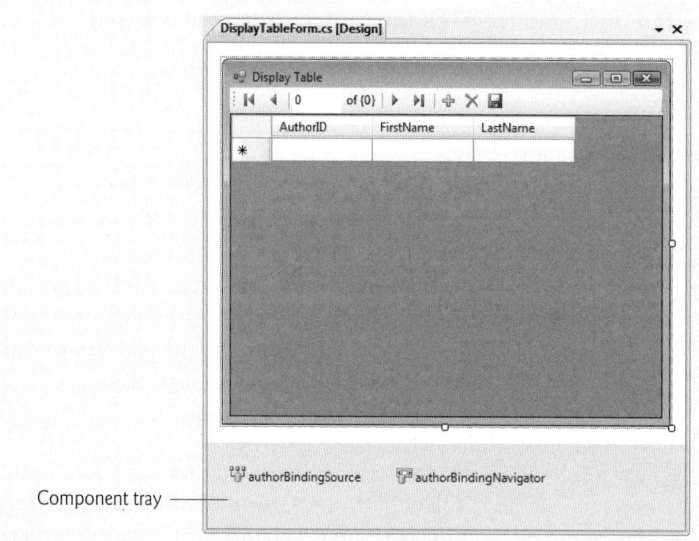

Fig. 21.23 | Component tray holds nonvisual components in **Design** view.

Step 3: Connect the BooksDataContext to the AuthorBindingSource

Now that we've created the back-end LINQ to SQL classes and the front-end `DataGrid-View` and `BindingNavigator`, we must connect them with a small amount of code. The `DataGridView` is already connected to the `BindingSource` by the IDE, so we simply need to connect the `BooksDataContext` you declared in the previous section and the `authorBindingSource` you created above. Figure 21.24 shows the small amount of code needed to move data back and forth between the database and GUI.

As mentioned in the previous section, we must use a `DataContext` object to interact with the database. The `BooksDataContext` class is automatically generated by the IDE to allow access to the `Books` database. Line 18 defines an object of this class named `database`.

```
 1    // Fig. 21.24: DisplayTableForm.cs
 2    // Displaying data from a database table in a DataGridView.
 3    using System;
 4    using System.Linq;
 5    using System.Windows.Forms;
 6
 7    namespace DisplayTable
 8    {
 9       public partial class DisplayTableForm : Form
10       {
11          // constructor
12          public DisplayTableForm()
13          {
14             InitializeComponent();
15          } // end constructor
16
17          // LINQ to SQL data context
18          private BooksDataContext database = new BooksDataContext();
19
20          // load data from database into DataGridView
21          private void DisplayTableForm_Load( object sender, EventArgs e )
22          {
23             // use LINQ to order the data for display
24             authorBindingSource.DataSource =
25                from author in database.Authors
26                orderby author.AuthorID
27                select author;
28          } // end method DisplayTableForm_Load
29
30          // click event handler for the Save Button in the
31          // BindingNavigator saves the changes made to the data
32          private void authorBindingNavigatorSaveItem_Click(
33             object sender, EventArgs e )
34          {
35             Validate(); // validate input fields
36             authorBindingSource.EndEdit(); // indicate edits are complete
37             database.SubmitChanges(); // write changes to database file
38          } // end method authorBindingNavigatorSaveItem_Click
39       } // end class DisplayTableForm
40    } // end namespace DisplayTable
```

Fig. 21.24 | Displaying data from a database table in a `DataGridView`.

Create the Form's Load handler by double clicking the title bar in **Design** view. We
allow data to move between the `DataContext` and the `BindingSource` by creating a LINQ

query that extracts data from the DataContext's Authors property (lines 25–27), which corresponds to the Authors table in the database. The BindingSource's **DataSource** *property* is set to the results of this query (line 24). The BindingSource uses its DataSource to extract data from the database and to populate the DataGridView.

Step 4: Saving Modifications Back to the Database

We'd like to save data back to the database if the user modifies it. By default, the Binding-Navigator's save Button (▣) is disabled. Enable it via the save Button's right-click menu or by using the **Properties** window to set its Enabled property to True. Then, double click the Button to create its event handler.

Saving the data entered into the DataGridView back to the database is a three-step process (lines 35–37). First, all controls on the form are validated (line 35)—if any of the controls have validation event handlers, those execute to determine whether the controls' contents are valid. Second, line 36 calls *EndEdit* on the BindingSource, which forces it to save any pending changes to its DataSource. Finally, with the data saved back to the LINQ to SQL classes, we call SubmitChanges on the BooksDataContext to store the changes in the database. For efficiency reasons, LINQ to SQL sends only data that has changed.

Step 5: Configuring the Database File to Persist Changes

By default, the original database file is copied to the project's bin directory—the location of the program's executable—each time you execute the program. To persist changes between program executions, select the database in the **Solution Explorer** and set the **Copy to Output Directory** property in the **Properties** window to **Copy if newer**.

Testing the Application

Run the application to verify that it works. The DataGridView should be filled with the author data, as shown in the screenshot. You can add and remove rows, and save your changes back to the database. Note that NULL values are not allowed in the database, and the data bindings consider an empty cell in the DataGridView to be NULL, not an empty string. Therefore, attempting to save the data with some of the fields empty will cause an exception to be thrown.

21.7 More Complex LINQ Queries and Data Binding

Now that you've seen how to display an entire database table in a DataGridView, we demonstrate how to execute more advanced queries against the database and display the results. Perform the following steps to build the example application, which executes custom queries against the Titles table of the Books database.

Step 1: Creating the Project

Create a new Windows Forms Application named DisplayQueryResult. Rename its C# file to DisplayQueryResultForm.cs. Rename the Form class to DisplayQueryResultForm when the IDE prompts you. Set the Form's **Text** property to Display Query Result.

Step 2: Creating the LINQ to SQL Classes

Follow the steps in Section 21.6.1 to add the Books database to the project and generate the LINQ to SQL classes.

Step 3: Creating a `DataGridView` to Display the `Titles` Table
Follow *Steps 1* and *2* in Section 21.6.2 to create the data source and the `DataGridView`. In this example, select the `Title` class (rather than the `Author` class) as the data source, and drag the **Title** node from the **Data Sources** window onto the form.

Step 4: Adding a ComboBox to the Form
Leave the Form's **Design** view open and add a ComboBox named `queriesComboBox` below the `DataGridView` on the Form. Set the ComboBox's Dock property to `Bottom` to make it fill the bottom part of the Form, and set its `DropDownStyle` property to `DropDownList`—this prevents the user from being able to type in the control. From this control users select options representing the queries to execute. Open the **String Collection Editor** by selecting **Edit Items** from the right-click or smart-tag menu of `queriesComboBox`. You can open the *smart-tag menu* by clicking the small arrowhead that appears in the upper-right corner of the control in **Design** view. The Visual C# IDE displays smart-tag menus for many GUI controls to facilitate common tasks. Add the following three items to `queriesComboBox`—one for each of the queries we'll create:

1. All titles
2. Titles with 2008 copyright
3. Titles ending with "How to Program"

Step 5: Programming an Event Handler for the ComboBox
Next you must write code that executes the appropriate query when the user selects an item from `queriesComboBox`. Double click `queriesComboBox` in **Design** view to generate a `queriesComboBox_SelectedIndexChanged` event handler (lines 46–80 of Fig. 21.25). In the event handler, we use a `switch` statement (lines 50–77) to set `titleBindingSource`'s `DataSource` property to a LINQ query that returns the correct set of data. Line 18 declares the `BooksDataContext` used as the subject of the LINQ queries. The data bindings created by the IDE update `titlesDataGridView` each time we change the `DataSource`. The *Move-First method* of the `BindingSource` (line 79) is used to move the focus to the first element each time a query executes.

```
1    // Fig. 21.25: DisplayQueryResultForm.cs
2    // Displaying the result of a user-selected query in a DataGridView.
3    using System;
4    using System.Linq;
5    using System.Windows.Forms;
6
7    namespace DisplayQueryResult
8    {
9       public partial class DisplayQueryResultForm : Form
10      {
11         // constructor
12         public DisplayQueryResultForm()
13         {
14            InitializeComponent();
15         } // end constructor
```

Fig. 21.25 | Displaying the result of a user-selected query in a `DataGridView`. (Part 1 of 3.)

```
16
17      // LINQ to SQL data context
18      private BooksDataContext database = new BooksDataContext();
19
20      // load data from database into DataGridView
21      private void DisplayQueryResultForm_Load(
22          object sender, EventArgs e )
23      {
24          // write SQL to standard output stream
25          database.Log = Console.Out;
26
27          // set the ComboBox to show the default query that
28          // selects all books from the Titles table
29          queriesComboBox.SelectedIndex = 0;
30      } // end method DisplayQueryResultForm_Load
31
32      // Click event handler for the Save Button in the
33      // BindingNavigator saves the changes made to the data
34      private void titleBindingNavigatorSaveItem_Click(
35          object sender, EventArgs e )
36      {
37          Validate(); // validate input fields
38          titleBindingSource.EndEdit(); // indicate edits are complete
39          database.SubmitChanges(); // write changes to database file
40
41          // when saving, return to "all titles" query
42          queriesComboBox.SelectedIndex = 0;
43      } // end method titleBindingNavigatorSaveItem_Click
44
45      // loads data into TitleBindingSource based on user-selected query
46      private void queriesComboBox_SelectedIndexChanged(
47          object sender, EventArgs e )
48      {
49          // set the data displayed according to what is selected
50          switch ( queriesComboBox.SelectedIndex )
51          {
52              case 0: // all titles
53                  // use LINQ to order the books by title
54                  titleBindingSource.DataSource =
55                      from title in database.Titles
56                      orderby title.BookTitle
57                      select title;
58                  break;
59              case 1: // titles with 2008 copyright
60                  // use LINQ to get titles with 2008
61                  // copyright and sort them by title
62                  titleBindingSource.DataSource =
63                      from title in database.Titles
64                      where title.Copyright == "2008"
65                      orderby title.BookTitle
66                      select title;
67                  break;
```

Fig. 21.25 | Displaying the result of a user-selected query in a DataGridView. (Part 2 of 3.)

```
68              case 2: // titles ending with "How to Program"
69                  // use LINQ to get titles ending with
70                  // "How to Program" and sort them by title
71                  titleBindingSource.DataSource =
72                      from title in database.Titles
73                      where title.BookTitle.EndsWith( "How to Program" )
74                      orderby title.BookTitle
75                      select title;
76                  break;
77          } // end switch
78
79          titleBindingSource.MoveFirst(); // move to first entry
80      } // end method queriesComboBox_SelectedIndexChanged
81   } // end class DisplayQueryResultForm
82 } // end namespace DisplayQueryResult
```

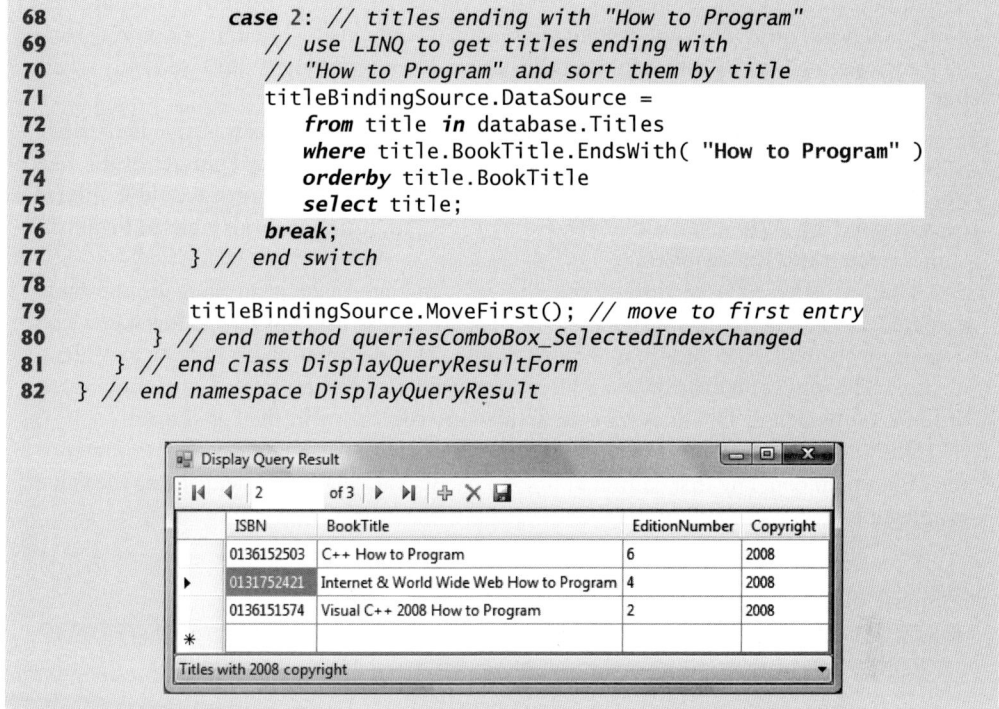

Fig. 21.25 | Displaying the result of a user-selected query in a `DataGridView`. (Part 3 of 3.)

Step 6: Customizing the Form's Load Event Handler
Create the Form's Load event handler by double clicking the title bar in **Design** view. Add a line setting the SelectedIndex of the queriesComboBox to 0 (line 29). This causes the program to show all titles when it executes.

Step 7: Saving Changes
Follow the instructions in the previous example to add a handler for the BindingNavigator's save Button (lines 34–43). Note that, except for changes to the names, the three lines are identical. The last statement (line 42) makes the DataGridView reset to the All titles query. Also, set the database's **Copy to Output Directory** property to **Copy if newer**, as was done in the preceding example.

Testing the Application
You may now run the application. As in the previous example, you can add and remove rows to and from the table, and save your changes to the database. Additionally, selecting one of the queries from the ComboBox will filter the results so that only some of the rows are displayed.

The BooksDataContext's Log Property
Line 25 sets the BooksDataContext database's **Log** property. When you set this property, the DataContext object logs all queries it runs on the database to the specified stream—in this case, Console.Out. Recall from Chapter 19 that Console.Out is the standard output

stream object. In a GUI application, "standard output" is sent to the IDE's **Output** window, shown in Fig. 21.26. The **Output** window can be opened while the program is running by selecting **View > Output** in the IDE. [*Note:* The output log is displayed only when running in debug mode.]

The SQL syntax in Fig. 21.26 is slightly different from the syntax we presented earlier in this chapter. Microsoft SQL Server uses a SQL variant known as Transact-SQL. The square brackets are used to quote table and column names, instead of the double quotes used in standard SQL. The SQL generated by LINQ to SQL quotes all table and column names, even if it is not required.

The identifier t0 used throughout the SQL in Fig. 21.26 is an alias for the table named dbo.Titles. This alias is defined in the FROM clause using SQL's AS keyword. The alias simply provides a shorter name for the table. The identifier dbo stands for "database owner." This represents the database user that is allowed to perform all operations on a SQL Server database. The lines starting with -- are comments in the Log output.

The @p0 seen in the third line of the second query is a placeholder for a parameter to the SQL statement. The first comment line for the second SQL statement shows the value of the parameter at the end of the line in square brackets (i.e., [2008]).

a) SQL generated by the **All titles** query.

b) SQL generated by the **Titles with 2008 copyright** query.

c) SQL generated by the **Titles ending with "How to Program"** query.

Fig. 21.26 | **Output** window of the **Display Query Result** application.

21.8 Retrieving Data from Multiple Tables with LINQ

In the two previous examples, we used data bindings to display data extracted using LINQ to SQL. In this section, we concentrate on LINQ to SQL features that simplify querying and combining data from multiple tables. You've already seen the SQL INNER JOIN operator in Section 21.4.4—LINQ to SQL provides similar capabilities and allows more complex operations as well. Figure 21.27 uses LINQ to SQL to combine and organize data from multiple tables.

```csharp
 1  // Fig. 21.27: JoiningTest.cs
 2  // Using LINQ to perform a join and aggregate data across tables.
 3  using System;
 4  using System.Linq;
 5
 6  namespace JoiningWithLINQ
 7  {
 8     public class JoiningTest
 9     {
10        public static void Main( string[] args )
11        {
12           // create database connection
13           BooksDataContext database = new BooksDataContext();
14
15           // get authors and ISBNs of each book they co-authored
16           var authorsAndISBNs =
17              from author in database.Authors
18              join book in database.AuthorISBNs
19                 on author.AuthorID equals book.AuthorID
20              orderby author.LastName, author.FirstName
21              select new { author.FirstName, author.LastName, book.ISBN };
22
23           Console.WriteLine( "Authors and ISBNs:" ); // display header
24
25           // display authors and ISBNs in tabular format
26           foreach ( var element in authorsAndISBNs )
27           {
28              Console.WriteLine( "\t{0,-10} {1,-10} {2,-10}",
29                 element.FirstName, element.LastName, element.ISBN );
30           } // end foreach
31
32           // get authors and titles of each book they co-authored
33           var authorsAndTitles =
34              from title in database.Titles
35              from book in title.AuthorISBNs
36              let author = book.Author
37              orderby author.LastName, author.FirstName, title.BookTitle
38              select new { author.FirstName, author.LastName,
39                 title.BookTitle };
40
41           Console.WriteLine( "\nAuthors and titles:" ); // header
42
```

Fig. 21.27 | Using LINQ to perform a join and aggregate data across tables. (Part 1 of 3.)

```
43          // display authors and titles in tabular format
44          foreach ( var element in authorsAndTitles )
45          {
46             Console.WriteLine( "\t{0,-10} {1,-10} {2}",
47                element.FirstName, element.LastName, element.BookTitle );
48          } // end foreach
49
50          // get authors and titles of each book
51          // they co-authored; group by author
52          var titlesByAuthor =
53             from author in database.Authors
54             orderby author.LastName, author.FirstName
55             let name = author.FirstName + " " + author.LastName
56             let titles =
57                from book in author.AuthorISBNs
58                orderby book.Title.BookTitle
59                select book.Title.BookTitle
60             select new { Name = name, Titles = titles };
61
62          Console.WriteLine( "\nTitles grouped by author:" ); // header
63
64          // display titles written by each author, grouped by author
65          foreach ( var author in titlesByAuthor )
66          {
67             // display author's name
68             Console.WriteLine( "\t" + author.Name + ":" );
69
70             // display titles written by that author
71             foreach ( var title in author.Titles )
72             {
73                Console.WriteLine( "\t\t" + title );
74             } // end inner foreach
75          } // end outer foreach
76       } // end Main
77    } // end class JoiningTest
78 } // end namespace JoiningWithLINQ
```

```
Authors and ISBNs:
        Greg      Ayer       0136053033
        Harvey    Deitel     0131752421
        Harvey    Deitel     0132222205
        Harvey    Deitel     0132404168
        Harvey    Deitel     0136053033
        Harvey    Deitel     013605305X
        Harvey    Deitel     013605322X
        Harvey    Deitel     0136151574
        Harvey    Deitel     0136152503
        Paul      Deitel     0131752421
        Paul      Deitel     0132222205
        Paul      Deitel     0132404168
        Paul      Deitel     0136053033
        Paul      Deitel     013605305X
```

Fig. 21.27 | Using LINQ to perform a join and aggregate data across tables. (Part 2 of 3.)

```
                Paul      Deitel    013605322X
                Paul      Deitel    0136151574
                Paul      Deitel    0136152503
                Dan       Quirk     0136151574
Authors and titles:
                Greg      Ayer      Simply Visual Basic 2008
                Harvey    Deitel    C How to Program
                Harvey    Deitel    C++ How to Program
                Harvey    Deitel    Internet & World Wide Web How to Program
                Harvey    Deitel    Java How to Program
                Harvey    Deitel    Simply Visual Basic 2008
                Harvey    Deitel    Visual Basic 2008 How to Program
                Harvey    Deitel    Visual C# 2008 How to Program
                Harvey    Deitel    Visual C++ 2008 How to Program
                Paul      Deitel    C How to Program
                Paul      Deitel    C++ How to Program
                Paul      Deitel    Internet & World Wide Web How to Program
                Paul      Deitel    Java How to Program
                Paul      Deitel    Simply Visual Basic 2008
                Paul      Deitel    Visual Basic 2008 How to Program
                Paul      Deitel    Visual C# 2008 How to Program
                Paul      Deitel    Visual C++ 2008 How to Program
                Dan       Quirk     Visual C++ 2008 How to Program
Titles grouped by author:
                Greg Ayer:
                        Simply Visual Basic 2008
                Harvey Deitel:
                        C How to Program
                        C++ How to Program
                        Internet & World Wide Web How to Program
                        Java How to Program
                        Simply Visual Basic 2008
                        Visual Basic 2008 How to Program
                        Visual C# 2008 How to Program
                        Visual C++ 2008 How to Program
                Paul Deitel:
                        C How to Program
                        C++ How to Program
                        Internet & World Wide Web How to Program
                        Java How to Program
                        Simply Visual Basic 2008
                        Visual Basic 2008 How to Program
                        Visual C# 2008 How to Program
                        Visual C++ 2008 How to Program
                Dan Quirk:
                        Visual C++ 2008 How to Program
```

Fig. 21.27 | Using LINQ to perform a join and aggregate data across tables. (Part 3 of 3.)

The code combines data from the three tables in the Books database and displays the relationships between the book titles and authors in three different ways. The LINQ to SQL classes used in this example were created using the steps described in Section 21.6.1. As in previous examples, the BooksDataContext object (declared in line 13) is needed to be able to query the database.

The first query in the example (lines 17–21) returns results identical to those in Fig. 21.19. It uses LINQ's ***join clause***, which functions like SQL's INNER JOIN operator—the generated SQL is nearly identical to the SQL given earlier in Section 21.4.4. As in the SQL example, only rows with the same AuthorID are joined together. Like the from clause, the join clause introduces a range variable—unlike the from clause, it specifies a criterion for joining. The join clause uses equals instead of the == comparison operator because the join criterion is not an arbitrary Boolean expression—you may only join based on equality. Like nested repetition statements, join clauses cause multiple range variables to be in scope—other clauses can access both range variables to combine data from multiple tables (lines 20–21).

The second query (lines 34–39) gives similar output, but it does not use the join query operator. Operations that would require a join in SQL often do not need one in LINQ to SQL, because it automatically creates properties based on foreign-key relationships. These properties enable you to easily access related rows in other tables. Line 35 uses the generated AuthorISBNs property of the Title class to query only the rows in the AuthorISBN table that link to that row of the Titles table. It does this by using multiple from clauses in the same query. In this example the inner from clause iterates over data related to the outer range variable, but the sequences iterated over may be completely unrelated. As with a join clause, both range variables may be used in later clauses. The author variable created in the let clause (line 36) refers to book.Author, demonstrating the automatically generated link between the AuthorISBN and Authors tables based on the foreign-key relationship between them.

Lines 53–60 contain the final query in the example. Instead of returning a flat result set, with data laid out in relational-style rows and columns, the results from this query are hierarchical. Each element in the results contains the name of an Author and a list of Titles that the author wrote. The LINQ query does this by using a nested query in the second let clause (lines 56–59). The outer query iterates over the authors in the database. The inner query (lines 57–59) takes a specific author and retrieves all titles that the author worked on. It does this by navigating the properties created by the foreign-key relationships in the database. The book range variable represents each pair of AuthorID and ISBN in the AuthorISBN table belonging to the author range variable of the outer query. It accesses the Title property of book to retrieve the row in the Titles table with that ISBN and then uses the BookTitle property to include the title of the book in the results. This list of titles is placed into the Titles property of the anonymous type created in the select clause, which also has a Name property that contains the author's full name. These results are then displayed using nested foreach statements (lines 65–75).

Relational databases cannot return this kind of hierarchical result set, so, unlike the previous two queries, it would be impossible to write a query like this in SQL. Before LINQ, you'd have had to retrieve the results in a flat table like the other two queries, then transform them into the desired format. LINQ does this work for you, allowing you to ignore the relational storage model and concentrate on the object structure that fits your application.

21.9 Creating a Master/Detail View Application

The previous examples demonstrated using LINQ to SQL to combine data from different tables and displaying data from a database in a GUI. It is often necessary to combine the two, as the example in this section does. Figure 21.28 demonstrates a ***master/detail*** *view*—one part of the interface (the master) allows you to select an entry, and another part (the details) displays detailed information about that entry. In this example, you select either a book title or an author, and the details displayed are the co-authors of the book or the titles the author has written, respectively.

```
 1   // Fig. 21.28: MasterDetailForm.cs
 2   // Using a DataGridView to display details based on a selection.
 3   using System;
 4   using System.Linq;
 5   using System.Windows.Forms;
 6
 7   namespace MasterDetail
 8   {
 9      public partial class MasterDetailForm : Form
10      {
11         public MasterDetailForm()
12         {
13            InitializeComponent();
14         } // end constructor
15
16         // connection to database
17         private BooksDataContext database = new BooksDataContext();
18
19         // this class helps us display each author's first
20         // and last name in the authors drop-down list
21         private class AuthorBinding
22         {
23            public Author Author { get; set; } // contained Author object
24            public string Name { get; set; } // author's full name
25         } // end class AuthorBinding
26
27         // initialize data sources when the Form is loaded
28         private void MasterDetailForm_Load( object sender, EventArgs e )
29         {
30            // display AuthorBinding.Name
31            authorComboBox.DisplayMember = "Name";
32
33            // set authorComboBox's DataSource to the list of authors
34            authorComboBox.DataSource =
35               from author in database.Authors
36               orderby author.LastName, author.FirstName
37               let name = author.FirstName + " " + author.LastName
38               select new AuthorBinding { Author = author, Name = name };
39
40            // display Title.BookTitle
41            titleComboBox.DisplayMember = "BookTitle";
42
43            // set titleComboBox's DataSource to the list of titles
44            titleComboBox.DataSource =
45               from title in database.Titles
46               orderby title.BookTitle
47               select title;
```

Fig. 21.28 | Using a DataGridView to display details based on a selection. (Part 1 of 3.)

```
48
49            // initially, display no "detail" data
50            booksBindingSource.DataSource = null;
51
52            // set the DataSource of the DataGridView to the BindingSource
53            booksDataGridView.DataSource = booksBindingSource;
54         } // end method MasterDetailForm_Load
55
56         // display titles that were co-authored by the selected author
57         private void authorComboBox_SelectedIndexChanged(
58            object sender, EventArgs e )
59         {
60            // get the selected Author object from the ComboBox
61            Author currentAuthor =
62               ( ( AuthorBinding ) authorComboBox.SelectedItem ).Author;
63
64            // set booksBindingSource's DataSource to the
65            // list of titles written by the selected author
66            booksBindingSource.DataSource =
67               from book in currentAuthor.AuthorISBNs
68               select book.Title;
69         } // end method authorComboBox_SelectedIndexChanged
70
71         // display the authors of the selected title
72         private void titleComboBox_SelectedIndexChanged(
73            object sender, EventArgs e )
74         {
75            // get the selected Title object from the ComboBox
76            Title currentTitle = ( Title ) titleComboBox.SelectedItem;
77
78            // set booksBindingSource's DataSource to the
79            // list of authors for the selected title
80            booksBindingSource.DataSource =
81               from book in currentTitle.AuthorISBNs
82               select book.Author;
83         } // end method titleComboBox_SelectedIndexChanged
84      } // end class MasterDetailForm
85   } // end namespace MasterDetail
```

a) **Master/Detail** application when it begins execution

Fig. 21.28 | Using a DataGridView to display details based on a selection. (Part 2 of 3.)

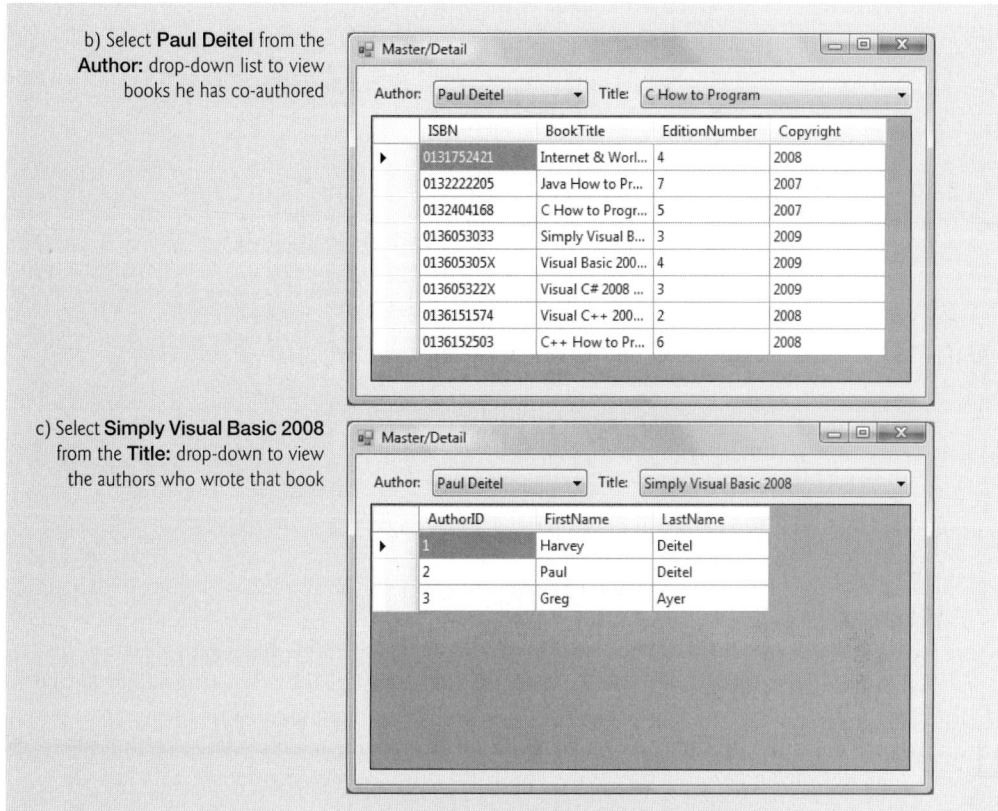

b) Select **Paul Deitel** from the **Author:** drop-down list to view books he has co-authored

c) Select **Simply Visual Basic 2008** from the **Title:** drop-down to view the authors who wrote that book

Fig. 21.28 | Using a DataGridView to display details based on a selection. (Part 3 of 3.)

In the previous examples, the IDE automatically generated the BindingSource, BindingNavigator and GUI elements when you dragged a data source onto the Form. While this works for simple applications, those with more complex operations involve writing more substantial amounts of code. Before explaining the code, we list the steps required to create the interface the code manipulates.

Step 1: Creating the Project
Create a new Windows Forms Application called MasterDetail. Name the source file and class as indicated in Fig. 21.28, and set the Form's Text property to **Master/Detail**.

Step 2: Creating LINQ to SQL Classes
Follow the instructions in Section 21.6.1 to add the Books database and create the LINQ to SQL classes to interact with the database.

Step 3: Creating GUI Elements
Add two Labels and two ComboBoxes to the top of the Form. Position them as shown in Fig. 21.29. The Label and ComboBox on the left should be named authorLabel and authorComboBox, respectively. The Label and ComboBox on the right should be named titleLabel and titleComboBox. Set the Text property of the Labels as indicated in the

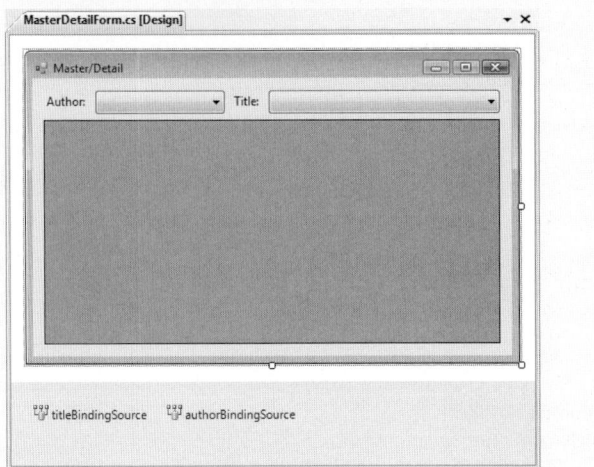

Fig. 21.29 | Finished design of **MasterDetail** application.

screenshot. Also change the `DropDownStyle` properties of the `ComboBox`es from `DropDown` to `DropDownList`.

Create a `DataGridView` called `booksDataGridView` to hold the details that are displayed. Unlike previous examples, do not automatically create it by dragging a data source from the **Data Sources** window, because this example sets the data source programmatically. Instead, manually add it from the **Toolbox**. Resize the `DataGridView` so that it fills the remainder of the `Form`. Because this control is only for viewing data, set its `ReadOnly` property to **True** using the **Properties** window.

Finally, we need to add a `BindingSource` named `booksBindingSource` from the **Data** section of the **Toolbox**, to act as an intermediary between `booksDataGridView` and `books-DataContext`. As in the previous examples, it does not appear as a visible component on the `Form`, but appears in the component tray. The `BindingSource` will be used as a data source for `booksDataGridView`—we will fill `booksBindingSource` with data from the `Authors` or `Titles` table, depending on which drop-down is selected. With the GUI creation complete, we can now write the code to provide the functionality we require.

The Master/Detail Application
When the code has been written, the **Master/Detail** application allows the user to select an author or book title from one of two drop-down lists, and view the details of the titles that author worked on or the authors of that book, respectively.

Class `MasterDetailForm` contains the nested class `AuthorBinding` (lines 21–25). Class definitions may be nested inside other classes. `AuthorBinding` is `private` because it should be accessed only from its containing class. We created the `AuthorBinding` class to allow us to associate a full `Author` object—the `Author` class is automatically generated by LINQ to SQL—with each row in the drop-down list, but have it display the author's full name. Recall that the author's name is stored as two separate fields in the database, so the `Author` class does not have single property that retrieves the full name. The `Name` property of the `AuthorBinding` class stores the author's full name, and the `Author` property stores the `Author` object that contains the author's information from the database.

The ComboBox's *DisplayMember property* is set to the String "Name" (line 31), which tells the ComboBox to use the Name property of AuthorBinding to determine what text to display for each AuthorBinding object. Lines 34–38 create an AuthorBinding object for each author and assign it to the authorComboBox's DataSource property. This makes authorComboBox create one entry per author. Recall from Section 10.17 that object initializers (e.g., line 38) can be used to initialize an object without calling a constructor.

There is no need to create a custom class to wrap the Title class, because it already has a property for what we want to display—the BookTitle property. The text in the ComboBox is set to be retrieved from the BookTitle property (line 41). Lines 44–47 create and assign the DataSource for titleComboBox—a sorted list of Title objects.

Initially, we don't want to display any data in the DataGridView. However, when the ComboBoxes are created and initialized with their DataSources, their SelectedIndexChanged event handlers are called, setting a DataSource for booksBindingSource (connected to booksDataGridView on line 53). To prevent this, we explicitly set the DataSource property to null (line 50)—this is done before connecting the DataGridView to avoid loading data that will just be thrown away when the DataSource is reset.

Simple GUI elements like ComboBoxes can be populated from a data source—in this case, the result of a LINQ to SQL query. However, the DataGridView is more complex and requires an intermediary class (a BindingSource) as its DataSource. We can change the columns and data displayed in booksDataGridView merely by changing the DataSource property of booksBindingSource—booksDataGridView will update the data and even column names automatically.

The authorComboBox_SelectedIndexChanged event handler (lines 57–69) performs two distinct operations. First, it retrieves the selected Author (lines 61–62). The ComboBox's SelectedItem property returns an object, so the SelectedItem property's value must be cast to the AuthorBinding class we used as the data source. The event handler then accesses the AuthorBinding's Author property to retrieve the wrapped Author object. Second, the event handler uses LINQ to retrieve the Title objects representing books the Author worked on (lines 67–68)—the mechanism for this was explained in the preceding example. The results of the LINQ query are assigned to the DataSource property of booksBindingSource (line 66)—note that the event handler for authorComboBox sets the DataSource to a data from the Titles table because we want to display Title rows associated with that Author.

The event handler for titleComboBox is structured identically to the authorComboBox one. The primary difference is that the author and title names are switched. Also, the first step is slightly simpler, because the Title class did not need to be wrapped to display correctly in the ComboBox.

21.10 Programming with LINQ to SQL: Address-Book Case Study

Our next example implements a simple address-book application that enables users to insert rows into, locate rows from and update the database AddressBook.mdf, which is included in the directory with this chapter's examples.

The AddressBook application (Fig. 21.30) provides a GUI through which users can query the database with LINQ. However, rather than displaying a database table in a DataGridView, this example presents data from a table one row at a time, using several

TextBoxes that display the values of each of the row's columns. A BindingNavigator allows you to control which row of the table is in view at any given time. The Binding-Navigator also allows you to add rows, delete rows, and save changes to the data. We discuss the application's functionality and the code that implements it momentarily. First we show the steps to create this application.

```
1   // Fig. 21.30: AddressBookForm.cs
2   // Manipulating an address book.
3   using System;
4   using System.Linq;
5   using System.Windows.Forms;
6
7   namespace AddressBook
8   {
9      public partial class AddressBookForm : Form
10     {
11        public AddressBookForm()
12        {
13           InitializeComponent();
14        } // end constructor
15
16        // LINQ to SQL data context
17        private AddressBookDataContext database =
18           new AddressBookDataContext();
19
20        // fill our addressBindingSource with all rows, ordered by name
21        private void BindDefault()
22        {
23           // use LINQ to create a data source from the database
24           addressBindingSource.DataSource =
25              from address in database.Addresses
26              orderby address.LastName, address.FirstName
27              select address;
28
29           addressBindingSource.MoveFirst(); // go to the first result
30           findTextBox.Clear(); // clear the Find TextBox
31        } // end method BindDefault
32
33        private void AddressBookForm_Load( object sender, EventArgs e )
34        {
35           BindDefault(); // fill binding with data from database
36        } // end method AddressBookForm_Load
37
38        // Click event handler for the Save Button in the
39        // BindingNavigator saves the changes made to the data
40        private void addressBindingNavigatorSaveItem_Click(
41           object sender, EventArgs e )
42        {
43           Validate(); // validate input fields
44           addressBindingSource.EndEdit(); // indicate edits are complete
45           database.SubmitChanges(); // write changes to database file
46
```

Fig. 21.30 | Manipulating an address book. (Part 1 of 2.)

```
47              BindDefault(); // change back to initial unfiltered data on save
48        } // end method addressBindingNavigatorSaveItem_Click
49
50        // load LINQ to create a data source that contains
51        // only people with the specified last name
52        private void findButton_Click( object sender, EventArgs e )
53        {
54            // use LINQ to create a data source that contains
55            // only people with the specified last name
56            addressBindingSource.DataSource =
57                from address in database.Addresses
58                where address.LastName == findTextBox.Text
59                orderby address.LastName, address.FirstName
60                select address;
61
62            addressBindingSource.MoveFirst(); // go to first result
63        } // end method findButton_Click
64
65        private void browseButton_Click( object sender, EventArgs e )
66        {
67            BindDefault(); // change back to initial unfiltered data
68        } // end method browseButton_Click
69    } // end class AddressBookForm
70 } // end namespace AddressBook
```

a) **AddressBook** application after adding four entries.   b) Searching for a specific last name.

c) Use the **Browse All Entries** Button to view all people in the address book.

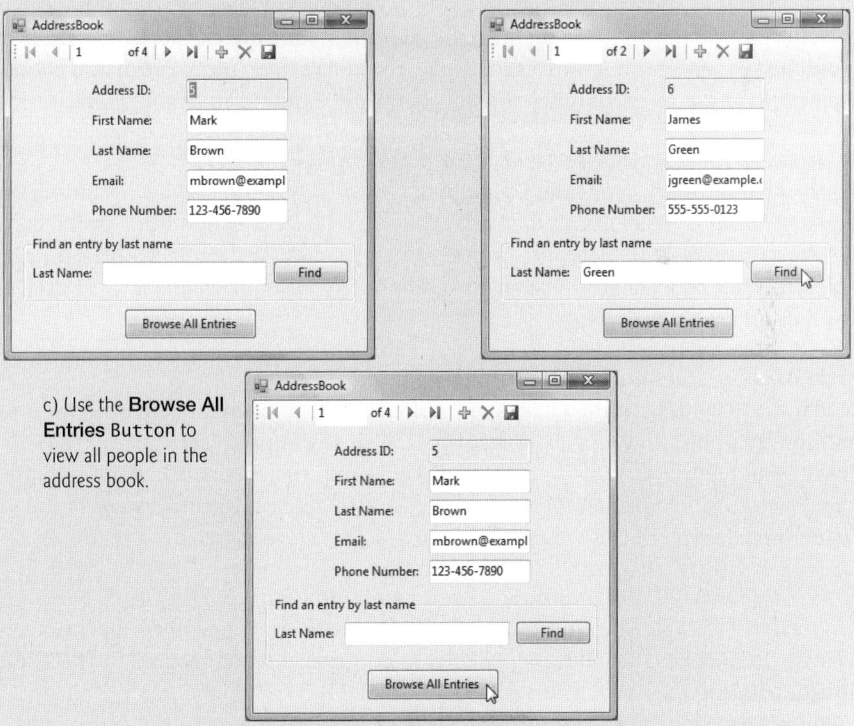

Fig. 21.30 | Manipulating an address book. (Part 2 of 2.)

Step 1: Creating the Project
Create a new Windows Forms Application named AddressBook. Rename the Form AddressBookForm and its source file AddressBookForm.cs, then set the Form's Text property to AddressBook.

Step 2: Creating LINQ to SQL Classes and Data Source
Follow the instructions in Section 21.6.1 to add a database to the project and generate the LINQ to SQL classes. For this example, add the AddressBook.mdf database from the Databases folder included with this chapter's examples and name the file AddressBook.dbml instead of Books.dbml. You must also add the Addresses table as a data source, as was done with the Authors table in *Step 1* of Section 21.6.2.

Step 3: Indicating that the IDE Should Create a Set of Labels and TextBoxes to Display Each Row of Data
In the earlier sections, you dragged a node from the **Data Sources** window to the Form to create a DataGridView bound to the data-source member represented by that node. The IDE allows you to specify the type of control(s) that it creates when you drag and drop a data-source member onto a Form. In **Design** view, click the Address node in the **Data Sources** window. Note that this becomes a drop-down list when you select it. Click the down arrow to view the items in the list. The item to the left of **DataGridView** is initially highlighted in blue, because the default control to be bound to a table is a DataGridView (as you saw in the earlier examples). Select the **Details** option in the drop-down list to indicate that the IDE should create a set of Label/TextBox pairs for each column-name/column-value pair when you drag and drop the Address node onto the Form. The drop-down list contains suggestions for controls to display the table's data, but you can also choose the **Customize...** option to select other controls that can be bound to a table's data.

Step 4: Dragging the Address Data-Source Node to the Form
Drag the Address node from the **Data Sources** window to the Form. This automatically creates a BindingNavigator and the Labels and TextBoxes corresponding to the columns of the database table. The fields are ordered alphabetically by default, with Email appearing directly after AddressID. Reorder the components, using **Design** view, so they are in the proper order shown in Fig. 21.30.

Step 5: Making the AddressID TextBox ReadOnly
The AddressID column of the Addresses table is an autoincremented identity column, so users should not be allowed to edit the values in this column. Select the TextBox for the AddressID and set its ReadOnly property to **True** using the **Properties** window. Note that you may need to click in an empty part of the Form to deselect the other Labels and TextBoxes before selecting the AddressID TextBox.

Step 6: Connecting the BindingSource to the DataContext
As in previous examples, we must connect the AddressBindingSource that controls the GUI with the AddressBookDataContext that controls the connection to the database. This is done using the BindDefault method (lines 21–31), which sets the AddressBindingSource's DataSource property to the result of a LINQ query on the Addresses table. The need for a separate function becomes apparent later, when we have two places that

need to set the DataSource to the result of that query. Line 30 uses a GUI element that will be created in subsequent steps—do not add this line until you create findTextBox in *Step 8* or the program will not compile.

The BindDefault method must be called from the Form's Load event handler for the data to be displayed when the application starts (line 35). As before, you create the Load event handler by double clicking the Form's title bar.

We must also create an event handler to save the changes to the database when the BindingNavigator's save Button is clicked (lines 40–48). Note that, besides the names of the variables, the three-statement save logic remains the same. We also call BindDefault after saving to re-sort the data and move back to the first element. Recall from Section 21.6 that to allow changes to the database to save between runs of the application, you must select the database in the **Solution Explorer**, then change its **Copy to Output Directory** property to **Copy if newer** in the **Properties** window.

The AddressBook database is configured to require values for the first name, last name, phone number or e-mail. In order to simplify the code, we have not checked for errors, but an exception (of type System.Data.SqlClient.SqlException) will be thrown if you attempt to save when any of the fields are empty.

Step 7: Running the Application

Run the application and experiment with the controls in the BindingNavigator at the top of the window. Like the previous examples, this example fills a BindingSource object (called addressBindingSource, specifically) with all the rows of a database table (i.e., Addresses). However, only a single row of the database appears at any given time. The CD- or DVD-like buttons of the BindingNavigator allow you to change the currently displayed row (i.e., change the values in each of the TextBoxes). The Buttons to add a row, delete a row and save changes also perform their designated tasks. Adding a row clears the TextBoxes and sets the TextBox to the right of **Address ID** to zero. Note that if starting with an empty database, the TextBoxes will be empty and editable even though there is no current entry—be sure to create a new entry with the add Button before you enter data or saving will have no effect. After entering several address-book entries, click the **Save** Button to record the new rows to the database—the **Address ID** field is automatically changed from zero to a unique number by the database. When you close and restart the application, you should be able to use the BindingNavigator controls to browse your entries.

Step 8: Adding Controls to Allow Users to Specify a Last Name to Locate

While the BindingNavigator allows you to browse the address book, it would be more convenient to be able to find a specific entry by last name. To add this functionality to the application, we must create controls to allow the user to enter a last name, then event handlers to actually perform the search.

Go to **Design** view and add to the Form a Label named findLabel, a TextBox named findTextBox, and a Button named findButton. Place these controls in a GroupBox named findGroupBox. Set the Text properties of these controls as shown in Fig. 21.30.

Step 9: Programming an Event Handler that Locates the User-Specified Last Name

Double click findButton to create a Click event handler for this Button. In the event handler, use LINQ to select only people with the last name entered in findTextBox and sort them by last name, then first name (lines 57–60). Start the application to test the new functionality. When you enter a last name and click **Find**, the `BindingNavigator` allows the user to browse only the rows containing the specified last name. This is because the data source bound to the `Form`'s controls (the result of the LINQ query) has changed and now contains only a limited number of rows. The database in this example is initially empty, so you'll need to add several records before testing the find capability.

Step 10: Allowing the User to Return to Browsing All Rows of the Database

To allow users to return to browsing all the rows after searching for specific rows, add a `Button` named browseAllButton below the findGroupBox. Set the `Text` property of browseAllButton to **Browse All Entries**. Double click browseAllButton to create a `Click` event handler. Have the event handler call `BindDefault` (line 67) to restore the data source to the full list of people. Also modify `BindDefault` so that it clears findTextBox (line 30).

Data Binding in the AddressBook Application

Dragging and dropping the `Address` node from the **Data Sources** window onto the AddressBookForm caused the IDE to generate several components in the component tray. These serve the same purposes as those generated for the earlier examples that use the Books database. In this example, addressBindingSource uses LINQ to SQL to manipulate the AddressBookDataContext's Addresses table. The BindingNavigator (named addressBindingNavigator) is bound to addressBindingSource, enabling the user to manipulate the Addresses table through the GUI. This binding is created by assigning addressBindingSource to addressBindingNavigator's **BindingSource** *property*. This is done automatically when the IDE creates them after you drag the Address data source onto the Form.

In each of the earlier examples using a `DataGridView` to display all the rows of a database table, the `DataGridView`'s DataSource property was set to the corresponding BindingSource object. In this example, you selected **Details** from the drop-down list for the Addresses table in the **Data Sources** window, so the values from a single row of the table appear on the Form in a set of TextBoxes. In this example, the IDE binds each TextBox to a specific column of the Addresses table in the AddressBookDataContext. To do this, the IDE sets the TextBox's **DataBindings.Text** *property*. You can view this property by clicking the plus sign next to **(DataBindings)** in the **Properties** window. Clicking the drop-down list for this property (as in Fig. 21.31) allows you to choose a BindingSource object and a property (i.e., column) within the associated data source to bind to the TextBox. Using a BindingSource keeps the data displayed in the TextBoxes synchronized, and allows the BindingNavigator to update them by changing the current row in the BindingSource.

Consider the `TextBox` that displays the `FirstName` value—named firstNameTextBox by the IDE. This control's DataBindings.Text property is set to the FirstName property of addressBindingSource (which refers to the Addresses table in the database). Thus, firstNameTextBox always displays the FirstName column's value in the currently selected row of the Addresses table. Each IDE-created TextBox on the Form is configured in a similar manner. Browsing the address book with addressBindingNavigator changes the current position in addressBindingSource, and thus changes the values displayed in each TextBox. Regardless of changes to the contents of the Addresses table in the database, the TextBoxes remain bound to the same properties of the table and always display the appropriate data. The TextBoxes do not display any values if addressBindingSource is empty.

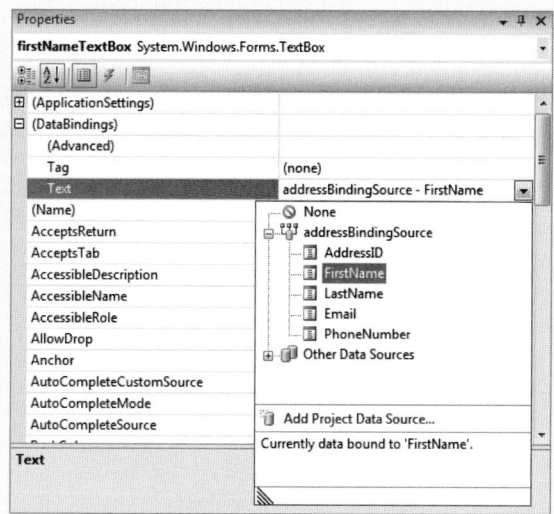

Fig. 21.31 | Data bindings for firstNameTextBox in the **AddressBook** application.

21.11 Wrap-Up

This chapter introduced relational databases, SQL, LINQ to SQL and the IDE's visual programming tools for working with databases. You examined the contents of a simple Books database and learned about the relationships among the tables in the database. You then learned basic SQL statements to retrieve data from, add new data to, delete data from and update data in a database.

We discussed the LINQ to SQL classes generated by the IDE, such as the DataContext that controls interactions with the database. We also explained that LINQ to SQL transforms the LINQ queries you write into SQL, which is then sent to the database.

Next, the chapter focused on using the IDE's tools and wizards to access and manipulate data sources like databases in GUI applications. You learned how to generate LINQ to SQL classes and how to use the IDE's drag-and-drop capabilities to display database tables in applications. We discussed the IDE's wizards that help you create fully functional applications requiring just a few lines of code.

In the next chapter, we demonstrate how to build web applications using Microsoft's ASP.NET technology. We also introduce the concept of a three-tier application, which is divided into three pieces that can reside on the same computer or be distributed among separate computers across a network such as the Internet. One of these tiers—the information tier—typically stores data in an DBMS like SQL Server.

21.12 Tools and Web Resources

Deitel has created an extensive LINQ Resource Center at www.deitel.com/LINQ that contains many links to additional information, including blogs by Microsoft LINQ team members, sample chapters, tutorials and videos.

A useful tool for learning LINQ is LINQPad (www.linqpad.net), which defines itself as a *code snippet IDE*. It allows you to execute any Visual Basic or C# expression, including

LINQ queries, and view their results. It also supports connecting to a SQL Server database and querying it using SQL and LINQ to SQL.

DbLinq is an open-source project to add LINQ support for DBMSs other than Microsoft SQL Server—including Oracle, MySQL, PostgreSQL and SQLite. The current development version can be downloaded from `code2code.net/DB_Linq/`.

ASP.NET 3.5 and ASP.NET AJAX

If any man will draw up his case, and put his name at the foot of the first page, I will give him an immediate reply. Where he compels me to turn over the sheet, he must wait my leisure.
—Lord Sandwich

Rule One: Our client is always right
Rule Two: If you think our client is wrong, see Rule One.
—Anonymous

A fair question should be followed by a deed in silence.
—Dante Alighieri

You'll come here and get books that will open your eyes, and your ears, and your curiosity, and turn you inside out or outside in.
—Ralph Waldo Emerson

OBJECTIVES

In this chapter you'll learn:

- Web-application development using ASP.NET.
- To create Web Forms.
- To create ASP.NET applications consisting of multiple Web Forms.
- To maintain state information about a user with session tracking and cookies.
- To use the **Web Site Administration Tool** to modify web application configuration settings.
- To control user access to web applications using forms authentication and ASP.NET login controls.
- To use databases in ASP.NET applications.
- To design a master page and content pages to create a uniform look-and-feel for a website.
- To use ASP.NET AJAX to improve the user interactivity of your web applications.

Outline

22.1 Introduction
22.2 Simple HTTP Transactions
22.3 Multitier Application Architecture
22.4 Creating and Running a Simple Web-Form Example
   22.4.1 Examining an ASPX File
   22.4.2 Examining a Code-Behind File
   22.4.3 Relationship Between an ASPX File and a Code-Behind File
   22.4.4 How the Code in an ASP.NET Web Page Executes
   22.4.5 Examining the XHTML Generated by an ASP.NET Application
   22.4.6 Building an ASP.NET Web Application
22.5 Web Controls
   22.5.1 Text and Graphics Controls
   22.5.2 AdRotator Control
   22.5.3 Validation Controls
22.6 Session Tracking
   22.6.1 Cookies
   22.6.2 Session Tracking with HttpSessionState
22.7 Case Study: Connecting to a Database in ASP.NET
   22.7.1 Building a Web Form That Displays Data from a Database
   22.7.2 Modifying the Code-Behind File for the Guestbook Application
22.8 Case Study: Secure Books Database Application
   22.8.1 Examining the Completed Secure Books Database Application
   22.8.2 Creating the Secure Books Database Application
22.9 ASP.NET AJAX
   22.9.1 Traditional Web Applications
   22.9.2 Ajax Web Applications
   22.9.3 Examining an ASP.NET AJAX Application
22.10 New ASP.NET 3.5 Data Controls
22.11 Wrap-Up
22.12 Web Resources

22.1 Introduction

In previous chapters, we used Windows Forms and WPF to develop Windows applications. In this chapter, we introduce *web-application development* with Microsoft's *Active Server Pages .NET* (*ASP.NET 3.5*) technology. Web-based applications create web content for web-browser clients. This web content includes Extensible HyperText Markup Language (XHTML), client-side scripting, images and binary data. If you are not familiar with XHTML, check out our XHTML resource center at www.deitel.com/xhtml/ for links to online tutorials and other resources.

We present several examples that demonstrate web-application development using *Web Forms*, *web controls* (also called *ASP.NET server controls*) and C# programming. Web Form files have the file-name extension *.aspx* and contain the web page's GUI. You customize Web Forms by adding web controls such as labels, textboxes, images, buttons and other GUI components. The Web Form file represents the web page that is sent to the client browser. From this point onward, we refer to Web Form files as *ASPX files*.

Every ASPX file created in Visual Studio has a corresponding class written in a .NET language, such as C#. This class contains event handlers, initialization code, utility methods and other supporting code. The file that contains this class is called the *code-behind file* and provides the ASPX file's programmatic implementation.

To develop the this chapter's examples, we used Microsoft Visual Web Developer 2008 Express Edition—an IDE designed for developing ASP.NET web applications. Visual Web Developer and Visual C# 2008 Express share many common features and visual programming tools that simplify building complex applications, such as those that access a database (presented in Sections 22.7 and 22.8). The full version of Visual Studio 2008 includes the functionality of Visual Web Developer, so the instructions we present for Visual Web Developer also apply to Visual Studio 2008. Note that you must install either Visual Web Developer 2008 Express (available from `http://www.microsoft.com/express/default.aspx`) or a complete version of Visual Studio 2008 to implement the programs in this chapter and Chapter 23, Windows Communication Foundation (WCF) Web Services. The site `www.deitel.com/books/csharpfp3/` provides instructions for running the ASP.NET 3.5 examples presented in this chapter, if you do not wish to re-create them.

22.2 Simple HTTP Transactions

In this section, we discuss what occurs behind the scenes when a user requests a web page in a browser. The HTTP protocol allows clients and servers to interact and exchange information in a uniform and reliable manner.

In its simplest form, a web page is nothing more than an XHTML document that describes to a web browser how to display and format the document's information. XHTML documents normally contain hyperlinks that link to different pages or to other parts of the same page. When the user clicks a hyperlink, the requested web page loads into the user's web browser. Similarly, the user can type the address of a page into the browser's address field.

URIs

HTTP uses URIs (Uniform Resource Identifiers) to identify data on the Internet. URIs that specify document locations are called URLs (Uniform Resource Locators). Common URLs refer to files, directories or objects that perform complex tasks, such as database lookups and Internet searches. If you know the URL of a publicly available resource or file anywhere on the web, you can access it through HTTP.

Parts of a URL

A URL contains information that directs a browser to the resource that the user wishes to access. Computers that run *web-server* software make such resources available. Let's examine the components of the URL

```
http://www.deitel.com/books/downloads.html
```

The `http://` indicates that the resource is to be obtained using the HTTP protocol. The middle portion, `www.deitel.com`, is the server's fully qualified *hostname*—the name of the server on which the resource resides. This computer usually is referred to as the *host*, because it houses and maintains resources. The hostname `www.deitel.com` is translated into an *IP address*—a unique numerical value that identifies the server much as a telephone number uniquely defines a particular phone line. More information on IP addresses is available at en.wikipedia.org/wiki/IP_address. This translation is performed by a *domain-name system (DNS) server*—a computer that maintains a database of hostnames and their corresponding IP addresses—and the process is called a *DNS lookup*.

The remainder of the URL (i.e., /books/downloads.html) specifies both the name of the requested resource (the XHTML document downloads.html) and its path, or location (/books), on the web server. The path could specify the location of an actual directory on the web server's file system. For security reasons, however, the path normally specifies the location of a *virtual directory*. The server translates the virtual directory into a real location on the server (or on another computer on the server's network), thus hiding the true location of the resource. Some resources are created dynamically using other information stored on the server computer, such as a database. The hostname in the URL for such a resource specifies the correct server; the path and resource information identify the resource with which to interact to respond to the client's request.

Making a Request and Receiving a Response

When given a URL, a web browser performs a simple HTTP transaction to retrieve and display the web page found at that address. Figure 22.1 illustrates the transaction, showing the interaction between the web browser (the client side) and the web-server application (the server side).

In Fig. 22.1, the web browser sends an HTTP request to the server. The request (in its simplest form) is

```
GET /books/downloads.html HTTP/1.1
```

The word **GET** is an *HTTP method* indicating that the client wishes to obtain a resource from the server. The remainder of the request provides the path name of the resource (e.g., an XHTML document) and the protocol's name and version number (HTTP/1.1). The client's request also contains some required and optional headers.

Any server that understands HTTP (version 1.1) can translate this request and respond appropriately. Figure 22.2 depicts the server responding to a request. The server first responds by sending a line of text that indicates the HTTP version, followed by a numeric code and a phrase describing the status of the transaction. For example,

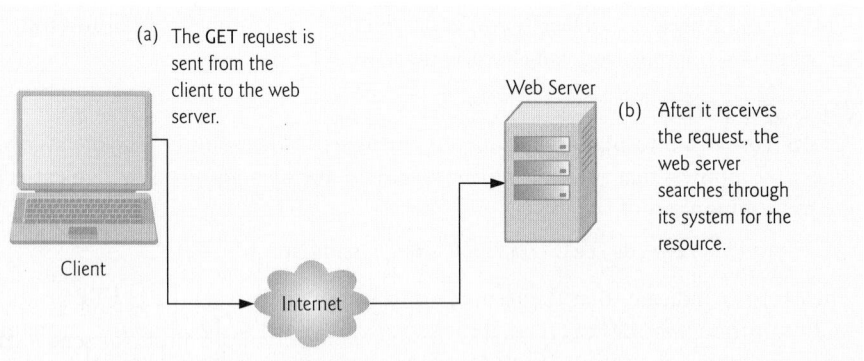

Fig. 22.1 | Client interacting with web server. *Step 1:* The GET request.

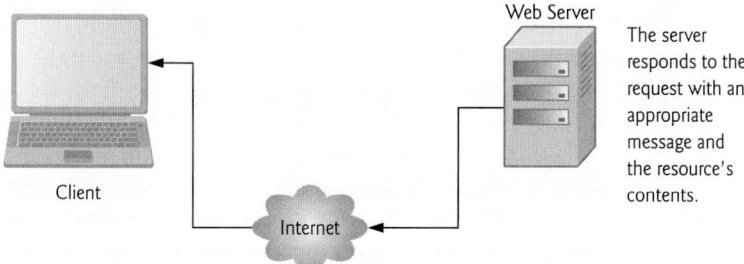

Fig. 22.2 | Client interacting with web server. *Step 2:* The HTTP response.

    HTTP/1.1 200 OK

indicates success, whereas

    HTTP/1.1 404 Not found

informs the client that the web server could not locate the requested resource. A complete list of numeric codes indicating the status of an HTTP transaction can be found at www.w3.org/Protocols/rfc2616/rfc2616-sec10.html.

HTTP Headers

The server then sends one or more *HTTP headers*, which provide additional information about the data that will be sent. In this case, the server is sending an XHTML text document, so one HTTP header for this example would read:

    Content-type: text/html

The information provided in this header specifies the *Multipurpose Internet Mail Extensions (MIME)* type of the content that the server is transmitting to the browser. MIME is an Internet standard that specifies data formats so that programs can interpret data correctly. For example, the MIME type text/plain indicates that the sent information is text that can be displayed directly, without any interpretation of the content as XHTML markup. Similarly, the MIME type image/jpeg indicates that the content is a JPEG image. When the browser receives this MIME type, it attempts to display the image. For a list of available MIME types, please see www.w3schools.com/media/media_mimeref.asp.

The header or set of headers is followed by a blank line, which indicates to the client browser that the server is finished sending HTTP headers. The server then sends the contents of the requested XHTML document (downloads.html). The client-side browser parses the XHTML markup it receives and *renders* (or displays) the results. The server normally keeps the connection open to process other requests from the client.

HTTP GET and POST Requests

The two most common *HTTP request types* (also known as *request methods*) are GET and POST. A GET request typically gets (or retrieves) information from a server. Common uses of GET requests are to retrieve an XHTML document or an image, or to fetch search results based on a user-submitted search term. A POST request typically posts (or sends) data to a server. Common uses of POST requests are to send form data or documents to a server.

An HTTP request often posts data to a *server-side form handler* that processes the data. For example, when a user performs a search or participates in a web-based survey, the web server receives the information specified in the XHTML form as part of the request. Get requests and POST requests can both be used to send form data to a web server, yet each request type sends the information differently.

A GET request sends information to the server in the URL, e.g., www.google.com/ search?q=deitel. In this case, search is the name of Google's server-side form handler, q is the name of a variable in Google's search form and deitel is the search term. A ? separates the *query string* from the rest of the URL in a request. A *name/value* pair is passed to the server with the *name* and the *value* separated by an equals sign (=). If more than one *name/value* pair is submitted, each pair is separated by an ampersand (&). The server uses data passed in a query string to retrieve an appropriate resource from the server. The server then sends a *response* to the client. A GET request may be initiated by submitting an XHTML form whose method attribute is set to "get", by typing the URL (possibly containing a query string) directly into the browser's address bar or through a normal hyperlink.

A POST request sends form data as part of the HTTP message, not as part of the URL. A GET request typically limits the query string (i.e., everything to the right of the ?) to a specific number of characters (2083 in Internet Explorer; more in other browsers), so it is often necessary to send large pieces of information using the POST method. The POST method is also sometimes preferred because it hides the submitted data from the user by embedding it in an HTTP message. If a form submits hidden input values along with user-submitted data, the POST method might generate a URL like www.searchengine.com/ search. The form data still reaches the server for processing, but the user does not see the exact information sent.

Software Engineering Observation 22.1

The data sent in a POST request is not part of the URL, and the user can't see the data by default. However, there are tools available that expose this data, so you should not assume that the data is secure just because a POST request is used.

Client-Side Caching

Browsers often *cache* (save on disk) web pages for quick reloading. If there are no changes between the version stored in the cache and the current version on the web, this speeds up your browsing experience. An HTTP response can indicate the length of time for which the content remains "fresh." If this amount of time has not been reached, the browser can avoid another request to the server. Otherwise, the browser requests the document from the server. Thus, the browser minimizes the amount of data that must be downloaded for you to view a web page. Browsers typically do not cache the server's response to a POST request, because the next POST might not return the same result. For example, in a survey, many users could visit the same web page and answer a question. The survey results could then be displayed for the user. Each new answer changes the overall results of the survey.

When you use a web-based search engine, the browser normally supplies the information you specify in an XHTML form to the search engine with a GET request. The search engine performs the search, then returns the results to you as a web page. Such pages are sometimes cached by the browser in case you perform the same search again.

22.3 Multitier Application Architecture

Web-based applications are *multitier applications* (sometimes referred to as *n-tier applications*). Multitier applications divide functionality into separate *tiers* (i.e., logical groupings of functionality). Although tiers can be located on the same computer, the tiers of web-based applications typically reside on separate computers. Figure 22.3 presents the basic structure of a three-tier web-based application.

The *information tier* (also called the *data tier* or the *bottom tier*) maintains data pertaining to the application. This tier typically stores data in a relational database management system (RDBMS). We discussed RDBMSs in Chapter 21. For example, a retail store might have a database for storing product information, such as descriptions, prices and quantities in stock. The same database also might contain customer information, such as user names, billing addresses and credit card numbers. This tier can contain multiple databases, which together comprise the data needed for our application.

The *middle tier* implements *business logic*, *controller logic* and *presentation logic* to control interactions between the application's clients and the application's data. The middle tier acts as an intermediary between data in the information tier and the application's clients. The middle-tier controller logic processes client requests (such as requests to view a product catalog) and retrieves data from the database. The middle-tier presentation logic then processes data from the information tier and presents the content to the client. Web applications typically present data to clients as XHTML documents.

Business logic in the middle tier enforces *business rules* and ensures that data is reliable before the server application updates the database or presents the data to users. Business rules dictate how clients can and cannot access application data, and how applications process data. For example, a business rule in the middle tier of a retail store's web-based application might ensure that all product quantities remain positive. A client request to set a negative quantity in the bottom tier's product-information database would be rejected by the middle tier's business logic.

The *client tier*, or *top tier*, is the application's user interface, which gathers input and displays output. Users interact directly with the application through the user interface (typically viewed in a web browser), keyboard and mouse. In response to user actions (e.g., clicking a hyperlink), the client tier interacts with the middle tier to make requests and to retrieve data from the information tier. The client tier then displays the data retrieved from the middle tier to the user. The client tier never directly interacts with the information tier.

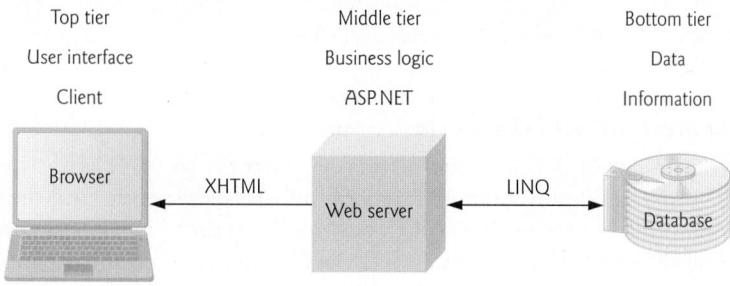

Fig. 22.3 | Three-tier architecture.

22.4 Creating and Running a Simple Web-Form Example

Our first example displays the web server's time of day in a browser window. When run, this program displays the text Current time on the web server:, followed by the web server's time. As mentioned previously, the program consists of two related files—an ASPX file (Fig. 22.4) and a C# code-behind file (Fig. 22.5). We first display the markup and code, then we carefully guide you through the step-by-step process of creating this program. [*Note:* The markup in Fig. 22.4 and other ASPX file listings in this chapter is the same as the markup that appears in Visual Web Developer, but we have reformatted the markup for presentation purposes to make the code more readable.]

Visual Web Developer generates all the markup shown in Fig. 22.4 when you set the web page's title, type text in the Web Form, drag a Label onto the Web Form and set the properties of the page's text and the Label. We discuss these steps in Section 22.4.6.

```
1   <%-- Fig. 22.4: WebTime.aspx --%>
2   <%-- A page that displays the current time in a Label. --%>
3   <%@ Page Language="C#" AutoEventWireup="true" CodeFile="WebTime.aspx.cs"
4      Inherits="WebTime" EnableSessionState="False" %>
5
6   <!DOCTYPE html PUBLIC "-//W3C//DTD XHTML 1.0 Transitional//EN"
7      "http://www.w3.org/TR/xhtml1/DTD/xhtml1-transitional.dtd">
8
9   <html xmlns="http://www.w3.org/1999/xhtml">
10  <head runat="server">
11     <title>A Simple Web Form Example</title>
12  </head>
13  <body>
14     <form id="form1" runat="server">
15     <div>
16        <h2>Current time on the web server:</h2>
17        <p>
18           <asp:Label ID="timeLabel" runat="server" BackColor="Black"
19              Font-Size="XX-Large" ForeColor="Yellow"
20              EnableViewState="False"></asp:Label>
21        </p>
22     </div>
23     </form>
24  </body>
25  </html>
```

Fig. 22.4 | ASPX file that displays the web server's time.

22.4.1 Examining an ASPX File

The ASPX file contains other information in addition to XHTML. Lines 1–2 are *ASP.NET comments* that indicate the figure number, the file name and the purpose of the file. ASP.NET comments begin with <%-- and terminate with --%>, and can span multiple lines. We added these comments to the file. Lines 3–4 use a *Page* directive (in an ASPX file a *directive* is delimited by <%@ and %>) to specify information needed by ASP.NET to process this file. The Page directive's *Language* attribute specifies C# as the code-behind file's language; the code-behind file (i.e., the ***CodeFile***) is WebTime.aspx.cs. Note that a code-behind file name usually consists of the full ASPX file name (e.g., WebTime.aspx) followed by the .cs extension.

The ***AutoEventWireup*** attribute (line 3) determines how Web Form event handling is recognized. When AutoEventWireup is set to true, ASP.NET automatically treats a method of name Page_*eventName* as an event handler for the specified event of the Page without having to explicitly define it as such. For example, ASP.NET uses the methods Page_Init and Page_Load in the code-behind file to handle the Page's Init and Load events, respectively. (We discuss these events later in the chapter.) When AutoEventWireup is set to false, you specify the methods that handle a Page's events using attributes in the Page directive just as you would any other web control. We explain how to specify methods as event handlers in ASPX markup in Section 22.6. By default, AutoEventWireup is set to true when you create a new ASP.NET website in C#.

The ***Inherits*** attribute (line 4) specifies the class in the code-behind file from which this ASP.NET class inherits—in this case, WebTime. We say more about Inherits momentarily. [*Note:* We explicitly set the ***EnableSessionState*** attribute (line 4) to False. We explain the significance of this attribute later in the chapter. The IDE sometimes generates attribute values (e.g., True and False) and control names (as you'll see later in the chapter) that do not adhere to our standard code capitalization conventions (i.e., true and false). However, unlike C# code, ASP.NET markup is not case sensitive, so using a different case is not problematic. To remain consistent with the code generated by the IDE, we do not modify these values in our code listings or in our accompanying discussions.]

For this first ASPX file, we provide a brief discussion of the XHTML markup. We do not discuss the majority of the XHTML contained in subsequent ASPX files. Lines 6–7 contain the document type declaration, which specifies the document element name (html) and the PUBLIC Uniform Resource Identifier (URI) for the DTD that defines the XHTML vocabulary.

Lines 9–10 contain the <html> and <head> start tags, respectively. XHTML documents have the root element html and markup information about the document in the head element. Note that the html element specifies the XML namespace of the document using the xmlns attribute. Also note the ***runat*** attribute in line 10, which is set to ***"server"***. This attribute indicates that when a client requests this ASPX file, ASP.NET processes the head element and its nested elements on the server and generates the corresponding XHTML, which is then sent to the client. In this case, the XHTML sent to the client will be identical to the markup in the ASPX file. However, as you'll see, ASP.NET can generate complex XHTML markup from simple elements in an ASPX file.

Line 11 sets the title of this web page. We demonstrate how to set the title through a property in the IDE shortly. Line 13 contains the <body> start tag, which begins the body of the XHTML document; the body contains the main content that the browser displays. The form that contains our XHTML text and controls is defined in lines 14–23. Again, the runat attribute in the form element indicates that this element executes on the server, which generates equivalent XHTML and sends it to the client. Lines 15–22 contain a div element that groups the elements of the form in a block of markup.

Line 16 is an h2 heading element that contains text indicating the purpose of the web page. As we demonstrate shortly, the IDE generates this element in response to typing text directly in the Web Form and selecting the text as a second-level heading.

Lines 17–21 contain a p element to mark up a paragraph of content in the browser. Lines 18–20 mark up a label web control. The properties that we set in the **Properties** window, such as Font-Size and BackColor (i.e., background color), are attributes here. The **ID** attribute (line 18) assigns a name to the control so that it can be manipulated programmatically in the code-behind file. We set the control's EnableViewState attribute (line 20) to False. We explain the significance of this attribute later in the chapter.

The **asp: tag prefix** in the declaration of the **Label** tag (line 18) indicates that the label is an ASP.NET web control, not an XHTML element. Each web control maps to a corresponding XHTML element (or group of elements)—when processing a web control on the server, ASP.NET generates XHTML markup that will be sent to the client to represent that control in a web browser.

Portability Tip 22.1

The same web control can map to different XHTML elements, depending on the client browser and the web control's property settings.

In this example, the asp:Label control maps to the XHTML **span** element (i.e., ASP.NET creates a span element to represent this control in the client's web browser). A span element contains text that is displayed in a web page. This particular element is used because span elements allow formatting styles to be applied to text. Several of the property values that were applied to our label are represented as part of the style attribute of the span element. You'll soon see what the generated span element's markup looks like.

The web control in this example contains the runat="server" attribute/value pair (line 18), because this control must be processed on the server so that the server can translate the control into XHTML that can be rendered in the client browser. If this attribute pair is not present, the asp:Label element is written as text to the client (i.e., the control is not converted into a span element and does not render properly).

22.4.2 Examining a Code-Behind File

Figure 22.5 presents the code-behind file. [*Note:* we have removed the unnecessary using statements that are automatically generated by Visual Web Developer when you create a new project.] Recall that the ASPX file in Fig. 22.4 references this file in line 3. Line 5 of Fig. 22.5 begins the declaration of class WebTime. Recall that a class declaration can span multiple source-code files and that the separate portions of the class declaration in each file are known as partial classes. The partial modifier in line 5 indicates that the code-behind file actually is a partial class.

```
1   // Fig. 22.5: WebTime.aspx.cs
2   // Code-behind file for a page that displays the current time.
3   using System;
4
5   public partial class WebTime : System.Web.UI.Page
6   {
7      // initializes the contents of the page
8      protected void Page_Init( object sender, EventArgs e )
9      {
```

Fig. 22.5 | Code-behind file for a page that displays the web server's time. (Part 1 of 2.)

```
10            // display the server's current time in timeLabel
11            timeLabel.Text = DateTime.Now.ToString( "hh:mm:ss" );
12        } // end method Page_Init
13    } // end class WebTime
```

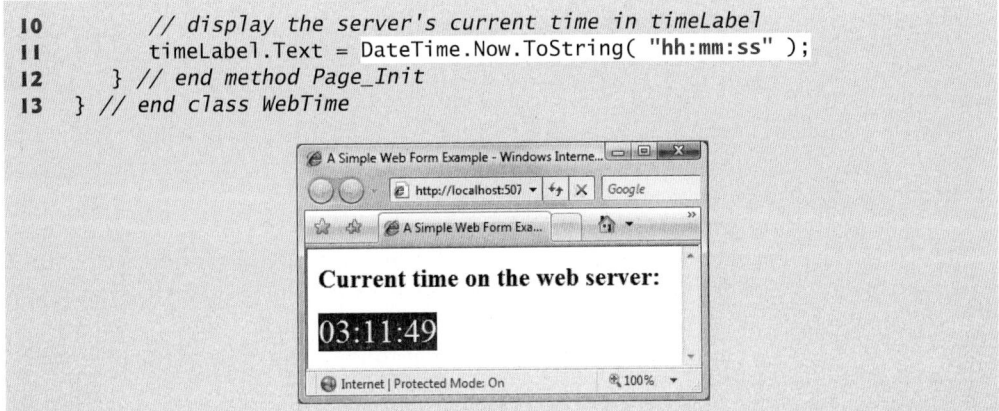

Fig. 22.5 | Code-behind file for a page that displays the web server's time. (Part 2 of 2.)

Line 5 indicates that WebTime inherits from class *Page* in namespace *System.Web.UI*. This namespace contains classes and controls that assist in building web-based applications. Class Page provides event handlers and objects necessary for creating web-based applications. In addition to class Page (from which all web applications directly or indirectly inherit), System.Web.UI also includes class *Control*—the base class that provides common functionality for all web controls.

Lines 8–12 define method *Page_Init*, which handles the page's *Init* event. This event—the first event raised after a page is requested—indicates that the page is ready to be initialized. The only initialization required for this page is setting timeLabel's Text property to the time on the server (i.e., the computer on which this code executes). The statement in line 11 retrieves the current time and formats it as hh:mm:ss. For example, 9 AM is formatted as 09:00:00, and 2:30 PM is formatted as 02:30:00. Notice that the code-behind file can access timeLabel (the ID of the Label in the ASPX file) programmatically, even though the file does not contain a declaration for a variable named timeLabel. You'll learn why momentarily.

22.4.3 Relationship Between an ASPX File and a Code-Behind File

How are the ASPX and code-behind files used to create the web page that is sent to the client? First, recall that class WebTime is the base class specified in line 4 of the ASPX file (Fig. 22.4). This class (partially declared in the code-behind file) inherits from Page, which defines the general functionality of a web page. Partial class WebTime inherits this functionality and defines some of its own (e.g., displaying the current time). The code-behind file contains the code to display the time, whereas the ASPX file contains the markup to define the GUI.

Before the ASPX file gets compiled, ASP.NET creates two partial classes behind the scenes. The code-behind file contains a partial class named WebTime, and ASP.NET generates another partial class that defines the remainder of class WebTime, based on the markup in the ASPX file. For example, WebTime.aspx defines a Label web control with ID timeLabel, so the generated partial class would contain a declaration for a Label control named timeLabel. Label is a web control defined in namespace *System.Web.UI.Web-Controls*, which contains web controls for designing a page's user interface. Web controls in this namespace derive from class *WebControl*. When compiled, the automatically generated partial class declaration containing web-control declarations combines with the code-behind file's partial class declaration to form the complete WebTime class. This explains why line 11 in method Page_Init of the code-behind file (Fig. 22.5) can access timeLabel, which is defined in lines 18–20 of the ASPX file (Fig. 22.4). The Page_Init method and the timeLabel control are actually members of the same class, but defined in separate partial classes.

The partial class generated by ASP.NET is based on the ASPX file that defines the page's visual representation. This new class inherits from class WebTime (as specified by the Inherits attribute of the Page directive), which defines the page's logic. The first time the web page is requested, this class is compiled, and an instance is created. This instance represents our page—it creates the XHTML that is sent to the client. The assembly for the compiled classes is placed within a subdirectory of

```
C:\WINDOWS\Microsoft.NET\Framework\v2.0.50727\
    Temporary ASP.NET Files\WebTime
```

on Windows XP. On Windows Vista, the assembly is placed in

```
C:\Users\User\AppData\Local\Temp\Temporary ASP.NET Files\webtime
```

Once an instance of the web page has been created, multiple clients can use it to access the page—no recompilation is necessary. The project will be recompiled only when you modify the application; changes are detected by the runtime environment, and the application is recompiled to reflect the altered content.

22.4.4 How the Code in an ASP.NET Web Page Executes

Let's look briefly at how the code for our web page executes. When an instance of the page is created, the *PreInit* event occurs first, invoking method *Page_PreInit*. Method Page_PreInit can be used to set a page's theme and look-and-feel (and perform other tasks that are beyond this chapter's scope). The Init event occurs next, invoking method Page_Init. Method Page_Init is used to initialize objects and other aspects of the page. After Page_Init executes, the *Load* event occurs, and the *Page_Load* event handler executes. Note that the Init event is raised only once (when the page is first requested), whereas the Load event is raised with every request. Although not present in this example, the PreInit and Load events are inherited from class Page. You will see examples of the Page_Load event handler later in the chapter. After the Load event handler finishes executing, the page processes events that are generated by the page's controls, such as user interactions with the GUI. When the Web Form object is ready for garbage collection (because the response has been generated and sent), an *Unload* event occurs, which calls the *Page_Unload* event handler. This event, too, is inherited from class Page. Page_Unload typically contains code that releases resources used by the page. Other events occur as well, but are typically used only by ASP.NET controls to render themselves. You can learn more about a Page's event lifecycle at msdn.microsoft.com/en-US/library/ms178472.aspx.

22.4.5 Examining the XHTML Generated by an ASP.NET Application

Figure 22.6 shows the XHTML generated by ASP.NET when a web browser requests WebTime.aspx (Fig. 22.4). To view this XHTML (when you run the application in

```
 1   <!-- Fig. 22.6: WebTime.html -->
 2   <!-- The XHTML generated when WebTime.aspx is loaded. -->
 3   <!DOCTYPE html PUBLIC "-//W3C//DTD XHTML 1.1//EN"
 4      "http://www.w3.org/TR/xhtml11/DTD/xhtml11.dtd">
 5
 6   <html xmlns="http://www.w3.org/1999/xhtml">
 7   <head>
 8      <title>A Simple Web Form Example</title>
 9   </head>
10   <body>
11      <form method="post" action="WebTime.aspx" id="form1">
12         <div>
13            <input type="hidden" name="__VIEWSTATE" id="__VIEWSTATE" value=
14               "/wEPDwUJODExMDE5NzY5ZGQ4n4mht8D7Eqxn73tM5LDnstPlCg==" />
15         </div>
16
17         <div>
18            <h2>Current time on the web server:</h2>
19            <p>
20               <span id="timeLabel" style="color:Yellow;
21                  background-color:Black;font-size:XX-Large;">
22                  03:11:49
23               </span>
24            </p>
25         </div>
26      </form>
27   </body>
28   </html>
```

Fig. 22.6 | XHTML response when the browser requests `WebTime.aspx`.

Section 22.4.6), select **View Source** from the **Page** menu (![Page]) in Internet Explorer (or **View > Page Source** if you are using Firefox). [*Note:* We added the XHTML comments in lines 1–2 and reformatted the XHTML for readability.]

The contents of this page are similar to those of the ASPX file. Lines 7–9 define a document header comparable to that in Fig. 22.4. Lines 10–27 define the body of the document. Line 11 begins the form, a mechanism for collecting user information and sending it to the web server. In this particular program, the user does not submit any data to the web server for processing; however, processing user data is a crucial part of many applications that is facilitated by forms. We demonstrate how to submit form data to the server in later examples.

XHTML forms can contain visual and nonvisual components. Visual components include clickable buttons and other GUI components with which users interact. Nonvisual components, called *hidden inputs*, store data, such as e-mail addresses, that the document author specifies. One of these hidden inputs is defined in lines 13–14. We discuss the precise meaning of this hidden input later in the chapter. Attribute *method* of the form element (line 11) specifies the method by which the web browser submits the form to the server. The *action* attribute identifies the name and location of the resource that will be requested when this form is submitted—in this case, `WebTime.aspx`. Recall that the form element defined in the ASPX file contained the runat="server" attribute/value pair (line 14 of Fig. 22.4). When the form is processed on the server, the runat attribute is removed.

The method and action attributes are added, and the resulting XHTML form is sent to the client browser.

In the ASPX file, the form's Label (i.e., timeLabel) is a web control. Here, we are viewing the XHTML created by our application, so the form contains a span element (lines 20–23 of Fig. 22.6) to represent the text in the label. In this particular case, ASP.NET maps the *Label* web control to an XHTML span element. The formatting options that were specified as properties of timeLabel, such as the font size and the color of the text in the *Label*, are now specified in the style attribute of the span element.

Notice that only those elements in the ASPX file marked with the runat="server" attribute–value pair are modified or replaced when the file is processed by the server. The literal XHTML elements, such as the h2 in line 18 of Fig. 22.6, are sent to the browser as they appear in the ASPX file (line 16 of Fig. 22.4).

22.4.6 Building an ASP.NET Web Application

Now that we have presented the ASPX file, the code-behind file and the resulting web page sent to the web browser, we outline the process by which we created this application. To build the WebTime application, perform the following steps in Visual Web Developer:

Step 1: Creating the Web Application Project
Select **File > New Web Site...** to display the **New Web Site** dialog (Fig. 22.7). In this dialog, select ***ASP.NET Web Site*** in the **Templates** pane. Below this pane are two fields in which you can specify the location and language of the web application you are creating. If it is not already selected, select **File System** from the drop-down list closest to **Location**. This indicates that the web application should be built on your local file system. You will be able to test the application using Visual Web Developer's internal ASP.NET Development Server, but you will not be able to access the application remotely over the Internet. Later, you can publish your application to a web server as an IIS application that uses HTTP. You should create your project in a directory named WebTime.

The **Language** drop-down list in the **New Web Site** dialog allows you to specify the language (e.g., Visual Basic or Visual C#) in which you'll write the code-behind file(s) for

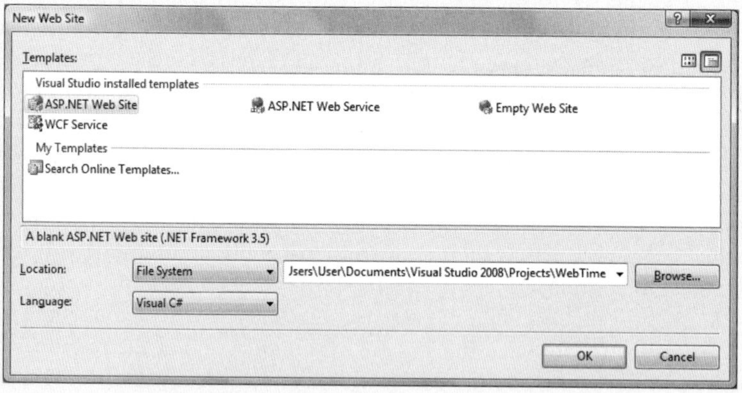

Fig. 22.7 | Creating an **ASP.NET Web Site** in Visual Web Developer.

the web application. Change the setting to Visual C#. Click **OK** to create the ASP.NET website. In addition to the directory in which your web-application files will be created, this action also creates a WebTime folder in the Visual Studio 2008\Projects subdirectory of your My Documents (Windows XP) or Documents (Windows Vista) directory. This folder contains the project's solution files (e.g., WebTime.sln). We do not provide solution files with the examples in this chapter. To open one of the website examples, select **File > Open Web Site** in Visual Web Developer, select the root folder where it resides, and click **Open**.

Step 2: Examining the Solution Explorer of the Newly Created Project
The next several figures describe the new project's content, beginning with the **Solution Explorer** shown in Fig. 22.8. Like Visual C# 2008 Express, Visual Web Developer creates several files when a new project is created. An ASPX file (i.e., Web Form) named Default.aspx is created for each new **ASP.NET Web Site** project. This file is open by default in the Web Forms Designer in **Source** mode when the project first loads (we discuss this momentarily). As mentioned previously, a code-behind file is included as part of the project. Visual Web Developer creates a code-behind file named Default.aspx.cs. To open the ASPX file's code-behind file, right click the ASPX file and select **View Code** or click the **View Code** button at the top of the **Solution Explorer**. Alternatively, you can expand the node for the ASPX file and double click the node for the code-behind file that appears (see Fig. 22.8). You can also choose to list all the files in the project individually (instead of nested) by clicking the **Nest Related Files** button—this option is turned on by default, so clicking the button toggles the option off.

The **Properties** and **Refresh** buttons in Visual Web Developer's **Solution Explorer** behave like those in Visual C# 2008 Express. Visual Web Developer's **Solution Explorer** also contains three additional buttons—**View Designer**, **Copy Web Site** and **ASP.NET Configuration**. The **View Designer** button allows you to open the Web Form in **Design** mode, which we discuss shortly. The **Copy Web Site** button opens a dialog that allows you to move the project's files to another location, such as a remote web server. This is useful if you are developing the application on your local computer but want to make it available to the public at a different location. Finally, the **ASP.NET Configuration** button takes you to the **Web Site Administration Tool**, where you can manipulate various settings and security options for your application. We discuss this tool in greater detail in Section 22.8.

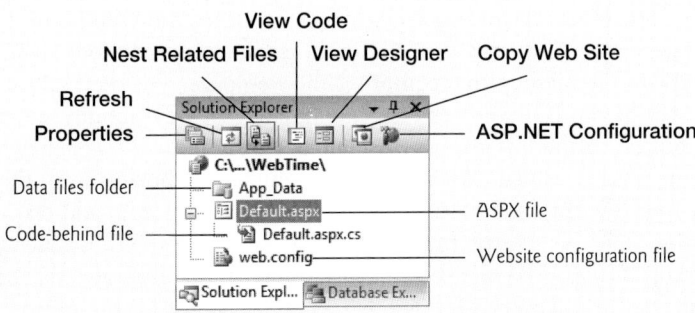

Fig. 22.8 | **Solution Explorer** window for project WebTime.

Step 3: Examining the Toolbox in Visual Web Developer

Figure 22.9 shows the **Toolbox** displayed in the IDE when the project loads. Figure 22.9(a) displays the beginning of the **Standard** list of web controls, and Fig. 22.9(b) displays the remaining web controls, as well as the list of **Data** controls used in ASP.NET. We discuss specific controls in Fig. 22.9 as they are used throughout the chapter. Notice that some controls in the **Toolbox** are similar to the Windows Forms or WPF controls presented earlier in the book.

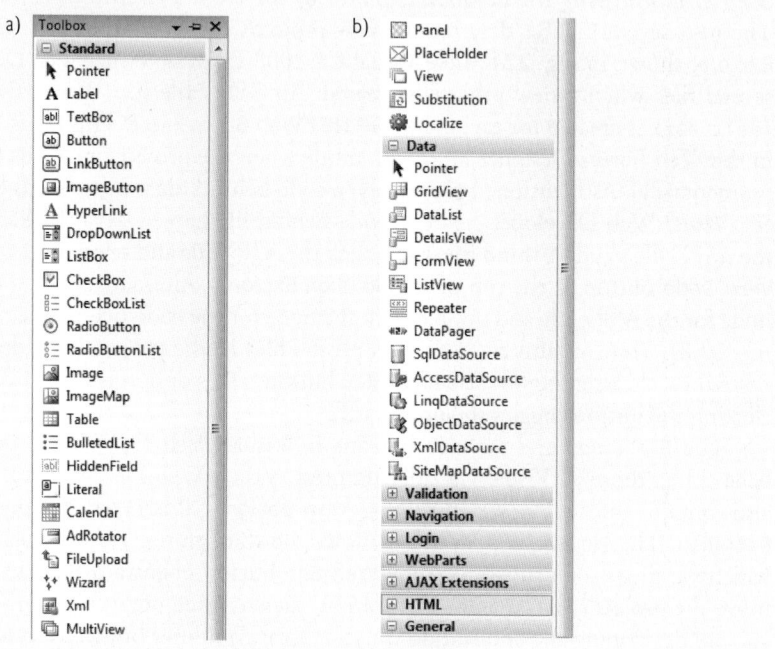

Fig. 22.9 | **Toolbox** in Visual Web Developer.

Step 4: Examining the Web Forms Designer

Figure 22.10 shows the Web Forms Designer in *Source* mode, which appears in the center of the IDE. When the project loads for the first time, the Web Forms Designer displays the autogenerated ASPX file (i.e., `Default.aspx`) in **Source** mode, which allows you to view and edit the markup that comprises the web page. The markup listed in Fig. 22.10 was created by the IDE and serves as a template that we'll modify shortly. Clicking the **Design** button in the lower-left corner of the Web Forms Designer switches to *Design* mode (Fig. 22.11), which allows you to drag and drop controls from the **Toolbox** on the Web Form. You can also type at the current cursor location to add text to the web page. We demonstrate this shortly. In response to such actions, the IDE generates the appropriate markup in the ASPX file. Notice that **Design** mode indicates the XHTML element where the cursor is currently located. Clicking the **Source** button returns the Web Forms Designer to **Source** mode, where you can see the generated markup. You can also view both the markup and the web-page design at the same time by using *Split* mode, as shown in Fig. 22.12.

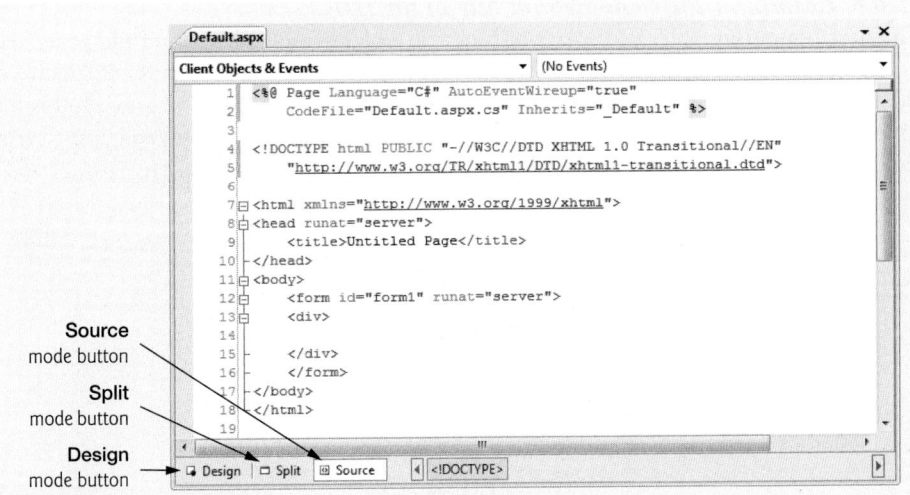

Source mode button

Split mode button

Design mode button

Fig. 22.10 | **Source** mode of the Web Forms Designer.

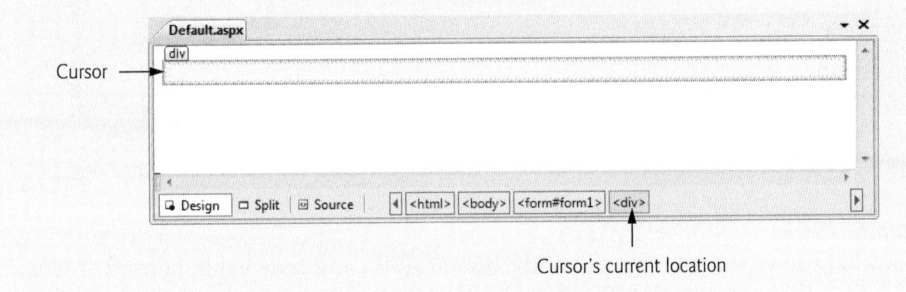

Cursor

Cursor's current location

Fig. 22.11 | **Design** mode of the Web Forms Designer.

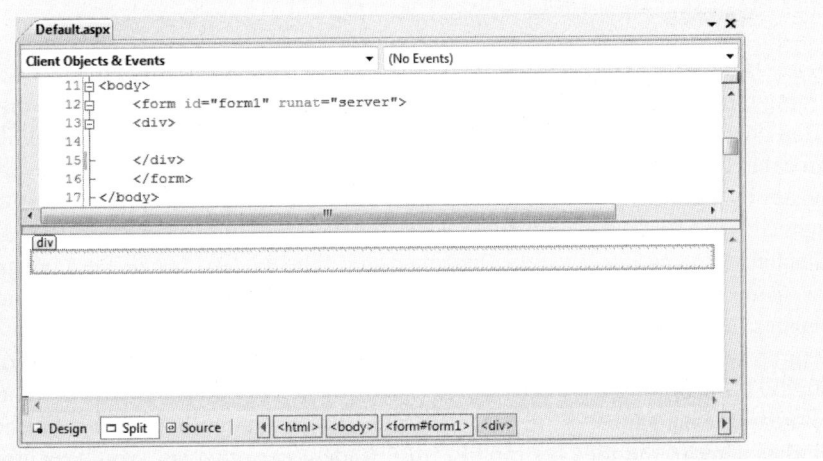

Fig. 22.12 | **Split** mode of Web Forms Designer.

Step 5: Examining the Code-Behind File in the IDE

The next figure (Fig. 22.13) displays Default.aspx.cs—the code-behind file generated by Visual Web Developer for Default.aspx. Right click the ASPX file in the **Solution Explorer** and select **View Code** to open the code-behind file. When it is first created, this file contains nothing more than a partial class declaration with an empty Page_Load event handler. We'll add the Page_Init event handler to this code momentarily.

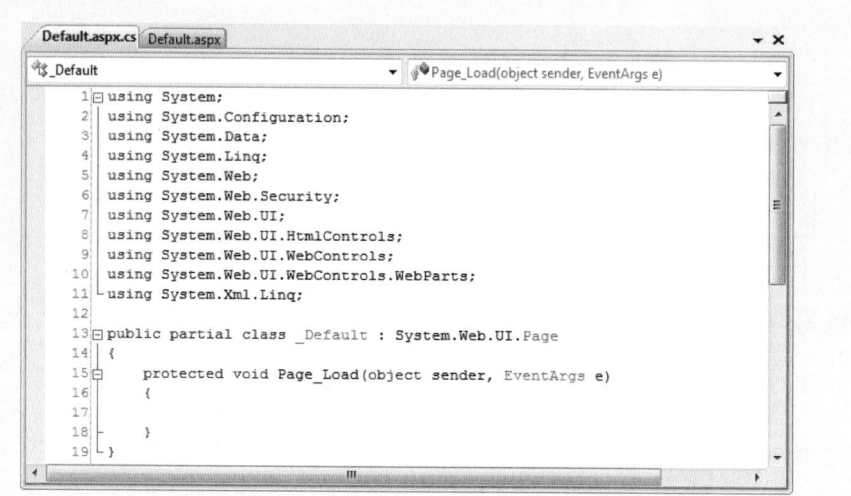

```csharp
 1  using System;
 2  using System.Configuration;
 3  using System.Data;
 4  using System.Linq;
 5  using System.Web;
 6  using System.Web.Security;
 7  using System.Web.UI;
 8  using System.Web.UI.HtmlControls;
 9  using System.Web.UI.WebControls;
10  using System.Web.UI.WebControls.WebParts;
11  using System.Xml.Linq;
12
13  public partial class _Default : System.Web.UI.Page
14  {
15      protected void Page_Load(object sender, EventArgs e)
16      {
17
18      }
19  }
```

Fig. 22.13 | Code-behind file for Default.aspx generated by Visual Web Developer.

Step 6: Renaming the ASPX File

Now that you've seen the contents of the default ASPX and code-behind files, let's rename these files. Right click the ASPX file in the **Solution Explorer** and select **Rename**. Enter the new file name WebTime.aspx and press *Enter*. This updates the name of both the ASPX file and the code-behind file. The IDE also automatically updates the Page directive's CodeFile attribute in WebTime.aspx.

Step 7: Renaming the Class in the Code-Behind File and Updating the ASPX File

Although renaming the ASPX file causes the name of the code-behind file to change, this action does not affect the name of the partial class declared in the code-behind file. To rename the partial class, you should use Visual Studio's refactoring tool, which automatically updates the existing references to this class in the rest of the project to reflect this change. Right click the class name in the partial class's declaration (line 13 in Fig. 22.13) and select **Refactor > Rename...** to open the **Rename** dialog (Fig. 22.14). Specify WebTime as the new class name and click **OK**. If the **Preview reference changes** option was checked, the **Preview Changes - Rename** dialog appears. Here, you can make sure that you wish to make all of the proposed changes, and you can uncheck any of the references that you do not wish to modify. Leave all of the checkboxes checked and click **Apply**. Note that the Inherits attribute of the Page directive in WebTime.aspx was automatically updated. This value and the class name in the code-behind file must be identical; otherwise, you'll get errors when you build the web application.

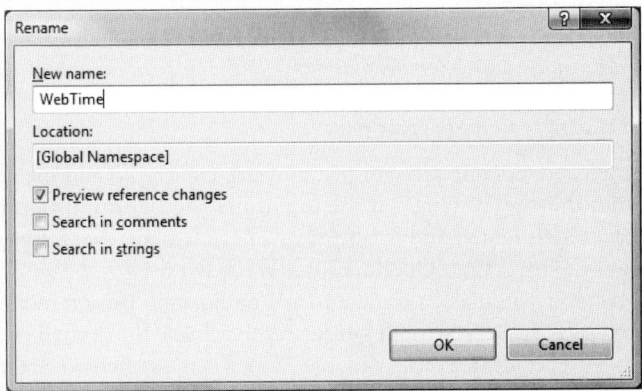

Fig. 22.14 | Rename dialog.

Step 8: Changing the Title of the Page

Before designing the content of the Web Form, we change its title from the default Untitled Page (line 9 of Fig. 22.10) to A Simple Web Form Example. To do so, open the ASPX file in **Source** mode and modify the text between the start and end <title> tags. Alternatively, you can modify the Web Form's *Title* property in the **Properties** window. To view the Web Form's properties, select DOCUMENT from the drop-down list in the **Properties** window; DOCUMENT is the name used to represent the Web Form in the **Properties** window.

Step 9: Designing the Page

Designing a Web Form is as simple as designing a Windows Form. To add controls to the page, you can drag and drop them from the **Toolbox** onto the Web Form in **Design** mode. Like the Web Form itself, each control is an object that has properties, methods and events. You can set these properties and events visually using the **Properties** window or programmatically in the code-behind file. However, unlike working with a Windows Form, you can type text directly on a Web Form at the cursor location or insert XHTML elements using menu commands.

Controls and other elements are placed sequentially on a Web Form, much as text and images are placed in a document using word-processing software like Microsoft Word. Controls are placed one after another in the order in which you drag and drop them onto the Web Form. The cursor indicates the point at which text and XHTML elements will be inserted. If you want to position a control between existing text or controls, you can drop the control at a specific position within the existing elements. You can also rearrange existing controls using drag-and-drop actions. The positions of controls and other elements are relative to the Web Form's upper-left corner. This type of layout is known as *relative positioning*.

An alternate type of layout is known as *absolute positioning*, in which controls are located exactly where they are dropped on the Web Form. You can enable absolute positioning in **Design** mode by selecting **Tools > Options...** to open the **Options** dialog. If it isn't checked already, check the **Show all settings** checkbox. Next, open the **HTML Designer > CSS Styling** node and ensure that the checkbox labeled **Change positioning to absolute for controls added using Toolbox, past or drag and drop** is selected.

Portability Tip 22.2

Absolute positioning is discouraged, because pages designed in this manner may not render correctly in different browsers or on computers with different screen resolutions and font sizes. This could cause absolutely positioned elements to overlap each other or display off-screen, requiring the client to scroll to see the full page content.

In this example, we use one piece of text and one Label. To add the text to the Web Form, click within the gray rectangle at the top of the Web Form in **Design** mode. Note that the rectangle is highlighted and is labeled as a div element. Next, type Current time on the web server:. Visual Web Developer is a *WYSIWYG* (*What You See Is What You Get*) editor—whenever you make a change to a Web Form in **Design** mode, the IDE creates the markup (visible in **Source** mode) necessary to achieve the desired visual effects seen in **Design** mode. After adding the text to the Web Form, switch to **Source** mode. You should see that the IDE added this text to the div element that appears in the ASPX file by default. Back in **Design** mode, highlight the text you added. From the **Block Format** drop-down list (see Fig. 22.15), choose **Heading 2** to format this text as a heading that will appear bold in a font slightly larger than the default. This action causes the IDE to enclose the newly added text in an h2 element. Finally, click to the right of the text and press the *Enter* key to move the cursor to a new paragraph. This action generates an empty p element in the ASPX file's markup. The IDE should now look like Fig. 22.15.

You can place a Label on a Web Form either by dragging and dropping or by double clicking the **Toolbox**'s **Label** control. Be sure the cursor is in the newly created paragraph, then add a Label that will be used to display the time. Using the **Properties** window, set the (ID) property of the Label to timeLabel. We delete timeLabel's text, because we set it programmatically in the code-behind file. When a Label does not contain text, the name

Block Format drop-down list

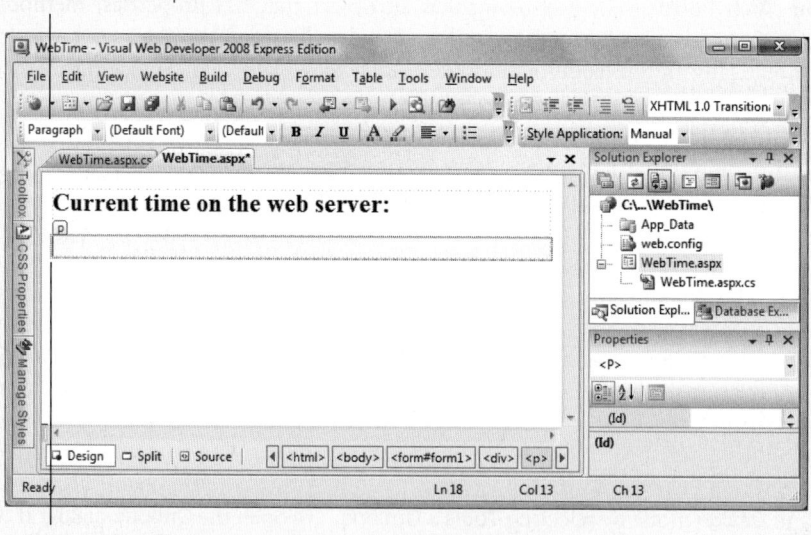

Cursor position after inserting a new paragraph by pressing *Enter*

Fig. 22.15 | WebTime.aspx after inserting text and a new paragraph.

is displayed in square brackets in the Web Forms Designer (Fig. 22.16) but is not displayed at execution time. The label name is a placeholder for design and layout purposes. We set timeLabel's BackColor, ForeColor and Font-Size properties to Black, Yellow and XX-Large, respectively. To change font properties, expand the Font node in the **Properties** window, then change each relevant property individually. Once the Label's properties are set in the **Properties** window, Visual Web Developer updates the ASPX file's contents. Figure 22.16 shows the IDE after these properties are set.

Next, set the Label's EnableViewState property to False. Finally, select DOCUMENT from the drop-down list in the **Properties** window and set the Web Form's Enable-SessionState property to False. We discuss both of these properties later in the chapter.

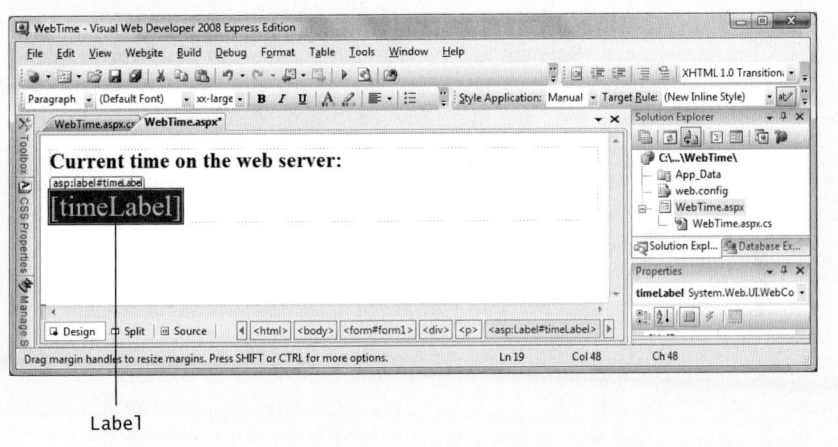

Label

Fig. 22.16 | WebTime.aspx after adding a Label and setting its properties.

Step 10: Adding Page Logic
Once the user interface has been designed, C# code must be added to the code-behind file to display the current time on the web server. Open WebTime.aspx.cs by double clicking its node in the **Solution Explorer**. In this example, we add a Page_Init event handler (lines 8–12 of Fig. 22.5) to the code-behind file. Recall that Page_Init handles the Init event and contains code to initialize the page. The statement in line 11 of Fig. 22.5 programmatically sets the text of timeLabel to the current time on the server.

Step 11: Running the Program
You can view the Web Form several ways. First, you can select **Debug > Start Without Debugging**, which runs the application by opening it in a browser window. If you created the ASP.NET application on the local file system, the URL shown in the browser will have the form http://localhost:*PortNumber*/WebTime/WebTime.aspx, where *PortNumber* is the assigned port on which the ASP.NET Development Server runs. This URL indicates that the WebTime project folder is being accessed through the test server running at local-host:*PortNumber*. When you select **Debug > Start Without Debugging**, a tray icon appears

in the bottom-right of your screen to show that the **ASP.NET Development Server** is running. The test server stops when you exit Visual Web Developer.

To debug your application, you can select **Debug > Start Debugging** to view the web page in a web browser with debugging enabled. You cannot debug a web application unless debugging is explicitly enabled by the ***web.config*** file—a file that stores configuration settings for an ASP.NET web application. You will rarely need to manually create or modify web.config. The first time you select **Debug > Start Debugging** in a project, a dialog appears and asks whether you want the IDE to modify the web.config file to enable debugging. After you click **OK**, the IDE enters **Running** mode. You can exit **Running** mode by selecting **Debug > Stop Debugging** in Visual Web Developer or, if you are using Internet Explorer, by closing the browser window in which the ASPX file is displayed. If you are using Firefox, closing the browser window will not stop debuggging.

To view a specific ASPX file, you can right click either the Web Forms Designer or the ASPX file name (in the **Solution Explorer**) and select ***View In Browser*** to load the page in a web browser. Right clicking the ASPX file in the **Solution Explorer** and selecting **Browse With...** also opens the page in a browser, but first allows you to specify the web browser that should display the page and its screen resolution.

Finally, you can run your application by opening a browser window and typing the web page's URL in the **Address** field. First start the **ASP.NET Development Server** by running the application using one of the methods described above. Then you can type the URL (including the *PortNumber* found in the test server's tray icon) in the browser to execute the application.

Note that all of these techniques for running the application compile the project for you. In fact, ASP.NET compiles your web page whenever it changes between HTTP requests. For example, suppose you browse the page, then modify the ASPX file or add code to the code-behind file. When you reload the page, ASP.NET recompiles the page on the server before returning the HTTP response to the browser. This important behavior of ASP.NET 3.5 ensures that clients always see the latest version of the page. You can manually compile a web page or an entire website by selecting ***Build Page*** or ***Build Site***, respectively, from the **Build** menu in Visual Web Developer.

Windows Firewall Settings

If you are using a local IIS web server to test web applications (rather than the built-in test server in Visual Web Developer) and would like to test your web applications over a network, you may need to change your Windows Firewall settings. For security reasons, Windows Firewall does not allow remote access to a web server on your local computer by default. To change this, open the Windows Firewall utility in the Windows Control Panel. Next, if you are using Windows Vista, click the **Exceptions** tab and ensure that the checkbox next to **World Wide Web Services (HTTP)** is checked. If you are using Windows XP, click the **Advanced** tab and select your network connection from the **Network Connection Settings** list, then click **Settings....** On the **Services** tab of the **Advanced Settings** dialog, ensure that **Web Server (HTTP)** is checked.

22.5 Web Controls

This section introduces several web controls located from the **Toolbox**'s **Standard** section (Fig. 22.9). Figure 22.17 summarizes several web controls used in the chapter examples.

Web control	Description
Label	Displays text that the user cannot edit.
TextBox	Gathers user input and displays text.
Button	Triggers an event when clicked.
HyperLink	Displays a hyperlink.
DropDownList	Displays a drop-down list of choices from which a user can select an item.
RadioButtonList	Groups radio buttons.
Image	Displays images (e.g., GIF, JPG and PNG).

Fig. 22.17 | Commonly used web controls.

22.5.1 Text and Graphics Controls

Figure 22.18 depicts a simple form for gathering user input. This example uses all the controls listed in Fig. 22.17, except Label, which you used in Section 22.4. The code in Fig. 22.18 was generated by Visual Web Developer in response to dragging controls onto the page in **Design** mode. To begin, create an **ASP.NET Web Site** named WebControls. [*Note:* This example does not contain any functionality—i.e., no action occurs when the user clicks **Register**. In subsequent examples, we demonstrate how to add functionality to many of these web controls.]

Before discussing the web controls used in this ASPX file, we explain the XHTML that creates the layout seen in Fig. 22.18. The page contains an h3 heading element (line 26), followed by a series of additional XHTML blocks. We place most of the web controls inside p elements (i.e., paragraphs), but we use an XHTML table element (lines 33–64) to organize the Image and TextBox controls in the user-information section of the page. In the preceding section, we described how to add heading elements and paragraphs visually without manipulating any XHTML in the ASPX file directly. Visual Web Developer allows you to add a table in a similar maner.

Adding an XHTML Table to a Web Form

To create a table with two rows and two columns in **Design** mode, select **Insert Table** from the **Table** menu to display the **Insert Table** dialog (Fig. 22.19). In the **Size** group box, change the values of **Rows** and **Columns** to 2. Click **OK** to close the **Insert Table** dialog and create the table. Once a table is created, controls and text can be added to particular cells to create a neatly organized layout. Alternatively, you can drag and drop a Table (in the **HTML** tab) onto the form and edit it in **Design mode** and the **Properties** window.

```
1   <%-- Fig. 22.18: WebControls.aspx --%>
2   <%-- Registration form that demonstrates web controls. --%>
3   <%@ Page Language="C#" AutoEventWireup="true"
4      CodeFile="WebControls.aspx.cs" Inherits="WebControls" %>
5
6   <!DOCTYPE html PUBLIC "-//W3C//DTD XHTML 1.0 Transitional//EN"
7      "http://www.w3.org/TR/xhtml1/DTD/xhtml1-transitional.dtd">
```

Fig. 22.18 | Web Form that demonstrates web controls. (Part 1 of 4.)

```
8
9   <html xmlns="http://www.w3.org/1999/xhtml">
10  <head runat="server">
11     <title>Web Controls Demonstration</title>
12     <style type="text/css">
13        .style1
14        {
15           color: #006699;
16        }
17        .style2
18        {
19           width: 100%;
20        }
21     </style>
22  </head>
23  <body>
24     <form id="form1" runat="server">
25     <div>
26        <h3>This is a sample registration form.</h3>
27        <p><i>Please fill in all fields and click Register.</i></p>
28        <p>
29           <asp:Image ID="userInformationImage" runat="server"
30              ImageUrl="~/Images/user.png" />
31           <span class="style1">Please fill out the fields below.</span>
32        </p>
33        <table class="style2">
34           <tr>
35              <td valign="top" style="width: 225px">
36                 <asp:Image ID="firstNameImage" runat="server"
37                    ImageUrl="~/Images/fname.png" />
38                 <asp:TextBox ID="firstNameTextBox" runat="server">
39                 </asp:TextBox>
40              </td>
41              <td valign="top">
42                 <asp:Image ID="lastNameImage" runat="server"
43                    ImageUrl="~/Images/lname.png" />
44                 <asp:TextBox ID="lastNameTextBox" runat="server">
45                 </asp:TextBox>
46              </td>
47           </tr>
48           <tr>
49              <td valign="top" style="width: 225px">
50                 <asp:Image ID="emailImage" runat="server"
51                    ImageUrl="~/Images/email.png" />
52                 <asp:TextBox ID="emailTextBox" runat="server">
53                 </asp:TextBox>
54              </td>
55              <td valign="top">
56                 <asp:Image ID="phoneImage" runat="server"
57                    ImageUrl="~/Images/phone.png" />
58                 <asp:TextBox ID="phoneTextBox" runat="server">
59                 </asp:TextBox>
```

Fig. 22.18 | Web Form that demonstrates web controls. (Part 2 of 4.)

```
60                    <br />
61                    Must be in the form (555) 555-5555.
62                 </td>
63              </tr>
64           </table>
65           <p>
66              <asp:Image ID="publicationsImage" runat="server"
67                 ImageUrl="~/Images/publications.png" /> 
68              <span class="style1">
69                 Which book would you like information about?</span>
70           </p>
71           <p>
72              <asp:DropDownList ID="booksDropDownList" runat="server">
73                 <asp:ListItem>Visual Basic 2008 How to Program</asp:ListItem>
74                 <asp:ListItem>Visual C# 2008 How to Program</asp:ListItem>
75                 <asp:ListItem>Java How to Program 6e</asp:ListItem>
76                 <asp:ListItem>C++ How to Program 5e</asp:ListItem>
77                 <asp:ListItem>C How to Program 5e</asp:ListItem>
78                 <asp:ListItem>Internet and World Wide Web How to Program 4e
79                    </asp:ListItem>
80              </asp:DropDownList>
81           </p>
82           <p>
83              <asp:HyperLink ID="booksHyperLink" runat="server"
84                 NavigateUrl="http://www.deitel.com" Target="_blank">
85                 Click here to view more information about our books
86              </asp:HyperLink>
87           </p>
88           <p>
89              <asp:Image ID="operatingSystemImage" runat="server"
90                 ImageUrl="~/Images/os.png" /> 
91              <span class="style1">Which operating system are you using?
92                 </span>
93           </p>
94           <p>
95              <asp:RadioButtonList ID="operatingSystemRadioButtonList"
96                 runat="server">
97                 <asp:ListItem>Windows Vista</asp:ListItem>
98                 <asp:ListItem>Windows XP</asp:ListItem>
99                 <asp:ListItem>Mac OS X</asp:ListItem>
100                <asp:ListItem>Linux</asp:ListItem>
101                <asp:ListItem>Other</asp:ListItem>
102             </asp:RadioButtonList>
103          </p>
104          <p>
105             <asp:Button ID="registerButton" runat="server"
106                Text="Register" />
107          </p>
108       </div>
109    </form>
110 </body>
111 </html>
```

Fig. 22.18 | Web Form that demonstrates web controls. (Part 3 of 4.)

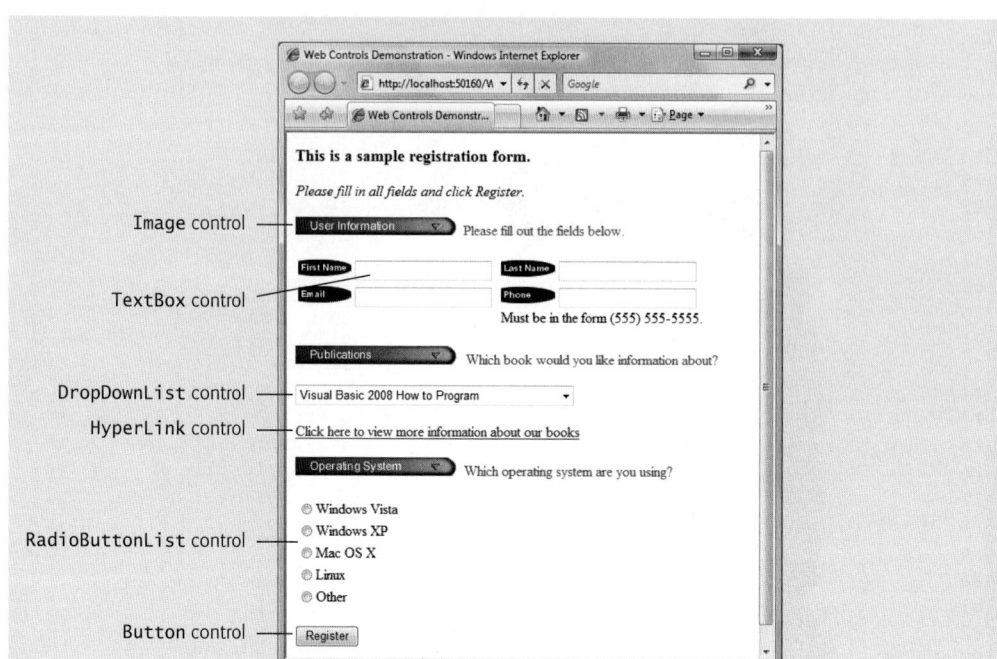

Fig. 22.18 | Web Form that demonstrates web controls. (Part 4 of 4.)

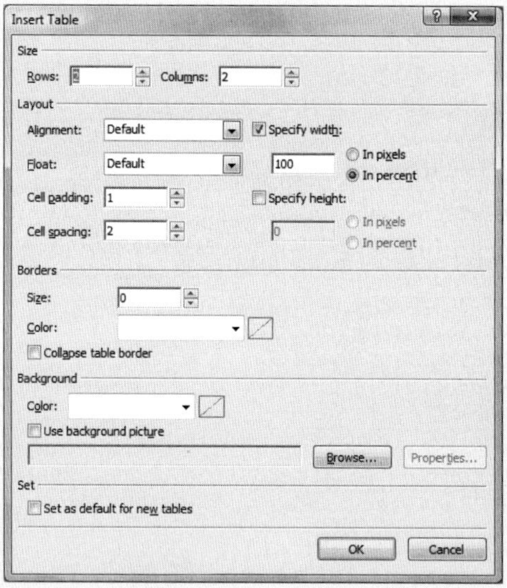

Fig. 22.19 | Insert Table dialog.

By default, a table cell's contents are aligned in the middle vertically. We changed the vertical alignment of all cells in the table (i.e., td elements) by setting the valign property to top in the **Properties** window. This causes the content of each table cell to align with the top of the cell. We also changed the width of the cells in the left column by modifying the style property in the **Properties** window. Click the ellipsis next to the style property to display the **Modify Style** dialog. This tool can be used to create a CSS style for formatting an XHTML element such as td. We'll discuss CSS styling of web content at the end of this section. In this case, we set the width (in the **Position** category) to 225px.

Setting the Color of Text on a Web Form

Notice that some of the instructions to the user on the form appear in a teal color. To set the color of a specific piece of text, highlight the text and select **Format > Font...**. In the **Font** dialog that appears, you can choose a color from those provided in the drop-down menu or click **More Colors...**. This displays the **More Colors** dialog, which offers a greater selection of colors and allows you to specify a custom color by clicking the **Colors...** button. Note that the IDE places the colored text in an XHTML span element (e.g., line 31) and applies the color using CSS styling.

Examining Web Controls on a Sample Registration Form

Lines 29–30 of Fig. 22.18 define an *Image* control, which inserts an image into a web page. The images used in this example are located in the Images subdirectory of this chapter's examples directory. You can download the examples from www.deitel.com/books/csharpfp3. Before an image can be displayed on a web page using an Image web control, the image must first be added to the project. We added an Images folder to this project by right clicking the location of the project in the **Solution Explorer**, selecting **New Folder** and entering the folder name Images. We then added each of the images used in the example to this folder by right clicking the folder, selecting **Add Existing Item...** and browsing for the files to add (located in the Images subfolder of this chapter's examples folder). You can also drag a folder full of images onto the project's location in the **Solution Explorer** to add the folder and all the images to the project.

The *ImageUrl* property (line 30) specifies the location of the image to display in the Image control. To select an image, click the ellipsis next to the ImageUrl property in the **Properties** window and use the **Select Image** dialog to browse for the desired image in the project's Images folder. When the IDE fills in the ImageUrl property based on your selection, it includes a tilde and forward slash (~/) at the beginning to indicate that the Images folder is in the root directory of the project. This syntax can be used only in server controls.

Lines 33–64 contain the table element created by the steps discussed previously. Each td element contains an Image control and a *TextBox* control, which allows you to obtain text from the user and display text to the user. For example, lines 38–39 define a TextBox control used to collect the user's first name.

Lines 72–80 define a *DropDownList*. This control is similar to the Windows Forms ComboBox control. Unlike the ComboBox, however, an ASP.NET DropDownList cannot be configured to allow users to type text. When a user clicks the drop-down list, it expands and displays a list from which the user can make a selection. Each item in the drop-down list is defined by a *ListItem* element (e.g., line 73). After dragging a DropDownList control onto a Web Form, you can add items to it using the **ListItem Collection Editor**. This process is similar to customizing a ListBox in a Windows application. In Visual Web Developer, you can access the **ListItem Collection Editor** by clicking the ellipsis next to the Items property of the DropDownList, or by using the **DropDownList Tasks** menu. You can open this menu by clicking the small arrowhead that appears in the upper-right corner of the control in **Design** mode (Fig. 22.20). This menu is called a *smart-tag menu*. Visual Web Developer displays smart-tag menus for many ASP.NET controls to facilitate common tasks. Clicking **Edit Items...** in the **DropDownList Tasks** menu opens the **ListItem Collection Editor**, which allows you to add ListItem elements to the DropDownList.

The *HyperLink* control (lines 83–86 of Fig. 22.18) adds a hyperlink to a web page. The *NavigateUrl* property (line 84) of this control specifies the resource (i.e., http://www.deitel.com) that is requested when a user clicks the hyperlink. Setting the *Target* property to _blank specifies that the requested web page should open in either a new window or a new tab, depending on the settings of the user's Internet browser. By default, HyperLink controls cause pages to open in the same browser window.

Lines 95–102 define a *RadioButtonList* control, which provides a series of radio buttons from which the user can select only one. Like options in a DropDownList, individual radio buttons are defined by ListItem elements. Note that, like the **DropDownList Tasks** smart-tag menu, the **RadioButtonList Tasks** smart-tag menu also provides an **Edit Items...** link to open the **ListItem Collection Editor**.

The final web control in Fig. 22.18 is a *Button* (lines 105–106). A Button web control represents a button that triggers an action when clicked. This control typically maps to an XHTML input element with attribute type set to "button". As stated earlier, clicking the **Register** button in this example does not do anything.

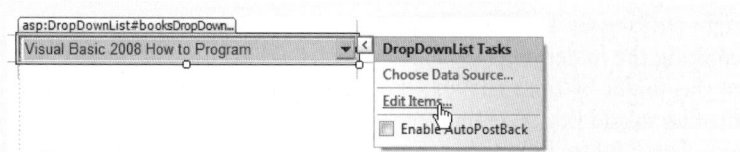

Fig. 22.20 | **DropDownList Tasks** smart-tag menu.

CSS Inline Styles and Embedded Style Sheets

When you specify how an XHTML element should display through the **Design** view, **Properties** window, or a wizard, Visual Web Developer often generates *CSS (Cascading Style Sheets™)* code to specify the presentation of the element. In the head element of your .aspx file, the *style* element defines *embedded style sheets* (lines 12–21). The style element's type attribute specifes the MIME type of its content. The body of the style sheet declares *CSS rules* (styles), each of which is composed of a *CSS selector* and a series of property specifications separated by semicolons (;) and enclosed in curly braces ({}). Each specification is composed of a property followed by a colon and a value (e.g., line 15). When you use one of the visual programming tools to define an XHTML element's appearance, Visual Web Developer sometimes creates a *style class*, which can be used as a selector by prefixing it with a period (e.g., line 13). The style class can then be applied to any element in the document by setting the XHTML attribute *class* (e.g., line 31). The style class style1 is used to color text (created from using the **Font** dialog), and style2 is used to format the table (created from using by the **Insert Table** dialog).

Another way to apply styles is to use *inline styles*, which are composed of a series of property specifications separated by semicolons. Inline styles declare an individual element's format using the XHTML attribute *style*. When we set the width of the cells in the left column of the table, Visual Web Developer generated inline styles (lines 35 and 49). These are interchangeable with embedded style sheets, and Visual Web Developer generates a mixture of both. You can also write your own CSS code in **Source** mode. For more CSS information, please visit our CSS Resource Center at www.deitel.com/CSS21/.

22.5.2 AdRotator Control

Web pages often contain product or service advertisements, which usually consist of images. Although website authors want to include as many sponsors as possible, web pages can display only a limited number of advertisements. To address this problem, ASP.NET provides the *AdRotator* web control for displaying advertisements. Using advertisement data located in an XML file, an AdRotator randomly selects an image to display and generates a hyperlink to the web page associated with that image. Browsers that do not support images display alternate text that is specified in the XML document. If a user clicks the image or substituted text, the browser loads the web page associated with that image.

Demonstrating the AdRotator Web Control

Figure 22.21 demonstrates the AdRotator web control. In this example, the "advertisements" that we rotate are the flags of 10 countries. When a user clicks the displayed flag image, the browser is redirected to a web page containing information about the country that the flag represents. If a user refreshes the browser or requests the page again, one of the ten flags is again chosen at random and displayed.

```
1   <%-- Fig. 22.21: FlagRotator.aspx --%>
2   <%-- A Web Form that displays flags using an AdRotator control. --%>
3   <%@ Page Language="C#" AutoEventWireup="false"
4      CodeFile="FlagRotator.aspx.cs" Inherits="FlagRotator" %>
5
6   <!DOCTYPE html PUBLIC "-//W3C//DTD XHTML 1.0 Transitional//EN"
7      "http://www.w3.org/TR/xhtml1/DTD/xhtml1-transitional.dtd">
8
9   <html xmlns="http://www.w3.org/1999/xhtml" >
10  <head runat="server">
11     <title>Flag Rotator</title>
12  </head>
13  <body background="Images/background.png">
14     <form id="form1" runat="server">
15     <div>
16        <h3>AdRotator Example</h3>
17        <p>
18           <asp:AdRotator ID="countryRotator" runat="server"
19              DataSourceID="adXmlDataSource" />
20           <asp:XmlDataSource ID="adXmlDataSource" runat="server"
21              DataFile="~/App_Data/AdRotatorInformation.xml">
22           </asp:XmlDataSource>
23        </p>
24     </div>
25     </form>
26  </body>
27  </html>
```

Fig. 22.21 | Web Form that demonstrates the AdRotator web control. (Part 1 of 2.)

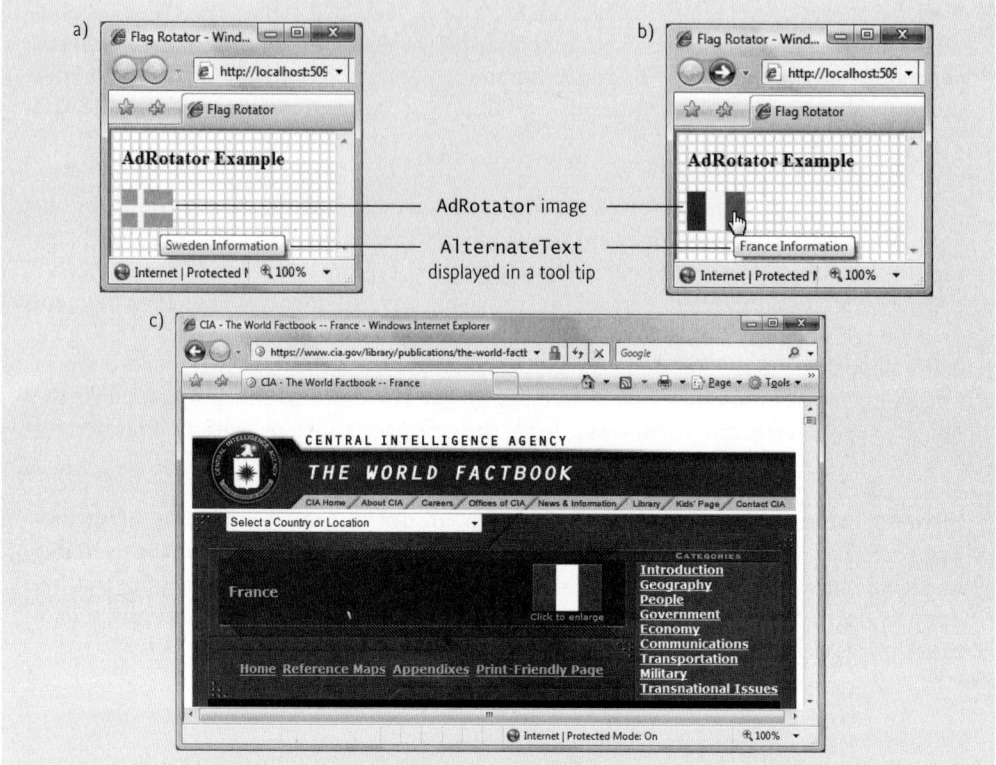

Fig. 22.21 | Web Form that demonstrates the AdRotator web control. (Part 2 of 2.)

The ASPX file in Fig. 22.21 is similar to that in Fig. 22.4. However, instead of XHTML text and a Label, this page contains XHTML text (the h3 element in line 16) and an AdRotator control named countryRotator (lines 18–19). This page also contains an XmlDataSource control (lines 20–22), which supplies the data to the AdRotator control. The background attribute of the page's body element (line 13) is set to the image background.png, located in the project's Images folder. To specify this file, click the ellipsis provided next to the Background property of DOCUMENT in the **Properties** window and use the resulting dialog to select background.png from the Images folder. The images and XML file used in this example are both located in the chapter's examples directory.

You do not need to add any code to the code-behind file, because the AdRotator control "does all the work." The output depicts two different requests. Figure 22.21(a) shows the first time the page is requested, when the Swedish flag is displayed. In the second request, as shown in Fig. 22.21(b), the French flag is displayed. Figure 22.21(c) depicts the web page that loads when you click the French flag.

Connecting Data to an AdRotator Control
An AdRotator control accesses an XML file to determine what advertisement (i.e., flag) image, hyperlink URL and alternate text to display and include in the page. To connect the AdRotator control to the XML file, we create an ***XmlDataSource*** control—one of several ASP.NET data controls (found in the **Data** section of the **Toolbox**) that encapsulate

data sources and make such data available for web controls. An `XmlDataSource` references an XML file containing data that will be used in an ASP.NET application. Later in the chapter, you'll learn more about data-bound web controls, as well as the `LinqDataSource` control, which retrieves data from a LINQ data context.

To build this example, we first add the XML file `AdRotatorInformation.xml` to the project. Each project created in Visual Web Developer contains an `App_Data` folder, which is intended to store all the data used by the project. Right click this folder in the **Solution Explorer** and select **Add Existing Item...**, then browse for `AdRotatorInformation.xml` in this chapter's examples folder. We provide this file in the chapter's examples directory in the subdirectory named `XMLFiles`.

Next, drag an `AdRotator` control from the **Toolbox** to the Web Form. The **AdRotator Tasks** smart-tag menu opens automatically. From this menu, select **<New Data Source...>** from the **Choose Data Source** drop-down list to start the **Data Source Configuration Wizard**. Select **XML File** as the data-source type. This causes the wizard to create an `XmlDataSource` with the `ID` specified in the bottom half of the wizard dialog. We set the `ID` of the control to `adXmlDataSource`. Click **OK** in the **Data Source Configuration Wizard** dialog. The **Configure Data Source - adXmlDataSource** dialog appears next. In this dialog's **Data File** section, click **Browse...** and, in the **Select XML File** dialog, locate and select the XML file you added to the `App_Data` folder. Click **OK** to exit this dialog, then click **OK** to exit the **Configure Data Source - adXmlDataSource** dialog. After completing these steps, the `AdRotator` is configured to use the XML file to determine which advertisements to display.

Examining an XML File Containing Advertisement Information

XML document `AdRotatorInformation.xml`—or any XML document used with an `AdRotator` control—must contain one ***Advertisements*** root element. Within that element can be as many ***Ad*** elements as you need. Each `Ad` element is similar to the following:

```
<Ad>
    <ImageUrl>Images/france.png</ImageUrl>
    <NavigateUrl>https://www.cia.gov/library/publications/
        the-world-factbook/geos/fr.html</NavigateUrl>
    <AlternateText>France Information</AlternateText>
    <Impressions>1</Impressions>
</Ad>
```

and provides information about an advertisement. Element ***ImageUrl*** specifies the path (location) of the advertisement's image, and element ***NavigateUrl*** specifies the URL for the web page that loads when a user clicks the advertisement. Note that we reformatted this `NavigateUrl` element above for presentation purposes. The actual XML file cannot contain any whitespace before, after, or in the middle of the URL. Otherwise, the whitespace will be considered part of the URL, and the target will not load properly.

The ***AlternateText*** element nested in each `Ad` element contains text that displays in place of the image when the browser cannot locate or render the image for some reason (i.e., the file is missing, or the browser is not capable of displaying it), or to assist the visually impaired. The `AlternateText` element's text is also a tool tip that the web browser displays when a user places the mouse pointer over the image (Fig. 22.21). The ***Impressions*** element specifies how often a particular image appears, relative to the other images. An advertisement that has a higher `Impressions` value displays more frequently than an advertisement with a lower value. In our example, the advertisements display with equal probability, because the value of each Impressions element is set to 1.

The advertisement XML file can also include other elements. For more information, visit msdn.microsoft.com/en-us/library/system.web.ui.webcontrols.adrotator. advertisementfile.aspx.

22.5.3 Validation Controls

This section introduces a different type of web control, called a *validation control* (or *validator*), which determines whether the data in another web control is in the proper format. For example, validators could determine whether a user has provided information in a required field or whether a zip-code field contains exactly five digits. Validators provide a mechanism for validating user input before it is processed. When the XHTML for our page is created, the validator is converted into *JavaScript* that performs the validation. JavaScript is a scripting language that enhances the functionality and appearance of web pages and is typically executed on the client. However, some clients disable scripting or do not support scripting, so validation must be performed on the server. ASP.NET validation controls can function on the client, on the server or both.

Validating Input in a Web Form

The example in this section prompts the user to enter a name, e-mail address and phone number. A website could use a form like this to collect contact information from site visitors. After the user enters any data, but before the data is sent to the web server, validators ensure that the user entered a value in each field and that the e-mail address and phone-number values are in an acceptable format. In this example, (555) 123-4567, 555-123-4567 and 123-4567 are all considered valid phone numbers. Once the data is submitted, the web server responds by displaying an appropriate message and an XHTML table repeating the submitted information. Note that a real business application would typically store the submitted data in a database or in a file on the server. We simply send the data back to the form to demonstrate that the server received the data.

Figure 22.22 presents the ASPX file. Like the Web Form in Fig. 22.18, this Web Form uses a table to organize the page's contents. Lines 32–33, 44–45 and 64–65 define TextBoxes for retrieving the user's name, e-mail address and phone number, respectively, and line 83 defines a **Submit** button. Lines 86–88 create a Label named outputLabel that displays the response from the server when the user successfully submits the form. Notice that outputLabel's *Visible* property is initially set to False (line 87), so the Label does not appear in the client's browser when the page loads for the first time.

```
 1   <%-- Fig. 22.22: Validation.aspx --%>
 2   <%-- Form that demonstrates using validators to validate user input. --%>
 3
 4   <%@ Page Language="C#" AutoEventWireup="true"
 5      CodeFile="Validation.aspx.cs" Inherits="Validation" %>
 6
 7   <!DOCTYPE html PUBLIC "-//W3C//DTD XHTML 1.0 Transitional//EN"
 8      "http://www.w3.org/TR/xhtml1/DTD/xhtml1-transitional.dtd">
```

Fig. 22.22 | Validators used in a Web Form that retrieves user contact information. (Part 1 of 4.)

```
 9
10   <html xmlns="http://www.w3.org/1999/xhtml">
11   <head runat="server">
12       <title>Demonstrating Validation Controls</title>
13       <style type="text/css">
14           .style1
15           {
16               width: 125px;
17               vertical-align: top;
18           }
19       </style>
20   </head>
21   <body>
22       <form id="form1" runat="server">
23       <div>
24           <p>
25               Please fill out the following form.<br /><i>All fields are
26               required and must contain valid information.</i>
27           </p>
28           <table style="width: 100%;">
29               <tr>
30                   <td class="style1">Name:</td>
31                   <td>
32                       <asp:TextBox ID="nameTextBox" runat="server">
33                       </asp:TextBox><br />
34                       <asp:RequiredFieldValidator ID="nameExistsValidator"
35                           runat="server" ControlToValidate="nameTextBox"
36                           ErrorMessage="Please enter your name."
37                           Display="Dynamic">
38                       </asp:RequiredFieldValidator>
39                   </td>
40               </tr>
41               <tr>
42                   <td class="style1">E-mail address:</td>
43                   <td>
44                       <asp:TextBox ID="emailTextBox" runat="server">
45                       </asp:TextBox> e.g., user@domain.com<br />
46                       <asp:RequiredFieldValidator ID="emailExistsValidator"
47                           runat="server" ControlToValidate="emailTextBox"
48                           ErrorMessage="Please enter your e-mail address."
49                           Display="Dynamic">
50                       </asp:RequiredFieldValidator>
51                       <asp:RegularExpressionValidator ID="emailFormatValidator"
52                           runat="server" ControlToValidate="emailTextBox"
53                           ErrorMessage=
54                               "Please enter an e-mail address in a valid format."
55                           ValidationExpression=
56                               "\w+([-+.']\w+)*@\w+([-.]\w+)*\.\w+([-.]\w+)*"
57                           Display="Dynamic">
58                       </asp:RegularExpressionValidator>
59                   </td>
60               </tr>
```

Fig. 22.22 | Validators used in a Web Form that retrieves user contact information. (Part 2 of 4.)

```
61              <tr>
62                  <td class="style1">Phone number:</td>
63                  <td>
64                      <asp:TextBox ID="phoneTextBox" runat="server">
65                      </asp:TextBox> e.g., (555) 555-5555<br />
66                      <asp:RequiredFieldValidator ID="phoneExistsValidator"
67                          runat="server" ControlToValidate="phoneTextBox"
68                          ErrorMessage="Please enter your phone number."
69                          Display="Dynamic">
70                      </asp:RequiredFieldValidator>
71                      <asp:RegularExpressionValidator ID="phoneFormatValidator"
72                          runat="server" ControlToValidate="phoneTextBox"
73                          ErrorMessage=
74                              "Please enter a phone number in a valid format."
75                          ValidationExpression=
76                              "(\(\d{3}\) ?)|(\d{3}-))?\d{3}-\d{4}"
77                          Display="Dynamic">
78                      </asp:RegularExpressionValidator>
79                  </td>
80              </tr>
81          </table>
82          <p>
83              <asp:Button ID="submitButton" runat="server" Text="Submit" />
84          </p>
85          <p>
86              <asp:Label ID="outputLabel" runat="server"
87                  Text="Thank you for your submission." Visible="False">
88              </asp:Label>
89          </p>
90      </div>
91      </form>
92  </body>
93  </html>
```

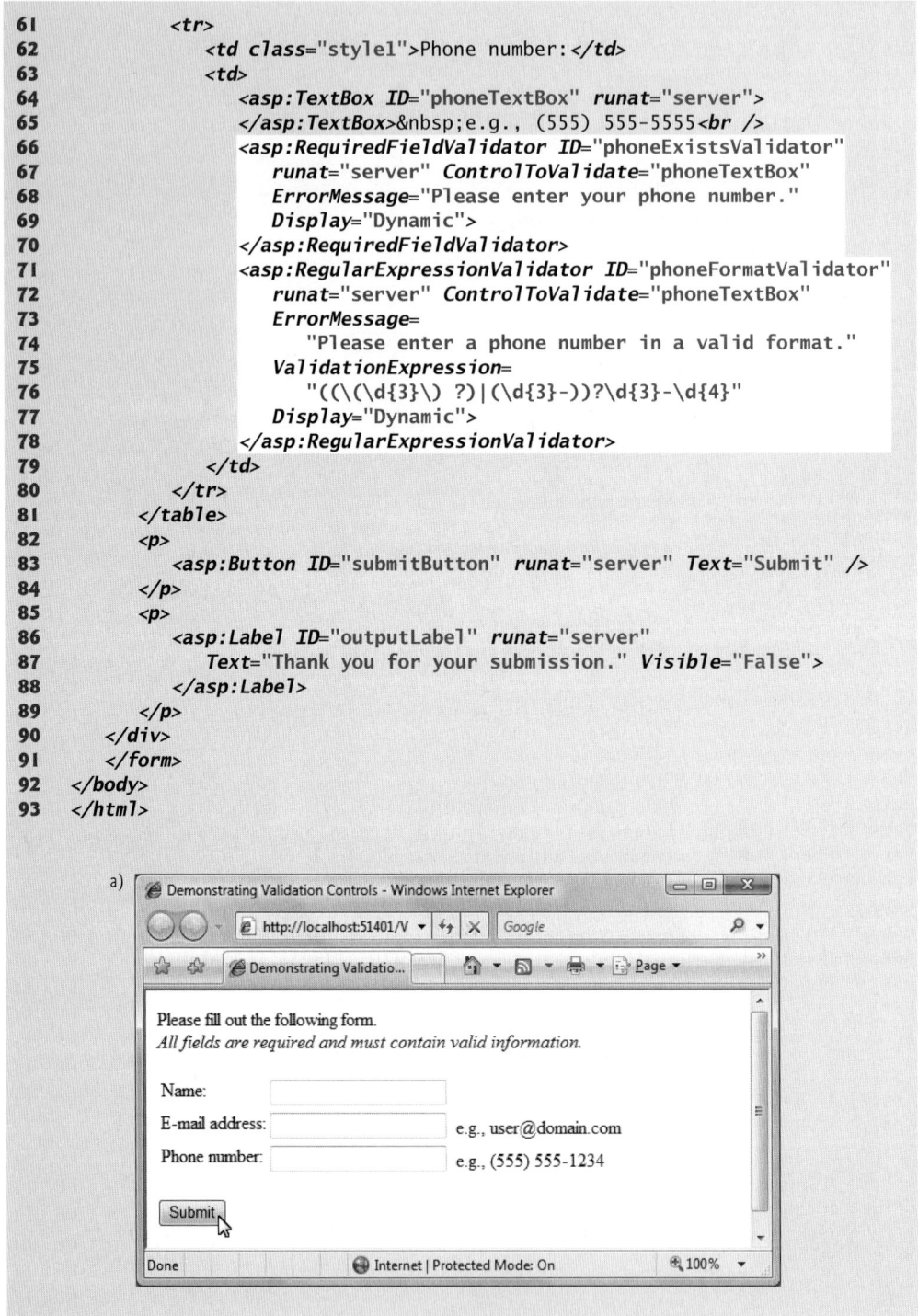

Fig. 22.22 | Validators used in a Web Form that retrieves user contact information. (Part 3 of 4.)

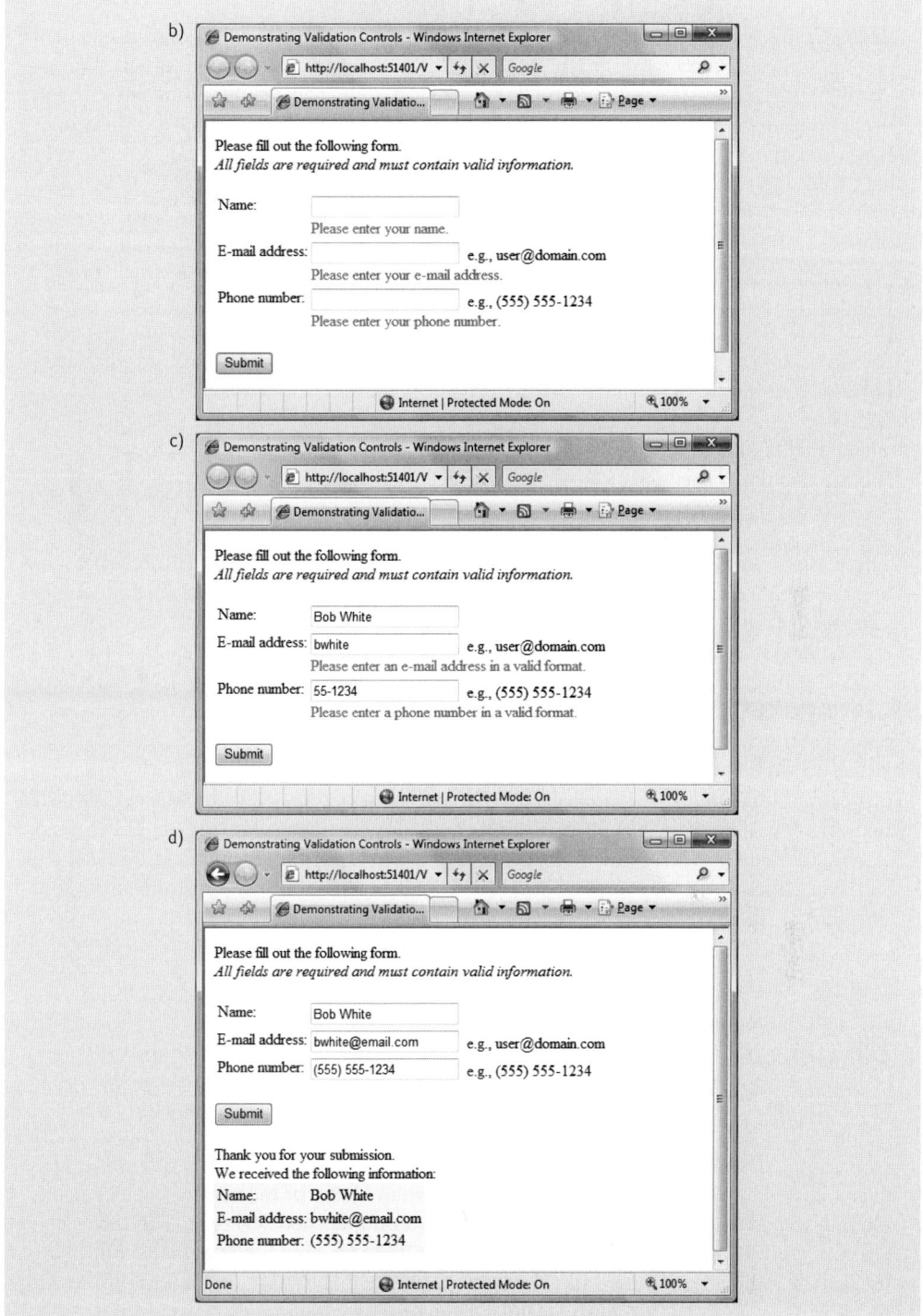

Fig. 22.22 | Validators used in a Web Form that retrieves user contact information. (Part 4 of 4.)

Using *RequiredFieldValidator* Controls

In this example, we use three *RequiredFieldValidator* controls (found in the **Validation** section of the **Toolbox**) to ensure that the name, e-mail address and phone-number Text-Boxes are not empty when the form is submitted. A RequiredFieldValidator makes an input control a required field. If such a field is empty, validation fails. For example, lines 34–38 define RequiredFieldValidator nameExistsValidator, which makes sure that nameTextBox is not empty. Line 35 associates nameTextBox with nameExistsValidator by setting the validator's *ControlToValidate* property to nameTextBox. This indicates that nameExistsValidator verifies the nameTextBox's contents. We set the value of this property (and the validator's other properties) by selecting the validator in **Design** mode and using the **Properties** window to specify property values. Property *ErrorMessage*'s text (line 36) is displayed on the Web Form if the validation fails. If the user does not input any data in nameTextBox and attempts to submit the form, the ErrorMessage text is displayed in red. Because we set the validator's *Display* property to Dynamic (line 37), the validator is displayed on the Web Form only when validation fails. Space is allocated dynamically when validation fails, causing the controls below the validator to shift downward to accommodate the ErrorMessage, as seen in Fig. 22.22(b).

Using *RegularExpressionValidator* Controls

This example also uses *RegularExpressionValidator* controls to match the e-mail address and phone number entered by the user against regular expressions (introduced in Chapter 18). These controls determine whether the e-mail address and phone number were each entered in a valid format. For example, lines 51–58 create a RegularExpressionVal-idator named emailFormatValidator. Line 52 sets property ControlToValidate to emailTextBox to indicate that emailFormatValidator verifies the emailTextBox's contents. Figure 22.22(c) demonstrates their responses when there is an error.

A RegularExpressionValidator's *ValidationExpression* property specifies the regular expression that validates the ControlToValidate's contents. Clicking the ellipsis next to property ValidationExpression in the **Properties** window displays the **Regular Expression Editor** dialog, which contains a list of **Standard expressions** for phone numbers, zip codes and other formatted information. You can also write your own custom expression. For the emailFormatValidator, we selected the standard expression **Internet e-mail address**, which uses the validation expression

```
\w+([-+.']\w+)*@\w+([-.]\w+)*\.\w+([-.]\w+)*
```

This regular expression indicates that an e-mail address is valid if the part of it before the @ symbol contains one or more word characters (i.e., alphanumeric characters or underscores), followed by zero or more strings comprised of a hyphen, plus sign, period or apostrophe and additional word characters. After the @ symbol, a valid e-mail address must contain one or more groups of word characters potentially separated by hyphens or periods, followed by a required period and another group of one or more word characters potentially separated by hyphens or periods. For example, bob.white@email.com, bob-white@my-email.com and bob's-personal.email@white.email.com are all valid. If the user enters an invalid email address in the emailTextBox and either clicks in a different text box or attempts to submit the form, the ErrorMessage text is displayed in red.

We also use `RegularExpressionValidator phoneFormatValidator` (lines 71–78) to ensure that the `phoneTextBox` contains a valid phone number before the form is submitted. In the **Regular Expression Editor** dialog, we select **U.S. phone number**, which assigns

$$((\backslash(\backslash d\{3\}\backslash) \ ?)|(\backslash d\{3\}-))?\backslash d\{3\}-\backslash d\{4\}$$

to the `ValidationExpression` property. This expression indicates that a phone number can contain a three-digit area code either in parentheses and followed by an optional space or without parentheses and followed by a required hyphen. After an optional area code, a phone number must contain three digits, a hyphen and another four digits. For example, (555) 123-4567, 555-123-4567 and 123-4567 are all valid phone numbers.

If all five validators are successful (i.e., each `TextBox` is filled in, and the e-mail address and phone number provided are valid), clicking the **Submit** button sends the form's data to the server. As shown in Fig. 22.22(d), the server then responds by displaying the submitted data in the `outputLabel` (lines 86–88).

Examining the Code-Behind File for a Web Form That Receives User Input

Figure 22.23 depicts the code-behind file for the ASPX file in Fig. 22.22. Notice that, although the form should have been validated on the client, this code-behind file validates the information in the request before processing it. This ensures that the form is validated even if the client has JavaScript disabled.

Web programmers using ASP.NET often design their web pages so that the current page reloads when the user submits the form; this enables the program to receive input, process it as necessary and display the results in the same page when it is loaded the second

```
1   // Fig. 22.23: Validation.aspx.cs
2   // Code-behind file for the form demonstrating validation controls.
3   using System;
4
5   public partial class Validation : System.Web.UI.Page
6   {
7      // Page_Load event handler executes when the page is loaded
8      protected void Page_Load( object sender, EventArgs e )
9      {
10        // if this is not the first time the page is loading
11        // (i.e., the user has already submitted form data)
12        if ( IsPostBack )
13        {
14           Validate(); // validate the form
15
16           // if the form is valid
17           if ( IsValid )
18           {
19              // retrieve the values submitted by the user
20              string name = nameTextBox.Text;
21              string email = emailTextBox.Text;
22              string phone = phoneTextBox.Text;
23
```

Fig. 22.23 | Code-behind file for a Web Form that obtains a user's contact information. (Part 1 of 2.)

```
24                   // create a table indicating the submitted values
25                   outputLabel.Text +=
26                      "<br />We received the following information:" +
27                      "<table style=\"background-color: yellow\">" +
28                      "<tr><td>Name:</td><td>" + name + "</td></tr>" +
29                      "<tr><td>E-mail address:</td><td>" + email +
30                      "</td></tr>" +
31                      "<tr><td>Phone number:</td><td>" + phone + "</td></tr>" +
32                      "</table>";
33
34                   outputLabel.Visible = true; // display the output message
35               } // end if
36           } // end if
37       } // end method Page_Load
38   } // end class Validation
```

Fig. 22.23 | Code-behind file for a Web Form that obtains a user's contact information. (Part 2 of 2.)

time. These pages usually contain a form that, when submitted, sends the values of all the controls to the server and causes the current page to be requested again. This event is known as a *postback*. Line 12 uses the *IsPostBack* property of class Page to determine whether the page is being loaded due to a postback. The first time that the web page is requested, IsPostBack is false, and the page displays only the form for user input. When the postback occurs (from the user clicking **Submit**), IsPostBack is true.

Server-side Web Form validation must be implemented programmatically. Line 14 calls the current Page's *Validate* method to validate the information in the request. This validates the information as specified by the validation controls in the Web Form. Line 17 uses the *IsValid* property of class Page to check whether all the validators succeeded. If this property is set to true (i.e., validation succeeded and the Web Form is valid), then we display the Web Form's information. Otherwise, the web page loads without any changes, except any validator that failed now displays its ErrorMessage. Note that you should always call method Validate before using property IsValid.

Lines 20–22 retrieve the values of nameTextBox, emailTextBox and phoneTextBox. When data is posted to the web server, the XHTML form's data becomes accessible to the web application through the properties of the various web controls. Lines 25–32 append to outputLabel's Text a line break, an additional message and an XHTML table containing the submitted data so the user knows that the server received the data correctly. In a real business application, the data would be stored in a database or file at this point in the application. Line 34 sets the outputLabel's Visible property to true, so that the user can see the thank-you message and submitted data.

Examining the Client-Side XHTML for a Web Form with Validation
If a validation control's *EnableClientScript* property is True (which it is by default), then the validator performs client-side validation as the user edits the Web Form. If you wish, you can view the XHTML and JavaScript sent to the client browser when Validation.aspx loads after the postback by selecting **Page > View Source** in Internet Explorer or **View > Page Source** in Firefox (other browsers have similar capabilities). As you look

through the code, you'll see several <script></script> elements which define the client-side JavaScript code that performs the validation. You do not need to be able to create or even understand this code—the functionality defined for the controls in our application is converted to working JavaScript by ASP.NET.

The EnableViewState attribute determines whether a web control's current state is remembered each time a postback occurs. The default value, True, indicates that the control's state at the last postback is retained. A hidden input in the XHTML generated for the page contains this information. This element is always named __*VIEWSTATE* and stores the controls' data as an encoded string. This data allows the server to determine whether anything about the control, such as its value, has changed since the last postback. For example, to determine whether a TextBox's TextChanged event should be raised on a postback, the server compares the control's current text to that specified by the __VIEWSTATE. If there's a difference, then the text has changed and the TextChanged event is raised.

Performance Tip 22.1

Setting EnableViewState *to* False *reduces the amount of data passed to the web server with each request.*

22.6 Session Tracking

Originally, critics accused the Internet and e-business of failing to provide the customized service typically experienced in "brick-and-mortar" stores. To address this problem, e-businesses began to establish mechanisms by which they could personalize users' browsing experiences, tailoring content to individual users while enabling them to bypass irrelevant information. Businesses achieve this level of service by tracking each customer's movement through the Internet and combining the collected data with information provided by the consumer, including billing information, personal preferences, interests and hobbies.

Personalization
Personalization makes it possible for e-businesses to communicate effectively with their customers and also improves users' ability to locate desired products and services. Companies that provide content of particular interest to users can establish relationships with customers and build on those relationships over time. Furthermore, by targeting consumers with personal offers, recommendations, advertisements, promotions and services, e-businesses create customer loyalty. Websites can use sophisticated technology to allow visitors to customize home pages to suit their individual needs and preferences. Similarly, online shopping sites often store personal information for customers, tailoring notifications and special offers to their interests. Such services encourage customers to visit sites more frequently and make purchases more regularly.

Privacy
A trade-off exists, however, between personalized e-business service and protection of privacy. Some consumers embrace the idea of tailored content, but others fear the possible adverse consequences if the info they provide to e-businesses is released or collected by tracking technologies. Consumers and privacy advocates ask: What if the e-business to which we give personal data sells or gives it to another organization without our knowledge? What if we do not want our actions on the Internet—a supposedly anonymous me-

dium—to be tracked and recorded by unknown parties? What if unauthorized parties gain access to sensitive private data, such as credit-card numbers or medical history? All of these are questions that must be debated and addressed by programmers, consumers, e-businesses and lawmakers alike.

Recognizing Clients

To provide personalized services to consumers, e-businesses must be able to recognize clients when they request information from a site. As we have discussed, the request/response system on which the web operates is facilitated by HTTP. Unfortunately, HTTP is a stateless protocol—it does not support persistent connections that would enable web servers to maintain state information regarding particular clients. This means that web servers cannot determine whether a request comes from a particular client or whether the same or different clients generate a series of requests. To circumvent this problem, sites can provide mechanisms by which they identify individual clients. A session represents a unique client on a website. If the client leaves a site and then returns later, the client will still be recognized as the same user. When the user closes the browser, the session ends. To help the server distinguish among clients, each client must identify itself to the server. Tracking individual clients, known as *session tracking*, can be achieved in a number of ways. One popular technique uses cookies (Section 22.6.1); another uses ASP.NET's HttpSession-State object (Section 22.6.2). Additional session-tracking techniques include the use of input form elements of type "hidden" and URL rewriting. Using "hidden" form elements, a Web Form can write session-tracking data into a form in the web page that it returns to the client in response to a prior request. When the user submits the form in the new web page, all the form data, including the "hidden" fields, is sent to the form handler on the web server. When a website performs URL rewriting, the Web Form embeds session-tracking information directly in the URLs of hyperlinks that the user clicks to send subsequent requests to the web server.

22.6.1 Cookies

Cookies provide web developers with a tool for personalizing web pages. A cookie is a piece of data stored in a small text file on the user's computer. A cookie maintains information about the client during and between browser sessions. The first time a user visits the website, the user's computer might receive a cookie; this cookie is then reactivated each time the user revisits that site. The collected information is intended to be an anonymous record containing data that is used to personalize the user's future visits to the site. For example, cookies can store a user's preferences for a site's appearance. When a user adds items to an online shopping cart or performs another task resulting in a request to the web server, the server receives a cookie containing the user's unique identifier. The server then uses the unique identifier to locate the shopping cart and perform any necessary processing.

In addition to identifying users, cookies also can indicate users' shopping preferences. When a Web Form receives a request from a client, the Web Form can examine the cookie(s) it sent to the client during previous communications, identify the users's preferences and immediately display products of interest to the client.

Every HTTP-based interaction between a client and a server includes a header containing information either about the request (when the communication is from the client to the server) or about the response (when the communication is from the server to the client). When a Web Form receives a request, the header includes information such as the request type (e.g., GET) and any cookies that have been sent previously from the server to be stored on the client machine. When the server formulates its response, the header information contains any cookies the server wants to store on the client computer and other information, such as the MIME type of the response.

The *expiration date* of a cookie determines how long the cookie remains on the client's computer. If you do not set an expiration date for a cookie, the web browser maintains the cookie for the duration of the browsing session. Otherwise, the web browser maintains the cookie until the expiration date occurs. When the browser requests a resource from a web server, cookies previously sent to the client by that web server are returned to the web server as part of the request formulated by the browser. Cookies are deleted when they *expire*.

Portability Tip 22.3

Users may disable cookies in their web browsers to help ensure their privacy. Such users will experience difficulty using web applications that depend on cookies to maintain state information.

Using Cookies to Provide Book Recommendations

The next web application demonstrates the use of cookies. The example contains two pages. In the first page (Figs. 22.24–22.25), users select a favorite programming language from a group of radio buttons and submit the XHTML form to the web server for processing. The web server responds by creating a cookie that stores a record of the chosen language, as well as the ISBN for a book on that topic. The server then returns an XHTML document to the browser, allowing the user either to select another favorite programming language or to view the second page in our application (Figs. 22.26 and 22.27), which lists recommended books pertaining to the programming language that the user selected previously. When the user clicks the **Click here to get book recommendations** hyperlink, the cookies previously stored on the client are read and used to form the list of book recommendations.

The ASPX file in Fig. 22.24 contains five radio buttons (lines 20–26) with the values **Visual Basic 2008**, **Visual C# 2008**, **C**, **C++**, and **Java**. Recall that you can set the values of radio buttons via the **ListItem Collection Editor**, which you open either by clicking the RadioButtonList's Items property in the **Properties** window or by clicking the **Edit Items...** link in the **RadioButtonList Tasks** smart-tag menu. The user selects a programming language by clicking one of the radio buttons. When the user clicks **Submit**, we'll create a cookie containing the selected language. Then we'll add this cookie to the HTTP response

```
1    <%-- Fig. 22.24: Options.aspx --%>
2    <%-- Allows client to select programming languages and access book --%>
3    <%-- recommendations. --%>
4    <%@ Page Language="C#" AutoEventWireup="true"
5       CodeFile="Options.aspx.cs" Inherits="Options" %>
6
7    <!DOCTYPE html PUBLIC "-//W3C//DTD XHTML 1.0 Transitional//EN"
8       "http://www.w3.org/TR/xhtml1/DTD/xhtml1-transitional.dtd">
9
```

Fig. 22.24 | ASPX file that presents a list of programming languages. (Part 1 of 3.)

```
10   <html xmlns="http://www.w3.org/1999/xhtml">
11   <head runat="server">
12      <title>Cookies</title>
13   </head>
14   <body>
15      <form id="form1" runat="server">
16      <div>
17         <asp:Label ID="promptLabel" runat="server" Font-Bold="True"
18            Font-Size="Large" Text="Select a programming language:">
19         </asp:Label>
20         <asp:RadioButtonList ID="languageList" runat="server">
21            <asp:ListItem>Visual Basic 2008</asp:ListItem>
22            <asp:ListItem>Visual C# 2008</asp:ListItem>
23            <asp:ListItem>C</asp:ListItem>
24            <asp:ListItem>C++</asp:ListItem>
25            <asp:ListItem>Java</asp:ListItem>
26         </asp:RadioButtonList>
27         <asp:Button ID="submitButton" runat="server" Text="Submit"
28            onclick="submitButton_Click" />
29      </div>
30      <div>
31         <asp:Label ID="responseLabel" runat="server" Font-Bold="True"
32            Font-Size="Large" Text="Welcome to cookies!" Visible="False">
33         </asp:Label>
34         <br /><br />
35         <asp:HyperLink ID="languageLink" runat="server"
36            NavigateUrl="~/Options.aspx" Visible="False">
37            Click here to choose another language.
38         </asp:HyperLink>
39         <br /><br />
40         <asp:HyperLink ID="recommendationsLink" runat="server"
41            NavigateUrl="~/Recommendations.aspx" Visible="False">
42            Click here to get book recommendations.
43         </asp:HyperLink>
44      </div>
45      </form>
46   </body>
47   </html>
```

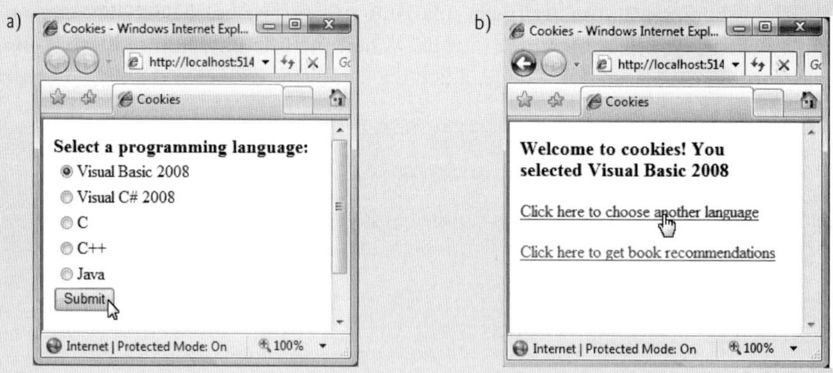

Fig. 22.24 | ASPX file that presents a list of programming languages. (Part 2 of 3.)

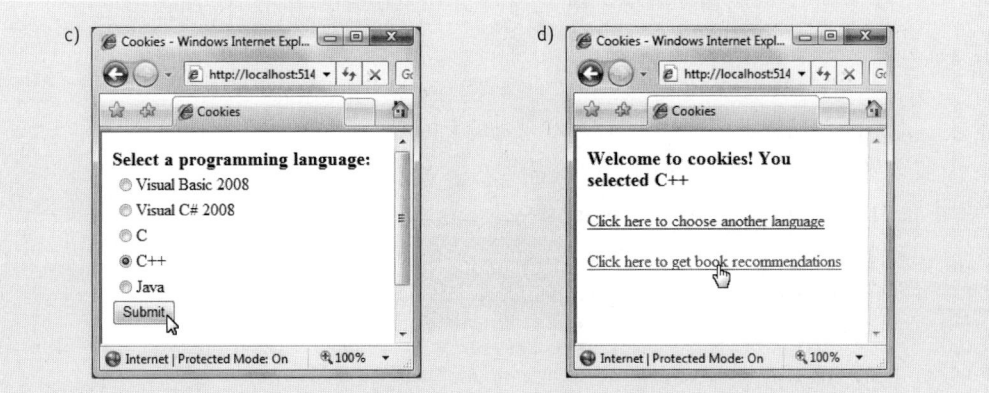

Fig. 22.24 | ASPX file that presents a list of programming languages. (Part 3 of 3.)

header, so the cookie will be stored on the user's computer. Each time the user chooses a language and clicks **Submit**, a cookie is written to the client. Each time the client requests information from our web application, the cookies are sent back to the server.

When the postback occurs, certain controls are hidden and others are displayed. The Label, RadioButtonList and Button used to select a language are hidden. Toward the bottom of the page, a Label and two HyperLinks are displayed. One link requests this page (lines 35–38), and the other requests Recommendations.aspx (lines 40–43). Clicking the first hyperlink (the one that requests the current page) does not cause a postback to occur. The file Options.aspx is specified in the NavigateUrl property of the hyperlink. When the hyperlink is clicked, a new request for this page occurs. Recall that earlier in the chapter, we set NavigateUrl to a remote website (http://www.deitel.com). To set this property to a page within the same ASP.NET application, click the ellipsis button next to the NavigateUrl property in the **Properties** window to open the **Select URL** dialog. Use this dialog to select a page within your project as the destination for the HyperLink.

Adding and Linking to a New Web Form

Setting the NavigateUrl property to a page in the current application requires that the destination page exist already. Thus, to set the NavigateUrl property of the second link (the one that requests the page with book recommendations) to Recommendations.aspx, you must first create this file by right clicking the project location in the **Solution Explorer** and selecting **Add New Item...** from the menu that appears. In the **Add New Item** dialog, select **Web Form** from the **Templates** pane and change the name of the file to Recommendations.aspx. Finally, check the box labeled **Place code in separate file** to indicate that the IDE should create a code-behind file for this ASPX file. Click **Add** to create the file. (We discuss the contents of this ASPX file and code-behind file shortly.) Once the Recommendations.aspx file exists, you can select it as the NavigateUrl value for a HyperLink in the **Select URL** dialog.

Writing Cookies in a Code-Behind File

Figure 22.25 presents the code-behind file for Options.aspx (Fig. 22.24). This code writes a cookie to the client machine when the user selects a programming language. The code-behind file also modifies the appearance of the page in response to a postback.

```csharp
1   // Fig. 22.25: Options.aspx.cs
2   // Processes user's selection of a programming language by displaying
3   // links and writing a cookie to the user's machine.
4   using System;
5   using System.Web;
6   using System.Collections.Generic;
7
8   public partial class Options : System.Web.UI.Page
9   {
10     // stores values to represent books as cookies
11     private Dictionary< string, string > books =
12       new Dictionary< string, string >();
13
14     // initializes the Dictionary when the Page initializes
15     protected void Page_Init( object sender, EventArgs e )
16     {
17       books.Add( "Visual Basic 2008", "0-13-606305-X" );
18       books.Add( "Visual C# 2008", "0-13-605322-X" );
19       books.Add( "C", "0-13-240416-8" );
20       books.Add( "C++", "0-13-615250-3" );
21       books.Add( "Java", "0-13-222220-5" );
22     } // end method Page_Init
23
24     // hide and display links to make additional selections or view
25     // recommendations, and write a cookie to record the user's selection
26     // when the form is submitted
27     protected void submitButton_Click ( object sender, EventArgs e )
28     {
29       // display appropriate message and hyperlinks
30       responseLabel.Visible = true;
31       languageLink.Visible = true;
32       recommendationsLink.Visible = true;
33
34       // hide controls for selecting a language
35       promptLabel.Visible = false;
36       languageList.Visible = false;
37       submitButton.Visible = false;
38
39       // if the user made a selection
40       if ( languageList.SelectedItem != null )
41       {
42         // get value of user's selection
43         string language = languageList.SelectedItem.Value;
44
45         string ISBN = books[ language ]; // get ISBN for given language
46
47         // create cookie using language-ISBN name-value pair
48         HttpCookie cookie = new HttpCookie( language, ISBN );
49
50         // add cookie to response to place it on the user's machine
51         Response.Cookies.Add( cookie );
52
```

Fig. 22.25 | Code-behind file that writes a cookie to the client. (Part 1 of 2.)

```
53              // display user's selection in responseLabel
54              responseLabel.Text += " You selected " + language + ".";
55         } // end if
56         else
57         {
58              // inform user that no selection was made
59              responseLabel.Text += " You didn't make a selection.";
60         } // end else
61      } // end method submitButton_Click
62   } // end class Options
```

Fig. 22.25 | Code-behind file that writes a cookie to the client. (Part 2 of 2.)

Lines 11–12 creates variable books as a *Dictionary*—a data structure that stores *key/value pairs*. A program uses the key to store and retrieve the associated value in the Dictionary. In this example, the keys are strings containing the programming languages' names, and the values are strings containing the ISBN numbers for the recommended books. For adding new entries, class Dictionary provides method *Add*, which takes a key and a value as arguments. A value that is added via method Add is placed in the Dictionary at a location determined by the key. In the Page_Init event handler (lines 15–22), five language/ISBN name/value pairs are added to Dictionary books. The value for a specific Dictionary entry can be determined by indexing the Dictionary with that value's key. The expression

> *dictionaryName*[*keyName*]

returns the value in the key/value pair in which *keyName* is the key. For example, the expression books[language] in line 45 returns the value that corresponds to the key contained in language. We discuss the Dictionary class in further detail in Chapter 27, Collections.

Clicking the **Submit** button creates a cookie if a language is selected and causes a postback to occur. In the ASPX file, we specify the event handler for **Submit** button's Click event by setting attribute onclick. The markup onclick="submitButton_Click" in the submitButton element's start tag indicates that method submitButton_Click handles its Click event (line 28 of Fig. 22.24). Setting the attribute on*EventName* for an element specifies the method that handles the associated event. For example, if AutoEventWireup was false in this example, we would have had to include oninit="Page_Init" in the Page directive to specify that method Page_Init handles the Page's Init event. [Note: Recall that ASPX markup is not case sensitive. Thus, either oninit or onInit would specify the event handler for the Init event.]

The submitButton_Click event handler (lines 27–61 of Fig. 22.25) hides the controls used to obtain the user's language selection and reveals the initially hidden controls responseLabel, languageLink, and recommendationsLink. Line 40 determines whether the user selected a language. If so, a new cookie object (of type *HttpCookie*) is created to store the language and its corresponding ISBN number (line 48). This cookie is then Added to the *Cookies* collection sent as part of the HTTP response header (line 51). The selected language is displayed in responseLabel (line 54). If no language was selected, text indicating that a selection was not made is displayed in responseLabel (line 59).

Displaying Book Recommendations Based on Cookie Values

After the postback of `Options.aspx`, the user may request a recommendation of books. The book-recommendations hyperlink forwards the user to `Recommendations.aspx` (Fig. 22.26), which displays recommendations based on the user's language selections.

```
1   <%-- Fig. 22.26: Recommendations.aspx --%>
2   <%-- Displays book recommendations using cookies. --%>
3   <%@ Page Language="C#" AutoEventWireup="true"
4      CodeFile="Recommendations.aspx.cs" Inherits="Recommendations" %>
5
6   <!DOCTYPE html PUBLIC "-//W3C//DTD XHTML 1.0 Transitional//EN"
7      "http://www.w3.org/TR/xhtml1/DTD/xhtml1-transitional.dtd">
8
9   <html xmlns="http://www.w3.org/1999/xhtml">
10  <head runat="server">
11     <title>Book Recommendations</title>
12  </head>
13  <body>
14     <form id="form1" runat="server">
15     <div>
16        <asp:Label ID="recommendationsLabel" runat="server"
17           Font-Bold="True" Font-Size="X-Large" Text="Recommendations">
18        </asp:Label>
19        <br /><br />
20        <asp:ListBox ID="booksListBox" runat="server" Height="125px"
21           Width="450px">
22        </asp:ListBox>
23        <br /><br />
24        <asp:HyperLink ID="languageLink" runat="server"
25           NavigateUrl="~/Options.aspx">
26           Click here to choose another language.
27        </asp:HyperLink>
28     </div>
29     </form>
30  </body>
31  </html>
```

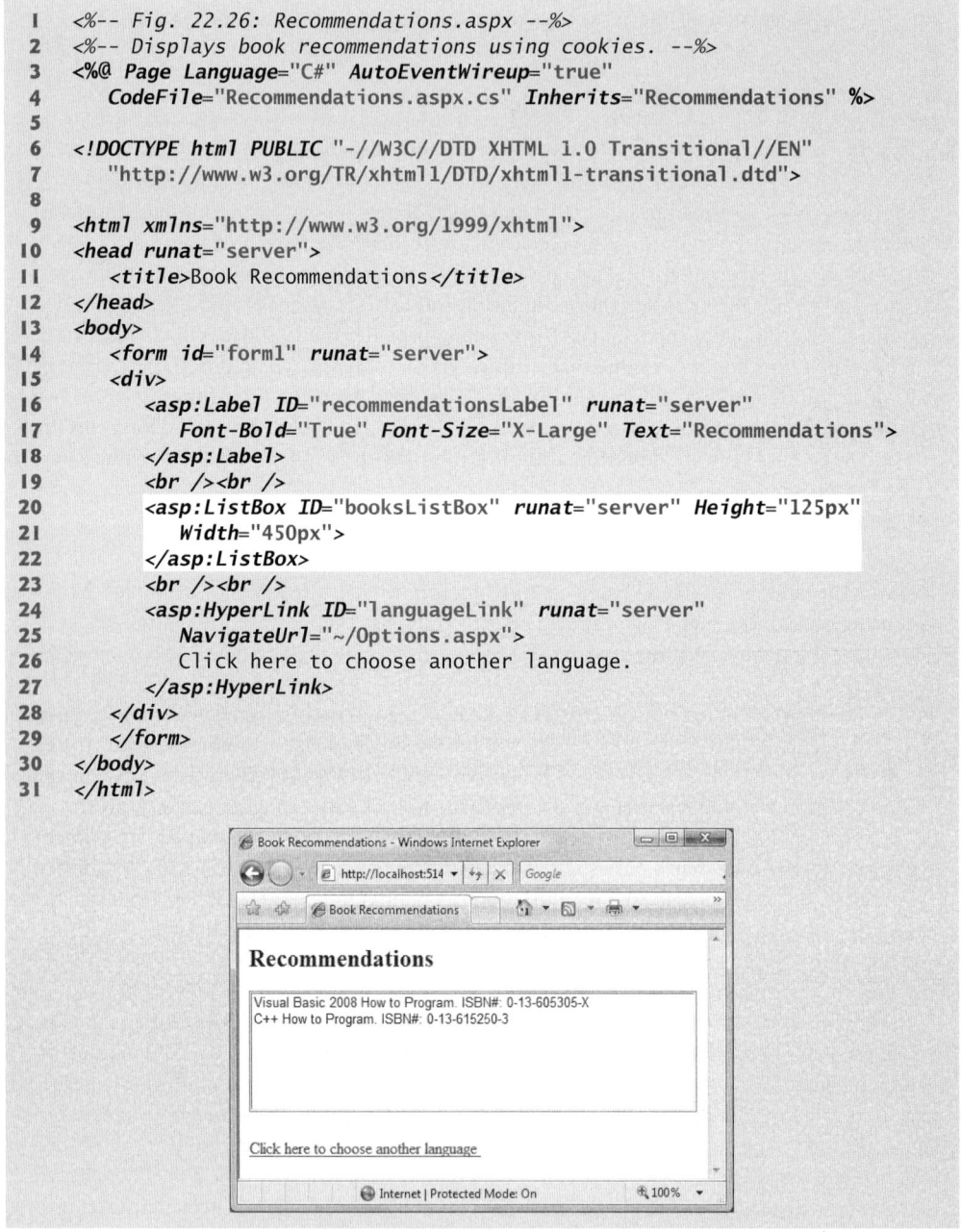

Fig. 22.26 | ASPX file that displays book recommendations based on cookies.

Recommendations.aspx contains a Label (lines 16–18), a ListBox (lines 20–22) and a HyperLink (lines 24–27). The Label displays the text **Recommendations** if the user selects one or more languages; otherwise, it displays **No Recommendations**. The ListBox displays the recommendations specified by the code-behind file (Fig. 22.27). The Hyper-Link allows the user to return to Options.aspx to select additional languages.

Code-Behind File That Creates Book Recommendations From Cookies

In Fig. 22.27, method Page_Init (lines 9–31) retrieves the cookies from the client, using the Request object's *Cookies* property (line 12). This returns a collection of type *Http-CookieCollection*, containing cookies that were previously written to the client. Cookies can be read by an application only if they were created in the domain in which the application is running—a web server can never access cookies created outside its domain. For example, a cookie created by the deitel.com web server cannot be read by a web server in any other domain. [*Note:* Depending on the settings in web.config and whether other pages store cookies, other cookie values may be displayed by this web application.]

```
1   // Fig. 22.27: Recommendations.aspx.cs
2   // Creates book recommendations based on cookies.
3   using System;
4   using System.f;
5
6   public partial class Recommendations : System.Web.UI.Page
7   {
8      // read cookies and populate ListBox with any book recommendations
9      protected void Page_Init(object sender, EventArgs e)
10     {
11        // retrieve client's cookies
12        HttpCookieCollection cookies = Request.Cookies;
13
14        // if there are cookies, list the appropriate books and ISBNs
15        if ( cookies.Count > 0 )
16        {
17           for ( int i = 0; i < cookies.Count; i++ )
18              booksListBox.Items.Add( cookies[ i ].Name +
19                 " How to Program. ISBN: " + cookies[ i ].Value );
20        } // end if
21        else
22        {
23           // if there are no cookies, then no language was chosen, so
24           // display appropriate message and clear and hide booksListBox
25           recommendationsLabel.Text = "No Recommendations";
26           booksListBox.Visible = false;
27
28           // modify languageLink because no language was selected
29           languageLink.Text = "Click here to choose a language.";
30        } // end else
31     } // end method Page_Init
32  } // end class Recommendations
```

Fig. 22.27 | Reading cookies from a client to determine book recommendations.

Line 15 determines whether at least one cookie exists. Lines 17–19 add the information in the cookie(s) to the booksListBox. The for statement retrieves the name and value of each cookie using i, the loop's control variable, to determine the current value in the cookie collection. The *Name* and *Value* properties of class HttpCookie, which contain the language and corresponding ISBN, respectively, are concatenated with " How to Program. ISBN: " and added to the ListBox. Lines 25–29 execute if no language was selected. We summarize some commonly used HttpCookie properties in Fig. 22.28.

Properties	Description
Domain	Returns a string containing the cookie's domain (i.e., the domain of the web server running the application that wrote the cookie). This determines which web servers can receive the cookie. By default, cookies are sent to the web server that originally sent the cookie. Changing the Domain property causes the cookie to be returned to a web server other than the one that originally wrote it.
Expires	Returns a DateTime object indicating when the browser can delete the cookie. You can delete a cookie by setting this property to be a DateTime in the past.
Name	Returns a string containing the cookie's name.
Path	Returns a string containing the path to a directory on the server (i.e., the Domain) to which the cookie applies. Cookies can be "targeted" to specific directories on the web server. By default, a cookie is returned only to applications operating in the same directory as the application that sent the cookie or a subdirectory of that directory. Changing the Path property causes the cookie to be returned to a directory other than the one from which it was originally written.
Secure	Returns a bool value indicating whether the cookie should be transmitted through a secure protocol. The value true causes a secure protocol to be used.
Value	Returns a string containing the cookie's value.

Fig. 22.28 | HttpCookie properties.

22.6.2 Session Tracking with HttpSessionState

Session-tracking capabilities are provided by the .NET class *HttpSessionState*. To demonstrate basic session-tracking techniques, we modified the example of Figs. 22.24–22.27 to use HttpSessionState objects. Figures 22.29–22.30 present the ASPX file and code-behind file for Options.aspx. Figures 22.32–22.33 present the ASPX file and code-behind file for Recommendations.aspx. Options.aspx is similar to the version presented in Fig. 22.24, but Fig. 22.29 contains two additional Labels (lines 35 and 37–38), which we discuss shortly.

In the WebTime example, we set the Web Form's EnableSessionState property to false. We could have also used this setting in our other examples, since we didn't need to use session tracking in any of them. However, because we wish to use session tracking in the following example, we *must* keep this property's default setting—True.

Every Web Form includes an HttpSessionState object, which is accessible through property *Session* of class Page. Throughout this section, we use property Session to manipulate our page's HttpSessionState object. When the web page is requested, an

```
 I   <%-- Fig. 22.29: Options.aspx --%>
 2   <%-- Allows client to select programming languages and access book --%>
 3   <%-- recommendations. --%>
 4   <%@ Page Language="C#" AutoEventWireup="true"
 5      CodeFile="Options.aspx.cs" Inherits="Options" %>
 6
 7   <!DOCTYPE html PUBLIC "-//W3C//DTD XHTML 1.0 Transitional//EN"
 8      "http://www.w3.org/TR/xhtml1/DTD/xhtml1-transitional.dtd">
 9
10   <html xmlns="http://www.w3.org/1999/xhtml">
11   <head runat="server">
12      <title>Sessions</title>
13   </head>
14   <body>
15      <form id="form1" runat="server">
16      <div>
17         <asp:Label ID="promptLabel" runat="server" Font-Bold="True"
18            Font-Size="Large" Text="Select a programming language:">
19         </asp:Label>
20         <asp:RadioButtonList ID="languageList" runat="server">
21            <asp:ListItem>Visual Basic 2008</asp:ListItem>
22            <asp:ListItem>Visual C# 2008</asp:ListItem>
23            <asp:ListItem>C</asp:ListItem>
24            <asp:ListItem>C++</asp:ListItem>
25            <asp:ListItem>Java</asp:ListItem>
26         </asp:RadioButtonList>
27         <asp:Button ID="submitButton" runat="server" Text="Submit"
28            onclick="submitButton_Click" />
29      </div>
30      <div>
31         <asp:Label ID="responseLabel" runat="server" Font-Bold="True"
32            Font-Size="Large" Text="Welcome to cookies!" Visible="False">
33         </asp:Label>
34         <br /><br />
35         <asp:Label ID="idLabel" runat="server" Visible="False"></asp:Label>
36         <br /><br />
37         <asp:Label ID="timeoutLabel" runat="server" Visible="False">
38         </asp:Label>
39         <br /><br />
40         <asp:HyperLink ID="languageLink" runat="server"
41            NavigateUrl="~/Options.aspx" Visible="False">
42            Click here to choose another language.
43         </asp:HyperLink>
44         <br /><br />
45         <asp:HyperLink ID="recommendationsLink" runat="server"
46            NavigateUrl="~/Recommendations.aspx" Visible="False">
47            Click here to get book recommendations.
48         </asp:HyperLink>
49      </div>
50      </form>
51   </body>
52   </html>
```

Fig. 22.29 | ASPX file that presents a list of programming languages. (Part 1 of 2.)

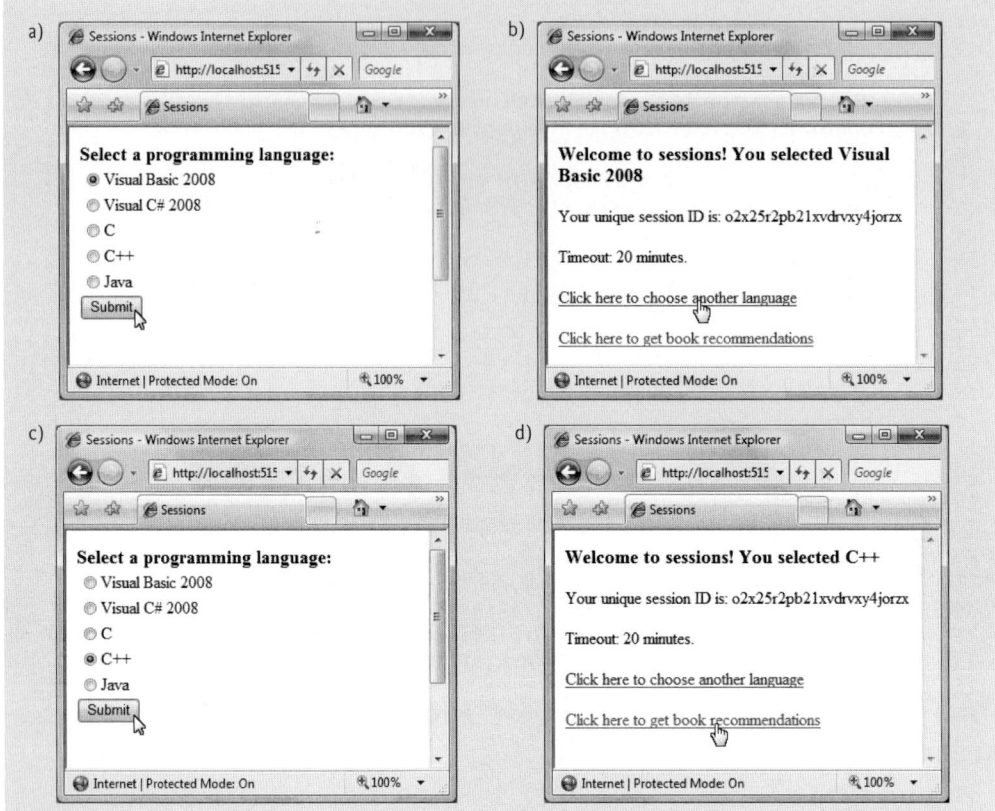

Fig. 22.29 | ASPX file that presents a list of programming languages. (Part 2 of 2.)

HttpSessionState object is created and assigned to the Page's Session property. As a result, we often refer to property Session as the Session object. Note that a distinct HttpSessionState resides on the server, whereas a cookie is stored on the user's client. Thus, using sessions is the more secure method of session tracking.

Adding Session Items
When the user presses **Submit** on the Web Form, submitButton_Click is invoked in the code-behind file (Fig. 22.30). Method submitButton_Click responds by causing a postback and adding a key/value pair to our Session object, specifying the language chosen and the ISBN for a book on that language. These key/value pairs are often referred to as *session items*. Each time the user clicks **Submit**, submitButton_Click adds a new session item to the HttpSessionState object. Because much of this example is identical to the last example, we concentrate on the new features.

> ### Software Engineering Observation 22.2
> *A Web Form should not use instance variables to maintain client state information, because each new request or postback is handled by a new instance of the page. Instead, maintain client state information in HttpSessionState objects, because such objects are specific to each client.*

Like a cookie, an HttpSessionState object can store name/value pairs. These session items are placed in an HttpSessionState object by calling method ***Add***. Line 48 calls Add to place the language and its corresponding recommended book's ISBN in the HttpSessionState object. If the application calls method Add to add an attribute that has the same name as an attribute previously stored in a session, the object associated with that attribute is replaced. Another common syntax for placing a session item in the HttpSessionState object is Session[*name*] = *value*. For example, we could have replaced line 48 with Session[language] = ISBN.

Software Engineering Observation 22.3

A benefit of using HttpSessionState objects (rather than cookies) is that they can store any type of object (not just strings) as attribute values. This provides you with increased flexibility in determining the type of state information to maintain for clients.

```
 1   // Fig. 22.30: Options.aspx.cs
 2   // Processes user's selection of a programming language by displaying
 3   // links and writing information in a Session object.
 4   using System;
 5   using System.Collections.Generic;
 6
 7   public partial class Options : System.Web.UI.Page
 8   {
 9      // stores values to represent books
10      private Dictionary< string, string > books =
11         new Dictionary< string, string >();
12
13      // initializes the Dictionary when the Page initializes
14      protected void Page_Init( object sender, EventArgs e )
15      {
16         books.Add( "Visual Basic 2008", "0-13-606305-X" );
17         books.Add( "Visual C# 2008", "0-13-605322-X" );
18         books.Add( "C", "0-13-240416-8" );
19         books.Add( "C++", "0-13-615250-3" );
20         books.Add( "Java", "0-13-222220-5" );
21      } // end method Page_Init
22
23      // hide and display links to make additional selections or view
24      // recommendations, and record the user's selection in the Session
25      // when the form is submitted
26      protected void submitButton_Click ( object sender, EventArgs e )
27      {
28         // display appropriate message and hyperlinks
29         responseLabel.Visible = true;
30         idLabel.Visible = true;
31         timeoutLabel.Visible = true;
32         languageLink.Visible = true;
33         recommendationsLink.Visible = true;
34
```

Fig. 22.30 | Creates a session item for each programming language selected by the user on the ASPX page. (Part I of 2.)

```
35          // hide controls for selecting a language
36          promptLabel.Visible = false;
37          languageList.Visible = false;
38          submitButton.Visible = false;
39
40          // if the user made a selection
41          if ( languageList.SelectedItem != null )
42          {
43              // get value of user's selection
44              string language = languageList.SelectedItem.Value;
45
46              string ISBN = books[ language ]; // get ISBN for given language
47
48              Session.Add( language, ISBN ); // add name/value pair to Session
49
50              // display user's selection in responseLabel
51              responseLabel.Text += " You selected " + language + ".";
52          } // end if
53          else
54          {
55              // inform user that no selection was made
56              responseLabel.Text += " You didn't make a selection.";
57          } // end else
58
59          idLabel.Text = "Your unique session ID is: " + Session.SessionID +
60              "."; // display session ID
61
62          // display amount of time before session times out
63          timeoutLabel.Text = "Timeout: " + Session.Timeout + " minutes.";
64      } // end method submitButton_Click
65  } // end class Options
```

Fig. 22.30 | Creates a session item for each programming language selected by the user on the ASPX page. (Part 2 of 2.)

The submitButton_Click event handler also retrieves information about the current client's session from the Session object's properties and displays this information in the web page. The ASP.NET application contains information about the HttpSessionState object for the current client. Property **SessionID** (line 59) contains the *unique session ID*—a sequence of random letters and numbers. The first time a client connects to the web server, a unique session ID is created for that client and a temporary cookie is written to the client so the server can identify the client on subsequent requests. An HttpSession-State can also be configured to run in cookie-less mode, in which case the unique session ID is embedded in the URL in the browser's address bar. When the client makes additional requests, the client's session ID from that temporary cookie is compared with the session IDs stored in the web server's memory to retrieve the client's HttpSessionState object. Property **Timeout** (line 63) specifies the maximum amount of time that an Http-SessionState object can be inactive before it is discarded. By default, a session times out after twenty minutes. Figure 22.31 lists some common HttpSessionState properties. For more information on class HttpSessionState, please visit msdn.microsoft.com/en-us/library/system.web.sessionstate.httpsessionstate.apsx.

Properties	Description
Count	Specifies the number of key/value pairs in the Session object.
IsNewSession	Indicates whether this is a new session (i.e., whether the session was created during loading of this page).
IsReadOnly	Indicates whether the Session object is read-only.
Keys	Returns a collection containing the Session object's keys.
SessionID	Returns the session's unique ID.
Timeout	Specifies the maximum number of minutes during which a session can be inactive (i.e., no requests are made) before the session expires. By default, this property is set to 20 minutes.

Fig. 22.31 | HttpSessionState properties.

Displaying Recommendations Based on Session Values

As in the cookies example, this application provides a link to Recommendations.aspx (Fig. 22.32), which displays a list of book recommendations based on the user's language selections. Lines 20–22 define a ListBox web control that is used to present the recommendations to the user.

```
1   <%-- Fig. 22.32: Recommendations.aspx --%>
2   <%-- Displays book recommendations using a Session object. --%>
3   <%@ Page Language="C#" AutoEventWireup="true"
4      CodeFile="Recommendations.aspx.cs" Inherits="Recommendations" %>
5
6   <!DOCTYPE html PUBLIC "-//W3C//DTD XHTML 1.0 Transitional//EN"
7      "http://www.w3.org/TR/xhtml1/DTD/xhtml1-transitional.dtd">
8
9   <html xmlns="http://www.w3.org/1999/xhtml">
10  <head runat="server">
11     <title>Book Recommendations</title>
12  </head>
13  <body>
14     <form id="form1" runat="server">
15     <div>
16        <asp:Label ID="recommendationsLabel" runat="server"
17           Font-Bold="True" Font-Size="X-Large" Text="Recommendations">
18        </asp:Label>
19        <br /><br />
20        <asp:ListBox ID="booksListBox" runat="server" Height="125px"
21           Width="450px">
22        </asp:ListBox>
23        <br /><br />
24        <asp:HyperLink ID="languageLink" runat="server"
25           NavigateUrl="~/Options.aspx">
26           Click here to choose another language.
27        </asp:HyperLink>
```

Fig. 22.32 | Session-based book recommendations displayed in a ListBox. (Part I of 2.)

```
28        </div>
29      </form>
30   </body>
31   </html>
```

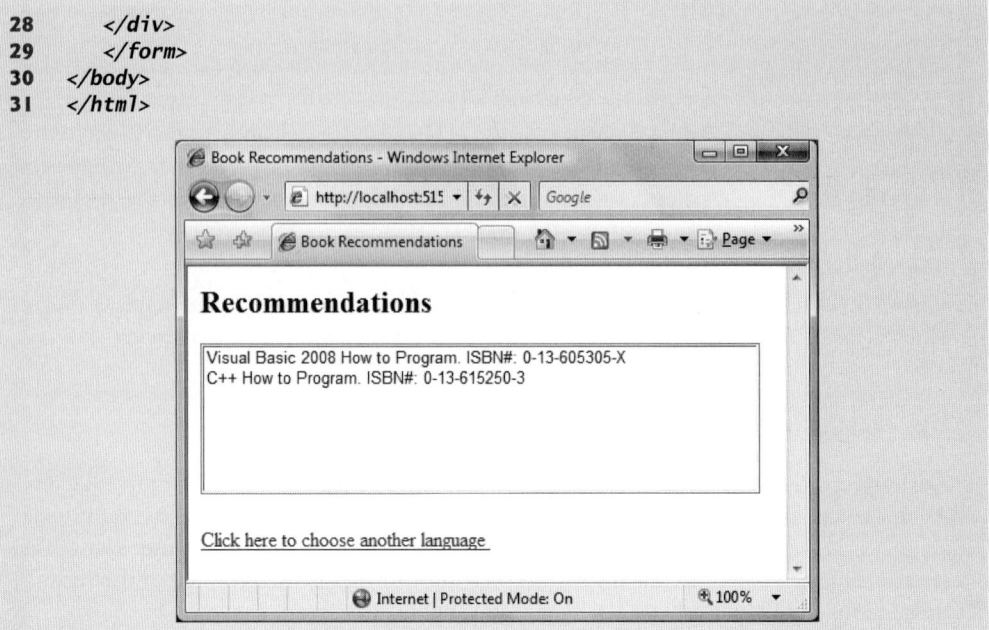

Fig. 22.32 | Session-based book recommendations displayed in a ListBox. (Part 2 of 2.)

Code-Behind File That Creates Book Recommendations from a Session

Figure 22.33 presents the code-behind file for Recommendations.aspx. Event handler Page_Init (lines 8–33) retrieves the session information. If a user has not selected a language on Options.aspx, our Session object's **Count** property will be 0. This property provides the number of session items contained in a Session object. If Session object's Count property is 0 (i.e., no language was selected), then we display the text **No Recommendations** and update the Text of the HyperLink back to Options.aspx.

If the user has chosen a language, the foreach statement in lines 13–19 iterates through a collection containing all the keys in the session—the **Keys** property of class HttpSessionState (line 13). The value in a key/value pair is retrieved from the Session object by indexing the Session object with the key name, using the same process by which we retrieved a value from our Dictionary line 46 of Fig. 22.30. Lines 17–18 concatenate the current key's string value (keyName) to the string " How to Program. ISBN: " and the value from the Session object for which keyName is the key. This string is the recommendation that appears in the ListBox.

```
1   // Fig. 22.33: Recommendations.aspx.cs
2   // Creates book recommendations based on a Session object.
3   using System;
4
5   public partial class Recommendations : System.Web.UI.Page
6   {
```

Fig. 22.33 | Session data used to provide book recommendations to the user. (Part 1 of 2.)

```
 7      // read Session items and populate ListBox with recommendations
 8      protected void Page_Init(object sender, EventArgs e)
 9      {
10         // if there are Session items, list the appropriate books and ISBNs
11         if ( Session.Count > 0 )
12         {
13            foreach ( string keyName in Session.Keys )
14            {
15               // use current key to display one of the session's
16               // name/value pairs
17               booksListBox.Items.Add( keyName + " How to Program. ISBN: " +
18                  Session[ keyName ] );
19            } // end foreach
20         } // end if
21         else
22         {
23            // if there are no items, then no language was chosen, so
24            // display appropriate message and clear and hide booksListBox
25            recommendationsLabel.Text = "No Recommendations";
26            booksListBox.Visible = false;
27
28            // modify languageLink because no language was selected
29            languageLink.Text = "Click here to choose a language.";
30         } // end else
31      } // end method Page_Init
32   } // end class Recommendations
```

Fig. 22.33 | Session data used to provide book recommendations to the user. (Part 2 of 2.)

22.7 Case Study: Connecting to a Database in ASP.NET

Many websites allow users to provide feedback about the website in a *guestbook*. Typically, users click a link on the website's home page to request the guestbook page. This page usually consists of an XHTML form that contains fields for the user's name, e-mail address, message/feedback and so on. Data submitted on the guestbook form is then stored in a database located on the web server's machine.

In this section, we create a guestbook Web Form application. This example's GUI is slightly more complex than that of earlier examples. It contains a *GridView* ASP.NET data control, as shown in Fig. 22.34, which displays all the entries in the guestbook in tabular format. We explain how to create and configure this data control shortly. Note that the GridView displays **abc** in **Design** mode to indicate string data that will be retrieved from a data source at runtime.

The XHTML form presented to the user consists of a name field, an e-mail address field and a message field. The form also contains a **Submit** button to send the data to the server and a **Clear** button to reset each of the fields on the form. The application stores the guestbook information in a SQL Server database called Guestbook.mdf located on the web server. (We provide this database in the Databases subdirectory of this chapter's examples directory. You can download the examples from www.deitel.com/books/csharpfp3.) Below the XHTML form, the GridView displays the data (i.e., guestbook entries) in the database's Messages table.

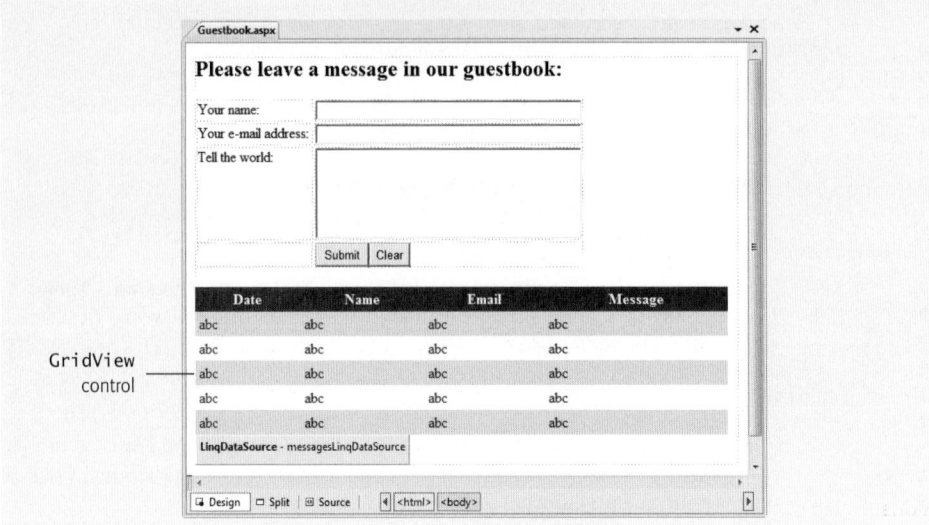

Fig. 22.34 | Guestbook application GUI in **Design** mode.

22.7.1 Building a Web Form That Displays Data from a Database

We now explain how to build this GUI and set up the data binding between the GridView control and the database. Many of these steps are similar to those performed in Chapter 21 to access and interact with a database in a Windows application. We present the ASPX file generated from the GUI later in this section, and we discuss the related code-behind file in the next subsection. To build the guestbook application, perform the following steps:

Step 1: Creating the Project
Create an **ASP.NET Web Site** named Guestbook and name the ASPX file Guestbook.aspx. Rename the class in the code-behind file Guestbook, and update the Page directive in the ASPX file accordingly.

Step 2: Creating the Form for User Input
In **Design** mode for the ASPX file, add the text Please leave a message in our guestbook: formatted as an h2 header. Insert an XHTML table with two columns and four rows, configured so that the text in each cell aligns with the top of the cell. Place the appropriate text (see Fig. 22.34) in the top three cells in the table's left column. Then place TextBoxes named nameTextBox, emailTextBox and messageTextBox in the top three table cells in the right column, each with widths of 300px. Set messageTextBox to be a multiline TextBox by the setting the TextMode property to MultiLine. Finally, add Buttons named submitButton and clearButton to the bottom-right table cell. Set the buttons' Text properties to Submit and Clear, respectively. We discuss the buttons' event handlers when we present the code-behind file.

Step 3: Adding a GridView Control to the Web Form
Add a GridView named messagesGridView that will display the guestbook entries. This control appears in the **Data** section of the **Toolbox**. The colors for the GridView are specified through the **Auto Format...** link in the **GridView Tasks** smart-tag menu that opens when

you place the GridView on the page. Clicking this link causes an **AutoFormat** dialog to open with several choices. In this example, we chose **Simple**. We show how to set the Grid-View's data source (i.e., where it gets the data to display in its rows and columns) shortly.

Step 4: Adding a Database to an ASP.NET Web Application

To use a SQL Server 2005 Express database file in an ASP.NET web application, you must first add the file to the project's App_Data folder. Right click this folder in the **Solution Explorer** and select **Add Existing Item....** Locate the Guestbook.mdf file in the Databases subdirectory of this chapter's examples directory, then click **Add**.

To create LINQ to SQL classes so that you can interact with the database using LINQ, right click the project in the **Solution Explorer** and select **Add New Item....** In the **Add New Item** dialog, select **LINQ to SQL Classes**, enter GuestbookDB.dbml as the **Name**, and click **Add**. A dialog appears asking if you would like to put your new LINQ to SQL classes in the App_Code folder; click **Yes**. If the **Object Relational Designer** does not open automatically, double click GuestbookDB.dbml in the **Solution Explorer**. Next, drag the Guestbook database's Messages table from the **Database Explorer** onto the **Object Relational Designer**. Finally, save your project by selecting **File > Save All**.

Step 5: Binding the GridView to the Messages Table of the Guestbook Database

Now that the Guestbook.mdf database is part of the project and we have created LINQ to SQL classes for interacting with it, we can configure the GridView to display the data in the database. Open the **GridView Tasks** smart-tag menu, then select **<New data source...>** from the **Choose Data Source** drop-down list. In the **Data Source Configuration Wizard** that appears, select LINQ. In this example, we use a *LinqDataSource* control that allows the application to interact with the Guestbook.mdf database through LINQ. Set the ID of the data source to messagesLinqDataSource and click **OK** to begin the **Configure Data Source** wizard. In the **Choose a Context Object** screen, select GuestbookDBDataContext from the drop-down list (Fig. 22.35), then click **Next >**.

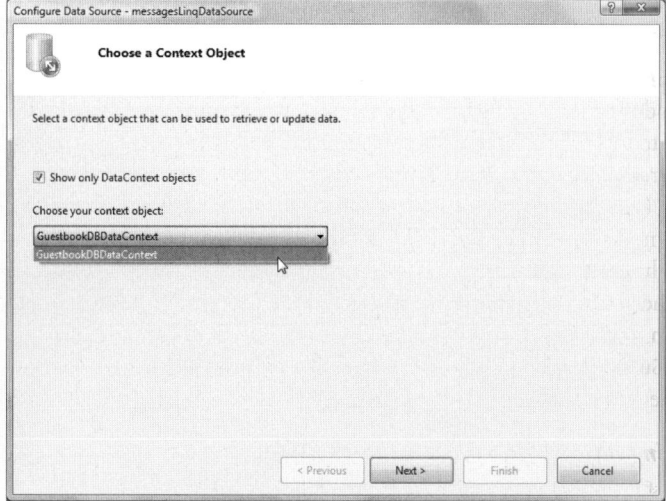

Fig. 22.35 | Configure **Data Source** dialog in Visual Web Developer.

The **Configure Data Selection** step (Fig. 22.36) allows you to specify which data the LinqDataSource should retrieve from the data context. Your choices on this page design a select LINQ query. The **Table** drop-down list identifies a table in the data context. The GuestbookDB data context contains one table named Messages, which is selected by default. If you haven't saved your project since creating your LINQ to SQL classes (*Step 4*), the list of tables will not appear. Next, in the **Select** pane, select the checkbox marked with an asterisk (*) to indicate that you want to retrieve all the columns in the Messages table. Click the **Advanced...** button, then check the box next to **Enable the LinqDataSource to perform automatic inserts**. This configures the LinqDataSource control to allow us to insert new data into the database. We discuss inserting new guestbook entries based on users' form submissions shortly. Click **Finish** to complete the wizard.

A control named messagesLinqDataSource now appears on the Web Form directly below the GridView (Fig. 22.37). This control is represented in **Design** mode as a gray box containing its type and name. It will *not* appear on the web page at runtime—the gray box simply provides a way to manipulate the control visually through **Design** mode. Also notice that the GridView now has column headers that correspond to the columns in the Messages table and that the rows each contain either a number (which signifies an auto-incremented column) or **abc** (which indicates string data). The actual data from the Guestbook.mdf database file will appear in these rows when you view the ASPX file in a web browser.

Step 6: Modifying the Columns of the Data Source Displayed in the GridView

It is not necessary for site visitors to see the MessageID column when viewing past guest-book entries—this column is merely a unique primary key required by the Messages table within the database. Thus, we modify the GridView so that this column does not display on the Web Form. In the **GridView Tasks** smart-tag menu, click **Edit Columns**. In the resulting **Fields** dialog (Fig. 22.38), select **MessageID** in the **Selected fields** pane, then click

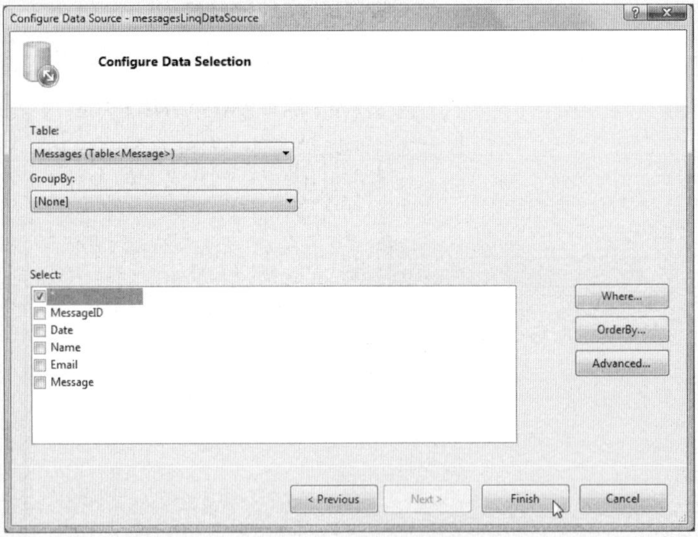

Fig. 22.36 | Configuring the query used by the LinqDataSource to retrieve data.

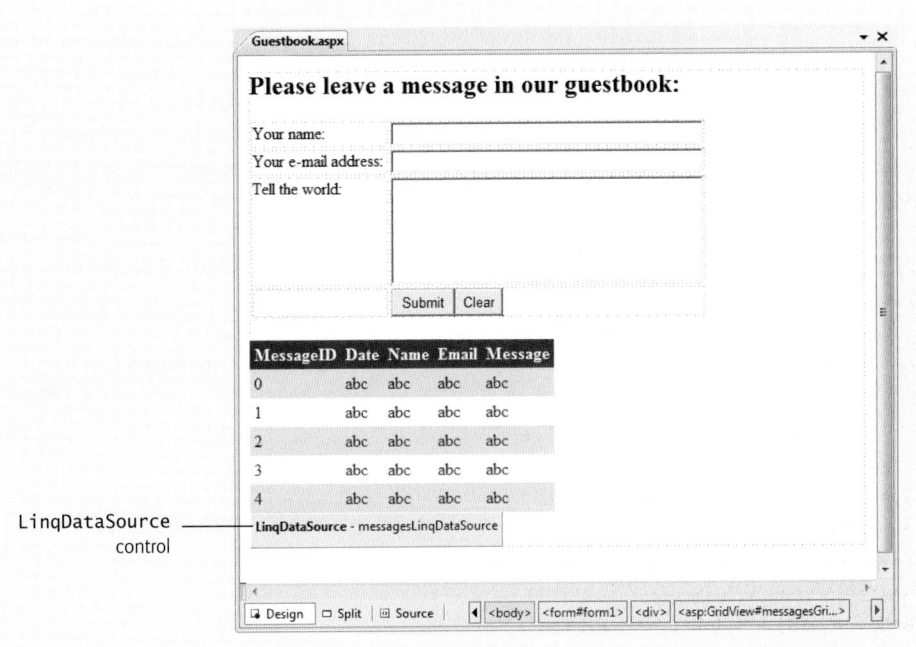

Fig. 22.37 | **Design** mode displaying LinqDataSource control for a GridView.

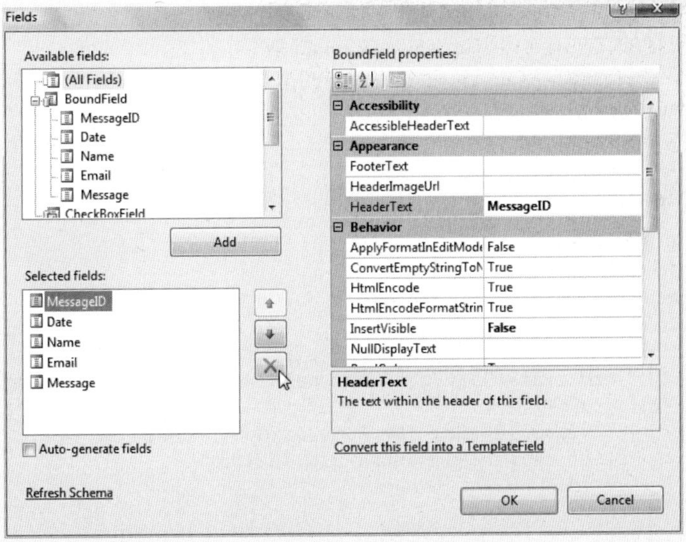

Fig. 22.38 | Removing the MessageID column from the GridView.

the **Delete** button (). This removes the MessageID column from the GridView. Click **OK** to return to the main IDE window. Next, select the **MessageText** field and change the HeaderText property to Message. The GridView should now appear as in Fig. 22.34.

ASPX File for a Web Form That Interacts with a Database

The ASPX file generated by the guestbook GUI (and messagesLinqDataSource control) is shown in Fig. 22.39. This file contains a large amount of generated markup. We discuss only those parts that are new or noteworthy for the current example. Lines 29–61 contain the XHTML and ASP.NET elements that comprise the form that gathers user input. The GridView control appears in lines 63–88. The <asp:GridView> start tag (lines 63–66) contains properties that set various aspects of the GridView's appearance and behavior, such as whether grid lines should be displayed between rows and columns. The **DataSourceID** property identifies the data source that is used to fill the GridView with data at runtime.

```
 1    <%-- Fig. 22.39: Guestbook.aspx --%>
 2    <%-- Guestbook web application with a form for users to submit --%>
 3    <%-- guestbook entries and a GridView to view existing entries. --%>
 4    <%@ Page Language="C#" AutoEventWireup="true"
 5       CodeFile="Guestbook.aspx.cs" Inherits="Guestbook" %>
 6
 7    <!DOCTYPE html PUBLIC "-//W3C//DTD XHTML 1.0 Transitional//EN"
 8       "http://www.w3.org/TR/xhtml1/DTD/xhtml1-transitional.dtd">
 9
10    <html xmlns="http://www.w3.org/1999/xhtml">
11    <head runat="server">
12       <title>Guestbook</title>
13       <style type="text/css">
14          .style1
15          {
16             width: 100%;
17          }
18          .style2
19          {
20             width: 150px;
21             vertical-align: top;
22          }
23       </style>
24    </head>
25    <body>
26       <form id="form1" runat="server">
27       <div>
28          <h2>Please leave a message in our guestbook: </h2>
29          <table class="style1">
30             <tr>
31                <td class="style2">Your name: </td>
32                <td>
33                   <asp:TextBox ID="nameTextBox" runat="server"
34                      Width="300px"></asp:TextBox>
35                </td>
36             </tr>
37             <tr>
38                <td class="style2">Your e-mail address: </td>
39                <td>
40                   <asp:TextBox ID="emailTextBox" runat="server"
41                      Width="300px"></asp:TextBox>
```

Fig. 22.39 | ASPX file for the guestbook application. (Part 1 of 3.)

```
42                </td>
43            </tr>
44            <tr>
45                <td class="style2">Tell the world:</td>
46                <td>
47                    <asp:TextBox ID="messageTextBox" runat="server"
48                        Height="100px" Rows="8" Width="300px"
49                        TextMode="MultiLine"></asp:TextBox>
50                </td>
51            </tr>
52            <tr>
53                <td class="style2"> </td>
54                <td>
55                    <asp:Button ID="submitButton" runat="server"
56                        onclick="submitButton_Click" Text="Submit" />
57                    <asp:Button ID="clearButton" runat="server"
58                        onclick="clearButton_Click" Text="Clear" />
59                </td>
60            </tr>
61        </table>
62        <p>
63            <asp:GridView ID="messagesGridView" runat="server"
64                AutoGenerateColumns="False" CellPadding="4"
65                DataKeyNames="MessageID" ForeColor="#333333" GridLines="None"
66                DataSourceID="messagesLinqDataSource" Width="600px">
67                <FooterStyle BackColor="#1C5E55" Font-Bold="True"
68                    ForeColor="White" />
69                <RowStyle BackColor="#E3EAEB" />
70                <Columns>
71                    <asp:BoundField DataField="Date" HeaderText="Date"
72                        SortExpression="Date" />
73                    <asp:BoundField DataField="Name" HeaderText="Name"
74                        SortExpression="Name" />
75                    <asp:BoundField DataField="Email" HeaderText="Email"
76                        SortExpression="Email" />
77                    <asp:BoundField DataField="MessageText"
78                        HeaderText="Message" SortExpression="MessageText" />
79                </Columns>
80                <PagerStyle BackColor="#666666" ForeColor="White"
81                    HorizontalAlign="Center" />
82                <SelectedRowStyle BackColor="#C5BBAF" Font-Bold="True"
83                    ForeColor="#333333" />
84                <HeaderStyle BackColor="#1C5E55" Font-Bold="True"
85                    ForeColor="White" />
86                <EditRowStyle BackColor="#7C6F57" />
87                <AlternatingRowStyle BackColor="White" />
88            </asp:GridView>
89            <asp:LinqDataSource ID="messagesLinqDataSource" runat="server"
90                ContextTypeName="GuestbookDBDataContext" EnableInsert="True"
91                TableName="Messages">
92            </asp:LinqDataSource>
93        </p>
94    </div>
```

Fig. 22.39 | ASPX file for the guestbook application. (Part 2 of 3.)

```
95      </form>
96  </body>
97  </html>
```

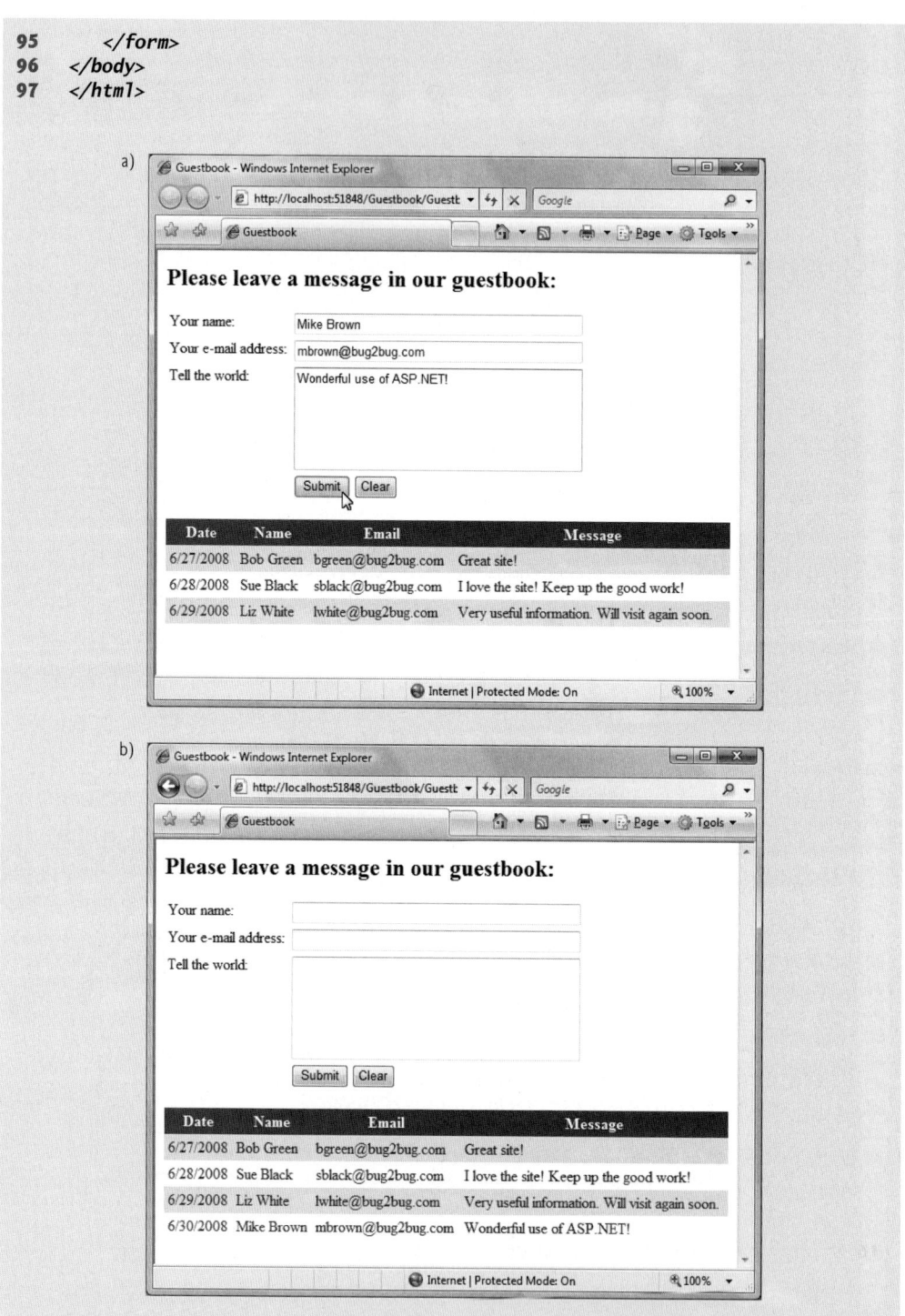

Fig. 22.39 | ASPX file for the guestbook application. (Part 3 of 3.)

Lines 70–79 define the GridView's Columns. Each column is represented as a ***Bound-Field***, because the values in the columns are bound to data in the data source (i.e., the Guestbook database's Messages table). Property DataField of each BoundField identifies the column in the data source to which a GridView column is bound. The HeaderText property indicates the text that appears as the column header. By default, this is the name of the column in the data source, but you can change this property as desired. For example, we use Message as the header for the MessageText column. The SortExpression property specifies the expression used to sort the GridView's elements when the user chooses to sort by the column. Because the GridView cannot be sorted in this example, we could have omitted this autogenerated code. Lines 80–87 contain nested elements that define the styles used to format the GridView's rows. The IDE configured these styles based on your selection of the **Simple** style in the **Auto Format** dialog for the GridView.

The messagesLinqDataSource is defined in lines 89–92 in Fig. 22.39. The ***Context-TypeName*** property (line 90) indicates the data context that the LinqDataSource interacts with. Recall that we specified this value earlier in this section using the **Configure Data Source** wizard. As determined by our actions in the same wizard, the ***TableName*** property in line 91 specifies the table from which to retrieve data. [*Note:* these properties are used to create a select LINQ query that is generated and executed implicitly by the LinqData-Source.] The EnableInsert property in line 90 is set to true, allowing the data source to insert records into the data context.

22.7.2 Modifying the Code-Behind File for the Guestbook Application

After building the Web Form and configuring the data controls used in this example, double click the **Submit** and **Clear** buttons in **Design** view to create their corresponding Click event handlers in the code-behind file (Fig. 22.40). The IDE generates empty event handlers, so we must add the appropriate code to make these buttons work properly. The event handler for clearButton (lines 36–41) clears each TextBox by setting its Text property to an empty string. This resets the form for a new guestbook submission.

```
 1   // Fig. 22.40: Guestbook.aspx.cs
 2   // Code-behind file that defines event handlers for the guestbook.
 3   using System;
 4   using System.Collections.Generic;
 5
 6   public partial class Guestbook : System.Web.UI.Page
 7   {
 8      // Submit Button adds a new guestbook entry to the database, clears
 9      // the form and displays the updated list of guestbook entries
10      protected void submitButton_Click( object sender, EventArgs e )
11      {
12         // create dictionary of parameters for inserting
13         Dictionary< string, string > parameters =
14            new Dictionary< string, string >();
15
16         // add current date and the user's name, e-mail address and
17         // message to dictionary of insert parameters
18         parameters.Add( "Date", DateTime.Now.ToShortDateString() );
```

Fig. 22.40 | Code-behind file for the guestbook application. (Part I of 2.)

```
19        parameters.Add( "Name", nameTextBox.Text );
20        parameters.Add( "Email", emailTextBox.Text );
21        parameters.Add( "MessageText", messageTextBox.Text );
22
23        // execute an insert LINQ statement to add a new entry to the
24        // Messages table in the Guestbook data context that contains the
25        // current date and the user's name, e-mail address and message
26        messagesLinqDataSource.Insert( parameters );
27
28        // clear the TextBoxes
29        clearButton_Click( sender, e );
30
31        // update the GridView with the new database table contents
32        messagesGridView.DataBind();
33     } // end method submitButton_Click
34
35     // Clear Button clears the Web Form's TextBoxes
36     protected void clearButton_Click( object sender, EventArgs e )
37     {
38        nameTextBox.Text = string.Empty;
39        emailTextBox.Text = string.Empty;
40        messageTextBox.Text = string.Empty;
41     } // end method clearButton_Click
42  } // end class Guestbook
```

Fig. 22.40 | Code-behind file for the guestbook application. (Part 2 of 2.)

Lines 10–33 contain submitButton's event handler, which adds the user's information to the Guestbook database's Messages table. To use the Web Form's TextBox values as the values to insert into the database, we must create a Dictionary of insert parameters. Lines 13–14 create a Dictionary object named parameters. Lines 18–21 populate the Dictionary with a key/value pair to represent each of the four insert parameters—the current date and the user's name, e-mail address, and message. Each parameter is represented by an entry in parameters whose key is the name of the field in the database and whose value is the field's value. Invoking the LinqDataSource method **Insert** (line 26) executes the insert LINQ command against the data context and adds a row to the Messages table. We pass the Dictionary object as an argument for the Insert method to specify the insert parameters. After the data is inserted into the database, line 29 clears the TextBoxes by calling the clearButton_Click event handler, and line 32 invokes messagesGridView's **DataBind** method to refresh the data that the GridView displays. This causes messagesLinqDataSource (the GridView's source) to execute its select command to obtain the Messages table's newly updated data.

22.8 Case Study: Secure Books Database Application

This case study presents a web application in which a user logs into a secure website to view a list of publications by a selected author. The application consists of several ASPX files. Section 22.8.1 presents the application and explains the purpose of each of its web pages. Section 22.8.2 provides step-by-step instructions to guide you through building the application and presents the markup in the ASPX files.

22.8.1 Examining the Completed Secure Books Database Application

This example uses a technique known as *forms authentication* to protect a page so that only users known to the website can access it. Such users are known as the site's members. Authentication is a crucial tool for sites that allow only members to enter the site or a portion of the site. In this application, website visitors must log in before they are allowed to view the publications in the Books database. The first page that a user would typically request is Login.aspx (Fig. 22.41). You will soon learn to create this page using a Login control, one of several *ASP.NET login controls* that help create secure applications using authentication. These controls are found in the **Login** section of the **Toolbox**.

The Login.aspx page allows a visitor to enter an existing user name and password to log into the site. A first-time visitor must click the link below the **Log In** button to create a new user before logging in. Doing so redirects the visitor to CreateNewUser.aspx (Fig. 22.42),

Fig. 22.41 | Login.aspx page of the secure books database application.

Fig. 22.42 | CreateNewUser.aspx page of the secure books database application.

which contains a CreateUserWizard control that presents the visitor with a user registration form. We discuss the CreateUserWizard control in further detail in Section 22.8.2. In Fig. 22.42, we use the password pa$$word for testing purposes—as you'll see, the CreateUserWizard requires that the password contain special characters for security purposes. Clicking **Create User** establishes a new user account. After creating the account, the user is automatically logged in and shown a success message (Fig. 22.43).

Clicking the **Continue** button on the confirmation page sends the user to Books.aspx (Fig. 22.44), which provides a drop-down list of authors and a table containing the ISBNs, titles, edition numbers and copyright years of books in the database. By default, all the books by **Harvey Deitel** are displayed. Links appear at the bottom of the table that allow

Fig. 22.43 | Message displayed to indicate that a user account was created successfully.

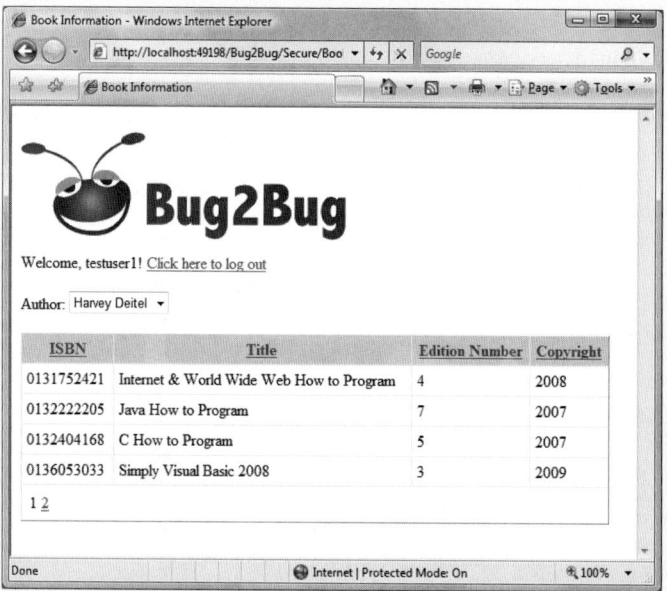

Fig. 22.44 | Books.aspx displaying books by **Harvey Deitel** (by default).

you to access additional pages of data. When the user chooses an author, a postback occurs, and the page is updated to display information about books written by the selected author (Fig. 22.45).

Note that once the user creates an account and is logged in, Books.aspx displays a welcome message customized for the particular logged-in user. As you will soon see, a LoginName control provides this functionality. After you add this control to the page, ASP.NET handles the details of determining the user name.

Clicking the **Click here to log out** link logs the user out, then sends the user back to Login.aspx (Fig. 22.46). This link is created by a LoginStatus control, which handles the log-out details. After logging out, the user would need to log in through Login.aspx to view the book listing again. The Login control on this page receives the username and password entered by a visitor. ASP.NET compares these values with usernames and passwords stored in a database on the server. If there is a match, the visitor is *authenticated*

Fig. 22.45 | Books.aspx displaying books by Greg Ayer.

Fig. 22.46 | Logging in using the Login control.

(i.e., the user's identity is confirmed). We explain the authentication process in detail in Section 22.8.2. When an existing user is successfully authenticated, Login.aspx redirects the user to Books.aspx (Fig. 22.44). If the user's login attempt fails, an appropriate error message is displayed (Fig. 22.47).

Notice that Login.aspx, CreateNewUser.aspx and Books.aspx share the same page header containing the fictitious company Bug2Bug's logo. We use a *master page* to achieve this common look-and-feel. As we demonstrate shortly, a master page defines common GUI elements that are inherited by each page in a set of *content pages*. Just as C# classes can inherit instance variables and methods from existing classes, content pages inherit visual elements from master pages—this is known as *visual inheritance*.

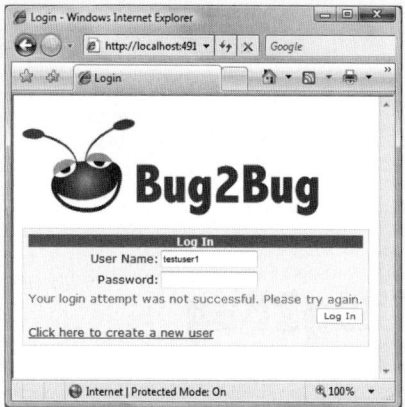

Fig. 22.47 | Error message displayed for an unsuccessful login attempt.

22.8.2 Creating the Secure Books Database Application

Now that you are familiar with how this application behaves, you'll learn how to create it from scratch. Thanks to the rich set of login and data controls provided by ASP.NET, you will have to write almost no C# code to create this application. Most of the functionality is specified through properties of controls, many of which are set through wizards and other visual programming tools. ASP.NET hides the details of authenticating users against a database of user names and passwords, displaying appropriate success or error messages and redirecting the user to the correct page based on the authentication results. We now discuss the steps you must perform to create the secure books database application.

Step 1: Creating the Website
Create a new **ASP.NET Web Site** with a folder named Bug2Bug. We'll explicitly create each ASPX file that we need in this application, so delete the IDE-generated Default.aspx file (and its corresponding code-behind file) by selecting Default.aspx in the **Solution Explorer** and pressing the *Delete* key. Click **OK** in the confirmation dialog to delete these files.

Step 2: Setting Up the Website's Folders
Before building any of the pages in the website, we create folders to organize its contents. First, create an Images folder by right clicking the location of the website in the **Solution Explorer** and selecting **New Folder**, then add the bug2bug.png file to it. This image can be

found in the Images subdirectory of this chapter's examples directory. Next, add the Books.mdf database file (located in the Databases subdirectory of this chapter's examples directory) to the project's App_Data folder. We show how to retrieve data from this database later in the section.

Step 3: Configuring the Application's Security Settings

In this application, we want to ensure that only authenticated users are allowed to access Books.aspx (created in *Step 9* and *Step 10*) to view the information in the database. Previously, we created all of our ASPX pages in the web application's root directory (e.g., http://localhost:*PortNumber*/*ProjectName*). By default, any website visitor (regardless of whether the visitor is authenticated) can view pages in the root directory. ASP.NET allows you to restrict access to particular folders of a website. We do not want to restrict access to the root of the website, however, because all users must be able to view Login.aspx and CreateNewUser.aspx to log in and create user accounts, respectively. Thus, if we want to restrict access to Books.aspx, it should reside in a directory other than the root directory. Create a folder named Secure. Later in the section, we will create Books.aspx in this folder. First, let's enable forms authentication in our application and configure the Secure folder to restrict access to authenticated users only.

Select **Website > ASP.NET Configuration** to open the ***Web Site Administration Tool*** in a web browser (Fig. 22.48). This tool allows you to configure various options that determine how your application behaves. Click either the **Security** link or the **Security** tab to open a web page in which you can set security options (Fig. 22.49), such as the type of authentication the application should use. In the **Users** column, click **Select authentication type**. On the resulting page (Fig. 22.50), select the radio button next to **From the internet** to indicate that users will log in via a form on the website in which they can enter a username and password (i.e., the application will use forms authentication). The default setting—**From a local network**—relies on users' Windows usernames and passwords for authentication purposes. Click the **Done** button to save this change.

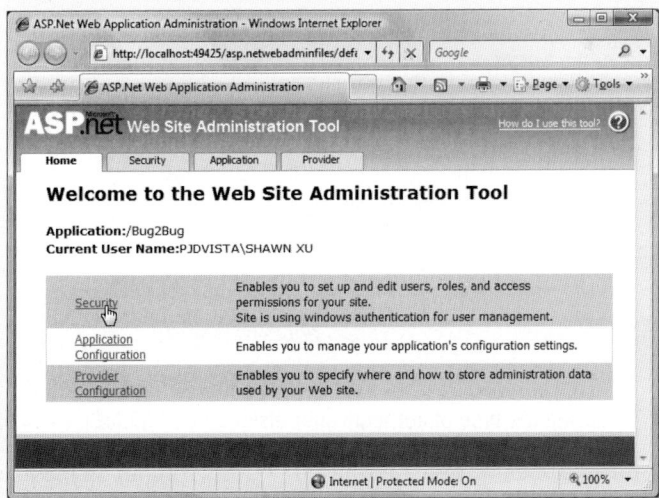

Fig. 22.48 | **Web Site Administration Tool** for configuring a web application.

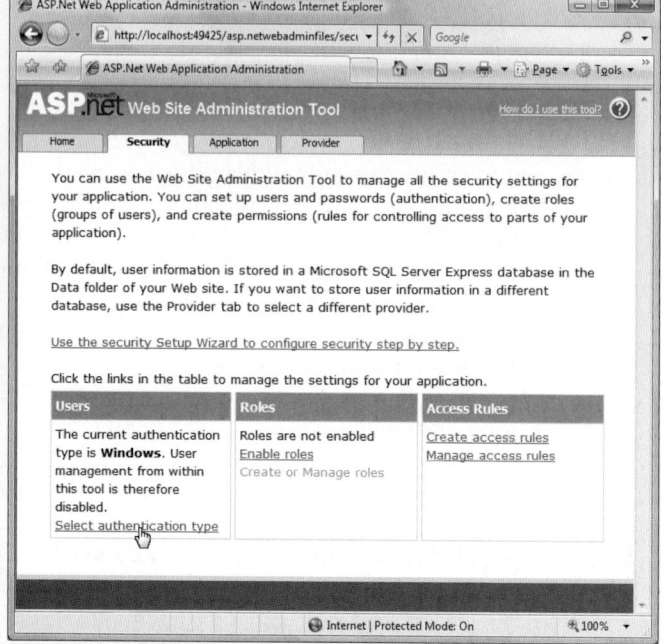

Fig. 22.49 │ **Security** page of the **Web Site Administration Tool**.

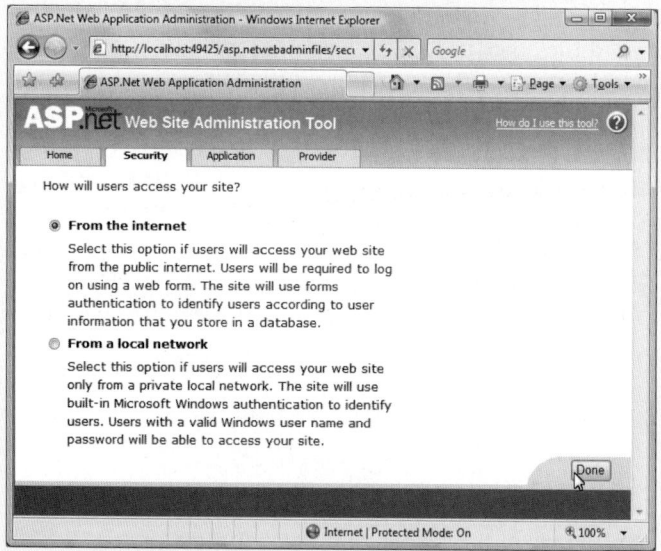

Fig. 22.50 │ Choosing the type of authentication used by an ASP.NET web application.

Now that forms authentication is enabled, the **Users** column on the main page of the **Web Site Administration Tool** (Fig. 22.51) provides links to create and manage users. As you saw in Section 22.8.1, our application provides the CreateNewUser.aspx page in which

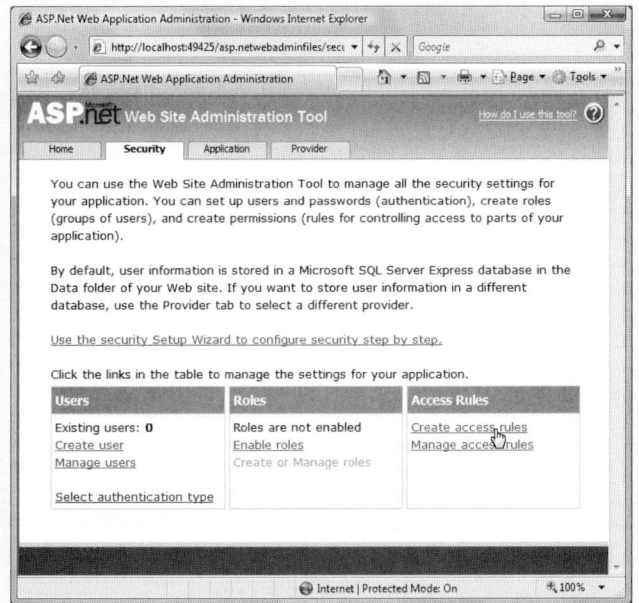

Fig. 22.51 | Main page of the **Web Site Administration Tool** after enabling forms authentication.

users can create their own accounts. Thus, while it is possible to create users through the **Web Site Administration Tool**, we do not do so here.

Even though no users exist at the moment, we configure the Secure folder to grant access only to authenticated users (i.e., deny access to all unauthenticated users). Click the **Create access rules** link in the **Access Rules** column of the **Web Site Administration Tool** (Fig. 22.51) to view the **Add New Access Rule** page (Fig. 22.52). This page is used to create an *access rule*—a rule that grants or denies access to a particular web-application directory for a specific user or group of users. Click the Secure directory in the left column of the page to identify the directory to which our access rule applies. In the middle column, select the radio button marked **Anonymous users** to specify that the rule applies to users who have not been authenticated. Finally, select **Deny** in the right column, labeled **Permission**, then click **OK**. This rule indicates that *anonymous users* (i.e., users who have not identified themselves by logging in) should be denied access to any pages in the Secure directory (e.g., Books.aspx). By default, anonymous users who attempt to load a page in the Secure directory are redirected to the Login.aspx page so that they can identify themselves. Note that, because we did not set up any access rules for the Bug2Bug root directory, anonymous users may still access pages there (e.g., Login.aspx, CreateNewUser.aspx). We create these pages momentarily.

Step 4: Examining the Autogenerated web.config Files
We have now configured the application to use forms authentication and created an access rule to ensure that only authenticated users can access the Secure folder. Before creating the website's content, we examine how the changes made through the **Web Site Adminis-**

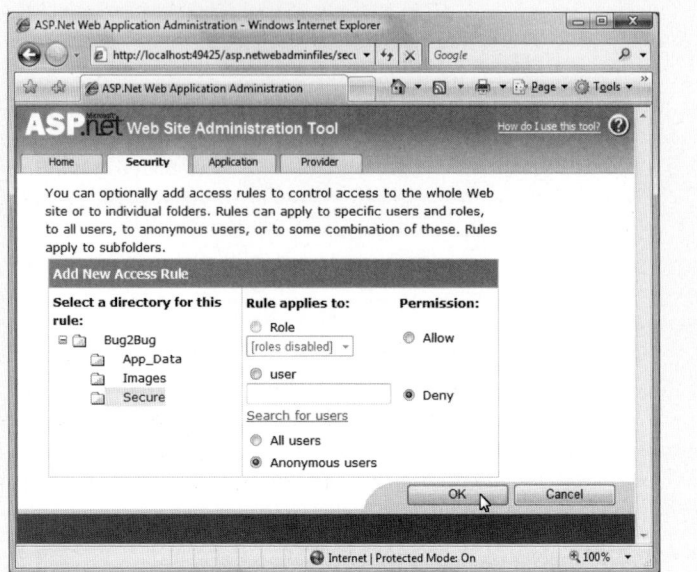

Fig. 22.52 | **Add New Access Rule** page used to configure directory access.

tration Tool appear in the IDE. Recall that web.config is an XML file used for application configuration, such as enabling debugging or storing database connection strings. Visual Web Developer generates two web.config files in response to our actions using the **Web Site Administration Tool**—one in the application's root directory and one in the Secure folder. [*Note:* You may need to click the **Refresh** button in the **Solution Explorer** to see these files.] In an ASP.NET application, a page's configuration settings are determined by the current directory's web.config file. The settings in this file take precedence over the settings in the root directory's web.config file.

After setting the authentication type for the web application, the IDE generates a web.config file at http://localhost:*PortNumber*/Bug2Bug/web.config, which contains an ***authentication*** element

```
<authentication mode="Forms" />
```

This element appears in the root directory's web.config file, so the setting applies to the entire website. The value "Forms" of the ***mode*** attribute specifies that we want to use forms authentication. Had we left the authentication type set to **From a local network** in the **Web Site Administration Tool**, the mode attribute would be set to "Windows".

After creating the access rule for the Secure folder, the IDE generates a second web.config file in that folder. This file contains an ***authorization*** element that indicates who is, and who is not, authorized to access this folder over the web. In this application, we want to allow only authenticated users to access the contents of the Secure folder, so the authorization element appears as

```
<authorization>
    <deny users="?" />
</authorization>
```

Rather than grant permission to each individual authenticated user, we deny access to those users who are not authenticated (i.e., those who have not logged in to the website). The *deny* element inside the authorization element specifies the users to whom we wish to deny access. When the users attribute's value is set to "?", all anonymous (i.e., unauthenticated) users are denied access to the folder. Thus, an unauthenticated user will not be able to load http://localhost:*PortNumber*/Bug2Bug/Secure/Books.aspx. Instead, such a user will be redirected to the Login.aspx page—when a user is denied access to a part of a site, ASP.NET by default sends the user to a page named Login.aspx in the application's root directory.

Step 5: Creating a Master Page
Now that you have established the application's security settings, you can create the application's web pages. We begin with the master page, which defines the elements we want to appear on each page. A master page is like a base class in a visual inheritance hierarchy, and content pages are like derived classes. The master page contains placeholders for custom content created in each content page. The content pages visually inherit the master page's content, then add content in place of the master page's placeholders.

For example, you might want to include a *navigation bar* (i.e., a series of buttons for navigating a website) on every page of a site. If the site encompasses a large number of pages, adding markup to create the navigation bar for each page can be time consuming. Moreover, if you subsequently modify the navigation bar, every page on the site that uses it must be updated. By creating a master page, you can specify the navigation-bar markup in one file and have it appear on all the content pages, with only a few lines of markup. If the navigation bar changes, only the master page changes—any content pages that use it are updated the next time the page is requested.

In this example, we want the Bug2Bug logo to appear as a header at the top of every page, so we will place an Image control in the master page. Each subsequent page we create will be a content page based on this master page and thus will include the header. To create a master page, right click the location of the website in the **Solution Explorer** and select **Add New Item....** In the **Add New Item** dialog, select **Master Page** from the template list and specify Bug2Bug.master as the file name. Master pages have the file-name extension *.master* and, like Web Forms, can optionally use a code-behind file to define additional functionality. In this example, we do not need to specify any code for the master page, so leave the box labeled **Place code in a separate file** unchecked. Click **Add** to create the page.

The IDE opens the master page in **Source** mode (Fig. 22.53) when the file is first created. [*Note:* We added a line break in the DOCTYPE element for presentation purposes.] The markup for a master page is almost identical to that of a Web Form. One difference is that a master page contains a *Master* directive (line 1 in Fig. 22.53), which specifies that this file defines a master page using the indicated Language for any code. Because we chose not to use a code-behind file, the master page also contains a *script* element (lines 6–8). Code that would usually be placed in a code-behind file can be placed in a script element. However, we could have omitted the script element from this page, because we do not need to write any additional code. Next, set the title of the page to Bug2Bug. Finally, notice that the master page contains two *ContentPlaceHolder* controls (lines 13–14 and 19–21 of Fig. 22.53). These serve as a placeholders for content that will be defined by a content page. You will see how to define content to replace ContentPlaceHolders shortly.

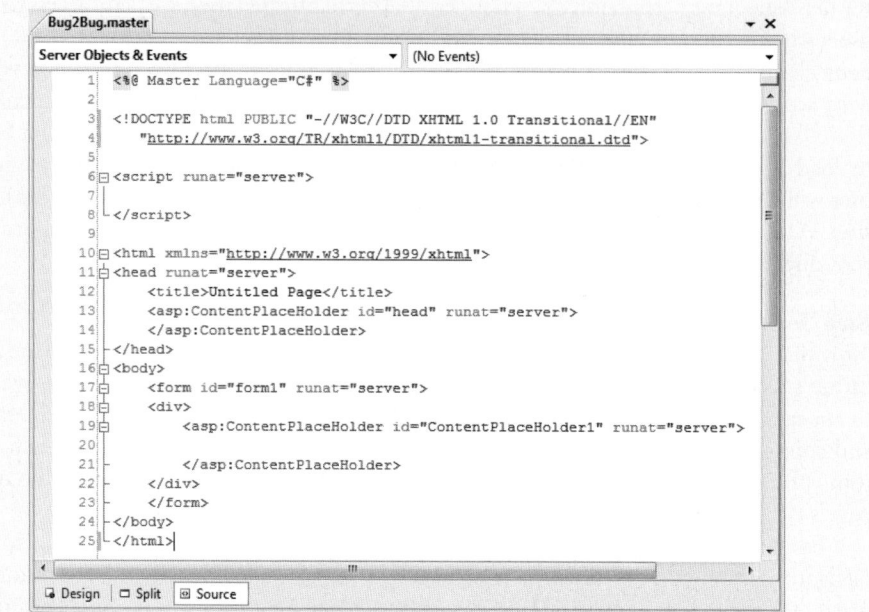

Fig. 22.53 | Master page in **Source** mode.

At this point, you can edit the master page in **Design** mode (Fig. 22.54) as if it were an ASPX file. Notice that the `ContentPlaceHolder` control (defined by lines 19–21 in Fig. 22.53) appears as a rectangle with a purple outline indicating the control's type and ID. Using the **Properties** window, change the ID of this control to bodyContent.

To create a header in the master page that will appear at the top of each content page, we insert a table into the master page. Place the cursor to the left of `ContentPlaceHolder` and select **Table > Insert Table**. In the **Insert Table** dialog, set **Rows** to 2 and **Columns** to 1. In the **Layout** section, specify a **Cell padding** of 0 and a **Cell spacing** of 0. Set both the width and height of the table to 100 percent. Make sure that the **Size** value in the **Borders** section is 0. Click **OK** to create a table that fills the page and contains two rows.

Change the `valign` property of the bottom table cell to `top`, so that its content vertically aligns with the top of the cell. Drag and drop the `ContentPlaceHolder` into this cell. Next, set the `Height` of the top table cell to 130. Add to this cell an `Image` control named `headerImage` with its `ImageUrl` property set to the `bug2bug.png` file in the project's

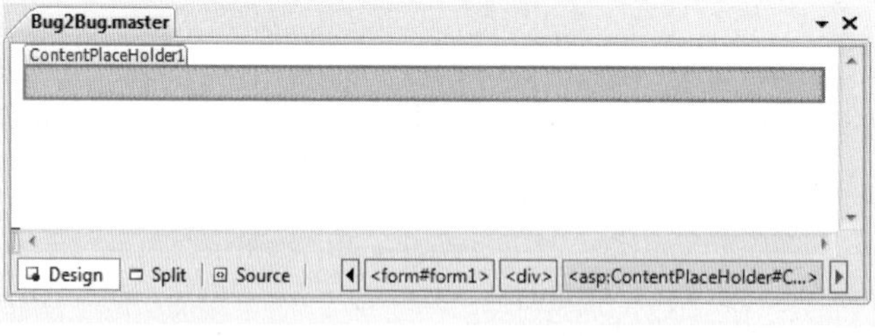

Fig. 22.54 | Master page in **Design** mode.

Images folder. Figure 22.55 shows the markup and **Design** view of the completed master page. As you will see in *Step 6*, a content page based on this master page displays the logo image defined here, as well as the content designed for that specific page (in place of the ContentPlaceHolder).

```
1   <%-- Fig. 22.55: Bug2Bug.Master --%>
2   <%-- Master page that defines commmon features of all pages in the --%>
3   <%-- secure books database application. --%>
4   <%@ Master Language="C#" %>
5
6   <!DOCTYPE html PUBLIC "-//W3C//DTD XHTML 1.0 Transitional//EN"
7      "http://www.w3.org/TR/xhtml1/DTD/xhtml1-transitional.dtd">
8
9   <script runat="server">
10
11  </script>
12
13  <html xmlns="http://www.w3.org/1999/xhtml">
14  <head runat="server">
15     <title>Bug2Bug</title>
16     <asp:ContentPlaceHolder id="head" runat="server">
17     </asp:ContentPlaceHolder>
18     <style type="text/css">
19      .style1
20      {
21         width: 100%;
22         height: 100%;
23      }
24     </style>
25  </head>
26  <body>
27     <form id="form1" runat="server">
28     <div>
29        <table cellpadding="0" cellspacing="0" class="style1">
30           <tr>
31              <td style="height: 130px;">
32                 <asp:Image ID="headerImage" runat="server"
33                    ImageUrl="~/Images/bug2bug.png" />
34              </td>
35           </tr>
36           <tr>
37              <td valign="top">
38                 <asp:ContentPlaceHolder id="bodyContent" runat="server">
39                 </asp:ContentPlaceHolder>
40              </td>
41           </tr>
42        </table>
43     </div>
44     </form>
45  </body>
46  </html>
```

Fig. 22.55 | Bug2Bug.master page that defines a logo image header for all pages in the secure books database application. (Part 1 of 2.)

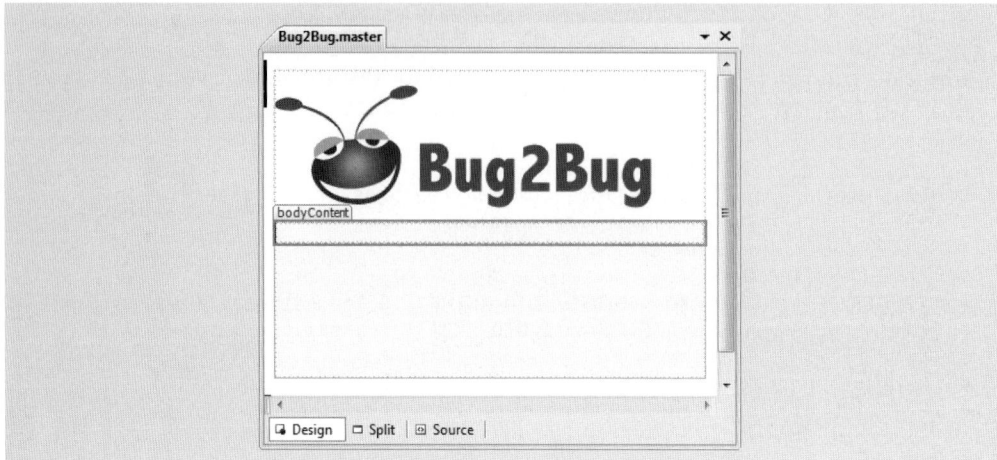

Fig. 22.55 | `Bug2Bug.master` page that defines a logo image header for all pages in the secure books database application. (Part 2 of 2.)

Step 6: Creating a Content Page

We now create a content page based on `Bug2Bug.master`. We begin by building `Create-NewUser.aspx`. To create this file, right click the master page in the **Solution Explorer** and select **Add Content Page**. This action causes a `Default.aspx` file, configured to use the master page, to be added to the project. Rename this file `CreateNewUser.aspx`, then open it in **Source** mode (Fig. 22.56). Note that this file contains a `Page` directive with a `Language` property, a `MasterPageFile` property and a `Title` property. The `Page` directive indicates the **`MasterPageFile`** that is used as a starting point for this new page's design. In this case, the `MasterPageFile` property is set to `"~/Bug2Bug.master"` to indicate that the current file is based on the master page we just created. The **`Title`** property specifies the title that will be displayed in the web browser's title bar when the content page is loaded. This value, which we set to `Create a New User`, replaces the value (i.e., `Bug2Bug`) set in the `title` element of the master page.

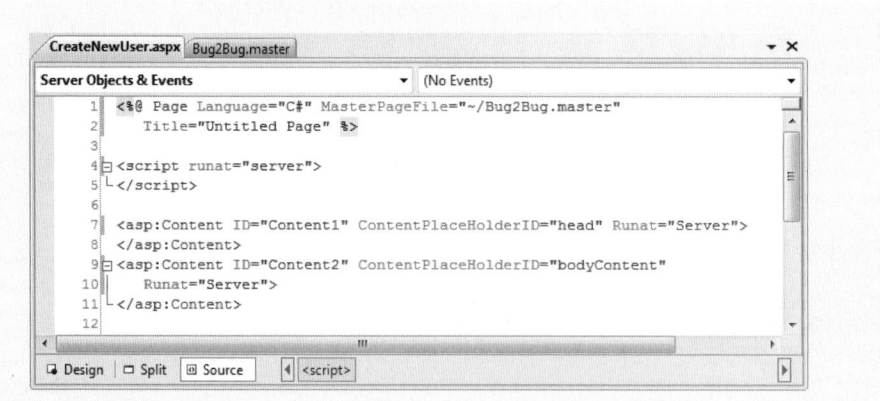

Fig. 22.56 | Content page `CreateNewUser.aspx` in **Source** mode.

Because CreateNewUser.aspx's Page directive specifies Bug2Bug.master as the page's MasterPageFile, the content page implicitly contains the contents of the master page, such as the DOCTYPE, html and body elements. The content-page file does not duplicate the XHTML elements found in the master page. Instead, the content page contains **Content** controls (e.g. lines 7–8 and 9–11 in Fig. 22.56), in which we will place page-specific content that will replace the master page's ContentPlaceHolders when the content page is requested. The ContentPlaceHolderID property of the Content control identifies the ContentPlaceHolder in the master page that the control should replace—in this case, head and bodyContent (lines 7 and 9, respectively).

The relationship between a content page and its master page is more evident in **Design** mode (Fig. 22.57). The gray-shaded region contains the contents of the master page Bug2Bug.master as they will appear in CreateNewUser.aspx when rendered in a web browser. The contents are grayed out in the IDE to indicate that they are uneditable, but they will display normally when you run the web application. The only editable part of this page is the bodyContent Content control, which appears in place of the master page's ContentPlaceHolder. The head Content control is for adding elements to the page's head element, and can only be edited in **Source** mode.

Fig. 22.57 | Content page CreateNewUser.aspx in **Design** mode.

Step 7: Adding a CreateUserWizard Control to a Content Page

Recall from Section 22.8.1 that CreateNewUser.aspx is the page in our website that allows first-time visitors to create user accounts. To provide this functionality, we use a **CreateUserWizard** control. Place the cursor inside the Content control in **Design** mode and double click CreateUserWizard in the **Login** section of the **Toolbox** to add it to the page at the current cursor position. You can also drag and drop the control onto the page. To change the CreateUserWizard's appearance, open the **CreateUserWizard Tasks** smart-tag menu and click **Auto Format**. Select the **Professional** color scheme.

As discussed previously, a CreateUserWizard provides a registration form that site visitors can use to create a user account. When you configure your website to use forms authentication (*Step 3*), ASP.NET creates a SQL Server database (named ASPNETDB.MDF and located in the App_Data folder) to store the usernames, passwords and other account information of the application's users. ASP.NET also enforces a default set of requirements for filling out the form. Each field on the form is required, the password must contain at least seven characters (including at least one nonalphanumeric character), and the two passwords entered must match. The form also asks for a security question and answer that can be used to identify a user in case the user needs to reset or recover the account's password.

After the user fills in the form's fields and clicks the **Create User** button to submit the account information, ASP.NET verifies that all the form's requirements were fulfilled and attempts to create the user account. If an error occurs (e.g., the username already exists), the CreateUserWizard displays a message below the form. If the account is created successfully, the form is replaced by a confirmation message and a button that allows the user to continue. You can view this confirmation message in **Design** mode by selecting **Complete** from the **Step** drop-down list in the **CreateUserWizard Tasks** smart-tag menu.

When a user account is created, ASP.NET automatically logs the user into the site (we say more about the login process shortly). At this point, the user is authenticated and allowed to access the Secure folder. After we create Books.aspx later in this section, we set the CreateUserWizard's ContinueDestinationPageUrl property to ~/Secure/ Books.aspx to indicate that the user should be redirected to Books.aspx after clicking the **Continue** button on the confirmation page.

Figure 22.58 presents the completed CreateNewUser.aspx file (reformatted for readability). Inside the Content control, the CreateUserWizard control is defined by the markup in lines 13–40. The start tag (lines 13–16) contains several properties that specify formatting styles for the control, as well as the ContinueDestinationPageUrl property, which you will set later in the chapter. Lines 36–39 specify the wizard's two steps— CreateUserWizardStep and CompleteWizardStep—in a WizardSteps element. Create-UserWizardStep and CompleteWizardStep are classes that encapsulate the details of creating a user and issuing a confirmation message. Finally, lines 17–35 contain elements that define additional styles used to format specific parts of the control.

The sample outputs in Fig. 22.58(a) and Fig. 22.58(b) demonstrate successfully creating a user account with CreateNewUser.aspx. We use the password pa$$word for testing purposes. This password satisfies the minimum-length and special-character requirement imposed by ASP.NET, but in a real application, you should use a password that is more difficult for someone to guess. Figure 22.58(c) illustrates the error message that appears when you attempt to create a second user account with the same username—ASP.NET requires that each username be unique.

```
 1    <%-- Fig. 22.58: CreateNewUser.aspx --%>
 2    <%-- Content page using a CreateUserWizard control to register users. --%>
 3    <%@ Page Language="C#" MasterPageFile="~/Bug2Bug.master"
 4       Title="Create a New User" %>
 5
 6    <script runat="server">
 7    </script>
 8
 9    <asp:Content ID="Content1" ContentPlaceHolderID="head" Runat="Server">
10    </asp:Content>
11    <asp:Content ID="Content2" ContentPlaceHolderID="bodyContent"
12       Runat="Server">
```

Fig. 22.58 | CreateNewUser.aspx page that provides a user registration form. (Part 1 of 3.)

```
13    <asp:CreateUserWizard ID="CreateUserWizard1" runat="server"
14       BackColor="#F7F6F3" BorderColor="#E6E2D8" BorderStyle="Solid"
15       BorderWidth="1px" Font-Names="Verdana" Font-Size="0.8em"
16       ContinueDestinationPageUrl="~/Secure/Books.aspx">
17       <SideBarStyle BackColor="#5D7B9D" BorderWidth="0px"
18          Font-Size="0.9em" VerticalAlign="Top" />
19       <SideBarButtonStyle BorderWidth="0px" Font-Names="Verdana"
20          ForeColor="White" />
21       <ContinueButtonStyle BackColor="#FFFBFF" BorderColor="#CCCCCC"
22          BorderStyle="Solid" BorderWidth="1px" Font-Names="Verdana"
23          ForeColor="#284775" />
24       <NavigationButtonStyle BackColor="#FFFBFF" BorderColor="#CCCCCC"
25          BorderStyle="Solid" BorderWidth="1px" Font-Names="Verdana"
26          ForeColor="#284775" />
27       <HeaderStyle BackColor="#5D7B9D" BorderStyle="Solid"
28          Font-Bold="True" Font-Size="0.9em" ForeColor="White"
29          HorizontalAlign="Center" />
30       <CreateUserButtonStyle BackColor="#FFFBFF" BorderColor="#CCCCCC"
31          BorderStyle="Solid" BorderWidth="1px" Font-Names="Verdana"
32          ForeColor="#284775" />
33       <TitleTextStyle BackColor="#5D7B9D" Font-Bold="True"
34          ForeColor="White" />
35       <StepStyle BorderWidth="0px" />
36       <WizardSteps>
37          <asp:CreateUserWizardStep runat="server" />
38          <asp:CompleteWizardStep runat="server" />
39       </WizardSteps>
40    </asp:CreateUserWizard>
41 </asp:Content>
```

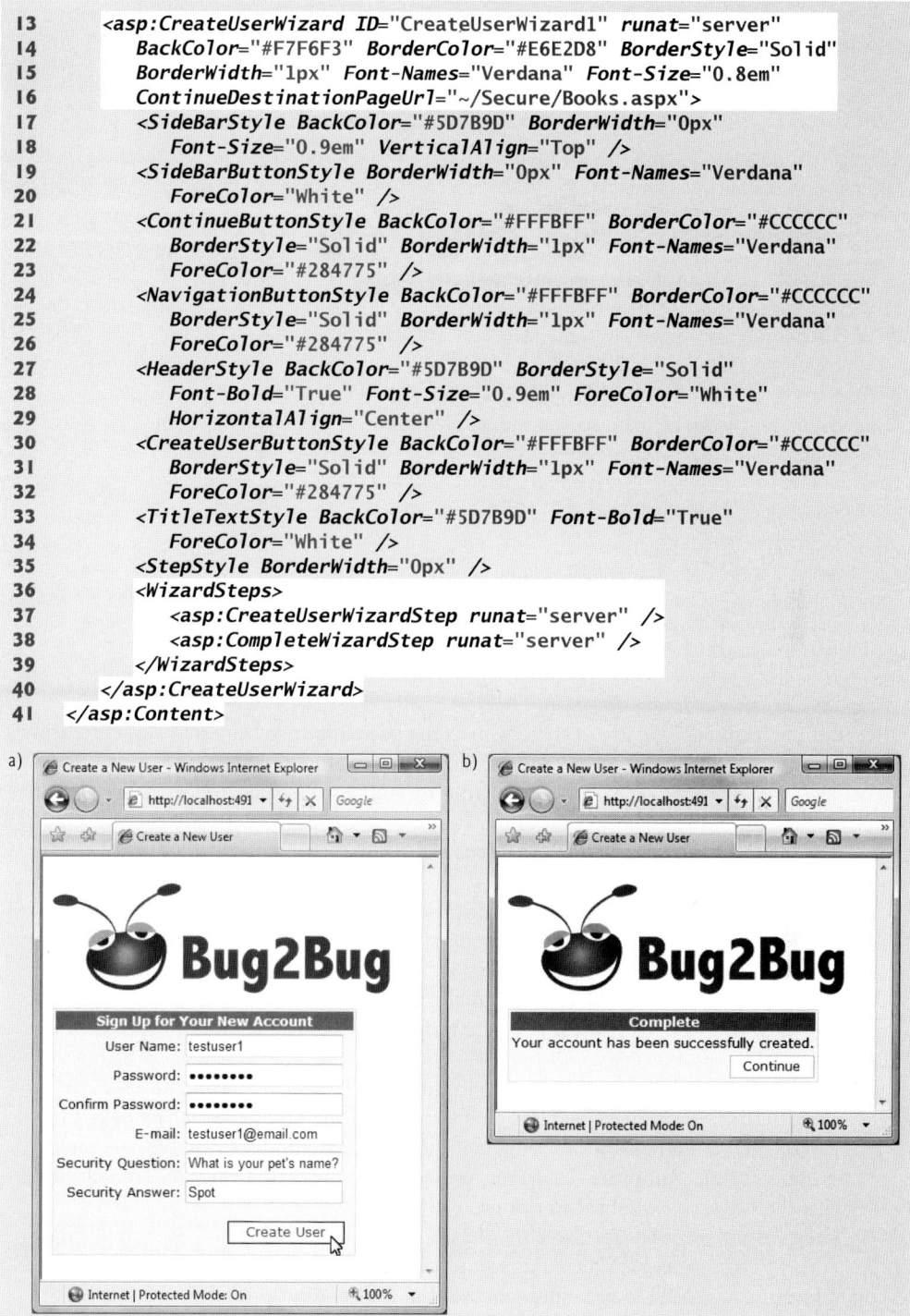

Fig. 22.58 | CreateNewUser.aspx page that provides a user registration form. (Part 2 of 3.)

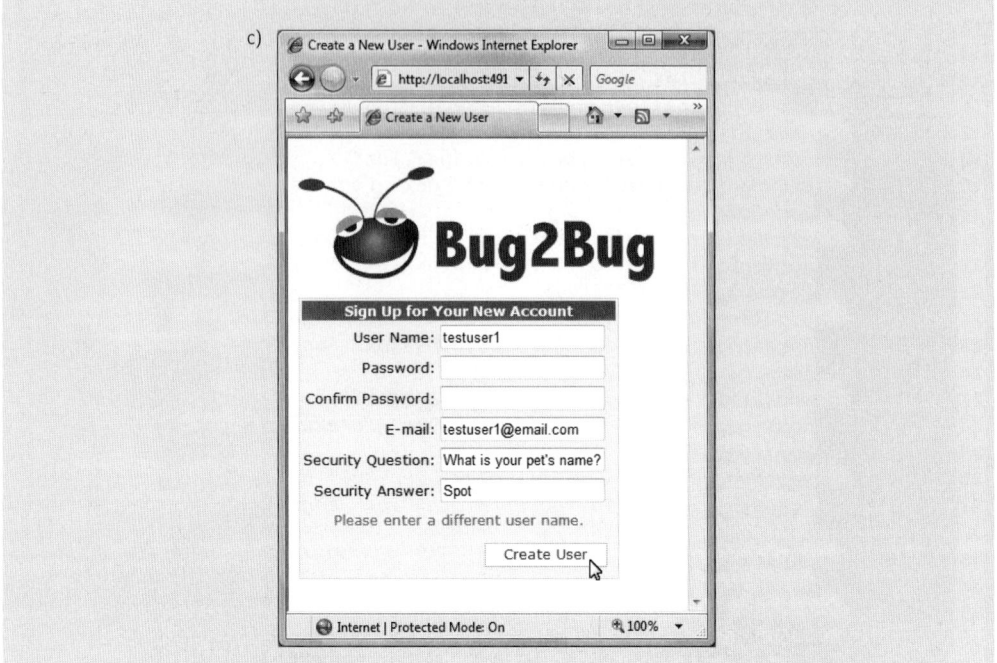

Fig. 22.58 | CreateNewUser.aspx page that provides a user registration form. (Part 3 of 3.)

Step 8: Creating a Login Page

Recall from Section 22.8.1 that Login.aspx is the page in our website that allows returning visitors to log into their user accounts. To create this functionality, add another content page named Login.aspx and set its title to Login. In **Design** mode, drag a *Login* control (located in the **Login** section of the **Toolbox**) to the page's Content control. Open the **Auto Format** dialog from the **Login Tasks** smart-tag menu and set the control's color scheme to **Professional**.

Next, configure the Login control to display a link to the page for creating new users. Set the Login control's CreateUserUrl property to CreateNewUser.aspx by clicking the ellipsis button to the right of this property in the **Properties** window and selecting the CreateNewUser.aspx file in the resulting dialog. Then set the CreateUserText property to Click here to create a new user. These property values cause a link to appear in the Login control.

Finally, change the value of the Login control's DisplayRememberMe property to False. By default, the control displays a checkbox and the text Remember me next time. This can be used to allow a user to remain authenticated beyond a single browser session on the user's current computer. However, we want to require that users log in each time they visit the site, so we disable this option.

The Login control encapsulates the details of logging a user into a web application (i.e., authenticating a user). When a user enters a username and password, then clicks the **Log In** button, ASP.NET determines whether the information provided matches that of an account in the membership database (i.e., ASPNETDB.MDF created by ASP.NET). If they match, the user is authenticated (i.e., the user's identity is confirmed), and the browser is redirected to the page specified by the Login control's DestinationPageUrl property. We set this property to the Books.aspx page after creating it in the next section. If the user's identity cannot be confirmed (i.e., the user is not authenticated), the Login control displays an error message (see Fig. 22.59), and the user can attempt to log in again.

```
 1   <%-- Figure 22.59: Login.aspx --%>
 2   <%-- Content page using a Login control that authenticates users. --%>
 3   <%@ Page Language="C#" MasterPageFile="~/Bug2Bug.master" Title="Login" %>
 4
 5   <script runat="server">
 6   </script>
 7
 8   <asp:Content ID="Content1" ContentPlaceHolderID="head" Runat="Server">
 9   </asp:Content>
10   <asp:Content ID="Content2" ContentPlaceHolderID="bodyContent"
11      Runat="Server">
12      <asp:Login ID="Login1" runat="server" BackColor="#F7F6F3"
13         BorderColor="#E6E2D8" BorderPadding="4" BorderStyle="Solid"
14         BorderWidth="1px" CreateUserText="Click here to create a new user"
15         CreateUserUrl="~/CreateNewUser.aspx" DisplayRememberMe="False"
16         Font-Names="Verdana" Font-Size="0.8em" ForeColor="#333333"
17         DestinationPageUrl="~/Secure/Books.aspx">
18         <TextBoxStyle Font-Size="0.8em" />
19         <LoginButtonStyle BackColor="#FFFBFF" BorderColor="#CCCCCC"
20            BorderStyle="Solid" BorderWidth="1px" Font-Names="Verdana"
21            Font-Size="0.8em" ForeColor="#284775" />
22         <InstructionTextStyle Font-Italic="True" ForeColor="Black" />
23         <TitleTextStyle BackColor="#5D7B9D" Font-Bold="True"
24            Font-Size="0.9em" ForeColor="White" />
25      </asp:Login>
26   </asp:Content>
```

Fig. 22.59 | Login.aspx content page using a Login control.

Figure 22.59 presents the completed `Login.aspx` page. Note that, as in `CreateNew-User.aspx`, the `Page` directive indicates that this content page inherits content from `Bug2Bug.master`. In the `Content` control that replaces the master page's `ContentPlace-Holder` with ID `bodyContent`, lines 12–25 create a `Login` control. Note the `CreateUser-Text` and `CreateUserUrl` properties (lines 14–15) that we set using the **Properties** window. Line 17 in the start tag for the `Login` control contains the `DestinationPageUrl` (you will set this property in the next step). The elements in lines 18–24 define various formatting styles applied to parts of the control. Note that all of the functionality related to actually logging the user in or displaying error messages is completely hidden from you.

When a user enters the username and password of an existing user account, ASP.NET authenticates the user and writes to the client an *encrypted* cookie containing information about the authenticated user. Encrypted data is data translated into a code that only the sender and receiver can understand—thereby keeping it private. The encrypted cookie contains a `string` username and a `bool` value that specifies whether this cookie should persist (i.e., remain on the client's computer) beyond the current session. Our application authenticates the user for only the current session.

Step 9: Creating a Content Page That Only Authenticated Users Can Access

A user who has been authenticated will be redirected to `Books.aspx`. We now create the `Books.aspx` file in the `Secure` folder—the folder for which we set an access rule denying access to anonymous users. If an unauthenticated user requests this file, the user will be redirected to `Login.aspx`. From there, the user can either log in or create a new account, both of which will authenticate the user, thus allowing the user to return to `Books.aspx`.

To create `Books.aspx`, right click the `Secure` folder in the **Solution Explorer** and select **Add New Item…**. In the resulting dialog, select **Web Form** and specify the file name `Books.aspx`. You'll need to write event handlers for this form, so check the checkbox **Place code in separate file**. Also check the checkbox **Select master page** to indicate that this page should be created as a content page that references a master page. Click **Add**. In the **Select a Master Page** dialog, select `Bug2Bug.master` and click **OK**. The IDE creates the file and opens it in **Source** mode. Change the `Page` directive's `Title` property to `Book Information`.

Step 10: Customizing the Secure Page

To customize the `Books.aspx` page for a particular user, we add a welcome message containing a *LoginName* control, which displays the current authenticated username. Open `Books.aspx` in **Design** mode. In the `Content` control, type `Welcome` followed by a comma and a space. Then drag a `LoginName` control from the **Toolbox** onto the page. When this page executes on the server, the text `[UserName]` that appears in this control in **Design** mode will be replaced by the current username. In **Source** mode, type an exclamation point (!) directly after the `LoginName` control (with no spaces in between). [*Note:* If you add the exclamation point in **Design** mode, the IDE may insert extra spaces or a line break between this character and the preceding control. Entering the ! in **Source** mode ensures that it appears adjacent to the user's name.]

Next, add a `LoginStatus` control, which will allow the user to log out of the website when finished viewing the listing of books in the database. A *LoginStatus* control renders on a web page in one of two ways—by default, if the user is not authenticated, the control displays a hyperlink with the text `Login`; if the user is authenticated, the control displays a hyperlink with the text `Logout`. Each link performs the stated action. Add a `LoginStatus` control to the page by dragging it from the **Toolbox** onto the page. In this example, any user who reaches this page must already be authenticated, so the control will always render as a Logout link. The **LoginStatus Tasks** smart-tag menu allows you switch between the control's **Views**. Select the **Logged In** view to see the Logout link. To change the actual text of this link, modify the control's LogoutText property to Click here to log out. Next, set the LogoutAction property to RedirectToLoginPage.

Step 11: Connecting the *CreateUserWizard* and *Login* Controls to the Secure Page
Now that we have created Books.aspx, we can specify that this is the page to which the CreateUserWizard and Login controls redirect users after they are authenticated. Open CreateNewUser.aspx in **Design** mode and set the CreateUserWizard control's Continue-DestinationPageUrl property to Books.aspx. Next, open Login.aspx and select Books.aspx as the DestinationPageUrl of the Login control.

At this point, you can run the web application by selecting **Debug > Start Without Debugging**. First, create a user account on CreateNewUser.aspx, then notice how the LoginName and LoginStatus controls appear on Books.aspx. Next, log out of the site and log back in using the account you just created. Note that if you terminate the application, you are automatically logged out. If you restart the application, you can log in using the user you created earlier, because it has been stored in the ASPNETDB.mdf database.

Step 12: Generating LINQ to SQL Classes Based on the *Books.mdf* Database
Now let's add the content (i.e., book information) to the secure page Books.aspx. This page will provide a DropDownList containing authors' names and a GridView displaying information about books written by the author selected in the DropDownList. A user will select an author from the DropDownList to cause the GridView to display information about only the books written by the selected author.

To work with the Books database through LINQ, we use the same approach as the preceding case study, in which we accessed the Guestbook database. First you need to generate the LINQ to SQL classes based on the Books database, which is provided in the Databases subfolder of this chapter's examples folder. Name the classes BooksDB.dbml When you drag the tables of the Books database onto the **Object Relation Designer** of BooksDB.dbml, you'll find that associations (represented by arrows) between the two tables are automatically generated (Fig. 22.60).

To obtain data from this data context, you'll use two LinqDataSource controls. In both case, however, the LinqDataSource control's built-in data selection functionality won't be versatile enough, so the implementation will be slightly different than in the preceding case study. In *Steps 13* and *14*, you'll learn to use a custom select LINQ statement to select the data of a LinqDataSource.

Step 13: Adding a *DropDownList* Containing Authors' First and Last Names
Now that we have created a BooksDBDataContext (one of the generated LINQ to SQL classes), we add controls to Books.aspx that will display the data on the web page. We first add the DropDownList from which users can select an author. Open Books.aspx in **Design** mode, then add the text Author: and a DropDownList control named authorsDropDownList in the page's Content control, below the existing content. The DropDownList initially displays the text [Unbound]. We now bind the list to a data source, so the list displays the author information in the Authors table of the Books database.

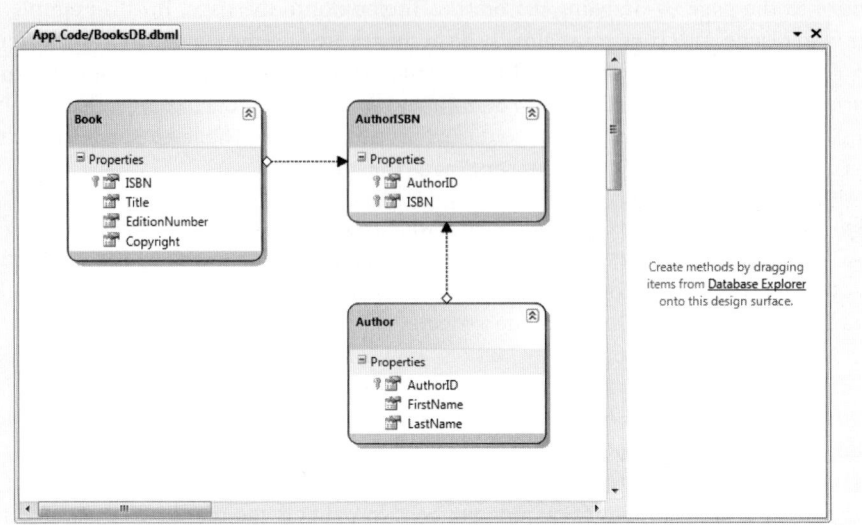

Fig. 22.60 | Object Relation Designer of Books database.

Because the **Configure Data Source** wizard only allows us to create LinqDataSources with simple select LINQ statements, we cannot use it here. Instead, add a LinqData-Source object below the DropDownList named authorsLinqDataSource. In the **Drop-DownList Tasks** smart-tag menu, click **Choose Data Source...** to start the **Data Source Configuration Wizard** (Fig. 22.61). Select authorsLinqDataSource from the **Select a data source** drop-down list in the first screen of the wizard. Set Name as the data field to display

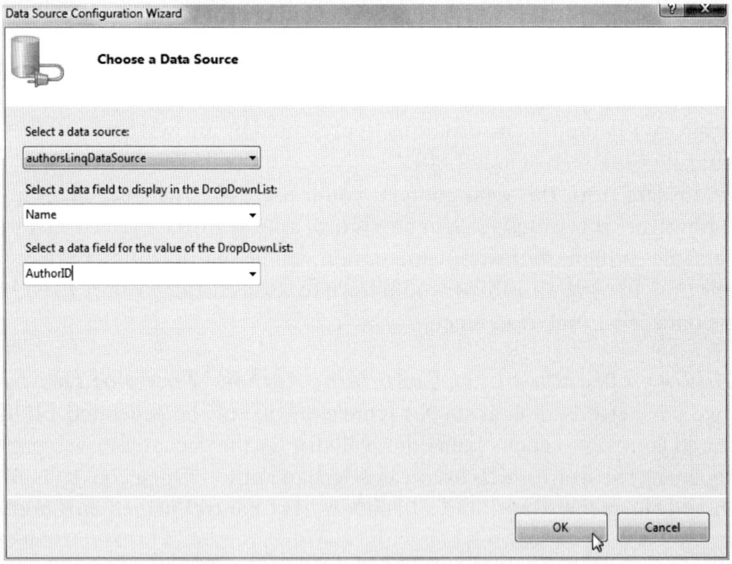

Fig. 22.61 | Choosing a data source for a DropDownList.

and `AuthorID` as the data field to use as the value. [*Note:* Because `authorsLinqDataSource` has no internally defined `select` query, you must manually type these values in; they will not appear in the drop-down list.] Thus, when `authorsDropDownList` is rendered in a web browser, the list items will display the names of the authors, but the underlying values associated with each item will be their database IDs. Click **OK** to bind the `DropDownList` to the specified data.

In the C# code-behind file (`Books.aspx.cs`), create an instance of `Books-DBDataContext` as an instance variable. In the **Design** view of `Books.aspx`, double click `authorsLinqDataSource`. Double-clicking a `LinqDataSource` control creates an event handler for its default event, the *Selecting* event. This event is raised every time the `Linq-DataSource` selects data from its data context, and can be used to implement custom `select` queries against the data context. To do so, set the *Result* property of the event handler's arguments object to be the custom LINQ query. The results of the query become the data source's data. In this case, we must create a custom anonymous type in the `select` clause with properties `Name` and `AuthorID` that contain the author's full name and ID. The LINQ query is

```
from author in booksDatabase.Authors
select new
{
    Name = author.FirstName + " " + author.LastName,
    author.AuthorID
}
```

The limitations of the **Configure Data Source** wizard prevent us from using a custom property such as `Name` (a combination of database fields `FirstName` and `LastName`, separated by a space) that isn't one of the data table's columns.

The last step in configuring the `DropDownList` on `Books.aspx` is to set the control's *AutoPostBack* property to `True`. This property indicates that a postback occurs each time the user selects an item in the `DropDownList`. As you will see shortly, this causes the page's `GridView` (created in the next step) to display new data.

Step 14: Creating a GridView to Display the Selected Author's Books
We now add a `GridView` to `Books.aspx` for displaying the book information by the author selected in the `authorsDropDownList`. Add a `GridView` named `booksGridView` below the other controls in the page's `Content` control.

To bind the `GridView` to data from the Books database, create a `LinqDataSource` named `booksLinqDataSource` beneath the `GridView`. Select `booksLinqDataSource` from the **Choose Data Source** drop-down list in the **GridView Tasks** smart-tag menu. Because `booksLinqDataSource` has no internally defined `select` query, the `GridView` will not automatically be configured.

To configure the columns of the `GridView` to display the appropriate data, select **Edit Columns...** from the **GridView Tasks** smart-tag menu to initiate the **Fields** dialog (Fig. 22.62). Uncheck the **Auto-generate fields** box to indicate that you'll manually define the fields to display. Create `BoundField`s with `HeaderText`s `ISBN`, `Title`, `Edition Number`, and `Copyright`. For each one except for `Edition Number`, the `SortExpression` and `Data-Field` properties should match the `HeaderText`. For `Edition Number`, the `SortExpression` and `DataField` should be `EditionNumber`—the name of the field in the database.

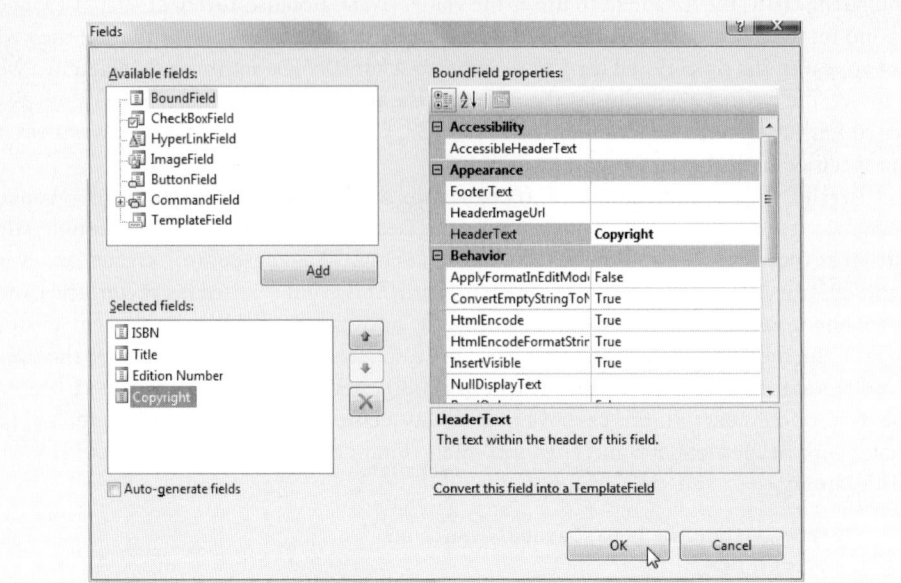

Fig. 22.62 | Creating GridView fields in the **Fields** dialog.

The SortExpression specifies the data field to sort by when the user chooses to sort by the column. Shortly, we'll enable sorting to allow users to sort this GridView.

To specify the select LINQ query for obtaining the data, double click booksLinq-DataSource to create an event handler for its Selecting event. Just as you did in the Selecting event handler for authorsLinqDataSource, set the Result property of the event-arguments object to be the LINQ query. In this case we must to use a select, which cannot be accomplished if you use the **Configure Data Source** wizard to specify the Linq-DataSource control's data selection. The LINQ query is

```
from book in booksDatabase.Titles
join isbn in booksDatabase.AuthorISBNs
on book.ISBN equals isbn.ISBN
where isbn.AuthorID.Equals( authorsDropDownList.SelectedValue )
select book
```

The GridView needs to update every time the user makes a new author selection. To implement this, double click the DropDownList to create an event handler for its default event, the SelectedIndexChanged event. Make the GridView update by invoking its DataBind method. Note that this works only if the DropDownList's AutoPostBack property is True. Otherwise, a request won't be made to the server when a selection is made, and so this event handler won't be executed. Furthermore, the DropDownList's EnableViewState property must be true (which it is by default) because ASP.NET must know what the previous selection was in order to determine whether it has changed.

Figure 22.63 shows the code for the completed code-behind file. Line 11 defines the data-context object that is used as the source of both data sources. Lines 14–24 and 27–36 define the two data source's Selecting events. Lastly, authorsDropDownList's SelectedIndexChanged event handler is defined in lines 39–43.

```
1   // Fig. 22.63: Books.aspx.cs
2   // Code-behind file that defines event handlers for the secure books
3   // database application.
4   using System;
5   using System.Linq;
6   using System.Web.UI.WebControls;
7
8   public partial class Secure_Books : System.Web.UI.Page
9   {
10      // instantiate data context queried by data sources
11      BooksDBDataContext booksDatabase = new BooksDBDataContext();
12
13      // runs a query and uses the result as authorsLinqDataSource's data
14      protected void authorsLinqDataSource_Selecting(
15         object sender, LinqDataSourceSelectEventArgs e )
16      {
17         // select LINQ query returning all authors' full names and IDs
18         e.Result = from authors in booksDatabase.Authors
19            select new
20               {
21                  Name = authors.FirstName + " " + authors.LastName,
22                  authors.AuthorID
23               };
24      } // end method authorsLinqDataSource_Selecting
25
26      // runs a query and uses the result as booksLinqDataSource's data
27      protected void booksLinqDataSource_Selecting(
28         object sender, LinqDataSourceSelectEventArgs e )
29      {
30         // select LINQ query return all books by the selected author
31         e.Result = from book in booksDatabase.Books
32            join isbn in booksDatabase.AuthorISBNs
33            on book.ISBN equals isbn.ISBN
34            where isbn.AuthorID.Equals( authorsDropDownList.SelectedValue )
35            select book;
36      } // end method booksLinqDataSource_Selecting
37
38      // updates the books list whenever the user selects a new author
39      protected void authorsDropDownList_SelectedIndexChanged(
40         object sender, EventArgs e )
41      {
42         booksGridView.DataBind(); // update the GridView
43      } // end method authorsDropDownList_SelectedIndexChanged
44   } // end class Secure_Books
```

Fig. 22.63 | Code-behind file that defines event handlers for the secure books database application.

Now that the GridView is tied to a data source, we modify several of the control's properties to adjust its appearance and behavior. Set the GridView's CellPadding property to 5, set the BackColor of the AlternatingRowStyle to LightYellow, and set the Back-Color of the HeaderStyle to LightGreen. Note that you can set these properties by typing these values into the **Properties** window instead of trying to locate the color in the **More**

Colors dialog. Next, change the Width of the control to 600px to ensure that long data values don't wrap to multiple lines.

Next, in the **GridView Tasks** smart-tag menu, check **Enable Sorting** to change the column headings in the GridView into hyperlinks that allow users to sort the data in the GridView using the sort expressions specified by each column. For example, clicking the Title heading in the web browser will sort the data in alphabetical order by title. Clicking this heading a second time will sort the data in reverse alphabetical order by title. ASP.NET hides the details required to achieve this functionality.

Finally, in the **GridView Tasks** smart-tag menu, check **Enable Paging**. This causes the GridView to split across multiple pages. The user can click the numbered links at the bottom of the GridView control to display a different page of data. GridView's **PageSize** property determines the number of entries per page. Set the PageSize property to 4 using the **Properties** window so that the GridView displays only four books per page. This technique for displaying data makes the site more readable and enables pages to load more quickly (because less data is displayed at one time). Note that, as with sorting data in a GridView, you do not need to add any code to achieve paging functionality. Figure 22.64 displays the completed Books.aspx file in **Design** mode.

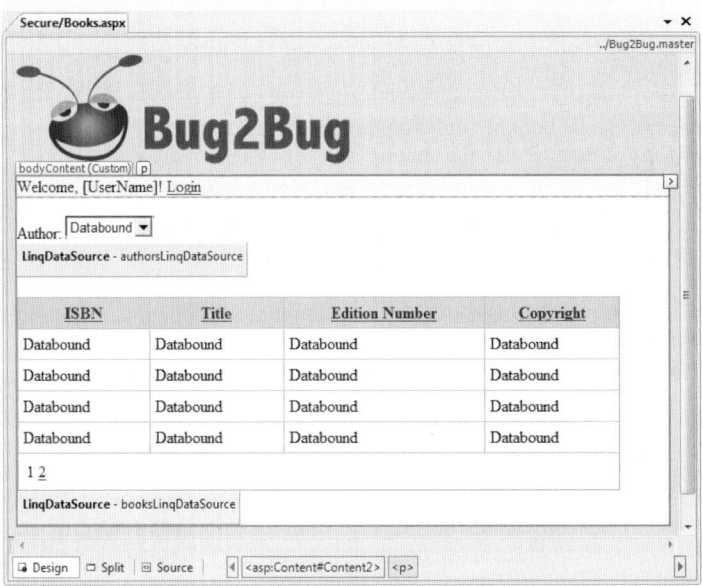

Fig. 22.64 | Completed Books.aspx in **Design** mode.

Step 17: Examining the Markup in Books.aspx

Figure 22.65 presents the markup in Books.aspx (reformatted for readability). Aside from the exclamation point in line 13, which we added manually in **Source** mode, all the remaining markup was generated by the IDE in response to the actions we performed in **Design** mode. The Content control (lines 9–53) defines page-specific content that will replace the ContentPlaceHolder named bodyContent. Recall that this control is located in the master page specified in line 3. Line 13 creates the LoginName control, which displays

```
 1   <%-- Fig. 22.65: Books.aspx --%>
 2   <%-- Displays information from the Books database. --%>
 3   <%@ Page Language="C#" MasterPageFile="~/Bug2Bug.master"
 4      AutoEventWireup="true" CodeFile="Books.aspx.cs"
 5      Inherits="Secure_Books" Title="Book Information" %>
 6
 7   <asp:Content ID="Content1" ContentPlaceHolderID="head" Runat="Server">
 8   </asp:Content>
 9   <asp:Content ID="Content2" ContentPlaceHolderID="bodyContent"
10      Runat="Server">
11      <p>
12         Welcome,
13         <asp:LoginName ID="LoginName1" runat="server" />!
14         <asp:LoginStatus ID="LoginStatus1" runat="server"
15            LogoutAction="RedirectToLoginPage"
16            LogoutText="Click here to log out." />
17      </p>
18      <p>
19         Author:
20         <asp:DropDownList ID="authorsDropDownList" runat="server"
21            DataSourceID="authorsLinqDataSource" DataTextField="Name"
22            DataValueField="AuthorID" AutoPostBack="True"
23            onselectedindexchanged=
24               "authorsDropDownList_SelectedIndexChanged">
25         </asp:DropDownList>
26         <asp:LinqDataSource ID="authorsLinqDataSource" runat="server"
27            onselecting="authorsLinqDataSource_Selecting">
28         </asp:LinqDataSource>
29      </p>
30      <p>
31         <asp:GridView ID="booksGridView" runat="server" AllowPaging="True"
32            AllowSorting="True" AutoGenerateColumns="False" CellPadding="5"
33            DataSourceID="booksLinqDataSource" PageSize="4"
34            Width="600px">
35            <Columns>
36               <asp:BoundField DataField="ISBN" HeaderText="ISBN"
37                  SortExpression="ISBN" />
38               <asp:BoundField DataField="Title" HeaderText="Title"
39                  SortExpression="Title" />
40               <asp:BoundField DataField="EditionNumber"
41                  HeaderText="Edition Number"
42                  SortExpression="EditionNumber" />
43               <asp:BoundField DataField="Copyright" HeaderText="Copyright"
44                  SortExpression="Copyright" />
45            </Columns>
46            <HeaderStyle BackColor="LightGreen" />
47            <AlternatingRowStyle BackColor="LightYellow" />
48         </asp:GridView>
49         <asp:LinqDataSource ID="booksLinqDataSource" runat="server"
50            onselecting="booksLinqDataSource_Selecting">
51         </asp:LinqDataSource>
52      </p>
53   </asp:Content>
```

Fig. 22.65 | Displays information from the Books database. (Part 1 of 3.)

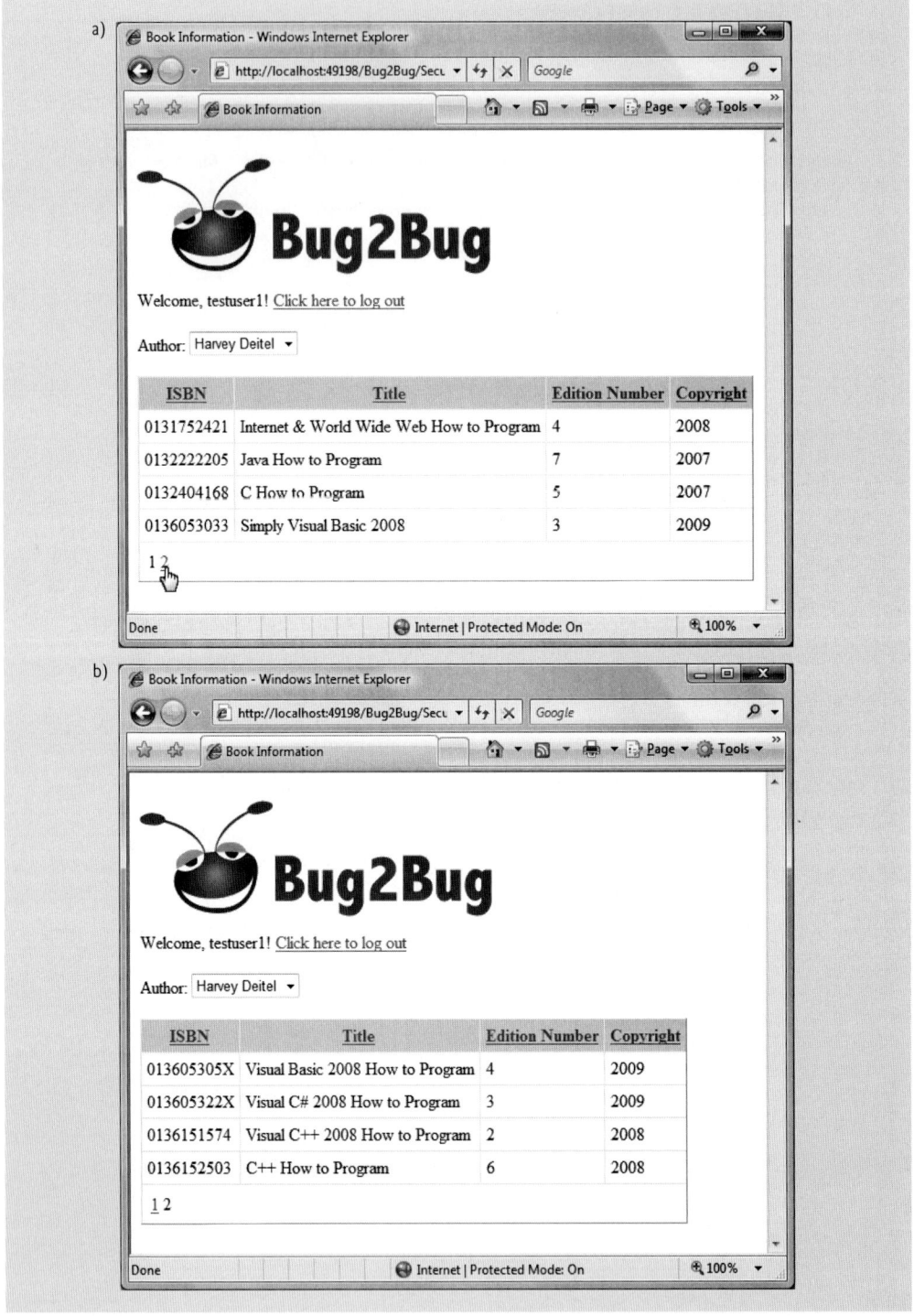

Fig. 22.65 | Displays information from the Books database. (Part 2 of 3.)

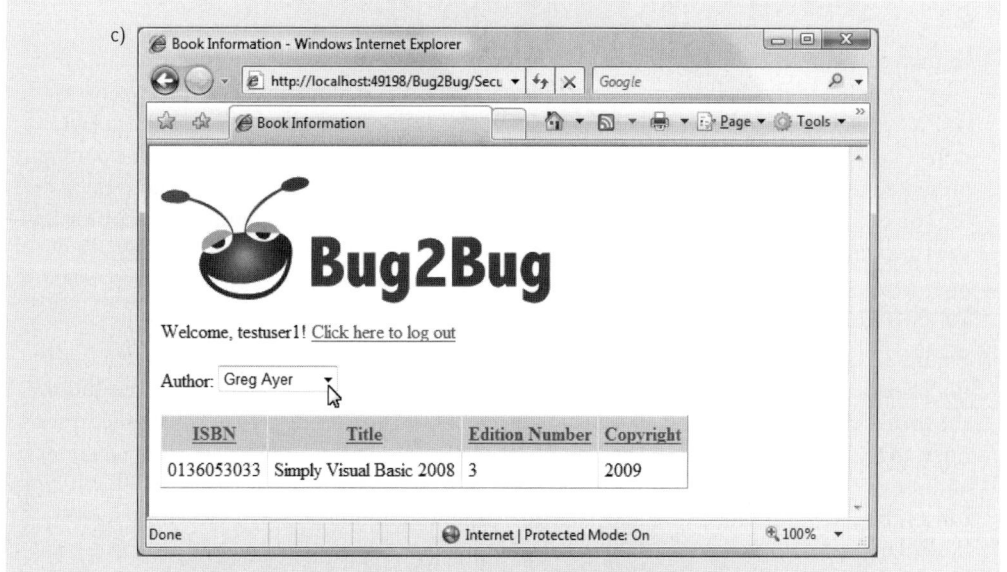

Fig. 22.65 | Displays information from the Books database. (Part 3 of 3.)

the authenticated user's name when the page is requested and viewed in a browser. Lines 14–16 create the LoginStatus control. Recall that we configured this control to redirect the user to the login page after logging out (i.e., clicking the hyperlink with the Logout-Text) by setting the LogoutAction property to RedirectToLoginPage (line 15).

Lines 20–25 define the DropDownList that displays the names of the authors in the Books database. Line 22 contains the control's AutoPostBack property, which indicates that changing the selected item in the list causes a postback to occur. The DataSourceID property in line 21 specifies that the DropDownList's items are created based on the data obtained through the authorsLinqDataSource (defined in lines 26–28).

Lines 31–48 create the GridView that displays information about the books written by the selected author. The start tag (lines 31–34) indicates that paging (with a page size of 4) and sorting are enabled in the GridView. Property AutoGenerateColumns indicates whether the columns in the GridView are generated automatically at runtime based on the fields in the data source. This property is set to False, reflecting our choice in the **Fields** dialog. The IDE-generated Columns element (lines 35–45) specifies the columns for the GridView using BoundFields. Lines 49–51 define the LinqDataSource used to fill the GridView with data. Recall that we configured the selections of both the LinqDataSource controls programmatically, so almost no properties are defined in the markup.

Figure 22.65(a) depicts the default appearance of Books.aspx in a web browser. By default, the author with AuthorID 1 (i.e., **Harvey Deitel**) is selected, and his books are displayed when the page first loads. Note that the GridView displays paging links below the data, because the number of rows of data in booksLinqDataSource is greater than the page size. Figure 22.65(b) shows the GridView after clicking the 2 link to view the second page of data. Figure 22.65(c) presents Books.aspx after the user selects a different author from the authorsDropDownList. The data fits on one page, so the GridView does not display paging links.

22.9 ASP.NET AJAX

In this section, you learn the difference between a traditional web application and an *Ajax (Asynchronous JavaScript and XML) web application*. You also learn how to use *ASP.NET AJAX* to quickly and easily improve the user experience for your web applications. To demonstrate ASP.NET AJAX capabilities, you enhance the validation example presented in Section 22.5.3 by displaying the submitted form information without reloading the entire page. The only noteworthy modifications to this web application appear in Validation.aspx file. You use Ajax-enabled controls to add this feature.

22.9.1 Traditional Web Applications

Figure 22.66 presents the typical interactions between the client and the server in a traditional web application, such as one that uses a user registration form. The user first fills in the form's fields, then submits the form (Fig. 22.66, *Step 1*). The browser generates a request to the server, which receives the request and processes it (*Step 2*). The server generates and sends a response containing the exact page that the browser renders (*Step 3*), which causes the browser to load the new page (*Step 4*) and temporarily makes the browser window blank. Note that the client *waits* for the server to respond and *reloads the entire page* with the data from the response (*Step 4*). While such a **synchronous request** is being processed on the server, the user cannot interact with the web page. Frequent long periods of waiting, due perhaps to Internet congestion, have led some users to refer to the World Wide Web as the "World Wide Wait." If the user interacts with and submits another form, the process begins again (*Steps 5–8*).

This model was designed for a web of hypertext documents—what some people call the "brochure web." As the web evolved into a full-scale applications platform, the model shown in Fig. 22.66 yielded "choppy" application performance. Every full-page refresh required users to reload the full page. Users began to demand a more responsive model.

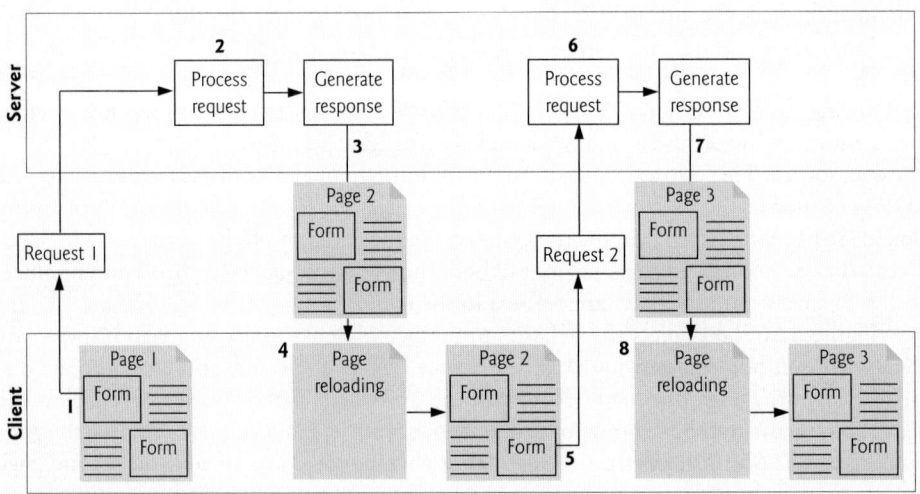

Fig. 22.66 | Traditional web application reloading the page for every user interaction.

22.9.2 Ajax Web Applications

Ajax web applications add a layer between the client and the server to manage communication between the two (Fig. 22.67). When the user interacts with the page, the client requests information from the server (*Step 1*). The request is intercepted by the ASP.NET AJAX controls and sent to the server as an ***asynchronous request*** (*Step 2*)—the user can continue interacting with the application in the client browser while the server processes the request. Other user interactions could result in additional requests to the server (*Steps 3 and 4*). Once the server responds to the original request (*Step 5*), the ASP.NET AJAX control that issued the request calls a client-side function to process the data returned by the server. This function—known as a ***callback function***—uses ***partial-page updates*** (*Step 6*) to display the data in the existing web page *without reloading the entire page*. At the same time, the server may be responding to the second request (*Step 7*) and the client browser may be starting another partial-page update (*Step 8*). The callback function updates only a designated part of the page. Such partial-page updates help make web applications more responsive, making them feel more like desktop applications. The web application does not load a new page while the user interacts with it. In the following section, you use ASP.NET AJAX controls to enhance the `Validation.aspx` page.

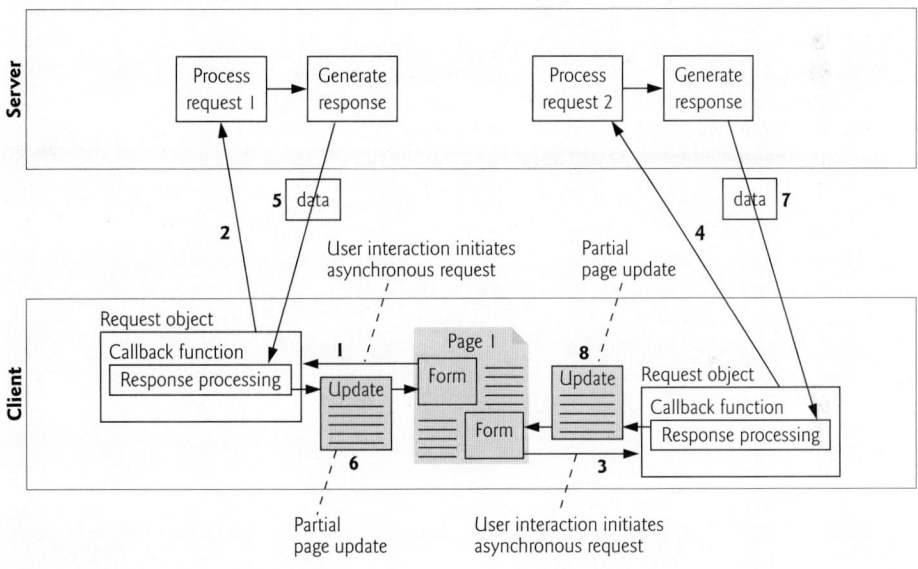

Fig. 22.67 | Ajax-enabled web application interacting with the server asynchronously.

22.9.3 Examining an ASP.NET AJAX Application

ASP.NET AJAX is built into .NET 3.5, and the ***AJAX Extensions package*** that implements basic Ajax functionality comes preinstalled in Visual Web Developer 2008. You'll notice that there is a tab of basic **AJAX Extensions** controls in the **Toolbox**. Microsoft also provides the ***ASP.NET AJAX Control Toolkit***, which contains rich, Ajax-enabled GUI controls. You can download the latest version of the Ajax Control Toolkit from www.asp.net/ajax/ajaxcontroltoolkit. Be sure to download the .NET Framework 3.5 version. The toolkit does not come with an installer, so you must extract the contents of the toolkit's ZIP file to your hard drive.

To make using the ASP.NET AJAX Control Toolkit more convenient, you'll want to add its controls to the **Toolbox** in Visual Web Developer (or in Visual Studio) so you can drag and drop controls onto your Web Forms. To do so, right click the **Toolbox** and choose **Add Tab.** Type AJAX Control Toolkit as the name of the new tab. Then right click the tab and select **Choose Items.** Next, click **Browse...** and navigate to the folder in which you extracted the toolkit and select AjaxControlToolkit.dll from the SampleWeb-Site\Bin subfolder. Finally, click **OK**, and a list of available Ajax controls will appear under the **AJAX Control Toolkit** tab when you are in **Design** mode.

To demonstrate ASP.NET AJAX capabilities we'll enhance the Validation application from Figs. 22.22–22.23. The only significant modifications to this application appear in its ASPX file. Thus, we do not present the new version of the code-behind file in this section. We'll use Ajax-enabled controls to add Ajax features to this application. Figure 22.68 is a modified Validation.aspx file that enhances the application by using the ToolkitScriptManager, TabContainer, UpdatePanel and ValidatorCalloutEx-tender controls.

```
 1   <%-- Fig. 22.68: Validation.aspx --%>
 2   <%-- Validation application enhanced with ASP.NET AJAX. --%>
 3   <%@ Page Language="C#" AutoEventWireup="true"
 4      CodeFile="Validation.aspx.cs" Inherits="Validation" %>
 5   <%@ Register assembly="AjaxControlToolkit"
 6      namespace="AjaxControlToolkit" tagprefix="ajax" %>
 7
 8   <!DOCTYPE html PUBLIC "-//W3C//DTD XHTML 1.0 Transitional//EN"
 9      "http://www.w3.org/TR/xhtml1/DTD/xhtml1-transitional.dtd">
10
11   <html xmlns="http://www.w3.org/1999/xhtml">
12   <head runat="server">
13      <title>Demonstrating Validation Controls</title>
14      <style type="text/css">
15         .style1
16         {
17            width: 100%;
18         }
19         .style2
20         {
21            text-align: right;
22            vertical-align: top;
23         }
24      </style>
25   </head>
26   <body>
27   <form id="form1" runat="server">
28   <ajax:ToolkitScriptManager ID="ToolkitScriptManager1" runat="server">
29   </ajax:ToolkitScriptManager>
30   <div>
```

Fig. 22.68 | Validation application enhanced by ASP.NET AJAX. (Part 1 of 5.)

```
31   <p>
32       Please fill out the following form.<br /><i>All fields are
33       required and must contain valid information.</i>
34   </p>
35   <ajax:TabContainer ID="TabContainer1" runat="server"
36       ActiveTabIndex="0" Width="500px">
37       <ajax:TabPanel runat="server" HeaderText="Name" ID="TabPanel1">
38          <ContentTemplate>
39          <table class="style1">
40              <tr>
41                  <td class="style2">First Name:</td>
42                  <td>
43                      <asp:TextBox ID="firstNameTextBox" runat="server">
44                      </asp:TextBox><br />
45                      <asp:RequiredFieldValidator
46                          ID="firstNameExistsValidator" runat="server"
47                          ControlToValidate="firstNameTextBox" Display="None"
48                          ErrorMessage="Please enter your first name.">
49                      </asp:RequiredFieldValidator>
50                      <ajax:ValidatorCalloutExtender
51                          ID="firstNameExistsCallout" runat="server"
52                          Enabled="True"
53                          TargetControlID="firstNameExistsValidator">
54                      </ajax:ValidatorCalloutExtender>
55                  </td>
56              </tr>
57              <tr>
58                  <td class="style2">Last Name:</td>
59                  <td>
60                      <asp:TextBox ID="lastNameTextBox" runat="server">
61                      </asp:TextBox><br />
62                      <asp:RequiredFieldValidator
63                          ID="lastNameExistsValidator" runat="server"
64                          ControlToValidate="lastNameTextBox" Display="None"
65                          ErrorMessage="Please enter your last name.">
66                      </asp:RequiredFieldValidator>
67                      <ajax:ValidatorCalloutExtender
68                          ID="lastNameExistsCallout" runat="server"
69                          Enabled="True"
70                          TargetControlID="lastNameExistsValidator">
71                      </ajax:ValidatorCalloutExtender>
72                  </td>
73              </tr>
74          </table>
75          </ContentTemplate>
76      </ajax:TabPanel>
77      <ajax:TabPanel ID="TabPanel2" runat="server" HeaderText="Contact">
78          <ContentTemplate>
79          <table class="style1">
80              <tr>
81                  <td class="style2">E-mail address:</td>
82                  <td>
83                      <asp:TextBox ID="emailTextBox" runat="server">
```

Fig. 22.68 | Validation application enhanced by ASP.NET AJAX. (Part 2 of 5.)

```
 84                </asp:TextBox> e.g., user@domain.com<br />
 85                <asp:RequiredFieldValidator
 86                   ID="emailExistsValidator" runat="server"
 87                   ErrorMessage="Please enter your e-mail address."
 88                   ControlToValidate="emailTextBox" Display="None">
 89                </asp:RequiredFieldValidator>
 90                <ajax:ValidatorCalloutExtender
 91                   ID="emailExistsCallout" runat="server"
 92                   Enabled="True"
 93                   TargetControlID="emailExistsValidator">
 94                </ajax:ValidatorCalloutExtender>
 95                <asp:RegularExpressionValidator
 96                   ID="emailFormatValidator" runat="server"
 97                   ErrorMessage="Please enter a valid e-mail address."
 98                   ControlToValidate="emailTextBox" Display="None"
 99                   ValidationExpression=
100                      "\w+([-+.']\w+)*@\w+([-.]\w+)*\.\w+([-.]\w+)*">
101                </asp:RegularExpressionValidator>
102                <ajax:ValidatorCalloutExtender ID="emailFormatCallout"
103                   runat="server" Enabled="True"
104                   TargetControlID="emailFormatValidator">
105                </ajax:ValidatorCalloutExtender>
106             </td>
107          </tr>
108          <tr>
109             <td class="style2">Phone number:</td>
110             <td>
111                <asp:TextBox ID="phoneTextBox" runat="server">
112                </asp:TextBox> e.g., (555) 555-5555<br />
113                <asp:RequiredFieldValidator ID="phoneExistsValidator"
114                   runat="server" ControlToValidate="phoneTextBox"
115                   ErrorMessage="Please enter your phone number."
116                   Display="None">
117                </asp:RequiredFieldValidator>
118                <ajax:ValidatorCalloutExtender ID="phoneExistsCallout"
119                   runat="server" Enabled="True"
120                   TargetControlID="phoneExistsValidator">
121                </ajax:ValidatorCalloutExtender>
122                <asp:RegularExpressionValidator
123                   ID="phoneFormatValidator" runat="server"
124                   ControlToValidate="phoneTextBox"
125                   ErrorMessage="Please enter a valid phone number."
126                   Display="None" ValidationExpression=
127                      "((\(\d{3}\) ?)|(\d{3}-))?\d{3}-\d{4}">
128                </asp:RegularExpressionValidator>
129                <ajax:ValidatorCalloutExtender ID="phoneFormatCallout"
130                   runat="server" Enabled="True"
131                   TargetControlID="phoneFormatValidator">
132                </ajax:ValidatorCalloutExtender>
133             </td>
134          </tr>
135       </table>
```

Fig. 22.68 | Validation application enhanced by ASP.NET AJAX. (Part 3 of 5.)

```
136              </ContentTemplate>
137            </ajax:TabPanel>
138         </ajax:TabContainer>
139         <p>
140            <asp:Button ID="submitButton" runat="server" Text="Submit" />
141         </p>
142         <asp:UpdatePanel ID="UpdatePanel1" runat="server">
143            <ContentTemplate>
144               <asp:Label ID="outputLabel" runat="server"
145                  Text="Thank you for your submission." Visible="False">
146               </asp:Label>
147            </ContentTemplate>
148            <Triggers>
149               <asp:AsyncPostBackTrigger ControlID="submitButton"
150                  EventName="Click" />
151            </Triggers>
152         </asp:UpdatePanel>
153      </div>
154   </form>
155   </body>
156   </html>
```

a) The user enters his or her first and last name and proceeds to the Contact tab.

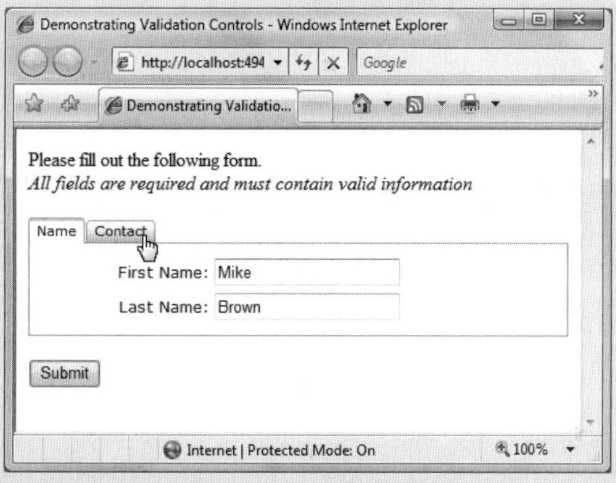

b) The user enters an e-mail address in an incorrect format and presses *Tab* to move to the next input field. A callout appears informing the user to enter an e-mail address in a valid format.

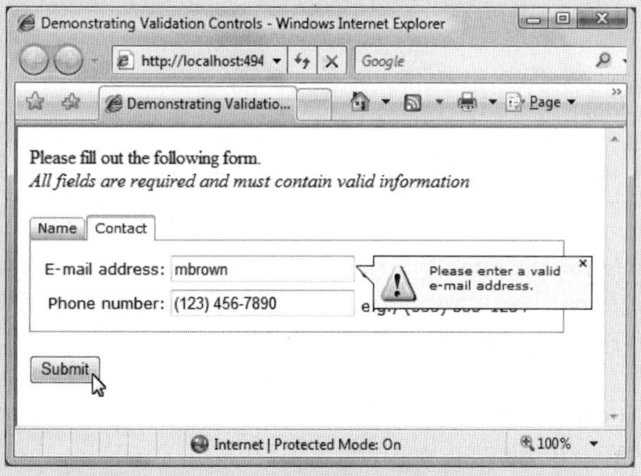

Fig. 22.68 | Validation application enhanced by ASP.NET AJAX. (Part 4 of 5.)

c) After the user
fills out the form
properly and clicks
the **Submit**
button, the
submitted data is
displayed at the
bottom of the page
with a partial-page
update.

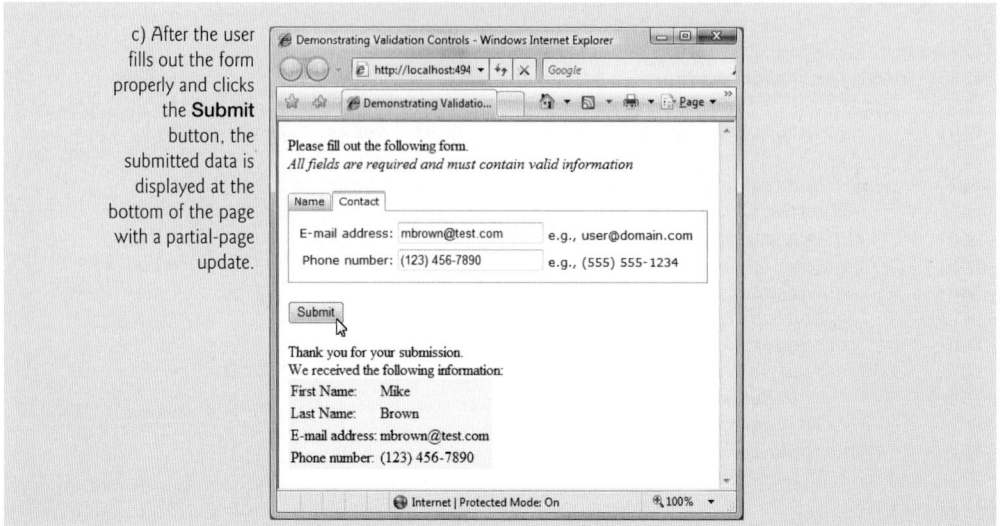

Fig. 22.68 | Validation application enhanced by ASP.NET AJAX. (Part 5 of 5.)

ScriptManager Control

The key control in every ASP.NET AJAX-enabled application is the *ScriptManager*, which manages the client-side scripts that enable asynchronous Ajax functionality. There can be only one ScriptManager per page. To incorporate controls from the AJAX Control Toolkit, use the *ToolkitScriptManager* (which derives from ScriptManager) that comes with the toolkit controls, rather than the standard ScriptManager control from the Ajax Extensions package. The ToolkitScriptManager bundles all the scripts associated with the controls of the ASP. NET AJAX Control Toolkit to optimize the application's performance. Drag the ToolkitScriptManager from the **AJAX Control Toolkit** tab in the **Toolbox** to the top of the page—a script manager must appear before any controls that use the scripts it manages. This generates lines 5–6 and lines 28–29. Lines 5–6 associate the Ajax-ControlToolkit assembly with a tag prefix, allowing us to use AJAX Control Toolkit elements. To improve readability, we have changed the prefix from cc1, which is what's assigned by default, to ajax. Lines 28–29 load the ToolkitScriptManager on the page.

Common Programming Error 22.1

Putting more than one instance of the ScriptManager control on a Web Form causes the application to throw an InvalidOperationException when the page is initialized.

Grouping Information in Tabs Using the TabContainer Control

The *TabContainer control* enables you to group information into tabs that are displayed only if they are selected. The information in an unselected tab won't be displayed. To create multiple tabs, drag the TabContainer control from the **AJAX Control Toolkit** tab in the **Toolbox** to your form. This creates a container for hosting tabs (lines 35–138). To add a tab, open the **TabContainer Tasks** smart-tag menu and select **Add Tab Panel**. This adds a *TabPanel object*—representing a tab—to the TabContainer. Change the TabPanel's HeaderText property to specify the tab's header. In this example, we created two tabs to separate the form's name information from its contact information (lines 37–76 and 77–137).

In **Design** view, you can navigate between tabs by holding *Ctrl* and clicking the tab header. You can drag and drop elements into the tab as you would anywhere else. In actuality, however, the content of a TabPanel must be defined inside its ContentTemplate element (e.g., lines 38–75 and 78–136). In this example, we created a layout table in each tab and moved the old input controls into the tabs. The name input field has been separated into first and last name.

Partial-Page Updates Using the UpdatePanel Control

The *UpdatePanel control* eliminates full-page refreshes by isolating a section of a page for a partial-page update. To implement a partial-page update, drag the UpdatePanel control from the **AJAX Extensions** tab in the **Toolbox** to your form. Then, drag into the UpdatePanel the controls to update (lines 142–152). For this example, drag the outputLabel element into the UpdatePanel. Just as in a TabPanel, the components that are managed by the UpdatePanel are defined within its ContentTemplate element in ASPX markup (lines 143–147).

To specify when an UpdatePanel should update, you need to define an *UpdatePanel trigger*. Click the ellipsis button next to the control's Triggers property in the **Properties** window. In the **UpdatePanelTrigger Collection Editor** dialog that appears (Fig. 22.69), click **Add** to add an *AsyncPostBackTrigger*. Set the ControlID property to submitButton and the EventName property to Click. Now, when the user clicks the **Submit** button, the UpdatePanel intercepts the request and makes an asynchronous request to the server instead. Then the response is inserted in the outputLabel element, and the UpdatePanel reloads the label to display the new text without refreshing the entire page.

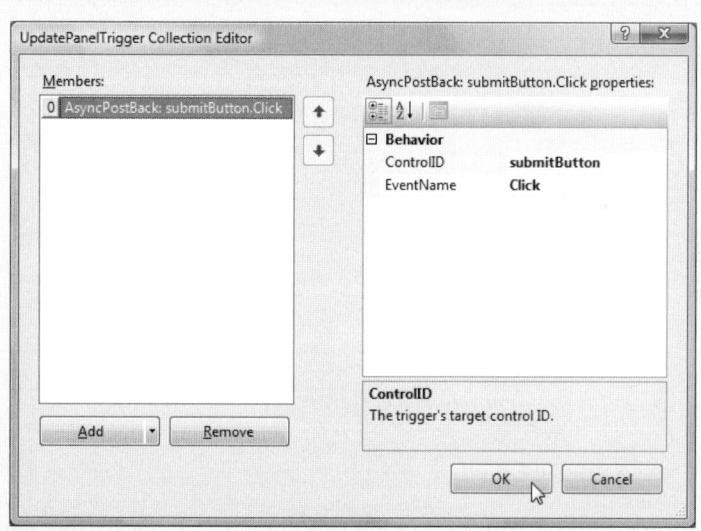

Fig. 22.69 | Creating a trigger for an UpdatePanel.

Adding Ajax Functionality to ASP.NET Validation Controls Using Ajax Extenders

Several controls in the Ajax Control Toolkit are *extenders*—components that enhance regular ASP.NET controls. Lines 50–54, 67–71, 90–94, 102–105, 118–121, and 129–

132 in Fig. 22.68 define *ValidatorCalloutExtender controls* that display error messages in small yellow callouts next to the input fields. To create a ValidatorCalloutExtender, you can either drag and drop it into the form, just as you do with any other control, or you can select the **Add Extender** option in a validator's smart-tag menu. In the **Extender Wizard** dialog that displays (Fig. 22.70), choose ValidatorCalloutExtender from the list of available extenders, specify its ID, and click **OK**.

Line 53 of Fig. 22.68 sets the first ValidatorCalloutExtender's TargetControlID property, which indicates the validator control from which the extender should obtain the error message to display. This is automatically determined if you created the extender through the **Extender Wizard**. The ValidatorCalloutExtenders display error messages with a nicer look-and-feel, so we no longer need the validator controls to display these messages on their own. For this reason, line 47 sets the Display property of the first validator to None. The remaining control validator controls and corresponding extenders are configured similarly.

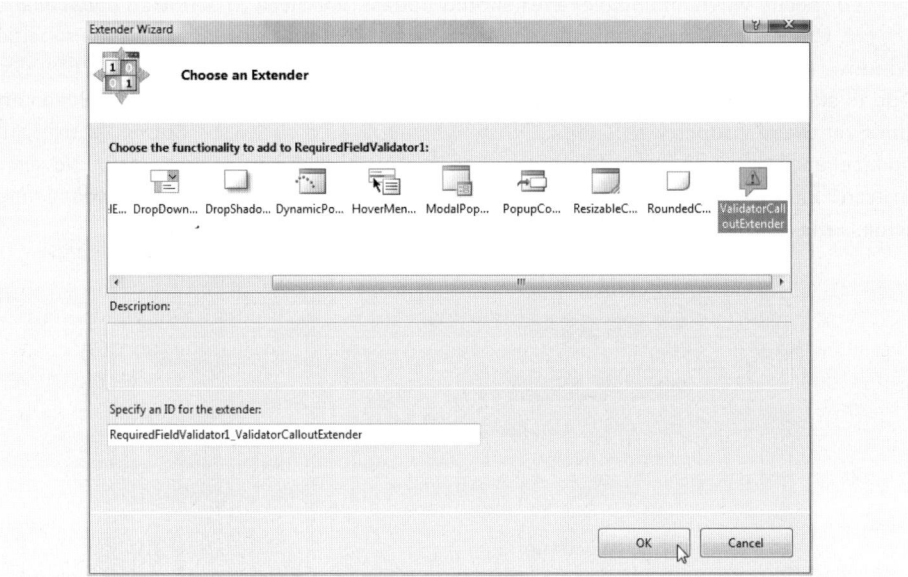

Fig. 22.70 | Creating a control extender using the **Extender Wizard**.

Additional ASP.NET Information

The Ajax Control Toolkit contains many other extenders and independent controls. You can check them out using the sample website included with the toolkit. The live version of the sample website can be found at www.asp.net/ajax/ajaxcontroltoolkit/samples/. For more information on ASP.NET AJAX, check out our ASP.NET AJAX Resource Center at www.deitel.com/aspdotnetajax.

22.10 New ASP.NET 3.5 Data Controls

ASP.NET 3.5 introduces two new server-side data controls, the ListView and the DataPager. The ListView is highly customizable control for displaying data. Its implementation is similar to that of a WPF `ListView`. You can define an assortment of templates such as `ItemsTemplate`, `SelectedItemTemplate`, `ItemSeparatorTemplate`, and `GroupTemplate` to customize how to display data. For more information about the ASP.NET `ListView` control please see `msdn.microsoft.com/en-us/library/bb398790.aspx`.

The `DataPager` control works alongside a data control, such as `GridView` or `ListView`, and customizes how it pages through data. With a data pager, you can customize the combination of page-navigation buttons (such as next, previous, or page numbers) that are displayed. For more information about the ASP.NET `DataPager` control, please see `msdn.microsoft.com/en-us/library/system.web.ui.webcontrols.datapager.aspx`.

22.11 Wrap-Up

In this chapter, we introduced web-application development using ASP.NET and Visual Web Developer 2008 Express. We began by discussing the simple HTTP transactions that take place when you request and receive a web page through a web browser. You then learned about the three tiers (i.e., the client or top tier, the business logic or middle tier and the information or bottom tier) that comprise most web applications.

Next, we explained the role of ASPX files (i.e., Web Form files) and code-behind files, and the relationship between them. We discussed how ASP.NET compiles and executes web applications so that they can be displayed as XHTML in a web browser. You also learned how to build an ASP.NET web application using Visual Web Developer.

The chapter demonstrated several common ASP.NET web controls used for displaying text and images on a Web Form. You learned how to use an `AdRotator` control to display randomly selected images. We also discussed validation controls, which allow you to ensure that user input on a web page satisfies certain requirements.

We discussed the benefits of maintaining a user's state information across multiple pages of a website. We then demonstrated how you can include such functionality in a web application using either cookies or session tracking with `HttpSessionState` objects.

We presented two case studies on building ASP.NET applications that interact with databases. First, we showed how to build a guestbook application that allows users to submit comments about a website. You learned how to save the user input in a SQL Server database and how to display past submissions on the web page.

The second case study presented a secure web application that requires users to log in before accessing information from the `Books` database (discussed in Chapter 21). You used the **Web Site Administration Tool** to configure the application to use forms authentication and prevent anonymous users from accessing the book information. This case study explained how to use the `Login`, `CreateUserWizard`, `LoginName` and `LoginStatus` controls to simplify user authentication. You also learned to create a uniform look-and-feel for a website using a master page and several content pages.

Finally, you learned the difference between a traditional web application and an Ajax web application. We introduced ASP.NET AJAX and Microsoft's Ajax Control Toolkit. You learned how to build an Ajax-enabled web application by using a `ScriptManager` and the Ajax-enabled controls of the Ajax Extensions package and the Ajax Control Toolkit.

In the next chapter, we introduce web services, which allow methods on one machine to call methods on other machines via common data formats and protocols, such as XML and HTTP. You'll see how web services promote software reusability and interoperability across multiple computers on a network such as the Internet.

22.12 Web Resources

We provide links to many online resources for ASP.NET and ASP.NET AJAX in our Resource Centers:

```
www.deitel.com/aspdotnet3.5/
www.deitel.com/aspdotnetajax/
```

Start your searches here for tutorials, articles, books, blogs, sample code, forums, training courses, videos, webcasts and more. For related technologies, see our complete list of Resource Centers at www.deitel.com/ResourceCenters.html.

Windows Communication Foundation (WCF) Web Services

A client is to me a mere unit, a factor in a problem.
—Sir Arthur Conan Doyle

...if the simplest things of nature have a message that you understand, rejoice, for your soul is alive.
—Eleonora Duse

Protocol is everything.
—Francoise Giuliani

They also serve who only stand and wait.
—John Milton

OBJECTIVES

In this chapter you'll learn:

- What a WCF service is.
- How to create WCF web services.
- How XML, JSON, XML-Based Simple Object Access Protocol (SOAP) and Representational State Transfer (REST) Architecture enable WCF web services.
- The elements that comprise WCF web services, such as service references, service endpoints, service contracts and service bindings.
- How to create a client that consumes a WCF web service.
- How to use WCF web services with Windows applications and web applications.
- How to use session tracking in WCF web services to maintain state information for the client.
- How to pass user-defined types to a WCF web service.

Outline

23.1 Introduction
23.2 WCF Services Basics
23.3 Simple Object Access Protocol (SOAP)
23.4 Representational State Transfer (REST)
23.5 JavaScript Object Notation (JSON)
23.6 Publishing and Consuming SOAP-Based Web Services
    23.6.1 Creating a WCF Web Service
    23.6.2 Code for the `WelcomeSOAPXMLService`
    23.6.3 Building a SOAP-Based Web Service
    23.6.4 Deploying the `WelcomeSOAPXMLService`
    23.6.5 Creating a Client to Consume the `WelcomeSOAPXMLService`
    23.6.6 Consuming the `WelcomeSOAPXMLService`
23.7 Publishing and Consuming REST-Based XML Web Services
    23.7.1 Creating a REST-Based XML Web Service
    23.7.2 Consuming a REST-Based XML Web Service
23.8 Publishing and Consuming REST-Based JSON Web Services
    23.8.1 Creating a REST-Based JSON Web Service
    23.8.2 Consuming a REST-Based JSON Web Service
23.9 Blackjack Web Service: Using Session Tracking in a SOAP-Based Web Service
    23.9.1 Creating a Blackjack Web Service
    23.9.2 Consuming the Blackjack Web Service
23.10 Airline Reservation Web Service: Database Access and Invoking a Service from ASP.NET
23.11 Equation Generator: Returning User-Defined Types
    23.11.1 Creating the REST-Based XML `EquationGenerator` Web Service
    23.11.2 Consuming the REST-Based XML `EquationGenerator` Web Service
    23.11.3 Creating the REST-Based JSON `EquationGenerator` Web Service
    23.11.4 Consuming the REST-Based JSON `EquationGenerator` Web Service
23.12 Wrap-Up
23.13 Deitel Web Services Resource Centers

23.1 Introduction

This chapter introduces *Windows Communication Foundation (WCF)* services. WCF is a set of technologies for building distributed systems in which system components communicate with one another over networks. In earlier versions of .NET, the various types of communication used different technologies and programming models. WCF uses a common framework for all communication between systems, so you need to learn only one programming model to use WCF.

This chapter focuses on WCF web services, which promote software reusability in distributed systems that typically execute across the Internet. A *web service* is a class that allows its methods to be called by methods on other machines via common data formats and protocols, such as XML (see Chapter 20), JSON (Section 23.5) and HTTP. In .NET, the over-the-network method calls are commonly implemented through *Simple Object Access Protocol (SOAP)* or the *Representational State Transfer (REST)* architecture. SOAP is an XML-based protocol describing how to mark up requests and responses so that they can be sent via protocols such as HTTP. SOAP uses a standardized XML-based format to enclose data in a message that can be sent between a client and a server. REST is a network architecture that uses the web's traditional request/response mechanisms such as GET and POST requests. REST-based systems do not require data to be wrapped in a special message format.

We build the WCF web services presented in this chapter in Visual Web Developer 2008 Express, and we create client applications that invoke these services using both Visual C# 2008 Express and Visual Web Developer 2008 Express. Full versions of Visual Studio 2008 include the functionality of both Express editions.

Requests to and responses from web services created with Visual Web Developer are typically transmitted via SOAP or REST, so any client capable of generating and processing SOAP or REST messages can interact with a web service, regardless of the language in which the web service is written. We say more about SOAP and REST in Section 23.3 and Section 23.4, respectively.

23.2 WCF Services Basics

Microsoft's Windows Communication Foundation (WCF) was created as a single platform to encompass many existing communication technologies. WCF increases productivity, because you learn only one straightforward programming model. Each WCF service can have one or more *endpoints*. An endpoint is the path through which a WCF client connects to a WCF service. Every endpoint has three key components—addresses, bindings and contracts (usually called the ABCs of a WCF service):

- An *address* represents the service's location, which includes the protocol (e.g., HTTP) and network address (e.g., www.deitel.com) used to access the service.

- A *binding* specifies how a client communicates with the service (e.g., SOAP, REST, and so on). Bindings can also specify other options, such as security constraints.

- A *contract* is an interface representing the service's properties and methods. The service's contract allows clients to interact with the service.

The machine on which the web service resides is referred to as a *web service host*. The client application that accesses the web service sends a method call over a network to the web service host, which processes the call and returns a response over the network to the application. This kind of distributed computing benefits systems in various ways. For example, an application without direct access to data on another system might be able to retrieve this data via a web service. Similarly, an application lacking the processing power necessary to perform specific computations could use a web service to take advantage of other systems' superior resources.

23.3 Simple Object Access Protocol (SOAP)

The Simple Object Access Protocol (SOAP) is a platform-independent protocol that uses XML to make remote procedure calls, typically over HTTP. You can view the SOAP specification at www.w3.org/TR/soap/. Each request and response is packaged in a *SOAP message*—XML markup containing the information that a web service requires to process the message. SOAP messages are written in XML so that they are computer readable, human readable and platform independent. Most *firewalls*—security barriers that restrict communication among networks—allow HTTP traffic to pass through, so that clients can browse the web by sending requests to and receiving responses from web servers. Thus, SOAP-based services can send and receive SOAP messages over HTTP connections with few limitations.

SOAP supports an extensive set of types. The *wire format* used to transmit requests and responses must support all types passed between the applications. SOAP types include the primitive types (e.g., int), as well as DateTime, XmlNode and others. SOAP can also transmit arrays of these types. In Section 23.11, you'll see that you can also transmit user-defined types in SOAP messages.

When a program invokes a method of a SOAP web service, the request and all relevant information are packaged in a SOAP message enclosed in a *SOAP envelope* and sent to the server on which the web service resides. When the web service receives this SOAP message, it parses the XML representing the message, then processes the message's contents. The message specifies the method that the client wishes to execute and the arguments the client passed to that method. Next, the web service calls the method with the specified arguments (if any) and sends the response back to the client in another SOAP message. The client parses the response to retrieve the method's result. In Section 23.6, you'll build and consume a basic SOAP web service.

23.4 Representational State Transfer (REST)

Representational State Transfer (REST) refers to an architectural style for implementing web services. Such web services are often called *RESTful web services*. Though REST itself is not a standard, RESTful web services are implemented using web standards. Each method in a RESTful web service is identified by a unique URL. Thus, when the server receives a request, it immediately knows what operation to perform. Such web services can be used in a program or directly from a web browser. The results of a particular operation may be cached locally by the browser when the service is invoked with a GET request. This can make subsequent requests for the same operation faster by loading the result directly from the browser's cache. Amazon's web services (aws.amazon.com) are RESTful, as are many others.

RESTful web services are alternatives to those implemented with SOAP. Unlike SOAP-based web services, the request and response of REST services are not wrapped in envelopes. REST is also not limited to returning data in XML format. It can use a variety of formats, such as XML, JSON, HTML, plain text and media files. In Sections 23.7–23.8, you'll build and consume basic RESTful web services.

23.5 JavaScript Object Notation (JSON)

JavaScript Object Notation (JSON) is an alternative to XML for representing data. JSON is a text-based data-interchange format used to represent objects in JavaScript as collections of name/value pairs represented as strings. It is commonly used in Ajax applications. JSON is a simple format that makes objects easy to read, create and parse, and allows programs to transmit data efficiently across the Internet because it is much less verbose than XML. Each JSON object is represented as a list of property names and values contained in curly braces, in the following format:

{ *propertyName1* : *value1*, *propertyName2* : *value2* }

Arrays are represented in JSON with square brackets in the following format:

[*value1*, *value2*, *value3*]

Each value in an array can be a string, a number, a JSON object, `true`, `false` or `null`. To appreciate the simplicity of JSON data, examine this representation of an array of address-book entries

```
[ { first: 'Cheryl', last: 'Black' },
  { first: 'James', last: 'Blue' },
  { first: 'Mike', last: 'Brown' },
  { first: 'Meg', last: 'Gold' } ]
```

Many programming languages now support the JSON data format.

23.6 Publishing and Consuming SOAP-Based Web Services

This section presents our first example of *publishing* (enabling for client access) and *consuming* (using) a web service. We begin with a SOAP-based web service.

23.6.1 Creating a WCF Web Service

To build a SOAP-based WCF web service in Visual Web Developer, you first create a project of type **WCF Service**. SOAP is the default protocol for WCF web services, so no special configuration is required to create them. Visual Web Developer then generates files for the WCF service code, an *SVC file* (`Service.svc`, which provides access to the service), and a **Web.config** file (which specifies the service's binding and behavior).

Visual Web Developer also generates code files for the *WCF service class* and any other code that is part of the WCF service implementation. In the service class, you define the methods that your WCF web service makes available to client applications.

23.6.2 Code for the `WelcomeSOAPXMLService`

Figures 23.1 and 23.2 present the code-behind files for the `WelcomeSOAPXMLService` WCF web service that you build in Section 23.6.3. When creating services in Visual Web Developer, you work almost exclusively in the code-behind files. The service provides a method that takes a name (represented as a `string`) as an argument and appends it to the welcome message that is returned to the client. We use a parameter in the method definition to demonstrate that a client can send data to a web service.

Figure 23.1 is the service's interface, which describes the service's contract—the set of methods and properties the client uses to access the service. The **ServiceContract** attribute (line 6) exposes a class that implements this interface as a WCF web service. The **OperationContract** attribute (line 10) exposes the `Welcome` method to clients for remote calls. Optional parameters can be assigned to these contracts to change the data format and method behavior, as we'll show in later examples. The `System.ServiceModel` namespace is imported (line 4) to use the `ServiceContract` and `OperationContract` attributes.

```
 1   // Fig. 23.1: IWelcomeSOAPXMLService.cs
 2   // WCF web service interface that returns a welcome message through SOAP
 3   // protocol and XML data format.
 4   using System.ServiceModel;
 5
 6   [ServiceContract]
 7   public interface IWelcomeSOAPXMLService
 8   {
 9      // returns a welcome message
10      [OperationContract]
11      string Welcome( string yourName );
12   } // end interface IWelcomeSOAPXMLService
```

Fig. 23.1 | WCF web service interface that returns a welcome message through SOAP protocol and XML format.

Figure 23.2 defines the class that implements the interface declared as the Service-Contract. Lines 7–11 define the method Welcome, which returns a string welcoming you to WCF web services. Next, we build the web service from scratch.

```
 1   // Fig. 23.2: WelcomeSOAPXMLService.cs
 2   // WCF web service that returns a welcome message using SOAP protocol and
 3   // XML data format.
 4   public class WelcomeSOAPXMLService : IWelcomeSOAPXMLService
 5   {
 6      // returns a welcome message
 7      public string Welcome( string yourName )
 8      {
 9         return string.Format( "Welcome to WCF Web Services"
10            + " with SOAP and XML, {0}!", yourName );
11      } // end method Welcome
12   } // end class WelcomeSOAPXMLService
```

Fig. 23.2 | WCF web service that returns a welcome message through the SOAP protocol and XML format.

23.6.3 Building a SOAP-Based Web Service

In the following steps, you create a **WCF Service** project for the WelcomeSOAPXMLService and test it using the built-in ASP.NET Development Server that comes with Visual Web Developer Express and Visual Studio.

Step 1: Creating the Project

To create a **WCF Service** project, select **File > New Web Site...** to display the **New Web Site** dialog (Fig. 23.3). Click **WCF Service** in the **Templates** pane. Select **File System** from the **Location** drop-down list to indicate that the files should be placed on your local hard disk. By default, Visual Web Developer places files on the local machine in a directory named WCFService1. Rename this folder to WelcomeSOAPXMLService. We modified the default path as well. Select **Visual C#** from the **Language** drop-down list to indicate that you'll use Visual C# as the language in the code-behind files. Click **OK** to create the project.

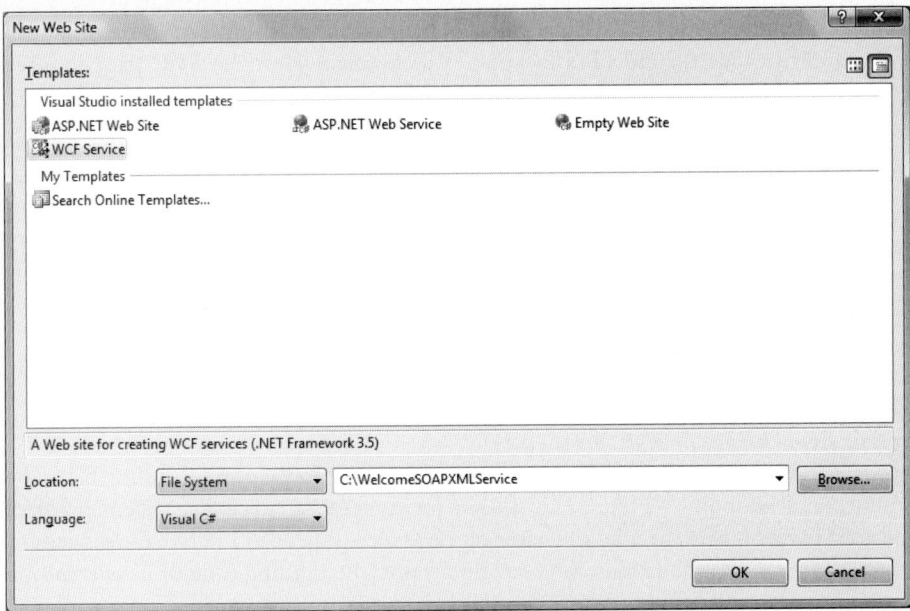

Fig. 23.3 | Creating a **WCF Service** in Visual Web Developer.

Step 2: Examining the Newly Created Project

After you create the project, the code-behind file Service.cs, which contains code for a simple web service, is displayed by default. If the code-behind file is not open, open it by double clicking the file in the **App_Code** directory listed in the **Solution Explorer**. By default, a new code-behind file implements an interface named IService that is marked with the ServiceContract and OperationContract attributes. In addition, the IService.cs file defines a class named CompositeType with a DataContract attribute (discussed in Section 23.8). The interface contains two sample service methods named GetData and GetDataUsingContract. The Service.cs contains the code that defines these methods.

Step 3: Modifying and Renaming the Code-Behind File

To create the WelcomeSOAPXMLService service developed in this section, modify IService.cs and Service.cs by replacing the sample code provided by Visual Web Developer with the code from the IWelcomeSOAPXMLService and WelcomeSOAPXMLService files (Figs. 23.1 and 23.2, respectively). Then rename the files to IWelcomeSOAPXMLService.cs and WelcomeSOAPXMLService.cs by right clicking each file in the Solution Explorer and choosing **Rename**.

Step 4: Examining the SVC File

The Service.svc file, when accessed through a web browser, provides information about the web service. However, if you open the SVC file on disk, note that it contains only the following directives

```
<%@ ServiceHost Language="C#" Debug="true" Service="Service"
    CodeBehind="~/App_Code/Service.cs" %>
```

to indicate the programming language in which the web service's code-behind file is written, the Debug attribute (enables a page to be compiled for debugging), the name of the service and the code-behind file's location. When you request the SVC page in a web browser, WCF uses this information to dynamically generate information used by the client to communicate with the web service.

Step 5: Modifying the SVC File

If you change the code-behind file name or the class name that defines the web service, you must modify the SVC file accordingly. Thus, after defining class WelcomeSOAPXMLService in the code-behind file WelcomeSOAPXMLService.cs, modify the SVC file as follows:

```
<%@ ServiceHost Language="C#" Debug="true"
    Service="WelcomeSOAPXMLService"
    CodeBehind="~/App_Code/WelcomeSOAPXMLService.cs" %>
```

Step 6: Examining the Web.config File

The Web.config file specifies the service's configuration information, including behaviors, bindings and endpoints. Figure 23.4 shows the system.serviceModel element of the Web.config file. Line 3 specifies the name of the service. Lines 6–11 define the service endpoint, where client applications connect. By default, the binding (line 6) is ***wsHttpBinding***, which means that data is transferred in a reliable manner over HTTP protocol using XML as the data format. This is the default binding for SOAP-based services. The contract attribute (line 7) specifies the name of the interface class. In later examples, we'll discuss the behaviors element (line 16–23).

```
 1  <system.serviceModel>
 2     <services>
 3        <service name="Service"
 4           behaviorConfiguration="ServiceBehavior">
 5           <!-- Service Endpoints -->
 6           <endpoint address="" binding="wsHttpBinding"
 7              contract="IService">
 8              <identity>
 9                 <dns value="localhost"/>
10              </identity>
11           </endpoint>
12           <endpoint address="mex" binding="mexHttpBinding"
13              contract="IMetadataExchange"/>
14        </service>
15     </services>
16     <behaviors>
17        <serviceBehaviors>
18           <behavior name="ServiceBehavior">
19              <serviceMetadata httpGetEnabled="true"/>
20              <serviceDebug includeExceptionDetailInFaults="false"/>
21           </behavior>
22        </serviceBehaviors>
23     </behaviors>
24  </system.serviceModel>
```

Fig. 23.4 | Default Web.config file's service model configuration for WCF service.

Step 7: Modifying the Web.config File

After changing the ServiceContract's code-behind file name, the web-service class name or interface name, you must change the Web.config file to reference the appropriate names. In Fig. 23.5, we change the service name from Service to WelcomeSOAPXMLSer-vice (line 3) and the contract from IService to IWelcomeSOAPXMLService (line 7).

```
 1  <system.serviceModel>
 2      <services>
 3          <service name="WelcomeSOAPXMLService"
 4              behaviorConfiguration="ServiceBehavior">
 5              <!-- Service Endpoints -->
 6              <endpoint address="" binding="wsHttpBinding"
 7                  contract="IWelcomeSOAPXMLService">
 8                  <identity>
 9                      <dns value="localhost"/>
10                  </identity>
11              </endpoint>
12              <endpoint address="mex" binding="mexHttpBinding"
13                  contract="IMetadataExchange"/>
14          </service>
15      </services>
16      <behaviors>
17          <serviceBehaviors>
18              <behavior name="ServiceBehavior">
19                  <serviceMetadata httpGetEnabled="true"/>
20                  <serviceDebug includeExceptionDetailInFaults="false"/>
21              </behavior>
22          </serviceBehaviors>
23      </behaviors>
24  </system.serviceModel>
```

Fig. 23.5 | Web.config file's service model configuration for WelcomeSOAPXMLService web service.

23.6.4 Deploying the WelcomeSOAPXMLService

To view the Service.svc file, you must set the .svc file as the project's start page by right clicking it in **Solution Explorer** and selecting **Set As Start Page**. Next, choose **Build Web Site** from the **Build** menu to ensure that the web service compiles without errors. You can also test the web service directly from Visual Web Developer by selecting **Start Debugging** from the **Debug** menu. The first time you do this, the **Debugging Not Enabled** dialog appears. Click **OK** if you want to enable debugging. Next, a browser window opens and displays information about the service. This information is generated dynamically when the SVC file is requested. Figure 23.6 shows a web browser displaying the Service.svc file for the WelcomeSOAPXMLService WCF web service.

Once the service is running, you can also access the SVC page from your browser by typing a URL of the following form in a web browser:

    http://localhost:*portNumber*/*virtualPath*/Service.svc

(See the actual URL in Fig. 23.6.) By default, the ASP.NET Development Server assigns a random port number to each website it hosts. You can change this behavior by going to

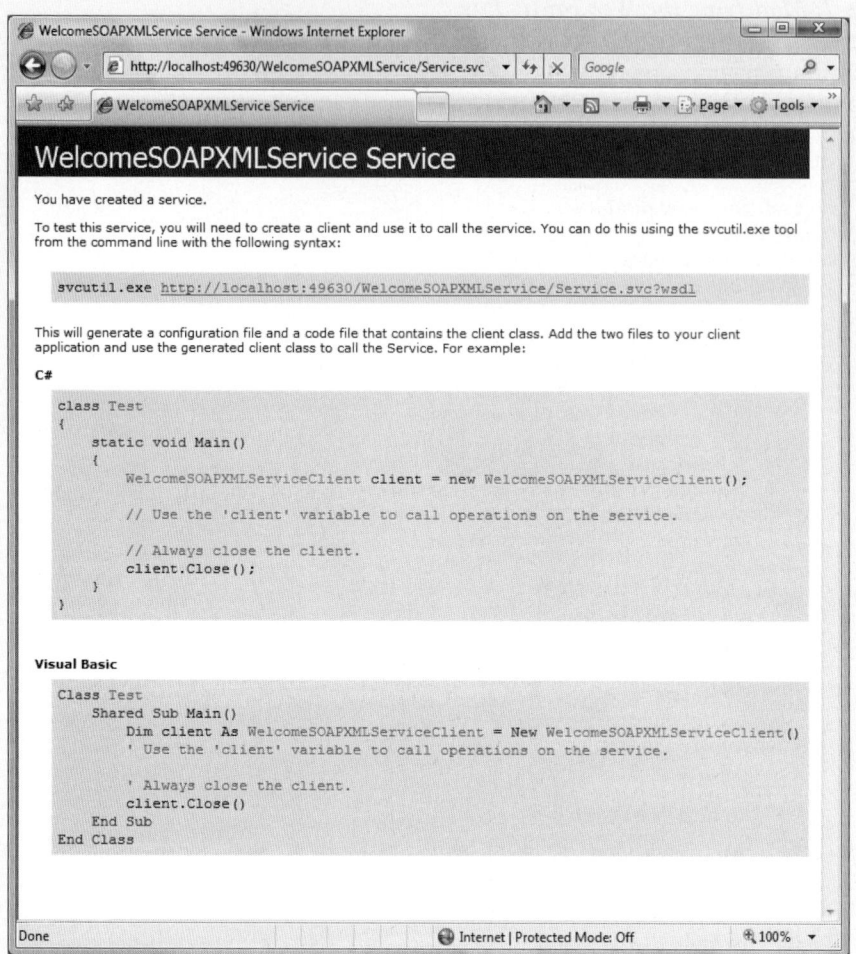

Fig. 23.6 | SVC file rendered in a web browser.

the **Solution Explorer** and clicking on the project name to view the **Properties** window (Fig. 23.7). Set the **Use dynamic ports** property to **False** and set the **Port number** property to the port number that you want to use, which can be any unused TCP port. Generally, you don't do this for web services that will be deployed to a real web server because web servers typically use port 80. You can also change the service's virtual path, perhaps to make the path shorter or more readable.

Web Services Description Language

To consume a web service, a client must determine the service's functionality and how to use it. For this purpose, web services normally contain a *service description*. This is an XML document that conforms to the *Web Service Description Language* (*WSDL*)—an XML vocabulary that defines the methods a web service makes available and how clients interact with them. The WSDL document also specifies lower-level information that clients might need, such as the required formats for requests and responses.

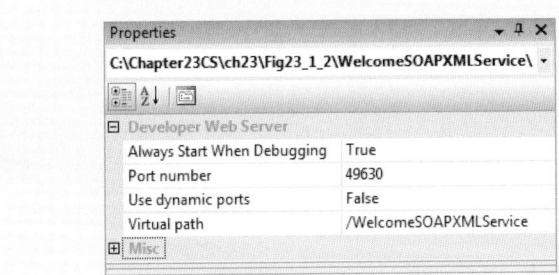

Fig. 23.7 | WCF web service **Properties** window.

WSDL documents help applications determine how to interact with the web services described in the documents. When viewed in a web browser, an SVC file presents a link to the service's WSDL document and information on using the utility *svcutil.exe* to generate test console applications. The svcutil.exe tool is included with Visual Studio 2008 and Visual Web Developer. We do not use svcutil.exe to test our services, opting instead to build our own test applications. When a client requests the SVC file's URL followed by ?wsdl, the server autogenerates the WSDL that describes the web service and returns the WSDL document. Copy the SVC URL (which ends with .svc) from the browser's address ComboBox in Fig. 23.6, as you'll need it in the next section to build the client application. Also, leave the web service running so the client can interact with it.

23.6.5 Creating a Client to Consume the WelcomeSOAPXMLService

Now that you've defined and deployed the web service, let's consume it from a client application. A .NET web-service client can be any type of .NET application, such as a Windows application, a console application or a web application, or it can be an application developed in a different language on an entirely different platform. You can enable a client application to consume a web service by *adding a service reference* to the client. Figure 23.8 diagrams the parts of a client for a SOAP-based web service after a service reference has been added. [*Note*: This section discusses Visual C# 2008 Express, but the discussion also applies to Visual Web Developer 2008 Express.]

An application that consumes a SOAP-based web service actually consists of two parts—a proxy class representing the web service and a client application that accesses the web service via a proxy object (i.e., an instance of the proxy class). A *proxy class* handles all the "plumbing" required for service method calls (i.e., the networking details and the formation of SOAP messages). Whenever the client application calls a web service's method, the application actually calls a corresponding method in the proxy class. This method has the same name and parameters as the web service's method that is being called, but formats the call to be sent as a request in a SOAP message. The web service receives this request as a SOAP message, executes the method call and sends back the result as another SOAP message. When the client application receives the SOAP message containing the response, the proxy class deserializes it and returns the results as the return value of the web-service method that was called. Figure 23.9 depicts the interactions among the client code, proxy class and web service. The proxy class is not shown in the project unless you click the **Show All Files** button in the **Solution Explorer**.

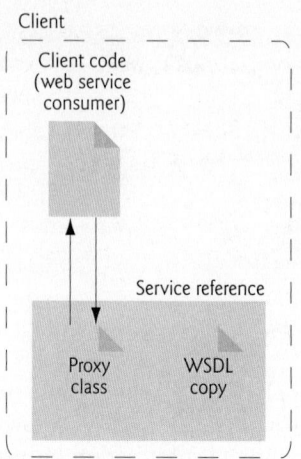

Fig. 23.8 | .NET WCF web service client after a web-service reference has been added.

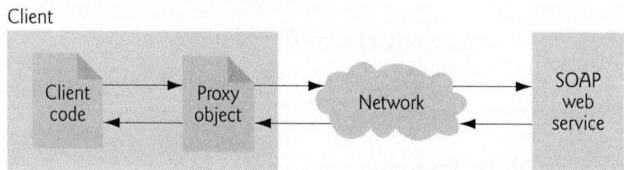

Fig. 23.9 | Interaction between a web-service client and a SOAP web service.

Many aspects of web-service creation and consumption—such as generating WSDL files and proxy classes—are handled by Visual Web Developer, Visual C# 2008 and WCF. Although developers are relieved of the tedious process of creating these files, they can still modify the files if necessary. This is required only when developing advanced web services—none of our examples require modifications to these files.

We now create a client and generate a proxy class that allows the client to access the WelcomeSOAPXMLService web service. First create a Windows application named WelcomeSOAPXMLClient in Visual C# 2008, then perform the following steps.

Step 1: Opening the Add Service Reference *Dialog*
Right click the project name in the **Solution Explorer** and select **Add Service Reference...** to display the **Add Service Reference** dialog.

Step 2: Specifying the Web Service's Location
In the dialog, enter the URL of WelcomeSOAPXMLService's .svc file (i.e., the URL you copied from Fig. 23.6) in the **Address** field. When you specify the service you want to consume, the IDE accesses the web service's WSDL information and copies it into a WSDL file that is stored in the client project's Service References folder. This file is visible when you view all of your project's files in the **Solution Explorer**. [*Note:* A copy of the WSDL file provides the client application with local access to the web service's description. To ensure

that the WSDL file is up to date, Visual C# 2008 provides an **Update Service Reference** option (available by right clicking the service reference in the **Solution Explorer**), which updates the files in the `Service References` folder.]

Many companies that provide web services simply distribute the exact URLs at which their web services can be accessed. The **Add Service Reference** dialog also allows you to search for services on your local machine or on the Internet.

Step 3: Renaming the Service Reference's Namespace
In the **Add Service Reference** dialog, rename the service reference's namespace by changing the **Namespace** field to `ServiceReference`.

Step 4: Adding the Service Reference
Click the **Ok** button to add the service reference.

Step 5: Viewing the Service Reference in the Solution Explorer
The **Solution Explorer** should now contain a **Service References** folder with a node showing the namespace you specified in *Step 3*.

23.6.6 Consuming the WelcomeSOAPXMLService

The application in Fig. 23.10 uses the `WelcomeSOAPXMLService` service to send a welcome message. You are already familiar with Visual C# applications that use `Labels`, `TextBoxes` and `Buttons`, so we focus our discussions on the web-services concepts in this chapter's applications.

```
1   // Fig. 23.10: WelcomeSOAPXMLForm.cs
2   // Client that consumes WelcomeSOAPXMLService.
3   using System;
4   using System.Windows.Forms;
5
6   namespace WelcomeSOAPXMLClient
7   {
8      public partial class WelcomeSOAPXMLForm : Form
9      {
10         // declare a reference to web service
11         private ServiceReference.WelcomeSOAPXMLServiceClient client;
12
13         public WelcomeSOAPXMLForm()
14         {
15            InitializeComponent();
16            client = new ServiceReference.WelcomeSOAPXMLServiceClient();
17         } // end constructor
18
19         // creates welcome message from text input and web service
20         private void submitButton_Click( object sender, EventArgs e )
21         {
22            MessageBox.Show( client.Welcome( textBox.Text ), "Welcome" );
23         } // end method submitButton_Click
24      } // end class WelcomeSOAPXMLForm
25   } // end namespace WelcomeSOAPXMLClient
```

Fig. 23.10 | Client that consumes `WelcomeSOAPXMLService`. (Part 1 of 2.)

a) User inputs name.

b) Message sent from **WelcomeSOAPXMLService**.

Fig. 23.10 | Client that consumes `WelcomeSOAPXMLService`. (Part 2 of 2.)

Line 11 defines `client` as a `ServiceReference.WelcomeSOAPXMLServiceClient` proxy object. Line 16 creates the proxy object. The event handler uses this object to call methods of the `WelcomeSOAPXMLService` web service. Line 22 invokes the `WelcomeSOAP-XMLService` web service's `Welcome` method. Note that the call is made via the local proxy object `client`, which then communicates with the web service on the client's behalf. If you downloaded the example from `www.deitel.com/books/csharpfp3/`, you may need to regenerate the proxy by updating the service reference because ASP.NET Development Server may use a different port number on your computer. To do so, right click **Ser-viceReference** in the **Service References** folder in the **Solution Explorer** and select the option **Configure Service Reference....** Then set the **Address** field to the service's URL and port number found in Section 23.6.4. Click the **OK** button to regenerate the project's service reference.

When the application runs, enter your name and click the **Submit** button. The application invokes the `Welcome` service method to perform the appropriate task and return the result, then displays the result in a `MessageBox`.

23.7 Publishing and Consuming REST-Based XML Web Services

In the previous section, we used a proxy object to pass data to and from a WCF web service using the SOAP protocol. In this section, we access a WCF web service using the REST architecture. We modify the `IWelcomeSOAPXMLService` example to return data in plain XML format. You can create a **WCF Service** project as you did in Section 23.6 to begin.

23.7.1 Creating a REST-Based XML Web Service

Step 1: Adding the WebGet Attribute
`IWelcomeRESTXMLService` interface (Fig. 23.11) is a modified version of the `IWelcome-SOAPXMLService` interface. The `Welcome` method's ***WebGet*** attribute (line 13) maps a method to a unique URL that can be accessed via an HTTP `GET` operation programmatically or in a web browser. To use the `WebGet` attribute, we import the `System.Service-`

```
 1   // Fig. 23.11: IWelcomeRESTXMLService.cs
 2   // WCF web service interface. A class that implements this interface
 3   // returns a welcome message through REST architecture and XML data
 4   // format.
 5   using System.ServiceModel;
 6   using System.ServiceModel.Web;
 7
 8   [ServiceContract]
 9   public interface IWelcomeRESTXMLService
10   {
11      // returns a welcome message
12      [OperationContract]
13      [WebGet( UriTemplate = "/welcome/{yourName}" )]
14      string Welcome( string yourName );
15   } // end interface IWelcomeRESTXMLService
```

Fig. 23.11 | WCF web-service interface. A class that implements this interface returns a welcome message through REST architecture and XML data format.

Model.Web namespace (line 6). WebGet's **UriTemplate** property (line 13) specifies the URI format that is used to invoke the method. You can access the Welcome method in a web browser by appending text that matches the UriTemplate definition to the end of the service's location, as in http://localhost:50000/WelcomeRESTXMLService/Service.svc/welcome/Bruce. WelcomeRESTXMLService (Fig. 23.12) is the class that implements the IWelcomeRESTXMLService interface; it is similar to the WelcomeSOAPXMLService class (Fig. 23.2).

```
 1   // Fig. 23.12: WelcomeRESTXMLService.cs
 2   // WCF web service that returns a welcome message using REST architecture
 3   // and XML data format.
 4   public class WelcomeRESTXMLService : IWelcomeRESTXMLService
 5   {
 6      // returns a welcome message
 7      public string Welcome( string yourName )
 8      {
 9         return string.Format( "Welcome to WCF Web Services"
10            + " with REST and XML, {0}!", yourName );
11      } // end method Welcome
12   } // end class WelcomeRESTXMLService
```

Fig. 23.12 | WCF web service that returns a welcome message using REST architecture and XML data format.

Step 2: Modifying the Web.config File
Figure 23.13 shows part of the default Web.config file modified to use REST architecture. First, the service binding in the endpoint element must be changed from wsHttpBinding to **webHttpBinding** (line 6) to respond to REST-based HTTP requests rather than SOAP-based messages. You must also add a new **behaviorConfiguration** (we called it REST-

```
 1   <system.serviceModel>
 2      <services>
 3         <service name="WelcomeRESTXMLService"
 4            behaviorConfiguration="ServiceBehavior">
 5            <!-- Service Endpoints -->
 6            <endpoint address="" binding="webHttpBinding"
 7               contract="IWelcomeRESTXMLService"
 8               behaviorConfiguration="RESTBehavior">
 9               <identity>
10                  <dns value="localhost"/>
11               </identity>
12            </endpoint>
13            <endpoint address="mex" binding="mexHttpBinding"
14               contract="IMetadataExchange"/>
15         </service>
16      </services>
17      <behaviors>
18         <serviceBehaviors>
19            <behavior name="ServiceBehavior">
20               <serviceMetadata httpGetEnabled="true"/>
21               <serviceDebug includeExceptionDetailInFaults="false"/>
22            </behavior>
23         </serviceBehaviors>
24         <endpointBehaviors>
25            <behavior name="RESTBehavior">
26               <webHttp />
27            </behavior>
28         </endpointBehaviors>
29      </behaviors>
30   </system.serviceModel>
```

Fig. 23.13 | WelcomeRESTXMLService Web.config file.

Behavior) at line 8 of the endpoint to define the endpoint's behavior. This behavior is configured in the endpointBehaviors section at lines 25–27. Line 25 specifies the name of the behavior being configured, and line 26 uses the *webHttp* element to specify that clients communicate with this service using standard HTTP requests and responses.

Figure 23.14 tests the WelcomeRESTXMLService's Welcome method in a web browser. The URL specifies the location of the Service.svc file and uses the URI template to invoke method Welcome with the argument Bruce. The browser displays the XML data response from WelcomeRESTXMLService. Next, you'll learn how to consume this service.

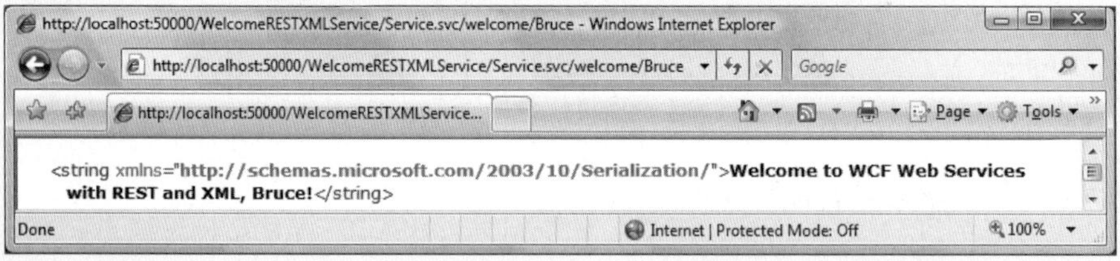

```
http://localhost:50000/WelcomeRESTXMLService/Service.svc/welcome/Bruce - Windows Internet Explorer

http://localhost:50000/WelcomeRESTXMLService/Service.svc/welcome/Bruce        Google

http://localhost:50000/WelcomeRESTXMLService...        Page    Tools

<string xmlns="http://schemas.microsoft.com/2003/10/Serialization/">Welcome to WCF Web Services
with REST and XML, Bruce!</string>

Done        Internet | Protected Mode: Off        100%
```

Fig. 23.14 | Response from WelcomeRESTXMLService in XML data format.

23.7.2 Consuming a REST-Based XML Web Service

WelcomeRESTXMLForm (Fig. 23.15) uses the System.Net namespace's **WebClient** class (line 13) to invoke the web service and receive its response. In lines 24–26, we associate Web-Client's DownloadStringCompleted event with a handler to indicate that the WebClient object has events associated with it.

```
 1   // Fig. 23.15: WelcomeRESTXMLForm.cs
 2   // Client that consumes the WelcomeRESTXMLService.
 3   using System;
 4   using System.Net;
 5   using System.Windows.Forms;
 6   using System.Xml.Linq;
 7
 8   namespace WelcomeRESTXMLClient
 9   {
10      public partial class WelcomeRESTXMLForm : Form
11      {
12         // object to invoke the WelcomeRESTXMLService
13         private WebClient client = new WebClient();
14
15         private XNamespace xmlNamespace =
16            XNamespace.Get(
17            "http://schemas.microsoft.com/2003/10/Serialization/" );
18
19         public WelcomeRESTXMLForm()
20         {
21            InitializeComponent();
22
23            // add DownloadStringCompleted event handler to WebClient
24            client.DownloadStringCompleted
25               += new DownloadStringCompletedEventHandler(
26               client_DownloadStringCompleted );
27         } // end constructor
28
29         // get user input and pass it to the web service
30         private void submitButton_Click( object sender, EventArgs e )
31         {
32            // send request to WelcomeRESTXMLService
33            client.DownloadStringAsync( new Uri(
34               "http://localhost:50000/WelcomeRESTXMLService/Service.svc/"
35               + "welcome/" + textBox.Text ) );
36         } // end method submitButton_Click
37
38         // process web service response
39         private void client_DownloadStringCompleted(
40            object sender, DownloadStringCompletedEventArgs e )
41         {
42            // check if any error occurred in retrieving service data
43            if ( e.Error == null )
44            {
```

Fig. 23.15 | Client that consumes the WelcomeRESTXMLService. (Part 1 of 2.)

```
45              // parse the returned XML string (e.Result)
46              XDocument xmlResponse = XDocument.Parse( e.Result );
47
48              // get the <string> element's value
49              MessageBox.Show( xmlResponse.Element(
50                  xmlNamespace + "string" ).Value, "Welcome" );
51          } // end if
52      } // end method client_DownloadStringCompleted
53  } // end class WelcomeRESTXMLForm
54 } // end namespace WelcomeRESTXMLClient
```

a) User inputs name.

b) Message sent from **WelcomeRESTXMLService**.

Fig. 23.15 | Client that consumes the WelcomeRESTXMLService. (Part 2 of 2.)

In this example, we process the WebClient's ***DownloadStringCompleted*** event, which occurs when the client receives the completed response from the web service. Line 33 calls the client object's ***DownloadStringAsync*** method to invoke the web service asynchronously. (There is also a synchronous DownloadString method that does not return until it receives the response.) The method's argument (i.e., the URL to invoke the web service) must be specified as an object of class ***Uri***. Class Uri's constructor receives a string representing a uniform resource identifier. [*Note:* The URL's port number must match the one issued to the web service by the ASP.NET Development Server.] When the call to the web service completes, the WebClient object raises the DownloadStringCompleted event. Its event handler has a parameter e of type ***DownloadStringCompletedEventArgs*** which contains the information returned by the web service. We can use this variable's properties to get the returned XML document (***e.Result***) and any errors that may have occurred during the process (***e.Error***). We then parse the XML response using XDocument method Parse (line 46). In lines 15–17, we specify the XML message's namespace (seen in Fig. 23.14), and use it to parse the service's XML response to display our welcome string in a MessageBox (lines 49–50).

23.8 Publishing and Consuming REST-Based JSON Web Services

We now build a RESTful web service that returns data in JSON format.

23.8.1 Creating a REST-Based JSON Web Service

By default, a web-service method with the WebGet attribute returns data in XML format. In Fig. 23.16, we modify the WelcomeRESTXMLService to return data in JSON format by setting WebGet's ***ResponseFormat*** property to WebMessageFormat.Json (line 13). (WebMessageFormat.XML is the default value.) For JSON serialization to work properly, the

```
 1   // Fig. 23.16: IWelcomeRESTJSONService.cs
 2   // WCF web service interface that returns a welcome message through REST
 3   // architecture and JSON format.
 4   using System.Runtime.Serialization;
 5   using System.ServiceModel;
 6   using System.ServiceModel.Web;
 7
 8   [ServiceContract]
 9   public interface IWelcomeRESTJSONService
10   {
11      // returns a welcome message
12      [OperationContract]
13      [WebGet( ResponseFormat = WebMessageFormat.Json,
14         UriTemplate = "/welcome/{yourName}" )]
15      TextMessage Welcome( string yourName );
16   } // end interface IWelcomeRESTJSONService
17
18   // class to encapsulate a string to send in JSON format
19   [DataContract]
20   public class TextMessage
21   {
22      // automatic property message
23      [DataMember]
24      public string Message {get; set; }
25   } // end class TextMessage
```

Fig. 23.16 | WCF web-service interface that returns a welcome message through REST architecture and JSON format.

objects being converted to JSON must have `public` properties. This enables the JSON serialization to create name/value pairs representing each `public` property and its corresponding value. The previous examples return `string` objects containing the responses. Even though `strings` are objects, `strings` do not have any `public` properties that represent their contents. So, lines 20–25 define a `TextMessage` class that encapsulates a `string` value and defines a `public` property `Message` to access that value. `System.Runtime.Serialization`'s **DataContract** attribute (line 19) exposes the `TextMessage` class for serialization to the client. Similarly, `System.Runtime.Serialization`'s **DataMember** attribute (line 23) exposes a property of this class for serialization to the client. This property will appear in the JSON object as a name/value pair. Only `DataMembers` of a `DataContract` are serialized

Figure 23.17 shows the implementation of the interface of Fig. 23.16. The `Welcome` method (lines 7–14) returns a `TextMessage` object, reflecting the changes we made to the interface class. This object is automatically serialized in JSON format (as a result of line 13 in Fig. 23.16) and sent to the client.

We can once again test the web service using a web browser, by accessing the `Service.svc` file (`http://localhost:50000/WelcomeRESTJSONService/Service.svc`) and appending the URI template (`welcome/yourName`) to the address. The response prompts you to download a file called *yourName*, which is a text file. This contains the JSON formatted data. By opening the file in a text editor such as Notepad (Fig. 23.18), you can see the service response as a JSON object. Notice that the property named `Message` has the welcome message as its value.

```
 1   // Fig. 23.17: WelcomeRESTJSONService.cs
 2   // WCF web service that returns a welcome message through REST
 3   // architecture and JSON format.
 4   public class WelcomeRESTJSONService : IWelcomeRESTJSONService
 5   {
 6      // returns a welcome message
 7      public TextMessage Welcome( string yourName )
 8      {
 9         // add welcome message to field of TextMessage object
10         TextMessage message = new TextMessage();
11         message.Message = string.Format( "Welcome to WCF Web Services" +
12            " with REST and JSON, {0}!", yourName );
13         return message;
14      } // end method Welcome
15   } // end class WelcomeRESTJSONService
```

Fig. 23.17 | WCF web service that returns a welcome message through REST architecture and JSON format.

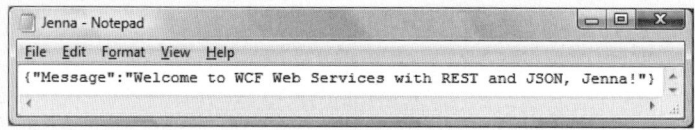

Fig. 23.18 | Response from WelcomeRESTJSONService in JSON data format.

23.8.2 Consuming a REST-Based JSON Web Service

We mentioned earlier that all types passed to and from web services can be supported by REST. Custom types that are sent to or from a REST web service are converted to XML or JSON data format. This process is referred to as *XML serialization* or *JSON serialization*, respectively. In Fig. 23.19, we consume the WelcomeRESTJSONService service using an object of the System.Runtime.Serialization.Json library's **DataContractJsonSerializer** class (lines 44–45).

To use the System.Runtime.Serialization.Json library and DataContractJsonSerializer class, you must include references to the System.ServiceModel.Web and System.Runtime.Serialization blies in the project. To do so, right click the project name, select **Add Reference** and add the System.ServiceModel.Web and System.Run-

```
 1   // Fig. 23.19: WelcomeRESTJSONForm.cs
 2   // Client that consumes WelcomeRESTJSONService.
 3   using System;
 4   using System.IO;
 5   using System.Net;
 6   using System.Runtime.Serialization.Json;
 7   using System.Text;
 8   using System.Windows.Forms;
 9
```

Fig. 23.19 | Client that consumes WelcomeRESTJSONService. (Part 1 of 3.)

```
10   namespace WelcomeRESTJSONClient
11   {
12      public partial class WelcomeRESTJSONForm : Form
13      {
14         // object to invoke the WelcomeRESTJSONService
15         private WebClient client = new WebClient();
16
17         public WelcomeRESTJSONForm()
18         {
19            InitializeComponent();
20
21            // add DownloadStringCompleted event handler to WebClient
22            client.DownloadStringCompleted
23               += new DownloadStringCompletedEventHandler(
24               client_DownloadStringCompleted );
25         } // end constructor
26
27         // get user input and pass it to the web service
28         private void submitButton_Click( object sender, EventArgs e )
29         {
30            // send request to WelcomeRESTJSONService
31            client.DownloadStringAsync( new Uri(
32               "http://localhost:50000/WelcomeRESTJSONService/Service.svc/"
33               + "welcome/" + textBox.Text ) );
34         } // end method submitButton_Click
35
36         // process web service response
37         private void client_DownloadStringCompleted(
38            object sender, DownloadStringCompletedEventArgs e )
39         {
40            // check if any error occurred in retrieving service data
41            if ( e.Error == null )
42            {
43               // deserialize response into a TextMessage object
44               DataContractJsonSerializer JSONSerializer =
45                  new DataContractJsonSerializer( typeof( TextMessage ) );
46               TextMessage message =
47                  ( TextMessage ) JSONSerializer.ReadObject( new
48                  MemoryStream( Encoding.Unicode.GetBytes( e.Result ) ) );
49
50               // display Message text
51               MessageBox.Show( message.Message, "Welcome" );
52            } // end if
53         } // end method client_DownloadStringCompleted
54      } // end class WelcomeRESTJSONForm
55
56      // TextMessage class representing a JSON object
57      [Serializable]
58      public class TextMessage
59      {
60         public string Message;
61      } // end class TextMessage
62   } // end namespace WelcomeRESTJSONClient
```

Fig. 23.19 | Client that consumes WelcomeRESTJSONService. (Part 2 of 3.)

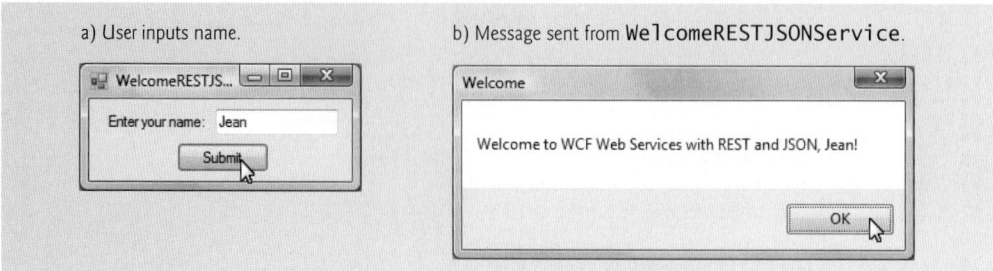

Fig. 23.19 | Client that consumes `WelcomeRESTJSONService`. (Part 3 of 3.)

time.Serialization blies. The `TextMessage` class (lines 58–61) maps the JSON response's fields for the `DataContractJsonSerializer` to deserialize. We add the ***Serializable*** attribute (line 57) to the `TextMessage` class to recognize it as a valid serializable object we can convert to and from JSON format. Also, this class on the client must have `public` data or properties that match the `public` data or properties in the corresponding class from the web service. Since we want to convert the JSON response into a `TextMessage` object, we set the `DataContractJsonSerializer`'s type parameter to `TextMessage` (line 45). In line 48, we use the `System.Text` namespace's `Encoding.Unicode.GetBytes` method to convert the JSON response to a Unicode encoded byte array, and encapsulate the byte array in a `MemoryStream` object so we can read data from the array using stream semantics. The bytes in the `MemoryStream` object are read by the `DataContractJsonSerializer` and deserialized into a `TextMessage` object (line 47).

23.9 Blackjack Web Service: Using Session Tracking in a SOAP-Based Web Service

In Chapter 22, we described the advantages of maintaining information about users to personalize their experiences. In particular, we discussed session tracking using cookies and `HttpSessionState` objects. Next, we incorporate session tracking into a SOAP-based WCF web service.

Suppose a client application needs to call several methods from the same web service, possibly several times each. In such a case, it can be beneficial for the web service to maintain state information for the client. Session tracking eliminates the need for information about the client to be passed between the client and the web service multiple times. For example, a web service providing access to local restaurant reviews would benefit from storing the client user's street address. Once the user's address is stored in a session variable, web service methods can return personalized, localized results without requiring that the address be passed in each method call. This not only improves performance but also requires less effort on your part—less information is passed in each method call.

23.9.1 Creating a Blackjack Web Service

Web services store session information to provide more intuitive functionality. Our next example is a SOAP-based web service that assists programmers in developing a blackjack card game. The web service provides methods to deal a card and to evaluate a hand of cards. After presenting the web service, we use it to serve as the dealer for a game of black-jack. The blackjack web service creates a session variable to maintain a unique deck of cards for each client application. Several clients can use the service at the same time, but method calls made by a specific client use only the deck stored in that client's session. Our example uses a simple subset of casino blackjack rules:

> Two cards each are dealt to the dealer and the player. The player's cards are dealt face up. Only the dealer's first card is dealt face up. Each card has a value. A card numbered 2 through 10 is worth its face value. Jacks, queens and kings each count as 10. Aces can count as 1 or 11—whichever value is more beneficial to the player (as we'll soon see). If the sum of the player's two initial cards is 21 (i.e., the player was dealt a card valued at 10 and an ace, which counts as 11 in this situation), the player has "blackjack" and immediately wins the game. Otherwise, the player can begin taking additional cards one at a time. These cards are dealt face up, and the player decides when to stop taking cards. If the player "busts" (i.e., the sum of the player's cards exceeds 21), the game is over, and the player loses. When the player is satisfied with the current set of cards, the player "stays" (i.e., stops taking cards), and the dealer's hidden card is revealed. If the dealer's total is 16 or less, the dealer must take another card; otherwise, the dealer must stay. The dealer must continue to take cards until the sum of the dealer's cards is greater than or equal to 17. If the dealer exceeds 21, the player wins. Otherwise, the hand with the higher point total wins. If the dealer and the player have the same point total, the game is a "push" (i.e., a tie), and no one wins.

The blackjack WCF web service's interface (Fig. 23.20) uses a ServiceContract with the **SessionMode** property set to Required (line 5). This means the service requires sessions to execute correctly. By default, the SessionMode property is set to Allowed. It can also be set to NotAllowed to disable sessions.

```
 1   // Fig. 23.20: IBlackjackService.cs
 2   // Blackjack game WCF web service interface.
 3   using System.ServiceModel;
 4
 5   [ServiceContract( SessionMode = SessionMode.Required )]
 6   public interface IBlackjackService
 7   {
 8      // deals a card that has not been dealt
 9      [OperationContract]
10      string DealCard();
11
12      // creates and shuffle the deck
13      [OperationContract]
14      void Shuffle();
15
16      // calculates value of a hand
17      [OperationContract]
18      int GetHandValue( string dealt );
19   } // end interface IBlackjackService
```

Fig. 23.20 | Blackjack game WCF web-service interface.

The web-service class (Fig. 23.21) provides methods to deal a card, shuffle the deck and determine the point value of a hand. For this example, we want a separate object of the BlackjackService class to handle each client session, so we can maintain a unique deck for each client. To do this, we must specify this behavior in the *ServiceBehavior* attribute (line 7). Setting the ServiceBehavior's *InstanceContextMode* property to PerSession creates a new instance of the class for each session. The InstanceContextMode property can also be set to PerCall or Single. PerCall uses a new object of the web-service class to handle every method call to the service. Single uses the same object of the web service class to handle all calls to the service.

```csharp
 1   // Fig. 23.21: BlackjackService.cs
 2   // Blackjack game WCF web service.
 3   using System;
 4   using System.Collections.Generic;
 5   using System.ServiceModel;
 6
 7   [ServiceBehavior( InstanceContextMode = InstanceContextMode.PerSession )]
 8   public class BlackjackService : IBlackjackService
 9   {
10      // create persistent session deck of cards object
11      List< string > deck = new List< string >();
12
13      // deals card that has not yet been dealt
14      public string DealCard()
15      {
16         string card = deck[ 0 ]; // get first card
17         deck.RemoveAt( 0 ); // remove card from deck
18         return card;
19      } // end method DealCard
20
21      // creates and shuffles a deck of cards
22      public void Shuffle()
23      {
24         Random randomObject = new Random(); // generates random numbers
25
26         deck.Clear(); // clears deck for new game
27
28         // generate all possible cards
29         for ( int face = 1; face <= 13; face++ ) // loop through faces
30            for ( int suit = 0; suit <= 3; suit++ ) // loop through suits
31               deck.Add( face + " " + suit ); // add card (string) to deck
32
33         // shuffles deck by swapping each card with another card randomly
34         for ( int i = 0; i < deck.Count; i++ )
35         {
36            // get random index
37            int newIndex = randomObject.Next( deck.Count - 1 );
38
39            // save current card in temporary variable
40            string temporary = deck[ i ];
41            deck[ i ] = deck[ newIndex ]; // copy randomly selected card
```

Fig. 23.21 | Blackjack game WCF web service. (Part 1 of 2.)

```
42
43              // copy current card back into deck
44              deck[ newIndex ] = temporary;
45           } // end for
46        } // end method Shuffle
47
48        // computes value of hand
49        public int GetHandValue( string dealt )
50        {
51           // split string containing all cards
52           string[] cards = dealt.Split( '\t' ); // get array of cards
53           int total = 0; // total value of cards in hand
54           int face; // face of the current card
55           int aceCount = 0; // number of aces in hand
56
57           // loop through the cards in the hand
58           foreach ( var drawn in cards )
59           {
60              // get face of card
61              face = Convert.ToInt32(
62                 drawn.Substring( 0, drawn.IndexOf( ' ' ) ) );
63
64              switch ( face )
65              {
66                 case 1: // if ace, increment aceCount
67                    ++aceCount;
68                    break;
69                 case 11: // if jack add 10
70                 case 12: // if queen add 10
71                 case 13: // if king add 10
72                    total += 10;
73                    break;
74                 default: // otherwise, add value of face
75                    total += face;
76                    break;
77              } // end switch
78           } // end foreach
79
80           // if there are any aces, calculate optimum total
81           if ( aceCount > 0 )
82           {
83              // if it is possible to count one ace as 11, and the rest
84              // as 1 each, do so; otherwise, count all aces as 1 each
85              if ( total + 11 + aceCount - 1 <= 21 )
86                 total += 11 + aceCount - 1;
87              else
88                 total += aceCount;
89           } // end if
90
91           return total;
92        } // end method GetHandValue
93     } // end class BlackjackService
```

Fig. 23.21 | Blackjack game WCF web service. (Part 2 of 2.)

We represent each card as a string consisting of a digit (i.e., 1–13) representing the card's face (e.g., ace through king), followed by a space and a digit (i.e., 0–3) representing the card's suit (e.g., clubs, diamonds, hearts or spades). For example, the jack of hearts is represented as "11 2", and the two of clubs as "2 0". After deploying the web service, we create a Windows Forms application that uses the BlackjackService's methods to implement a blackjack game.

Method DealCard (lines 14–19) removes a card from the deck and sends it to the client. Without using session tracking, the deck of cards would need to be passed back and forth with each method call. Using session state makes the method easy to call (it requires no arguments) and avoids the overhead of sending the deck over the network multiple times.

Method DealCard (lines 14–19) manipulates the current user's deck (the List of strings defined at line 11). From the user's deck, DealCard obtains the current top card (line 16), removes the top card from the deck (line 17) and returns the card's value as a string (line 18).

Method Shuffle (lines 22–46) fills the List object representing a deck of cards and shuffles it. Lines 29–31 generate strings in the form "*face suit*" to represent each card in a deck. Lines 34–45 shuffle the deck by swapping each card with another randomly selected card in the deck.

Method GetHandValue (lines 49–92) determines the total value of cards in a hand by trying to attain the highest score possible without going over 21. Recall that an ace can be counted as either 1 or 11, and all face cards count as 10.

As you'll see in Fig. 23.22, the client application maintains a hand of cards as a string in which each card is separated by a tab character. Line 52 of Fig. 23.21 tokenizes the hand of cards (represented by dealt) into individual cards by calling string method Split and passing to it the tab character. Split uses the delimiter characters to separate tokens in the string. Lines 58–78 count the value of each card. Lines 61–62 retrieve the first integer— the face—and uses that value in the switch statement (lines 64–77). If the card is an ace, the method increments variable aceCount (line 67). We discuss how this variable is used shortly. If the card is an 11, 12 or 13 (jack, queen or king), the method adds 10 to the total value of the hand (line 72). If the card is anything else, the method increases the total by that value (line 75).

Because an ace can represent 1 or 11, additional logic is required to process aces. Lines 81–89 process the aces after all the other cards. If a hand contains several aces, only one ace can be counted as 11 (if two aces each are counted as 11, the hand would have a losing value of at least 22). The condition in line 85 determines whether counting one ace as 11 and the rest as 1 results in a total that does not exceed 21. If this is possible, line 86 adjusts the total accordingly. Otherwise, line 88 adjusts the total, counting each ace as 1.

Method GetHandValue maximizes the value of the current cards without exceeding 21. Imagine, for example, that the dealer has a 7 and receives an ace. The new total could be either 8 or 18. However, GetHandValue always maximizes the value of the cards without going over 21, so the new total is 18.

23.9.2 Consuming the Blackjack Web Service

Now we use our blackjack web service in a Windows application (Fig. 23.22). This application uses an instance of BlackjackServiceClient (declared in line 14 and created in line 48) to represent the dealer. The web service keeps track of the player's and the dealer's cards (i.e., all the cards that have been dealt). As in Section 23.6.5, you must add a service reference to your project so it can access the web service. The code and images for this example are provided with the chapter's examples, which can be downloaded from our website www.deitel.com/books/csharpfp3.

```csharp
 1   // Fig. 23.22: BlackjackForm.cs
 2   // Blackjack game that uses the BlackjackService web service.
 3   using System;
 4   using System.Drawing;
 5   using System.Windows.Forms;
 6   using System.Collections.Generic;
 7   using System.Resources;
 8
 9   namespace BlackjackClient
10   {
11      public partial class BlackjackForm : Form
12      {
13         // reference to web service
14         private ServiceReference.BlackjackServiceClient dealer;
15
16         // string representing the dealer's cards
17         private string dealersCards;
18
19         // string representing the player's cards
20         private string playersCards;
21
22         // list of PictureBoxes for card images
23         private List< PictureBox > cardBoxes;
24         private int currentPlayerCard; // player's current card number
25         private int currentDealerCard; // dealer's current card number
26
27         private ResourceManager pictureLibrary =
28            BlackjackClient.Properties.Resources.ResourceManager;
29
30         // enum representing the possible game outcomes
31         public enum GameStatus
32         {
33            PUSH, // game ends in a tie
34            LOSE, // player loses
35            WIN, // player wins
36            BLACKJACK // player has blackjack
37         } // end enum GameStatus
38
39         public BlackjackForm()
40         {
41            InitializeComponent();
42         } // end constructor
43
44         // sets up the game
45         private void Blackjack_Load( object sender, EventArgs e )
46         {
```

Fig. 23.22 | Blackjack game that uses the BlackjackService web service. (Part 1 of 8.)

```
47          // instantiate object allowing communication with web service
48          dealer = new ServiceReference.BlackjackServiceClient();
49
50          // put PictureBoxes into cardBoxes List
51          cardBoxes = new List<PictureBox>(); // create list
52          cardBoxes.Add( pictureBox1 );
53          cardBoxes.Add( pictureBox2 );
54          cardBoxes.Add( pictureBox3 );
55          cardBoxes.Add( pictureBox4 );
56          cardBoxes.Add( pictureBox5 );
57          cardBoxes.Add( pictureBox6 );
58          cardBoxes.Add( pictureBox7 );
59          cardBoxes.Add( pictureBox8 );
60          cardBoxes.Add( pictureBox9 );
61          cardBoxes.Add( pictureBox10 );
62          cardBoxes.Add( pictureBox11 );
63          cardBoxes.Add( pictureBox12 );
64          cardBoxes.Add( pictureBox13 );
65          cardBoxes.Add( pictureBox14 );
66          cardBoxes.Add( pictureBox15 );
67          cardBoxes.Add( pictureBox16 );
68          cardBoxes.Add( pictureBox17 );
69          cardBoxes.Add( pictureBox18 );
70          cardBoxes.Add( pictureBox19 );
71          cardBoxes.Add( pictureBox20 );
72          cardBoxes.Add( pictureBox21 );
73          cardBoxes.Add( pictureBox22 );
74      } // end method BlackjackForm_Load
75
76      // deals cards to dealer while dealer's total is less than 17,
77      // then computes value of each hand and determines winner
78      private void DealerPlay()
79      {
80          // reveal dealer's second card
81          string[] cards = dealersCards.Split( '\t' );
82          DisplayCard( 1, cards[1] );
83
84          string nextCard;
85
86          // while value of dealer's hand is below 17,
87          // dealer must take cards
88          while ( dealer.GetHandValue( dealersCards ) < 17 )
89          {
90              nextCard = dealer.DealCard(); // deal new card
91              dealersCards += '\t' + nextCard; // add new card to hand
92
93              // update GUI to show new card
94              MessageBox.Show( "Dealer takes a card" );
95              DisplayCard( currentDealerCard, nextCard );
96              ++currentDealerCard;
97          } // end while
98
```

Fig. 23.22 | Blackjack game that uses the `BlackjackService` web service. (Part 2 of 8.)

```
 99          int dealersTotal = dealer.GetHandValue( dealersCards );
100          int playersTotal = dealer.GetHandValue( playersCards );
101
102          // if dealer busted, player wins
103          if ( dealersTotal > 21 )
104          {
105             GameOver( GameStatus.WIN );
106          } // end if
107          else
108          {
109             // if dealer and player have not exceeded 21,
110             // higher score wins; equal scores is a push.
111             if ( dealersTotal > playersTotal ) // player loses game
112                GameOver( GameStatus.LOSE );
113             else if ( playersTotal > dealersTotal ) // player wins game
114                GameOver( GameStatus.WIN );
115             else // player and dealer tie
116                GameOver( GameStatus.PUSH );
117          } // end else
118       } // end method DealerPlay
119
120       // displays card represented by cardValue in specified PictureBox
121       public void DisplayCard( int card, string cardValue )
122       {
123          // retrieve appropriate PictureBox
124          PictureBox displayBox = cardBoxes[ card ];
125
126          // if string representing card is empty,
127          // set displayBox to display back of card
128          if ( string.IsNullOrEmpty( cardValue ) )
129          {
130             displayBox.Image =
131                ( Image ) pictureLibrary.GetObject( "cardback" );
132             return;
133          } // end if
134
135          // retrieve face value of card from cardValue
136          string face =
137             cardValue.Substring( 0, cardValue.IndexOf( ' ' ) );
138
139          // retrieve the suit of the card from cardValue
140          string suit =
141             cardValue.Substring( cardValue.IndexOf( ' ' ) + 1 );
142
143          char suitLetter; // suit letter used to form image file name
144
145          // determine the suit letter of the card
146          switch ( Convert.ToInt32( suit ) )
147          {
148             case 0: // clubs
149                suitLetter = 'c';
150                break;
```

Fig. 23.22 | Blackjack game that uses the BlackjackService web service. (Part 3 of 8.)

```
151              case 1: // diamonds
152                 suitLetter = 'd';
153                 break;
154              case 2: // hearts
155                 suitLetter = 'h';
156                 break;
157              default: // spades
158                 suitLetter = 's';
159                 break;
160           } // end switch
161
162           // set displayBox to display appropriate image
163           displayBox.Image = ( Image ) pictureLibrary.GetObject(
164              "_" + face + suitLetter );
165        } // end method DisplayCard
166
167        // displays all player cards and shows
168        // appropriate game status message
169        public void GameOver( GameStatus winner )
170        {
171           string[] cards = dealersCards.Split( '\t' );
172
173           // display all the dealer's cards
174           for ( int i = 0; i < cards.Length; i++ )
175              DisplayCard( i, cards[ i ] );
176
177           // display appropriate status image
178           if ( winner == GameStatus.PUSH ) // push
179              statusPictureBox.Image =
180                 ( Image ) pictureLibrary.GetObject( "tie" );
181           else if ( winner == GameStatus.LOSE ) // player loses
182              statusPictureBox.Image =
183                 ( Image ) pictureLibrary.GetObject( "lose" );
184           else if ( winner == GameStatus.BLACKJACK )
185              // player has blackjack
186              statusPictureBox.Image =
187                 ( Image ) pictureLibrary.GetObject( "blackjack" );
188           else // player wins
189              statusPictureBox.Image =
190                 ( Image ) pictureLibrary.GetObject( "win" );
191
192           // display final totals for dealer and player
193           dealerTotalLabel.Text =
194              "Dealer: " + dealer.GetHandValue( dealersCards );
195           playerTotalLabel.Text =
196              "Player: " + dealer.GetHandValue( playersCards );
197
198           // reset controls for new game
199           stayButton.Enabled = false;
200           hitButton.Enabled = false;
201           dealButton.Enabled = true;
202        } // end method GameOver
203
```

Fig. 23.22 | Blackjack game that uses the BlackjackService web service. (Part 4 of 8.)

```
204        // deal two cards each to dealer and player
205        private void dealButton_Click( object sender, EventArgs e )
206        {
207           string card; // stores a card temporarily until added to a hand
208
209           // clear card images
210           foreach ( PictureBox cardImage in cardBoxes )
211              cardImage.Image = null;
212
213           statusPictureBox.Image = null; // clear status image
214           dealerTotalLabel.Text = string.Empty; // clear dealer total
215           playerTotalLabel.Text = string.Empty; // clear player total
216
217           // create a new, shuffled deck on the web service host
218           dealer.Shuffle();
219
220           // deal two cards to player
221           playersCards = dealer.DealCard(); // deal first card to player
222           DisplayCard( 11, playersCards ); // display card
223           card = dealer.DealCard(); // deal second card to player
224           DisplayCard( 12, card ); // update GUI to display new card
225           playersCards += '\t' + card; // add second card to player's hand
226
227           // deal two cards to dealer, only display face of first card
228           dealersCards = dealer.DealCard(); // deal first card to dealer
229           DisplayCard( 0, dealersCards ); // display card
230           card = dealer.DealCard(); // deal second card to dealer
231           DisplayCard( 1, string.Empty ); // display card face down
232           dealersCards += '\t' + card; // add second card to dealer's hand
233
234           stayButton.Enabled = true; // allow player to stay
235           hitButton.Enabled = true; // allow player to hit
236           dealButton.Enabled = false; // disable Deal Button
237
238           // determine the value of the two hands
239           int dealersTotal = dealer.GetHandValue( dealersCards );
240           int playersTotal = dealer.GetHandValue( playersCards );
241
242           // if hands equal 21, it is a push
243           if ( dealersTotal == playersTotal && dealersTotal == 21 )
244              GameOver( GameStatus.PUSH );
245           else if ( dealersTotal == 21 ) // if dealer has 21, dealer wins
246              GameOver( GameStatus.LOSE );
247           else if ( playersTotal == 21 ) // player has blackjack
248              GameOver( GameStatus.BLACKJACK );
249
250           // next dealer card has index 2 in cardBoxes
251           currentDealerCard = 2;
252
253           // next player card has index 13 in cardBoxes
254           currentPlayerCard = 13;
255        } // end method dealButton
256
```

Fig. 23.22 | Blackjack game that uses the BlackjackService web service. (Part 5 of 8.)

```
257        // deal another card to player
258        private void hitButton_Click( object sender, EventArgs e )
259        {
260            string card = dealer.DealCard(); // deal new card
261            playersCards += '\t' + card; // add new card to player's hand
262
263            DisplayCard( currentPlayerCard, card ); // display card
264            ++currentPlayerCard;
265
266            // determine the value of the player's hand
267            int total = dealer.GetHandValue( playersCards );
268
269            // if player exceeds 21, house wins
270            if ( total > 21 )
271                GameOver( GameStatus.LOSE );
272            else if ( total == 21 ) // if player has 21, dealer's turn
273            {
274                hitButton.Enabled = false;
275                DealerPlay();
276            } // end if
277        } // end method hitButton_Click
278
279        // play the dealer's hand after the player chooses to stay
280        private void stayButton_Click( object sender, EventArgs e )
281        {
282            stayButton.Enabled = false; // disable Stay Button
283            hitButton.Enabled = false; // disable Hit Button
284            dealButton.Enabled = true; // enable Deal Button
285            DealerPlay(); // player chose to stay, so play the dealer's hand
286        } // end method stayButton_Click
287    } // end class BlackjackForm
288 } // end namespace BlackjackClient
```

a) Initial cards dealt to the player and the dealer when the user presses the **Deal** button.

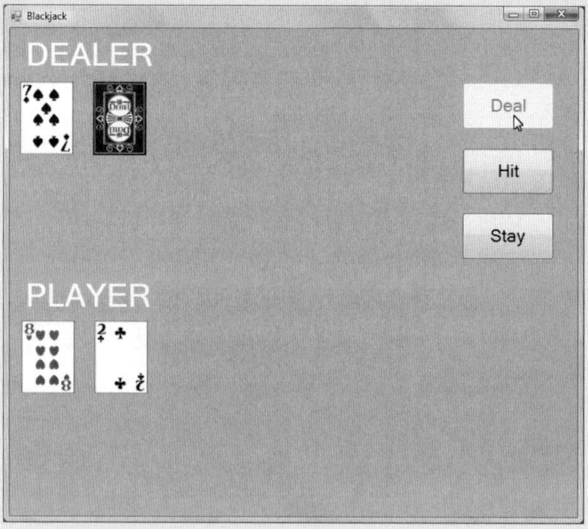

Fig. 23.22 | Blackjack game that uses the BlackjackService web service. (Part 6 of 8.)

b) Cards after the player presses the **Hit** button once, then the **Stay** button. In this case, the player wins the game with a higher total than the dealer.

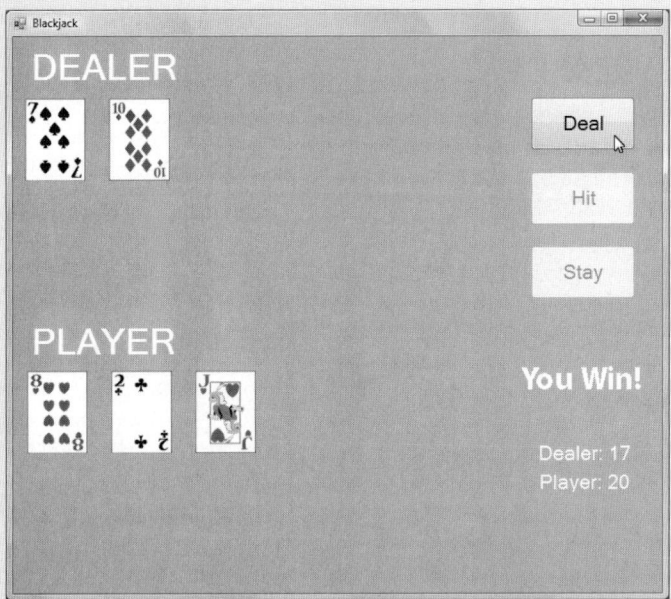

c) Cards after the player presses the **Hit** button once, then the **Stay** button. In this case, the player busts (exceeds 21) and the dealer wins the game.

Fig. 23.22 | Blackjack game that uses the BlackjackService web service. (Part 7 of 8.)

d) Cards after the player presses the **Deal** button. In this case, the player wins with Blackjack because the first two cards are an ace and a card with a value of 10 (a jack in this case).

e) Cards after the player presses the **Stay** button. In this case, the player and dealer push—they have the same card total.

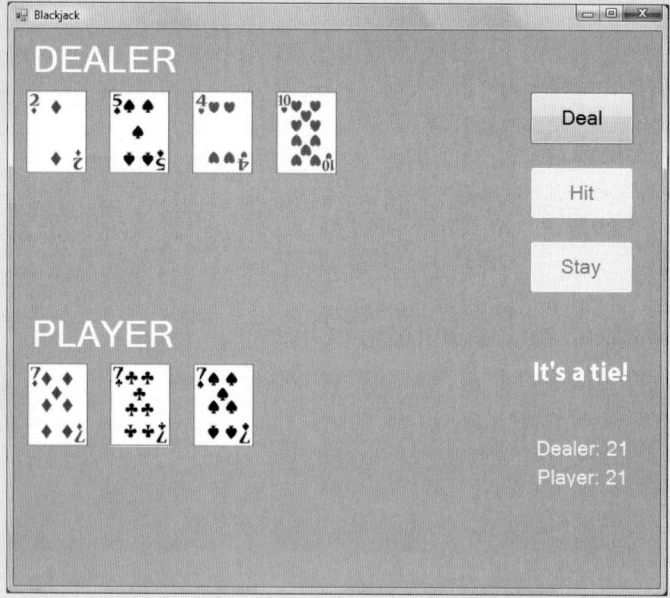

Fig. 23.22 | Blackjack game that uses the `BlackjackService` web service. (Part 8 of 8.)

Each player has 11 `PictureBoxes`—the maximum number of cards that can be dealt without exceeding 21 (i.e., four aces, four twos and three threes). These `PictureBoxes` are placed in a `List` (lines 52–73), so we can index the `List` during the game to determine which `PictureBox` should display a particular card image. In lines 27–28, we create a `ResourceManager` to access the library of card images.

Method `GameOver` (lines 169–202) shows an appropriate message in the status `PictureBox` and displays the final point totals of both the dealer and the player. These values are obtained by calling the web service's `GetHandValue` method in lines 194 and 196. Method `GameOver` receives as an argument a member of the `GameStatus` enumeration (defined in lines 31–37). The enumeration represents whether the player tied, lost or won the game; its four members are `PUSH`, `LOSE`, `WIN` and `BLACKJACK`.

When the player clicks the **Deal** button, the event handler (lines 205–255) clears the `PictureBoxes` and the `Labels` displaying the final point totals. Line 218 shuffles the deck by calling the web service's `Shuffle` method, then the player and dealer receive two cards each (returned by calls to the web service's `DealCard` method in lines 221, 223, 228 and 230). Lines 239–240 evaluate both the dealer's and player's hands by calling the web service's `GetHandValue` method. If the player and the dealer both obtain scores of 21, the program calls method `GameOver`, passing `GameStatus.PUSH`. If only the player has 21 after the first two cards are dealt, the program passes `GameStatus.BLACKJACK` to method `GameOver`. If only the dealer has 21, the program passes `GameStatus.LOSE` to method `GameOver`.

If `dealButton_Click` does not call `GameOver`, the player can take more cards by clicking the **Hit** button. The event handler for this button is in lines 258–277. Each time a player clicks **Hit**, the program deals the player one more card (line 260), displaying it in the GUI. Line 267 evaluates the player's hand. If the player exceeds 21, the game is over, and the player loses. If the player has exactly 21, the player cannot take any more cards, and method `DealerPlay` (lines 78–118) is called, causing the dealer to keep taking cards until the dealer's hand has a value of 17 or more (lines 88–97). If the dealer exceeds 21, the player wins (line 105); otherwise, the values of the hands are compared, and `GameOver` is called with the appropriate argument (lines 111–116).

Clicking the **Stay** button indicates that a player does not want to be dealt another card. The event handler for this button (lines 280–286) disables the **Hit** and **Stay** buttons, then calls method `DealerPlay`.

Method `DisplayCard` (lines 121–165) updates the GUI to display a newly dealt card. The method takes as arguments an integer representing the index of the `PictureBox` in the `List` that must have its image set, and a `string` representing the card. An empty `string` indicates that we wish to display the card face down. If method `DisplayCard` receives a `string` that's not empty, the program extracts the face and suit from the `string` and uses this information to find the correct image. The `switch` statement (lines 146–160) converts the number representing the suit to an `int` and assigns the appropriate character literal to `suitLetter` (c for clubs, d for diamonds, h for hearts and s for spades). The character in `suitLetter` is used to complete the image's file name (lines 163–164).

23.10 Airline Reservation Web Service: Database Access and Invoking a Service from ASP.NET

Our prior examples accessed web services from Windows Forms applications. You can just as easily use web services in ASP.NET web applications. In fact, because web-based businesses are becoming increasingly prevalent, it is common for web applications to consume web services. Figures 23.23 and 23.24 present the interface and class, respectively, for an airline reservation service that receives information regarding the type of seat a customer wishes to reserve, checks a database to see if such a seat is available and, if so, makes a reservation. Later in this section, we present an ASP.NET web application that allows a customer to specify a reservation request, then uses the airline reservation web service to attempt to execute the request. The code and database used in this example are provided with the chapter's examples, which can be downloaded from www.deitel.com/books/csharpfp3.

```
 1   // Fig. 23.23: IReservationService.cs
 2   // Airline reservation WCF web service interface.
 3   using System.ServiceModel;
 4
 5   [ServiceContract]
 6   public interface IReservationService
 7   {
 8      // reserves a seat
 9      [OperationContract]
10      bool Reserve( string seatType, string classType );
11   } // end interface IReservationService
```

Fig. 23.23 | Airline reservation WCF web-service interface.

```
 1   // Fig. 23.24: ReservationService.cs
 2   // Airline reservation WCF web service.
 3   using System.Linq;
 4
 5   public class ReservationService : IReservationService
 6   {
 7      // create ticketsDB object to access Tickets database
 8      private TicketsDataContext ticketsDB = new TicketsDataContext();
 9
10      // checks database to determine whether matching seat is available
11      public bool Reserve( string seatType, string classType )
12      {
13         // LINQ query to find seats matching the parameters
14         var result =
15            from seat in ticketsDB.Seats
16            where ( seat.Taken == false ) && ( seat.SeatType == seatType )
17               && ( seat.SeatClass == classType )
18            select seat;
19
20         // get first available seat
21         Seat firstAvailableSeat = result.FirstOrDefault();
22
23         // if seat is available seats, mark it as taken
24         if ( firstAvailableSeat != null )
25         {
```

Fig. 23.24 | Airline reservation WCF web service. (Part 1 of 2.)

```
26              firstAvailableSeat.Taken = true; // mark the seat as taken
27              ticketsDB.SubmitChanges(); // update
28              return true; // seat was reserved
29          } // end if
30
31          return false; // no seat was reserved
32      } // end method Reserve
33  } // end class ReservationService
```

Fig. 23.24 | Airline reservation WCF web service. (Part 2 of 2.)

In Chapter 21, you learned how to use LINQ to SQL to extract data from a database. We added the Tickets.mdf database and corresponding LINQ to SQL classes to create a DataContext object (line 8) for our ticket reservation system. Tickets.mdf database contains the Seats table with four columns—the seat number (1–10), the seat type (Window, Middle or Aisle), the class type (Economy or First) and a column containing either 1 (true) or 0 (false) to indicate whether the seat is taken.

This web service has a single method—Reserve (lines 11–32)—which searches the seat database (Tickets.mdf) to locate a seat matching a user's request. If it finds an appropriate seat, Reserve updates the database, makes the reservation and returns true; otherwise, no reservation is made, and the method returns false. Note that the statements in lines 14–18 and lines 22–29, which query and update the database, use LINQ to SQL.

Reserve receives two parameters—a string representing the seat type (i.e., Window, Middle or Aisle) and a string representing the class type (i.e., Economy or First). Lines 14–18 retrieve the seat numbers of any available seats matching the requested seat and class type with the results of a query. In line 21, we access the query result's *FirstOrDefault* method to get the first available seat if there is one, or a null value if there is not. In line 24, if firstAvailableSeat is not null, there was at least one seat that matched the user's request. In this case, the web service reserves the first matching seat. Line 26 marks the seat as taken and line 27 submits the changes to the database. Method Reserve returns true (line 28) to indicate that the reservation was successful. If there are no matching seats, Reserve returns false (line 31) to indicate that no seats matched the user's request.

Creating a Web Form to Interact with the Airline Reservation Web Service

Figure 23.25 presents the code for an ASP.NET page through which users can select seat types. This page allows users to reserve a seat on the basis of its class (Economy or First) and location (Aisle, Middle or Window) in a row of seats. The page then uses the airline reservation web service to carry out user requests. If the database request is not successful, the user is instructed to modify the request and try again. When you create this ASP.NET application, remember to add a service reference to the ReservationService.

This page defines two DropDownList objects and a Button. One DropDownList (lines 21–26) displays all the seat types from which users can select. The second (lines 29–32) provides choices for the class type. Users click the Button named reserveButton (lines 35–37) to submit requests after making selections from the DropDownLists. The page also defines an initially blank Label named errorLabel (lines 39–40), which displays an appropriate message if no seat matching the user's selection is available.

```
 1   <%-- Fig. 23.25: ReservationClient.aspx                      --%>
 2   <%-- Web Form that allows users to reserve seats on a plane. --%>
 3   <%@ Page Language="C#" AutoEventWireup="true"
 4      CodeFile="ReservationClient.aspx.cs" Inherits="ReservationClient" %>
 5
 6   <!DOCTYPE html PUBLIC "-//W3C//DTD XHTML 1.1//EN"
 7      "http://www.w3.org/TR/xhtml11/DTD/xhtml11.dtd">
 8
 9   <html xmlns="http://www.w3.org/1999/xhtml" >
10   <head runat="server">
11      <title>Ticket Reservation</title>
12   </head>
13   <body>
14      <form id="form1" runat="server">
15      <div>
16         <asp:Label ID="instructionsLabel" runat="server"
17            Text="Please select the seat type and class to reserve:">
18         </asp:Label>
19         <br /><br />
20         <%-- seat options --%>
21         <asp:DropDownList ID="seatList" runat="server"
22            Height="22px" Width="100px">
23            <asp:ListItem>Aisle</asp:ListItem>
24            <asp:ListItem>Middle</asp:ListItem>
25            <asp:ListItem>Window</asp:ListItem>
26         </asp:DropDownList>
27              
28         <%-- class options --%>
29         <asp:DropDownList ID="classList" runat="server" Width="100px">
30            <asp:ListItem>Economy</asp:ListItem>
31            <asp:ListItem>First</asp:ListItem>
32         </asp:DropDownList>
33              
34         <%-- submits selections to server --%>
35         <asp:Button ID="reserveButton" runat="server" Height="24px"
36            OnClick="reserveButton_Click"
37            Text="Reserve" Width="102px" />
38         <br /><br />
39         <asp:Label ID="errorLabel" runat="server" ForeColor="#C00000"
40            Height="19px" Width="343px"></asp:Label>
41      </div>
42      </form>
43   </body>
44   </html>
```

Fig. 23.25 | ASPX file that takes reservation information.

Lines 8–9 of Fig. 23.26 create a ReservationServiceClient proxy object. When the user clicks **Reserve** (Fig. 23.27), the reserveButton_Click event handler (lines 12–34 of Fig. 23.26) executes, and the page reloads. The event handler calls the web service's Reserve method and passes to it the selected seat and class type as arguments (lines 15–16). If Reserve returns true, the application hides the GUI controls and displays a message thanking the user for making a reservation (line 26); otherwise, the application

```
1   // Fig. 23.26: ReservationClient.aspx.cs
2   // ReservationClient code behind file.
3   using System;
4
5   public partial class ReservationClient : System.Web.UI.Page
6   {
7      // object of proxy type used to connect to ReservationService
8      private ServiceReference.ReservationServiceClient ticketAgent =
9         new ServiceReference.ReservationServiceClient();
10
11     // attempt to reserve the selected type of seat
12     protected void reserveButton_Click( object sender, EventArgs e )
13     {
14        // if the ticket is reserved
15        if ( ticketAgent.Reserve( seatList.SelectedItem.Text,
16           classList.SelectedItem.Text ) )
17        {
18           // hide other controls
19           instructionsLabel.Visible = false;
20           seatList.Visible = false;
21           classList.Visible = false;
22           reserveButton.Visible = false;
23           errorLabel.Visible = false;
24
25           // display message indicating success
26           Response.Write( "Your reservation has been made. Thank you." );
27        } // end if
28        else // service method returned false, so signal failure
29        {
30           // display message in the initially blank errorLabel
31           errorLabel.Text = "This type of seat is not available. " +
32              "Please modify your request and try again.";
33        } // end else
34     } // end method reserveButton_Click
35  } // end class ReservationClient
```

Fig. 23.26 | ReservationClient code-behind file.

notifies the user that the type of seat requested is not available and instructs the user to try again (lines 31–32). You can use the techniques presented in Chapter 22 to build this Web Form. Figure 23.27 shows several user interactions with this web application.

a) Selecting a seat.

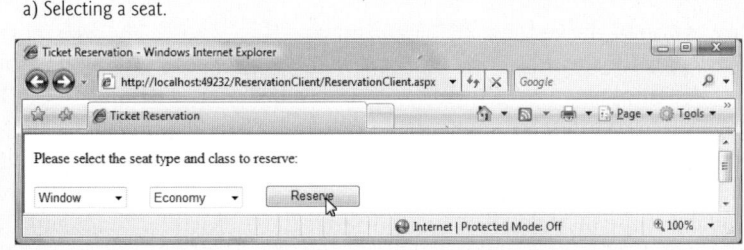

Fig. 23.27 | Ticket reservation web-application sample execution. (Part 1 of 2.)

b) Seat is reserved successfully.

Your reservation has been made. Thank you.

c) Attempting to reserve another seat.

Please select the seat type and class to reserve:

Aisle   Economy   Reserve

d) No seats match the requested type and class.

Please select the seat type and class to reserve:

Window   Economy   Reserve
This type of seat is not available. Please modify your
request and try again.

Fig. 23.27 | Ticket reservation web-application sample execution. (Part 2 of 2.)

23.11 Equation Generator: Returning User-Defined Types

With the exception of the WelcomeRESTJSONService (Fig. 23.17), the web services we've demonstrated all received and returned primitive-type instances. It is also possible to process instances of complete user-defined types in a web service. These types can be passed to or returned from web-service methods.

This section presents an EquationGenerator web service that generates random arithmetic equations of type Equation. The client is a math-tutoring application that inputs information about the mathematical question that the user wishes to attempt (addition, subtraction or multiplication) and the skill level of the user (1 specifies equations using numbers from 1 to 10, 2 specifies equations involving numbers from 10 to 100, and 3 specifies equations containing numbers from 100 to 1000). The web service then generates an equation consisting of random numbers in the proper range. The client application receives the Equation and displays the sample question to the user.

Defining Class Equation

We define class Equation in Fig. 23.28. Lines 33–53 define a constructor that takes three arguments—two ints representing the left and right operands and a string that represents the arithmetic operation to perform. The constructor sets the Equation's properties, then calculates the appropriate result. The parameterless constructor (lines 26–30) calls the three-argument constructor (lines 33–53) and passes default values.

```
 1    // Fig. 23.28: Equation.cs
 2    // Class Equation that contains information about an equation.
 3    using System.Runtime.Serialization;
 4
 5    [DataContract]
 6    public class Equation
 7    {
 8       // automatic property to access the left operand
 9       [DataMember]
10       private int Left { get; set; }
11
12       // automatic property to access the right operand
13       [DataMember]
14       private int Right { get; set; }
15
16       // automatic property to access the result of applying
17       // an operation to the left and right operands
18       [DataMember]
19       private int Result { get; set; }
20
21       // automatic property to access the operation
22       [DataMember]
23       private string Operation { get; set; }
24
25       // required default constructor
26       public Equation()
27          : this( 0, 0, "add" )
28       {
29          // empty body
30       } // end default constructor
31
32       // three-argument constructor for class Equation
33       public Equation( int leftValue, int rightValue, string type )
34       {
35          Left = leftValue;
36          Right = rightValue;
37
38          switch ( type ) // perform appropriate operation
39          {
```

Fig. 23.28 | Class Equation that contains information about an equation. (Part 1 of 2.)

```
40                  case "add": // addition
41                      Result = Left + Right;
42                      Operation = "+";
43                      break;
44                  case "subtract": // subtraction
45                      Result = Left - Right;
46                      Operation = "-";
47                      break;
48                  case "multiply": // multiplication
49                      Result = Left * Right;
50                      Operation = "*";
51                      break;
52          } // end switch
53      } // end three-argument constructor
54
55      // return string representation of the Equation object
56      public override string ToString()
57      {
58          return string.Format( "{0} {1} {2} = {4}", Left, Operation,
59              Right, Result );
60      } // end method ToString
61
62      // property that returns a string representing left-hand side
63      [DataMember]
64      private string LeftHandSide
65      {
66          get
67          {
68              return string.Format( "{0} {1} {2}", Left, Operation,
69                  Right );
70          } // end get
71          set
72          {
73              // empty body
74          } // end set
75      } // end property LeftHandSide
76
77      // property that returns a string representing right-hand side
78      [DataMember]
79      private string RightHandSide
80      {
81          get
82          {
83              return Result.ToString();
84          } // end get
85          set
86          {
87              // empty body
88          } // end set
89      } // end property RightHandSide
90  } // end class Equation
```

Fig. 23.28 | Class Equation that contains information about an equation. (Part 2 of 2.)

Class Equation defines properties LeftHandSide (lines 64–75), RightHandSide (lines 79–89), Left (line 10), Right (line 14), Result (line 19) and Operation (line 23). The web service client does not need to modify the values of properties LeftHandSide and RightHandSide. However, a property can be serialized only if it has both a get and a set accessor—even if the set accessor has an empty body. Each property is preceded by the DataMember attribute to indicate that it should be serialized. LeftHandSide (lines 64–75) returns a string representing everything to the left of the equals (=) sign in the equation, and RightHandSide (lines 79–89) returns a string representing everything to the right of the equals (=) sign. Left (line 10) returns the int to the left of the operator (known as the left operand), and Right (lines 14) returns the int to the right of the operator (known as the right operand). Result (line 19) returns the solution to the equation, and Operation (line 23) returns the operator in the equation. The client in this case study does not use the RightHandSide property, but we included it in case future clients choose to use it. Method ToString (lines 56–60) returns a string representation of the equation.

23.11.1 Creating the REST-Based XML EquationGenerator Web Service

Figures 23.29–23.30 present the EquationGeneratorService's interface and class for creating randomly generated Equations. Method GenerateEquation (lines 9–26 of Fig. 23.30) takes two parameters—a string representing the mathematical operation ("add", "subtract" or "multiply") and a string representing the difficulty level. The difficulty level is a string because variables for UriTemplate path segments must be of type

```
I    // Fig. 23.29: IEquationGeneratorService.cs
2    // WCF REST service interface to create random equations based on a
3    // specified operation and difficulty level.
4    using System.ServiceModel;
5    using System.ServiceModel.Web;
6
7    [ServiceContract]
8    public interface IEquationGeneratorService
9    {
10       // method to generate a math equation
11       [OperationContract]
12       [WebGet( UriTemplate = "equation/{operation}/{level}" )]
13       Equation GenerateEquation( string operation, string level );
14    } // end interface IEquationGeneratorService
```

Fig. 23.29 | WCF REST service interface to create random equations based on a specified operation and difficulty level.

```
I    // Fig. 22.30: EquationGeneratorService.cs
2    // WCF REST service to create random equations based on a
3    // specified operation and difficulty level.
4    using System;
5
```

Fig. 23.30 | WCF REST service to create random equations based on a specified operation and difficulty level. (Part 1 of 2.)

```
 6   public class EquationGeneratorService : IEquationGeneratorService
 7   {
 8      // method to generate a math equation
 9      public Equation GenerateEquation( string operation, string level )
10      {
11         // calculate maximum and minimum number to be used
12         int maximum =
13            Convert.ToInt32( Math.Pow( 10, Convert.ToInt32( level ) ) );
14         int minimum =
15            Convert.ToInt32( Math.Pow( 10, Convert.ToInt32( level ) - 1 ) );
16
17         Random randomObject = new Random(); // generate random numbers
18
19         // create Equation consisting of two random
20         // numbers in the range minimum to maximum
21         Equation newEquation = new Equation(
22            randomObject.Next( minimum, maximum ),
23            randomObject.Next( minimum, maximum ), operation );
24
25         return newEquation;
26      } // end method GenerateEquation
27   } // end class EquationGeneratorService
```

Fig. 23.30 | WCF REST service to create random equations based on a specified operation and difficulty level. (Part 2 of 2.)

string. When line 25 of Fig. 23.30 returns the Equation, it is serialized as XML by default and sent to the client. We'll do this with JSON as well in Section 23.11.3. Recall from Section 23.7.1 that you must modify the Web.config file to enable REST support as well.

23.11.2 Consuming the REST-Based XML EquationGenerator Web Service

The MathTutor application (Fig. 23.31) calls the EquationGenerator web service's GenerateEquation method to create an Equation object. The tutor then displays the left-hand side of the Equation and waits for user input.

```
 1   // Fig. 23.31: MathTutorForm.cs
 2   // Math tutor using EquationGeneratorServiceXML to create equations.
 3   using System;
 4   using System.Net;
 5   using System.Windows.Forms;
 6   using System.Xml.Linq;
 7
 8   namespace MathTutorXML
 9   {
10      public partial class MathTutorForm : Form
11      {
```

Fig. 23.31 | Math tutor using EquationGeneratorServiceXML to create equations. (Part 1 of 4.)

```
12      private string operation = "add"; // the default operation
13      private int level = 1; // the default difficulty level
14      private string leftHandSide; // the left side of the equation
15      private int result; // the answer
16      private XNamespace xmlNamespace =
17         XNamespace.Get( "http://schemas.datacontract.org/2004/07/" );
18
19      // object used to invoke service
20      private WebClient service = new WebClient();
21
22      public MathTutorForm()
23      {
24         InitializeComponent();
25
26         // add DownloadStringCompleted event handler to WebClient
27         service.DownloadStringCompleted
28            += new DownloadStringCompletedEventHandler(
29            service_DownloadStringCompleted );
30      } // end constructor
31
32      // generates new equation when user clicks button
33      private void generateButton_Click( object sender, EventArgs e )
34      {
35         // send request to EquationGeneratorServiceXML
36         service.DownloadStringAsync( new Uri(
37            "http://localhost:49732/EquationGeneratorServiceXML" +
38            "/Service.svc/equation/" + operation + "/" + level ) );
39      } // end method generateButton_Click
40
41      // process web service response
42      private void service_DownloadStringCompleted(
43         object sender, DownloadStringCompletedEventArgs e )
44      {
45         // check if any errors occurred in retrieving service data
46         if ( e.Error == null )
47         {
48            // parse response and get LeftHandSide and Result values
49            XDocument xmlResponse = XDocument.Parse( e.Result );
50            leftHandSide = xmlResponse.Element(
51               xmlNamespace + "Equation" ).Element(
52               xmlNamespace + "LeftHandSide" ).Value;
53            result = Convert.ToInt32( xmlResponse.Element(
54               xmlNamespace + "Equation" ).Element(
55               xmlNamespace + "Result" ).Value );
56
57            // display left side of equation
58            questionLabel.Text = leftHandSide;
59            okButton.Enabled = true; // enable okButton
60            answerTextBox.Enabled = true; // enable answerTextBox
61         } // end if
62      } // end method client_DownloadStringCompleted
63
```

Fig. 23.31 | Math tutor using EquationGeneratorServiceXML to create equations. (Part 2 of 4.)

```
64          // check user's answer
65          private void okButton_Click( object sender, EventArgs e )
66          {
67              if ( !string.IsNullOrEmpty( answerTextBox.Text ) )
68              {
69                  // get user's answer
70                  int userAnswer = Convert.ToInt32( answerTextBox.Text );
71
72                  // determine whether user's answer is correct
73                  if ( result == userAnswer )
74                  {
75                      questionLabel.Text = string.Empty; // clear question
76                      answerTextBox.Clear(); // clear answer
77                      okButton.Enabled = false; // disable OK button
78                      MessageBox.Show( "Correct! Good job!", "Result" );
79                  } // end if
80                  else
81                  {
82                      MessageBox.Show( "Incorrect. Try again.", "Result" );
83                  } // end else
84              } // end if
85          } // end method okButton_Click
86
87          // set the operation to addition
88          private void additionRadioButton_CheckedChanged( object sender,
89              EventArgs e )
90          {
91              if ( additionRadioButton.Checked )
92                  operation = "add";
93          } // end method additionRadioButton_CheckedChanged
94
95          // set the operation to subtraction
96          private void subtractionRadioButton_CheckedChanged( object sender,
97              EventArgs e )
98          {
99              if ( subtractionRadioButton.Checked )
100                 operation = "subtract";
101         } // end method subtractionRadioButton_CheckedChanged
102
103         // set the operation to multiplication
104         private void multiplicationRadioButton_CheckedChanged(
105             object sender, EventArgs e )
106         {
107             if ( multiplicationRadioButton.Checked )
108                 operation = "multiply";
109         } // end method multiplicationRadioButton_CheckedChanged
110
111         // set difficulty level to 1
112         private void levelOneRadioButton_CheckedChanged( object sender,
113             EventArgs e )
114         {
```

Fig. 23.31 | Math tutor using EquationGeneratorServiceXML to create equations. (Part 3 of 4.)

```
115            if ( levelOneRadioButton.Checked )
116               level = 1;
117         } // end method levelOneRadioButton_CheckedChanged
118
119         // set difficulty level to 2
120         private void levelTwoRadioButton_CheckedChanged( object sender,
121            EventArgs e )
122         {
123            if ( levelTwoRadioButton.Checked )
124               level = 2;
125         } // end method levelTwoRadioButton_CheckedChanged
126
127         // set difficulty level to 3
128         private void levelThreeRadioButton_CheckedChanged( object sender,
129            EventArgs e )
130         {
131            if ( levelThreeRadioButton.Checked )
132               level = 3;
133         } // end method levelThreeRadioButton_CheckedChanged
134      } // end class MathTutorForm
135   } // end namespace MathTutorXML
```

a) Generating a level 1 addition equation.

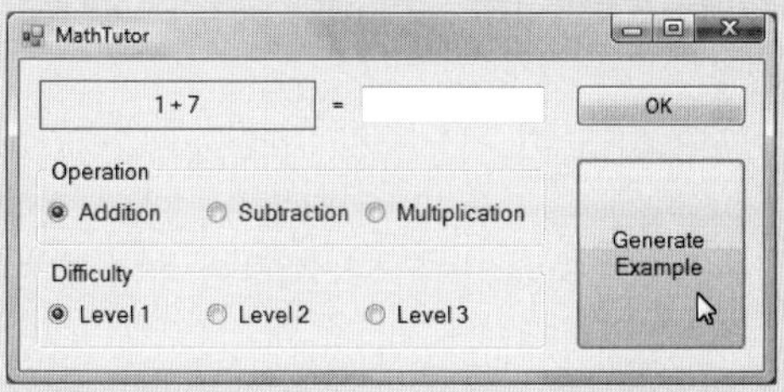

b) Answering the question incorrectly.

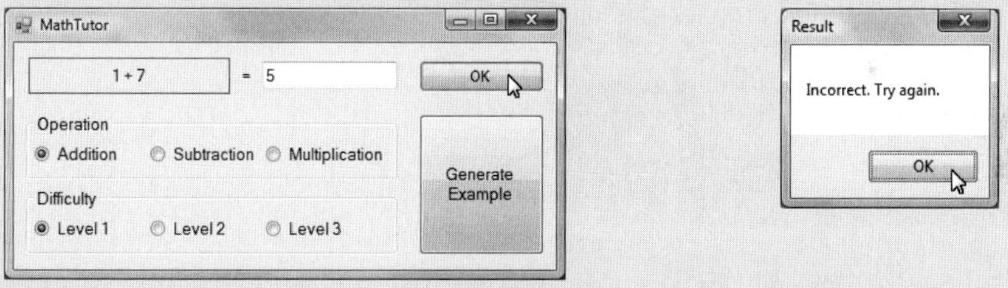

c) Answering the question correctly.

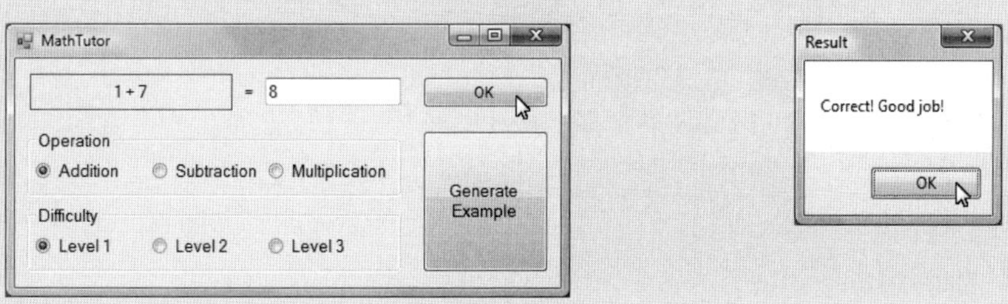

Fig. 23.31 | Math tutor using `EquationGeneratorServiceXML` to create equations. (Part 4 of 4.)

The default setting for the difficulty level is 1, but the user can change this by choosing a level from the RadioButtons in the GroupBox labeled **Difficulty**. Clicking any of the levels invokes the corresponding RadioButton's CheckedChanged event handler (lines 112–133), which sets integer level to the level selected by the user. Although the default setting for the question type is **Addition**, the user also can change this by selecting one of the RadioButtons in the GroupBox labeled **Operation**. Doing so invokes the corresponding operation's event handlers in lines 88–109, which assigns to string operation the string corresponding to the user's selection.

Line 20 defines the WebClient that is used to invoke the web service. Event handler generateButton_Click (lines 33–39) invokes EquationGeneratorService method GenerateEquation (line 36–38) asynchronously using the web service's UriTemplate specified at line 12 in Fig. 23.29. When the response arrives, the DownloadStringCompleted event handler (lines 42–62) parses the XML response (line 49), uses XDocument's Element method to obtain the left side of the equation (lines 50–52) and stores the result (lines 53–55). We define the XML response's namespace in lines 16–17 as an XNamespace to parse the XML response. Then, the handler displays the left-hand side of the equation in questionLabel (line 58) and enables okButton so that the user can enter an answer. When the user clicks **OK**, okButton_Click (lines 65–85) checks whether the user provided the correct answer.

23.11.3 Creating the REST-Based JSON EquationGenerator Web Service

You can set the web service to return JSON data instead of XML. Figure 23.32 is a modified IEquationGeneratorService interface for a service that returns an Equation in JSON format. The ResponseFormat property (line 12) is added to the WebGet attribute and set to WebMessageFormat.Json. We don't show the implementation of this interface here, because it is identical to that of Fig. 23.30. This shows how flexible WCF can be.

```
 1   // Fig. 23.32: IEquationGeneratorService.cs
 2   // WCF REST service interface to create random equations based on a
 3   // specified operation and difficulty level.
 4   using System.ServiceModel;
 5   using System.ServiceModel.Web;
 6
 7   [ServiceContract]
 8   public interface IEquationGeneratorService
 9   {
10      // method to generate a math equation
11      [OperationContract]
12      [WebGet( ResponseFormat = WebMessageFormat.Json,
13         UriTemplate = "equation/{operation}/{level}" )]
14      Equation GenerateEquation( string operation, string level );
15   } // end interface IEquationGeneratorService
```

Fig. 23.32 | WCF REST service interface to create random equations based on a specified operation and difficulty level.

23.11.4 Consuming the REST-Based JSON `EquationGenerator` Web Service

A modified `MathTutor` application (Fig. 23.33) accesses the URI of the `EquationGenerator` web service to get the JSON object (lines 35–37). We define a JSON representation of an `Equation` object for the serializer in Fig. 23.34. The JSON object is deserialized using the `System.Runtime.Serialization.Json` namespace's `DataContractJsonSerializer` (lines 48–49) and converted into an `Equation` object. We use the `LeftHandSide` field of the deserialized object (line 55) to display the left side of the equation and the `Result` field (line 67) to obtain the answer.

```
1   // Fig. 23.33: MathTutorForm.cs
2   // Math tutor using EquationGeneratorServiceJSON to create equations.
3   using System;
4   using System.IO;
5   using System.Net;
6   using System.Runtime.Serialization.Json;
7   using System.Text;
8   using System.Windows.Forms;
9
10  namespace MathTutorJSON
11  {
12     public partial class MathTutorForm : Form
13     {
14        private string operation = "add"; // the default operation
15        private int level = 1; // the default difficulty level
16        private Equation currentEquation;   // represents the Equation
17
18        // object used to invoke service
19        private WebClient service = new WebClient();
20
21        public MathTutorForm()
22        {
23           InitializeComponent();
24
25           // add DownloadStringCompleted event handler to WebClient
26           service.DownloadStringCompleted
27              += new DownloadStringCompletedEventHandler(
28              service_DownloadStringCompleted );
29        } // end constructor
30
31        // generates new equation when user clicks button
32        private void generateButton_Click( object sender, EventArgs e )
33        {
34           // send request to EquationGeneratorServiceJSON
35           service.DownloadStringAsync( new Uri(
36              "http://localhost:50103/EquationGeneratorServiceJSON" +
37              "/Service.svc/equation/" + operation + "/" + level ) );
38        } // end method generateButton_Click
39
```

Fig. 23.33 | Math tutor using `EquationGeneratorServiceJSON` to create equations. (Part 1 of 4.)

```
40    // process web service response
41    private void service_DownloadStringCompleted(
42       object sender, DownloadStringCompletedEventArgs e )
43    {
44       // check if any errors occurred in retrieving service data
45       if ( e.Error == null )
46       {
47          // deserialize response into an Equation object
48          DataContractJsonSerializer JSONSerializer =
49             new DataContractJsonSerializer( typeof( Equation ) );
50          currentEquation =
51             ( Equation ) JSONSerializer.ReadObject( new
52             MemoryStream( Encoding.Unicode.GetBytes( e.Result ) ) );
53
54          // display left side of equation
55          questionLabel.Text = currentEquation.LeftHandSide;
56          okButton.Enabled = true; // enable okButton
57          answerTextBox.Enabled = true; // enable answerTextBox
58       } // end if
59    } // end method client_DownloadStringCompleted
60
61    // check user's answer
62    private void okButton_Click( object sender, EventArgs e )
63    {
64       if ( !string.IsNullOrEmpty( answerTextBox.Text ) )
65       {
66          // determine whether user's answer is correct
67          if ( currentEquation.Result ==
68             Convert.ToInt32( answerTextBox.Text ) )
69          {
70             questionLabel.Text = string.Empty; // clear question
71             answerTextBox.Clear(); // clear answer
72             okButton.Enabled = false; // disable OK button
73             MessageBox.Show( "Correct! Good job!", "Result" );
74          } // end if
75          else
76          {
77             MessageBox.Show( "Incorrect. Try again.", "Result" );
78          } // end else
79       } // end if
80    } // end method okButton_Click
81
82    // set the operation to addition
83    private void additionRadioButton_CheckedChanged( object sender,
84       EventArgs e )
85    {
86       if ( additionRadioButton.Checked )
87          operation = "add";
88    } // end method additionRadioButton_CheckedChanged
89
```

Fig. 23.33 | Math tutor using EquationGeneratorServiceJSON to create equations. (Part 2 of 4.)

```
 90            // set the operation to subtraction
 91            private void subtractionRadioButton_CheckedChanged( object sender,
 92               EventArgs e )
 93            {
 94               if ( subtractionRadioButton.Checked )
 95                  operation = "subtract";
 96            } // end method subtractionRadioButton_CheckedChanged
 97
 98            // set the operation to multiplication
 99            private void multiplicationRadioButton_CheckedChanged(
100               object sender, EventArgs e )
101            {
102               if ( multiplicationRadioButton.Checked )
103                  operation = "multiply";
104            } // end method multiplicationRadioButton_CheckedChanged
105
106            // set difficulty level to 1
107            private void levelOneRadioButton_CheckedChanged( object sender,
108               EventArgs e )
109            {
110               if ( levelOneRadioButton.Checked )
111                  level = 1;
112            } // end method levelOneRadioButton_CheckedChanged
113
114            // set difficulty level to 2
115            private void levelTwoRadioButton_CheckedChanged( object sender,
116               EventArgs e )
117            {
118               if ( levelTwoRadioButton.Checked )
119                  level = 2;
120            } // end method levelTwoRadioButton_CheckedChanged
121
122            // set difficulty level to 3
123            private void levelThreeRadioButton_CheckedChanged( object sender,
124               EventArgs e )
125            {
126               if ( levelThreeRadioButton.Checked )
127                  level = 3;
128            } // end method levelThreeRadioButton_CheckedChanged
129         } // end class MathTutorForm
130      } // end namespace MathTutorJSON
```

a) Generating a level 2 multiplication equation.

Fig. 23.33 | Math tutor using EquationGeneratorServiceJSON to create equations. (Part 3 of 4.)

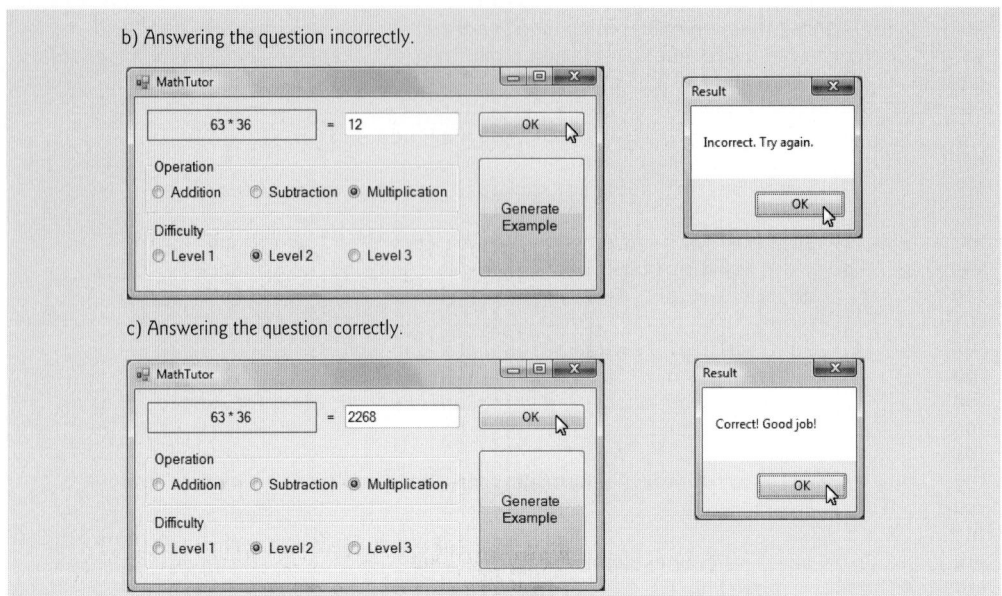

Fig. 23.33 | Math tutor using `EquationGeneratorServiceJSON` to create equations. (Part 4 of 4.)

```
1   // Fig. 23.34: Equation.cs
2   // Equation class representing a JSON object.
3   using System;
4
5   namespace MathTutorJSON
6   {
7      [Serializable]
8      class Equation
9      {
10        public int Left = 0;
11        public string LeftHandSide = null;
12        public string Operation = null;
13        public int Result = 0;
14        public int Right = 0;
15        public string RightHandSide = null;
16     } // end class Equation
17  } // end namespace MathTutorJSON
```

Fig. 23.34 | `Equation` class representing a JSON object.

23.12 Wrap-Up

This chapter introduced web services—a set of technologies for building distributed systems in which system components communicate with one another over networks. You learned that a web service is a class that allows client software to call the web service's methods remotely via common data formats and protocols, such as XML, JSON, HTTP, SOAP and REST. We also discussed several benefits of distributed computing with web services.

We discussed how Visual C# 2008 Express, Visual Web Developer 2008 Express, and WCF facilitate publishing and consuming web services. You learned how to define web services and methods using both SOAP protocol and REST architecture, and how to return data in both XML and JSON formats. You consumed SOAP-based web services using proxy classes to call the web service's methods. You also consumed REST-based web services using class WebClient. We built both Windows applications and ASP.NET web applications as web-service clients. After explaining the mechanics of web services through our Welcome examples, we demonstrated more sophisticated web services that use session tracking, database access and user-defined types.

23.13 Deitel Web Services Resource Centers

To learn more about web services, check out our web services Resource Centers at:

```
www.deitel.com/WebServices/
www.deitel.com/RESTWebServices/
```

You'll find articles, samples chapters and tutorials that discuss XML, web-services specifications, SOAP, WSDL, UDDI, .NET web services, consuming XML web services, and web-services architecture. You'll learn how to build your own Yahoo! maps mashup and applications that work with the Yahoo! Music Engine. You'll find information about Amazon's web services including the Amazon E-Commerce Service (ECS), Amazon historical pricing, Amazon Mechanical Turk, Amazon S3 (Simple Storage Service) and the Scalable Simple Queue Service (SQS). You'll learn how to use web services from several other companies including eBay, Google and Microsoft. You'll find REST web services best practices and guidelines. You'll also learn how to use REST web services with other technologies including SOAP, Rails, Windows Communication Foundation (WCF) and more. You can view the complete list of Deitel Resource Centers at www.deitel.com/ResourceCenters.html.

24

Silverlight, Rich Internet Applications and Multimedia

OBJECTIVES

In this chapter you'll learn:

- What Silverlight is and how it relates to Windows Presentation Foundation.
- To use Silverlight controls to create Rich Internet Applications.
- To create custom Silverlight controls.
- To use animation for enhanced GUIs.
- To display and manipulate images.
- To use Silverlight with Flickr's web services to build an online photo-searching application.
- To create Silverlight deep zoom applications.
- To include audio and video in Silverlight applications.

Outline

24.1 Introduction

24.2 Platform Overview

24.3 Silverlight Runtime and Tools Installation

24.4 Building a Silverlight **WeatherViewer** Application

    24.4.1 GUI Layout

    24.4.2 Obtaining and Displaying Weather Forecast Data

    24.4.3 Custom Controls

24.5 Animations and the **FlickrViewer**

24.6 Images and Deep Zoom

    24.6.1 Getting Started With Deep Zoom Composer

    24.6.2 Creating a Silverlight Deep Zoom Application

24.7 Audio and Video

24.8 Isolated Storage

24.9 Silverlight Demos and Web Resources

24.10 Wrap-Up

24.1 Introduction

Silverlight™ is Microsoft's platform for building *Rich Internet Applications (RIAs)*—web applications comparable in responsiveness and rich user interactivity to desktop applications. Silverlight is a robust, cross-platform, cross-browser subset of the .NET platform that competes with RIA technologies such as Adobe Flash and Flex and Sun's JavaFX, and complements Microsoft's ASP.NET and ASP.NET AJAX (which we discussed in Chapter 22). Since Silverlight is a subset of WPF, developers familiar with programming WPF applications are able to adapt quickly to creating Silverlight applications.

Multimedia may be the largest revolution in the history of the computer industry. We who entered the field decades ago used computers primarily to perform arithmetic calculations at high speed. As the field evolved, we began to see computers' data-manipulation capabilities as perhaps far more important. The "sizzle" of Silverlight is *multimedia*—the use of images, graphics, animation, sound and video to make applications "come alive." Silverlight includes strong multimedia support, including state-of-the-art high-definition video streaming. Microsoft also provides a service called Silverlight Streaming (streaming.live.com) for distributing multimedia-intensive Silverlight applications.

Multimedia programming offers many new challenges. The field is already enormous and growing rapidly. Most new computers sold today are "multimedia ready," with CD-RW and DVD drives, audio boards and special video capabilities. Today's desktop and laptop computers are so powerful that they can store and play DVD-quality sound and video, and we anticipate further advances in the programmable multimedia capabilities available through programming languages. One thing we've learned is to plan for the "impossible"—in the computer and communications fields, the "impossible" has repeatedly become reality.

Among users who want graphics, many now want three-dimensional, high-resolution graphics. True three-dimensional imaging may become available within the next decade.

Imagine having high-resolution "theater-in-the-round"—three-dimensional television. Sporting and entertainment events will appear to take place in your living room! And, you'll be able to zoom in as if you had the best seats in the house! Medical students worldwide will use web applications to see operations being performed thousands of miles away, as if they were occurring in the same room. People will be able to learn how to drive with extremely realistic driving simulators in their homes before they get behind the wheel. The possibilities are exciting and endless.

Multimedia demands extraordinary computing power. Until recently, affordable computers with that kind of power were not available. Today's ultrapowerful processors make effective multimedia possible and economical. The computer and communications industries will be primary beneficiaries of the multimedia revolution. Users will be willing to pay for the faster processors, larger memories and wider communications bandwidths that support demanding multimedia applications, just as they're willing to pay more for high-definition television today. Ironically, users may not have to pay more, because the fierce competition in these industries continues to drive prices down.

We need tools that make creating multimedia applications easy. Most programming languages do not incorporate such capabilities. WPF and Silverlight, through the .NET 3.5 class libraries, provide extensive multimedia facilities that enable you to start developing powerful multimedia applications immediately. Among these facilities is *deep zoom*, which allows the user to view high-resolution images over the web as if they were stored on the local computer. Users can interactively "explore" a high-resolution image by zooming in and out and panning—while maintaining the original image's quality. Silverlight supports deep zoom images as large as one billion by one billion pixels.

Visit our Silverlight 2 Resource Center at `www.deitel.com/silverlight20/` for the latest Silverlight information and additional Silverlight web resources. There you'll find Silverlight demos, articles, tutorials, downloads, sample code, training courses, forums, FAQs, books, eBooks, sample chapters and more. Section 24.9 also overviews several Silverlight demo sites. All Silverlight code examples in this chapter were implemented using Silverlight 2 Beta 2. As new versions of Silverlight are released, updates for the examples will be posted at `www.deitel.com/books/csharpfp3/`.

24.2 Platform Overview

Silverlight runs as a browser plug-in for Internet Explorer, Firefox and Safari on recent versions of Microsoft Windows and Mac OS X. The system requirements for the runtime can be found at `microsoft.com/silverlight/resources/install.aspx?v=2.0#sysreq`. Silverlight is also available on Linux systems via the Mono Project's Moonlight, which is located at `mono-project.com/Moonlight`.

Like WPF applications, Silverlight applications consist of user interfaces described in XAML and code-behind files containing application logic. The XAML used in Silverlight is a subset of that used in WPF.

The subset of the .NET Framework available in Silverlight 2 includes APIs for collections, input/output, generics, multithreading, globalization, XML and LINQ. It also includes APIs for interacting with JavaScript and the elements in a web page, and APIs for local storage data to help you create more robust web-based applications.

Silverlight 2 is an implementation of the .NET Platform, so you can create Silverlight applications in .NET languages such as Visual C# and Visual Basic. You can also use Iron-

Ruby and IronPython, but these require the Silverlight Dynamic Languages SDK from www.codeplex.com/sdlsdk/. Silverlight makes it easy for .NET programmers to create applications that run in web browsers.

Silverlight 2's graphics and GUI capabilities are a subset of the Windows Presentation Foundation (WPF) framework. Some capabilities supported in Silverlight include GUI elements, layout management, graphics, animation and multimedia. There are also styles and template-based "skinning" capabilities to manage the look-and-feel of a Silverlight user interface. Like WPF, Silverlight provides a powerful data-binding model that makes it easy to display data from objects, collections, databases, XML and even other GUI controls. Silverlight 2 also provides rich networking support, enabling you to write browser-based applications that invoke web services and use other networking technologies.

24.3 Silverlight Runtime and Tools Installation

Silverlight runs in web browsers as a plug-in. To view websites programmed in Silverlight, you need the *Silverlight 2 Runtime* plug-in from www.microsoft.com/silverlight/resources/installationFiles.aspx?v=2.0. After installing the plug-in, go to Microsoft's Silverlight Gallery website at silverlight.net/themes/silverlight/community/gallerydetail.aspx?cat=6 to try some sample applications. See Section 24.9 for more Silverlight demo and resource websites.

At the time of this writing, Silverlight 2 development is not yet supported in Microsoft's Visual Studio Express editions. When the final version of Service Pack 1 is released for the Express Editions, it will include Silverlight compatibility, but until then you'll need a complete version of Visual Studio 2008 to build a Silverlight application. In addition, the Visual Web Developer feature must be installed. Trial versions are available from msdn.microsoft.com/en-us/vstudio/products/aa700831.aspx. You'll also need the Silverlight Tools Beta 2 for Visual Studio 2008 from go.microsoft.com/fwlink/?LinkId=120319. Download and execute the file silverlight_chainer.exe, then follow the on-screen instructions to install the tools for developing Silverlight 2 applications in Visual Studio 2008. Watch www.deitel.com/books/csharpfp3/ for updates.

If you don't have access to a complete version of Visual Studio 2008, Microsoft also provides the *Silverlight 2 SDK Beta 2*. You can get the SDK by going to the website www.microsoft.com/downloads/ and searching for "Silverlight 2 SDK." The SDK provides documentation, sample code and tools to help you build applications for Silverlight 2 Beta 2. We do not cover the SDK in this book.

24.4 Building a Silverlight WeatherViewer Application

Silverlight is a subset of WPF, so the two share many capabilities. Since Silverlight produces Internet applications instead of desktop applications, the setup of a Silverlight project is different from that of WPF.

A basic Silverlight application has two XAML files—Page.xaml and App.xaml. Page.xaml defines the application's GUI, and its code-behind file Page.xaml.cs declares the GUI event handlers and other methods required by the application. App.xaml declares your application's shared resources that can be applied to various GUI elements. The code-behind file App.xaml.cs defines application-level event handlers, such as an event handler for unhandled exceptions. Content in these files can be used by all the application's pages. Since our example applications each contain only a single page, we do not use `App.xaml` and `App.xaml.cs` in this chapter.

Differences Between WPF and Silverlight

To create a new Silverlight project, select **File > New Project...** in Visual Studio 2008. In the **Project types** window under **Visual C#**, select the **Silverlight** option. Then in the **Templates** window, select **Silverlight Application**. When you've entered the information, click **OK**. An **Add Silverlight Application** dialog appears, asking how you would like to host your application. Select the **Add a new Web to the solution for hosting the control** option. This creates a web project to test the application. The **Dynamically generate an HTML test page to host Silverlight within this project** option (which we do not discuss) creates an HTML document for testing the application without the use of a web project. In the **Project Type** drop-down menu, select **Web Site**. Keep the default **Name** and click **OK**.

The `Page.xaml` file displayed in the XAML tab of Visual Studio (Fig. 24.1) is similar to the default XAML for a WPF application. In a WPF application, the root XAML element is a `Window`. In Silverlight, the root element is a ***UserControl***. The default `UserControl` has a class name specified with the ***x:Class*** attribute (line 1), specifies the namespaces (lines 2–3) to provide access to the Silverlight controls throughout the XAML, and has a `Width` and `Height` of 400 and 300 pixels, respectively. These numbers are system-independent pixel measurements, where each pixel represents 1/96th of an inch. Lines 5–7 are the default `Grid` layout container. Unlike a WPF application, the ***x:Name***

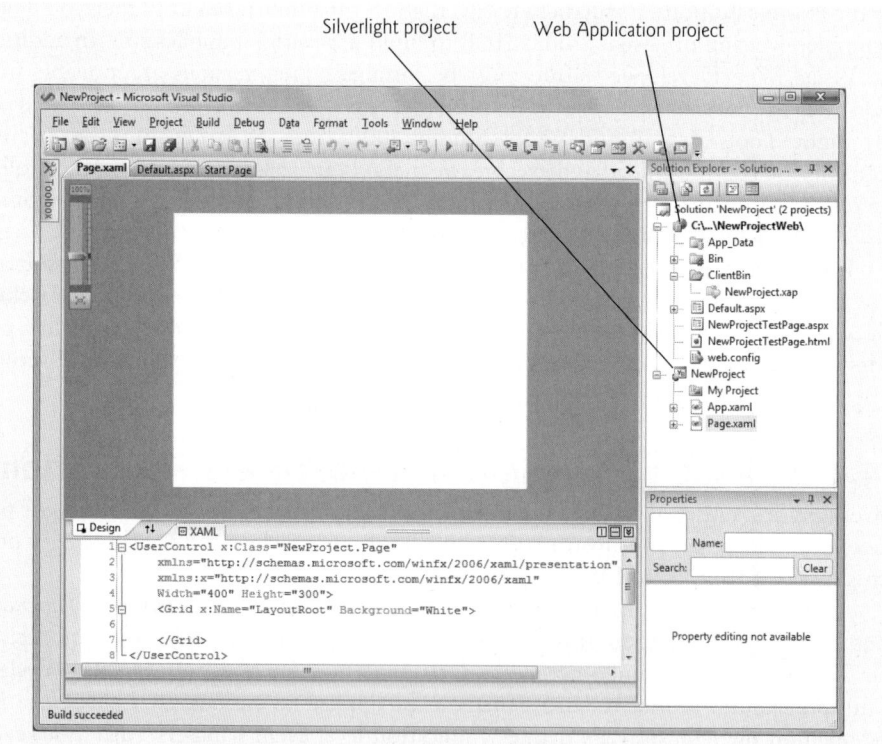

Fig. 24.1 | New Silverlight application in Visual Studio.

(the name used in code to manipulate the control) and Background attributes are set by default in a Silverlight application.

A compiled Silverlight application is packaged by the IDE as a *.xap* file containing the application and its supporting resources (such as images or other files used by the application). The web page that hosts the Silverlight application references the Silverlight plug-in and the application's .xap file. The Silverlight plug-in then executes the application. The test web application that was created for you contains the file NewProjectTest-Page.aspx, which loads and executes the Silverlight application. To ensure that this page is used by the test application when you run the project, right click the NewProject-Test.aspx file in your **Solution Explorer** and click **Set As Start Page.**

A Silverlight application must be hosted in a web page. The **Web Application Project** is one option used to test the Silverlight application in a web browser. Building the solution automatically copies the compiled application into the **Web Application Project.** You can then test it using the built-in web server in Visual Studio. After the application is built in the IDE, this part of the application contains the .xap file that was described in the preceding paragraph.

Note that the first time you start debugging a Silverlight application, a **Debugging Not Enabled** dialog appears. It states that debugging is not enabled in the **Web.config** file. If you would like to run your project in debug mode, you can select the **Modify the Web.Config file to enable debugging** option.

At the time of this writing the **Design** view is read-only and the **Properties** window is not yet enabled for Silverlight development with the Silverlight Tools Beta 2 for Visual Studio 2008. For this reason, much of the code you write in this chapter will be in the context of the XAML files. You can drag and drop Silverlight controls from the **Toolbox** into the XAML view, rather than typing the elements yourself. You can also use Microsoft Expression Blend 2.5 or later for an interactive **Design** view of your web application. Expression Blend is beyond the scope of this chapter. Trial and preview versions are available from www.microsoft.com/expression/.

Introduction to the WeatherViewer Application
Our **WeatherViewer** application (Fig. 24.2) allows the user to input a zip code and invokes a web service to get weather information for that location. The application receives weath-

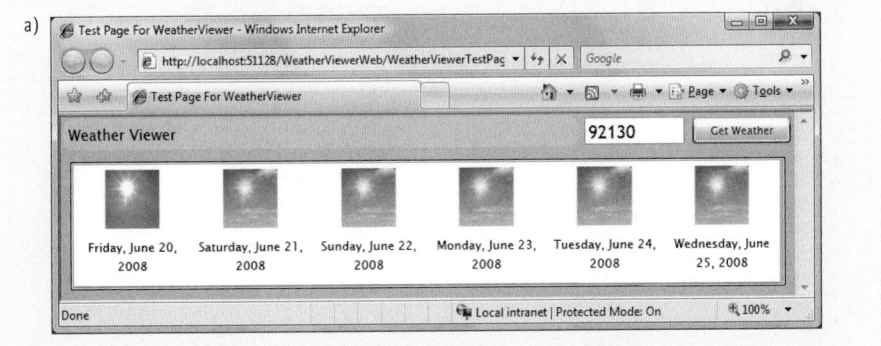

Fig. 24.2 | **WeatherViewer** application displays a six-day weather forecast. The program can also display detailed information for a selected day. (Part 1 of 2.)

b)
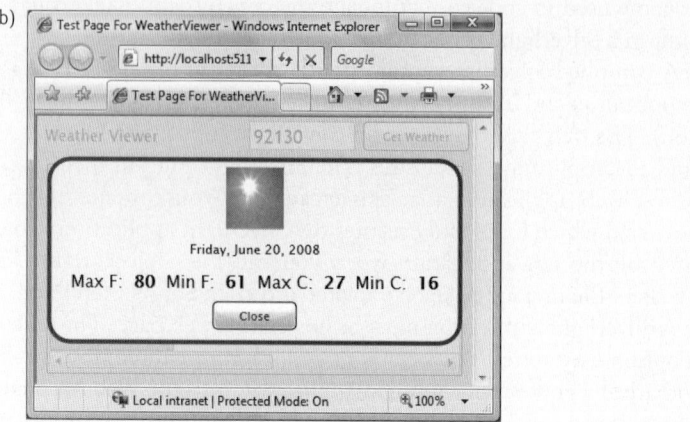

Fig. 24.2 | **WeatherViewer** application displays a six-day weather forecast. The program can also display detailed information for a selected day. (Part 2 of 2.)

er data from www.webservicex.net—a site offering several web services that return XML information. This application uses LINQ to XML to process the weather data that is returned by the web service. The application also includes a custom control that displays more specific weather information for a single day of the week. Figure 24.2 shows a preview of the application after the user enters a zip code and clicks a specific day to see its weather details. You can test the example online at www.deitel.com/books/csharpfp3/.

24.4.1 GUI Layout

The main layout controls of WPF described in Chapter 16—Grid, StackPanel and Canvas—are also available in Silverlight. The XAML for the layout of the **WeatherViewer** application is shown in Fig. 24.3. This application uses nested Grid controls to lay out its elements.

```
1    <!-- Fig. 24.3: WeatherViewer.xaml -->
2    <!-- WeatherViewer displays day-by-day weather data (XAML). -->
3    <UserControl xmlns:Weather="clr-namespace:WeatherViewer"
4       x:Class="WeatherViewer.WeatherViewerPage"
5       xmlns="http://schemas.microsoft.com/winfx/2006/xaml/presentation"
6       xmlns:x="http://schemas.microsoft.com/winfx/2006/xaml">
7       <Grid x:Name="LayoutRoot" Background="LightSkyBlue">
8          <Grid.RowDefinitions>
9             <RowDefinition Height="35" />
10            <RowDefinition />
11         </Grid.RowDefinitions>
12
13         <Grid>
14            <Grid.ColumnDefinitions>
15               <ColumnDefinition Width="*" />
16               <ColumnDefinition Width="110" />
```

Fig. 24.3 | **WeatherViewer** displays day-by-day weather data (XAML). (Part 1 of 3.)

```
17          <ColumnDefinition Width="110" />
18       </Grid.ColumnDefinitions>
19
20       <!-- Border containing the title "Weather Viewer" -->
21       <Border Grid.Column="0" CornerRadius="10"
22          Background="LightGray" Margin="2">
23          <TextBlock Text="Weather Viewer" Padding="6" />
24       </Border>
25
26       <!-- zip code goes into this text box -->
27       <TextBox x:Name="inputTextBox" Grid.Column="1" FontSize="18"
28          Margin="4" TextChanged="inputTextBox_TextChanged" />
29
30       <!-- click to invoke web service -->
31       <Button x:Name="submitButton" Content="Get Weather"
32          Grid.Column="2" Margin="4" Click="submitButton_Click" />
33    </Grid>
34
35    <!-- contains weather images for several upcoming days -->
36    <ListBox x:Name="forecastList" Grid.Row="1" Margin="10"
37       SelectionChanged="forecastList_SelectionChanged">
38       <ListBox.ItemsPanel>
39          <ItemsPanelTemplate>
40             <!-- arrange items horizontally -->
41             <StackPanel Orientation="Horizontal" />
42          </ItemsPanelTemplate>
43       </ListBox.ItemsPanel>
44
45       <ListBox.ItemTemplate>
46          <DataTemplate>
47             <!-- represents item for a single day -->
48             <StackPanel Width="120" Orientation="Vertical"
49                HorizontalAlignment="Center">
50
51                <!-- displays image for a single day -->
52                <Image Source="{Binding WeatherImage}"
53                   Margin="5" Width="55" Height="58" />
54
55                <!-- displays the day of the week -->
56                <TextBlock Text="{Binding DayOfWeek}"
57                   TextAlignment="Center" FontSize="12"
58                   Margin="5" TextWrapping="Wrap" />
59             </StackPanel>
60          </DataTemplate>
61       </ListBox.ItemTemplate>
62    </ListBox>
63
64    <!-- custom control for displaying detailed information -->
65    <Weather:WeatherDetailsView x:Name="completeDetails"
66       Visibility="Collapsed" Grid.RowSpan="2" />
67    </Grid>
68 </UserControl>
```

Fig. 24.3 | **WeatherViewer** displays day-by-day weather data (XAML). (Part 2 of 3.)

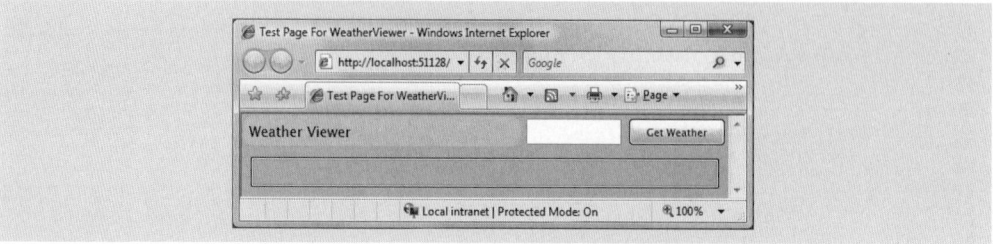

Fig. 24.3 | **WeatherViewer** displays day-by-day weather data (XAML). (Part 3 of 3.)

Lines 8–11 contain the RowDefinitions of the main Grid. Lines 14–18 contain the ColumnDefinitions of a nested Grid element which displays the top row of the page containing the light gray title Border, the search TextBox and the search Button, as shown in the screen capture in Fig. 24.3.

Line 23 defines the TextBlock's **Padding** property, which specifies the distance between the edge of the element and its contained text. Lines 36–62 define the **ListBox** used on the main page to display each day's weather image. Line 41 defines the StackPanel that is used as a template by the ListBox's **ItemsPanel**, allowing the ListBox's items to display horizontally. Lines 48–59 define a StackPanel for each individual item, displaying the weather Image and the TextBlock containing the day of the week vertically oriented. This StackPanel is nested in the **ItemTemplate** property of the ListBox which allows you to define the look of a single item in the list. Lines 52 and 56 bind data from the web service's XML response to the two elements that display weather information.

Lines 65–66 create a WeatherDetailsView custom control element. The code for the custom control appears later in the chapter. This control's Visibility property is initially set to Collapsed, so it is not visible when the page loads. The Visibility of a control defines whether it is rendered on the screen. We also set the Grid.RowSpan property to 2. By taking up two rows, the GUI is blocked when the custom control is displayed, so the user can no longer interact with the main page until the control is closed. Notice that WeatherDetailsView is in the namespace Weather. This namespace (defined in line 3 of the XAML file) allows you to use the custom control in the application. The custom control must be referenced through the namespace, since it is not a predefined control. If we did not define the namespace, there would be no way to reference WeatherDetailsView.

24.4.2 Obtaining and Displaying Weather Forecast Data

The **WeatherViewer** example uses Silverlight's web services, LINQ to XML and data-binding capabilities. The application's code-behind file appears in Fig. 24.4.

```
1   // Fig. 24.4: WeatherViewer.xaml.cs
2   // WeatherViewer displays day-by-day weather data (code-behind).
3   using System;
4   using System.Linq;
5   using System.Net;
6   using System.Windows;
7   using System.Windows.Controls;
```

Fig. 24.4 | **WeatherViewer** displays day-by-day weather data (code-behind). (Part 1 of 3.)

```
 8    using System.Windows.Input;
 9    using System.Xml.Linq;
10
11    namespace WeatherViewer
12    {
13       public partial class WeatherViewerPage : UserControl
14       {
15          // object to invoke the web service
16          private WebClient weatherService = new WebClient();
17
18          // constructor
19          public WeatherViewerPage()
20          {
21             InitializeComponent();
22
23             weatherService.DownloadStringCompleted +=
24                new DownloadStringCompletedEventHandler(
25                weatherService_DownloadStringCompleted );
26          } // end constructor
27
28          // when user clicks submit button, invoke web service
29          private void submitButton_Click( object sender, RoutedEventArgs e )
30          {
31             string zipcode = inputTextBox.Text; // get zipcode
32             this.Cursor = Cursors.Wait; // wait cursor
33
34             // webserviceX.net's WeatherForcast web service URL
35             string forecastURL = "http://www.webservicex.net/" +
36                "WeatherForecast.asmx/GetWeatherByZipCode?ZipCode=" +
37                zipcode;
38
39             // asynchronously invoke the web service
40             weatherService.DownloadStringAsync( new Uri( forecastURL ) );
41          } // end method submitButton_Click
42
43          // when download is complete for web-service result
44          private void weatherService_DownloadStringCompleted( object sender,
45             DownloadStringCompletedEventArgs e )
46          {
47             if ( e.Error == null && e.Result.Contains( "Day" ) )
48                DisplayWeatherForecast( e.Result );
49
50             this.Cursor = Cursors.Arrow; // arrow cursor
51          } // end method weatherService_DownloadStringCompleted
52
53          // display the received weather data
54          private void DisplayWeatherForecast( string xmlData )
55          {
56             // parse the XML data for use with LINQ
57             XDocument weatherXML = XDocument.Parse( xmlData );
58
59             XNamespace weatherNamespace =
60                XNamespace.Get( "http://www.webservicex.net" );
```

Fig. 24.4 | **WeatherViewer** displays day-by-day weather data (code-behind). (Part 2 of 3.)

```
61
62          // convert XML into WeatherData objects using XML literals
63          var weatherInformation =
64              from item in weatherXML.Descendants(
65                  weatherNamespace + "WeatherData" )
66              where !item.IsEmpty
67              select new WeatherData()
68              {
69                  DayOfWeek = item.Element(
70                      weatherNamespace + "Day" ).Value,
71                  WeatherImage = item.Element(
72                      weatherNamespace + "WeatherImage" ).Value,
73                  HighFahrenheit = item.Element(
74                      weatherNamespace + "MaxTemperatureF" ).Value,
75                  LowFahrenheit = item.Element(
76                      weatherNamespace + "MinTemperatureF" ).Value,
77                  HighCelsius = item.Element(
78                      weatherNamespace + "MaxTemperatureC" ).Value,
79                  LowCelsius = item.Element(
80                      weatherNamespace + "MinTemperatureC" ).Value
81              };
82
83          // bind forecastList.ItemSource to the weatherInformation
84          forecastList.ItemsSource = weatherInformation;
85      } // end method DisplayWeatherForecast
86
87      // displays the custom control
88      private void forecastList_SelectionChanged( object sender,
89          SelectionChangedEventArgs e )
90      {
91          // specify the WeatherData object containing the details
92          if ( forecastList.SelectedItem != null )
93              completeDetails.DataContext = forecastList.SelectedItem;
94
95          // show the complete weather details
96          completeDetails.Visibility = Visibility.Visible;
97      } // end method forecastList_SelectionChanged
98
99      // remove displayed weather information when input zip code changes
100     private void inputTextBox_TextChanged( object sender,
101         TextChangedEventArgs e )
102     {
103         forecastList.ItemsSource = null;
104     } // end method inputTextBox_TextChanged
105  } // end class WeatherViewerPage
106 } // end namespace WeatherViewer
```

Fig. 24.4 | **WeatherViewer** displays day-by-day weather data (code-behind). (Part 3 of 3.)

The code for the main page of the **WeatherViewer** invokes the web service and binds all the necessary data to the proper elements of the page. Notice that we import the System.Xml.Linq namespace (line 9), which enables the LINQ to XML that is used in the example. You must also add a reference to this assembly. To do so, right click the **Weather-Viewer** project in the **Solution Explorer** and select **Add Reference....** In the dialog that appears, locate the assembly System.Xml.Linq in the .NET tab and click OK. Lines 59–60 define the namespace for the XML returned by the web service and allows the application to access the data.

Error-Prevention Tip 24.1

When invoking a web service that returns XML, ensure that the namespace you specify in your code precisely matches the namespace specified in the returned XML. Otherwise, the elements in the returned XML will not be recognized in your code.

This application also uses the class WeatherData (line 67) that includes all the necessary weather information for a single day of the week. We created this class for you. It contains six weather-information properties—DayOfWeek, WeatherImage, HighFahrenheit, LowFahrenheit, HighCelsius and LowCelsius. To add the code for this class to the project, right click the **WeatherViewer** project in the **Solution Explorer** and select **Add > Existing Item...**. Find the file WeatherData.cs in this chapter's examples folder and click **OK**. We use this class to bind the necessary information to the ListBox and the custom control in our application. Note that if this were a WPF application, we could use an anonymous class here instead of our WeatherData class. However, in Silverlight applications, you cannot bind to anonymous types, which is why we needed to create the new class.

Using the WebClient Class to Invoke a Web Service

The application's submitButton_click event handler grabs the zip code entered by the user in the TextBox (line 31), formats the web-service URL with the zip code (lines 35–37) and asynchronously invokes the web service (line 40). We use the WebClient class to use the web service and retrieve the desired information.

Line 40 calls the weatherService object's DownloadStringAsync method to invoke the web service. The web service's location must be specified as an object of class Uri. Class Uri's constructor receives a string representing a uniform resource identifier, such as "http://www.deitel.com". When the web service returns its result, the WebClient object raises the DownloadStringCompleted event. Its event handler (lines 44–51) has a parameter e of type DownloadStringCompletedEventArgs which contains information returned by the web service. We can use this variable's properties to get the returned XML (e.Result) and any errors that may have occurred during the process (e.Error).

Using LINQ to XML to Process the Weather Data

Once the WebClient has received the response, the application checks for an error and ensures that the result contains the desired information (line 47). If the user enters an invalid zip code, the service responds without error and sends back XML that does not contain a weather forecast. If the XML contains the string "Day", then we know the response includes relevant weather forecast data. A sample of the web service's XML response appears in Fig. 24.5. The web service returns XML data that describes the high and low temperatures for the corresponding city over a period of several days. The data for each day also contains a link to an image that represents the weather for that day. If there is no error, the application calls the DisplayWeatherForecast method (defined in lines 54–85).

We use class XDocument's Parse method (line 57) to convert a string—containing the contents of the XML response—to an XDocument to use in the LINQ to XML query (lines 64–81). The query gathers the weather information and sets the corresponding

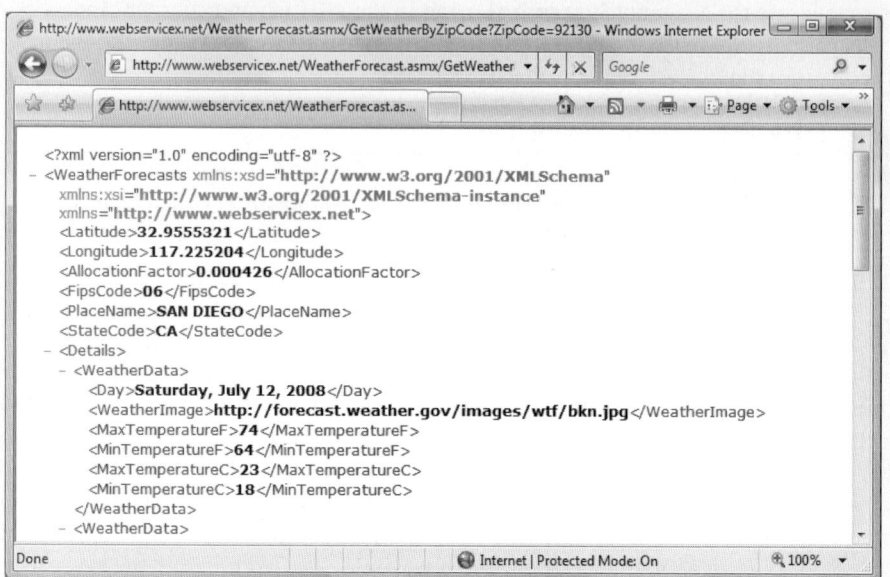

Fig. 24.5 | Sample web-service XML response.

values for a `WeatherData` object. The LINQ query gathers more information from the XML than is initially displayed on the main page of the application. This is because the selected object is also passed to the custom control, where more detailed information about the weather is displayed.

Using Data Binding to Display the Weather Data
We first bind the results of the `weatherInformation` LINQ query to the `ListBox` (line 84). This displays the summary of the six-day weather forecast. When the user selects a particular day, we bind the `WeatherData` object for the selected day to the custom control, which displays the details for that day. The `ListBox`'s `SelectionChanged` event handler (lines 88–97) sets the `DataContext` of our custom control (line 93) to the `WeatherData` object for the selected day. The method also changes the custom control's `Visibility` to `Visible`, so the user can see the weather details.

24.4.3 Custom Controls

There are many ways to customize controls in Silverlight, including WPF's `Styles` and `ControlTemplates`. As with WPF, if deeper customization is desired, you can create *custom controls* by using the `UserControl` element as a template. The **WeatherViewer** example creates a custom control that displays detailed weather information for a particular day of the week. The control has a simple GUI and is displayed when you change your selection in the `ListBox` on the main page.

To add a new `UserControl` to the project, right click the project in the **Solution Explorer** and select **Add > New Item...**. Select the **Silverlight User Control** template and name the file (Fig. 24.6). In the case of the **WeatherViewer** example, our custom control was named `WeatherDetailsView`.

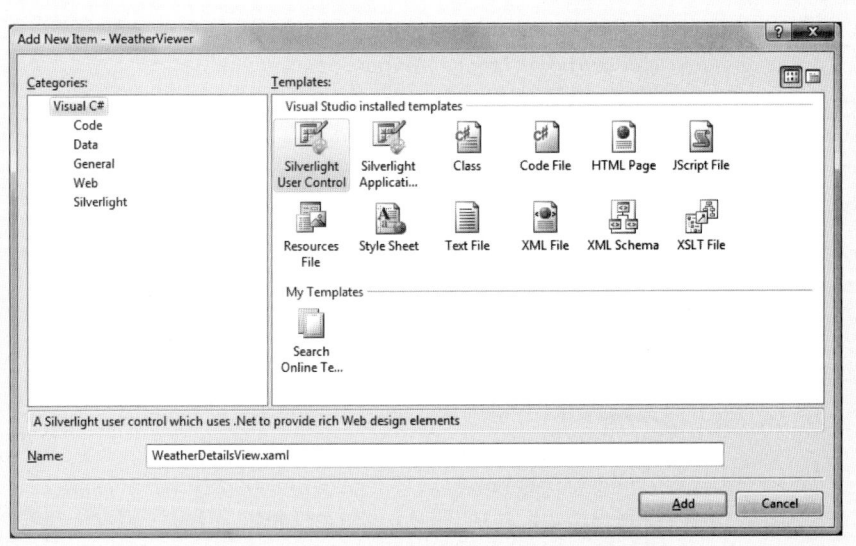

Fig. 24.6 | Adding a new `UserControl` to a Silverlight application.

Once added to the project, the `UserControl` can be coded similar to any other Silverlight application. The XAML code for the GUI appears in Fig. 24.7.

```
1   <!-- Fig. 24.7: WeatherDetailsView.xaml -->
2   <!-- WeatherViewer's WeatherDetailsView custom control (XAML). -->
3   <UserControl x:Class="WeatherViewer.WeatherDetailsView"
4      xmlns="http://schemas.microsoft.com/winfx/2006/xaml/presentation"
5      xmlns:x="http://schemas.microsoft.com/winfx/2006/xaml">
6      <Grid>
7         <!-- background semitransparent rectangle -->
8         <Rectangle HorizontalAlignment="Stretch" Fill="Aquamarine"
9            VerticalAlignment="Stretch" Opacity="0.8" />
10
11        <!-- Border containing all the elements of the control -->
12        <Border CornerRadius="20" Background="AliceBlue"
13           BorderBrush="Blue" BorderThickness="4"
14           Width="400" Height="175">
15
16           <!-- StackPanel contains all the displayed weather info -->
17           <StackPanel>
18              <!-- the day and the corresponding weather image -->
19              <Image Source="{Binding WeatherImage}" Margin="5" Width="55"
20                 Height="58" />
21              <TextBlock Text="{Binding DayOfWeek}" Margin="5"
22                 TextAlignment="Center" FontSize="12"
23                 TextWrapping="Wrap" />
```

Fig. 24.7 | **WeatherViewer**'s `WeatherDetailsView` custom control (XAML). (Part 1 of 2.)

```
24
25              <!-- displays the temperature info in C and F -->
26              <StackPanel HorizontalAlignment="Center"
27                 Orientation="Horizontal">
28                 <TextBlock Text="Max F:" Margin="5" FontSize="16"/>
29                 <TextBlock Text="{Binding HighFahrenheit}"
30                    Margin="5" FontSize="16" FontWeight="Bold"/>
31                 <TextBlock Text="Min F:" Margin="5" FontSize="16"/>
32                 <TextBlock Text="{Binding LowFahrenheit}"
33                    Margin="5" FontSize="16" FontWeight="Bold"/>
34                 <TextBlock Text="Max C:" Margin="5" FontSize="16"/>
35                 <TextBlock Text="{Binding HighCelsius}"
36                    Margin="5" FontSize="16" FontWeight="Bold"/>
37                 <TextBlock Text="Min C:" Margin="5" FontSize="16"/>
38                 <TextBlock Text="{Binding LowCelsius}"
39                    Margin="5" FontSize="16" FontWeight="Bold"/>
40              </StackPanel>
41
42              <!-- closes the control to go back to the main page -->
43              <Button x:Name="closeButton" Content="Close" Width="80"
44                 Click="closeButton_Click"/>
45           </StackPanel>
46        </Border>
47     </Grid>
48  </UserControl>
```

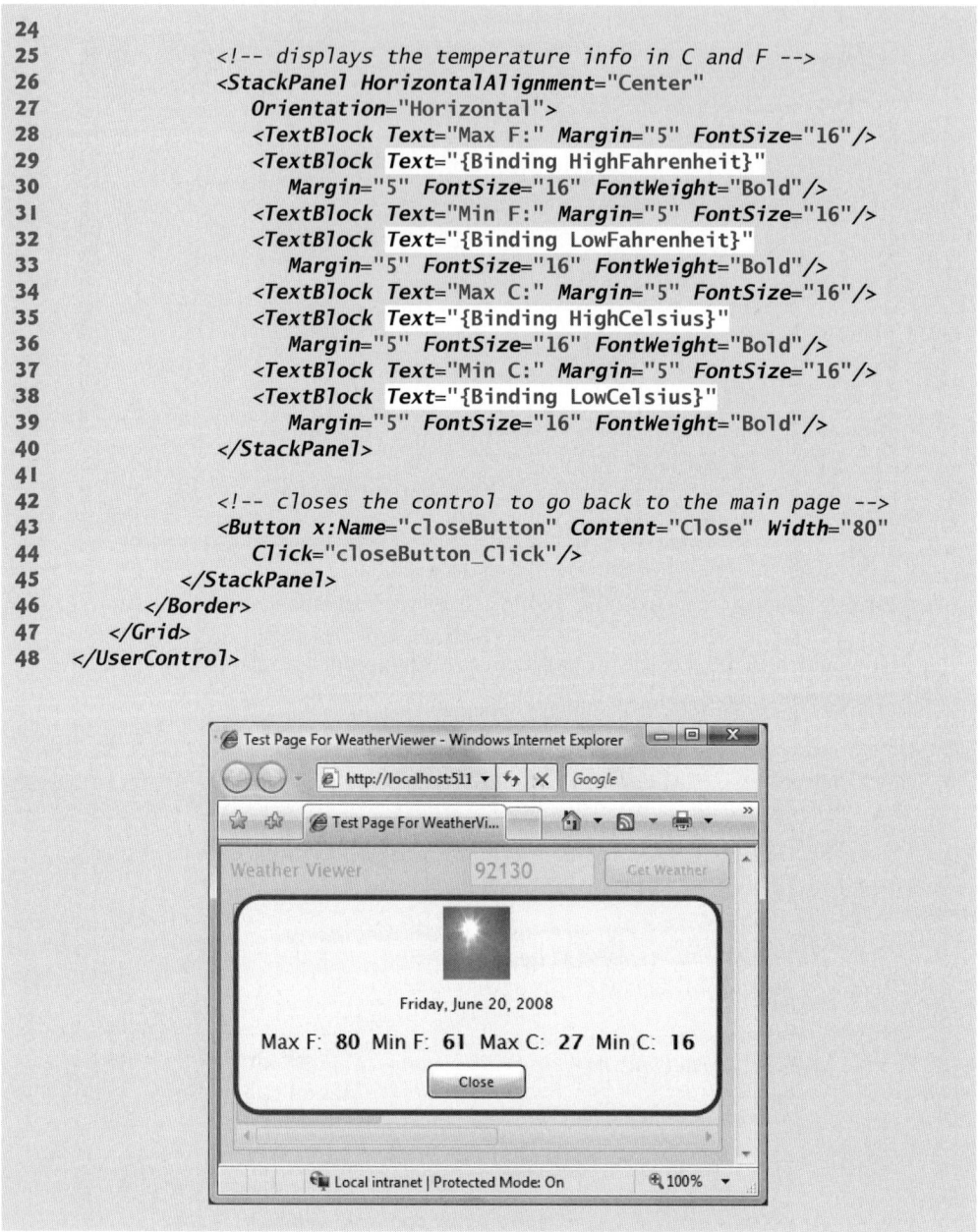

Fig. 24.7 | WeatherViewer's WeatherDetailsView custom control (XAML). (Part 2 of 2.)

This control contains two StackPanels embedded in a Grid. Since the aquamarine Rectangle (lines 8–9) in the background has an Opacity of 0.8, you can see that the control is treated as another element "on top of" the main page. Figure 24.8 shows the code-behind file for this control. The Button's Click event handler collapses the control, so the user can continue interacting with the main page of the application.

```
 1   // Fig. 24.8: WeatherDetailsView.xaml.cs
 2   // WeatherViewer's WeatherDetailsView custom control (code-behind).
 3   using System.Windows;
 4   using System.Windows.Controls;
 5
 6   namespace WeatherViewer
 7   {
 8      public partial class WeatherDetailsView : UserControl
 9      {
10         // constructor
11         public WeatherDetailsView()
12         {
13            InitializeComponent();
14         } // end constructor
15
16         // close the details view
17         private void closeButton_Click( object sender, RoutedEventArgs e )
18         {
19            this.Visibility = Visibility.Collapsed;
20         } // end method closeButton_Click
21      } // end class WeatherDetailsView
22   } // end namespace WeatherViewer
```

Fig. 24.8 | **WeatherViewer**'s WeatherDetailsView custom control (code-behind).

24.5 Animations and the FlickrViewer

Animations in Silverlight are defined in Storyboards, which are created as Resources of a control and contain one or more animation elements. When a Storyboard's Begin method is called, the embedded animations begin executing. Silverlight's supported animations include DoubleAnimations, PointAnimations and ColorAnimations.

FlickrViewer *Example*

Our **FlickrViewer** example (a sample screen capture is shown in Fig. 24.9) uses a web service provided by the public photo-sharing site Flickr. The application allows you to search by tag for photos that users worldwide have uploaded to Flickr. *Tagging*—or labeling content—is part of the collaborative nature of Web 2.0. A *tag* is any user-generated word or phrase that helps organize web content. Tagging items with self-chosen words or phrases creates a strong identification of the content. Flickr uses tags on uploaded files to improve its photo-search service, giving the user better results. To run this example on your computer, you need to obtain your own Flickr API key at www.flickr.com/services/api/keys/ and add it to the FlickrViewer.xaml.cs file (which we discuss shortly). This key is a unique string of characters and numbers that enables Flickr to track usage of their APIs. You can test the example online at www.deitel.com/books/csharpfp3/.

The application displays thumbnails of up to twenty results and allows you to click a thumbnail to view its full-sized image. As you change your selection, the application animates out the previously selected image and animates in the new one. The Border shrinks until the current Image is no longer visible, then expands to display the new selection.

As shown in Fig. 24.9, you can type one or more tags (e.g., "deitel flowers") into the application's TextBox. When you click the **Search** Button, the application invokes the

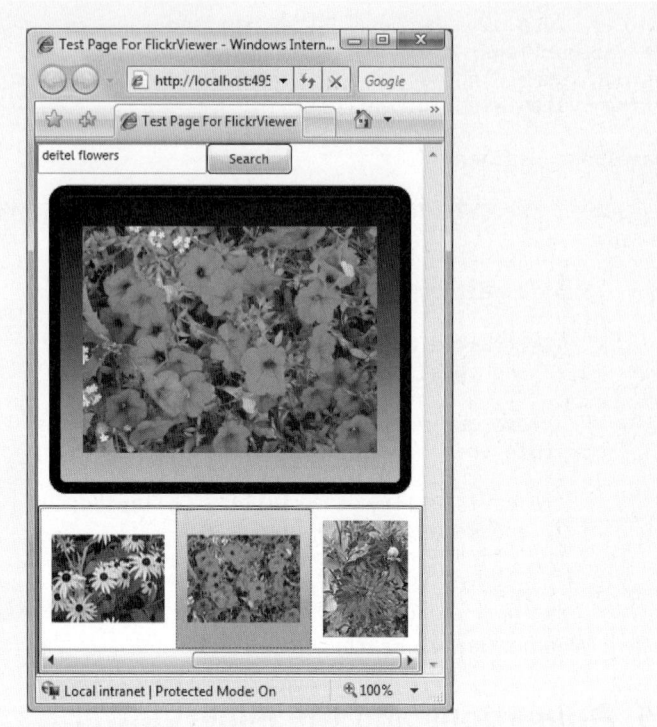

Fig. 24.9 | FlickrViewer allows users to search photos by tag.

Flickr web service, which responds with an XML document containing links to the photos that match the tags. The application parses the XML and displays thumbnails of these photos. The application's XAML is shown in Fig. 24.10.

Lines 13–27 define the Grid's Resources, which contain two Storyboard elements to animate the large image in and out. The animateIn Storyboard (lines 15–19) contains a DoubleAnimation that animates the Height property of the largeCoverImage's Border. Though this animation is a From/To/By animation, the To property is not set. We set this value in the code-behind to allow the border to fill the available space in the window regardless of the browser window size. The animateOut Storyboard (lines 22–26) shrinks the Border until the image inside is no longer visible.

The rest of the layout is similar to that of the **WeatherViewer**. Lines 7–11 define the main Grid's three rows. The first row contains a StackPanel with an embedded search TextBox and a Button (lines 30–34). The second row contains the Border with an embedded Image (lines 37–49) to display the large version of the selected thumbnail. The third row contains the ListBox (lines 52–65), which displays the thumbnails of the photos returned from Flickr. This ListBox is organized and coded in the same way as in the **WeatherViewer**, except that the DataTemplate contains only one Image—one of the photos returned by the web service.

The screen capture in Fig. 24.10 shows the empty layout of the **FlickrViewer** before a search query has been made. The code-behind for the application can be seen in Fig. 24.11. This example uses web services and LINQ to XML.

```xml
 1   <!-- Fig. 24.10: FlickrViewer.xaml -->
 2   <!-- FlickrViewer allows users to search for tagged photos (XAML). -->
 3   <UserControl x:Class="FlickrViewer.FlickrViewerPage"
 4      xmlns="http://schemas.microsoft.com/winfx/2006/xaml/presentation"
 5      xmlns:x="http://schemas.microsoft.com/winfx/2006/xaml">
 6      <Grid x:Name="LayoutRoot">
 7         <Grid.RowDefinitions>
 8            <RowDefinition Height="Auto" />
 9            <RowDefinition x:Name="imageRow" />
10            <RowDefinition Height="Auto" />
11         </Grid.RowDefinitions>
12
13         <Grid.Resources>
14            <!-- enlarge the Border to display a new image -->
15            <Storyboard x:Name="animateIn" Completed="animateIn_Completed"
16               Storyboard.TargetName="largeCoverImage">
17               <DoubleAnimation x:Name="animate"
18                  Storyboard.TargetProperty="Height" Duration="0:0:0.45" />
19            </Storyboard>
20
21            <!-- collapse the Border in preparation for a new image -->
22            <Storyboard x:Name="animateOut" Completed="animateOut_Completed"
23               Storyboard.TargetName="largeCoverImage">
24               <DoubleAnimation Storyboard.TargetProperty="Height" To="60"
25                  Duration="0:0:0.25" />
26            </Storyboard>
27         </Grid.Resources>
28
29         <!-- the search box and button for user interaction -->
30         <StackPanel Grid.Row="0" Orientation="Horizontal">
31            <TextBox x:Name="searchBox" Width="150" />
32            <Button x:Name="searchButton" Content="Search" Width="75"
33               Click="searchButton_Click" />
34         </StackPanel>
35
36         <!-- Border that contains the large main image -->
37         <Border Grid.Row="1" x:Name="largeCoverImage" Height="60"
38            BorderBrush="Black" BorderThickness="10" CornerRadius="10"
39            Padding="20" Margin="10" HorizontalAlignment="Center">
40            <Border.Background>
41               <LinearGradientBrush StartPoint="0,0" EndPoint="0,1">
42                  <GradientStop Offset="0" Color="Black" />
43                  <GradientStop Offset="1" Color="LightGray" />
44               </LinearGradientBrush>
45            </Border.Background>
46
47            <!-- display the image that the user selected -->
48            <Image Source="{Binding}" Stretch="Uniform" />
49         </Border>
50
51         <!-- Listbox displays thumbnails of the search results -->
52         <ListBox x:Name="thumbsListBox" HorizontalAlignment="Center"
53            SelectionChanged="thumbsListBox_SelectionChanged" Grid.Row="2">
```

Fig. 24.10 | **FlickrViewer** allows users to search for tagged photos (XAML). (Part 1 of 2.)

```
54              <ListBox.ItemsPanel>
55                 <ItemsPanelTemplate>
56                    <StackPanel Orientation="Horizontal"/>
57                 </ItemsPanelTemplate>
58              </ListBox.ItemsPanel>
59
60              <ListBox.ItemTemplate>
61                 <DataTemplate>
62                    <Image Source="{Binding}" Margin="10" />
63                 </DataTemplate>
64              </ListBox.ItemTemplate>
65           </ListBox>
66        </Grid>
67     </UserControl>
```

Fig. 24.10 | **FlickrViewer** allows users to search for tagged photos (XAML). (Part 2 of 2.)

```
1   // Fig. 24.11: FlickrViewer.xaml.cs
2   // FlickrViewer allows users to search for photos (code-behind).
3   using System;
4   using System.Linq;
5   using System.Net;
6   using System.Windows;
7   using System.Windows.Controls;
8   using System.Xml.Linq;
9
10  namespace FlickrViewer
11  {
12     public partial class FlickrViewerPage : UserControl
13     {
14        // Flickr API key
15        private const string KEY = "Your API key goes here as string";
16
17        // object used to invoke Flickr web service
18        private WebClient flickr = new WebClient();
19
20        // constructor
21        public FlickrViewerPage()
22        {
```

Fig. 24.11 | **FlickrViewer** allows users to search for photos (code-behind). (Part 1 of 3.)

```
23          InitializeComponent();
24          flickr.DownloadStringCompleted += new
25             DownloadStringCompletedEventHandler(
26             flickr_DownloadStringCompleted );
27       } // end constructor
28
29       // when the photo selection has changed
30       private void thumbsListBox_SelectionChanged( object sender,
31          SelectionChangedEventArgs e )
32       {
33          // set the height back to a value so that it can be animated
34          largeCoverImage.Height = largeCoverImage.ActualHeight;
35
36          animateOut.Begin(); // begin shrinking animation
37       } // end method thumbsListBox_SelectionChanged
38
39       // once the nested image is no longer visible
40       private void animateOut_Completed( object sender, EventArgs e )
41       {
42          if ( thumbsListBox.SelectedItem != null )
43          {
44             // grab the URL of the selected item's full image
45             string photoURL =
46                thumbsListBox.SelectedItem.ToString().Replace(
47                "_t.jpg", ".jpg" );
48
49             largeCoverImage.DataContext = photoURL;
50
51             animate.To = imageRow.ActualHeight - 20;
52             animateIn.Begin();
53          } // end if
54       } // end method animateOut_Completed
55
56       // this makes sure that the border will resize with the window
57       private void animateIn_Completed( object sender, EventArgs e )
58       {
59          largeCoverImage.Height = double.NaN; // image height = *
60       } // end method animateIn_Completed
61
62       // begin the search when the user clicks the search button
63       private void searchButton_Click( object sender, RoutedEventArgs e )
64       {
65          // Flickr's web-service URL for searches
66          var flickrURL = string.Format("http://api.flickr.com/services" +
67             "/rest/?method=flickr.photos.search&api_key={0}&tags={1}" +
68             "&tag_mode=all&per_page=20&privacy_filter=1", KEY,
69             searchBox.Text.Replace( " " , "," ) );
70
71          // invoke the web service
72          flickr.DownloadStringAsync( new Uri( flickrURL ) );
73
74          // disable the search button
75          searchButton.Content = "Loading...";
```

Fig. 24.11 | **FlickrViewer** allows users to search for photos (code-behind). (Part 2 of 3.)

```
76          searchButton.IsEnabled = false;
77       } // end method searchButton_Click
78
79       // once we have received the XML file from Flickr
80       private void flickr_DownloadStringCompleted( object sender,
81          DownloadStringCompletedEventArgs e )
82       {
83          searchButton.Content = "Search";
84          searchButton.IsEnabled = true;
85
86          if ( e.Error == null )
87          {
88             // parse the data with LINQ
89             XDocument flickrXML = XDocument.Parse( e.Result );
90
91             // gather information on all photos
92             var flickrPhotos =
93                from photo in flickrXML.Descendants( "photo" )
94                let id = photo.Attribute( "id" ).Value
95                let secret = photo.Attribute( "secret" ).Value
96                let server = photo.Attribute( "server" ).Value
97                let farm = photo.Attribute( "farm" ).Value
98                select string.Format(
99                   "http://farm{0}.static.flickr.com/{1}/{2}_{3}_t.jpg",
100                  farm, server, id, secret);
101
102            // set thumbsListBox's item source to the URLs we received
103            thumbsListBox.ItemsSource = flickrPhotos;
104         } // end if
105      } // end method flickr_DownloadStringCompleted
106   } // end class FlickrViewerPage
107 } // end namespace FlickrViewer
```

Fig. 24.11 | FlickrViewer allows users to search for photos (code-behind). (Part 3 of 3.)

Line 15 defines a constant string for the API key that is required to use the Flickr API. To run this application insert your Flickr API key here.

Recall that the To property of the DoubleAnimation in the animateIn Storyboard is set programatically. Line 51 sets the To property to the Height of the page's second row (minus 20 to account for the Border's Margin), animating the Height to the largest possible value while keeping the Border completely visible on the page.

For animations to function properly, the properties being animated must contain numeric values—relative values "*" and "Auto" do not work. So before animateOut begins, we assign the value largeImageCover.ActualHeight to the Border's Height (line 34). When the Border is not being animated, we want it to take up as much space as possible on screen while still being resizable based on the changing size of the browser window. Line 59 resets the Border's Height back to double.NaN, which allows the border to be resized with the window.

Notice that when you click a new picture you have not previously viewed, the Border's Height increases without displaying a new picture inside. This is because the animation begins before the application can download the entire image. The picture is not displayed until its download is complete. If you click the thumbnail of an image you've viewed previously, it displays properly, because the image has already been downloaded to your system and cached by the browser. Viewing the image again causes it to be loaded from the browser's cache rather than over the web.

Lines 92–100 of Fig. 24.11 use a LINQ query to gather the necessary information from the attributes of the photo elements in the XML returned by the web service. A sample of the XML response is shown in Fig. 24.12. The four values collected are used to form the URL to the online photos. The "_t" before the ".jpg" in each URL indicates that we want the thumbnail of the photo rather than the full-sized file. These URLs are passed to the ItemsSource of thumbsListBox, which displays all the thumbnails at the bottom of the page. To load the large Image, use the URL of the thumbnail and remove the "_t" from the link (lines 45–47), then change the source of the Image element in the Border (line 49). Notice that the data binding in lines 48 and 62 of Fig. 24.10 uses the simple "{Binding}" syntax. We can use this syntax because we bind a single string to the object rather than a class with separate properties.

```
1    <?xml version="1.0" encoding="utf-8" ?>
2    <rsp stat="ok">
3       <photos page="1" pages="1" perpage="20" total="5">
4          <photo id="2608518732" owner="8832668@N04" secret="76dab8eb42"
5             server="3185" farm="4" title="Red Flowers 1" ispublic="1"
6             isfriend="0" isfamily="0" />
7          <photo id="2608518654" owner="8832668@N04" secret="57d35c8f64"
8             server="3293" farm="4" title="Lavender Flowers" ispublic="1"
9             isfriend="0" isfamily="0" />
10         <photo id="2608518890" owner="8832668@N04" secret="98fcb5fb42"
11            server="3121" farm="4" title="Yellow Flowers" ispublic="1"
12            isfriend="0" isfamily="0" />
13         <photo id="2608518370" owner="8832668@N04" secret="0099e12778"
14            server="3076" farm="4" title="Fuscia Flowers" ispublic="1"
15            isfriend="0" isfamily="0" />
16         <photo id="2607687273" owner="8832668@N04" secret="4b630e31ba"
17            server="3283" farm="4" title="Red Flowers 2" ispublic="1"
18            isfriend="0" isfamily="0" />
19      </photos>
20   </rsp>
```

Fig. 24.12 | Sample XML response from the Flickr APIs.

24.6 Images and Deep Zoom

One feature in Silverlight that is not in WPF is the *MultiScaleImage*. In most desktop applications, you'll have no trouble viewing and zooming in on a high-resolution image. Doing this over the Internet is problematic, however, because transferring large images usually takes significant time, which prevents web-based applications from having the feel of desktop applications.

This problem is addressed by Silverlight's *deep zoom* capabilities, which use Multi-ScaleImages to allow you to zoom far into an image in a web browser while maintaining quality. One of the best demonstrations of this technology is the Hard Rock Cafe's memorabilia page (memo.hardrock.com), which uses Silverlight's deep zoom capabilities to display a large collage of rock-and-roll memorabilia. You can zoom in on any individual item to see its high-resolution image. The photographs were taken at such high resolution that you can actually see fingerprints on the surfaces of some of the guitars!

Deep zoom works by sending only the necessary image data for the part of the image you are viewing to your machine. To split an image or collage of images into the Silverlight-ready format used by `MultiScaleImages`, you use the ***Deep Zoom Composer*** (available from `silverlight.net/GetStarted/`). The original images are split into smaller pieces to support various zoom levels. This enables the server to send smaller chunks of the picture rather than the entire file. If you zoom in close to an image, the server sends only the small section that you are viewing at its highest available resolution (which depends on the resolution of the original image). If you zoom out, the server sends only a lower-resolution version of the image. In either case, the server sends just enough data to give the user a rich image-viewing experience.

A `MultiScaleImage`'s `Source` is an XML document—created by Deep Zoom Composer. The `MultiScaleImage` uses the data in the XML to display an image or collage of images. A `MultiScaleSubImage` of a `MultiScaleImage` contains information on a single image in a collage.

The DeepZoomCoverCollage *Example*

Our **DeepZoomCoverCollage** application contains a high-resolution collage of 11 of our book covers. You can test the example online at `www.deitel.com/books/csharpfp3/`. You can zoom in and out and pan the image with simple keystroke and mouse-click combinations. Figure 24.13 shows screen captures of the application. Figure 24.13(a) shows the

a) The full deep zoom collage

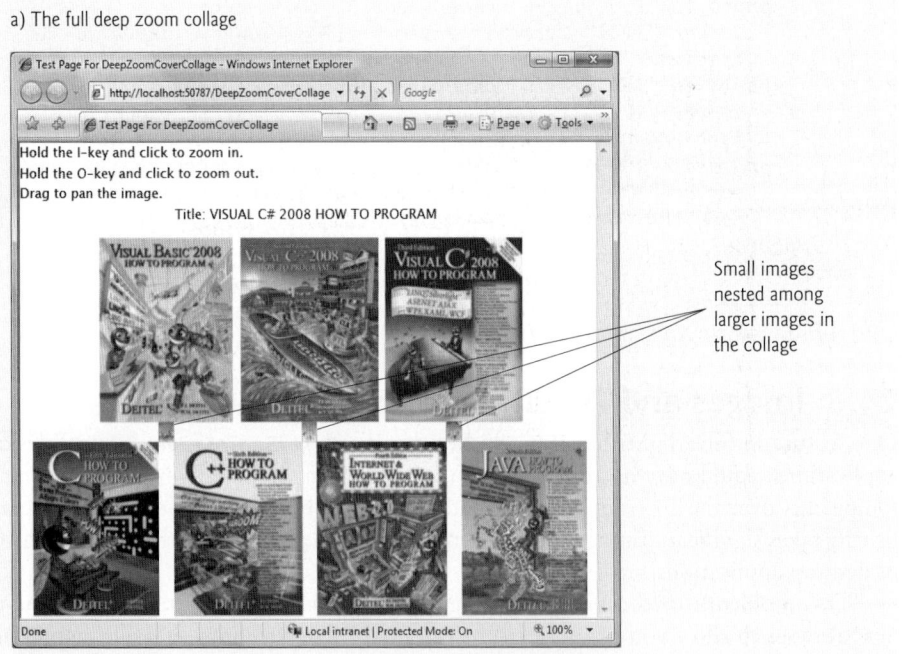

Fig. 24.13 | Main page of the **DeepZoomCoverCollage**. (Part 1 of 2.)

b) Zoomed in on a small cover in the middle of the collage

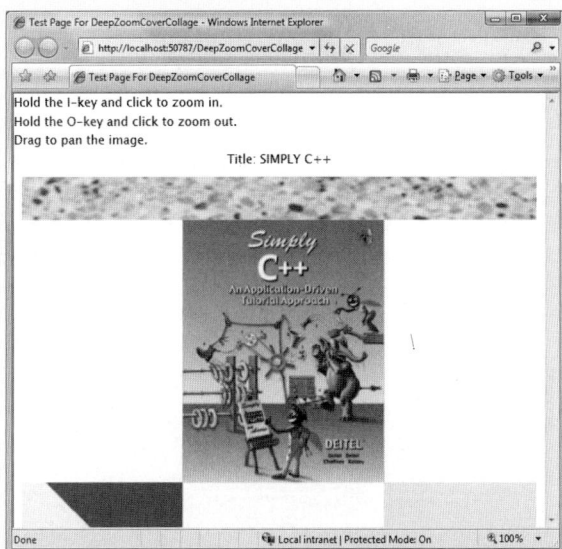

c) Deep zoom showing the details of the Visual C++ How to Program cover

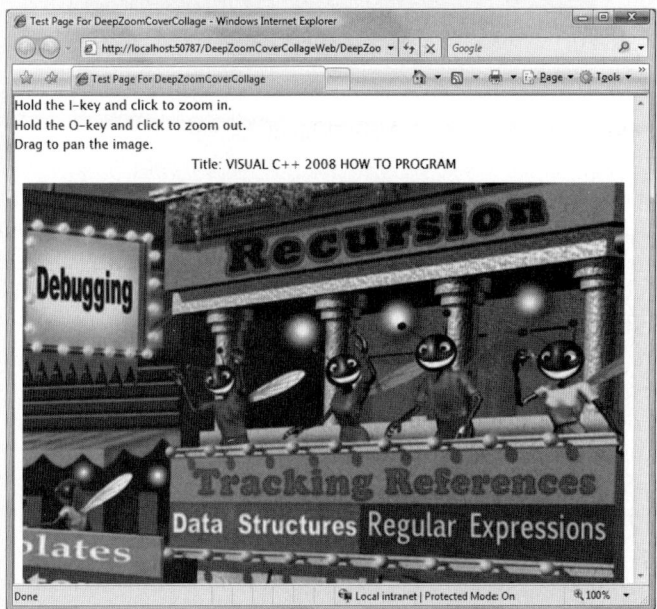

Fig. 24.13 | Main page of the **DeepZoomCoverCollage**. (Part 2 of 2.)

application when it's first loaded with all 11 cover images displayed. Seven large images and three small images are clearly visible. One cover is hidden within one of these eleven covers. Test-run the program to see if you can find it. Figure 24.13(b) shows the application after we've zoomed in closely on the leftmost small cover image. As you can see in the second screen capture, the small cover image still comes up clearly, because it was originally created in the Deep Zoom Composer with a high-resolution image. Figure 24.13(c) shows the application with an even deeper zoom on a different cover. Rather than being pixelated, the image displays the details of the original picture.

24.6.1 Getting Started With Deep Zoom Composer

To create the collection of files that is used by `MultiScaleImage`, you need to import the image or set of images into Deep Zoom Composer. When you first open the program, create a new project through the **File** menu, and specify the project's **Name** and **Location**. We named the project **CoverCollage** and saved it to the **Location** `C:\examples\ch24\Deep-ZoomProject`. Figure 24.14 shows the **New Project** dialog.

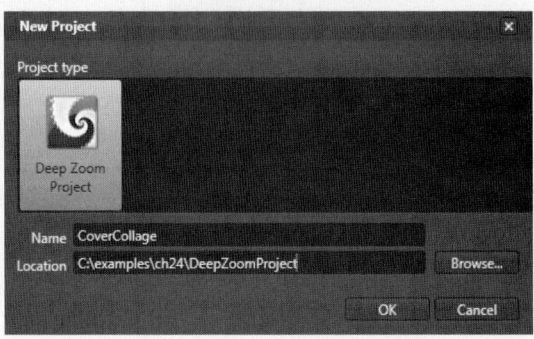

Fig. 24.14 | Deep Zoom Composer's **New Project** dialog.

The **Import** tab in Deep Zoom Composer is displayed by default. It enables you to add the image(s) that you want in the collage. Click the **Add Image...** button to add your images. (We provided our book-cover images with this chapter's examples in the `Cover Images` folder.) Once you've added your images, you'll see their thumbnails on the right side of the window. A larger version of the selected image appears in the middle of the window. Figure 24.15 shows the window with the **Import** tab open after the book-cover images have been imported to the project.

For our **CoverCollage** example, we use high-resolution `.jpg` images. Deep Zoom Composer also supports `.tif`, `.bmp` and `.png` formats. After importing the images, you can go to the **Compose** tab to organize them on your collage.

Drag the thumbnail of each desired image onto the main canvas of the window. When you drag a file into the collage, its thumbnail is grayed out in the side bar and you cannot add it to the collage again. Figure 24.16 shows what the composer looks like, once you bring files into the project.

When images are in the composition, you can move the images to the canvas and resize them to be as large or small as you want. Deep Zoom Composer has features such as snapping and alignment tools that help you lay out the images. The yellow pins throughout the collage in Fig. 24.16(a) indicate that there are small images at those locations. You can zoom in on the composition by scrolling the mouse wheel to see the smaller images. Figure 24.16(b) shows the smaller cover that one of the yellow pins indicates. A small screen in the bottom-left corner shows the entire collage and a white rectangular outline indicating the view displayed in the window.

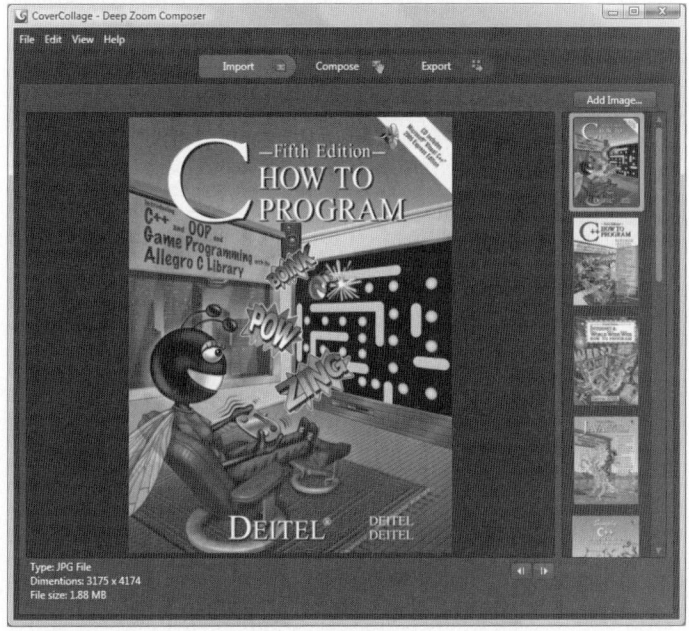

Fig. 24.15 | Deep Zoom Composer showing the imported image files.

a) Deep Zoom Composer showing the entire composition

Fig. 24.16 | Deep Zoom Composer showing the editable composition. (Part 1 of 2.)

b) Zoomed in on the composition in Deep Zoom Composer

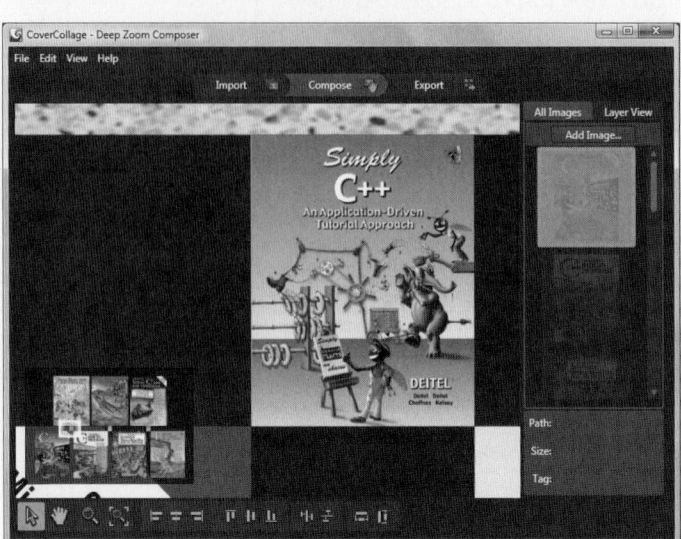

Fig. 24.16 | Deep Zoom Composer showing the editable composition. (Part 2 of 2.)

The panel on the right showing all the images also has a **Layer View** option, which indicates the layer ordering of all the composition's images. This view is used to control the order of overlapping images. The layers can be rearranged to allow you to place certain images on top of others.

Once you have a completed collage, go to the **Export** tab to export the files to be used by a MultiScaleImage in your application. Figure 24.17 shows the contents of the window under the **Export** tab.

You'll need to name the project. For this example, name the project **CoverCollage-Collection** and keep the default **Export Location**. The files are exported to a new folder inside the directory that you created earlier for the Deep Zoom Composer project. By default, Deep Zoom Composer selects the **Export as Collection** option using a PNG file format. By exporting as a collection instead of a composition, subimage information is included in the output XML files. Change the file format to **JPEG** and keep the **Quality** at 95—lower values result in smaller file sizes and lower-quality images. Also by default, the composer selects the **Export Images and Silverlight Project** output type. Select the **Export Images** option, since we are using the export in our own Silverlight project. Note that Deep Zoom Composer allows you to export a Silverlight C# project, which provides the functionality that we discuss in this chapter. We have created a new project instead of using the autogenerated project for discussion purposes. Once the images are done exporting, you'll be ready to import these files into a Silverlight project and use them to create a deep zoom application.

24.6.2 Creating a Silverlight Deep Zoom Application

Deep zoom images are created in Silverlight projects by using the MultiScaleImage element, which takes an XML file as its source. A MultiScaleImage can be treated similarly

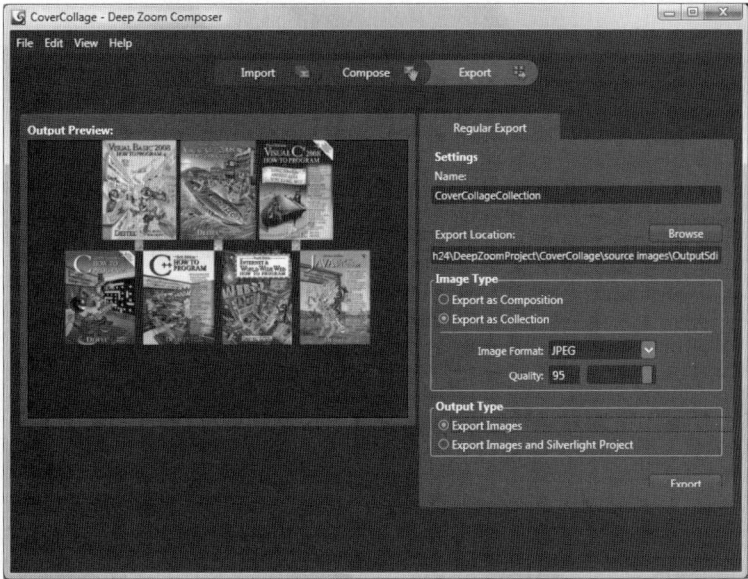

Fig. 24.17 | Deep Zoom Composer's exporting capabilities.

to a simple `Image` element in the XAML code. Earlier in the chapter we showed you screen captures of the **DeepZoomCoverCollage** example. Figure 24.18 is the XAML code that produces the layout of this application.

The main page contains only a `StackPanel` with embedded `TextBlocks` that display instructions, a `TextBlock` to display the selected book's title and the `MultiScaleImage` to display the collage we created in the previous section. To use the collage, you must add the entire **CoverCollageCollection** folder to your web application project. If you kept the default Deep Zoom Composer export location, this folder can be found in the `Cover-Collage` project's folder under the subfolder `\source images\OutputSdi\`. Use Windows Explorer to copy the `CoverCollageCollection` folder into the web application's `Cli-entBin` folder (`C:\examples\ch24\DeepZoomCoverCollage\DeepZoomCoverCollageWeb\ClientBin\`). Right click **ClientBin** under the **DeepZoomCoverCollageWeb** project in the **Solution Explorer** in Visual Studio and click **Refresh Folder**. If the folder was copied correctly, you should see a **CoverCollageCollection** folder (Fig. 24.19). You can now refer to this collection in your application.

```
1   <!-- Fig. 24.18: DeepZoomCoverCollage.xaml -->
2   <!-- DeepZoomCoverCollage employs Silverlight's deep zoom (XAML). -->
3   <UserControl x:Class="DeepZoomCoverCollage.DeepZoomCoverCollagePage"
4      xmlns="http://schemas.microsoft.com/winfx/2006/xaml/presentation"
5      xmlns:x="http://schemas.microsoft.com/winfx/2006/xaml">
6      x:Name="mainPage" KeyDown="mainPage_KeyDown" KeyUp="mainPage_KeyUp">
7      <Grid x:Name="LayoutRoot">
8
```

Fig. 24.18 | **DeepZoomCoverCollage** employs Silverlight's deep zoom (XAML). (Part 1 of 2.)

```
 9          <!-- instructions on how to interact with the page -->
10          <StackPanel Orientation="Vertical">
11             <TextBlock Text="Hold the I-key and click to zoom in." />
12             <TextBlock Text="Hold the O-key and click to zoom out." />
13             <TextBlock Text="Drag to pan the image."  />
14
15             <TextBlock x:Name="titleTextBlock" Text="Title:"
16                HorizontalAlignment="Center" />
17
18             <!-- deep zoom collage that was created in Composer -->
19             <MultiScaleImage x:Name="Image" Margin="10"
20                Source="/CoverCollageCollection/dzc_output.xml"
21                MouseLeave="Image_MouseLeave" MouseMove="Image_MouseMove"
22                MouseLeftButtonDown="Image_MouseLeftButtonDown"
23                MouseLeftButtonUp="Image_MouseLeftButtonUp" />
24          </StackPanel>
25       </Grid>
26    </UserControl>
```

Fig. 24.18 | **DeepZoomCoverCollage** employs Silverlight's deep zoom (XAML). (Part 2 of 2.)

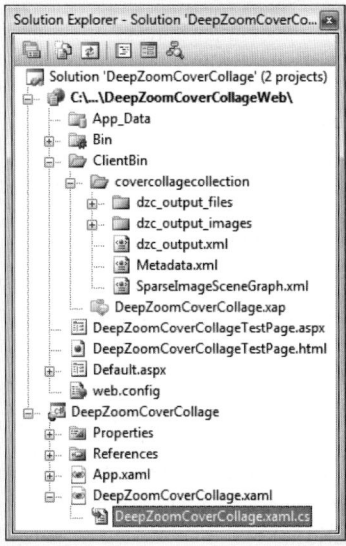

Fig. 24.19 | **Solution Explorer** after the deep zoom files have been added to the project.

Once the necessary files are in the project, they can be used by the `MultiScaleImage` element that displays the deep zoom image. Line 20 of Fig. 24.18 sets the source of the `MultiScaleImage` to `"/CoverCollageCollection/dzc_output.xml"`. The source address in this case is relative to the **ClientBin**, meaning that the application searches for the given path in the **ClientBin** folder of the project. Now that the `MultiScaleImage` is ready, we can program the application's event handlers for zooming and panning the image, and for displaying a book's title when its cover is clicked (Fig. 24.20).

Line 8 imports the LINQ to XML namespace. We use a LINQ query to find the title of the cover image the user selects. We have several instance variables that help us determine which operation is to occur when you click the mouse.

Zooming a *MultiScaleImage*

To zoom in or out with a MultiScaleImage, we call its ***ZoomAboutLogicalPoint*** method (lines 74 and 78–79), which takes a zoom factor, an *x*-coordinate and a *y*-coordinate as parameters. A zoom factor of 1 keeps the image at its current size. Values less than 1 zoom out and values greater than 1 zoom in. The method zooms toward or away from the coordinates passed to the method. The coordinates need to be absolute points divided by the entire collage's Width. To convert the absolute coordinates raised by a mouse event to these coordinates, we use MultiScaleImage's ***ElementToLogicalPoint*** method (line 70), which takes the Point's absolute coordinates as parameters.

```
1   // Fig. 24.20: DeepZoomCoverCollage.xaml.cs
2   // DeepZoomCoverCollage employs Silverlight's deep zoom (code-behind).
3   using System;
4   using System.IO;
5   using System.Linq;
6   using System.Windows;
7   using System.Windows.Controls;
8   using System.Windows.Input;
9   using System.Xml.Linq;
10
11  namespace DeepZoomCoverCollage
12  {
13     public partial class DeepZoomCoverCollagePage : UserControl
14     {
15        private const double ZOOMFACTOR = 2.0;
16
17        private bool zoomIn = false; // true if I button is pressed
18        private bool zoomOut = false; // true if O button is pressed
19        private bool mouseDown = false; // true if mouse button is down
20        private Point currentPosition; // position of viewport when clicked
21        private Point dragOffset; // mouse offset used for panning
22
23        // constructor
24        public DeepZoomCoverCollagePage()
25        {
26           InitializeComponent();
27        } // end constructor
28
29        // when a key is pressed, set the correct variables to true
30        private void mainPage_KeyDown( object sender, KeyEventArgs e )
31        {
32           if ( e.Key == Key.I ) // button pressed is I
33           {
34              zoomIn = true; // prepare to zoom in
35           } // end if
```

Fig. 24.20 | **DeepZoomCoverCollage** employs Silverlight's deep zoom (code-behind). (Part 1 of 4.)

```
36          else if ( e.Key == Key.O ) // button pressed is O
37          {
38             zoomOut = true; // prepare to zoom out
39          } // end else if
40       } // end method mainPage_KeyDown
41
42       // when a key is released, set the correct variables to false
43       private void mainPage_KeyUp( object sender, KeyEventArgs e )
44       {
45          if ( e.Key == Key.I ) // button released is I
46          {
47             zoomIn = false; // don't zoom in
48          } // end if
49          else if ( e.Key == Key.O ) // button released is O
50          {
51             zoomOut = false; // don't zoom out
52          } // end else if
53       } // end method mainPage_KeyUp
54
55       // when the mouse leaves the area of the image we don't want to pan
56       private void Image_MouseLeave( object sender, MouseEventArgs e )
57       {
58          mouseDown = false; // if mouse leaves area, no more panning
59       } // end method Image_MouseLeave
60
61       // handle events when user clicks the mouse
62       private void Image_MouseLeftButtonDown( object sender,
63          MouseButtonEventArgs e )
64       {
65          mouseDown = true; // mouse button is down
66          currentPosition = Image.ViewportOrigin; // viewport position
67          dragOffset = e.GetPosition( Image ); // mouse position
68
69          // logical position (between 0 and 1) of mouse
70          Point click = Image.ElementToLogicalPoint( dragOffset );
71
72          if ( zoomIn ) // zoom in when I key is pressed
73          {
74             Image.ZoomAboutLogicalPoint( ZOOMFACTOR, click.X, click.Y );
75          } // end if
76          else if ( zoomOut ) // zoom out when O key is pressed
77          {
78             Image.ZoomAboutLogicalPoint( 1 / ZOOMFACTOR,
79                click.X, click.Y );
80          } // end else if
81
82          // determine which book cover was pressed to display the title
83          int index = SubImageIndex( click );
84
85          if ( index > -1 )
86          {
```

Fig. 24.20 | DeepZoomCoverCollage employs Silverlight's deep zoom (code-behind). (Part 2 of 4.)

```
87           titleTextBlock.Text = string.Format(
88              "Title: {0}", GetTitle( index ) );
89        }
90        else // user clicked a blank space
91        {
92           titleTextBlock.Text = "Title:";
93        } // end else
94     } // end method Image_MouseLeftButtonDown
95
96     // if the mouse button is released, we don't want to pan anymore
97     private void Image_MouseLeftButtonUp( object sender,
98        MouseButtonEventArgs e )
99     {
100       mouseDown = false; // no more panning
101    } // end method Image_MouseLeftButtonUp
102
103    // handle when the mouse moves: panning
104    private void Image_MouseMove( object sender, MouseEventArgs e )
105    {
106       // if no zoom occurs, we want to pan
107       if ( mouseDown && !zoomIn && !zoomOut )
108       {
109          Point click = new Point(); // records point to move to
110          click.X = currentPosition.X - Image.ViewportWidth * (
111             e.GetPosition( Image ).X - dragOffset.X ) /
112             Image.ActualWidth;
113          click.Y = currentPosition.Y - Image.ViewportWidth * (
114             e.GetPosition( Image ).Y - dragOffset.Y ) /
115             Image.ActualWidth;
116          Image.ViewportOrigin = click; // pans the image
117       } // end if
118    } // end method Image_MouseMove
119
120    // returns the index of the clicked subimage
121    private int SubImageIndex( Point click )
122    {
123       // go through images such that images on top are processed first
124       for ( int i = Image.SubImages.Count - 1; i >= 0; i-- )
125       {
126          // select a single subimage
127          MultiScaleSubImage subImage = Image.SubImages[ i ];
128
129          // create a rect around the area of the cover
130          double scale = 1 / subImage.ViewportWidth;
131          Rect area = new Rect( -subImage.ViewportOrigin.X * scale,
132             -subImage.ViewportOrigin.Y * scale, scale, scale /
133             subImage.AspectRatio );
134
135          if ( area.Contains( click ) )
136          {
```

Fig. 24.20 | **DeepZoomCoverCollage** employs Silverlight's deep zoom (code-behind). (Part 3 of 4.)

```
137            return i; // return the index of the clicked cover
138          } // end if
139       } // end for
140       return -1; // if no cover was clicked, return -1
141    } // end method SubImageIndex
142
143    // returns the title of the subimage with the given index
144    private string GetTitle( int index )
145    {
146       // XDocument that contains info on all subimages in the collage
147       XDocument xmlDocument = XDocument.Load( "Metadata.xml" );
148
149       // LINQ to XML to find the title based on index of clicked image
150       var bookTitle =
151          from info in xmlDocument.Descendants( "Image" )
152          let order = Convert.ToInt32( info.Element( "ZOrder" ).Value )
153          where order == index + 1
154          select info.Element( "FileName" ).Value;
155
156       string title = bookTitle.Single(); // gets book title
157
158       // only want title of book, not the rest of the file name
159       title = Path.GetFileName( title );
160
161       // make slight changes to the file name
162       title = title.Replace( ".jpg", string.Empty );
163       title = title.Replace( "pp", "++" );
164       title = title.Replace( "sharp", "#" );
165
166       // display the title on the page
167       return title.ToUpper();
168    } // end method GetTitle
169  } // end class DeepZoomCoverCollagePage
170 } // end namespace DeepZoomCoverCollage
```

Fig. 24.20 | DeepZoomCoverCollage employs Silverlight's deep zoom (code-behind). (Part 4 of 4.)

Panning a MultiScaleImage

The viewport of a MultiScaleImage represents the portion of the image that is rendered on screen. To pan, change the **ViewportOrigin** property—which returns a point representing the top-left corner of the viewport with respect to the collage's top-left corner—of the MultiScaleImage (line 116). Figures 24.21–24.22 demonstrate what values are returned by various MultiScaleImage properties. Assume the "container" of Fig. 24.21 is the viewport while the "image" is the entire collage. By keeping track of the offset between where the user initially clicked (line 67) and where the user has dragged the mouse, we can calculate where we need to move the origin (lines 110–115) to shift the image.

To determine the new x-coordinate of the ViewportOrigin, we first find the difference between the x-coordinates of the current mouse position (e.GetPosition(Image).X) and the mouse position where the user initially clicked (dragOffset.X), which we'll refer to as the mouse offset. To convert this value to one we can use for the ViewportOrigin, we need

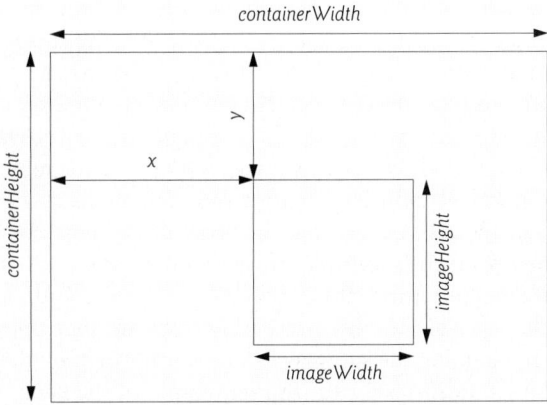

Fig. 24.21 | Various values used to by `MultiScaleImage`'s properties.

Property	Value
ViewportOrigin	$\left(\dfrac{-x}{imageWidth}, \dfrac{-y}{imageWidth}\right)$
ViewportWidth	$\dfrac{containerWidth}{imageWidth}$
AspectRatio	$\dfrac{imageWidth}{imageHeight}$
ActualWidth	$containerWidth$

Fig. 24.22 | Ratios returned by MultiScaleImage's properties.

to divide it by the width of the collage—which we cannot get directly. The `MultiScale-Image`'s *ViewportWidth* property returns the ratio of the viewport's width and the collage's width (*containerWidth* and *imageWidth* in Fig. 24.21, respectively). A `MultiScaleImage`'s `ActualWidth` property returns the width of the piece of the collage rendered on-screen (containerWidth). Multiplying the mouse offset by the `ViewportWidth` and dividing by the `ActualWidth` returns the ratio of the mouse offset and the collage's width. We then subtract this value from the `ViewportOrigin`'s original *x*-coordinate to obtain the new value. A similar calculation is performed for the *y*-coordinate (keep in mind we still use `ActualWidth` in this calculation since both of `ViewportOrigin`'s coordinates are given in terms of the width).

Determining the Title of the Clicked Cover
Determining a clicked image's book title requires the `Metadata.xml` file created by Deep Zoom Composer. In the **Solution Explorer**, find this XML file in the collection folder we imported and drag the file to your Silverlight deep zoom project so that you can use it in a LINQ query later in the application. The file contains information on where each subimage is located in the collage.

To determine which cover the user clicked, we create a **Rect** object (lines 131–133) for each subimage that represents the on-screen area that the image occupies. A Rect defines a rectangular area on the page. If the Point returned by the mouse-click event is inside the Rect, the user clicked the cover in that Rect. We can use Rect method **Contains** to determine whether the click was inside the rectangle. If a cover was clicked, method SubImageIndex returns the index of the subimage. Otherwise the method returns -1.

A MultiScaleSubImage's properties return the same ratios as a MultiScaleImage's properties (Figs. 24.21–24.22), except that the "container" represents the entire collage while the "image" represents the subimage. Since the ElementToLogicalPoint method of a MultiScaleImage element returns points based on a scaled coordinate system with the origin at the top-left corner of the collage, we want to create Rect objects using the same coordinate system. By dividing the subimage's ViewportOrigin by the subimage's ViewportWidth, we obtain coordinates for the top-left corner of the Rect. To find the Rect's Width, we take the inverse of the subimage's ViewportWidth. We can then use the subimage's AspectRatio to obtain the Height from the Width.

Next, we use the subimage's index in a LINQ to XML query to locate the subimage's information in the Metadata.xml document (lines 151–154). Each subimage in the collage has a unique numeric ZOrder property, which corresponds to the order in which the images are rendered on screen—the cover with a ZOrder of 1 is drawn first (behind the rest of the covers), while the cover with a ZOrder of 11 is drawn last (on top of all other covers). This ordering also corresponds to the order of the subimages in the collection Image.SubImages and therefore corresponds with the index that we found in the SubImageIndex method. To determine which cover was clicked, we can compare the returned index with the ZOrder of each subimage in the collection using our LINQ to XML query. We add 1 to the returned index (line 153), because the indices in a collection start at 0 while the ZOrder properties of the subimages start at 1.

We then obtain the title from the subimage's original file name (lines 159–164) and display the title above the deep zoom image (lines 87–88). The If statement in line 85 checks whether any of the sub-images fit our criteria. If a sub-image was clicked, we use the **Single** method (line 156) on our LINQ query result to get the one (and only) returned string. This method returns the element itself (in this case, the string). If none of the covers were clicked, then no title is displayed (line 92).

24.7 Audio and Video

Silverlight uses the MediaElement element to embed audio or video files into your application. The source for MediaElements can be either a file stored with the Silverlight application or a source on the Internet. MediaElement supports playback in the following encoded formats (more information is available at msdn.microsoft.com/en-us/library/cc189080(vs.95).aspx):

- Video: WMV1, WMV2, WMV3, WMVA, WMVC1
- Audio: WMA7, WMA8, WMA9, MP3

Silverlight also supports high-definition video. While Silverlight is compatible with only Windows media files, Microsoft's Expression Encoder can be used to convert files into a supported format. Other encoders that can convert to Windows media format will work as well, including the free online media encoder at media-convert.com/

MediaElements can be in one of the following states—Buffering, Closed, Paused, Opening, Playing or Stopped. A MediaElement's state can be determined from its *CurrentState* property. When in the Buffering state, the MediaElement is loading the media in preparation for playback. When in the Closed state, the MediaElement contains no media and displays a transparent frame. When in the Opening state, the MediaElement is attempting to load the media from the given source.

Our **VideoSelector** application (Fig. 24.23) shows some of Silverlight's media-playing capabilities. This application obtains its video sources from a user-created XML file and displays small previews of those videos on the left side of the screen. When you click a preview, the application loads that video in the application's main area. The application plays the audio only for the video in the main area. You can test the example online at www.deitel.com/books/csharpfp3/.

```
 1   <!-- Fig. 24.23: VideoSelector.xaml -->
 2   <!-- VideoSelector lets users watch several videos at once (XAML). -->
 3   <UserControl x:Class="VideoSelector.VideoSelectorPage"
 4      xmlns="http://schemas.microsoft.com/winfx/2006/xaml/presentation"
 5      xmlns:x="http://schemas.microsoft.com/winfx/2006/xaml">
 6      <Grid x:Name="LayoutRoot">
 7         <Grid.ColumnDefinitions>
 8            <ColumnDefinition Width="Auto" />
 9            <ColumnDefinition />
10         </Grid.ColumnDefinitions>
11
12         <Grid.Resources>
13            <!-- Fades the main screen in, displaying the new video -->
14            <Storyboard x:Name="fadeIn" Storyboard.TargetName="screen">
15               <DoubleAnimation Storyboard.TargetProperty="Opacity"
16                  From="0" To="1" Duration="0:0:0.5" />
17            </Storyboard>
18
19            <!-- Fades the main screen out when a new video is selected -->
20            <Storyboard x:Name="fadeOut" Storyboard.TargetName="screen"
21               Completed="fadeOut_Completed">
22               <DoubleAnimation Storyboard.TargetProperty="Opacity"
23                  From="1" To="0" Duration="0:0:0.5" />
24            </Storyboard>
25         </Grid.Resources>
26
27         <!-- ListBox containing all available videos -->
28         <ListBox x:Name="previewListBox"
29            SelectionChanged="previewListBox_SelectionChanged">
30            <ListBox.ItemsPanel>
31               <ItemsPanelTemplate>
32                  <StackPanel Orientation="Vertical" />
33               </ItemsPanelTemplate>
34            </ListBox.ItemsPanel>
35         </ListBox>
36
```

Fig. 24.23 | **VideoSelector** lets users watch several videos at once (XAML). (Part 1 of 2.)

```
37        <!-- Rectangle object with a video brush showing the main video -->
38        <Rectangle x:Name="screen" Grid.Column="1">
39           <Rectangle.Fill>
40              <VideoBrush x:Name="brush" Stretch="Uniform" />
41           </Rectangle.Fill>
42        </Rectangle>
43     </Grid>
44  </UserControl>
```

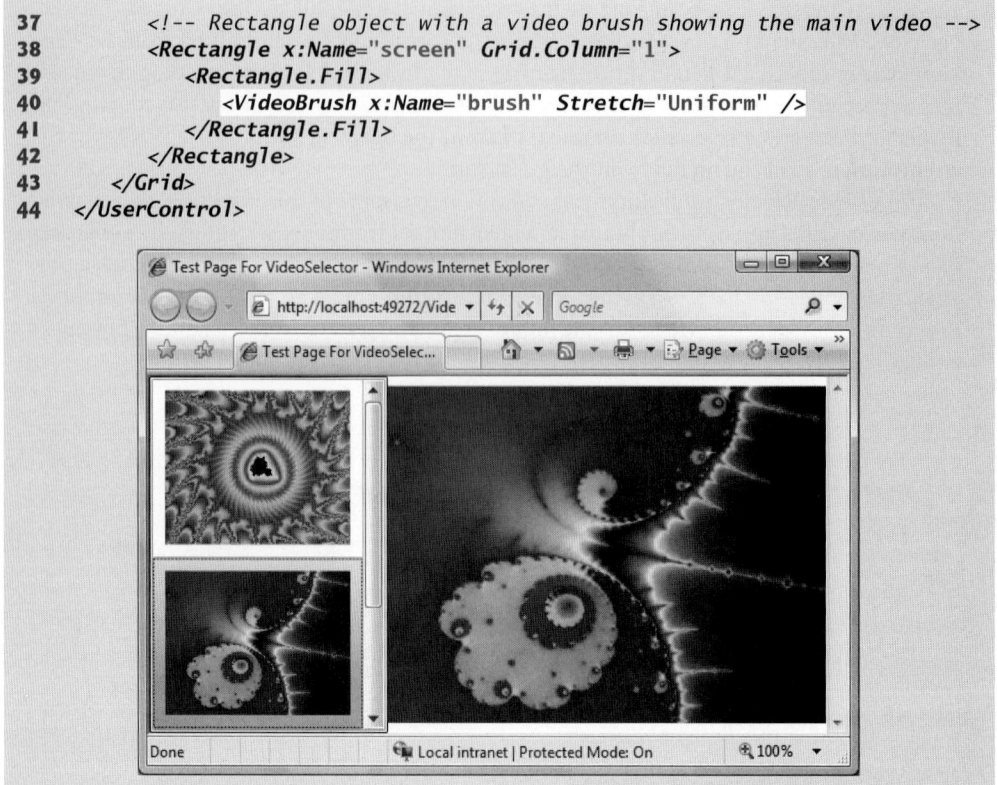

Fig. 24.23 | VideoSelector lets users watch several videos at once (XAML). (Part 2 of 2.)

The videos for this example were downloaded from the Wikimedia Commons website (`commons.wikimedia.org`) and are in the public domain. This site contains many image, sound and video files that you can use in your programs—not all are in the public domain. The videos in the screen capture in Fig. 24.23 were obtained under the science videos section at

        `commons.wikimedia.org/wiki/Category:Science_videos`

The files were `.ogg` files that we converted to `.wmv` files using the online video converter at `media-convert.com/`.

The application displays one preview video on the side of the page for each source defined in a user-created XML file (discussed shortly). The GUI contains a `Grid` with two `Column`s. The first `Column` contains a `ListBox` that allows you to scroll through previews of the videos (lines 28–35). The second `Column` contains a `Rectangle` element with a `VideoBrush` for its `Fill` (lines 38–42). A *VideoBrush* displays a video as a graphics object's `Fill`—similar to an `ImageBrush`. The `SetSource` method of `VideoBrush` takes a `MediaElement` as a parameter and sets the video to be played in the brush.

The `Grid` element contains two `Storyboard` `Resource`s, which contain the main video's fade-in and fade-out animations (lines 12–25). These animations are `DoubleAnimations` that target the `Opacity` property of the `Rectangle` that displays the video. To make the Rectangle display the selected video, we'll change the VideoBrush's source to the video the user clicks.

When the page loads, the application performs several initialization tasks. It first loads a new MediaElement for each source that is included in the sources.xml file (Fig. 24.24). We query this XML file using LINQ to XML. To specify your own list of videos, you must edit our sources.xml file, or create a new one and add it to the project. To do this, open a new XML file by right clicking the application project—in this case **VideoSelector**—in the **Solution Explorer** and go to **Add > New Item...**. Select **Visual C#** in the **Categories** section of the window, then select **XML File** in the **Templates** section. Change the file's **Name** to **sources.xml** and click **Add**. Open the file to begin editing it. The sample file in Fig. 24.24 shows the format required to list the sources of the desired videos.

The XML document defines a videos root element that may contain any number of video children. Each video element contains a uri element whose value is the source for the corresponding MediaElement. Simply replace the value in the uri tag(s) with the path to your video(s). These videos also need to be included in your **Web Project**'s **Client Bin** if you want to play them from the same location as the Silverlight application. If your sources link to online videos, then you don't need to add anything else to your project. To add these files, right click the **Client Bin** folder in the **Web Project** associated with your Silverlight application (**VideoSelectorWeb**) in the **Solution Explorer** and select **Add Existing Item...**. Locate the videos you want to add and click **Add**. Now that we've added the necessary files to the project, we can continue with the code-behind file shown in Fig. 24.25.

```
 1    <?xml version="1.0" encoding="utf-8" ?>
 2
 3    <!-- Fig. 24.24: sources.xml -->
 4    <!-- VideoSelector's list of video sources. -->
 5    <videos>
 6       <video> <!-- each video child contains a uri source property -->
 7          <uri>/newfractal.wmv</uri> <!-- source for first video -->
 8       </video>
 9       <video>
10          <uri>/fractal.wmv</uri> <!-- source for second video -->
11       </video>
12       <video>
13          <uri>/bailey.wmv</uri> <!-- source for third video -->
14       </video>
15    </videos>
```

Fig. 24.24 | VideoSelector's list of video sources.

```
 1    // Fig. 24.25: VideoSelector.xaml.cs
 2    // VideoSelector lets users watch several videos (code-behind).
 3    using System;
 4    using System.Linq;
 5    using System.Windows;
 6    using System.Windows.Controls;
 7    using System.Windows.Media;
 8    using System.Xml.Linq;
```

Fig. 24.25 | VideoSelector lets users watch several videos (code-behind). (Part 1 of 3.)

```
 9
10   namespace VideoSelector
11   {
12      public partial class VideoSelectorPage : UserControl
13      {
14         private MediaElement currentVideo = new MediaElement();
15
16         // constructor
17         public VideoSelectorPage()
18         {
19            InitializeComponent();
20
21            // sources.xml contains the sources for all the videos
22            XDocument sources = XDocument.Load( "sources.xml" );
23
24            // LINQ to XML to create new MediaElements
25            var videos =
26               from video in sources.Descendants( "video" )
27               where video.Element( "uri" ).Value != string.Empty
28               select new MediaElement()
29               {
30                  Source = new Uri( video.Element( "uri" ).Value,
31                     UriKind.RelativeOrAbsolute ),
32                  Width = 150,
33                  Margin = new Thickness( 10 ),
34                  IsMuted = true
35               };
36
37            // send all videos to the ListBox
38            previewListBox.ItemsSource = videos;
39         } // end constructor
40
41         // when the user makes a new selection
42         private void previewListBox_SelectionChanged( object sender,
43            SelectionChangedEventArgs e )
44         {
45            fadeOut.Begin(); // begin fade out animation
46         } // end method previewListBox_SelectionChanged
47
48         // change the video if there is a new selection
49         private void fadeOut_Completed( object sender, EventArgs e )
50         {
51            // if there is a selection
52            if ( previewListBox.SelectedItem != null )
53            {
54               // grab the new video to be played
55               MediaElement newVideo =
56                  ( MediaElement ) previewListBox.SelectedItem;
57
58               // if new video has finished playing, restart it
59               if ( newVideo.CurrentState == MediaElementState.Paused )
60               {
61                  newVideo.Stop();
```

Fig. 24.25 | **VideoSelector** lets users watch several videos (code-behind). (Part 2 of 3.)

```
62                  newVideo.Play();
63              } // end if
64
65              currentVideo.IsMuted = true; // mute the old video
66              newVideo.IsMuted = false; // play audio for main video
67
68              currentVideo = newVideo; // set the currently playing video
69              brush.SetSource( newVideo ); // set source of video brush
70          } // end if
71
72          fadeIn.Begin(); // begin fade in animation
73      } // end method fadeOut_Completed
74    } // end class VideoSelectorPage
75 } // end namespace VideoSelector
```

Fig. 24.25 | **VideoSelector** lets users watch several videos (code-behind). (Part 3 of 3.)

The **VideoSelector** uses LINQ to XML to determine which videos to display in the side bar. Line 22 defines the XDocument that loads sources.xml. Lines 25–35 contain a LINQ query that gets each video element from the XML file. For each video element that has a non-empty uri element, the query creates a new MediaElement with that uri as its Source. If your video is in the same location as the application or any subdirectory of that location, you may use a relative Source value. Otherwise, you need to use an absolute Source, which specifies the full path of the video. Notice the *UriKind.RelativeOr-Absolute* argument for the MediaElement's source, which allows us to prepare for either type of URI since we will not know which is being used until runtime. We set each element's Width, Margin and *IsMuted* properties to specify how the videos appear and perform when the application loads. Setting a MediaElement's IsMuted property to true (line 34) mutes its audio—the default value is false—so that we do not hear the audio from all videos at once. We then feed the videos to the ItemsSource (line 38) of the ListBox to display the preview videos.

The application uses previewListBox's SelectionChanged event handler to determine which video the user wants to view in the main area. When this event occurs, we begin the fade-out animation (line 45). After the fade-out animation completes, the application determines which video was clicked by grabbing previewListBox's SelectedItem object and stores it in a MediaElement variable (line 55–56).

When a video has finished playing, it ends up in the Paused state. Lines 59–63 ensure that the selected video is restarted if it is in this state. We then mute the audio of the old video and enable the audio of the selected video (lines 65 and 66, respectively). Next, we set the source for the VideoBrush of the Rectangle's Fill to the selected video (line 69). Finally, we begin the fade-in animation to show the new video in the main area (line 72).

24.8 Isolated Storage

Just as web applications can store data on a client's computer via cookies, Silverlight allows applications to store data on client computers. This feature, called *isolated storage*, is used to save user-specific data associated with one or more Silverlight applications from a single domain. These files can store any kind of data that the application needs, such as the user's preferences for the application. The current limit for isolated data storage on a client machine is 1 MB; however, the application can request a higher quota, and Silverlight will automatically prompt the user to approve the request. The quota is for all applications from one domain, not each individual application. The isolated storage is shared among all Silverlight applications from a given domain.

Applications use isolated storage to store data in a *virtual file system*. The file system is considered virtual because it is not stored at a specific location on the client computer. Rather, storage files—called *stores*—contain the information on the physical location of the data. The same isolated storage is used by all browsers on the client's computer. For example, if a client accesses a Silverlight application from Internet Explorer, then accesses the same application from Firefox, the application running in Firefox has access to any data stored in the isolated storage when the application was running in Internet Explorer (and vice versa). This system is particularly useful in offering cross-browser operability of Silverlight applications, since the user's browser has no effect on the site's ability to retrieve the data. More information on isolated storage can be found at

> msdn.microsoft.com/en-us/library/bdts8hk0(VS.95).aspx

24.9 Silverlight Demos and Web Resources

A great way to get into the "Silverlight world" is to visit the growing number of demo sites and general resource sites on the web.

www.deitel.com/ResourceCenters/Microsoft/Silverlight20/tabid/2985/Default.aspx
Start your search here for Silverlight 2.0 resources, including sample applications, articles, blogs, videos, tutorials, downloads, training courses, forums, FAQs, books, eBooks, sample chapters and more.

www.silverlight.net/Showcase/
Hundreds of Silverlight applications and demos. Includes Developer Express (a layout-management tool for creating advanced web applications powered by Silverlight), Silverlight Virtual Earth Draw Tools, The Bragosphere, Silverlight.net (mouse-gesture recognition), Media Player, ABC Shop Online, Movie Trailers, Buddy Knavery (adventure game), Suboost (for adding tags and subtitles to videos), Fragmenti (puzzle game), AllMusic Streaming, Shidonni (virtual world for children), Dortik Solitaire Games, AgLite Effects (animation library), EyeRollerWEB (this widget displays a face whose eyes follow mouse moves around a web page), Silverlight Weather Widget and Knight's Tour Classic Chess Puzzle.

silverlight.net/community/gallerydetail.aspx?cat=6&sort=1
Dozens of Silverlight 2 samples, including Disco Floor (smooth animation), Color Picker Control, Binary Clock, Shiver Mario, DeepView Lite (to share your DeepZoom data), Spider Solitaire Game, Silverlight Klotski (sliding block puzzle), MinoPlayer, SilverLander: A Silverlight 2 Game, Silverlight Controls demo (DropDownList, TreeView, Popup Dialogs and more), Image Snipper, LINQ Food Finder, Syndication-RSS/Atom Feed Reader, Silverlight Control Demo Sample (24 Silverlight 2 controls), Silverlight Airline Sample, Silverlight Surface, Clock VB.NET and Clock C#, Bumble Beegger (2D Silverlight action game), Digital Clock, and Tetrislight.

www.vectorform.com/silverlight/
Vectorform Labs Silverlight Examples. Samples include Tile Navigation (allows user to select different videos using an animated GUI), Video Player (Microsoft Surface), and Breakout.

`blogs.msdn.com/tims/archive/2007/07/07/from-a-to-z-50-silverlight-applications.aspx`

Tim Sneath of Microsoft put together a list of 50 sample Silverlight applications from numerous websites, including 2D Physics Simulation, Grand Piano, Silverlight Mind Map, 3D Teapot Demo, Infragistics Controls Demo, Silverlight Pad, Amazon Search Visualization, JavaScript/.NET Chess, Silverlight Playground, AOL Social Mail Gadget, Laugh-o-Sphere, Silverlight Rocks, Binary Clock, LiveStation, SilverNibbles, Popfly, Telerik RadControls 3D Cube, Disco Dance Floor, Windows Journal-to-Silverlight Converter, Windows Vista Simulator, XamlWebPad, Gradient Animations, and Silverlight Chess Game Replay (playback of a few full games of chess).

`memorabilia.hardrock.com/`

Silverlight demo: Hard Rock Memorabilia. This site allows users to view all of the memorabilia items on display in the Hard Rock Cafes worldwide (clicking on an item will zoom it in).

`www.youtube.com/results?search_query=silverlight+2&search_type=&aq=f`

Silverlight 2 videos and demos on YouTube. The videos are anywhere from one to ten minutes long. Includes Silverlight 2 Control Unit Tests (demonstration from MIX conference), Deep Zoom, iTunes as Silverlight media Display (a Silverlight application that mimics iTunes), the Silverlight announcement by Bill Gates, Silverlight Talking, the Silverlight video for the MIX08 conference and more.

`sessions.visitmix.com/?selectedSearch=CT01`

Video: "Building Rich Internet Applications Using Microsoft Silverlight," with Mike Harsh and Joe Stegman at MIX08. The video, roughly 80 minutes long, discusses and demos Silverlight. Topics include an overview of Silverlight, getting started with Silverlight, building an application, networking, XML, controls, data binding, control templating, custom controls, custom layouts, OpenFile Dialog, HTML integration, Deep Zoom and more.

24.10 Wrap-Up

In this chapter, you learned how to use Silverlight (a cross-platform, cross-browser subset of .NET) to build Rich Internet Applications (RIAs) in Visual Studio 2008. We began by introducing the **WeatherViewer** application to portray some of the key features of a new Silverlight application. Since Silverlight is a subset of WPF, the two have similar programming environments with slight minor variations. The GUI of any Silverlight page is created by a XAML file in the project. All event handlers and other methods are created in the code-behind files.

With the **WeatherViewer** example, we showed that you can use web services, LINQ to XML and data binding to create a web application with desktoplike capabilities. We also showed you how to create a custom control by using a UserControl as a template. Unlike Styles and ControlTemplates, custom controls allow you to manipulate the control's functionality rather than just the visual aspects. The GUI and code-behind of a custom control are created as if it were a new page in the application.

We showed you our **FlickrViewer** example, which, similar to the **WeatherViewer**, shows how to use web services to enhance the capabilities of your application—specifically in this example with the Image element. This application combines a web service—provided by Flickr—and animations to create a photo-searching website.

You learned about Silverlight's deep zoom capabilities. You saw how to use Deep Zoom Composer and Silverlight to create your own deep zoom application. We showed how to implement zooming, panning, and subimage recognition in the code-behind file of your application using MultiScaleImage and MultiScaleSubImage.

Silverlight supports audio and video playback using the MediaElement. This class supports embedding Windows media format files into the application. We introduced our **VideoSelector** application to show how to program MediaElements in your application. The example also showed the VideoBrush being applied to the Fill of a Rectangle (applicable to any graphics object) to display the video within the graphic.

We introduced the concept of isolated storage, which allows the application to store user-specific data on the client machine or on the server. These files are stored in a virtual file system and can be used to save state information. In the next chapter, you'll learn how to build dynamic data structures that can grow or shrink at execution time.

25

Data Structures

Much that I bound,
I could not free;
Much that I freed
returned to me.
—Lee Wilson Dodd

"Will you walk a little
faster?" said a whiting
to a snail,
"There's a porpoise close
behind us, and he's treading
on my tail."
—Lewis Carroll

There is always room at the
top.
—Daniel Webster

Push on—keep moving.
—Thomas Morton

I think that I shall never see
A poem lovely as a tree.
—Joyce Kilmer

OBJECTIVES

In this chapter you'll learn:

- To form linked data structures using references, self-referential classes and recursion.

- How boxing and unboxing enable simple-type values to be used where **object**s are expected in a program.

- To create and manipulate dynamic data structures, such as linked lists, queues, stacks and binary trees.

- Various important applications of linked data structures.

- To create reusable data structures with classes, inheritance and composition.

Outline

25.1 Introduction
25.2 Simple-Type `structs`, Boxing and Unboxing
25.3 Self-Referential Classes
25.4 Linked Lists
25.5 Stacks
25.6 Queues
25.7 Trees
    25.7.1 Binary Search Tree of Integer Values
    25.7.2 Binary Search Tree of `IComparable` Objects
25.8 Wrap-Up

25.1 Introduction

This chapter continues our four-chapter treatment of data structures. Most of the *data structures* that we have studied thus far have had fixed sizes, such as one- and two-dimensional arrays. Previously, we also introduced the dynamically resizable `List<T>` collection (Chapter 9). This chapter enhances our discussion of *dynamic data structures* that grow and shrink at execution time. Linked lists are collections of data items "lined up in a row" or "chained together"—users can make insertions and deletions anywhere in a linked list. Stacks are important in compilers and operating systems; insertions and deletions are made at only one end—its *top*. Queues represent waiting lines; insertions are made at the back (also referred to as the *tail*) of a queue, and deletions are made from the front (also referred to as the *head*) of a queue. *Binary trees* facilitate high-speed searching and sorting of data, efficient elimination of duplicate data items, representation of file-system directories and compilation of expressions into machine language. These data structures have many other interesting applications as well.

We'll discuss each of these major types of data structures and implement programs that create and manipulate them. We use classes, inheritance and composition to create and package these data structures for reusability and maintainability. In Chapter 26, we introduce generics, which allow you to declare data structures that can be automatically adapted to contain data of any type. In Chapter 27, we discuss C#'s predefined classes that implement various data structures.

25.2 Simple-Type `structs`, Boxing and Unboxing

The data structures we discuss in this chapter store `object` references. However, as you'll soon see, we are able to store both simple- and reference-type values in these data structures. This section discusses the mechanisms that enable simple-type values to be manipulated as objects.

Simple-Type *structs*
Each simple type (Appendix B, Simple Types) has a corresponding *struct* in namespace `System` that declares the simple type. These structs are called `Boolean`, `Byte`, `SByte`, `Char`,

Decimal, Double, Single, Int32, UInt32, Int64, UInt64, Int16 and UInt16. Types declared with keyword struct are implicitly value types.

Simple types are actually aliases for their corresponding structs, so a variable of a simple type can be declared using either the keyword for that simple type or the struct name—e.g., int and Int32 are interchangeable. The methods related to a simple type are located in the corresponding struct (e.g., method Parse, which converts a string to an int value, is located in struct Int32). Refer to the documentation for the corresponding struct type to see the methods available for manipulating values of that type.

Boxing and Unboxing Conversions

All simple-type structs inherit from class *ValueType* in namespace System. Class ValueType inherits from class object. Thus, any simple-type value can be assigned to an object variable; this is referred to as a *boxing conversion* and enables simple types to be used anywhere objects are expected. In a boxing conversion, the simple-type value is copied into an object so that the simple-type value can be manipulated as an object. Boxing conversions can be performed either explicitly or implicitly as shown in the following statements:

```
int i = 5; // create an int value
object object1 = ( object ) i; // explicitly box the int value
object object2 = i; // implicitly box the int value
```

After executing the preceding code, both object1 and object2 refer to two different objects that contain a copy of the integer value in int variable i.

An *unboxing conversion* can be used to explicitly convert an object reference to a simple value, as shown in the following statement:

```
int int1 = ( int ) object1; // explicitly unbox the int value
```

Explicitly attempting to unbox an object reference that does not refer to the correct simple value type causes an *InvalidCastException*.

In Chapter 26, Generics, and Chapter 27, Collections, we discuss C#'s generics and generic collections. As you'll see, generics eliminate the overhead of boxing and unboxing conversions by enabling us to create and use collections of specific value types.

25.3 Self-Referential Classes

A *self-referential class* contains a reference member that refers to an object of the same class type. For example, the class declaration in Fig. 25.1 defines the shell of a self-referential class named Node. This type has two properties—integer Data and Node reference Next. Next references an object of type Node, an object of the same type as the one being declared here—hence, the term "self-referential class." Next is referred to as a *link* (i.e., Next can be used to "tie" an object of type Node to another object of the same type).

Self-referential objects can be linked together to form useful data structures, such as lists, queues, stacks and trees. Figure 25.2 illustrates two self-referential objects linked together to form a linked list. A backslash (representing a null reference) is placed in the link member of the second self-referential object to indicate that the link does not refer to another object. The backslash is for illustration purposes; it does not correspond to the backslash character in C#. A null link normally indicates the end of a data structure.

```
 1    // Fig. 25.1: Fig26_01.cs
 2    // Self-referential Node class declaration.
 3    class Node
 4    {
 5       public int Data { get; set; } // store integer data
 6       public Node Next { get; set; } // store reference to next Node
 7
 8       public Node( int dataValue )
 9       {
10          // constructor body
11       } // end constructor
12    } // end class node
```

Fig. 25.1 | Self-referential Node class declaration.

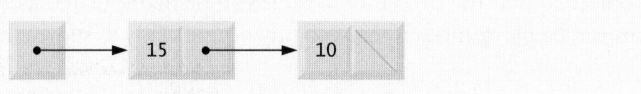

Fig. 25.2 | Self-referential class objects linked together.

 Common Programming Error 25.1

Not setting the link in the last node of a list to null is a logic error.

Creating and maintaining dynamic data structures requires ***dynamic memory alloca-tion***—a program's ability to obtain more memory space at execution time to hold new nodes and to release space no longer needed. As you learned in Section 10.9, C# programs do not explicitly release dynamically allocated memory—rather, the CLR performs automatic garbage collection.

The new operator is essential to dynamic memory allocation. Operator new takes as an operand the type of the object being dynamically allocated and returns a reference to an object of that type. For example, the statement

```
Node nodeToAdd = new Node( 10 );
```

allocates the appropriate amount of memory to store a Node and stores a reference to this object in nodeToAdd. If no memory is available, new throws an OutOfMemoryException. The constructor argument 10 specifies the Node object's data.

The following sections discuss lists, stacks, queues and trees. These data structures are created and maintained with dynamic memory allocation and self-referential classes.

 Good Programming Practice 25.1

When creating a large number of objects, test for an OutOfMemoryException. Perform appropriate error processing if the requested memory is not allocated.

25.4 Linked Lists

A *linked list* is a linear collection (i.e., a sequence) of self-referential class objects, called *nodes*, connected by reference links—hence, the term "linked" list. A program accesses a linked list via a reference to the first node of the list. Each subsequent node is accessed via the link-reference member stored in the previous node. By convention, the link reference in the last node of a list is set to null to mark the end of the list. Data is stored in a linked list dynamically—that is, each node is created as necessary. A node can contain data of any type, including references to objects of other classes. Stacks and queues are also linear data structures—in fact, they are constrained versions of linked lists. Trees are nonlinear data structures.

Lists of data can be stored in arrays, but linked lists provide several advantages. A linked list is appropriate when the number of data elements to be represented in the data structure is unpredictable. Unlike a linked list, the size of a conventional C# array cannot be altered, because the array size is fixed at creation time. Conventional arrays can become full, but linked lists become full only when the system has insufficient memory to satisfy dynamic memory allocation requests.

Performance Tip 25.1
An array can be declared to contain more elements than the number of items expected, possibly wasting memory. Linked lists provide better memory utilization in these situations, because they can grow and shrink at execution time.

Performance Tip 25.2
After locating the insertion point for a new item in a sorted linked list, inserting an element in the list is fast—only two references have to be modified. All existing nodes remain at their current locations in memory.

Programmers can maintain linked lists in sorted order simply by inserting each new element at the proper point in the list (locating the proper insertion point does take time). They do not need to move existing list elements.

Performance Tip 25.3
The elements of an array are stored contiguously in memory to allow immediate access to any array element—the address of any element can be calculated directly from its index. Linked lists do not afford such immediate access to their elements—an element can be accessed only by traversing the list from the front.

Normally linked-list nodes are not stored contiguously in memory. Rather, the nodes are logically contiguous. Figure 25.3 illustrates a linked list with several nodes.

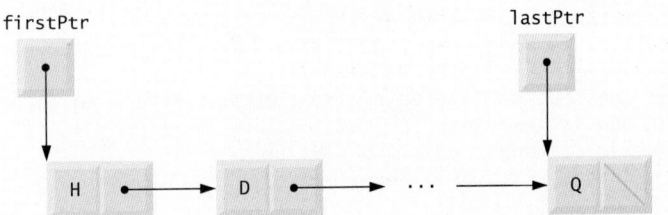

Fig. 25.3 | Linked list graphical representation.

Performance Tip 25.4

Using linked data structures and dynamic memory allocation (instead of arrays) for data structures that grow and shrink at execution time can save memory. Keep in mind, however, that reference links occupy space, and dynamic memory allocation incurs the overhead of method calls.

Linked-List Implementation

The program of Figs. 25.4 and 25.5 uses an object of class List to manipulate a list of miscellaneous object types. The Main method of class ListTest (Fig. 25.5) creates a list of objects, inserts objects at the beginning of the list using List method InsertAtFront, inserts objects at the end of the list using List method InsertAtBack, deletes objects from the front of the list using List method RemoveFromFront and deletes objects from the end of the list using List method RemoveFromBack. After each insertion and deletion operation, the program invokes List method Display to output the current list contents. If an attempt is made to remove an item from an empty list, an EmptyListException occurs. A detailed discussion of the program follows.

Performance Tip 25.5

Insertion and deletion in a sorted array can be time consuming—all the elements following the inserted or deleted element must be shifted appropriately.

The program consists of four classes—ListNode (Fig. 25.4, lines 8–30), List (lines 33–147), EmptyListException (lines 150–172) and ListTest (Fig. 25.5). The classes in Fig. 25.4 create a linked-list library (defined in namespace LinkedListLibrary) that can be reused throughout this chapter. You should place the code of Fig. 25.4 in its own class library project, as we described in Section 10.14.

```
1   // Fig. 25.4: LinkedListLibrary.cs
2   // ListNode, List and EmptyListException class declarations.
3   using System;
4
5   namespace LinkedListLibrary
6   {
7      // class to represent one node in a list
8      class ListNode
9      {
10        // automatic read-only property Data
11        public object Data { get; private set; }
12
13        // automatic property Next
14        public ListNode Next { get; set; }
15
16        // constructor to create ListNode that refers to dataValue
17        // and is last node in list
18        public ListNode( object dataValue )
19           : this( dataValue, null )
20        {
21        } // end default constructor
```

Fig. 25.4 | ListNode, List and EmptyListException class declarations. (Part 1 of 4.)

```
22
23          // constructor to create ListNode that refers to dataValue
24          // and refers to next ListNode in List
25          public ListNode( object dataValue, ListNode nextNode )
26          {
27             Data = dataValue;
28             Next = nextNode;
29          } // end constructor
30       } // end class ListNode
31
32       // class List declaration
33       public class List
34       {
35          private ListNode firstNode;
36          private ListNode lastNode;
37          private string name; // string like "list" to display
38
39          // construct empty List with specified name
40          public List( string listName )
41          {
42             name = listName;
43             firstNode = lastNode = null;
44          } // end constructor
45
46          // construct empty List with "list" as its name
47          public List()
48             : this( "list" )
49          {
50          } // end default constructor
51
52          // Insert object at front of List. If List is empty,
53          // firstNode and lastNode will refer to same object.
54          // Otherwise, firstNode refers to new node.
55          public void InsertAtFront( object insertItem )
56          {
57             if ( IsEmpty() )
58                firstNode = lastNode = new ListNode( insertItem );
59             else
60                firstNode = new ListNode( insertItem, firstNode );
61          } // end method InsertAtFront
62
63          // Insert object at end of List. If List is empty,
64          // firstNode and lastNode will refer to same object.
65          // Otherwise, lastNode's Next property refers to new node.
66          public void InsertAtBack( object insertItem )
67          {
68             if ( IsEmpty() )
69                firstNode = lastNode = new ListNode( insertItem );
70             else
71                lastNode = lastNode.Next = new ListNode( insertItem );
72          } // end method InsertAtBack
73
```

Fig. 25.4 | ListNode, List and EmptyListException class declarations. (Part 2 of 4.)

```
74      // remove first node from List
75      public object RemoveFromFront()
76      {
77          if ( IsEmpty() )
78              throw new EmptyListException( name );
79
80          object removeItem = firstNode.Data; // retrieve data
81
82          // reset firstNode and lastNode references
83          if ( firstNode == lastNode )
84              firstNode = lastNode = null;
85          else
86              firstNode = firstNode.Next;
87
88          return removeItem; // return removed data
89      } // end method RemoveFromFront
90
91      // remove last node from List
92      public object RemoveFromBack()
93      {
94          if ( IsEmpty() )
95              throw new EmptyListException( name );
96
97          object removeItem = lastNode.Data; // retrieve data
98
99          // reset firstNode and lastNode references
100         if ( firstNode == lastNode )
101             firstNode = lastNode = null;
102         else
103         {
104             ListNode current = firstNode;
105
106             // loop while current node is not lastNode
107             while ( current.Next != lastNode )
108                 current = current.Next; // move to next node
109
110             // current is new lastNode
111             lastNode = current;
112             current.Next = null;
113         } // end else
114
115         return removeItem; // return removed data
116     } // end method RemoveFromBack
117
118     // return true if List is empty
119     public bool IsEmpty()
120     {
121         return firstNode == null;
122     } // end method IsEmpty
123
124     // output List contents
125     public void Display()
126     {
```

Fig. 25.4 | ListNode, List and EmptyListException class declarations. (Part 3 of 4.)

```
127            if ( IsEmpty() )
128            {
129               Console.WriteLine( "Empty " + name );
130            } // end if
131            else
132            {
133               Console.Write( "The " + name + " is: " );
134
135               ListNode current = firstNode;
136
137               // output current node data while not at end of list
138               while ( current != null )
139               {
140                  Console.Write( current.Data + " " );
141                  current = current.Next;
142               } // end while
143
144               Console.WriteLine( "\n" );
145            } // end else
146         } // end method Display
147      } // end class List
148
149      // class EmptyListException declaration
150      public class EmptyListException : Exception
151      {
152         // parameterless constructor
153         public EmptyListException()
154            : base( "The list is empty" )
155         {
156            // empty constructor
157         } // end EmptyListException constructor
158
159         // one-parameter constructor
160         public EmptyListException( string name )
161            : base( "The " + name + " is empty" )
162         {
163            // empty constructor
164         } // end EmptyListException constructor
165
166         // two-parameter constructor
167         public EmptyListException( string exception, Exception inner )
168            : base( exception, inner )
169         {
170            // empty constructor
171         } // end EmptyListException constructor
172      } // end class EmptyListException
173   } // end namespace LinkedListLibrary
```

Fig. 25.4 | ListNode, List and EmptyListException class declarations. (Part 4 of 4.)

Encapsulated in each List object is a linked list of ListNode objects. Class ListNode (Fig. 25.4, lines 8–30) contains two properties—Data and Next. Data can refer to any object. [*Note:* Typically, a data structure will contain data of only one type, or data of any type derived from one base type.] In this example, we use data of various types derived from object to demonstrate that our List class can store data of any type. Next stores a reference to the next ListNode object in the linked list. The ListNode constructors (lines 18–21 and 25–29) enable us to initialize a ListNode that will be placed at the end of a List or before a specific ListNode in a List, respectively. A List accesses the ListNode member variables via properties Next (line 14) and Data (line 11), respectively.

Class List (lines 33–147) contains private instance variables firstNode (a reference to the first ListNode in a List) and lastNode (a reference to the last ListNode in a List). The constructors (lines 40–44 and 47–50) initialize both references to null and enable us to specify the List's name for output purposes. InsertAtFront (lines 55–61), InsertAt-Back (lines 66–72), RemoveFromFront (lines 75–89) and RemoveFromBack (lines 92–116) are the primary methods of class List. Method IsEmpty (lines 119–122) is a *predicate method* that determines whether the list is empty (i.e., the reference to the first node of the list is null). Predicate methods typically test a condition and do not modify the object on which they are called. If the list is empty, method IsEmpty returns true; otherwise, it returns false. Method Display (lines 125–146) displays the list's contents. A detailed discussion of class List's methods follows Fig. 25.5.

Class EmptyListException (lines 150–172) defines an exception class that we use to indicate illegal operations on an empty List.

Class ListTest (Fig. 25.5) uses the linked-list library to create and manipulate a linked list. [*Note:* In the project containing Fig. 25.5, you must add a reference to the class library containing the classes in Fig. 25.4. If you use our existing example, you may need to update this reference.] Line 11 creates a new List object and assigns it to variable list. Lines 14–17 create data to add to the list. Lines 20–27 use List insertion methods to insert these values and use List method Display to output the contents of list after each insertion. Note that the values of the simple-type variables are implicitly boxed in lines 20, 22 and 24 where object references are expected. The code inside the try block (lines 33–50) removes objects via List deletion methods, outputs each removed object and outputs list after every deletion. If there is an attempt to remove an object from an empty list, the catch at lines 51–54 catches the EmptyListException and displays an error message.

```
 1   // Fig. 25.5: ListTest.cs
 2   // Testing class List.
 3   using System;
 4   using LinkedListLibrary;
 5
 6   // class to test List class functionality
 7   class ListTest
 8   {
 9      public static void Main( string[] args )
10      {
11         List list = new List(); // create List container
12
13         // create data to store in List
14         bool aBoolean = true;
15         char aCharacter = '$';
16         int anInteger = 34567;
17         string aString = "hello";
```

Fig. 25.5 | Testing class List. (Part 1 of 3.)

```
18
19          // use List insert methods
20          list.InsertAtFront( aBoolean );
21          list.Display();
22          list.InsertAtFront( aCharacter );
23          list.Display();
24          list.InsertAtBack( anInteger );
25          list.Display();
26          list.InsertAtBack( aString );
27          list.Display();
28
29          // use List remove methods
30          object removedObject;
31
32          // remove data from list and display after each removal
33          try
34          {
35             removedObject = list.RemoveFromFront();
36             Console.WriteLine( removedObject + " removed" );
37             list.Display();
38
39             removedObject = list.RemoveFromFront();
40             Console.WriteLine( removedObject + " removed" );
41             list.Display();
42
43             removedObject = list.RemoveFromBack();
44             Console.WriteLine( removedObject + " removed" );
45             list.Display();
46
47             removedObject = list.RemoveFromBack();
48             Console.WriteLine( removedObject + " removed" );
49             list.Display();
50          } // end try
51          catch ( EmptyListException emptyListException )
52          {
53             Console.Error.WriteLine( "\n" + emptyListException );
54          } // end catch
55       } // end Main
56    } // end class ListTest
```

```
The list is: True

The list is: $ True

The list is: $ True 34567

The list is: $ True 34567 hello

$ removed
The list is: True 34567 hello

True removed
The list is: 34567 hello
```

Fig. 25.5 | Testing class List. (Part 2 of 3.)

```
hello removed
The list is: 34567

34567 removed
Empty list
```

Fig. 25.5 | Testing class List. (Part 3 of 3.)

Method InsertAtFront

Over the next several pages, we discuss each of the methods of class List in detail. Method InsertAtFront (Fig. 25.4, lines 55–61) places a new node at the front of the list. The method consists of three steps:

1. Call IsEmpty to determine whether the list is empty (line 57).

2. If the list is empty, set both firstNode and lastNode to refer to a new ListNode initialized with insertItem (line 58). The ListNode constructor at lines 18–21 of Fig. 25.4 calls the ListNode constructor at lines 25–29, which sets property data to refer to the object passed as the first argument and sets the next property's reference to null.

3. If the list is not empty, the new node is "linked" into the list by setting firstNode to refer to a new ListNode object initialized with insertItem and firstNode (line 60). When the ListNode constructor (lines 25–29) executes, it sets properties Data to refer to the object passed as the first argument and performs the insertion by setting the Next reference to the ListNode passed as the second argument.

In Fig. 25.6, part (a) shows a list and a new node during the InsertAtFront operation and before the new node is linked into the list. The dashed lines and arrows in part (b) illustrate *Step 3* of the InsertAtFront operation, which enables the node containing 12 to become the new list front.

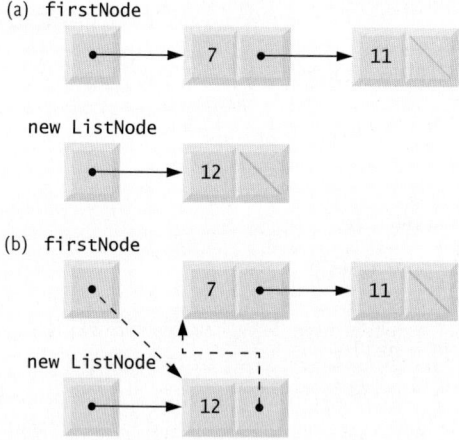

Fig. 25.6 | InsertAtFront operation.

Method **InsertAtBack**

Method InsertAtBack (Fig. 25.4, lines 85–91) places a new node at the back of the list. The method consists of three steps:

1. Call IsEmpty to determine whether the list is empty (line 68).

2. If the list is empty, set both firstNode and lastNode to refer to a new ListNode initialized with insertItem (line 68). The ListNode constructor at lines 18–21 calls the ListNode constructor at lines 25–29, which sets property Data to refer to the object passed as the first argument and sets the Next reference to null.

3. If the list is not empty, link the new node into the list by setting lastNode and lastNode.Next to refer to a new ListNode object initialized with insertItem (line 71). When the ListNode constructor (lines 18–21) executes, it calls the constructor at lines 25–29, which sets property Data to refer to the object passed as an argument and sets the Next reference to null.

In Fig. 25.7, part (a) shows a list and a new node during the InsertAtBack operation; before the new node has been linked into the list. The dashed lines and arrows in part (b) illustrate *Step 3* of method InsertAtBack, which enables a new node to be added to the end of a list that is not empty.

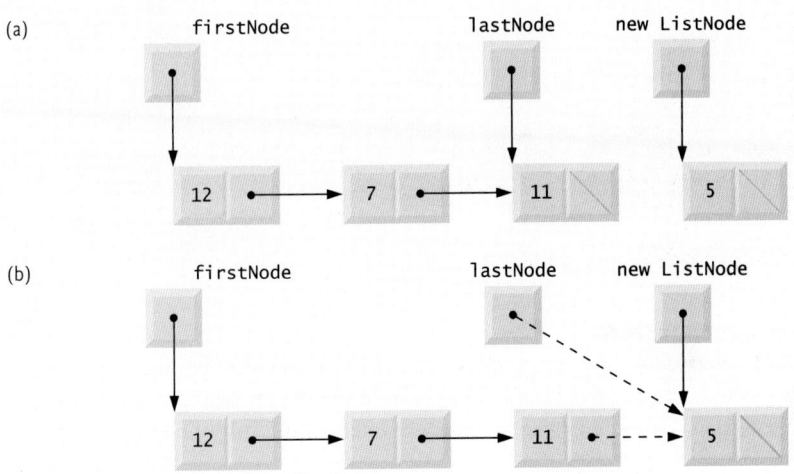

Fig. 25.7 | InsertAtBack operation.

Method **RemoveFromFront**

Method RemoveFromFront (Fig. 25.4, lines 75–89) removes the front node of the list and returns a reference to the removed data. The method throws an EmptyListException (line 78) if the programmer tries to remove a node from an empty list. Otherwise, the method returns a reference to the removed data. After determining that a List is not empty, the method consists of four steps to remove the first node:

1. Assign firstNode.Data (the data being removed from the list) to variable removeItem (line 80).

2. If the objects to which firstNode and lastNode refer are the same object, the list has only one element, so the method sets firstNode and lastNode to null (line 84) to remove the node from the list (leaving the list empty).

3. If the list has more than one node, the method leaves reference lastNode as is and assigns firstNode.Next to firstNode (line 86). Thus, firstNode references the node that was previously the second node in the List.

4. Return the removeItem reference (line 88).

In Fig. 25.8, part (a) illustrates a list before a removal operation. The dashed lines and arrows in part (b) show the reference manipulations.

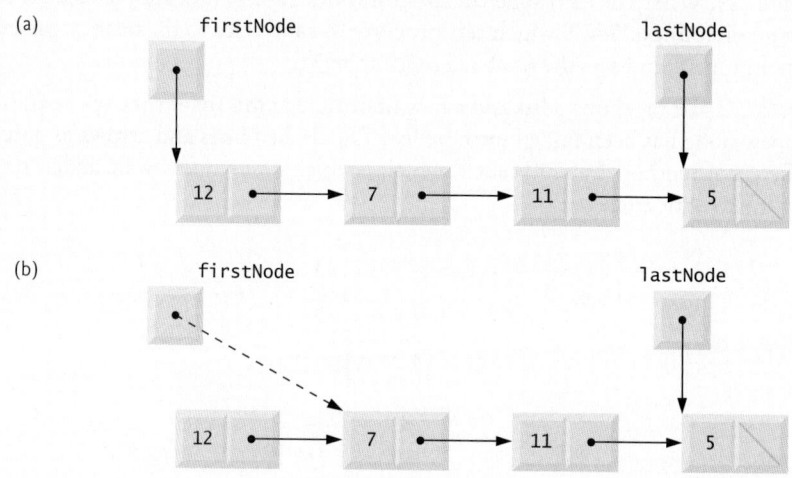

Fig. 25.8 | RemoveFromFront operation.

Method RemoveFromBack
Method RemoveFromBack (Fig. 25.4, lines 92–116) removes the last node of a list and returns a reference to the removed data. The method throws an EmptyListException (line 95) if the program attempts to remove a node from an empty list. The method consists of several steps:

1. Assign lastNode.Data (the data being removed from the list) to variable removeItem (line 97).

2. If firstNode and lastNode refer to the same object (line 100), the list has only one element, so the method sets firstNode and lastNode to null (line 101) to remove that node from the list (leaving the list empty).

3. If the list has more than one node, create ListNode variable current and assign it firstNode (line 104).

4. Now "walk the list" with current until it references the node before the last node. The while loop (lines 107–112) assigns current.Next to current as long as current.Next is not equal to lastNode.

5. After locating the second-to-last node, assign current to lastNode (line 111) to update which node is last in the list.

6. Set current.Next to null (line 112) to remove the last node from the list and terminate the list at the current node.

7. Return the removeItem reference (line 115).

In Fig. 25.9, part (a) illustrates a list before a removal operation. The dashed lines and arrows in part (b) show the reference manipulations.

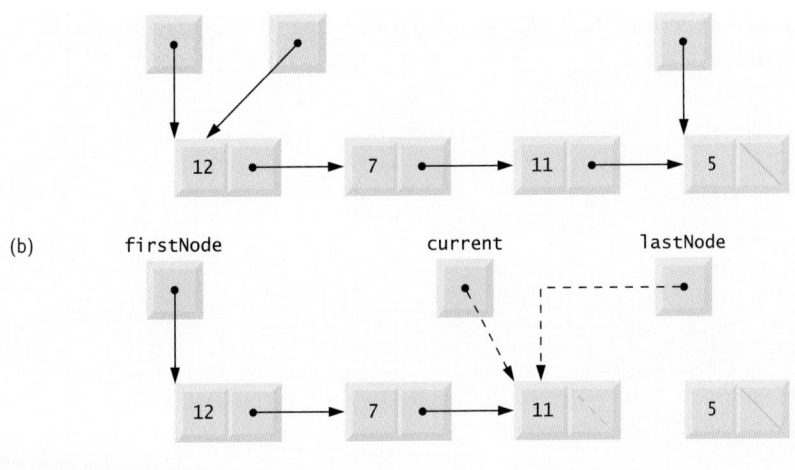

Fig. 25.9 | RemoveFromBack operation.

Method Display

Method Display (Fig. 25.4, lines 125–146) first determines whether the list is empty (line 127). If so, Display displays a string consisting of the string "Empty " and the list's name, then returns control to the calling method. Otherwise, Display outputs the data in the list. The method writes a string consisting of the string "The ", the list's name and the string " is: ". Then line 135 creates ListNode variable current and initializes it with firstNode. While current is not null, there are more items in the list. Therefore, the method displays current.Data (line 140), then assigns current.Next to current (line 141) to move to the next node in the list.

Linear and Circular Singly Linked and Doubly Linked Lists

The kind of linked list we have been discussing is a *singly linked list*—it begins with a reference to the first node, and each node contains a reference to the next node "in sequence." This list terminates with a node whose reference member has the value null. A singly linked list may be traversed in only one direction.

A *circular, singly linked list* (Fig. 25.10) begins with a reference to the first node, and each node contains a reference to the next node. The "last node" does not contain a null reference; rather, the reference in the last node points back to the first node, thus closing the "circle."

A *doubly linked list* (Fig. 25.11) allows traversals both forward and backward. Such a list is often implemented with two "start references"—one that refers to the first element of the list to allow front-to-back traversal of the list and one that refers to the last element to allow back-to-front traversal. Each node has both a forward reference to the next node in the list and a backward reference to the previous node. If your list contains an alphabetized telephone directory, for example, a search for someone whose name begins with a letter near the front of the alphabet might begin from the front of the list. A search for someone whose name begins with a letter near the end of the alphabet might begin from the back.

In a *circular, doubly linked list* (Fig. 25.12), the forward reference of the last node refers to the first node, and the backward reference of the first node refers to the last node, thus closing the "circle."

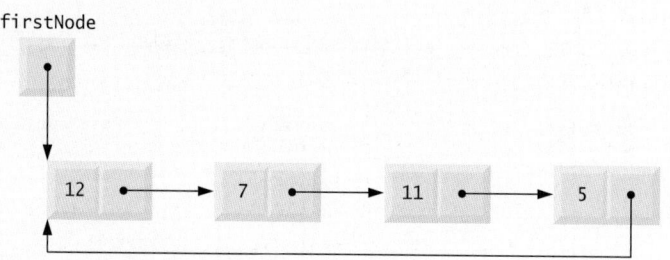

Fig. 25.10 | Circular, singly linked list.

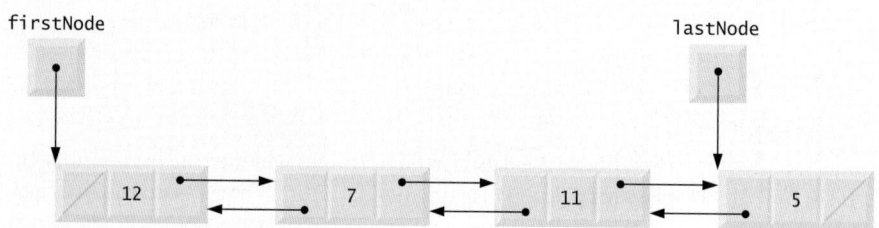

Fig. 25.11 | Doubly linked list.

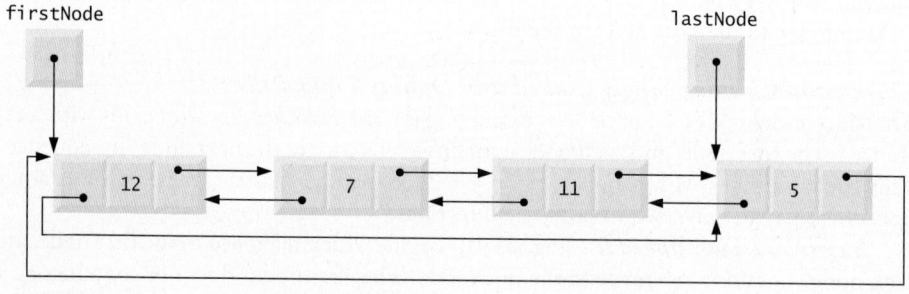

Fig. 25.12 | Circular, doubly linked list.

25.5 Stacks

A *stack* is a constrained version of a linked list—it receives new nodes and releases nodes only at the top. For this reason, a stack is referred to as a *last-in, first-out (LIFO)* data structure.

The primary operations to manipulate a stack are *push* and *pop*. Operation push adds a new node to the top of the stack. Operation pop removes a node from the top of the stack and returns the data item from the popped node.

Stacks have many interesting applications. For example, when a program calls a method, the called method must know how to return to its caller, so the return address is pushed onto the method-call stack. If a series of method calls occurs, the successive return values are pushed onto the stack in last-in, first-out order so that each method can return to its caller. Stacks support recursive method calls in the same manner that they do conventional nonrecursive method calls.

The System.Collections namespace contains class Stack for implementing and manipulating stacks that can grow and shrink during program execution. Chapters 26–27 discuss class System.Collections.Stack.

In our next example, we take advantage of the close relationship between lists and stacks to implement a stack class by reusing a list class. We demonstrate two different forms of reusability. First, we implement the stack class by inheriting from class List of Fig. 25.4. Then we implement an identically performing stack class through composition by including a List object as a private member of a stack class.

Stack Class That Inherits from List

The program of Figs. 25.13 and 25.14 creates a stack class by inheriting from class List of Fig. 25.4 (line 8). We want the stack to have methods Push, Pop, IsEmpty and Display. Essentially, these are the methods InsertAtFront, RemoveFromFront, IsEmpty and Display of class List. Of course, class List contains other methods (such as InsertAtBack and RemoveFromBack) that we would rather not make accessible through the public interface of the stack. It is important to remember that all methods in the public interface of class List are also public methods of the derived class StackInheritance (Fig. 25.13).

```
1   // Fig. 25.13: StackInheritanceLibrary.cs
2   // Implementing a stack by inheriting from class List.
3   using LinkedListLibrary;
4
5   namespace StackInheritanceLibrary
6   {
7      // class StackInheritance inherits class List's capabilities
8      public class StackInheritance : List
9      {
10        // pass name "stack" to List constructor
11        public StackInheritance()
12           : base( "stack" )
13        {
14        } // end constructor
15
```

Fig. 25.13 | Implementing a stack by inheriting from class List. (Part 1 of 2.)

```
16          // place dataValue at top of stack by inserting
17          // dataValue at front of linked list
18          public void Push( object dataValue )
19          {
20              InsertAtFront( dataValue );
21          } // end method Push
22
23          // remove item from top of stack by removing
24          // item at front of linked list
25          public object Pop()
26          {
27              return RemoveFromFront();
28          } // end method Pop
29      } // end class StackInheritance
30  } // end namespace StackInheritanceLibrary
```

Fig. 25.13 | Implementing a stack by inheriting from class List. (Part 2 of 2.)

The implementation of each StackInheritance method calls the appropriate List method—method Push calls InsertAtFront, method Pop calls RemoveFromFront. Class StackInheritance does not define methods IsEmpty and Display, because StackInheritance inherits these methods from class List into StackInheritance's public interface. Note that class StackInheritance uses namespace LinkedListLibrary (Fig. 25.4); thus, the class library that defines StackInheritance must have a reference to the LinkedList-Library class library.

StackInheritanceTest's Main method (Fig. 25.14) uses class StackInheritance to create a stack of objects called stack (line 12). Lines 15–18 define four values that will be pushed onto the stack and popped off it. The program pushes onto the stack (lines 21, 23, 25 and 27) a bool containing true, a char containing '$', an int containing 34567 and a string containing "hello". An infinite while loop (lines 33–38) pops the elements from the stack. When the stack is empty, method Pop throws an EmptyListException, and the program displays the exception's stack trace, which shows the program-execution stack at the time the exception occurred. The program uses method Display (inherited by StackInheritance from class List) to output the contents of the stack after each operation. Note that class StackInheritanceTest uses namespace LinkedListLibrary (Fig. 25.4) and namespace StackInheritanceLibrary (Fig. 25.13); thus, the solution for class StackInheritanceTest must have references to both class libraries.

```
1   // Fig. 25.14: StackInheritanceTest.cs
2   // Testing class StackInheritance.
3   using System;
4   using StackInheritanceLibrary;
5   using LinkedListLibrary;
6
7   // demonstrate functionality of class StackInheritance
8   class StackInheritanceTest
9   {
```

Fig. 25.14 | Testing class StackInheritance. (Part 1 of 3.)

```
10      public static void Main( string[] args )
11      {
12          StackInheritance stack = new StackInheritance();
13
14          // create objects to store in the stack
15          bool aBoolean = true;
16          char aCharacter = '$';
17          int anInteger = 34567;
18          string aString = "hello";
19
20          // use method Push to add items to stack
21          stack.Push( aBoolean );
22          stack.Display();
23          stack.Push( aCharacter );
24          stack.Display();
25          stack.Push( anInteger );
26          stack.Display();
27          stack.Push( aString );
28          stack.Display();
29
30          // remove items from stack
31          try
32          {
33              while ( true )
34              {
35                  object removedObject = stack.Pop();
36                  Console.WriteLine( removedObject + " popped" );
37                  stack.Display();
38              } // end while
39          } // end try
40          catch ( EmptyListException emptyListException )
41          {
42              // if exception occurs, write stack trace
43              Console.Error.WriteLine( emptyListException.StackTrace );
44          } // end catch
45      } // end Main
46  } // end class StackInheritanceTest
```

```
The stack is: True

The stack is: $ True

The stack is: 34567 $ True

The stack is: hello 34567 $ True

hello popped
The stack is: 34567 $ True

34567 popped
The stack is: $ True
```

Fig. 25.14 | Testing class StackInheritance. (Part 2 of 3.)

```
$ popped
The stack is: True

True popped
Empty stack
    at LinkedListLibrary.List.RemoveFromFront()
        in C:\examples\ch26\Fig26_04\LinkedListLibrary\
        LinkedListLibrary\LinkedListLibrary.cs:line 78
    at StackInheritanceLibrary.StackInheritance.Pop()
        in C:\examples\ch26\Fig26_13\StackInheritanceLibrary\
        StackInheritanceLibrary\StackInheritance.cs:line 27
    at StackInheritanceTest.Main(String[] args)
        in C:\examples\ch26\Fig26_14\StackInheritanceTest\
        StackInheritanceTest\StackInheritanceTest.cs:line 35
```

Fig. 25.14 | Testing class StackInheritance. (Part 3 of 3.)

Stack Class That Contains a Reference to a List

Another way to implement a stack class is by reusing a list class through composition. The class in Fig. 25.15 uses a private object of class List (line 10) in the declaration of class StackComposition. Composition enables us to hide the methods of class List that should not be in our stack's public interface by providing public interface methods only to the required List methods. This class implements each stack method by delegating its work to an appropriate List method. StackComposition's methods call List methods InsertAtFront, RemoveFromFront, IsEmpty and Display. In this example, we do not show class StackCompositionTest, because the only difference in this example is that we change the name of the stack class from StackInheritance to StackComposition. If you execute the application from the code on the CD that accompanies this book, you'll see that the output is identical.

```
1   // Fig. 25.15: StackCompositionLibrary.cs
2   // StackComposition declaration with composed List object.
3   using LinkedListLibrary;
4
5   namespace StackCompositionLibrary
6   {
7       // class StackComposition encapsulates List's capabilities
8       public class StackComposition
9       {
10          private List stack;
11
12          // construct empty stack
13          public StackComposition()
14          {
15              stack = new List( "stack" );
16          } // end constructor
17
18          // add object to stack
19          public void Push( object dataValue )
20          {
```

Fig. 25.15 | StackComposition class encapsulates functionality of class List. (Part 1 of 2.)

```
21              stack.InsertAtFront( dataValue );
22          } // end method Push
23
24          // remove object from stack
25          public object Pop()
26          {
27              return stack.RemoveFromFront();
28          } // end method Pop
29
30          // determine whether stack is empty
31          public bool IsEmpty()
32          {
33              return stack.IsEmpty();
34          } // end method IsEmpty
35
36          // output stack contents
37          public void Display()
38          {
39              stack.Display();
40          } // end method Display
41      } // end class StackComposition
42  } // end namespace StackCompositionLibrary
```

Fig. 25.15 | StackComposition class encapsulates functionality of class List. (Part 2 of 2.)

25.6 Queues

Another commonly used data structure is the queue. A queue is similar to a checkout line in a supermarket—the cashier services the person at the beginning of the line first. Other customers enter the line only at the end and wait for service. Queue nodes are removed only from the head (or front) of the queue and are inserted only at the tail (or end). For this reason, a queue is a *first-in, first-out* (*FIFO*) data structure. The insert and remove operations are known as *enqueue* and *dequeue*.

Queues have many uses in computer systems. Computers with only a single processor can service only one application at a time. Each application requiring processor time is placed in a queue. The application at the front of the queue is the next to receive service. Each application gradually advances to the front as the applications before it receive service.

Queues are also used to support *print spooling*. For example, a single printer might be shared by all users of a network. Many users can send print jobs to the printer, even when the printer is already busy. These print jobs are placed in a queue until the printer becomes available. A program called a *spooler* manages the queue to ensure that as each print job completes, the next one is sent to the printer.

Information packets also wait in queues in computer networks. Each time a packet arrives at a network node, it must be routed to the next node along the path to the packet's final destination. The routing node routes one packet at a time, so additional packets are enqueued until the router can route them.

A file server in a computer network handles file-access requests from many clients throughout the network. Servers have a limited capacity to service requests from clients. When that capacity is exceeded, client requests wait in queues.

Queue Class That Inherits from List

The program of Figs. 25.16 and 25.17 creates a queue class by inheriting from a list class. We want the QueueInheritance class (Fig. 25.16) to have methods Enqueue, Dequeue, IsEmpty and Display. Essentially, these are the methods InsertAtBack, RemoveFrom-Front, IsEmpty and Display of class List. Of course, the list class contains other methods (such as InsertAtFront and RemoveFromBack) that we would rather not make accessible through the public interface to the queue class. Remember that all methods in the public interface of the List class are also public methods of the derived class QueueInheritance.

The implementation of each QueueInheritance method calls the appropriate List method—method Enqueue calls InsertAtBack and method Dequeue calls RemoveFrom-Front. Calls to IsEmpty and Display invoke the base-class versions that were inherited from class List into QueueInheritance's public interface. Note that class QueueInheritance uses namespace LinkedListLibrary (Fig. 25.4); thus, the class library for QueueInheritance must have a reference to the LinkedListLibrary class library.

Class QueueInheritanceTest's Main method (Fig. 25.17) creates a QueueInheritance object called queue. Lines 15–18 define four values that will be enqueued and dequeued. The program enqueues (lines 21, 23, 25 and 27) a bool containing true, a char containing '$', an int containing 34567 and a string containing "hello". Note that

```
 1    // Fig. 25.16: QueueInheritanceLibrary.cs
 2    // Implementing a queue by inheriting from class List.
 3    using LinkedListLibrary;
 4
 5    namespace QueueInheritanceLibrary
 6    {
 7       // class QueueInheritance inherits List's capabilities
 8       public class QueueInheritance : List
 9       {
10          // pass name "queue" to List constructor
11          public QueueInheritance()
12             : base( "queue" )
13          {
14          } // end constructor
15
16          // place dataValue at end of queue by inserting
17          // dataValue at end of linked list
18          public void Enqueue( object dataValue )
19          {
20             InsertAtBack( dataValue );
21          } // end method Enqueue
22
23          // remove item from front of queue by removing
24          // item at front of linked list
25          public object Dequeue()
26          {
27             return RemoveFromFront();
28          } // end method Dequeue
29       } // end class QueueInheritance
30    } // end namespace QueueInheritanceLibrary
```

Fig. 25.16 | Implementing a queue by inheriting from class List.

class QueueInheritanceTest uses namespace LinkedListLibrary and namespace QueueInheritanceLibrary; thus, the solution for class StackInheritanceTest must have references to both class libraries.

An infinite while loop (lines 36–41) dequeues the elements from the queue in FIFO order. When there are no objects left to dequeue, method Dequeue throws an EmptyListException, and the program displays the exception's stack trace, which shows the program-execution stack at the time the exception occurred. The program uses method Display (inherited from class List) to output the contents of the queue after each operation. Note that class QueueInheritanceTest uses namespace LinkedListLibrary (Fig. 25.4) and namespace QueueInheritanceLibrary (Fig. 25.16); thus, the solution for class QueueInheritanceTest must have references to both class libraries.

```
1   // Fig. 25.17: QueueTest.cs
2   // Testing class QueueInheritance.
3   using System;
4   using QueueInheritanceLibrary;
5   using LinkedListLibrary;
6
7   // demonstrate functionality of class QueueInheritance
8   class QueueTest
9   {
10      public static void Main( string[] args )
11      {
12         QueueInheritance queue = new QueueInheritance();
13
14         // create objects to store in the queue
15         bool aBoolean = true;
16         char aCharacter = '$';
17         int anInteger = 34567;
18         string aString = "hello";
19
20         // use method Enqueue to add items to queue
21         queue.Enqueue( aBoolean );
22         queue.Display();
23         queue.Enqueue( aCharacter );
24         queue.Display();
25         queue.Enqueue( anInteger );
26         queue.Display();
27         queue.Enqueue( aString );
28         queue.Display();
29
30         // use method Dequeue to remove items from queue
31         object removedObject = null;
32
33         // remove items from queue
34         try
35         {
36            while ( true )
37            {
38               removedObject = queue.Dequeue();
```

Fig. 25.17 | Testing class QueueInheritance. (Part 1 of 2.)

```
39              Console.WriteLine( removedObject + " dequeued" );
40              queue.Display();
41          } // end while
42      } // end try
43      catch ( EmptyListException emptyListException )
44      {
45          // if exception occurs, write stack trace
46          Console.Error.WriteLine( emptyListException.StackTrace );
47      } // end catch
48  } // end Main
49 } // end class QueueTest
```

```
The queue is: True

The queue is: True $

The queue is: True $ 34567

The queue is: True $ 34567 hello

True dequeued
The queue is: $ 34567 hello

$ dequeued
The queue is: 34567 hello

34567 dequeued
The queue is: hello

hello dequeued
Empty queue
   at LinkedListLibrary.List.RemoveFromFront()
      in C:\examples\ch26\Fig26_04\LinkedListLibrary\
      LinkedListLibrary\LinkedListLibrary.cs:line 78
   at QueueInheritanceLibrary.QueueInheritance.Dequeue()
      in C:\examples\ch26\Fig26_16\QueueInheritanceLibrary\
      QueueInheritanceLibrary\QueueInheritance.cs:line 28
   at QueueTest.Main(String[] args)
      in C:\examples\ch26\Fig26_17\QueueTest\
      QueueTest\QueueTest.cs:line 38
```

Fig. 25.17 | Testing class `QueueInheritance`. (Part 2 of 2.)

25.7 Trees

Linked lists, stacks and queues are *linear data structures* (i.e., *sequences*). A *tree* is a non-linear, two-dimensional data structure with special properties. Tree nodes contain two or more links.

Basic Terminology

With *binary trees* (Fig. 25.18), each tree node contains two links (none, one or both of which may be null). The *root node* is the first node in a tree. Each link in the root node refers to a *child*. The *left child* is the first node in the *left subtree*, and the *right child* is the first node in the *right subtree*. The children of a specific node are called *siblings*. A

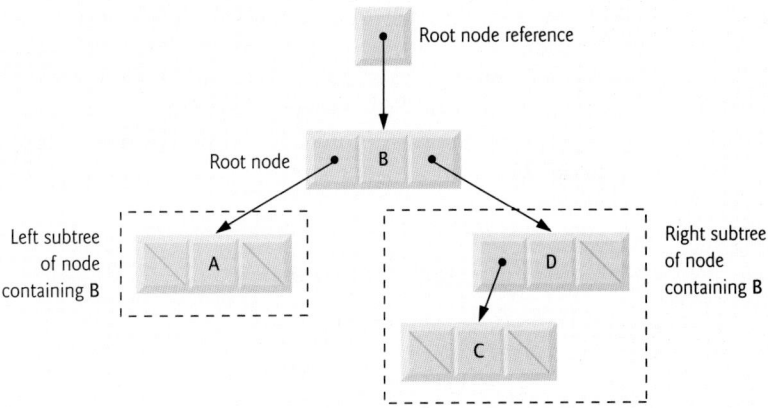

Fig. 25.18 | Binary-tree graphical representation.

node with no children is called a *leaf node*. Computer scientists normally draw trees from the root node down—exactly the opposite of the way most trees grow in nature.

 Common Programming Error 25.2

Not setting to null the links in leaf nodes of a tree is a common logic error.

Binary Search Trees

In our binary-tree example, we create a special binary tree called a *binary search tree*. A binary search tree (with no duplicate node values) has the characteristic that the values in any left subtree are less than the value in the subtree's *parent node*, and the values in any right subtree are greater than the value in the subtree's parent node. Figure 25.19 illustrates a binary search tree with 9 integer values. Note that the shape of the binary search tree that corresponds to a set of data can depend on the order in which the values are inserted into the tree.

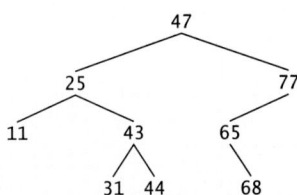

Fig. 25.19 | Binary search tree containing 9 values.

25.7.1 Binary Search Tree of Integer Values

The application of Figs. 25.20 and 25.21 creates a binary search tree of integers and traverses it (i.e., walks through all its nodes) in three ways—using recursive *inorder, preorder* and *postorder* traversals. The program generates 10 random numbers and inserts each into the tree. Figure 25.20 defines class `Tree` in namespace `BinaryTreeLibrary` for reuse purposes. Figure 25.21 defines class `TreeTest` to demonstrate class `Tree`'s functionality. Method `Main` of class `TreeTest` instantiates an empty `Tree` object, then randomly generates 10 integers and inserts each value in the binary tree by calling `Tree` method `Insert-Node`. The program then performs preorder, inorder and postorder traversals of the tree. We'll discuss these traversals shortly.

```
1   // Fig. 25.20: BinaryTreeLibrary.cs
2   // Declaration of class TreeNode and class Tree.
3   using System;
4
5   namespace BinaryTreeLibrary
6   {
7      // class TreeNode declaration
8      class TreeNode
9      {
10        // automatic property LeftNode
11        public TreeNode LeftNode { get; set; }
12
13        // automatic property Data
14        public int Data { get; set; }
15
16        // automatic property RightNode
17        public TreeNode RightNode { get; set; }
18
19        // initialize Data and make this a leaf node
20        public TreeNode( int nodeData )
21        {
22           Data = nodeData;
23           LeftNode = RightNode = null; // node has no children
24        } // end constructor
25
26        // insert TreeNode into Tree that contains nodes;
27        // ignore duplicate values
28        public void Insert( int insertValue )
29        {
30           if ( insertValue < Data ) // insert in left subtree
31           {
32              // insert new TreeNode
33              if ( LeftNode == null )
34                 LeftNode = new TreeNode( insertValue );
35              else // continue traversing left subtree
36                 LeftNode.Insert( insertValue );
37           } // end if
38           else if ( insertValue > Data ) // insert in right subtree
39           {
40              // insert new TreeNode
41              if ( RightNode == null )
42                 RightNode = new TreeNode( insertValue );
```

Fig. 25.20 | Declaration of class `TreeNode` and class `Tree`. (Part 1 of 3.)

```
43                else // continue traversing right subtree
44                   RightNode.Insert( insertValue );
45             } // end else if
46          } // end method Insert
47       } // end class TreeNode
48
49       // class Tree declaration
50       public class Tree
51       {
52          private TreeNode root;
53
54          // construct an empty Tree of integers
55          public Tree()
56          {
57             root = null;
58          } // end constructor
59
60          // Insert a new node in the binary search tree.
61          // If the root node is null, create the root node here.
62          // Otherwise, call the insert method of class TreeNode.
63          public void InsertNode( int insertValue )
64          {
65             if ( root == null )
66                root = new TreeNode( insertValue );
67             else
68                root.Insert( insertValue );
69          } // end method InsertNode
70
71          // begin preorder traversal
72          public void PreorderTraversal()
73          {
74             PreorderHelper( root );
75          } // end method PreorderTraversal
76
77          // recursive method to perform preorder traversal
78          private void PreorderHelper( TreeNode node )
79          {
80             if ( node != null )
81             {
82                // output node Data
83                Console.Write( node.Data + " " );
84
85                // traverse left subtree
86                PreorderHelper( node.LeftNode );
87
88                // traverse right subtree
89                PreorderHelper( node.RightNode );
90             } // end if
91          } // end method PreorderHelper
92
93          // begin inorder traversal
94          public void InorderTraversal()
95          {
```

Fig. 25.20 | Declaration of class TreeNode and class Tree. (Part 2 of 3.)

```
 96                    InorderHelper( root );
 97             } // end method InorderTraversal
 98
 99             // recursive method to perform inorder traversal
100             private void InorderHelper( TreeNode node )
101             {
102                 if ( node != null )
103                 {
104                     // traverse left subtree
105                     InorderHelper( node.LeftNode );
106
107                     // output node data
108                     Console.Write( node.Data + " " );
109
110                     // traverse right subtree
111                     InorderHelper( node.RightNode );
112                 } // end if
113             } // end method InorderHelper
114
115             // begin postorder traversal
116             public void PostorderTraversal()
117             {
118                 PostorderHelper( root );
119             } // end method PostorderTraversal
120
121             // recursive method to perform postorder traversal
122             private void PostorderHelper( TreeNode node )
123             {
124                 if ( node != null )
125                 {
126                     // traverse left subtree
127                     PostorderHelper( node.LeftNode );
128
129                     // traverse right subtree
130                     PostorderHelper( node.RightNode );
131
132                     // output node Data
133                     Console.Write( node.Data + " " );
134                 } // end if
135             } // end method PostorderHelper
136      } // end class Tree
137 } // end namespace BinaryTreeLibrary
```

Fig. 25.20 | Declaration of class TreeNode and class Tree. (Part 3 of 3.)

Class TreeNode (lines 8–47 of Fig. 25.20) is a self-referential class containing three properties—LeftNode and RightNode of type TreeNode and Data of type int. Initially, every TreeNode is a leaf node, so the constructor (lines 20–24) initializes references left-Node and rightNode to null. We discuss TreeNode method Insert (lines 28–46) shortly.

Class Tree (lines 50–136 of Fig. 25.20) manipulates objects of class TreeNode. Class Tree has as private data root (line 52)—a reference to the root node of the tree. The class contains public method InsertNode (lines 63–69) to insert a new node in the tree and public methods PreorderTraversal (lines 72–75), InorderTraversal (lines 94–97) and

```
 1   // Fig. 25.21: TreeTest.cs
 2   // Testing class Tree with a binary tree.
 3   using System;
 4   using BinaryTreeLibrary;
 5
 6   // class TreeTest declaration
 7   public class TreeTest
 8   {
 9      // test class Tree
10      public static void Main( string[] args )
11      {
12         Tree tree = new Tree();
13         int insertValue;
14
15         Console.WriteLine( "Inserting values: " );
16         Random random = new Random();
17
18         // insert 10 random integers from 0-99 in tree
19         for ( int i = 1; i <= 10; i++ )
20         {
21            insertValue = random.Next( 100 );
22            Console.Write( insertValue + " " );
23
24            tree.InsertNode( insertValue );
25         } // end for
26
27         // perform preorder traversal of tree
28         Console.WriteLine( "\n\nPreorder traversal" );
29         tree.PreorderTraversal();
30
31         // perform inorder traversal of tree
32         Console.WriteLine( "\n\nInorder traversal" );
33         tree.InorderTraversal();
34
35         // perform postorder traversal of tree
36         Console.WriteLine( "\n\nPostorder traversal" );
37         tree.PostorderTraversal();
38         Console.WriteLine();
39      } // end Main
40   } // end class TreeTest
```

```
Inserting values:
39 69 94 47 50 72 55 41 97 73

Preorder traversal
39 69 47 41 50 55 94 72 73 97

Inorder traversal
39 41 47 50 55 69 72 73 94 97

Postorder traversal
41 55 50 47 73 72 97 94 69 39
```

Fig. 25.21 | Testing class Tree with a binary tree.

PostorderTraversal (lines 116–119) to begin traversals of the tree. Each of these methods calls a separate recursive utility method to perform the traversal operations on the internal representation of the tree. The Tree constructor (lines 55–58) initializes root to null to indicate that the tree initially is empty.

Tree method InsertNode (lines 63–69) first determines whether the tree is empty. If so, line 66 allocates a new TreeNode, initializes the node with the integer being inserted in the tree and assigns the new node to root. If the tree is not empty, InsertNode calls TreeNode method Insert (lines 28–46), which recursively determines the location for the new node in the tree and inserts the node at that location. *A node can be inserted only as a leaf node in a binary search tree.*

The TreeNode method Insert compares the value to insert with the data value in the root node. If the insert value is less than the root-node data, the program determines whether the left subtree is empty (line 33). If so, line 34 allocates a new TreeNode, initializes it with the integer being inserted and assigns the new node to reference leftNode. Otherwise, line 36 recursively calls Insert for the left subtree to insert the value into the left subtree. If the insert value is greater than the root-node data, the program determines whether the right subtree is empty (line 41). If so, line 42 allocates a new TreeNode, initializes it with the integer being inserted and assigns the new node to reference rightNode. Otherwise, line 44 recursively calls Insert for the right subtree to insert the value in the right subtree.

Methods InorderTraversal, PreorderTraversal and PostorderTraversal call helper methods InorderHelper (lines 100–113), PreorderHelper (lines 78–91) and PostorderHelper (lines 122–135), respectively, to traverse the tree and display the node values. The purpose of the helper methods in class Tree is to allow the programmer to start a traversal without needing to obtain a reference to the root node first, then call the recursive method with that reference. Methods InorderTraversal, PreorderTraversal and PostorderTraversal simply take private variable root and pass it to the appropriate helper method to initiate a traversal of the tree. For the following discussion, we use the binary search tree shown in Fig. 25.22.

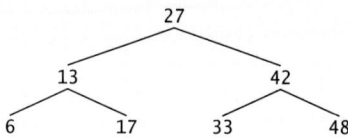

Fig. 25.22 | Binary search tree.

Inorder Traversal Algorithm
Method InorderHelper (lines 100–113) defines the steps for an inorder traversal. Those steps are as follows:

1. If the argument is null, do not process the tree.
2. Traverse the left subtree with a call to InorderHelper (line 105).
3. Process the value in the node (line 108).
4. Traverse the right subtree with a call to InorderHelper (line 111).

The inorder traversal does not process the value in a node until the values in that node's left subtree are processed. The inorder traversal of the tree in Fig. 25.22 is

```
6 13 17 27 33 42 48
```

Note that the inorder traversal of a binary search tree displays the node values in ascending order. The process of creating a binary search tree actually sorts the data (when coupled with an inorder traversal)—thus, this process is called the *binary-tree sort*.

Preorder Traversal Algorithm

Method `PreorderHelper` (lines 78–91) defines the steps for a preorder traversal. Those steps are as follows:

1. If the argument is `null`, do not process the tree.
2. Process the value in the node (line 83).
3. Traverse the left subtree with a call to `PreorderHelper` (line 86).
4. Traverse the right subtree with a call to `PreorderHelper` (line 89).

The preorder traversal processes the value in each node as the node is visited. After processing the value in a given node, the preorder traversal processes the values in the left subtree, then the values in the right subtree. The preorder traversal of the tree in Fig. 25.22 is

```
27 13 6 17 42 33 48
```

Postorder Traversal Algorithm

Method `PostorderHelper` (lines 122–135) defines the steps for a postorder traversal. Those steps are as follows:

1. If the argument is `null`, do not process the tree.
2. Traverse the left subtree with a call to `PostorderHelper` (line 127).
3. Traverse the right subtree with a call to `PostorderHelper` (line 130).
4. Process the value in the node (line 133).

The postorder traversal processes the value in each node after the values of all that node's children are processed. The postorder traversal of the tree in Fig. 25.22 is

```
6 17 13 33 48 42 27
```

Duplicate Elimination

A binary search tree facilitates *duplicate elimination.* While building a tree, the insertion operation recognizes attempts to insert a duplicate value, because a duplicate follows the same "go left" or "go right" decisions on each comparison as the original value did. Thus, the insertion operation eventually compares the duplicate with a node containing the same value. At this point, the insertion operation might simply discard the duplicate value.

Searching a binary tree for a value that matches a key value is fast, especially for *tightly packed* binary trees. In a tightly packed binary tree, each level contains about twice as many elements as the previous level. Figure 25.22 is a tightly packed binary tree. A binary search tree with n elements has a minimum of $\log_2 n$ levels. Thus, at most $\log_2 n$ comparisons are required either to find a match or to determine that no match exists. Searching a (tightly packed) 1000-element binary search tree requires at most 10 comparisons, because

$2^{10} > 1000$. Searching a (tightly packed) 1,000,000-element binary search tree requires at most 20 comparisons, because $2^{20} > 1,000,000$.

25.7.2 Binary Search Tree of IComparable Objects

The binary-tree example in Section 25.7.1 works nicely when all the data is of type int. Suppose that you want to manipulate a binary tree of double values. You could rewrite the TreeNode and Tree classes with different names and customize the classes to manipulate double values. Similarly, for each data type you could create customized versions of classes TreeNode and Tree. This results in a proliferation of code, which can become difficult to manage and maintain.

Ideally, we would like to define the functionality of a binary tree once and reuse it for many data types. Languages like Java™ and C# provide polymorphic capabilities that enable all objects to be manipulated in a uniform manner. Using such capabilities enables us to design a more flexible data structure. The new version of C#, C# 2.0, provides these capabilities with generics (Chapter 26).

In our next example, we take advantage of C#'s polymorphic capabilities by implementing TreeNode and Tree classes that manipulate objects of any type that implements interface *IComparable* (namespace System). It is imperative that we be able to compare objects stored in a binary search, so we can determine the path to the insertion point of a new node. Classes that implement IComparable define method *CompareTo*, which compares the object that invokes the method with the object that the method receives as an argument. The method returns an int value less than zero if the calling object is less than the argument object, zero if the objects are equal and a positive value if the calling object is greater than the argument object. Also, both the calling and argument objects must be of the same data type; otherwise, the method throws an ArgumentException.

The program of Figs. 25.23 and 25.24 enhances the program from Section 25.7.1 to manipulate IComparable objects. One restriction on the new versions of classes TreeNode and Tree in Fig. 25.23 is that each Tree object can contain objects of only one data type (e.g., all strings or all doubles). If a program attempts to insert multiple data types in the same Tree object, ArgumentExceptions will occur. We modified only five lines of code in class TreeNode (lines 14, 20, 28, 30 and 38) and one line of code in class Tree (line 63) to enable processing of IComparable objects. With the exception of lines 30 and 38, all other changes simply replaced the type int with the type IComparable. Lines 30 and 38 previously used the < and > operators to compare the value being inserted with the value in a given node. These lines now compare IComparable objects via the interface's CompareTo method, then test the method's return value to determine whether it is less than zero (the calling object is less than the argument object) or greater than zero (the calling object is greater than the argument object), respectively. [*Note:* If this class were written using generics, the type of data, int or IComparable could be replaced at compile time by any other type that implements the necessary operators and methods.]

```
1   // Fig. 25.23: BinaryTreeLibrary2.cs
2   // Declaration of class TreeNode and class Tree.
3   using System;
```

Fig. 25.23 | Declaration of class TreeNode and class Tree. (Part 1 of 4.)

```
4
5    namespace BinaryTreeLibrary2
6    {
7       // class TreeNode declaration
8       class TreeNode
9       {
10          // automatic property LeftNode
11          public TreeNode LeftNode { get; set; }
12
13          // automatic property Data
14          public IComparable Data { get; set; }
15
16          // automatic property RightNode
17          public TreeNode RightNode { get; set; }
18
19          // initialize Data and make this a leaf node
20          public TreeNode( IComparable nodeData )
21          {
22             Data = nodeData;
23             LeftNode = RightNode = null; // node has no children
24          } // end constructor
25
26          // insert TreeNode into Tree that contains nodes;
27          // ignore duplicate values
28          public void Insert( IComparable insertValue )
29          {
30             if ( insertValue.CompareTo(Data) < 0 ) // insert in left subtree
31             {
32                // insert new TreeNode
33                if ( LeftNode == null )
34                   LeftNode = new TreeNode( insertValue );
35                else // continue traversing left subtree
36                   LeftNode.Insert( insertValue );
37             } // end if
38             else if ( insertValue.CompareTo( Data ) > 0 ) // insert in right
39             {
40                // insert new TreeNode
41                if ( RightNode == null )
42                   RightNode = new TreeNode( insertValue );
43                else // continue traversing right subtree
44                   RightNode.Insert( insertValue );
45             } // end else if
46          } // end method Insert
47       } // end class TreeNode
48
49       // class Tree declaration
50       public class Tree
51       {
52          private TreeNode root;
53
54          // construct an empty Tree of integers
55          public Tree()
56          {
```

Fig. 25.23 | Declaration of class TreeNode and class Tree. (Part 2 of 4.)

```
57              root = null;
58          } // end constructor
59
60          // Insert a new node in the binary search tree.
61          // If the root node is null, create the root node here.
62          // Otherwise, call the insert method of class TreeNode.
63          public void InsertNode( IComparable insertValue )
64          {
65              if ( root == null )
66                  root = new TreeNode( insertValue );
67              else
68                  root.Insert( insertValue );
69          } // end method InsertNode
70
71          // begin preorder traversal
72          public void PreorderTraversal()
73          {
74              PreorderHelper( root );
75          } // end method PreorderTraversal
76
77          // recursive method to perform preorder traversal
78          private void PreorderHelper( TreeNode node )
79          {
80              if ( node != null )
81              {
82                  // output node Data
83                  Console.Write( node.Data + " " );
84
85                  // traverse left subtree
86                  PreorderHelper( node.LeftNode );
87
88                  // traverse right subtree
89                  PreorderHelper( node.RightNode );
90              } // end if
91          } // end method PreorderHelper
92
93          // begin inorder traversal
94          public void InorderTraversal()
95          {
96              InorderHelper( root );
97          } // end method InorderTraversal
98
99          // recursive method to perform inorder traversal
100         private void InorderHelper( TreeNode node )
101         {
102             if ( node != null )
103             {
104                 // traverse left subtree
105                 InorderHelper( node.LeftNode );
106
107                 // output node data
108                 Console.Write( node.Data + " " );
109
```

Fig. 25.23 | Declaration of class TreeNode and class Tree. (Part 3 of 4.)

```
110          // traverse right subtree
111          InorderHelper( node.RightNode );
112       } // end if
113    } // end method InorderHelper
114
115    // begin postorder traversal
116    public void PostorderTraversal()
117    {
118       PostorderHelper( root );
119    } // end method PostorderTraversal
120
121    // recursive method to perform postorder traversal
122    private void PostorderHelper( TreeNode node )
123    {
124       if ( node != null )
125       {
126          // traverse left subtree
127          PostorderHelper( node.LeftNode );
128
129          // traverse right subtree
130          PostorderHelper( node.RightNode );
131
132          // output node Data
133          Console.Write( node.Data + " " );
134       } // end if
135    } // end method PostorderHelper
136  } // end class Tree
137 } // end namespace BinaryTreeLibrary
```

Fig. 25.23 | Declaration of class `TreeNode` and class `Tree`. (Part 4 of 4.)

Class `TreeTest` (Fig. 25.24) creates three `Tree` objects to store `int`, `double` and `string` values, all of which the .NET Framework defines as `IComparable` types. The program populates the trees with the values in arrays `intArray` (line 12), `doubleArray` (line 13) and `stringArray` (lines 14–15), respectively.

```
1  // Fig. 25.24: TreeTest.cs
2  // Testing class Tree with IComparable objects.
3  using System;
4  using BinaryTreeLibrary2;
5
6  // class TreeTest declaration
7  public class TreeTest
8  {
9     // test class Tree
10    public static void Main( string[] args )
11    {
12       int[] intArray = { 8, 2, 4, 3, 1, 7, 5, 6 };
13       double[] doubleArray = { 8.8, 2.2, 4.4, 3.3, 1.1, 7.7, 5.5, 6.6 };
14       string[] stringArray = { "eight", "two", "four",
15          "three", "one", "seven", "five", "six" };
```

Fig. 25.24 | Testing class `Tree` with `IComparable` objects. (Part 1 of 3.)

```
16
17        // create int Tree
18        Tree intTree = new Tree();
19        populateTree( intArray, intTree, "intTree" );
20        traverseTree( intTree, "intTree" );
21
22        // create double Tree
23        Tree doubleTree = new Tree();
24        populateTree( doubleArray, doubleTree, "doubleTree" );
25        traverseTree( doubleTree, "doubleTree" );
26
27        // create string Tree
28        Tree stringTree = new Tree();
29        populateTree( stringArray, stringTree, "stringTree" );
30        traverseTree( stringTree, "stringTree" );
31     } // end Main
32
33     // populate Tree with array elements
34     private static void populateTree( Array array, Tree tree, string name )
35     {
36        Console.WriteLine( "\n\n\nInserting into " + name + ":" );
37
38        foreach ( IComparable data in array )
39        {
40           Console.Write( data + " " );
41           tree.InsertNode( data );
42        } // end foreach
43     } // end method populateTree
44
45     // insert perform traversals
46     private static void traverseTree( Tree tree, string treeType )
47     {
48        // perform preorder traversal of tree
49        Console.WriteLine( "\n\nPreorder traversal of " + treeType );
50        tree.PreorderTraversal();
51
52        // perform inorder traversal of tree
53        Console.WriteLine( "\n\nInorder traversal of " + treeType );
54        tree.InorderTraversal();
55
56        // perform postorder traversal of tree
57        Console.WriteLine( "\n\nPostorder traversal of " + treeType );
58        tree.PostorderTraversal();
59     } // end method traverseTree
60  } // end class TreeTest
```

```
Inserting into intTree:
8 2 4 3 1 7 5 6

Preorder traversal of intTree
8 2 1 4 3 7 5 6
```

Fig. 25.24 | Testing class Tree with IComparable objects. (Part 2 of 3.)

```
Inorder traversal of intTree
1 2 3 4 5 6 7 8

Postorder traversal of intTree
1 3 6 5 7 4 2 8


Inserting into doubleTree:
8.8 2.2 4.4 3.3 1.1 7.7 5.5 6.6

Preorder traversal of doubleTree
8.8 2.2 1.1 4.4 3.3 7.7 5.5 6.6

Inorder traversal of doubleTree
1.1 2.2 3.3 4.4 5.5 6.6 7.7 8.8

Postorder traversal of doubleTree
1.1 3.3 6.6 5.5 7.7 4.4 2.2 8.8


Inserting into stringTree:
eight two four three one seven five six

Preorder traversal of stringTree
eight two four five three one seven six

Inorder traversal of stringTree
eight five four one seven six three two

Postorder traversal of stringTree
five six seven one three four two eight
```

Fig. 25.24 | Testing class `Tree` with `IComparable` objects. (Part 3 of 3.)

Method `PopulateTree` (lines 34–43) receives as arguments an `Array` containing the initializer values for the `Tree`, a `Tree` in which the array elements will be placed and a `string` representing the `Tree` name, then inserts each `Array` element into the `Tree`. Method `TraverseTree` (lines 46–59) receives as arguments a `Tree` and a `string` representing the `Tree` name, then outputs the preorder, inorder and postorder traversals of the `Tree`. Note that the inorder traversal of each `Tree` outputs the data in sorted order regardless of the data type stored in the `Tree`. Our polymorphic implementation of class `Tree` invokes the appropriate data type's `CompareTo` method to determine the path to each value's insertion point by using the standard binary-search-tree insertion rules. Also, notice that the `Tree` of `string`s appears in alphabetical order.

25.8 Wrap-Up

In this chapter, you learned that simple types are value-type `struct`s but can still be used anywhere `object`s are expected in a program due to boxing and unboxing conversions. You learned that linked lists are collections of data items that are "linked together in a chain." You also learned that a program can perform insertions and deletions anywhere in a linked list (though our implementation performed insertions and deletions only at the ends of the list). We demonstrated that the stack and queue data structures are constrained versions of lists. For stacks, you saw that insertions and deletions are made only at the top—so stacks are known as last-in, first out (LIFO) data structures. For queues, which represent waiting lines, you saw that insertions are made at the tail and deletions are made from the head—so queues are known as first-in, first out (FIFO) data structures. We also presented the binary tree data structure. You saw a binary search tree that facilitated high-speed searching and sorting of data and efficient duplicate elimination. In the next chapter, we introduce generics, which allow you to declare a family of classes and methods that implement the same functionality on any type.

26

Generics

…our special individuality, as distinguished from our generic humanity.
—Oliver Wendell Holmes, Sr.

Every man of genius sees the world at a different angle from his fellows.
—Havelock Ellis

Born under one law, to another bound.
—Lord Brooke

OBJECTIVES

In this chapter you'll learn:

- To create generic methods that perform identical tasks on arguments of different types.

- To create a generic `Stack` class that can be used to store objects of any class or interface type.

- To understand how to overload generic methods with nongeneric methods or with other generic methods.

- To understand the `new()` constraint of a type parameter.

- To apply multiple constraints to a type parameter.

Outline

26.1 Introduction
26.2 Motivation for Generic Methods
26.3 Generic-Method Implementation
26.4 Type Constraints
26.5 Overloading Generic Methods
26.6 Generic Classes
26.7 Wrap-Up

26.1 Introduction

In Chapter 25, we presented data structures that stored and manipulated object references. This chapter continues our multi-chapter discussion on data structures. You could store any object in our data structures. One inconvenient aspect of storing object references occurs when retrieving them from a collection. An application normally needs to process specific types of objects. As a result, the object references obtained from a collection typically need to be downcast to an appropriate type to allow the application to process the objects correctly. In addition, data of value types (e.g., int and double) must be boxed to be manipulated with object references, which increases the overhead of processing such data. Also, processing all data as type object limits the C# compiler's ability to perform type checking.

Though we can easily create data structures that manipulate any type of data as objects (as we did in Chapter 25), it would be nice if we could detect type mismatches at compile time—this is known as *compile-time type safety*. For example, if a Stack should store only int values, attempting to push a string onto that Stack should cause a compile-time error. Similarly, a Sort method should be able to compare elements that are all guaranteed to have the same type. If we create type-specific versions of class Stack class and method Sort, the C# compiler would certainly be able to ensure compile-time type safety. However, this would require that we create many copies of the same basic code.

This chapter discusses *generics*, which provide the means to create the general models mentioned above. *Generic methods* enable you to specify, with a single method declaration, a set of related methods. *Generic classes* enable you to specify, with a single class declaration, a set of related classes. Similarly, *generic interfaces* enable you to specify, with a single interface declaration, a set of related interfaces. Generics provide compile-time type safety. [*Note:* You can also implement generic structs and delegates. For more information, see the C# language specification.] So far in this book, we have used the generic types List (Chapter 9), Dictionary (Chapter 19) and Func<A,R> (Chapter 19).

We can write a generic method for sorting an array of objects, then invoke the generic method separately with an int array, a double array, a string array and so on, to sort each different type of array. The compiler performs *type checking* to ensure that the array passed to the sorting method contains only elements of the same type. We can write a single generic Stack class that manipulates a stack of objects, then instantiate Stack objects for a stack of ints, a stack of doubles, a stack of strings and so on. The compiler performs type checking to ensure that the Stack stores only elements of the same type.

This chapter presents examples of generic methods and generic classes. It also considers the relationships between generics and other C# features, such as overloading.

Chapter 27, Collections, discusses the .NET Framework's generic and nongeneric collections classes. A collection is a data structure that maintains a group of related objects or values. The .NET Framework collection classes use generics to allow you to specify the exact types of object that a particular collection will store.

26.2 Motivation for Generic Methods

Overloaded methods are often used to perform similar operations on different types of data. To understand the motivation for generic methods, let's begin with an example (Fig. 26.1) that contains three overloaded DisplayArray methods (lines 23–29, lines 32–38 and lines 41–47). These methods display the elements of an int array, a double array and a char array, respectively. Soon, we'll reimplement this program more concisely and elegantly using a single generic method.

```
 1   // Fig. 26.1: OverloadedMethods.cs
 2   // Using overloaded methods to display arrays of different types.
 3   using System;
 4
 5   class OverloadedMethods
 6   {
 7      static void Main( string[] args )
 8      {
 9         // create arrays of int, double and char
10         int[] intArray = { 1, 2, 3, 4, 5, 6 };
11         double[] doubleArray = { 1.1, 2.2, 3.3, 4.4, 5.5, 6.6, 7.7 };
12         char[] charArray = { 'H', 'E', 'L', 'L', 'O' };
13
14         Console.WriteLine( "Array intArray contains:" );
15         DisplayArray( intArray ); // pass an int array argument
16         Console.WriteLine( "Array doubleArray contains:" );
17         DisplayArray( doubleArray ); // pass a double array argument
18         Console.WriteLine( "Array charArray contains:" );
19         DisplayArray( charArray ); // pass a char array argument
20      } // end Main
21
22      // output int array
23      private static void DisplayArray( int[] inputArray )
24      {
25         foreach ( int element in inputArray )
26            Console.Write( element + " " );
27
28         Console.WriteLine( "\n" );
29      } // end method DisplayArray
30
31      // output double array
32      private static void DisplayArray( double[] inputArray )
33      {
34         foreach ( double element in inputArray )
35            Console.Write( element + " " );
36
```

Fig. 26.1 | Using overloaded methods to display arrays of different types. (Part 1 of 2.)

```
37            Console.WriteLine( "\n" );
38       } // end method DisplayArray
39
40       // output char array
41       private static void DisplayArray( char[] inputArray )
42       {
43          foreach ( char element in inputArray )
44             Console.Write( element + " " );
45
46          Console.WriteLine( "\n" );
47       } // end method DisplayArray
48    } // end class OverloadedMethods
```

```
Array intArray contains:
1 2 3 4 5 6

Array doubleArray contains:
1.1 2.2 3.3 4.4 5.5 6.6 7.7

Array charArray contains:
H E L L O
```

Fig. 26.1 | Using overloaded methods to display arrays of different types. (Part 2 of 2.)

The program begins by declaring and initializing three arrays—six-element int array intArray (line 10), seven-element double array doubleArray (line 11) and five-element char array charArray (line 12). Then, lines 14–19 output the arrays.

When the compiler encounters a method call, it attempts to locate a method declaration that has the same method name and parameters that match the argument types in the method call. In this example, each DisplayArray call exactly matches one of the Display-Array method declarations. For example, line 15 calls DisplayArray with intArray as its argument. At compile time, the compiler determines argument intArray's type (i.e., int[]), attempts to locate a method named DisplayArray that specifies a single int[] parameter (which it finds at lines 23–29) and sets up a call to that method. Similarly, when the compiler encounters the DisplayArray call at line 17, it determines argument double-Array's type (i.e., double[]), then attempts to locate a method named DisplayArray that specifies a single double[] parameter (which it finds at lines 32–38) and sets up a call to that method. Finally, when the compiler encounters the DisplayArray call at line 19, it determines argument charArray's type (i.e., char[]), then attempts to locate a method named DisplayArray that specifies a single char[] parameter (which it finds at lines 41–47) and sets up a call to that method.

Study each DisplayArray method. Note that the array element type (int, double or char) appears in two locations in each method—the method header (lines 23, 32 and 41) and the foreach statement header (lines 25, 34 and 43). If we replace the element types in each method with a generic name (such as T for "type") then all three methods would look like the one in Fig. 26.2. It appears that if we can replace the array element type in each of the three methods with a single "generic type parameter," then we should be able to declare one DisplayArray method that can display the elements of *any* array. The method in Fig. 26.2 will not compile, because its syntax is not correct. We declare a generic Display-Array method with the proper syntax in Fig. 26.3.

```
1    private static void DisplayArray( T[] inputArray )
2    {
3        foreach ( T element in inputArray )
4            Console.Write( element + " " );
5
6        Console.WriteLine( "\n" );
7    } // end method DisplayArray
```

Fig. 26.2 | `DisplayArray` method in which actual type names are replaced by convention with the generic name T.

26.3 Generic-Method Implementation

If the operations performed by several overloaded methods are identical for each argument type, the overloaded methods can be more compactly and conveniently coded using a generic method. You can write a single generic-method declaration that can be called at different times with arguments of different types. Based on the types of the arguments passed to the generic method, the compiler handles each method call appropriately.

Figure 26.3 reimplements the application of Fig. 26.1 using a generic `DisplayArray` method (lines 24–30). Note that the `DisplayArray` method calls in lines 16, 18 and 20 are identical to those of Fig. 26.1, the outputs of the two applications are identical and the code in Fig. 26.3 is 17 lines shorter than that in Fig. 26.1. As illustrated in Fig. 26.3, generics enable us to create and test our code once, then reuse it for many different types of data. This demonstrates the expressive power of generics.

Line 24 begins method `DisplayArray`'s declaration. All generic method declarations have a *type-parameter list* delimited by angle brackets (< T > in this example) that follows

```
1    // Fig. 26.3: GenericMethod.cs
2    // Using overloaded methods to display arrays of different types.
3    using System;
4    using System.Collections.Generic;
5
6    class GenericMethod
7    {
8        public static void Main( string[] args )
9        {
10           // create arrays of int, double and char
11           int[] intArray = { 1, 2, 3, 4, 5, 6 };
12           double[] doubleArray = { 1.1, 2.2, 3.3, 4.4, 5.5, 6.6, 7.7 };
13           char[] charArray = { 'H', 'E', 'L', 'L', 'O' };
14
15           Console.WriteLine( "Array intArray contains:" );
16           DisplayArray( intArray ); // pass an int array argument
17           Console.WriteLine( "Array doubleArray contains:" );
18           DisplayArray( doubleArray ); // pass a double array argument
19           Console.WriteLine( "Array charArray contains:" );
20           DisplayArray( charArray ); // pass a char array argument
21       } // end Main
22
```

Fig. 26.3 | Using overloaded methods to display arrays of different types. (Part 1 of 2.)

```
23        // output array of all types
24        private static void DisplayArray< T >( T[] inputArray )
25        {
26           foreach ( T element in inputArray )
27              Console.Write( element + " " );
28
29           Console.WriteLine( "\n" );
30        } // end method DisplayArray
31    } // end class GenericMethod
```

```
Array intArray contains:
1 2 3 4 5 6

Array doubleArray contains:
1.1 2.2 3.3 4.4 5.5 6.6 7.7

Array charArray contains:
H E L L O
```

Fig. 26.3 | Using overloaded methods to display arrays of different types. (Part 2 of 2.)

the method's name. Each type-parameter list contains one or more *type parameters,* separated by commas. A type parameter is an identifier that is used in place of actual type names. The type parameters can be used to declare the return type, the parameter types and the local variable types in a generic method declaration; the type parameters act as placeholders for *type arguments* that represent the types of data that will be passed to the generic method. A generic method's body is declared like that of any other method. Note that the type-parameter names throughout the method declaration must match those declared in the type-parameter list. For example, line 26 declares element in the foreach statement as type T, which matches the type parameter (T) declared in line 24. Also, a type parameter can be declared only once in the type-parameter list but can appear more than once in the method's parameter list. Type-parameter names need not be unique among different generic methods.

Common Programming Error 26.1

If you forget to include the type-parameter list when declaring a generic method, the compiler will not recognize the type-parameter names when they are encountered in the method. This results in compilation errors.

Method DisplayArray's type-parameter list (line 24) declares type parameter T as the placeholder for the array-element type that DisplayArray will output. Note that T appears in the parameter list as the array-element type (line 24). The foreach statement header (line 26) also uses T as the element type. These are the same two locations where the overloaded DisplayArray methods of Fig. 26.1 specified int, double or char as the element type. The remainder of DisplayArray is identical to the version presented in Fig. 26.1.

Good Programming Practice 26.1

It is recommended that type parameters be specified as individual capital letters. Typically, a type parameter that represents the type of an element in an array (or other collection) is named E for "element" or T for "type."

As in Fig. 26.1, the program of Fig. 26.3 begins by declaring and initializing six-element int array intArray (line 11), seven-element double array doubleArray (line 12) and five-element char array charArray (line 13). Then each array is output by calling DisplayArray (lines 16, 18 and 20)—once with argument intArray, once with argument doubleArray and once with argument charArray.

When the compiler encounters a method call such as line 16, it analyzes the set of methods (both nongeneric and generic) that might match the method call, looking for a method that best matches the call. If there are no matching methods, or if there is more than one best match, the compiler generates an error. If you have any uncertainty on which of your methods will be called, the complete details of method-call resolution can be found in Section 14.5.5.1 of the Ecma C# Language Specification

> www.ecma-international.org/publications/standards/Ecma-334.htm

or Section 7.4.3 of the Microsoft C# Language Specification 3.0

> msdn.microsoft.com/en-us/vcsharp/aa336809.aspx

In the case of line 16, the compiler determines that the best match occurs if the type parameter T in lines 24 and 26 of method DisplayArray's declaration is replaced with the type of the elements in the method call's argument intArray (i.e., int). Then, the compiler sets up a call to DisplayArray with the int as the *type argument* for the type parameter T. This is known as the *type-inferencing* process. The same process is repeated for the calls to method DisplayArray in lines 18 and 20.

Common Programming Error 26.2

If the compiler cannot find a single nongeneric or generic method declaration that is a best match for a method call, or if there are multiple best matches, a compilation error occurs.

You can also use *explicit type arguments* to indicate the exact type that should be used to call a generic function. For example, line 16 could be written as

```
DisplayArray< int >( intArray ); // pass an int array argument
```

The preceding method call explicitly provides the type argument (int) that should be used to replace type parameter T in lines 24 and 26 of the DisplayArray method's declaration.

For each variable declared with a type parameter, the compiler also determines whether the operations performed on such a variable are allowed for all types that the type parameter can assume. The only operation performed on the array elements in this example is to output the string representation of the elements. Line 27 performs an implicit conversion for every value-type array element and an implicit ToString call on every reference-type array element. Since all objects have a ToString method, the compiler is satisfied that line 27 performs a valid operation for any array element.

By declaring DisplayArray as a generic method in Fig. 26.3, we eliminated the need for the overloaded methods of Fig. 26.1, saving 17 lines of code and creating a reusable method that can output the string representations of the elements in *any* one-dimensional array, not just arrays of int, double or char elements.

26.4 Type Constraints

In this section, we present a generic Maximum method that determines and returns the largest of its three arguments (all of the same type). The generic method in this example uses the type parameter to declare both the method's return type and its parameters. Normally, when comparing values to determine which one is greater, you would use the > operator. However, this operator is not overloaded for use with every type that is built into the .NET Framework Class Library or that might be defined by extending those types. Generic code is restricted to performing operations that are guaranteed to work for every possible type. Thus, an expression like variable1 < variable2 is not allowed unless the compiler can ensure that the operator < is provided for every type that will ever be used in the generic code. Similarly, you cannot call a method on a generic-type variable unless the compiler can ensure that all types that will ever be used in the generic code support that method.

IComparable< T > Interface

It is possible to compare two objects of the same type if that type implements the generic interface IComparable< T > (of namespace System). A benefit of implementing interface IComparable< T > is that IComparable< T > objects can be used with the sorting and searching methods of classes in the System.Collections.Generic namespace—we discuss those methods in Chapter 27, Collections. The structures in the .NET Framework Class Library that correspond to the simple types all implement this interface. For example, the structure for simple type double is Double and the structure for simple type int is Int32—both Double and Int32 implement the IComparable interface. Types that implement IComparable< T > must declare a CompareTo method for comparing objects. For example, if we have two ints, int1 and int2, they can be compared with the expression:

```
int1.CompareTo( int2 )
```

Method CompareTo must return 0 if the objects are equal, a negative integer if int1 is less than int2 or a positive integer if int1 is greater than int2. It is the responsibility of the programmer who declares a type that implements IComparable< T > to declare method CompareTo such that it compares the contents of two objects of that type and returns the appropriate result.

Specifying Type Constraints

Even though IComparable objects can be compared, they cannot be used with generic code by default, because not all types implement interface IComparable< T >. However, we can restrict the types that can be used with a generic method or class to ensure that they meet certain requirements. This feature—known as a *type constraint*—restricts the type of the argument supplied to a particular type parameter. Figure 26.4 declares method Maximum (lines 20–34) with a type constraint that requires each of the method's arguments to be of type IComparable< T >. This restriction is important, because not all objects can be compared. However, all IComparable< T > objects are guaranteed to have a CompareTo method that can be used in method Maximum to determine the largest of its three arguments.

Generic method Maximum uses type parameter T as the return type of the method (line 20), as the type of method parameters x, y and z (line 20), and as the type of local variable max (line 23). Generic method Maximum's *where* clause (after the parameter list in line 21) specifies the type constraint for type parameter T. In this case, the clause where T : IComparable< T > indicates that this method requires the type arguments to implement interface IComparable< T >. If no type constraint is specified, the default type constraint is object.

```
 1   // Fig. 26.4: MaximumTest.cs
 2   // Generic method Maximum returns the largest of three objects.
 3   using System;
 4
 5   class MaximumTest
 6   {
 7      public static void Main( string[] args )
 8      {
 9         Console.WriteLine( "Maximum of {0}, {1} and {2} is {3}\n",
10            3, 4, 5, Maximum( 3, 4, 5 ) );
11         Console.WriteLine( "Maximum of {0}, {1} and {2} is {3}\n",
12            6.6, 8.8, 7.7, Maximum( 6.6, 8.8, 7.7 ) );
13         Console.WriteLine( "Maximum of {0}, {1} and {2} is {3}\n",
14            "pear", "apple", "orange",
15            Maximum( "pear", "apple", "orange" ) );
16      } // end Main
17
18      // generic function determines the
19      // largest of the IComparable objects
20      private static T Maximum< T >( T x, T y, T z )
21         where T : IComparable< T >
22      {
23         T max = x; // assume x is initially the largest
24
25         // compare y with max
26         if ( y.CompareTo( max ) > 0 )
27            max = y; // y is the largest so far
28
29         // compare z with max
30         if ( z.CompareTo( max ) > 0 )
31            max = z; // z is the largest
32
33         return max; // return largest object
34      } // end method Maximum
35   } // end class MaximumTest
```

```
Maximum of 3, 4 and 5 is 5

Maximum of 6.6, 8.8 and 7.7 is 8.8

Maximum of pear, apple and orange is pear
```

Fig. 26.4 | Generic method Maximum returns the largest of three objects.

C# provides several kinds of type constraints. A *class constraint* indicates that the type argument must be an object of a specific base class or one of its subclasses. An *interface constraint* indicates that the type argument's class must implement a specific interface. The type constraint in line 20 is an interface constraint, because IComparable< T > is an interface. You can specify that the type argument must be a reference type or a value type by using the *reference-type constraint* (**class**) or the *value-type constraint* (**struct**), respectively. Finally, you can specify a *constructor constraint*—**new()**—to indicate that the generic code can use operator new to create new objects of the type represented by the type parameter. If a type parameter is specified with a constructor constraint, the type argument's class must provide a public parameterless or default constructor to ensure that objects of the class can be created without passing constructor arguments; otherwise, a compilation error occurs.

It is possible to apply *multiple constraints* to a type parameter. To do so, simply provide a comma-separated list of constraints in the where clause. If you have a class constraint, reference-type constraint or value-type constraint, it must be listed first—only one of these types of constraints can be used for each type parameter. Interface constraints (if any) are listed next. The constructor constraint is listed last (if there is one).

Analyzing the Code

Method Maximum assumes that its first argument (x) is the largest and assigns it to local variable max (line 23). Next, the if statement at lines 26–27 determines whether y is greater than max. The condition invokes y's CompareTo method with the expression y.CompareTo(max). If y is greater than max, then y is assigned to variable max (line 27). Similarly, the statement at lines 30–31 determines whether z is greater than max. If so, line 31 assigns z to max. Then, line 33 returns max to the caller.

In Main (lines 7–16), line 10 calls Maximum with the integers 3, 4 and 5. Generic method Maximum is a match for this call, but its arguments must implement interface IComparable< T > to ensure that they can be compared. Type int is a synonym for struct Int32, which implements interface IComparable< int >. Thus, ints (and other simple types) are valid arguments to method Maximum.

Line 12 passes three double arguments to Maximum. Again, this is allowed because double is a synonym for the Double struct, which implements IComparable< double >. Line 15 passes Maximum three strings, which are also IComparable< string > objects. Note that we intentionally placed the largest value in a different position in each method call (lines 10, 12 and 15) to show that the generic method always finds the maximum value, regardless of its position in the argument list and regardless of the inferred type argument.

26.5 Overloading Generic Methods

A generic method may be *overloaded*. Each overloaded method must have a unique signature (as discussed in Chapter 7. A class can provide two or more generic methods with the same name but different method parameters. For example, we could provide a second version of generic method DisplayArray (Fig. 26.3) with the additional parameters lowIndex and highIndex that specify the portion of the array to output.

A generic method can be overloaded by nongeneric methods with the same method name. When the compiler encounters a method call, it searches for the method declaration that best matches the method name and the argument types specified in the call. For example, generic method DisplayArray of Fig. 26.3 could be overloaded with a version specific to strings that outputs the strings in neat, tabular format. If the compiler cannot match a method call to either a nongeneric method or a generic method, or if there is ambiguity due to multiple possible matches, the compiler generates an error.

26.6 Generic Classes

The concept of a data structure (e.g., a stack) that contains data elements can be understood independently of the element type it manipulates. A generic class provides a means for describing a class in a type-independent manner. We can then instantiate type-specific objects of the generic class. This capability is an opportunity for software reusability.

Once you have a generic class, you can use a simple, concise notation to indicate the actual type(s) that should be used in place of the class's type parameter(s). At compilation time, the compiler ensures your code's type safety, and the runtime system replaces type parameters with type arguments to enable your client code to interact with the generic class.

One generic Stack class, for example, could be the basis for creating many Stack classes (e.g., "Stack of double," "Stack of int," "Stack of char," "Stack of Employee"). Figure 26.5 presents a generic Stack class declaration. This class should not be confused with the provided System.Collections.Stack class in C#. A generic class declaration is similar to a nongeneric class declaration, except that the class name is followed by a type-parameter list (line 5) and, optionally, a constraint on its type parameter. Type parameter T represents the element type the Stack will manipulate. As with generic methods, the type-parameter list of a generic class can have one or more type parameters separated by commas. Type parameter T is used throughout the Stack class declaration (Fig. 26.5) to represent the element type. Class Stack declares variable elements as an array of type T (line 8). This array (created at line 21) will store the Stack's elements. [*Note:* This example implements a Stack as an array. As you have seen in Chapter 25, Stacks also are commonly implemented as linked lists.]

```
1   // Fig. 26.5: Stack.cs
2   // Generic class Stack.
3   using System;
4
5   class Stack< T >
6   {
7      private int top; // location of the top element
8      private T[] elements; // array that stores stack elements
9
10     // parameterless constructor creates a stack of the default size
11     public Stack()
12        : this( 10 ) // default stack size
13     {
14        // empty constructor; calls constructor at line 18 to perform init
15     } // end stack constructor
16
17     // constructor creates a stack of the specified number of elements
18     public Stack( int stackSize )
19     {
20        if ( stackSize > 0 ) // validate stackSize
21           elements = new T[ stackSize ]; // create stackSize elements
22        else
23           throw new ArgumentException( "Stack size must be positive." );
24
```

Fig. 26.5 | Generic class Stack. (Part 1 of 2.)

```
25              top = -1; // stack initially empty
26          } // end stack constructor
27
28          // push element onto the stack; if unsuccessful,
29          // throw FullStackException
30          public void Push( T pushValue )
31          {
32              if ( top == elements.Length - 1 ) // stack is full
33                  throw new FullStackException( string.Format(
34                      "Stack is full, cannot push {0}", pushValue ) );
35
36              ++top; // increment top
37              elements[ top ] = pushValue; // place pushValue on stack
38          } // end method Push
39
40          // return the top element if not empty,
41          // else throw EmptyStackException
42          public T Pop()
43          {
44              if ( top == -1 ) // stack is empty
45                  throw new EmptyStackException( "Stack is empty, cannot pop" );
46
47              --top; // decrement top
48              return elements[ top + 1 ]; // return top value
49          } // end method Pop
50      } // end class Stack
```

Fig. 26.5 | Generic class Stack. (Part 2 of 2.)

Class Stack has two constructors. The parameterless constructor (lines 11–15) passes the default stack size (10) to the one-argument constructor, using the syntax this (line 12) to invoke another constructor in the same class. The one-argument constructor (lines 18–26) validates the stackSize argument and creates an array of the specified stackSize (if it is greater than 0) or throws an exception, otherwise.

Method Push (lines 30–38) first determines whether an attempt is being made to push an element onto a full Stack. If so, lines 33–34 throw a FullStackException (declared in Fig. 26.6). If the Stack is not full, line 36 increments the top counter to indicate the new top position, and line 37 places the argument in that location of array elements.

Method Pop (lines 42–49) first determines whether an attempt is being made to pop an element from an empty Stack. If so, line 45 throws an EmptyStackException (declared in Fig. 26.7). Otherwise, line 47 decrements the top counter to indicate the new top position, and line 48 returns the original top element of the Stack.

Classes FullStackException (Fig. 26.6) and EmptyStackException (Fig. 26.7) each provide a parameterless constructor, a one-argument constructor of exception classes (as discussed in Section 13.8) and a two-argument constructor for creating a new exception using an existing one. The parameterless constructor sets the default error message while the other two constructors set custom error messages.

As with generic methods, when a generic class is compiled, the compiler performs type checking on the class's type parameters to ensure that they can be used with the code in the generic class. The constraints determine the operations that can be performed on the type parameters. The runtime system replaces the type parameters with the actual types at runtime. For class Stack (Fig. 26.5), no type constraint is specified, so the default type constraint, object, is used. The scope of a generic class's type parameter is the entire class.

```
1   // Fig. 26.6: FullStackException.cs
2   // FullStackException indicates a stack is full.
3   using System;
4
5   class FullStackException : Exception
6   {
7       // parameterless constructor
8       public FullStackException() : base( "Stack is full" )
9       {
10          // empty constructor
11      } // end FullStackException constructor
12
13      // one-parameter constructor
14      public FullStackException( string exception ) : base( exception )
15      {
16          // empty constructor
17      } // end FullStackException constructor
18
19      // two-parameter constructor
20      public FullStackException( string exception, Exception inner )
21          : base( exception, inner )
22      {
23          // empty constructor
24      } // end FullStackException constructor
25  } // end class FullStackException
```

Fig. 26.6 | FullStackException indicates a stack is full.

```
1   // Fig. 26.7: EmptyStackException.cs
2   // EmptyStackException indicates a stack is empty.
3   using System;
4
5   class EmptyStackException : Exception
6   {
7       // parameterless constructor
8       public EmptyStackException() : base( "Stack is empty" )
9       {
10          // empty constructor
11      } // end EmptyStackException constructor
12
13      // one-parameter constructor
14      public EmptyStackException( string exception ) : base( exception )
15      {
16          // empty constructor
17      } // end EmptyStackException constructor
18
```

Fig. 26.7 | EmptyStackException indicates a stack is empty. (Part 1 of 2.)

```
19        // two-parameter constructor
20        public EmptyStackException( string exception, Exception inner )
21           : base( exception, inner )
22        {
23           // empty constructor
24        } // end EmptyStackException constructor
25     } // end class EmptyStackException
```

Fig. 26.7 | EmptyStackException indicates a stack is empty. (Part 2 of 2.)

Now, let's consider an application (Fig. 26.8) that uses the Stack generic class. Lines 13–14 declare variables of type Stack< double > (pronounced "Stack of double") and Stack< int > (pronounced "Stack of int"). The types double and int are the Stack's type arguments. The compiler replaces the type parameters in the generic class so that the compiler can perform type checking. Method Main instantiates objects doubleStack of size 5 (line 18) and intStack of size 10 (line 19), then calls methods TestPushDouble (lines 28–48), TestPopDouble (lines 51–73), TestPushInt (lines 76–96) and TestPopInt (lines 99–121) to manipulate the two Stacks in this example.

```
1     // Fig. 26.8: StackTest.cs
2     // Testing generic class Stack.
3     using System;
4
5     class StackTest
6     {
7        // create arrays of doubles and ints
8        private static double[] doubleElements =
9           new double[]{ 1.1, 2.2, 3.3, 4.4, 5.5, 6.6 };
10       private static int[] intElements =
11          new int[]{ 1, 2, 3, 4, 5, 6, 7, 8, 9, 10, 11 };
12
13       private static Stack< double > doubleStack; // stack stores doubles
14       private static Stack< int > intStack; // stack stores int objects
15
16       public static void Main( string[] args )
17       {
18          doubleStack = new Stack< double >( 5 ); // stack of doubles
19          intStack = new Stack< int >( 10 ); // stack of ints
20
21          TestPushDouble(); // push doubles onto doubleStack
22          TestPopDouble(); // pop doubles from doubleStack
23          TestPushInt(); // push ints onto intStack
24          TestPopInt(); // pop ints from intStack
25       } // end Main
26
27       // test Push method with doubleStack
28       private static void TestPushDouble()
29       {
```

Fig. 26.8 | Testing generic class Stack. (Part 1 of 4.)

```
30          // push elements onto stack
31          try
32          {
33             Console.WriteLine( "\nPushing elements onto doubleStack" );
34
35             // push elements onto stack
36             foreach ( var element in doubleElements )
37             {
38                Console.Write( "{0:F1} ", element );
39                doubleStack.Push( element ); // push onto doubleStack
40             } // end foreach
41          } // end try
42          catch ( FullStackException exception )
43          {
44             Console.Error.WriteLine();
45             Console.Error.WriteLine( "Message: " + exception.Message );
46             Console.Error.WriteLine( exception.StackTrace );
47          } // end catch
48       } // end method TestPushDouble
49
50       // test Pop method with doubleStack
51       private static void TestPopDouble()
52       {
53          // pop elements from stack
54          try
55          {
56             Console.WriteLine( "\nPopping elements from doubleStack" );
57
58             double popValue; // store element removed from stack
59
60             // remove all elements from stack
61             while ( true )
62             {
63                popValue = doubleStack.Pop(); // pop from doubleStack
64                Console.Write( "{0:F1} ", popValue );
65             } // end while
66          } // end try
67          catch ( EmptyStackException exception )
68          {
69             Console.Error.WriteLine();
70             Console.Error.WriteLine( "Message: " + exception.Message );
71             Console.Error.WriteLine( exception.StackTrace );
72          } // end catch
73       } // end method TestPopDouble
74
75       // test Push method with intStack
76       private static void TestPushInt()
77       {
78          // push elements onto stack
79          try
80          {
81             Console.WriteLine( "\nPushing elements onto intStack" );
82
```

Fig. 26.8 | Testing generic class Stack. (Part 2 of 4.)

```
83              // push elements onto stack
84              foreach ( var element in intElements )
85              {
86                  Console.Write( "{0} ", element );
87                  intStack.Push( element ); // push onto intStack
88              } // end foreach
89          } // end try
90          catch ( FullStackException exception )
91          {
92              Console.Error.WriteLine();
93              Console.Error.WriteLine( "Message: " + exception.Message );
94              Console.Error.WriteLine( exception.StackTrace );
95          } // end catch
96      } // end method TestPushInt
97
98      // test Pop method with intStack
99      private static void TestPopInt()
100     {
101         // pop elements from stack
102         try
103         {
104             Console.WriteLine( "\nPopping elements from intStack" );
105
106             int popValue; // store element removed from stack
107
108             // remove all elements from stack
109             while ( true )
110             {
111                 popValue = intStack.Pop(); // pop from intStack
112                 Console.Write( "{0} ", popValue );
113             } // end while
114         } // end try
115         catch ( EmptyStackException exception )
116         {
117             Console.Error.WriteLine();
118             Console.Error.WriteLine( "Message: " + exception.Message );
119             Console.Error.WriteLine( exception.StackTrace );
120         } // end catch
121     } // end method TestPopInt
122 } // end class StackTest
```

```
Pushing elements onto doubleStack
1.1 2.2 3.3 4.4 5.5 6.6
Message: Stack is full, cannot push 6.6
   at Stack`1.Push(T pushValue) in
      C:\Examples\ch27\Fig27_05_08\Stack\Stack\Stack.cs:line 33
   at StackTest.TestPushDouble() in
      C:\Examples\ch27\Fig27_05_08\Stack\Stack\StackTest.cs:line 39

Popping elements from doubleStack
5.5 4.4 3.3 2.2 1.1
```

Fig. 26.8 | Testing generic class Stack. (Part 3 of 4.)

```
Message: Stack is empty, cannot pop
   at Stack`1.Pop() in
      C:\Examples\ch27\Fig27_05_08\Stack\Stack\Stack.cs:line 45
   at StackTest.TestPopDouble() in
      C:\Examples\ch27\Fig27_05_08\Stack\Stack\StackTest.cs:line 63

Pushing elements onto intStack
1 2 3 4 5 6 7 8 9 10 11
Message: Stack is full, cannot push 11
   at Stack`1.Push(T pushValue) in
      C:\Examples\ch27\Fig27_05_08\Stack\Stack\Stack.cs:line 33
   at StackTest.TestPushInt() in
      C:\Examples\ch27\Fig27_05_08\Stack\Stack\StackTest.cs:line 87

Popping elements from intStack
10 9 8 7 6 5 4 3 2 1
Message: Stack is empty, cannot pop
   at Stack`1.Pop() in
      C:\Examples\ch27\Fig27_05_08\Stack\Stack\Stack.cs:line 45
   at StackTest.TestPopInt() in
      C:\Examples\ch27\Fig27_05_08\Stack\Stack\StackTest.cs:line 111
```

Fig. 26.8 | Testing generic class Stack. (Part 4 of 4.)

Method TestPushDouble (lines 28–48) invokes method Push to place the double values 1.1, 2.2, 3.3, 4.4 and 5.5 stored in array doubleElements onto doubleStack. The foreach statement terminates when the test program attempts to Push a sixth value onto doubleStack (which is full, because doubleStack can store only five elements). In this case, the method throws a FullStackException (Fig. 26.6) to indicate that the Stack is full. Lines 42–47 catch this exception and display the message and stack-trace information. The stack trace indicates the exception that occurred and shows that Stack method Push generated the exception at line 33 of the file Stack.cs (Fig. 26.5). The trace also shows that method Push was called by StackTest method TestPushDouble at line 39 of StackTest.cs. This information enables you to determine the methods that were on the method-call stack at the time that the exception occurred. Because the program catches the exception, the C# runtime environment considers the exception to have been handled, and the program can continue executing.

Method TestPopDouble (lines 51–73) invokes Stack method Pop in an infinite while loop to remove all the values from the stack. Note in the output that the values are popped off in last-in, first-out order—this, of course, is the defining characteristic of stacks. The while loop (lines 61–65) continues until the stack is empty. An EmptyStackException occurs when an attempt is made to pop from the empty stack. This causes the program to proceed to the catch block (lines 67–72) and handle the exception, so the program can continue executing. When the test program attempts to Pop a sixth value, the doubleStack is empty, so method Pop throws an EmptyStackException.

Method TestPushInt (lines 76–96) invokes Stack method Push to place values onto intStack until it is full. Method TestPopInt (lines 99–121) invokes Stack method Pop to remove values from intStack until it is empty. Once again, note that the values pop off in last-in, first-out order.

Creating Generic Methods to Test Class Stack< T >

Note that the code in methods TestPushDouble and TestPushInt is almost identical for pushing values onto a Stack< double > or a Stack< int >, respectively. Similarly the code in methods TestPopDouble and TestPopInt is almost identical for popping values from a Stack< double > or a Stack< int >, respectively. This presents another opportunity to use generic methods. Figure 26.9 declares generic method TestPush (lines 32–53) to perform the same tasks as TestPushDouble and TestPushInt in Fig. 26.8—that is, Push values onto a Stack< T > . Similarly, generic method TestPop (lines 55–77) performs the same tasks as TestPopDouble and TestPopInt in Fig. 26.8—that is, Pop values off a Stack< T >. Note that the output of Fig. 26.9 precisely matches the output of Fig. 26.8.

```csharp
1   // Fig. 26.9: StackTest.cs
2   // Testing generic class Stack.
3   using System;
4   using System.Collections.Generic;
5
6   class StackTest
7   {
8      // create arrays of doubles and ints
9      private static double[] doubleElements =
10        new double[] { 1.1, 2.2, 3.3, 4.4, 5.5, 6.6 };
11     private static int[] intElements =
12        new int[] { 1, 2, 3, 4, 5, 6, 7, 8, 9, 10, 11 };
13
14     private static Stack< double > doubleStack; // stack stores doubles
15     private static Stack< int > intStack; // stack stores int objects
16
17     public static void Main( string[] args )
18     {
19        doubleStack = new Stack< double >( 5 ); // stack of doubles
20        intStack = new Stack< int >( 10 ); // stack of ints
21
22        // push doubles onto doubleStack
23        TestPush( "doubleStack", doubleStack, doubleElements );
24        // pop doubles from doubleStack
25        TestPop( "doubleStack", doubleStack );
26        // push ints onto intStack
27        TestPush( "intStack", intStack, intElements );
28        // pop ints from intStack
29        TestPop( "intStack", intStack );
30     } // end Main
31
32     // test Push method
33     private static void TestPush< T >( string name, Stack< T > stack,
34        IEnumerable< T > elements )
35     {
36        // push elements onto stack
37        try
38        {
39           Console.WriteLine( "\nPushing elements onto " + name );
```

Fig. 26.9 | Testing generic class Stack. (Part I of 3.)

```
40
41          // push elements onto stack
42          foreach ( var element in elements )
43          {
44             Console.Write( "{0} ", element );
45             stack.Push( element ); // push onto stack
46          } // end foreach
47       } // end try
48       catch ( FullStackException exception )
49       {
50          Console.Error.WriteLine();
51          Console.Error.WriteLine( "Message: " + exception.Message );
52          Console.Error.WriteLine( exception.StackTrace );
53       } // end catch
54    } // end method TestPush
55
56    // test Pop method
57    private static void TestPop< T >( string name, Stack< T > stack )
58    {
59       // push elements onto stack
60       try
61       {
62          Console.WriteLine( "\nPopping elements from " + name );
63
64          T popValue; // store element removed from stack
65
66          // remove all elements from stack
67          while ( true )
68          {
69             popValue = stack.Pop(); // pop from stack
70             Console.Write( "{0} ", popValue );
71          } // end while
72       } // end try
73       catch ( EmptyStackException exception )
74       {
75          Console.Error.WriteLine();
76          Console.Error.WriteLine( "Message: " + exception.Message );
77          Console.Error.WriteLine( exception.StackTrace );
78       } // end catch
79    } // end TestPop
80 } // end class StackTest
```

```
Pushing elements onto doubleStack
1.1 2.2 3.3 4.4 5.5 6.6
Message: Stack is full, cannot push 6.6
   at Stack`1.Push(T pushValue) in
      C:\Examples\ch27\Fig27_09\Stack\Stack\Stack.cs:line 33
   at StackTest.TestPush[T](String name, Stack`1 stack, IEnumerable`1
      elements) in C:\Examples\ch27\Fig27_09\Stack\Stack\StackTest.cs:line 45

Popping elements from doubleStack
5.5 4.4 3.3 2.2 1.1
```

Fig. 26.9 | Testing generic class Stack. (Part 2 of 3.)

```
Message: Stack is empty, cannot pop
   at Stack`1.Pop() in
      C:\Examples\ch27\Fig27_09\Stack\Stack\Stack.cs:line 45
   at StackTest.TestPop[T](String name, Stack`1 stack) in
      C:\Examples\ch27\Fig27_09\Stack\Stack\StackTest.cs:line 69

Pushing elements onto intStack
1 2 3 4 5 6 7 8 9 10 11
Message: Stack is full, cannot push 11
   at Stack`1.Push(T pushValue) in
      C:\Examples\ch27\Fig27_09\Stack\Stack\Stack.cs:line 33
   at StackTest.TestPush[T](String name, Stack`1 stack, IEnumerable`1
      elements) in C:\Examples\ch27\Fig27_09\Stack\Stack\StackTest.cs:line 45

Popping elements from intStack
10 9 8 7 6 5 4 3 2 1
Message: Stack is empty, cannot pop
   at Stack`1.Pop() in
      C:\Examples\ch27\Fig27_09\Stack\Stack\Stack.cs:line 45
   at StackTest.TestPop[T](String name, Stack`1 stack) in
      C:\Examples\ch27\Fig27_09\Stack\Stack\StackTest.cs:line 69
```

Fig. 26.9 | Testing generic class Stack. (Part 3 of 3.)

Method Main (lines 17–30) creates the Stack< double > (line 19) and Stack< int > (line 20) objects. Lines 23–29 invoke generic methods TestPush and TestPop to test the Stack objects.

Generic method TestPush (lines 33–54) uses type parameter T (specified at line 33) to represent the data type stored in the Stack. The generic method takes three arguments—a string that represents the name of the Stack object for output purposes, an object of type Stack< T > and an IEnumerable< T >—the type of elements that will be Pushed onto Stack< T >. Note that the compiler enforces consistency between the type of the Stack and the elements that will be pushed onto the Stack when Push is invoked, which is the type argument of the generic method call. Generic method TestPop (lines 57–79) takes two arguments—a string that represents the name of the Stack object for output purposes and an object of type Stack< T >.

26.7 Wrap-Up

This chapter introduced generics. We discussed how generics ensure compile-time type safety by checking for type mismatches at compile time. You learned that the compiler will allow generic code to compile only if all operations performed on the type parameters in the generic code are supported for all types that could be used with the generic code. You also learned how to declare generic methods and classes using type parameters. We demonstrated how to use a type constraint to specify the requirements for a type parameter—a key component of compile-time type safety. We discussed several kinds of type constraints, including reference-type constraints, value-type constraints, class constraints, interface constraints and constructor constraints. You learned that a constructor constraint indicates that the type argument must provide a public parameterless or default constructor so that objects of that type can be created with new. We also discussed how to implement multiple type constraints for a type parameter. Finally, we showed how generics improve code reuse. In the next chapter, we demonstrate the .NET Framework Class Library's collection classes, interfaces and algorithms. Collection classes are pre-built data structures that you can reuse in your applications, saving you time. We present both generic collections and the older, nongeneric collections.

Collections

OBJECTIVES

In this chapter you'll learn:

- The nongeneric and generic collections that are provided by the .NET Framework.

- To use class Array's static methods to manipulate arrays.

- To use enumerators to "walk through" a collection.

- To use the foreach statement with the .NET collections.

- To use nongeneric collection classes ArrayList, Stack, and Hashtable.

- To use generic collection classes SortedDictionary and LinkedList.

Outline

27.1 Introduction
27.2 Collections Overview
28.3 Class `Array` and Enumerators
27.4 Nongeneric Collections
    28.4.1 Class `ArrayList`
    28.4.2 Class `Stack`
    28.4.3 Class `Hashtable`
27.5 Generic Collections
    28.5.1 Generic Class `SortedDictionary`
    28.5.2 Generic Class `LinkedList`
27.6 Wrap-Up

27.1 Introduction

Chapter 25 discussed how to create and manipulate data structures. The discussion was "low level," in the sense that we painstakingly created each element of each data structure dynamically with new and modified the data structures by directly manipulating their elements and references to their elements. For the vast majority of applications, there is no need to build custom data structures. Instead, you can use the prepackaged data-structure classes provided by the .NET Framework. These classes are known as *collection classes*—they store collections of data. Each instance of one of these classes is a *collection* of items. Some examples of collections are the cards you hold in a card game, the songs stored in your computer, the real-estate records in your local registry of deeds (which map book numbers and page numbers to property owners), and the players on your favorite sports team.

Collection classes enable programmers to store sets of items by using existing data structures, without concern for how they are implemented. This is a nice example of code reuse. Programmers can code faster and expect excellent performance, maximizing execution speed and minimizing memory consumption. In this chapter, we discuss the collection interfaces that list the capabilities of each collection type, the implementation classes and the *enumerators* that "walk through" collections.

The .NET Framework provides three namespaces dedicated to collections. Namespace `System.Collections` contains collections that store references to `objects`. We included these because there is a large amount of legacy code in industry that uses these collections. Most new applications should use the collections in the *System.Collections.Generic* namespace, which contains generic classes—such as the `List<T>` and `Dictionary<K, V>` classes you learned previously—to store collections of specified types. The *System.Collections.Specialized* namespace contains several collections that support specific types, such as `strings` and bits. You can learn more about this namespace at `msdn.microsoft.com/en-us/library/system.collections.specialized.aspx`. The collections in these namespaces provide standardized, reusable components; you do not need to write your own collection classes. These collections are written for broad reuse. They are tuned for rapid execution and for efficient use of memory. As new data structures and algorithms are developed that fit this framework, a large base of programmers already will be familiar with the interfaces and algorithms implemented by those data structures.

27.2 Collections Overview

All collection classes in the .NET Framework implement some combination of the collection interfaces. These interfaces declare the operations to be performed generically on various types of collections. Figure 27.1 lists some of the interfaces of the .NET Framework collections. All the interfaces in Fig. 27.1 are declared in namespace System.Collections and have generic analogs in namespace System.Collections.Generic. Implementations of these interfaces are provided within the framework. Programmers may also provide implementations specific to their own requirements.

In earlier versions of C#, the .NET Framework primarily provided the collection classes in the System.Collections and System.Collections.Specialized namespaces. These classes stored and manipulated object references. You could store any object in a collection. One inconvenient aspect of storing object references occurs when retrieving them from a collection. An application normally needs to process specific types of objects. As a result, the object references obtained from a collection typically need to be downcast to an appropriate type to allow the application to process the objects correctly.

The .NET Framework also includes the System.Collections.Generic namespace, which uses the generics capabilities we introduced in Chapter 26. Many of these new classes are simply generic counterparts of the classes in namespace System.Collections. This means that you can specify the exact type that will be stored in a collection. You also receive the benefits of compile-time type checking—the compiler ensures that you're using appropriate types with your collection and, if not, issues compile-time error messages. Also, once you specify the type stored in a collection, any item you retrieve from the collection will have the correct type. This eliminates the need for explicit type casts that can throw InvalidCastExceptions at execution time if the referenced object is not of the appropriate type. This also eliminates the overhead of explicit casting, improving efficiency and type safety. Generic collections are especially useful for storing structs, since they eliminate the overhead of boxing and unboxing.

Interface	Description
ICollection	The interface from which interfaces IList and IDictionary inherit. Contains a Count property to determine the size of a collection and a CopyTo method for copying a collection's contents into a traditional array.
IList	An ordered collection that can be manipulated like an array. Provides an indexer for accessing elements with an int index. Also has methods for searching and modifying a collection, including Add, Remove, Contains and IndexOf.
IDictionary	A collection of values, indexed by an arbitrary "key" object. Provides an indexer for accessing elements with an object index and methods for modifying the collection (e.g., Add, Remove). IDictionary property Keys contains the objects used as indices, and property Values contains all the stored objects.
IEnumerable	An object that can be enumerated. This interface contains exactly one method, GetEnumerator, which returns an IEnumerator object (discussed in Section 27.3). ICollection implements IEnumerable, so all collection classes implement IEnumerable directly or indirectly.

Fig. 27.1 | Some common collection interfaces.

In this chapter, we demonstrate six collection classes—*Array*, *ArrayList*, *Stack*, *Hashtable*, generic *SortedDictionary*, and generic *LinkedList*—plus built-in array capabilities. Namespace System.Collections provides several other data structures, including *BitArray* (a collection of true/false values), *Queue* and *SortedList* (a collection of key/value pairs that are sorted by key and can be accessed either by key or by index). Figure 27.2 summarizes many of the collection classes. We also discuss the IEnumerator interface. Collection classes can create enumerators that allow programmers to walk through the collections. Although these enumerators have different implementations, they all implement the IEnumerator interface so that they can be processed polymorphically. As we'll soon see, the foreach statement is simply a convenient notation for using an enumerator. In the next section, we begin our discussion by examining enumerators and the capabilities for array manipulation.

Class	Implements	Description
System namespace:		
Array	IList	The base class of all conventional arrays. See Section 27.3.
System.Collections namespace:		
ArrayList	IList	Mimics conventional arrays, but will grow or shrink as needed to accommodate the number of elements. See Section 27.4.1.
BitArray	ICollection	A memory-efficient array of bools.
Hashtable	IDictionary	An unordered collection of key/value pairs that can be accessed by key. See Section 27.4.3.
Queue	ICollection	A first-in, first-out collection. See Section 25.6.
SortedList	IDictionary	A generic Hashtable that sorts data by keys and can be accessed either by key or by index.
Stack	ICollection	A last-in, first-out collection. See Section 27.4.2.
System.Collections.Generic namespace:		
Dictionary< K, V >	IDictionary< K, V >	A generic, unordered collection of key/value pairs that can be accessed by key.
LinkedList< T >	ICollection< T >	A doubly linked list. See Section 27.5.2.
List< T >	IList< T >	A generic ArrayList.
Queue< T >	ICollection< T >	A generic Queue.

Fig. 27.2 | Some collection classes of the .NET Framework. (Part 1 of 2.)

Class	Implements	Description
SortedDictionary< K, V >	IDictionary< K, V >	A Dictionary that sorts the data by the keys in a binary tree. See Section 27.5.1.
SortedList< K, V >	IDictionary< K, V >	A generic SortedList.
Stack< T >	ICollection< T >	A generic Stack.

[*Note: All collection classes directly or indirectly implement* ICollection *and* IEnumerable *(or the equivalent generic interfaces* ICollection< T > *and* IEnumerable< T > *for generic collections).*]

Fig. 27.2 | Some collection classes of the .NET Framework. (Part 2 of 2.)

27.3 Class Array and Enumerators

Chapter 8 presented basic array-processing capabilities. All arrays implicitly inherit from abstract base class Array (namespace System); this class defines property Length, which specifies the number of elements in the array. In addition, class Array provides static methods that provide algorithms for processing arrays. Typically, class Array overloads these methods—for example, Array method Reverse can reverse the order of the elements in an entire array or can reverse the elements in a specified range of elements in an array. For a complete list of class Array's static methods visit:

msdn.microsoft.com/en-us/library/system.array.aspx

Figure 27.3 demonstrates several static methods of class Array.

```
1   // Fig. 28.3: UsingArray.cs
2   // Array class static methods for common array manipulations.
3   using System;
4   using System.Collections;
5
6   // demonstrate algorithms of class Array
7   public class UsingArray
8   {
9      private static int[] intValues = { 1, 2, 3, 4, 5, 6 };
10     private static double[] doubleValues = { 8.4, 9.3, 0.2, 7.9, 3.4 };
11     private static int[] intValuesCopy;
12
13     // method Main demonstrates class Array's methods
14     public static void Main( string[] args )
15     {
16        intValuesCopy = new int[ intValues.Length ]; // defaults to zeroes
17
18        Console.WriteLine( "Initial array values:\n" );
19        PrintArrays(); // output initial array contents
20
21        // sort doubleValues
22        Array.Sort( doubleValues );
```

Fig. 27.3 | Array class used to perform common array manipulations. (Part 1 of 3.)

```
23
24        // copy intValues into intValuesCopy
25        Array.Copy( intValues, intValuesCopy, intValues.Length );
26
27        Console.WriteLine( "\nArray values after Sort and Copy:\n" );
28        PrintArrays(); // output array contents
29        Console.WriteLine();
30
31        // search for 5 in intValues
32        int result = Array.BinarySearch( intValues, 5 );
33        if ( result >= 0 )
34           Console.WriteLine( "5 found at element {0} in intValues",
35              result );
36        else
37           Console.WriteLine( "5 not found in intValues" );
38
39        // search for 8763 in intValues
40        result = Array.BinarySearch( intValues, 8763 );
41        if ( result >= 0 )
42           Console.WriteLine( "8763 found at element {0} in intValues",
43              result );
44        else
45           Console.WriteLine( "8763 not found in intValues" );
46     } // end Main
47
48     // output array content with enumerators
49     private static void PrintArrays()
50     {
51        Console.Write( "doubleValues: " );
52
53        // iterate through the double array with an enumerator
54        IEnumerator enumerator = doubleValues.GetEnumerator();
55
56        while ( enumerator.MoveNext() )
57           Console.Write( enumerator.Current + " " );
58
59        Console.Write( "\nintValues: " );
60
61        // iterate through the int array with an enumerator
62        enumerator = intValues.GetEnumerator();
63
64        while ( enumerator.MoveNext() )
65           Console.Write( enumerator.Current + " " );
66
67        Console.Write( "\nintValuesCopy: " );
68
69        // iterate through the second int array with a foreach statement
70        foreach ( var element in intValuesCopy )
71           Console.Write( element + " " );
72
73        Console.WriteLine();
74     } // end method PrintArrays
75  } // end class UsingArray
```

Fig. 27.3 | Array class used to perform common array manipulations. (Part 2 of 3.)

```
Initial array values:

doubleValues: 8.4 9.3 0.2 7.9 3.4
intValues: 1 2 3 4 5 6
intValuesCopy: 0 0 0 0 0 0

Array values after Sort and Copy:

doubleValues: 0.2 3.4 7.9 8.4 9.3
intValues: 1 2 3 4 5 6
intValuesCopy: 1 2 3 4 5 6

5 found at element 4 in intValues
8763 not found in intValues
```

Fig. 27.3 | Array class used to perform common array manipulations. (Part 3 of 3.)

The using directives in lines 3–4 include the namespaces System (for classes Array and Console) and System.Collections (for interface IEnumerator, which we discuss shortly). References to the assemblies for these namespaces are implicitly included in every application, so we do not need to add any new references to the project file.

Our test class declares three static array variables (lines 9–11). The first two lines initialize intValues and doubleValues to an int and double array, respectively. Static variable intValuesCopy is intended to demonstrate the Array's Copy method, so it is left with the default value null—it does not yet refer to an array.

Line 16 initializes intValuesCopy to an int array with the same length as array int-Values. Line 19 calls the PrintArrays method (lines 49–74) to output the initial contents of all three arrays. We discuss the PrintArrays method shortly. We can see from the output of Fig. 27.3 that each element of array intValuesCopy is initialized to the default value 0.

Line 22 uses static Array method **Sort** to sort array doubleValues. When this method returns, the array contains its original elements sorted in ascending order.

Line 25 uses static Array method **Copy** to copy elements from array intValues to array intValuesCopy. The first argument is the array to copy (intValues), the second argument is the destination array (intValuesCopy) and the third argument is an int representing the number of elements to copy (in this case, intValues.Length specifies all elements).

Lines 32 and 40 invoke static Array method **BinarySearch** to perform binary searches on array intValues. Method BinarySearch receives the *sorted* array in which to search and the key for which to search. The method returns the index in the array at which it finds the key (or a negative number if the key was not found). Notice that BinarySearch assumes that it receives a sorted array. Its behavior on an unsorted array is unpredictable.

Common Programming Error 27.1

Passing an unsorted array to BinarySearch is a logic error—the value returned is undefined.

The PrintArrays method (lines 49–74) uses class Array's methods to loop though each array. In line 54, the GetEnumerator method obtains an enumerator for array dou-bleValues. Recall that Array implements the **IEnumerable** interface. All arrays inherit implicitly from Array, so both the int[] and double[] array types implement IEnumerable interface method **GetEnumerator**, which returns an enumerator that can iterate over the collection. Interface **IEnumerator** (which all enumerators implement) defines methods

MoveNext and *Reset* and property *Current*. MoveNext moves the enumerator to the next element in the collection. The first call to MoveNext positions the enumerator at the first element of the collection. MoveNext returns true if there is at least one more element in the collection; otherwise, the method returns false. Method Reset positions the enumerator before the first element of the collection. Methods MoveNext and Reset throw an *InvalidOperationException* if the contents of the collection are modified in any way after the enumerator is created. Property Current returns the object at the current location in the collection.

Common Programming Error 27.2

If a collection is modified after an enumerator is created for that collection, the enumerator immediately becomes invalid—any methods called with the enumerator after this point throw InvalidOperationExceptions. For this reason, enumerators are said to be "fail fast."

When an enumerator is returned by the GetEnumerator method in line 54, it is initially positioned *before* the first element in Array doubleValues. Then when line 56 calls MoveNext in the first iteration of the while loop, the enumerator advances to the first element in doubleValues. The while statement in lines 56–57 loops over each element until the enumerator passes the end of doubleValues and MoveNext returns false. In each iteration, we use the enumerator's Current property to obtain and output the current array element. Lines 62–65 iterate over array intValues.

Notice that PrintArrays is called twice (lines 19 and 28), so GetEnumerator is called twice on doubleValues. The GetEnumerator method (lines 54 and 62) always returns an enumerator positioned before the first element. Also notice that the IEnumerator property Current is read-only. Enumerators cannot be used to modify the contents of collections, only to obtain the contents.

Lines 70–71 use a foreach statement to iterate over the collection elements like an enumerator. In fact, the foreach statement behaves exactly like an enumerator. Both loop over the elements of an array one by one in consecutive order. Neither allows you to modify the elements during the iteration. This is not a coincidence. The foreach statement implicitly obtains an enumerator via the GetEnumerator method and uses the enumerator's MoveNext method and Current property to traverse the collection, just as we did explicitly in lines 54–57. For this reason, we can use the foreach statement to iterate over *any* collection that implements the IEnumerable interface—not just arrays. We demonstrate this functionality in the next section when we discuss class ArrayList.

Other static Array methods include *Clear* (to set a range of elements to 0, false or null), *CreateInstance* (to create a new array of a specified type), *IndexOf* (to locate the first occurrence of an object in an array or portion of an array), *LastIndexOf* (to locate the last occurrence of an object in an array or portion of an array) and *Reverse* (to reverse the contents of an array or portion of an array).

27.4 Nongeneric Collections

The System.Collections namespace in the .NET Framework Class Library is the primary source for nongeneric collections. These classes provide standard implementations of many of the data structures discussed in Chapter 25 with collections that store references of type object. In this section, we demonstrate classes ArrayList, Stack and Hashtable.

27.4.1 Class ArrayList

In most programming languages, conventional arrays have a fixed size—they cannot be changed dynamically to conform to an application's execution-time memory requirements. In some applications, this fixed-size limitation presents a problem for programmers. They must choose between using fixed-size arrays that are large enough to store the maximum number of elements the application may require and using dynamic data structures that can grow and shrink the amount of memory required to store data in response to the changing requirements of an application at execution time.

The .NET Framework's *ArrayList* collection class mimics the functionality of conventional arrays and provides dynamic resizing of the collection through the class's methods. At any time, an ArrayList contains a certain number of elements less than or equal to its *capacity*—the number of elements currently reserved for the ArrayList. An application can manipulate the capacity with ArrayList property Capacity. [*Note:* New applications should use the generic List<T> class introduced in Chapter 9.]

Performance Tip 27.1

As with linked lists, inserting additional elements into an ArrayList whose current size is less than its capacity is a fast operation.

Performance Tip 27.2

It is a slow operation to insert an element into an ArrayList that needs to grow larger to accommodate a new element. An ArrayList that is at its capacity must have its memory reallocated and the existing values copied into it.

Performance Tip 27.3

If storage is at a premium, use method TrimToSize of class ArrayList to trim an ArrayList to its exact size. This will optimize an ArrayList's memory use. Be careful—if the application needs to insert additional elements, the process will be slower, because the ArrayList must grow dynamically (trimming leaves no room for growth).

ArrayLists store references to objects. All classes derive from class object, so an ArrayList can contain objects of any type. Figure 27.4 lists some useful methods and properties of class ArrayList.

Method or property	Description
Add	Adds an object to the ArrayList and returns an int specifying the index at which the object was added.
Capacity	Property that gets and sets the number of elements for which space is currently reserved in the ArrayList.
Clear	Removes all the elements from the ArrayList.
Contains	Returns true if the specified object is in the ArrayList; otherwise, returns false.

Fig. 27.4 | Some methods and properties of class ArrayList. (Part 1 of 2.)

Method or property	Description
Count	Read-only property that gets the number of elements stored in the ArrayList.
IndexOf	Returns the index of the first occurrence of the specified object in the ArrayList.
Insert	Inserts an object at the specified index.
Remove	Removes the first occurrence of the specified object.
RemoveAt	Removes an object at the specified index.
RemoveRange	Removes a specified number of elements starting at a specified index in the ArrayList.
Sort	Sorts the ArrayList.
TrimToSize	Sets the Capacity of the ArrayList to the number of elements the ArrayList currently contains (Count).

Fig. 27.4 | Some methods and properties of class ArrayList. (Part 2 of 2.)

Figure 27.5 demonstrates class ArrayList and several of its methods. Class ArrayList belongs to the System.Collections namespace (line 4). Lines 8–11 declare two arrays of strings (colors and removeColors) that we'll use to fill two ArrayList objects. Recall from Section 10.11 that constants must be initialized at compile time, but readonly variables can be initialized at execution time. Arrays are objects created at execution time, so we declare colors and removeColors with readonly—not const—to make them unmodifiable. When the application begins execution, we create an ArrayList with an initial capacity of one element and store it in variable list (line 16). The foreach statement in lines 19–20 adds the five elements of array colors to list via ArrayList's **Add** method, so list grows to accommodate these new elements. Line 24 uses ArrayList's overloaded constructor to create a new ArrayList initialized with the contents of array removeColors, then assigns it to variable removeList. This constructor can initialize the contents of an ArrayList with the elements of any ICollection passed to it. Many of the collection classes have such a constructor. Notice that the constructor call in line 24 performs the task of lines 19–20.

```
1   // Fig. 28.5: ArrayListTest.cs
2   // Using class ArrayList.
3   using System;
4   using System.Collections;
5
6   public class ArrayListTest
7   {
8      private static readonly string[] colors =
9         { "MAGENTA", "RED", "WHITE", "BLUE", "CYAN" };
10     private static readonly string[] removeColors =
11        { "RED", "WHITE", "BLUE" };
```

Fig. 27.5 | Using class ArrayList. (Part 1 of 3.)

```
12
13      // create ArrayList, add colors to it and manipulate it
14      public static void Main( string[] args )
15      {
16          ArrayList list = new ArrayList( 1 ); // initial capacity of 1
17
18          // add the elements of the colors array to the ArrayList list
19          foreach ( var color in colors )
20              list.Add( color ); // add color to the ArrayList list
21
22          // add elements in the removeColors array to
23          // the ArrayList removeList with the ArrayList constructor
24          ArrayList removeList = new ArrayList( removeColors );
25
26          Console.WriteLine( "ArrayList: " );
27          DisplayInformation( list ); // output the list
28
29          // remove from ArrayList list the colors in removeList
30          RemoveColors( list, removeList );
31
32          Console.WriteLine( "\nArrayList after calling RemoveColors: " );
33          DisplayInformation( list ); // output list contents
34      } // end Main
35
36      // displays information on the contents of an array list
37      private static void DisplayInformation( ArrayList arrayList )
38      {
39          // iterate through array list with a foreach statement
40          foreach ( var element in arrayList )
41              Console.Write( "{0} ", element ); // invokes ToString
42
43          // display the size and capacity
44          Console.WriteLine( "\nSize = {0}; Capacity = {1}",
45              arrayList.Count, arrayList.Capacity );
46
47          int index = arrayList.IndexOf( "BLUE" );
48
49          if ( index != -1 )
50              Console.WriteLine( "The array list contains BLUE at index {0}.",
51                  index );
52          else
53              Console.WriteLine( "The array list does not contain BLUE." );
54      } // end method DisplayInformation
55
56      // remove colors specified in secondList from firstList
57      private static void RemoveColors( ArrayList firstList,
58          ArrayList secondList )
59      {
60          // iterate through second ArrayList like an array
61          for ( int count = 0; count < secondList.Count; count++ )
62              firstList.Remove( secondList[ count ] );
63      } // end method RemoveColors
64  } // end class ArrayListTest
```

Fig. 27.5 | Using class ArrayList. (Part 2 of 3.)

```
ArrayList:
MAGENTA RED WHITE BLUE CYAN
Size = 5; Capacity = 8
The array list contains BLUE at index 3.

ArrayList after calling RemoveColors:
MAGENTA CYAN
Size = 2; Capacity = 8
The array list does not contain BLUE.
```

Fig. 27.5 | Using class `ArrayList`. (Part 3 of 3.)

Line 27 calls method `DisplayInformation` (lines 37–54) to output the contents of the `list`. This method uses a `foreach` statement to traverse the elements of an `ArrayList`. As we discussed in Section 27.3, the `foreach` statement is a convenient shorthand for calling `ArrayList`'s `GetEnumerator` method and using an enumerator to traverse the elements of the collection. Also, line 40 infers that the iteration variable's type is `object` because class `ArrayList` is nongeneric and stores references to `objects`.

We use the **Count** and **Capacity** properties in line 45 to display the current number of elements and the maximum number of elements that can be stored without allocating more memory to the `ArrayList`. The output of Fig. 27.5 indicates that the `ArrayList` has capacity 8.

In line 47, we invoke method **IndexOf** to determine the position of the `string` "BLUE" in `arrayList` and store the result in local variable `index`. `IndexOf` returns -1 if the element is not found. The `if` statement in lines 49–53 checks if `index` is -1 to determine whether `arrayList` contains "BLUE". If it does, we output its index. `ArrayList` also provides method **Contains**, which simply returns `true` if an object is in the `ArrayList`, and `false` otherwise. Method `Contains` is preferred if we do not need the index of the element.

Performance Tip 27.4

`ArrayList` *methods* `IndexOf` *and* `Contains` *each perform a linear search, which is a costly operation for large* `ArrayLists`. *If the* `ArrayList` *is sorted, use* `ArrayList` *method* `BinarySearch` *to perform a more efficient search. Method* `BinarySearch` *returns the index of the element, or a negative number if the element is not found.*

After method `DisplayInformation` returns, we call method `RemoveColors` (lines 57–63) with the two `ArrayLists`. The `for` statement in lines 61–62 iterates over `ArrayList` `secondList`. Line 62 uses an indexer to access an `ArrayList` element—by following the `ArrayList` reference name with square brackets (`[]`) containing the desired index of the element. An `ArgumentOutOfRangeException` occurs if the specified index is not both greater than 0 and less than the number of elements currently stored in the `ArrayList` (specified by the `ArrayList`'s `Count` property).

We use the indexer to obtain each of `secondList`'s elements, then remove each one from `firstList` with the **Remove** method. This method deletes a specified item from an `ArrayList` by performing a linear search and removing (only) the first occurrence of the specified object. All subsequent elements shift toward the beginning of the `ArrayList` to fill the emptied position.

After the call to `RemoveColors`, line 33 again outputs the contents of `list`, confirming that the elements of `removeList` were, indeed, removed.

27.4.2 Class Stack

The Stack class implements a stack data structure and provides much of the functionality that we defined in our own implementation in Section 26.5. Refer to that section for a discussion of stack data-structure concepts. We created a test application in Fig. 26.14 to demonstrate the StackInheritance data structure that we developed. We adapt Fig. 25.14 in Fig. 27.6 to demonstrate the .NET Framework collection class Stack. [*Note:* New applications requiring a stack class should use the generic Stack<T> class.]

```
 1   // Fig. 28.6: StackTest.cs
 2   // Demonstrating class Stack.
 3   using System;
 4   using System.Collections;
 5
 6   public class StackTest
 7   {
 8      public static void Main( string[] args )
 9      {
10         Stack stack = new Stack(); // default Capacity of 10
11
12         // create objects to store in the stack
13         bool aBoolean = true;
14         char aCharacter = '$';
15         int anInteger = 34567;
16         string aString = "hello";
17
18         // use method Push to add items to (the top of) the stack
19         stack.Push( aBoolean );
20         PrintStack( stack );
21         stack.Push( aCharacter );
22         PrintStack( stack );
23         stack.Push( anInteger );
24         PrintStack( stack );
25         stack.Push( aString );
26         PrintStack( stack );
27
28         // check the top element of the stack
29         Console.WriteLine( "The top element of the stack is {0}\n",
30            stack.Peek() );
31
32         // remove items from stack
33         try
34         {
35            while ( true )
36            {
37               object removedObject = stack.Pop();
38               Console.WriteLine( removedObject + " popped" );
39               PrintStack( stack );
40            } // end while
41         } // end try
```

Fig. 27.6 | Demonstrating class Stack. (Part 1 of 2.)

```
42          catch ( InvalidOperationException exception )
43          {
44              // if exception occurs, output stack trace
45              Console.Error.WriteLine( exception );
46          } // end catch
47      } // end Main
48
49      // display the contents of a stack
50      private static void PrintStack( Stack stack )
51      {
52          if ( stack.Count == 0 )
53              Console.WriteLine( "stack is empty\n" ); // the stack is empty
54          else
55          {
56              Console.Write( "The stack is: " );
57
58              // iterate through the stack with a foreach statement
59              foreach ( var element in stack )
60                  Console.Write( "{0} ", element ); // invokes ToString
61
62              Console.WriteLine( "\n" );
63          } // end else
64      } // end method PrintStack
65  } // end class StackTest
```

```
The stack is: True

The stack is: $ True

The stack is: 34567 $ True

The stack is: hello 34567 $ True

The top element of the stack is hello

hello popped
The stack is: 34567 $ True

34567 popped
The stack is: $ True

$ popped
The stack is: True

True popped
stack is empty

System.InvalidOperationException: Stack empty.
   at System.Collections.Stack.Pop()
   at StackTest.Main(String[] args) in C:\examples\ch28\
       fig28_06\StackTest\StackTest.cs:line 37
```

Fig. 27.6 | Demonstrating class Stack. (Part 2 of 2.)

The `using` directive in line 4 allows us to use the `Stack` class with its unqualified name from the `System.Collections` namespace. Line 10 creates a `Stack`. As one might expect, class `Stack` has methods `Push` and `Pop` to perform the basic stack operations.

Method `Push` takes an `object` as an argument and inserts it at the top of the `Stack`. If the number of items on the `Stack` (the `Count` property) is equal to the capacity at the time of the `Push` operation, the `Stack` grows to accommodate more `object`s. Lines 19–26 use method `Push` to add four elements (a `bool`, a `char`, an `int` and a `string`) to the stack and invoke method `PrintStack` (lines 50–64) after each `Push` to output the contents of the stack. Notice that this nongeneric `Stack` class can store only references to `object`s, so each of the value-type items—the `bool`, the `char` and the `int`—is implicitly boxed before it is added to the `Stack`. (Namespace `System.Collections.Generic` provides a generic `Stack` class that has many of the same methods and properties used in Fig. 27.6. This version eliminates the overhead of boxing and unboxing simple types.)

Method `PrintStack` (lines 50–64) uses `Stack` property `Count` (implemented to fulfill the contract of interface `ICollection`) to obtain the number of elements in `stack`. If the stack is not empty (i.e., `Count` is not equal to 0), we use a `foreach` statement to iterate over the stack and output its contents by implicitly invoking the `ToString` method of each element. The `foreach` statement implicitly invokes `Stack`'s `GetEnumerator` method, which we could have called explicitly to traverse the stack via an enumerator.

Method **Peek** returns the value of the top stack element but does not remove the element from the `Stack`. We use `Peek` at line 30 to obtain the top object of the `Stack`, then output that object, implicitly invoking the object's `ToString` method. An `InvalidOperationException` occurs if the `Stack` is empty when the application calls `Peek`. (We do not need an exception-handling block because we know the stack is not empty here.)

Method `Pop` takes no arguments—it removes and returns the object currently on top of the `Stack`. An infinite loop (lines 35–40) pops objects off the stack and outputs them until the stack is empty. When the application calls `Pop` on the empty stack, an `InvalidOperationException` is thrown. The `catch` block (lines 42–46) outputs the exception, implicitly invoking the `InvalidOperationException`'s `ToString` method to obtain its error message and stack trace.

Common Programming Error 27.3

Attempting to Peek or Pop an empty Stack (a Stack whose Count property is 0) causes an InvalidOperationException.

Although Fig. 27.6 does not demonstrate it, class `Stack` also has method `Contains`, which returns `true` if the `Stack` contains the specified object, and returns `false` otherwise.

27.4.3 Class Hashtable

When an application creates objects of new or existing types, it needs to manage those objects efficiently. This includes sorting and retrieving objects. Sorting and retrieving information with arrays is efficient if some aspect of your data directly matches the key value and if those keys are unique and tightly packed. If you have 100 employees with nine-digit social security numbers and you want to store and retrieve employee data by using the social security number as a key, it would nominally require an array with 1,000,000,000 elements, because there are 1,000,000,000 unique nine-digit numbers. If you have an array that large, you could get high performance storing and retrieving employee records by simply using the social security number as the array index, but it would be a large waste of memory.

Many applications have this problem—either the keys are of the wrong type (i.e., not nonnegative integers), or they are of the right type but are sparsely spread over a large range.

What is needed is a high-speed scheme for converting keys such as social security numbers and inventory part numbers to unique array indices. Then, when an application needs to store something, the scheme could convert the application key rapidly to an index and the record of information could be stored at that location in the array. Retrieval occurs the same way—once the application has a key for which it wants to retrieve the data record, the application simply applies the conversion to the key, which produces the array index where the data resides in the array and retrieves the data.

The scheme we describe here is the basis of a technique called *hashing*, in which we store data in a data structure called a *hash table*. Why the name? Because, when we convert a key into an array index, we literally scramble the bits, making a "hash" of the number. The number actually has no real significance beyond its usefulness in storing and retrieving this particular data record.

A glitch in the scheme occurs when there are *collisions* (i.e., two different keys "hash into" the same cell, or element, in the array). Since we cannot sort two different data records to the same space, we need to find an alternative home for all records beyond the first that hash to a particular array index. One scheme for doing this is to "hash again" (i.e., to reapply the hashing transformation to the key to provide a next candidate cell in the array). The hashing process is designed so that with just a few hashes, an available cell will be found.

Another scheme uses one hash to locate the first candidate cell. If the cell is occupied, successive cells are searched linearly until an available cell is found. Retrieval works the same way—the key is hashed once, the resulting cell is checked to determine whether it contains the desired data. If it does, the search is complete. If it does not, successive cells are searched linearly until the desired data is found.

The most popular solution to hash-table collisions is to have each cell of the table be a hash "bucket"—typically, a linked list of all the key/value pairs that hash to that cell. This is the solution that the .NET Framework's **Hashtable** class implements.

The *load factor* affects the performance of hashing schemes. The load factor is the ratio of the number of objects stored in the hash table to the total number of cells of the hash table. As this ratio gets higher, the chance of collisions tends to increase.

Performance Tip 27.5

*The load factor in a hash table is a classic example of a **space/time trade-off**: By increasing the load factor, we get better memory utilization, but the application runs slower due to increased hashing collisions. By decreasing the load factor, we get better application speed because of reduced hashing collisions, but we get poorer memory utilization because a larger portion of the hash table remains empty.*

Recognizing the value of hashing, the .NET Framework provides class Hashtable to enable programmers to easily employ hashing in applications. This concept is profoundly important in our study of object-oriented programming. Classes encapsulate and hide complexity (i.e., implementation details) and offer user-friendly interfaces. Crafting classes to do this properly is one of the most valued skills in the field of object-oriented programming.

A *hash function* performs a calculation that determines where to place data in the hash table. The hash function is applied to the key in a key/value pair of objects. Class Hashtable can accept any object as a key. For this reason, class object defines method GetHashCode, which all objects inherit. Most classes that are candidates to be used as keys in a hash table override this method to provide one that performs efficient hash-code calculations for a specific type. For example, a string has a hash-code calculation that is based on the contents of the string. Figure 27.7 uses a Hashtable to count the number of occurrences of each word in a string. [*Note:* New applications should use generic class Dictionary< K, V > (introduced in Section 19.4 rather than Hashtable.]

Lines 4–6 contain using directives for namespaces System (for class Console), System.Text.RegularExpressions (for class Regex, discussed in Chapter 18) and System.Collections (for class Hashtable). Class HashtableTest declares three static methods. Method CollectWords (lines 20–46) inputs a string and returns a Hashtable in which each value stores the number of times that word appears in the string and the word is used for the key. Method DisplayHashtable (lines 49–60) displays the Hashtable passed to it in column format. The Main method (lines 10–17) simply invokes CollectWords (line 13), then passes the Hashtable returned by CollectWords to DisplayHashtable in line 16.

```
1   // Fig. 28.7: HashtableTest.cs
2   // Application counts the number of occurrences of each word in a string
3   // and stores them in a hash table.
4   using System;
5   using System.Text.RegularExpressions;
6   using System.Collections;
7
8   public class HashtableTest
9   {
10     public static void Main( string[] args )
11     {
12        // create hash table based on user input
13        Hashtable table = CollectWords();
14
15        // display hash-table content
16        DisplayHashtable( table );
17     } // end Main
18
19     // create hash table from user input
20     private static Hashtable CollectWords()
21     {
22        Hashtable table = new Hashtable(); // create a new hash table
23
24        Console.WriteLine( "Enter a string: " ); // prompt for user input
25        string input = Console.ReadLine(); // get input
```

Fig. 27.7 | Application counts the number of occurrences of each word in a string and stores them in a hash table. (Part 1 of 2.)

```
26
27          // split input text into tokens
28          string[] words = Regex.Split( input, @"\s+" );
29
30          // processing input words
31          foreach ( var word in words )
32          {
33             string wordKey = word.ToLower(); // get word in lowercase
34
35             // if the hash table contains the word
36             if ( table.ContainsKey( wordKey ) )
37             {
38                table[ wordKey ] = ( ( int ) table[ wordKey ] ) + 1;
39             } // end if
40             else
41                // add new word with a count of 1 to hash table
42                table.Add( wordKey, 1 );
43          } // end foreach
44
45          return table;
46       } // end method CollectWords
47
48       // display hash-table content
49       private static void DisplayHashtable( Hashtable table )
50       {
51          Console.WriteLine( "\nHashtable contains:\n{0,-12}{1,-12}",
52             "Key:", "Value:" );
53
54          // generate output for each key in hash table
55          // by iterating through the Keys property with a foreach statement
56          foreach ( var key in table.Keys )
57             Console.WriteLine( "{0,-12}{1,-12}", key, table[ key ] );
58
59          Console.WriteLine( "\nsize: {0}", table.Count );
60       } // end method DisplayHashtable
61    } // end class HashtableTest
```

```
Enter a string:
As idle as a painted ship upon a painted ocean

Hashtable contains:
Key:        Value:
painted     2
a           2
upon        1
as          2
ship        1
idle        1
ocean       1

size: 7
```

Fig. 27.7 | Application counts the number of occurrences of each word in a `string` and stores them in a hash table. (Part 2 of 2.)

Method CollectWords (lines 20–46) begins by initializing local variable table with a new Hashtable (line 22) that has a default maximum load factor of 1.0. When the number of items in the Hashtable becomes greater than the number of cells times the load factor, the capacity is increased automatically. (This implementation detail is invisible to clients of the class.) Lines 24–25 prompt the user and input a string. We use static method Split of class Regex in line 28 to divide the string by its whitespace characters. This creates an array of "words," which we then store in local variable words.

The foreach statement in lines 31–43 loops over every element of array words. Each word is converted to lowercase with string method *ToLower*, then stored in variable wordKey (line 33). Then line 36 calls Hashtable method *ContainsKey* to determine whether the word is in the hash table (and thus has occurred previously in the string). If the Hashtable does not contain an entry for the word, line 42 uses Hashtable method Add to create a new entry in the hash table, with the lowercase word as the key and an object containing 1 as the value. Note that autoboxing occurs when the application passes integer 1 to method Add, because the hash table stores both the key and value in references to type object.

Common Programming Error 27.4

Using the Add method to add a key that already exists in the hash table causes an ArgumentException.

If the word is already a key in the hash table, line 38 uses the Hashtable's indexer to obtain and set the key's associated value (the word count) in the hash table. We first downcast the value obtained by the get accessor from an object to an int. This unboxes the value so that we can increment it by 1. Then, when we use the indexer's set accessor to assign the key's associated value, the incremented value is implicitly reboxed so that it can be stored in the hash table.

Notice that invoking the get accessor of a Hashtable indexer with a key that does not exist in the hash table obtains a null reference. Using the set accessor with a key that does not exist in the hash table creates a new entry, as if you had used the Add method.

Line 45 returns the hash table to the Main method, which then passes it to method DisplayHashtable (lines 49–60), which displays all the entries. This method uses read-only property *Keys* (line 56) to get an ICollection that contains all the keys. Because ICollection extends IEnumerable, we can use this collection in the foreach statement in lines 56–57 to iterate over the keys of the hash table. This loop accesses and outputs each key and its value in the hash table using the iteration variable and table's get accessor. Each key and its value is displayed in a field width of -12. The negative field width indicates that the output is left justified. Note that a hash table is not sorted, so the key/value pairs are not displayed in any particular order. Line 59 uses Hashtable property *Count* to get the number of key/value pairs in the Hashtable.

Lines 56–57 could have also used the foreach statement with the Hashtable object itself, instead of using the Keys property. If you use a foreach statement with a Hashtable object, the iteration variable will be of type *DictionaryEntry*. The enumerator of a Hashtable (or any other class that implements *IDictionary*) uses the DictionaryEntry structure to store key/value pairs. This structure provides properties Key and Value for retrieving the key and value of the current element. If you do not need the key, class Hashtable also provides a read-only *Values* property that gets an ICollection of all the values stored in the Hashtable. We can use this property to iterate through the values stored in the Hashtable without regard for where they are stored.

Problems with Nongeneric Collections

In the word-counting application of Fig. 27.7, our Hashtable stores its keys and data as object references, even though we store only string keys and int values by convention. This results in some awkward code. For example, line 38 was forced to unbox and box the int data stored in the Hashtable every time it incremented the count for a particular key. This is inefficient. A similar problem occurs in line 56—the iteration variable of the foreach statement is an object reference. If we need to use any of its string-specific methods, we need an explicit downcast.

This can cause subtle bugs. Suppose we decide to improve the readability of Fig. 27.7 by using the indexer's set accessor instead of the Add method to add a key/value pair in line 42, but accidentally type:

```
table[ wordKey ] = wordKey; // initialize to 1
```

This statement will create a new entry with a string key and string value instead of an int value of 1. Although the application will compile correctly, this is clearly incorrect. If a word appears twice, line 38 will try to downcast this string to an int, causing an InvalidCastException at execution time. The error that appears at execution time will indicate that the problem is at line 38, where the exception occurred, *not* at line 42. This makes the error more difficult to find and debug, especially in large software applications where the exception may occur in a different file—and even in a different assembly.

In Chapter 26, we introduced generics. In the next section, we demonstrate how to use generic collections.

27.5 Generic Collections

The System.Collections.Generic namespace in the .NET Framework Class Library contains generic classes that allow us to create collections of specific types. As you saw in Fig. 27.2, many of the classes are simply generic versions of nongeneric collections. A couple classes implement new data structures. In this section, we demonstrate generic collections SortedDictionary and LinkedList.

27.5.1 Generic Class SortedDictionary

A *dictionary* is the general term for a collection of key/value pairs. A hash table is one way to implement a dictionary. The .NET Framework provides several implementations of dictionaries, both generic and nongeneric, all of which implement the IDictionary interface (described in Fig. 27.1). The application in Fig. 27.8 is a modification of Fig. 27.7 that uses the generic class *SortedDictionary*. Generic class SortedDictionary does not use a hash table, but instead stores its key/value pairs in a binary search tree. (We discuss binary trees in depth in Section 26.7.) As the class name suggests, the entries in Sorted-Dictionary are sorted in the tree by key. When the key implements generic interface IComparable, the SortedDictionary uses the results of IComparable method CompareTo to sort the keys. Notice that despite these implementation details, we use the same public

methods, properties and indexers with classes `Hashtable` and `SortedDictionary` in the
same ways. In fact, except for the generic-specific syntax, Fig. 27.8 looks remarkably similar to Fig. 27.7. This is the beauty of object-oriented programming.

```
 1   // Fig. 28.12: SortedDictionaryTest.cs
 2   // Application counts the number of occurrences of each word in a string
 3   // and stores them in a generic sorted dictionary.
 4   using System;
 5   using System.Text.RegularExpressions;
 6   using System.Collections.Generic;
 7
 8   public class SortedDictionaryTest
 9   {
10      public static void Main( string[] args )
11      {
12         // create sorted dictionary based on user input
13         SortedDictionary< string, int > dictionary = CollectWords();
14
15         // display sorted dictionary content
16         DisplayDictionary( dictionary );
17      } // end Main
18
19      // create sorted dictionary from user input
20      private static SortedDictionary< string, int > CollectWords()
21      {
22         // create a new sorted dictionary
23         SortedDictionary< string, int > dictionary =
24            new SortedDictionary< string, int >();
25
26         Console.WriteLine( "Enter a string: " ); // prompt for user input
27         string input = Console.ReadLine(); // get input
28
29         // split input text into tokens
30         string[] words = Regex.Split( input, @"\s+" );
31
32         // processing input words
33         foreach ( var word in words )
34         {
35            string wordKey = word.ToLower(); // get word in lowercase
36
37            // if the dictionary contains the word
38            if ( dictionary.ContainsKey( wordKey ) )
39            {
40               ++dictionary[ wordKey ];
41            } // end if
42            else
43               // add new word with a count of 1 to the dictionary
44               dictionary.Add( wordKey, 1 );
45      } // end foreach
46
```

Fig. 27.8 | Application counts the number of occurrences of each word in a `string` and stores
them in a generic sorted dictionary. (Part I of 2.)

```
47              return dictionary;
48          } // end method CollectWords
49
50          // display dictionary content
51          private static void DisplayDictionary< K, V >(
52              SortedDictionary< K, V > dictionary )
53          {
54              Console.WriteLine( "\nSorted dictionary contains:\n{0,-12}{1,-12}",
55                  "Key:", "Value:" );
56
57              // generate output for each key in the sorted dictionary
58              // by iterating through the Keys property with a foreach statement
59              foreach ( K key in dictionary.Keys )
60                  Console.WriteLine( "{0,-12}{1,-12}", key, dictionary[ key ] );
61
62              Console.WriteLine( "\nsize: {0}", dictionary.Count );
63          } // end method DisplayDictionary
64      } // end class SortedDictionaryTest
```

```
Enter a string:
We few, we happy few, we band of brothers

Sorted dictionary contains:
Key:        Value:
band        1
brothers    1
few,        2
happy       1
of          1
we          3

size: 6
```

Fig. 27.8 | Application counts the number of occurrences of each word in a string and stores them in a generic sorted dictionary. (Part 2 of 2.)

Line 6 contains a using directive for the System.Collections.Generic namespace, which contains class SortedDictionary. The generic class SortedDictionary takes two type arguments—the first specifies the type of key (i.e., string) and the second the type of value (i.e., int). We have simply replaced the word Hashtable in line 13 and lines 23–24 with SortedDictionary< string, int > to create a dictionary of int values keyed with strings. Now, the compiler can check and notify us if we attempt to store an object of the wrong type in the dictionary. Also, because the compiler now knows that the data structure contains int values, there is no longer any need for the downcast in line 40. This allows line 40 to use the much more concise prefix increment (++) notation. These are the only changes made to methods Main and CollectWords but they result in code that can be checked for type safety at compile time.

Static method DisplayDictionary (lines 51–63) has been modified to be completely generic. It takes type parameters K and V. These parameters are used in line 52 to indicate that DisplayDictionary takes a SortedDictionary with keys of type K and values of type V. We use type parameter K again in line 59 as the type of the iteration key. This use of generics is a marvelous example of code reuse. If we decide to change the application to count the number of times each character appears in a string, method `DisplayDictionary` could receive an argument of type `SortedDictionary< char, int >` without modification. Note that the key-value pairs displayed are now ordered by key, as shown in Fig. 27.8.

Performance Tip 27.6

Because class `SortedDictionary` keeps its elements sorted in a binary tree, obtaining or inserting a key/value pair takes O(log n) time, which is fast compared to linear searching, then inserting.

Common Programming Error 27.5

Invoking the `get` accessor of a `SortedDictionary` indexer with a key that does not exist in the collection causes a `KeyNotFoundException`. This behavior is different from that of the `Hashtable` indexer's `get` accessor, which would return `null`.

27.5.2 Generic Class `LinkedList`

Chapter 25 began our discussion of data structures with the concept of a linked list. We end our discussion with the .NET Framework's generic *LinkedList* class. The `LinkedList` class is a doubly linked list—we can navigate the list both backward and forward with nodes of generic class *LinkedListNode*. Each node contains property *Value* and read-only properties *Previous* and *Next*. The `Value` property's type matches `LinkedList`'s single type parameter because it contains the data stored in the node. The `Previous` property gets a reference to the preceding node in the linked list (or `null` if the node is the first of the list). Similarly, the `Next` property gets a reference to the subsequent reference in the linked list (or `null` if the node is the last of the list). We demonstrate a few linked-list manipulations in Fig. 27.9.

```
1    // Fig. 28.9: LinkedListTest.cs
2    // Using LinkedLists.
3    using System;
4    using System.Collections.Generic;
5
6    public class LinkedListTest
7    {
8       private static readonly string[] colors = { "black", "yellow",
9          "green", "blue", "violet", "silver" };
10      private static readonly string[] colors2 = { "gold", "white",
11         "brown", "blue", "gray" };
12
13      // set up and manipulate LinkedList objects
14      public static void Main( string[] args )
15      {
16         LinkedList< string > list1 = new LinkedList< string >();
17
18         // add elements to first linked list
19         foreach ( var color in colors )
20            list1.AddLast( color );
21
22         // add elements to second linked list via constructor
```

Fig. 27.9 | Using `LinkedList`s. (Part 1 of 3.)

```
23            LinkedList< string > list2 = new LinkedList< string >( colors2 );
24
25            Concatenate( list1, list2 ); // concatenate list2 onto list1
26            PrintList( list1 ); // display list1 elements
27
28            Console.WriteLine( "\nConverting strings in list1 to uppercase\n" );
29            ToUppercaseStrings( list1 ); // convert to uppercase string
30            PrintList( list1 ); // display list1 elements
31
32            Console.WriteLine( "\nDeleting strings between BLACK and BROWN\n" );
33            RemoveItemsBetween( list1, "BLACK", "BROWN" );
34
35            PrintList( list1 ); // display list1 elements
36            PrintReversedList( list1 ); // display list in reverse order
37        } // end Main
38
39        // display list contents
40        private static void PrintList< T >( LinkedList< T > list )
41        {
42            Console.WriteLine( "Linked list: " );
43
44            foreach ( T value in list )
45                Console.Write( "{0} ", value );
46
47            Console.WriteLine();
48        } // end method PrintList
49
50        // concatenate the second list on the end of the first list
51        private static void Concatenate< T >( LinkedList< T > list1,
52            LinkedList< T > list2 )
53        {
54            // concatenate lists by copying element values
55            // in order from the second list to the first list
56            foreach ( T value in list2 )
57                list1.AddLast( value ); // add new node
58        } // end method Concatenate
59
60        // locate string objects and convert to uppercase
61        private static void ToUppercaseStrings( LinkedList< string > list )
62        {
63            // iterate over the list by using the nodes
64            LinkedListNode< string > currentNode = list.First;
65
66            while ( currentNode != null )
67            {
68                string color = currentNode.Value; // get value in node
69                currentNode.Value = color.ToUpper(); // convert to uppercase
70
71                currentNode = currentNode.Next; // get next node
72            } // end while
73        } // end method ToUppercaseStrings
74
```

Fig. 27.9 | Using LinkedLists. (Part 2 of 3.)

```
75      // delete list items between two given items
76      private static void RemoveItemsBetween< T >( LinkedList< T > list,
77         T startItem, T endItem )
78      {
79         // get the nodes corresponding to the start and end item
80         LinkedListNode< T > currentNode = list.Find( startItem );
81         LinkedListNode< T > endNode = list.Find( endItem );
82
83         // remove items after the start item
84         // until we find the last item or the end of the linked list
85         while ( ( currentNode.Next != null ) &&
86            ( currentNode.Next != endNode ) )
87         {
88            list.Remove( currentNode.Next ); // remove next node
89         } // end while
90      } // end method RemoveItemsBetween
91
92      // display reversed list
93      private static void PrintReversedList< T >( LinkedList< T > list )
94      {
95         Console.WriteLine( "Reversed List:" );
96
97         // iterate over the list by using the nodes
98         LinkedListNode< T > currentNode = list.Last;
99
100        while ( currentNode != null )
101        {
102           Console.Write( "{0} ", currentNode.Value );
103           currentNode = currentNode.Previous; // get previous node
104        } // end while
105
106        Console.WriteLine();
107     } // end method PrintReversedList
108  } // end class LinkedListTest
```

```
Linked list:
black yellow green blue violet silver gold white brown blue gray

Converting strings in list1 to uppercase

Linked list:
BLACK YELLOW GREEN BLUE VIOLET SILVER GOLD WHITE BROWN BLUE GRAY

Deleting strings between BLACK and BROWN

Linked list:
BLACK BROWN BLUE GRAY
Reversed List:
GRAY BLUE BROWN BLACK
```

Fig. 27.9 | Using LinkedLists. (Part 3 of 3.)

The using directive in line 4 allows us to use the LinkedList class by its unqualified name. Lines 16–23 create LinkedLists list1 and list2 of strings and fill them with the contents of arrays colors and colors2, respectively. Note that LinkedList is a generic class that has one type parameter for which we specify the type argument string in this example (lines 16 and 23). We demonstrate two ways to fill the lists. In lines 19–20, we use the foreach statement and method *AddLast* to fill list1. The AddLast method creates a new LinkedListNode (with the given value available via the Value property) and appends this node to the end of the list. There is also an AddFirst method that inserts a node at the beginning of the list. Line 23 invokes the constructor that takes an IEnumerable< string > parameter. All arrays implicitly inherit from the generic interfaces IList and IEnumerable with the type of the array as the type argument, so the string array colors2 implements IEnumerable< string >. The type parameter of this generic IEnumerable matches the type parameter of the generic LinkedList object. This constructor call copies the contents of the array colors2 to list2.

Line 25 calls generic method Concatenate (lines 51–58) to append all elements of list2 to the end of list1. Line 26 calls method PrintList (lines 40–48) to output list1's contents. Line 29 calls method ToUppercaseStrings (lines 61–73) to convert each string element to uppercase, then line 30 calls PrintList again to display the modified strings. Line 33 calls method RemoveItemsBetween (lines 76–90) to remove the elements between "BLACK" and "BROWN"—not including either. Line 35 outputs the list again, then line 36 invokes method PrintReversedList (lines 93–107) to display the list in reverse order.

Generic method Concatenate (lines 51–58) iterates over list2 with a foreach statement and calls method AddLast to append each value to the end of list1. The LinkedList class's enumerator loops over the values of the nodes, not the nodes themselves, so the iteration variable has type T. Notice that this creates a new node in list1 for each node in list2. One LinkedListNode cannot be a member of more than one LinkedList. Any attempt to add a node from one LinkedList to another generates an InvalidOperationException. If you want the same data to belong to more than one LinkedList, you must make a copy of the node for each list.

Generic method PrintList (lines 40–48) similarly uses a foreach statement to iterate over the values in a LinkedList, and outputs them. Method ToUppercaseStrings (lines 61–73) takes a linked list of strings and converts each string value to uppercase. This method replaces the strings stored in the list, so we cannot use an enumerator (via a foreach statement) as in the previous two methods. Instead, we obtain the first LinkedListNode via the First property (line 64), and use a while statement to loop through the list (lines 66–72). Each iteration of the while statement obtains and updates the contents of currentNode via property Value, using string method *ToUpper* to create an uppercase version of string color. At the end of each iteration, we move the current node to the next node in the list by assigning currentNode to the node obtained by its own Next property (line 71). The Next property of the last node of the list gets null, so when the while statement iterates past the end of the list, the loop exits.

Notice that it does not make sense to declare ToUppercaseStrings as a generic method, because it uses the string-specific methods of the values in the nodes. Methods PrintList (lines 40–48) and Concatenate (lines 51–58) do not need to use any string-specific methods, so they can be declared with generic type parameters to promote maximal code reuse.

Generic method `RemoveItemsBetween` (lines 76–90) removes a range of items between two nodes. Lines 80–81 obtain the two "boundary" nodes of the range by using method *Find*. This method performs a linear search on the list and returns the first node that contains a value equal to the passed argument. Method `Find` returns `null` if the value is not found. We store the node preceding the range in local variable `currentNode` and the node following the range in `endNode`.

The `while` statement in lines 85–89 removes all the elements between `currentNode` and `endNode`. On each iteration of the loop, we remove the node following `currentNode` by invoking method *Remove* (line 88). Method `Remove` takes a `LinkedListNode`, splices that node out of the `LinkedList`, and fixes the references of the surrounding nodes. After the `Remove` call, `currentNode`'s `Next` property now gets the node *following* the node just removed, and that node's `Previous` property now gets `currentNode`. The `while` statement continues to loop until there are no nodes left between `currentNode` and `endNode`, or until `currentNode` is the last node in the list. (Note that there is also an overloaded version of method `Remove` that performs a linear search for the specified value and removes the first node in the list that contains it.)

Method `PrintReversedList` (lines 93–107) displays the list backward by navigating the nodes manually. Line 98 obtains the last element of the list via the *Last* property and stores it in `currentNode`. The while statement in lines 100–104 iterates through the list backward by moving the `currentNode` reference to the previous node at the end of each iteration, then exiting when we move past the beginning of the list. Note how similar this code is to lines 64–72, which iterated through the list from the beginning to the end.

27.6 Wrap-Up

This chapter introduced the .NET Framework collection classes. You learned about the hierarchy of interfaces that many of the collection classes implement. You saw how to use class `Array` to perform array manipulations. You learned that the `System.Collections` and `System.Collections.Generic` namespaces contain many nongeneric and generic collection classes, respectively. We presented the nongeneric classes `ArrayList`, `Stack` and `Hashtable` as well as generic classes `SortedDictionary` and `LinkedList`. In doing so, we discussed data structures in greater depth. We discussed dynamically expanding collections, hashing schemes, and two implementations of a dictionary. You saw the advantages of generic collections over their nongeneric counterparts.

You also learned how to use enumerators to traverse these data structures and obtain their contents. We demonstrated the `foreach` statement with many of the classes of the .NET Framework Class Library, and explained that this works by using enumerators "behind-the-scenes" to traverse the collections.

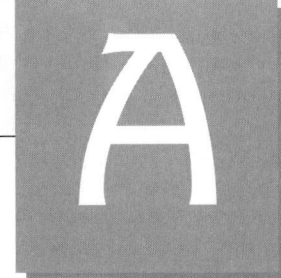

Operator Precedence Chart

Operators are shown in decreasing order of precedence from top to bottom with each level of precedence separated by a horizontal line. The associativity of the operators is shown in the right column.

Operator	Type	Associativity
.	member access	left-to-right
()	method call	
[]	element access	
++	postfix increment	
--	postfix decrement	
new	object creation	
typeof	get System.Type object for a type	
sizeof	get size in bytes of a type	
checked	checked evaluation	
unchecked	unchecked evaluation	
+	unary plus	right-to-left
-	unary minus	
!	logical negation	
~	bitwise complement	
++	prefix increment	

Fig. A.1 | Operator precedence chart (Part 1 of 2.).

Operator	Type	Associativity
--	prefix decrement	
(*type*)	cast	
*	multiplication	left-to-right
/	division	
%	remainder	
+	addition	left-to-right
-	subtraction	
>>	right shift	left-to-right
<<	left shift	
<	less than	left-to-right
>	greater than	
<=	less than or equal to	
>=	greater than or equal to	
is	type comparison	
as	type conversion	
!=	is not equal to	left-to-right
==	is equal to	
&	logical AND	left-to-right
^	logical XOR	left-to-right
|	logical OR	left-to-right
&&	conditional AND	left-to-right
||	conditional OR	left-to-right
??	null coalescing	right-to-left
?:	conditional	right-to-left
=	assignment	right-to-left
*=	multiplication assignment	
/=	division assignment	
%=	remainder assignment	
+=	addition assignment	
-=	subtration assignment	
<<=	left shift assignment	
>>=	right shift assignment	
&=	logical AND assignment	
^=	logical XOR assignment	
|=	logical OR assignment	

Fig. A.1 | Operator precedence chart (Part 2 of 2.).

B

Simple Types

Type	Size in bits	Value range	Standard
bool	8	true or false	
byte	8	0 to 255, inclusive	
sbyte	8	−128 to 127, inclusive	
char	16	'\u0000' to '\uFFFF' (0 to 65535), inclusive	Unicode
short	16	−32768 to 32767, inclusive	
ushort	16	0 to 65535, inclusive	
int	32	−2,147,483,648 to 2,147,483,647, inclusive	
uint	32	0 to 4,294,967,295, inclusive	
float	32	*Approximate negative range:* −3.4028234663852886E+38 to −1.40129846432481707E−45 *Approximate positive range:* 1.40129846432481707E−45 to 3.4028234663852886E+38 *Other supported values:* positive and negative zero positive and negative infinity not-a-number (NaN)	IEEE 754 IEC 60559
long	64	−9,223,372,036,854,775,808 to 9,223,372,036,854,775,807, inclusive	
ulong	64	0 to 18,446,744,073,709,551,615, inclusive	

Fig. B.1 | Simple types. (Part 1 of 2.)

Type	Size in bits	Value range	Standard
double	64	*Approximate negative range:* −1.7976931348623157E+308 to −4.94065645841246544E−324 *Approximate positive range:* 4.94065645841246544E−324 to 1.7976931348623157E+308 *Other supported values:* positive and negative zero positive and negative infinity not-a-number (NaN)	IEEE 754 IEC 60559
decimal	128	*Negative range:* −79,228,162,514,264,337,593,543,950,335 (−7.9E+28) to −1.0E−28 *Positive range:* 1.0E−28 to 79,228,162,514,264,337,593,543,950,335 (7.9E+28)	

Fig. B.1 | Simple types. (Part 2 of 2.)

Additional Simple Type Information

- This appendix is based on information from Sections 4.1.4–4.1.8 of Microsoft's version of the *C# Language Specification* and Sections 11.1.4–11.1.8 of the ECMA-334 (the ECMA version of the *C# Language Specification*). These documents are available from the following websites:

  ```
  msdn.microsoft.com/en-us/vcsharp/aa336809.aspx
  www.ecma-international.org/publications/standards/Ecma-334.htm
  ```

- Values of type float have seven digits of precision.

- Values of type double have 15–16 digits of precision.

- Values of type decimal are represented as integer values that are scaled by a power of 10. Values between −1.0 and 1.0 are represented exactly to 28 digits.

- For more information on IEEE 754 visit grouper.ieee.org/groups/754/. For more information on Unicode, see Appendix G, Unicode®.

C

Number Systems

OBJECTIVES

In this appendix you'll learn:

- To understand basic number systems concepts, such as base, positional value and symbol value.

- To understand how to work with numbers represented in the binary, octal and hexadecimal number systems.

- To abbreviate binary numbers as octal numbers or hexadecimal numbers.

- To convert octal numbers and hexadecimal numbers to binary numbers.

- To convert back and forth between decimal numbers and their binary, octal and hexadecimal equivalents.

- To understand binary arithmetic and how negative binary numbers are represented using two's complement notation.

Outline

C.1 Introduction

C.2 Abbreviating Binary Numbers as Octal and Hexadecimal Numbers

C.3 Converting Octal and Hexadecimal Numbers to Binary Numbers

C.4 Converting from Binary, Octal or Hexadecimal to Decimal

C.5 Converting from Decimal to Binary, Octal or Hexadecimal

C.6 Negative Binary Numbers: Two's Complement Notation

C.1 Introduction

In this appendix, we introduce the key number systems that programmers use, especially when they are working on software projects that require close interaction with machine-level hardware. Projects like this include operating systems, computer networking software, compilers, database systems and applications requiring high performance.

When we write an integer such as 227 or –63 in a program, the number is assumed to be in the decimal (base 10) number system. The digits in the decimal number system are 0, 1, 2, 3, 4, 5, 6, 7, 8 and 9. The lowest digit is 0 and the highest digit is 9—one less than the base of 10. Internally, computers use the binary (base 2) number system. The binary number system has only two digits, namely 0 and 1. Its lowest digit is 0 and its highest digit is 1—one less than the base of 2.

As we'll see, binary numbers tend to be much longer than their decimal equivalents. Programmers who work in assembly languages and in high-level languages like C# that enable programmers to reach down to the machine level, find it cumbersome to work with binary numbers. So two other number systems—the octal number system (base 8) and the hexadecimal number system (base 16)—are popular primarily because they make it convenient to abbreviate binary numbers.

In the octal number system, the digits range from 0 to 7. Because both the binary number system and the octal number system have fewer digits than the decimal number system, their digits are the same as the corresponding digits in decimal.

The hexadecimal number system poses a problem because it requires 16 digits—a lowest digit of 0 and a highest digit with a value equivalent to decimal 15 (one less than the base of 16). By convention, we use the letters A through F to represent the hexadecimal digits corresponding to decimal values 10 through 15. Thus in hexadecimal we can have numbers like 876 consisting solely of decimal-like digits, numbers like 8A55F consisting of digits and letters and numbers like FFE consisting solely of letters. Occasionally, a hexadecimal number spells a common word such as FACE or FEED—this can appear strange to programmers accustomed to working with numbers. The digits of the binary, octal, decimal and hexadecimal number systems are summarized in Fig. C.1–Fig. C.2.

Each of these number systems uses positional notation—each position in which a digit is written has a different positional value. For example, in the decimal number 937 (the 9, the 3 and the 7 are referred to as symbol values), we say that the 7 is written in the ones position, the 3 is written in the tens position and the 9 is written in the hundreds position. Note that each of these positions is a power of the base (base 10) and that these powers begin at 0 and increase by 1 as we move left in the number (Fig. C.3).

Binary digit	Octal digit	Decimal digit	Hexadecimal digit
0	0	0	0
1	1	1	1
	2	2	2
	3	3	3
	4	4	4
	5	5	5
	6	6	6
	7	7	7
		8	8
		9	9
			A (decimal value of 10)
			B (decimal value of 11)
			C (decimal value of 12)
			D (decimal value of 13)
			E (decimal value of 14)
			F (decimal value of 15)

Fig. C.1 | Digits of the binary, octal, decimal and hexadecimal number systems.

Attribute	Binary	Octal	Decimal	Hexadecimal
Base	2	8	10	16
Lowest digit	0	0	0	0
Highest digit	1	7	9	F

Fig. C.2 | Comparing the binary, octal, decimal and hexadecimal number systems.

Positional values in the decimal number system			
Decimal digit	9	3	7
Position name	Hundreds	Tens	Ones
Positional value	100	10	1
Positional value as a power of the base (10)	10^2	10^1	10^0

Fig. C.3 | Positional values in the decimal number system.

For longer decimal numbers, the next positions to the left would be the thousands position (10 to the 3rd power), the ten-thousands position (10 to the 4th power), the hundred-thousands position (10 to the 5th power), the millions position (10 to the 6th power), the ten-millions position (10 to the 7th power) and so on.

In the binary number 101, the rightmost 1 is written in the ones position, the 0 is written in the twos position and the leftmost 1 is written in the fours position. Each position is a power of the base (base 2) and that these powers begin at 0 and increase by 1 as we move left in the number (Fig. C.4). So, $101 = 1 * 2^2 + 0 * 2^1 + 1 * 2^0 = 4 + 0 + 1 = 5$.

For longer binary numbers, the next positions to the left would be the eights position (2 to the 3rd power), the sixteens position (2 to the 4th power), the thirty-twos position (2 to the 5th power), the sixty-fours position (2 to the 6th power) and so on.

In the octal number 425, we say that the 5 is written in the ones position, the 2 is written in the eights position and the 4 is written in the sixty-fours position. Note that each of these positions is a power of the base (base 8) and that these powers begin at 0 and increase by 1 as we move left in the number (Fig. C.5).

For longer octal numbers, the next positions to the left would be the five-hundred-and-twelves position (8 to the 3rd power), the four-thousand-and-ninety-sixes position (8 to the 4th power), the thirty-two-thousand-seven-hundred-and-sixty-eights position (8 to the 5th power) and so on.

In the hexadecimal number 3DA, we say that the A is written in the ones position, the D is written in the sixteens position and the 3 is written in the two-hundred-and-fifty-sixes position. Note that each of these positions is a power of the base (base 16) and that these powers begin at 0 and increase by 1 as we move left in the number (Fig. C.6).

For longer hexadecimal numbers, the next positions to the left would be the four-thousand-and-ninety-sixes position (16 to the 3rd power), the sixty-five-thousand-five-hundred-and-thirty-sixes position (16 to the 4th power) and so on.

Positional values in the binary number system			
Binary digit	1	0	1
Position name	Fours	Twos	Ones
Positional value	4	2	1
Positional value as a power of the base (2)	2^2	2^1	2^0

Fig. C.4 | Positional values in the binary number system.

Positional values in the octal number system			
Decimal digit	4	2	5
Position name	Sixty-fours	Eights	Ones
Positional value	64	8	1
Positional value as a power of the base (8)	8^2	8^1	8^0

Fig. C.5 | Positional values in the octal number system.

Positional values in the hexadecimal number system			
Decimal digit	3	D	A
Position name	Two-hundred-and-fifty-sixes	Sixteens	Ones
Positional value	256	16	1
Positional value as a power of the base (16)	16^2	16^1	16^0

Fig. C.6 | Positional values in the hexadecimal number system.

C.2 Abbreviating Binary Numbers as Octal and Hexadecimal Numbers

The main use for octal and hexadecimal numbers in computing is for abbreviating lengthy binary representations. Figure C.7 highlights the fact that lengthy binary numbers can be expressed concisely in number systems with higher bases than the binary number system.

Decimal number	Binary representation	Octal representation	Hexadecimal representation
0	0	0	0
1	1	1	1
2	10	2	2
3	11	3	3
4	100	4	4
5	101	5	5
6	110	6	6
7	111	7	7
8	1000	10	8
9	1001	11	9
10	1010	12	A
11	1011	13	B
12	1100	14	C
13	1101	15	D
14	1110	16	E
15	1111	17	F
16	10000	20	10

Fig. C.7 | Decimal, binary, octal and hexadecimal equivalents.

A particularly important relationship that both the octal number system and the hexa-decimal number system have to the binary system is that the bases of octal and hexadec-imal (8 and 16 respectively) are powers of the base of the binary number system (base 2). Consider the following 12-digit binary number and its octal and hexadecimal equivalents. See if you can determine how this relationship makes it convenient to abbreviate binary numbers in octal or hexadecimal. The answer follows the numbers.

Binary number	Octal equivalent	Hexadecimal equivalent
100011010001	4321	8D1

To see how the binary number converts easily to octal, simply break the 12-digit binary number into groups of three consecutive bits each and write those groups over the corresponding digits of the octal number as follows:

100	011	010	001
4	3	2	1

Note that the octal digit you have written under each group of three bits corresponds precisely to the octal equivalent of that 3-digit binary number, as shown in Fig. C.7.

The same kind of relationship can be observed in converting from binary to hexadec-imal. Break the 12-digit binary number into groups of four consecutive bits each and write those groups over the corresponding digits of the hexadecimal number as follows:

1000	1101	0001
8	D	1

Notice that the hexadecimal digit you wrote under each group of four bits corre-sponds precisely to the hexadecimal equivalent of that 4-digit binary number as shown in Fig. C.7.

C.3 Converting Octal and Hexadecimal Numbers to Binary Numbers

In the previous section, we saw how to convert binary numbers to their octal and hexadec-imal equivalents by forming groups of binary digits and simply rewriting them as their equivalent octal digit values or hexadecimal digit values. This process may be used in re-verse to produce the binary equivalent of a given octal or hexadecimal number.

For example, the octal number 653 is converted to binary simply by writing the 6 as its 3-digit binary equivalent 110, the 5 as its 3-digit binary equivalent 101 and the 3 as its 3-digit binary equivalent 011 to form the 9-digit binary number 110101011.

The hexadecimal number FAD5 is converted to binary simply by writing the F as its 4-digit binary equivalent 1111, the A as its 4-digit binary equivalent 1010, the D as its 4-digit binary equivalent 1101 and the 5 as its 4-digit binary equivalent 0101 to form the 16-digit 1111101011010101.

C.4 Converting from Binary, Octal or Hexadecimal to Decimal

We are accustomed to working in decimal, and therefore it is often convenient to convert a binary, octal, or hexadecimal number to decimal to get a sense of what the number is "really" worth. Our diagrams in Section C.1 express the positional values in decimal. To convert a number to decimal from another base, multiply the decimal equivalent of each digit by its positional value and sum these products. For example, the binary number 110101 is converted to decimal 53, as shown in Fig. C.8.

To convert octal 7614 to decimal 3980, we use the same technique, this time using appropriate octal positional values, as shown in Fig. C.9.

To convert hexadecimal AD3B to decimal 44347, we use the same technique, this time using appropriate hexadecimal positional values, as shown in Fig. C.10.

C.5 Converting from Decimal to Binary, Octal or Hexadecimal

The conversions in Section C.4 follow naturally from the positional notation conventions. Converting from decimal to binary, octal, or hexadecimal also follows these conventions.

Converting a binary number to decimal					
Postional values:	32	16	8	4	2	1
Symbol values:	1	1	0	1	0	1
Products:	1*32=32	1*16=16	0*8=0	1*4=4	0*2=0	1*1=1
Sum:	= 32 + 16 + 0 + 4 + 0s + 1 = 53					

Fig. C.8 | Converting a binary number to decimal.

Converting an octal number to decimal			
Positional values:	512	64	8	1
Symbol values:	7	6	1	4
Products	7*512=3584	6*64=384	1*8=8	4*1=4
Sum:	= 3584 + 384 + 8 + 4 = 3980			

Fig. C.9 | Converting an octal number to decimal.

Converting a hexadecimal number to decimal			
Postional values:	4096	256	16	1
Symbol values:	A	D	3	B
Products	A*4096=40960	D*256=3328	3*16=48	B*1=11
Sum:	= 40960 + 3328 + 48 + 11 = 44347			

Fig. C.10 | Converting a hexadecimal number to decimal.

Suppose we wish to convert decimal 57 to binary. We begin by writing the positional values of the columns right to left until we reach a column whose positional value is greater than the decimal number. We do not need that column, so we discard it. Thus, we first write:

Positional values: 64   32   16   8   4   2   1

Then we discard the column with positional value 64, leaving:

Positional values: 32   16   8   4   2   1

Next we work from the leftmost column to the right. We divide 32 into 57 and observe that there is one 32 in 57 with a remainder of 25, so we write 1 in the 32 column. We divide 16 into 25 and observe that there is one 16 in 25 with a remainder of 9 and write 1 in the 16 column. We divide 8 into 9 and observe that there is one 8 in 9 with a remainder of 1. The next two columns each produce quotients of 0 when their positional values are divided into 1, so we write 0s in the 4 and 2 columns. Finally, 1 into 1 is 1, so we write 1 in the 1 column. This yields:

Positional values: 32   16   8   4   2   1
Symbol values: 1   1   1   0   0   1

and thus decimal 57 is equivalent to binary 111001.

To convert decimal 103 to octal, we begin by writing the positional values of the columns until we reach a column whose positional value is greater than the decimal number. We do not need that column, so we discard it. Thus, we first write:

Positional values: 512   64   8   1

Then we discard the column with positional value 512, yielding:

Positional values: 64   8   1

Next we work from the leftmost column to the right. We divide 64 into 103 and observe that there is one 64 in 103 with a remainder of 39, so we write 1 in the 64 column. We divide 8 into 39 and observe that there are four 8s in 39 with a remainder of 7 and write 4 in the 8 column. Finally, we divide 1 into 7 and observe that there are seven 1s in 7 with no remainder, so we write 7 in the 1 column. This yields:

Positional values: 64   8   1
Symbol values: 1   4   7

and thus decimal 103 is equivalent to octal 147.

To convert decimal 375 to hexadecimal, we begin by writing the positional values of the columns until we reach a column whose positional value is greater than the decimal number. We do not need that column, so we discard it. Thus, we first write:

Positional values: 4096   256   16   1

Then we discard the column with positional value 4096, yielding:

Positional values: 256   16   1

Next we work from the leftmost column to the right. We divide 256 into 375 and observe that there is one 256 in 375 with a remainder of 119, so we write 1 in the 256 column. We divide 16 into 119 and observe that there are seven 16s in 119 with a remainder of 7 and write 7 in the 16 column. Finally, we divide 1 into 7 and observe that there are seven 1s in 7 with no remainder, so we write 7 in the 1 column. This yields:

```
Positional values:   256     16      1
Symbol values:        1       7       7
```

and thus decimal 375 is equivalent to hexadecimal 177.

C.6 Negative Binary Numbers: Two's Complement Notation

The discussion so far in this appendix has focused on positive numbers. In this section, we explain how computers represent negative numbers using *two's complement notation*. First we explain how the two's complement of a binary number is formed, then we show why it represents the negative value of the given binary number.

Consider a machine with 32-bit integers. Suppose

```
int value = 13;
```

The 32-bit representation of value is

```
00000000 00000000 00000000 00001101
```

To form the negative of value we first form its *one's complement* by applying C#'s bitwise complement operator (~):

```
onesComplementOfValue = ~value;
```

Internally, ~value is now value with each of its bits reversed—ones become zeros and zeros become ones, as follows:

```
value:
00000000 00000000 00000000 00001101
```

```
~value  (i.e., value's ones complement):
11111111 11111111 11111111 11110010
```

To form the two's complement of value, we simply add 1 to value's one's complement. Thus

```
Two's complement of value:
11111111 11111111 11111111 11110011
```

Now if this is in fact equal to −13, we should be able to add it to binary 13 and obtain a result of 0. Let us try this:

```
  00000000 00000000 00000000 00001101
 +11111111 11111111 11111111 11110011
-------------------------------------
  00000000 00000000 00000000 00000000
```

The carry bit coming out of the leftmost column is discarded and we indeed get 0 as a result. If we add the one's complement of a number to the number, the result would be all 1s. The key to getting a result of all zeros is that the twos complement is one more than the one's complement. The addition of 1 causes each column to add to 0 with a carry of 1. The carry keeps moving leftward until it is discarded from the leftmost bit, and thus the resulting number is all zeros.

Computers actually perform a subtraction, such as

```
x = a - value;
```

by adding the two's complement of `value` to a, as follows:

```
x = a + (~value + 1);
```

Suppose a is 27 and `value` is 13 as before. If the two's complement of `value` is actually the negative of `value`, then adding the two's complement of value to a should produce the result 14. Let us try this:

```
a (i.e., 27)       00000000 00000000 00000000 00011011
+(~value + 1)    +11111111 11111111 11111111 11110011
                 -----------------------------------
                   00000000 00000000 00000000 00001110
```

which is indeed equal to 14.

ATM Case Study Code

D.1 ATM Case Study Implementation

This appendix contains the complete working implementation of the ATM system that we designed in the nine Software Engineering Case Study sections in Chapters 1, 3–8, 10 and 12. The implementation comprises 655 lines of C# code. We consider the 11 classes in the order in which we identified them in Section 4.12 (with the exception of Transaction, which was introduced in Chapter 12 as the base class of classes BalanceInquiry, Withdrawal and Deposit):

- ATM
- Screen
- Keypad
- CashDispenser
- DepositSlot
- Account
- BankDatabase
- Transaction
- BalanceInquiry
- Withdrawal
- Deposit

We apply the guidelines discussed in Section 10.22 and Section 12.9 to code these classes based on how we modeled them in the UML class diagrams of Fig. 12.21 and Fig. 12.22. To develop the bodies of class methods, we refer to the activity diagrams presented in Section 6.9 and the communication and sequence diagrams presented in Section 8.14. Note that our ATM design does not specify all the program logic and may not specify all the attributes and operations required to complete the ATM implementation. This is a normal part of the object-oriented design process. As we implement the system, we complete the program logic and add attributes and behaviors as necessary to construct the ATM system specified by the requirements document in Section 3.9.

We conclude the discussion by presenting a test harness (ATMCaseStudy in Section D.13) that creates an object of class ATM and starts it by calling its Run method. Recall that we are developing a first version of the ATM system that runs on a personal computer and uses the keyboard and monitor to approximate the ATM's keypad and screen. Also, we simulate the actions of the ATM's cash dispenser and deposit slot. We attempt to implement the system so that real hardware versions of these devices could be integrated without significant code changes. [*Note:* For the purpose of this simulation, we have provided two predefined accounts in class BankDatabase. The first account has the account number 12345 and the PIN 54321. The second account has the account number 98765 and the PIN 56789. You should use these accounts when testing the ATM.]

D.2 Class ATM

Class ATM (Fig. D.1) represents the ATM as a whole. Lines 5–11 implement the class's attributes. We determine all but one of these attributes from the UML class diagrams of Fig. 12.21 and Fig. 12.22. Line 5 declares the bool attribute userAuthenticated from Fig. 12.22. Line 6 declares an attribute not found in our UML design—int attribute currentAccountNumber, which keeps track of the account number of the current authenticated user. Lines 7–11 declare reference-type instance variables corresponding to the ATM class's associations modeled in the class diagram of Fig. 12.21. These attributes allow the ATM to access its parts (i.e., its Screen, Keypad, CashDispenser and DepositSlot) and interact with the bank's account information database (i.e., a BankDatabase object).

```
1   // ATM.cs
2   // Represents an automated teller machine.
3   public class ATM
4   {
5      private bool userAuthenticated; // true if user is authenticated
6      private int currentAccountNumber; // user's account number
7      private Screen screen; // reference to ATM's screen
8      private Keypad keypad; // reference to ATM's keypad
9      private CashDispenser cashDispenser; // ref to ATM's cash dispenser
10     private DepositSlot depositSlot; // reference to ATM's deposit slot
11     private BankDatabase bankDatabase; // ref to account info database
12
13     // enumeration that represents main menu options
14     private enum MenuOption
15     {
16        BALANCE_INQUIRY = 1,
17        WITHDRAWAL = 2,
18        DEPOSIT = 3,
19        EXIT_ATM = 4
20     } // end enum MenuOption
21
22     // parameterless constructor initializes instance variables
23     public ATM()
24     {
```

Fig. D.1 | Class ATM represents the ATM. (Part 1 of 4.)

```
25          userAuthenticated = false; // user is not authenticated to start
26          currentAccountNumber = 0; // no current account number to start
27          screen = new Screen(); // create screen
28          keypad = new Keypad(); // create keypad
29          cashDispenser = new CashDispenser(); // create cash dispenser
30          depositSlot = new DepositSlot(); // create deposit slot
31          bankDatabase = new BankDatabase(); // create account info database
32       } // end constructor
33
34       // start ATM
35       public void Run()
36       {
37          // welcome and authenticate users; perform transactions
38          while ( true ) // infinite loop
39          {
40             // loop while user is not yet authenticated
41             while ( !userAuthenticated )
42             {
43                screen.DisplayMessageLine( "\nWelcome!" );
44                AuthenticateUser(); // authenticate user
45             } // end while
46
47             PerformTransactions(); // for authenticated user
48             userAuthenticated = false; // reset before next ATM session
49             currentAccountNumber = 0; // reset before next ATM session
50             screen.DisplayMessageLine( "\nThank you! Goodbye!" );
51          } // end while
52       } // end method Run
53
54       // attempt to authenticate user against database
55       private void AuthenticateUser()
56       {
57          // prompt for account number and input it from user
58          screen.DisplayMessage( "\nPlease enter your account number: " );
59          int accountNumber = keypad.GetInput();
60
61          // prompt for PIN and input it from user
62          screen.DisplayMessage( "\nEnter your PIN: " );
63          int pin = keypad.GetInput();
64
65          // set userAuthenticated to boolean value returned by database
66          userAuthenticated =
67             bankDatabase.AuthenticateUser( accountNumber, pin );
68
69          // check whether authentication succeeded
70          if ( userAuthenticated )
71             currentAccountNumber = accountNumber; // save user's account #
72          else
73             screen.DisplayMessageLine(
74                "Invalid account number or PIN. Please try again." );
75       } // end method AuthenticateUser
76
```

Fig. D.1 | Class ATM represents the ATM. (Part 2 of 4.)

```
77      // display the main menu and perform transactions
78      private void PerformTransactions()
79      {
80         Transaction currentTransaction; // transaction being processed
81         bool userExited = false; // user has not chosen to exit
82
83         // loop while user has not chosen exit option
84         while ( !userExited )
85         {
86            // show main menu and get user selection
87            int mainMenuSelection = DisplayMainMenu();
88
89            // decide how to proceed based on user's menu selection
90            switch ( ( MenuOption ) mainMenuSelection )
91            {
92               // user chooses to perform one of three transaction types
93               case MenuOption.BALANCE_INQUIRY:
94               case MenuOption.WITHDRAWAL:
95               case MenuOption.DEPOSIT:
96                  // initialize as new object of chosen type
97                  currentTransaction =
98                     CreateTransaction( mainMenuSelection );
99                  currentTransaction.Execute(); // execute transaction
100                 break;
101              case MenuOption.EXIT_ATM: // user chose to terminate session
102                 screen.DisplayMessageLine( "\nExiting the system..." );
103                 userExited = true; // this ATM session should end
104                 break;
105              default: // user did not enter an integer from 1-4
106                 screen.DisplayMessageLine(
107                    "\nYou did not enter a valid selection. Try again." );
108                 break;
109           } // end switch
110        } // end while
111     } // end method PerformTransactions
112
113     // display the main menu and return an input selection
114     private int DisplayMainMenu()
115     {
116        screen.DisplayMessageLine( "\nMain menu:" );
117        screen.DisplayMessageLine( "1 - View my balance" );
118        screen.DisplayMessageLine( "2 - Withdraw cash" );
119        screen.DisplayMessageLine( "3 - Deposit funds" );
120        screen.DisplayMessageLine( "4 - Exit\n" );
121        screen.DisplayMessage( "Enter a choice: " );
122        return keypad.GetInput(); // return user's selection
123     } // end method DisplayMainMenu
124
125     // return object of specified Transaction derived class
126     private Transaction CreateTransaction( int type )
127     {
128        Transaction temp = null; // null Transaction reference
129
```

Fig. D.1 | Class ATM represents the ATM. (Part 3 of 4.)

```
130          // determine which type of Transaction to create
131          switch ( ( MenuOption ) type )
132          {
133             // create new BalanceInquiry transaction
134             case MenuOption.BALANCE_INQUIRY:
135                temp = new BalanceInquiry( currentAccountNumber,
136                   screen, bankDatabase);
137                break;
138             case MenuOption.WITHDRAWAL: // create new Withdrawal transaction
139                temp = new Withdrawal( currentAccountNumber, screen,
140                   bankDatabase, keypad, cashDispenser);
141                break;
142             case MenuOption.DEPOSIT: // create new Deposit transaction
143                temp = new Deposit( currentAccountNumber, screen,
144                   bankDatabase, keypad, depositSlot);
145                break;
146          } // end switch
147
148          return temp;
149       } // end method CreateTransaction
150    } // end class ATM
```

Fig. D.1 | Class ATM represents the ATM. (Part 4 of 4.)

Lines 14–20 declare an enumeration that corresponds to the four options in the ATM's main menu (i.e., balance inquiry, withdrawal, deposit and exit). Lines 23–32 declare class ATM's constructor, which initializes the class's attributes. When an ATM object is first created, no user is authenticated, so line 25 initializes userAuthenticated to false. Line 26 initializes currentAccountNumber to 0 because there is no current user yet. Lines 27–30 instantiate new objects to represent the parts of the ATM. Recall that class ATM has composition relationships with classes Screen, Keypad, CashDispenser and DepositSlot, so class ATM is responsible for their creation. Line 31 creates a new BankDatabase. As you'll soon see, the BankDatabase creates two Account objects that can be used to test the ATM. [*Note:* If this were a real ATM system, the ATM class would receive a reference to an existing database object created by the bank. However, in this implementation, we are only simulating the bank's database, so class ATM creates the BankDatabase object with which it interacts.]

Implementing the Operation
The class diagram of Fig. 12.22 does not list any operations for class ATM. We now implement one operation (i.e., public method) in class ATM that allows an external client of the class (i.e., class ATMCaseStudy; Section D.13) to tell the ATM to run. ATM method Run (lines 35–52) uses an infinite loop (lines 38–51) to repeatedly welcome a user, attempt to authenticate the user and, if authentication succeeds, allow the user to perform transactions. After an authenticated user performs the desired transactions and exits, the ATM resets itself, displays a goodbye message and restarts the process for the next user. We use an infinite loop here to simulate the fact that an ATM appears to run continuously until the bank turns it off (an action beyond the user's control). An ATM user can exit the system, but cannot turn off the ATM completely.

Inside method Run's infinite loop, lines 41–45 cause the ATM to repeatedly welcome and attempt to authenticate the user as long as the user has not been authenticated (i.e., the condition !userAuthenticated is true). Line 43 invokes method Display-MessageLine of the ATM's screen to display a welcome message. Like Screen method DisplayMessage designed in the case study, method DisplayMessageLine (declared in lines 14–17 of Fig. D.2) displays a message to the user, but this method also outputs a newline after displaying the message. We add this method during implementation to give class Screen's clients more control over the placement of displayed messages. Line 44 invokes class ATM's private utility method AuthenticateUser (declared in lines 55–75) to attempt to authenticate the user.

Authenticating the User

We refer to the requirements document to determine the steps necessary to authenticate the user before allowing transactions to occur. Line 58 of method AuthenticateUser invokes method DisplayMessage of the ATM's screen to prompt the user to enter an account number. Line 59 invokes method GetInput of the ATM's keypad to obtain the user's input, then stores this integer in local variable accountNumber. Method AuthenticateUser next prompts the user to enter a PIN (line 62), and stores the PIN in local variable pin (line 63). Next, lines 66–67 attempt to authenticate the user by passing the accountNumber and pin entered by the user to the bankDatabase's AuthenticateUser method. Class ATM sets its userAuthenticated attribute to the bool value returned by this method—userAuthenticated becomes true if authentication succeeds (i.e., the accountNumber and pin match those of an existing Account in bankDatabase) and remains false otherwise. If userAuthenticated is true, line 71 saves the account number entered by the user (i.e., accountNumber) in the ATM attribute currentAccountNumber. The other methods of class ATM use this variable whenever an ATM session requires access to the user's account number. If userAuthenticated is false, lines 73–74 call the screen's DisplayMessageLine method to indicate that an invalid account number and/or PIN was entered, so the user must try again. Note that we set currentAccountNumber only after authenticating the user's account number and the associated PIN—if the database cannot authenticate the user, currentAccountNumber remains 0.

After method Run attempts to authenticate the user (line 44), if userAuthenticated is still false (line 41), the while loop body (lines 41–45) executes again. If userAuthenticated is now true, the loop terminates, and control continues with line 47, which calls class ATM's private utility method PerformTransactions.

Performing Transactions

Method PerformTransactions (lines 78–111) carries out an ATM session for an authenticated user. Line 80 declares local variable Transaction, to which we assign a BalanceInquiry, Withdrawal or Deposit object representing the ATM transaction currently being processed. Note that we use a Transaction variable here to allow us to take advantage of polymorphism. Also, note that we name this variable after the role name included in the class diagram of Fig. 4.23—currentTransaction. Line 81 declares another local variable—a bool called userExited that keeps track of whether the user has chosen to exit. This variable controls a while loop (lines 84–110) that allows the user to execute an unlimited number of transactions before choosing to exit. Within this loop, line 87 displays the main menu and obtains the user's menu selection by calling ATM utility method DisplayMainMenu (declared in lines 114–123). This method displays the main menu by invoking methods of the ATM's screen and returns a menu selection obtained from the user through the ATM's keypad. Line 87 stores the user's selection, returned by `DisplayMain-Menu`, in local variable `mainMenuSelection`.

After obtaining a main menu selection, method `PerformTransactions` uses a `switch` statement (lines 90–109) to respond to the selection appropriately. If `mainMenuSelection` is equal to the underlying value of any of the three enum members representing transaction types (i.e., if the user chose to perform a transaction), lines 97–98 call utility method `CreateTransaction` (declared in lines 126–149) to return a newly instantiated object of the type that corresponds to the selected transaction. Variable `currentTransaction` is assigned the reference returned by method `CreateTransaction`, then line 99 invokes method `Execute` of this transaction to execute it. We discuss `Transaction` method `Execute` and the three `Transaction` derived classes shortly. Note that we assign to the `Transaction` variable `currentTransaction` an object of one of the three `Transaction` derived classes so that we can execute transactions. For example, if the user chooses to perform a balance inquiry, (`MenuOption`) `mainMenuSelection` (line 90) matches the case label `MenuOption.BALANCE_INQUIRY`, and `CreateTransaction` returns a `BalanceInquiry` object (lines 97–98). Thus, `currentTransaction` refers to a `BalanceInquiry` and invoking `currentTransaction.Execute()` (line 99) results in `BalanceInquiry`'s version of `Execute` being called polymorphically.

Creating Transactions

Method `CreateTransaction` (lines 126–149) uses a `switch` statement (lines 131–146) to instantiate a new `Transaction` derived class object of the type indicated by the parameter `type`. Recall that method `PerformTransactions` passes `mainMenuSelection` to method `CreateTransaction` only when `mainMenuSelection` contains a value corresponding to one of the three transaction types. So parameter `type` (line 126) receives one of the values `MenuOption.BALANCE_INQUIRY`, `MenuOption.WITHDRAWAL` or `MenuOption.DEPOSIT`. Each case in the `switch` statement instantiates a new object by calling the appropriate `Transaction` derived class constructor. Note that each constructor has a unique parameter list, based on the specific data required to initialize the derived class object. A `BalanceInquiry` (lines 135–136) requires only the account number of the current user and references to the ATM's `screen` and the `bankDatabase`. In addition to these parameters, a `Withdrawal` (lines 139–140) requires references to the ATM's `keypad` and `cashDispenser`, and a `Deposit` (lines 143–144) requires references to the ATM's `keypad` and `depositSlot`. We discuss the transaction classes in detail in Sections D.9–D.12.

After executing a transaction (line 99 in method `PerformTransactions`), `userExited` remains `false`, and the `while` loop in lines 84–110 repeats, returning the user to the main menu. However, if a user does not perform a transaction and instead selects the main menu option to exit, line 103 sets `userExited` to `true`, causing the condition in line 84 of the `while` loop (`!userExited`) to become `false`. This `while` is the final statement of method `PerformTransactions`, so control returns to line 47 of the calling method `Run`. If the user enters an invalid main menu selection (i.e., not an integer in the range 1–4), lines 106–107 display an appropriate error message, `userExited` remains `false` (as set in line 81) and the user returns to the main menu to try again.

When method `PerformTransactions` returns control to method `Run`, the user has chosen to exit the system, so lines 48–49 reset the ATM's attributes `userAuthenticated` and `currentAccountNumber` to `false` and `0`, respectively, to prepare for the next ATM user. Line 50 displays a goodbye message to the current user before the ATM welcomes the next user.

D.3 Class Screen

Class Screen (Fig. D.2) represents the screen of the ATM and encapsulates all aspects of displaying output to the user. Class Screen simulates a real ATM's screen with the computer monitor and outputs text messages using standard console output methods Console.Write and Console.WriteLine. In the design portion of this case study, we endowed class Screen with one operation—DisplayMessage. For greater flexibility in displaying messages to the Screen, we now declare three Screen methods—DisplayMessage, DisplayMessageLine and DisplayDollarAmount.

Method DisplayMessage (lines 8–11) takes a string as an argument and prints it to the screen using Console.Write. The cursor stays on the same line, making this method appropriate for displaying prompts to the user. Method DisplayMessageLine (lines 14–17) does the same using Console.WriteLine, which outputs a newline to move the cursor to the next line. Finally, method DisplayDollarAmount (lines 20–23) outputs a properly formatted dollar amount (e.g., $1,234.56). Line 22 uses method Console.Write to output a decimal value formatted as currency with a dollar sign, two decimal places and commas to increase the readability of large dollar amounts.

```
1   // Screen.cs
2   // Represents the screen of the ATM
3   using System;
4
5   public class Screen
6   {
7      // displays a message without a terminating carriage return
8      public void DisplayMessage( string message )
9      {
10         Console.Write( message );
11     } // end method DisplayMessage
12
13     // display a message with a terminating carriage return
14     public void DisplayMessageLine( string message )
15     {
16         Console.WriteLine( message );
17     } // end method DisplayMessageLine
18
19     // display a dollar amount
20     public void DisplayDollarAmount( decimal amount )
21     {
22         Console.Write( "{0:C}", amount );
23     } // end method DisplayDollarAmount
24  } // end class Screen
```

Fig. D.2 | Class Screen represents the screen of the ATM.

D.4 Class Keypad

Class Keypad (Fig. D.3) represents the keypad of the ATM and is responsible for receiving all user input. Recall that we are simulating this hardware, so we use the computer's keyboard to approximate the keypad. We use method Console.ReadLine to obtain keyboard input from the user. A computer keyboard contains many keys not found on the ATM's

```
 1    // Keypad.cs
 2    // Represents the keypad of the ATM.
 3    using System;
 4
 5    public class Keypad
 6    {
 7       // return an integer value entered by user
 8       public int GetInput()
 9       {
10          return Convert.ToInt32( Console.ReadLine() );
11       } // end method GetInput
12    } // end class Keypad
```

Fig. D.3 | Class Keypad represents the ATM's keypad.

keypad. We assume that the user presses only the keys on the computer keyboard that also appear on the keypad—the keys numbered 0–9 and the *Enter* key.

Method GetInput (lines 8–11) invokes Convert method ToInt32 to convert the input returned by Console.ReadLine (line 10) to an int value. [*Note:* Method ToInt32 can throw a FormatException if the user enters non-integer input. Because the real ATM's keypad permits only integer input, we simply assume that no exceptions will occur. See Chapter 13, Exception Handling, for information on catching and processing exceptions.] Recall that ReadLine obtains all the input used by the ATM. Class Keypad's GetInput method simply returns the integer input by the user. If a client of class Keypad requires input that satisfies some particular criteria (i.e., a number corresponding to a valid menu option), the client must perform the appropriate error checking.

D.5 Class CashDispenser

Class CashDispenser (Fig. D.4) represents the cash dispenser of the ATM. Line 6 declares constant INITIAL_COUNT, which indicates the number of $20 bills in the cash dispenser when the ATM starts (i.e., 500). Line 7 implements attribute billCount (modeled in Fig. 12.22), which keeps track of the number of bills remaining in the CashDispenser at any time. The constructor (lines 10–13) sets billCount to the initial count. [*Note:* We assume that the process of adding more bills to the CashDispenser and updating the bill-Count occur outside the ATM system.] Class CashDispenser has two public methods—DispenseCash (lines 16–21) and IsSufficientCashAvailable (lines 24–31). The class trusts that a client (i.e., Withdrawal) calls method DispenseCash only after establishing that sufficient cash is available by calling method IsSufficientCashAvailable. Thus, DispenseCash simulates dispensing the requested amount of cash without checking whether sufficient cash is available.

Method IsSufficientCashAvailable (lines 24–31) has a parameter amount that specifies the amount of cash in question. Line 27 calculates the number of $20 bills required to dispense the specified amount. The ATM allows the user to choose only withdrawal amounts that are multiples of $20, so we convert amount to an integer value and divide it by 20 to obtain the number of billsRequired. Line 30 returns true if the Cash-Dispenser's billCount is greater than or equal to billsRequired (i.e., enough bills are available) and false otherwise (i.e., not enough bills). For example, if a user wishes to

```
 1    // CashDispenser.cs
 2    // Represents the cash dispenser of the ATM
 3    public class CashDispenser
 4    {
 5       // the default initial number of bills in the cash dispenser
 6       private const int INITIAL_COUNT = 500;
 7       private int billCount; // number of $20 bills remaining
 8
 9       // parameterless constructor initializes billCount to INITIAL_COUNT
10       public CashDispenser()
11       {
12          billCount = INITIAL_COUNT; // set billCount to INITIAL_COUNT
13       } // end constructor
14
15       // simulates dispensing the specified amount of cash
16       public void DispenseCash( decimal amount )
17       {
18          // number of $20 bills required
19          int billsRequired = ( ( int ) amount ) / 20;
20          billCount -= billsRequired;
21       } // end method DispenseCash
22
23       // indicates whether cash dispenser can dispense desired amount
24       public bool IsSufficientCashAvailable( decimal amount )
25       {
26          // number of $20 bills required
27          int billsRequired = ( ( int ) amount ) / 20;
28
29          // return whether there are enough bills available
30          return ( billCount >= billsRequired );
31       } // end method IsSufficientCashAvailable
32    } // end class CashDispenser
```

Fig. D.4 | Class CashDispenser represents the ATM's cash dispenser.

withdraw $80 (i.e., billsRequired is 4), but only three bills remain (i.e., billCount is 3), the method returns false.

Method DispenseCash (lines 16–21) simulates cash dispensing. If our system were hooked up to a real hardware cash dispenser, this method would interact with the hardware device to physically dispense the cash. Our simulated version of the method simply decreases the billCount of bills remaining by the number required to dispense the specified amount (line 20). Note that it is the responsibility of the client of the class (i.e., Withdrawal) to inform the user that cash has been dispensed—CashDispenser does not interact directly with Screen.

D.6 Class DepositSlot

Class DepositSlot (Fig. D.5) represents the deposit slot of the ATM. This class simulates the functionality of a real hardware deposit slot. DepositSlot has no attributes and only one method—IsDepositEnvelopeReceived (lines 7–10)—which indicates whether a deposit envelope was received.

```
 1   // DepositSlot.cs
 2   // Represents the deposit slot of the ATM
 3   public class DepositSlot
 4   {
 5      // indicates whether envelope was received (always returns true,
 6      // because this is only a software simulation of a real deposit slot)
 7      public bool IsDepositEnvelopeReceived()
 8      {
 9         return true; // deposit envelope was received
10      } // end method IsDepositEnvelopeReceived
11   } // end class DepositSlot
```

Fig. D.5 | Class DepositSlot represents the ATM's deposit slot.

Recall from the requirements document that the ATM allows the user up to two minutes to insert an envelope. The current version of method IsDepositEnvelopeReceived simply returns true immediately (line 9), because this is only a software simulation, so we assume that the user inserts an envelope within the required time frame. If an actual hardware deposit slot were connected to our system, method IsDepositEnvelopeReceived would be implemented to wait for a maximum of two minutes to receive a signal from the hardware deposit slot indicating that the user has indeed inserted a deposit envelope. If IsDepositEnvelopeReceived were to receive such a signal within two minutes, the method would return true. If two minutes were to elapse and the method still had not received a signal, then the method would return false.

D.7 Class Account

Class Account (Fig. D.6) represents a bank account. Each Account has four attributes (modeled in Fig. 12.22)—accountNumber, pin, availableBalance and totalBalance. Lines 5–8 implement these attributes as private instance variables. For each of the instance variables accountNumber, availableBalance and totalBalance, we provide a property with the same name as the attribute, but starting with a capital letter. For example, property AccountNumber corresponds to the accountNumber attribute modeled in Fig. 12.22. Clients of this class do not need to modify the accountNumber instance variable, so AccountNumber is declared as a read-only property (i.e., it provides only a get accessor).

Class Account has a constructor (lines 11–18) that takes an account number, the PIN established for the account, the initial available balance and the initial total balance as arguments. Lines 14–17 assign these values to the class's attributes (i.e., instance variables). Note that Account objects would normally be created externally to the ATM system. However, in this simulation, the Account objects are created in the BankDatabase class (Fig. D.7).

```
 1   // Account.cs
 2   // Class Account represents a bank account.
 3   public class Account
 4   {
 5      private int accountNumber; // account number
 6      private int pin; // PIN for authentication
```

Fig. D.6 | Class Account represents a bank account. (Part I of 3.)

```
7     private decimal availableBalance; // available withdrawal amount
8     private decimal totalBalance; // funds available + pending deposit
9
10    // four-parameter constructor initializes attributes
11    public Account( int theAccountNumber, int thePIN,
12       decimal theAvailableBalance, decimal theTotalBalance )
13    {
14       accountNumber = theAccountNumber;
15       pin = thePIN;
16       availableBalance = theAvailableBalance;
17       totalBalance = theTotalBalance;
18    } // end constructor
19
20    // read-only property that gets the account number
21    public int AccountNumber
22    {
23       get
24       {
25          return accountNumber;
26       } // end get
27    } // end property AccountNumber
28
29    // read-only property that gets the available balance
30    public decimal AvailableBalance
31    {
32       get
33       {
34          return availableBalance;
35       } // end get
36    } // end property AvailableBalance
37
38    // read-only property that gets the total balance
39    public decimal TotalBalance
40    {
41       get
42       {
43          return totalBalance;
44       } // end get
45    } // end property TotalBalance
46
47    // determines whether a user-specified PIN matches PIN in Account
48    public bool ValidatePIN( int userPIN )
49    {
50       return ( userPIN == pin );
51    } // end method ValidatePIN
52
53    // credits the account (funds have not yet cleared)
54    public void Credit( decimal amount )
55    {
56       totalBalance += amount; // add to total balance
57    } // end method Credit
58
```

Fig. D.6 | Class Account represents a bank account. (Part 2 of 3.)

```
59    // debits the account
60    public void Debit( decimal amount )
61    {
62       availableBalance -= amount; // subtract from available balance
63       totalBalance -= amount; // subtract from total balance
64    } // end method Debit
65  } // end class Account
```

Fig. D.6 | Class Account represents a bank account. (Part 3 of 3.)

public *Read-Only Properties of Class* Account
Read-only property AccountNumber (lines 21–27) provides access to an Account's accountNumber instance variable. We include this property in our implementation so that a client of the class (e.g., BankDatabase) can identify a particular Account. For example, BankDatabase contains many Account objects, and it can access this property on each of its Account objects to locate the one with a specific account number.

Read-only properties AvailableBalance (lines 30–36) and TotalBalance (lines 39–45) allow clients to retrieve the values of private decimal instance variables available-Balance and totalBalance, respectively. Property AvailableBalance represents the amount of funds available for withdrawal. Property TotalBalance represents the amount of funds available, plus the amount of deposited funds pending confirmation of cash in deposit envelopes or clearance of checks in deposit envelopes.

public *Methods of Class* Account
Method ValidatePIN (lines 48–51) determines whether a user-specified PIN (i.e., parameter userPIN) matches the PIN associated with the account (i.e., attribute pin). Recall that we modeled this method's parameter userPIN in the UML class diagram of Fig. 7.22. If the two PINs match, the method returns true; otherwise, it returns false.

Method Credit (lines 54–57) adds an amount of money (i.e., parameter amount) to an Account as part of a deposit transaction. Note that this method adds the amount only to instance variable totalBalance (line 56). The money credited to an account during a deposit does not become available immediately, so we modify only the total balance. We assume that the bank updates the available balance appropriately at a later time, when the amount of cash in the deposit envelope has be verified and the checks in the deposit envelope have cleared. Our implementation of class Account includes only methods required for carrying out ATM transactions. Therefore, we omit the methods that some other bank system would invoke to add to instance variable availableBalance to confirm a deposit or to subtract from attribute totalBalance to reject a deposit.

Method Debit (lines 60–64) subtracts an amount of money (i.e., parameter amount) from an Account as part of a withdrawal transaction. This method subtracts the amount from both instance variable availableBalance (line 62) and instance variable totalBalance (line 63), because a withdrawal affects both balances.

D.8 Class BankDatabase
Class BankDatabase (Fig. D.7) models the bank database with which the ATM interacts to access and modify a user's account information. We determine one reference-type attribute for class BankDatabase based on its composition relationship with class Account. Re-

call from Fig. 12.21 that a BankDatabase is composed of zero or more objects of class Account. Line 5 declares attribute accounts—an array that will store Account objects—to implement this composition relationship. Class BankDatabase has a parameterless constructor (lines 8–15) that initializes accounts with new Account objects (lines 13–14). Note that the Account constructor (Fig. D.6, lines 11–18) has four parameters—the account number, the PIN assigned to the account, the initial available balance and the initial total balance.

```csharp
 1  // BankDatabase.cs
 2  // Represents the bank account information database
 3  public class BankDatabase
 4  {
 5     private Account[] accounts; // array of the bank's Accounts
 6
 7     // parameterless constructor initializes accounts
 8     public BankDatabase()
 9     {
10        // create two Account objects for testing and
11        // place them in the accounts array
12        accounts = new Account[ 2 ]; // create accounts array
13        accounts[ 0 ] = new Account( 12345, 54321, 1000.00M, 1200.00M );
14        accounts[ 1 ] = new Account( 98765, 56789, 200.00M, 200.00M );
15     } // end constructor
16
17     // retrieve Account object containing specified account number
18     private Account GetAccount( int accountNumber )
19     {
20        // loop through accounts searching for matching account number
21        foreach ( Account currentAccount in accounts )
22        {
23           if ( currentAccount.AccountNumber == accountNumber )
24              return currentAccount;
25        } // end foreach
26
27        // account not found
28        return null;
29     } // end method GetAccount
30
31     // determine whether user-specified account number and PIN match
32     // those of an account in the database
33     public bool AuthenticateUser( int userAccountNumber, int userPIN)
34     {
35        // attempt to retrieve the account with the account number
36        Account userAccount = GetAccount( userAccountNumber );
37
38        // if account exists, return result of Account function ValidatePIN
39        if ( userAccount != null )
40           return userAccount.ValidatePIN( userPIN ); // true if match
41        else
42           return false; // account number not found, so return false
43     } // end method AuthenticateUser
```

Fig. D.7 | Class BankDatabase represents the bank's account information database. (Part I of 2.)

```
44
45        // return available balance of Account with specified account number
46        public decimal GetAvailableBalance( int userAccountNumber )
47        {
48            Account userAccount = GetAccount( userAccountNumber );
49            return userAccount.AvailableBalance;
50        } // end method GetAvailableBalance
51
52        // return total balance of Account with specified account number
53        public decimal GetTotalBalance( int userAccountNumber )
54        {
55            Account userAccount = GetAccount(userAccountNumber);
56            return userAccount.TotalBalance;
57        } // end method GetTotalBalance
58
59        // credit the Account with specified account number
60        public void Credit( int userAccountNumber, decimal amount )
61        {
62            Account userAccount = GetAccount( userAccountNumber );
63            userAccount.Credit( amount );
64        } // end method Credit
65
66        // debit the Account with specified account number
67        public void Debit( int userAccountNumber, decimal amount )
68        {
69            Account userAccount = GetAccount( userAccountNumber );
70            userAccount.Debit( amount );
71        } // end method Debit
72    } // end class BankDatabase
```

Fig. D.7 | Class BankDatabase represents the bank's account information database. (Part 2 of 2.)

Recall that class BankDatabase serves as an intermediary between class ATM and the actual Account objects that contain users' account information. Thus, methods of class BankDatabase invoke the corresponding methods and properties of the Account object belonging to the current ATM user.

private Utility Method GetAccount
We include private utility method GetAccount (lines 18–29) to allow the BankDatabase to obtain a reference to a particular Account within the accounts array. To locate the user's Account, the BankDatabase compares the value returned by property AccountNumber for each element of accounts to a specified account number until it finds a match. Lines 21–25 traverse the accounts array. If currentAccount's account number equals the value of parameter accountNumber, the method returns currentAccount. If no account has the given account number, then line 28 returns null.

public Methods
Method AuthenticateUser (lines 33–43) proves or disproves the identity of an ATM user. This method takes a user-specified account number and a user-specified PIN as arguments and indicates whether they match the account number and PIN of an Account in the database. Line 36 calls method GetAccount, which returns either an Account with

userAccountNumber as its account number or null to indicate that userAccountNumber is invalid. If GetAccount returns an Account object, line 40 returns the bool value returned by that object's ValidatePIN method. Note that BankDatabase's AuthenticateUser method does not perform the PIN comparison itself—rather, it forwards userPIN to the Account object's ValidatePIN method to do so. The value returned by Account method ValidatePIN (line 40) indicates whether the user-specified PIN matches the PIN of the user's Account, so method AuthenticateUser simply returns this value (line 40) to the client of the class (i.e., ATM).

The BankDatabase trusts the ATM to invoke method AuthenticateUser and receive a return value of true before allowing the user to perform transactions. BankDatabase also trusts that each Transaction object created by the ATM contains the valid account number of the current authenticated user and that this account number is passed to the remaining BankDatabase methods as argument userAccountNumber. Methods GetAvailableBalance (lines 46–50), GetTotalBalance (lines 53–57), Credit (lines 60–64) and Debit (lines 67–71) therefore simply retrieve the user's Account object with utility method GetAccount, then invoke the appropriate Account method on that object. We know that the calls to GetAccount within these methods will never return null, because userAccountNumber must refer to an existing Account. Note that GetAvailableBalance and GetTotalBalance return the values returned by the corresponding Account properties. Also, note that methods Credit and Debit simply redirect parameter amount to the Account methods they invoke.

D.9 Class Transaction

Class Transaction (Fig. D.8) is an abstract base class that represents the notion of an ATM transaction. It contains the common features of derived classes BalanceInquiry, Withdrawal and Deposit. This class expands on the "skeleton" code first developed in Section 12.9. Line 3 declares this class to be abstract. Lines 5–7 declare the class's private instance variables. Recall from the class diagram of Fig. 12.22 that class Transaction contains the property AccountNumber that indicates the account involved in the Transaction. Line 5 implements the instance variable accountNumber to maintain the AccountNumber property's data. We derive attributes screen (implemented as instance variable userScreen in line 6) and bankDatabase (implemented as instance variable database in line 7) from class Transaction's associations, modeled in Fig. 12.21. All transactions require access to the ATM's screen and the bank's database.

Class Transaction has a constructor (lines 10–16) that takes the current user's account number and references to the ATM's screen and the bank's database as arguments. Because Transaction is an abstract class (line 3), this constructor is never called directly to instantiate Transaction objects. Instead, this constructor is invoked by the constructors of the Transaction derived classes via constructor initializers.

```
1   // Transaction.cs
2   // Abstract base class Transaction represents an ATM transaction.
3   public abstract class Transaction
4   {
```

Fig. D.8 | abstract base class Transaction represents an ATM transaction. (Part 1 of 2.)

```
 5        private int accountNumber; // account involved in the transaction
 6        private Screen userScreen; // reference to ATM's screen
 7        private BankDatabase database; // reference to account info database
 8
 9        // three-parameter constructor invoked by derived classes
10        public Transaction( int userAccount, Screen theScreen,
11           BankDatabase theDatabase )
12        {
13           accountNumber = userAccount;
14           userScreen = theScreen;
15           database = theDatabase;
16        } // end constructor
17
18        // read-only property that gets the account number
19        public int AccountNumber
20        {
21           get
22           {
23              return accountNumber;
24           } // end get
25        } // end property AccountNumber
26
27        // read-only property that gets the screen reference
28        public Screen UserScreen
29        {
30           get
31           {
32              return userScreen;
33           } // end get
34        } // end property UserScreen
35
36        // read-only property that gets the bank database reference
37        public BankDatabase Database
38        {
39           get
40           {
41              return database;
42           } // end get
43        } // end property Database
44
45        // perform the transaction (overridden by each derived class)
46        public abstract void Execute(); // no implementation here
47     } // end class Transaction
```

Fig. D.8 | abstract base class Transaction represents an ATM transaction. (Part 2 of 2.)

Class Transaction has three public read-only properties—AccountNumber (lines 19–25), UserScreen (lines 28–34) and Database (lines 37–43). Derived classes of Transaction inherit these properties and use them to gain access to class Transaction's private instance variables. Note that we chose the names of the UserScreen and Database properties for clarity—we wanted to avoid property names that are the same as the class names Screen and BankDatabase, which can be confusing.

Class `Transaction` also declares abstract method `Execute` (line 46). It does not make sense to provide an implementation for this method in class `Transaction`, because a generic transaction cannot be executed. Thus, we declare this method to be abstract, forcing each `Transaction` concrete derived class to provide its own implementation that executes the particular type of transaction.

D.10 Class `BalanceInquiry`

Class `BalanceInquiry` (Fig. D.9) inherits from `Transaction` and represents an ATM balance inquiry transaction (line 3). `BalanceInquiry` does not have any attributes of its own, but it inherits `Transaction` attributes `accountNumber`, `screen` and `bankDatabase`, which are accessible through `Transaction`'s `public` read-only properties. The `BalanceInquiry` constructor (lines 6–8) takes arguments corresponding to these attributes and forwards them to `Transaction`'s constructor by invoking the constructor initializer with keyword `base` (line 8). The body of the constructor is empty.

Class `BalanceInquiry` overrides `Transaction`'s abstract method `Execute` to provide a concrete implementation (lines 11–27) that performs the steps involved in a balance inquiry. Lines 14–15 obtain the specified `Account`'s available balance by invoking the `GetAvailableBalance` method of the inherited property `Database`. Note that line 15 uses the inherited property `AccountNumber` to get the account number of the current user. Line

```
 1    // BalanceInquiry.cs
 2    // Represents a balance inquiry ATM transaction
 3    public class BalanceInquiry : Transaction
 4    {
 5       // five-parameter constructor initializes base class variables
 6       public BalanceInquiry( int userAccountNumber,
 7          Screen atmScreen, BankDatabase atmBankDatabase )
 8          : base( userAccountNumber, atmScreen, atmBankDatabase ) {}
 9
10       // performs transaction; overrides Transaction's abstract method
11       public override void Execute()
12       {
13          // get the available balance for the current user's Account
14          decimal availableBalance =
15             Database.GetAvailableBalance( AccountNumber );
16
17          // get the total balance for the current user's Account
18          decimal totalBalance = Database.GetTotalBalance( AccountNumber );
19
20          // display the balance information on the screen
21          UserScreen.DisplayMessageLine( "\nBalance Information:" );
22          UserScreen.DisplayMessage( " - Available balance: " );
23          UserScreen.DisplayDollarAmount( availableBalance );
24          UserScreen.DisplayMessage( "\n - Total balance: " );
25          UserScreen.DisplayDollarAmount( totalBalance );
26          UserScreen.DisplayMessageLine( "" );
27       } // end method Execute
28    } // end class BalanceInquiry
```

Fig. D.9 | Class `BalanceInquiry` represents a balance inquiry ATM transaction.

18 retrieves the specified Account's total balance. Lines 21–26 display the balance information on the ATM's screen using the inherited property UserScreen. Recall that DisplayDollarAmount takes a decimal argument and outputs it to the screen formatted as a dollar amount with a dollar sign. For example, if a user's available balance is 1000.50M, line 23 outputs $1,000.50. Note that line 26 inserts a blank line of output to separate the balance information from subsequent output (i.e., the main menu repeated by class ATM after executing the BalanceInquiry).

D.11 Class Withdrawal

Class Withdrawal (Fig. D.10) extends Transaction and represents an ATM withdrawal transaction. This class expands on the "skeleton" code for this class developed in Fig. 12.24. Recall from the class diagram of Fig. 12.22 that class Withdrawal has one attribute, amount, which line 5 declares as a decimal instance variable. Fig. 12.21 models associations between class Withdrawal and classes Keypad and CashDispenser, for which lines 6–7 implement reference attributes keypad and cashDispenser, respectively. Line 10 declares a constant corresponding to the cancel menu option.

Class Withdrawal's constructor (lines 13–21) has five parameters. It uses the constructor initializer to pass parameters userAccountNumber, atmScreen and atmBankDatabase to base class Transaction's constructor to set the attributes that Withdrawal inherits from Transaction. The constructor also takes references atmKeypad and atmCashDispenser as parameters and assigns them to reference-type attributes keypad and cashDispenser, respectively.

```csharp
1   // Withdrawal.cs
2   // Class Withdrawal represents an ATM withdrawal transaction.
3   public class Withdrawal : Transaction
4   {
5      private decimal amount; // amount to withdraw
6      private Keypad keypad; // reference to Keypad
7      private CashDispenser cashDispenser; // reference to cash dispenser
8
9      // constant that corresponds to menu option to cancel
10     private const int CANCELED = 6;
11
12     // five-parameter constructor
13     public Withdrawal( int userAccountNumber, Screen atmScreen,
14        BankDatabase atmBankDatabase, Keypad atmKeypad,
15        CashDispenser atmCashDispenser )
16        : base( userAccountNumber, atmScreen, atmBankDatabase )
17     {
18        // initialize references to keypad and cash dispenser
19        keypad = atmKeypad;
20        cashDispenser = atmCashDispenser;
21     } // end constructor
22
23     // perform transaction, overrides Transaction's abstract method
24     public override void Execute()
25     {
```

Fig. D.10 | Class Withdrawal represents an ATM withdrawal transaction. (Part 1 of 3.)

```
26            bool cashDispensed = false; // cash was not dispensed yet
27
28            // transaction was not canceled yet
29            bool transactionCanceled = false;
30
31            // loop until cash is dispensed or the user cancels
32            do
33            {
34               // obtain the chosen withdrawal amount from the user
35               int selection = DisplayMenuOfAmounts();
36
37               // check whether user chose a withdrawal amount or canceled
38               if ( selection != CANCELED )
39               {
40                  // set amount to the selected dollar amount
41                  amount = selection;
42
43                  // get available balance of account involved
44                  decimal availableBalance =
45                     Database.GetAvailableBalance( AccountNumber );
46
47                  // check whether the user has enough money in the account
48                  if ( amount <= availableBalance )
49                  {
50                     // check whether the cash dispenser has enough money
51                     if ( cashDispenser.IsSufficientCashAvailable( amount ) )
52                     {
53                        // debit the account to reflect the withdrawal
54                        Database.Debit( AccountNumber, amount );
55
56                        cashDispenser.DispenseCash( amount ); // dispense cash
57                        cashDispensed = true; // cash was dispensed
58
59                        // instruct user to take cash
60                        UserScreen.DisplayMessageLine(
61                           "\nPlease take your cash from the cash dispenser." );
62                     } // end innermost if
63                     else // cash dispenser does not have enough cash
64                        UserScreen.DisplayMessageLine(
65                           "\nInsufficient cash available in the ATM." +
66                           "\n\nPlease choose a smaller amount." );
67                  } // end middle if
68                  else // not enough money available in user's account
69                     UserScreen.DisplayMessageLine(
70                        "\nInsufficient cash available in your account." +
71                        "\n\nPlease choose a smaller amount." );
72               } // end outermost if
73               else
74               {
75                  UserScreen.DisplayMessageLine( "\nCanceling transaction..." );
76                  transactionCanceled = true; // user canceled the transaction
77               } // end else
78            } while ( ( !cashDispensed ) && ( !transactionCanceled ) );
```

Fig. D.10 | Class Withdrawal represents an ATM withdrawal transaction. (Part 2 of 3.)

```
79      } // end method Execute
80
81      // display a menu of withdrawal amounts and the option to cancel;
82      // return the chosen amount or 6 if the user chooses to cancel
83      private int DisplayMenuOfAmounts()
84      {
85          int userChoice = 0; // variable to store return value
86
87          // array of amounts to correspond to menu numbers
88          int[] amounts = { 0, 20, 40, 60, 100, 200 };
89
90          // loop while no valid choice has been made
91          while ( userChoice == 0 )
92          {
93              // display the menu
94              UserScreen.DisplayMessageLine( "\nWithdrawal options:" );
95              UserScreen.DisplayMessageLine( "1 - $20" );
96              UserScreen.DisplayMessageLine( "2 - $40" );
97              UserScreen.DisplayMessageLine( "3 - $60" );
98              UserScreen.DisplayMessageLine( "4 - $100" );
99              UserScreen.DisplayMessageLine( "5 - $200" );
100             UserScreen.DisplayMessageLine( "6 - Cancel transaction" );
101             UserScreen.DisplayMessage(
102                 "\nChoose a withdrawal option (1-6): " );
103
104             // get user input through keypad
105             int input = keypad.GetInput();
106
107             // determine how to proceed based on the input value
108             switch ( input )
109             {
110                 // if the user chose a withdrawal amount (i.e., option
111                 // 1, 2, 3, 4, or 5), return the corresponding amount
112                 // from the amounts array
113                 case 1: case 2: case 3: case 4: case 5:
114                     userChoice = amounts[ input ]; // save user's choice
115                     break;
116                 case CANCELED: // the user chose to cancel
117                     userChoice = CANCELED; // save user's choice
118                     break;
119                 default:
120                     UserScreen.DisplayMessageLine(
121                         "\nInvalid selection. Try again." );
122                     break;
123             } // end switch
124         } // end while
125
126         return userChoice;
127     } // end method DisplayMenuOfAmounts
128 } // end class Withdrawal
```

Fig. D.10 | Class Withdrawal represents an ATM withdrawal transaction. (Part 3 of 3.)

Overriding abstract Method Execute

Class Withdrawal overrides Transaction's abstract method Execute with a concrete implementation (lines 24–79) that performs the steps involved in a withdrawal. Line 26 declares and initializes a local bool variable cashDispensed. This variable indicates whether cash has been dispensed (i.e., whether the transaction has completed successfully) and is initially false. Line 29 declares and initializes to false a bool variable transactionCanceled to indicate that the transaction has not yet been canceled by the user.

Lines 32–78 contain a do...while statement that executes its body until cash is dispensed (i.e., until cashDispensed becomes true) or until the user chooses to cancel (i.e., until transactionCanceled becomes true). We use this loop to continuously return the user to the start of the transaction if an error occurs (i.e., the requested withdrawal amount is greater than the user's available balance or greater than the amount of cash in the cash dispenser). Line 35 displays a menu of withdrawal amounts and obtains a user selection by calling private utility method DisplayMenuOfAmounts (declared in lines 83–127). This method displays the menu of amounts and returns either an int withdrawal amount or an int constant CANCELED to indicate that the user has chosen to cancel the transaction.

Displaying Options With private Utility Method DisplayMenuOfAmounts

Method DisplayMenuOfAmounts (lines 83–127) first declares local variable userChoice (initially 0) to store the value that the method will return (line 85). Line 88 declares an integer array of withdrawal amounts that correspond to the amounts displayed in the withdrawal menu. We ignore the first element in the array (index 0), because the menu has no option 0. The while statement at lines 91–124 repeats until userChoice takes on a value other than 0. We will see shortly that this occurs when the user makes a valid selection from the menu. Lines 94–102 display the withdrawal menu on the screen and prompt the user to enter a choice. Line 105 obtains integer input through the keypad. The switch statement at lines 108–123 determines how to proceed based on the user's input. If the user selects 1, 2, 3, 4 or 5, line 114 sets userChoice to the value of the element in the amounts array at index input. For example, if the user enters 3 to withdraw $60, line 114 sets userChoice to the value of amounts[3]—i.e., 60. Variable userChoice no longer equals 0, so the while at lines 91–124 terminates, and line 126 returns userChoice. If the user selects the cancel menu option, line 117 executes, setting userChoice to CANCELED and causing the method to return this value. If the user does not enter a valid menu selection, lines 120–121 display an error message, and the user is returned to the withdrawal menu.

The if statement at line 38 in method Execute determines whether the user has selected a withdrawal amount or chosen to cancel. If the user cancels, line 75 displays an appropriate message to the user before control is returned to the calling method—ATM method PerformTransactions. If the user has chosen a withdrawal amount, line 41 assigns local variable selection to instance variable amount. Lines 44–45 retrieve the available balance of the current user's Account and store it in a local decimal variable availableBalance. Next, the if statement at line 48 determines whether the selected amount is less than or equal to the user's available balance. If it is not, lines 69–71 display an error message. Control then continues to the end of the do...while statement, and the loop repeats because both cashDispensed and transactionCanceled are still false. If the user's balance is high enough, the if statement at line 51 determines whether the cash dispenser has enough money to satisfy the withdrawal request by invoking the cashDispenser's IsSufficientCashAvailable method. If this method returns false, lines

64–66 display an error message, and the do…while statement repeats. If sufficient cash is available, the requirements for the withdrawal are satisfied, and line 54 debits the user's account in the database by amount. Lines 56–57 then instruct the cash dispenser to dispense the cash to the user and set cashDispensed to true. Finally, lines 60–61 display a message to the user to take the dispensed cash. Because cashDispensed is now true, control continues after the do…while statement. No additional statements appear below the loop, so the method returns control to class ATM.

D.12 Class Deposit

Class Deposit (Fig. D.11) inherits from Transaction and represents an ATM deposit transaction. Recall from the class diagram of Fig. 12.22 that class Deposit has one attribute, amount, which line 5 declares as a decimal instance variable. Lines 6–7 create reference attributes keypad and depositSlot that implement the associations between class Deposit and classes Keypad and DepositSlot, modeled in Fig. 12.21. Line 10 declares a constant CANCELED that corresponds to the value a user enters to cancel a deposit transaction.

Class Deposit contains a constructor (lines 13–21) that passes three parameters to base class Transaction's constructor using a constructor initializer. The constructor also has parameters atmKeypad and atmDepositSlot, which it assigns to the corresponding reference instance variables (lines 19–20).

```
1   // Deposit.cs
2   // Represents a deposit ATM transaction.
3   public class Deposit : Transaction
4   {
5       private decimal amount; // amount to deposit
6       private Keypad keypad; // reference to the Keypad
7       private DepositSlot depositSlot; // reference to the deposit slot
8
9       // constant representing cancel option
10      private const int CANCELED = 0;
11
12      // five-parameter constructor initializes class's instance variables
13      public Deposit( int userAccountNumber, Screen atmScreen,
14          BankDatabase atmBankDatabase, Keypad atmKeypad,
15          DepositSlot atmDepositSlot )
16          : base( userAccountNumber, atmScreen, atmBankDatabase )
17      {
18          // initialize references to keypad and deposit slot
19          keypad = atmKeypad;
20          depositSlot = atmDepositSlot;
21      } // end five-parameter constructor
22
23      // perform transaction; overrides Transaction's abstract method
24      public override void Execute()
25      {
26          amount = PromptForDepositAmount(); // get deposit amount from user
27
```

Fig. D.11 | Class Deposit represents an ATM deposit transaction. (Part 1 of 2.)

```
28          // check whether user entered a deposit amount or canceled
29          if ( amount != CANCELED )
30          {
31             // request deposit envelope containing specified amount
32             UserScreen.DisplayMessage(
33                "\nPlease insert a deposit envelope containing " );
34             UserScreen.DisplayDollarAmount( amount );
35             UserScreen.DisplayMessageLine( " in the deposit slot." );
36
37             // retrieve deposit envelope
38             bool envelopeReceived = depositSlot.IsDepositEnvelopeReceived();
39
40             // check whether deposit envelope was received
41             if ( envelopeReceived )
42             {
43                UserScreen.DisplayMessageLine(
44                   "\nYour envelope has been received.\n" +
45                   "The money just deposited will not be available " +
46                   "until we \nverify the amount of any " +
47                   "enclosed cash, and any enclosed checks clear." );
48
49                // credit account to reflect the deposit
50                Database.Credit( AccountNumber, amount );
51             } // end inner if
52             else
53                UserScreen.DisplayMessageLine(
54                   "\nYou did not insert an envelope, so the ATM has " +
55                   "canceled your transaction." );
56          } // end outer if
57          else
58             UserScreen.DisplayMessageLine( "\nCanceling transaction..." );
59       } // end method Execute
60
61       // prompt user to enter a deposit amount to credit
62       private decimal PromptForDepositAmount()
63       {
64          // display the prompt and receive input
65          UserScreen.DisplayMessage(
66             "\nPlease input a deposit amount in CENTS (or 0 to cancel): " );
67          int input = keypad.GetInput();
68
69          // check whether the user canceled or entered a valid amount
70          if ( input == CANCELED )
71             return CANCELED;
72          else
73             return input / 100.00M;
74       } // end method PromptForDepositAmount
75    } // end class Deposit
```

Fig. D.11 | Class Deposit represents an ATM deposit transaction. (Part 2 of 2.)

Overriding abstract Method Execute

Method Execute (lines 24–59) overrides abstract method Execute in base class Transaction with a concrete implementation that performs the steps required in a deposit transaction. Line 26 prompts the user to enter a deposit amount by invoking private utility method PromptForDepositAmount (declared in lines 62–74) and sets attribute amount to the value returned. Method PromptForDepositAmount asks the user to enter a deposit amount as an integer number of cents (because the ATM's keypad does not contain a decimal point; this is consistent with many real ATMs) and returns the decimal value representing the dollar amount to be deposited.

Getting Deposit Amount with private Utility Method PromptForDepositAmount
Lines 65–66 in method PromptForDepositAmount display a message asking the user to input a deposit amount as a number of cents or "0" to cancel the transaction. Line 67 receives the user's input from the keypad. The if statement at lines 70–73 determines whether the user has entered a deposit amount or chosen to cancel. If the user chooses to cancel, line 71 returns constant CANCELED. Otherwise, line 73 returns the deposit amount after converting the int number of cents to a dollar-and-cents amount by dividing by the decimal literal 100.00M. For example, if the user enters 125 as the number of cents, line 73 returns 125 divided by 100.00M, or 1.25—125 cents is $1.25.

The if statement at lines 29–58 in method Execute determines whether the user has chosen to cancel the transaction instead of entering a deposit amount. If the user cancels, line 58 displays an appropriate message, and the method returns. If the user enters a deposit amount, lines 32–35 instruct the user to insert a deposit envelope with the correct amount. Recall that Screen method DisplayDollarAmount outputs a decimal value formatted as a dollar amount (including the dollar sign).

Line 38 sets a local bool variable to the value returned by depositSlot's IsDepositEnvelopeReceived method, indicating whether a deposit envelope has been received. Recall that we coded method IsDepositEnvelopeReceived (lines 7–10 of Fig. D.5) to always return true, because we are simulating the functionality of the deposit slot and assume that the user always inserts an envelope in a timely fashion (i.e., within the two-minute time limit). However, we code method Execute of class Deposit to test for the possibility that the user does not insert an envelope—good software engineering demands that programs account for all possible return values. Thus, class Deposit is prepared for future versions of IsDepositEnvelopeReceived that could return false. Lines 43–50 execute if the deposit slot receives an envelope. Lines 43–47 display an appropriate message to the user. Line 50 credits the user's account in the database with the deposit amount. Lines 53–55 execute if the deposit slot does not receive a deposit envelope. In this case, we display a message stating that the ATM has canceled the transaction. The method then returns without crediting the user's account.

D.13 Class ATMCaseStudy

Class ATMCaseStudy (Fig. D.12) simply allows us to start, or "turn on," the ATM and test the implementation of our ATM system model. Class ATMCaseStudy's Main method (lines 6–10) simply instantiates a new ATM object named theATM (line 8) and invokes its Run method (line 9) to start the ATM.

D.14 Wrap-Up

Now that we have presented the complete ATM implementation, you can see that many issues arose during implementation for which we did not provide detailed UML diagrams.

```
1   // ATMCaseStudy.cs
2   // Application for testing the ATM case study.
3   public class ATMCaseStudy
4   {
5      // Main method is the application's entry point
6      public static void Main( string[] args )
7      {
8         ATM theATM = new ATM();
9         theATM.Run();
10     } // end method Main
11  } // end class ATMCaseStudy
```

Fig. D.12 | Class ATMCaseStudy starts the ATM.

This is not uncommon in an object-oriented design and implementation experience. For example, many attributes listed in the class diagrams were implemented as C# properties so that clients of the classes could gain controlled access to the underlying private instance variables. We did not make all of these properties during our design process, because there was nothing in the requirements document or our design process to indicate that certain attributes would eventually need to be accessed outside of their classes.

We also encountered various issues with simulating hardware. A real-world ATM is a hardware device that does not have a complete computer keyboard. One problem with using a computer keyboard to simulate the keypad is that the user can enter non-digits as input. We did not spend much time dealing with such issues, because this problem is not possible in a real ATM, which has only a numeric keypad. However, having to think about issues like this is a good thing. Quite typically, software designs for complete systems involve simulating hardware devices like the cash dispenser and keypad. Despite the fact that some aspects of our ATM may seem contrived, in real-world systems, hardware design and implementation often occurs in parallel with software design and implementation. In such cases, the software cannot be implemented in final form because the hardware is not yet ready. So, software developers must simulate the hardware, as we have done in this case study.

Congratulations on completing the entire software engineering ATM case study! We hope you found this experience to be valuable and that it reinforced many of the concepts that you learned in Chapters 1–12. We would sincerely appreciate your comments, criticisms and suggestions. You can reach us at deitel@deitel.com. We will respond promptly.

UML 2: Additional Diagram Types

E.1 Introduction

If you read the optional Software Engineering Case Study sections in Chapters 3–8, 10 and 12, you should now have a comfortable grasp of the UML diagram types that we use to model our ATM system. The case study is intended for use in first- or second-semester courses, so we limit our discussion to a concise subset of the UML. The UML 2 provides a total of 13 diagram types. The end of Section 3.9 summarizes the six diagram types that we use in the case study. This appendix lists and briefly defines the seven remaining diagram types.

E.2 Additional Diagram Types

The following are the seven diagram types that we have chosen not to use in our Software Engineering Case Study.

- *Object diagrams* model a "snapshot" of the system by modeling a system's objects and their relationships at a specific point in time. Each object represents an instance of a class from a class diagram, and several objects may be created from one class. For our ATM system, an object diagram could show several distinct Account objects side by side, illustrating that they are all part of the bank's account database.

- *Component diagrams* model the *artifacts* and *components*—resources (which include source files)—that make up the system.

- *Deployment diagrams* model the rsystem's runtime requirements (such as the computer or computers on which the system will reside), memory requirements, or other devices the system requires during execution.

- *Package diagrams* model the hierarchical structure of *packages* (which are groups of classes) in the system at compile time and the relationships that exist between the packages.

- *Composite structure diagrams* model the internal structure of a complex object at runtime. New in UML 2, they allow system designers to hierarchically decompose a complex object into smaller parts. Composite structure diagrams are beyond the scope of our case study. They are more appropriate for larger industrial applications, which exhibit complex groupings of objects at execution time.

- *Interaction overview diagrams*, new in UML 2, provide a summary of control flow in the system by combining elements of several types of behavioral diagrams (e.g., activity diagrams, sequence diagrams).

- *Timing diagrams*, also new in UML 2, model the timing constraints imposed on stage changes and interactions between objects in a system.

To learn more about these diagrams and advanced UML topics, please visit www.uml.org and the web resources listed at the end of Section 3.9.

ASCII Character Set

	0	1	2	3	4	5	6	7	8	9
0	nul	soh	stx	etx	eot	enq	ack	bel	bs	ht
1	nl	vt	ff	cr	so	si	dle	dc1	dc2	dc3
2	dc4	nak	syn	etb	can	em	sub	esc	fs	gs
3	rs	us	sp	!	"	#	$	%	&	'
4	(	)	*	+	,	-	.	/	0	1
5	2	3	4	5	6	7	8	9	:	;
6	<	=	>	?	@	A	B	C	D	E
7	F	G	H	I	J	K	L	M	N	O
8	P	Q	R	S	T	U	V	W	X	Y
9	Z	[	\	]	^	_	'	a	b	c
10	d	e	f	g	h	i	j	k	l	m
11	n	o	p	q	r	s	t	u	v	w
12	x	y	z	{			}	~	del		

Fig. F.1 | ASCII Character Set.

The digits at the left of the table are the left digits of the decimal equivalent (0–127) of the character code, and the digits at the top of the table are the right digits of the character code. For example, the character code for "F" is 70, and the character code for "&" is 38.

Most users of this book are interested in the ASCII character set used to represent English characters on many computers. The ASCII character set is a subset of the Unicode character set used by C# to represent characters from most of the world's languages. For more information on the Unicode character set, see Appendix G.

Unicode®

OBJECTIVES

In this appendix you'll learn:

- The mission of the Unicode Consortium.
- The design basis of Unicode.
- The three Unicode encoding forms: UTF-8, UTF-16 and UTF-32.
- Characters and glyphs.
- The advantages and disadvantages of using Unicode.

Outline

G.1 Introduction
G.2 Unicode Transformation Formats
G.3 Characters and Glyphs
G.4 Advantages/Disadvantages of Unicode
G.5 Using Unicode
G.6 Character Ranges

G.1 Introduction

The use of inconsistent character *encodings* (i.e., numeric values associated with characters) in the developing of global software products causes serious problems, because computers process information as numbers. For instance, the character "a" is converted to a numeric value so that a computer can manipulate that piece of data. Many countries and corporations have developed their own encoding systems that are incompatible with the encoding systems of other countries and corporations. For example, the Microsoft Windows operating system assigns the value 0xC0 to the character "A with a grave accent"; the Apple Macintosh operating system assigns that same value to an upside-down question mark. This results in the misrepresentation and possible corruption of data when it is not processed as intended.

In the absence of a widely implemented universal character-encoding standard, global software developers had to *localize* their products extensively before distribution. Localization includes the language translation and cultural adaptation of content. The process of localization usually includes significant modifications to the source code (such as the conversion of numeric values and the underlying assumptions made by programmers), which results in increased costs and delays releasing the software. For example, some English-speaking programmers might design global software products assuming that a single character can be represented by one byte. However, when those products are localized for Asian markets, the programmer's assumptions are no longer valid; thus, the majority, if not the entirety, of the code needs to be rewritten. Localization is necessary with each release of a version. By the time a software product is localized for a particular market, a newer version, which needs to be localized as well, may be ready for distribution. As a result, it is cumbersome and costly to produce and distribute global software products in a market where there is no universal character-encoding standard.

In response to this situation, the *Unicode Standard*, an encoding standard that facilitates the production and distribution of software, was created. The Unicode Standard outlines a specification to produce consistent encoding of the world's characters and symbols. Software products that handle text encoded in the Unicode Standard need to be localized, but the localization process is simpler and more efficient, because the numeric values need not be converted and the assumptions made by programmers about the character encoding are universal. The Unicode Standard is maintained by a nonprofit organization called the *Unicode Consortium*, whose members include Apple, IBM, Microsoft, Oracle, Sun Microsystems, Sybase and many others.

When the Consortium envisioned and developed the Unicode Standard, they wanted an encoding system that was *universal, efficient, uniform* and *unambiguous*. A universal encoding system encompasses all commonly used characters. An efficient encoding system allows text files to be parsed easily. A uniform encoding system assigns fixed values to all characters. An unambiguous encoding system represents a given character in a consistent manner. These four terms are referred to as the Unicode Standard *design basis*.

G.2 Unicode Transformation Formats

Although Unicode incorporates the limited ASCII character set (i.e., a collection of characters), it encompasses a more comprehensive character set. In ASCII each character is represented by a byte containing 0s and 1s. One byte is capable of storing the binary numbers from 0 to 255. Each character is assigned a number between 0 and 255; thus, ASCII-based systems can support only 256 characters, a tiny fraction of world's characters. Unicode extends the ASCII character set by encoding the vast majority of the world's characters. The Unicode Standard encodes all of those characters in a uniform numerical space from 0 to 10FFFF hexadecimal. An implementation will express these numbers in one of several transformation formats, choosing the one that best fits the particular application at hand.

Three such formats are in use, called *UTF-8*, *UTF-16* and *UTF-32*, depending on the size of the units—in bits—being used. UTF-8, a variable-width encoding form, requires one to four bytes to express each Unicode character. UTF-8 data consists of 8-bit bytes (sequences of one, two, three or four bytes depending on the character being encoded) and is well suited for ASCII-based systems, where there is a predominance of one-byte characters (ASCII represents characters as one byte). Currently, UTF-8 is widely implemented in UNIX systems and in databases.

The variable-width UTF-16 encoding form expresses Unicode characters in units of 16 bits (i.e., as two adjacent bytes, or a short integer in many machines). Most characters of Unicode are expressed in a single 16-bit unit. However, characters with values above FFFF hexadecimal are expressed with an ordered pair of 16-bit units called *surrogates*. Surrogates are 16-bit integers in the range D800 through DFFF, which are used solely for the purpose of "escaping" into higher-numbered characters. Approximately one million characters can be expressed in this manner. Although a surrogate pair requires 32 bits to represent characters, it is space efficient to use these 16-bit units. Surrogates are rare characters in current implementations. Many string-handling implementations are written in terms of UTF-16. [*Note:* Details and sample code for UTF-16 handling are available on the Unicode Consortium website at `www.unicode.org`.]

Implementations that require significant use of rare characters or entire scripts encoded above FFFF hexadecimal should use UTF-32, a 32-bit, fixed-width encoding form that usually requires twice as much memory as UTF-16 encoded characters. The major advantage of the fixed-width UTF-32 encoding form is that it expresses all characters uniformly, so it is easy to handle in arrays.

There are few guidelines that state when to use a particular encoding form. The best encoding form to use depends on computer systems and business protocols, not on the data itself. Typically, the UTF-8 encoding form should be used where computer systems and business protocols require data to be handled in 8-bit units, particularly in legacy systems being upgraded, because it often simplifies changes to existing programs. For this reason, UTF-8 has become the encoding form of choice on the Internet. Likewise, UTF-16 is the encoding form of choice on Microsoft Windows applications. UTF-32 is likely to become more widely used in the future, as more characters are encoded with values above FFFF hexadecimal. Also, UTF-32 requires less sophisticated handling than UTF-

16 in the presence of surrogate pairs. Figure G.1 shows the different ways in which the three encoding forms handle character encoding.

Character	UTF-8	UTF-16	UTF-32
Latin Capital Letter A	0x41	0x0041	0x00000041
Greek Capital Letter Alpha	0xCD 0x91	0x0391	0x00000391
CJK Unified Ideograph-4e95	0xE4 0xBA 0x95	0x4E95	0x00004E95
Old Italic Letter A	0xF0 0x80 0x83 0x80	0xDC00 0xDF00	0x00010300

Fig. G.1 | Correlation between the three encoding forms.

G.3 Characters and Glyphs

The Unicode Standard consists of characters, written components (i.e., alphabetic letters, numerals, punctuation marks, accent marks, and so on) that can be represented by numeric values. Examples of characters include: U+0041 Latin capital letter A. In the first character representation, U+*yyyy* is a *code value*, in which U+ refers to Unicode code values, as opposed to other hexadecimal values. The *yyyy* represents a four-digit hexadecimal number of an encoded character. Code values are bit combinations that represent encoded characters. Characters are represented with *glyphs*, various shapes, fonts and sizes for displaying characters. There are no code values for glyphs in the Unicode Standard. Examples of glyphs are shown in Fig. G.2.

The Unicode Standard encompasses the alphabets, ideographs, syllabaries, punctuation marks, *diacritics*, mathematical operators and so on that comprise the written languages and scripts of the world. A diacritic is a special mark added to a character to distinguish it from another letter or to indicate an accent (e.g., in Spanish, the tilde "~" above the character "n"). Currently, Unicode provides code values for 94,140 character representations, with more than 880,000 code values reserved for future expansion.

Fig. G.2 | Various glyphs of the character A.

G.4 Advantages/Disadvantages of Unicode

The Unicode Standard has several significant advantages that promote its use. One is its impact on the performance of the international economy. Unicode standardizes the characters for the world's writing systems to a uniform model that promotes transferring and sharing data. Programs developed using such a schema maintain their accuracy, because each character has a single definition (i.e., *a* is always U+0061, % is always U+0025). This enables corporations to manage the high demands of international markets by processing different writing systems at the same time. Also, all characters can be managed in an identical manner, thus avoiding any confusion caused by different character-code architectures. Moreover, managing data in a consistent manner eliminates data corruption, because data can be sorted, searched and manipulated via a consistent process.

Another advantage of the Unicode Standard is portability (i.e., the ability to execute software on disparate computers or with disparate operating systems). Most operating systems, databases, programming languages and web browsers currently support, or are planning to support, Unicode. Additionally, Unicode includes more characters than any other character set in common use (although it does not yet include all of the world's characters).

A disadvantage of the Unicode Standard is the amount of memory required by UTF-16 and UTF-32. ASCII character sets are 8 bits in length, so they require less storage than the default 16-bit Unicode character set. However, the *double-byte character set (DBCS)* and the *multibyte character set (MBCS)* that encode Asian characters (ideographs) require two to four bytes, respectively. In such instances, the UTF-16 or the UTF-32 encoding forms may be used with little hindrance to memory and performance.

G.5 Using Unicode

Visual Studio uses Unicode UTF-16 encoding to represent all characters. Figure G.3 uses C# to display the text "Welcome to Unicode!" in eight different languages: English, French, German, Japanese, Portuguese, Russian, Spanish and Traditional Chinese.

The first welcome message (lines 19–23) contains the hexadecimal codes for the English text. The **Code Charts** page on the Unicode Consortium website contains a document that lists the code values for the **Basic Latin** block (or category), which includes the English alphabet. The hexadecimal codes in lines 19–21 equate to "Welcome." When using Unicode characters in C#, the format \u*yyyy* is used, where *yyyy* represents the hexadecimal Unicode encoding. For example, the letter "W" (in "Welcome") is denoted by \u0057.

```
1   // Fig. G.3: UnicodeForm.cs
2   // Unicode enconding demonstration.
3   using System;
4   using System.Windows.Forms;
5
6   namespace UnicodeDemo
7   {
8      public partial class UnicodeForm : Form
9      {
10        public UnicodeForm()
11        {
12           InitializeComponent();
13        }
14
15        // assign Unicode strings to each Label
16        private void UnicodeForm_Load( object sender, EventArgs e )
17        {
18           // English
19           char[] english = { '\u0057', '\u0065', '\u006C',
20              '\u0063', '\u006F', '\u006D', '\u0065', '\u0020',
21              '\u0074', '\u006F', '\u0020' };
```

Fig. G.3 | Windows application demonstrating Unicode encoding. (Part 1 of 3.)

```
22              englishLabel.Text = new string( english ) +
23                 "Unicode" + '\u0021';
24
25              // French
26              char[] french = { '\u0042', '\u0069', '\u0065',
27                 '\u006E', '\u0076', '\u0065', '\u006E', '\u0075',
28                 '\u0065', '\u0020', '\u0061', '\u0075', '\u0020' };
29              frenchLabel.Text = new string( french ) +
30                 "Unicode" + '\u0021';
31
32              // German
33              char[] german = { '\u0057', '\u0069', '\u006C',
34                 '\u006B', '\u006F', '\u006D', '\u006D', '\u0065',
35                 '\u006E', '\u0020', '\u007A', '\u0075', '\u0020' };
36              germanLabel.Text = new string( german ) +
37                 "Unicode" + '\u0021';
38
39              // Japanese
40              char[] japanese = { '\u3078', '\u3087', '\u3045',
41                 '\u3053', '\u305D', '\u0021' };
42              japaneseLabel.Text = "Unicode" + new string( japanese );
43
44              // Portuguese
45              char[] portuguese = { '\u0053', '\u0065', '\u006A',
46                 '\u0061', '\u0020', '\u0062', '\u0065', '\u006D',
47                 '\u0020', '\u0076', '\u0069', '\u006E', '\u0064',
48                 '\u006F', '\u0020', '\u0061', '\u0020' };
49              portugueseLabel.Text = new string( portuguese ) +
50                 "Unicode" + '\u0021';
51
52              // Russian
53              char[] russian = { '\u0414', '\u043E', '\u0431',
54                 '\u0440', '\u043E', '\u0020', '\u043F', '\u043E',
55                 '\u0436', '\u0430', '\u043B', '\u043E', '\u0432',
56                 '\u0430', '\u0442', '\u044A', '\u0020', '\u0432', '\u0020' };
57              russianLabel.Text = new string( russian ) +
58                 "Unicode" + '\u0021';
59
60              // Spanish
61              char[] spanish = { '\u0042', '\u0069', '\u0065',
62                 '\u006E', '\u0076', '\u0065', '\u006E', '\u0069',
63                 '\u0064', '\u006F', '\u0020', '\u0061', '\u0020' };
64              spanishLabel.Text = new string( spanish ) +
65                 "Unicode" + '\u0021';
66
67              // Simplified Chinese
68              char[] chinese = { '\u6B22', '\u8FCE', '\u4F7F',
69                 '\u7528', '\u0020' };
70              chineseLabel.Text = new string( chinese ) +
71                 "Unicode" + '\u0021';
72          } // end method UnicodeForm_Load
73       } // end class UnicodeForm
74    } // end namespace UnicodeDemo
```

Fig. G.3 | Windows application demonstrating Unicode encoding. (Part 2 of 3.)

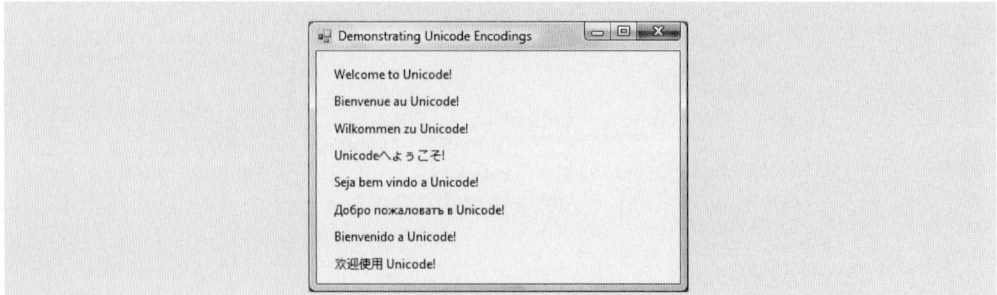

Fig. G.3 | Windows application demonstrating Unicode encoding. (Part 3 of 3.)

Line 9 contains the hexadecimal for the *space* character (\u0020). The hexadecimal value for the word "to" is on line 21, and the word "Unicode" is on line 23. "Unicode" is not encoded because it is a registered trademark and has no equivalent translation in most languages. Line 23 also contains the \u0021 notation for the exclamation mark (!).

The remaining welcome messages (lines 26–71) contain the hexadecimal codes for the other seven languages. The code values used for the French, German, Portuguese and Spanish text are located in the **Basic Latin** block, the code values used for the Traditional Chinese text are located in the **CJK Unified Ideographs** block, the code values used for the Russian text are located in the **Cyrillic** block and the code values used for the Japanese text are located in the **Hiragana** block.

[*Note:* To render the Asian characters in an application under Windows XP, you need to install the proper language files on your computer. To do this, open the **Regional Options** dialog from the **Control Panel** (**Start > Settings > Control Panel**). At the bottom of the **General** tab is a list of languages. Check the **Japanese** and the **Traditional Chinese** checkboxes and press **Apply**. Follow the directions of the install wizard to install the languages. For more information, visit www.unicode.org/help/display_problems.html.]

G.6 Character Ranges

The Unicode Standard assigns code values, which range from 0000 (**Basic Latin**) to E007F (**Tags**), to the written characters of the world. Currently, there are code values for 94,140 characters. To simplify the search for a character and its associated code value, the Unicode Standard generally groups code values by *script* and function (i.e., Latin characters are grouped in a block, mathematical operators are grouped in another block, and so on). As a rule, a script is a single writing system that is used for multiple languages (e.g., the Latin script is used for English, French, Spanish, and so on). The **Code Charts** page on the Unicode Consortium website lists all the defined blocks and their respective code values. Figure G.4 lists some blocks (scripts) from the website and their range of code values.

Script	Range of code values
Arabic	U+0600–U+06FF
Basic Latin	U+0000–U+007F

Fig. G.4 | Some character ranges. (Part 1 of 2.)

Script	Range of code values
Bengali (India)	U+0980–U+09FF
Cherokee (Native America)	U+13A0–U+13FF
CJK Unified Ideographs (East Asia)	U+4E00–U+9FAF
Cyrillic (Russia and Eastern Europe)	U+0400–U+04FF
Ethiopic	U+1200–U+137F
Greek	U+0370–U+03FF
Hangul Jamo (Korea)	U+1100–U+11FF
Hebrew	U+0590–U+05FF
Hiragana (Japan)	U+3040–U+309F
Khmer (Cambodia)	U+1780–U+17FF
Lao (Laos)	U+0E80–U+0EFF
Mongolian	U+1800–U+18AF
Myanmar	U+1000–U+109F
Ogham (Ireland)	U+1680–U+169F
Runic (Germany and Scandinavia)	U+16A0–U+16FF
Sinhala (Sri Lanka)	U+0D80–U+0DFF
Telugu (India)	U+0C00–U+0C7F
Thai	U+0E00–U+0E7F

Fig. G.4 | Some character ranges. (Part 2 of 2.)

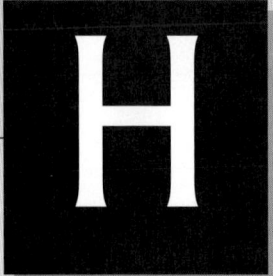

H

Using the Visual C# 2008 Debugger

OBJECTIVES

In this appendix you'll learn:

- To use breakpoints to pause program execution and allow you to examine the values of variables.

- To set, disable and remove breakpoints.

- To use the **Continue** command to continue execution from a breakpoint.

- To use the **Locals** window to view and modify variable values.

- To use the **Watch** window to evaluate expressions.

- To use the **Step Into**, **Step Out** and **Step Over** commands to execute a program line by line.

- To use the debugging features **Edit and Continue** and **Just My Code**™ debugging.

Outline

H.1 Introduction

H.2 Breakpoints and the **Continue** Command

H.3 *DataTips* and Visualizers

H.4 The **Locals** and **Watch** Windows

H.5 Controlling Execution Using the **Step Into**, **Step Over**, **Step Out** and **Continue** Commands

H.6 Other Debugging Features

    H.6.1 Edit and **Continue**

    H.6.2 Exception Assistant

    H.6.3 Just My Code™ Debugging

    H.6.4 Other Debugger Features

H.1 Introduction

In this appendix, you'll learn about tools and techniques that can be used to address compilation errors and logic errors. In Chapter 3, you were introduced to syntax errors—violations of Visual C#'s language rules. Syntax errors are a type of *compilation error*—an error that prevents code from compiling. Logic errors, also called *bugs*, do not prevent a program from compiling successfully, but can cause a running program to produce erroneous results or terminate prematurely. Most compiler vendors, like Microsoft, package their IDEs with a tool called a *debugger*. Debuggers allow you to monitor the execution of your programs to locate and remove logic errors. A program must successfully compile before it can be used in the debugger. The debugger allows you to suspend program execution, examine and set variable values and much more. In this appendix, we introduce the Visual C# 2008 IDE and debugger features for fixing errors in your programs.

H.2 Breakpoints and the Continue Command

While compilation errors can be found automatically by the compiler, it can be much more difficult to determine the cause of logic errors. To help with this, we investigate the concept of *breakpoints*. Breakpoints are special markers that can be set at any executable line of code. They cannot be placed on comments or whitespace. When a running program reaches a breakpoint, execution pauses, allowing you to examine the values of variables to help determine whether logic errors exist. For example, you can examine the value of a variable that stores a calculation's result to determine whether the calculation was performed correctly. You can also examine the value of an expression.

    To illustrate the debugger features, we use the program in Figs. H.1–H.2 that creates and manipulates an Account (Fig. H.1) object. This example is based on concepts from Chapter 4, so it does not use features that are presented after Chapter 4. Execution begins in Main (lines 8–41 of Fig. H.2). Line 10 creates an Account object with an initial balance of $50.00. Account's constructor (lines 10–13 of Fig. H.1) accepts one argument, which specifies the Account's initial balance. Lines 13–14 of Fig. H.2 output the initial account balance using Account property Balance. Lines 18–20 prompt the user for and input the withdrawalAmount. Lines 22–24 subtract the withdrawal amount from the Account's balance using its Debit method. Line 27 displays the new balance. Next, lines 30–40 perform similar steps to credit the account.

```csharp
1   // Fig. H.1: Account.cs
2   // Account class with a Debit method that withdraws money from account.
3   using System;
4
5   public class Account
6   {
7      private decimal balance; // instance variable that stores the balance
8
9      // constructor
10     public Account( decimal initialBalance )
11     {
12        Balance = initialBalance; // set balance using property
13     } // end Account constructor
14
15     // credits (adds) an amount to the account
16     public void Credit( decimal amount )
17     {
18        Balance = Balance + amount; // add amount to balance
19     } // end method Credit
20
21     // debit (subtracts) an amount from the account
22     public void Debit( decimal amount )
23     {
24        if ( amount > Balance )
25           Console.WriteLine( "Debit amount exceeded account balance." );
26
27        if ( amount <= Balance )
28           Balance = Balance - amount; // subtract amount from balance
29     } // end method Debit
30
31     // property to get the balance
32     public decimal Balance
33     {
34        get
35        {
36           return balance;
37        } // end get
38        set
39        {
40           // validate that value is greater than or equal to 0;
41           // if it is not, balance is left unchanged
42           if ( value >= 0 )
43              balance = value;
44        } // end set
45     } // end property Balance
46  } // end class Account
```

Fig. H.1 | Account class with a Debit method that withdraws money from account.

```
 1    // Fig. H.2: AccountTest.cs
 2    // Creating and manipulating an Account object.
 3    using System;
 4
 5    public class AccountTest
 6    {
 7       // Main method begins execution of C# application
 8       public static void Main( string[] args )
 9       {
10          Account account1 = new Account( 50.00M ); // create Account object
11
12          // display initial balance of account object
13          Console.WriteLine( "account1 balance: {0:C}",
14             account1.Balance );
15
16          decimal withdrawalAmount; // withdrawal amount entered by user
17
18          Console.Write( "Enter withdrawal amount for account1: " );
19          // obtain user input
20          withdrawalAmount = Convert.ToDecimal( Console.ReadLine() );
21
22          Console.WriteLine( "\nsubtracting {0:C} from account1 balance",
23             withdrawalAmount );
24          account1.Debit( withdrawalAmount ); // subtract amount from account1
25
26          // display balance
27          Console.WriteLine( "account1 balance: {0:C}", account1.Balance );
28          Console.WriteLine();
29
30          Console.Write( "Enter credit amount for account1: " );
31          // obtain user input
32          decimal creditAmount = Convert.ToDecimal( Console.ReadLine() );
33
34          Console.WriteLine( "\nadding {0:C} to account1 balance",
35             creditAmount );
36          account1.Credit( creditAmount );
37
38          // display balance
39          Console.WriteLine( "account1 balance: {0:C}", account1.Balance );
40          Console.WriteLine();
41       } // end Main
42    } // end AccountTest
```

```
account1 balance: $50.00
Enter withdrawal amount for account1: 25

subtracting $25.00 from account1 balance
account1 balance: $25.00

Enter credit amount for account1: 33

adding $33.00 to account1 balance
account1 balance: $58.00
```

Fig. H.2 | Creating and manipulating an Account object.

In the following steps, you'll use breakpoints and debugger commands to examine variable withdrawalAmount's value (declared in Fig. H.2) while the program executes.

1. *Inserting breakpoints in Visual C#.* First, ensure that AccountTest.cs is open in the IDE's code editor. To insert a breakpoint, left click inside the *margin indicator bar* (the gray margin at the left of the code window in Fig. H.3) next to the line of code at which you wish to break, or right click that line of code and select **Breakpoint > Insert Breakpoint**. Additionally, you can also press *F9* when your cursor is on the line to toggle the breakpoint. You may set as many breakpoints as you like. Set breakpoints at lines 18, 24 and 41 of your code. [*Note:* If you have not already done so, have the code editor display line numbers by opening **Tools > Options...**, navigating to **Text Editor > C#** and selecting the **Line numbers** checkbox.] A solid circle appears in the margin indicator bar where you clicked, and the entire code statement is highlighted, indicating that breakpoints have been set (Fig. H.3). When the program runs, the debugger suspends execution at any line that contains a breakpoint. The program then enters *break mode*. Breakpoints can be set before running a program, both in break mode and during execution. To show a list of all breakpoints in a project, select **Debug > Windows > Breakpoints**. This feature is available only in the full version of Visual Studio 2008.

2. *Beginning the debugging process.* After setting breakpoints in the code editor, select **Build > Build Account** to compile the program, then select **Debug > Start**

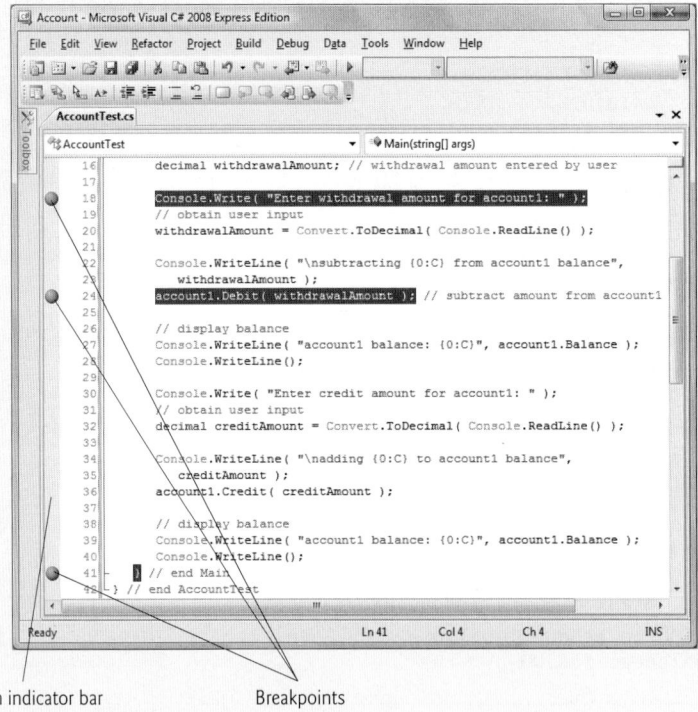

Margin indicator bar   Breakpoints

Fig. H.3 | Setting breakpoints.

Debugging (or press the *F5* key) to begin the debugging process. While debugging a console application, the **Command Prompt** window appears (Fig. H.4), allowing program interaction (input and output).

3. *Examining program execution.* Program execution pauses at the first breakpoint (line 18), and the IDE becomes the active window (Fig. H.5). The yellow arrow to the left of line 18, also called the *Instruction Pointer*, indicates that this line contains the next statement to execute. The IDE also highlights the line as well.

4. *Using the* **Continue** *command to resume execution.* To resume execution, select **Debug > Continue** (or press the *F5* key). The **Continue** *command* executes the statements from the current point in the program to the next breakpoint or the end of Main, whichever comes first. It is also possible to drag the *Instruction Pointer* to another line in the same method to resume execution starting at that position. If you want to run the application only until a specific line, you can place your cursor on that line and then use the **Run To Cursor** *command* to execute the program until that line. Here, we use the **Continue** command, and the program continues executing and pauses for input at line 20. Enter 25 in the **Command Prompt** window as the withdrawal amount. When you press *Enter*, the program executes until it stops at the next breakpoint (line 24). Notice that when you place the mouse pointer over the variable name withdrawalAmount, its value is displayed in a *Quick Info box* (Fig. H.6). As you'll see, this can help you spot logic errors in your programs.

5. *Continuing program execution.* Use the **Debug > Continue** command to execute line 24. The program then asks you to input a credit (deposit) amount. Enter 33, then press *Enter*. The program displays the result of its calculation (Fig. H.7).

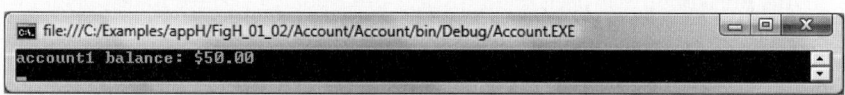

Fig. H.4 | Account program running.

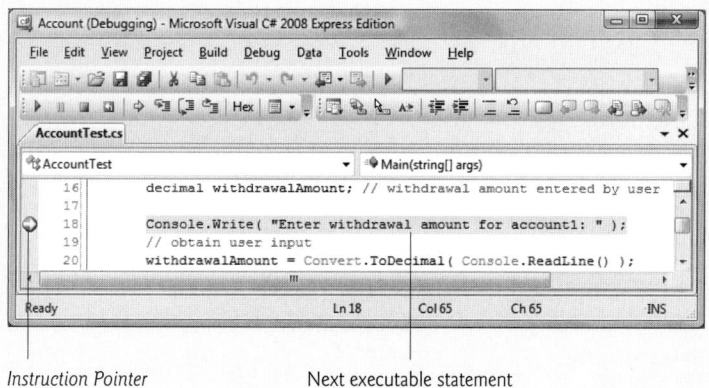

Instruction Pointer   Next executable statement

Fig. H.5 | Program execution suspended at the first breakpoint.

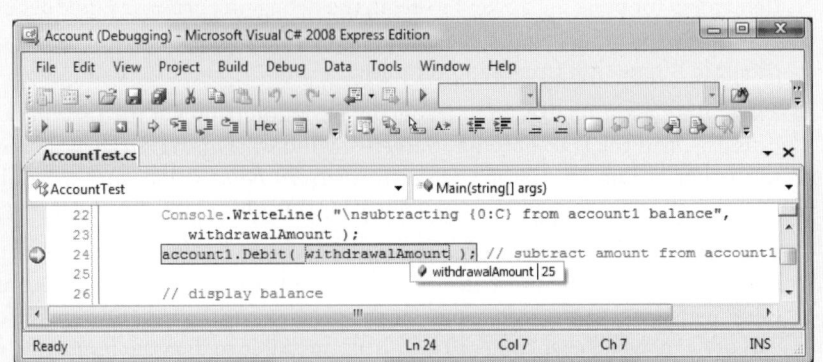

Fig. H.6 | *Quick Info* box displays value of variable `withdrawalAmount`.

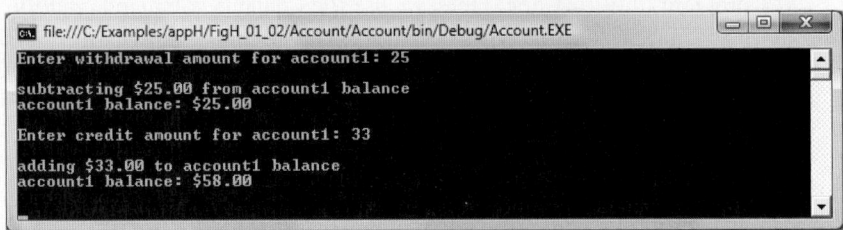

Fig. H.7 | Sample execution of `Account.EXE` in debug mode.

6. *Disabling a breakpoint.* To *disable a breakpoint*, right click a line of code in which the breakpoint has been set and select **Breakpoint > Disable Breakpoint**. The disabled breakpoint is indicated by a hollow circle (Fig. H.8)—the breakpoint can be

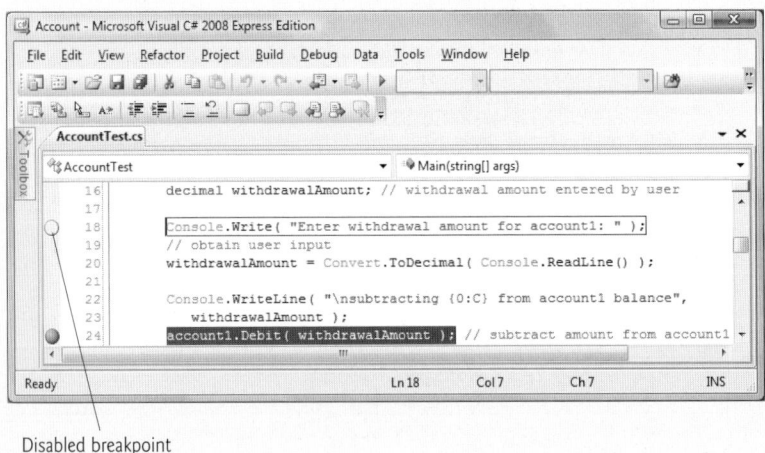

Disabled breakpoint

Fig. H.8 | Disabled breakpoint.

reenabled by right clicking the line marked by the hollow circle and selecting **Breakpoint > Enable Breakpoint**.

7. *Removing a breakpoint.* To remove a breakpoint that you no longer need, right click the line of code on which the breakpoint has been set and select **Breakpoint > Delete Breakpoint**. You also can remove a breakpoint by clicking the circle in the margin indicator bar or pressing *F9* when the cursor is on the line.

8. *Finishing program execution.* Select **Debug > Continue** to execute the program to completion. Then delete all the breakpoints.

H.3 *DataTips* and **Visualizers**

You already know how to use the *Quick Info* window to view a variable's value. However, often you may want to check the status of an `object`. For example, you may want to check the `Text` value of a `TextBox` control. When you hover the mouse over a reference-type variable, the *DataTip* window appears (Fig. H.9). When you hover over the + sign in the *DataTip*, the *DataTip* window gives information about the object's data. There are some limitations—references must instance variables or local variables, and expressions involving method calls cannot be evaluated.

For the `Account` object, this means that you can see the `balance` inside it (as well as the `Balance` property used to access it). Just like the *Quick Info* window, you can also

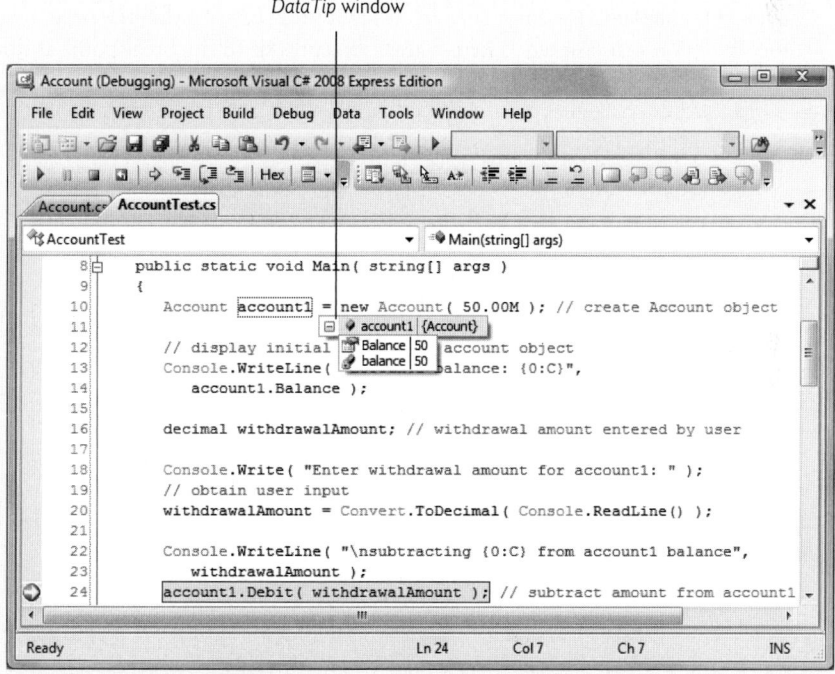

Fig. H.9 | A *DataTip* displayed for the `account1` variable.

change the value of a property or variable inside it by clicking on one of the values listed, then typing the new value.

DataTips do not intuitively display information for all variables. For example, a variable representing an XML document cannot be viewed in its natural form using most debugging tools. For such types, *visualizers* can be useful. Visualizers are specialized windows to view certain types of data. They are shown through *DataTip* windows by clicking the small magnifying glass next to a variable name. There are three predefined visualizers—advanced programmers may create additional ones. The **Text Visualizer** lets you see `string` values with all their formatting included. The **XML Visualizer** formats XML objects into a color-coded format. Finally, the **HTML Visualizer** parses HTML code (in `string` or XML form) into a web page, which is displayed in the small window.

H.4 The Locals and Watch Windows

In the preceding section, you learned how to use the *Quick Info* and *DataTip* features to examine the variable's value. In this section, you'll learn how to use the **Locals window** to view all variables that are in use while your program is running. You'll also use the **Watch window** to examine the values of expressions.

1. *Inserting breakpoints.* Set a breakpoint at line 24 (Fig. H.10) in the source code by left clicking in the margin indicator bar to the left of line 24. Use the same technique to set breakpoints at lines 27 and 28 as well.

2. *Starting debugging.* Select **Debug > Start Debugging**. Type 25 at the **Enter withdrawal amount for account1:** prompt (Fig. H.11) and press *Enter* so that the program reads the value you just entered. The program executes until the breakpoint at line 24.

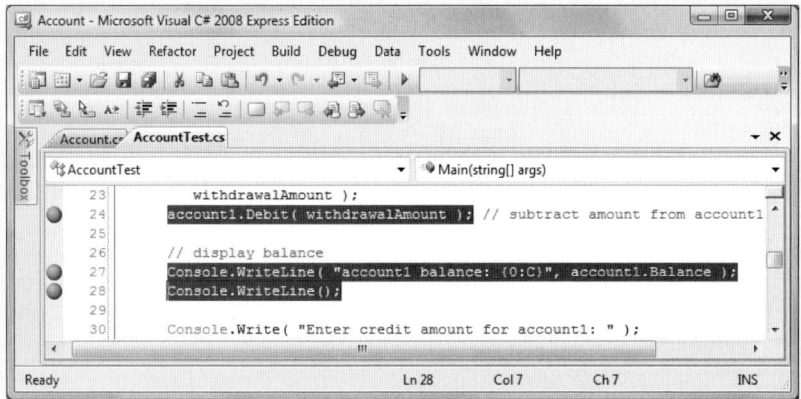

Fig. H.10 | Setting breakpoints at lines 24, 27 and 28.

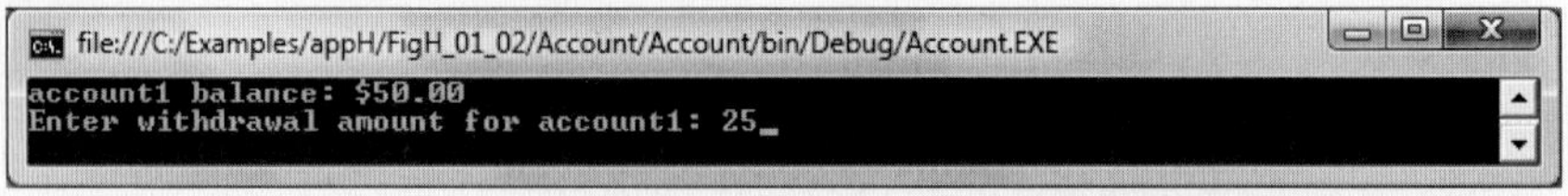

Fig. H.11 | Entering the withdrawal amount before the breakpoint is reached.

3. *Suspending program execution.* When the program reaches line 24, the IDE suspends program execution and switches the program into break mode (Fig. H.12). At this point, the statement in line 20 (Fig. H.2) has input the withdrawal-Amount that you entered (25), the statement in lines 22–23 has output that the program is subtracting that amount from the account1 balance and the statement in line 24 is the next statement that executes.

4. *Examining data.* Once the program enters break mode, you can explore the local variable values using the **Locals** window. To view this window, select **Debug > Windows > Locals**. Click the plus to the left of account1 in the **Locals** window's **Name** column (Fig. H.13). This allows you to view each of account1's instance variable values individually, including the value for balance (50). Note that the **Locals** window displays a class' properties as data, which is why you see both the Balance property and the balance instance variable in the **Locals** window. In addition, the current value of local variable withdrawalAmount (25) is also displayed.

5. *Evaluating arithmetic and boolean expressions.* You can evaluate arithmetic and bool expressions using the **Watch** window. Select **Debug > Windows > Watch** to display the window (Fig. H.14). In the **Name** column's first row (which should be blank initially), type (withdrawalAmount + 10) * 5, then press *Enter*. The value 175 is displayed (Fig. H.14). In the **Name** column's next row in the **Watch** window, type withdrawalAmount == 200, then press *Enter*. This expression deter-

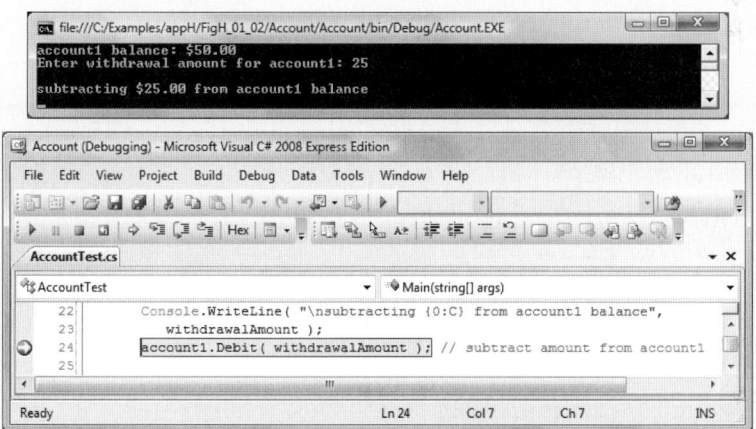

Fig. H.12 | Program execution pauses when debugger reaches the breakpoint at line 24.

Name	Value	Type
args	{string[0]}	string[]
account1	{Account}	Account
Balance	50	decimal
balance	50	decimal
withdrawalAmount	25	decimal
creditAmount	0	decimal

Fig. H.13 | Examining local variables.

mines whether the value contained in withdrawalAmount is 200. Expressions containing the == symbol are boolean expressions. The value returned is false (Fig. H.14), because withdrawalAmount does not currently contain the value 200.

6. *Resuming execution.* Select **Debug > Continue** to resume execution. Line 24 executes, subtracting the account with the withdrawal amount, and the program enters break mode again at line 27. Select **Debug > Windows > Locals**. The updated balance instance variable and Balance property value are now displayed (Fig. H.15). The values in red in the window are those that have just been modified.

7. *Modifying values.* Based on the value input by the user (25), the account balance output by the program should be 25. However, you can use the **Locals** window to change variable values during program execution. This can be valuable for experimenting with different values and for locating logic errors in programs. In the **Locals** window, click the **Value** field in the balance row to select the value 25. Type 37, then press *Enter*. The debugger changes the value of balance (and the Balance property as well), then displays its new value in red (Fig. H.16). Now select **Debug > Continue** to execute lines 27–28. Notice that the new value of balance is displayed in the **Command Prompt** window.

8. *Stopping the debugging session.* Select **Debug > Stop Debugging**. Delete all breakpoints, which can be done by pressing *Ctrl-Shift-F9*.

Evaluating an arithmetic expression — (withdrawalAmount + 10) * 5 ... 175 ... decimal

Evaluating a bool expression — withdrawalAmount == 200 ... false ... bool

Fig. H.14 | Examining the values of expressions.

Name	Value	Type
args	{string[0]}	string[]
account1	{Account}	Account
Balance	25	decimal
balance	25	decimal
withdrawalAmount	25	decimal
creditAmount	0	decimal

Updated value of the balance variable appears in red on the screen

Fig. H.15 | Displaying the value of local variables.

Name	Value	Type
args	{string[0]}	string[]
account1	{Account}	Account
Balance	37	decimal
balance	37	decimal
withdrawalAmount	25	decimal
creditAmount	0	decimal

Value modified in the debugger

Fig. H.16 | Modifying the value of a variable.

H.5 Controlling Execution Using the Step Into, Step Over, Step Out and Continue Commands

Sometimes you need to execute a program line by line to find and fix logic errors. Stepping through a portion of your program this way can help you verify that a method's code executes correctly. The commands you learn in this section allow you to execute a method line by line, execute all of a method's statements or execute only its remaining statements (if you have already executed some statements in the method).

1. *Setting a breakpoint.* Set a breakpoint at line 24 by left clicking in the margin indicator bar (Fig. H.17).

2. *Starting the debugger.* Select **Debug > Start Debugging**. Enter the value 25 at the **Enter withdrawal amount for account1:** prompt. Program execution halts when the program reaches the breakpoint at line 24.

3. *Using the Step Into command.* The **Step Into** *command* executes the next statement in the program (the yellow highlighted line of Fig. H.18) and immediately halts. If the statement to execute is a method call, control transfers to the called method. The **Step Into** command allows you to follow execution into a method and confirm its execution by individually executing each statement inside the method. Select **Debug > Step Into** (or press *F11*) to enter the Debit method (Fig. H.19).

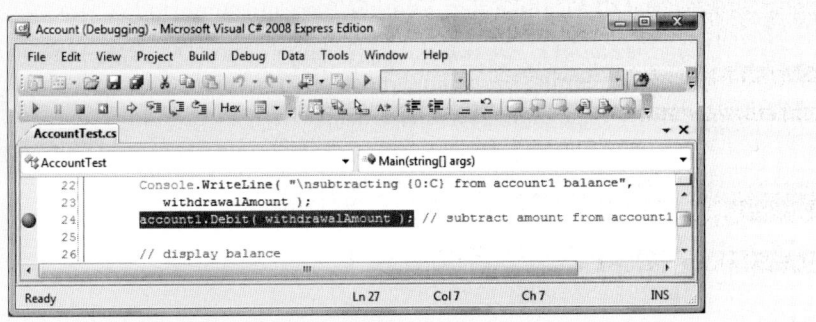

Fig. H.17 | Setting a breakpoint in the program.

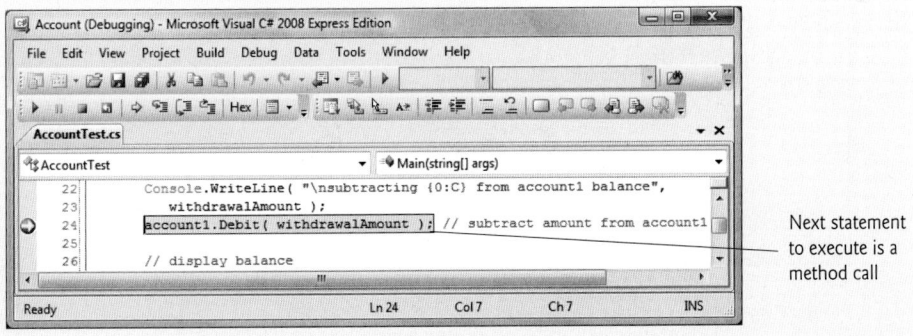

Fig. H.18 | **Step Into** command enters the Debit method.

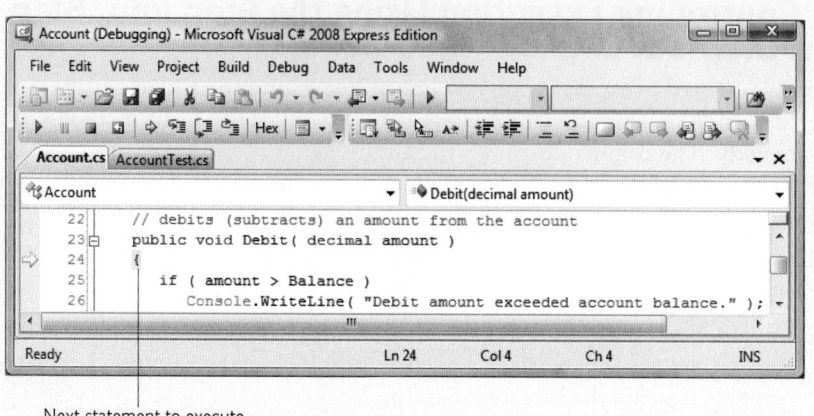

Next statement to execute

Fig. H.19 | Stepping into the Debit method.

4. *Using the Step Over command.* Select **Debug > Step Over** (or press *F10*) to enter the Debit method's body and transfer control to line 25 (Fig. H.20). The **Step Over** *command* behaves like the **Step Into** command when the next statement to execute does not contain a method call or access a property. You'll see how the **Step Over** command differs from the **Step Into** command in *Step 10*.

5. *Using the Step Out command.* Select **Debug > Step Out** or press *Shift-F11* to execute the remaining statements in the method and return control to the calling method. Often, in lengthy methods, you may want to look at a few key lines of code, then continue debugging the caller's code. The **Step Out** *command* executes the remainder of a method and returns to the caller.

6. *Setting a breakpoint.* Set a breakpoint (Fig. H.21) at line 28 of Fig. H.2. This breakpoint is used in the next step.

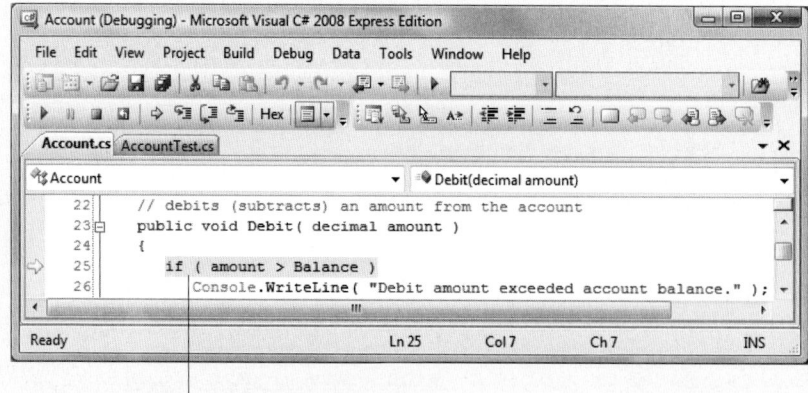

Control is transferred to the next statement

Fig. H.20 | Stepping over a statement in the Debit method.

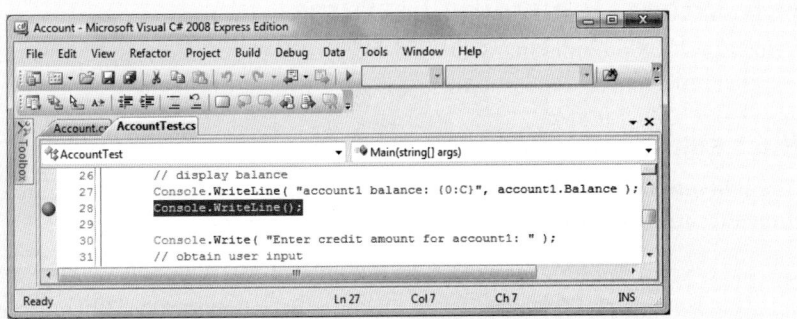

Fig. H.21 | Setting a second breakpoint in the program.

7. *Using the Continue command.* Select **Debug > Continue** to execute until the next breakpoint is reached at line 20. This feature saves time when you do not want to step line by line through many lines of code to reach the next breakpoint.

8. *Stopping the debugger.* Select **Debug > Stop Debugging** to stop debugging.

9. *Starting the debugger.* Before we can demonstrate the next debugger feature, you must restart the debugger. Start it, as you did in *Step 2*, and enter the same value (25). The debugger pauses execution at line 24.

10. *Using the Step Over command.* Select **Debug > Step Over** (Fig. H.22). Recall that this command behaves like the **Step Into** command when the next statement to execute does not contain a method call. If the next statement to execute contains a method call, the called method executes in its entirety (without pausing execution at any statement inside the method—unless there is a breakpoint in the method), and the arrow advances to the next executable line (after the method call) in the current method. In this case, the debugger executes line 24 in Main (Fig. H.2), which calls the Debit method. Then the debugger pauses execution at line 27, the next executable statement.

11. *Stopping the debugger.* Select **Debug > Stop Debugging**. Remove all remaining breakpoints.

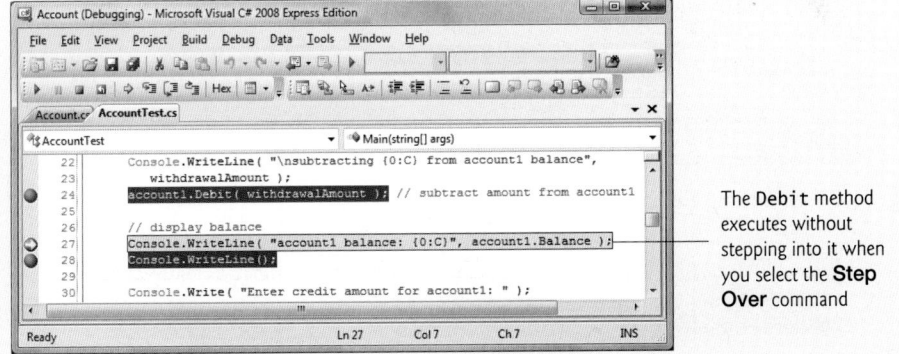

The Debit method executes without stepping into it when you select the **Step Over** command

Fig. H.22 | Using the debugger's **Step Over** command.

H.6 Other Debugging Features

Visual C# 2008 provides many other debugging features that simplify the testing and debugging process. We discuss some of these features in this section.

H.6.1 Edit and Continue

The **Edit and Continue** feature allows you to modify your code in debug mode, then continue executing the program without having to recompile your code.

1. *Setting a breakpoint.* Set a breakpoint at line 18 in your example (Fig. H.23).

2. *Starting the debugger.* Select **Debug > Start Debugging**. When execution begins, the account1 balance is displayed. The debugger enters break mode when it reaches the breakpoint at line 18.

3. *Changing the input prompt text.* Suppose you wish to modify the input prompt text to provide the user with a range of values for variable withdrawalAmount. Rather than stopping the debugging process, add the text "(from 1 to 49):" to the end of "Enter withdrawal amount for account1" at line 18 in the code view window. Select **Debug > Continue**. The application prompts you for input using the updated text (Fig. H.24).

In this example, we wanted to make a change in the text for our input prompt before line 18 executes. However, if you want to make a change to a line that has already executed, you must select a prior statement in your code from which to continue execution.

1. *Setting a breakpoint.* Delete the breakpoint at line 18 and set a new breakpoint at line 22 (Fig. H.25).

2. *Starting the debugger.* Delete the "(from 1 to 49)" text you just added in the previous steps. Select **Debug > Start Debugging**. When execution begins, the

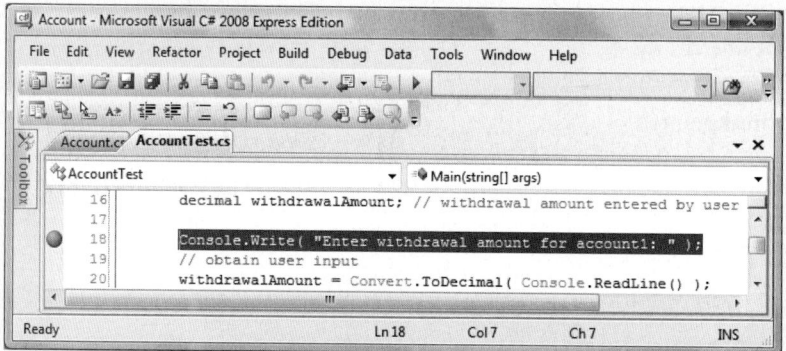

Fig. H.23 | Setting a breakpoint at line 18.

Fig. H.24 | Application prompt displaying the updated text.

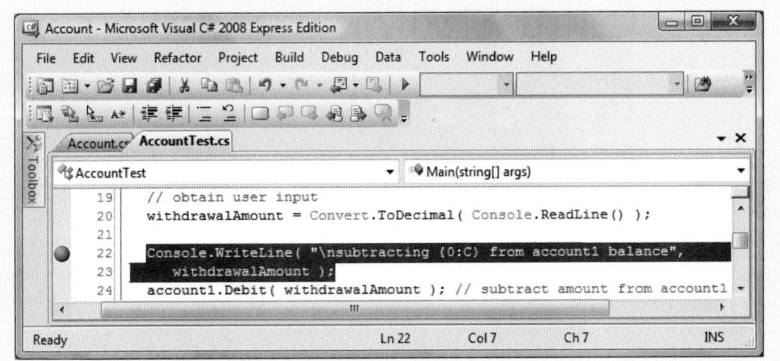

Fig. H.25 | Setting a breakpoint at line 22.

prompt **Enter withdrawal amount for account1:** appears. Enter the value 22 at the prompt (Fig. H.26). The debugger enters break mode at line 22 (Fig. H.26).

3. *Changing the input prompt text.* Let's say that you once again wish to modify the input-prompt text to provide the user with a range of values for variable `with-drawalAmount`. Add the text `"(from 1 to 49):"` to the end of `"Enter withdraw-al amount for account1"` in line 18 inside the code view window.

4. *Setting the next statement.* For the program to update the input-prompt text correctly, you must set the execution point to a previous line of code. Right click in line 18 and select **Set Next Statement** from the menu that appears (Fig. H.27). Alternatively, you can also drag the yellow arrow that is displayed in the left margin.

5. Select **Debug > Continue**. The application prompts you again for input, using the updated text (Fig. H.28).

6. *Stopping the debugger.* Select **Debug > Stop Debugging**.

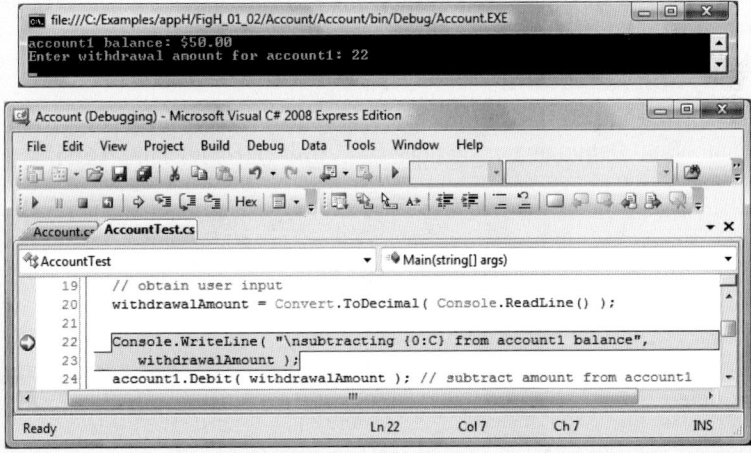

Fig. H.26 | Stopping execution at the breakpoint in line 22.

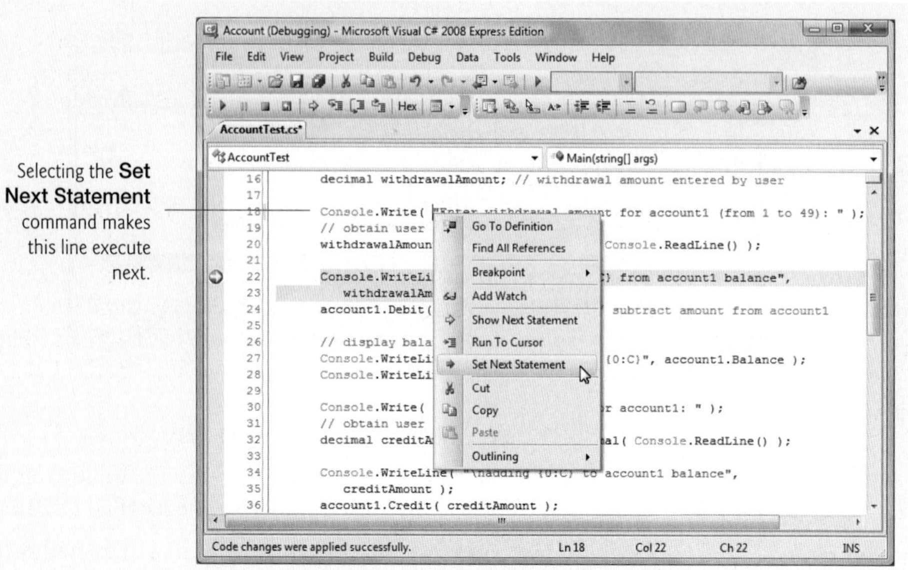

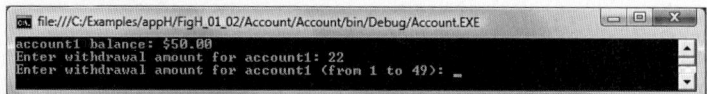

Selecting the **Set
Next Statement**
command makes
this line execute
next.

Fig. H.27 | Setting the next statement to execute.

Fig. H.28 | Program execution continues with updated prompt text.

Certain types of changes are not allowed with the **Edit and Continue** feature, once the
program begins execution. These include changing class names, adding or removing
method parameters, adding `public` fields to a class and adding or removing methods. If a
particular change that you make to your program is not allowed during the debugging process, Visual C# displays a dialog box as shown in Fig. H.29.

H.6.2 Exception Assistant

Another debugging feature is the **Exception Assistant**. You can run a program by selecting
either **Debug > Start Debugging** or **Debug > Start Without Debugging**. If you select the op-

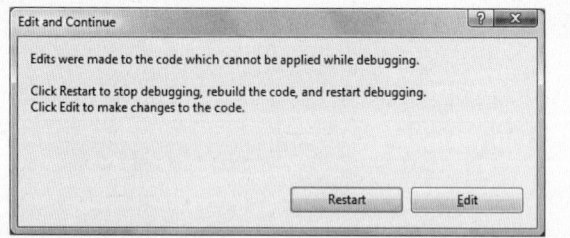

Fig. H.29 | Dialog box stating that program edits are not allowed during program execution.

tion **Debug > Start Debugging** and the runtime environment detects uncaught exceptions, the application pauses, and a window called the **Exception Assistant** appears, indicating where the exception occurred, the exception type and links to helpful information on handling the exception. We discuss the **Exception Assistant** in detail in Section 13.4.3.

H.6.3 Just My Code™ Debugging

Throughout this book, we produce increasingly substantial programs that often include a combination of code written by the programmer and code generated by Visual Studio. The IDE-generated code can be difficult to understand—fortunately, you rarely need to look at this code. Visual Studio 2008 provides a debugging feature called **Just My Code**™ that allows programmers to test and debug only the portion of the code they have written. When this option is enabled, the debugger always steps over method calls to methods of classes that you did not write.

To enable this option, in the **Options** dialog, select the **Debugging** category to view the available debugging tools and options. Then click the checkbox that appears next to the **Enable Just My Code (Managed only)** option (Fig. H.30) to enable or disable this feature.

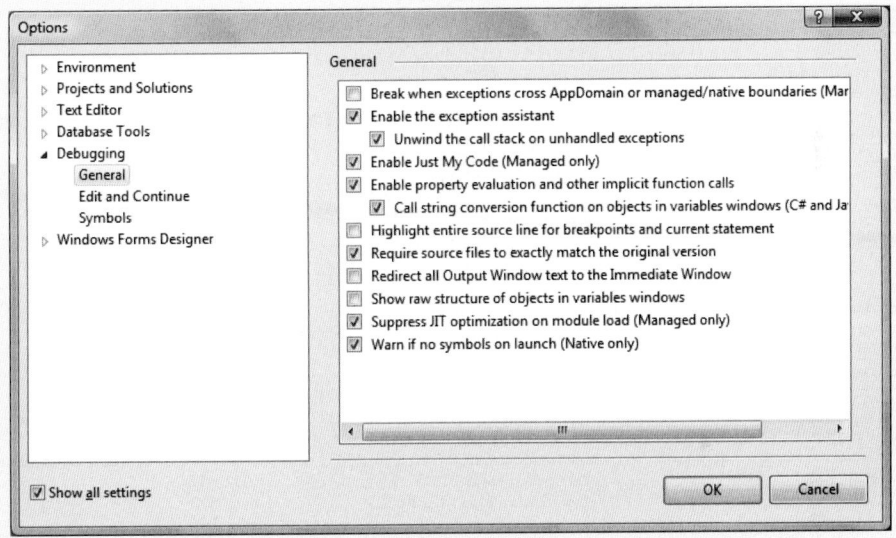

Fig. H.30 | Enabling the **Just My Code** debugging feature in Visual C#.

H.6.4 Other Debugger Features

The debugger for the full version of Visual Studio 2008 offers additional features, such as tracepoints and more, which you can learn about at msdn.microsoft.com/en-us/library/sc65sadd.aspx.

Index

[*Note:* Page references for defining occurrences of terms appear in ***bold italic***.]

Symbols

∧, boolean logical exclusive OR 180, *182*
    truth table 183
_ SQL wildcard character *828*
--, predecrement/postdecrement 148
--, prefix/postfix decrement 148, 149
-, private visibility symbol *102*
-, subtraction 70, 71
!, logical negation 180, *182*
    truth table 183
!=, not equals 72, 74
? quantifier (regular expressions) *719*
?:, ternary conditional operator 131, 150
. metacharacter (regular expressions) 723
"", empty string *106*
{, left brace 53
{n,} quantifier (regular expressions) 723
{n,m} quantifier (regular expressions) 723
{n} quantifier (regular expressions) 723
}, right brace 53
@ verbatim string character 691
@ XPath attribute symbol *794*
*, multiplication 70, 71
*, multiplication operator 798
*, quantifier (regular expressions) 723
/ forward slash in end tags *596*
/ XPath root selector 793
/, division 70, 71
/* */ delimited comment 50
//, single-line comment 50
\, escape character 65
\", double-quote escape sequence 65
\d character class (digit) (regular
    expressions) 720, 729
\D character class (non-digit) (regular
    expressions) 720
\n, newline escape sequence 65
\r, carriage-return escape sequence 65
\S character class (non-whitespace)
    (regular expressions) 720
\s character class (whitespace) (regular
    expressions) 720, 729
\t, horizontal tab escape sequence 65
\uyyyy notation 1192
\W character class (non-word character)
    (regular expressions) 720
\w character class (word character)
    (regular expressions) 720
&, boolean logical AND 180, *182*
&, menu access shortcut 532, 534
&&, conditional AND *180*, 181
    truth table 181
%, remainder 70, 71

%, SQL wildcard character *828*
+ quantifier (regular expressions) *722*
+, addition 70, 71
+, concatenation operator 700
+, public visibility symbol *93*
++, prefix/postfix increment 148
++, preincrement/postincrement 148
+=, addition assignment operator 147
<, less than 72
<!--...--> XML comment tags 600
<? and ?> XML processing instruction
    delimiters *793*
<%-- and --%> for delimiting ASP.NET
    comments *868*
<%@ and %> for delimiting ASP.NET
    directives *868*
<=, less than or equal 72
<>, angle brackets for XML elements *596*
=, assignment operator 69
==, comparison operator 694
==, is equal to 72
=>, lambda operator *357*
>, greater than 72
>=, greater than or equal to 72
| alternation (regular expression) *719*
|, boolean logical inclusive OR 180, *182*
||, conditional OR 180, *181*
    truth table *181*

A

A more complex regular expression 723
abbreviating assignment expressions 147
abnormally terminate a program 250
Abs method of Math 195
absolute addressing (XPath) *793*
absolute positioning *879*
absolute Source 1055
absolute value 195
abstract base class 452
abstract class 410, *415*, 416, 434, 452
abstract data type (ADT) *340*
abstract keyword 387, *415*
abstract method *415*, 417, 420
abstract operation in the UML *448*
AcceptButton property of class Form
    489
AcceptsReturn property of class
    TextBox 501
access modifier 90, 98, 362
    internal 315
    private 315, 374
    protected 315, *374*
    protected internal *374*
    public *90*, 315, 374

access rule in ASP.NET *931*
access shortcut 532
accessor *99*
Account class
    ATM case study 83, 117, 121, 152,
        153, 284, 285, 287, 289
Account class (ATM case study) 230,
    367
Account class with a constructor to
    initialize instance variable balance
    111
Account class with a Debit method that
    withdraws money from account 1198
accounts-receivable file 735
action 130, 134, 340
action attribute of XHTML element
    form *873*
action expression in the UML *127*, 188
action of an object 187
action oriented *13*
action state in the UML *127*, 188
action state symbol *127*
actions (verbs) *5*
activation in a UML sequence diagram
    287
Activation property of class ListView
    566
activation record *203*
active control *497*
active tab *25*
active window *488*, 1201
ActiveLinkColor property of class
    LinkLabel 546
ActiveMdiChild property of class Form
    577, 578
activity *127*
activity (UML) *83*, *186*, 190
activity diagram 127, 129, 130, 163
    do...while statement 170
    for statement 164
    if statement 129
    if...else statement 130
    in the UML 134
    sequence statement 127
    switch statement 177
    while statement 135
activity diagram (UML) *83*, 187, 189,
    191
actor in use case (UML) *81*
ActualWidth property of
    MultiScaleImage element *1049*
Ad XML element in an AdRotator
    advertisement file *891*
add a database to a project 836
Add Connection dialog *836*

add custom control to a form 591
Add method of class ArrayList 1126, *1127*
Add method of class Dictionary(Of K, V) *744*, *905*
Add method of class Hashtable *1136*
Add method of class HttpSessionState *911*
Add method of class List<T> *304*
Add method of class ObjectCollection *551*
Add method of class PointCollection *659*
Add method of class XContainer *815*
Add method of UIElementCollection class *621*
Add Tab menu item 572
Add User Control... option in Visual Studio .NET 590
Add Windows Form... option in Visual Studio 576
AddDay method of structure DateTime *545*
Adding a file to a Visual Studio project 662
adding a service reference to a project in Visual C# 2008 Express 974
adding a service reference to a project in Visual Web Developer *973*
addition 70
AddLast method of class LinkedList *1143*
address of a WCF service *965*
AddYears method of structure DateTime *545*
ADO.NET 835
Adobe Flash 1017
Adobe Flex 1017
Adobe® Photoshop™ Elements 44
AdRotator ASP.NET web control *889*, 890
ADT (abstract data type) 340
Advanced Research Projects Agency (ARPA) 5
advertisement 899
Advertisements XML element in an AdRotator advertisement file *891*
AfterSelected event of class TreeView 561
aggregation *120*
AJAX (Asynchronous Javascript and XML) *952*
AJAX Extensions package *953*
AJAX web application *952*
algebraic notation 70
algorithm 135
all XML Schema element *789*
AllowsTransparency property of Window control *636*
Alphabetic icon 32
alphabetizing 694
Alt key 525
Alt key shortcut 532
Alt property of class KeyEventArgs 526, 528
AlternateText element in an AdRotator advertisement file *891*
alternation, | (regular expression) *719*
analysis 14

analysis stage of the software life cycle 80
ancestor node of a DOM tree *799*
anchor a control *498*
Anchor property of class Control 499
anchoring a control 498
Anchoring demonstration 499
AND SQL operator *834*
angle bracket (<>) for XML elements *596*
Angle property of class AxisAngleRotation3D *686*
anonymous function *357*
anonymous object-creation expression *360*
anonymous type *301*, *360*
    Equals method 361
    ToString method 360
anonymous type in LINQ *361*
anonymous user *931*
Any extension method of interface IEnumerable<T> *301*, 811
App.xaml *610*
App.xaml (Silverlight) 1019
App.xaml.cs (Silverlight) 1019
App.xaml.vb *610*
Appearance property of class CheckBox 507
Append method of class StringBuilder 706
AppendFormat method of class StringBuilder 707, 708
AppendText method of class File 737
Apple Computer, Inc. 1189
application *19*, 53
Application class *537*
Application counts the number of occurrences of each word in a string and stores them in a generic sorted dictionary 1138
Application counts the number of occurrences of each word in a string and stores them in a hash table 1134
Application to test class Craps 214
Application to test class MaximumFinder 199
Application to test class MethodOverload 221
Application to test class ReferenceAndOutputParameters 228
Application to test class Scope 219
Application.Current.Shutdown method *628*
Application.Exit method 552
Application.xaml StartupUri property *610*, 611
application-development process 340
Applicaton class
    Exit method *536*
Applying an XSLT style sheet to an XML document 815
Applying transforms to a Polygon 666
arbitrary number of arguments 279
args parameter of Main method 280
argument promotion *203*
argument to a method 55, 93
ArgumentException class 1136
ArgumentOutOfRangeException 692, 700, 708

ArgumentOutOfRangeException class 1129
arithmetic operators 70
arithmetic overflow *340*
ARPA (Advanced Research Projects Agency) 5
ARPAnet *6*
ArrangeIcons value of enumeration MdiLayout *579*
array *239*
    Length property *240*
    pass an array element to a method 257
    pass an array to a method 257
array-access expression *239*
Array class 291, *1121*, 1122, 1124
Array class static methods for common array manipulations 1122
array-creation expression *241*
array initializer *243*
    for jagged array 269
    for rectangular array 269
    nested *269*
array-access expression
    for jagged arrays 269
    for rectangular arrays 269
ArrayList class *1121*, *1126*, 1127
    property Capacity 1126
    property Count 1127
arrays as references 259
arrow 128
arrowhead in a UML sequence diagram 287, 288
article.xml displayed by Internet Explorer 601
artifact in the UML *1185*
as operator 811
as operator (downcasting) 430
ASC in SQL *829*, 830
ascending modifier of a LINQ orderby clause *297*
ascending order 798
    ASC in SQL *829*, 830
ASCII (American Standard Code for Information Interchange) 1190
ASCII (American Standard Code for Information Interchange) character set 178, 1187
ASCII character, test for 528
asp
    tag prefix *870*
ASP.NET *7*
    Page event lifecycle *872*
ASP.NET 3.5 7, *862*
ASP.NET AJAX *952*
ASP.NET AJAX Control Toolkit *953*
ASP.NET comment *868*
ASP.NET Development Server 968
ASP.NET login control *925*
ASP.NET server control *862*
ASP.NET validation control *892*
ASP.NET Web Site in Visual Web Developer *874*
aspect ratio *680*
ASPX file *863*
ASPX file for the guestbook application. 920

ASPX file that displays book recommendations based on cookies. 906

ASPX file that displays the Web server's time 868

ASPX file that presents a list of programming languages 901, 909

ASPX file that takes reservation information 1000

.aspx filename extension *862*

assembly (compiled code) 60

assign a value to a variable 69

Assigning base class and derived class references to base class and derived class variables 413

assignment operator, = *69*, 71

assignment operators *147*

assignment statement *69*

associate
    left to right 150
    right to left 143, 150

association (in the UML) *14*, *118*, 119, 120, 364, 365
    name 118

associativity of operators *71*, 75, 150
    left to right 76
    right to left 71, 76

asterisk (*) in a SQL SELECT 827

asterisk (*) occurrence indicator *781*

asynchronous call *286*

asynchronous request *953*

AsyncPostBackTrigger class *959*

ATM (automated teller machine) case study 76, 81

ATM class (ATM case study) 117, 118, 119, 152, 153, 155, 186, 230, 283, 284, 285, 286, 287, 362

ATM system 81, 82, 116, 117, 151, 186, 230, 362

attached property (WPF) *616*

ATTLIST attribute-list declaration (DTD) *781*

attribute 364, 365
    compartment in a class diagram 154
    declaration in the UML 155, 156
    in the UML 92, 118, 122, 152, 153, *155*, 186, 190
    name in the UML 155

attribute (in the UML) 450
    in the UML *12*

attribute (XAML) 608

attribute (XML) *604*

attribute element *789*

attribute-list declaration *781*

Attribute method of class XElement *810*

attribute node 794

attribute of a class 13
    in the UML *12*

attribute value in XML *604*

attributes *5*

authenticating a user *927*

authentication element in Web.config *932*

AuthorISBN table of Books database 822, 824

authorization element in Web.config *932*

Authors table of Books database 822

auto-implemented property *104*

AutoEventWireup attribute of ASP.NET page *869*

auto-hide 28

auto-implemented properties 747

autoincremented database column *822*

automated teller machine (ATM) 76, 81
    user interface 77

automatic garbage collection 468

automatically implemented property *104*

AutoPopDelay property of class ToolTip 518

AutoPostBack property of a DropDownList ASP.NET control *945*

AutoScroll property of class Form 489

AutoScroll property of class Panel 504

AutoSize property of TextBox *41*

average 135, 137

Axis property of class AxisAngleRotation3D *686*

AxisAngleRotation3D class *686*
    Angle property *686*
    Axis property *686*

B

BackColor property of a form *39*

BackColor property of class Control 497

background color 39

Background property of TextBlock element *662*

Background property of WPF controls 630

BackgroundImage property of class Control 497

backslash, (\) *64*, 65

backward reference 1074

BalanceInquiry class (ATM case study) 117, 120, 152, 153, 155, 187, 188, 230, 283, 284, 285, 286, 287, 363, 446, 447, 448, 449

Ballmer, Steve 8

bandwidth 6, 1018

BankDatabase class (ATM case study) 117, 121, 152, 230, 231, 283, 284, 285, 287, 289, 362, 365

bar chart 246

Bar chart printing application 247

bar of asterisks 246

base
    chaining 398
    for constructor initializers 387
    for invoking overridden methods 397
    keyword 375, 387, 397, 400

base attribute of element extension *789*

base case 223

base class *371*, 447
    constructor 378
    default constructor 378
    direct *371*, 373
    indirect *371*, 373
    method overridden in a derived class 398

Base class for GUIs in our file-processing applications 745

base type (XML Schema) *789*

BasePlusCommissionEmployee class declaration 402

BasePlusCommissionEmployee class represents an employee that receives a base salary in addition to a commission 381

BasePlusCommissionEmployee class that extends CommissionEmployee 425

BasePlusCommissionEmployee has access to CommissionEmployee's private data via its public properties 396

BasePlusCommissionEmployee inherits from class CommissionEmployee 386

BasePlusCommissionEmployee inherits from CommissionEmployee and has access to CommissionEmployee's protected members 391

BasicShapes example 654

Begin method of class Storyboard 1031

behavior 13, 229

behavior of a system 186, 187, 190

behavior of the system 285

behaviorConfiguration Web.config configuration *977*

behaviors *5*

behaviors in the UML *12*

Berners-Lee, Tim 6

BevelBitmapEffect class *673*
    BevelWidth property *674*

BevelWidth property of class BevelBitmapEffect *674*

bidirectional navigability in the UML *363*

binary (base 2) number system 1150

binary arithmetic operators 143

binary digit *733*

binary operator *69*, 70, 182

binary search tree *1083*, *1088*

binary tree *1060*, 1083, 1089

binary tree sort *1089*

BinaryFormatter class *766*
    Deserialize method *766*
    Serialize method 773

BinarySearch method of class Array *1124*

BinarySearch method of class ArrayList 1129

Binding class (WPF) *644*
    ElementName property *644*
    IsAsync property *650*
    Path property *644*
    Source property *644*

binding of a WCF service *965*

BindingNavigator class *838*
    BindingSource property *858*

BindingSource class *838*
    DataSource property *840*, 853
    EndEdit method *840*
    MoveFirst method *841*

BindingSource property of class BindingNavigator *858*

bit *733*

bit (size of unit) 1190

bit manipulation 733

BitArray class *1121*
bitmap graphics *595*
BitmapEffect property of a WPF GUI element *673*
BitmapEffectGroup class *673*
bitwise operators 509
bitwise Xor operator 541
BizTalk 608
blackjack 984
Blackjack game WCF web service. 986
blank line 52
block 199
block of statements *133*, 142
blogs.msdn.com/charlie/archive/2006/10/05/Links-to-LINQ.aspx 294
blueprint 5
BMP (Windows bitmap) 44
body
    of a class declaration 53
    of a loop 134
    of a method *54*
    of an if statement 71
Bohm, C. 127
Booch, Grady 15
Books database 822
    table relationships 825
bool attribute *153*
bool simple type *131*, 1147
boolean expression *131*
boolean logical AND, & 180, *182*
boolean logical exclusive OR, ^ 180, *182*
    truth table 183
boolean logical inclusive OR, | *182*
Boolean struct *1060*
Border element 613, 674, 1024
BorderStyle property of class Panel 504
bottom tier *867*
boundary of control 589
BoundField ASP.NET element *923*
bounds checking *250*
Box class definition represents a box with length, width and height dimensions with indexers 319
boxing 1132, 1136
boxing conversion *1061*
braces ({ and }) 133, 142, 161, 170
braces not required 175
braces, { } 243
break keyword *174*
break mode *1200*
break statement 174, 178
    exiting a for statement 178
breakpoint *1197*
    disabling *1202*
    inserting 1200, 1204
bricks-and-mortar store 899
brittle software *394*
Browse... button 36
brush 659
Brush class (WPF) 630
    ImageBrush class 636
Brush property of class DiffuseMaterial *685*
bubbling events (WPF) *625*
buffer *736*
BufferedStream class *736*
buffering *736*

Buffering state of MediaElement element 1051
bug *1197*
Bug2Bug.master page that defines a logo image header for all pages in the secure books database application 935
Build menu 25
Build Page command in Visual Web Developer *882*
Build Site command in Visual Web Developer *882*
"building blocks" 13
built-in array capabilities 1121
built-in data types 787
Business letter marked up as XML 602
business logic *867*
business rule *867*
button 486
Button ASP.NET web control *888*
Button class 487, 502
    Click event 502
    FlatStyle property 502
    Text property 502
Button control 9, 1024
    Click event *621*, 623
    Windows Forms 613
    WPF *613*, 621, 630
Button properties and events 502
Button property of class MouseEventArgs 523
ButtonBase class *502*
buttons 8
By property of class DoubleAnimation *680*
byte *734*
byte simple type 1147
Byte struct *1060*

C

C format specifier *114*, 168, 379, 383
C programming language *3*
.cs file name extension 53
C# keywords 52
C# Language Specification
    www.ecma-international.org/publications/standards/Ecma-334.htm 4, *17*
C# programming language *4*
C++ *3*
cache *835*, *866*
    use in LINQ to SQL 835
Calculating values to be placed into the elements of an array 244
calculations 85, 127
CalendarForeColor property of class DateTimePicker 543
CalendarMonthBackground property of class DateTimePicker 543
call stack 476
callback function *953*
calling method (caller) *90*
camel casing *68*
Camera property of class Viewport3D *685*
CancelButton property of class Form 489
CanExecute event of CommandBinding class *628*

CanExecute method of ICommand interface *626*
Canvas control 656
Canvas control (WPF) *617*
    Left attached property *617*, 618
    SetLeft method *618*
    SetTop method *618*
    Top attached property *617*, 618
    ZIndex attached property *617*
capacity of a collection *1126*
Capacity property of class ArrayList 1126, *1129*
Capacity property of class List<T> 304, *306*
Capacity property of class StringBuilder 704
Card class 713
Card class represents a playing card 251
card games 251, 713
Card shuffling and dealing application 254
Card shuffling and dealing simulation 714
carriage return 65
carry bit 1157
Cascade value of enumeration MdiLayout *579*
cascaded method calls *354*
cascaded window *579*
case *174*, 175
    keyword *174*
case sensitive *53*
CashDispenser class (ATM case study) 117, 119, 152, 153, 230, 289
casino 207, 212
cast
    downcast *412*
cast operator 142, 204, 216
catch
    general catch clause *464*
catch all exception types 464
catch an exception *461*
catch block (or handler) *464*
catch block with no exception type 464
catch block with no identifier 464
catch-related errors 467
Categorized icon *32*
CDATA keyword (DTD) *781*
Ceiling method of Math 195
CenterX property of class ScaleTransform 675
CenterY property of class ScaleTransform 675
char
    simple type 68
char array 692
char simple type 1147
Char struct 689
    CompareTo method 713
    IsDigit method 712
    IsLetter method 713
    IsLetterOrDigit method 713
    IsLower method 713
    IsPunctuation method 713
    IsSymbol method 713
    IsUpper method 713
    IsWhiteSpace method 713

Char struct (cont.)
    static character-testing methods
      and case-conversion methods 711
    ToLower method 713
    ToUpper method 713
character 206, *733*
    constant *178*
character class (regular expressions) *720*
character class subtraction *724*
character constant *690*
character data in XML *781*
character entity reference 781
character set *733*, 1190
Character struct *1060*
check box *502*
CheckBox class 487, *507*
    Appearance property 507
    Checked property 507
    CheckedChanged event 507
    CheckState property 507
    CheckStateChanged event 507
    Text property 507
    ThreeState property *507*
CheckBox control 674
    WPF 630
CheckBox properties and events 507
CheckBoxes property of class ListView
    566, 566
CheckBoxes property of class TreeView
    561
Checked event handler 659
Checked event of RadioButton control
    621, 623
Checked property of class CheckBox 507
Checked property of class RadioButton
    510
Checked property of class
    ToolStripMenuItem 535, *540*
Checked property of class TreeNode 561
CheckedChanged event of class
    CheckBox 507
CheckedChanged event of class
    RadioButton 511
CheckedIndices property of class
    CheckedListBox 554
CheckedItems property of class
    CheckedListBox 554
CheckedListBox class 531, *549*, 553
    CheckedIndices property 554
    CheckedItems property 554
    GetItemChecked method 554
    ItemCheck event *553*, 554
    SelectionMode property 554
CheckedListBox properties and events
    554
CheckOnClick property of class
    ToolStripMenuItem 535
CheckState property of class CheckBox
    507
CheckStateChanged event of class
    CheckBox 507
child element (XML) *601*, 604
child node 560, *1082*
child node (XML)
    of a DOM tree *799*
child window *576*
child window maximized 578
child window minimized 578
children (in DOM tree) 799

Children property of Panel control
    621
Choose Data Source dialog *836*
Choose Items... option in Visual Studio
    591
circular, doubly linked list *1074*
circular, singly linked list *1073*
clarity 2
class *5*, 12, 13, 154, 193, 230, 234, 362
    class keyword 90
    declaration 52, 53
    declare a method *89*
    instance variable *88*, 97, *196*
    instantiating an object *89*
    name *52*, 53, 341, 364
    user defined *52*
class average 135
class cannot extend a sealed class 432
class constraint *1105*
Class declaration with a method that has a
    parameter 94
Class declaration with one method 90
class diagram
    for the ATM system model 121, 123
    in the UML *83*, *118*, 120, 151, 154,
      362, 365
class diagram (in the UML) 230, 449,
    450, 451
class hierarchy *371*, 416
class keyword 90
class library *4*, 338, 341, *372*, 405
Class that overloads operators for adding,
    subtracting and multiplying complex
    numbers 443
Class View (Visual Studio .NET) 347
"class-wide" information *332*
class XHTML attribute *888*
Classes
    565, *887*
    Application *537*
    ArgumentException 1136
    ArgumentOutOfRangeException
      1129
    Array 291, *1121*, 1122, *1124*, *1125*
    ArrayList 1121, *1126*, *1127*, 1129
    AxisAngleRotation3D *686*
    BevelBitmapEffect *674*
    BinaryFormatter *766*
    Binding *644*
    BindingNavigator *838*
    BindingSource *838*
    BitArray *1121*
    BitmapEffectGroup *673*
    Border 613, 674
    Brush 630
    BufferedStream *736*
    Button 9, 502, *888*
    ButtonBase *502*
    Canvas *617*, 656
    CheckBox *507*, 674
    CheckedListBox 531, *549*, 553
    CollectionView *649*
    ColorAnimation 680, 1031
    ColumnDefinition 1024
    ComboBox 531, *556*
    CommandBinding *628*
    Console 735, 736

Classes (cont.)
    ContentControl *609*, 613, *933*
    ContentPlaceHolder *933*
    ContentPresenter *609*, 613, *640*,
      642
    Control *497*, 497, 499, 588, *871*
    ControlTemplate *640*, 674, 1028
    Convert *69*, 282
    DataContext *836*
    DataContractJsonSerializer
      982, 982
    DataGridView *836*
    DataTemplate *647*
    DateTimePicker *542*
    Delegate *494*
    Dictionary *744*, *745*, 1121
    Dictionary(Of K, V) *744*, *745*,
      905, 1121
    DiffuseMaterial *684*, *685*
    DirectionalLight *685*
    Directory *736*, 741
    DirectoryInfo *571*, *736*
    DispatcherTimer *638*
    DivideByZeroException *460*,
      462, 467
    DockPanel 613
    DoubleAnimation *680*, 1031
    DownloadStringCompletedEven
      tArgs *980*, 1027
    DropDownList *887*, *945*
    Ellipse *655*
    EmissiveMaterial 684
    EventArgs 491, 622
    EventSetter *634*
    Exception *466*
    ExecutionEngineException *467*
    Expander 613
    File *736*, 737, 741, *745*
    FileInfo *571*
    FileStream *736*
    Font *509*
    Form 489, 577, 578
    FormatException *461*, 463
    GradientStop *664*
    Graphics *525*, *559*
    Grid *615*, *616*, 1024
    GridView *646*, *915*, *948*
    GridViewColumn *647*
    GridViewCumn *646*
    GroupBox *503*, *615*
    Hashtable 1121, *1133*, 1134, *1136*
    HttpCookie *905*, 908
    HttpCookieCollection *907*
    HttpSessionState *908*, 910, 911,
      911, 912, 913, 914
    Image *887*, 1024
    ImageBrush 636
    ImageList *561*, 566
    IndexOutOfRangeException 250
    InvalidCastException 430,
      1061, 1120, 1137
    InvalidOperationException
      1125, 1132, 1143
    ItemCheckEventArgs 554
    KeyEventArgs *525*, 526, 528
    KeyNotFoundException 1140
    Label *23*, *35*, *610*
    LinearGradientBrush *662*

Classes (cont.)
LinkedList 1121, *1140*, *1143*
LinkedListNode *1140*
LinkLabel 531, *545*, 546
LinqDataSource *917*
List 1121
List<T> *303*, 304, 306, 1121
ListBox 531, *549*, 913, *1024*
ListItem *887*
ListView *565*, *566*, 960
ListViewItem *567*
Login *940*
LoginName *942*
LoginStatus *942*
Match 690, 717, *718*
MatchCollection 718
Math 194, 195
MediaElement *662*
MemoryStream *736*
MenuItem *630*
MenuStrip *532*
MeshGeometry3D *683*
Model3DGroup *683*
ModelVisual3D *683*
MonthCalendar *541*
MouseButtonEventArgs *622*
MouseDown 622
MouseEventArgs *523*
MouseLeftButtonDown *622*, 625
MouseLeftButtonUp *622*, 625
MouseMove 622
MouseRightButtonDown *622*
MouseRightButtonUp *622*
MouseUp 622
MouseWheel 622
MouseWheelEventArgs 622
MulticastDelegate *494*
MultiScaleImage *1037*
MultiScaleSubImage *1038*
NullReferenceException *467*
NumericUpDown 487, *520*
object *376*, 406
ObjectCollection *550*, *551*, *552*
OpenFileDialog *759*, *760*
OutOfMemoryException *467*, 1062
Page *871*, 898, 908
PaintEventArgs *588*
Panel *503*, 504, *621*
Path *565*, *744*
PerspectiveCamera *685*
PictureBox 515, 580
Point 659
Point3D *685*
PointAnimation 680, 1031
PointCollection *659*
Polygon *656*
Polyline *656*
PreviewMouseLeftButtonDown *625*
PreviewMouseLeftButtonUp *625*
Process *546*
Queue *1121*
RadialGradientBrush *662*, 674
RadioButton *507*, 510, *621*
Random 207, 667
Rectangle *654*
Regex *718*, 724

Classes (cont.)
RegularExpressionValidator *896*
RequiredFieldValidator *896*
ResourceManager *517*, 997
Resources *517*
RichTextBox *626*
RotateTransform *665*
RotateTransform3D *686*
RoutedCommand *626*
RoutedEventArgs 622, 623
RowDefinition 1024
SaveFileDialog 749
ScaleTransform *665*, 675
ScriptManager *958*
Separator *630*
Setter *634*, 642
SkewTransform *665*, 675
Slider *634*
SolidBrush *525*
SolidColorBrush 659
SortedDictionary 1122, *1137*, 1139
SortedList *1121*, 1122
Stack 1107, *1121*, 1122, 1130
StackOverflowException *467*
StackPanel *615*, 1024
Storyboard *679*, 1031
Stream *736*, *765*
StreamReader *736*
StreamWriter *736*
string 689
StringBuilder 689, 702, 703, 706, 707, 708
Style *634*, 1028
SystemException *467*
TabContainer *958*
TabControl *571*
TabPage *572*
TabPanel *958*
TextBlock 1024
TextBox *41*, 487, *623*, *887*
TextReader 736
TextWriter 736
Timer *588*
TimeSpan *638*
ToolStripMenuItem *532*, *534*
ToolTip *518*, 518
TreeNode *560*, 561
TreeView 531, *560*, 561, 803
TreeViewEventArgs *561*
Trigger *642*
Type 407, *430*
UIElementCollection *621*
UInt32 *1061*
UnauthorizedAccessException 565
UpdatePanel *959*
Uri 980, 1027
UserControl *588*, *1020*, 1028
ValidatorCalloutExtender *960*
ValueType *711*, *1061*
Vector3D *685*
VideoBrush *1052*
Viewport3D *683*
WeatherData 1027
WebClient 979, 1027
WebControl *872*

Classes (cont.)
Window *609*, 618, 637
WrapPanel 613
XAttribute *810*
XComment *811*
XContainer *809*, *815*
XDocument *800*, 1027
XDocumentType *810*
XElement *800*, *810*
XmlDataProvider *650*
XmlReader *598*
XName *802*
XNamespace *810*, *812*, 1010
XNode *811*
XObject *811*
XProcessingInstruction *811*
XslCompiledTransform *817*
XText *811*
Clear method of class Array *1125*
Clear method of class ArrayList 1126
Clear method of class Dictionary *745*
Clear method of class Graphics *559*
Clear method of class List<T> 304
Clear method of class ObjectCollection *552*
Clear method of class PointCollection *659*
Clear method of UIElementCollection class *621*
ClearSelected method of class ListBox 550
ClearType xl
CLI (Common Language Infrastructure) *8*
click a Button 490
click a button 502
Click event handler 659
Click event of Button control *621*, 623
Click event of class Button 502
Click event of class PictureBox 515
Click event of class ToolStripMenuItem *534*, 536
clicking *20*
Clicks property of class MouseEventArgs 523
client code 412
Client interacting with server and web server. *Step 1* The GET request 864
Client interacting with server and web server. *Step 2* The HTTP response 865
client of a class *13*, 229, 285, 339
Client that consumes the WelcomeRESTXMLService 979
Client that consumes WelcomeSOAPXMLService 975
client tier *867*
ClipRectangle property of class PaintEventArgs *588*, 589
clock 588
cloning objects shallow copy *407*
close a project 25
close a window 490
close box *11*, 46, 47
Close method of class Form 489
Closed state of MediaElement element 1051

CLR (Common Language Runtime) *8*, 468, 482
CML (Chemical Markup Language) 597
code-behind file *863*
code reuse 371, 1119
code snippets *105*
code snippets (IDE)
　switch 217
code value (Unicode) *1191*
code walkthrough 50
code-behind class (WPF) 609, 611
Code-behind file for a page that updates the time every minute 870
Code-behind file for a Web Form that obtains a user's contact information. 897
Code-behind file for the guestbook application 923
Code-behind file that defines event handlers for the secure books database application 947
Code-behind file that writes a cookie to the client. 904
CodeFile attribute in a Page directive *869*
coin tossing 207
collaboration diagram in the UML *83*, *285*
collaboration in the UML *282*, 283, 286
collapse a tree 31
Collapse method of class TreeNode 562
collapse node 560
collection 303, 1099, *1119*
collection class *1119*
collection initializers *308*
CollectionView class (WPF) *649*
CollectionViewSource.Get-DefaultView method *649*
collision *1133*
Color property of class DirectionalLight *685*
Color property of class GradientStop *664*
Color structure *525*
ColorAnimation class 680, 1031
column 268
Column attached property of Grid control *616*
column of a database table *821*, 822
ColumnDefinition class 1024
ColumnDefinition class associated with Grid control *615*
ColumnDefinitions property of Grid control *615*
columns of a two-dimensional array *268*
ColumnSpan attached property of Grid control *616*
ComboBox class 487, 531, *556*
　DisplayMember property *853*
　DropDownStyle property 556, *557*
　Items property 556, *557*
　MaxDropDownItems property *556*
　SelectedIndex property 556, *557*
　SelectedIndexChanged event *557*, 853
　SelectedItem property *557*
　Sorted property 557

ComboBox control
　SelectedIndexChanged event handler 841
ComboBox control (WPF) 630
ComboBox demonstration 556
ComboBox properties and an event 556
ComboBox used to draw a selected shape 557
ComboBoxStyle enumeration *557*
　DropDown value *557*
　DropDownList value *557*
　Simple value *557*
comma (,) 165
comma in an argument list 66
comma-separated list 165
　of parameters 198
　of arguments *66*, 68
command binding (WPF) *628*
command library (WPF) 626
command-line argument *197*, *280*, 282
Command Prompt *50*, 280
CommandBinding class (WPF) *628*
　CanExecute event *628*
　Executed event *628*
　PreviewCanExecute event *628*
　PreviewExecuted event *628*
CommandBindings property of Window control *628*
commands (WPF) *625*
comment 50
CommissionEmployee class represents a commission employee 376, 394, 400
CommissionEmployee class that extends Employee 424
CommissionEmployee with protected instance variables 389
Common Language Infrastructure (CLI) *8*
Common Language Runtime (CLR) 8, 468, 482
Common Programming Errors overview xxx
communication diagram in the UML *83*, *285*, 286
CompareTo method
　of IComparable *1104*
　of interface IComparable 442
CompareTo method of IComparable *1090*
CompareTo method of struct Char 713
Comparing integers using if statements, equality operators and relational operators 72
comparison operator 442
comparison operators *71*
compilation error *1197*
Compilation errors generated by BasePlusCommissionEmployee 388
compile 55
compile-time type safety *1098*
compiling 1060
complex content in XML Schema *788*
ComplexNumber class 443
complexType XML Schema element *786*
component *3*, *486*, 488
component diagram in the UML *1185*

component in the UML *14*, *1185*
component selection drop-down list *33*
component tray *518*, *838*
composite key *821*
composite structure diagram in the UML *1186*
composition *119*, 119, 120, 122, *328*, 372, 374
Composition demonstration 331
compound assignment operators 147, 150
compound interest 166
compound-interest
　calculating with for 167
Computing the sum of the elements of an array 246
Concat method of class string 700
concatenate strings 334
concrete class *415*
concrete derived class 420
condition 169
conditional AND (&&) operator 299
conditional AND, && *180*, 182
　truth table 181
conditional expression *131*, 312
conditional operator, ?: 131, 150
conditional OR, || 180, *181*
　truth table *181*
confusing the equality operator == with the assignment operator = 71
connect to a database 836
consistent state 312, 322
console application *50*, 55
Console class 735, 736
　ReadLine method 93
console window *50*, 64, 65
Console.Write method *65*
Console.WriteLine method *55*, 64
const
　keyword 178, *196*, 245
const keyword 336
constant *178*, 196, 245
　declare 245
　must be initialized 245
constant integral expression *170*, 177
constant string expression *170*, 177
Constants
　Nan of structure Double *460*, 482
　NegativeInfinity of structure Double *460*
　PositiveInfinity of structure Double *460*
constituent controls *588*
constrained version of a linked list 1075
constructor 107
　naming 108
　parameter list 108
constructor constraint (new()) *1105*
constructor initializer *324*, 387
　with keyword base 387
constructors cannot specify a return type 109
consuming a web service *967*
container 487, *489*
container element (XML) *601*
Contains method of class ArrayList 1126, *1129*
Contains method of class List<T> 304, *306*

Contains method of class Stack 1132
Contains method of Rect structure *1050*
ContainsKey method of class Dictionary(Of K, V) *744*
ContainsKey method of Hashtable *1136*
Content ASP.NET control *937*
content control (WPF) *609*
content page in ASP.NET *928*
Content property of class ModelVisual3D *683*
Content property of ContentPresenter class *642*
ContentControl class (WPF) *609*, 613
ContentPlaceHolder ASP.NET control *933*
ContentPresenter class (WPF) *640*
    Content property *642*
Contents command of **Help** 34
context node (XPath) *797*
context-sensitive help *34*
ContextTypeName property of LinqDataSource ASP.NET data control *923*
contextual keyword 100
contextual keywords 52, *53*
Continue command (debugger) *1201*
continue keyword *178*
continue statement 178, 179
    terminating an iteration of a for statement 179
contract of a WCF service *965*
control *23*, 31, 488
control (WPF) *609*, 639
control boundary 589
Control class *497*, 588, *871*
    Anchor property 499
    BackColor property 497
    BackgroundImage property 497
    Dock property 499
    Enabled property 497, *498*
    Focused property 497
    Font property 497
    ForeColor property 497
    Hide method 497
    KeyDown event *525*, 526
    KeyPress event *525*, 526
    KeyUp event *525*, 526
    Location property 499
    MaximumSize property 499
    MinimumSize property 499
    MouseDown event 523
    MouseEnter event 523
    MouseHover event 523
    MouseLeave event 523
    MouseMove event 523
    MouseUp event 523
    OnPaint method *588*
    Padding property 499
    Select method *497*
    Show method 497
    Size property 499
    TabIndex property *497*
    TabStop property 497
    Text property 497
    Visible property 497
control layout and properties 497

Control property of class KeyEventArgs 526, 528
control statement 128, 130, 158
    nesting 129
    stacking 129
control structure 127
control template (WPF) *639*
control variable *158*, 159, 160, 162
controller logic *867*
Controls *9*
    AdRotator *889*
    Border 613
    Butto 621
    Button *613*, 630, *888*
    Canvas *617*
    CheckBox 630
    ComboBox 630
    Content *937*
    ContentControl *609*, 613
    DataPager *961*
    DockPanel 613
    Expander 613
    Form 609
    Grid 609, *615*, 616
    GridView *646*, *915*
    GroupBox 9, *615*
    HyperLink *888*
    Image *887*
    ImageBrush 636
    Label *23*, *35*, 40, *610*
    LinqDataSource *917*
    ListBox 913
    ListView *644*, 960
    Login 925, *940*
    LoginName *942*
    LoginStatus *942*
    Menu *630*
    MenuItem *630*
    Panel 9, *609*
    PictureBox *23*, *35*, 43
    RadioButton 9, *613*, 630
    RadioButtonList *888*
    RegularExpressionValidator *896*
    RequiredFieldValidator *896*
    RichTextBox *626*
    ScriptManager *958*
    Separator *630*
    Slider *634*
    StackPanel *615*
    TabContainer *958*
    TextBlock *647*
    TextBox *623*
    ToolBar *630*
    ToolBarTray *630*
    ToolkitScriptManager *958*
    ValidatorCalloutExtender *960*
    Window *609*, 618, 637
    WrapPanel 613
Controls property of class GroupBox *504*, 504
Controls property of class Panel 504
ControlTemplate class (WPF) *640*, 674, 1028
    TargetType property *640*
    Triggers property *642*
ControlToValidate property of an ASP.NET validation control *896*

ControlToValidate property of class RegularExpressionValidator *896*
converge on a base case 223
Convert 72
convert
    a binary number to decimal 1155
    a hexadecimal number to decimal 1155
    an integral value to a floating-point value 204
    an octal number to decimal 1155
Convert class *69*, 282
    ToDecimal method *114*
    ToInt32 method 282
cookie *900*, 901, 907, 908
    deletion 901
    domain 908
    expiration *901*
    expiration date *901*
    header 900, 901
Cookies collection of the Response object *905*
Cookies property of Request object *907*
Copy method of class Array *1124*
Copy method of class File 737
copying objects
    shallow copy *407*
CopyTo method of class string 692
Corel® Paint Shop Pro® 44
Cos method of Math 195
cosine 195
Count extension method of interface IEnumerable<T> *301*
Count method (LINQ) 744
Count property of Hashtable *1136*
Count property of class ArrayList 1127, *1129*
Count property of class HttpSessionState 913, *914*
Count property of class List<T> *304*
counter-controlled repetition 141, 144, 158, 160
    with the for repetition statement 160
    with the while repetition statement 159
CoverCollage Deep Zoom Composer project 1040
craps (casino game) 207, 212
Craps class simulates the dice game craps 212
create a class library 341
Create a **GradeBook** object and call its DisplayMessage method 91
create a reusable class 341
create an object of a class 92
Create and manipulate a **GradeBook** object 101
Create and manipulate an **Account** object 112
Create and write to a sequential-access file 749
Create **GradeBook** object and pass a string to its DisplayMessage method 94

Create GradeBook object using a
 rectangular array of grades 278
Create GradeBook object using an array
 of grades 267
create GradeBook object, input grades
 and display grade report 176
Create method of class File 737
create new classes from existing class
 declarations 376
CreateDirectory method of class
 Directory 736, 737
CreateInstance method of class
 Array 1125
CreateNewUser.aspx page that
 provides a user registration form 938
Creates a session item for each
 programming language selected by the
 user on the ASPX page. 911
CreateText method of class File 737
CreateUserWizard ASP.NET login
 control 937
creating a child Form to be added to an
 MDI Form 576
Creating a **Class Library** Project 343
creating a generic method 1114
Creating a WCF Service in Visual Web
 Developer 969
creating and initializing an array 242
Creating and manipulating an Account
 object 1199
creating GradeBook object 138, 143
Credit-inquiry program 760
cropping *680*
.cs file-name extension 30
CSS (Cascading Style Sheets) *888*
CSS rule *888*
CSS selector *888*
Ctrl key 525
Ctrl key 174
Ctrl + z 174
Current property of IEnumerator
 1125
current time 590
CurrentState property of
 MediaElement element *1051*
CurrentValue property of class
 ItemCheckEventArgs 554
cursor 55, 64
custom control 588, *1028*
Custom control added to a Form 591
Custom control added to the ToolBox
 591
Custom control creation 588, 591
custom controls *587*
Custom palette 39
Custom tab *39*
Custom value of enumeration
 DateTimePickerFormat *542*
CustomFormat property of class
 DateTimePicker *542*, 543
customize a Form 31
customize Visual Studio IDE 26
Customizing gradients 664

D

D format specifier 114, 246
D2 format specifier 312
dangling-else problem *132*

data abstraction *339*
data binding 680, *836*
data binding (WPF) *644*
 to LINQ 644
data hierarchy *734*
data in support of actions 340
data independence *7*
Data menu 25
data provider (WPF) *650*
data representation *340*
data source 295
Data Source Configuration Wizard
 837
Data Sources window *837*
data structure *239*, *1060*
data template (WPF) *647*
data tier *867*
data validation *103*
data view (WPF) *649*
database 25, *735*, *820*, 826
 add to a project 836
 saving changes in LINQ to SQL 840
 schema 822
Database Explorer window *837*
database management system (DBMS)
 735, *820*
database schema *822*, 835
database table *821*
DataBind method of a GridView
 ASP.NET control *924*
DataBindings.Text property of class
 TextBox *858*
DataContext class *836*
 Log property *843*
 SubmitChanges method *836*, 840
DataContext of WPF controls *647*
DataContract attribute *981*
DataContractJsonSerializer class
 982
DataGridView class *836*
DataMember attribute 981, *1005*
DataPager ASP.NET data control 961
DataSource property of class
 BindingSource *840*, 853
DataSourceID property of a GridView
 ASP.NET control *920*
DataTemplate class (WPF) *647*
DataTip *1203*
data-type attribute (XPath) *798*
Date class
 declaration 328
Date property of class DateTimePicker
 542, 543
DateChanged event of class
 MonthCalendar *542*
DateTime structure *590*
 AddDay method *545*
 AddYears method *545*
 DayOfWeek property *545*
 Now property *590*
 ToLongDateString method *545*
 ToLongTimeString method *590*
DateTimePicker class *542*
 CalendarForeColor property 543
 CalendarMonthBackground
 property 543
 CustomFormat property *542*, 543
 Date property *542*, 543
 Format property *542*, 543

DateTimePicker class (cont.)
 MaxDate property 543, *545*
 MinDate property 543, *545*
 ShowCheckBox property 543
 ShowUpDown property 543
 TimeOfDay property *542*, 543
 Value property *542*, 543, *545*
 ValueChanged event *542*, 543
DateTimePickerFormat enumeration
 542
 Custom value *542*
 Long value *542*
 Short value *542*
 Time value *542*
DayOfWeek enumeration *545*
DayOfWeek property of structure
 DateTime *545*
DB2 820
DBCS (double byte character set) *1192*
DbLinq 860
DBMS (database management system)
 735, *820*
dealing 251
Debug menu 25
debugger *1197*
 break mode 1200
 breakpoint *1197*
 Continue command *1201*
 defined *1197*
 Instruction Pointer *1201*
 Locals window *1204*
 logic error 1197
 margin indicator bar *1200*
 Step Into command *1207*
 Step Out command *1208*
 Step Over command *1208*
 suspending program execution 1204
 Watch window *1204*, 1205
debugging 25
Debugging Not Enabled dialog 1021
decimal 110, 111
decimal (base 10) number system 1150
decimal digit *733*
decimal point 143
decimal simple type 68, *110*, 1148
DecimalPlaces property of class
 NumericUpDown *520*
decision 71, 129
decision in the UML 188
decision symbol *129*
DeckOfCards class represents a deck of
 playing cards 252
declaration *67*
 class 52, *53*
 method *54*
Declaration of class TreeNode and class
 Tree 1084, 1090
declarative programming *294*, *595*, 608
declare a constant 245
declare a method of a class *89*
decrement *158*
decrement operator, -- 148, 149
deep zoom *1018*, 1037
Deep Zoom Composer *1038*
 Compose tab 1040
 Export tab 1042
 Import tab 1040
 Layer View 1042

DeepZoomCoverCollage example 1038
default
  case in a switch 174
  keyword 174
default case 210
default constructor 327, 378
default event of a control *494*
default initial value of a field *101*
default namespace *607*
  demonstration 607
default namespace (XAML) 609
default settings 10
default type constraint (object) of a type parameter 1109
default value 151
Default Web.config file's service model configuration for WCF service. 970
deferred execution *308*
definitely assigned *137*, 215
deitel@deitel.com 2
delegate *354*, *493*, 765
  Delegate class *494*
  MulticastDelegate class *494*
  registering an event handler *493*
Delegate class *494*
delegate keyword *354*, *494*
Delete method of class Directory 737
Delete method of class File 737, *745*
DELETE SQL statement 826, *834*
deletion 1064
delimited comments *50*
Demonstrate basic regular expressions 718
Demonstrate using character classes and quantifiers 720
Demonstrating a user-defined exception class 483
Demonstrating class Stack 1130
Demonstrating keyboard events 526
deny element in Web.config *933*
dependency property (WPF) *635*, 642
  attached property *616*
dependent condition 182
deployment diagram in the UML *1185*
Deposit class (ATM case study) 117, 120, 152, 153, 230, 284, 285, 290, 363, 446, 447, 448
DepositSlot class (ATM case study) 117, 119, 152, 230, 285, 363
dequeue operation of queue 340, *1079*
derived class *371*, 447, 448
DESC in SQL 829, *829*
descendant node of a DOM tree 799
Descendants method of class XContainer *809*
descending modifier of a LINQ orderby clause *297*
descending order
  DESC in SQL *829*
descriptive words and phrases (OOD/UML case study) 152, 154
deselected state *510*
Deserialize method of class BinaryFormatter *766*
deserialized object *766*
design mode *38*, 46
Design mode in Visual Web Developer *876*

design process 14, 76, 82, 231, 236
design specification *82*
Design view *23*, 610
Design view (Silverlight) 1021
destructor 332
diacritic *1191*
dialog 22
DialogResult enumeration *515*, *753*
Dialogs
  Font 41
  New Project *22*, 24, 36
  Project Location *36*
diamond *127*, 129
dice game 212
dictionary *1137*
Dictionary(Of K, V) generic class *744*, *905*, 1121
  Add method *744*
  Clear method *745*
  ContainsKey method *744*
  Keys property *745*
  Remove method *745*
DictionaryEntry structure *1136*
DiffuseMaterial class 684, *685*
  Brush property *685*
digit 68, 1150
digit character class (\d) *720*
direct base class 371, 373
direct events, (WPF) *625*
Direction property of class DirectionalLight *685*
DirectionalLight class *685*
  Color property *685*
  Direction property *685*
directive in ASP.NET *868*
Directory class *736*, 741
  CreateDirectory method *736*
  GetFiles method *741*
Directory class methods (partial list) 737
DirectoryInfo class *571*, *736*
  Exists method *571*
  FullName property *571*
  GetDirectories method *571*
  GetFiles method *571*
  Name property *571*
  Parent property *571*
disabling a breakpoint *1202*
DispatcherTimer class *638*
  Interval property *638*
  IsEnabled property *638*
  Tick event *638*
Display order in which base class and derived class constructors are called 404
display output 85
Display property of an ASP.NET validation control *896*
DisplayArray generic method 1101
DisplayArray method in which actual type names are replaced by convention with the generic name E 1101
Displaying data from a database table in a DataGridView 839
displaying line numbers in the IDE 57
Displaying multiple lines of text with string formatting 65
Displaying multiple lines with a single statement 64

Displaying one line of text with multiple statements 63
Displaying the result of a user-selected query in a DataGridView 841
Displaying the sum of two numbers input from the keyboard 67
DisplayMember property of class ComboBox *853*
DisplayMemberBinding property of GridViewColumn class *647*
Displays information from the Books database 949
DisplayWeatherForecast method of class WeatherViewerPage 1027
Dispose method of interface IDisposable 442, 475
distance between values (random numbers) 211
Distinct extension method of interface IEnumerable<T> *301*
Distinct query operator (LINQ) 744
distributed computing 965
divide by zero 460, 462
DivideByZeroException class *460*, 462, 464, 467
division 70
division by zero is undefined 340
.dll file 343
.dll file name extension *60*
DNS (domain name system) server *864*
DNS lookup *864*
do keyword *168*
do...while repetition statement 128, 168, 169, 170
dock a control *498*
Dock property of class Control 499
docking demonstration 499
DockPanel control (WPF) 613
  LastChildFill property 613
Document navigation using XNode and axis properties 803
Document Object Model (DOM) tree 799
Document property of class XObject *811*
document root *793*
document type declaration 869
Document Type Definition (DTD) *598*, 603, 780
  for a business letter 780
DOM (Document Object Model) tree 799
  ancestor node 799
  child node 799
  descendant node 799
  parent node 799
  root node 800
  sibling node 799
DOM parser 799
domain name system (DNS) server *864*
Domain property of HttpCookie class 908
DOS 2
dotted line in the UML 128
Double 1104
double-byte character set (DBCS) *1192*
(double) cast 142
double-clicking *20*
double equals, == 71

double-precision floating-point number *110*

double quote (") 55, 64, 65

double quotes ("") to delineate a string 604

double-selection statement 128

double simple type *68*, 141, 1148

`Double struct` *1061*

`Double.NaN` *460*, 482

`double.NaN` constant 1036

`Double.NegativeInfinity` *460*

`Double.PositiveInfinity` *460*

`DoubleAnimation class` *680*, 1031

    By property *680*

    Duration property *680*

    From property *680*

    To property *680*

doubly linked list *1074*

down-arrow button 39

downcast 430, 1137

downcasting *412*

`DownloadStringAsync` method of class `WebClient` 1027

`DownloadStringCompletedEvent-Args class` *980*, 1027

    Error property 1027

    Result property 1027

`DragMove` method of `Window` control *637*

Draw event of class `ToolTip` 518

draw on control 589

`DrawEllipse` method of class `Graphics` *560*

Drawing Polylines and Polygons 657

`DrawPie` method of class `Graphics` *560*

`DrawPolygons` example 656

`DrawRectangle` method of class `Graphics` *560*

`DrawStars` example 666

drop-down list 487, *556*

`DropDown` value of enumeration `ComboBoxStyle` *557*

`DropDownList` ASP.NET web control *887*

`DropDownList` value of enumeration `ComboBoxStyle` *557*

`DropDownStyle` property of class `ComboBox` 556, *557*

`DropShadowBitmapEffect class` *673*

    ShadowDepth property *674*

    Softness property *674*

DTD (Document Type Definition) *598*, 603

.dtd filename extension *604*

DTD repository 780

dummy value *139*

duplicate elimination *1089*

`Duration` property of class `DoubleAnimation` *680*

dynamic binding *429*

dynamic content *4*

dynamic data structures *1060*

dynamic memory allocation *1062*, 1064

dynamic resizing *293*

dynamic resizing of a `List` collection 304

dynamic resource (WPF) *634*

dynamically linked library *60*, *343*

E

E format specifier 114

e-mail (electronic mail) 6

Ecma International 9

ECMA-334: C# Language Specification 4

Edit and Continue *1210*

Edit menu 25

editable list 557

efficient (Unicode design basis) *1189*

Electric Rain's ZAM3D 683

electronic mail (e-mail) 6

element (XAML) 608

element (XML) *596*

ELEMENT element type declaration (DTD) *780*

`Element` method of class `XContainer` *810*

element of an array *239*

element of chance 207

element type declaration *780*

element XML Schema element *786*

`ElementName` property of `Binding` class *644*

`Elements` method of class `XContainer` *803*

`Elements` method of class `XElement` *803*

`ElementToLogicalPoint` method of `MultiScaleImage` element *1045*

elided UML diagram *118*

eligible for destruction *332*

eligible for garbage collection *332*, 335

eliminate resource leak 469

`Ellipse` element *655*

ellipsis button *41*

`else` 130

embedded style sheet *888*

`EmissiveMaterial` class 684

Employee abstract base class 420, 438

Employee class with `FirstName`, `LastName` and `MonthlySalary` properties 298

Employee class with references to other objects 330

Employee hierarchy test application 427

empty element 604

EMPTY keyword (DTD) *782*

empty statement 133

empty statement (semicolon by itself) *75*, 170

empty string

    "" *106*

    string.Empty *106*

`EmptyStackException` indicates a stack is empty 1109

en.wikipedia.org/wiki/IP_address 864

Enable Paging setting for an ASP.NET GridView *948*

Enable Sorting setting for an ASP.NET GridView *948*

`EnableClientScript` property of an ASP.NET validation control *898*

`Enabled` property of class `Control` 497, *498*

`EnableSessionState` property of a Web Form 869, *881*

`EnableViewState` property of an ASP.NET web control 870, *881*, 899

encapsulation *13*, 103, 432

encoding *1189*

encoding in xml declaration *599*

encrypted data *942*

"end of data entry" 139

end-of-file (EOF) indicator *174*

end-of-file marker *735*

end tag *596*

end tag (XAML) 608

`EndEdit` method of class `BindingSource` *840*

endpoint (of a WCF service) *965*

`EndPoint` property of class `LinearGradientBrush` *664*

`EndsWith` method of class `string` 696, 697

enqueue operation of queue 340, *1079*

`EnsureCapacity` method of class `StringBuilder` 704

Enter (or *Return*) key 38

enter data from the keyboard 487

entity

    & 781

    ' 781

    > 781

    < 781

    " 781

entity-relationship diagram *825*

entry point of an application *196*

enum *215*

    keyword 215

enumeration *215*

enumeration constant *215*

Enumerations

    XmlNodeType *811*

enumerations

    ComboBoxStyle *557*

    DateTimePickerFormat *542*

    DayOfWeek *545*

    MdiLayout *579*

    SelectionMode *550*

enumerator *1119*, 1124

    fail fast 1125

    of a LinkedList 1143

equal likelihood 209

`Equals` method of an anonymous type 361

`Equals` method of class `object` 406

`Equals` method of class `string` 694

Error List window *62*

Error-Prevention Tip overview xxx

error-processing code 458

`Error` property of class `Console` 735

`Error` property of class `DownloadStringCompletedEvent Args` *980*, 1027

`ErrorMessage` property of an ASP.NET validation control *896*

escape character *64*, 833

escape sequence *65*, 68

    newline, \n 65, 68

event 186, *490*

event argument 491

event driven *490*

event-driven programming 2

event handler *490*

event handling *490*

    WPF 618

event handling model 490
event multicasting *494*
event receiver *493*
event routing (WPF) 623
event sender *493*
EventArgs class 491, 622
events *4*
events at an interval 588
EventSetter class (WPF) *634*
Examples
   A more complex regular expression 723
   A simple XAML document 608
   Account class with a constructor to initialize instance variable balance 111
   Account class with a Debit method that withdraws money from account 1198
   Adding a new UserControl to a Silverlight application 1029
   Addition.cs 67
   Anchoring demonstration 499
   Animating a 3-D object 681
   Animating the width and height of a video 678
   Append method of class StringBuilder 706
   Application counts the number of occurrences of each word in a string and stores them in a generic sorted dictionary 1138
   Application counts the number of occurrences of each word in a string and stores them in a hash table 1134
   Application to test class Craps 214
   Application to test class MaximumFinder 199
   Application to test class MethodOverload 221
   Application to test class ReferenceAndOutput-Parameters 228
   Application to test class Scope 219
   Applying an XSLT style sheet to an XML document 815
   Applying brushes to various XAML elements 659
   Applying transforms to a Polygon 666
   article.xml displayed by Internet Explorer 601
   ASPX file for the guestbook application. 920
   ASPX file that displays book recommendations based on cookies. 906
   ASPX file that displays the Web server's time 868
   ASPX file that presents a list of programming languages 901, 909
   ASPX file that takes reservation information 1000
   Assigning base class and derived class references to base class and derived class variables 413
   Bar chart printing application 247

Examples (cont.)
   Base class for GUIs in our file-processing applications 745
   BasePlusCommissionEmployee class declaration 402
   BasePlusCommissionEmployee class represents an employee that receives a base salary in addition to a commission 381
   BasePlusCommissionEmployee class that extends CommissionEmployee 425
   BasePlusCommissionEmployee has access to CommissionEmployee's private data via its public properties 396
   BasePlusCommissionEmployee inherits from class CommissionEmployee 386
   BasePlusCommissionEmployee inherits from CommissionEmployee and has access to CommissionEmployee's protected members 391
   Blackjack game WCF web service 986
   Box class definition represents a box with length, width and height dimensions with indexers 319
   break statement exiting a for statement 178
   Bug2Bug.master page that defines a logo image header for all pages in the secure books database application 935
   Business letter marked up as XML 602
   Calculating values to be placed into the elements of an array 244
   Card class 713
   Card class represents a playing card 251
   Card dealing and shuffling simulation 714
   Card shuffling and dealing application 254
   Changing the axis of rotation for a 3-D animation 686
   Changing the tab spacing 611
   Char's static character-testing methods and case-conversion methods 711
   Class declaration with a method that has a parameter 94
   Class declaration with one method 90
   Class that overloads operators for adding, subtracting and multiplying complex numbers 443
   Client that consumes the WelcomeRESTXMLService 979
   Client that consumes WelcomeSOAPXMLService 975
   Code-behind class and GUI display of a simple text editor 628
   Code-behind class for Painter 618

Examples (cont.)
   Code-behind file for a page that updates the time every minute 870
   Code-behind file for a Web Form that obtains a user's contact information. 897
   Code-behind file for the guestbook application 923
   Code-behind file that defines event handlers for the secure books database application 947
   Code-behind file that writes a cookie to the client 904
   Color chooser application showing the use of styles (code-behind) 633
   Color chooser application showing the use of styles (XAML) 631
   ComboBox used to draw a selected shape 557
   CommissionEmployee class represents a commission employee 376, 394, 400
   CommissionEmployee class that extends Employee 424
   CommissionEmployee with protected instance variables 389
   Common built-in commands from WPF command library 626
   Common controls used for layout 612
   Common mouse and keyboard events 622
   Comparison.cs 72
   Composition demonstration 331
   compound-interest calculations with for 167
   Computing the sum of the elements of an array 246
   Concat static method 700
   continue statement terminating an iteration of a for statement 179
   counter-controlled repetition with the for repetition statement 160
   counter-controlled repetition with the while repetition statement 159
   Craps class simulates the dice game craps 212
   Create a GradeBook object and call its DisplayMessage method 91
   Create and manipulate a GradeBook object 101
   Create and manipulate an Account object 112
   Create and write to a sequential-access file 749
   Create GradeBook object and pass a string to its DisplayMessage method 94
   Create GradeBook object using a rectangular array of grades 278
   Create GradeBook object using an array of grades 267
   create GradeBook object, input grades and display grade report 176

Examples (cont.)

CreateNewUser.aspx page that provides a user registration form 938

Creates a session item for each programming language selected by the user on the ASPX page. 911

Creating a **Console Application** with the **New Project** dialog 56

Creating a WCF Service in Visual Web Developer 969

Creating an array 242

Creating and manipulating an Account object 1199

Creating custom windows and using timers (code-behind) 637

Creating custom windows and using timers (XAML) 636

creating GradeBook object 138, 143

Creating menus and toolbars, and using commands (XAML) 627

Credit-inquiry program 760

Customizing gradients 664

Date class declaration 328

DeckOfCards class represents a deck of playing cards 252

Declaration of class TreeNode and class Tree 1084, 1090

Deep Zoom Composer showing the editable composition 1041

Deep Zoom Composer showing the imported image files 1041

Deep Zoom Composer's exporting capabilities 1043

Deep Zoom Composer's **New Project** dialog 1040

DeepZoomCoverCollage employs Silverlight's deep zoom (code-behind) 1045

DeepZoomCoverCollage employs Silverlight's deep zoom (XAML) 1043

Default namespaces demonstration 607

Default Web.config file's service model configuration for WCF service. 970

Defining a Polygon representing a star in XAML 666

Defining gradients in XAML 663

Defining Polylines and Polygons in XAML 656

Demonstrate basic regular expressions 718

Demonstrate object initializers using class Time. 350

Demonstrate using character classes and quantifiers 720

Demonstrating a user-defined exception class 483

Demonstrating class Stack 1130

Demonstrating extension methods. 352

Demonstrating keyboard events 526

Directory class methods (partial list) 737

Examples (cont.)

Display order in which base class and derived class constructors are called 404

DisplayArray method in which actual type names are replaced by convention with the generic name E 1101

Displaying data from a database table in a DataGridView 839

Displaying multiple lines of text with string formatting 65

Displaying multiple lines with a single statement 64

Displaying one line of text with multiple statements 63

Displaying the result of a user-selected query in a DataGridView 841

Displaying the sum of two numbers input from the keyboard 67

Displays information from the Books database 949

do...while repetition statement 169

Document navigation using XNode and axis properties 803

Document Type Definition (DTD) for a business letter 780

Drawing basic shapes in XAML 654

Drawing Polylines and Polygons 657

Employee abstract base class 420, 438

Employee class with FirstName, LastName and MonthlySalary properties 298

Employee class with references to other objects 330

Employee hierarchy test application 427

EmptyStackException indicates a stack is empty 1109

File class methods (partial list) 737

finally blocks always execute, even when no exception occurs 470

Finished design of **MasterDetail** application 852

FlickrViewer allows users to search for photos (code-behind) 1034

FlickrViewer allows users to search for tagged photos (XAML) 1033

FlickrViewer allows users to search photos by tag 1032

FormatException and DivideByZeroException handlers 462

Formatting fonts in XAML code 653

FullStackException indicates a stack is full 1109

Generic class Stack 1107

Generic List<T> collection demonstration 304

Generic method Maximum returns the largest of three objects 1105

Grade book using an array to store test grades 264

Grade book using rectangular array to store grades 274

Examples (cont.)

GradeBook class that contains a private instance variable, and a public property to get and set its value 97

GradeBook class uses switch statement 171

GradeBook class using counter-controlled repetition 135

GradeBook class using sentinel-controlled repetition 140

GradeBook class with a constructor to initialize the course name 107

GradeBook class with an auto-implemented property 104

GradeBook constructor used to specify the course name at the time each GradeBook object is created 108

GUI of color chooser application at initialization 636

HourlyEmployee class that extends Employee 422

IDE with an open console application 56, 57, 59

Implementing a queue by inheriting from class List 1080

Implementing a stack by inheriting from class List 1075

Important methods of class HttpCookie 908

Indexers provide access to an object's members 321

Inheritance examples 372, 373

Inheritance hierarchy for university CommunityMembers 373

Initializing jagged and rectangular arrays 271

Initializing the elements of an array with an array initializer 243

Integer division without exception handling 459

IntelliSense feature of Visual C# Express 58

IntelliSense support for extension methods. 353

Interaction between a web service client and a web service 974

Invoice class implements IPayable 436

IPayable interface declaration 435

Levels of value determination system 635

LINQ to Objects using a List<T> 306

LINQ to Objects using an array of Employee objects 299

LINQ to Objects using an Integer array 295

LINQ usage throughout the book 293

ListNode, List and EmptyListException class declarations 1064

ListView display with no data template 647

ListView displaying files and folders 567

logical operators 184

Examples (cont.)

Login.aspx content page using a Login control 941

Main page of the **DeepZoomCoverCollage** 1038

Manipulating an address book 854

Math tutor using EquationGeneratorService-XML to create equations 1006

MDI child FrmChild 583

MDI parent window class 580

Members declared internal in a class are accessible by other classes in the same assembly 346

NegativeNumberException represents exceptions caused by illegal operations performed on negative numbers 481

.NET web service client after web service reference has been added 974

New Project dialog 610

New Silverlight application in Visual Studio 1020

Overloaded constructors used to initialize Time2 objects 326

Overloaded method declarations 220

Overloaded methods with identical signatures 222

Overloading operators for complex numbers 445

Parameter Info window 59

Passing an array reference by value and by reference 260

Passing arrays and individual array elements to methods 257

Poll analysis application 249

Private members of class Time1 are not accessible 315

Program to display hidden text in a password box 502

Quantifiers used in regular expressions 723

Reading an XML document and displaying it in a TextBox 800

Reading cookies from a client to determine book recommendations. 907

Reading sequential-access files 755

readonly instance variable in a class 337

readonly variable initialized with a constructor argument 337

Record for sequential-access file-processing applications 747

Recursive Factorial method 225

Reference, output and value parameters 227

Renaming the program file in the **Properties** window 58

Roll a six-sided die 6000 times 209, 248

Routed events example (code-behind) 624

Routed events example (XAML) 623

SalariedEmployee class that extends Employee 421, 439

Sample new-format input for the XMLCombine application 814

Examples (cont.)

Sample old-format input for the XMLCombine application 813

Sample web service XML response 1028

Sample XML response from the Flickr APIs 1037

Schema-valid XML document describing a list of books 784

Scope class demonstrates instance and local variable scopes 218

Searching for characters and substrings in strings 697

Self-referential Node class declaration 1062

Sequential file created using serialization 768

Sequential file read using deserialzation 773

Session data used to provide book recommendations to the user. 914

Session-based book recommendations displayed in a ListBox. 913

Shifted and scaled random integers 208

Solution Explorer after the Deep Zoom files have been added to the project 1044

Some methods of class ArrayList 1126

Some methods of class List<T> 304

Stack unwinding and Exception class properties 477

StackComposition class encapsulates functionality of class List 1078

StartsWith and EndsWith methods 694, 696

Static member demonstration 334

static method Concat 700

Static variable used to maintain a count of the number of Employee objects in memory 333

string constructors 691

string indexer, Length properties and CopyTo method 692

string test to determine equality 694

StringBuilder class constructors 703

StringBuilder method AppendFormat 707

StringBuilder size manipulation 704

StringBuilder text insertion and removal 708

StringBuilder text replacement 710

StringBuilder's AppendFormat method 707

Substrings generated from strings 699

summing integers with the for statement 165

Syntax errors indicated by the IDE 62

Examples (cont.)

test application for class Analysis 146

Testing class BasePlusCommission-Employee 384, 392, 398

Testing class CommissionEmployee 380

Testing class List 1068

Testing class QueueInheritance 1081

Testing class StackInheritance 1076

Testing class Tree with a binary tree 1087

Testing class Tree with IComparable objects 1093

Testing generic class Stack 1110, 1114

Tests interface IPayable with disparate classes 441

Text-displaying application 51

The default Button 639

The logical and visual trees for a default Button 639

this used implicitly and explicitly to refer to members of an object 316

Time1 class declaration in a namespace 342

Time1 class declaration maintains the time in 24-hour format 311

Time1 object used in an application 313, 344

Time2 class declaration with overloaded constructors 322

Transforming an XML document and splicing its contents with another 812

Tree structure for the document article.xml 800

TreeView used to display directories 563

TV GUI showing the versatility of WPF customization (code-behind) 676

UserControl defined clock 589

User-defined method Maximum 198

Using a DataGridView to display details based on a selection 849

Using a PictureBox to display images 516

Using anonymous types. 360

Using Array class to perform common array manipulations 1122

Using CheckBoxes to change font styles 508

Using class ArrayList 1127

Using command-line arguments to initialize an array 281

Using control templates (code-behind) 642

Using control templates (XAML) 640

Using data binding (code-behind) 646

Using data binding (XAML) 644

Using data templates (XAML) 648

Examples (cont.)

Using delegates to pass functions as arguments. 355

Using GroupBoxes and Panels to arrange Buttons 505

Using lambda expressions 357

Using LinkedLists 1140

Using LINQ to perform a join and aggregate data across tables 845

Using LINQ to search directories and determine file types 741

using nested control statements 145

Using overloaded methods to display arrays of different types 1099, 1101

using prefix increment and postfix increment operators 149

Using RadioButtons to set message-window options 511

Using Regex methods Replace and Split 729

Using the foreach statement to total integers in an array 255

Using variable-length argument lists 279

Validate user information using regular expressions 725

Validation application enhanced by ASP.NET AJAX 954

Validators used in a Web Form that retrieves user contact information. 892

VideoSelector lets users watch several videos (code-behind) 1053

VideoSelector lets users watch several videos at once (XAML) 1051

VideoSelector's list of video sources 1053

Visual C# console application 56, 57, 59

WCF REST service to create random equations based on a specified operation and difficulty level 1005

WCF web service interface that returns a welcome message through SOAP protocol and XML format 968

WCF web service that returns a welcome message through the SOAP protocol and XML format 968

WCF web service using REST architecture and JSON data format 981

WCF web service using REST architecture and XML data format 977

WeatherViewer application displays an image of the weather for several upcoming days. The program can also display detailed information for one particular day 1021

WeatherViewer displays day-by-day weather data (code-behind) 1024

WeatherViewer displays day-by-day weather data (XAML) 1022

Examples (cont.)

WeatherViewer's WeatherDetailsView custom control (code-behind) 1031

WeatherViewer's WeatherDetailsView custom control (XAML) 1029

Web Form that demonstrates the AdRotator web control 889

Web Form that demonstrates web control 883

Web.config file's service model configuration for WelcomeSOAPXMLService web service 971

Welcome2.cs 63

Welcome3.cs 64

Welcome4.cs 65

XAML of a painter application 613

XAML view 610

XHTML response when the browser requests WebTime.aspx 873

XML document containing book information 794

XML document that describes various sports 791

XML document using the laptop element defined in computer.xsd 789

XML file generated by XMLCombine 814

XML namespaces demonstration 605

XML Schema document defining simple and complex types 788

XML Schema document for book.xml 785

XML used to mark up an article 599

XSL document that transforms sorting.xml into XHTML 795

XSLT that creates elements and attributes in an XHTML document 792

exception *457*

Exception Assistant *465*

Exception Assistant 1213

Exception class *466*, 467, 473, 476

exception handler *457*, 467

Exceptions 250

ArgumentException 1136

ArgumentOutOfRangeException 1129

IndexOutOfRangeException 250

InvalidCastException 430, 1120, 1137

InvalidOperationException 1125, 1132, 1143

KeyNotFoundException 1140

.exe file name extension *60*

executable *60*

execute an application 55

Execute method of ICommand interface *626*

Executed event of CommandBinding class *628*

ExecutionEngineException class *467*

exhausting memory 226

Exists method of class Directory 737

Exists method of class DirectoryInfo *571*

Exit method of class Application *536*, 552

exit point of a control statement 129

Exp method of Math 195

expand a tree 31

Expand method of class TreeNode 562

expand node 560

ExpandAll method of class TreeNode 562

Expander control (WPF) 613

Expat XML Parser *598*

expiration date of a cookie *901*

Expires property of HttpCookie class 908

explicit conversion *143*

explicit type argument *1103*

exponential method 195

exponentiation operator 166

expression *69*

Expression Blend *596*

expression lambda *359*

extend a class *371*

extend an XML Schema data type 789

extender *959*

extensibility *7*, 412

Extensible Application Markup Language (XAML) *594*

Extensible HyperText Markup Language (XHTML) 596, *790*, 862, 863

extensible language *15*, *92*

Extensible Markup Language (XML) 594, 972

Extensible Stylesheet Language (XSL) *599*, 608, *790*

extension element base attribute *789*

extension method *351*

extension XML Schema element *789*

external DTD *603*

F

F format specifier 114, 143

F2 format specifier 379, 383

factorial 223

Factorial method 224

false keyword 130, 131

fault-tolerant program *457*

field *97*, *734*

field of a class 13

field width *166*

fields *196*, 217

FIFO (first-in, first-out) 340

file 735

as a collection of bytes 735

File class *736*, 741

Delete method *745*

File class methods (partial list) 737

File menu 25

File-name extensions .cs 30

File Name property of a file in the **Solution Explorer** *57*

FileAccess enumeration 754

FileInfo class *571*
  FullName property *571*
  Name property *571*
Filename extensions
  .aspx *862*
  .master *933*
file-position pointer 760
files 733
FileStream class *736*, 753, 760, 773
Fill property of a shape element *654*
Fill value of Stretch property *680*
FillEllipse method of class
  Graphics *525*, *560*
FillPie method of class Graphics *560*
FillRectangle method of class
  Graphics *560*
filter a collection using LINQ *293*
filtering array elements 357
final state in the UML 128, 188
final value 159
Finalize method
  of class object 407
finally block *464*, 469
finally blocks always execute, even
  when no exception occurs 470
Find method of class LinkedList *1144*
Finished design of **MasterDetail**
  application 852
firewall *966*
First extension method of interface
  IEnumerable<T> *301*
first-in, first-out (FIFO) data structure
  340, *1079*
FirstDayOfWeek property of class
  MonthCalendar 542
FirstNode property of class TreeNode
  561
FirstOrDefault extension method of
  interface IEnumerable<T> 999
#FIXED keyword (DTD) *781*
fixed text 69
  in a format string *66*
flag *139*
FlagsAttribute *526*
FlatStyle property of class Button 502
Flickr 1031
Flickr API key 1031
FlickrViewer example 1031
float simple type 68, *110*, 1147
Float struct *1061*
floating-point literal *110*
floating-point number 139, 141
  division 143
  double precision *110*
  double simple type *110*
  float simple type *110*
  single precision *110*
floating-point *110*
floating-point literal
  double by default 110
Floor method of Math 195
flow of control 134, 141
  in the if statement 129
  in the if...else statement 130
  in the while statement 134
flow-based layout *612*
focus *488*
Focused property of class Control 497

Font class *509*
  Style property *509*
Font dialog *41*
Font property of a Label *41*
Font property of class Control 497
Font property of class Form 489
font size 41
font style 41, 507
Font window 42
FontFamily property of TextBlock
  element *653*
Fonts
  Arial 653
  Courier New 654
  Segoe UI 654
  Tahoma 654
  Times New Roman 653
FontSize property of TextBlock
  element *654*
FontStyle enumeration *509*
FontStyle property of TextBlock
  element *654*
FontWeight property of TextBlock
  element *654*
for repetition statement 128, 160, 161,
  163, 164, 165, 166
  activity diagram 164
  example 163
  header *161*
foreach statement *255*, 1125, 1129,
  1132
  on rectangular arrays 277
ForeColor property of class Control
  497
Foreground property of TextBlock
  element *662*
foreign key *824*, 826
  LINQ to SQL 835
forkeyword *160*
form *23*
form background color 39
Form class 489
  AcceptButton property 489
  ActiveMdiChild property 578
  AutoScroll property 489
  CancelButton property 489
  Close method 489
  Font property 489
  FormBorderStyle property 489,
    500
  Hide method 489
  IsMdiChild property 578
  IsMdiContainer property *576*,
    578
  LayoutMdi method 578, *579*
  Load event 489
  MaximumSize property *500*
  MdiChildActivate event 578
  MdiChildren property 578
  MdiParent property *576*, 578
  MinimumSize property *500*
  Padding property *498*
  Show method 489
  Text property 489
Form control (Windows Forms) 609
Form properties, methods and events 489
Form title bar 38
Form1.cs 46
formal parameter *198*

format item *66*
Format menu 26
Format method of String *312*
Format property of class
  DateTimePicker *542*, 543
format specifier *114*
format specifier table 114
Format specifiers
  C *114*, 168, 379, 383
  D 114, 246
  D2 312
  E 114
  F 114, 143
  F2 379, 383
  G 114
  N 114
  X 114
format string *66*
FormatException and
  DivideByZeroException handlers
  462
FormatException class *461*, 463, 464
FormatString 707
formatted output
  field width *166*
  left justify *166*
  right justify *166*
formatting
  display formatted data 65
FormBorderStyle property of a Form
  500
FormBorderStyle property of class
  Form 489
forms authentication *925*
forward reference 1074
forward slash character (/) in end tags
  596, 794
fragile software *394*
from clause of a LINQ query *295*
From property of class
  DoubleAnimation *680*
FROM SQL clause 826
FullName property of class
  DirectoryInfo *571*
FullName property of class FileInfo
  571
FullPath property of class TreeNode
  561
FullStackException indicates a stack
  is full 1109
fully qualified class name 96, 205, 342,
  345
Func class 765
function 13
function key *528*

G

G format specifier 114
game playing 206
garbage collection 468
garbage collector *331*, *332*
general catch clause *464*
general class average problem 139
generalization in the UML *447*
generating LINQ to SQL classes 837
generic class *303*, *1098*, 1107
Generic class Stack 1107

Generic classes
   Dictionary 1121
   LinkedList 1121, *1140*
   LinkedListNode *1140*
   List 1121
   Queue 1121
   SortedDictionary 1122, *1137*, 1139
   SortedList 1122
   Stack 1122
generic interface *1098*
Generic List<T> collection
   demonstration 304
generic method *302*, *1098*, 1101
   creating 1114
   implementation 1101
Generic method Maximum returns the
   largest of three objects 1105
generic type *296*
generics *1098*, 1120
   class *1098*
   class constraint *1105*
   compile-time type safety *1098*
   constructor constraint (new()) *1105*
   default type constraint (object) of a
     type parameter 1109
   interface *1098*
   interface constraint *1105*
   method 1101
   overloading 1106
   reference type constraint class
     1105
   reusability 1107
   scope of a type parameter 1109
   specifying type constraints *1104*
   Stack class 1107
   type argument *296*, *1103*, 1110
   type checking *1098*
   type constraint of a type parameter
     1104, 1104
   type parameter *302*, *1102*
   type parameter list *302*, *1101*
   value type constraint struct *1105*
   where clause *1104*
Geometry property of class
   GeometryModel3D *683*
GeometryModel3D class *683*
   Geometry property *683*
   Material property *684*
get accessor of a property *88*, 99, 102
GET HTTP request *864*
get keyword *100*
get request 866
GetCreationTime method of class
   Directory 737
GetCreationTime method of class
   File 737
GetDefaultView method of
   CollectionViewSource class *649*
GetDirectories method of class
   Directory 565, 737
GetDirectories method of class
   DirectoryInfo *571*
GetEnumerator method of interface
   IEnumerable *1124*
GetExtension method of class Path
   744
GetFiles method of class Directory
   737, *741*

GetFiles method of class
   DirectoryInfo *571*
GetHashCode method of class Object
   1134
GetHashCode method of class object
   407
GetItemChecked method of class
   CheckedListBox 554
GetLastAccessTime method of class
   Directory 737
GetLastAccessTime method of class
   File 737
GetLastWriteTime method of class
   Directory 737
GetLastWriteTime method of class
   File 737
GetLength method of an array 272
GetNodeCount method of class
   TreeNode 562
GetObject method of class
   ResourceManager *517*
GetPosition method of
   MouseEventArgs class *622*
GetSelected method of class ListBox
   550, *551*
GetType method of class object 407,
   430
GIF (Graphic Interchange Format) *44*
global namespace *96*
glyph 1191
Good Programming Practices overview
   xxx
goto elimination 126
goto statement *126*
Grade book using an array to store test
   grades 264
Grade book using rectangular array to
   store grades 274
GradeBook class that contains a
   private instance variable, and a
   public property to get and set its
   value 97
GradeBook class uses switch statement
   171
GradeBook class using counter-
   controlled repetition 135
GradeBook class using sentinel-
   controlled repetition 140
GradeBook class with a constructor to
   initialize the course name 107
GradeBook class with an auto-
   implemented property 104
GradeBook constructor used to specify
   the course name at the time each
   GradeBook object is created 108
gradient *662*
GradientStop class *664*
   Color property *664*
   Offset property *664*
graph information 246
Graphic Interchange Format (GIF) 44
graphical user interface (GUI) 22, 205,
   486
graphics 1017
Graphics class *525*, 559
   Clear method *559*
   DrawEllipse method *560*
   DrawPie method *560*
   DrawRectangle method *560*

Graphics class (cont.)
   FillEllipse method *525*, *560*
   FillPie method *560*
   FillRectangle method *560*
Graphics property of class
   PaintEventArgs *588*, 589
greedy quantifier *722*
Grid control (WPF) 609, *615*, 1024
   Column attached property *616*
   ColumnDefinition class *615*
   ColumnDefinitions property *615*
   ColumnSpan attached property *616*
   Resources property 1031
   Row attached property *616*
   RowDefinition class *615*
   RowDefinitions property *615*
   RowSpan attached property *616*
GridView ASP.NET data control *915*
GridView control (WPF) *646*
GridViewColumn class (WPF) *646*
   DisplayMemberBinding property
     647
GroupBox class (Windows Forms) 9,
   503, 615
   Controls property *504*
   Text property 504
GroupBox class (WPF) *615*
GroupBox control (WPF)
   Header property *615*
GroupBox properties 504
grouper.ieee.org/groups/754/
   1148
guard condition 129
guard condition in the UML 188
guestbook on a website *915*
GUI (graphical user interface) *22*, 486
GUI control 486
GUI control, basic examples 487

H

handle an event 493
handle an exception *461*
Handled property of class
   KeyEventArgs 526
Handled property of class
   KeyPressEventArgs 526
Handled property of RoutedEventArgs
   class *623*
has-a relationship *328*, *372*
has-a relationship (composition) *119*
HasChildren property of class
   MenuStrip 535
HasElements property of class
   XElement *803*
hash function *1134*
hash table *1133*
hashing *1133*
Hashtable class *1121*, *1133*, 1134
   ContainsKey method *1136*
   Count property *1136*
   method Add *1136*
   property Values *1136*
head element 869
head of a queue *1060*, 1079
Header property of GroupBox control
   615
Height property of structure Size *500*

Height property of WPF GUI elements 654
Hejlsberg, Anders 4
Help menu 26, *33*
helper method *176*, 1088
HelpLink property of Exception 477
hexadecimal (base 16) number system 1150
hidden
    element 900
    field 900
"hidden" fields 217
hidden form element 900
hidden input in an XHTML form *873*
hide implementation details 314, 339, 340
Hide method of class Control 497
Hide method of class Form 489
hiding implementation details 1133
hierarchy 601
horizontal tab 65
HorizontalAlignment property of WPF controls *612*
host *863*
hostname *863*
hot key 532
HourlyEmployee class that extends Employee 422
How Do I? command 34
HTML (HyperText Markup Language) *6*
html element 869
HTML Visualizer *1204*
HTTP (HyperText Transfer Protocol) *6*, 900
    being used with firewalls 966
HTTP (Hypertext Transfer Protocol)
    header 865
    method *864*
    request type *865*
    transaction 864
http://www.w3.org/2000/10/ XMLSchema (XML Schema URI) *785*
HttpCookie class *905*, 908
    Domain property 908
    Expires property 908
    Name property 908
    Path property 908
    Secure property 908
    Value property 908
HttpCookieCollection class *907*
HttpSessionState class *908*, 910, 911, 912, 913, 914
    Counts property 913
    IsNewSession property 913
    IsReadOnly property 913
    Keys property 913, 914
    SessionID property 912, 913
    Timeout property 912, 913
HyperLink ASP.NET web control *888*
HyperText Markup Language (HTML) 6
HyperText Transfer Protocol (HTTP) *6*, 866, 900

I

IBM Corporation 1189
IBM DB2 820
ICollection interface 1120

ICommand interface (WPF) *626*
    CanExecute method *626*
    Execute method *626*
IComparable interface 442, *1090*
IComparable<T> interface *1104*
    CompareTo method *1104*
IComponent interface 442, *488*
icon 26
ID attribute of an ASP.NET Web control *870*
IDE (Integrated Development Environment) 19
identifier *53*, 67
identity column in a database table *822*, 833
IDictionary interface 1120
IDisposable interface 442, 475
    Dispose method 442
IEC 60559 1147
IEEE 754 1147
IEnumerable interface
    method GetEnumerator *1124*
IEnumerable<T> interface *297*, 835, 1120, *1124*
    Any extension method *301*, 811
    Count extension method *301*
    Distinct extension method *301*
    First extension method *301*
    FirstOrDefault extension method *999*
IEnumerator interface 443, *1124*
if single-selection statement *71*, 128, 129, 170
    activity diagram 129
if...else double-selection statement 128, 130, 141, 170
    activity diagram 130
ignoring element zero 250
IList interface 1120
image 1017
Image ASP.NET web control *887*
Image Collection Editor 566
Image element 1024
Image property of class PictureBox 515
Image property of PictureBox *43*
image resource *517*
ImageBrush element *662*
    ImageSource property *662*
ImageBrush element (WPF) 636
ImageIndex property of class ListViewItem *567*
ImageIndex property of class TreeNode 561
ImageList class *561*, 566
    Images property *566*
ImageList property of class TabControl 573
ImageList property of class TreeView 561
Images property of class ImageList *566*
ImageSource property of ImageBrush element *662*
ImageUrl element in an AdRotator advertisement file *891*
ImageUrl property of an Image web control *887*
immutable 334
immutable string 692

imperative programming *294*
implement
    an interface *410*, *433*, 439
    multiple interfaces 437
implementation-dependent code 314
implementation inheritance *418*
implementation of a function 420
implementation phase 452
implementation process 231, 362
implementing a dispose method (link to MSDN article) 442
Implementing a queue by inheriting from class List 1080
Implementing a stack by inheriting from class List 1075
implicit conversion *143*
implicit conversions between simple types 204
implicitly typed local variable *256*, 302
implicityly typed local variable *256*
#IMPLIED keyword (DTD) *781*
Important methods of class HttpCookie 908
Impressions element in an AdRotator advertisement file *891*
In property of class Console 735
increment *158*, 165
    a control variable 159
    expression 179
    of a for statement 163
increment and decrement operators 148
increment operator, ++ 148
Increment property of class NumericUpDown *520*
indefinite repetition *139*
indentation 54, 130, 132
    indent size 54
independent software vendor (ISV) 405
index *239*
Index command of **Help** 34
Index property of class ItemCheckEventArgs 554
Index property of class ToolStripMenuItem 535
index zero *240*
indexer *318*, 320, 692
    of a Hashtable 1136
    of an ArrayList 1129
Indexers provide access to an object's members 321
IndexOf method of class Array *1125*
IndexOf method of class ArrayList 1127, *1129*
IndexOf method of class List<T> 304
IndexOf method of class string 697, 699
IndexOfAny method of class string 697
IndexOutOfRangeException class *250*, 467
IndexType 318
indirect base class 371, 373
infer a local variable's type 256
infinite loop 134, 142, 162, 163, 226
infinite recursion *226*
infinity symbol 825
information hiding *13*, *99*, 339, 432
information tier *867*
inherit from class Control 589

inherit from Windows Form control 588
inheritance *13*, *371*, 376, 405, 446, 447,
    450, 451, 452
    examples 372
    hierarchy *373*
    hierarchy for university
        CommunityMembers 373
    implementation vs. interface
        inheritance *418*
    multiple 371
    single *371*
Inheritance hierarchy for class Shape 374
inheritance with exceptions 467
Inherits attribute of ASP.NET page
    869
Init event of an ASP.NET Web page
    871
initial state *128*
initial state in the UML *186*, 188
initial value of an attribute 155
initial value of control variable *158*
InitialDelay property of class
    ToolTip 518
initialization 165
initializer list *243*
Initializing jagged and rectangular arrays
    271
initializing readonly arrays 1127
Initializing the elements of an array with
    an array initializer 243
initializing two-dimensional arrays in
    declarations 271
inline style *888*
inlining method calls *432*
INNER JOIN SQL operator 826, *831*, 845
InnerException property of
    Exception *476*, 480
innermost square brackets 250
inorder traversal of a binary tree *1083*
input *24*
input data from the keyboard 85
input/output operations 127
InputGestures property of
    RoutedCommand class *626*
Insert method of class ArrayList
    1127
Insert method of class List<T> *304*
Insert method of LinqDataSource
    ASP.NET data control *924*
Insert Separator option 534
Insert Snippet window 105
INSERT SQL statement 826, *832*
inserting a breakpoint 1200
inserting separators in a menu 534
insertion point 1063, 1064
instance (non-static) method 335
instance of a class 97
instance variable *88*, 97, 111, 196
InstanceContextMode property of
    ServiceBehavior attribute *986*
instantiate an object of a class 5, *13*
instantiating an object of a class *89*
Instruction Pointer *1201*
int simple type *68*, 141, 148, 1147
Int16 struct *1061*
Int32 1104
integer 66
    division 70, 139
    mathematics 340

integer (cont.)
    quotient 70
    value 68
integer array 243
Integer division without exception
    handling 459
integer division yields an integer result
    142
Integer struct *1061*
Integrated Development Environment
    (IDE) 19
IntelliSense 58, 295, 353, 354, 597, 821,
    835
    support for extension methods 353
interaction between a web service client
    and a web service 974
interaction diagram in the UML *285*
interaction overview diagram in the UML
    1186
interactions among objects 282, 286, 340
interest rate 166
interface *13*, *297*, 410, 434, 440
    declaration *433*
    inheritance *418*
interface constraint *1105*
interface keyword *433*, 440
Interfaces
    ICollection 1120
    ICommand *626*
    IComparable 442, *1090*, *1104*
    IComponent 442, *488*
    IDictionary 1120
    IDisposable 442, 475
    IEnumerable 1120, *1124*
    IEnumerable<T> *297*, 835
    IEnumerator 443, *1124*
    IList 1120
    IQueryable<T> *835*
    ISerializable *767*
interfaces
    IComparable *1104*
internal
    access modifier *345*
    keyword *345*
internal data representation 340
internal member 346
internal web browser *21*
Internet *6*, 7
Internet Explorer 601
Internet Protocol (IP) 6
Interval property of class Timer *588*
Interval property of
    DispatcherTimer class *638*
InvalidCastException 430, *1061*
InvalidCastException class 1120,
    1137
InvalidOperationException class
    1125, 1132, 1143
Invoice class implements IPayable
    436
invoke a method *106*
IP (Internet Protocol) *6*
IP address *864*
IPayable interface declaration 435
IQueryable<T> interface *835*
is-a relationship *372*, 411
is operator *430*

IsAsync property of Binding class *650*
IsAsynchronous property of
    ObjectDataProvider class *650*
IsAsynchronous property of
    XmlDataProvider class *650*
IsDigit method of struct Char 712
IsEnabled property of
    DispatcherTimer class *638*
ISerializable interface *767*
IsLetter method of struct Char 713
IsLetterOrDigit method of struct
    Char 713
IsLower method of struct Char 713
IsMdiChild property of class Form 578
IsMdiContainer property of class Form
    576, 578
IsMouseOver property of WPF controls
    642
IsMuted property of MediaElement
    element *1055*
IsNewSession property of
    HttpSessionState class 913
isolated storage *1055*
IsPostBack property of Page class *898*
IsPunctuation method of struct
    Char 713
IsReadOnly property of
    HttpSessionState class 913
IsSymbol method of struct Char 713
IsUpper method of struct Char 713
IsValid property of Page class *898*
IsWhiteSpace method of struct Char
    713
Italic FontStyle 654
ItemActivate event of class ListView
    566
ItemCheck event of class
    CheckedListBox *553*, 554
ItemCheckEventArgs class 554
    CurrentValue property 554
    Index property 554
    NewValue property 554
Items property of class ComboBox 556,
    557
Items property of class ListBox *550*,
Items property of class ListView 566
ItemSize property of class TabControl
    573
ItemsPanel property of ListBox
    control *1024*
ItemsSource property of ListBox
    control 1037
ItemsSource property of ListView
    645
ItemTemplate property of ListBox
    control *1024*
ItemTemplate property of ListView
    control *647*
iteration
    of a loop *158*, 165, 179
iteration statement 128
iteration variable *255*
iterative 226
iterative model *80*
iterator 417
    class *417*

J

Jacobson, Ivar 15
Jacopini, G. 127
jagged array **268**, 269, 271
Java programming language **4**
JavaScript **892**
JavaScript Object Notation (JSON) **966**
JIT (just-in-time) compiler **8**
join clause of a LINQ query **848**
joining database tables **825**, 831
    LINQ to SQL 845
Joint Photographic Experts Group
    (JPEG) 44
JPEG (Joint Photographic Experts
    Group) 44
JSON (JavaScript Object Notation) **966**
JSON serialization **982**
Just My Code **1213**
just-in-time (JIT) compiler **8**

K

key code **528**
key data 528
key event **525**, 526
key value 528, 1089
key-value pair **905**
keyboard 66, 487
keyboard shortcut **532**
KeyboardEventArgs class (WPF) 622
KeyChar property of class
    KeyPressEventArgs **525**
KeyCode property of class
    KeyEventArgs 526
KeyData property of class
    KeyEventArgs 526
KeyDown event
    WPF 622
KeyDown event of class Control **525**,
    526
KeyEventArgs class **525**
    Alt property 526, 528
    Control property 526, 528
    Handled property 526
    KeyCode property 526
    KeyData property 526
    KeyValue property 526
    Modifiers property 526
    Shift property 526, 528
KeyEventArgs properties 526
KeyNotFoundException class 1140
Keypad class (ATM case study) 83, 117,
    119, 230, 283, 284, 285, 288, 363
KeyPress event of class Control **525**,
    526
KeyPressEventArgs class **525**
    Handled property 526
    KeyChar property **525**, 526
KeyPressEventArgs properties 526
keys
    function **528**
    modifier **525**
Keys enumeration **525**
Keys property of class Dictionary **745**
Keys property of Hashtable **1136**
Keys property of HttpSessionState
    class 913, **914**
KeyUp event (WPF) 622
KeyUp event of class Control **525**, 526

KeyValue property of class
    KeyEventArgs 526
Keywords **52**, 128
    abstract 387, **415**
    base 375, 387, 397, 400
    bool **131**
    break **174**
    case **174**
    char **68**
    class **52**, 90
    const 178, **196**, **245**, 336
    continue **178**
    decimal **68**, **110**
    default **174**
    delegate **354**, **494**
    do **168**
    double **110**
    else 130
    enum **215**
    false **131**
    float **68**
    for **160**
    get **100**
    if **71**, 129, 130
    interface **433**
    internal 315, **345**
    is **430**
    namespace 341
    new **92**, 107, 241, 242, 270
    null 101, **106**, 151, 241
    operator **444**
    out **226**, 228
    override **251**, **379**, 387
    params **279**
    private **98**, 315, 362, 374
    protected 315, **374**
    protected internal **374**
    Public **90**, 315, 374
    public **53**, 90, 98, 362
    readonly **336**
    ref **226**, 227, 257
    return **100**, 202
    sealed **432**
    set **100**
    static **166**
    struct 105, **710**
    this **316**, 317, 318, 335
    true **131**
    value (contextual) **100**
    var **256**
    virtual **387**
    void **54**, 90
    while 134, 168
Koenig, Andrew 457

L

Label 41
label 500
Label control **23**, **35**, 40, 487, 500
    Windows Forms 610
    WPF **610**
label in a switch **174**, 175
lambda expression **357**, 765
    expression lambda **359**
    lambda operator **357**
    statement lambda **359**
lambda operator **357**

Language attribute in a Page directive
    868
language independence 8
Language Integrated Query (LINQ) 256,
    293
language interoperability **8**
LargeImageList property of class
    ListView 566, **567**
last-in-first-out (LIFO) order 1113
Last property of class LinkedList
    1144
LastChildFill property of DockPanel
    control 613
last-in, first-out (LIFO) data structure
    1075
LastIndexOf method of class Array
    1125
LastIndexOf method of class string
    697, 699
LastIndexOfAny method of class
    string 697
last-in-first-out (LIFO) **202**
last-in-first-out (LIFO) data structure 339
LastNode property of class TreeNode
    561
late binding **429**
layout container (WPF) **609**, 612, 621
layout, control 497
LayoutMdi method of class Form 578,
    579
lazy quantifier **722**
leaf node in a binary search tree **1083**,
    1088
Left attached property of Canvas
    control **617**, 618
left brace, { **53**, 54, 67
left child **1082**
left justify output **166**
left subtree **1082**, 1088
Length property of an array 240
Length property of class string 692,
    693
Length property of class
    StringBuilder 704
let clause of a LINQ query **307**
let query operator (LINQ) **728**
letter **733**
level of indentation 130
lexicographical comparison **694**
lifeline of an object in a UML sequence
    diagram **287**
LIFO (last-in, first-out) 202, 339
LIFO (last-in-first-out) order 1113
LIKE SQL clause **828**, 830
Line element **655**
line numbers 57
linear collection 1062
linear data structure **1082**
LinearGradientBrush element **662**
    EndPoint property **664**
    StartPoint property **664**
link 1063, 1082
link for a self-referential class **1061**
LinkArea property of class LinkLabel
    546
LinkBehavior property of class
    LinkLabel 546
LinkClicked event of class LinkLabel
    545, 546

LinkColor property of class LinkLabel 546
linked list 1060, *1062*, 1063
linked list data structure *1060*
linked list in sorted order 1063
LinkedList generic class 1121, 1140, *1140*
   AddFirst method 1143
   AddLast method *1143*
   method Find *1144*
   method Remove *1144*
   property First 1143
   property Last *1144*
LinkedListNode class
   property Next *1140*
   property Previous *1140*
   property Value *1140*
LinkedListNode generic class *1140*
LinkLabel class 531, *545*
   ActiveLinkColor property 546
   LinkArea property 546
   LinkBehavior property 546
   LinkClicked event 545, 546
   LinkColor property 546
   LinkVisited property 546
   Text property 546
   UseMnemonic property 546
   VisitedLinkColor property 546
LinkLabel properties and an event 546
LinkVisited property of class LinkLabel 546
LINQ (Language Integrated Query) *293*, 724, 725, 741
   anonymous type *301*
   ascending modifier *297*
   Count method 744
   deferred execution *308*
   descending modifier *297*
   Distinct query operator 744
   explicitly typed range variable 725
   from clause *295*
   let clause *307*, *728*
   LINQ to Objects *293*
   LINQ to SQL 294
   LINQ to XML 294
   orderby clause *297*
   provider *294*
   query expression *293*
   range variable *295*
   select clause *296*
   where clause *296*
LINQ (Language-Integrated Query)
   anonymous type *361*
   join clause *848*
   LINQ to Objects 821
   LINQ to SQL *821*
   LINQ to XML *779*, 800
LINQ provider *294*
LINQ Resource Center (www.deitel.com/LINQ) 859
LINQ to Objects *293*, 741, 811, 821
   using a List<T> 306
   using an array of Employee objects 299
   using an Integer array 295
LINQ to SQL 294, *821*
   cache 835
   conversion from LINQ query to SQL query 835

LINQ to SQL (cont.)
   data binding *836*
   DataContext class *836*
   foreign keys 835
   generating classes 837
   primary keys 835
   saving changes back to a database 840
LINQ to XML 294, *779*, 800, 1022
LINQ usage throughout the book 293
LINQ, data binding to 644
LinqDataSource ASP.NET data control *917*
LINQPad (www.linqpad.net) 859
Linux 3
list, editable 557
List<T> generic class *303*, 997, 1121
   Add method *304*
   Capacity property 304, *306*
   Clear method 304
   Contains method 304, *306*
   Count property *304*
   IndexOf method 304
   Insert method *304*
   Remove method 304, *306*
   RemoveAt method 304, *306*
   RemoveRange method 304
   Sort method 304
   TrimExcess method 304
ListBox control 487, 531, *549*, *1024*
   ClearSelected method 550
   GetSelected method 550, *551*
   Items property *550*
   ItemsPanel property *1024*
   ItemsSource property 1037
   ItemTemplate property *1024*
   MultiColumn property 550
   SelectedIndex property 550, *551*
   SelectedIndexChanged event 550
   SelectedIndices property 550, *551*
   SelectedItem property *550*
   SelectedItems property 550, *551*
   SelectionMode property *549*, 550
   Sorted property 550
ListBox properties, method and event 550
ListBox web control 913
ListItem class *887*
ListNode, List and EmptyListException class declarations 1064
ListView ASP.NET data control 960
ListView clacontrolss
   MultiSelect property *566*
ListView control *565*
   Activation property *566*
   CheckBoxes property *566*
   ItemActivate event 566
   Items property 566
   LargeImageList property 566, *567*
   SelectedItems property 566
   SmallImageList property 566, *567*
   View property *566*
ListView control (WPF)
   ItemsSource property *645*
   ItemTemplate property *647*
   SelectedItem property *644*

ListView control (WPF)Classes *644*
ListView displaying files and folders 567
ListView properties and events 566
ListViewItem class *567*
   ImageIndex property *567*
literals
   decimal *110*
   floating point *110*
   int 110
live-code approach xxx, *2*
Load event of an ASP.NET web page *872*
Load event of class Form 489
load factor *1133*
Load method of class XDocument *802*
Load method of class XslCompiledTransform *817*
local variable *96*, 137, 217, 218, 317
local variable "goes out of scope" 733
localization 1189
localize an application *1189*
LocalName property of class XName *802*
Locals window *1204*
Location property of class Control 499
Location property of TextDecoration element *654*
Log method of Math 195, 196
Log property of class DataContext *843*
logarithm 195
logic error 69, 161, 1197
logical negation !
   operator truth table 183
logical negation, ! 183
logical operators 180, 182, 184
logical output operation *736*
logical point *664*
logical tree (WPF) *639*
logical XOR, ^ *182*
Login ASP.NET control 925, *940*
login control in ASP.NET *925*
Login.aspx content page using a Login control 941
LoginName ASP.NET login control *942*
LoginStatus ASP.NET login control *942*
long simple type 1147
Long struct *1061*
long-term retention of data 733
Long value of enumeration DateTimePickerFormat *542*
Look-and-Feel Observations overview xxxi
LookDirection property of class PerspectiveCamera *685*
lookless control (WPF) *639*
loop 135, 137
   body 165, 169
   counter 158
   infinite *134*, 142
loop-continuation condition *158*, 159, 160, 161, 162, 163, 165, 168, 169, 179, 250
lowercase letter 52

M

m-by-*n* array *269*
magnetic disk 733
magnetic tape 733

Main method 54, 55, 67, 92
maintainability 1060
make your point (game of craps) 212
making decisions 85
Manipulating an address book 854
many-to-many relationship 826
many-to-one relationship *121*
margin indicator bar *1200*
Margin property of GUI elements 1055
Margin property of WPF controls *612*
markup extension (XAML) *634*, 641, 644
markup in XML *595*
mask the user input 501
Master directive *933*
.master filename extension *933*
master page in ASP.NET *928*
master/detail view *848*
MasterPageFile property of a Page directive *936*
match attribute *793*
Match class 690, 717, *718*
    Success property *728*
Match method of class Regex *718*
MatchCollection class 718
Matches method of class Regex 718
Material property of GeometryModel3D class *684*
MaterialGroup class 684
Math class 194, 195
    Abs method 195
    Ceiling method 195
    Cos method 195
    E constant *196*
    Exp method 195
    Floor method 195
    Log method 195, 196
    Max method 195
    Min method 195
    PI constant *196*
    Pow method 167, 168, 194, 196
    Sin method 196
    Sqrt method 195, 196, 203, 482
    Tan method 196
Math tutor using EquationGeneratorServiceXML to create equations 1006
MathML 596
Max method of Math 195
MaxDate property of class DateTimePicker 543, *545*
MaxDate property of class MonthCalendar 542
MaxDropDownItems property of class ComboBox *556*
MaxHeight property of WPF controls *612*
Maximum method 197
Maximum property of class NumericUpDown *520*
MaximumSize property of class Control 499
MaximumSize property of class Form *500*
maxOccurs XML Schema attribute *786*
MaxSelectionCount property of class MonthCalendar 542
MaxWidth property of WPF controls *612*
MBCS (multi-byte character set) *1192*

.mdf file extension 822
MDI (Multiple Document Interface) *576*
MDI (multiple document interface) window *487*
MDI child FrmChild 583
MDI parent and MDI child properties, method and event 578
MDI parent window class 580
MDI title bar 577
MdiChildActivate event of class Form 578
MdiChildren property of class Form 577, 578
MdiLayout enumeration *579*, 580
    ArrangeIcons value *579*
    Cascade value *579*
    TileHorizontal value *579*
    TileVertical value *579*
MdiParent property of class Form *576*, 578
MdiWindowListItem property of class MenuStrip *579*
MediaElement element *662*, 1050
    IsMuted property *1055*
    Source property *662*
    Stretch property *680*
    Width property 1055
member access (.) operator 167, 194, 333
member access operator *92*
member of a class *58*
Members declared internal in a class are accessible by other classes in the same assembly 346
MemberwiseClone method of class object 407
memory consumption 1119
memory leak *332*, *468*
MemoryStream class *736*
menu 25, 486, 531
menu access shortcut 532
menu access shortcut, create *532*
menu bar *25*, 486
menu bar in Visual Studio IDE 25
Menu control (WPF) *630*
menu item *25*, 531
menu, ellipsis convention 536
menu, expanded and checked 532
MenuItem control (WPF) *630*
MenuItem property MdiList example 579
MenuItems property of class MenuStrip 535
MenuItems property of class ToolStripMenuItem 535
Menus
    Build 25
    Data 25
    Debug 25
    Edit 25
    File 25
    Format 26
    Help 26, *33*
    Project 25
    Tools 26
    View 25, 28
    Window 26
menus *25*
MenuStrip class *532*
    HasChildren property 535

MenuStrip class (cont.)
    MdiWindowListItem property *579*
    MenuItems property 535
    RightToLeft property 535
MenuStrip properties and events 535
merge in the UML 188
Merge records from Tables 831
merge symbol in the UML 134
MeshGeometry3D class *683*
    Positions property *683*
    TextureCoordinates property *685*
    TriangleIndices property *683*
message (sent to an object) *88*
message in the UML *282*, 285, 286, 287
message passing in the UML 287
Message property of Exception *466*, 473, 476
messages between objects 13
metacharacter (regular expression) *719*
method *13*, 54, 93
    call *88*
    declaration 54
    header *91*
    parameter 95
    parameter list *95*
    return type *90*
    static *166*
method attribute of XHTML element form *873*
method call 198
method call stack *203*, 476, *1075*
method declaration 198
method overloading *193*, *220*
method parameter list 279
Methods
    DownloadStringAsync (WebClient) *980*
methods *5*
methods implicitly sealed 432
Microsoft 1189
    Access 820
    Office 820
    SQL Server 820
    SQL Server 2005 Express *820*
Microsoft ASP.NET 1017
Microsoft ASP.NET AJAX 1017
Microsoft C# quick tour
    msdn.microsoft.com/en-us/ vcsharp/aa336809.aspx 17
Microsoft Developers Network (MSDN) *21*
Microsoft Expression Blend 1021
Microsoft Expression Encoder 1050
Microsoft Intermediate Language (MSIL) *8*, 60
Microsoft .NET 7
Microsoft Paint 44
Microsoft XML Core Services (MSXML) *598*, 601
middle tier *867*
MIME (Multipurpose Internet Mail Extensions) *865*, 901
Min method of Math 195
MinDate property of class DateTimePicker 543, *545*
MinDate property of class MonthCalendar 542

MinHeight property of WPF controls *612*

minimized and maximized child window 578

Minimized constant of WindowState class *642*

Minimum property of class NumericUpDown *520*

MinimumSize property of class Control 499

MinimumSize property of class Form *500*

minInclusive XML Schema element *789*

minOccurs XML Schema attribute *786*

minus box 31

minus sign (–) for container elements in Internet Explorer 601

minus sign (–) indicating private visibility in the UML 362

MinWidth property of WPF controls *612*

modal dialog *753*

mode attribute of element authentication in Web.config *932*

model of a software system 118, 155, 449

Model3DGroup class *683*

ModelVisual3D class *683*
    Content property *683*
    Transform property *686*

modifier key *525*

Modifiers property of class KeyEventArgs 526

modulus operator (%) *70*

monetary calculations 168

Mono project for developing .NET applications on Linux, Windows and Mac OS X *22*

Mono Project's Moonlight 1018

MonthCalendar class *541*
    DateChanged event *542*
    FirstDayOfWeek property 542
    MaxDate property 542
    MaxSelectionCount property 542
    MinDate property 542
    MonthlyBoldedDates property 542
    SelectionEnd property 542
    SelectionRange property 542
    SelectionStart property 542

MonthlyBoldedDates property of class MonthCalendar 542

More Windows... option in Visual Studio .NET 579

mouse *20*, 487

mouse click *522*

mouse event *522*, 523

mouse move *522*

mouse pointer 27

MouseButtonEventArgs class (WPF) *622*

MouseDown event 622

MouseDown event handler 659

MouseDown event of class Control 523

MouseEnter event of class Control 523

MouseEventArgs class *523*
    Button property 523
    Clicks property 523
    GetPosition method *622*

MouseEventArgs class (cont.)
    X property 523
    Y property 523

MouseEventArgs class (WPF) *622*

MouseEventArgs properties 523

MouseEventHandler delegate *523*

MouseHover event of class Control 523

MouseLeave event of class Control 523

MouseLeftButtonDown event (WPF) *622*, 625

MouseLeftButtonUp event (WPF) *622*, 625

MouseMove event (WPF) *622*

MouseMove event of class Control 523

MouseRightButtonDown event (WPF) *622*

MouseRightButtonUp event (WPF) *622*

MouseUp event 622

MouseUp event of class Control 523

MouseWheel event (WPF) 622

MouseWheelEventArgs class (WPF) 622

Move method of class Directory 737

Move method of class File 737

MoveFirst method of class BindingSource *841*

MoveNext method of IEnumerator *1125*

MSDN (Microsoft Developer Network) 52, 194, 205

MSDN (Microsoft Developers Network *21*

msdn.microsoft.com/en-us/library/aa719441.aspx 339

msdn.microsoft.com/en-us/library/fs2xkftw.aspx 442

msdn.microsoft.com/en-us/library/ms229335.aspx 52, 194, 205, 206, 339

msdn.microsoft.com/en-us/library/sc65sadd.aspx 1213

msdn.microsoft.com/en-us/library/system.array.aspx 1122

msdn.microsoft.com/en-us/library/system.collections.specialized.aspx 1119

msdn.microsoft.com/en-us/library/system.idisposable.aspx 442

msdn.microsoft.com/en-us/library/system.object_members.aspx 406

msdn.microsoft.com/en-us/library/system.random.aspx 207

msdn.microsoft.com/en-us/vcsharp/aa336809.aspx 468, 1103

MSIL (Microsoft Intermediate Language) 8

MSXML (Microsoft XML Core Services) *598*, 601

mulit-byte character set (MBCS) *1192*

multicast delegate *494*

multicast event 494

MulticastDelegate class *494*

MultiColumn property of class ListBox 550

multidimensional array 268

MultiExtended value of enumeration SelectionMode *550*

Multiline property of class TabControl 573

Multiline property of class TextBox 501

multimedia *1017*

Multiple Document Interface (MDI) *576*

multiple document interface (MDI) window *487*

multiple inheritance 371

multiple-selection statement 128

multiplication, * *70*

multiplicative operators: *, / and % 143

multiplicity *118*, 119

Multipurpose Internet Mail Extensions (MIME) *865*, 901

MultiScaleImage element *1037*
    ActualWidth property *1049*
    ElementToLogicalPoint method *1045*
    ViewportOrigin property *1048*
    ViewportWidth property *1049*
    ZoomAboutLogicalPoint method *1045*

MultiScaleSubImage class *1038*

MultiSelect property of class ListView *566*

MultiSimple value of enumeration SelectionMode *550*

multitier application *867*

mutual exclusion *510*

mutually exclusive options 510

MySQL 820

N

N format specifier 114

n-tier application *867*

name attribute (XPath) *798*

name collision *342*

name conflict *342*

name node-set function *798*

Name property of class DirectoryInfo *571*

Name property of class FileInfo *571*

Name property of class HttpCookie *908*

Name property of class XElement *802*

Name property of RoutedCommand class 626

name XML Schema attribute *786*

named constant *245*

namespace *51*, 193, 205
    prefix 789
    prefix XML *605*
    XAML 609
    XML 605

namespace 341
    declaration *341*
    keyword 341

Namespace property of class XName *814*

Namespaces
    of the .NET Framework Class Library 205
    System 207

Namespaces (cont.)
    System.Collections 206, *1075*,
    1104, 1119
    System.Collections.Generic
    206, 303, 744, *1119*, 1139
    System.Collections.
    Specialized *1119*
    System.Data 205, 206
    System.Data.Linq 205
    System.Diagnostics *546*
    System.FlagsAttribute *526*
    System.IO 205, 736
    System.Runtime.Serializatio
    n.Formatters.Binary *766*
    System.Runtime.
    Serialization.Json *982*
    System.Text 206, 689
    System.Text.Regular.
    Expressions 718
    System.Text.
    RegularExpressions 690
    System.Web 206
    System.Web.UI *871*
    System.Web.UI.WebControls
    871
    System.Windows.Controls 205
    System.Windows.Forms 205, 489
    System.Windows.Input 205
    System.Windows.Media 205
    System.Windows.Shapes 205
    System.Xml 206, *800*
    System.Xml.Linq *800*, 1026
    System.Xml.XPath *809*
    System.Xml.Xsl *817*
namespaces
    System.Diagnostics *546*
    System.IO 736
naming collision *604*
NaN constant of structure Double *460*,
    482
natural logarithm 195
navigability arrow in the UML *362*
NavigateUrl element in an AdRotator
    advertisement file *891*
NavigateUrl property of a HyperLink
    control *888*
navigation bar on a website *933*
NegativeInfinity constant of
    structure Double *460*
NegativeNumberException represents
    exceptions caused by illegal operations
    performed on negative numbers 481
nested array initializer 269
nested class 345, 852
nested class definition 852
nested control statements 144, 210
nested element *601*
nested element (XAML) 608
nested for statement 247, 271, 272, 273
nested foreach statement 272
nested if...else selection statement 131,
    132
nested message in the UML *287*
nested parentheses 70
.NET
    Framework *8*
    initiative *7*
.NET-aware language 8
.NET Framework 1099

.NET Framework 3.5 1120
.NET Framework Class Library *8*, *51*,
    194, 205, 338, 442, 1104
.NET Framework documentation 52
.NET platform *4*
.NET WCF web service client after web
    service reference has been added 974
New keyword 360
new keyword 241, 242, 270
new operator *92*, 107, 1062
New Project dialog *22*, 24, 36, 610
new project in Visual Studio 25
new() (constructor constraint) *1105*
newline character 65
newline escape sequence, \n 65, 68
NewProjectTestPage.aspx 1021
newsgroup 20
NewValue property of class
    ItemCheckEventArgs 554
Next method of class Random *207*, 208,
    210
Next property of class LinkedListNode
    1140
NextBytes method of class Random *667*
NextNode property of class TreeNode
    561
NextNode property of class XNode *812*
node *560*
    child *560*
    expand and collapse 560
    parent *560*
    root *560*
    sibling *560*
node (in DOM tree) 799
node-set function *798*
node set of an xsl
    for-each element *794*
nodes in a linked list *1062*
Nodes method of class XContainer *811*
Nodes property of class TreeNode 561
Nodes property of class TreeView 561
NodeType property of class XObject 811
non-static class member 335
None value for Stretch property *680*
None value of enumeration
    SelectionMode *550*
nonlinear data structures 1063
nonvalidating XML parser *598*
normalizing a database *831*
not selected state *510*
NOT SQL operator *834*
note (in the UML) 128
Notepad 546
noun phrase in requirements document
    116, 151
nouns in a system specification *13*
Now property of structure DateTime *590*
null keyword 101, *106*, 151, 241
null reference 1061, 1073
NullReferenceException class *467*
NumericUpDown control 487, *520*
    DecimalPlaces property *520*
    Increment property *520*
    Maximum property *520*
    Minimum property *520*
    ReadOnly property *522*
    UpDownAlign property 520
    Value property 520
    ValueChanged event 521

NumericUpDown properties and events
    520

O

object *3*, 5
    send a message 106
object (or instance) *12*, 285
Object Browser (Visual Studio .NET)
    347
object class 371, *376*, 406
    Equals method 406
    Finalize method 407
    GetHashCode method 407
    GetType method 407, *430*
    MemberwiseClone method 407
    ReferenceEquals method 407
    ToString method 379, 407
object creation expression *92*, 108
object diagram in the UML *1185*
object initializer *348*
object initializer list *350*
Object Management Group (OMG) *15*
object methods that are inherited
    directly or indirectly by all classes 406
object of a class 88
object of a derived class 412
object of a derived class is instantiated 399
object orientation 11
object-oriented analysis and design
    (OOAD) 14, 15
object-oriented design (OOD) *12*, 76,
    116, 151, 155, 229, 362
object-oriented language *13*
object-oriented programming (OOP) 2,
    3, *13*, 15, 76, 311, 371
OOP (object-oriented programming) 3,
    13
Object Relational Designer window
    837
object serialization *766*
object technology *5*
ObjectCollection class *550*
ObjectCollection collection
    Add method *551*
    Clear method *552*
    RemoveAt method *551*
ObjectDataProvider class (WPF) *650*
    IsAsynchronous property *650*
Oblique FontStyle 654
occurrence indicator *781*
octal number system (base 8) 1150
ODF (Open Document Format) 597
off-by-one error *161*
Offset property of class GradientStop
    664
OMG (Object Management Group) 15
omit-xml-declaration attribute *793*
ON SQL clause *831*
one statement per line 75
one-to-many relationship *121*, *825*
one-to-one relationship *120*
One value of enumeration
    SelectionMode *550*
one's complement 1157
ones position 1150
OnPaint method of class Control 587,
    588

OOAD (object-oriented analysis and design) 14, 15
OOD (object-oriented design) xxviii, 76, 82, 116, 151, 155, 229, 362
OOP (object-oriented programming) 76, 311, 371
OOXML (Office Open XML) 597
opacity mask *668*
Opacity property of GUI elements 1030
OpacityMask property of WPF GUI elements *675*
Open method of class File 737
OpenFileDialog class *759*, *760*
opening a project 25
Opening state of MediaElement element 1051
OpenRead method of class File 737
OpenText method of class File 737
OpenWrite method of class File 737
operand 143
operands of a binary operator 69
operation compartment in a UML class diagram 230
operation in the UML *13*, 93, 118, 229, 230, 234, 364, 366, 450
operation parameter in the UML 96, 230, 234, 235
OperationContract attribute *967*, 969
operations of an abstract data type *340*
operator 70
operator keyword 444
operator overloading *443*
operator precedence 71
   operator precedence chart 143
   rules *71*
Operator precedence chart appendix 1145
Operators *357*
   ^, boolean logical exclusive OR 180, *182*
   --, prefix decrement/postfix decrement 148, 149
   !, logical negation 180, *182*
   ?:, ternary conditional 131, 150
   ?:, ternary conditional operator 131, 150
   &, boolean logical AND 180, *182*
   &&, conditional AND *180*, 181
   ++, prefix increment/postfix increment 148, 149
   +=, addition assignment *147*
   = *69*, 71
   |, boolean logical inclusive OR 180, *182*
   ||, conditional OR 180, *181*
   arithmetic *70*
   as 430, 811
   binary *69*, 70
   boolean logical AND, & 180, *182*
   boolean logical exclusive OR, ^ 180, *182*
   boolean logical inclusive OR, | *182*
   cast *142*, 216
   compound assignment 147, 150
   conditional AND, && *180*, 182, 299
   conditional OR, || 180, *181*, 182
   conditional, ?: *131*, 150

Operators (cont.)
   decrement operator, -- 148
   decrement, -- 148, 149
   increment and decrement 148
   increment, ++ 148
   logical negation, ! 183
   logical operators *180*, 182
   logical XOR, ^ *182*
   member access (.) 167, 333
   multiplicative: *, / and % *143*
   new *92*, 107
   postfix decrement *148*
   postfix increment *148*
   prefix decrement *148*
   prefix increment *148*
   remainder, % *70*
optical disk 733
optimizing compiler 168
OR SQL operator *834*
Oracle Corporation 820, 1189
order attribute *798*
ORDER BY SQL clause 826, *829*, 830
orderby clause of a LINQ query *297*
   ascending modifier *297*
   descending modifier *297*
ordering of records 826
Orientation of WrapPanel control 613
Orientation property of StackPanel control *615*
orthographic projection *675*
out keyword *226*, 228
out-of-bounds array index 250
out-of-range array index 467
Out property of class Console 735
OutOfMemoryException class *467*, 1062
output *24*, 64
output parameter *226*
overload a method 220
overloaded constructors *321*
Overloaded constructors used to initialize Time2 objects 326
overloaded method 1099
Overloaded method declarations 220
overloaded methods 59
Overloaded methods with identical signatures 222
overloading generic methods 1106
Overloading operators for complex numbers 445
override a base class method *374*, 379
override keyword 251, *379*, 387

P

package *1185*
package diagram in the UML *1185*
Padding property of class Control 499
Padding property of class Form *498*
Padding property of GUI elements *1024*
Page class *871*, 898, 908
   Session property 908
Page directive in ASP.NET *868*
Page event lifecycle (ASP.NET) *872*
page layout software 689
Page_Init event handler *871*
Page_Load event handler *872*
Page_PreInit event handler *872*

Page_Unload event handler *872*
Page.xaml 1019
Page.xaml.cs 1019
PageSize property of a GridView ASP.NET control *948*
PaintEventArgs class *588*
   ClipRectangle property *588*
   Graphics property *588*
PaintEventArgs properties 589
palette *39*
Panel control 9, 487, *503*
   AutoScroll property 504
   BorderStyle property 504
   Children property *621*
   Controls property 504
   WPF *609*
Panel properties 504
Panel with scrollbars 505
parameter *93*, 95
   output *226*
parameter in the UML 96, 230, 234, 235
Parameter Info window *59*
parameter list *95*, 108
parameterless constructor *324*, 326, 327, *1106*
params keyword *279*
parent element *601*
parent menu 532
parent node *560*, 1083
parent node of a DOM tree *799*
Parent property of class DirectoryInfo *571*
Parent property of class XObject *811*
parent window *576*
parent/child relationships between data 601
parentheses *54*, 70
   nested *70*
Parse method of class XDocument *1027*
parsed character data *781*
parser *597*
partial class *489*, 870
Partial modifier 870
partial page update *953*
Pascal casing *53*
pass an array element to a method 257
pass an array to a method 257
pass-by-reference *226*
pass-by-value *226*, 257
Passing an array reference by value and by reference 260
Passing arrays and individual array elements to methods 257
passing options to a program with command-line arguments 282
password TextBox *500*
Path class *565*, *744*
   GetExtension method *744*
Path property of Binding class *644*
Path property of HttpCookie class 908
path to a resource 864
pattern matching *828*
pattern of 0s and 1s 734
Paused state of MediaElement element 1051
Payable interface hierarchy UML class diagram 435
payroll file 735
payroll system 734

#PCDATA keyword (DTD) *781*
Peek method of class Stack *1132*
PerCall setting of
    InstanceContextMode property
    986
percent (%) SQL wildcard character 828
perform a calculation 85
perform a task 91
Performance Tips overview xxx
permission setting 567
PerSession setting of
    InstanceContextMode property
    986
persistent data *733*
persistent information 900
personalization *899*
perspective projection *675*
PerspectiveCamera class *685*
    LookDirection property *685*
    Position property *685*
    UpDirection property *685*
physical output operation *736*
PI (processing instruction) 791
PictureBox control *23*, *35*, 43, 515,
    580
    Click event 515
    Image property 515
    SizeMode property 515
PictureBox properties and event 515
pin icon 28
platform independence *8*
Playing state of MediaElement
    element 1051
plus box 31
plus sign (+) for container elements in
    Internet Explorer 601
plus sign (+) indicating public visibility in
    the UML 362
plus sign (+) occurrence indicator *781*
PNG (Portable Network Graphics) *44*
Point class 659
Point3D class *685*
PointAnimation class 680, 1031
PointCollection class *659*
    Add method *659*
    Clear method *659*
Points property of Polyline and
    Polyon elements *659*
Poll analysis application 249
Polygon element *656*
    Points property *659*
Polyline element *656*
    Points property *659*
polymorphic programming 417
polymorphic screen manager 411
polymorphically process Invoices and
    Employees 440
polymorphism 178, 407, *409*, 410, 446
pop data off a stack *202*
Pop method of class Stack 1132
pop stack operation *1075*
portability 8, 1192
Portability Tips overview xxxi
Portable Network Graphics (PNG) 44
porting *8*
position number 239
Position property of class
    PerspectiveCamera *685*
positional notation 1150

positional value 1151
positional values in the decimal number
    system 1151
Positions property of class
    MeshGeometry3D *683*
PositiveInfinity constant of
    structure Double *460*
postback event of an ASP.NET page *898*
postfix decrement operator *148*
postfix increment operator *148*, 163
PostgreSQL 820
postorder traversal of a binary tree *1084*
Pow method of Math 167, 168, 194, 196
power (exponent) 196
power of 3 larger than 100 134
precedence 75, 150
    arithmetic operators 71
    chart 71
precedence chart 143
precedence chart appendix 1145
precision
    formatting a floating-point number
        143
    of double values 1148
    of float values 1148
precision of a floating-point value *110*
predicate *296*, 827
predicate method *1068*
prefix decrement operator *148*
prefix increment operator *148*
PreInit event of an ASP.NET web page
    872
preorder traversal of a binary tree *1083*
prepackaged data structures 1119
presentation logic *867*
presentation XAML namespace (XAML)
    609
PreviewCanExecute event of
    CommandBinding class *628*
PreviewExecuted event of
    CommandBinding class *628*
PreviewMouseLeftButtonDown event
    (WPF) *625*
PreviewMouseLeftButtonUp event
    (WPF) *625*
Previous property of class
    LinkedListNode *1140*
PreviousNode property of class XNode
    812
PrevNode property of class TreeNode
    561
primary key *821*, 825, 826
primary keys in LINQ to SQL 835
principal 166
principle of least privilege *336*
print spooling *1079*
privacy protection 899
private
    access modifier 315, 362
    keyword 362
    static class member 333
private access modifier *98*, 374
Private members of class Time1 are not
    accessible 315
private visibility in the UML 362
probability 207
procedural programming language *13*
Process class *546*
    Start method *546*

processing instruction (PI) *791*
    target *793*
    value *793*
processor *597*
program execution stack *203*
program in the general 409
program in the specific 409
Program to display hidden text in a
    password box 502
program, suspend 1197
programming languages
    C 3
    C++ 3
    Java 4
    Visual C# 4
    Visual C++ 7
project *21*, 22
Project Location dialog *36*
Project menu 25
projection *296*
prolog (XML) *600*
promotion *143*, 166, 899
promotion rules *203*
prompt 68
properties 96
Properties window *32*, 33, 38, 42, 610,
    879
property *88*, 322
property declaration *99*
property for a Form or control *32*
property of an object *5*
Property property of Trigger class *642*
proprietary class 405
protected
    access modifier 315
protected access modifier 374
protected internal access modifier
    374
proxy class for a web service *973*
pseudorandom number *207*, 211
public
    access modifier 90, 98, 362
    class 53
    interface *311*
    keyword 53, 98, 362, 366
    member of a derived class 375
    method 312, 315
    method encapsulated in an object
        314
    service *311*
    static class members 333
    static method 333
public access modifier 374
public default constructor *107*
public visibility in the UML 362
publishing a web service *967*
push data onto a stack *202*
Push method of class Stack 1132
push stack operation *1075*

Q

qualified name *831*
quantifier (regular expression) *719*
Quantifiers used in regular expressions
    723
query *293*, 822
query expression (LINQ) *293*

query string **866**
question mark (?) occurrence indicator **781**
queue **340**, 1060, 1079
Queue class **1121**
queue data structure **1060**
Queue generic class 1121
Quick Info box **1201**

R

RadialGradientBrush element **662**, 674
radians 195
radio button **502**, 510
radio button group **510**
radio buttons, using with TabPage 576
RadioButton control 9, **507**, 510, 659, 674
   Checked event **621**, 623
   Checked property 510
   CheckedChanged event 511
   Text property 510
RadioButton control (WPF) **613**, 630
RadioButton properties and events 510
RadioButtonList ASP.NET web control **888**
Random class 207, 667
   Next method **207**, 208, 210
   NextBytes method **667**
random number generation 251, 713
random numbers 211
   in a range 211
   scaling factor **207**, 211
   seed value **207**, 211
   shifting value 211
range variable
   explicitly typed 725
range variable of a LINQ query **295**
rapid application development (RAD) **338**
raster-based graphics **595**, **652**
Rational Software Corporation 15, 82
Rational Unified Process™ 82
RDBMS (relational database management system) 867
Read method of class Console 736
Reading an XML document and displaying it in a TextBox 800
Reading cookies from a client to determine book recommendations. 907
Reading sequential-access files 755
ReadLine method of class Console **69**, 93, 174, 736
readonly
   keyword **336**
readonly instance variable in a class 337
read-only property 232
ReadOnly property of class NumericUpDown **522**
ReadOnly property of class TextBox 501
readonly variable initialized with a constructor argument 337
real number 141
realization in the UML **435**
reclaim memory 335
recognizing clients 900
record **734**

Record for sequential-access file-processing applications 747
record key **735**
recover from an error 250
Rect structure **1050**
   Contains method **1050**
Rectangle element **654**
rectangular array **268**, 270
Rectangular array with three rows and four columns 269, 270
recursion **193**, 565
recursion step 223
recursive call 223
recursive descent **798**
Recursive evaluation
   of 5! 224
recursive evaluation 224
recursive factorial 223
Recursive Factorial method 225
recursive method 223
ref keyword **226**, 227, 257
refer to an object **106**
reference **105**
reference manipulation 1060
reference type **105**, 239
reference type constraint class **1105**
Reference, output and value parameters 227
ReferenceEquals method of object 407
Regex class 690, **718**, 724
   Match method 718
   Matches method 718
   Replace method **730**
   Split method **731**
regular expression **717**
   ? quantifier **723**
   {n,} quantifier 723
   {n,m} quantifier **723**
   {n} quantifier **723**
   * quantifier **723**
   \D character class **720**
   \d character class **720**
   \s character class **720**
   \W character class **720**
   \w character class **720**
   + quantifier **723**
   character class **720**
   greedy quantifier **722**
   lazy quantifier **722**
   validating user input 724
   whitespace character **720**
   word character **720**
RegularExpressionValidator
   ASP.NET validation control **896**
reinventing the wheel 51
relational database **820**, 821
relational database management system (RDBMS) 867
relational database table 821
relational operators **71**
relative addressing (XPath) **794**
relative positioning **879**
relative Source 1055
release resource 469
release unmanaged resources 442
remainder 70
remainder operator, % 70

Remove method of class ArrayList 1127, **1129**
Remove method of class Dictionary **745**
Remove method of class LinkedList **1144**
Remove method of class List<T> 304, **306**
Remove method of class StringBuilder 708
RemoveAt method of class ArrayList 1127
RemoveAt method of class List<T> 304, **306**
RemoveAt method of class ObjectCollection **551**
RemoveAt method of UIElementCollection class 621
RemoveRange method of class ArrayList 1127
RemoveRange method of class List<T> 304
rendering XHTML in a web browser **865**
RenderTransform property of WPF GUI elements **667**
RepeatBehavior property of class Storyboard **686**
   Forever value **686**
repetition
   counter controlled 141, 144
   sentinel controlled 139, 141, 142
repetition statement 127, **128**, 134
   do...while 128, 168, 170, 170
   for 128, 164
   foreach 128
   while 128, **134**, 135, 137, 141
repetition terminates 134
Replace method of class Regex **730**
Replace method of class string 701, 702
Replace method of class StringBuilder 709
Representational State Transfer (REST) 7, **965**, 966
Request class
   Cookies property 907
request method **865**
Request object in ASP.NET 907
#REQUIRED keyword (DTD) **781**
RequiredFieldValidator ASP.NET validation control **896**
requirements **14**, 80
requirements document 12, **76**, 80, 82
requirements gathering **80**
reserved word **52**, 128
Reset of IEnumerator **1125**
ReshowDelay property of class ToolTip 518
Resize method of class Array 293, 303
resolution independence **595**, 612
resolution-independent pixel **652**
resource **517**
resource (WPF) **631**
   dynamic resource **634**
   static resource **634**
resource binding (WPF) **634**, 640
resource leak **331**, **468**

`ResourceManager` class *517*, 997
    `GetObject` method *517*
`Resources` class *517*
`Resources` property of `Grid` control 1031
`Resources` property of WPF controls *634*
`ResponseFormat` property of the `WebGet` attribute *980*, 1010
responses to a survey 249
RESTful web services *966*
restriction on built-in XML Schema data type *788*, 789
result of an uncaught exception *465*
`Result` property of class `DownloadStringCompletedEventArgs` 1027
`Result` property of `DownloadStringCompletedEventArgs` *980*
`Result` property of `LinqDataSourceSelectEventArgs` class *945*
result tree (XSLT) *790*
resumption model of exception handling *465*
rethrow an exception *474*
`return` keyword *100*, 202
return message in the UML 288
`return` statement *100*, 223
return type (in the UML) 230, 236
return type of a method *90*
reusability 1060, 1107
reusable component 372
reusable software components 205
reuse 14, 51
`Reverse` method of class `Array` *1125*
RIA (Rich Internet Application) 594
Rich Internet Application (RIA) 594, *1017*
`RichTextBox` control (WPF) *626*
right brace, } 54, 67, 137, 141
right child *1082*
right justify output *166*
right subtree *1082*, 1088
`RightToLeft` property of class `MenuStrip` 535
Ritchie, Dennis 3
robust 69
robust application *457*
role name in the UML *119*
Roll a six-sided die 6000 times 209, 248
rolling two dice 212
root element (XAML) 608, 609
root element (XML) *596*, 601, 603
root node *560*, *1082*
root node of a DOM tree *800*
root node, create 562
`Root` property of class XDocument *802*
`RotateTransform` class *665*
`RotateTransform3D` class *686*
round a floating-point number for display purposes 143
rounded rectangle (for representing a state in a UML state diagram) *186*
rounding a number 70, 139, 168, 195
routed events (WPF) *623*
    bubbling events *625*
    direct events *625*
    tunneling events *625*

`RoutedCommand` class (WPF) *626*
    `InputGestures` property *626*
    `Name` property 626
`RoutedEventArgs` class 622, 623
`RoutedEventArgs` class (WPF)
    `Handled` property *623*
    `Source` property *623*
`Row` attached property of `Grid` control *616*
row of a database table *821*, 825, 826, 827, 828, 832, 833
`RowDefinition` class 1024
`RowDefinition` class associated with `Grid` control *615*
`RowDefinitions` property of `Grid` control *615*
rows of a two-dimensional array *268*
`RowSpan` attached property of `Grid` control *616*
Rule of Entity Integrity 825
Rule of Referential Integrity 825
rules of operator precedence 71
Rumbaugh, James 15
Run command in Windows 546
run mode *46*
run-time logic error 69
Run to Cursor command (debugger) *1201*
`runat` ASP.NET attribute *869*
running an application 546
runtime system 1107

S

`SalariedEmployee` class that extends `Employee` 421, 439
Sample new-format input for the `XMLCombine` application 814
Sample old-format input for the `XMLCombine` application 813
Save Project dialog *36*
`SaveFileDialog` class 749
saving changes back to a database in LINQ to SQL 840
savings account 166
`sbyte` simple type 1147
`SByte` struct *1060*
`ScaleTransform` class *665*, 675
    `CenterX` property *675*
    `CenterY` property *675*
    `ScaleX` property *675*
    `ScaleY` property *675*
`ScaleX` property of `ScaleTransform` class *675*
`ScaleY` property of `ScaleTransform` class *675*
scaling factor (random numbers) 207, 211
schema 783
schema (database) *822*
Schema (XML) *598*
schema invalid document *784*
schema repository *780*
schema valid XML document *784*
schema-valid XML document describing a list of books 784
`schema` XML Schema element *785*
scope *162*
    `static` variable 333

Scope class demonstrates instance and local variable scopes 218
scope of a declaration *217*
scope of a type parameter 1109
Screen class (ATM case study) 117, 119, 230, 283, 284, 285, 287, 288, 289, 363
screen cursor 55, 64, 65
screen-manager program 411
script (Unicode) *1194*
`script` element in ASP.NET *933*
`ScriptManager` control *958*
scrollbar *32*, 486
scrollbars 8
`ScrollBars` property of class `TextBox` 501
scrollbox *32*
SDI (Single Document Interface) *576*
`sealed`
    class 432
    keyword *432*
    method 432
Search command of **Help** 34
search engine 866
searching 1060
Searching for characters and substrings in `strings` 697
secondary storage device *733*
`Secure` property of `HttpCookie` class 908
secure protocol 908
seed value (random numbers) 207, 211
`Seek` method of class `Stream` *765*
`SeekOrigin` enumeration *765*
Segoe UI font xl
`select` attribute (XPath) *798*
`select` attribute of `xsl:for-each` element *794*
`select` clause of a LINQ query *296*
`Select` method of class `Control` *497*
Select Resource dialog *43*
SELECT SQL keyword *826*, 828, 829, 830
selected state *510*
`SelectedImageIndex` property of class `TreeNode` 561
`SelectedIndex` property of class `ComboBox` 556, *557*
`SelectedIndex` property of class `ListBox` 550, *551*
`SelectedIndex` property of class `TabControl` 573
`SelectedIndexChanged` event handler `ComboBox` class 841
`SelectedIndexChanged` event of class `ComboBox` 557, *557*, 853
`SelectedIndexChanged` event of class `ListBox` *550*
`SelectedIndexChanged` event of class `TabControl` 573
`SelectedIndices` property of class `ListBox` 550, *551*
`SelectedItem` property of class `ComboBox` *557*
`SelectedItem` property of class `ListBox` *550*
`SelectedItem` property of `ListView` control *644*

SelectedItems property of class
   ListBox 550, *551*
SelectedItems property of class
   ListView 566
SelectedNode property of class
   TreeView 561
SelectedTab property of class
   TabControl 573
selecting an item from a menu 490
selecting an item with the mouse *20*
selecting data from a table 822
Selecting event of LinqDataSource
   ASP.NET data control *945*
selection 128
selection criteria *827*
selection statement 127, *128*
   if 128, 129, 170
   if...else 128, 130, 141, 170
   switch 128, 170, 176
SelectionEnd property of class
   MonthCalendar 542
SelectionMode enumeration *550*
   MultiExtended value *550*
   MultiSimple value *550*
   None value *550*
   One value *550*
SelectionMode property of class
   CheckedListBox 554
SelectionMode property of class
   ListBox *549*, 550
SelectionRange property of class
   MonthCalendar 542
SelectionStart property of class
   MonthCalendar 542
self-documenting code *68*
self-referential class *1061*, 1062
Self-referential Node class declaration
   1062
self-referential object 1061
semicolon (;) *55*, 67, 74
send a message to an object 106
sentinel-controlled repetition *139*, 141,
   142
sentinel value *139*, 142
separator bar *534*
Separator control (WPF) *630*
sequence *1082*
sequence diagram in the UML *83*, *285*
sequence of items 1062
sequence of messages in the UML *286*
sequence statement *127*
sequence structure 127
sequence-structure activity diagram 127
sequential-access file 748
sequential execution 126
sequential file *735*
Sequential file created using serialization
   768
Sequential file read using deserialzation
   773
[Serializable] attribute *766*
Serializable attribute 984
serialization *982*
Serialize method of class
   BinaryFormatter *766*, 773
serialized object *766*, *767*
server response *866*
server-side form handler *866*
service description for a web service *972*

service of a class 315
Service references
   adding a service reference to a project
      in Visual C# 2008 Express 974
Service.svc 967
ServiceBehavior attribute *986*
ServiceContract attribute *967*, 969
session 900
Session data used to provide book
   recommendations to the user. 914
session item *910*
Session property of Page class *908*
session tracking *900*
   in web services 984
Session-based book recommendations
   displayed in a ListBox. 913
SessionID property of
   HttpSessionState class *912*, 913
SessionMode property of
   ServiceContract attribute *985*
set accessor of a property *88*, 99, 102
set keyword *100*
SET SQL clause *834*
SetLeft method of Canvas control *618*
Setter class (WPF) *634*, 642
   TargetName property *642*
SetTop method of Canvas control *618*
ShadowDepth property of class
   DropShadowBitmapEffect *674*
shallow copy *407*
Shape class hierarchy 373
shift *207*
Shift key 525
Shift property of class KeyEventArgs
   526, 528
Shifted and scaled random integers 208
shifting value (random numbers) *207*,
   211
short-circuit evaluation *182*
short simple type 1147
Short value of enumeration
   DateTimePickerFormat *542*
shortcut key 532
ShortcutKeyDisplayString property
   of class ToolStripMenuItem *534*,
   536
ShortcutKeys property of class
   ToolStripMenuItem *533*, 536
shortcuts with the & symbol 534
Show All Files icon *30*
Show method of class Control 497
Show method of class Form 489, 576, 584
ShowCheckBox property of class
   DateTimePicker 543
ShowDialog method of class
   OpenFileDialog *759*, *760*
ShowDialog method of class
   SaveFileDialog 753
ShowShortcutKeys property of class
   ToolStripMenuItem *534*, 536
ShowUpDown property of class
   DateTimePicker 543
shuffling 251
Shutdown of Application.Current
   628
sibling *1082*
sibling node *560*
sibling node of a DOM tree *799*
side effect *182*, 226

signal value *139*
signature of a method *221*
Silverlight *1017*
   Border element 1024
   Button control 1024
   ColorAnimation class 1031
   ColumnDefinition class 1024
   ControlTemplate control 1028
   DoubleAnimation class 1031
   Grid control 1024
   Image element 1024
   ListBox control *1024*
   MediaElement element 1050
   MultiScaleImage element *1037*
   MultiScaleSubImage class *1038*
   PointAnimation class 1031
   Rect structure *1050*
   Resource Center 1018
   RowDefinition class 1024
   Silverlight Streaming 1017
   Silverlight Tools for Visual Studio
      2008 1019
   StackPanel control 1024
   Storyboard class 1031
   Style class 1028
   Support in Visual Studio express
      editions 1019
   TextBlock element 1024
   TextBox control 1024
   UserControl control *1020*
   VideoBrush class *1052*
   WeatherDetailsView custom
      control 1024, 1028
Silverlight 2 Runtime *1019*
Silverlight 2 SDK Beta 2 *1019*
Silverlight demos 1056
simple condition *180*
simple content in XML Schema *788*
simple name *341*
Simple Object Access Protocol (SOAP) 7,
   965, 966
simple type *68*, 151, 203, 788
Simple Types
   bool 1147
   byte 1147
   char 68, 1147
   decimal *68*, *110*, 1148
   double *110*, 141, 1148
   float *68*, *110*, 1147
   int 67, 68, 141, 148, 1147
   long 1147
   names are keywords 68
   sbyte 1147
   short 1147
   table of 1147
   uint 1147
   ulong 1147
   ushort 1147
Simple value of enumeration
   ComboBoxStyle *557*
simpleContent XML Schema element
   789
simpleType XML Schema element *789*
Sin method of Math 196
sine 196
Single Document Interface (SDI) *576*
single-entry/single-exit control statements
   129
single inheritance 371

`Single` method of `IEnumerable`
  interface *1050*
single-precision floating-point number
  110
single-quote character (') 604, 828
single-selection statement 128, 129
`Single` setting of
  `InstanceContextMode` property
  986
single-clicking the mouse *20*
single-line comment *50*
single-selection statement
  `if` 129
singly linked list *1073*
`Size` property of class `Control` 499
`Size` structure *500*
  `Height` property *500*
  `Width` property *500*
`SizeMode` property of class `PictureBox`
  515
`SizeMode` property of `PictureBox` *44*
sizing handle 38
sizing handle, enabled *38*
`SkewTransform` class *665*, 675
`Slider` control (WPF) *634*
`SmallImageList` property of class
  `ListView` 566, *567*
smart tag menu *841*
smart tag menu in Visual Web Developer
  888
snap line *500*
snap lines in Visual Studio 2008 *500*
SOAP (Simple Object Access Protocol) *7*,
  965, 966
  envelope *966*
  message *966*
`Softness` property of
  `DropShadowBitmapEffect` class
  674
software asset 14
software component 8
software engineering
  encapsulation 103
Software Engineering Observations
  overview xxxi
software life cycle *80*
software reuse 8, 339, 341, 371
solid circle 128
solid circle (for representing an initial
  state in a UML diagram) in the UML
  186, 188
solid circle enclosed in an open circle (for
  representing the end of a UML activity
  diagram) 188
solid circle surrounded by a hollow circle
  128
solid diamond (representing
  composition) in the UML *119*
`SolidBrush` class *525*
`SolidColorBrush` class 659
solution (in the IDE) *21*
Solution Explorer 610, 1026
Solution Explorer window *30*
Some methods of class `ArrayList` 1126
Some methods of class `List<T>` 304
`Sort` method of class `Array` *1124*
`Sort` method of class `ArrayList` 1127
`Sort` method of class `List<T>` 304

sorted array 1064
`Sorted` property of class `ComboBox` 557
`Sorted` property of class `ListBox` 550
`SortedDictionary` generic class 1122,
  1137, 1139
`SortedList` generic class *1121*, 1122
sorting 1060
sorting in XSL 798
sound 1017
source code 405
Source mode in Visual Web Developer
  876
`Source` property of `Binding` class *644*
`Source` property of `Exception` 477
`Source` property of `MediaElement`
  element *662*
`Source` property of `RoutedEventArgs`
  class *623*
source tree (XSLT) *790*
sources.xml 1053
space/time trade-off *1133*
`span` XHTML element *870*, 874
special character 68, *690*
special symbol *733*
specialization in the UML *447*
`SpecularMaterial` class 684
`Split` method of class `Regex` *731*, 1136
Split mode in Visual Web Developer *876*
spooler *1079*
spooling *1079*
SQL 293, *820*, 822, 826, 832
  DELETE statement 826, *834*
  FROM clause 826
  INNER JOIN operator 826, *831*, 845
  INSERT statement 826, *832*
  LIKE clause *828*
  ON clause *831*
  ORDER BY clause 826, *829*, 830
  SELECT query *826*, 828, 829, 830
  SET clause *834*
  UPDATE statement 826
  VALUES clause *832*
  WHERE clause *827*
SQL keyword 826
SQL Server *820*
`Sqrt` method of class `Math` 482
`Sqrt` method of `Math` 195, 196, 203
square brackets, `[]` *240*, 250
square root 196
stack *202*, *339*, *1075*, 1107
`Stack` class *1121*, 1130
stack data structure *1060*
stack frame *203*
`Stack` generic class 1107, 1122
  `Stack< double>` 1116
  `Stack<int>` 1116
stack overflow *203*
stack trace *460*
stack unwinding 477
Stack unwinding and `Exception` class
  properties 477
`StackComposition` class encapsulates
  functionality of class `List` 1078
`StackOverflowException` class *467*
`StackPanel` control (WPF) *615*, 1024
  `Orientation` property *615*
`StackTrace` property of `Exception`
  476, 477, 480

*Standard ECMA-334: C# Language
  Specification*
  www.ecma-international.org/
    publications/standards/
    Ecma-334.htm 4, *17*
standard error stream object *736*
standard input stream object *735*
standard input/output object *55*
standard input/output stream (`Console`)
  55
standard output stream object *736*, 843
standard reusable component *372*
standard time format 313
standard XAML namespace (XAML) *609*
standardized, interchangeable parts 14
`Start` method of class `Process` *546*
Start Page *19*
start tag *596*, 604
start tag (XAML) 608
`StartPoint` property of class
  `LinearGradientBrush` *664*
`StartsWith` and `EndsWith` methods
  696
`StartsWith` method of class `string`
  307, 696
startup project *30*
`StartupUri` property of
  `Application.xaml` *610*, 611
state *83*
state button *507*
state in the UML *83*, 188
state machine diagram for some of the
  states of the ATM object 186
state machine diagram in the UML *83*,
  186
state of an object 152, 186
stateless protocol 900
statement *55*, *91*
statement lambda *359*
Statements
  `yield return` 766
statements
  `break` 174, 178
  `continue` *178*
  control statements 128
  control-statement nesting *129*
  control-statement stacking *129*
  `do...while` 128, 168, 170
  double selection *128*
  empty *75*
  empty statement 133
  `for` 128, 160, 161, 163, 164, 165,
    166
  `if` *71*, 128, 129, 170
  `if...else` 128, 130, 141, 170
  multiple selection *128*
  nested *144*
  nested `if...else` *131*, 132
  repetition *127*, 128, 134
  `return` 202
  selection *127*, 128
  single selection *128*
  `switch` 128, 170, 176
  `switch` multiple-selection statement
    210
  `throw` *473*
  `try` *466*
  `using` 475
  `while` 128, 135, 137, 141

static
  class member 332
  method 92, *166*
  variable *332*, 333
static binding *432*
Static member demonstration 334
static method cannot access non-
  static class members 335
static method Concat 700
static resource (WPF) *634*
static variable scope 333
Static variable used to maintain a count of
  the number of Employee objects in
  memory 333
Step Into command (debugger) *1207*
Step Out command (debugger) *1208*
Step Over command (debugger) *1208*
stereotype in the UML *102*
Stopped state of MediaElement
  element 1051
stores (Isolated storage) *1056*
Storyboard class *679*, 1031
  Begin method 1031
  RepeatBehavior property *686*
  TargetName property *680*
  TargetProperty property *680*
straight-line form *70*
stream
  standard error *736*
  standard input *735*
  standard output *736*
Stream class 736, *736*
  Seek method *765*
stream of bytes *735*
StreamReader class *736*
StreamWriter class *736*
Stretch property of multimedia
  elements *680*
  Fill value *680*
  None value *680*
  Uniform value *680*
  UniformToFill value *680*
StretchImage value 44
string *55*, 206
string
  verbatim *549*
string array 241
string class 689
  Concat method 700
  constructors 691
  CopyTo method 692
  EndsWith method 696, 697
  Equals method 694
  format method *312*
  immutable 692
  IndexOf method 697, 699
  IndexOfAny method 697
  LastIndexOf method 697, 699
  LastIndexOfAny method 697, 699
  Length property 692, 693
  method ToLower *1136*
  method ToUpper *1143*
  Replace method 701, 702
  StartsWith method *307*, 696
  Substring method 699
  ToLower method 701, 702
  ToUpper method *307*, 701, 702
  Trim method 701, 702
  verbatim string literal 201

String Collection Editor in Visual
  Studio .NET 551
string concatenation *200*, 334
string constant *690*
string constructors 691
string format specifiers 114
string indexer 693
string indexer, Length property and
  CopyTo method 692
string literal *690*
string XML Schema data type 787
string.Empty *106*
StringBuilder class 689, 702
  Append method 706
  AppendFormat method 707
  Capacity property 704
  constructors 703
  EnsureCapacity method 704
  Length property 704
  Remove method 708
  Replace method 709
  ToString method 703
StringBuilder constructors 703
StringBuilder size manipulation 704
StringBuilder text replacement 710
Stroke property of WPF shapes *654*
StrokeThickness property of WPF
  shapes *654*
strongly typed languages *151*
Stroustrup, Bjarne 3, 457
struct 1061
struct 105, *1060*
struct keyword *710*
structs
  Boolean *1060*
  Byte *1060*
  Character *1060*
  Decimal *1061*
  Double *1061*
  Int16 *1061*
  Int32 *1061*
  Int64 *1061*
  Single *1061*
  UInt16 *1061*
  UInt64 *1061*
structure of a system 155, 186
structured programming 5, *126*, 180
Structured Query Language (SQL) *820*,
  822, 826
structures
  DateTime *590*
style (WPF) *631*
style class *888*
Style class (WPF) *634*, 1028
  TargetType property *634*
  Triggers property *642*
Style property of class Font *509*
style sheet *601*
style XHTML attribute *888*
style XHTML element *888*
stylesheet start tag *793*
SubImageIndex method of class
  DeepZoomCoverCollage 1050
submenu 531
SubmitChanges method of class
  DataContext *836*, 840
Substring method of class string 699
substrings generated from strings 699
subtraction 70

Success property of class Match *728*
sum function (XSL) *798*
summing integers with the for statement
  165
Sun JavaFX 1017
Sun Microsystems, Inc. 1189
surrogates (Unicode) *1190*
survey 250
suspend a program 1197
SVC file *967*
svcutil.exe 973
switch code snippet (IDE) 217
switch expression 174
switch keyword
  Keywords
    switch *174*
switch logic 178
switch multiple-selection statement
  128, 170, 176, 210
  activity diagram with break
    statements 177
  case label 174, 175
  controlling expression *174*
  default label *174*, 210
Sybase 820
Sybase, Inc. 1189
synchronous call *285*
synchronous request *952*
syntax error 55, *62*, 1197
syntax error underlining 62
syntax-color highlighting *57*
system *82*
system behavior *82*
SYSTEM keyword in XML *603*
System namespace 51, 207, 689
system requirements *80*
system structure *82*
System.Collections namespace 206,
  1075, 1104, 1119
System.Collections.Generic
  namespace 206, 303, 744, *1119*, 1139
System.Collections.Specialized
  namespace *1119*
System.Data namespace 205, 206
System.Data.Linq namespace 205
System.Diagnostics namespace *546*
System.FlagsAttribute namespace
  526
System.IO namespace 205, 736
System.Runtime.Serialization.
  Formatters.Binary namespace
  766
System.Runtime.Serialization.
  Json namespace 982
System.Text namespace 206, 689
System.Text.RegularExpressions
  namespace 690
System.Web namespace 206
System.Web.UI namespace *871*
System.Web.UI.WebControls
  namespace *871*
System.Windows.Controls
  namespace 205
System.Windows.Forms namespace
  205, 489
System.Windows.Input namespace
  205
System.Windows.Media namespace
  205

System.Windows.Shapes namespace 205

System.Xml namespace 206, **800**

System.Xml.Linq namespace **800**, 1026

System.Xml.XPath namespace **809**

System.Xml.Xsl namespace **817**

SystemException class **467**, 482

T

tab 486

tab (in a window) **21**

tab character, \t 52, 65

Tab key **54**

tab stops 54, 65

Tabbed pages in Visual Studio .NET 572

tabbed window 25

TabContainer Ajax Control Toolkit control **958**

TabControl class **571**
    ImageList property 573
    ItemSize property 573
    Multiline property 573
    SelectedIndex property 573
    SelectedIndexChanged event 573
    SelectedTab property 573
    TabCount property 573
    TabPages property **572**, 573

TabControl with TabPages example 572

TabControl, adding a TabPage 573

TabCount property of class TabControl 573

TabIndex property of class Control **497**

table 268, 821

table element 268

table of simple types 1147

table of values **268**

TableName property of LinqDataSource ASP.NET data control **923**

TabPage class **572**
    Text property **572**

TabPage, add to TabControl 572

TabPage, using radio buttons 576

TabPages added to a TabControl 573

TabPages property of class TabControl **572**, 573

TabPanel class **958**

TabStop property of class Control 497

tabular format 243

tag **1031**

tagging **1031**

tail of a queue **1060**, 1079

Tan method of Math 196

tangent 196

Target property of a HyperLink control **888**

TargetControlID property of ValidatorCalloutExtender control **960**

TargetName property of class Storyboard **680**

TargetName property of Setter class **642**

targetNamespace XML Schema attribute **786**

TargetProperty property of class Storyboard **680**

TargetSite property of Exception 477

TargetType property of ControlTemplate class **640**

TargetType property of Style class **634**

TCP/IP (Transmission Control Protocol/Internet Protocol) **6**

template **22**

template binding (WPF) **641**

Template property of WPF controls **640**

temporary 142

temporary data storage 733

termination housekeeping **332**

termination model of exception handling **465**

ternary operator **131**

test application for class Analysis 146

test harness **267**

Testing class BasePlusCommissionEmployee 384, 392, 398

Testing class CommissionEmployee 380

Testing class List 1068

Testing class QueueInheritance 1081

Testing class StackInheritance 1076

Testing class Tree with a binary tree 1087

Testing class Tree with IComparable objects 1093

Testing generic class Stack 1110, 1114

Tests interface IPayable with disparate classes 441

text editor 689

text file 799

text node-set function **798**

Text property **38**, 42

Text property of class Button 502

Text property of class CheckBox 507

Text property of class Control 497

Text property of class Form 489

Text property of class GroupBox 504

Text property of class LinkLabel 546

Text property of class RadioButton 510

Text property of class TabPage **572**

Text property of class TextBox 501

Text property of class ToolStripMenuItem 536

Text property of class TreeNode 561

Text Visualizer 1204

TextAlign property of a Label **41**

TextBlock control (WPF) **647**

TextBlock element 652, 1024
    Background property 662
    FontFamily property **653**
    FontSize property **654**
    FontStyle property **654**
    FontWeight property **654**
    Foreground property 662
    TextDecorations property **654**

textbox 8

TextBox ASP.NET web control **887**

TextBox control 487, 500, **623**, 665, 1024
    AcceptsReturn property 501
    DataBindings.Text property **858**
    Multiline property 501
    ReadOnly property 501

TextBox control (cont.)
    ScrollBars property 501
    Text property 501
    TextChanged event 501
    UseSystemPasswordChar property **501**

TextChanged event of class TextBox 501

TextDecoration element **654**
    Baseline **654**
    Location property **654**
    Overline **654**
    Strikethrough **654**
    Underline **654**

TextDecorations property of TextBlock element **654**

Text-displaying application 51

TextReader class 736

TextureCoordinates property of class MeshGeometry3D **685**

TextWriter class 736

this
    keyword 316, 317, 318, 335
    reference **316**
    to call another constructor of the same class 324

this used implicitly and explicitly to refer to members of an object 316

three-dimensional, high-resolution, color graphics 1017

ThreeState property of class CheckBox **507**

throw an exception **458**, 464, 465

throw point **461**, 465

throw statement **473**

Tick event of class Timer **588**

Tick event of DispatcherTimer class **638**

tier in a multitier application **867**

tightly packed binary tree **1089**

tiled window **579**

TileHorizontal value of enumeration MdiLayout **579**

TileVertical value of enumeration MdiLayout **579**

time and date 590

Time value of enumeration DateTimePickerFormat **542**

Time1 class declaration in a namespace 342

Time1 class declaration maintains the time in 24-hour format 311

Time1 object used in an application 313, 344

Time2 class declaration with overloaded constructors 322

TimeOfDay property of class DateTimePicker **542**, 543

Timeout property of HttpSessionState class **912**, 913

Timer class **588**, 638
    Interval property **588**
    Tick event **588**

TimeSpan class **638**

timing diagram in the UML **1186**

title bar 38

title bar, MDI parent and child 577

Title property of a Page directive **936**

Title property of a Web Form **879**

`Titles` table of Books database 822, 823
`To` property of `DoubleAnimation` class **680**
`ToDecimal` method of class `Convert` **114**
`ToInt32` method of class `Convert` **69**, 72, 282
`ToLongDateString` method of structure `DateTime` **545**
`ToLongTimeString` method of structure `DateTime` **590**
`ToLower` method of class `string` 701, 702, **1136**
`ToLower` method of struct `Char` 713
tool bar 486
tool tip **27**, 891
toolbar **26**
`ToolBar` control (WPF) **630**
toolbar icon **26**
`ToolBarTray` control (WPF) **630**
Toolbox 31, 610, 879
`ToolkitScriptManager` control **958**
Tools menu 26
`ToolStripMenuItem`
   `Click` event 536
`ToolStripMenuItem` class **532**
   `Checked` property 535, **540**
   `CheckOnClick` property 535
   `Click` event **534**
   `Index` property 535
   `MenuItems` property 535
   `ShortcutKeyDisplayString` property **534**, 536
   `ShortcutKeys` property **533**, 536
   `ShowShortcutKeys` property **534**, 536
   `Text` property 536
`ToolStripMenuItem` properties and an event 535
`ToolTip` class **518**
   `AutoPopDelay` property 518
   `Draw` event 518
   `InitialDelay` property 518
   `ReshowDelay` property 518
`ToolTip` properties and events 518
`Top` attached property of `Canvas` control **617**, 618
top-level class 345
top of a stack **1060**
top tier **867**
`ToString` method of an anonymous type 360
`ToString` method of class `object` 379, 407
`ToString` method of class `StringBuilder` 703, 706
`ToString` method of class`Exception` 480
`ToUpper` method of class `string` **307**, 701, 702, **1143**
`ToUpper` method of struct `Char` 713
trace **1113**
tracking customers 899
`Transaction` class (ATM case study) 447, 448, 449, 452
Transact-SQL 844
transfer of control 126
transform **665**

`Transform` method of class `XslCompiledTransform` **817**
`Transform` property of class `ModelVisual3D` **686**
Transforming an XML document and splicing its contents with another 812
transition **128**
transition arrow **127**, 129, 130, 135
transition arrow in the UML 134
transition between states in the UML **187**
`TranslateTransform` class **665**
Transmission Control Protocol/Internet Protocol (TCP/IP) **6**
traversals forwards and backwards 1074
traverse a tree 1088
traverse an array **271**
tree **560**, **1082**
tree structure 602
Tree structure for the document `article.xml` 800
`TreeNode` class **560**, 561
   `Checked` property 561
   `Collapse` method 562
   `Expand` method 562
   `ExpandAll` method 562
   `FirstNode` property 561
   `FullPath` property 561
   `GetNodeCount` method 562
   `ImageIndex` property 561
   `LastNode` property 561
   `NextNode` property 561
   `Nodes` property 561
   `PrevNode` property 561
   `SelectedImageIndex` property 561
   `Text` property 561
`TreeNode` Editor 562
`TreeNode` properties and methods 561
`TreeView` class 531, **560**, 803
   `AfterSelected` event 561
   `CheckBoxes` property 561
   `ImageList` property 561
   `Nodes` property 561
   `SelectedNode` property 561
`TreeView` displaying a sample tree 560
`TreeView` properties and an event 561
`TreeView` used to display directories 563
`TreeViewEventArgs` class **561**
`TriangleIndices` property of class `MeshGeometry3D` **683**
trigger (WPF) **642**
trigger an event 487
`Trigger` class (WPF) **642**
   `Property` property **642**
   `Value` property **642**
trigger of `UpdatePanel` ASP.NET AJAX Extensions control **959**
`Triggers` property of `ControlTemplate` class **642**
`Triggers` property of `Style` class **642**
trigonometric cosine 195
trigonometric sine 196
trigonometric tangent 196
`Trim` method of class `string` 701
`TrimExcess` method of class `List<T>` 304
`TrimToSize` method of class `ArrayList` 1127
`true` 130, 131

truncate 70, 139
truth table **181**
truth tables
   for operator ^ 182
   for operator ! 183
   for operator && 181
   for operator || 181
`try` block **464**
`try` statement **466**
`TryParse` method of structure `Int32` **463**
tunneling events (WPF) **625**
TV GUI showing the versatility of WPF customization (code-behind) 676
two-dimensional array **268**
two-dimensional data structure 1082
two's complement 1157
twos position 1152
type 67, 68
type argument **296**, **1102**, **1103**, 1110
type attribute in a processing instruction **793**
type checking **1098**
`Type` class 407, **430**
type constraint **1104**
   specifying **1104**
type inference **1103**
type parameter **302**, **1102**, 1107, 1116
   scope 1109
type parameter list **1101**, 1107
type XML Schema attribute **786**
type-parameter list **302**
typesetting system 689
typing in a `TextBox` 490

U

U+*yyyy* (Unicode notational convention) 1191
`UIElementCollection` class **621**
   `Add` method **621**
   `Clear` method **621**
   `RemoveAt` method 621
`uint` simple type 1147
`UInt16` struct **1061**
`UInt64` struct **1061**
`ulong` simple type 1147
UML (the)
   abstract operation **448**
   activity diagram 127, 129, 130, 134, 163, 169
   arrow 128
   attribute 450
   class diagram **92**, 449, 450, 451
   diamond 129
   dotted line **128**
   final state **128**
   generalization **447**
   guard condition **129**
   merge symbol **134**
   modeling properties 102
   note **128**
   operation 450
   private visibility 362
   public visibility 362
   solid circle **128**
   solid circle surrounded by a hollow circle 128

UML (the) (cont.)
   specialization *447*
   stereotype *102*
UML (Unified Modeling Language) *12*,
   15, 76, 82, 118, 154, 155, 447
   diagram 82
UML Activity Diagram
   solid circle (for representing an initial
     state) in the UML 188
   solid circle enclosed in an open circle
     (for representing the end of an
     activity) in the UML 188
UML class diagram 373
   attribute compartment 154
   operation compartment 230
UML Partners *15*
UML Sequence Diagram
   activation *287*
   arrowhead 287, 288
   lifeline *287*
UML State Diagram
   rounded rectangle (for representing a
     state) in the UML *186*
   solid circle (for representing an initial
     state) in the UML *186*
UML Use Case Diagram
   actor *81*
   use case 82
unambiguous (Unicode design basis)
   1189
unary cast operator 142
unary operator *143*, 183
UnauthorizedAccessException class
   565
unbounded value 786
unboxing conversion *1061*
uncaught exception *464*
underscore (_) SQL wildcard character
   828
uneditable text or icons 487
unhandled exception *464*
Unicode character set 151, 178, *690*
Unicode Consortium *1189*
Unicode Standard *1189*
Unicode Standard design basis 1190
   efficient *1189*
   unambiguous *1189*
   uniform *1189*
   universal 1189
Unicode® *734*
Unified Modeling Language (UML) 12,
   15, 76, 82, 118, 154, 155, 447
uniform (Unicode design basis) *1189*
Uniform Resource Identifier (URI) *606*,
   863
Uniform Resource Locator (URL) *606*,
   863
Uniform Resource Name (URN) *606*
Uniform value for Stretch property
   680
UniformToFill value for Stretch
   property *680*
unique session ID of an ASP.NET client
   912
universal (Unicode design principle) 1189
universal-time format 311, 312, 313
UNIX 3
Unload event of an ASP.NET page *872*
unmanaged resource 442

unqualified name *205*, 217, 341
unwind a method from the call stack *480*
UPDATE SQL statement 826, *833*
UpdatePanel ASP.NET AJAX
   Extensions control *959*
UpdatePanel trigger *959*
UpDirection property of class
   PerspectiveCamera *685*
UpDownAlign property of class
   NumericUpDown 520
uppercase letter 53, 68
Uri 980
URI (Uniform Resource Identifier) *606*,
   863
Uri class 1027
UriKind.RelativeOrAbsolute value
   for Uri type property *1055*
UriTemplate property of WebGet
   attribute *977*
URL (Uniform Resource Locator) *606*,
   863
   rewriting 900
URN (Uniform Resource Name) *606*
use case diagram in the UML *81*, 82
use case in the UML *81*, 82
use case modeling *81*
UseMnemonic property of class
   LinkLabel 546
user-defined classes 52
user-defined types in web services *1002*
user interface 867
UserControl control *588*, *1020*, 1028
UserControl defined clock 589
user-defined exception class *481*
user-defined method Maximum 198
user-defined types 13, 787
UseSystemPasswordChar property of
   class TextBox *501*
ushort simple type 1147
Using a DataGridView to display details
   based on a selection 849
Using a PictureBox to display images
   516
Using CheckBoxes to change font styles
   508
Using class ArrayList 1127
Using command-line arguments to
   initialize an array 281
using declaration 342
using directive *51*, 96, 205, 341, 345
Using foreach statement to total
   integers in an array 255
Using GroupBoxes and Panels to
   arrange Buttons 505
Using lambda expressions 357
Using LinkedLists 1140
Using LINQ to perform a join and
   aggregate data across tables 845
Using LINQ to search directories and
   determine file types 741
using nested control statements 145
Using overloaded methods to display
   arrays of different types 1099, 1101
using prefix increment and postfix
   increment operators 149
Using RadioButtons to set message-
   window options 511
Using Regex methods Replace and
   Split 729

using statement 475
Using string indexer, Length property
   and CopyTo method 692
Using variable-length argument lists 279
UsingAnimations example 677
UsingBrushes example 659
UsingGradients example 662
UTF-8 1190
UTF-16 *1190*
UTF-32 *1190*
utility method *176*

V

valid identifier 67
valid XML document *598*, 780
Validate property of Page class *898*
Validate user information using regular
   expressions 725
validating XML parser *598*
Validation application enhanced by
   ASP.NET AJAX 954
validation control *892*
ValidationExpression property of a
   RegularExpressionValidator
   control *896*
validator *892*
ValidatorCalloutExtender control
   960
Validators used in a Web Form that
   retrieves user contact information. 892
validity checking 113
Value *811*
value contextual keyword *100*
Value property of class
   DateTimePicker *542*, 543, *545*
Value property of class
   LinkedListNode *1140*
Value property of class NumericUpDown
   520
Value property of class XElement *803*
Value property of class XText *811*
Value property of HttpCookie class *908*
Value property of Trigger class *642*
value type *105*, 239
   struct 105
value type constraint struct *1105*
ValueChanged event of class
   DateTimePicker *542*, 543
ValueChanged event of class
   NumericUpDown 521
Values property of class Hashtable
   1136
VALUES SQL clause *832*
ValueType class *711*, *1061*
var keyword *256*
variable
   declaration statement *67*
   name 67
variable is not modifiable 336
variable-length argument list *279*
variable scope 162
vector-based graphics *652*
Vector3D class *685*
vector-based graphics *595*
verb phrase in requirements document
   230
verbatim string *549*

verbatim string literal 201
verbatim string syntax(@) 691
version attribute (XSL) **793**
version in xml declaration **599**
VerticalAlignment property of WPF controls **612**
video 1017
VideoBrush class **1052**
VideoSelector example 1051
VideoSelectorWeb 1053
View In Browser command in Visual Web Developer **882**
View menu 25, 28
View property of class ListView **566**, 566
Viewport3D class **683**
    Camera property **685**
ViewportOrigin property of MultiScaleImage element **1048**
ViewportWidth property of MultiScaleImage element **1049**
__VIEWSTATE hidden input **899**
virtual
    keyword **387**
virtual directory **864**
virtual file system **1056**
virtualization software **3**
visibility in the UML **362**
visibility marker in the UML **362**
Visibility property of GUI elements 1024
    Collapsed state 1024
    Visible state 1028
Visibility property of WPF GUI elements **657**
    Collapsed state **657**
    Hidden state **657**
    Visible state **657**
visibility symbols in the UML **93**, 102
Visible property of an ASP.NET web control **892**
Visible property of class Control 497
VisitedLinkColor property of class LinkLabel 546
Visual C++ 7
visual inheritance **928**
visual programming 19, 489
Visual property of class VisualBrush **662**
Visual Studio
    component tray **518**
Visual Studio .NET Class View 347
Visual Studio .NET Object Browser 347
Visual Studio 2008
    Quick Info box **1201**
visual tree (WPF) **639**
Visual Web Developer
    WCF Web Service project 968
VisualBrush class **662**
    Visual property **662**
visualizer (debugger) **1204**
Visualizers
    HTML Visualizer *1204*
    Text Visualizer *1204*
    XML Visualizer *1204*
vocabulary (XML) **7**, **597**
VoiceXML 597
void keyword 54, 90

W

W3C (World Wide Web Consortium) **6**, **596**
W3C XML Schema **598**
waiting line 1060
walk the list 1072
Watch window (debugger) **1204**, 1205
waterfall model **80**
WCF
    DataContract attribute 981
    DataMember attribute 981
    OperationContract attribute **967**
    ResponseFormat property of the WebGet attribute **980**
    Serializable attribute 984
    ServiceContract attribute 967
    UriTemplate property of WebGet attribute **977**
    WebGet attribute 976
WCF REST service to create random equations based on a specified operation and difficulty level 1005
WCF service class 967
WCF service endpoint **965**
WCF web service interface that returns a welcome message through SOAP protocol and XML format 968
WCF Web Service project in Visual Web Developer 968
WCF Web Service project type **967**
WCF web service that returns a welcome message through the SOAP protocol and XML format 968
Weather namespace 1024
WeatherData class 1027
WeatherDetailsView custom control 1024, 1028
WeatherViewer example 1021
Web 2.0 1031
web application 1017
Web Application Project 1021
Web control **862**
Web Form **862**, 900, 901, 910
Web Form that demonstrates the AdRotator web control 889
Web Form that demonstrates web controls 883
web server **863**
Web service **964**
web service
    processing user-defined types 1002
Web Service Description Language (WSDL) **972**
web service host **965**
Web Site Administration Tool 929
Web.config file 967
Web.config ASP.NET configuration file **882**
Web.config file's service model configuration for WelcomeSOAPXMLService web service 971
web-application development **862**
WebClient class 979, 1027
    DownloadStringAsync method **980**, 1027
    DownloadStringCompleted event **980**, 1027
WebControl class **872**

WebGet attribute 976
webHttp Web.config property **978**
webHttpBinding Web.config binding setting **977**
WebMessageFormat.Json setting of ResponseFormat property 980, 1010
WebMessageFormat.Xml setting of ResponseFormat property 980
WebserviceX.NET (www.webservicex.net) 1022
Websites
    Deitel's Silverlight Resource Center (www.deitel.com/Silverlight/) 1018
    en.wikipedia.org/wiki/IP_address 864
    Flickr API Key (www.flickr.com/services/api/keys/) 1031
    grouper.ieee.org/groups/754/ 1148
    Hard Rock Memorabilia (memo.hardrock.com) 1037
    Isolated storage information (msdn.microsoft.com/en-us/library/bdts8hk0(VS.95).aspx) 1056
    Media-Convert free online video converter (media-convert.com/) 1050, 1052
    MediaElement supported formats (msdn.microsoft.com/en-us/library/cc189080(vs.95).aspx) 1050
    Mono Project's Moonlight (mono-project.com/Moonlight) 1018
    msdn.microsoft.com/en-us/library/system.array.aspx 1122
    msdn.microsoft.com/en-us/library/system.collections.specialized.aspx 1119
    msdn.microsoft.com/en-us/library/system.object_members.aspx 406
    Sample Beta2 Applications (silverlight.net/themes/silverlight/community/gallerydetail.aspx?cat=6) 1019
    Silverlight 2 Runtime (www.microsoft.com/silverlight/resources/installationFiles.aspx?v=2.0) 1019
    Silverlight Runtime system requirements (microsoft.com/silverlight/resources/install.aspx?v=2.0#sysreq) 1018
    Silverlight Streaming (streaming.live.com) 1017
    Silverlight Tools Beta 2 (go.microsoft.com/fwlink/?LinkId=120319) 1019

Websites (cont.)
 Updates to Silverlight
  Examples(www.deitel.com/
  books/cshcsharpfp3/) 1018
 Visual Studio 2008 Trial Version
  (msdn.microsoft.com/
  en-us/vstudio/products/
  aa700831.aspx) 1019
 Wikimedia Commons
  (commons.wikimedia.org)
  1052
 Wikimedia Commons Science
  Videos
  (commons.wikimedia.org/
  wiki/
  Category:Science_videos)
  1052
 www.uml.org 128
 www.w3.org/Protocols/
  rfc2616/
  rfc2616-sec10.html 865
well-formed XML document *598*
where clause *1104*
where clause of a LINQ query *296*
WHERE SQL clause 826, *827*, 828, 830,
  833, 834
while keyword 168
while repetition statement 128, *134*,
  135, 137, 141
  activity diagram in the UML 135
whitespace *52*, 55, 75
  characters *52*
whitespace character (regular expressions)
  702, *720*
whole/part relationship 119
widget *486*
Width property of MediaElement
  element 1055
Width property of structure Size *500*
Width property of WPF GUI elements
  654
Wikimedia Commons 1052
Wiltamuth, Scott 4
window auto hide *28*
Window control (WPF) *609*, 618, 637
  AllowsTransparency property
   636
  CommandBindings property *628*
  DragMove method *637*
  WindowState property *642*
  WindowStyle property *636*
window gadget *486*
Window menu 26
window tab 25
Windows
  Font 42
  Properties *32*, 33, 38, 42
  Solution Explorer *30*
Windows bitmap (BMP) 44
Windows Communication Foundation
  (WCF) 964
Windows Control Library project 747
Windows Explorer 549
Windows Form *487*
Windows Form Designer *23*
Windows Forms application *22*
Windows operating system *3*
Windows Presentation Foundation
  (WPF) *594*, 652

Windows XP 22
WindowState property of Window
  control *642*
WindowState.Minimized constant
  642
WindowStyle property of Window
  control *636*
wire format 966
Withdrawal class (ATM case study) 117,
  118, 120, 152, 153, 188, 230, 284,
  285, 287, 288, 289, 364, 365, 366,
  446, 447, 448, 449, 452
word character (regular expressions) *720*
word processor 689, 697
workflow *127*
workflow of an object in the UML 187
World Wide Web (WWW) 6
World Wide Web Consortium (W3C) *6*,
  596
WPF (Windows Presentation
  Foundation) *594*, 623
  App.xaml *610*
  App.xaml.vb *610*
  AxisAngleRotation3D class *686*
  Background property 630
  BevelBitmapEffect class *673*
  Binding class *644*
  BitmapEffectGroup class *673*
  Border control 613
  Border element 674
  Brush class 630
  Button control *613*, 621, 630
  Canvas class 656
  Canvas control *617*
  CheckBox control 630, 674
  code-behind class 609, 611
  CollectionView class *649*
  ColorAnimation class 680
  ComboBox control 630
  command binding *628*
  command library 626
  CommandBinding class *628*
  commands *625*
  content control *609*
  ContentControl control *609*, 613
  ContentPresenter class *640*
  control *609*, 639
  control template *639*
  control template, control template
   (WPF) 640
  ControlTemplate class *640*, 674
  data binding *644*
  data provider *650*
  data template *647*
  data view *649*
  DataContext property *647*
  DataTemplate class *647*
  dependency property *635*, 642
  DiffuseMaterial class *684*, *685*
  DirectionalLight class *685*
  DockPanel control 613
  DoubleAnimation class *680*
  DropShadowBitmapEffect class
   673
  Ellipse element *655*
  EmissiveMaterial class 684
  event handling 618
  EventSetter class *634*
  Expander control 613

WPF (Windows Presentation
  Foundation) (cont.)
  GeometryModel3D class *683*
  GradientStop class *664*
  Grid control 609, *615*
  GridView control *646*
  GridViewColumn control *646*
  GroupBox control *615*
  HorizontalAlignment property
   612
  ICommand interface *626*
  ImageBrush element *662*
  IsMouseOver property *642*
  KeyboardEventArgs class 622
  KeyDown event 622
  KeyUp event 622
  Label control *610*
  layout container *609*, 621
  layout control 612
  Line element *655*
  LinearGradientBrush element
   662
  ListView control *644*
  logical tree *639*
  lookless control *639*
  Margin property *612*
  MaterialGroup class 684
  MaxHeight property *612*
  MaxWidth property *612*
  MediaElement element *662*
  Menu control *630*
  MenuItem control *630*
  MeshGeometry3D class *683*
  MinHeight property *612*
  MinWidth property *612*
  Model3DGroup class *683*
  ModelVisual3D class *683*
  MouseButtonEventArgs class *622*
  MouseEventArgs class *622*
  MouseLeftButtonDown event *622*,
   625
  MouseLeftButtonUp event *622*,
   625
  MouseMove event *622*
  MouseRightButtonDown event
   622
  MouseRightButtonUp event *622*
  MouseWheel event 622
  MouseWheelEventArgs class 622
  ObjectDataProvider class *650*
  Panel control *609*
  PerspectiveCamera class *685*
  PointAnimation class 680
  Polygon element *656*
  Polyline element *656*
  PreviewMouseLeftButtonDown
   event *625*
  PreviewMouseLeftButtonUp
   event *625*
  RadialGradientBrush element
   662, 674
  RadioButton control *613*, 630,
   659, 674
  Rectangle element *654*
  resource *631*
  resource binding *634*, 640
  Resources property *634*
  RichTextBox control *626*
  RotateTransform class *665*

WPF (Windows Presentation
    Foundation) (cont.)
    RotateTransform3D class *686*
    routed events *623*
    RoutedCommand class *626*
    RoutedEventArgs class 622, 623
    ScaleTransform class *665*, 675
    Separator control *630*
    Setter class *634*, 642
    SkewTransform class *665*, 675
    Slider control *634*
    SolidColorBrush class 659
    SpecularMaterial class 684
    StackPanel control *615*
    Storyboard class *679*
    style *631*
    Style class *634*
    template binding *641*
    Template property *640*
    TextBlock control *647*
    TextBlock element *652*
    TextBox control *623*, 665
    ToolBar control *630*
    ToolBarTray control *630*
    TranslateTransform class *665*
    trigger *642*
    Trigger class *642*
    VerticalAlignment property *612*
    Viewport3D class *683*
    visual tree *639*
    VisualBrush class *662*
    Window control *609*, 618, 637
    WrapPanel control 613
    XmlDataProvider class *650*
WPF bitmap effect *668*, 673
WrapPanel control (WPF) 613
    Orientation property 613
Write method of class Console *64*, 736
WriteLine method of class Console 54,
    64, 736
WriteLine method of class
    StreamWriter *754*
WSDL (Web Service Description
    Language) 597, *972*, 974
wsHttpBinding setting of Web.config
    binding property *970*
WWW (World Wide Web) *6*
www.adobe.com 44
www.corel.com 44
www.deitel.com 17
www.deitel.com/books/csharpfp3/
    xxxv, 2, 822, 1019)
www.deitel.com/LINQ 859
www.deitel.com/LINQ/ 308
www.deitel.com/newsletter/
    subscribe.html 2
www.deitel.com/
    ResourceCenters.html 2
www.deitel.com/UML/ 128
www.deitel.com/
    VisualCSharp2008/ 17
www.ecma-international.org/
    publications/standards/
    Ecma-334.htm 1103
www.erain.com/products/zam3d/
    DefaultPDC.asp 683

www.microsoft.com/express/
    default.aspx 863
www.microsoft.com/express/sql
    820
www.mono-project.com 22
www.nasa.gov/multimedia/hd/
    index.html 668
www.oasis-open.org 780
www.omg.org 15
www.prenhall.com/deitel 17
www.unicode.org 734
www.w3.org 6
www.w3.org/2000/10/XMLSchema
    786
www.w3.org/XML/Schema 783
www.w3.org/XML/Schema.html 782
www.w3schools.com/schema/
    default.asp 783
www.xml.org 780
WYSIWYG (What You See Is What You
    Get) editor *880*

X

X format specifier 114
X property of class MouseEventArgs 523
x:Class attribute (XAML) *609*
x:Class attribute of a UserControl
    1020
x:Name attribute of a control *1020*
Xalan XSLT processor *791*
XAML (Extensible Application Markup
    Language) *594*, 1018, 1019
    attribute 608
    default namespace 609
    element 608
    end tag 608
    markup extension *634*, 641, 644
    namespace 609
    nested element 608
    presentation XAML namespace *609*
    root element 608
    standard XAML namespace *609*
    start tag 608
    x:Class attribute *609*
XAML view *610*
.xap *1021*
XAttribute class *810*
XBRL (Extensible Business Reporting
    Language) 597
XComment class *811*
XContainer class *809*
    Add method *815*
    Descendants method *809*
    Element method *810*
    Elements method *803*
    Nodes method *811*
XDocument class *800*, 1027
    Load method *802*
    Parse method 1027
    Root property *802*
XDocumentType class *810*
XElement class *800*
    Attribute method *810*
    Elements method *803*
    HasElements property *803*
    Name property *802*
    Value property *803*
Xerces parser from Apache 598

Xerox Palo Alto Research Center (PARC)
    3
XHTML (Extensible HyperText Markup
    Language) 596, *790*, 862, 863
XHTML response when the browser
    requests WebTime.aspx 873
XML (Extensible Markup Language) 7,
    594, 972
    attribute *604*
    attribute value *604*
    child element *601*
    container element *601*
    declaration *599*, 602
    document 644
    element *596*
    empty element 604
    end tag *596*
    instance document *788*, 789
    node *602*
    parent element *601*
    parser 597
    processor *597*
    prolog *600*
    root *602*
    root element *596*
    start tag *596*
    vocabulary *597*
XML document containing book
    information 794
XML document that describes various
    sports 791
XML document using the laptop
    element defined in computer.xsd
    789
.xml file extension *597*
XML file generated by XMLCombine 814
xml namespace prefix 605
XML namespaces demonstration 605
XML Path Language (XPath) *790*
XML Schema *598*, 608, *783*, 786
    complex types *786*
    simple types *786*
XML Schema document defining simple
    and complex types 788
XML Schema document for book.xml
    785
XML Schema URI (http://
    www.w3.org/2000/10/
    XMLSchema) 785
XML used to mark up an article 599
XML Visualizer 1204
XML vocabulary *7*
XML Working Group of the W3C 596
XmlDataProvider class (WPF) *650*
    IsAsynchronous property *650*
XmlDataSource ASP.NET control *890*
XmlNodeType enumeration *811*
xmlns attribute in XML *606*, 607
xmlns namespace prefix 605
XmlReader class *598*
XName class *802*
    LocalName property *802*
    Namespace property *814*
XNamespace class 810, *812*, 1010
XNode class *811*
    NextNode property *812*
    PreviousNode property *812*
    XPathSelectElements extension
        method *809*

XObject class *811*
    Document property *811*
    NodeType property *811*
    Parent property *811*
Xor bitwise operator 541
XPath 790, 809
XPath (XML Path Language) *790*
XPathSelectElements extension
    method of class XNode *809*
XProcessingInstruction class *811*
.xsd filename extension *784*
XSL (Extensible Stylesheet Language)
    599, 608, *790*
    variable *798*
XSL document that transforms
    sorting.xml into XHTML 795
.xsl filename extension *793*
XSL-FO (XSL Formatting Objects) *790*

XSL Formatting Objects (XSL-FO) *790*
XSL style sheet *790*, 798
XSL template *793*
xsl template element *793*
XSL Transformations (XSLT) 790
xsl:for-each element *794*
xsl:output element *793*
xsl:text element *797*
xsl:value-of element *794*
XslCompiledTransform class *817*
    Load method *817*
    Transform method *817*
XSLT processor 791
XSLT that creates elements and attributes
    in an XHTML document 792
XText class *811*
    Value property *811*

Y

Y property of class MouseEventArgs 523
yield return statement 766

Z

zero-based counting 161
zeroth element *240*
ZIndex attached property of Canvas
    control *617*
ZoomAboutLogicalPoint method of
    MultiScaleImage element *1045*

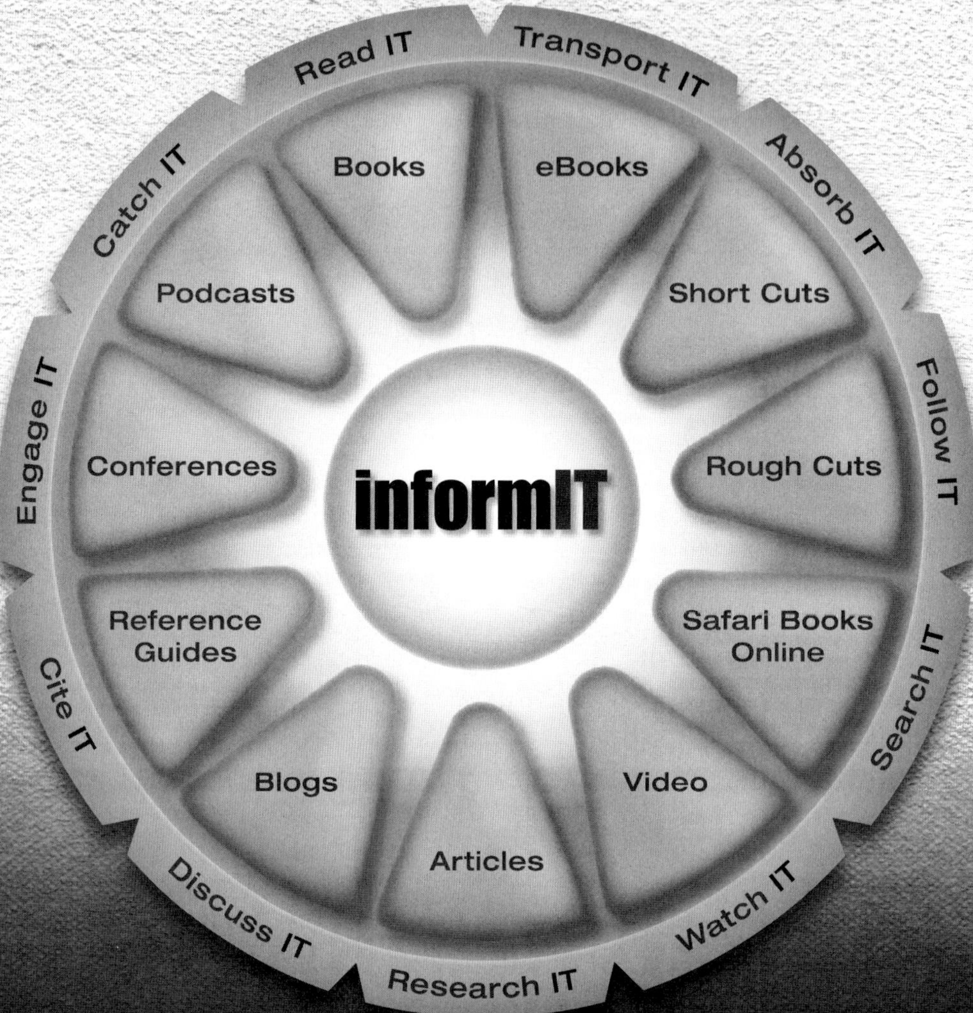

FREE Online Edition

Your purchase of **C# 2008 for Programmers** includes access to a free online edition for 45 days through the Safari Books Online subscription service. Nearly every Prentice Hall book is available online through Safari Books Online, along with more than 5,000 other technical books and videos from publishers such as Addison-Wesley Professional, Cisco Press, Exam Cram, IBM Press, O'Reilly, Que, and Sams.

SAFARI BOOKS ONLINE allows you to search for a specific answer, cut and paste code, download chapters, and stay current with emerging technologies.

Activate your FREE Online Edition at www.informit.com/safarifree

> **STEP 1:** Enter the coupon code: TUMFJGA.

> **STEP 2:** New Safari users, complete the brief registration form.
> Safari subscribers, just log in.

If you have difficulty registering on Safari or accessing the online edition,
please e-mail customer-service@safaribooksonline.com